22nd Conference on Computational Natural Language Learning (CoNLL 2018)

Brussels, Belgium
31 October - 1 November 2018

ISBN: 978-1-5108-7413-8

CoNLL 2018

The 22nd Conference on Computational Natural Language Learning

Proceedings of the Conference

October 31 - November 1, 2018
Brussels, Belgium

Sponsors

Order copies of this and other ACL proceedings from:

Association for Computational Linguistics (ACL)
209 N. Eighth Street
Stroudsburg, PA 18360
USA
Tel: +1-570-476-8006
Fax: +1-570-476-0860
acl@aclweb.org

Introduction

The 2018 Conference on Computational Natural Language Learning (CoNLL) is the 22nd in the series of annual meetings organized by SIGNLL, the ACL special interest group on natural language learning. CoNLL 2018 will be held on October 31 - November 1, 2018, and is co-located with the 2018 Conference on Empirical Methods in Natural Language Processing (EMNLP) in Brussels, Belgium.

CoNLL 2018 followed the tradition of previous CoNLL conferences in inviting only long papers, in order to accommodate papers with experimental material and detailed analysis. The final, camera-ready submissions were allowed a maximum of nine content pages plus unlimited pages of references and supplementary material.

CoNLL 2018 received a record number of 295 submissions in total, out of which 5 had to be rejected for formal reasons and 16 were withdrawn by the authors during the review period. Of the remaining 274 papers, 57 papers were chosen to appear in the conference program, with an overall acceptance rate of 20.8%. One of these was withdrawn after the notification, resulting in 56 papers for the final program: 16 were selected for oral presentation, and the remaining 40 for poster presentation plus lightning oral presentation. All 56 papers appear here in the conference proceedings.

CoNLL 2018 features two invited speakers, Asifa Majid (University of York) and Max Welling (University of Amsterdam / CIFAR). As in recent years, it also features two shared tasks: one on Universal Morphological Reinflection and one on Multilingual Parsing from Raw Text to Universal Dependencies. Papers accepted for the shared tasks are published in companion volumes of the CoNLL 2018 proceedings.

We would like to thank all the authors who submitted their work to CoNLL 2018, and the program committee for helping us select the best papers out of many high-quality submissions. We are grateful to the many program committee members who did a thorough job reviewing our submissions. Due to the the growing size of of the conference, we also had area chairs, for the first time, supporting the CoNLL organization. We were fortunate to have 12 excellent areas chairs who assisted us greatly in selecting the best programme:

Marine Carpuat, University of Maryland, USA
Paul Cook, University of New Brunswick, USA
Vera Demberg, Saarland University, Germany
Graham Neubig, Carnegie Mellon University, USA
Sebastian Pado, University of Stuttgart, Germany
Siva Reddy, Stanford University, USA
Roi Reichart, Technion, Israel
Alan Ritter, Ohio State University, USA
Tim Rocktäschel, University of Oxford, UK
Mehrnoosh Sadrzadeh, Queen Mary University of London, UK
Sameer Singh, University of California, Irvine USA
Yulia Tsvetkov, Carnegie Mellon University, USA

We are immensely thankful to Julia Hockenmaier and to the members of the SIGNLL board for their valuable advice and assistance in putting together this year's program. We also thank Ben Verhoeven, for maintaining the CoNLL 2018 website and Miikka Silfverberg for preparing the proceedings for the main conference. Finally, we would like to thank our hard working assistants, Phong Le and Edoardo Ponti, for their great support with the conference administration and publicity.

Finally, our gratitude goes to our sponsors, Google Inc. and Textkernel, for supporting the conference financially.

We hope you enjoy the conference!

Anna Korhonen and Ivan Titov

CoNLL 2018 conference co-chairs

Conference chairs:

Anna Korhonen, University of Cambridge
Ivan Titov, University of Edinburgh / University of Amsterdam

Invited speakers:

Asifa Maji, University of York
Max Welling, University of Amsterdam / CIFAR

Area chairs:

Marine Carpuat, University of Maryland, USA
Paul Cook, University of New Brunswick, USA
Vera Demberg, Saarland University, Germany
Graham Neubig, Carnegie Mellon University, USA
Sebastian Pado, University of Stuttgart, Germany
Siva Reddy, Stanford University, USA
Roi Reichart, Technion, Israel
Alan Ritter, Ohio State University, USA
Tim Rocktäschel, University of Oxford, UK
Mehrnoosh Sadrzadeh, Queen Mary University of London, UK
Sameer Singh, University of California, Irvine USA
Yulia Tsvetkov, Carnegie Mellon University, USA

Publication chair:

Miikka Silfverberg, University of Colorado, USA

Administration chair:

Phong Le, University of Edinburgh, UK

Publicity / sponsorship chair:

Edoardo Ponti, University of Cambridge, UK

Program Committee:

Omri Abend, Željko Agić, Roee Aharoni, Alan Akbik, Afra Alishahi, Stefanos Angelidis, Marianna Apidianaki, Kenji Araki, Wilker Aziz, Ashutosh Baheti, Fan Bai, Simon Baker, Omid Bakhshandeh, Miguel Ballesteros, Joost Bastings, Timo Baumann, Yonatan Belinkov, Iz Beltagy, Anja Belz, Jonathan Berant, Taylor Berg-Kirkpatrick, Raffaella Bernardi, Yevgeni Berzak, Alexandra Birch, Arianna Bisazza, Yonatan Bisk, Philippe Blache, Bernd Bohnet, Gerlof Bouma, Samuel Bowman, S.R.K. Branavan, Chloé Braud, Daniel Cer, Snigdha Chaturvedi, Boxing Chen, Danqi Chen, Xinchi Chen, Jianpeng Cheng, Christos Christodoulopoulos, Grzegorz Chrupała, Shay B. Cohen, Trevor Cohn, Danish Contractor, Caio Corro, Marta R. Costa-jussà, Ryan Cotterell, Tim Van de Cruys, Joachim Daiber, Amitava Das, Rajarshi Das, Steve DeNeefe, Thomas Demeester, Pascal Denis, Shuoyang Ding, Georgiana Dinu, Simon Dobnik, Jesse Dodge, Li Dong, Doug Downey, Gabriel Doyle, Markus Dreyer, Maximillian Droog-Hayes, Xinya Du, Kevin Duh, Nadir Durrani, Michael Elhadad, Micha Elsner, Federico Fancellu, Afsaneh Fazly, Marcello Federico, Christian Federmann, Yansong Feng, Raquel Fernández, Katja Filippova,

Andrea K. Fischer, Jeffrey Flanigan, Annie Foret, George Foster, Stefan L. Frank, Stella Frank, Dan Garrette, Mehdi Ghanimifard, Dafydd Gibbon, Daniel Gildea, Roxana Girju, Yoav Goldberg, Dan Goldwasser, Matthew R. Gormley, Yvette Graham, Edward Grefenstette, Nitish Gupta, Gholamreza Haffari, Keith Hall, William L. Hamilton, Kazuma Hashimoto, Hua He, Luheng He, Aurélie Herbelot, Dirk Hovy, Renfen Hu, Tim Hunter, Alvin Grissom II, Marco Idiart, Srinivasan Iyer, Laura Jehl, Robin Jia, Anders Johannsen, Alexander Johansen, Richard Johansson, Mandar Joshi, Katharina Kann, Dimitri Kartsaklis, Daisuke Kawahara, Tushar Khot, Yoon Kim, Milton King, Eliyahu Kiperwasser, Svetlana Kiritchenko, Sigrid Klerke, Roman Klinger, Thomas Kober, Philipp Koehn, Ioannis Konstas, Julia Kreutzer, Jayant Krishnamurthy, Germán Kruszewski, Marco Kuhlmann, Sachin Kumar, Jonathan K. Kummerfeld, Oier Lopez de Lacalle, Ni Lao, Yoong Keok Lee, Jochen L. Leidner, Roger Levy, Martha Lewis, Xi Victoria Lin, Xiao Ling, Wei Lu, Suresh Manandhar, Diego Marcheggiani, Yuval Marton, Diana McCarthy, David McClosky, Stephen McGregor, R. Thomas Mccoy, Pasquale Minervini, Jeff Mitchell, Daichi Mochihashi, Marie-Francine Moens, Nasrin Mostafazadeh, Smaranda Muresan, Kenton Murray, Ajay Nagesh, Preslav Nakov, Jason Naradowsky, Shashi Narayan, Massimo Nicosia, Xing Niu, Brendan O'Connor, Kemal Oflazer, Ulrike Pado, Alexis Palmer, Martha Palmer, Alexander Panchenko, Ali Hakimi Parizi, Panupong Pasupat, Michael J. Paul, Laura Perez-Beltrachini, Hieu Pham, Yuval Pinter, Barbara Plank, Massimo Poesio, Ella Rabinovich, Preethi Raghavan, Afshin Rahimi, Carlos Ramisch, Marek Rei, Steffen Remus, Xiang Ren, Sebastian Riedel, Martin Riedl, Laura Rimell, Brian Roark, Laurent Romary, Michael Roth, Joseph Le Roux, Alla Rozovskaya, Sebastian Ruder, Andreas Rücklé, Kenji Sagae, Ivan Sanchez, Ryohei Sasano, Carolina Scarton, Christian Scheible, Marten van Schijndel, William Schuler, Philip Schulz, Roy Schwartz, Djamé Seddah, Abigail See, Rico Sennrich, Minjoon Seo, Ehsan Shareghi, Wei Shi, Carina Silberer, Kevin Small, Daniil Sorokin, Vivek Srikumar, Miloš Stanojević, Gabriel Stanovsky, Mark Steedman, Pontus Stenetorp, Karl Stratos, Yu Su, Huan Sun, Partha Talukdar, Christoph Teichmann, Oren Tsur, Oscar Täckström, Patrick Verga, Aline Villavicencio, Andreas Vlachos, Svitlana Volkova, Sabine Schulte im Walde, William Yang Wang, Taro Watanabe, Julie Weeds, Dirk Weissenborn, Johannes Welbl, Michael Wiegand, Gijs Wijnholds, Dekai Wu, Kun Xu, Mohamed Yahya, Bishan Yang, Weiwei Yang, François Yvon, Congle Zhang, Victor Zhong, Shi Zong, Willem Zuidema

Table of Contents

Conference Program

Wednesday, October 31, 2018

08:45–09:00   *Opening remarks*

09:00–10:30   *CoNLL Shared Task: Multilingual Parsing from Raw Text to Universal Dependencies*

10:30–11:00   *Coffee break*

11:00–12:30   *CoNLL–SIGMORPHON 2018 Shared Task: Universal Morphological Reinflection*

12:30–14:00   *Lunch*

Invited Talk by Max Welling

14:00–15:00   Inductive Bias in Deep Learning

Session 1

15:00–15:15   *Embedded-State Latent Conditional Random Fields for Sequence Labeling*
Dung Thai, Sree Harsha Ramesh, Shikhar Murty, Luke Vilnis and Andrew McCallum

15:15–15:30   *Continuous Word Embedding Fusion via Spectral Decomposition*
Tianfan Fu, Cheng Zhang and Stephan Mandt

15:30–16:00   *Coffee break*

16:00–17:30   *Poster session 1*

Dual Latent Variable Model for Low-Resource Natural Language Generation in Dialogue Systems
Van-Khanh Tran and Le-Minh Nguyen

Churn Intent Detection in Multilingual Chatbot Conversations and Social Media
Christian Abbet, Meryem M'hamdi, Athanasios Giannakopoulos, Robert West, Andreea Hossmann, Michael Baeriswyl and Claudiu Musat

Learning Text Representations for 500K Classification Tasks on Named Entity Disambiguation
Ander Barrena, Aitor Soroa and Eneko Agirre

Hierarchical Attention Based Position-Aware Network for Aspect-Level Sentiment Analysis
Lishuang Li, Yang Liu and AnQiao Zhou

Bidirectional Generative Adversarial Networks for Neural Machine Translation
Zhirui Zhang, Shujie Liu, Mu Li, Ming Zhou and Enhong Chen

Latent Entities Extraction: How to Extract Entities that Do Not Appear in the Text?
Eylon Shoshan and Kira Radinsky

Generalizing Procrustes Analysis for Better Bilingual Dictionary Induction
Yova Kementchedjhieva, Sebastian Ruder, Ryan Cotterell and Anders Søgaard

Simple Unsupervised Keyphrase Extraction using Sentence Embeddings
Kamil Bennani-Smires, Claudiu Musat, Andreea Hossmann, Michael Baeriswyl and Martin Jaggi

Thursday, November 1, 2018

Session 2

09:00–09:15   *A Temporally Sensitive Submodularity Framework for Timeline Summarization*
Sebastian Martschat and Katja Markert

09:15–09:30   *Chinese Poetry Generation with a Salient-Clue Mechanism*
Xiaoyuan Yi, Ruoyu Li and Maosong Sun

09:30–09:45   *Multi-Modal Sequence Fusion via Recursive Attention for Emotion Recognition*
Rory Beard, Ritwik Das, Raymond W. M. Ng, P. G. Keerthana Gopalakrishnan, Luka Eerens, Pawel Swietojanski and Ondrej Miksik

Session 4

Inductive Bias in Deep Learning

Max Welling

Deep learning is often considered a 'black box' predictor, that is, a highly flexible mapping from input variables to target variables which is hard to interpret. In almost all other scientific disciplines researchers build highly intuitive models with few variables in which decades of accumulated expertise is embedded. Not surprisingly, black box models need a lot of data to be successful as predictors while generative models need much less data. One natural question to ask is if we can inject more inductive bias in black box models, such as deep neural networks.

We will look at two different ways to achieve this. First, data often has certain symmetries, i.e. a satellite image will have no useful information in the orientation of the objects of interest. This is of course similar to the fact that in natural images there is typically no useful information in the absolute location of the objects. Convolutions implement the latter inductive bias and lead to very significant gains in terms of data efficiency. We will argue that there may be other symmetries present in data (such as orientation) which can also be hardcoded in a deep architecture and result in data efficiency gains. We will illustrate this idea in pathology slide analysis.

A second way to inject inductive bias into predictors is to consider the data generating process of the data. I will argue that for certain tasks, such as image reconstruction, the generative process can be directly embedded into the classifier by, at every layer of the network, comparing the data generated by the current reconstruction with the observations and feeding the difference back into the network. We will illustrate the resulting model, which we call the "Recurrent Inference Machine" on the task MRI image reconstruction.

Keynote Talk

Semantic Spaces Across Diverse Languages

Asifa Majid

Across diverse disciplines there is a wide-spread assumption that natural languages are equally express-ible: anything that can be thought can be said. In fact, words are held to label categories that exist independently of language, such that language merely captures these pre-existing categories. In this talk, I will illustrate through cross-linguistic comparison across diverse domains that named distinctions are not nearly as self-evident as they may seem on first examination. Even for basic perceptual experiences, languages vary in which notions they lexicalise, and which concepts are coded at all. Crucially, in order to develop a universal theory of semantics, scholars must first seriously engage with the cultural variation found worldwide.

Embedded-State Latent Conditional Random Fields
for Sequence Labeling

Dung Thai Sree Harsha Ramesh Shikhar Murty Luke Vilnis Andrew McCallum
College of Information and Computer Sciences
University of Massachusetts Amherst
{dthai, shramesh, smurty, luke, mccallum}@cs.umass.edu

Abstract

Complex textual information extraction tasks are often posed as sequence labeling or *shallow parsing*, where fields are extracted using local labels made consistent through probabilistic inference in a graphical model with constrained transitions. Recently, it has become common to locally parametrize these models using rich features extracted by recurrent neural networks (such as LSTM), while enforcing consistent outputs through a simple linear-chain model, representing Markovian dependencies between successive labels. However, the simple graphical model structure belies the often complex non-local constraints between output labels. For example, many fields, such as a first name, can only occur a fixed number of times, or in the presence of other fields. While RNNs have provided increasingly powerful context-aware local features for sequence tagging, they have yet to be integrated with a global graphical model of similar expressivity in the output distribution. Our model goes beyond the linear chain CRF to incorporate multiple hidden states per output label, but parametrizes their transitions parsimoniously with low-rank log-potential scoring matrices, effectively learning an embedding space for hidden states. This augmented latent space of inference variables complements the rich feature representation of the RNN, and allows exact global inference obeying complex, learned non-local output constraints. We experiment with several datasets and show that the model outperforms baseline CRF+RNN models when global output constraints are necessary at inference-time, and explore the interpretable latent structure.

1 Introduction

As with many other prediction tasks involving complex structured outputs, such as image segmentation (Chen et al., 2018), machine transla-
tion (Bahdanau et al., 2015), and speech recognition (Hinton et al., 2012), deep neural networks (DNNs) for sequence labeling and shallow parsing have become standard tools for for information extraction (Collobert et al., 2011; Lample et al., 2016). In the language of structured prediction, DNNs process the input sequence to produce a rich *local* parametrization for the output prediction model. However, output variables obey a variety of hard and soft constraints — for example, in sequence tagging tasks such as named entity recognition, I-PER cannot follow B-ORG.

Interestingly, even with such powerful local featurization, the DNN model does not automatically capture a mode of the output distribution through local decisions alone, and can violate these constraints. Successful applications of DNNs to sequence tagging gain from incorporating a simple linear chain probabilistic graphical model to enforce consistent output predictions (Collobert et al., 2011; Lample et al., 2016), and more generally the addition of a graphical model to enforce output label consistency is common practice for other tasks such as image segmentation (Chen et al., 2018).

Previous work in DNN-featurized sequence tagging with graphical models for information extraction has limited its output structure modeling to these simple local Markovian dependencies. In this work, we explore the addition of latent variables to the prediction model, and through a parsimonious factorized parameter structure, perform representation learning of hidden state embeddings in the graphical model, complementary to the standard practice of representation learning in the local potentials of the segmentation model. By factorizing the log-potentials of the hidden state transition matrices, we are able to learn large numbers of hidden states without overfitting, while the latent dynamics add the capability to learn global

1

Proceedings of the 22nd Conference on Computational Natural Language Learning (CoNLL 2018), pages 1–10
Brussels, Belgium, October 31 - November 1, 2018. ©2018 Association for Computational Linguistics

Figure 1: An example result from the CLEF eHealth dataset. The soft output constraint suggests tagging patient status as *Myshift/Others* if there already is a *Myshift_Status* tag. Note that we have the same phrase tagged as *Myshift_Status* in the training dataset.

constraints on the overall prediction, without sacrificing efficient exact inference.

While soft and hard global constraints have a rich history in sequence tagging (Koo et al., 2010; Rush and Collins, 2012; Anzaroot et al., 2014), they have been underexplored in the context of neural-network based feature extraction models. In response, we present a latent-variable CRF model with a novel mechanism for learning latent constraints without overfitting, using low-rank embeddings of large-cardinality latent variables. For example, these non-local constraints appear in fine-grained nested field extraction, which requires hierarchical consistency between the subtags of an entity. Further, information extraction and slot filling tasks often require domain specific constraints — for example, we must avoid extracting the same field multiple times. A good combination of input featurization and output modeling is needed to capture these structural dependencies.

In this work we present a method for sequence labeling in which representation learning is applied not only to inputs, but also to output space, in the form of a lightly parameterized transition function between a large number of latent states. We introduce a hidden state variable and learn the model dynamics in the hidden state space rather than the label state space. This relaxes the Markov assumption between output labels and allows the model to learn global constraints. To avoid the quadratic blowup in parameters with the size of the latent state space, we factorize the transition log-potentials into a low-rank matrix, avoiding overfitting by effectively learning parsimonious embedded representations of the latent states. While the low rank *log*-potential matrix does not improve test-time inference speed, we can perform exact Viterbi inference to compute the labeling sequence. Figure 1 shows an example where our model finds the correct labeling sequence while a standard DNN+CRF model fails, by obeying a global constraint learned from the training data.

We examine the performance of the Embedded-State Latent CRF on two datasets: citation extraction on the UMass Citations dataset and medical record field extraction on the CLEF dataset. We observe improved performance in both tasks, whose outputs obey complex structural dependencies that are not able to be captured by RNN featurization. Our biggest improvement comes in the medical domain, where the small training set gives our parsimonious approach to output representation learning an extra advantage.

2 Proposed Model

2.1 Problem Formulation

We consider the sequence labeling task, defined as follows. Given an input text sequence with T tokens $\mathbf{x} = \{x_1, x_2, ..., x_T\}$, find a corresponding output sequence $\mathbf{y} = \{y_1, y_2, ..., y_T\}$ where each output symbol y_i is one of N possible output labels. There are structural dependencies between the output labels, and resolving such dependencies is necessary for good performance.

2.2 Background

The input featurization in our model is similar to previously mentioned existing methods for tagging with DNNs (Collobert et al., 2011). We represent each input token x_t with a word embedding w_t. We then feed the embedded sequence $\mathbf{w} = \{w_1, w_2, ..., w_T\}$ into a bidirectional LSTM (Graves and Schmidhuber, 2005). As a result, each input x_t is associated with a contextualized feature vector $f_t = [\overrightarrow{f_t}; \overleftarrow{f_t}] \in \mathbb{R}^d$ where $\overrightarrow{f_t}$ and $\overleftarrow{f_t}$ represent the left and right context at time step t of the sequence.

In this work, we concern ourselves with the mapping from these input features to a distribution over output label sequences.

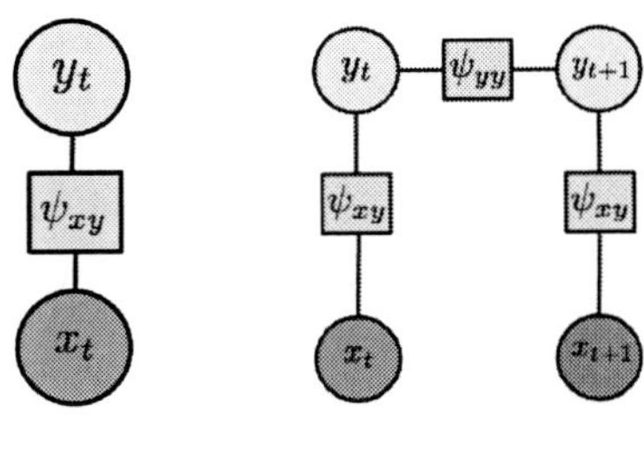

(a) Softmax   (b) Linear-Chain CRF

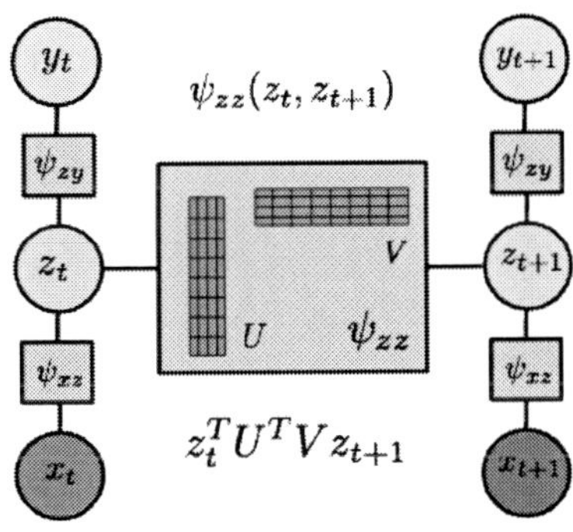

(c) Embedded-State Latent CRF

Figure 2: Comparing PGMs for tag prediction.

A straightforward solution is to use a feed-forward network to map the feature vector to the corresponding label. From a probabilistic perspective, this method is equivalent to the probabilistic graphical model in Fig.2a. Here, the goal is to estimate the posterior distribution:

$$\mathbb{P}(\mathbf{y} \mid \mathbf{x}) = \prod_{i=1}^{T} P(y_t \mid x_t) = \prod_{i=1}^{T} \psi(y_t; x_t) \quad (1)$$

where the joint distribution over the sequence is fully factorized, i.e. there is no structural dependency between y_t and the distribution $P(y_t \mid x_t)$ is parameterized by a deep neural network $\psi(y_t; x_t) = feed\_forward(f_t, y_t)$. This model ignores all the structural dependencies between the output labels during prediction, though not featurization, and has been found unsuitable for structured prediction tasks on sequences (Collobert et al., 2011).

In order to enforce some local output consistency, Collobert et al. (2011) introduce a linear chain Conditional Random Field (CRF) layer to the model (Fig.2b). They define the energy func-

tion for a particular configuration as follows

$$\mathcal{E}(\mathbf{y} \mid \mathbf{x}) = \sum_{t=1}^{T} \psi_{xy}(x_t, y_t) + \psi_{yy}(y_t, y_{t+1}) \quad (2)$$

where the local log-potentials ψ_{xy} are parameterized by a DNN, and (for their application) the edge log-potentials ψ_{yy} are parameterized by an input-independent parameter matrix, modeling the intra-state dependencies under a Markovian assumption, giving the data log-likelihood as

$$\log \mathbb{P}(\mathbf{y} \mid \mathbf{x}) = \mathcal{E}(\mathbf{y} \mid \mathbf{x}) - \log \sum_{\mathbf{y}'} \exp(\mathcal{E}(\mathbf{y}' \mid \mathbf{x})) \quad (3)$$

Collobert et al. (2011) show a +1.71 performance gain in Named-Entity Recognition (NER) by explicitly enforcing these local structural dependencies. However, the Markov assumption is limiting, and much of the gain comes from enforcing deterministic hard constraints of the segmentation encoding (e.g. *I-ORG* cannot go after *B-PER*). Similar types of local gains come from hierarchical tagging schemes (e.g. *I-DATE* should be tagged as *I-VENUE/DATE* if it appears inside the *I-VENUE/** segment). We would like to model, and learn, global, semantically meaningful soft constraints, e.g. *BOOKTITLE* should become *TITLE* if another *TITLE* does not appear in the same citation (Anzaroot et al., 2014). The state transition dynamics of the linear-chain CRF model are limited by a restriction to interaction between N output labels. The information-rich features $f_t \in \mathbb{R}^d$ input to the local potential are restricted to a local preference over the N labels in output space, failing to exploit the full power of the underlying feature space.

2.3 Embedded-State Latent CRF

Our proposed model, the embedded-state latent CRF, is shown in Figure 2c. We introduce a sequence of hidden states $\mathbf{z} = \{z_1, z_2, ..., z_T\}$ where z_t is one of M possible discrete hidden states and $M >> N$. Similarly, the corresponding energy for a particular joint configuration over $\mathbf{y}$ and $\mathbf{z}$ is

$$\mathcal{E}(\mathbf{y}, \mathbf{z} \mid \mathbf{x}) = \sum_{t=1}^{T} \psi_{xz}(x_t, z_t) + \psi_{yz}(y_t, z_t)$$
$$+ \psi_{zz}(z_t, z_{t+1}) \quad (4)$$

where $\psi_{xz}(x_t, z_t)$, $\psi_{yz}(y_t, z_t)$ are the local interaction log-potentials between the input features and hidden states, and the hidden states and output states, respectively. The hidden state dynamics come from the log-scores $\psi_{zz}(z_t, z_{t+1})$ for transitioning between hidden state z_t to z_{t+1}. The posterior distribution over output labels can be computed by summing over all possible configurations of $\mathbf{z}$

$$\mathbb{P}(\mathbf{y} \mid \mathbf{x}) = \frac{1}{Z} \sum_{\mathbf{z}} \exp\left(\mathcal{E}(\mathbf{y}, \mathbf{z} \mid \mathbf{x})\right) \quad (5)$$

where $Z = \sum_{\mathbf{y}'} \sum_{\mathbf{z}'} \exp\left(\mathcal{E}(\mathbf{y}', \mathbf{z}' \mid \mathbf{x})\right)$ is the partition function. The local log-potentials $\psi_{xz}(x_t, z_t)$ are produced by an affine transform from the RNN feature extractor, and the output potentials $\psi_{zy}(z_t, y_t)$ are many-to-one mappings from the hidden state, with learned potentials but pre-allocated numbers of states for each output label.

Factorized transition log-potentials We empirically observe that introducing a large number of hidden states can lead to overfitting, due to over-parameterization of the output dependencies. For example, *JOURNAL* often co-occurs with *PAGES* but *JOURNAL* is not strictly accompanied by *PAGES* (Anzaroot et al., 2014). Therefore, we regularize the state transition log-potential with a low-rank constraint, forming an embedding matrix wherein state transition interaction scores are mediated through low-dimensional *state embeddings* rather than a fully unconstrained parameter matrix. Instead of learning $A \in \mathbb{R}^{M \times M}$, a full-rank hidden state transition potential, we learn a low-rank model $A = U^T V$ where U and V are two *rank-k* matrices. This reduces the number of parameters from M^2 to $2Mk$ (where $k << M$) and shares statistical strength when learning transitions between similar states.

Inference. The brute-force computation of the posterior distribution using (5) is intractable, especially with the large number of hidden states. Fortunately, both the energy and the partition function can be computed efficiently using tree belief propagation. Due to the deterministic mapping from hidden states to outputs, we can simply fold the local input *and* output potentials $\psi_{xz}(x_t, z_t)$ and $\psi_{yz}(y_t, z_t)$ into the edge potentials and perform the forward-backward algorithm as in a standard linear-chain CRF. This deterministic mapping also lets us enforce hard transition constraints while retaining exact inference. Furthermore, since our implementation is in PyTorch

(Paszke et al., 2017), we only need to implement the forward pass, as automatic differentiation (back-propagation) is equivalent to the backward pass (Eisner, 2016).

MAP inference. At test time, we run the Viterbi algorithm to search for the best configuration over $\mathbf{z}$ rather than over $\mathbf{y}$. Mapping from the hidden state z_t to the output label y_t is deterministic given the output state embedding.

3 Related Work

Much deep learning research concerns itself with learning to represent the structure of input space in a way that is highly predictive of the output. In this work, while using state-of-the-art sequence tagging baselines for input representation learning, we concern ourselves with learning the global structure of the output space of label sequences, as well as fine-grained local distinctions in output space. While representation learning in the form of fine-grained, discrete, latent state transitions in the output space has been explored in this context (e.g. various latent-variable conditional random fields (Quattoni et al., 2007; Sutton et al., 2007; Morency et al., 2007) and latent structured support vector machines (Yu and Joachims, 2009)), we enable the use of many more hidden states without overfitting by factorizing the log-potential transition matrices and modeling the log-scores of latent state interactions as products of low-dimensional embeddings, effectively performing feature learning in output space.

A simple linear-chain CRF over the labels was used in early applications of deep learning to sequence tagging (Collobert et al., 2011), as well as the most recent high-performing segmentation models for named entity recognition (Lample et al., 2016). Outside of NLP, in tasks such as computer vision, certain classes of fully-connected graphical models over the output pixels have been used for multi-dimensional smoothing (Adams et al., 2010; Krähenbühl and Koltun, 2011), borrowing techniques for the graphics literature.

However, none of these models performs representation learning in the output space, as in the case of our proposed embedded latent-state model. Srikumar and Manning (2014) propose a similar factorized representation of output labels and their transitions, but only apply this to pairwise transitions of output labels and not latent dynamics of the whole sequence, while we believe the biggest gains are to be found by marrying representation learning techniques with latent variable methods.

In the graphical models literature, the most similar work to ours is the Latent-Dynamic CRF of Morency et al. (2007), who propose the same graphical model structure, without the deep input featurization, or more importantly, the learned embedded factorization of transition scores. Additionally, that work uses a deterministic mapping of equal numbers of hidden states to output labels, while we have a hard-constrained (hidden states to output variables are always many-to-one), but learned, potential with different outputs pre-allocated different numbers of states based on corpus frequency.

Many graphical models have been proposed for natural language processing under hard and soft global constraints, e.g. (Koo et al., 2010; Anzaroot et al., 2014; Vilnis et al., 2015), many based on dual decomposition (Rush and Collins, 2012). However, the constraints are often fixed, and even when learned (Anzaroot et al., 2014; Vilnis et al., 2015), the learning is done simply on constraint weights generated from pre-made templates, the construction of which requires domain knowledge.

Finally, Structured Prediction Energy Networks (Belanger and McCallum, 2016; Belanger et al., 2017) have been used for NLP tasks such as semantic role labeling, but they perform approximate inference through gradient descent on a learned energy function over labelings, effectively a fully-connected graphical model, while our model sits more clearly within the framework of graphical models, permitting exact inference with only nonconvex learning, common to all latent-variable models.

4 Experiments

We experiment on two datasets with a rich output label space, the UMass Citations dataset (Anzaroot and McCallum, 2013) and the CLEF eHealth dataset (Suominen et al., 2015). Both of the datasets have a hierarchical label space, enforced by hard transition constraints, making this a form of shallow parsing (Anzaroot et al., 2014), with additional soft constraints in the label space due to the interdependent nature of the fields being extracted.

4.1 Datasets

4.1.1 UMass Citations

We experiment with citation field extraction on the UMass Citations dataset (Anzaroot and McCallum, 2013), a collection of 2476 richly labeled citation strings, each tagged in a hierarchical manner, across a set of 38 entities demarcating both coarse-grained labeled segments, such as title, date, authors and venue, as well as fine-grained inner segments where applicable. The data follows a train/dev/test split of 1454, 655 and 367 citations, with 231085 total tokens. For example, a person's last name could be tagged as AUTHORS/PERSON/PERSON-LAST or VENUE/EDITOR/PERSON/PERSON-LAST depending on whether the person is the author of the cited TITLE or an editor of the publication VENUE. Similarly, year could be tagged as either DATE/YEAR or VENUE/DATE/YEAR depending on whether it is the cited work's publication date or the publication date of the venue of the cited work.

4.1.2 CLEF eHealth

We perform our second set of sequence labeling experiments on the NICTA Synthetic Nursing Handover dataset (Suominen et al., 2015) for clinical information extraction, consisting of 101 documents totaling 32122 tokens.

It is a synthetic dataset of handover records, which contain patient profiles as written by a registered nurse (RN) working in the medical ward and delivering verbal handovers to another nurse at a shift change by the patients bedside. A document is typically 100-300 words long, and the included handover information contains five coarse entities i.e, PATIENTINTRODUCTION, MYSHIFT, APPOINTMENTS, MEDICATION and FUTURECARE. Similar to the setup of the citation field extraction task described in Section 4.1.1, each of these coarse categories has a further level of nested finer labels and the entities to be identified are all hierarchical in nature. For example, the PATIENTINTRODUCTION section contains entities such as PATIENTINTRODUCTION/LASTNAME and PATIENTINTRODUCTION/UNDERDR_LASTNAME, the APPOINTMENTS section contains APPOINTMENT/PROCEDURE_CLINICIANLASTNAME, and MEDICATION contains MEDICATION/DOSAGE and MEDICATION/MEDICINE. There are a total of 35 such fine-grained entities. In addition to the hard-constrained hierarchical structure of the labels, the task also exhibits interesting global constraints, such as only tagging the first occurrence of the patient's gender, or the convention of labeling the most brief description of a nurse's shift status as MYSHIFT/STATUS, while the details of the shift are tagged as MYSHIFT/OTHER. In such cases, information extraction benefits from modeling output label dependencies, as we show in the results section.

4.2 Training Details

Our baseline is the BiLSTM+CRF model from Lample et al. (2016), employing a bidirectional LSTM with 500 hidden units for input featurization to capture long-range dependencies in the input space. Since we do not focus on input featurization, we do not use character-level embeddings in the baseline model.

Both the baseline model and our EL-CRF model were implemented in PyTorch. For training our models, we use the hyper-parameter settings from the LSTM+CRF model of Lample et al. (2016). Although, we did explore different optimizer techniques to enhance SGD such as Adam (Kingma and Ba, 2015), Averaged SGD (Polyak and Juditsky, 1992) and YellowFin (Zhang et al., 2017), none of them performed as well as mini-batch SGD with a batch-size of 1. We also employed gradient clipping to a norm of 5.0, a learning rate of 0.01, learning rate decay of 0.05, dropout with $p = 0.5$, and early stopping, tuned on the citation development data. We initialized our word level embeddings using pre-trained 100 dimensional Glove embeddings (Pennington et al., 2014), which gave better performance on our tasks than the skip-n-gram embeddings (Ling et al., 2015) used in the original work of Lample et al. (2016). The datasets were pre-processed to zero-replace all occurrences of numbers. Finally, we experimented with both IOBES and IOB tagging schemes, with IOB demonstrating higher performance on our tasks.

Embedding size We tune the embedding size (rank constraint) for the hidden state matrix A, varying from 10 to 40, alongside the neural network parameters, and report results when fixing the other hyperparameters and varying embedding size, similar to ablation analysis. Table 4 shows the impact of different embedding sizes on the performance of the model. We found that a size of

20 works best for both datasets, confirming the importance of the rank-constrained log-potential when using large-cardinality hidden variables.

Mapping tags to hidden states We find that the mapping between tags and hidden states greatly influences the performance of the model. We experimented with several heuristics (e.g., individual IOB tag count ratio and entity count ratio), and found that allocating a number of hidden states proportional to the entity count gives us the best performance.

4.2.1 Evaluation

We report field-level F1 scores as computed using the `conlleval.pl` script.

Since the train/validation/test splits were clearly defined for the UMass Citation dataset, we trained the models on the training split, tuned the hyper-parameters on the validation split and report the scores on the test dataset. However, as there were only 101 documents in the CLEF eHealth dataset, we report the Leave-One-Out (LOO) cross-validation F1 scores for this dataset i.e., we trained 101 models each with a different held-out document, merged the respective test outputs, and computed the F1 score on this merged output.

4.3 Results

Table 1 shows that overall performance on the UMass Citation dataset using the embedded-state latent CRF (95.18) is marginally better than the baseline BiLSTM+CRF model (95.07). However, examining the entities with the largest F1 score improvement in Table 2, we see that they are mostly within the VENUE section, which has long-range constraints with other sections, giving evidence of the model's ability to learn constraints from the citation dataset.

Dataset	CRF	EL-CRF	+
UMASS CITATION	95.07	95.18	**0.11**
CLEF EHEALTH	68.66	70.32	**1.66**

Table 1: Entity-level F1 scores of the embedded-state latent CRF and BiLSTM+CRF baseline.

Table 1 demonstrates that EL-CRF outperforms the BiLSTM+CRF on both datasets, with larger gains on the much smaller CLEF data. Table 3 shows the top-gaining entities include MEDICATION_MEDICINE and MEDICATION_DOSAGE,

Label	CRF	EL-CRF	+	S
V/DEPARTMENT	66.67	100	**33.33**	1
V/STATUS	77.78	87.5	**9.72**	9
V/E/P/ PERSON_MIDDLE	83.33	91.67	**8.34**	11
REFERENCE_ID	85.11	93.02	**7.91**	22
V/SERIES	55.17	61.54	**6.37**	12
V/ADDRESS	78.85	84.31	**5.46**	46

Table 2: Top 5 entities in terms of F1 improvement on the UMass Citation Dataset. The column *S* shows the support for a given entity in the test dataset. Key for contracted entity names: V: VENUE, E: EDITOR, P: PERSON

Label	CRF	EL-CRF	+	S
P/DR/GIVENNAMES/ INITIALS	33.33	64.29	**30.96**	15
A/PROCEDURE/ TIME	34.78	53.66	**18.88**	28
M/MEDICINE	55.28	71.1	**15.82**	157
FA/WARNING/ ABNORMALRESULT	0	11.43	**11.43**	59
M/DOSAGE	9.09	18.75	**9.66**	37

Table 3: Top 5 entities in terms of F1 improvement on the CLEF eHealth dataset. Key for contracted entity names: P/DR: PATIENT_INTRODUCTION/UNDER_DR, A: APPOINTMENT, M: MEDICATION, FA: FUTURE_ALERT

due to the global constraint that those entities always co-occur.

5 Qualitative Analysis

In this section, we provide qualitative evidence that the embedded-state latent CRF learns constraints which are not captured by the standard CRF.

First, we pick a few representative examples from the UMass Citations dataset and discuss when our model is able to correctly determine the label sequence based on the output constraints. In addition to the the hard constraints arising from hierarchical segmentation, this dataset also exhibits empirical pairwise constraints between fields e.g. two different authors' first names cannot be placed next to each other. Figure 3 demonstrates that the CRF model fails to enforce such constraints.

Another constraint we observe in the citation data

Factor Size	UMass Citation	CLEF eHealth
10	94.92	70.06
20	**95.18**	**71.51**
30	94.91	69.92
40	94.88	70.33
Full Rank	95.13	71.11

Table 4: Comparison of F1 scores obtained by varying the *factor_size* parameter, and setting the other model and neural network parameters from the model with the best cross validation.

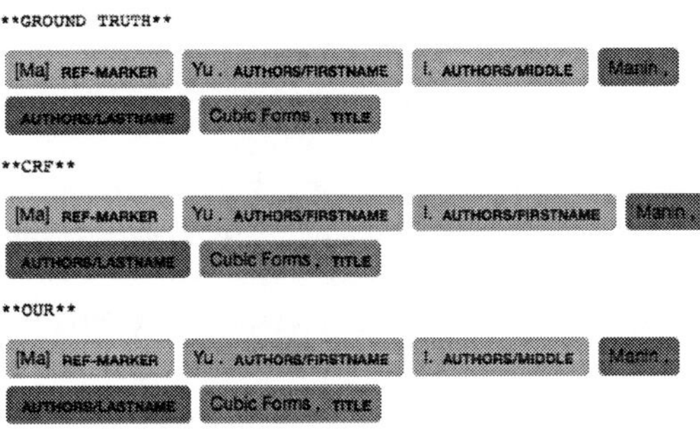

Figure 3: Authors name constraint violation

is that the *Venue/Series* tag only appears once per citation if *Venue/Booktitle* is also present. Our model obeys this constraint and marks the whole span as *Title* instead of breaking it into *Title* and *Venue/Series*, even though the input text for that segment in isolation could represent a valid series (Figure4).

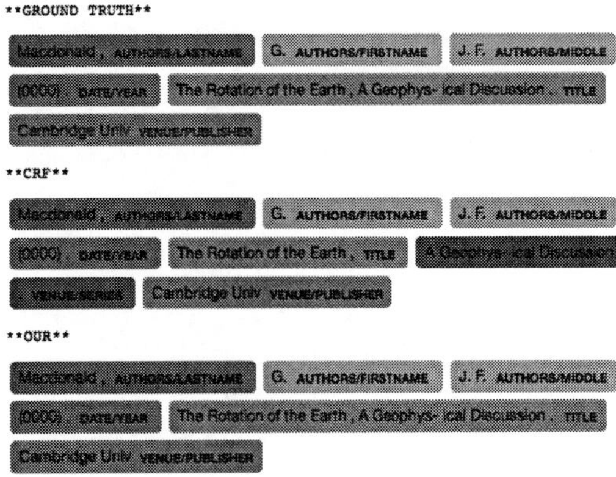

Figure 4: Title should not co-occur with series.

Sometimes output structural dependencies are not able to resolve ambiguity in the labeling sequence. In Figure 5 our model correctly predicts the presence of a *Venue/Booktitle* and a *Venue/Series*, but it fails to correctly assign the entity labels.

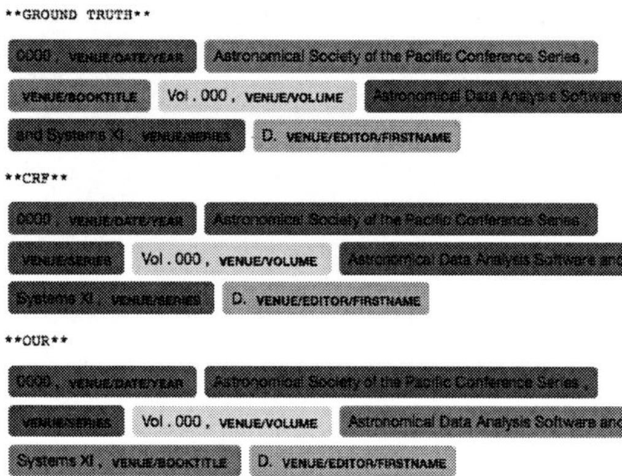

Figure 5: There is at most one series per citation.

The CLEF eHealth dataset holds a different set of constraints than the citation data, and its input sequences are not strong local indicators of the labeling sequence. Therefore, our model shows stronger performance over the Markovian baseline for this dataset. Some of the constraints concern the number of entities per document. For example, we only tag the first occurrence of a gender indicator e.g. *he*, *she*, *her*, etc., or the most general status of a nurse's shift.

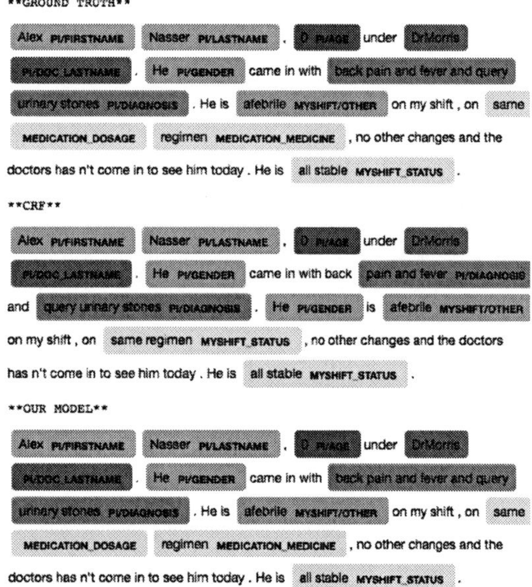

Figure 6: The gender indicator constraint and nurse's shift status constraint in the CLEF eHealth dataset.

Finally, a T-SNE (Maaten and Hinton, 2008) clustering on the embedding vectors of the output tags, shown in Figure 7, demonstrates that output structural dependencies can be reflected in tag embedding space.

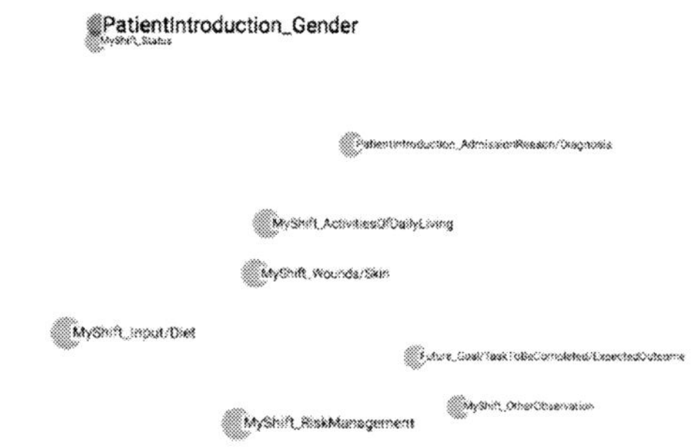

Figure 7: A part of the T-SNE clustering of the tag embedding from the CLEF eHealth dataset. The two tag PATIENTINTRODUCTION_GENDER and MYSHIFT_STATUS are under the similar constraint of being tagged only once per document.

6 Conclusion & Future Work

We present a latent variable model which not only parametrizes local potentials with the learned features from a deep neural network, but learns embedded representations in a large hidden state space, leveraging feature learning in both the input and output representations. Experimental results demonstrate that our model can learn global structural dependencies in the presence of ambiguities that cannot be resolved by local featurization of the input sequence. We find interpretable structure in the output state embeddings.

Future work will apply our model to larger datasets with more complex dependencies, and introduce multiple latent states per time-step, enabling exponentially more expressivity in output states at the cost of exact inference. We will also explore approximate inference methods, such as expectation propagation, to speed up message passing in the regime of low-rank log-potentials.

References

Andrew Adams, Jongmin Baek, and Myers Abraham Davis. 2010. Fast high-dimensional filtering using the permutohedral lattice. In *Computer Graphics Forum*, volume 29, pages 753–762. Wiley Online Library.

Sam Anzaroot and Andrew McCallum. 2013. A new dataset for fine-grained citation field extraction.

Sam Anzaroot, Alexandre Passos, David Belanger, and Andrew McCallum. 2014. Learning soft linear constraints with application to citation field extraction. *arXiv preprint arXiv:1403.1349*.

Dzmitry Bahdanau, Kyunghyun Cho, and Yoshua Bengio. 2015. Neural machine translation by jointly learning to align and translate. *ICLR*.

David Belanger and Andrew McCallum. 2016. Structured prediction energy networks. In *International Conference on Machine Learning*, pages 983–992.

David Belanger, Bishan Yang, and Andrew McCallum. 2017. End-to-end learning for structured prediction energy networks. *ICML*.

Liang-Chieh Chen, George Papandreou, Iasonas Kokkinos, Kevin Murphy, and Alan L Yuille. 2018. Deeplab: Semantic image segmentation with deep convolutional nets, atrous convolution, and fully connected crfs. *PAMI*.

Ronan Collobert, Jason Weston, Léon Bottou, Michael Karlen, Koray Kavukcuoglu, and Pavel Kuksa. 2011. Natural language processing (almost) from scratch. *Journal of Machine Learning Research*, 12(Aug):2493–2537.

Jason Eisner. 2016. Inside-outside and forward-backward algorithms are just backprop (tutorial paper). In *Proceedings of the Workshop on Structured Prediction for NLP*, pages 1–17.

Alex Graves and Jürgen Schmidhuber. 2005. Framewise phoneme classification with bidirectional lstm networks. In *Neural Networks, 2005. IJCNN'05. Proceedings. 2005 IEEE International Joint Conference on*, volume 4, pages 2047–2052. IEEE.

Geoffrey Hinton, Li Deng, Dong Yu, George E Dahl, Abdel-rahman Mohamed, Navdeep Jaitly, Andrew Senior, Vincent Vanhoucke, Patrick Nguyen, Tara N Sainath, et al. 2012. Deep neural networks for acoustic modeling in speech recognition: The shared views of four research groups. *IEEE Signal Processing Magazine*, 29(6):82–97.

Diederik P Kingma and Jimmy Ba. 2015. Adam: A method for stochastic optimization. *ICLR*.

Terry Koo, Alexander M Rush, Michael Collins, Tommi Jaakkola, and David Sontag. 2010. Dual decomposition for parsing with non-projective head automata. In *EMNLP*.

Philipp Krähenbühl and Vladlen Koltun. 2011. Efficient inference in fully connected crfs with gaussian edge potentials. In *Advances in neural information processing systems*, pages 109–117.

Guillaume Lample, Miguel Ballesteros, Sandeep Subramanian, Kazuya Kawakami, and Chris Dyer. 2016. Neural architectures for named entity recognition. *ACL*.

Wang Ling, Yulia Tsvetkov, Silvio Amir, Ramon Fernandez, Chris Dyer, Alan W Black, Isabel Trancoso, and Chu-Cheng Lin. 2015. Not all contexts are created equal: Better word representations with variable attention. In *Proceedings of the 2015 Conference on Empirical Methods in Natural Language Processing*, pages 1367–1372.

Laurens van der Maaten and Geoffrey Hinton. 2008. Visualizing data using t-sne. *Journal of machine learning research*, 9(Nov):2579–2605.

Louis-Philippe Morency, Ariadna Quattoni, and Trevor Darrell. 2007. Latent-dynamic discriminative models for continuous gesture recognition. In *Computer Vision and Pattern Recognition, 2007. CVPR'07. IEEE Conference on*, pages 1–8. IEEE.

Adam Paszke, Sam Gross, Soumith Chintala, Gregory Chanan, Edward Yang, Zachary DeVito, Zeming Lin, Alban Desmaison, Luca Antiga, and Adam Lerer. 2017. Automatic differentiation in pytorch. In *NIPS-W*.

Jeffrey Pennington, Richard Socher, and Christopher Manning. 2014. Glove: Global vectors for word representation. In *Proceedings of the 2014 conference on empirical methods in natural language processing (EMNLP)*, pages 1532–1543.

Boris T Polyak and Anatoli B Juditsky. 1992. Acceleration of stochastic approximation by averaging. *SIAM Journal on Control and Optimization*, 30(4):838–855.

Ariadna Quattoni, Sybor Wang, Louis-Philippe Morency, Morency Collins, and Trevor Darrell. 2007. Hidden conditional random fields. *IEEE transactions on pattern analysis and machine intelligence*, 29(10).

Alexander M Rush and MJ Collins. 2012. A tutorial on dual decomposition and lagrangian relaxation for inference in natural language processing. *Journal of Artificial Intelligence Research*, 45:305–362.

Vivek Srikumar and Christopher D Manning. 2014. Learning distributed representations for structured output prediction. In *Advances in Neural Information Processing Systems*, pages 3266–3274.

Hanna Suominen, Liyuan Zhou, Leif Hanlen, and Gabriela Ferraro. 2015. Benchmarking clinical speech recognition and information extraction: new data, methods, and evaluations. *JMIR medical informatics*, 3(2).

Charles Sutton, Andrew McCallum, and Khashayar Rohanimanesh. 2007. Dynamic conditional random fields: Factorized probabilistic models for labeling and segmenting sequence data. *Journal of Machine Learning Research*, 8(Mar):693–723.

Luke Vilnis, David Belanger, Daniel Sheldon, and Andrew McCallum. 2015. Bethe projections for non-local inference. *arXiv preprint arXiv:1503.01397*.

Chun-Nam John Yu and Thorsten Joachims. 2009. Learning structural svms with latent variables. In *Proceedings of the 26th annual international conference on machine learning*, pages 1169–1176. ACM.

Jian Zhang, Ioannis Mitliagkas, and Christopher Ré. 2017. Yellowfin and the art of momentum tuning. *arXiv preprint arXiv:1706.03471*.

Continuous Word Embedding Fusion via Spectral Decomposition

Tianfan Fu
Georgia Institute of Technology
Atlanta, GA, USA
tfu42@gatech.edu

Cheng Zhang
Microsoft Research Cambridge
Cambridge, CB1 2FB, UK
cheng.zhang@microsoft.com

Stephan Mandt
Los Angeles, CA, USA
stephan.mandt@gmail.com

Abstract

Word embeddings have become a mainstream tool in statistical natural language processing. Practitioners often use pre-trained word vectors, which were trained on large generic text corpora, and which are readily available on the web. However, pre-trained word vectors oftentimes lack important words from specific domains. It is therefore often desirable to extend the vocabulary and embed new words into a set of pre-trained word vectors. In this paper, we present an efficient method for including new words from a specialized corpus, containing new words, into pre-trained generic word embeddings. We build on the established view of word embeddings as matrix factorizations to present a spectral algorithm for this task. Experiments on several domain-specific corpora with specialized vocabularies demonstrate that our method is able to embed the new words efficiently into the original embedding space. Compared to competing methods, our method is faster, parameter-free, and deterministic.

1 Introduction

There has been a recent surge of neural word embedding models (Mikolov et al., 2013a,b). These models have been shown to perform well in a variety of NLP problems, such as word similarity and relational analogy tasks. Word embeddings play a crucial role in diverse fields such as computer vision (Hwang and Sigal, 2014), news classification (Kenter and De Rijke, 2015; Phung and De Vine, 2015), machine translation (Zou et al., 2013; Wu et al., 2014), and have been extended in various ways (Rudolph et al., 2016; Bamler and Mandt, 2017; Peters et al., 2018).

Instead of training word embeddings from scratch, practitioners often resort to high-quality, pre-trained word embeddings which can be downloaded from the web. These embeddings were trained on massive corpora, such as online news. The downside is that their vocabulary is often restricted, and by nature, is very generic. An open question remains of how to optimally include new words from highly specialized text corpora into an existing word embedding fit. Such transfer learning has several advantages. First, one saves the computational burden of learning high-quality word vectors from scratch. Second, one can already rely on the fact that the majority of word embedding vectors are semantically meaningful. Third, as we show in this paper, there are deterministic and parameter-free approaches that fulfill this goal, making the scheme robust and reproducible.

For a practical application, imagine that we are given a small corpus, such as a collection of scientific articles, and our goal is to include the associated vocabulary into a pre-trained set of word vectors which were learned on Google Books or Wikipedia. The scientific corpus contains both common words (e.g., "propose", "experiment") and domain-specific words, such as "submodular" and "sublinear". However, this specialized corpus can be safely assumed to be too small to train a word embedding model from scratch. Alternatively, we could merge the domain-specific corpus with a large generic corpus and train the entire word-embedding from scratch, but this would be computationally demanding and non-reproducible due to the non-convexity of the underlying optimization problem. In this paper, we show how to include the specialized vocabulary into the generic set of word vectors without having to re-train the model on the large vocabulary, simply relying on linear algebra.

A naive baseline method is to fix the pre-trained

Proceedings of the 22nd Conference on Computational Natural Language Learning (CoNLL 2018), pages 11–20
Brussels, Belgium, October 31 - November 1, 2018. ©2018 Association for Computational Linguistics

word vectors and only update the new ones. We found that this approach suffers from local optima and sensitive to hyper-parameters; therefore it is not reliable in practice. In contrast, our approach is not based on gradient descent and therefore more robust, deterministic, and parameter-free.

In this paper, we propose a Spectral Online Word Embedding (**SOWE**) algorithm for integrating new words into a pre-trained word embedding fit. Our approach is based on online matrix factorization. In more detail, our main contributions are as follows:

- We propose a Spectral Online Word Embedding (SOWE) method to include new words into a pre-trained set of word vectors. This approach does naturally not suffer from optimization problems, such as initialization, parameter tuning, and local optima.

- Our approach approximately reduces to an online matrix factorization problem. We provide a bound on the approximation error and show that this error does not scale with the vocabulary size (Theorem 1).

- The complexity of proposed method scales linearly with the size of vocabulary and quadratically with embedding dimension, making the approach feasible in large-scale applications.

- We evaluate our method on two domain specific corpora. Experimental results show that our method is able to embed new vocabulary faster than the baseline method while obtaining more meaningful embeddings. It is also parameter-free and deterministic, making the approach easily reproducible.

2 Related Work

Our paper departs from word embeddings learned via the skip-gram method, and shows how the vocabulary can be extended in an online fashion, using methods from linear algebra. As such, our approach relates to word embeddings, online learning, and the singular value decomposition (SVD).

Skip-Gram Model   Our model builds on word embeddings trained via the skip-gram model with negative sampling (SGNS), proposed by Mikolov et al. (2013a,b). These papers proposed a scalable training algorithm based on negative sampling.

The model predicts a target word in the middle of a sentence based on its surrounding words (contexts). Each target word / context word is associated with a feature vector whose entries are latent, and are treated as parameters to be learned. This model is efficient to train via stochastic gradient descent; its resulting word vectors provide state-of-the-art results on various linguistic tasks (Liu et al., 2015; Pickhardt et al., 2014). The skip-gram model was influential both in the machine learning and related communities.

Levy and Goldberg (2014) showed that word2vec can be viewed as an implicit matrix factorization of the pointwise mutual information matrix (PMI) of word distributions. The authors present a closed-form solution based on a singular value decomposition of a sparse version of this matrix, termed SPPMI. In this paper, we extend on this view and present an efficient online learning algorithm based on a decomposition of SPPMI matrix which departs form pre-trained word embeddings.

Online Word Embeddings   Kiros et al. (2015) propose adding new words into an existing embedding space using a projection method to warm-start learning the new words. The authors assumed that there already exist well-trained word vectors from a large underlying vocabulary, and present a method that projects word vectors from an old space to a new space, where the projection matrix is learned from known words.

Bojanowski et al. (2016) exploited character-level features. Concretely, they train a character-n-gram model to locate the new word vector near the existing word with similar root. Le and Mikolov (2014) introduced paragraph-level vectors (instead of word-level), a fixed-length feature representations for variable-length texts. When embedding new paragraphs, old paragraph vectors are frozen, and the new ones are updated. Furthermore, Luo et al. (2015) proposed an efficient online method to address the memory issue encountered when learning word embeddings based on nonnegative matrix factorization.

Online SVD   We already discussed word embeddings via implicit matrix factorization (IMF) above. This method is based on a truncated SVD on a square matrix whose size is the vocabulary size. As this paper combines this idea with online learning, we review related word on online singular value decompositions.

Online SVD (incremental SVD) is a classical problem in numerical linear algebra (Datta, 2010), and is intensively used in recommendation systems (Sarwar et al., 2002; Brand, 2003) and subspace learning (Li, 2004). Online SVD only possesses an approximate solution. Recently some methods have been proposed to reduce the involved approximation error (Shamir, 2015; Allen-Zhu and Li, 2016) based on iterative learning. In this paper, we use the same online SVD method as in Sarwar et al. (2002), which owns a closed-form solution.

3 Method

We present our spectral word embedding method to efficiently insert new words from an extended vocabulary into pre-trained word embeddings, without having to re-train the model on the extended vocabulary. We first introduce some relevant background with respect to word embedding via implicit matrix factorization (Section 3.1) before presenting our method (Section 3.2) and theoretical consideration (Section 3.3).

Notation In this paper, the vocabulary of the existing pre-trained word embedding is called *base vocabulary*, whose size is m. After adding new words, we call the whole vocabulary the *extended vocabulary*; its size is $n \equiv m + m'$, where m' is the number of unique new words. We assume $m' \ll m$, so $\mathcal{O}(n) = \mathcal{O}(m)$. Furthermore, let d denote the embedding dimension. As will be explained below, let S_0, S_{full} denote the SPPMI matrices of the base and extended vocabularies, respectively. The subscript "full", thus, always refers to the extended vocabulary.

3.1 Background: Word Embedding via Implicit Matrix Factorization (IMF)

The basis of our approach is the skip-gram model with negative sampling (SGNS), also called word2vec (Mikolov et al., 2013a,b). Let D denote the set of all observed of word-context pairs. Furthermore, $\#(w, c)$ denotes the number of times the pair (w, c) appears in D, and $\vec{w}$ and $\vec{c}$ are the word and context embeddings.

The objective that SGNS minimizes is

$$L = \sum_{w \in V_w} \sum_{c \in V_c} \left\{ \#(w, c) \log \sigma(\vec{w} \cdot \vec{c}) \right. \tag{1}$$
$$\left. + k \cdot \mathbb{E}_{c_N \sim p_D}[\log \sigma(-\vec{w} \cdot \vec{c}_N)] \right\}.$$

In the limit of large d, Levy and Goldberg (2014) found the following closed-form solution to Eq 1: $x = \vec{w} \cdot \vec{c} = \log\left(\frac{\#(w,c)\cdot|D|}{\#(w)\,\#(c)}\right) - \log k$.

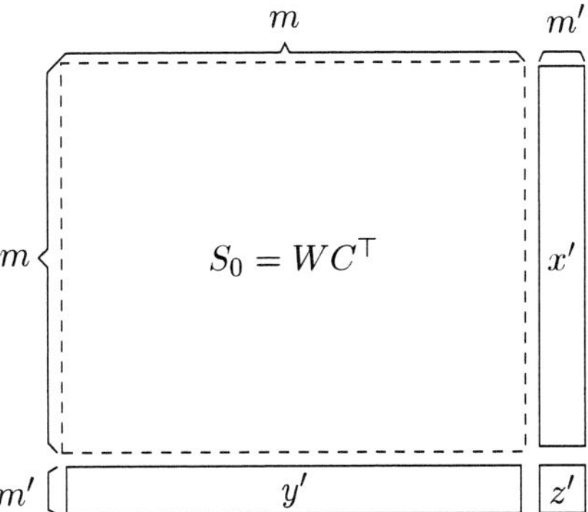

Figure 1: Block-structure of the Pointwise Mutual Information Matrix considered in this paper, and its block-structure for extended vocabulary. It corresponds to Equation (6).

The first term can be seen as an empirical estimate of Pointwise Mutual Information (PMI): $\text{PMI}(w, c) = \log\left(\frac{P(w,c)}{P(w)P(c)}\right)$. Thus, the matrix M that SGNS factorizes can be constructed from $M_{ij} = \text{PMI}(w_i, c_j) - \log k$. For computational convenience, Levy and Goldberg (2014) suggested a sparse and consistent alternative called Shifted Positive PMI (SPPMI):

$$\text{SPPMI}(w, c) = \max(\text{PMI}(w, c) - \log k, 0). \tag{2}$$

Levy and Goldberg (2014) showed that using such sparse representation, word and context embeddings could be efficiently obtained using a truncated singular value decomposition.

As will be explained in the next section, our approach builds on the intuition that word2vec implicitly factorizes the SPPMI matrix. Given pre-trained word and context vectors, we ask for an efficient way of extending the vocabulary and re-adjusting these vectors accordingly.

3.2 SOWE: Spectral Online Word Embedding

Our method takes advantages of the implicit matrix factorization method for efficiently embedding previously unseen words. Given a pre-trained word embedding, we firstly transform it to the SVD form. Using such form, under mild approximation, we can utilize efficient online SVD (Sarwar et al., 2002) to obtain the word embeddings for the extended vocabulary.

Figure 1 presents a sketch of the problem that we want to solve. We start from a $(m+m') \times (m+m')$ matrix in the extended vocabulary space, for which

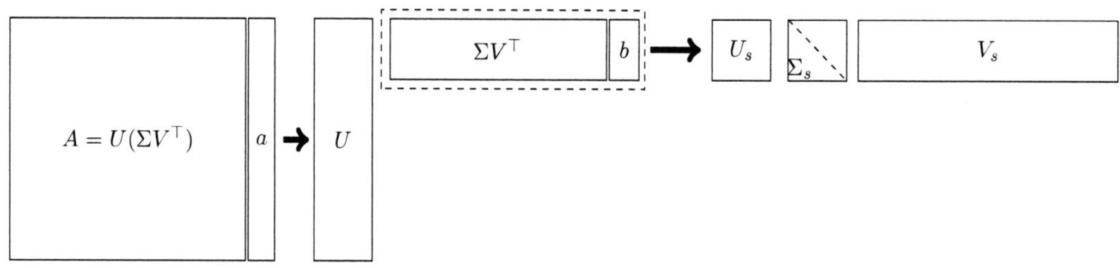

Figure 2: A sketch of the matrix manipulations carried out in online SVD (Algorithm 2). Given the truncated SVD of $A \approx U\Sigma V^\top$ and new columns a, we first compute b, the projection of a on U, i.e., $b = U^\top a$. Then we concatenate $Z = \Sigma V^\top$ and b via $V' = [Z, b]^\top$. Finally, we do rank-d truncated SVD on V', i.e, $[V_s, \Sigma_s, Us] = \text{tSVD}(V', d)$. Final result is $[UU_s, \Sigma_s, V_s] = \text{tSVD}([A, a], d)$.

Algorithm 1 Spectral Online Word Embedding (SOWE)

Input: Old word/context vectors W and C with $S_0 \equiv WC^\top$, co-occurrence matrices involving new vocabulary x', y', and z' (see Fig. 1).

Output: Word/context vectors $W_{\text{full}}, C_{\text{full}}$ for extended vocabulary.

1: **SVD of $WC^\top$ via QR decomposition.**
2: $U, R_1 \leftarrow \text{QR}(W)$ // $O(md^2)$
3: $V, R_2 \leftarrow \text{QR}(C)$ // $O(md^2)$
4: $U_0, \Sigma, V_0 \leftarrow \text{SVD}(R_1 R_2^\top)$ // $O(d^3)$
5: $U \leftarrow UU_0$ // $O(md^2)$
6: $V \leftarrow VV_0$ // $O(md^2)$
7: **Horizontal and vertical Online SVD.**
8: $U', \Sigma', V' \leftarrow \text{OSVD}([U\Sigma V^\top, x'])$
9: $U_{\text{full}}, \Sigma_{\text{full}}, V_{\text{full}} \leftarrow \text{OSVD}(\begin{bmatrix} U'\Sigma'V'^\top \\ [y', z'] \end{bmatrix})$.
10: **Return new embeddings.**
11: $W_{\text{full}} \leftarrow U_{\text{full}} \cdot \sqrt{\Sigma_{\text{full}}}$,
12: $C_{\text{full}} \leftarrow V_{\text{full}} \cdot \sqrt{\Sigma_{\text{full}}}$

---

we seek an approximate factorization. We assume that we already have a factorization of the upper-left submatrix of size $m \times m$, implicitly obtained from word2vec or related word embedding algorithms. We seek an efficient linear algebra algorithm that, given the block-structure, results in a factorization of the whole matrix in linear time in m. This will be detailed below.

Overview The following steps summarize our overall proposed procedure.

- We start by assuming that our word embedding algorithm came from a factorization of the pointwise mutual information matrix of word frequencies. Thus, $S_0 \approx WC^\top$.

- In order to make use of efficient only SVD, we need to convert this matrix product into an SVD form. This can be done in $O(m)$ time and results in $WC^\top = U\Sigma V^\top$ (Section 3.2.1).

- Next, we need to estimate all elements in the extended pointwise mutual information matrix, see Figure 1. We first estimate the dominant block (section 3.2.2 (i)), and show that it can be approximated by our previously obtained SVD. We then estimate the remaining blocks (section 3.2.2 (ii)). For the latter, we need to estimate the frequencies of the new words relative to the old words.

- We are now in a position to efficiently compute a new SVD for the extended pointwise mutual information matrix, $U_{\text{full}}\Sigma_{\text{full}}V_{\text{full}}^\top$, using online SVD. The operational costs are still $O(m)$ ((iii) in Section 3.2.2).

- Finally we define our new embedding matrices as $W_{\text{full}} = U_{\text{full}}\sqrt{\Sigma_{\text{full}}}$ and $C_{\text{full}} = V_{\text{full}}\sqrt{\Sigma_{\text{full}}}$, which completes our algorithm.

These steps will be explained in more detail below.

3.2.1 SVD from Word-Context Vectors

The first step in our algorithm is to obtain a singular value decomposition (SVD) of the old vocabulary's approximate PMI matrix S_0. Our working hypothesis is that our pre-trained word and context embedding matrices W and C are already approximately factorizing this matrix,

$$S_0 \approx WC^\top. \tag{3}$$

Levy and Goldberg (2014) showed that this factorization is correct in the limit of a large enough embedding dimension d, but is only approximately true otherwise. In this paper, we will use Eq. 3 as a working hypothesis.

Computing an SVD from S_0 would usually be an operation that costs $O(m^2)$, thus would scale quadratically in the vocabulary size. In such factorization would be not practical, since m is typically of the order of hundred thousands. Instead, we show next that, given a low-rank factorization of S_0 in terms of W and C renders this cost *linear* in the vocabulary size, making such an approach practical. The following procedure corresponds to steps 1-6 in Algorithm 1.

A truncated SVD (tSVD) of S_0 with rank d can be obtained from QR decompositions (Golub and Loan, 1996) of W and C as follows:

$$U', R_1 = \mathrm{QR}(W); \quad V', R_2 = \mathrm{QR}(C)$$

This results in $S_0 = U' R_1 R_2^\top V'^\top$. In a second step, we apply an SVD to $R_1 R_2^\top$:

$$U'', \Sigma, V'' = \mathrm{SVD}(R_1 R_2^\top).$$

The costs of this are small, as $R_{1,2}$ are $d \times d$ matrices. Since the composition of two orthogonal matrices is still orthogonal, we obtain the SVD of S_0 as $U = U' U''$, $V = V' V''$. Note that this transformation is exact since in our approximation, $S_0 = W C^\top$ was already of rank d. Thus, $W C^\top = U \Sigma V^\top$. The complexity of this operation is $O(m d^2)$, which concludes the first step.

3.2.2 Utilizing Online SVD to Embed Extended Vocabulary

The next steps amout to adding new words to the old embeddings by adding rows and columns to the original SPPMI matrix, and efficiently factorizing it via online SVD.

Given a representation of the old block of the PMI matrix in terms of an SVD, our next task is to compute the new elements of this matrix that correspond to the extended vocabulary of m' words, with $m' \ll m$. We denote this matrix $S_{\mathrm{full}} \in \mathbb{R}^{(m+m') \times (m+m')}$, and it has the following block structure (see also Fig. 1):

$$S_{\mathrm{full}} \triangleq \begin{pmatrix} S' & x' \\ y'^\top & z' \end{pmatrix}. \tag{4}$$

In the following three steps, we describe how to estimate and efficiently factorize this matrix.

(i) Approximating the main block In a first step, we approximate the main block S' of the SPPMI matrix (Eq. 4). We show that to a first approximation, this is just the SPPMI matrix of the original vocabulary, hence $S' \approx S_0$.

Algorithm 2 Recap: Online SVD (OSVD)

Input: Rank-d truncated SVD (tSVD) of $A \in \mathbb{R}^{m \times n}$: $U, \Sigma, V = \mathrm{tSVD}(A, d)$, where $a \in \mathbb{R}^{m \times m'}, U \in \mathbb{R}^{m \times d}, V \in \mathbb{R}^{n \times d}, \Sigma \in \mathbb{R}^{d \times d}$, $\{d, m'\} \ll \{m, n\}$.

Output: Rank-d truncated SVD of $[A, a]$:
1: $U^*, \Sigma^*, V^* \leftarrow \mathrm{tSVD}([A, a], d)$
2: **Compute projection of new matrix to U.**
3: $b \leftarrow U^\top a$.   // $O(ndm')$
4: $Z \leftarrow \Sigma V^\top$ // $O(nd)$
5: $V' \leftarrow [Z, b]^\top$.   // $O(nd^2)$
6: **Apply tSVD to projection.**
7: $V_s, \Sigma_s, Us \leftarrow \mathrm{tSVD}(V', d)$.
8:   // $O((n + m')d^2) \approx O(nd^2)$
9: **Return the results.**
10: $U^* \leftarrow U U_s, \Sigma^* \leftarrow \Sigma_s, V^* \leftarrow V_s$.   // $O(nd^2)$

To set up the SPPMI matrix, the following formula has to be applied to the observed co-occurrence counts $\#(w, c)$ between all word and context words in the extended vocabulary:

$$\max \left\{ \log \left(\frac{\#(w, c) \cdot |D|}{\#(w)\,\#(c)} \right) - \log k, 0 \right\} \tag{5}$$

Besides the co-occurrence counts, this also involves the absolute frequencies $\#(w)$ and $\#(c)$ of words and context vectors in the extended vocabulary, as well as the total number of counts $|D|$. Note that all these quantities enter only on a logarithmic scale.

The co-occurrence counts $\#(w, c)$ are the same for the SPPMI matrices of the original and full vocabularies. What differs slightly are the absolute counts $\#(w)$, $\#(c)$, and $|D|$ (these are slightly higher in the extended corpus). However, since we assumed that the original training corpus was much bigger than the corpus containing the new words, we can safely assume that the change in $\log \#(w)$, $\log \#(c)$, and $\log |D|$ is negligible (we will further specify and analyze this approximation in our section 3.3). Thus, $S' \approx S_0$. Furthermore, since we have shown in section 3.2.1 that $S_0 = U \Sigma V^\top$, this results in

$$S_{\mathrm{full}} \approx \begin{pmatrix} U \Sigma V^\top & x' \\ y'^\top & z' \end{pmatrix}. \tag{6}$$

(ii) Adding rows and columns The matrices $x', y' \in \mathbb{R}^{m \times m'}$ in Eq. 6 are tall-and-skinny matrices that contain information about cross co-ocurrences between old and new words, and $z' \in \mathbb{R}^{m' \times m'}$ are the co-occurrences of new words in the new vocabulary. Next, we will describe how to estimate these quantities, taking into account that we don't have access to the original training corpus that was used to learn the word embeddings of the old vocabulary.

As follows, we focus on x' as an example (estimating y' works analogously). In this case, we observe the co-occurrence counts $\#(w, c)$ between words w from the base vocabulary in the context of context words c from the new vocabulary. To compute the SPPMI (2), we then apply Eq. 5 to all obtained counts. This results in x'. The remaining problem is that $\#(w)$ and $|D|$ are unknown to us, and some heuristics have to be found to circumvent this problem.

First, notice that $\frac{\#(w)}{|D|}$ corresponds to the word frequencies in the original corpus. Furthermore, we are only interested in $\log \frac{\#(w)}{|D|}$. The logarithm is less sensitive to the result of the estimation of this quantity.

When using pre-trained word embeddings, the embedding vectors are typically ranked according to their frequency. We estimated the word frequency based based on their frequencies on the smaller corpus. For words from the old vocabulary that are not present in the new corpus, we interpolated using an exponential model, taking their frequency rankings into account.

Another heuristic has to be found to approximate z', in which case $\#(w)$ and $\#(c)$ are available, but $|D|$ is unknown. Here, we assume that the new words are about as rare as the rarest words in the old vocabulary, setting $\#(w)/|D|$ to the frequency of the least frequent word in corpus. This specifies the extended SPPMI matrix. Next, we show how to efficiently re-factorize it.

(iii) Factorizing the Extended SPPMI Matrix
Finally, the approximated SPPMI matrix is efficiently factorized using online SVD.

This can not be carried out in a single step, because the online SVD method sketched in Algorithm 2 only supports the addition *either* rows *or* columns (here presented for columns). Thus, we first concatenate $U\Sigma V^\top$ and x' horizontally and perform a rank d truncated SVD. In a second step, we concatenate the resulting singular value decomposition vertically with the concatenation of y' and z' to obtain a truncated SVD of the full SPPMI matrix. Algorithm 2 gives the details; for more details we refer to (Sarwar et al., 2002). This results in an approximate SVD for the full matrix. Word and

context embeddings can be obtained trivially from the SVD.

Finally, let us discuss the complexity of the method. The online SVD subroutine dominates the complexity of our approach, as it scales as $O(nd^2)$. In all steps, the costs remain linear in the vocabulary size. This makes our approach scalable and convenient to use. In contrast, when carrying out an SVD from scratch to compute the word and context embeddings, we would have a quadratic scaling in the vocabulary size, which would be impractical.

3.3 Theoretical Analysis

In this section, we show that under certain assumptions, the difference between approximate SPMMI matrix S'_{full} (Equation 6) and SPMMI matrix S_{full} (Equation 4) is bounded. This justifies the previous assumption that we can substitute S'_{full} for S_{full}. Now we want to show theoretically that this is a reasonable approximation. First, we make some assumptions.

Assumption 1. *There exists a constant $c_1 > 0$ such that number of nonzero (nnz) entries in $m \times m$ SPPMI matrix can be upper-bounded by $c_1 m$, i.e., $nnz(SPPMI) \leq c_1 m$.*

Remark 1. *It is reasonable to assume that in Shifted Positive PPMI matrix, most of the words are only closely related to a small number of other words.*

Assumption 2. *Every entry in co-occurrence matrix can be bounded by $c_2 > 0$, i.e., $\#(w, c) \leq c_2$ for $\forall\, w, c$.*

This is always satisfied, since the number of observed co-occurrences is always bounded.

Assumption 3. *For $m \times m$ SPPMI matrix, there exists a constant $c_3 > 0$ such that the number of w and c occur in corpus D at least $c_3 m$ times, i.e., $\min\{c_i, w_i\} \geq c_3\sqrt{m}$ for $\forall\, i$.*

Now, we provide our main theoretical result.

Theorem 1. *Under Assumption 1, 2 and 3, the gap between S'_{full} and S_{full} in Frobenius norm can be bounded by a constant $c_4 = \frac{3\sqrt{c_1}c_2}{c_3}$, i.e., $\|S'_{full} - S_{full}\|_F \leq c_4$.*

This results implies that the difference between S'_{full} and S_{full} is bounded by a constant independent of the vocabulary size. Since in large-scale word embedding models the size of the vocabulary is typically 10^5 or even 10^6, the relative difference between these two matrices can be negligible. We

Dataset	Method	Loss for new	Loss for all	time
NIPS	FOUN	-1.47 ± 0.004e5	-1.7026 ± 0.00004e7	103.8
	FOUN+anneal	-1.46 ± 0.006e5	-1.7026 ± 0.00006e7	103.3
	SOWE (ours)	-1.52e5	-1.7031e7	**47.1**
Economic News	FOUN	-8.64 ± 0.007e4	-1.6907 ± 0.000007e7	84.3
	FOUN+anneal	-8.63 ± 0.01e4	-1.6907 ± 0.00001e7	87.8
	SOWE (ours)	-8.65e4	-1.6904e7	**45.79**

Table 1: Performance on NIPS Abstract and Economic News. The unit of running time is second. We report the average value of 10 independent runs for FOUN and standard deviation in brackets only for "loss for new". For FOUN, "loss for all words" is the sum of "loss for new words" and "loss that are only related to old words"(which is a constant). So standard deviation of "loss for all" is equal to "loss for all".

provide the proof of the theorem in supplementary materials.

4 Experiment

In this section, we show empirical results where we compare our proposed SOWE with other continuous word embedding algorithms.We first present some generic settings of our experiments, followed by quantitative and qualitative baseline comparisons. Compared to the baselines, we find that our method is more efficient and finds more semantically meaningful embeddings. Our method takes less than one minute to insert about 1,000 domain-specific words (e.g., machine learning related words from NIPS abstracts) into a pre-trained embedding model with more than 180,000 words.

Experimental Setup Our approach departs from pre-trained word vectors from a generic training corpus. We downloaded publicly available pre-trained word embeddings and two small text corpora from specific domains. Our goal is to insert the domain-specific words that do not already appear in the original vocabulary efficiently into the embeddings.

First, we report on basic settings for our experiments. The pre-trained embedding model based on English Wikipedia is available online [1]. It contains 183,870 words. The embedding dimension is 300. The small, domain-specific corpora that we considered were the following ones: (1) "NIPS Abstracts": this data set contains abstracts of all the NIPS papers from 2014 to 2016. The data set contains 981 new words. (2) "Economy News": This data set contains news articles, containing 868 new words. These two corpora are much smaller than base corpus. For both the base corpus and the new corpus, the text was pre-processed using a

---

[1] http://u.cs.biu.ac.il/~yogo/data/ syntemb/bow5.words.bz2

window of 5 tokens on each side of the target word, where stop-words and non-textual elements were removed, and sentence splitting and tokenization were applied.

Baselines: FOUN and FOUN+annealing A natural idea for inserting new words into a pre-estisting word embedding fit is to fix the old word/context vectors, and only to update the new ones. This is our baseline method, referred in the following as "Fix Old, Update New" (**FOUN**). The approach uses the word2vec objective and employs stochastic gradient descent for training. We employ Robbins-Monro learning schedules (Robbins and Monro, 1951), setting the stepsize at the t-th step as $\epsilon_t = a(t + \gamma)^{-0.51}$. We used grid-search to find optimal parameters on all considered data sets, and found $k = 5$, $\gamma = 1e4$, $a = 1/10$ (for different tasks) to be optimal. Due to the involved randomness in the baseline approach, we conducted 10 independent trials using different random seeds for each results and reported the average results. For "FOUN+annealing" we used the same settings as in FOUN, but added random zero-mean Gaussian noise to the gradient. To this end, we employed a version of Stochastic Gradient Langevin Dynamics (Welling and Teh, 2011), where we scaled down the noise by a factor of 0.01.

Loss minimization and runtime We considered the word2vec loss on the extended vocabulary and evaluated the value of the loss function on the embedding vectors obtained form the different methods under consideration. The associated loss values and runtimes are reported in Table 1 for the "NIPS Abstracts", and for "Economy News". We found both approaches yield similar values of the loss function. (In our experiments below, however, we will show that our obtained word vectors seem to reflect the semantics of the original corpus better.) As a clear improvement, we found that our method

Method	Nearest Neighbor
FOUN	joyous haworth legionnaires kristiansand cade dingo gaozu mightywords budged freret pepco
FOUN+annealing	emmerich hotham totnes crescendo emt demesne family-friendly rutter khazars dijon isidro
SOWE (ours)	midcap ultralow jawboning cdw lennar sucres moviefone terest supercenters ious wci

Table 2: Nearest Neighbors of "**eurodollars**" in extended vocabulary.

Method	Nearest Neighbor
FOUN	mattias valmiki invalided mailman malkovich bufo khufu dijon propagating madman
FOUN + annealing	interrogative bouncers jf time-dependent invalidating bmo enameled subgroup brenda anal keller
SOWE (ours)	cannot nonsmooth cnns coreset svrg sublinear denoising lstm interpretability

Table 3: Nearest Neighbors of "**submodular**" in extended vocabulary. We measure the distance using cosine distance.

Method	EN-WS-353-SIM	EN-MTurk-771	EN-MEN-TR-3k	EN-RW-STANFORD	EN-WS-353-ALL
Ideal	69.94	57.45	64.43	43.26	65.14
FOUN	65.13	54.67	57.47	42.99	64.02
FOUN+anneal	64.99	54.89	**57.50**	42.73	64.01
SOWE (ours)	**66.48**	**55.49**	56.56	**42.92**	**64.82**

Table 4: Performance on word similarity task using text8 dataset. "ideal" means the matrix factorization method proposed in Levy and Goldberg (2014). FOUN and FOUN+annealing are the baseline that we are comparing with.

Method	capital-common-countries	nationality-adjective	family.txt	Syntactic
Ideal	49.60%	50.55%	55.23%	30.49%
FOUN	45.73%	50.63%	55.01%	**30.30%**
FOUN + anneal	44.70%	49.97%	**55.03%**	30.26%
SOWE (ours)	**46.43%**	**50.71%**	50.43%	29.38%

Table 5: Performance on word analogy task using text8 dataset. "ideal" means learning the word embedding with the full extended vocabulary from scratch. Here, the matrix factorization method proposed in Levy and Goldberg (2014) is used on the S_{full}. FOUN and FOUN+annealing are the baseline that we are comparing with.

Method	split number	capital-common-countries	nationality-adjective	family.txt	Syntactic
Ideal		64.74%	64.49%	62.32%	39.18%
FOUN		64.45±0.25 %	62.43±0.38%	61.29±0.44%	38.73±0.58 %
FOUN + anneal	20	64.26±0.38%	64.10±0.47 %	61.73±1.83 %	38.94±0.77%
SOWE (ours)		64.26±0.79%	64.22±0.47%	60.09±0.32%	38.20±0.72%
FOUN		59.80±1.27 %	60.93±1.76%	59.23±1.88%	38.47±1.23 %
FOUN + anneal	10	58.84±1.82%	59.93±1.90 %	59.77±2.00%	38.19±1.47%
SOWE (ours)		59.89±3.85%	60.86±1.02%	58.84±0.85%	38.00±1.83%
FOUN		51.88±4.03 %	52.10±2.94%	51.83±3.11%	33.33±2.09 %
FOUN + anneal	5	52.20±6.03%	52.08±3.96 %	54.01±3.88 %	33.84±2.11%
SOWE (ours)		51.14±%3.74	49.50±2.83%	50.84±1.44%	31.82±2.73 %

Table 6: Performance on word analogy task using existing embedding results and text8 dataset with different folds of splits. In the row "Ideal", we use the well-trained word embedding results downloaded from Internet. FOUN and FOUN+annealing are the baseline that we are comparing with.

is faster than the baseline, yielding a factor of 8 times speedup. We consider the baseline method to be converged when the loss value of the current epoch is close (smaller than a threshold) to that of the previous epoch, where the threshold is 1e2 for NIPS abstract and Economics News.

Qualitative Nearest Neighbor Test To test whether the learned embedding vectors are semantically meaningful, we chose some words from the new vocabulary and reported their nearest neighbors in the extended vocabulary. We expect the nearest neighbors to have a close semantic meanings. We chose cosine similarity as a means to measure distance between words.

We chose the words "eurodollars" as a query for "Economic News" and "submodular" for "NIPS Abstracts". The results are reported in Table 2 and 3. In the case of economics, we see that our algorithm recovered meaningful words such as "midcap" and "ultralow". The baseline methods failed to return meaningful results with respect to the query. One possible reason is that the baseline's underlying optimization algorithm got trapped in a poor local optimum. In the case of NIPS abstracts (Table 3), our SOWE method results in words such as "nonsmooth" and "coreset" which are highly related to the query "submodular", while the FOUN-based methods fail. Our approach thus outperforms the baseline in providing meaningful relationships between the pre-trained word vectors and the newly embedded ones. More examples are provided in the Appendix.

Evaluations on NLP Tasks Additionally, we evaluated the proposed method on some downstream NLP tasks, such as pairwise word similarity. To this end, we used datasets that contain word pairs associated with human-assigned similarity scores [2]. The word vectors are evaluated by ranking the pairs according to their cosine similarities, and measuring the correlation (Spearmans ρ) with the human ratings.

We excluded the word pairs of the similarity test from the original vocabulary and trained word2vec with the associated reduced vocabulary on several corpora. We then added the test words using the three competing methods (SOWE, FOUN, and FOUN+anneal). The fourth algorithm "Ideal" amounts to evaluating the test on the generic pre-trained word embeddings from the web. The results on the word similarity task are shown in Table 4. Our method obtains the best performance on four out of five word similarity tasks.

Word analogy tests consists of questions of the form "a is to a* as b is to b*", where b* must be completed (Mikolov et al., 2013b). We performed such word analogy tests; our results are reported in Table 5. We observe that SOWE outperform FOUN-based methods in two out of four cases.

Word Analogy Analysis with Varying Number of Folds We further split the corpus into folds to evaluate the word analogy task, where we varied the size of the folds. Here, we choose the most frequent 20,000 words in text8 and then split the vocabulary into $k \in \{5, 10, 20\}$ folds. All folds but one were considered as base vocabulary, and one fold was considered as new vocabulary. We used implicit matrix factorization on all but one fold, and added the last fold's vocabulary using the different methods under comparison (FOUN, FOUN+anneal and SOWE). We repeated this procedure k times and report means and standard deviations in Table 6. Our method achieves results comparable with the baselines.

5 Conclusion

We proposed a deterministic spectral algorithm for inserting new words into a pre-trained word embedding model. The approach is based on a small corpus (containing the new words) and the pre-trained word embedding vectors. Under well-specified assumptions, this vocabulary extension can be formulated as an online matrix factorization problem. This scheme scales linearly with the original vocabulary size, and quadratically with the embedding dimensions. Compared to baselines that involve optimizing the original word2vec loss with the old word vectors fixed, our method is parameter-free, does not suffer from optimization problems such as local optima, and as such easier to handle. We further provided an analysis on the involved approximation error and showed that it is bounded. While we found only slight improvements over the baseline methods in terms of quality of the word vectors, more work needs to be done to explore tradeoffs of the involved approaches.

---

[2] We used code and data from https://github.com/k-kawakami/embedding-evaluation

References

Zeyuan Allen-Zhu and Yuanzhi Li. 2016. LazySVD: Even Faster SVD Decomposition Yet Without Agonizing Pain. In *Proceedings of the 30th Conference on Neural Information Processing Systems, NIPS '16*. Full version available at http://arxiv.org/abs/1607.03463.

Robert Bamler and Stephan Mandt. 2017. Dynamic word embeddings. In *International Conference on Machine Learning*, pages 380–389.

Piotr Bojanowski, Edouard Grave, Armand Joulin, and Tomas Mikolov. 2016. Enriching word vectors with subword information. *arXiv preprint arXiv:1607.04606*.

Matthew Brand. 2003. Fast online svd revisions for lightweight recommender systems. In *Proceedings of the 2003 SIAM International Conference on Data Mining*, pages 37–46. SIAM.

Biswa Nath Datta. 2010. *Numerical linear algebra and applications*. SIAM.

Gene H. Golub and Charles F. Van Loan. 1996. *Matrix computations (3. ed.)*. Johns Hopkins University Press.

Sung Ju Hwang and Leonid Sigal. 2014. A unified semantic embedding: Relating taxonomies and attributes. *Neural Information Processing Systems*, pages 271–279.

Tom Kenter and Maarten De Rijke. 2015. Short text similarity with word embeddings. pages 1411–1420.

Ryan Kiros, Yukun Zhu, Ruslan R Salakhutdinov, Richard Zemel, Raquel Urtasun, Antonio Torralba, and Sanja Fidler. 2015. Skip-thought vectors. In *Advances in neural information processing systems*, pages 3294–3302.

Quoc Le and Tomas Mikolov. 2014. Distributed representations of sentences and documents. In *Proceedings of the 31st International Conference on Machine Learning (ICML-14)*, pages 1188–1196.

Omer Levy and Yoav Goldberg. 2014. Neural word embedding as implicit matrix factorization. In *Advances in Neural Information Processing Systems*, pages 2177–2185.

Yongmin Li. 2004. On incremental and robust subspace learning. *Pattern Recognition*, 37(7):1509–1518.

Pengfei Liu, Xipeng Qiu, and Xuanjing Huang. 2015. Learning context-sensitive word embeddings with neural tensor skip-gram model. pages 1284–1290.

Hongyin Luo, Zhiyuan Liu, Huanbo Luan, and Maosong Sun. 2015. Online learning of interpretable word embeddings. In *Proceedings of the 2015 Conference on Empirical Methods in Natural Language Processing*, pages 1687–1692.

Tomas Mikolov, Kai Chen, Greg Corrado, and Jeffrey Dean. 2013a. Efficient estimation of word representations in vector space. *arXiv preprint arXiv:1301.3781*.

Tomas Mikolov, Ilya Sutskever, Kai Chen, Greg S Corrado, and Jeff Dean. 2013b. Distributed representations of words and phrases and their compositionality. In *Advances in neural information processing systems*, pages 3111–3119.

Matthew E Peters, Mark Neumann, Mohit Iyyer, Matt Gardner, Christopher Clark, Kenton Lee, and Luke Zettlemoyer. 2018. Deep contextualized word representations. *arXiv preprint arXiv:1802.05365*.

Viet Phung and Lance De Vine. 2015. A study on the use of word embeddings and pagerank for vietnamese text summarization. page 7.

Rene Pickhardt, Thomas Gottron, Martin Korner, Paul Georg Wagner, Till Speicher, and Steffen Staab. 2014. A generalized language model as the combination of skipped n-grams and modified kneser ney smoothing. *meeting of the association for computational linguistics*, pages 1145–1154.

Herbert Robbins and Sutton Monro. 1951. A stochastic approximation method. *Annals of Mathematical Statistics*, 22(3):400–407.

Maja Rudolph, Francisco Ruiz, Stephan Mandt, and David Blei. 2016. Exponential family embeddings. In *Advances in Neural Information Processing Systems*, pages 478–486.

Badrul Sarwar, George Karypis, Joseph Konstan, and John Riedl. 2002. Incremental singular value decomposition algorithms for highly scalable recommender systems. In *Fifth International Conference on Computer and Information Science*, pages 27–28. Citeseer.

Ohad Shamir. 2015. A stochastic pca and svd algorithm with an exponential convergence rate. *international conference on machine learning*, pages 144–152.

Max Welling and Yee W Teh. 2011. Bayesian learning via stochastic gradient langevin dynamics. In *Proceedings of the 28th International Conference on Machine Learning (ICML-11)*, pages 681–688.

Haiyang Wu, Daxiang Dong, Xiaoguang Hu, Dianhai Yu, Wei He, Hua Wu, Haifeng Wang, and Ting Liu. 2014. Improve statistical machine translation with context-sensitive bilingual semantic embedding model. pages 142–146.

Will Y Zou, Richard Socher, Daniel M Cer, and Christopher D Manning. 2013. Bilingual word embeddings for phrase-based machine translation. pages 1393–1398.

Dual Latent Variable Model for Low-Resource Natural Language Generation in Dialogue Systems

Van-Khanh Tran[1,2] and Le-Minh Nguyen[1]

[1]Japan Advanced Institute of Science and Technology, JAIST
1-1 Asahidai, Nomi, Ishikawa, 923-1292, Japan
{tvkhanh, nguyenml}@jaist.ac.jp
[2]University of Information and Communication Technology, ICTU
Thai Nguyen University, Vietnam
tvkhanh@ictu.edu.vn

Abstract

Recent deep learning models have shown improving results to natural language generation (NLG) irrespective of providing sufficient annotated data. However, a modest training data may harm such models' performance. Thus, how to build a generator that can utilize as much of knowledge from a low-resource setting data is a crucial issue in NLG. This paper presents a variational neural-based generation model to tackle the NLG problem of having limited labeled dataset, in which we integrate a variational inference into an encoder-decoder generator and introduce a novel auxiliary auto-encoding with an effective training procedure. Experiments showed that the proposed methods not only outperform the previous models when having sufficient training dataset but also show strong ability to work acceptably well when the training data is scarce.

1 Introduction

Natural language generation (NLG) plays an critical role in Spoken dialogue systems (SDSs) with the NLG task is mainly to convert a meaning representation produced by the dialogue manager, *i.e.*, dialogue act (DA), into natural language responses. SDSs are typically developed for various specific domains, *i.e.*, flight reservations (Levin et al., 2000), buying a tv or a laptop (Wen et al., 2015b), searching for a hotel or a restaurant (Wen et al., 2015a), and so forth. Such systems often require well-defined ontology datasets that are extremely time-consuming and expensive to collect. There is, thus, a need to build NLG systems that can work acceptably well when the training data is in short supply.

There are two potential solutions for above-mentioned problems, which are *domain adaptation* training and *model designing for low-resource* training. First, *domain adaptation* training which

aims at learning from sufficient source domain a model that can perform acceptably well on a different target domain with a limited labeled target data. Domain adaptation generally involves two different types of datasets, one from a source domain and the other from a target domain. Despite providing promising results for low-resource setting problems, the methods still need an adequate training data at the source domain site.

Second, *model designing for low-resource setting* has not been well studied in the NLG literature. The generation models have achieved very good performances irrespective of providing sufficient labeled datasets (Wen et al., 2015b,a; Tran et al., 2017; Tran and Nguyen, 2017). However, small training data easily result in worse generation models in the supervised learning methods. Thus, this paper presents an explicit way to construct an effective low-resource setting generator.

In summary, we make the following contributions, in which we: (i) propose a variational approach for an NLG problem which benefits the generator to not only outperform the previous methods when there is a sufficient training data but also perform acceptably well regarding low-resource data; (ii) present a variational generator that can also adapt faster to a new, unseen domain using a limited amount of in-domain data; (iii) investigate the effectiveness of the proposed method in different scenarios, including ablation studies, scratch, domain adaptation, and semi-supervised training with varied proportion of dataset.

2 Related Work

Recently, the RNN-based generators have shown improving results in tackling the NLG problems in task oriented-dialogue systems with varied proposed methods, such as HLSTM (Wen et al., 2015a), SCLSTM (Wen et al., 2015b), or espe-

Proceedings of the 22nd Conference on Computational Natural Language Learning (CoNLL 2018), pages 21–30
Brussels, Belgium, October 31 - November 1, 2018. ©2018 Association for Computational Linguistics

cially RNN Encoder-Decoder models integrating with attention mechanism, such as Enc-Dec (Wen et al., 2016b), and RALSTM (Tran and Nguyen, 2017). However, such models have proved to work well only when providing a sufficient in-domain data since a modest dataset may harm the models' performance.

In this context, one can think of a potential solution where the domain adaptation learning is utilized. The source domain, in this scenario, typically contains a sufficient amount of annotated data such that a model can be efficiently built, while there is often little or no labeled data in the target domain. A phrase-based statistical generator (Mairesse et al., 2010) using graphical models and active learning, and a multi-domain procedure (Wen et al., 2016a) via data counterfeiting and discriminative training. However, a question still remains as how to build a generator that can directly work well on a scarce dataset.

Neural variational framework for generative models of text have been studied extensively. Chung et al. (2015) proposed a recurrent latent variable model for sequential data by integrating latent random variables into hidden state of an RNN. A hierarchical multi scale recurrent neural networks was proposed to learn both hierarchical and temporal representation (Chung et al., 2016), while Bowman et al. (2015) presented a variational autoencoder for unsupervised generative language model. Sohn et al. (2015) proposed a deep conditional generative model for structured output prediction, whereas Zhang et al. (2016) introduced a variational neural machine translation that incorporated a continuous latent variable to model underlying semantics of sentence pairs. To solve the exposure-bias problem (Bengio et al., 2015) Zhang et al. (2017); Shen et al. (2017) proposed a seq2seq purely convolutional and deconvolutional autoencoder, Yang et al. (2017) proposed to use a dilated CNN decoder in a latent-variable model, or Semeniuta et al. (2017) proposed a hybrid VAE architecture with convolutional and deconvolutional components.

3   Dual Latent Variable Model

3.1   Variational Natural Language Generator

We make an assumption about the existing of a continuous latent variable z from a underlying semantic space of DA-Utterance pairs $(\mathbf{d}, \mathbf{u})$, so that we explicitly model the space together with

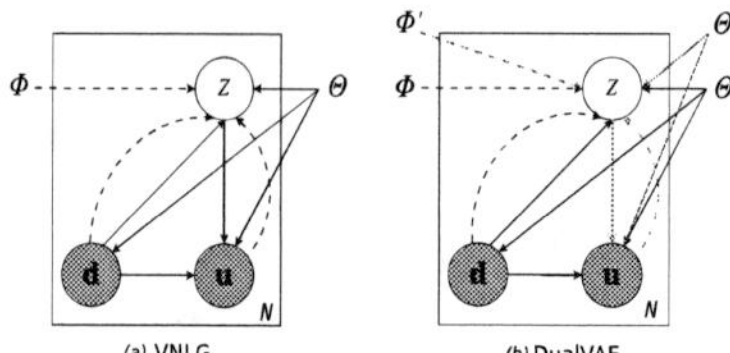

Figure 1: Illustration of proposed variational models as a directed graph. *(a)* VNLG: joint learning both variational parameters ϕ and generative model parameters θ. *(b)* DualVAE: red and blue arrows form a standard VAE (parameterized by ϕ' and θ') as an auxiliary auto-encoding to the VNLG model denoted by red and black arrows.

variable $\mathbf{d}$ to guide the generation process, *i.e.*, $p(\mathbf{u}|z, \mathbf{d})$. The original conditional probability $p(\mathbf{y}|\mathbf{d})$ modeled by a vanilla encoder-decoder network is thus reformulated as follows:

$$p(\mathbf{u}|\mathbf{d}) = \int_z p(\mathbf{u}, z|\mathbf{d})\mathbf{d}_z = \int_z p(\mathbf{u}|z, \mathbf{d})p(z|\mathbf{d})\mathbf{d}_z$$

$$(1)$$

This latent variable enables us to model the underlying semantic space as a global signal for generation. However, the incorporating of latent variable into the probabilistic model arises two difficulties in *(i)* modeling the intractable posterior inference $p(z|\mathbf{d}, \mathbf{u})$ and *(ii)* whether or not the latent variables z can be modeled effectively in case of low-resource setting data.

To address the difficulties, we propose an encoder-decoder based variational model to natural language generation (VNLG) by integrating a variational autoencoder (Kingma and Welling, 2013) into an encoder-decoder generator (Tran and Nguyen, 2017). Figure 1-*(a)* shows a graphical model of VNLG. We then employ deep neural networks to approximate the prior $p(z|\mathbf{d})$, true posterior $p(z|\mathbf{d}, \mathbf{u})$, and decoder $p(\mathbf{u}|z, \mathbf{d})$. To tackle the first issue, the intractable posterior is approximated from both the DA and utterance information $q_\phi(z|\mathbf{d}, \mathbf{u})$ under the above assumption. In contrast, the prior is modeled to condition on the DA only $p_\theta(z|\mathbf{d})$ due to the fact that the DA and utterance of a training pair usually share the same semantic information, *i.e.*, a given DA *inform*(name='*ABC*'; area='*XYZ*') contains key information of the corresponding utterance "The hotel *ABC* is in *XYZ* area". The underlying semantic space with having more information encoded from both the prior and the posterior provides the generator a potential solution to tackle the second issue. Lastly, in generative process, given an observation

DA **d** the output **u** is generated by the decoder network $p_\theta(\mathbf{u}|z, \mathbf{d})$ under the guidance of the global signal z which is drawn from the prior distribution $p_\theta(z|\mathbf{d})$. According to (Sohn et al., 2015), the variational lower bound can be recomputed as:

$$\mathcal{L}(\theta, \phi, \mathbf{d}, \mathbf{u}) = -KL(q_\phi(z|\mathbf{d}, \mathbf{u})\|p_\theta(z|\mathbf{d}))$$
$$+ \mathbb{E}_{q_\phi(z|\mathbf{d}, \mathbf{u})}[\log p_\theta(\mathbf{u}|z, \mathbf{d})] \leq \log p(\mathbf{u}|\mathbf{d}) \quad (2)$$

3.1.1 Variational Encoder Network

The encoder consists of two networks: (*i*) a Bidirectional LSTM (BiLSTM) which encodes the sequence of slot-value pairs $\{\mathbf{sv}_i\}_{i=1}^{T_{DA}}$ by separate parameterization of slots and values (Wen et al., 2016b); and (*ii*) a shared CNN/RNN Utterance Encoder which encodes the corresponding utterance. The encoder network, thus, produces both the DA representation $\mathbf{h_D}$ and the utterance representation $\mathbf{h_U}$ vectors which flow into the inference and decoder networks, and the posterior approximator, respectively (see Suppl. 1.1).

3.1.2 Variational Inference Network

This section models both the prior $p_\theta(z|\mathbf{d})$ and the posterior $q_\phi(z|\mathbf{d}, \mathbf{u})$ by utilizing neural networks.

Neural Posterior Approximator: We approximate the intractable posterior distribution of z to simplify the posterior inference, in which we first projects both DA and utterance representations onto the latent space:

$$\mathbf{h}_z' = g(\mathbf{W}_z[\mathbf{h_D}; \mathbf{h_U}] + b_z) \quad (3)$$

where $\mathbf{W}_z \in \mathbb{R}^{d_z \times (d_{\mathbf{h_D}} + d_{\mathbf{h_U}})}$, $b_z \in \mathbb{R}^{d_z}$ are matrix and bias parameters respectively, d_z is the dimensionality of the latent space, and we set $g(.)$ to be ReLU in our experiments. We then approximate the posterior as:

$$q_\phi(z|\mathbf{d}, \mathbf{u}) = \mathcal{N}(z; \mu_1(\mathbf{h}_z'), \sigma_1^2(\mathbf{h}_z')\boldsymbol{I}) \quad (4)$$

with mean μ_1 and standard variance σ_1 are the outputs of the neural network as follows:

$$\mu_1 = \mathbf{W}_{\mu_1}\mathbf{h}_z' + b_{\mu_1}, \log \sigma_1^2 = \mathbf{W}_{\sigma_1}\mathbf{h}_z' + b_{\sigma_1} \quad (5)$$

where $\mu_1, \log \sigma_1^2$ are both d_z dimension vectors.

Neural Prior: We model the prior as follows:

$$p_\theta(z|\mathbf{d}) = \mathcal{N}(z; \mu_1'(\mathbf{d}), \sigma_1'^2(\mathbf{d})\boldsymbol{I}) \quad (6)$$

where μ_1' and σ_1' of the prior are neural models only based on the Dialogue Act representation, which are the same as those of the posterior $q_\phi(z|\mathbf{d}, \mathbf{u})$ in Eq. 3 and 5, except for the absence of $\mathbf{h_U}$. To obtain a representation of the latent variable z, we re-parameterize it as follows: $\mathbf{h}_z = \mu_1 + \sigma_1 \odot \epsilon$ where $\epsilon \sim \mathcal{N}(0, \boldsymbol{I})$.

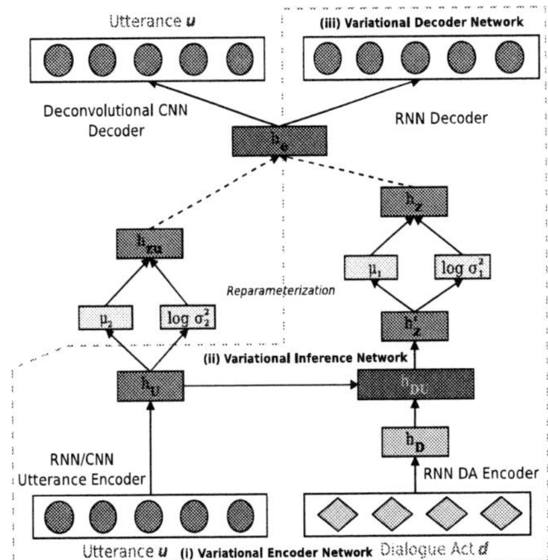

Figure 2: The Dual latent variable model consists of two VAE models: (*i*) a VNLG (red-dashed box) is to generate utterances and (*ii*) a Variational CNN-DCNN is an auxiliary auto-encoding model (left side). The RNN/CNN Utterance Encoder is shared between the two VAEs.

Note here that the parameters for the prior and the posterior are independent of each other. Moreover, during decoding we set $\mathbf{h}_z$ to be the mean of the prior $p_\theta(z|\mathbf{d})$, i.e., μ_1' due to the absence of the utterance **u**. In order to integrate the latent variable $\mathbf{h}_z$ into the decoder, we use a non-linear transformation to project it onto the output space for generation: $\mathbf{h}_e = g(\mathbf{W}_e\mathbf{h}_z + b_e)(7)$, where $\mathbf{h}_e \in \mathbb{R}^{d_e}$.

3.1.3 Variational Decoder Network

Given a DA **d** and the latent variable z, the decoder calculates the probability over the generation **u** as a joint probability of ordered conditionals:

$$p(\mathbf{u}|z, \mathbf{d}) = \prod_{t=1}^{T_\mathbf{U}} p(\mathbf{u}_t|\mathbf{u}_{<t}, z, \mathbf{d}) \quad (8)$$

where $p(\mathbf{u}_t|\mathbf{u}_{<t}, z, \mathbf{d}) = g'(\text{RALSTM}(\mathbf{u}_t, \mathbf{h}_{t-1}, \mathbf{d}_t)$. The RALSTM cell (Tran and Nguyen, 2017) is slightly modified in order to integrate the representation of latent variable, i.e., $\mathbf{h}_e$, into the computational cell (see Suppl. 1.3), in which the latent variable can affect the hidden representation through the gates. This allows the model can indirectly take advantage of the underlying semantic information from the latent variable z. In addition, when the model learns unseen dialogue acts, the semantic representation $\mathbf{h}_e$ can benefit the generation process (see Table 1).

We finally obtain the VNLG model with RNN Utterance Encoder (R-VNLG) or with CNN Utterance Encoder (C-VNLG).

3.2 Variational CNN-DCNN Model

This standard VAE model (left side in Figure 2) acts as an auxiliary auto-encoding for utterance (used at training time) to the VNLG generator. The model consists of two components. While the *shared* CNN Utterance Encoder with the VNLG model is to compute the latent representation vector $\mathbf{h}_U$ (see Suppl. 1.1.3), a Deconvolutional CNN Decoder to decode the latent representation $\mathbf{h}_e$ back to the source text (see Suppl. 2.1). Specifically, after having the vector representation $\mathbf{h}_U$, we apply another linear regression to obtain the distribution parameter $\mu_2 = \mathbf{W}_{\mu_2}\mathbf{h}_U + b_{\mu_2}$ and $\log \sigma_2^2 = \mathbf{W}_{\sigma_2}\mathbf{h}_U + b_{\sigma_2}$. We then re-parameterize them to obtain a latent representation $\mathbf{h}_{zu} = \mu_2 + \sigma_2 \odot \epsilon$, where $\epsilon \sim \mathcal{N}(0, \mathbf{I})$. In order to integrate the latent variable $\mathbf{h}_{zu}$ into the DCNN Decoder, we use the *shared* non-linear transformation as in Eq. 7 (denoted by the black-dashed line in Figure 2) as: $\mathbf{h}_e = g(\mathbf{W}_e\mathbf{h}_{zu} + b_e)$.

The entire resulting model, named DualVAE, by incorporating the VNLG with the Variational CNN-DCNN model, is depicted in Figure 2.

4 Training Dual Latent Variable Model

4.1 Training VNLG Model

Inspired by work of Zhang et al. (2016), we also employ the Monte-Carlo method to approximate the expectation of the posterior in Eq. 2, *i.e.* $\mathbb{E}_{q_\phi(z|\mathbf{d},\mathbf{u})}[.] \simeq \frac{1}{M}\sum_{m=1}^{M} \log p_\theta(\mathbf{u}|\mathbf{d}, \mathbf{h}_z^{(m)})$ where M is the number of samples. In this work, the joint training objective $\mathcal{L}_{\text{VNLG}}$ for a training instance pair $(\mathbf{d}, \mathbf{u})$ is formulated as:

$$\mathcal{L}(\theta, \phi, \mathbf{d}, \mathbf{u}) \simeq -KL(q_\phi(z|\mathbf{d}, \mathbf{u})||p_\theta(z|\mathbf{d}))$$
$$+ \frac{1}{M} \sum_{m=1}^{M} \sum_{t=1}^{T_U} \log p_\theta(\mathbf{u}_t|\mathbf{u}_{<t}, \mathbf{d}, \mathbf{h}_z^{(m)}) \tag{9}$$

where $\mathbf{h}_z^{(m)} = \mu + \sigma \odot \epsilon^{(m)}$, and $\epsilon^{(m)} \sim \mathcal{N}(0, \mathbf{I})$, and θ and ϕ denote decoder and encoder parameters, respectively. The first term is the KL divergence between two Gaussian distribution, and the second term is the approximation expectation. We simply set $M = 1$ which degenerates the second term to the objective of conventional generator. Since the objective function in Eq. 9 is differentiable, we can jointly optimize the parameter θ and variational parameter ϕ using standard gradient ascent techniques. However, the KL divergence loss tends to be significantly small during training (Bowman et al., 2015). As a results,

the decoder does not take advantage of information from the latent variable z. Thus, we apply the KL cost annealing strategy that encourages the model to encode meaningful representations into the latent vector z, in which we gradually anneal the KL term from 0 to 1. This helps our model to achieve solutions with non-zero KL term.

4.2 Training Variational CNN-DCNN Model

The objective function $\mathcal{L}_{\text{CNN-DCNN}}$ of the Variational CNN-DCNN model is the standard VAE lower bound and maximized as follows:

$$\mathcal{L}(\theta', \phi', \mathbf{u}) = -KL(q_{\phi'}(z|\mathbf{u})||p_{\theta'}(z))$$
$$+ \mathbb{E}_{q_{\phi'}(z|\mathbf{u})}[\log p_{\theta'}(\mathbf{u}|z)] \leq \log p(\mathbf{u}) \tag{10}$$

where θ' and ϕ' denote decoder and encoder parameters, respectively. During training, we also consider a denoising autoencoder where we slightly modify the input by swapping some arbitrary word pairs.

4.3 Joint Training Dual VAE Model

To allow the model explore and balance maximizing the variational lower bound between the Variational CNN-DCNN model and VNLG model, an objective is joint training as follows:

$$\mathcal{L}_{\text{DualVAE}} = \mathcal{L}_{\text{VNLG}} + \alpha\mathcal{L}_{\text{CNN-DCNN}} \tag{11}$$

where α controls the relative weight between two variational losses. During training, we anneal the value of α from 1 to 0, so that the dual latent variable learned can gradually focus less on reconstruction objective of the CNN-DCNN model, only retain those features that are useful for the generation objective.

4.4 Joint Cross Training Dual VAE Model

To allow the dual VAE model explore and encode useful information of the Dialogue Act into the latent variable, we further take a cross training between two VAEs by simply replacing the RALSTM Decoder of the VNLG model with the DCNN Utterance Decoder and its objective training $\mathcal{L}_{\text{DA-DCNN}}$ as:

$$\mathcal{L}(\theta', \phi, \mathbf{d}, \mathbf{u}) \simeq -KL(q_\phi(z|\mathbf{d}, \mathbf{u})||p_{\theta'}(z|\mathbf{d}))$$
$$+ \mathbb{E}_{q_\phi(z|\mathbf{d},\mathbf{u})}[\log p_{\theta'}(\mathbf{u}|z, \mathbf{d})], \tag{12}$$

and a joint cross training objective is employed:

$$\mathcal{L}_{\text{CrossVAE}} = \mathcal{L}_{\text{VNLG}}$$
$$+ \alpha(\mathcal{L}_{\text{CNN-DCNN}} + \mathcal{L}_{\text{DA-DCNN}}) \tag{13}$$

5 Experiments

We assessed the proposed models on four different original NLG domains: finding a restaurant and hotel (Wen et al., 2015a), or buying a laptop and television (Wen et al., 2016b).

5.1 Evaluation Metrics and Baselines

The generator performances were evaluated using the two metrics: the BLEU and the slot error rate ERR by adopting code from an NLG toolkit*. We compared the proposed models against strong baselines which have been recently published as NLG benchmarks of those datasets, including (i) gating models such as HLSTM (Wen et al., 2015a), and SCLSTM (Wen et al., 2015b); and (ii) attention models such as Enc-Dec (Wen et al., 2016b), RALSTM (Tran and Nguyen, 2017).

5.2 Experimental Setups

In this work, the CNN Utterance Encoder consists of $L = 3$ layers, which for a sentence of length $T = 73$, embedding size $d = 100$, stride length $s = \{2, 2, 2\}$, number of filters $k = \{300, 600, 100\}$ with filter sizes $h = \{5, 5, 16\}$, results in feature maps $\mathbf{V}$ of sizes $\{35 \times 300, 16 \times 600, 1 \times 100\}$, in which the last feature map corresponds to latent representation vector $\mathbf{h_U}$.

The hidden layer size and beam width were set to be 100 and 10, respectively, and the models were trained with a 70% of keep dropout rate. We performed 5 runs with different random initialization of the network, and the training process is terminated by using early stopping. For the variational inference, we set the latent variable size to be 300. We used Adam optimizer with the learning rate is initially set to be 0.001, and after 5 epochs the learning rate is decayed every epoch using an exponential rate of 0.95.

6 Results and Analysis

We performed the models in different scenarios as follows: (i) *scratch* training where models trained from scratch using 10% (*scr10*), 30% (*scr30*), and 100% (*scr100*) amount of in-domain data; and (ii) domain *adaptation* training where models pre-trained from scratch using all source domain data, then fine-tuned on the target domain using only 10% amount of the target data. Overall, the proposed models can work well in scenarios

*https://github.com/shawnwun/RNNLG

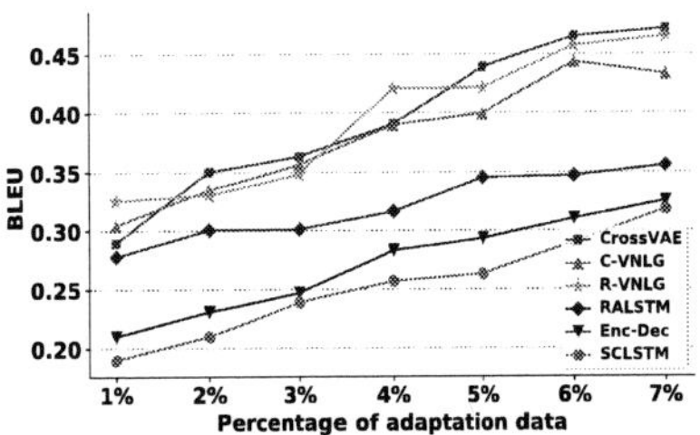

Figure 3: Performance on Laptop domain with varied limited amount, from 1% to 7%, of the adaptation training data when adapting models pre-trained on [Restaurant+Hotel] union dataset.

of low-resource setting data. The proposed models obtained state-of-the-art performances regarding both the evaluation metrics across all domains in all training scenarios.

6.1 Integrating Variational Inference

We compare the encoder-decoder RALSTM model to its modification by integrating with variational inference (R-VNLG and C-VNLG) as demonstrated in Figure 3 and Table 1.

It clearly shows that the variational generators not only provide a compelling evidence on adapting to a new, unseen domain when the target domain data is scarce, *i.e.*, from 1% to 7% (Figure 3) but also preserve the power of the original RALSTM on generation task since their performances are very competitive to those of RALSTM (Table 1, *scr100*). Table 1, *scr10* further shows the necessity of the integrating in which the VNLGs achieved a significant improvement over the RALSTM in *scr10* scenario where the models trained from *scratch* with only a limited amount of training data (10%). These indicate that the proposed variational method can learn the underlying semantic of the existing DA-utterance pairs, which are especially useful information for low-resource setting.

Furthermore, the R-VNLG model has slightly better results than the C-VNLG when providing sufficient training data in *scr100*. In contrast, with a modest training data, in *scr10*, the latter model demonstrates a significant improvement compared to the former in terms of both the BLEU and ERR scores by a large margin across all four dataset. Take Hotel domain, for example, the C-VNLG model (79.98 BLEU, 8.67% ERR) has better results in comparison to the R-VNLG (73.78 BLEU, 15.43% ERR) and RAL-

	Model	Hotel		Restaurant		Tv		Laptop	
		BLEU	ERR	BLEU	ERR	BLEU	ERR	BLEU	ERR
scr100	HLSTM	0.8488	2.79%	0.7436	0.85%	0.5240	2.65%	0.5130	1.15%
	SCLSTM	0.8469	3.12%	0.7543	0.57%	0.5235	2.41%	0.5109	0.89%
	ENCDEC	0.8537	4.78%	0.7358	2.98%	0.5142	3.38%	0.5101	4.24%
	RALSTM	**0.8965**	0.58%	*0.7779*	*0.20%*	*0.5373*	*0.49%*	*0.5231*	*0.50%*
	R-VNLG (Ours)	0.8851	0.57%	0.7709	0.36%	0.5356	0.73%	0.5210	0.59%
	C-VNLG (Ours)	0.8811	*0.49%*	0.7651	**0.06%**	0.5350	0.88%	0.5192	*0.56%*
	DualVAE (Ours)	0.8813	**0.33%**	0.7695	0.29%	0.5359	0.81%	0.5211	0.91%
	CrossVAE (Ours)	*0.8926*	0.72%	**0.7786**	0.54%	**0.5383**	0.48%	**0.5240**	**0.50%**
scr10	HLSTM	0.7483	8.69%	0.6586	6.93%	0.4819	9.39%	0.4813	7.37%
	SCLSTM	0.7626	17.42%	0.6446	16.93%	0.4290	31.87%	0.4729	15.89%
	ENCDEC	0.7370	23.19%	0.6174	23.63%	0.4570	21.28%	0.4604	29.86%
	RALSTM	0.6855	22.53%	0.6003	17.65%	0.4009	22.37%	0.4475	24.47%
	R-VNLG (Ours)	0.7378	15.43%	0.6417	15.69%	0.4392	17.45%	0.4851	10.06%
	C-VNLG (Ours)	0.7998	8.67%	0.6838	*6.86%*	0.5040	5.31%	0.4932	3.56%
	DualVAE (Ours)	*0.8022*	**6.61%**	*0.6926*	7.69%	*0.5110*	**3.90%**	*0.5016*	*2.44%*
	CrossVAE (Ours)	**0.8103**	**6.20%**	**0.6969**	**4.06%**	**0.5152**	**2.86%**	**0.5085**	**2.39%**
scr30	HLSTM	0.8104	6.39%	0.7044	2.13%	0.5024	5.82%	0.4859	6.70%
	SCLSTM	0.8271	6.23%	0.6825	4.80%	0.4934	7.97%	0.5001	3.52%
	ENCDEC	0.7865	9.38%	0.7102	13.47%	0.5014	9.19%	0.4907	10.72%
	RALSTM	0.8334	4.23%	0.7145	2.67%	0.5124	3.53%	0.5106	2.22%
	C-VNLG (Ours)	*0.8553*	2.64%	0.7256	*0.96%*	0.5265	**0.66%**	*0.5117*	2.15%
	DualVAE (Ours)	0.8534	*1.54%*	*0.7301*	2.32%	*0.5288*	1.05%	0.5107	*0.93%*
	CrossVAE (Ours)	**0.8585**	**1.37%**	**0.7479**	**0.49%**	**0.5307**	*0.82%*	**0.5154**	**0.81%**

Table 1: Results evaluated on four domains by training models from *scratch* with *10%*, *30%*, and *100%* in-domain data, respectively. The results were averaged over 5 randomly initialized networks. The **bold** and *italic* faces denote the best and second best models in each training scenario, respectively.

STM (68.55 BLEU, 22.53% ERR). Thus, the rest experiments focus on the C-VNLG since it shows obvious sign for constructing a dual latent variable models dealing with low-resource in-domain data. We leave the R-VNLG for future investigation.

6.2 Ablation Studies

The ablation studies (Table 1) demonstrate the contribution of each model components, in which we incrementally train the baseline RALSTM, the C-VNLG (= RALSTM + Variational inference), the DualVAE (= C-VNLG + Variational CNN-DCNN), and the CrossVAE (= DualVAE + Cross training) models. Generally, while all models can work well when there are sufficient training datasets, the performances of the proposed models also increase as increasing the model components. The trend is consistent across all training cases no matter how much the training data was provided. Take, for example, the *scr100* scenario in which the CrossVAE model mostly outperformed all the previous strong baselines with regard to the BLEU and the slot error rate ERR scores.

On the other hand, the previous methods showed extremely impaired performances regarding low BLEU score and high slot error rate ERR when training the models from *scratch* with only 10% of in-domain data (*scr10*). In contrast, by integrating the variational inference, the C-VNLG model, for example in Hotel domain, can significantly improve the BLEU score from 68.55 to 79.98, and also reduce the slot error rate ERR by a large margin, from 22.53 to 8.67, compared to the RALSTM baseline. Moreover, the proposed models have much better performance over the previous ones in the *scr10* scenario since the CrossVAE, and the DualVAE models mostly obtained the best and second best results, respectively. The CrossVAE model trained on *scr10* scenario, in some cases, achieved results which close to those of the HLSTM, SCLSTM, and ENCDEC models trained on all training data (*scr100*) scenario. Take, for example, the most challenge dataset Laptop, in which the DualVAE and CrossVAE obtained competitive results regarding the BLEU score, at 50.16 and 50.85 respectively, which close to those of the HLSTM (51.30 BLEU), SCLSTM (51.09 BLEU), and ENCDEC (51.01 BLEU), while the results regardless the slot error rate ERR scores are also close to those of the previous or even better in some cases, for example DualVAE (2.44 ERR), CrossVAE (2.39 ERR),

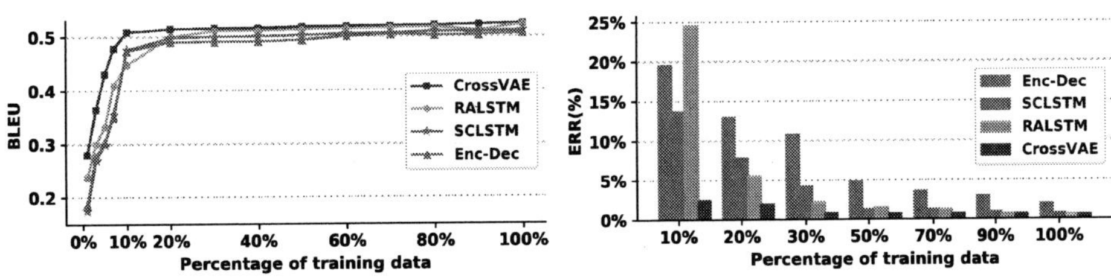

Figure 4: Performance comparison of the models trained on Laptop domain.

and ENCDEC (4.24 ERR). There are also some cases in TV domain where the proposed models (in *scr10*) have results close to or better over the previous ones (trained on *scr100*). These indicate that the proposed models can encode useful information into the latent variable efficiently to better generalize to the unseen dialogue acts, addressing the second difficulty with low-resource data.

The *scr30* section further confirms the effectiveness of the proposed methods, in which the Cross-VAE and DualVAE still mostly rank the best and second-best models compared with the baselines. The proposed models also show superior ability in leveraging the existing small training data to obtain very good performances, which are in many cases even better than those of the previous methods trained on 100% of in-domain data. Take Tv domain, for example, in which the CrossVAE in *scr30* achieves a good result regarding BLEU and slot error rate ERR score, at 53.07 BLEU and 0.82 ERR, that are not only competitive to the RALSTM (53.73 BLEU, 0.49 ERR), but also outperform the previous models in *scr100* training scenario, such as HLSTM (52.40 BLEU, 2.65 ERR), SCLSTM (52.35 BLEU, 2.41 ERR), and ENCDEC (51.42 BLEU, 3.38 ERR). This further indicates the need of the integrating with variational inference, the additional auxiliary auto-encoding, as well as the joint and cross training.

6.3 Model comparison on unseen domain

In this experiment, we trained four models (ENCDEC, SCLSTM, RALSTM, and CrossVAE) from *scratch* in the most difficult unseen Laptop domain with an increasingly varied proportion of training data, start from 1% to 100%. The results are shown in Figure 4. It clearly sees that the BLEU score increases and the slot error ERR decreases as the models are trained on more data. The CrossVAE model is clearly better than the previous models (ENCDEC, SCLSTM, RALSTM) in all cases. While the performance of the Cross-VAE, RALSTM model starts to saturate around 30% and 50%, respectively, the ENCDEC model

seems to continue getting better as providing more training data. The figure also confirms that the CrossVAE trained on 30% of data can achieve a better performance compared to those of the previous models trained on 100% of in-domain data.

6.4 Domain Adaptation

We further examine the domain scalability of the proposed methods by training the CrossVAE and SCLSTM models on *adaptation* scenarios, in which we first trained the models on out-of-domain data, and then fine-tuned the model parameters by using a small amount (10%) of in-domain data. The results are shown in Table 2.

Both SCLSTM and CrossVAE models can take advantage of "*close*" dataset pairs, *i.e.*, Restaurant ↔ Hotel, and Tv ↔ Laptop, to achieve better performances compared to those of the "*different*" dataset pairs, *i.e.* Latop ↔ Restaurant. Moreover, Table 2 clearly shows that the SCLSTM (denoted by ♭) is limited to scale to another domain in terms of having very low BLEU and high ERR scores. This adaptation scenario along with the *scr10* and *scr30* in Table 1 demonstrate that the SCLSTM can not work when having a low-resource setting of in-domain training data.

On the other hand, the CrossVAE model again show ability in leveraging the out-of-domain data to better adapt to a new domain. Especially in the case where Laptop, which is a most difficult unseen domain, is the target domain the Cross-VAE model can obtain good results irrespective of low slot error rate ERR, around 1.90%, and high BLEU score, around 50.00 points. Surprisingly, the CrossVAE model trained on *scr10* scenario in some cases achieves better performance compared to those in adaptation scenario first trained with 30% out-of-domain data (denoted by ♮) which is also better than the adaptation model trained on 100% out-of-domain data (denoted by ξ).

Preliminary experiments on semi-supervised training were also conducted, in which we trained the CrossVAE model with the same 10% in-domain *labeled* data as in the other scenarios and

Target Source	Hotel		Restaurant		Tv		Laptop	
	BLEU	ERR	BLEU	ERR	BLEU	ERR	BLEU	ERR
Hotel[♭]	-	-	0.6243	11.20%	0.4325	29.12%	0.4603	22.52%
Restaurant[♭]	0.7329	29.97%	-	-	0.4520	24.34%	0.4619	21.40%
Tv[♭]	0.7030	25.63%	0.6117	12.78%	-	-	0.4794	11.80%
Laptop[♭]	0.6764	39.21%	0.5940	28.93%	0.4750	14.17%	-	-
Hotel[♯]	-	-	0.7138	2.91%	0.5012	5.83%	0.4949	1.97%
Restaurant[♯]	0.7984	4.04%	-	-	0.5120	3.26%	0.4947	1.87%
Tv[♯]	0.7614	5.82%	0.6900	5.93%	-	-	0.4937	1.91%
Laptop[♯]	0.7804	5.87%	0.6565	6.97%	0.5037	3.66%	-	-
Hotel[ξ]	-	-	0.6926	3.56%	0.4866	11.99%	0.5017	3.56%
Restaurant[ξ]	0.7802	3.20%	-	-	0.4953	3.10%	0.4902	4.05%
Tv[ξ]	0.7603	8.69%	0.6830	5.73%	-	-	0.5055	2.86%
Laptop[ξ]	0.7807	8.20%	0.6749	5.84%	0.4988	5.53%	-	-
CrossVAE (*scr10*)	0.8103	6.20%	0.6969	4.06%	0.5152	2.86%	0.5085	2.39%
CrossVAE (*semi-U50-L10*)	0.8144	6.12%	0.6946	3.94%	0.5158	2.95%	0.5086	1.31%

Table 2: Results evaluated on **Target** domains by *adaptation* training SCLSTM model from 100% (denoted as ♭) of Source data, and the CrossVAE model from 30% (denoted as ♯), 100% (denoted as ξ) of Source data. The scenario used only 10% amount of the **Target** domain data. The last two rows show results by training the CrossVAE model on the *scr10* and semi-supervised learning, respectively.

50% in-domain *unlabeled* data by keeping only the utterances **u** in a given input pair of dialogue act-utterance (**d**, **u**), denoted by *semi-U50-L10*. The results showed CrossVAE's ability in leveraging the unlabeled data to achieve slightly better results compared to those in *scratch* scenario. All these stipulate that the proposed models can perform acceptably well in training cases of *scratch*, domain *adaptation*, and *semi-supervised* where the in-domain training data is in short supply.

6.5 Comparison on Generated Outputs

We present top responses generated for different scenarios from TV (Table 3) and Laptop (Table 4), which further show the effectiveness of the proposed methods.

On the one hand, previous models trained on *scr10*, *scr30* scenarios produce a diverse range of the outputs' error types, including missing, misplaced, redundant, wrong slots, or spelling mistake information, resulting in a very high score of the slot error rate ERR. The ENCDEC, HLSTM and SCLSTM models in Table 3-**DA 1**, for example, tend to generate outputs with redundant slots (*i.e.*, *SLOT_HDMIPORT*, *SLOT_NAME*, *SLOT_FAMILY*), missing slots (*i.e.*, [17 family], [4 hdmi port -s]), or even in some cases produce irrelevant slots (*i.e.*, *SLOT_AUDIO*, *eco rating*), resulting in inadequate utterances.

On the other hand, the proposed models can effectively leverage the knowledge from only few of the existing training instances to better generalize to the unseen dialogue acts, leading to satisfactory responses. For example in Table 3, the proposed methods can generate adequate number of the required slots, resulting in fulfilled utterances (DualVAE-10, CrossVAE-10, DualVAE-30, CrossVAE-30), or acceptable outputs with much fewer error information, *i.e.*, mis-ordered slots in the generated utterances (C-VNLG-30).

For a much easier dialogue act in Table 3-**DA 2**, previous models still produce some error outputs, whereas the proposed methods seem to form some specific slots into phrase in concise outputs. For example, instead of generating "the *proteus 73* is a *television*" phrase, the proposed models tend to concisely produce "the *proteus 73 television*". The trend is mostly consistent to those in Table 4.

7 Conclusion and Future Work

We present an approach to low-resource NLG by integrating the variational inference and introducing a novel auxiliary auto-encoding. Experiments showed that the models can perform acceptably well using a scarce dataset. The ablation studies demonstrate that the variational generator contributes to learning the underlying semantic of DA-utterance pairs, while the variational CNN-DCNN plays an important role of encoding useful information into the latent variable. In the future, we further investigate the proposed models with adversarial training, semi-supervised, or unsupervised training.

Acknowledgements

This work was supported by the JST CREST Grant Number JPMJCR1513, the JSPS KAKENHI Grant number 15K16048 and the grant of a collaboration between JAIST and TIS.

Model	Generated Responses from TV Domain
DA 1	compare(name='*typhon 45*'; hdmiport='2'; family='*l2*'; name='*hades 48*'; hdmiport='4'; family='*l7*')
Reference 1	Compared to *typhon 45* which has *2 hdmi port -s* and is in the *L2 product family*, *hades 48* has *4 hdmi port -s* and is in the *L7 product family*. Which one do you prefer ?
ENCDEC-10	the *typhon 45* is in the *l2 product family* and has *2 hdmi port -s* and is in the *l7 product family* with *4 hdmi port -s*, the *hades 48* is in the *SLOT_FAMILY* product family with a *SLOT_AUDIO*.
HLSTM-10	the *typhon 45* is a great *eco rating*, the *hades 48* is in the *l2 family* with *2 hdmi port -s*. [l7 family] [4 hdmi port -s]
SCLSTM-10	the *typhon 45* is the *hades 48* with *2 hdmi port* in the *l2 family*, the *SLOT_NAME* has *4 hdmi port -s* and *SLOT_HDMIPORT* hdmi port. [l7 family]
C-VNLG-10	the *typhon 45* has *2 hdmi port -s* and the *hades 48* is in the *l2 family* and has *4 hdmi port -s*. [l7 family]
DualVAE-10	the *typhon 45* has *2 hdmi port -s* and is in the *l2 family* while the *hades 48* has *4 hdmi port -s* and is in the *l7 family*. [OK]
CrossVAE-10	the *typhon 45* is in the *l2 family* with *2 hdmi port -s* while the *hades 48* has *4 hdmi port -s* and is in the *l7 family*. [OK]
ENCDEC-30	the *typhon 45* has *2 hdmi port -s*, the *hades 48* has *4 hdmi port -s*, the *SLOT_NAME* has *SLOT_HDMIPORT* hdmi port. [l2 family] [l7 family]
HLSTM-30	the *typhon 45* is in the *l2 product family* with *2 hdmi port -s*, whereas the *hades 48* has *4 hdmi port*. [l7 family]
SCLSTM-30	the *typhon 45* has *2 hdmi port -s*, the *hades 48* is in the *l2 product family*. [l7 family] [4 hdmi port -s]
C-VNLG-30	the *typhon 45* has *2 hdmi port -s*, the *hades 48* is in the *l2 product family* and has *4 hdmi port -s* in *l7 family*.
DualVAE-30	which do you prefer, the *typhon 45* in the *l2 product family* with *2 hdmi port -s* . the *hades 48* is in the *l7 family* with *4 hdmi port -s*. [OK]
CrossVAE-30	the *typhon 45* has *2 hdmi port -s* and in the *l2 family* while the *hades 48* has *4 hdmi port -s* and is in the *l7 family*. which item do you prefer. [OK]
DA 2	recommend(name='*proteus 73*'; type='*television*'; price='*1500 dollars*'; audio='*nicam stereo*'; hdmiport='2')
Reference 2	*proteus 73* is a nice *television*. its price is *1500 dollars*, its audio is *nicam stereo*, and it has *2 hdmi port -s*.
ENCDEC-10	the *proteus 73* is a great *television* with a *nicam stereo* and *2 hdmi port -s* [1500 dollars]
HLSTM-10	the *proteus 73* is a *television* with *2 hdmi port -s* and comes with a *nicam stereo* and costs *1500 dollars* [OK]
SCLSTM-10	the *proteus 73* is a nice *television* with *nicam stereo* and *2 hdmi port -s* [1500 dollars]
C-VNLG-10	the *proteus 73 television* has a *nicam stereo* and *2 hdmi port -s* and costs *1500 dollars* [OK]
DualVAE-10	the *proteus 73 television* has a *nicam stereo* and *2 hdmi port -s* and costs *1500 dollars* [OK]
CrossVAE-10	the *proteus 73 television* has *2 hdmi port -s* and a *nicam stereo* and costs *1500 dollars* [OK]
ENCDEC-30	the *proteus 73 television* has *2 hdmi port -s* and *nicam stereo* audio for *1500 dollars* [OK]
HLSTM-30	the *proteus 73 television* has a *nicam stereo* and *2 hdmi port -s* and is priced at *1500 dollars* [OK]
SCLSTM-30	the *proteus 73* is a nice *television* with *nicam stereo* and *2 hdmi port -s* . it is priced at *1500 dollars* [OK]
C-VNLG-30	the *proteus 73 television* has *2 hdmi port -s* , *nicam stereo* audio , and costs *1500 dollars* [OK]
DualVAE-30	the *proteus 73 television* has *2 hdmi port -s* and *nicam stereo* audio and costs *1500 dollars* [OK]
CrossVAE-30	the *proteus 73 television* has *2 hdmi port -s* and *nicam stereo* audio and costs *1500 dollars* [OK]

Table 3: Comparison of top **Tv** responses generated for different models in different scenarios. Errors are marked in colors ([missing], misplaced, redundant, wrong, spelling mistake information). [OK] denotes successful generation. Model-X where X is amount of training data, *i.e.* 10%, 30%, or 100%.

Model	Generated Responses from Laptop Domain
DA	compare(name='*satellite pallas 21*'; battery='*4 hour*'; drive='*500 gb*'; name='*satellite dinlas 18*'; battery='*3.5 hour*'; drive='*1 tb*')
Reference	compared to satellite *pallas 21* which can last *4 hour* and has a *500 gb drive* , *satellite dinlas 18* can last *3.5 hour* and has a *1 tb drive* . which one do you prefer
Enc-Dec-10	the *satellite pallas 21* has a *500 gb drive* , the *satellite dinlas 18* has a *4 hour battery* life and a *3.5 hour battery* life and a *SLOT_BATTERY* battery life and a *1 tb drive*
HLSTM-10	the *satellite pallas 21* has a *4 hour battery* life and a *500 gb drive* . which one do you prefer [satellite pallas 18] [3.5 hour battery] [1 tb drive]
SCLSTM-10	the *satellite pallas 21* has a *4 hour battery* , and has a *3.5 hour battery* life and a *500 gb drive* and a *1 tb drive* [satellite dinlas 18]
C-VNLG-10	the *satellite pallas 21* has a *500 gb drive* and a *4 hour battery* life . the *satellite dinlas 18* has a *3.5 hour battery* life and a *SLOT_BATTERY* battery life [1 tb drive]
DualVAE-10	the *satellite pallas 21* has a *4 hour battery* life and a *500 gb drive* and the *satellite dinlas 18* with a *3.5 hour battery* life and *is good for business computing* . which one do you prefer [1 tb drive]
CrossVAE-10	the *satellite pallas 21* with *500 gb* and a *1 tb drive* . the *satellite dinlas 18* with a *4 hour battery* and a *SLOT_DRIVE* drive . which one do you prefer [3.5 hour battery]
Enc-Dec-30	the *satellite pallas 21* has a *500 gb drive* with a *1 tb drive* and is the *satellite dinlas 18* with a *SLOT_DRIVE* drive for *4 hour -s* . which one do you prefer [3.5 hour battery]
HLSTM-30	the *satellite pallas 21* is a *500 gb drive* with a *4 hour battery* life . the *satellite dinlas 18* has a *3.5 hour battery* life . which one do you prefer [1 tb drive]
SCLSTM-30	the *satellite pallas 21* has a *500 gb drive* . the *satellite dinlas 18* has a *4 hour battery* life . the *SLOT_NAME* has a *3.5 hour battery* life . which one do you prefer [1 tb drive]
C-VNLG-30	which one do you prefer the *satellite pallas 21* with a *4 hour battery* life , the *satellite dinlas 18* has a *500 gb drive* and a *3.5 hour battery* life and a 1 tb drive . which one do you prefer
DualVAE-30	*satellite pallas 21* has a *500 gb drive* and a *4 hour battery* life while the *satellite dinlas 18* with a *3.5 hour battery* life and a *1 tb drive* . [OK]
CrossVAE-30	the *satellite pallas 21* has a *500 gb drive* with a *4 hour battery* life . the *satellite dinlas 18* has a *1 tb drive* and a *3.5 hour battery* life . which one do you prefer [OK]

Table 4: Comparison of top **Laptop** responses generated for different models in different scenarios. Errors are marked in colors ([missing], misplaced, redundant, wrong, spelling information). [OK] denotes successful generation. Model-X where X is amount of training data, *i.e.* 10%, 30%, or 100%.

References

Samy Bengio, Oriol Vinyals, Navdeep Jaitly, and Noam Shazeer. 2015. Scheduled sampling for sequence prediction with recurrent neural networks. In *Advances in Neural Information Processing Systems*, pages 1171–1179.

Samuel R. Bowman, Luke Vilnis, Oriol Vinyals, Andrew M. Dai, Rafal Józefowicz, and Samy Bengio. 2015. Generating sentences from a continuous space. *CoRR*, abs/1511.06349.

Junyoung Chung, Sungjin Ahn, and Yoshua Bengio. 2016. Hierarchical multiscale recurrent neural networks. *arXiv preprint arXiv:1609.01704*.

Junyoung Chung, Kyle Kastner, Laurent Dinh, Kratarth Goel, Aaron C Courville, and Yoshua Bengio. 2015. A recurrent latent variable model for sequential data. In *Advances in neural information processing systems*, pages 2980–2988.

Diederik P Kingma and Max Welling. 2013. Auto-encoding variational bayes. *arXiv preprint arXiv:1312.6114*.

Esther Levin, Shrikanth Narayanan, Roberto Pieraccini, Konstantin Biatov, Enrico Bocchieri, Giuseppe Di Fabbrizio, Wieland Eckert, Sungbok Lee, A Pokrovsky, Mazin Rahim, et al. 2000. The at&t-darpa communicator mixed-initiative spoken dialog system. In *Sixth International Conference on Spoken Language Processing*.

François Mairesse, Milica Gašić, Filip Jurčíček, Simon Keizer, Blaise Thomson, Kai Yu, and Steve Young. 2010. Phrase-based statistical language generation using graphical models and active learning. In *Proceedings of the 48th Annual Meeting of the Association for Computational Linguistics*, ACL '10, pages 1552–1561, Stroudsburg, PA, USA. Association for Computational Linguistics.

Stanislau Semeniuta, Aliaksei Severyn, and Erhardt Barth. 2017. A hybrid convolutional variational autoencoder for text generation. *arXiv preprint arXiv:1702.02390*.

Dinghan Shen, Yizhe Zhang, Ricardo Henao, Qinliang Su, and Lawrence Carin. 2017. Deconvolutional latent-variable model for text sequence matching. *arXiv preprint arXiv:1709.07109*.

Kihyuk Sohn, Honglak Lee, and Xinchen Yan. 2015. Learning structured output representation using deep conditional generative models. In *Advances in Neural Information Processing Systems*, pages 3483–3491.

Van-Khanh Tran and Le-Minh Nguyen. 2017. Natural language generation for spoken dialogue system using rnn encoder-decoder networks. In *Proceedings of the 21st Conference on Computational Natural Language Learning (CoNLL 2017)*, pages 442–451, Vancouver, Canada. Association for Computational Linguistics.

Van-Khanh Tran, Le-Minh Nguyen, and Satoshi Tojo. 2017. Neural-based natural language generation in dialogue using rnn encoder-decoder with semantic aggregation. In *Proceedings of the 18th Annual SIGdial Meeting on Discourse and Dialogue*, pages 231–240, Saarbrcken, Germany. Association for Computational Linguistics.

Tsung-Hsien Wen, Milica Gašić, Dongho Kim, Nikola Mrkšić, Pei-Hao Su, David Vandyke, and Steve Young. 2015a. Stochastic Language Generation in Dialogue using Recurrent Neural Networks with Convolutional Sentence Reranking. In *Proceedings SIGDIAL*. Association for Computational Linguistics.

Tsung-Hsien Wen, Milica Gasic, Nikola Mrksic, Lina M Rojas-Barahona, Pei-Hao Su, David Vandyke, and Steve Young. 2016a. Multi-domain neural network language generation for spoken dialogue systems. *arXiv preprint arXiv:1603.01232*.

Tsung-Hsien Wen, Milica Gašic, Nikola Mrkšic, Lina M Rojas-Barahona, Pei-Hao Su, David Vandyke, and Steve Young. 2016b. Toward multi-domain language generation using recurrent neural networks.

Tsung-Hsien Wen, Milica Gašić, Nikola Mrkšić, Pei-Hao Su, David Vandyke, and Steve Young. 2015b. Semantically conditioned lstm-based natural language generation for spoken dialogue systems. In *Proceedings of EMNLP*. Association for Computational Linguistics.

Zichao Yang, Zhiting Hu, Ruslan Salakhutdinov, and Taylor Berg-Kirkpatrick. 2017. Improved variational autoencoders for text modeling using dilated convolutions. *arXiv preprint arXiv:1702.08139*.

B. Zhang, D. Xiong, J. Su, H. Duan, and M. Zhang. 2016. Variational Neural Machine Translation. *ArXiv e-prints*.

Yizhe Zhang, Dinghan Shen, Guoyin Wang, Zhe Gan, Ricardo Henao, and Lawrence Carin. 2017. Deconvolutional paragraph representation learning. In *Advances in Neural Information Processing Systems*, pages 4172–4182.

A Trio Neural Model for Dynamic Entity Relatedness Ranking

Tu Ngoc Nguyen
L3S Research Center
tunguyen@L3S.de

Tuan Tran
Robert Bosch GmbH
anhtuan.tran2@de.bosch.com

Wolfgang Nejdl
L3S Research Center
nejdl@L3S.de

Abstract

Measuring entity relatedness is a fundamental task for many natural language processing and information retrieval applications. Prior work often studies entity relatedness in static settings and an unsupervised manner. However, entities in real-world are often involved in many different relationships, consequently entity-relations are very dynamic over time. In this work, we propose a neural network-based approach for *dynamic* entity relatedness, leveraging the *collective attention* as supervision. Our model is capable of learning rich and different entity representations in a joint framework. Through extensive experiments on large-scale datasets, we demonstrate that our method achieves better results than competitive baselines.

1 Introduction

Measuring semantic relatedness between entities is an inherent component in many text mining applications. In search and recommendation, the ability to suggest most related entities to the entity-bearing query has become a standard feature of popular Web search engines (Blanco et al., 2013). In natural language processing, entity relatedness is an important factor for various tasks, such as entity linking (Hoffart et al., 2012) or word sense disambiguation (Moro et al., 2014).

However, prior work on semantic relatedness often neglects the time dimension and consider entities and their relationships as static. In practice, many entities are highly ephemeral (Jiang et al., 2016), and users seeking information related to those entities would like to see fresh information. For example, users looking up the entity Taylor Lautner during 2008–2012 might want to be recommended with entities such as The Twilight Saga, due to Lautner's well-known performance in the film series; however the same query

in August 2016 should be served with entities related to his appearances in more recent films such as "Scream Queens", "Run the Tide". In addition, much of previous work resorts to deriving semantic relatedness from co-occurrence -based computations or heuristic functions without direct optimization to the final goal. We believe that desirable framework should see entity semantic relatedness as not separate but an integral part of the process, for instance in a supervised manner.

In this work, we address the problem of ***entity relatedness ranking***, that is, designing the semantic relatedness models that are optimized for ranking systems such as top-k entity retrieval or recommendation. In this setting, the goal is not to quantify the semantic relatedness between two entities based on their occurrences in the data, but to optimize the partial order of the related entities in the top positions. This problem differs from traditional entity ranking (Kang et al., 2015) in that the entity rankings are driven by user queries and are optimized to their (ad-hoc) information needs, while entity relatedness ranking also aims to uncover the meanings of the the relatedness from the data. In other words, while conventional entity semantic relatedness learns from data (editors or content providers' perspectives), and entity ranking learns from the user's perspective, the entity relatedness ranking takes the trade-off between these views. Such a hybrid approach can benefit applications such as exploratory entity search (Miliaraki et al., 2015), where users have a specific goal in mind, but at the same time are opened to other related entities.

We also tackle the issue of *dynamic ranking* and design the supervised-learning model that takes into account the temporal contexts of entities, and proposes to leverage *collective attention* from public sources. As an illustration, when one looks into the Wikipedia page of Taylor Lautner, each navi-

Proceedings of the 22nd Conference on Computational Natural Language Learning (CoNLL 2018), pages 31–41
Brussels, Belgium, October 31 - November 1, 2018. ©2018 Association for Computational Linguistics

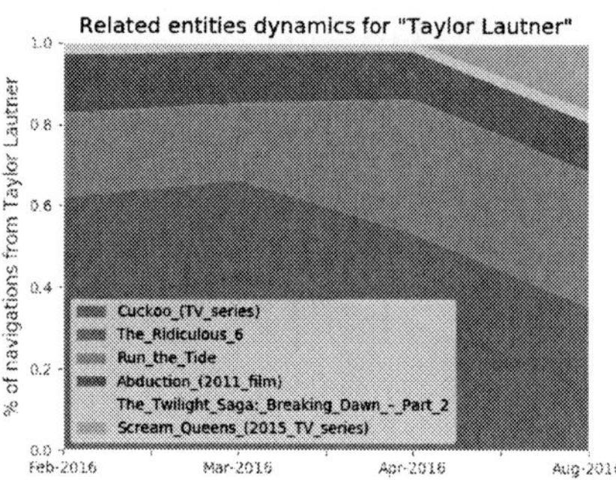

Figure 1: The dynamics of collective attention for related entities of Taylor Lautner in 2016.

gation to other Wikipedia pages indicates the user interest in the corresponding target entity given her initial interest in Lautner. Collectively, the navigation traffic observed over time is a good proxy to the shift of public attention to the entity (Figure 1).

In addition, while previous work mainly focuses on one aspect of the entities such as textual profiles or linking graphs , we propose a *trio neural* model that learns the low level representations of entities from three different aspects: Content, structures and time aspects. For the time aspect, we propose a convolutional model to *embed* and *attend* to local patterns of the past temporal signals in the Euclidean space. Experiments show that our trio model outperforms traditional approaches in ranking correlation and recommendation tasks. Our contributions are summarized as follows.

- We present the first study of dynamic entity relatedness ranking using collective attention.

- We introduce an attention-based convolutional neural networks (CNN) to capture the temporal signals of an entity.

- We propose a joint framework to incorporate multiple views of the entities, both from content provider and from user's perspectives, for entity relatedness ranking.

2 Related Work

2.1 Entity Relatedness and Recommendation

Most of existing semantic relatedness measures (e.g. derived from Wikipedia) can be divided into the following two major types: (1) *text*-based, (2) *graph*-based. For the first, traditional methods mainly focus on a high-dimensional semantic space based on occurrences of words (Gabrilovich and Markovitch (2007, 2009)) or concepts (Aggarwal and Buitelaar (2014)). In recent years, embedding methods that learn low-dimensional word representations have been proposed. Hu et al. (2015) leverages entity embedding on knowledge graphs to better learn the distributional semantics. Ni et al. (2016) use an adapted version of Word2Vec, where each entity in a Wikipedia page is considered as a term. For the *graph*-based approaches, these measures usually take advantage of the hyperlink structure of entity graph (Witten and Milne, 2008; Guo and Barbosa, 2014). Recent graph embedding techniques (e.g., Deep-Walk (Perozzi et al., 2014)) have not been directly used for entity relatedness in Wikipedia, yet its performance is studied and shown very competitive in recent related work (Zhao et al., 2015; Ponza et al., 2017).

Entity relatedness is also studied in connection with the entity recommendation task. The Spark (Blanco et al., 2013) system firstly introduced the task for Web search, Yu et al. (2014); Zhang et al. (2016a) exploit user click logs and entity pane logs for global and personalized entity recommendation. However, these approaches are optimized to user information needs, and also does not target the *global* and *temporal* dimension. Recently, Zhang et al. (2016b); Tran et al. (2017) proposed time-aware *probabilistic* approaches that combine 'static' entity relatedness with temporal factors from different sources. Nguyen et al. (2018) studied the task of time-aware ranking for entity aspects and propose an ensemble model to address the sub-features competing problem.

2.2 Neural Network Models

Neural Ranking. Deep neural ranking among IR and NLP can be generally divided into two groups: representation-focused and interaction-focused models. The *representation-focused* approach (Huang et al., 2013) independently learns a representation for each ranking element (e.g., query and document) and then employ a similarity function. On the other hand, the *interaction-focused* models are designed based on the early interactions between the ranking pairs as the input of network. For instance, Lu and Li (2013); Guo et al. (2016) build interactions (i.e., local matching signals) between two pieces of text and trains a feed-forward network for computing the matching score. This enables the model to capture various interactions between ranking elements, while with former, the model has only the chance of isolated observation of input elements.

Attention networks. In recent years, attention-based NN architectures, which learn to focus their "attention" to specific parts of the input, have shown promising results on various NLP tasks. For most cases, attentions are applied on *sequential models* to capture *global* context (Luong et al., 2015). An attention mechanism often relies on a *context* vector that facilitates outputting a "summary" over all (deterministic soft) or a sample (stochastic hard) of input states. Recent work proposed a CNN with attention-based framework to model *local* context representations of textual pairs (Yin et al., 2016), or to combine with LSTM to model *time-series* data (Ordóñez and Roggen, 2016; Lin et al., 2017) for classification and trend prediction tasks.

3 Problem

3.1 Preliminaries

We denote as named entities any real-world objects registered in a database. Each entity has a textual document (e.g. content of a home page), and a sequence of references to other entities (e.g., obtained from semantic annotations), called the entity *link profile*. All link profiles constitute an entity linking graph. In addition, two types of information are included to form the entity collective attention.

Temporal signals. Each entity can be associated with a number of properties such as view counts, content edits, etc. Given an entity e and a time point n, given D properties, the temporal signals set, in the form of a (univariate or multivariate) *time series* $X \in \mathbf{R}^{D \times T}$ consists of T real-valued vector $x_{n-T}, \cdots, x_{n-1}$, where $x_t \in \mathbf{R}^D$ captures the past signals of e at time point t.

Entity Navigation. In many systems, the user navigation between two entities is captured, e.g., search engines can log the total click-through of documents of the target entity presented in search results of a query involving the source entity. Following learning to rank approaches (Kang et al., 2015), we use this information as the ground truth in our supervised models. Given two entities e_1, e_2, the navigation signal from e_1 to e_2 at time point t is denoted by $y^t_{\{e_1, e_2\}}$.

3.2 Problem Definition

In our setting, it is not required to have a predefined, static function quantifying the semantic relatedness between two entities. Instead, it can capture a family of functions F where the prior distribution relies on time parameter. We formalize the concepts below.

Dynamic Entity Relatedness between two entities e_s, e_t, where e_s is the source entity and e_t is the target entity, in a given time t, is a function (denoted by $f_t(e_s, e_t)$) with the following properties.

- asymmetric: $f_t(e_i, e_j) \neq f_t(e_j, e_i)$

- non-negativity: $f(e_i, e_j) \geq 0$

- indiscernibility of identicals: $e_i = e_j \rightarrow f(e_i, e_j) = 1$

Dynamic Entity Relatedness Ranking. Given a source entity e_s and time point t, rank the candidate entities e_t's by their semantic relatedness.

4 Approach Overview

4.1 Datasets and Their Dynamics

In this work we use Wikipedia data as the case study for our entity relatedness ranking problem due to its rich knowledge and dynamic nature. It is worth noting that despite experimenting on Wikipedia, our framework is universal can be applied to other sources of entity with available temporal signals and entity navigation. We use Wikipedia pages to represent entities and page views as the temporal signals (details in section 6.1).

Clickstream. For entity navigation, we use the clickstream dataset generated from the Wikipedia webserver logs from February until September, 2016. These datasets contain an accumulation of transitions between two Wikipedia articles with their respective counts on a monthly basis. We study only actual pages (e.g. excluding disambiguation or redirects). In the following, we provide the first analysis of the clickstream data to gain insights into the temporal dynamics of the entity collective attention in Wikipedia.

Figure 2a illustrates the distribution of entities by click frequencies, and the correlation of top popular entities (measured by total navigations) across different months is shown in Figure 2b. In general, we observe that the user navigation activities in the top popular entities are very dynamic,

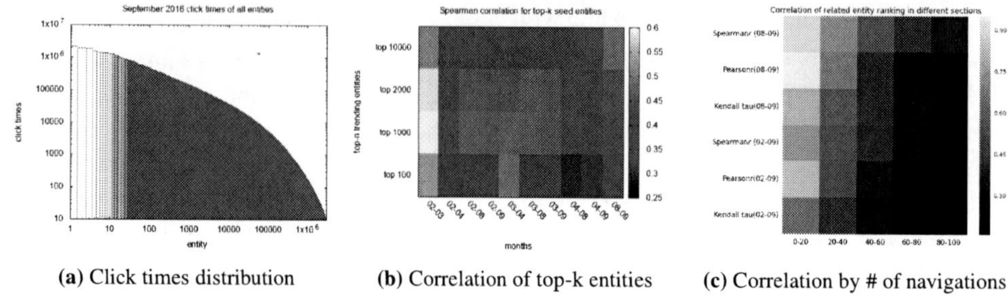

(a) Click times distribution   **(b)** Correlation of top-k entities   **(c)** Correlation by # of navigations

Figure 2: Click (navigation) times distribution and ranking correlation of entities in September 2016.

	% new e_s	% with new e_t	% w. new e_t in top-30	# new e_t (avg.)
08-2016	24.31	71.18	15.54	18.25
04-2016	30.61	66.72	53.44	42.20

Table 1: Statistics on the dynamic of clickstream, e_s denote source entities, e_t related entities.

and changes substantially with regard to time. Figure 2c visualizes the dynamics of related entities toward different ranking sections (e.g., from rank 0 to rank 20) of different months, in terms of their correlation scores. It can be interpreted that the entities that stay in top-20 most related ones tend to be more correlated than entities in bottom-20 when considering top-100 related entities.

As we show in Table 1, there are 24.31% of entities in top-10,000 most active entities of September 2006 do not appear in the same list the previous month. And 30.61% are new compared with 5 months before. In addition, there are 71% of entities in top-10,000 having navigations to new entities compared to the previous month, with approx. 18 new entities are navigated to, on average. Thus, the datasets are naturally very dynamic and sensitive to change. The substantial amount of missing *past* click logs on the **newly-formed relationships** also raises the necessity of an dynamic measuring approach.

Figure 3 shows the overall architecture of our framework, which consists of three major components: *time-*, *graph-* and *content*-based networks. Each component can be considered as a separate sub-ranking network. Each network accepts a tuple of three elements/representations as an input in a *pair-wise* fashion, i.e., the source entity e_s, the target entity e_t with higher rank (denoted as $e_{(+)}$) and the one with lower rank (denoted as $e_{(-)}$). For the *content* network, each element is a sequence of terms, coming from entity textual representation. For the *graph* network, we learn the embed-

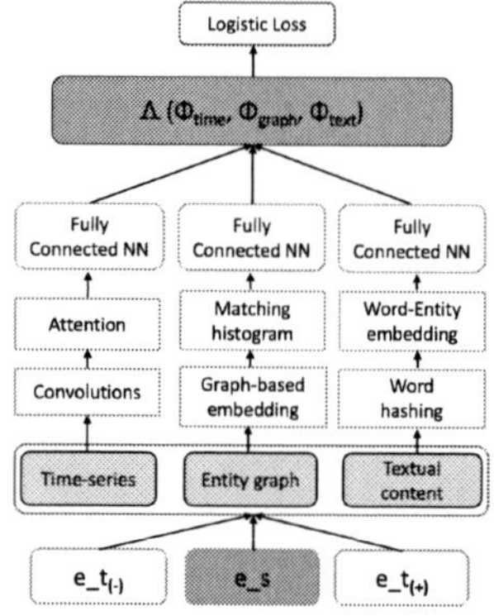

Figure 3: The trio neural model for entity ranking.

dings from the entity linking graph. For the *time* network, we propose a new convolutional model learning from the entity temporal signals. More detailed are described as follows.

4.2 Neural Ranking Model Overview

The entity relatedness ranking can be handled by a point-wise ranking model that learns to predict relatedness score directly. However, as the navigational frequency distribution is often *skewed* at top, supervisions guided by long-tail navigations would be prone to errors. Hence instead of learning explicitly a calibrated scoring function, we opt for a *pair-wise* ranking approach. When applying to ranking top-k entities, this approach has the advantage of correctly predicting partial orders of different relatedness functions f_t at any time points regardless of their non-transitivity (Cheng et al., 2012).

This work builds upon the idea of *interaction*-based deep neural models, i.e. learning soft semantic matches from the source-target entity pairs. Note that, we do not aim for a Siamese architecture (Chopra et al., 2005) (i.e., in *representation*-based models), where the weight parameters

34

are shared across networks. The reason is that, the conventional kind of network produces a *symmetric* relation, violating the **asymmetric** property of the relatedness function f_t (section 3.2). Concretely, each deep network ψ consists of an input layer z_0, $n-1$ hidden layers and an output layer z_n. Each hidden layer z_i is a fully-connected network that computes the transformation: $z_i = \sigma(\mathbf{w}_i \cdot z_{i-1} + b_i)$, where $\mathbf{w}_i$ and b_i are the weight matrix and bias at hidden layer i, σ is a non-linear function such as the rectified linear unit(ReLU). The final score under the trio setup is summed from multiple networks.

$$\phi(<e_s, e_{(+)}, e_{(-)}>) = \phi_{time} + \phi_{graph} + \phi_{content} \tag{1}$$

In the next section we describe the input representations z_0 for each network.

5 Entity Relatedness Ranking

5.1 Content-based representation learning

To learn the entity representation from its content, we rely on entity textual document (*word*-based) as well as its link profile (*entity*-based) (section 3.1). Since the vocabulary size of entities and words is often very large, conventional one-hot vector representation becomes expensive. Hence, we adopt the *word hashing* technique from (Huang et al., 2013), that breaks a term into character *trigraphs* and thus can dramatically reduce the size of the vector dimensionality. We then rely on embeddings to learn the distributed representations and build up the soft semantic interactions via input concatenation. Let $\mathsf{E} : \mathscr{V} \to \mathbb{R}^m$ be the embedding function, $\mathscr{V}$ is the vocabulary and m is the embedding size. $\mathsf{w} : \mathscr{V} \to \mathbb{R}$, is the weighting function that learns the global term importance and a weighted element-wise sum of word embedding vectors -*compositionality* function $\oplus$, the word-based representation for entity e is hence $\oplus_{i=1}^{|e_w|}(\mathsf{E}(w_i), \mathsf{w}(w_i))$. For entity-based representation, we break down the *surface form* of a linked entity into bag-of-words and apply analogously. The concatenation of the two representations for the tuple $<e_s, e_{(+)}, e_{(-)}>$ is then input to the deep feed-forward network.

5.2 Graph-based representation

To obtain the graph embedding for each entity, we adopt the idea of DeepWalk (Perozzi et al., 2014), which learns the embedding by predicting the ver-

tex sequence generated by random walk. Concretely, given an entity e, we learn to predict the sequence of entity references $\mathbb{S}_e$ – which can be considered as the *graph-wise* context in the Skip-gram model. We then adopt the matching histogram mapping in (Guo et al., 2016) for the *soft interaction* of the ranking model. Specifically, denote the bag of entities representation of e_s as $\mathbb{C}_{e_s}$, and that of e_t as $\mathbb{C}_{e_t}$; we discretize the soft matching (calculated by cosine similarity of the embedding vectors) of each entity pair in $(\mathbb{C}_{e_s}, \mathbb{C}_{e_t})$ into different bins. The logarithmic numbers of the count values of each bin then constitute the interaction vector. This soft-interaction in a way is similar in the idea with the traditional link-based model (Witten and Milne, 2008), where the relatedness measure is based on the overlapping of incoming links.

5.3 Attention-based CNN for temporal representation

For learning representation from entity temporal signals, the intuition is to model the low-level *temporal correlation* between two *multivariate* time series. Specifically, we learn to embed these time series of equal size T into an Euclidean space, such that similar pairs are close to each other. Our embedding function takes the form of a convolutional neural network (CNN), shown in Figure 4. The architecture rests on four basic layers: a 1-D convolutional (that restricts the slide only along the time window dimension, following (Zheng et al., 2014)), a batch-norm, an attention-based and a fully connected layer.

Convolution layer: A 1-D convolution operation involves applying a filter $\mathbf{w}_f \in \mathbf{R}^{1 \times w \times D}$ (i.e., a matrix of weight parameters) to each subsequence X_e^i of window size m to produce a new abstraction.

$$q_i = \mathbf{w}_f \mathsf{L}_{t:t+m-1,D}^i + b; \; s_i = BN(q_i); \; h_i = ReLU(s_i) \tag{2}$$

where $\mathsf{L}_{t:t+w-1,D}^i$ denotes the concatenation of w vectors in the lookup layer representing the subsequence X_e^i, b is a bias term. The convolutional layer is followed by a batch normalization (BN) layer (Ioffe and Szegedy, 2015), to speed up the convergence and help improve generalization.

Attention Mechanism: We apply an attention layer on the convolutional outputs. Conceptually, attention mechanisms allow NN models to focus selectively on only the important fea-

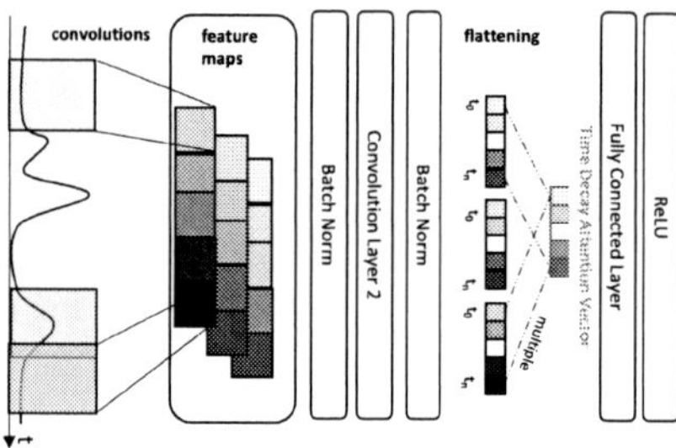

Figure 4: The attentional CNN for time series representation.

tures, based on the attention weights that often derived from the interaction with the target or within the input itself (self-attention) (Vaswani et al., 2017). We adopt the former approach, with the intuition that the time-spatial patterns should not be treated equally, but the ones near the studied time should gain more focus. To ensure that each feature in $\mathbb{F}_i^c$ that associates with different timestamps are rewarded differently, the attention weights are guided by a time-decay weight function, in a *recency*-favor fashion. More formally, let $A \in \mathbf{R}^{T-w+1\times 1}$ be the time *context* vector and $\mathbb{F}_i^c \in \mathbf{R}^{1\times(T-w+1)}$ the output of convolution for X. Then the kth column of the re-weighted feature map $\mathbb{F}_i^h$ is derived by:

$$\mathbb{F}_i^h[:,k] = A[k] \cdot \mathbb{F}_i^c[:,k], k = 1 \cdots T - w + 1 \quad (3)$$

The time context vector a is generated by a decay weight function, since each column k in the vector is associated with a time t_k which is $T - k + w$ time units away from studied time t.

Decay weight function: we leverage the Polynomial Curve for the function. $PD(t_i, t) = \frac{1}{(t-t_i)^\alpha+1}$, whereas α defines the decay rate. It is worth noting that when α is increased, the attention layer acts just like a *pooling* one [1]. Stacking up multiple convolutional layers is possible, in this case $|A|$ is the size of the previous layer. The attention layer is only applied to the **last** convolution layer in our architecture. The output of the attention layer is then passed to a fully-connected layer with non-linear activation to obtain the **temporal representation**.

---

[1] Note that, for clear visualization, we put *flattening* before attention layer in Figure 4

5.4 Learning and Optimization

Finally, we describe the optimization and training procedure of our network. We use a Logarithmic loss that can lead to better probability estimation at the cost of accuracy [2]. Our network minimizes the cross-entropy loss function as follows:

$$L = -\frac{1}{N} \sum_{i=1}^{N} [P_{\{e_s,e_1,e_2\}_i} \log \bar{y}_i$$
$$+ (1 - P_{\{e_s,e_1,e_2\}_i}) \log(1 - \bar{y}_i)] + \lambda |\theta|_2^2 \quad (4)$$

where N is the training size, $\bar{y}$ is the output of the sigmoid layer on the predicted label. θ contains all the parameters of the network and $\lambda |\theta|_2^2$ is the L2 regularization. $P_{\{e_s,e_{(+)}.e_{(-)}\}_i}$ is the probability that $e_{(+)}$ is ranked higher than $e_{(-)}$ derived from entity navigation, $P_{\{e_s,e_{(+)},e_{(-)}\}_i} = y_{\{e_s,e_{(+)}\}}^{t(i)} / (y_{\{e_s,e_{(+)}\}}^{t(i)} + y_{\{e_s,e_{(-)}\}}^{t(i)})$, where $t(i)$ is the observed time point of the training instance i. The network parameters are updated using Adam optimizer (Kingma and Ba, 2014).

6 Experiments

6.1 Dataset

To recap from Section 4.1, we use the click stream datasets in 2016. We also use the corresponding Wikipedia article dumps, with over 4 million entities represented by actual pages. Since the length of the content of an Wikipedia article is often long, in this work, we make use of only its **abstract** section. To obtain temporal signals of the entity, we use page view statistics of Wikipedia articles and aggregate the counts by month. We fetch the data from June, 2014 up until the studied time, which results in the length of 27 months.

Seed entities and related candidates. To extract popular and trending entities, we extract from the clickstream data the top 10,000 entities based on the number of navigations from major search engines (*Google* and *Bing)*, at the studied time. Getting the subset of related entity candidates – for efficiency purposes– has been well-addressed in related work (Guo and Barbosa, 2014; Ponza et al., 2017). In this work, we do not leverage a method and just assume the use of an appropriate one. In the experiment, we resort to choose only

---

[2] Other ranking-based loss such as Hinge loss favours over sparsity and accuracy (in the sense of direct punishing misclassification via margins) at the cost of probability estimation. The logistic loss distinguishes better between examples whose supervision scores are close.

	Counts
Total seed entities	10,000
Total entities	1,420,819
Candidate per entities (avg.)	142
Training seed entities	8,000
Dev. seed entities	1,000
Test seed entities	1,000
Training pairs	100,650K
Dev. pairs	12,420K
Test pairs	12,590K

Table 2: Statistics of the dataset.

candidates which are visited from the seed entities at studied time. We filtered out entity-candidate pairs with too few navigations (less than 10) and considered the top-100 candidates.

6.2 Models for Comparison

In this paper, we compare our models against the following baselines.

Wikipedia Link-based (WLM): Witten and Milne (2008) proposed a low-cost measure of semantic relatedness based on Wikipedia entity graph, inspired by Normalized Google Distance.

DeepWalk (DW): DeepWalk (Perozzi et al., 2014) learned representations of vertices in a graph with a random walk generator and language modeling. We chose not to compare with the matrix factorization approach in (Zhao et al., 2015), as even though it allows the incorporation of different relation types (i.e., among entity, category and word), the iterative computation cost over large graphs is very expensive. When consider only entity-entity relation, the performance is reported rather similar to DW.

Entity2Vec Model (E2V): or entity embedding learning using Skip-Gram (Mikolov et al., 2013) model. E2V utilizes textual information to capture latent word relationships. Similar to Zhao et al. (2015); Ni et al. (2016), we use Wikipedia articles as training corpus to learn word vectors and reserved hyperlinks between entities.

ParaVecs (PV): Le and Mikolov (2014); Dai et al. (2015) learned document/entity vectors via the distributed memory (**ParaVecs-DM**) and distributed bag of words (**ParaVecs-DBOW**) models, using hierarchical softmax. We use Wikipedia articles as training corpus to learn entity vectors.

RankSVM: Ceccarelli et al. (2013) learned entity relatedness from a set of 28 **handcrafted features**, using the traditional learning-to-rank method, RankSVM. We put together additional well-known temporal features (Kanhabua et al., 2014; Zhang et al., 2016b) (i.e., time series cross correlation, trending level and predicted popularity based on *page views*) and report the results of the extended feature set.

For our approach, we tested different combinations of *content* (denoted as **Content$_{Emb}$**), *graph*, (**Graph$_{Emb}$**) and *time* (**TS-CNN-Att**) networks. We also test the *content* and *graph* networks with **pretrained** entity representations (i.e., ParaVecs-DM and DeepWalk).

6.3 Experimental Setup

Evaluation procedures. The time granularity is set to months. The studied time t_n of our experiments is September 2016. From the seed queries, we use 80% for training, 10% for development and 10% for testing, as shown in Table 2. Note that, for the **time-aware** setting and to avoid leakage and bias as much as possible, the data for training and development (including supervision) are up until time $t_n - 1$. In specific, for content and graph data, only $t_n - 1$ is used.

Metrics. We use 2 correlation coefficient methods, Pearson and Spearman, which have been used often throughout literature, cf. (Dallmann et al., 2016; Ponza et al., 2017). The Pearson index focuses on the difference between predicted-vs-correct relatedness scores, while Spearman focuses on the ranking order among entity pairs. Our work studies on the strength of the dynamic relatedness between entities, hence we focus more on Pearson index. However, traditional correlation metrics do not consider the positions in the ranked list (correlations at the top or bottom are treated equally). For this reason, we adjust the metric to consider the rankings at specific top-k positions, which consequently can be used to measure the correlation for only top items in the ranking (based to the ground truth). In addition, we use Normalized Discounted Cumulative Gain (NDCG) measure to evaluate the recommendation tasks.

Implementation details. All neural models are implemented in TensorFlow. Initial learning rate is tuned amongst {1.e-2, 1.e-3, 1.e-4, 1.e-5}. The batch size is tuned amongst {50, 100, 200}. The weight matrices are initialized with samples from the uniform distribution (Glorot and Bengio, 2010). Models are trained for maximum 25 epochs. The hidden layers for each network are among {2, 3, 4}, while for hidden nodes are {128, 256, 512}. Dropout rate is set from {0.2, 0.3, 0.5}. The pretrained DW is empirically set to 128 dimensions, and 200 for PV. For CNN, the filter number are in $\{10, 20, 30\}$, window size in $\{4, 5, 6\}$, convolutional layers in $\{1, 2, 3\}$ and decay rate α in $\{1.0, 1.5, \cdots, 7.5\}$. 2 conv- layers with window size 5 and 4, number of filters of 20 and 25 respectively are used for decay hyperparameter analysis.

6.4 Experimental Tasks

We evaluate our proposed method in two different scenarios: (1) Relatedness ranking and (2) Entity recommendation. The first task evaluates how well we can **mimic** the ranking via the entity navigation. Here we use the raw number of navigations in Wikipedia clickstream. The second task is formulated as: *given an entity, suggest the top-k most related entities to it right now*. Since there is no standard ground-truth for this temporal task, we constructed two relevance ground-truths. The **first** one is the *proxy* ground-truth, with relevance grade is *automatically* assigned from the (top-100) most navigated target entities. The graded relevance score is then given as the *reversed* rank order. For this, all entities in the test set are used. The **second** one is based on the human judgments with 5-level graded relevance scale, i.e., from 4 - highly relevant to 0 - not (temporally) relevant. Two human experts evaluate on the subset of 20 entities (randomly sampled from the test set), with 600 entity pairs (approx. 30 per seed, using *pooling* method). The ground-truth size is comparable the widely used ground-truth for *static* relatedness assessment, KORE (Hoffart et al., 2012). The Cohen's Kappa agreement is 0.72. Performance of the best-performed models on this dataset is then tested with paired *t*-test against the WLM baseline.

6.5 Results on Relatedness Ranking

We report the performance of the relatedness ranking on the left side of Table 3, with the Pearson and Spearman metrics. Among existing baselines, we observe that link-based approaches i.e., WLM and DeepWalk perform better than others for top-k correlation. Whereas, temporal models yield substantial improvement overall. Specifically, the TS-CNN-Att performs better than the no-attention model in most cases, improves 11% for Pearson@10, and 3% when considering the total rank. Our trio model performs well overall, gives best results for total rank. The duo models (combine base with either pretrained DW or PV) also deliver improvements over the sole temporal ones. We also observer additional gains while combining of temporal base with pretrained DW and PV altogether.

6.6 Results on Entity Recommendation

Here we report the results on the nDCG metrics. Table 3 (right-side) demonstrates the results for two ground-truth settings (proxy and human). We can observe the good performance of the baselines for this task over conventional temporal models, significantly for *proxy* setting. It can be explained that, 'static' entity relations are ranked high in the non time-aware baselines, hence are still rewarded when considering a fine-grained grading scale (100 level). The margin becomes smaller when comparing in *human* setting, with the standard 5-level scale. All the models with pretrained representations perform poorly. It shows that for this task, early interaction-based approach is more suitable than purely based on representation.

6.7 Additional Analysis

We present an anecdotic example of top-selected entities for Kingsman: The Golden Circle in Table 4. While the content-based model favors old relations like the preceding movies, TS-CNN puts popular actress Halle Berry or the recent released X-men: Apocalypse on top. The latter is not ideal as there is not a solid relationship between the two movies. One implication is that the two entities are ranked high is more because of the popularity of themselves than the strength of the relationship toward the source entity. The Trio model addresses the issue by taking other perspectives into account, and also balances out the recency and long-term factors, gives the best ranking performance.

Analysis on decay hyper-parameter. We give a study on the effect of decay parameter on performance. Figure 5a illustrates the results on $Pearson_{all}$ and nDCG@10 for the *trio* model. It can be seen that while nDCG slightly increases, Pearson score peaks while α in the range $[1.5, 3.5]$. Additionally, we show the convergence analysis on α for TS-CNN-Att in Figure 6. Bigger α tends to converge faster, but to a significant higher loss when α is over 5.5 (omitted from the Figure).

Performances on different entity types. We demonstrate in Figures 5b and 5c the model performances on the *person* and *event* types. WLM performs poorer for the latter, that can be interpreted as link-based methods tend to slowly adapt

	Pearson $\times 100$				$\rho \times 100$	nDCG (proxy)			nDCG (human)		
Model	@10	@30	@50	all	all	@3	@10	@20	@3	@10	@20
Baselines											
WLM	27.6	28.3	24.0	19.4	12.1	0.63	0.59	0.62	0.50	0.46	0.52
RankSVM	28.5	34.7	31.4	20.7	27.5	0.65	0.61	0.64	0.52	0.61	0.65
Entity2Vec	18.6	22.0	21.8	20.5	18.7	0.62	0.60	0.61	0.54	0.53	0.54
DeepWalk	31.3	30.9	21.4	17.6	10.1	0.41	0.43	0.47	0.34	0.38	0.45
ParaVecs-DBOW	18.6	22.0	21.8	20.5	16.0	0.62	0.60	0.61	0.50	0.50	0.55
ParaVecs-DM	19.0	23.0	23.2	22.3	18.3	0.66	0.63	0.63	0.49	0.52	0.58
Model Ablation											
TS-CNN	51.9	51.0	43.0	35.8	26.5	0.41	0.43	0.47	0.40	0.43	0.48
TS-CNN-Att (**Base**)	57.9	49.7	44.7	37.1	24.9	0.43	0.44	0.49	0.38	0.45	0.50
Base+PV	<u>60.6</u>	44.2	41.4	36.4	11.2	0.41	0.43	0.47	0.49	0.51	0.55
Base+DW	43.5	36.5	35.7	32.7	31.0	0.44	0.48	0.53	0.47	0.51	0.52
Base+PV+DW	56.9	46.1	43.4	32.9	28,4	0.41	0.44	0.48	0.49	0.54	0.57
$Content_{Emb}+Graph_{Emb}$	48.9	40.1	49.9	37.5	27.9	0.67	0.62	0.70	0.61	0.69	0.65
Base+$Content_{Emb}$	**67.1**	<u>54.2</u>	**53.4**	<u>43.7</u>	26.5	0.67	0.69	0.71	0.61	0.72	0.74
Base+$Graph_{Emb}$	55.2	50.2	41.3	31.5	<u>35.5</u>	<u>0.71</u>	<u>0.75</u>	<u>0.78</u>	<u>0.65</u>∓	<u>0.78</u>∓	<u>0.81</u>∓
Trio	58.6	**54.3**	<u>50.2</u>	**45.4**	**43.5**	**0.75**	**0.78**	**0.83**	**0.74**∓	**0.82**∓	**0.85**∓

Table 3: Performance of different models on task (1) Pearson, Spearman's ρ ranking correlation, and task (2) recommendation (measured by nDCG). Bold and underlined numbers indicate best and second-to-best results. ∓ shows statistical significant over WLM ($p < 0.05$).

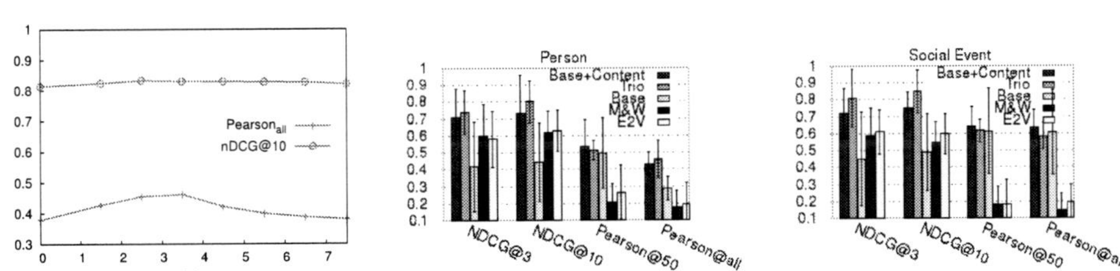

(a) Decay parameter for time-series embedding. **(b)** Model performances for *person*-type entities. **(c)** Model performances for *social event*-type entities.

Figure 5: Performance results for variation of decay parameter and different entity types.

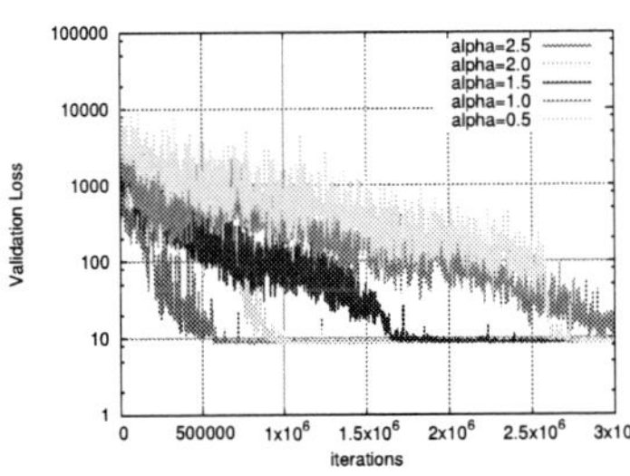

Figure 6: Convergence of decay parameters.

	Models		
PV-DM	**TS-CNN-Att**	**Temp+PV**	**Trio**
Secret Service	Halle Berry	*Elton John*	Mark Strong
Spider-Man	*X-Men*	Taron Egerton	Jeff Bridges
Taron Egerton	Jeff Bridges	Edward Holcroft	Julianne More

Table 4: Different top-k rankings for entity *Kingsman: The Golden Circle*. Italic means irrelevance.

for recent trending entities. The temporal models seem to capture these entites better.

7 Conclusion

In this work, we presented a trio neural model to solve the dynamic entity relatedness ranking problem. The model jointly learns rich representations of entities from textual content, graph and temporal signals. We also propose an effective CNN-based attentional mechanism for learning the temporal representation of an entity. Experiments on ranking correlations and top-k recommendation tasks demonstrate the effectiveness of our approach over existing baselines. For future work, we aim to incorporate more temporal signals, and investigate on different 'trainable' attention mechanisms to go beyond the time-based decay, for instance by incorporating latent topics.

Acknowledgments. This work is funded by the ERC Advanced Grant ALEXANDRIA (grant no. 339233). We thank the reviewers for the suggestions on the content and structure of the paper.

References

Nitish Aggarwal and Paul Buitelaar. 2014. Wikipedia-based distributional semantics for entity relatedness. In *2014 AAAI Fall Symposium Series*.

Roi Blanco, Berkant Barla Cambazoglu, Peter Mika, and Nicolas Torzec. 2013. Entity recommendations in web search. In *ISWC*, pages 33–48. Springer.

Diego Ceccarelli, Claudio Lucchese, Salvatore Orlando, Raffaele Perego, and Salvatore Trani. 2013. Learning relatedness measures for entity linking. In *Proceedings of the 22nd ACM international conference on Information & Knowledge Management*, pages 139–148. ACM.

Weiwei Cheng, Eyke Hüllermeier, Willem Waegeman, and Volkmar Welker. 2012. Label ranking with partial abstention based on thresholded probabilistic models. In F. Pereira, C. J. C. Burges, L. Bottou, and K. Q. Weinberger, editors, *Advances in Neural Information Processing Systems 25*, pages 2501–2509. Curran Associates, Inc.

Sumit Chopra, Raia Hadsell, and Yann LeCun. 2005. Learning a similarity metric discriminatively, with application to face verification. In *Computer Vision and Pattern Recognition, 2005. CVPR 2005. IEEE Computer Society Conference on*, volume 1, pages 539–546. IEEE.

Andrew M Dai, Christopher Olah, and Quoc V Le. 2015. Document embedding with paragraph vectors. *arXiv preprint arXiv:1507.07998*.

Alexander Dallmann, Thomas Niebler, Florian Lemmerich, and Andreas Hotho. 2016. Extracting semantics from random walks on wikipedia: Comparing learning and counting methods.

Evgeniy Gabrilovich and Shaul Markovitch. 2007. Computing semantic relatedness using wikipedia-based explicit semantic analysis. In *Proceedings of the 20th International Joint Conference on Artifical Intelligence*, IJCAI'07, pages 1606–1611, San Francisco, CA, USA. Morgan Kaufmann Publishers Inc.

Evgeniy Gabrilovich and Shaul Markovitch. 2009. Wikipedia-based semantic interpretation for natural language processing. *Journal of Artificial Intelligence Research*, 34:443–498.

Xavier Glorot and Yoshua Bengio. 2010. Understanding the difficulty of training deep feedforward neural networks. In *Proceedings of the thirteenth international conference on artificial intelligence and statistics*, pages 249–256.

Jiafeng Guo, Yixing Fan, Qingyao Ai, and W Bruce Croft. 2016. A deep relevance matching model for ad-hoc retrieval. In *Proceedings of the 25th ACM International on Conference on Information and Knowledge Management*, pages 55–64. ACM.

Zhaochen Guo and Denilson Barbosa. 2014. Robust entity linking via random walks. In *Proceedings of the 23rd ACM International Conference on Conference on Information and Knowledge Management*, pages 499–508. ACM.

Johannes Hoffart, Stephan Seufert, Dat Ba Nguyen, Martin Theobald, and Gerhard Weikum. 2012. Kore: keyphrase overlap relatedness for entity disambiguation. In *Proceedings of the 21st ACM international conference on Information and knowledge management*, pages 545–554. ACM.

Zhiting Hu, Poyao Huang, Yuntian Deng, Yingkai Gao, and Eric Xing. 2015. Entity hierarchy embedding. In *Proceedings of the 53rd Annual Meeting of the Association for Computational Linguistics and the 7th International Joint Conference on Natural Language Processing (Volume 1: Long Papers)*, volume 1, pages 1292–1300.

Po-Sen Huang, Xiaodong He, Jianfeng Gao, Li Deng, Alex Acero, and Larry Heck. 2013. Learning deep structured semantic models for web search using clickthrough data. In *Proceedings of the 22nd ACM international conference on Conference on information & knowledge management*, pages 2333–2338. ACM.

Sergey Ioffe and Christian Szegedy. 2015. Batch normalization: Accelerating deep network training by reducing internal covariate shift. In *International Conference on Machine Learning*, pages 448–456.

Tingsong Jiang, Tianyu Liu, Tao Ge, Lei Sha, Baobao Chang, Sujian Li, and Zhifang Sui. 2016. Towards time-aware knowledge graph completion. In *Proceedings of COLING 2016, the 26th International Conference on Computational Linguistics: Technical Papers*, pages 1715–1724.

Changsung Kang, Dawei Yin, Ruiqiang Zhang, Nicolas Torzec, Jianzhang He, and Yi Chang. 2015. Learning to rank related entities in web search. *Neurocomputing*, 166:309–318.

Nattiya Kanhabua, Tu Ngoc Nguyen, and Claudia Niederée. 2014. What triggers human remembering of events? a large-scale analysis of catalysts for collective memory in wikipedia. In *Digital Libraries (JCDL), 2014 IEEE/ACM Joint Conference on*, pages 341–350. IEEE.

Diederik P Kingma and Jimmy Ba. 2014. Adam: A method for stochastic optimization. *arXiv preprint arXiv:1412.6980*.

Quoc Le and Tomas Mikolov. 2014. Distributed representations of sentences and documents. In *International Conference on Machine Learning*, pages 1188–1196.

Tao Lin, Tian Guo, and Karl Aberer. 2017. Hybrid neural networks for learning the trend in time series.

Zhengdong Lu and Hang Li. 2013. A deep architecture for matching short texts. In *Advances in Neural Information Processing Systems*, pages 1367–1375.

Minh-Thang Luong, Hieu Pham, and Christopher D Manning. 2015. Effective approaches to attention-based neural machine translation. *arXiv preprint arXiv:1508.04025*.

Tomas Mikolov, Ilya Sutskever, Kai Chen, Greg S Corrado, and Jeff Dean. 2013. Distributed representations of words and phrases and their compositionality. In *Advances in neural information processing systems*, pages 3111–3119.

Iris Miliaraki, Roi Blanco, and Mounia Lalmas. 2015. From selena gomez to marlon brando: Understanding explorative entity search. In *Proceedings of the 24th International Conference on World Wide Web*, pages 765–775. International World Wide Web Conferences Steering Committee.

Andrea Moro, Alessandro Raganato, and Roberto Navigli. 2014. Entity linking meets word sense disambiguation: a unified approach. *Transactions of the Association for Computational Linguistics*, 2:231–244.

Tu Ngoc Nguyen, Nattiya Kanhabua, and Wolfgang Nejdl. 2018. Multiple models for recommending temporal aspects of entities. In *The Semantic Web - 15th International Conference, ESWC 2018, Heraklion, Crete, Greece, June 3-7, 2018, Proceedings*, pages 462–480.

Yuan Ni, Qiong Kai Xu, Feng Cao, Yosi Mass, Dafna Sheinwald, Hui Jia Zhu, and Shao Sheng Cao. 2016. Semantic documents relatedness using concept graph representation. In *Proceedings of the Ninth ACM International Conference on Web Search and Data Mining*, WSDM '16, pages 635–644, New York, NY, USA. ACM.

Francisco Javier Ordóñez and Daniel Roggen. 2016. Deep convolutional and lstm recurrent neural networks for multimodal wearable activity recognition. *Sensors*, 16(1):115.

Bryan Perozzi, Rami Al-Rfou, and Steven Skiena. 2014. Deepwalk: Online learning of social representations. In *Proceedings of the 20th ACM SIGKDD international conference on Knowledge discovery and data mining*, pages 701–710. ACM.

Marco Ponza, Paolo Ferragina, and Soumen Chakrabarti. 2017. A two-stage framework for computing entity relatedness in wikipedia. In *Proceedings of the 2017 ACM on Conference on Information and Knowledge Management*, CIKM '17, pages 1867–1876, New York, NY, USA. ACM.

Nam Khanh Tran, Tuan Tran, and Claudia Niederée. 2017. Beyond time: Dynamic context-aware entity recommendation. In *European Semantic Web Conference*, pages 353–368. Springer.

Ashish Vaswani, Noam Shazeer, Niki Parmar, Jakob Uszkoreit, Llion Jones, Aidan N Gomez, Łukasz Kaiser, and Illia Polosukhin. 2017. Attention is all you need. In *Advances in Neural Information Processing Systems*, pages 5998–6008.

Ian H Witten and David N Milne. 2008. An effective, low-cost measure of semantic relatedness obtained from wikipedia links.

Wenpeng Yin, Hinrich Schütze, Bing Xiang, and Bowen Zhou. 2016. Abcnn: Attention-based convolutional neural network for modeling sentence pairs. *Transactions of the Association of Computational Linguistics*, 4(1):259–272.

Xiao Yu, Hao Ma, Bo-June Paul Hsu, and Jiawei Han. 2014. On building entity recommender systems using user click log and freebase knowledge. In *Proceedings of WSDM*, pages 263–272. ACM.

Fuzheng Zhang, Nicholas Jing Yuan, Defu Lian, Xing Xie, and Wei-Ying Ma. 2016a. Collaborative knowledge base embedding for recommender systems. In *Proceedings of the 22nd ACM SIGKDD international conference on knowledge discovery and data mining*, pages 353–362. ACM.

Lei Zhang, Achim Rettinger, and Ji Zhang. 2016b. A probabilistic model for time-aware entity recommendation. In *International Semantic Web Conference*, pages 598–614. Springer.

Yu Zhao, Zhiyuan Liu, and Maosong Sun. 2015. Representation learning for measuring entity relatedness with rich information. In *Twenty-Fourth International Joint Conference on Artificial Intelligence*.

Yi Zheng, Qi Liu, Enhong Chen, Yong Ge, and J Leon Zhao. 2014. Time series classification using multi-channels deep convolutional neural networks. In *International Conference on Web-Age Information Management*, pages 298–310. Springer.

A Unified Neural Network Model for Geolocating Twitter Users

Mohammad Ebrahimi, Elaheh ShafieiBavani, Raymond Wong, Fang Chen
University of New South Wales, Sydney, Australia
Data61 CSIRO, Sydney, Australia
`{mohammade,elahehs,wong,fang}@cse.unsw.edu.au`

Abstract

Locations of social media users are important to many applications such as rapid disaster response, targeted advertisement, and news recommendation. However, many users do not share their exact geographical coordinates due to reasons such as privacy concerns. The lack of explicit location information has motivated a growing body of research in recent years looking at different automatic ways of determining the user's primary location. In this paper, we propose a unified user geolocation method which relies on a fusion of neural networks. Our joint model incorporates different types of available information including tweet text, user network, and metadata to predict users' locations. Moreover, we utilize a bidirectional LSTM network augmented with an attention mechanism to identify the most location indicative words in textual content of tweets. The experiments demonstrate that our approach achieves state-of-the-art performance over two Twitter benchmark geolocation datasets. We also conduct an ablation study to evaluate the contribution of each type of information in user geolocation performance.

1 Introduction

Knowing physical locations involved in social media data helps us to understand what is happening in real life, to bridge the online and offline worlds, and to develop applications for supporting real-life demands. For example, we can monitor public health of residents (Cheng et al., 2010), recommend local events (Yuan et al., 2013) or attractive places (Noulas et al., 2012) to tourists, identify locations of emergency (Ao et al., 2014) or even disasters (Lingad et al., 2013), and summarize regional topics (Rakesh et al., 2013). Even though platforms such as Twitter allow users to geolocate their posts to reveal their locations either manually or with the help of GPS, it is reported that less than 1% of Twitter data has geo-coordinates provided (Jurgens, 2013). Moreover, location information on Twitter is far from being complete and accurate. For instance, self-declared home information in many user profiles is inaccurate or even invalid (Hecht et al., 2011). The lack of explicit location information in the majority of tweets has motivated a growing body of research in recent years looking at different automatic ways of determining the user's primary location (i.e., *user geolocation*) and/or - as a proxy for the former - the location from which tweets have been posted (Ajao et al., 2015).

Geolocation methods usually train a model on a small set of users whose locations are known (e.g., through GPS-based geotagging), and predict locations of other users using the resulting model. These models broadly fall into three categories: text-based (Eisenstein et al., 2010; Wing and Baldridge, 2011; Roller et al., 2012), network-based (Jurgens, 2013; Compton et al., 2014; Jurgens et al., 2015), and hybrid methods that combine text, user network, and metadata information (Rahimi et al., 2015b,a; Jayasinghe et al., 2016; Miura et al., 2016) with the aim of achieving state-of-the-art performance.

In this paper, we present a neural network-based system that we developed for user geolocation in Twitter. Our model combines different sources of information including tweet text, metadata, and user network. We employ a neural network model to generate a dense vector representation for each field and then use the concatenation of these representations as the feature for classification. Our main contributions can be summarized as follows:

1. We propose a unified user geolocation method that relies on a fusion of neural networks, incorporating different types of avail-

Proceedings of the 22nd Conference on Computational Natural Language Learning (CoNLL 2018), pages 42–53
Brussels, Belgium, October 31 - November 1, 2018. ©2018 Association for Computational Linguistics

able information: tweet message, users' social relationships, and metadata fields embedded in tweets and profiles.

2. For modeling the tweet text (and textual metadata fields), we use bidirectional Long Short-Term Memory (LSTM) networks augmented with a context-aware attention mechanism (Yang et al., 2016), which helps to identify the most location indicative words.

3. Through the empirical studies on two standard Twitter datasets, we demonstrate that the proposed method outperforms other state-of-the-art approaches in addressing the problem of user geolocation.

4. We train an individual model for each information field, and analyze the contribution of each component in the geolocation process.

The rest of the paper is organized as follows. We review the related work in Section 2. Utilized data is described in Section 3. Section 4 explains the proposed approach. The experimental results are given in Section 5, and finally, we conclude the paper and outline possible future work in Section 6.

2   Related Work

2.1   Text-based Methods

Text-based methods utilize the geographical bias of language use in social media for geolocation. These methods have widely used probability distributions of words over locations. Maximum likelihood estimation approaches (Cheng et al., 2010, 2013) and language modeling approaches minimizing KL-divergence (Roller et al., 2012) have succeeded in predicting user locations using word distributions. Topic modeling approaches to extract latent topics with geographical regions (Eisenstein et al., 2010; Hong et al., 2012; Ahmed et al., 2013; Yuan et al., 2013) have also been explored considering word distributions.

Supervised learning methods with word features are also popular in text-based geoinference. Multinomial Naïve Bayes (Han et al., 2012, 2014; Wing and Baldridge, 2011), logistic regression (Wing and Baldridge, 2014; Han et al., 2014), hierarchical logistic regression (Wing and Baldridge, 2014), and multi-layer neural network with stacked denoising autoencoder (Liu and Inkpen, 2015) have realized geolocation predic-

tion from text. A semi-supervised learning approach has been proposed by Cha et al. (2015) using a sparse-coding and dictionary learning. Hulden et al. (2015) have used a kernel-based method to smooth linguistic features over very small grid sizes and consequently alleviate data sparseness. Chi et al. (2016) have employed Multinomial Naïve Bayes and focused on the use of textual features (i.e., location indicative words, GeoNames gazetteers, user mentions, and hashtags) for geolocation inference. More recently, Rahimi et al. (2017b) have proposed a neural network-based geolocation approach. They used the parameters of the hidden layer of the neural network as word and phrase embeddings, and performed a nearest neighbor search on a sample of city names and dialect terms.

While having good results, text-based approaches are often limited to those users who generate text that contains geographic references (Jurgens, 2013).

2.2   Network-based Methods

Network-based methods rely on the geospatial homophily of interactions (of several kinds) between users. An early work by Davis Jr et al. (2011) proposed an approach in which the location of a given user is inferred by simply taking the most-frequently seen location among its social network. Jurgens (2013) have extended the idea of location inference as label propagation over some form of friendship graph by interpreting location labels spatially. Locations are then inferred using an iterative, multi-pass procedure. This method has been further extended by Compton et al. (2014) to take into account edge weights in the social network, and to limit the propagation of noisy locations. They weigh locations as a function of how many times users interacted there, hence favoring locations of friends with evidence of a close relationship. Jurgens et al. (2015) have released a framework for nine network-based geolocation methods targeting Twitter.

The main limitation of network-based models is that they completely fail to geolocate users who are not connected to geolocated components of the graph (i.e., isolated users).

2.3   Hybrid Methods

Several attempts have been made to combine different sources of information for geolocating social media users. Li et al. (2012) have proposed a geolocation method by integrating both friendship and content information in a probabilistic model.

Rahimi et al. (2015b) showed that geolocation predictions from text can effectively be used as a back-off for disconnected users in a network-based approach. In another work by Rahimi et al. (2015a), a hybrid approach has been proposed by propagating information on a graph built from user mentions in Twitter messages, together with dongle nodes corresponding to the results of a text-based geolocation method. Ebrahimi et al. (2017, 2018b) have presented a hybrid approach by incorporating both text and network information, and shown that the filtering of highly mentioned users in the social graph can improve the geolocation performance. Rahimi et al. (2017b) have proposed a text geoloation method based on neural network and incorporated it into their network-based approach (Rahimi et al., 2015a). Wang et al. (2017) have introduced a collective geographical embedding algorithm to embed multiple information sources into a low dimensional space, such that the distance in the embedding space reflects the physical distance in the real world.

Metadata such as location fields have also been used as effective clues to predict the user's location (Hecht et al., 2011). Different geoinference approaches have been proposed to consider text and metadata information simultaneously, such as dynamically weighted ensemble method (Mahmud et al., 2012), and stacking approach (Han et al., 2014). Jayasinghe et al. (2016) have proposed a cascade ensemble approach by combining text-based, metadata-based, and network-based geolocation methods. Additionally, their approach makes use of several dedicated services, such as GeoNames gazetteers, time zone to GeoName mappings, IP country resolver and customized scrapers for social media websites.

Miura et al. (2016) have trained a neural network utilizing the fastText n-gram model (Joulin et al., 2016) on tweet text, user location, user description, and user timezone. They have utilized several mapping services using external resources, such as GeoNames and time zone boundaries for feature preprocessing. This model has been further extended by Miura et al. (2017) to also consider user network information for geolocation.

Thomas and Hennig (2017) have proposed a geolocation method that relies on the combination of individual neural networks trained on text and metadata fields. Ebrahimi et al. (2018a) have proposed a word embedding-based approach to predict the geographic proximity of connected users in the social graph based on their linguistic similarities. The calculated similarity scores have been used for weighting edges between users in the graph. Tweet content and metadata is also combined with an ensemble learning method to geolocate isolated users in the graph.

3 Data

We have used two benchmark Twitter geolocation datasets in our experiments:

- **TWITTERUS** is a dataset compiled by (Roller et al., 2012), which contains 38M tweets from 450K users in the United States. Out of 450K users, 10K are reserved for the development set and another 10K for the test set. The ground truth location of each user is set to its first geotag in the dataset. To make city prediction possible in this dataset, we additionally assigned city centers to ground truth geotags using the city category of Han et al. (2012).

- **WNUT** is a user-level dataset from the geolocation prediction shared task of WNUT 2016 (Han et al., 2016). The dataset covers 13M tweets from 3362 cities worldwide, and consists of 1M training users, 10K development users, and 10K test users. The ground truth location of a user is decided by majority voting of the closest city center.

Note that the metadata of a tweet includes not only the tweet message (text) but also a variety of information such as tweet publication time, and user account data such as location and timezone. The organizers have provided full metadata for the test sets but only the tweet IDs for training and development sets. We collect metadata for training/development tweets using the Twitter API[1].

4 The Proposed Approach

Figure 1 illustrates an overview of the proposed model for user geolocation. We make use of the following sources of information to train our model: 1) Tweet text; 2) User network; and 3)

---

[1]We were able to obtain approximately 71-75% of the full datasets. The remaining tweets are no longer available, mainly because users deleted these messages and/or accessibility changes in Twitter.

Metadata including user-declared location, user description, user name, timezone, user language, tweet creation time, user UTC offset, links (URL domains), and application source.

Each field is processed by a separate sub-network to generate a feature vector representation R_j. These feature vectors are then concatenated to build a final user representation $\hat{R}$ which is fed into a linear classification layer:

$$\hat{R} = R_1 \parallel ... \parallel R_N \tag{1}$$

$$r = softmax(W_r \hat{R} + b_r) \tag{2}$$

where N is the number of features (11 in total), $r \in \mathbb{R}^R$ is the hidden representation at the penultimate layer. W_r is a weight matrix and b_r is a bias vector. r is fully connected to the output layer and activated by softmax to generate a probability distribution over the classes. We employ the cross-entropy loss as the objective function. Let M be the number of examples (i.e., users) and c be the number of classes (i.e., regions), then the cross-entropy loss is defined by:

$$L = -\sum_{i=1}^{M}\sum_{j=1}^{c} y_i^{\,j} \log(\tilde{y}_i^{\,j}) \tag{3}$$

where $y_i, i = 1, ..., M$ is the ground-truth vector, $\tilde{y}_i$ is the predicted probability vector, and $\tilde{y}_i^{\,j}$ is the probability that user i resides in region j. We minimize the objective function through Stochastic Gradient Descent (SGD) over shuffled mini-batches with Adam (Kingma and Ba, 2014).

We design several sub-networks to provide vectorized representation for each raw field. For processing the tweet text, we utilize word embeddings (Mikolov et al., 2013) and bidirectional Long Short-Term Memory (LSTM) unit (Hochreiter and Schmidhuber, 1997) augmented with a context-aware attention mechanism (Yang et al., 2016) (Section 4.1). We construct a @-mention graph as a representation of users' interactions, and utilize this graph to extract the user network. We then use an embedding layer with attention mechanism to create the final user network representation (Section 4.2).

We divide metadata fields into two classes: textual, and categorical. For representing textual metadata fields (i.e., location, description, user name, and timezone), we use word embeddings and bidirectional LSTM networks with attention

mechanism. We treat other metadata fields (language, tweet time, UTC offset, links, and source) as categorical features, and convert them to one-hot encodings which are then fed forward to a dense layer (Section 4.3). In the following subsections, we describe details of each component.

4.1 Text Component

Figure 2(a) demonstrates the architecture of text sub-network. It takes the sequence of words in the tweet $T = \{w_1, w_2, ..., w_n\}$ as input. An embedding layer is used to project the words to a low-dimensional vector space $\mathbb{R}^E$, where E is the size of the embedding layer. We initialize the weights of the embedding layer using our pretrained word embeddings (Section 5.1). The embeddings of tweet words are then forwarded to an LSTM layer. An LSTM takes as input the words of a tweet and produces the word annotations $H = (h_1, h_2, ..., h_n)$, where h_i is the hidden state of the LSTM at time-step i, summarizing all the information of the sentence up to w_i. We use bidirectional LSTM (BiLSTM) in order to get annotations for each word that summarize the information from both directions of the message. A bidirectional LSTM consists of a forward LSTM, $\overrightarrow{f}$, that reads the sentence from w_1 to w_T, and a backward LSTM, $\overleftarrow{f}$, that reads the sentence from w_T to w_1. We obtain the final annotation for each word w_i, by concatenating the annotations from both directions:

$$h_i = \overrightarrow{h_i} \parallel \overleftarrow{h_i}, h_i \in \mathbb{R}^{2L} \tag{4}$$

where $\parallel$ denotes the concatenation operation and L the size of each LSTM. In order to amplify the contribution of important words in the final representation, we use a context-aware attention mechanism (Yang et al., 2016), that aggregates all the intermediate hidden states using their relative importance. An attention mechanism assigns a weight a_i to each word annotation, which reflects its importance. We compute the representation of the tweet text, R_{text}, as the weighted sum of all the word annotations using the attention weights. This attention mechanism introduces a context vector u_h that helps to identify the informative words and it is randomly initialized and jointly learned with the rest of the attention layer weights. Formally, R_{text} is defined as:

$$R_{text} = \sum_{i=1}^{|T|} a_i h_i, \quad R_{text} \in \mathbb{R}^{2L} \tag{5}$$

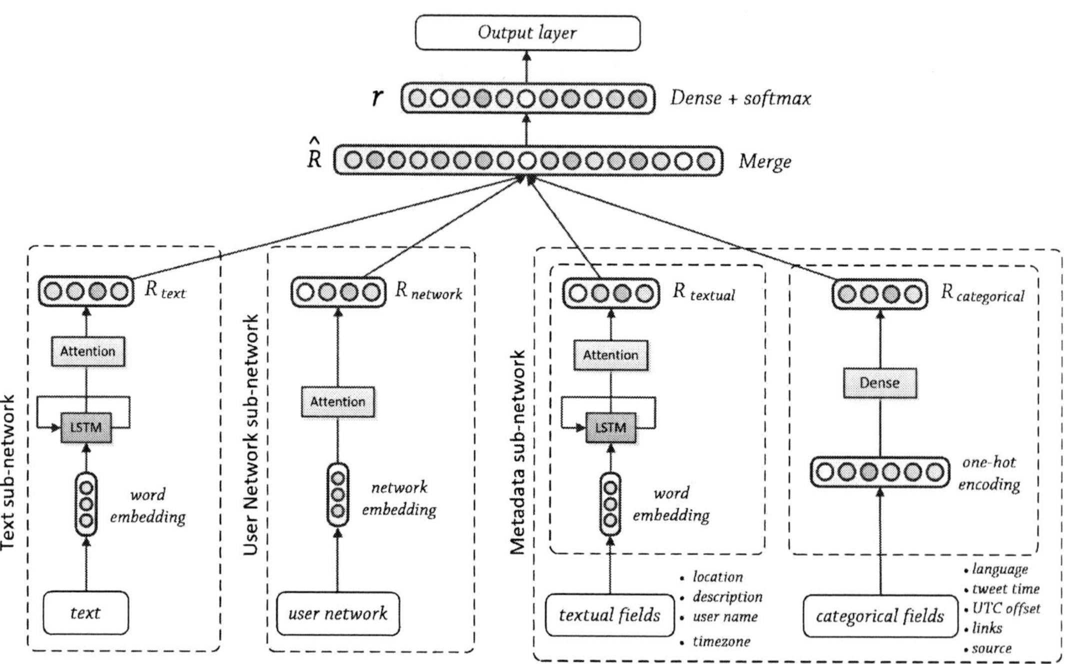

Figure 1: Overview of the proposed approach

$$a_i = \frac{exp(e_i{}^\top u_h)}{\sum_{t=1}^{|T|} exp(e_t{}^\top u_h)}, \quad \sum_{i=1}^{|T|} a_i = 1 \qquad (6)$$

$$e_i = tanh(W_h h_i + b_h), \quad e_i \in [-1, 1] \qquad (7)$$

where W_h, b_h and u_h are the layer's weights.

We use batch normalization (Ioffe and Szegedy, 2015) for normalizing inputs in order to reduce internal covariate shift. The risk of overfitting by co-adapting units is reduced by implementing dropout (Srivastava et al., 2014) between individual neural network layers.

4.2 User Network Component

As a representation of users' social relationships, we construct an undirected graph from interactions among Twitter users based on @-mentions in their tweets (Rahimi et al., 2015b). In this graph, nodes are all users in the dataset (train and test), as well as other external users mentioned in their tweets, and undirected edges are created between two users if either user mentioned the other. This unidirectional setting results in large numbers of edges. To make the process more tractable, we remove all nodes corresponding to external users with degree less than 3 (i.e., external users who have been mentioned by less than 3 different users in a training set).

Figure 2(b) illustrates an overview of the user network component. After filtering the graph, we consider the adjacent nodes (i.e., immediate linked users) of each training user as its network. The user network $N = \{u_1, u_2, ..., u_n\}$ is given as input to an embedding layer. Embedding of user network $E_N = (e_1, e_2, ..., e_n)$ is then fed to an attention layer to compute the final representation of user network, $R_{network}$:

$$R_{network} = \sum_{i=1}^{T} a_i e_i, \quad R_{network} \in \mathbb{R}^{2L} \qquad (8)$$

where a_i is the weight assigned to embedding e_i by the attention mechanism (Equation 6).

4.3 Metadata Component

According to (Guo and Berkhahn, 2016), the embeddings of categorical variables can reduce the network size while capturing the intrinsic properties of the categorical variables. Hence, we convert metadata fields with a finite set of elements (UTC offset, links, user language, tweet publication time, and application source) to one-hot encodings, which are then forwarded to a dense layer with Rectified Linear Units (ReLU) activation function.

The user UTC offset is an integer in seconds representation (e.g., -18000), and the tweet publication time is given in UTC time , e.g., Fri Mar 02

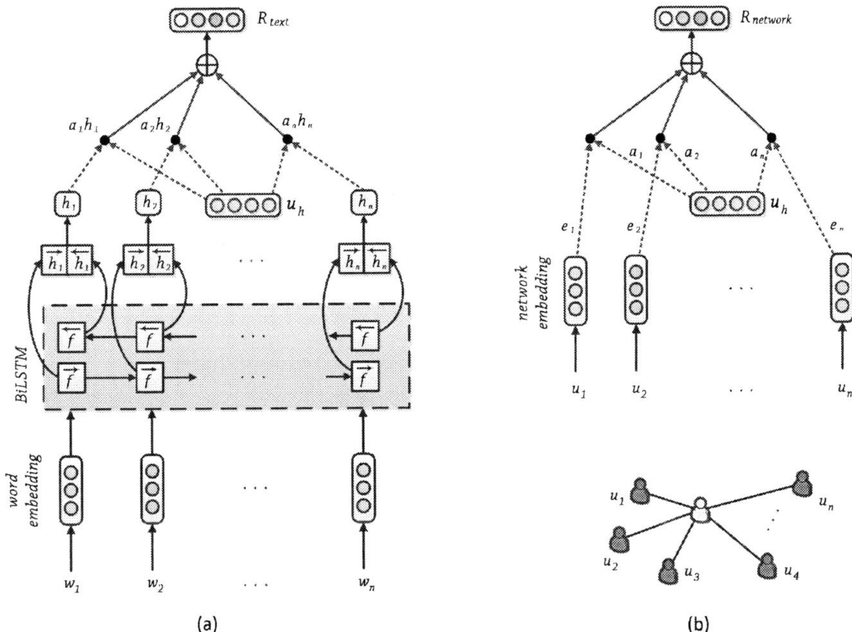

Figure 2: Architectures of the proposed sub-networks for (a) Tweet text, and (b) User network . $\oplus$ shows element-wise addition.

12:19:40 +0000 2012. We convert user UTC offset into hours representation (e.g., $-18000/3600 = -5$). For tweet publication time, we use only time of the day information (e.g., 12:19) and split it into multiple bins. Specifically, we interpret every 10 minutes as a bin (144 bins in total). The intuition is that tweets originated from a particular location (e.g., Germany) favor certain bins, and this preference of bins should be different to tweets from a distant location (e.g., Japan) (Lau et al., 2017).

For metadata fields containing texts (i.e., user description, user location, user name, and time-zone), we use an embedding layer and consequently forward the results to an LSTM layer. The attention mechanism is also employed to provide the final representation of textual metadata fields. Again batch normalization and dropout is applied between individual layers to avoid overfitting.

5 Experimental Results

5.1 Experiment Settings

In the text sub-network, words are input to the model as n-dimensional word embeddings. We pre-trained word embeddings using word2vec (Mikolov et al., 2013) over tweet text of the full training data. The model was trained using the Skip-gram architecture and negative sampling (k = 5) for five iterations, with a context window of 5 and subsampling factor of 0.001. It is note-worthy that to be part of the vocabulary, words should occur at least five times in the corpus. We chose word embeddings of size 200/300 for TWIT-TERUS/WNUT datasets because smaller embeddings experimentally showed to capture not as much detail and resulted in a lower accuracy. Larger word embeddings, on the other hand, made the model too complex to train. In the preprocessing step, we used replacement tokens for URLs, mentions and numbers. However, we did not replace hashtags as doing so experimentally demonstrated to decrease the accuracy.

The layers and the embeddings in our sub-networks have parameters like embedding dimension, LSTM unit size, and attention context vector size. We chose optimal values for these parameters in terms of accuracy with a grid search using the development sets of TwitterUS and WNUT. The selected parameters values are reported in Table 1. It should be noted that the main reason for selecting smaller values for the TWITTERUS dataset is its larger size (in terms of tweet number) comparing to the WNUT dataset. We set the hyper-parameters of our final model as follows: batch size = 256, learning rate = 0.001, epochs = 5. The dropout rate between layers is set to 0.2.

Model	Embedding size		LSTM unit size		Attention vector size	
	TwitterUS	**WNUT**	**TwitterUS**	**WNUT**	**TwitterUS**	**WNUT**
Tweet text	200	300	100	200	200	400
User network	200	400	100	200	200	400
Location	100	200	100	200	200	400
Description	100	200	100	200	200	400
User name	100	200	100	200	200	400
Timezone	100	200	100	200	200	400

Table 1: Parameter settings of the proposed models.

5.2 Evaluation Metrics

We evaluate our approach in the following three commonly used metrics for user geolocation:

- *Acc@161*: The percentage of predicted locations which are within a 161km (100 mile) radius of the actual location (Cheng et al., 2010). This metric is a proxy for accuracy within a metro area.

- *Mean error*: The mean value of error distances in predicted locations (Eisenstein et al., 2010).

- *Median error*: The median value of error distances in predictions (Eisenstein et al., 2010).

Note that higher numbers are better for Acc@161 but lower numbers are better for mean and median errors.

5.3 Results

Table 2 presents the performance of user geolocation methods over TwitterUS and WNUT[2] datasets.

The results show that our proposed method achieves the best performance in terms of all evaluation metrics. The main reason is the effective representation of text, metadata, and network information, and unifying them through a fusion of neural networks.

5.4 Ablation Study

To evaluate the contribution of each component in indicating the user's location, we train an individual neural network model for each field. To this end, we feed the final representation of each subnetwork to a fully-connected dense layer, activated by softmax function. We use stochastic gradient descent over shuffled mini-batches with Adam (Kingma and Ba, 2014) and cross-entropy loss as objective function for classification. The parameters of all models are set as follows: batch size = 256, epochs = 5, dropout=0.2, and learning rate = 0.001. Table 3 shows the performance breakdown for each model over the WNUT dataset.

The results conclude that user-declared location in tweet metadata is the most informative field for geolocating users, and model trained on this source achieves the best single source performance. This model can correctly geolocate 44.9% of users with a median error of 41.0km.

Using only tweet text, our model can predict the correct location for 34.9% of all users with a median error of 169.3km. It is noteworthy that this model outperforms the text-based approach IBM.1 (Chi et al., 2016) in terms of all metrics by a large margin.

User network model can correctly geolocate only 18.4% of users. However, our experiments show that excluding user network information declines the performance of the final model in terms of accuracy by 5.1%. Models using other metadata fields provide an accuracy between 2.7% to 10.6%, with description field being the most informative one. Tweet publication time, on the other hand, has the minimum accuracy in predicting user's location. However, mining the temporal patterns of users' posting habits can potentially provide useful information for geolocation inference.

We have also reported the results of our model when it takes only the metadata fields as inputs. The metadata-based model can correctly geolocate 46.1% of the users with a mean error of 1318.3km, and a median error of 37.9km. It shows the ef-

---

[2]For WNUT, we have reported the results of participating teams in user-level location prediction task.

		TWITTERUS			WNUT			
	Category	Acc@161	Mean	Median	Accuracy	Acc@161	Mean	Median
WB-UNIFORM (Wing and Baldridge, 2014)	TB	49	703	170	-	-	-	-
WB-KDTREE (Wing and Baldridge, 2014)	TB	48	686	191	-	-	-	-
MDN-SHARED (Rahimi et al., 2017a)	TB	42	655	216	-	-	-	-
MLP+KDTREE (Rahimi et al., 2017b)	TB	54	562	121	-	-	-	-
MLP+K-MEAN (Rahimi et al., 2017b)	TB	55	581	91	-	-	-	-
LP-RAHIMI (Rahimi et al., 2015b)	NB	37	747	431	-	-	-	-
LP-NA (Rahimi et al., 2016)	NB	50	610	144	-	-	-	-
MADCELB (Rahimi et al., 2015a)	NB	54	709	117	-	-	-	-
MADCELW (Rahimi et al., 2015a)	NB	54	705	116	-	-	-	-
LP-LR (Rahimi et al., 2015b)	Hyb	50	620	157	-	-	-	-
MADCELW-LR (Rahimi et al., 2015a)	Hyb	60	529	78	-	-	-	-
MADCELW-MLP (Rahimi et al., 2017b)	Hyb	61	515	77	-	-	-	-
GEOCEL-BK (Ebrahimi et al., 2017)	Hyb	66	438	56	-	-	-	-
DREXEL.2	?	-	-	-	7.9	-	6161.4	4000.2
DREXEL.1	?	-	-	-	8.0	-	6053.3	5714.9
AIST	?	-	-	-	9.8	-	4002.4	1711.1
IBM.1 (Chi et al., 2016)	TB	-	-	-	22.5	-	2860.2	630.2
DREXEL.3	?	-	-	-	35.2	-	3124.4	262.7
FUJIXEROX.3 (Miura et al., 2016)	Hyb	-	-	-	45.1	-	1084.3	28.2
FUJIXEROX.1 (Miura et al., 2016)	Hyb	-	-	-	46.4	-	963.8	21.0
FUJIXEROX.2 (Miura et al., 2016)	Hyb	-	-	-	47.6	-	1122	16.1
CSIRO.3 (Jayasinghe et al., 2016)	Hyb	-	-	-	50.1	-	2242.4	30.6
CSIRO.2 (Jayasinghe et al., 2016)	Hyb	-	-	-	52.0	-	2071.5	23.1
CSIRO.1 (Jayasinghe et al., 2016)	Hyb	-	-	-	52.6	-	1929	21.7
THOMAS (Thomas and Hennig, 2017)	Hyb	-	-	-	53.0	-	839	14.9
PROPOSED APPROACH	Hyb	**70.8**	**313.2**	**40.1**	**56.7**	**72.3**	**731.5**	**0**

Table 2: Performance of Text-based (TB), Network-based (NB), and Hybrid (Hyb) geolocation methods over TWITTERUS and WNUT datasets ("-" signifies that no results were published for the given dataset, and "?" signifies that the participant team has not provided descriptions of the proposed system). We have also reported the *Accuracy* of our proposed approach on WNUT dataset to make our results comparable with the existing methods.

fectiveness of utilized metadata fields for user geolocation. Meanwhile, a deeper analysis of metadata fields can further improve the performance of user location prediction. As an example, customized scrapers for social media websites like FourSquare, Swarm, Path, Facebook, and Instagram can be employed as described by (Jayasinghe et al., 2016) to increase the geolocation accuracy.

5.5 Error Analysis

As reported in Table 2, our proposed approach achieves quite low median errors over the TWITTERUS and WNUT datasets (i.e., 40.1km and 0km, respectively). However, there are some cases with large error distances, which make the mean errors much larger than median errors. Our analysis shows that some notable error distances are related to the following cases: (1) Users from remote areas for which less supervisions are available; (2) Users from small cities/states are misclassified to be in the neighboring larger cities/states; (3) Users from some neighboring cities/states are also misclassified between the two cities/states, which might be the result of business and entertainment connections between them.

Our ablation study demonstrates that the location field highly contributes to the geolocation per-

Model	Accuracy	Mean	Median
Tweet text	34.9	1674.1	169.3
User network	18.4	2551.7	789.8
Metadata fields	46.1	1318.3	37.9
- Location	44.9	3515.0	41.0
- Description	10.6	5540.7	3005.4
- Timezone	6.4	5203.6	5181.0
- User name	6.1	5836.1	3966.7
- UTC offset	5.3	6305.9	3727.8
- User language	4.6	9077.1	8585.4
- Links	4.5	6543.2	6691.6
- Source application	4.4	6950.3	6937.7
- Tweet time	2.7	11138.3	10165.5

Table 3: Performance breakdown for each component over WNUT dataset

formance. However, some prediction errors arise when location fields are incorrect. We found two main cases that result in incorrect location fields: (1) Users who move to a new place (i.e., house) but do not update their locations; (2) Users who visit a new place (e.g., as tourists) and temporarily update their locations. Our proposed model cannot handle these types of errors, since it only supports single location field. A future direction is to extend the current architecture to track location changes and deal with temporal states such as traveling.

Previous network-based methods (Jurgens, 2013; Compton et al., 2014) have demonstrated the effectiveness of users' social relationships for geolocation inference. However, our ablation study shows relatively low accuracy for the user network component. One main reason is that our model is less sophisticated (but more scalable) comparing to the mentioned network-based methods, since it only considers the immediate connected nodes as the network for each user. As a future work of this study, node/graph embeddings such as DeepWalk (Perozzi et al., 2014) can be employed to provide better representation of users' social relationships, and consequently improve the accuracy of network component.

6 Conclusion and Future Work

In this paper, we have proposed a unified user geolocation method which relies on a fusion of neural networks. Our joint model effectively utilizes different sources of information including tweet message, users' social relationships, and metadata fields embedded in tweets and profiles. In particular, we employed a neural network model to generate a dense vector representation for each information field and then used the concatenation of these representations as the feature for classification. For modeling tweet message and textual metadata fields, we utilized a bidirectional LSTM network augmented with an attention mechanism to identify the most location indicative words.

We have conducted comprehensive experiments on two standard Twitter geolocation datasets, and demonstrated that our method achieves the best performance in terms of all three evaluation metrics. In an ablation study, we have also trained individual models to investigate the usefulness of each information field in predicting the locations of Twitter users.

As a future work, it would be intriguing to utilize customized scrapers for social media websites (Jayasinghe et al., 2016) to further improve the performance of our geolocation model. It is noteworthy that the proposed model could be modified to infer other user demographic attributes such as gender and age.

Tweet publication time include both date and time, however, only time information is exploited in this work to infer users' geolocations. A future direction is to leverage tweeting behavior over dates for user geolocation. The intuition is that local residents would occasionally post tweets about their home city in a long-term manner, while tourists tend to tweet a lot while visiting the city. Hence, their different tweeting patterns can be easily revealed using date information from their tweet timestamps.

Acknowledgments

We would like to thank the anonymous reviewers for their valuable feedbacks to improve this paper.

References

Amr Ahmed, Liangjie Hong, and Alexander J Smola. 2013. Hierarchical geographical modeling of user locations from social media posts. In *Proceedings of the 22nd international conference on World Wide Web (WWW 2013)*, pages 25–36. ACM.

Oluwaseun Ajao, Jun Hong, and Weiru Liu. 2015. A survey of location inference techniques on twitter. *Journal of Information Science*, 41(6):855–864.

Ji Ao, Peng Zhang, and Yanan Cao. 2014. Estimating the locations of emergency events from twitter streams. *Procedia Computer Science*, 31:731–739.

Miriam Cha, Youngjune Gwon, and HT Kung. 2015. Twitter geolocation and regional classification via sparse coding. In *Proceedings of the 9th International Conference on Weblogs and Social Media (ICWSM 2015)*, pages 582–585.

Zhiyuan Cheng, James Caverlee, and Kyumin Lee. 2010. You are where you tweet: a content-based approach to geo-locating twitter users. In *Proceedings of the 19th ACM International Conference Information and Knowledge Management (CIKM 2010)*, pages 759–768. ACM.

Zhiyuan Cheng, James Caverlee, and Kyumin Lee. 2013. A content-driven framework for geolocating microblog users. *ACM Transactions on Intelligent Systems and Technology (TIST)*, 4(1):2.

Lianhua Chi, Kwan Hui Lim, Nebula Alam, and Christopher J Butler. 2016. Geolocation prediction in twitter using location indicative words and textual features. In *Proceedings of the 2nd Workshop on Noisy User-generated Text (WNUT 2016)*, pages 227–234. ACL.

Ryan Compton, David Jurgens, and David Allen. 2014. Geotagging one hundred million twitter accounts with total variation minimization. In *Proceedings of the 2014 IEEE International Conference on Big-Data (BigData 2014)*, pages 393–401. IEEE.

Clodoveu A Davis Jr, Gisele L Pappa, Diogo Rennó Rocha de Oliveira, and Filipe de L Arcanjo. 2011. Inferring the location of twitter messages based on user relationships. *Transactions in GIS*, 15(6):735–751.

Mohammad Ebrahimi, Elaheh ShafieiBavani, Raymond Wong, and Fang Chen. 2017. Exploring celebrities on inferring user geolocation in twitter. In *Proceedings of the 21st Pacific-Asia Conference on Knowledge Discovery and Data Mining (PAKDD 2017)*, pages 395–406. Springer.

Mohammad Ebrahimi, Elaheh ShafieiBavani, Raymond Wong, and Fang Chen. 2018a. Leveraging local interactions for geolocating social media users. In *Proceedings of the 22nd Pacific-Asia Conference on Knowledge Discovery and Data Mining (PAKDD 2018)*, pages 803–815. Springer.

Mohammad Ebrahimi, Elaheh ShafieiBavani, Raymond Wong, and Fang Chen. 2018b. Twitter user geolocation by filtering of highly mentioned users. *Journal of the Association for Information Science and Technology (JASIST)*, 69(7):879–889.

Jacob Eisenstein, Brendan O'Connor, Noah A Smith, and Eric P Xing. 2010. A latent variable model for geographic lexical variation. In *Proceedings of the 2010 Conference on Empirical Methods in Natural Language Processing (EMNLP 2010)*, pages 1277–1287. ACL.

Cheng Guo and Felix Berkhahn. 2016. Entity embeddings of categorical variables. *CoRR*, abs/1604.06737.

Bo Han, Paul Cook, and Timothy Baldwin. 2012. Geolocation prediction in social media data by finding location indicative words. In *Proceedings of the 24th International Conference on Computational Linguistics (COLING 2012)*, pages 1045–1062. ACL.

Bo Han, Paul Cook, and Timothy Baldwin. 2014. Text-based twitter user geolocation prediction. *Journal of Artificial Intelligence Research (JAIR)*, 49:451–500.

Bo Han, AI Hugo, Afshin Rahimi, Leon Derczynski, and Timothy Baldwin. 2016. Twitter geolocation prediction shared task of the 2016 workshop on noisy user-generated text. In *Proceedings of the 2nd Workshop on Noisy User-generated Text (WNUT 2016)*, pages 213–217. ACL.

Brent Hecht, Lichan Hong, Bongwon Suh, and Ed H Chi. 2011. Tweets from justin bieber's heart: the dynamics of the location field in user profiles. In *Proceedings of the SIGCHI Conference on Human Factors in Computing Systems*, pages 237–246. ACM.

Sepp Hochreiter and Jürgen Schmidhuber. 1997. Long short-term memory. *Neural Computation*, 9(8):1735–1780.

Liangjie Hong, Amr Ahmed, Siva Gurumurthy, Alexander J Smola, and Kostas Tsioutsiouliklis. 2012. Discovering geographical topics in the twitter stream. In *Proceedings of the 21st International Conference on World Wide Web (WWW 2012)*, pages 769–778. ACM.

Mans Hulden, Miikka Silfverberg, and Jerid Francom. 2015. Kernel density estimation for text-based geolocation. In *Proceedings of the 29th Conference on Artificial Intelligence (AAAI 2015)*, pages 145–150.

Sergey Ioffe and Christian Szegedy. 2015. Batch normalization: Accelerating deep network training by reducing internal covariate shift. In *Proceedings of the 37th International Conference on Machine Learning (ICML 2015)*, pages 448–456.

Gaya Jayasinghe, Brian Jin, James Mchugh, Bella Robinson, and Stephen Wan. 2016. Csiro data61 at the wnut geo shared task. In *Proceedings of the 2nd Workshop on Noisy User-generated Text (WNUT 2016)*, pages 218–226. ACL.

Armand Joulin, Edouard Grave, Piotr Bojanowski, and Tomas Mikolov. 2016. Bag of tricks for efficient text classification. *arXiv preprint arXiv:1607.01759*.

David Jurgens. 2013. That's what friends are for: Inferring location in online social media platforms based on social relationships. In *Proceedings of the 7th International Conference on Weblogs and Social Media (ICWSM 2013)*, volume 13, pages 273–282.

David Jurgens, Tyler Finethy, James McCorriston, Yi Tian Xu, and Derek Ruths. 2015. Geolocation prediction in twitter using social networks: A critical analysis and review of current practice. In *Proceedings of the 9th International Conference on Web and Social Media (ICWSM 2015)*, volume 15, pages 188–197.

Diederik P Kingma and Jimmy Ba. 2014. Adam: A method for stochastic optimization. *CoRR*, abs/1412.6980.

Jey Han Lau, Lianhua Chi, Khoi-Nguyen Tran, and Trevor Cohn. 2017. End-to-end network for twitter geolocation prediction and hashing. In *Proceedings of the 8th International Joint Conference on Natural Language Processing (IJCNLP 2017)*, pages 744–753.

Rui Li, Shengjie Wang, Hongbo Deng, Rui Wang, and Kevin Chen-Chuan Chang. 2012. Towards social user profiling: unified and discriminative influence model for inferring home locations. In *Proceedings of the 18th ACM SIGKDD International Conference on Knowledge Discovery and Data Mining (KDD 2012)*, pages 1023–1031. ACM.

John Lingad, Sarvnaz Karimi, and Jie Yin. 2013. Location extraction from disaster-related microblogs. In *Proceedings of the 22nd International Conference on World Wide Web (WWW 2013)*, pages 1017–1020. ACM.

Ji Liu and Diana Inkpen. 2015. Estimating user location in social media with stacked denoising autoencoders. In *Proceedings of the 14th Annual Conference of the North American Chapter of the Association for Computational Linguistics - Human Language Technologies (NAACL-HLT 2015)*, pages 201–210. ACL.

Jalal Mahmud, Jeffrey Nichols, and Clemens Drews. 2012. Where is this tweet from? inferring home locations of twitter users. In *Proceedings of the 6th International Conference on Web and Social Media (ICWSM 2012)*, volume 12, pages 511–514.

Tomas Mikolov, Kai Chen, Greg Corrado, and Jeffrey Dean. 2013. Efficient estimation of word representations in vector space. *arXiv preprint arXiv:1301.3781*.

Yasuhide Miura, Motoki Taniguchi, Tomoki Taniguchi, and Tomoko Ohkuma. 2016. A simple scalable neural networks based model for geolocation prediction in twitter. In *Proceedings of the 2nd Workshop on Noisy User-generated Text (WNUT 2016)*, volume 9026924, pages 235–239. ACL.

Yasuhide Miura, Motoki Taniguchi, Tomoki Taniguchi, and Tomoko Ohkuma. 2017. Unifying text, metadata, and user network representations with a neural network for geolocation prediction. In *Proceedings of the 55th Annual Meeting of the Association for Computational Linguistics (ACL 2017)*, volume 1, pages 1260–1272. ACL.

Anastasios Noulas, Salvatore Scellato, Neal Lathia, and Cecilia Mascolo. 2012. Mining user mobility features for next place prediction in location-based services. In *Proceedings of the 12th IEEE International Conference on Data mining (ICDM 2012)*, pages 1038–1043. IEEE.

Bryan Perozzi, Rami Al-Rfou, and Steven Skiena. 2014. Deepwalk: Online learning of social representations. In *Proceedings of the 20th ACM SIGKDD International Conference on Knowledge Discovery and Data Mining (KDD 2014)*, pages 701–710. ACM.

Afshin Rahimi, Timothy Baldwin, and Trevor Cohn. 2017a. Continuous representation of location for geolocation and lexical dialectology using mixture density networks. In *Proceedings of the 2017 Conference on Empirical Methods in Natural Language Processing (EMNLP 2017)*, pages 167–176. ACL.

Afshin Rahimi, Trevor Cohn, and Timothy Baldwin. 2015a. Twitter user geolocation using a unified text and network prediction model. In *Proceedings of the 53rd Annual Meeting of the Association for Computational Linguistics - 7th International Joint Conference on Natural Language Processing (ACL-IJCNLP 2015)*, pages 630–636. ACL.

Afshin Rahimi, Trevor Cohn, and Timothy Baldwin. 2016. pigeo: A python geotagging tool. In *Proceedings of the 54st Annual Meeting of the Association for Computational Linguistics (ACL 2014): System Demonstrations*, pages 127–132. ACL.

Afshin Rahimi, Trevor Cohn, and Timothy Baldwin. 2017b. A neural model for user geolocation and lexical dialectology. In *Proceedings of the 55th Annual Meeting of the Association for Computational Linguistics (Volume 2: Short Papers) (ACL 2017)*, volume 2, pages 209–216. ACL.

Afshin Rahimi, Duy Vu, Trevor Cohn, and Timothy Baldwin. 2015b. Exploiting text and network context for geolocation of social media users. In *Proceedings of the 14th Annual Conference of the North American Chapter of the Association for Computational Linguistics - Human Language Technologies (NAACL-HLT 2015)*, pages 1362–1367. ACL.

Vineeth Rakesh, Chandan K Reddy, and Dilpreet Singh. 2013. Location-specific tweet detection and topic summarization in twitter. In *Proceedings of the 2013 IEEE/ACM International Conference on Advances in Social Networks Analysis and Mining (ASONAM 2013)*, pages 1441–1444. ACM.

Stephen Roller, Michael Speriosu, Sarat Rallapalli, Benjamin Wing, and Jason Baldridge. 2012. Supervised text-based geolocation using language models on an adaptive grid. In *Proceedings of the 2012 Joint Conference on Empirical Methods in Natural Language Processing and Computational Natural Language Learning (EMNLP-CONLL 2012)*, pages 1500–1510. ACL.

Nitish Srivastava, Geoffrey Hinton, Alex Krizhevsky, Ilya Sutskever, and Ruslan Salakhutdinov. 2014. Dropout: A simple way to prevent neural networks from overfitting. *The Journal of Machine Learning Research (JMLR)*, 15(1):1929–1958.

Philippe Thomas and Leonhard Hennig. 2017. Twitter geolocation prediction using neural networks. In *International Conference of the German Society for Computational Linguistics and Language Technology*, pages 248–255. Springer.

Fengjiao Wang, Chun-Ta Lu, Yongzhi Qu, and S Yu Philip. 2017. Collective geographical embedding for geolocating social network users. In *Proceedings of the 21th Pacific-Asia Conference on Knowledge Discovery and Data Mining (PAKDD 2017)*, pages 599–611. Springer.

Benjamin Wing and Jason Baldridge. 2011. Simple supervised document geolocation with geodesic grids. In *Proceedings of the 49th Annual Meeting of the Association for Computational Linguistics: Human Language Technologies-Volume 1 (ACL-HLT 2011)*, pages 955–964. ACL.

Benjamin Wing and Jason Baldridge. 2014. Hierarchical discriminative classification for text-based geolocation. In *Proceedings of the 2014 Conference on Empirical Methods in Natural Language Processing (EMNLP 2014)*, pages 336–348. ACL.

Zichao Yang, Diyi Yang, Chris Dyer, Xiaodong He, Alex Smola, and Eduard Hovy. 2016. Hierarchical attention networks for document classification. In *Proceedings of the 15th Conference of the North American Chapter of the Association for Computational Linguistics: Human Language Technologies (NAACL-HLT 2016)*, pages 1480–1489. ACL.

Quan Yuan, Gao Cong, Zongyang Ma, Aixin Sun, and Nadia Magnenat Thalmann. 2013. Who, where, when and what: discover spatio-temporal topics for twitter users. In *Proceedings of the 19th ACM SIGKDD International Conference on Knowledge Discovery and Data Mining (ACM-SIGKDD 2013)*, pages 605–613. ACM.

Corpus-driven Thematic Hierarchy Induction

Ilia Kuznetsov and **Iryna Gurevych**

Ubiquitous Knowledge Processing Lab (UKP-TUDA) and Research Training Group AIPHES
Department of Computer Science
Technische Universität Darmstadt
`http://www.ukp.tu-darmstadt.de/`

Abstract

Thematic role hierarchy is a linguistic tool used to describe interactions between semantic roles and their syntactic realizations. Despite decades of dedicated research and numerous thematic hierarchy suggestions in the literature, this concept has not been used in NLP so far due to incompatibility and limited scope of existing hierarchies. We introduce an empirical framework for thematic hierarchy induction and evaluate several role ranking strategies on English and German corpus data. We hypothesize that inducing a thematic hierarchy is feasible, that a hierarchy can be induced from small amounts of data and that resulting hierarchies apply cross-lingually. We evaluate these assumptions empirically.

1 Introduction

Semantic roles are one of the core concepts in NLP, and automatic semantic role labeling (SRL) is a major task with applications in question answering (Shen and Lapata, 2007), machine translation (Liu and Gildea, 2010) and information extraction (Christensen et al., 2010). The goal of SRL is to label the semantic arguments of a predicate (e.g. a verb) with roles from a pre-defined role inventory. Conceptually, role assignment in SRL can be split in two steps: local labeling estimates the likelihood of a certain semantic argument bearing a certain role; global optimization takes context-dependent *role interactions* into account and enforces certain theoretically motivated constraints (e.g. "each role must appear only once per predication").

State of the art in SRL is held by the systems based on deep neural networks (Marcheggiani and Titov, 2017; He et al., 2017). While achieving remarkable quality on benchmark datasets, modern systems show a considerable $\approx$10-point performance drop when applied out-of-domain. This issue is aggravated by the fact that deep neural networks require significant amounts of training data, and SRL annotations are expensive to produce. While local role assignment can be augmented using unlabeled data (e.g. via pre-trained word and character embeddings), context-dependent role interaction is an SRL-specific phenomenon and can only be learned from annotated SRL corpora.

Aiming to reduce the training data requirements for SRL, we revisit the notion of **thematic hierarchy** (TH), a compact *delexicalized* way to model context-dependent role interactions. Thematic hierarchies assume that given a syntactic hierarchy (e.g. *subject $\prec^1$ object $\prec$ oblique*) semantic roles can be ranked in a way that higher ranked roles take higher ranked syntactic positions. One example of phenomena captured by THs is the choice of subject: given a thematic hierarchy `Agent` $\prec$ ... $\prec$ `Instrument`, an `Instrument` can only become subject if the `Agent` is not present, e.g. *"[John]$_{Ag}$ broke the window with a [hammer]$_{In}$"* $\rightarrow$ *"A [hammer]$_{In}$ broke the window"*.

THs have received considerable attention in linguistic literature, but were so far impractical for use in NLP and SRL due to incompatibility and limited scope of the existing hierarchies. As a first step towards including THs into the NLP tool inventory we suggest an empirical framework for inducing THs from role-annotated corpora. Since VerbNet (Schuler, 2006) is the only SRL framework that operates with thematic roles, we choose it as our basis and perform experiments on the PropBank corpus (Palmer et al., 2005) enriched with VerbNet role labels via SemLink (Bonial et al., 2013).

The contributions of this paper are as follows:

- We suggest a method for global thematic hierarchy induction from corpus data;

---

[1]We use $\prec$ for rank precedence, and / for ties

Proceedings of the 22nd Conference on Computational Natural Language Learning (CoNLL 2018), pages 54–64
Brussels, Belgium, October 31 - November 1, 2018. ©2018 Association for Computational Linguistics

- We propose several thematic and syntactic ranking models and evaluate them on English and German data;
- We show that thematic hierarchies can be induced and applied cross-lingually while leaving room for improvement; we further show that thematic hierarchy induction is data-efficient and can produce a high-quality hierarchy using just a fraction of training data.

2 Related work

2.1 Semantic roles and the Lexicon

Semantic roles in the modern sense have been introduced in 1960s as a way to account for variation in syntactic behavior of verbs which can not be explained by purely syntactic means (Gruber, 1965; Fillmore, 1968). A commonly used motivational example contrasts the use of verbs *hit* and *break*: while both are regular transitive verbs, *hit* does not allow construction (4); and construction (5) is ungrammatical in both cases.

(1) [John]$_X$ broke/hit the [window]$_Y$ with a [stone]$_Z$.

(2) [John]$_X$ broke/hit the [window]$_Y$.

(3) A [stone]$_Z$ broke/hit the [window]$_Y$.

(4) The [window]$_Y$ broke/*hit.

(5) The [window]$_Y$ *broke/*hit with a [stone]$_Z$.

There exist several principled ways to describe the syntactic behavior of arguments in the lexicon. Available constructions can be defined individually on **verb sense** basis. This strategy is precise but highly redundant, since verbs show substantial similarities in syntactic behavior; besides, it does not generalize to the out-of-vocabulary (OOV) predicates.

A step towards a more general representation is **verb class** grouping (Levin, 1993): verbs senses can be grouped into verb classes with syntactic behavior shared among the members of the class. For example, syntactically *break* behaves like *crash*, *shred* and *split*, while *hit* behaves like *bash* and *whack* in the corresponding verb senses. This significantly reduces the lexicon redundancy and allows treatment of the OOV verbs if the verb class can be determined. A similar level of granularity is used by the major SRL frameworks: FrameNet SRL (Das et al., 2010) and, to some extent, Prop-Bank SRL (Roth and Woodsend, 2014).

Semantic arguments share similarities across verb classes, giving rise to the notion of general semantic roles. While there exists no consensus on the inventory of semantic roles, a subset shared by the most theoretical approaches includes roles such as Agent (the active sentient initiator of the event), Theme (the most affected participant), Result (the outcome of the event), Instrument (the instrument used) etc. Semantic roles show similar behavior across languages and can be thought of as grammatically relevant universal categories humans use to conceptualize real-world events. Following common terminology, we further refer to *general, predicate-independent* semantic roles as **thematic roles**. This level of granularity is, for example, used by VerbNet (Schuler, 2006).

Thematic roles' syntactic behavior depends on the presence of other thematic roles in the sentence: as our example above demonstrates, an Instrument can only take the subject position if the Agent is not present (3); and Theme can only become subject if both Agent and Instrument are not expressed (4-5). A widely used modeling tool to account for context dependency is the **thematic hierarchy** (TH): given a syntactic prominence scale (e.g. *subject* $\prec$ *oblique... $\prec$ object*), one can assume that there exists a universal ranking of thematic roles, which is homomorphic to the syntactic ranking (e.g. Agent $\prec$ Instrument $\prec$ Theme). The top-ranking semantic argument gets assigned to the highest available syntactic position, the second-ranking gets the second-highest position, etc.

THs are a compact delexicalized way to describe semantic roles' syntactic behavior at the grammar level, which could reduce data requirements and improve generalization capability of SRL systems. However, THs from the literature come from varying theoretical backgrounds, are based on different syntactic formalisms and operate with different role inventories. Most of these THs are justified via basic (often synthetic) language examples, aiming to verify a certain theory cross-lingually rather than to describe the language use in a compact way.

2.2 Major SRL Frameworks

The choice of linguistic theory in SRL is mostly dictated by the availability of training data. Prop-Bank SRL is based on the PropBank corpus (Palmer et al., 2005) which utilizes a set of predicate-specific core roles (A0-5) and a set of general, predicate-independent adjunct roles (AM-TMP, AM-LOC etc.). Core roles are defined on verb sense level. An effort is made to ensure consistency in assigning A0 (Agent-like) and A1 (Patient-like). The rest of the core arguments (A2-5) are verb sense-specific; no finer-grained distinctions between roles are made.

PropBank annotation is closely tied to syntax. FrameNet (Baker et al., 1998) takes a different stance and focuses on accurate and detailed representation of event semantics. Verbs (as well as lexemes from other categories) are grouped into *frames* so that members of the same frame share a set of fine-grained frame-specific semantic roles (e.g. Impactee, Force, Buyer, Goods).

Both PropBank and FrameNet SRL operate on the verb sense/verb class generalization level. VerbNet (Schuler, 2006) groups verbs into Levin-inspired verb classes and defines sets of general, lexicon-level thematic roles and constructions for each class. It is the only SRL formalism that operates with a thematic role set. VerbNet role sets and verb class information are mapped to the PropBank corpus annotations via SemLink (Bonial et al., 2013).

2.3 Thematic roles in SRL

So far only few studies have considered VerbNet-level granularity in SRL and we are not aware of SRL systems specifically designed to exploit the thematic role generalizations. Zapirain et al. (2008) compare PropBank and VerbNet performance using a simple SRL system and conclude that PropBank labels generally perform better; however, they do not use any additional modeling possibilities offered by VerbNet's general, predicate-independent role set. Loper et al. (2007) show that replacing verb-specific PropBank roles A2-5 with the corresponding VerbNet roles improves the SRL performance. Merlo and van der Plas (2009) report a statistical analysis of PropBank and VerbNet annotations and conclude that while PropBank role inventory better correlates with syntax and is therefore easier to learn, VerbNet thematic roles are more informative and better generalize to new verb instances. Finally, a recent comparison on German data by Hartmann et al. (2017) positions VerbNet inventory above FrameNet and below PropBank in terms of complexity and generalization capabilities; however, the experiment is again based on the *mateplus* system (Roth and Woodsend, 2014) designed with PropBank generalization level in mind.

2.4 Semantic Proto-Roles

A related line of work is Semantic Proto Role Labeling (SPRL) (Reisinger et al., 2015; White et al., 2017) which, following Dowty (1991), discards the notion of atomic semantic role inventory and replaces it with Proto-Agent and Proto-Patient **property sets**. While our study utilizes traditional atomic role inventories, we see SPRL as a compatible parallel line of work and believe that additional benefits can be gained by combining the two views on syntax-semantics interface. In particular, Reisinger et al. (2015) investigate the alignment between Dowty-style role properties and VerbNet thematic roles and show that VerbNet Agents tend to bear Dowty's instigated, awareness and volitional properties, while Themes are more likely to change posession, change state, etc.

2.5 Thematic hierarchies

Numerous THs have been proposed in the linguistic literature, e.g. Agent ≺ Instrument ≺ Theme (Fillmore, 1968); see (Levin and Rappaport Hovav, 2005) for an overview. These hierarchies are rarely applicable for NLP since they originate from different theoretical backgrounds and are usually focused on a narrow set of linguistic phenomena (e.g. subject selection), aiming to provide a cross-linguistically valid hierarchy based on a set of manually constructed examples. In contrast, our approach is data-driven and aims to describe the general syntactic behavior of thematic roles. While an optimal TH that would successfully describe semantic roles' behavior across languages might not exist (and would imply the existence of a universal role inventory and grammar), our evidence suggests that this concept is at least partially applicable.

To the best of our knowledge, there exists no prior work explicitly aiming at discovering thematic hierarchies in corpora. However, the hierarchy-related effects are reported in some studies. For example, White et al. (2017) observe on a reduced role set that VerbNet roles disprefer the violations of thematic/syntactic hierarchy alignment. Sun et al. (2009) experiment on thematic rank prediction for PropBank A0 and A1, but extend their analysis neither to VerbNet thematic roles, nor to the PropBank A2-5.

2.6 Syntactic formalisms

Cross-lingual applicability has traditionally been a strong component in semantic role theory, and universality is one of the common desiderata for a thematic hierarchy. This, however, implies the existence of a universal syntactic prominence scale.

From the NLP perspective, the closest to universal syntactic representation for which automatic parsers are available is the Universal Dependencies (UD) representation. Universal Dependencies (Nivre et al., 2016) is a recent initiative aimed at creating a single dependency-based formalism suited for describing syntactic structure in a language-independent way. It encompasses freely available treebanks for more than 60 languages, and universal dependency parsing is an active research area (Zeman et al., 2017). Based on that, we make an effort to ground our study in UD syntax for English. Since neither gold UD annotations, nor a deterministic converter are available, for German we use the TIGER dependency syntax representation (Dipper et al., 2001).

3 Hierarchical Linking model

3.1 Model

We suggest a simple model to describe the interface between syntactic and thematic rankings. An SRL corpus can be seen as a collection of sentences with corresponding **predications**, where each predication has a **target** (e.g. verb) and a set of **arguments** labeled with semantic roles.

Let $a_1...a_n \in A$ be the set of arguments in the predication p; $r(a_i)$ be the role label af the argument a_i, and $d(a_i)$ be the path between the predicate and the argument in the dependency parse tree of the sentence. A **syntactic ranker** S provides a syntactic rank $s_i = S(d(a_i))$ for each argument a_i in A based on the path, and a **thematic ranker** T provides a thematic rank $t_i = T(r(a_i))$ based on the argument's role. For each pair of arguments (a_i, a_j) we expect their syntactic ranks to align with their thematic ranks, i.e.

$$\forall i \neq j : sign(t_i - t_j) = sign(s_i - s_j)$$

The model per se does not imply the existence of a global ranking and allows flexible ranker definition. It allows ties in both syntactic and thematic rankings.

We use accuracy to assess how well a given syntactic-semantic ranker pair reflects the actual

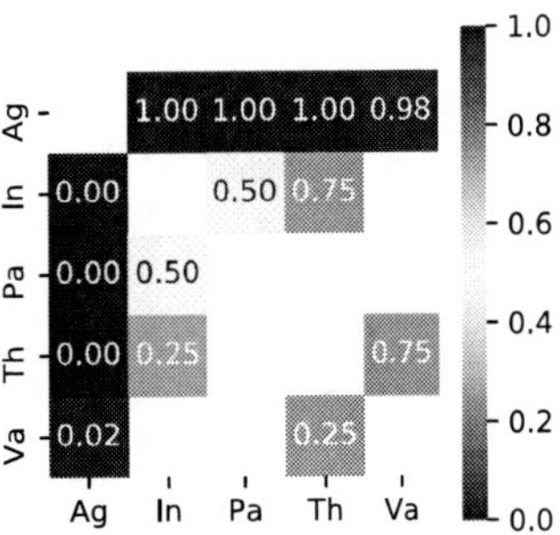

Figure 1: Preference matrix

argument ranks found in data. Given a set of test predications $p_1, p_2...p_k \in P$ with the argument sets $A^1, A^2...A^k$, we measure the correspondence between syntactic and semantic ranking over the argument pairs (a_i^k, a_j^k) via accuracy defined as

$$\frac{\#(sign(t_i^k - t_j^k) = sign(s_i^k - s_j^k))}{\#total\_pairs}$$

To avoid the majority class bias, we measure accuracy for each role pair and use macro-averaged accuracy over pairs as the final score. A straightforward alternative to our evaluation metric would be the Kendall rank correlation coefficient, which, based on our preliminary experiments, tends to overemphasize the performance on most frequent role pairs.

4 Thematic Hierarchy Induction

This paper investigates several thematic ranking strategies. As a running example we use a small role set: `Agent (Ag)`, `Patient (Pa)`, `Instrument (In)`, `Theme (Th)` and `Value (Va)`. For now we assume the following syntactic hierarchy: *subj ≺ iobj ≺ nmod ≺ obj ≺ other*.

Local ranker The simplest way to model role ranking is to extract the average syntactic rank for each role based on the data, and then, given a test pair, assign ranks based on average syntactic rank.

role	Ag	Pa	In	Th	Va
$mean(s)$	1.01	2.58	1.72	3.95	3.74

Table 1: Mean syntactic rank per role (1-5)

Pairwise ranker Given that roles often strongly prefer a certain syntactic position (also see (White

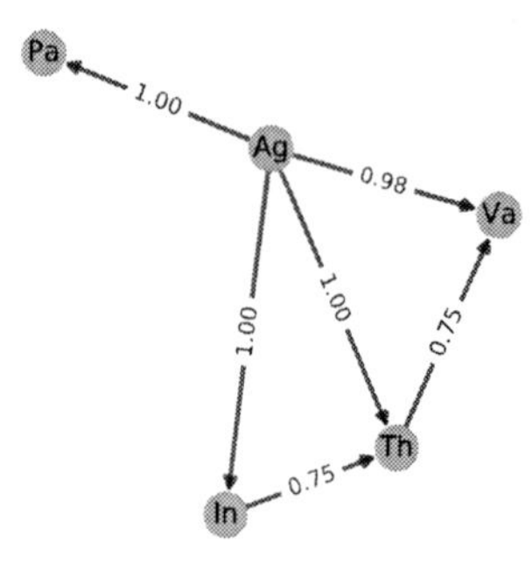

Figure 2: Preference graph

et al., 2016)), local ranking is a reasonable baseline strategy. However, it fails to account for the context dependency of thematic roles' syntactic realization. The next step is to construct a **pairwise preference matrix**: for each pair of roles encountered in training data we calculate the proportion of times role r_i receives a higher syntactic rank than role r_j. For our role set this results in the matrix shown on Fig. 1.

The preference matrix, for example, shows that Agent clearly dominates all the roles, Instrument ranks over Theme, and Value is below Theme.

Global ranker The pairwise ranking approach takes context into account. However, some role pairs only co-occur rarely. In such cases no pairwise ranking information is available to the model. Finding a global TH based on pairwise preferences is an example of a **rank aggregation** problem which can be solved via constrained ILP optimization on a **preference graph** (Conitzer et al., 2006). We represent the pairwise preference matrix as a graph $G = (v, e)$ where each vertex v represents a role, the edge weight is the preference strength measured as $\#(r_i \prec r_j)/\#(r_i, r_j)$. The edge direction is from higher- to lower-ranking role. If we assume a global ordering of the roles, we can induce the global ranking via transitivity relations. For example (Fig. 2), Instrument never appears with Value in our training data; however, by transitivity via Theme we can assume that Instrument ranks over Value.

Given the preference graph $G = (v, e)$, let w_{ij} be the weight of the edge between v_i and v_j. Let $x_{ij} \in 0, 1$ denote that we rank vertice v_i above v_j.

The goal is then to maximize $\sum_{i,j} x_{ij} w_{ij}$ subject to two groups of constraints. First, we prohibit two nodes to rank above each other, but allow ties, by enforcing $\forall_{i,j} : x_{ij} + x_{ji} \leq 1$. Second, we enforce transitivity, i.e. if r_i is ranked above r_j, and r_j is ranked above r_k, then r_i must be ranked above r_k, formally $\forall_{i,j,k}, i \neq j \neq k : x_{ij} + x_{jk} - x_{ik} \leq 1$. We solve the ILP problem using the off-the-shelf *pulp* optimizer (Mitchell et al., 2011).

For our restricted example, optimization produces the following global hierarchy: Ag $\prec$ In $\prec$ Th $\prec$ Va/Pa. This hierarchy ranks Instrument above Value by transitivity, however, in case of Patient and Value no preference can be inferred from the graph, so they receive the same thematic rank.

5 Experiments

5.1 Datasets and Restrictions

For our experiments on English, we use SemLink (Bonial et al., 2013), a manually constructed resource that enriches PropBank's (Palmer et al., 2005) semantic role annotations with VerbNet's (Schuler, 2006) thematic role labels. We use the Universal Dependencies converter (Schuster and Manning, 2016) to transform original PropBank syntactic annotation to UD. PropBank semantic role annotation and the corresponding SemLink reference are constituents-based. However, UD is a dependency formalism, and we employ a number of heuristics to align original PropBank annotations with the CoNLL-2009 datasets (Hajič et al., 2009) to recover the head node positions. We employ additional transformations, filtering out the predications in which not all PropBank core roles got aligned to the VerbNet thematic roles.

For German, we use the recently introduced SR3de dataset (Mújdricza-Maydt et al., 2016; Hartmann et al., 2017) which explicitly provides VerbNet annotations on top of SALSA corpus (Burchardt et al., 2006). There exist no gold UD annotations for the SALSA corpus, and we use the SALSA's default TIGER syntactic formalism (Dipper et al., 2001) in our experiments.

Following previous work, we employ certain restrictions on our data. Since thematic roles in both VerbNet and SR3de are only defined for verbal predicates, we restrict the scope of our study to verbs. We only consider direct dependents of the verbs in active voice, and since having access to the full argument set is important to study con-

dataset	#sent	#tok	#pred	#arg
EN (PropBank→SemLink)				
train	16 603	446 641	21 276	44 333
test	1 031	27 751	1 336	2 761
dev	550	15 157	684	1422
DE (SR3de VerbNet)				
train	898	20 277	905	1 992
test	240	4 738	245	532
dev	117	2 429	119	266

Table 2: Dataset statistics

text dependency, we only consider the predications where all arguments are direct dependents of the verb in the UD dependency tree. Since we are interested in relative ranking, only predications that contain more than one semantic argument are considered in the study.

Dataset statistics for English and German (after filtering) are summarized in Table 2. In all experiments we induce a TH and related statistics from the training data and evaluate it on the test data, using the split from the CoNLL SRL shared tasks.

5.2 Syntactic ranker

For simplicity in this paper we only experiment with two syntactic rankers per language. A common syntactic prominence scale assumed in linguistic literature is *subject* $\prec$ *object* $\prec$ *indirect object* $\prec$ *oblique*. This scale has to be adapted to the UD and TIGER labeling schemes. For each language we evaluate two syntactic rankings: one that positions *objects* above *indirect objects* and *obliques*, and one that positions *objects* below.

For English, we rank the UD syntactic relations as follows (**SE1**): *nsubj / csubj* $\prec$ *iobj* $\prec$ *nmod* $\prec$ *ccomp / dobj* $\prec$ *other*; where *nmod* corresponds to oblique and *other* is used for any other syntactic relation. An alternative ranking positions *dobj* directly after the subject (**SE2**): *nsubj / csubj* $\prec$ *ccomp / dobj* $\prec$ *iobj* $\prec$ *nmod* $\prec$ *other*.

For German, the following ranking of TIGER syntactic relations is employed (**SD1**): *SB* $\prec$ *DA* $\prec$ *OP / MO / OG/ OC* $\prec$ *OA / OA2 / CVC* $\prec$ *other*; where *SB* is the subject, *DA* is dative object, *OP / MO / OG / OC* correspond to oblique relations, and *OA / OA2 / CVC* to direct object relations (see (Dipper et al., 2001) for detailed description). Similarly, we evaluate the performance of the ranking that positions the direct object after the subject (**SD2**): *SB* $\prec$ *OA / OA2 / CVC* $\prec$ *DA* $\prec$ *OP / MO / OG / OC* $\prec$ *other*.

	synt	glob	pair	loc	RND	UB
EN	SE1	.869	.887	.867	.509	.927
EN	SE2	**.930**	**.929**	**.913**	.500	**.932**
DE	SD1	.655	.726	.637	.471	.818
DE	SD2	**.790**	**.820**	**.820**	.456	**.920**

Table 3: Thematic ranker evaluation, incl. random ranker (RND) and upper bound (UB); bold - best result over syntactic rankers, underlined - best result over thematic rankers

5.3 Bounds

We construct the **upper bound** for the hierarchy induction by evaluating a global ranker trained on the test dataset. The upper bound reflects the data properties, as well as the maximal alignment accuracy that can be achieved with the selected syntactic ranker. The **lower bound** is constructed by evaluating 100 random thematic rankers which rank roles according to a random (but consistent) hierarchy, and averaging the result.

5.4 Data utilization setup

To evaluate how effective the proposed rankers use the training data, we conduct a series of experiments with reduced dataset sizes using the following protocol. The training dataset is shuffled and split into $n = 100$ slices. A ranker is consecutively trained on the first $m \in 1..n$ slices and evaluated against the full test dataset. The procedure is repeated $k = 100$ times to eliminate the effect of data order, and the results per slice are averaged.

6 Results

6.1 General Accuracy and Syntactic Ranker

To get an overall impression of the ranking quality, we first compare the performance of thematic rankers with respect to syntactic rankers and available datasets. The results of this comparison are summarized in Table 3 and show that syntactic rankers positioning the object second in the hierarchy (SE2 and SD2) lead to better alignment on both datasets and have a higher upper bound. We report the results on these rankers for the rest of the paper.

For English the global hierarchy-based ranker approaches the upper bound, closely followed by the pairwise ranker. The accuracy on German data is lower and the pairwise and local rankers outperform the global hierarchy-based ranker. We revisit this observation in 6.5.

	EN-test	DE-test
UB	.932	.920
EN-train	.930	.787
DE-train	.852	.790
RND	.500	.456

Table 5: Cross-lingual evaluation, global ranker

Role pair	score	#(train)
Recipient - Topic	0.35	338
Source - Theme	0.46	246
Location - Theme	0.53	400
Material - Product	0.67	29
Result - Theme	0.67	30
Experiencer - Stimulus	0.74	922
Destination - Theme	0.86	401
Instrument - Theme	0.88	110
Recipient - Theme	0.89	419
Attribute - Experiencer	0.90	166

Table 6: Global ranker accuracy, English

[The top table:]

EN	Agent $\prec$ Cause/Instrument/Experiencer $\prec$ Pivot $\prec$ Theme $\prec$ Patient $\prec$ Material/Source/Asset $\prec$ Product $\prec$ Recipient/Beneficiary/Destination/Location $\prec$ Value/Stimulus/Topic/Result/Predicate/Goal/InitialLocation/Attribute/Extent	
DE	Agent $\prec$ Experiencer $\prec$ Stimulus/Pivot $\prec$ Cause $\prec$ Theme $\prec$ Patient $\prec$ Topic $\prec$ Instrument $\prec$ Beneficiary/InitialLocation $\prec$ Result $\prec$ Product/Goal $\prec$ Destination/Attribute $\prec$ Recipient $\prec$ Value/Time/CoAgent/Locus/Manner/Source/Trajectory/Location/Duration/Path/Extent	

Table 4: Induced hierarchies

6.2 Qualitative analysis

The result of hierarchy induction is a global ranking of thematic roles. Table 4 shows full rankings extracted for English and German data. While some correspondence to the hierarchies proposed in literature is evident (e.g. for English Agent $\prec$ Instrument $\prec$ Theme, similar to (Fillmore, 1968)), a direct comparison is impossible due to the differences in role definitions and underlying syntactic formalisms. Notice the high number of ties: some roles never co-occur (either by chance or by design) or occur on the same syntactic rank (e.g. *oblique*) so there is no evidence for preference even if we enforce transitivity.

6.3 Cross-lingual hierarchy induction

The induced hierarchies for English and German bear certain similarities, which raises the question on cross-lingual applicability of the hierarchies. This analysis is only possible because the VerbNet and SR3de role inventories are mostly compatible with few exceptions (Mújdricza-Maydt et al., 2016). Table 5 contrasts the performance of THs induced from English and German training data, and evaluated on German and English test data respectively. While the cross-lingual performance is expectedly lower than the monolingual performance, it outperforms the random baseline by a large margin, suggesting the potential for cross-lingual hierarchy induction.

6.4 Data utilization

One can assume that constructing a global hierarchy should require less training data due to the ef-fective utilisation of transitivity. We evaluate this assumption empirically. Fig. 3 reports the performance of rankers with access to different amounts of training data for English and German. The results on English data show that global hierarchy-based ranker effectively utilizes the training data and can be trained using just fractions of the original training dataset.

The accuracy measurements on German are less conclusive: the local ranker generally performs best and learns fastest. We attribute this to the fact that filtered SR3de is an order of magnitude smaller than the PropBank/SemLink dataset. For pairwise and global rankers as many role pairs as possible should be observed at least once to establish the pairwise preference. This holds for PropBank/SemLink (all role pairs from test data seen at least once after observing 20% of the training data, on average), however, for filtered SR3de, even given the full training data, only 83% of role pairs from the test set have been seen at least once.

6.5 Error analysis

Our evaluation procedure allows detailed insights into the performance of the models. To illustrate, we extract the role pairs from English and German data with ranking accuracy below 1.0.

Table 6 lists the ranking inconsistencies produced by the global ranker for English. We can

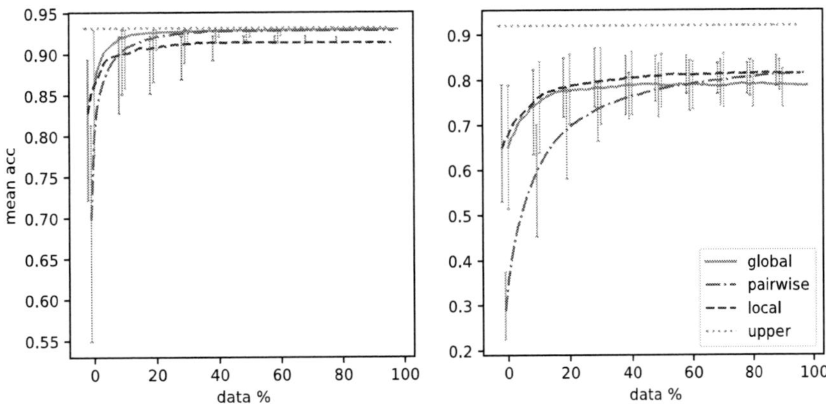

Figure 3: Data utilization for English (left) and German (right) along with max/min values

Role pair	score	#(train)
Attribute - Source	0.00	0
Beneficiary - Manner	0.00	0
Beneficiary - Value	0.00	1
Extent - Goal	0.00	2
Goal - Recipient	0.00	12
Instrument - Result	0.00	3
Locus - Topic	0.12	3
Recipient - Theme	0.40	26
Recipient - Topic	0.50	5
Pivot - Theme	0.67	57

Table 7: Global ranker accuracy, German

see that false ranking might be caused by the lack of training examples (e.g. `Material` vs. `Product`, `Theme` vs. `Result`). We also observe complications with positioning the `Theme` on the hierarchy. In many cases the misalignment is due to non-standard use of thematic roles, e.g. `Location` as subject in `wsj_2322:7` [*the delay$_{Loc}$ resulted from difficulties$_{Th}$*]. Another common reason for false alignments is the syntactic ranker. For example, in `wsj_2372:1` [*the Senate$_{Ag}$ voted 87-7$_{Res}$ to approve$_{Th}$...*] the `Result` is connected to the predicate via an *advmod* relation, and `Theme` is *xcomp*, both ranked equally (*other*) by our syntactic ranker.

Error analysis on the much smaller German dataset (Table 7) reveals the sparsity-related issues: most of the role pairs that tend to get misaligned do not, or only rarely appear in the training data, heavily influencing the score. As on English data, many misalignments are due to simplicity of the syntactic ranker.

7 Discussion

7.1 Importance of the syntactic ranker

The choice of syntactic ranking has a drastic effect on the resulting TH and the alignment quality, even if only direct syntactic dependents and a limited set of relations are taken into account. Realistically there might exist an arbitrary set of paths connecting arguments to predicates. UD as syntactic formalism is also subject to rapid change. Inducing a **joint syntactic and thematic hierarchy** that maximizes the overall alignment quality is a crucial direction for future work with potential benefits for SRL and syntactic parsing. Although we show that THs can be induced with an arbitrary dependency formalism, a **cross-lingual UD-based study** would be another extension to our work.

7.2 SRL integration

To utilize and evaluate the potential of thematic hierarchies for role interaction modeling, **SRL integration** is necessary. This, however, is not a trivial task: the absolute majority of semantic role labeling systems are designed with PropBank or FrameNet SRL formalism in mind and are not tailored to general VerbNet-style semantic roles and verb class-level disambiguation. A dedicated VerbNet SRL system would enable this assessment, and applying THs to such a system is an important future work direction.

7.3 Robustness to parsing errors

This paper focuses on TH induction using predefined syntactic annotation: a corpus annotated with semantic roles without an underlying syntactic layer is a rare occurence. However, for practical applications and for the cases when an SRL corpus is provided without syntactic annotations, it would be important to evaluate how effectively THs can be induced given parsing errors in training *and* in test data.

7.4 Data selection

We have demonstrated that THs can be induced from small portions of training data. The large discrepancy in the scores on the first data slices seen on Fig. 3 suggests that some data instances are more informative for TH induction. This raises the question whether it is possible to automatically **select useful training instances**, supported by the evidence from previous work in SRL (Peterson et al., 2014). One obvious strategy would be to make sure that the hierarchy inducer is presented as many role pairs as early as possible. Approximating this objective in an unsupervised way would reduce the amount of data needed to induce a high-quality thematic hierarchy.

7.5 The need for a global hierarchy

Our results regarding the **necessity of a global hierarchy** which ranks *all* the roles are inconclusive. While global ranking reaches the best quality for English, on the German data pairwise and local ranking approaches perform best. Although we attribute the latter to sparsity, more German data would be needed to evaluate this hypothesis. In particular, this can be achieved by relaxing some of the constraints we impose on the data.

8 Conclusion

This paper has presented an empirical framework for thematic hierarchy induction and evaluation. We have suggested several syntactic and thematic ranking strategies and a method to induce global thematic hierarchies from corpus data. Analysis on English and German data shows that hierarchy induction is feasible, data-efficient and has potential for cross-lingual applications. Promising directions for future work include joint modeling of syntactic and thematic ranking, selecting informative training instances and evaluating the utility of global hierarchies on extended language material.

Acknowledgements

This work has been supported by the German Research Foundation as part of the Research Training Group AIPHES (grant No. GRK 1994/1), QA-EduInf project (grant GU 798/18-1 and grant RI 803/12-1) and FAZIT Stiftung.

References

Collin F. Baker, Charles J. Fillmore, and John B. Lowe. 1998. The Berkeley FrameNet project. In *Proceedings of the 17th International Conference on Computational Linguistics*, volume 1, pages 86–90, Montreal, Quebec, Canada. Association for Computational Linguistics.

Claire Bonial, Kevin Stowe, and Martha Palmer. 2013. Renewing and revising SemLink. In *Proceedings of the 2nd Workshop on Linked Data in Linguistics (LDL-2013): Representing and linking lexicons, terminologies and other language data*, pages 9–17. Association for Computational Linguistics.

Aljoscha Burchardt, Katrin Erk, Anette Frank, Andrea Kowalski, Sebastian Pado, and Manfred Pinkal. 2006. The SALSA corpus: A German corpus resource for lexical semantics. In *Proceedings of the Fifth International Conference on Language Resources and Evaluation (LREC'06)*, pages 969–974. European Language Resources Association (ELRA).

Janara Christensen, Mausam, Stephen Soderland, and Oren Etzioni. 2010. Semantic role labeling for open information extraction. In *Proceedings of the NAACL HLT 2010 First International Workshop on Formalisms and Methodology for Learning by Reading*, FAM-LbR '10, pages 52–60, Stroudsburg, PA, USA. Association for Computational Linguistics.

Vincent Conitzer, Andrew Davenport, and Jayant Kalagnanam. 2006. Improved bounds for computing kemeny rankings. In *Proceedings of the 21st National Conference on Artificial Intelligence - Volume 1*, AAAI'06, pages 620–626. AAAI Press.

Dipanjan Das, Nathan Schneider, Desai Chen, and Noah A. Smith. 2010. Probabilistic frame-semantic parsing. In *Human Language Technologies: The 2010 Annual Conference of the North American Chapter of the Association for Computational Linguistics*, HLT '10, pages 948–956, Stroudsburg, PA, USA. Association for Computational Linguistics.

Stefanie Dipper, Thorsten Brants, Wolfgang Lezius, Oliver Plaehn, and George Smith. 2001. The TIGER treebank. In *Proceedings of the Workshop on Treebanks and Linguistic Theories*, pages 24–41.

David Dowty. 1991. Thematic proto-roles and argument selection. *Language*, 76(3):474–496.

Charles J. Fillmore. 1968. The Case for Case. In Emmon Bach and Robert T. Harms, editors, *Universals in Linguistic Theory*, pages 1–88. Holt, Rinehart and Winston, New York.

Jeffrey S. Gruber. 1965. *Studies in Lexical Relations.* Ph.D. thesis, MIT, Cambridge, MA.

Jan Hajič, Massimiliano Ciaramita, Richard Johansson, Daisuke Kawahara, Maria Antònia Martí, Lluís Màrquez, Adam Meyers, Joakim Nivre, Sebastian Padó, Jan Štěpánek, Pavel Straňák, Mihai Surdeanu, Nianwen Xue, and Yi Zhang. 2009. The CoNLL-2009 Shared Task: Syntactic and Semantic Dependencies in Multiple Languages. In *Proceedings of the Thirteenth Conference on Computational Natural Language Learning: Shared Task*, CoNLL '09, pages 1–18, Stroudsburg, PA, USA. Association for Computational Linguistics.

Silvana Hartmann, Éva Mújdricza-Maydt, Ilia Kuznetsov, Iryna Gurevych, and Anette Frank. 2017. Assessing SRL frameworks with automatic training data expansion. In *Proceedings of the 11th Linguistic Annotation Workshop*, pages 115–121. Association for Computational Linguistics.

Luheng He, Kenton Lee, Mike Lewis, and Luke Zettlemoyer. 2017. Deep semantic role labeling: What works and what's next. In *Proceedings of the 55th Annual Meeting of the Association for Computational Linguistics (Volume 1: Long Papers)*, pages 473–483. Association for Computational Linguistics.

Beth Levin. 1993. *English Verb Classes and Alternations: A Preliminary Investigation.* University of Chicago Press.

Beth Levin and Malka Rappaport Hovav. 2005. *Argument Realization.* Research Surveys in Linguistics. Cambridge University Press.

Ding Liu and Daniel Gildea. 2010. Semantic role features for machine translation. In *Proceedings of the 23rd International Conference on Computational Linguistics (Coling 2010)*, pages 716–724. Coling 2010 Organizing Committee.

Edward Loper, Szu ting Yi, and Martha Palmer. 2007. Combining lexical resources: Mapping between propbank and verbnet. In *Proceedings of the 7th International Workshop on Computational Linguistics*, Tilburg, the Netherlands.

Diego Marcheggiani and Ivan Titov. 2017. Encoding sentences with graph convolutional networks for semantic role labeling. In *Proceedings of the 2017 Conference on Empirical Methods in Natural Language Processing*, pages 1507–1516, Copenhagen, Denmark. Association for Computational Linguistics.

Paola Merlo and Lonneke van der Plas. 2009. Abstraction and generalisation in semantic role labels: Propbank, verbnet or both? In *Proceedings of the Joint Conference of the 47th Annual Meeting of the ACL and the 4th International Joint Conference on Natural Language Processing of the AFNLP*, pages 288–296. Association for Computational Linguistics.

Stuart Mitchell, Michael OSullivan, and Iain Dunning. 2011. Pulp: a linear programming toolkit for python.

Éva Mújdricza-Maydt, Silvana Hartmann, Iryna Gurevych, and Anette Frank. 2016. Combining semantic annotation of word sense & semantic roles: A novel annotation scheme for VerbNet roles on German language data. In *Proceedings of the Tenth International Conference on Language Resources and Evaluation (LREC 2016)*. European Language Resources Association (ELRA).

Joakim Nivre, Marie-Catherine de Marneffe, Filip Ginter, Yoav Goldberg, Jan Hajič, Christopher D. Manning, Ryan T. McDonald, Slav Petrov, Sampo Pyysalo, Natalia Silveira, Reut Tsarfaty, and Daniel Zeman. 2016. Universal dependencies v1: A multilingual treebank collection. In *Proceedings of the Tenth International Conference on Language Resources and Evaluation LREC 2016*. European Language Resources Association (ELRA).

Martha Palmer, Daniel Gildea, and Paul Kingsbury. 2005. The proposition bank: An annotated corpus of semantic roles. *Computational Linguistics*, 31(1):71–106.

Daniel Peterson, Martha Palmer, and Shumin Wu. 2014. Focusing annotation for semantic role labeling. In *Proceedings of the Ninth International Conference on Language Resources and Evaluation (LREC'14)*, Reykjavik, Iceland. European Language Resources Association (ELRA).

Drew Reisinger, Rachel Rudinger, Francis Ferraro, Craig Harman, Kyle Rawlins, and Benjamin Van Durme. 2015. Semantic Proto-Roles. *Transactions of the Association for Computational Linguistics*, 3:475–488.

Michael Roth and Kristian Woodsend. 2014. Composition of word representations improves semantic role labelling. In *Proceedings of the 2014 Conference on Empirical Methods in Natural Language Processing (EMNLP)*, pages 407–413. Association for Computational Linguistics.

Karin Kipper Schuler. 2006. *VerbNet: A Broad-Coverage, Comprehensive Verb Lexicon.* Ph.D. thesis, University of Pennsylvania.

Sebastian Schuster and Christopher D. Manning. 2016. Enhanced English universal dependencies: An improved representation for natural language understanding tasks. In *Proceedings of the Tenth International Conference on Language Resources and Evaluation (LREC 2016)*. European Language Resources Association (ELRA).

Dan Shen and Mirella Lapata. 2007. Using semantic roles to improve question answering. In *Proceedings of the 2007 Joint Conference on Empirical Methods in Natural Language Processing and Computational Natural Language Learning (EMNLP-CoNLL)*, pages 12–21, Prague, Czech Republic. Association for Computational Linguistics.

Weiwei Sun, Zhifang Sui, and Meng Wang. 2009. Prediction of thematic rank for structured semantic role labeling. In *Proceedings of the ACL-IJCNLP 2009 Conference Short Papers*, pages 253–256. Association for Computational Linguistics.

Aaron Steven White, Kyle Rawlins, and Benjamin Van Durme. 2017. The Semantic Proto-Role Linking Model. In *Proceedings of the 15th Conference of the European Chapter of the Association for Computational Linguistics*, volume 2, pages 92–98. Association for Computational Linguistics.

Aaron Steven White, Drew Reisinger, Rachel Rudinger, Kyle Rawlins, and Benjamin Van Durme. 2016. Computational linking theory. *arXiv*, abs/1610.02544.

Benat Zapirain, Eneko Agirre, and Lluìs Marquez. 2008. Robustness and generalization of role sets: PropBank vs. VerbNet. In *Proceedings of the 46th Annual Meeting of the Association for Computational Linguistics*, June, pages 550–558. Association for Computational Linguistics.

Daniel Zeman, Martin Popel, Milan Straka, Jan Hajič, Joakim Nivre, Filip Ginter, Juhani Luotolahti, Sampo Pyysalo, Slav Petrov, Martin Potthast, Francis Tyers, Elena Badmaeva, Memduh Gokirmak, Anna Nedoluzhko, Silvie Cinkova, Jan Hajič jr., Jaroslava Hlavacova, Václava Kettnerová, Zdenka Uresova, Jenna Kanerva, Stina Ojala, Anna Missilä, Christopher D. Manning, Sebastian Schuster, Siva Reddy, Dima Taji, Nizar Habash, Herman Leung, Marie-Catherine de Marneffe, Manuela Sanguinetti, Maria Simi, Hiroshi Kanayama, Valeria dePaiva, Kira Droganova, Héctor Martínez Alonso, Çağrı Çöltekin, Umut Sulubacak, Hans Uszkoreit, Vivien Macketanz, Aljoscha Burchardt, Kim Harris, Katrin Marheinecke, Georg Rehm, Tolga Kayadelen, Mohammed Attia, Ali Elkahky, Zhuoran Yu, Emily Pitler, Saran Lertpradit, Michael Mandl, Jesse Kirchner, Hector Fernandez Alcalde, Jana Strnadová, Esha Banerjee, Ruli Manurung, Antonio Stella, Atsuko Shimada, Sookyoung Kwak, Gustavo Mendonca, Tatiana Lando, Rattima Nitisaroj, and Josie Li. 2017. Conll 2017 shared task: Multilingual parsing from raw text to universal dependencies. In *Proceedings of the CoNLL 2017 Shared Task: Multilingual Parsing from Raw Text to Universal Dependencies*, pages 1–19. Association for Computational Linguistics.

Adversarially Regularising Neural NLI Models
to Integrate Logical Background Knowledge

Pasquale Minervini
University College London
p.minervini@cs.ucl.ac.uk

Sebastian Riedel
University College London
s.riedel@cs.ucl.ac.uk

Abstract

Adversarial examples are inputs to machine learning models designed to cause the model to make a mistake. They are useful for understanding the shortcomings of machine learning models, interpreting their results, and for regularisation. In NLP, however, most example generation strategies produce input text by using known, pre-specified semantic transformations, requiring significant manual effort and in-depth understanding of the problem and domain. In this paper, we investigate the problem of automatically generating adversarial examples that violate a set of given First-Order Logic constraints in Natural Language Inference (NLI). We reduce the problem of identifying such adversarial examples to a combinatorial optimisation problem, by maximising a quantity measuring the degree of violation of such constraints and by using a language model for generating linguistically-plausible examples. Furthermore, we propose a method for adversarially regularising neural NLI models for incorporating background knowledge. Our results show that, while the proposed method does not always improve results on the SNLI and MultiNLI datasets, it significantly and consistently increases the predictive accuracy on adversarially-crafted datasets – up to a 79.6% relative improvement – while drastically reducing the number of background knowledge violations. Furthermore, we show that adversarial examples *transfer* among model architectures, and that the proposed adversarial training procedure improves the robustness of NLI models to adversarial examples.

1 Introduction

An open problem in Artificial Intelligence is quantifying the extent to which algorithms exhibit intelligent behaviour (Levesque, 2014). In Machine Learning, a standard procedure consists in esti-

mating the *generalisation error*, i.e. the prediction error over an independent test sample (Hastie et al., 2001). However, machine learning models can succeed simply by recognising patterns that happen to be predictive on instances in the test sample, while ignoring deeper phenomena (Rimell and Clark, 2009; Paperno et al., 2016).

Adversarial examples are inputs to machine learning models designed to cause the model to make a mistake (Szegedy et al., 2014; Goodfellow et al., 2014). In Natural Language Processing (NLP) and Machine Reading, generating adversarial examples can be really useful for understanding the shortcomings of NLP models (Jia and Liang, 2017; Kannan and Vinyals, 2017) and for regularisation (Minervini et al., 2017).

In this paper, we focus on the problem of generating adversarial examples for Natural Language Inference (NLI) models in order to gain insights about the inner workings of such systems, and regularising them. NLI, also referred to as Recognising Textual Entailment (Fyodorov et al., 2000; Condoravdi et al., 2003; Dagan et al., 2005), is a central problem in language understanding (Katz, 1972; Bos and Markert, 2005; van Benthem, 2008; MacCartney and Manning, 2009), and thus it is especially well suited to serve as a benchmark task for research in machine reading. In NLI, a model is presented with two sentences, a *premise p* and a *hypothesis h*, and the goal is to determine whether p semantically entails h.

The problem of acquiring large amounts of labelled data for NLI was addressed with the creation of the SNLI (Bowman et al., 2015) and MultiNLI (Williams et al., 2017) datasets. In these processes, annotators were presented with a *premise p* drawn from a corpus, and were required to generate three new sentences (*hypotheses*) based on p, according to the following criteria: *a)* Entailment – h is definitely true given p (p

Proceedings of the 22nd Conference on Computational Natural Language Learning (CoNLL 2018), pages 65–74
Brussels, Belgium, October 31 - November 1, 2018. ©2018 Association for Computational Linguistics

entails h); *b)* Contradiction – h is definitely not true given p (p contradicts h); and *c)* Neutral – h might be true given p. Given a premise-hypothesis sentence pair (p, h), a NLI model is asked to classify the relationship between p and h – i.e. either *entailment*, *contradiction*, or *neutral*. Solving NLI requires to fully capture the sentence meaning by handling complex linguistic phenomena like lexical entailment, quantification, co-reference, tense, belief, modality, and lexical and syntactic ambiguities (Williams et al., 2017).

In this work, we use adversarial examples for: *a)* identifying cases where models violate existing background knowledge, expressed in the form of *logic rules*, and *b)* training models that are *robust* to such violations.

The underlying idea in our work is that NLI models should adhere to a set of structural constraints that are intrinsic to the human reasoning process. For instance, *contradiction* is inherently *symmetric*: if a sentence p contradicts a sentence h, then h contradicts p as well. Similarly, entailment is both *reflexive* and *transitive*. It is reflexive since a sentence a is always entailed by (i.e. is true given) a. It is also transitive, since if a is entailed by b, and b is entailed by c, then a is entailed by c as well.

Example 1 (Inconsistency). Consider three sentences a, b and c each describing a situation, such as: *a)* "The girl plays", *b)* "The girl plays with a ball", and *c)* "The girl plays with a red ball". Note that if a is entailed by b, and b is entailed by c, then also a is entailed by c. If a NLI model detects that b entails a, c entails b, but c does not entail a, we know that it is making an error (since its results are inconsistent), even though we may not be aware of the sentences a, b, and c and the true semantic relationships holding between them. $\triangle$

Our adversarial examples are different from those used in other fields such as computer vision, where they typically consist in small, semantically invariant perturbations that result in drastic changes in the model predictions. In this paper, we propose a method for generating adversarial examples that cause a model to violate preexisting background knowledge (Section 4), based on reducing the generation problem to a combinatorial optimisation problem. Furthermore, we outline a method for incorporating such background knowledge into models by means of an *adversarial training* procedure (Section 5).

Our results (Section 8) show that, even though the proposed adversarial training procedure does not sensibly improve accuracy on SNLI and MultiNLI, it yields significant relative improvement in accuracy (up to 79.6%) on adversarial datasets. Furthermore, we show that adversarial examples *transfer* across models, and that the proposed method allows training significantly more robust NLI models.

2 Background

Neural NLI Models. In NLI, in particular on the Stanford Natural Language Inference (SNLI) (Bowman et al., 2015) and MultiNLI (Williams et al., 2017) datasets, neural NLI models – end-to-end differentiable models that can be trained via gradient-based optimisation – proved to be very successful, achieving state-of-the-art results (Rocktäschel et al., 2016; Parikh et al., 2016; Chen et al., 2017).

Let $\mathcal{S}$ denote the set of all possible sentences, and let $a = (a_1, \ldots, a_{\ell_a}) \in \mathcal{S}$ and $b = (b_1, \ldots, b_{\ell_b}) \in \mathcal{S}$ denote two input sentences – representing the premise and the hypothesis – of length ℓ_a and ℓ_b, respectively. In neural NLI models, all words a_i and b_j are typically represented by k-dimensional *embedding vectors* $\mathbf{a}_i, \mathbf{b}_j \in \mathbb{R}^k$. As such, the sentences a and b can be encoded by the sentence *embedding matrices* $\mathbf{a} \in \mathbb{R}^{k \times \ell_a}$ and $\mathbf{b} \in \mathbb{R}^{k \times \ell_b}$, where the columns $\mathbf{a}_i$ and $\mathbf{b}_j$ respectively denote the embeddings of words a_i and b_j.

Given two sentences $a, b \in \mathcal{S}$, the goal of a NLI model is to identify the semantic relation between a and b, which can be either *entailment*, *contradiction*, or *neutral*. For this reason, given an instance, neural NLI models compute the following conditional probability distribution over all three classes:

$$p_\Theta(\,\cdot\,\mid a, b) = \text{softmax}(\text{score}_\Theta(\mathbf{a}, \mathbf{b})) \quad (1)$$

where $\text{score}_\Theta : \mathbb{R}^{k \times \ell_a} \times \mathbb{R}^{k \times \ell_b} \to \mathbb{R}^3$ is a model-dependent *scoring function* with parameters Θ, and $\text{softmax}(\mathbf{x})_i = \exp\{x_i\}/\sum_j \exp\{x_j\}$ denotes the softmax function.

Several scoring functions have been proposed in the literature, such as the conditional Bidirectional LSTM (cBiLSTM) (Rocktäschel et al., 2016), the Decomposable Attention Model (DAM) (Parikh et al., 2016), and the Enhanced LSTM model (ESIM) (Chen et al., 2017). One desirable quality of the scoring function score_Θ is that it should be *differentiable* with respect to the model parameters Θ, which allows the neural NLI model to be trained from data via back-propagation.

Model Training. Let $\mathcal{D} = \{(x_1, y_1), \ldots, (x_m, y_m)\}$ represent a NLI dataset, where x_i denotes the i-th premise-hypothesis sentence pair, and $y_i \in \{1, \ldots, K\}$ their relationship, where $K \in \mathbb{N}$ is the number of possible relationships – in the case of NLI, $K = 3$. The model is trained by minimising a *cross-entropy loss* $\mathcal{J}_{\mathcal{D}}$ on $\mathcal{D}$:

$$\mathcal{J}_{\mathcal{D}}(\mathcal{D}, \Theta) = -\sum_{i=1}^{m}\sum_{k=1}^{K} \mathbb{1}\{y_i = k\} \log(\hat{y}_{i,k}) \quad (2)$$

where $\hat{y}_{i,k} = p_{\Theta}(y_i = k \mid x_i)$ denotes the probability of class k on the instance x_i inferred by the neural NLI model as in Eq. (1).

In the following, we analyse the behaviour of neural NLI models by means of *adversarial examples* – inputs to machine learning models designed to cause the model to commit mistakes. In computer vision models, adversarial examples are created by adding a very small amount of noise to the input (Szegedy et al., 2014; Goodfellow et al., 2014): these perturbations do not change the semantics of the images, but they can drastically change the predictions of computer vision models. In our setting, we define an adversary whose goal is finding *sets* of NLI instances where the model fails to be consistent with available background knowledge, encoded in the form of First-Order Logic (FOL) rules. In the following sections, we define the corresponding optimisation problem, and propose an efficient solution.

3   Background Knowledge

For analysing the behaviour of NLI models, we verify whether they agree with the provided background knowledge, encoded by a set of FOL rules. Note that the three NLI classes – *entailment, contradiction,* and *neutrality* – can be seen as *binary logic predicates*, and we can define FOL formulas for describing the formal relationships that hold between them.

In the following, we denote the predicates associated with entailment, contradiction, and neutrality as ent, con, and neu, respectively. By doing so, we can represent semantic relationships between sentences via logic atoms. For instance, given three sentences $s_1, s_2, s_3 \in \mathcal{S}$, we can represent

NLI Rules	
$\mathbf{R_1}$	$\top \Rightarrow \text{ent}(X_1, X_1)$
$\mathbf{R_2}$	$\text{con}(X_1, X_2) \Rightarrow \text{con}(X_2, X_1)$
$\mathbf{R_3}$	$\text{ent}(X_1, X_2) \Rightarrow \neg\text{con}(X_2, X_1)$
$\mathbf{R_4}$	$\text{neu}(X_1, X_2) \Rightarrow \neg\text{con}(X_2, X_1)$
$\mathbf{R_5}$	$\text{ent}(X_1, X_2) \wedge \text{ent}(X_2, X_3) \Rightarrow \text{ent}(X_1, X_3)$

Table 1: First-Order Logic rules defining desired properties of NLI models: X_i are universally quantified variables, and operators $\wedge$, $\neg$, and $\top$ denote logic conjunction, negation, and tautology.

the fact that s_1 entails s_2 and s_2 contradicts s_3 by using the logic atoms $\text{ent}(s_1, s_2)$ and $\text{con}(s_2, s_3)$.

Let $X_1, \ldots, X_n$ be a set of universally quantified variables. We define our background knowledge as a set of FOL rules, each having the following body $\Rightarrow$ head form:

$$\text{body}(X_1, \ldots, X_n) \Rightarrow \text{head}(X_1, \ldots, X_n), \quad (3)$$

where body and head represent the *premise* and the *conclusion* of the rule – if body holds, head holds as well. In the following, we consider the rules $\mathbf{R_1}, \ldots, \mathbf{R_5}$ outlined in Table 1. Rule $\mathbf{R_1}$ enforces the constraint that entailment is reflexive; rule $\mathbf{R_2}$ that contradiction should always be symmetric (if s_1 contradicts s_2, then s_2 contradicts s_1 as well); rule $\mathbf{R_5}$ that entailment is transitive; while rules $\mathbf{R_3}$ and $\mathbf{R_4}$ describe the formal relationships between the *entailment, neutral,* and *contradiction* relations.

In Section 4 we propose a method to automatically generate sets of sentences that violate the rules outlined in Table 1 – effectively generating *adversarial examples*. Then, in Section 5 we show how we can leverage such adversarial examples by generating them on-the-fly during training and using them for regularising the model parameters, in an *adversarial training* regime.

4   Generating Adversarial Examples

In this section, we propose a method for efficiently *generating* adversarial examples for NLI models – i.e. examples that make the model violate the background knowledge outlined in Section 3.

4.1   Inconsistency Loss

We cast the problem of generating adversarial examples as an optimisation problem. In particular, we propose a continuous *inconsistency loss* that measures the *degree* to which a set of sentences causes a model to violate a rule.

Example 2 (Inconsistency Loss). Consider the rule $\mathbf{R_2}$ in Table 1, i.e. $\mathrm{con}(X_1, X_2) \Rightarrow \mathrm{con}(X_2, X_1)$. Let $s_1, s_2 \in \mathcal{S}$ be two sentences: this rule is violated if, according to the model, a sentence s_1 contradicts s_2, but s_2 does not contradict s_1. However, if we just use the final decision made by the neural NLI model, we can simply check whether the rule is violated by two given sentences, without any information on the *degree* of such a violation.

Intuitively, for the rule being *maximally violated*, the conditional probability associated to $\mathrm{con}(s_1, s_2)$ should be *very high* (≈ 1), while the one associated to $\mathrm{con}(s_2, s_1)$ should be *very low* (≈ 0). We can measure the extent to which the rule is violated – which we refer to as *inconsistency loss $\mathcal{J}_{\mathcal{I}}$* – by checking whether the probability of the body of the rule is higher than the probability of its head:

$$\mathcal{J}_{\mathcal{I}}(S = \{X_1 \mapsto s_1, X_2 \mapsto s_2\})$$
$$= [p_\Theta(\mathrm{con} \mid s_1, s_2) - p_\Theta(\mathrm{con} \mid s_2, s_1)]_+$$

where S is a *substitution set* that maps the variables X_1 and X_2 in $\mathbf{R_2}$ to the sentences s_1 and s_2, $[x]_+ = \max(0, x)$, and $p_\Theta(\mathrm{con} \mid s_i, s_j)$ is the (conditional) probability that s_i contradicts s_j according to the neural NLI model. Note that, in accordance with the logic implication, the inconsistency loss reaches its global minimum when the probability of the body is close to zero – i.e. the *premise* is false – and when the probabilities of both the body and the head are close to one – i.e. the *premise* and the *conclusion* are both true. $\triangle$

We now generalise the intuition in Ex. 2 to any FOL rule. Let $r = (\mathrm{body} \Rightarrow \mathrm{head})$ denote an arbitrary FOL rule in the form described in Eq. (3), and let $\mathrm{vars}(r) = \{X_1, \ldots, X_n\}$ denote the set of universally quantified variables in the rule r.

Furthermore, let $S = \{X_1 \mapsto s_1, \ldots, X_n \mapsto s_n\}$ denote a *substitution set*, i.e. a mapping from variables in $\mathrm{vars}(r)$ to sentences $s_1, \ldots, s_n \in \mathcal{S}$. The inconsistency loss associated with the rule r on the substitution set S can be defined as:

$$\mathcal{J}_{\mathcal{I}}(S) = [p(S; \mathrm{body}) - p(S; \mathrm{head})]_+ \quad (4)$$

where $p(S; \mathrm{body})$ and $p(S; \mathrm{head})$ denote the probability of body and head of the rule, after replacing the variables in r with the corresponding

sentences in S. The motivation for the loss in Eq. (4) is that logic implications can be understood as "whenever the body is true, the head has to be true as well". In terms of NLI models, this translates as "the probability of the head should at least be as large as the probability of the body".

For calculating the inconsistency loss in Eq. (4), we need to specify how to calculate the probability of head and body. The probability of a single ground atom is given by querying the neural NLI model, as in Eq. (1). The head contains a single atom, while the body can be a conjunction of multiple atoms. Similarly to Minervini et al. (2017), we use the Gödel t-norm, a continuous generalisation of the conjunction operator in logic (Gupta and Qi, 1991), for computing the probability of the body of a clause:

$$p_\Theta(a_1 \wedge a_2) = \min\{p_\Theta(a_1), p_\Theta(a_2)\}$$

where a_1 and a_2 are two clause atoms.

In this work, we cast the problem of generating adversarial examples as an optimisation problem: we search for the substitution set $S = \{X_1 \mapsto s_1, \ldots, X_n \mapsto s_n\}$ that maximises the inconsistency loss in Eq. (4), thus (maximally) violating the available background knowledge.

4.2 Constraining via Language Modelling

Maximising the inconsistency loss in Eq. (4) may not be sufficient for generating meaningful adversarial examples: they can lead neural NLI models to violate available background knowledge, but they may not be well-formed and meaningful.

For such a reason, in addition to maximising the inconsistency loss, we also constrain the *perplexity* of generated sentences by using a neural language model (Bengio et al., 2000). In this work, we use a LSTM (Hochreiter and Schmidhuber, 1997) neural language model $p_{\mathcal{L}}(w_1, \ldots, w_t)$ for generating low-perplexity adversarial examples.

4.3 Searching in a Discrete Space

As mentioned earlier in this section, we cast the problem of automatically generating adversarial examples – i.e. examples that cause NLI models to violate available background knowledge – as an optimisation problem. Specifically, we look for substitutions sets $S = \{X_1 \mapsto s_1, \ldots, X_n \mapsto s_n\}$ that jointly: *a)* maximise the *inconsistency loss* described in Eq. (4), and *b)* are composed by sentences with a low perplexity, as defined by the neural language model in Section 4.2.

The search objective can be formalised by the following optimisation problem:

$$\underset{S}{\text{maximise}} \quad \mathcal{J}_\mathcal{I}(S)$$
$$\text{subject to} \quad \log p_\mathcal{L}(S) \leq \tau \tag{5}$$

where $\log p_\mathcal{L}(S)$ denotes the log-probability of the sentences in the substitution set S, and τ is a threshold on the perplexity of generated sentences.

For generating low-perplexity adversarial examples, we take inspiration from Guu et al. (2017) and generate the sentences by editing prototypes extracted from a corpus. Specifically, for searching substitution sets whose sentences jointly have a high probability and are highly adversarial, as measured the inconsistency loss in Eq. (4), we use the following procedure, also described in Appendix A.4: *a)* we first sample sentences close to the data manifold (i.e. with a low perplexity), by either sampling from the training set or from the language model; *b)* we then make small variations to the sentences – analogous to adversarial images, which consist in small perturbations of training examples – so to optimise the objective in Eq. (5).

When editing prototypes, we consider the following perturbations: *a)* change one word in one of the input sentences; *b)* remove one parse subtree from one of the input sentences; *c)* insert one parse sub-tree from one sentence in the corpus in the parse tree of one of the input sentences.

Note that the generation process can easily lead to ungrammatical or implausible sentences; however, these will be likely to have a high perplexity according to the language model (Section 4.2), and thus they will be ruled out by the search algorithm.

5 Adversarial Regularisation

We now show one can use the adversarial examples to regularise the training process. We propose training NLI models by jointly: *a)* minimising the data loss (Eq. (2)), and *b)* minimising the inconsistency loss (Eq. (4)) on a set of generated adversarial examples (substitution sets).

More formally, for training, we jointly minimise the cross-entropy loss defined on the data $\mathcal{J}_\mathcal{D}(\Theta)$ and the inconsistency loss on a set of generated adversarial examples $\max_S \mathcal{J}_\mathcal{I}(S; \Theta)$, resulting in the following optimisation problem:

$$\underset{\Theta}{\text{minimise}} \quad \mathcal{J}_\mathcal{D}(\mathcal{D}, \Theta) + \lambda \max_S \mathcal{J}_\mathcal{I}(S; \Theta)$$
$$\text{subject to} \quad \log p_\mathcal{L}(S) \leq \tau \tag{6}$$

Premise	A man in a suit walks through a train station.
Hypothesis	Two boys ride skateboard.
Type	**Contradiction**
Premise	Two boys ride skateboard.
Hypothesis	A man in a suit walks through a train station.
Type	**Contradiction**
Premise	Two people are surfing in the ocean.
Hypothesis	There are people outside.
Type	**Entailment**
Premise	There are people outside.
Hypothesis	Two people are surfing in the ocean.
Type	**Neutral**

Table 2: Sample sentences from an Adversarial NLI Dataset generated using the DAM model, by maximising the inconsistency loss $\mathcal{J}_\mathcal{I}$.

where $\lambda \in \mathbb{R}_+$ is a hyperparameter specifying the trade-off between the data loss $\mathcal{J}_\mathcal{D}$ (Eq. (2)), and the inconsistency loss $\mathcal{J}_\mathcal{I}$ (Eq. (4)), measured on the generated substitution set S.

In Eq. (6), the regularisation term $\max_S \mathcal{J}_\mathcal{I}(S; \Theta)$ has the task of *generating* the adversarial substitution sets by maximising the inconsistency loss. Furthermore, the constraint $\log p_\mathcal{L}(S) \leq \tau$ ensures that the perplexity of generated sentences is lower than a threshold τ. For this work, we used the max aggregation function. However, other functions can be used as well, such as the sum or mean of multiple inconsistency losses.

For minimising the regularised loss in Eq. (6), we alternate between two optimisation processes – generating the adversarial examples (Eq. (5)) and minimising the regularised loss (Eq. (6)). The algorithm is outlined in Appendix A.4: at each iteration, after generating a set of adversarial examples S, it computes the gradient of the regularised loss in Eq. (6), and updates the model parameters via a gradient descent step.

6 Creating Adversarial NLI Datasets

We crafted a series of datasets for assessing the robustness of the proposed regularisation method to adversarial examples. Starting from the SNLI test set, we proceeded as follows. We selected the k instances in the SNLI test set that maximise the inconsistency loss in Eq. (4) with respect to the rules in $\mathbf{R_1}$, $\mathbf{R_2}$, $\mathbf{R_3}$, and $\mathbf{R_4}$ in Table 1. We refer to the generated datasets as $\mathcal{A}_m^k$, where m identifies the model used for selecting the sentence pairs, and k denotes number of examples in the dataset.

For generating each of the $\mathcal{A}_{\mathrm{m}}^{k}$ datasets, we proceeded as follows. Let $\mathcal{D} = \{(x_1, y_i), \ldots, (x_n, y_n)\}$ be a NLI dataset (such as SNLI), where each instance $x_i = (p_i, h_i)$ is a premise-hypothesis sentence pair, and y_i denotes the relationship holding between p_i and h_i. For each instance $x_i = (p_i, h_i)$, we consider two substitution sets: $S_i = \{X_1 \mapsto p_i, X_2 \mapsto h_i\}$ and $S_i' = \{X_1 \mapsto h_i, X_2 \mapsto p_i\}$, each corresponding to a mapping from variables to sentences.

We compute the *inconsistency score* associated to each instance x_i in the dataset $\mathcal{D}$ as $\mathcal{J}_{\mathcal{I}}(S_i) + \mathcal{J}_{\mathcal{I}}(S_i')$. Note that the inconsistency score only depends on the premise p_i and hypothesis h_i in each instance x_i, and it does not depend on its label y_i.

After computing the inconsistency scores for all sentence pairs in $\mathcal{D}$ using a model m, we select the k instances with the highest inconsistency score, we create two instances $x_i = (p_i, h_i)$ and $\hat{x}_i = (h_i, p_i)$, and add both (x_i, y_i) and $(\hat{x}_i, \hat{y}_i)$ to the dataset $\mathcal{A}_{\mathrm{m}}^{k}$. Note that, while y_i is already known from the dataset $\mathcal{D}$, $\hat{y}_i$ is unknown. For this reason, we find $\hat{y}_i$ by manual annotation.

7 Related Work

Adversarial examples are receiving a considerable attention in NLP; their usage, however, is considerably limited by the fact that semantically invariant input perturbations in NLP are difficult to identify (Buck et al., 2017).

Jia and Liang (2017) analyse the robustness of extractive question answering models on examples obtained by adding adversarially generated distracting text to SQuAD (Rajpurkar et al., 2016) dataset instances. Belinkov and Bisk (2017) also notice that character-level Machine Translation are overly sensitive to random character manipulations, such as typos. Hosseini et al. (2017) show that simple character-level modifications can drastically change the toxicity score of a text. Iyyer et al. (2018) proposes using paraphrasing for generating adversarial examples. Our model is fundamentally different in two ways: *a)* it does not need labelled data for generating adversarial examples – the inconsistency loss can be maximised by just making an NLI model produce inconsistent results, and *b)* it incorporates adversarial examples during the training process, with the aim of training more robust NLI models.

Adversarial examples are also used for assessing the robustness of computer vision mod-

Model		Original		Regularised	
		Valid.	Test	Valid.	Test
MultiNLI	cBiLSTM	61.52	63.95	**66.98**	**66.68**
	DAM	72.78	73.28	**73.57**	**73.51**
	ESIM	73.66	75.22	**75.72**	**75.80**
SNLI	cBiLSTM	81.41	80.99	**82.27**	**81.12**
	DAM	86.96	86.29	**87.08**	**86.43**
	ESIM	87.83	87.25	**87.98**	**87.55**

Table 3: Accuracy on the SNLI and MultiNLI datasets with different neural NLI models *before* (left) and *after* (right) adversarial regularisation.

Model	Rule	$\|\mathbf{B}\|$	$\|\mathbf{B} \wedge \neg\mathbf{H}\|$	Violations (%)
cBiLSTM	$\mathbf{R_1}$	1,098,734	261,064	23.76 %
	$\mathbf{R_2}$	174,902	80,748	46.17 %
	$\mathbf{R_3}$	197,697	24,294	12.29 %
	$\mathbf{R_4}$	176,768	33,435	18.91 %
DAM	$\mathbf{R_1}$	1,098,734	956	00.09 %
	$\mathbf{R_2}$	171,728	28,680	16.70 %
	$\mathbf{R_3}$	196,042	11,599	05.92 %
	$\mathbf{R_4}$	181,597	29,635	16.32 %
ESIM	$\mathbf{R_1}$	1,098,734	10,985	01.00 %
	$\mathbf{R_2}$	177,950	17,518	09.84 %
	$\mathbf{R_3}$	200,852	6,482	03.23 %
	$\mathbf{R_4}$	170,565	17,190	10.08 %

Table 4: Violations (%) of rules $\mathbf{R_1}, \mathbf{R_2}, \mathbf{R_3}, \mathbf{R_4}$ from Table 1 on the SNLI training set, yield by cBiLSTM, DAM, and ESIM.

els (Szegedy et al., 2014; Goodfellow et al., 2014; Nguyen et al., 2015), where they are created by adding a small amount of noise to the inputs that does not change the semantics of the images, but drastically changes the model predictions.

8 Experiments

We trained DAM, ESIM and cBiLSTM on the SNLI corpus using the hyperparameters provided in the respective papers. The results provided by such models on the SNLI and MultiNLI validation and tests sets are provided in Table 3. In the case of MultiNLI, the validation set was obtained by removing 10,000 instances from the training set (originally composed by 392,702 instances), and the test set consists in the *matched* validation set.

Background Knowledge Violations. As a first experiment, we count the how likely our model is to violate rules $\mathbf{R_1}, \mathbf{R_2}, \mathbf{R_3}, \mathbf{R_4}$ in Table 1.

In Table 4 we report the number sentence pairs in the SNLI training set where DAM, ESIM and cBiLSTM violate $\mathbf{R_1}, \mathbf{R_2}, \mathbf{R_3}, \mathbf{R_4}$. In the $\|\mathbf{B}\|$ column we report the number of times the body

Model \ Dataset	$\mathcal{A}_{\mathrm{DAM}}^{100}$	$\mathcal{A}_{\mathrm{DAM}}^{500}$	$\mathcal{A}_{\mathrm{DAM}}^{1000}$	$\mathcal{A}_{\mathrm{ESIM}}^{100}$	$\mathcal{A}_{\mathrm{ESIM}}^{500}$	$\mathcal{A}_{\mathrm{ESIM}}^{1000}$	$\mathcal{A}_{\mathrm{cBiLSTM}}^{100}$	$\mathcal{A}_{\mathrm{cBiLSTM}}^{500}$	$\mathcal{A}_{\mathrm{cBiLSTM}}^{1000}$
DAM$^{\mathcal{AR}}$	**83.33**	**79.15**	**79.37**	**71.35**	**72.19**	**70.05**	**93.00**	**88.99**	**86.00**
DAM	47.40	47.93	51.66	55.73	60.94	60.88	81.50	77.37	75.28
ESIM$^{\mathcal{AR}}$	**89.06**	**86.00**	**85.08**	**78.12**	**76.04**	**73.32**	**96.50**	**91.92**	**88.52**
ESIM	72.40	74.59	76.92	52.08	58.65	60.78	87.00	84.34	82.05
cBiLSTM$^{\mathcal{AR}}$	**85.42**	**80.39**	**78.74**	**73.96**	**70.52**	**65.39**	**92.50**	**88.38**	**83.62**
cBiLSTM	56.25	59.96	61.75	47.92	53.23	53.73	51.50	52.83	53.24

Table 5: Accuracy of unregularised and regularised neural NLI models DAM, cBiLSTM, and ESIM, and their adversarially regularised versions DAM$^{\mathcal{AR}}$, cBiLSTM$^{\mathcal{AR}}$, and ESIM$^{\mathcal{AR}}$, on adversarial datasets $\mathcal{A}_{\mathrm{m}}^{k}$.

of the rule holds, according to the model. In the $|\mathbf{B} \wedge \neg\mathbf{H}|$ column we report the number of times where the body of the rule holds, but the head does not – which is clearly a violation of available rules.

We can see that, in the case of rule $\mathbf{R_1}$ (reflexivity of entailment), DAM and ESIM make a relatively low number of violations – namely 0.09 and 1.00 %, respectively. However, in the case of cBiLSTM, we can see that, each sentence $s \in \mathcal{S}$ in the SNLI training set, with a 23.76 % chance, s does not entail itself – which violates our background knowledge.

With respect to $\mathbf{R_2}$ (symmetry of contradiction), we see that none of the models is completely consistent with the available background knowledge. Given a sentence pair $s_1, s_2 \in \mathcal{S}$ from the SNLI training set, if – according to the model – s_1 contradicts s_2, a significant number of times (between 9.84% and 46.17%) the same model also infers that s_2 *does not* contradict s_1. This phenomenon happens 16.70 % of times with DAM, 9.84 % of times with ESIM, and 46.17 % with cBiLSTM: this indicates that all considered models are prone to violating $\mathbf{R_2}$ in their predictions, with ESIM being the more robust.

In Appendix A.2 we report several examples of such violations in the SNLI training set. We select those that maximise the inconsistency loss described in Eq. (4), violating rules $\mathbf{R_2}$ and $\mathbf{R_3}$. We can notice that the presence of inconsistencies is often correlated with the length of the sentences. The model tends to detect entailment relationships between longer (i.e., possibly more specific) and shorter (i.e., possibly more general) sentences.

8.1 Generation of Adversarial Examples

In the following, we analyse the automatic generation of sets of adversarial examples that make the model violate the existing background knowl-

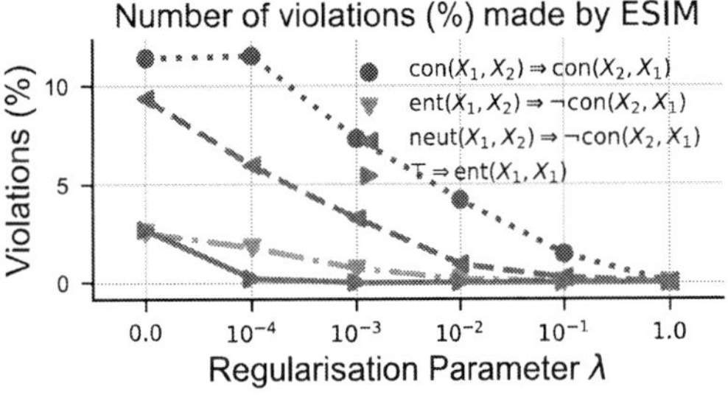

Figure 1: Number of violations (%) to rules in Table 1 made by ESIM on the SNLI test set.

edge. We search in the space of sentences by applying perturbations to sampled sentence pairs, using a language model for guiding the search process. The generation procedure is described in Section 4.

The procedure was especially effective in generating adversarial examples – a sample is shown in Table 6. We can notice that, even though DAM and ESIM achieve results close to human level performance on SNLI, they are likely to fail when faced with linguistic phenomena such as negation, hyponymy, and antonymy. Gururangan et al. (2018) recently showed that NLI datasets tend to suffer from annotation artefacts and limited linguistic variations: this allows NLI models to achieve nearly-human performance by capturing repetitive patterns and idiosyncrasies in a dataset, without being able of effectively capturing textual entailment. This is visible, for instance, in example 5 of Table 6, where the model fails to capture the hyponymy relation between "male" and "man", incorrectly predicting an entailment in place of a neutral relationship. Furthermore, it is clear that models lack commonsense knowledge, such as the relation between "pushing" and "carrying" (example 1), and being outside and swimming (example 2). Generating such adversarial

		Adversarial Example	Prediction	Inconsistency
1	s_1	A man in uniform is pushing a medical bed.	$s_1 \dashrightarrow s_2$, $s_2 \xrightarrow{0.93} s_1$	$.01 \rightsquigarrow .92$
	s_2	a man is ~~pushing~~ carrying something.		
1	s_1	A dog swims in the water	$s_1 \dashrightarrow s_2$, $s_2 \xrightarrow{0.99} s_1$	$.00 \rightsquigarrow .99$
	s_2	A dog is ~~swimming~~ outside.		
2	s_1	A young man is sledding down a snow covered hill on a green sled.	$s_1 \xrightarrow{0.98} s_2$, $s_2 \xrightarrow{1.00} s_1$	$.00 \rightsquigarrow .97$
	s_1	A man is ~~sledding~~ down to meet his daughter.		
3	s_1	A woman sleeps on the ground. A boy and girl play in a pool.	$s_1 \xrightarrow{0.94} s_2$, $s_2 \xrightarrow{0.85} s_1$	$.00 \rightsquigarrow .82$
	s_2	Two kids are happily playing in a swimming pool.		
4	s_1	The school is having a special event in order to show the american culture on how other cultures are dealt with in parties.	$s_1 \xrightarrow{0.96} s_2$, $s_2 \xrightarrow{0.66} s_1$	$.01 \rightsquigarrow .63$
	s_2	A ~~school~~ dog is hosting an event.		
5	s_1	A boy is drinking out of a water fountain shaped like a woman.	$s_1 \dashrightarrow s_2$, $s_2 \dashrightarrow s_3$, $s_1 \xrightarrow{0.97} s_3$	$.00 \rightsquigarrow .94$
	s_2	A male is getting a drink of water.		
	s_3	A ~~male~~ man is getting a drink of water.		

Table 6: Inconsistent results produced by DAM on automatically generated adversarial examples. The notation ~~segment one~~ segment two denotes that the corruption process removes "segment one" and introduced "segment two" in the sentence, and $s_1 \xrightarrow{p} s_2$ indicates that DAM classifies the relation between s_1 and s_2 as *contradiction*, with probability p. We use different colours for representing the contradiction, entailment and neutral classes. Examples 1, 2, 3, and 4 violate the rule $\mathbf{R_2}$, while example 5 violates the rule $\mathbf{R_5}$. $.00 \rightsquigarrow .99$ indicates that the corruption process increases the inconsistency loss from .00 to .99, and the red boxes are used for indicating mistakes made by the model on the adversarial examples.

examples provides us with useful insights on the inner workings of neural NLI models, that can be leveraged for improving the robustness of state-of-the-art models.

8.2 Adversarial Regularisation

We evaluated whether our approach for integrating logical background knowledge via adversarial training (Section 5) is effective at reducing the number of background knowledge violations, without reducing the predictive accuracy of the model. We started with pre-trained DAM, ESIM, and cBiLSTM models, trained using the hyperparameters published in their respective papers.

After training, each model was then fine-tuned for 10 epochs, by minimising the adversarially regularised loss function introduced in Eq. (6). Table 3 shows results on the SNLI and MultiNLI development and test set, while Fig. 1 shows the number of violations for different values of λ, where regularised models are much more likely to make predictions that are consistent with the available background knowledge.

We can see that, despite the drastic reduction of background knowledge violations, the improvement may not be significant, supporting the idea that models achieving close-to-human performance on SNLI and MultiNLI may be capturing annotation artefacts and idiosyncrasies in such

datasets (Gururangan et al., 2018).

Evaluation on Adversarial Datasets. We evaluated the proposed approach on 9 adversarial datasets $\mathcal{A}_m^k$, with $k \in \{100, 500, 1000\}$, generated following the procedure described in Section 6 – results are summarised in Table 5. We can see that the proposed adversarial training method significantly increases the accuracy on the adversarial test sets. For instance, consider $\mathcal{A}_{\text{DAM}}^{100}$: prior to regularising ($\lambda = 0$), DAM achieves a very low accuracy on this dataset – i.e. 47.4%. By increasing the regularisation parameter $\lambda \in \{10^{-4}, 10^{-3}, 10^{-2}, 10^{-1}\}$, we noticed sensible accuracy increases, yielding relative accuracy improvements up to 75.8% in the case of DAM, and 79.6% in the case of cBiLSTM.

From Table 5 we can notice that adversarial examples *transfer* across different models: an unregularised model is likely to perform poorly also on adversarial datasets generated by using different models, with ESIM being the more robust model to adversarially generated examples. Furthermore, we can see that regularised models are generally more robust to adversarial examples, even when those were generated using different model architectures. For instance we can see that, while cBiLSTM is vulnerable also to adversarial examples generated using DAM and ESIM, its adversarially regularised version cBiLSTM^{AR} is generally more robust to any sort of adversarial examples.

9 Conclusions

In this paper, we investigated the problem of automatically generating adversarial examples that violate a set of given First-Order Logic constraints in NLI. We reduced the problem of identifying such adversarial examples to an optimisation problem, by maximising a continuous relaxation of the violation of such constraints, and by using a language model for generating linguistically-plausible examples. Furthermore, we proposed a method for adversarially regularising neural NLI models for incorporating background knowledge.

Our results showed that the proposed method consistently yields significant increases to the predictive accuracy on adversarially-crafted datasets – up to a 79.6% relative improvement – while drastically reducing the number of background knowledge violations. Furthermore, we showed that adversarial examples transfer across model architectures, and the proposed adversarial training procedure produces generally more robust models. The source code and data for reproducing our results is available online, at https://github.com/uclmr/adversarial-nli/.

Acknowledgements

We are immensely grateful to Jeff Mitchell, Johannes Welbl, and the whole UCL Machine Reading research group for all useful discussions, inputs, and ideas. This work has been supported by an Allen Distinguished Investigator Award, and a Marie Curie Career Integration Award.

References

Yonatan Belinkov and Yonatan Bisk. 2017. Synthetic and natural noise both break neural machine translation. *CoRR*, abs/1711.02173.

Yoshua Bengio, Réjean Ducharme, and Pascal Vincent. 2000. A neural probabilistic language model. In *Advances in Neural Information Processing Systems 13, Papers from Neural Information Processing Systems (NIPS) 2000*, pages 932–938. MIT Press.

Johan van Benthem. 2008. A brief history of natural logic. In M. Chakraborty, B. Löwe, M. Nath Mitra, and S. Sarukki, editors, *Logic, Navya-Nyaya and Applications: Homage to Bimal Matilal*. College Publications.

Johan Bos and Katja Markert. 2005. Recognising textual entailment with logical inference. In *HLT/EMNLP 2005, Human Language Technology Conference and Conference on Empirical Methods in Natural Language Processing, Proceedings of the Conference*, pages 628–635. The Association for Computational Linguistics.

Samuel R. Bowman, Gabor Angeli, Christopher Potts, and Christopher D. Manning. 2015. A large annotated corpus for learning natural language inference. In *Proceedings of the 2015 Conference on Empirical Methods in Natural Language Processing, EMNLP 2015*, pages 632–642. The Association for Computational Linguistics.

Christian Buck, Jannis Bulian, Massimiliano Ciaramita, Andrea Gesmundo, Neil Houlsby, Wojciech Gajewski, and Wei Wang. 2017. Ask the right questions: Active question reformulation with reinforcement learning. *CoRR*, abs/1705.07830.

Qian Chen, Xiaodan Zhu, Zhen-Hua Ling, Si Wei, Hui Jiang, and Diana Inkpen. 2017. Enhanced LSTM for natural language inference. In *Proceedings of the 55th Annual Meeting of the Association for Computational Linguistics, ACL 2017*, pages 1657–1668. Association for Computational Linguistics.

Cleo Condoravdi, Dick Crouch, Valeria de Paiva, Reinhard Stolle, and Daniel G. Bobrow. 2003. Entailment, intensionality and text understanding. In *Proceedings of the HLT-NAACL 2003 Workshop on Text Meaning*, pages 38–45.

Ido Dagan, Oren Glickman, and Bernardo Magnini. 2005. The PASCAL recognising textual entailment challenge. In *Machine Learning Challenges, Evaluating Predictive Uncertainty, Visual Object Classification and Recognizing Textual Entailment, First PASCAL Machine Learning Challenges Workshop, MLCW 2005*, volume 3944 of *LNCS*, pages 177–190. Springer.

Yaroslav Fyodorov, Yoad Winter, and Nissim Francez. 2000. A natural logic inference system. In *Proceedings of the of the 2nd Workshop on Inference in Computational Semantics*.

Ian J. Goodfellow, Jonathon Shlens, and Christian Szegedy. 2014. Explaining and harnessing adversarial examples. *CoRR*, abs/1412.6572.

M. M. Gupta and J. Qi. 1991. Theory of t-norms and fuzzy inference methods. *Fuzzy Sets Syst.*, 40(3):431–450.

Suchin Gururangan, Swabha Swayamdipta, Omer Levy, Roy Schwartz, Samuel R. Bowman, and Noah A. Smith. 2018. Annotation artifacts in natural language inference data. *CoRR*, abs/1803.02324.

Kelvin Guu, Tatsunori B. Hashimoto, Yonatan Oren, and Percy Liang. 2017. Generating sentences by editing prototypes. *CoRR*, abs/1709.08878.

Trevor Hastie, Robert Tibshirani, and Jerome Friedman. 2001. *The Elements of Statistical Learning*. Springer Series in Statistics. Springer New York Inc.

Sepp Hochreiter and Jürgen Schmidhuber. 1997. Long short-term memory. *Neural Computation*, 9(8):1735–1780.

Hossein Hosseini, Baicen Xiao, and Radha Poovendran. 2017. Deceiving google's cloud video intelligence API built for summarizing videos. In *2017 IEEE Conference on Computer Vision and Pattern Recognition Workshops, CVPR Workshops*, pages 1305–1309. IEEE Computer Society.

Mohit Iyyer, John Wieting, Kevin Gimpel, and Luke Zettlemoyer. 2018. Adversarial example generation with syntactically controlled paraphrase networks. *CoRR*, abs/1804.06059.

Robin Jia and Percy Liang. 2017. Adversarial examples for evaluating reading comprehension systems. In *Proceedings of the 2017 Conference on Empirical Methods in Natural Language Processing, EMNLP 2017*, pages 2011–2021. Association for Computational Linguistics.

Anjuli Kannan and Oriol Vinyals. 2017. Adversarial evaluation of dialogue models. *CoRR*, abs/1701.08198.

J.J. Katz. 1972. *Semantic theory*. Studies in language. Harper & Row.

Hector J. Levesque. 2014. On our best behaviour. *Artif. Intell.*, 212:27–35.

Bill MacCartney and Christopher D Manning. 2009. An extended model of natural logic. In *Proceedings of the of the Eighth International Conference on Computational Semantics*, Tilburg, Netherlands.

Pasquale Minervini, Thomas Demeester, Tim Rocktäschel, and Sebastian Riedel. 2017. Adversarial sets for regularising neural link predictors. In *Proceedings of the Thirty-Third Conference on Uncertainty in Artificial Intelligence, UAI 2017*. AUAI Press.

Anh Mai Nguyen, Jason Yosinski, and Jeff Clune. 2015. Deep neural networks are easily fooled: High confidence predictions for unrecognizable images. In *IEEE Conference on Computer Vision and Pattern Recognition, CVPR 2015*, pages 427–436. IEEE Computer Society.

Denis Paperno, Germán Kruszewski, Angeliki Lazaridou, Quan Ngoc Pham, Raffaella Bernardi, Sandro Pezzelle, Marco Baroni, Gemma Boleda, and Raquel Fernández. 2016. The LAMBADA dataset: Word prediction requiring a broad discourse context. In *Proceedings of the 54th Annual Meeting of the Association for Computational Linguistics, ACL 2016*. The Association for Computer Linguistics.

Ankur P. Parikh, Oscar Täckström, Dipanjan Das, and Jakob Uszkoreit. 2016. A decomposable attention model for natural language inference. In (Su et al., 2016), pages 2249–2255.

Pranav Rajpurkar, Jian Zhang, Konstantin Lopyrev, and Percy Liang. 2016. Squad: 100, 000+ questions for machine comprehension of text. In (Su et al., 2016), pages 2383–2392.

Laura Rimell and Stephen Clark. 2009. Porting a lexicalized-grammar parser to the biomedical domain. *Journal of Biomedical Informatics*, 42(5):852–865.

Tim Rocktäschel, Edward Grefenstette, Karl Moritz Hermann, Tomas Kocisky, and Phil Blunsom. 2016. Reasoning about entailment with neural attention. In *International Conference on Learning Representations (ICLR)*.

Jian Su et al., editors. 2016. *Proceedings of the 2016 Conference on Empirical Methods in Natural Language Processing, EMNLP 2016*. The Association for Computational Linguistics.

Christian Szegedy, Wojciech Zaremba, Ilya Sutskever, Joan Bruna, Dumitru Erhan, Ian Goodfellow, and Rob Fergus. 2014. Intriguing properties of neural networks. In *International Conference on Learning Representations*.

Adina Williams, Nikita Nangia, and Samuel R. Bowman. 2017. A broad-coverage challenge corpus for sentence understanding through inference. *CoRR*, abs/1704.05426.

From Strings to Other Things:
Linking the Neighborhood and Transposition effects in Word Reading

Stéphan Tulkens and **Dominiek Sandra** and **Walter Daelemans**

CLiPS - Computational Linguistics Group
Department of Linguistics
University of Antwerp
{stephan.tulkens,dominiek.sandra,walter.daelemans}@uantwerpen.be

Abstract

We investigate the relation between the transposition and deletion effects in word reading, i.e., the finding that readers can successfully read "SLAT" as "SALT", or "WRK" as "WORK", and the neighborhood effect. In particular, we investigate whether lexical orthographic neighborhoods take into account transposition and deletion in determining neighbors. If this is the case, it is more likely that the neighborhood effect takes place early during processing, and does not solely rely on similarity of internal representations. We introduce a new neighborhood measure, rd20, which can be used to quantify neighborhood effects over arbitrary feature spaces. We calculate the rd20 over large sets of words in three languages using various feature sets and show that feature sets that do not allow for transposition or deletion explain more variance in Reaction Time (RT) measurements. We also show that the rd20 can be calculated using the hidden state representations of an Multi-Layer Perceptron, and show that these explain less variance than the raw features. We conclude that the neighborhood effect is unlikely to have a perceptual basis, but is more likely to be the result of items co-activating after recognition. All code is available at:
www.github.com/clips/conll2018

1 Introduction

Despite their many disagreements and differences, a common thread among many models of word reading is that they attempt to explain differences in reading speeds by assuming that similarity between words modulate reading speed. There is good reason for this assumption; many experiments have shown that responses on trials are modulated by a word's similarity to other words, be it semantic (Rodd et al., 2002, 2004), orthographic (Andrews, 1997; Perea and Pollat-

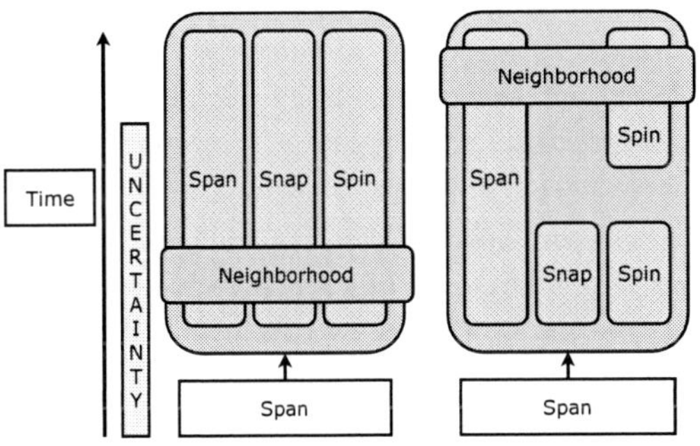

Figure 1: This diagram shows the two positions contrasted in this paper. The left model is the early model, in which the neighborhood effect arises before perceptual uncertainty is resolved; this causes transposition and substitution neighbors to count as neighbors. In the late model, the neighborhood effect only arises after perceptual uncertainty is resolved, and transposition and substitution neighbors do not count towards the neighborhood.

sek, 1998), or phonological similarity (Van Orden, 1987; Rastle and Brysbaert, 2006).

In psycholinguistic research on word reading, this has led to the common practice of including a measure of orthographic neighborhood similarity as a control variable, as these neighborhood measures explain variance in word reading even when controlling for frequency and length (Coltheart, 1977; Yarkoni et al., 2008).

Orthographic neighborhood measures are usually operationalized using edit distance metrics, such as the Levenshtein distance (Levenshtein, 1966). The most well-known measure of neighborhood size is Coltheart's N (Coltheart, 1977), which is the number of types within a substitution distance of 1. Yarkoni et al. (2008) show that N is nearly always 0 for longer words, as long words tend are less frequent, and present an alternative to N, called old20, which is the mean Levenshtein distance to the 20 closest neighbors. old20 corre-

Proceedings of the 22nd Conference on Computational Natural Language Learning (CoNLL 2018), pages 75–85
Brussels, Belgium, October 31 - November 1, 2018. ©2018 Association for Computational Linguistics

lates well with reaction time (RT) measures on two experiments, and explains more variance than N after accounting for length and frequency, and is therefore considered superior to N, and often used as a *de facto* replacement for N (Yarkoni et al., 2008).

Despite its ubiquity as a control variable, the cause for the neighborhood effect is unknown or disputed (Perea, 2015). One aspect, which we explore in the current work, is that it is currently unknown whether the neighborhood effect is *early* or *late*. If the neighborhood effect is *early*, it is caused by the visual stimulus co-activating multiple representations. If it is *late*, the effect is caused by an already activated representation co-activating similar representations.

Of particular interest regarding this question is the finding that skilled readers are remarkably proficient in reading words that contain transposed letters, e.g. "SLAT" versus "SALT" (Davis and Bowers, 2006; Grainger, 2008), or words from which letters are deleted, e.g. "WRK" and "WORK" (Schoonbaert and Grainger, 2004). In this work, we refer to these two effects in tandem as *flexible letter encoding*. Examples of models that try to explain flexible letter encoding include the open bigram family of models (Whitney, 2001; Grainger and Van Heuven, 2004; Schoonbaert and Grainger, 2004; Whitney and Cornelissen, 2008), the SOLAR model (Davis, 2001), the overlap model (Gomez et al., 2008), and, most recently, the spatial coding model (Davis, 2010b).

Taking into consideration both the neighborhood effect and flexible letter encoding, we define the following research question: are the neighborhoods also defined using flexible letter encoding? That is, if we know that readers activate "SALT" upon reading "SLAT", does this also imply that the lexical neighborhood of "THREE" includes "THERE"?

To answer this question, we calculate the neighborhood density using a variety of feature sets, including features that do not allow for flexible letter encoding, and those that do. If lexical neighborhoods calculated using flexible letter encodings account for less variance in word reading times than neighborhoods based on slot-based features, we can surmise that it is more likely that the neighborhood effect is late in origin. This follows from the fact that flexible letter encodings are most likely to be an intermediate encoding step to-

wards a concrete internal representation. Hence, if neighborhoods with flexible letter encodings explain less variance, flexible letter encoding most likely does not play a role in the neighborhood effect. This, in turn implies that the neighborhood effect is likely a late effect, and is caused by concrete representations co-activating similar representations. These two positions are contrasted in Figure 1.

2 Main Contributions

To quantify the effect of different forms of representations and their respective neighborhoods, we introduce the Representation Distance 20 (rd20), a generalization of old20 which operates on arbitrary feature spaces.

We first replicate the original findings of Yarkoni et al. (2008) regarding old20 and N on Dutch, British English, and French lexical databases. As old20 uses the Levenshtein metric, which encodes flexible letter position by allowing deletions and transpositions, the neighborhoods defined by old20 in principle support the idea of flexible letter encoding.

Comparing to old20 and N, we show that rd20 can be used to create neighborhood measures for various feature sets. Furthermore, we use regression models to quantify the relation between word length, frequency and rd20 on the one hand, and Reaction Times (RT) in lexical decision experiments on the other. We do this for four different feature sets on all aforementioned lexical databases. Two of the four feature sets are slot-based feature sets used in older models of computational psycholinguistics, and two of them are used by models that assume some kind of flexible letter encoding. We can therefore use rd20 to assess the effect of the representational assumptions in models of flexible letter encoding, as well as provide a direct comparison to old20.

We show that rd20 using one hot encoded letter features explains slightly more variance in lexical decision experiments than old20. The fact that rd20 takes much less time to compute and is more flexible in the choice of inputs shows that it is a practical alternative to old20. Additionally, we show that the rd20 of feature sets which specifically encode letters in a flexible manner explains far less variance in RT than the rd20 of encodings which do not support flexible letter encoding. This leads us to hypothesize that lexical neighborhoods are not defined using flexible letter encoding, and that, consequently, the neighborhood effect itself is a late effect, that is, an effect caused by co-activation of similar representations, and not caused by the visual likeness of stimuli.

To provide additional evidence regarding the statement that the neighborhood effect follows from internal representations, we perform an experiment using Multi-Layer Perceptrons. After training the network on each feature set, we calculate rd20 of the hidden states of these networks, and use these distances as a predictor in a linear regression experiment

2.1 Representation Distance 20

Representation Distance 20 (rd20) is a measure that does not assume a particular representational format, and thus applies to any kind of vector representation. It is therefore well-suited to quantifying the effect feature sets have on lexical decision experiments.

The rd20 for a featurized word x given a set of featurized words X, where $x \in X$, is defined as follows:

$$s(x, X) = sort(cos(x, X)) \qquad (1)$$

Where $sort$ is a sorting operator, cos is the cosine distance, x is featurized item, and X is the set of featurized items. We then take the mean of the 20 first items, excluding the item itself.

$$\text{rd20}(x, X) = \frac{\sum_{i=1}^{21} s(x, X)^i}{20} \qquad (2)$$

We use the 20 closest neighbors to be able to compare to old20, which also uses 20 neighbors. As Yarkoni et al. (2008) note, the value of 20 is quite arbitrary, and values between 5 and 50 seem to work well for most experiments. Because rd20 uses the cosine distance, it directly applies to any vector representation. It is therefore suitable for inspecting both external phenomena, i.e. featurized string representations, and internal representations, e.g. weight matrices of neural networks.

3   Materials

This section describes the materials used in the paper: the corpora, reaction time datasets, and the various feature sets.

3.1   Corpora

Throughout the paper we use three different lexical databases derived from subtitle corpora as the source of our words and frequency counts. For Dutch we use SUBTLEX-NL (Keuleers et al., 2010a), for English we use SUBTLEX-UK (Van Heuven et al., 2014), and for French we use Lexique 3 (New et al., 2007). Frequency counts from subtitle corpora account for substantially more variance in Reaction Time measurements, and are based on far larger corpora, than previously available databases (Brysbaert and New, 2009; Brysbaert and Cortese, 2011), such as CELEX (Baayen et al., 1993) and previous versions of Lexique (New et al., 2001).

For all three languages, we use reaction times (RT) from megastudies (Seidenberg and Waters, 1989). For Dutch we extract the reaction times from the Dutch Lexicon Project 2 (DLP) (Keuleers et al., 2010b; Brysbaert et al., 2016), for English we use the British Lexicon project (BLP) (Keuleers et al., 2012), and for French we use the French Lexicon project (FLP) (Ferrand et al., 2010). As with the subtitle corpora, these megastudies provide us with a more accurate estimate of Reaction Times than previous studies with a smaller number of participants and a smaller set of items.

We extract a subset of these corpora according to the following procedure: for each language, we take all words from the SUBTLEX corpora and lexicon projects, removing any words which were shorter than 2 characters, or words which contained non-alphabetic characters, such as '#' and '-'. We then remove any words from the lexicon project database which are not in the SUBTLEX database, such that the words extracted from the lexicon project were a subset of those in the SUBTLEX database.

Additionally, for all languages we remove any diacritic markers, transforming e.g. the French word 'très' to 'tres'. This was done because not all feature sets can appropriately featurize these diacritic markers.

For each language, this leaves us with a set of SUBTLEX words, for which we only have frequency counts, and a set of words from the lexicon project, for which we have both frequency counts and Reaction Time measurements. The sizes of the resulting corpora are listed in Table 1.

	Dutch	English	French
SUBTLEX	117,789	157,378	115,550
Lexicon project	24,908	28,530	36,677

Table 1: The number of words left over in the SUBTLEX and Lexicon projects after filtering. Note that we removed any words from the Lexicon project which were not in the SUBTLEX database, so that the words from the lexicon project are an exact subset of those in the SUBTLEX database.

3.2 Features

We use four different orthographic feature sets. All the feature sets were previously implemented in `wordkit` (Tulkens et al., 2018).

3.2.1 Slots

The two slot-based feature encodings are created by left-justifying strings, padding them with spaces to the length of the longest word in our corpus, and then replacing each letter in each resulting slot by a feature vector. These feature vectors are then concatenated to create a final feature vector. As noted in the introduction, these types of encodings are thought to be unrealistic (Grainger and Van Heuven, 2004; Davis and Bowers, 2006), as they predict that words which are not aligned have low similarity. The words "STAR" and "TAR", for example, have a similarity of 0 according to a naive slot-based encoding. Despite this shortcoming, the influence of slot-based encodings on contemporary models of word reading can not be understated (Miikkulainen, 1997; McClelland and Rumelhart, 1981; Harm and Seidenberg, 2004; Coltheart et al., 2001).

One hot encoded characters One hot encoded character featurization assigns a single orthogonal vector to each character, and hence assumes that there is no underlying similarity, visual or otherwise, between letters. This encoding is closest to the encoding implicitly used by the Levenshtein distance, and used by old20. In this encoding we treat the space character as a separate character, and not as a zero vector.

Fourteen segment encoding The fourteen segment encoding was first introduced by Rumelhart and Siple (1974), and is used in the original version of the Interactive Activation model (McClelland and Rumelhart, 1981). As its name implies, it uses fourteen binary segments, each of which denotes a specific vertical, horizontal, or diago-

nal line segment. Because the encoding is subsymbolic, words with different letters in the same slot might still have some overlap in their similarity. In this encoding, we treat the space character as a zero vector.

3.2.2 Wickelgraphs

Wickelgraphs were first introduced as Wickelphones in the context of phonological representations (Seidenberg and McClelland, 1989) and are named after, and based on the work of, Wickelgren (1969). As we saw above, slot-based encodings predict that words which are not aligned are completely dissimilar. Wickelgraphs attempt to overcome this downside by representing words as sets of contiguous $n$grams, where n is usually set to 3, and $n - 1$ padding characters are added to the start and end of each word. For example, the word "SALT" has the following wickelgraph representation: {##S, #SA, SAL, ALT, LT#, T##}.

3.2.3 Weighted Open bigrams

Another way of representing flexible letter coding in reading is the open bigram family of feature encodings. Open bigrams were first proposed by Whitney (2001) to account for readers' resilience to letter transposition effects, although earlier accounts of transposition-like encodings can be found in work by Mozer (1987). For a criticism of open bigrams, see work by Davis (2010a) and Kinoshita and Norris (2013).

Open bigrams are constructed by taking the ordered set of 2-combinations of all letters in a word. For example, the word 'SALT' becomes {SA, SL, ST, AL, AT, LT} in an open bigram encoding scheme. This scheme can account for transposition and deletion effects because most bigrams survive the transposition or deletion of two letters.

The weighted open bigram scheme attaches a weight to each bigram combination depending on the distance between the constituent letters of the bigram in the word (Schoonbaert and Grainger, 2004; Whitney and Cornelissen, 2008; Whitney, 2001). This encoding scheme was introduced to account for the observation that participants experience more inhibition to transpositions which are further apart. Following Whitney et al. (2012) we used weights of 1.0, .7, and .2 for bigrams with 0, 1, or 2 intervening letters in all our experiments. Bigrams with more than 2 intervening letters get a weight of 0, and are therefore discarded in the distance computation.

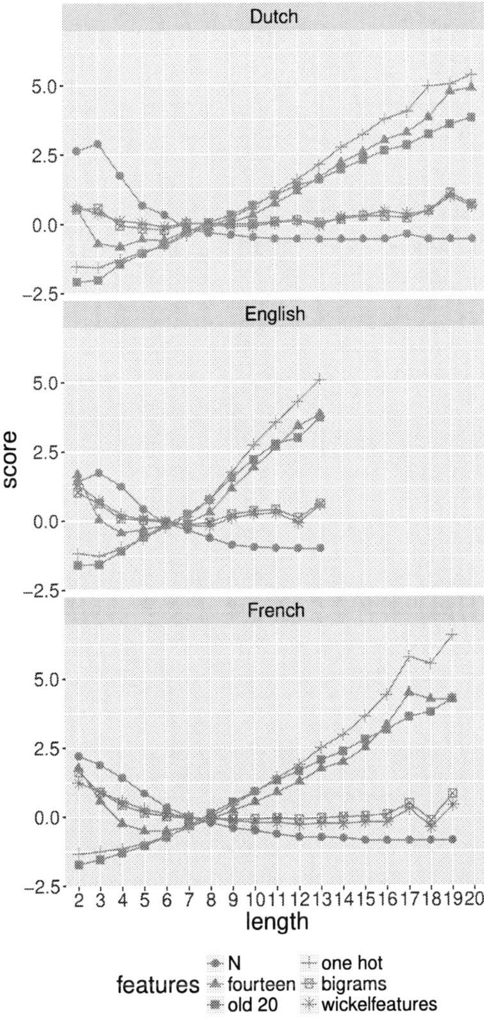

Figure 2: rd20, N and old20, plotted against word length for three languages. The figure shows the measures behave the same across languages. The y-axes denote the scaled quantities, as the old20 and N measures are expressed on a different scale than the various rd20 measures.

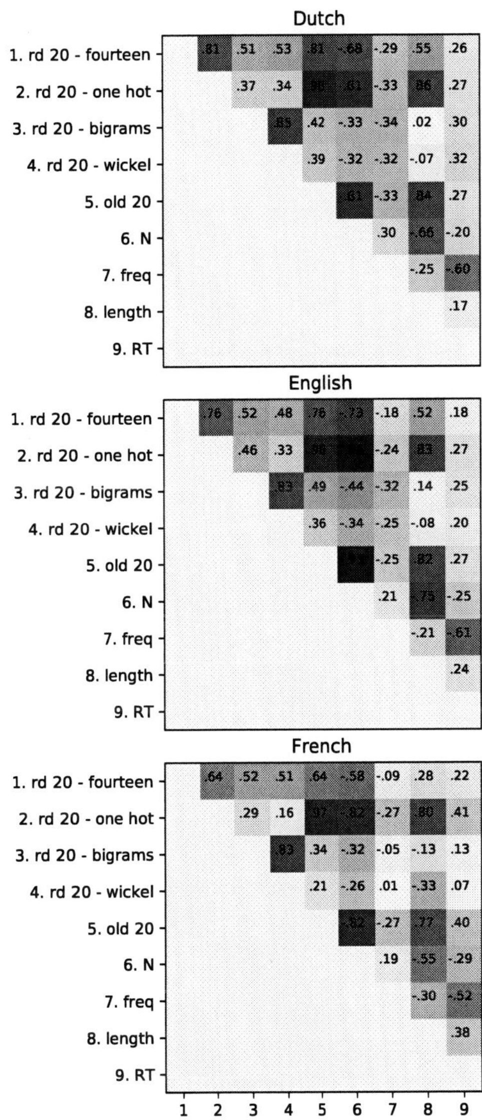

Figure 3: The correlations between the control variables (length and frequency), the various distance measures, and RT. All correlations are significant ($p < .05$).

4 Experiment 1: empirical validation of rd20

Using the materials defined in Section 3, we carry out comparative experiments of old20, N, and the rd20 of the four feature sets described above.

Figure 2 shows the word length versus the mean distance for each of the measures for all three languages. The figure shows that old20 and the measures based on slot-based encodings correlate strongly with length, while flexible encodings do not correlate with length. We observe the same pattern of performance for all three languages. As a similar pattern of performance was observed in Yarkoni et al. (2008), we consider this to be an empirical validation of our datasets.

Figure 3 shows the Spearman correlations between the different predictor variables (length, frequency), and the various measures for all languages. As the figure indicates, the pattern of correlations is consistent across all surveyed languages, and only differs in magnitude, not direction. Additionally, because the results corre-

	Predictor	Dutch			English			French		
		β	R^2_{adj}	ΔR^2_{adj}	β	R^2_{adj}	ΔR^2_{adj}	β	R^2_{adj}	ΔR^2_{adj}
base	length	.025	.252	.0	.083	.344	.0	.263	.314	.0
	freq	-.494			-.558			-.414		
rd20 - fourteen	length	-.058	.270	.018	.053	.346	.002	.209	.339	.025
	freq	-.472			-.553			-.421		
	score	.161			.059			.164		
rd20 - one hot	length	-.305	.292	**.040**	-.066	.353	**.011**	.003	.353	**.039**
	freq	-.459			-.552			-.417		
	score	.397			.181			.326		
rd20 - bigrams	length	.044	.273	.021	.079	.349	.005	.292	.342	.028
	freq	-.438			-.536			-.401		
	score	.154			.076			.167		
rd20 - wickel	length	.006	.289	.037	.096	.351	.007	.333	.350	.036
	freq	-.417			-.533			-.397		
	score	.206			.088			.200		
old20	length	-.240	.283	.022	-.051	.352	.008	.035	.349	.035
	freq	-.457			-.550			-.412		
	score	.329			.166			.295		
N	length	.087	.259	.007	.078	.344	.000	.261	.314	.0
	freq	-.510			-.557			-.414		
	score	.110			-.007			-.005		

Table 2: The coefficients, explained variance, and change in explained variance of the regression analyses. The rd20 measure using one hot features explains the most variance across all languages, although the difference is not significant for English.

spond with those from Yarkoni et al. (2008), this provides additional evidence for old20 and our datasets. Given that old20 is considered to be a good neighborhood measure, and the various rd20 measures show the same type of effects, i.e., effects in the same direction, this indirectly validates rd20 as a good measure.

As an aside, while we see the same direction of effects as in Yarkoni et al. (2008), we do see that the magnitude of the correlations between the scores and RT are lower for all corpora, which was reported to be .612 for the English Lexicon Project stimuli used in Yarkoni et al. (2008).

4.1 Regression analyses

In addition to the zero-order correlations above, we also conduct stepwise regression analyses. We use the RT values from the various lexicon projects, as explained in Section 3 as dependent variables, and consider the length, frequency, and the distance measures as independent variables. We first start by adding the control variables, length and frequency in this case. Then, for each defined measure, we add the score predictor as an

additional variable, while measuring the effect this addition has on model fit.

The difference between the adjusted R-squared, or R^2_{adj} from here on, of the model with the control variables and the model with the extra predictor is called the ΔR^2_{adj}, and explains how much additional variance is explained by the added predictor. Because all measures were calculated using the same data, we can simply compare the ΔR^2_{adj} of each of the regression models to determine the effect of that particular measure.

The results of the regression analyses are shown in Table 2. The rows above the horizontal line show the base model, i.e. the model with only the control variables as predictors, while the rows below the line denote the various statistics of the different models with respect to the base model.

All score predictors for each model but the N model show positive effect of score on RT, indicating that words in denser neighborhoods, i.e. words with a *lower* average distance to nearest neighbors, have shorter Reaction Times. These scores thus predict a positive effect of neighborhood density.

For N we expect a negative correlation, as the

measure is inverted, i.e. words with denser neighborhoods have higher figures. Nevertheless we see a positive effect of N for Dutch, which is unexpected.

In all three corpora the one hot encoded features explain the most variance out of all the measures, with the wickelfeatures following in second place for Dutch and French, and OLD20 following in second place for English. To see if these difference were significant, we bootstrapped the difference between the R^2_{adj} estimates of one hot encoded rd20 and other feature sets with an α of .05. For Dutch, we bootstrapped the differences between the one hot encoded and wickelfeatures; which led to intervals of [0.0004, 0.0058], indicating a significant, albeit really small, difference between the one hot encoded and wickelfeatures. For English and French, we compared old20 to both the rd20 of the one hot and the wickelfeatures. Because of multiple comparisons, we used Bonferroni correction to correct our α of .05 to .025. For English, the confidence interval of the bootstrapped differences between the one hot encoding and wickelgraphs was [-0.0028, -.0003], indicating significance, while the same confidence interval for one hot encoding and old20 was [0.0003, 0.0020], again indicating a significant difference. For French, the confidence intervals for the differences between one hot encoding and wickelgraphs were [-0.0011, 0.0032], indicating a nonsignificant difference, while the confidence interval for the differences between one hot encoding and old20 was [0.0029, 0.0061], again indicating significance.

In a practical sense, the significance is not that important: as all of these values are really small, there seems to be little reason to prefer one of the metrics over the other. That is, even though the difference between old 20 and the rd20 of a one hot encoded representation is significant, the difference in explained variance is so small to not really matter.

Theoretically, these results point towards a smaller role for transposition effects than previously assumed, for two reasons:

First, given that the main difference between the one-hot encoded features and the Levenshtein-based old20 is that the Levenshtein metric allows for transpositions and deletions, we can view the difference in explained variance between these two measures as the *net transposition effect*. If

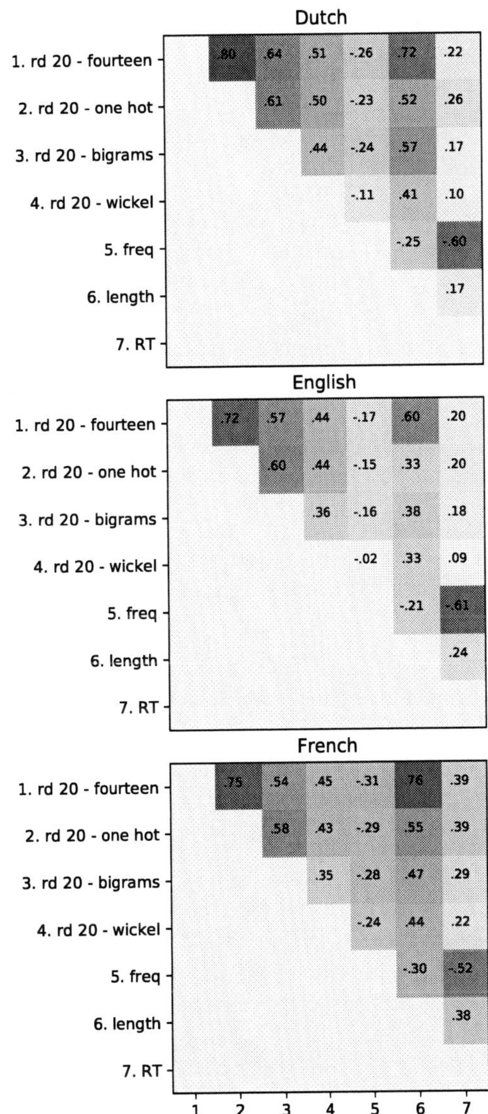

Figure 4: The correlations between the control variables, length and frequency, and the various distance measures for representations learned by the MLP.

transpositions and deletions played a large role during lexical access, then we would expect to see a large positive net transposition effect. In our experiments, we see exactly the opposite: a small but significant negative net transposition effect in all corpora. Second, we observe that the bigrams, the feature set specifically constructed for modeling transposition effects during word reading, explains less variance than the slot-based encodings in all cases.

Both of these results lead us to hypothesize that

	Predictor	Dutch			English			French		
		β	R^2_{adj}	ΔR^2_{adj}	β	R^2_{adj}	ΔR^2_{adj}	β	R^2_{adj}	ΔR^2_{adj}
base	length	.025	.252	.0	.08	.344	.0	.263	.315	.0
	freq	-.493			-.55			-.414		
fourteen	length	-.054	.257	.005	.031	.348	.004	.143	.327	.012
	freq	-.484			-.556			-.400		
	score	.110			.083			.168		
one hot	length	-.068	.274	**.022**	.041	.356	**.012**	.144	.347	**.032**
	freq	-.475			-.551			-.390		
	score	.179			.119			.221		
bigrams	length	.020	.252	.0	.061	.346	.002	.23	.319	.004
	freq	-.492			-.554			-.403		
	score	.008			.051			.075		
wickel	length	.008	.254	.002	.067	.345	.001	.256	.315	.000
	freq	-.493			-.560			-.412		
	score	.041			.047			.016		

Table 3: The coefficients, adjusted explained variance, and change in adjusted explained variance of the regression analyses on the hidden state representations learned by an MLP.

transposition and deletions play a smaller role in defining lexical neighborhoods than previously assumed.

5 Experiment 2: internal Representations

In the previous experiment, we showed that rd20 can be used to assess the neighborhood of featurized words. Calculating the rd20 over the raw features, however, assumes that our internal representations are exemplars instead of learned abstract representations, such as those found in a neural network. To assess whether rd20 can also be used with hidden state representations, we performed an additional experiment using a Multi-Layer Perceptron (MLP).

For each feature set, we trained an MLP to predict the identity of the word based on the input features, which is similar to experiments conducted by Dandurand et al. (2010). Each MLP had one hidden layer with 500 hidden units and a Sigmoid activation function, while the output layer had a softmax activation function, and a dimensionality of the vocabulary size. We used cross-entropy as a loss function, and optimized using Adam (Kingma and Ba, 2014). Our training regime was as follows: we shuffled before each epoch, and then presented all featurized words to the MLP. As in the previous experiment, we used the whole corpus for each language during training. We trained each model until convergence, where we defined convergence as there being no change in the loss for 20 epochs in a row. After convergence, we calculated the accuracy score for each of the models in each language. Each of the models achieved an accuracy of .95 or higher, showing that each model has correctly learned to predict nearly every word.

We then presented the words for which we had RTs (i.e. the words which were both in the SUBTLEX database and in the Lexicon Project for each language) to the network again, and stored the hidden unit activations in response to the input. Following the neural network literature (e.g. (Elman, 1991)), we assume these internal representations are the representations learned during the task of attempting to predict the word identity. We then calculated rd20 for each representation, and used these as input to the same analyses as the previous experiment.

Comparing the MLP results in Figure 4 to the results from Figure 3, we see that the MLP has a normalizing effect; as far as these statistics are concerned, the differences between the different feature sets have become smaller. The most prominent change is that all rd20 measures now correlate with length, whereas before only the rd20 based on slot-based values correlated with length. Similarly, the rd20 based on the one hot features did not correlate with the rd20 based on the bigram and wickelgraphs in experiment 1, but does correlate in the present experiment.

We also conducted regression analyses, using

the distances between the hidden layer representations as a predictor, as in experiment 1. Table 3 shows the results of these regression analyses. These analyses confirm that the MLP has a normalizing effect; whereas the effect of frequency and length differed in magnitude and sign between feature sets in Experiment 1, nearly all feature sets see a positive effect of length and a negative effect of frequency. The regression analysis shows that the R^2_{adj} was generally lower for the representations in the MLP, with the wickelgraphs especially suffering in comparison to Experiment 1.

6 Discussion and conclusion

Jointly, our experiments show that one hot encoded characters outperform other feature representations in explaining variance beyond frequency and length. In Experiment 1, we showed that transposition effects play a smaller role than previously thought; rd20 over a one hot encoded character representation explains significantly, albeit small amounts, more variance than old20. The rd20 of open bigrams, a feature set specifically constructed for a representation which takes into account transposition effects, does not explain a lot of variance. Returning to the main research question of this paper, i.e. whether the neighborhood effect is influenced by transposition neighbors, our evidence shows that it more likely the case that they do not.

Counter to what we found, experiments have shown that human subjects *do* take into account transposition neighbors in their neighborhoods (Davis et al., 2009; Acha and Perea, 2008). This raises an interesting conundrum, and shows that more research is required.

Furthermore, while the effect of denser neighborhoods was uniformly positive throughout all experiments and measures, this is not the case in human processing, where dense neighborhoods can sometimes have an inhibitory effect due to competition (Perea, 2015).

This leads us to another point of concern: the theoretical status of the neighborhood metric, be it old20, N, or rd20. Should these metrics be conceived of as purely diagnostic instruments, or as full-fledged, albeit limited, models of word processing? As our research shows, varying the neighborhood metric allows us to advance theoretical claims, like any model would allow us to do. In the future, we would like to investigate how

much of a model one can build out of the neighborhood metric.

Experiment 2 shows the validity of using rd20 on internal representations learned by a neural network. This opens up new avenues for research, and allows us to quantitatively determine the effect of neighborhood density in neural networks on behavioral measures.

7 Implementation details

All statistical analyses were carried out using R (Team et al., 2013), some of the Figures were made in ggplot2 (Wickham et al., 2008). rd20, old20 and N were implemented in Python (Van Rossum and Drake Jr, 1995), using Numpy (Walt et al., 2011), while the MLP was implemented using PyTorch (Paszke et al., 2017). Some Figures were made in Matplotlib (Hunter, 2007).

8 Acknowledgments

The first author is supported by a PhD scholarship from the FWO Research Foundation - Flanders. We would like to thank Robert Grimm and Giovanni Cassani for help with the statistical analysis and general comments. Additionally, we would like to thank the reviewers for helpful comments and suggestions, which improved the paper a lot.

References

Joana Acha and Manuel Perea. 2008. The effect of neighborhood frequency in reading: Evidence with transposed-letter neighbors. *Cognition*, 108(1):290–300.

Sally Andrews. 1997. The effect of orthographic similarity on lexical retrieval: Resolving neighborhood conflicts. *Psychonomic Bulletin & Review*, 4(4):439–461.

R Harald Baayen, Richard Piepenbrock, and Rijn van H. 1993. The CELEX lexical data base on CD-ROM.

Marc Brysbaert and Michael J Cortese. 2011. Do the effects of subjective frequency and age of acquisition survive better word frequency norms? *Quarterly Journal of Experimental Psychology*, 64(3):545–559.

Marc Brysbaert and Boris New. 2009. Moving beyond kučera and francis: A critical evaluation of current word frequency norms and the introduction of a new and improved word frequency measure for american english. *Behavior research methods*, 41(4):977–990.

Marc Brysbaert, Michaël Stevens, Paweł Mandera, and Emmanuel Keuleers. 2016. The impact of word prevalence on lexical decision times: Evidence from the dutch lexicon project 2. *Journal of Experimental Psychology: Human Perception and Performance*, 42(3):441.

Max Coltheart. 1977. Access to the internal lexicon. *The psychology of reading*.

Max Coltheart, Kathleen Rastle, Conrad Perry, Robyn Langdon, and Johannes Ziegler. 2001. Drc: a dual route cascaded model of visual word recognition and reading aloud. *Psychological review*, 108(1):204.

Frédéric Dandurand, Jonathan Grainger, and Stéphane Dufau. 2010. Learning location-invariant orthographic representations for printed words. *Connection Science*, 22(1):25–42.

Colin J Davis. 2010a. Solar versus seriol revisited. *European Journal of Cognitive Psychology*, 22(5):695–724.

Colin J Davis. 2010b. The spatial coding model of visual word identification. *Psychological Review*, 117(3):713.

Colin J Davis and Jeffrey S Bowers. 2006. Contrasting five different theories of letter position coding: Evidence from orthographic similarity effects. *Journal of Experimental Psychology: Human Perception and Performance*, 32(3):535.

Colin J Davis, Manuel Perea, and Joana Acha. 2009. Re (de) fining the orthographic neighborhood: The role of addition and deletion neighbors in lexical decision and reading. *Journal of Experimental Psychology: Human Perception and Performance*, 35(5):1550.

Colin John Davis. 2001. *The self-organising lexical acquisition and recognition (SOLAR) model of visual word recognition*. Ph.D. thesis, ProQuest Information & Learning.

Jeffrey L Elman. 1991. Distributed representations, simple recurrent networks, and grammatical structure. *Machine learning*, 7(2-3):195–225.

Ludovic Ferrand, Boris New, Marc Brysbaert, Emmanuel Keuleers, Patrick Bonin, Alain Méot, Maria Augustinova, and Christophe Pallier. 2010. The french lexicon project: Lexical decision data for 38,840 french words and 38,840 pseudowords. *Behavior Research Methods*, 42(2):488–496.

Pablo Gomez, Roger Ratcliff, and Manuel Perea. 2008. The overlap model: a model of letter position coding. *Psychological review*, 115(3):577.

Jonathan Grainger. 2008. Cracking the orthographic code: An introduction. *Language and cognitive processes*, 23(1):1–35.

Jonathan Grainger and Walter JB Van Heuven. 2004. Modeling letter position coding in printed word perception.

Michael W Harm and Mark S Seidenberg. 2004. Computing the meanings of words in reading: cooperative division of labor between visual and phonological processes. *Psychological review*, 111(3):662.

J. D. Hunter. 2007. Matplotlib: A 2d graphics environment. *Computing In Science & Engineering*, 9(3):90–95.

Emmanuel Keuleers, Marc Brysbaert, and Boris New. 2010a. Subtlex-nl: A new measure for dutch word frequency based on film subtitles. *Behavior research methods*, 42(3):643–650.

Emmanuel Keuleers, Kevin Diependaele, and Marc Brysbaert. 2010b. Practice effects in large-scale visual word recognition studies: A lexical decision study on 14,000 dutch mono-and disyllabic words and nonwords. *Frontiers in Psychology*, 1:174.

Emmanuel Keuleers, Paula Lacey, Kathleen Rastle, and Marc Brysbaert. 2012. The british lexicon project: Lexical decision data for 28,730 monosyllabic and disyllabic english words. *Behavior research methods*, 44(1):287–304.

Diederik P Kingma and Jimmy Ba. 2014. Adam: A method for stochastic optimization. *arXiv preprint arXiv:1412.6980*.

Sachiko Kinoshita and Dennis Norris. 2013. Letter order is not coded by open bigrams. *Journal of memory and language*, 69(2):135–150.

Vladimir I Levenshtein. 1966. Binary codes capable of correcting deletions, insertions, and reversals. In *Soviet physics doklady*, volume 10, pages 707–710.

James L McClelland and David E Rumelhart. 1981. An interactive activation model of context effects in letter perception: I. an account of basic findings. *Psychological review*, 88(5):375.

Risto Miikkulainen. 1997. Dyslexic and category-specific aphasic impairments in a self-organizing feature map model of the lexicon. *Brain and language*, 59(2):334–366.

Michael C Mozer. 1987. *Early parallel processing in reading: A connectionist approach*. Lawrence Erlbaum Associates, Inc.

Boris New, Marc Brysbaert, Jean Veronis, and Christophe Pallier. 2007. The use of film subtitles to estimate word frequencies. *Applied psycholinguistics*, 28(4):661–677.

Boris New, Christophe Pallier, Ludovic Ferrand, and Rafael Matos. 2001. Une base de données lexicales du français contemporain sur internet: Lexique//a lexical database for contemporary french: Lexique. *L'année psychologique*, 101(3):447–462.

Adam Paszke, Sam Gross, Soumith Chintala, Gregory Chanan, Edward Yang, Zachary DeVito, Zeming Lin, Alban Desmaison, Luca Antiga, and Adam Lerer. 2017. Automatic differentiation in pytorch.

Manuel Perea. 2015. Neighborhood effects in visual word recognition and reading. *The Oxford Handbook of Reading*, page 76.

Manuel Perea and Alexander Pollatsek. 1998. The effects of neighborhood frequency in reading and lexical decision. *Journal of Experimental Psychology: Human Perception and Performance*, 24(3):767.

Kathleen Rastle and Marc Brysbaert. 2006. Masked phonological priming effects in english: Are they real? do they matter? *Cognitive Psychology*, 53(2):97–145.

Jennifer Rodd, Gareth Gaskell, and William Marslen-Wilson. 2002. Making sense of semantic ambiguity: Semantic competition in lexical access. *Journal of Memory and Language*, 46(2):245–266.

Jennifer M Rodd, M Gareth Gaskell, and William D Marslen-Wilson. 2004. Modelling the effects of semantic ambiguity in word recognition. *Cognitive Science*, 28(1):89–104.

David E Rumelhart and Patricia Siple. 1974. Process of recognizing tachistoscopically presented words. *Psychological review*, 81(2):99.

Sofie Schoonbaert and Jonathan Grainger. 2004. Letter position coding in printed word perception: Effects of repeated and transposed letters. *Language and Cognitive Processes*, 19(3):333–367.

Mark S Seidenberg and James L McClelland. 1989. A distributed, developmental model of word recognition and naming. *Psychological review*, 96(4):523.

Mf S Seidenberg and GS Waters. 1989. Reading words aloud-a mega study.

R Core Team et al. 2013. R: A language and environment for statistical computing.

Stphan Tulkens, Dominiek Sandra, and Walter Daelemans. 2018. Wordkit: a python package for orthographic and phonological featurization. In *Proceedings of the Eleventh International Conference on Language Resources and Evaluation (LREC 2018)*, Paris, France. European Language Resources Association (ELRA).

Walter JB Van Heuven, Pawel Mandera, Emmanuel Keuleers, and Marc Brysbaert. 2014. Subtlex-uk: A new and improved word frequency database for british english. *Quarterly Journal of Experimental Psychology*, 67(6):1176–1190.

Guy C Van Orden. 1987. A rows is a rose: Spelling, sound, and reading. *Memory & cognition*, 15(3):181–198.

Guido Van Rossum and Fred L Drake Jr. 1995. *Python reference manual*. Centrum voor Wiskunde en Informatica Amsterdam.

Stéfan van der Walt, S Chris Colbert, and Gael Varoquaux. 2011. The numpy array: a structure for efficient numerical computation. *Computing in Science & Engineering*, 13(2):22–30.

Carol Whitney. 2001. How the brain encodes the order of letters in a printed word: The seriol model and selective literature review. *Psychonomic Bulletin & Review*, 8(2):221–243.

Carol Whitney, Daisy Bertrand, and Jonathan Grainger. 2012. On coding the position of letters in words. *Experimental psychology*.

Carol Whitney and Piers Cornelissen. 2008. Seriol reading. *Language and Cognitive Processes*, 23(1):143–164.

Wayne A Wickelgren. 1969. Context-sensitive coding, associative memory, and serial order in (speech) behavior. *Psychological Review*, 76(1):1.

Hadley Wickham, Winston Chang, et al. 2008. ggplot2: An implementation of the grammar of graphics. *R package version 0.7, URL: http://CRAN. R-project. org/package= ggplot2*.

Tal Yarkoni, David Balota, and Melvin Yap. 2008. Moving beyond colthearts n: A new measure of orthographic similarity. *Psychonomic Bulletin & Review*, 15(5):971–979.

Global Attention for Name Tagging

Boliang Zhang, Spencer Whitehead, Lifu Huang and Heng Ji
Computer Science Department
Rensselaer Polytechnic Institute
`{zhangb8,whites5,huangl7,jih}@rpi.edu`

Abstract

Many name tagging approaches use local contextual information with much success, but fail when the local context is ambiguous or limited. We present a new framework to improve name tagging by utilizing local, document-level, and corpus-level contextual information. We retrieve document-level context from other sentences within the same document and corpus-level context from sentences in other topically related documents. We propose a model that learns to incorporate document-level and corpus-level contextual information alongside local contextual information via global attentions, which dynamically weight their respective contextual information, and gating mechanisms, which determine the influence of this information. Extensive experiments on benchmark datasets show the effectiveness of our approach, which achieves state-of-the-art results for Dutch, German, and Spanish on the CoNLL-2002 and CoNLL-2003 datasets.[1].

1 Introduction

Name tagging, the task of automatically identifying and classifying named entities in text, is often posed as a sentence-level sequence labeling problem where each token is labeled as being part of a name of a certain type (*e.g.*, location) or not (Chinchor and Robinson, 1997; Tjong Kim Sang and De Meulder, 2003). When labeling a token, local context (*i.e.*, surrounding tokens) is crucial because the context gives insight to the semantic meaning of the token. However, there are many instances in which the local context is ambiguous or lacks sufficient content. For example, in Figure 1, the query sentence discusses "Zywiec" selling a

product and profiting from these sales, but the local contextual information is ambiguous as more than one entity type could be involved in a sale. As a result, the baseline model mistakenly tags "Zywiec" as a person (PER) instead of the correct tag, which is organization (ORG). If the model has access to supporting evidence that provides additional, clearer contextual information, then the model may use this information to correct the mistake given the ambiguous local context.

```
Baseline:
So far this year [PER Zywiec], whose full name
is Zaklady Piwowarskie w Zywcu SA, has netted six
million zlotys on sales of 224 million zlotys.

Our model (Document-level + Corpus-level Attention):
So far this year [ORG Zywiec], whose full name
is Zaklady Piwowarskie w Zywcu SA, has netted six
million zlotys on sales of 224 million zlotys.

Document-level Supporting Evidence:
Van Boxmeer also said [ORG Zywiec] would be boosted
by its recent shedding of soft drinks which only
accounted for about three percent of the firm's
overall sales and for which 7.6 million zlotys in
provisions had already been made.

Polish brewer [ORG Zywiec]'s 1996 profit slump may
last into next year due in part to hefty
depreciation charges, but recent high investment
should help the firm defend its 10-percent market
share, the firm's chief executive said.

Corpus-level Supporting Evidence:
The [ORG Zywiec] logo includes all of the most
important historical symbols of the brewery and
Poland itself.

[LOC Zywiec] is a town in south-central
Poland 32,242 inhabitants (as of November 2007).
```

Figure 1: Example from the baseline and our model with some supporting evidence.

Additional context may be found from other sentences in the same document as the query sentence (**document-level**). In Figure 1, the sentences in the document-level supporting evidence provide clearer clues to tag "Zywiec" as ORG, such as the references to "Zywiec" as a "firm". A concern of leveraging this information is the amount of noise that is introduced. However, across all the

---

[1]The programs are publicly available for research purpose: `https://github.com/boliangz/global_attention_ner`

Proceedings of the 22nd Conference on Computational Natural Language Learning (CoNLL 2018), pages 86–96
Brussels, Belgium, October 31 - November 1, 2018. ©2018 Association for Computational Linguistics

data in our experiments (Section 3.1), we find that an average of 35.43% of named entity mentions in each document are repeats and, when a mention appears more than once in a document, an average of 98.78% of these mentions have the same type. Consequently, one may use the document-level context to overcome the ambiguities of the local context while introducing little noise.

Although a significant amount of named entity mentions are repeated, 64.57% of the mentions are unique. In such cases, the sentences at the document-level cannot serve as a source of additional context. Nevertheless, one may find additional context from sentences in other documents in the corpus (**corpus-level**). Figure 1 shows some of the corpus-level supporting evidence for "Zywiec". In this example, similar to the document-level supporting evidence, the first sentence in this corpus-level evidence discusses the branding of "Zywiec", corroborating the ORG tag. Whereas the second sentence introduces noise because it has a different topic than the current sentence and discusses the Polish town named "Zywiec", one may filter these noisy contexts, especially when the noisy contexts are accompanied by clear contexts like the first sentence.

We propose to utilize local, document-level, and corpus-level contextual information to improve name tagging. Generally, we follow the *one sense per discourse* hypothesis introduced by Yarowsky (2003). Some previous name tagging efforts apply this hypothesis to conduct majority voting for multiple mentions with the same name string in a discourse through a cache model (Florian et al., 2004) or post-processing (Hermjakob et al., 2017). However, these rule-based methods require manual tuning of thresholds. Moreover, it's challenging to explicitly define the scope of discourse. We propose a new neural network framework with global attention to tackle these challenges. Specifically, for each token in a query sentence, we propose to retrieve sentences that contain the same token from the document-level and corpus-level contexts (*e.g.*, document-level and corpus-level supporting evidence for "Zywiec" in Figure 1). To utilize this additional information, we propose a model that, first, produces representations for each token that encode the local context from the query sentence as well as the document-level and corpus-level contexts from the retrieved sentences. Our model uses a *document-level at-*

tention and *corpus-level attention* to dynamically weight the document-level and corpus-level contextual representations, emphasizing the contextual information from each level that is most relevant to the local context and filtering noise such as the irrelevant information from the mention "[LOC Zywiec]" in Figure 1. The model learns to balance the influence of the local, document-level, and corpus-level contextual representations via gating mechanisms. Our model predicts a tag using the local, gated-attentive document-level, and gated-attentive corpus-level contextual representations, which allows our model to predict the correct tag, ORG, for "Zywiec" in Figure 1.

The major contributions of this paper are: First, we propose to use multiple levels of contextual information (local, document-level, and corpus-level) to improve name tagging. Second, we present two new attentions, document-level and corpus-level, which prove to be effective at exploiting extra contextual information and achieve the state-of-the-art.

2   Model

We first introduce our baseline model. Then, we enhance this baseline model by adding document-level and corpus-level contextual information to the prediction process via our document-level and corpus-level attention mechanisms, respectively.

2.1   Baseline

We consider name tagging as a sequence labeling problem, where each token in a sequence is tagged as the beginning (B), inside (I) or outside (O) of a name mention. The tagged names are then classified into predefined entity types. In this paper, we only use the person (PER), organization (ORG), location (LOC), and miscellaneous (MISC) types, which are the predefined types in CoNLL-02 and CoNLL-03 name tagging dataset (Tjong Kim Sang and De Meulder, 2003).

Our baseline model has two parts: 1) Encoding the sequence of tokens by incorporating the preceding and following contexts using a bi-directional long short-term memory (Bi-LSTM) (Graves et al., 2013), so each token is assigned a local contextual embedding. Here, following Ma and Hovy (2016a), we use the concatenation of pre-trained word embeddings and character-level word representations composed by a convolutional neural network (CNN) as input to the Bi-LSTM. 2) Using a Conditional Random Fields (CRFs) output layer to render predictions for each token, which can efficiently capture dependencies among name tags (*e.g.*, "I-LOC" cannot follow "B-ORG").

The Bi-LSTM CRF network is a strong baseline due to its remarkable capability of modeling contextual information and label dependencies. Many recent efforts combine the Bi-LSTM CRF network with language modeling (Liu et al., 2017; Peters et al., 2017, 2018) to boost the name tagging performance. However, they still suffer from the limited contexts within individual sequences. To overcome this limitation, we introduce two attention mechanisms to incorporate document-level and corpus-level supporting evidence.

2.2 Document-level Attention

Many entity mentions are tagged as multiple types by the baseline approach within the same document due to ambiguous contexts (14.43% of the errors in English, 18.55% in Dutch, and 17.81% in German). This type of error is challenging to address as most of the current neural network based approaches focus on evidence within the sentence when making decisions. In cases where a sentence is short or highly ambiguous, the model may either fail to identify names due to insufficient information or make wrong decisions by using noisy context. In contrast, a human in this situation may seek additional evidence from other sentences within the same document to improve judgments.

In Figure 1, the baseline model mistakenly tags "Zywiec" as PER due to the ambiguous context "whose full name is...", which frequently appears around a person's name. However, contexts from other sentences in the same document containing "Zywiec" (*e.g.*, s_q and s_r in Figure 2), such as "'s 1996 profit..." and "would be boosted by its recent shedding...", indicate that "Zywiec" ought to be tagged as ORG. Thus, we incorporate the document-level supporting evidence with the following attention mechanism (Bahdanau et al., 2015).

Formally, given a document $D = \{s_1, s_2, ...\}$, where $s_i = \{w_{i1}, w_{i2}, ...\}$ is a sequence of words, we apply a Bi-LSTM to each word in s_i, generating local contextual representations $h_i = \{\mathbf{h}_{i1}, \mathbf{h}_{i2}, ...\}$. Next, for each w_{ij}, we retrieve the sentences in the document that contain w_{ij} (*e.g.*,

s_q and s_r in Figure 2) and select the local contextual representations of w_{ij} from these sentences as supporting evidence, $\tilde{h}_{ij} = \{\tilde{\mathbf{h}}_{ij}^1, \tilde{\mathbf{h}}_{ij}^2, ...\}$ (*e.g.*, $\tilde{\mathbf{h}}_{qj}$ and $\tilde{\mathbf{h}}_{rk}$ in Figure 2), where h_{ij} and $\tilde{h}_{ij}$ are obtained with the same Bi-LSTM. Since each representation in the supporting evidence is not equally valuable to the final prediction, we apply an attention mechanism to weight the contextual representations of the supporting evidence:

$$e_{ij}^k = \mathbf{v}^\top \tanh \left(W_h \mathbf{h}_{ij} + W_{\tilde{h}} \tilde{\mathbf{h}}_{ij}^k + \mathbf{b}_e \right) ,$$

$$\alpha_{ij}^k = \text{Softmax} \left(e_{ij}^k \right) ,$$

where $\mathbf{h}_{ij}$ is the local contextual representation of word j in sentence s_i and $\tilde{\mathbf{h}}_{ij}^k$ is the k-th supporting contextual representation. W_h, $W_{\tilde{h}}$ and $\mathbf{b}_e$ are learned parameters. We compute the weighted average of the supporting representations by

$$\tilde{\mathbf{H}}_{ij} = \sum_{k=1} \alpha_{ij}^k \tilde{\mathbf{h}}_{ij}^k ,$$

where $\tilde{\mathbf{H}}_{ij}$ denotes the contextual representation of the supporting evidence for w_{ij}.

For each word w_{ij}, its supporting evidence representation, $\tilde{\mathbf{H}}_{ij}$, provides a summary of the other contexts where the word appears. Though this evidence is valuable to the prediction process, we must mitigate the influence of the supporting evidence since the prediction should still be made primarily based on the query context. Therefore, we apply a gating mechanism to constrain this influence and enable the model to decide the amount of the supporting evidence that should be incorporated in the prediction process, which is given by

$$\mathbf{r}_{ij} = \sigma(W_{\tilde{H},r}\tilde{\mathbf{H}}_{ij} + W_{h,r}\mathbf{h}_{ij} + \mathbf{b}_r) ,$$

$$\mathbf{z}_{ij} = \sigma(W_{\tilde{H},z}\tilde{\mathbf{H}}_{ij} + W_{h,z}\mathbf{h}_{ij} + \mathbf{b}_z) ,$$

$$\mathbf{g}_{ij} = \tanh(W_{h,g}\mathbf{h}_{ij} + \mathbf{z}_{ij} \odot (W_{\tilde{H},g}\tilde{\mathbf{H}}_{ij} + \mathbf{b}_g)) ,$$

$$\mathbf{D}_{ij} = \mathbf{r}_{ij} \odot \mathbf{h}_{ij} + (1 - \mathbf{r}_{ij}) \odot \mathbf{g}_{ij} ,$$

where all W, $\mathbf{b}$ are learned parameters and $\mathbf{D}_{ij}$ is the gated supporting evidence representation for w_{ij}.

2.3 Topic-aware Corpus-level Attention

The document-level attention fails to generate supporting evidence when the name appears only once in a single document. In such situations, we analogously select supporting sentences from the entire corpus. Unfortunately, different from

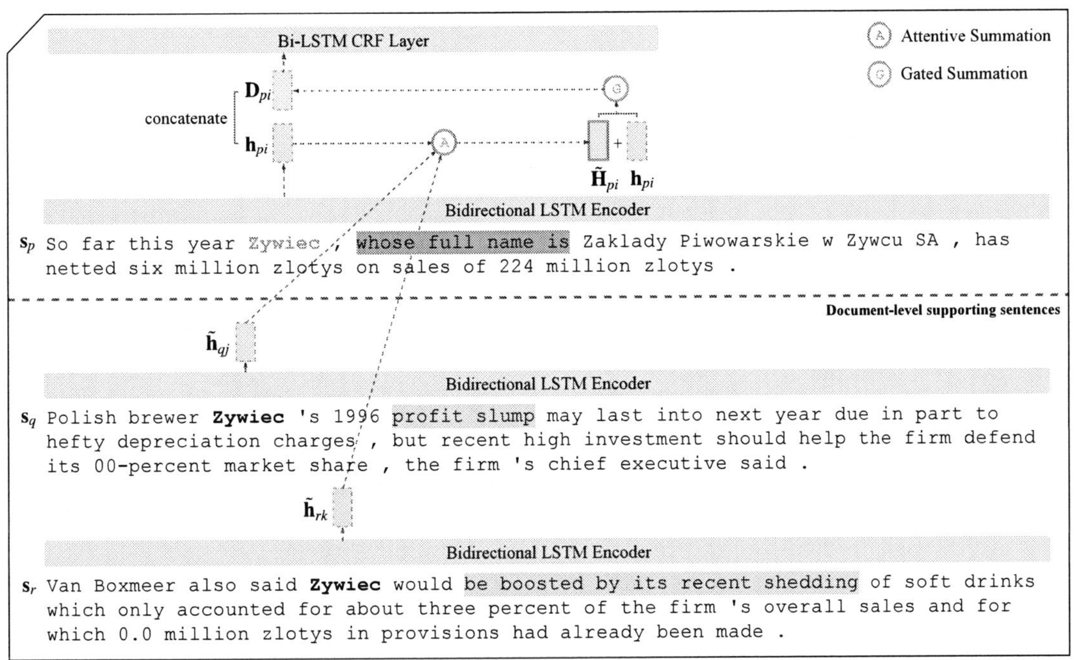

Figure 2: Document-level Attention Architecture. (Within-sequence context in red incorrectly indicates the name as PER, and document-level context in green correctly indicates the name as ORG.)

the sentences that are naturally topically relevant within the same documents, the supporting sentences from the other documents may be about distinct topics or scenarios, and identical phrases may refer to various entities with different types, as in the example in Figure 1. To narrow down the search scope from the entire corpus and avoid unnecessary noise, we introduce a topic-aware corpus-level attention which clusters the documents by topic and carefully selects topically related sentences to use as supporting evidence.

We first apply Latent Dirichlet allocation (LDA) (Blei et al., 2003) to model the topic distribution of each document and separate the documents into N clusters based on their topic distributions.[2] As in Figure 3, we retrieve supporting sentences for each word, such as "Zywiec", from the topically related documents and employ another attention mechanism (Bahdanau et al., 2015) to the supporting contextual representations, $\hat{h}_{ij} = \{\hat{\mathbf{h}}_{ij}^1, \hat{\mathbf{h}}_{ij}^2, ...\}$ (e.g., $\tilde{\mathbf{h}}_{xi}$ and $\tilde{\mathbf{h}}_{yi}$ in Figure 3). This yields a weighted contextual representation of the corpus-level supporting evidence, $\hat{\mathbf{H}}_{ij}$, for each w_{ij}, which is similar to the document-level supporting evidence representation, $\tilde{\mathbf{H}}_{ij}$, described in

section 2.2. We use another gating mechanism to combine $\hat{\mathbf{H}}_{ij}$ and the local contextual representation, $\mathbf{h}_{ij}$, to obtain the corpus-level gated supporting evidence representation, $\mathbf{C}_{ij}$, for each w_{ij}.

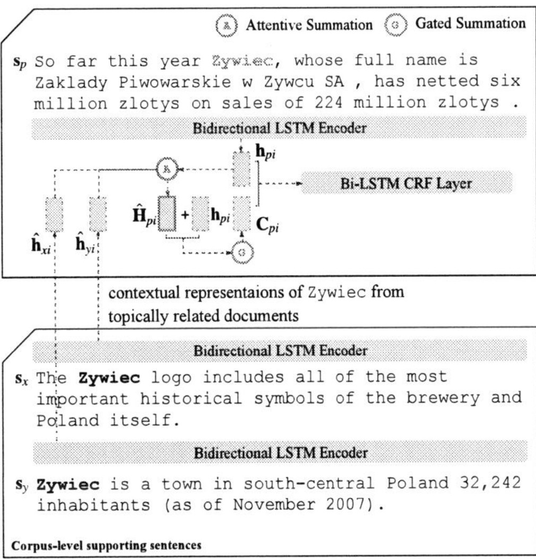

Figure 3: Corpus-level Attention Architecture.

---

[2] $N = 20$ in our experiments.

2.4 Tag Prediction

For each word w_{ij} of sentence s_i, we concatenate its local contextual representation $\mathbf{h}_{ij}$, document-level gated supporting evidence representation $\mathbf{D}_{ij}$, and corpus-level gated supporting evidence representation $\mathbf{C}_{ij}$ to obtain its final representation. This representation is fed to another Bi-LSTM to further encode the supporting evidence and local contextual features into an unified representation, which is given as input to an affine-CRF layer for label prediction.

3 Experiments

3.1 Dataset

We evaluate our methods on the CoNLL-2002 and CoNLL-2003 name tagging datasets (Tjong Kim Sang and De Meulder, 2003). The CoNLL-2002 dataset contains name tagging annotations for Dutch (NLD) and Spanish (ESP), while the CoNLL-2003 dataset contains annotations for English (ENG) and German (DEU). Both datasets have four pre-defined name types: person (PER), organization (ORG), location (LOC) and miscellaneous (MISC).[3]

Code	Train	Dev.	Test
NLD	202,931 (13,344)	37,761 (2,616)	68,994 (3,941)
ESP	264,715 (18,797)	52,923 (4,351)	51,533 (3,558)
ENG	204,567 (23,499)	51,578 (5,942)	46,666 (5,648)
DEU	207,484 (11,651)	51,645 (4,669)	52,098 (3,602)

Table 1: # of tokens in name tagging datasets statistics. # of names is given in parentheses.

We select at most four document-level supporting sentences and five corpus-level supporting sentences.[4] Since the document-level attention method requires input from each individual document, we do not evaluate it on the CoNLL-2002 Spanish dataset which lacks document delimiters. We still evaluate the corpus-level attention on the Spanish dataset by randomly splitting the dataset into documents (30 sentences per document). Although randomly splitting the sentences does not yield perfect topic modeling clusters, experiments show the corpus-level attention still outperforms the baseline (Section 3.3).

---

[3]The miscellaneous category consists of names that do not belong to the other three categories.

[4]Both numbers are tuned from 1 to 10 and selected when the model performs best on the development set.

Hyper-parameter	Value
CharCNN Filter Number	25
CharCNN Filter Widths	[2, 3, 4]
Lower Bi-LSTM Hidden Size	100
Lower Bi-LSTM Dropout Rate	0.5
Upper Bi-LSTM Hidden Size	100
Learning Rate	0.005
Batch Size	N/A*
Optimizer	SGD (Bottou, 2010)

* Each batch is a document. The batch size varies as the different document length.

Table 2: Hyper-parameters.

3.2 Experimental Setup

For word representations, we use 100-dimensional pre-trained word embeddings and 25-dimensional randomly initialized character embeddings. We train word embeddings using the word2vec package.[5] English embeddings are trained on the English Giga-word version 4, which is the same corpus used in (Lample et al., 2016). Dutch, Spanish, and German embeddings are trained on corresponding Wikipedia articles (2017-12-20 dumps). Word embeddings are fine-tuned during training.

Table 2 shows our hyper-parameters. For each model with an attention, since the Bi-LSTM encoder must encode the local, document-level, and/or corpus-level contexts, we pre-train a Bi-LSTM CRF model for 50 epochs, add our document-level attention and/or corpus-level attention, and then fine-tune the augmented model. Additionally, Reimers and Gurevych (2017) report that neural models produce different results even with same hyper-parameters due to the variances in parameter initialization. Therefore, we run each model ten times and report the mean as well as the maximum F1 scores.

3.3 Performance Comparison

We compare our methods to three categories of baseline name tagging methods:

- **Vanilla Name Tagging** Without any additional resources and supervision, the current state-of-the-art name tagging model is the Bi-LSTM-CRF network reported by Lample et al. (2016) and Ma and Hovy (2016b), whose difference lies in using a LSTM or CNN to encode characters. Our methods fall in this category.

- **Multi-task Learning** Luo et al. (2015); Yang et al. (2017) apply multi-task learning to boost

---

[5]https://github.com/tmikolov/word2vec

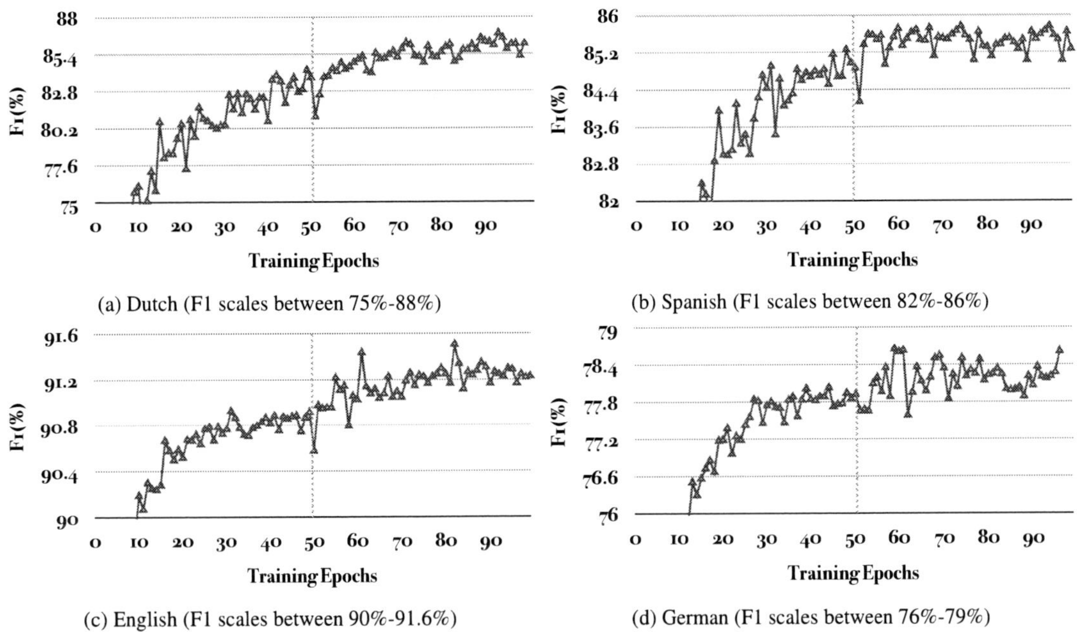

(a) Dutch (F1 scales between 75%-88%)   (b) Spanish (F1 scales between 82%-86%)

(c) English (F1 scales between 90%-91.6%)   (d) German (F1 scales between 76%-79%)

Figure 4: Average F1 score for each epoch of the ten runs of our model with both document-level and corpus-level attentions. Epochs 1-50 are the pre-training phase and 51-100 are the fine-tuning phase.

name tagging performance by introducing additional annotations from related tasks such as entity linking and part-of-speech tagging.

- **Join-learning with Language Model** Peters et al. (2017); Liu et al. (2017); Peters et al. (2018) leverage a pre-trained language model on a large external corpus to enhance the semantic representations of words in the local corpus. Peters et al. (2018) achieve a high score on the CoNLL-2003 English dataset using a giant language model pre-trained on a 1 Billion Word Benchmark (Chelba et al., 2013).

Table 3 presents the performance comparison among the baselines, the aforementioned state-of-the-art methods, and our proposed methods. Adding only the document-level attention offers a F1 gain of between 0.37% and 1.25% on Dutch, English, and German. Similarly, the addition of the corpus-level attention yields a F1 gain between 0.46% to 1.08% across all four languages. The model with both attentions outperforms our baseline method by 1.60%, 0.56%, and 0.79% on Dutch, English, and German, respectively. Using a paired t-test between our proposed model and the baselines on 10 randomly sampled subsets, we find that the improvements are statistically significant ($p \leq 0.015$) for all settings and all languages.

By incorporating the document-level and corpus-level attentions, we achieve state-of-the-art performance on the Dutch (NLD), Spanish (ESP) and German (DEU) datasets. For English, our methods outperform the state-of-the-art methods in the "Vanilla Name Tagging" category. Since the document-level and corpus-level attentions introduce redundant and topically related information, our models are compatible with the language model enhanced approaches. It is interesting to explore the integration of these two methods, but we leave this to future explorations.

Figure 4 presents, for each language, the learning curves of the full models (*i.e.*, with both document-level and corpus-level attentions). The learning curve is computed by averaging the F1 scores of the ten runs at each epoch. We first pre-train a baseline Bi-LSTM CRF model from epoch 1 to 50. Then, starting at epoch 51, we incorporate the document-level and corpus-level attentions to fine-tune the entire model. As shown in Figure 4, when adding the attentions at epoch 51, the F1 score drops significantly as new parameters are introduced to the model. The model gradually adapts to the new information, the F1 score rises, and the full model eventually outperforms the pre-trained model. The learning curves strongly prove the effectiveness of our proposed methods.

91

Code	Model		F1 (%)
NLD	(Gillick et al., 2015)	reported	82.84
	(Lample et al., 2016)	reported	81.74
	(Yang et al., 2017)	reported	85.19
	Our Baseline	mean	85.43
		max	85.80
	Doc-lvl Attention	mean	86.82
		max	87.05
	Corpus-lvl Attention	mean	86.41
		max	86.88
	Both	mean	87.14
		max	**87.40**
		Δ	**+1.60**
ESP	(Gillick et al., 2015)	reported	82.95
	(Lample et al., 2016)	reported	85.75
	(Yang et al., 2017)	reported	85.77
	Our Baseline	mean	85.33
		max	85.51
	Corpus-lvl Attention	mean	85.77
		max	**86.01**
		Δ	**+0.50**
ENG	(Luo et al., 2015)	reported	91.20
	(Lample et al., 2016)	reported	90.94
	(Ma and Hovy, 2016b)	reported	91.21
	(Liu et al., 2017)	reported	91.35
	(Peters et al., 2017)	reported	91.93
	(Peters et al., 2018)	reported	**92.22**
	Our Baseline	mean	90.97
		max	91.23
	Doc-lvl Attention	mean	91.43
		max	91.60
	Corpus-lvl Attention	mean	91.41
		max	91.71
	Both	mean	91.64
		max	**91.81**
		Δ	**+0.58**
DEU	(Gillick et al., 2015)	reported	76.22
	(Lample et al., 2016)	reported	78.76
	Our Baseline	mean	78.15
		max	78.42
	Doc-lvl Attention	mean	78.90
		max	79.19
	Corpus-lvl Attention	mean	78.53
		max	78.88
	Both	mean	78.83
		max	**79.21**
		Δ	**+0.79**

Table 3: Performance of our methods versus the baseline and state-of-the-art models.

We also compare our approach with a simple rule-based propagation method, where we use token-level majority voting to make labels consistent on document-level and corpus-level. The score of document-level propagation on English is 90.21% (F1), and the corpus-level propagation is 89.02% which are both lower than the BiLSTM-CRF baseline 90.97%.

3.4 Qualitative Analysis

Table 5 compares the name tagging results from the baseline model and our best models. All examples are selected from the development set.

In the Dutch example, "Granada" is the name of a city in Spain, but also the short name of "Granada Media". Without ORG related context, "Granada" is mistakenly tagged as LOC by the baseline model. However, the document-level and corpus-level supporting evidence retrieved by our method contains the ORG name "Granada Media", which strongly indicates "Granada" to be an ORG in the query sentence. By adding the document-level and corpus-level attentions, our model successfully tags "Granada" as ORG.

In example 2, the OOV word "Kaczmarek" is tagged as ORG in the baseline output. In the retrieved document-level supporting sentences, PER related contextual information, such as the pronoun "he", indicates "Kaczmarek" to be a PER. Our model correctly tags "Kaczmarek" as PER with the document-level attention.

In the German example, "Grünen" (Greens) is an OOV word in the training set. The character embedding captures the semantic meaning of the stem "Grün" (Green) which is a common non-name word, so the baseline model tags "Grünen" as O (outside of a name). In contrast, our model makes the correct prediction by incorporating the corpus-level attention because in the related sentence from the corpus "Bundesvorstandes der Grünen" (Federal Executive of the Greens) indicates "Grünen" to be a company name.

3.5 Remaining Challenges

By investigating the remaining errors, most of the named entity type inconsistency errors are eliminated, however, a few new errors are introduced due to the model propagating labels from negative instances to positive ones. Figure 5 presents a negative example, where our model, being influenced by the prediction "[B-ORG Indianapolis]" in the supporting sentence, incorrectly predicts "Indianapolis" as ORG in the query sentence. A potential solution is to apply sentence classification (Kim, 2014; Ji and Smith, 2017) to the documents, divide the document into fine-grained clusters of sentences, and select supporting sentences within the same cluster.

In morphologically rich languages, words may have many variants. When retrieving supporting evidence, our exact query word match criterion misses potentially useful supporting sentences that contain variants of the word. Normalization and

#1 Dutch	
Baseline	[B-LOC Granada] overwoog vervolgens een bod op Carlton uit te brengen, maar daar ziet het concern nu van af. *Granada then considered issuing a bid for Carlton, but the concern now sees it.*
Our model	[B-ORG Granada] overwoog vervolgens een bod op Carlton uit te brengen, maar daar ziet het concern nu van af.
D-lvl sentences	[B-ORG Granada] [I-ORG Media] neemt belangen in United News. *Granada Media takes interests in United News.*
C-lvl sentences	Het Britse concern [B-ORG Granada] [I-ORG Media] heeft voor 1,75 miljard pond sterling (111 miljard Belgische frank) aandelen gekocht van United News Media. *The British group Granada Media has bought shares of GBP 1.75 trillion (111 billion Belgian francs) from United News Media.*
#2 English	
Baseline	Initially Poland offered up to 75 percent of Ruch but in March [ORG Kaczmarek] cancelled the tender and offered a minority stake with an option to increase the equity.
Our model	Initially Poland offered up to 75 percent of Ruch but in March [PER Kaczmarek] cancelled the tender and offered a minority stake with an option to increase the equity.
D-lvl sentences	[PER Kaczmarek] said in May he was unhappy that only one investor ended up bidding for Ruch.
#3 German	
Baseline	Diese Diskussion werde ausschlaggebend sein für die Stellungnahme der **Grünen** in dieser Frage. *This discussion will be decisive for the opinion of the Greens on this question.*
Our model	Diese Diskussion werde ausschlaggebend sein für die Stellungnahme der [B-ORG Grünen] in dieser Frage.
C-lvl sentences	Auch das Mitglied des Bundesvorstandes der [B-ORG Grünen], Helmut Lippelt, sprach sich für ein Berufsheer au. *Helmut Lippelt, a member of the Federal Executive of the Greens, also called for a professional army.*
#4 Negative Example	
Reference	[B-LOC Indianapolis] 1996-12-06
Our model	[B-ORG Indianapolis] 1996-12-06
D-lvl sentence	The injury-plagued [B-ORG Indianapolis] [I-ORG Colts] lost another quarterback on Thursday but last year's AFC finalists rallied together to shoot down the Philadelphia Eagles 37-10 in a showdown of playoff contenders.

* D-lvl sentences: document-level supporting sentences.

* C-lvl sentences: corpus-level supporting sentences.

Figure 5: Comparison of name tagging results between the baseline and our methods.

morphological analysis can be applied in this case to help fetch supporting sentences.

4 Related Work

Name tagging methods based on sequence labeling have been extensively studied recently. Huang et al. (2015) and Lample et al. (2016) proposed a neural architecture consisting of a bi-directional long short-term memory network (Bi-LSTM) encoder and a conditional random field (CRF) output layer (Bi-LSTM CRF). This architecture has been widely explored and demonstrated to be effective for sequence labeling tasks. Efforts incorporated character level compositional word embeddings, language modeling, and CRF re-ranking into the Bi-LSTM CRF architecture which improved the performance (Ma and Hovy, 2016a; Liu et al., 2017; Sato et al., 2017; Peters et al., 2017, 2018). Similar to these studies, our approach is also based on a Bi-LSTM CRF architecture. However, considering the limited contexts within each individual sequence, we design two attention mechanisms to further incorporate topically related contextual information on both the document-level and corpus-level.

There have been efforts in other areas of information extraction to exploit features beyond individual sequences. Early attempts (Mikheev et al., 1998; Mikheev, 2000) on MUC-7 name tagging dataset used document centered approaches. A number of approaches explored document-level features (*e.g.*, temporal and co-occurrence patterns) for event extraction (Chambers and Jurafsky, 2008; Ji and Grishman, 2008; Liao and Grishman, 2010; Do et al., 2012; McClosky and Manning, 2012; Berant et al., 2014; Yang and Mitchell, 2016). Other approaches leveraged features from external resources (*e.g.*, Wiktionary or FrameNet) for low resource name tagging and event extraction (Li et al., 2013; Huang et al., 2016; Liu et al., 2016; Zhang et al., 2016; Cotterell and Duh, 2017; Zhang et al., 2017; Huang et al., 2018). Yaghoobzadeh and Schütze (2016) aggregated corpus-level contextual information of each entity to predict its type and Narasimhan et al. (2016) incorporated contexts from external information sources (*e.g.*, the documents that contain the desired information) to resolve ambiguities. Compared with these studies, our work incorporates both document-level and corpus-level contextual information with attention mechanisms, which is a more advanced and efficient way to capture meaningful additional features. Additionally, our model is able to learn how to regulate the influence of the information outside the local context using gating mechanisms.

5 Conclusions and Future Work

We propose document-level and corpus-level attentions for name tagging. The document-level attention retrieves additional supporting evidence from other sentences within the document to enhance the local contextual information of the query word. When the query word is unique in the document, the corpus-level attention searches for topically related sentences in the corpus. Both attentions dynamically weight the retrieved contextual information and emphasize the information most relevant to the query context. We present gating mechanisms that allow the model to regulate the influence of the supporting evidence on the predictions. Experiments demonstrate the effectiveness of our approach, which achieves state-of-the-art results on benchmark datasets.

We plan to apply our method to other tasks, such as event extraction, and explore integrating language modeling into this architecture to further boost name tagging performance.

Acknowledgments

This work was supported by the U.S. DARPA AIDA Program No. FA8750-18-2-0014, LORELEI Program No. HR0011-15-C-0115, Air Force No. FA8650-17-C-7715, NSF IIS-1523198 and U.S. ARL NS-CTA No. W911NF-09-2-0053. The views and conclusions contained in this document are those of the authors and should not be interpreted as representing the official policies, either expressed or implied, of the U.S. Government. The U.S. Government is authorized to reproduce and distribute reprints for Government purposes notwithstanding any copyright notation here on.

References

Dzmitry Bahdanau, Kyunghyun Cho, and Yoshua Bengio. 2015. Neural machine translation by jointly learning to align and translate. In *Proceedings of the 2015 International Conference on Learning Representations*.

Jonathan Berant, Vivek Srikumar, Pei-Chun Chen, Abby Vander Linden, Brittany Harding, Brad Huang, Peter Clark, and Christopher D Manning. 2014. Modeling biological processes for reading comprehension. In *Proceedings of the 2014 Conference on Empirical Methods in Natural Language Processing*.

David M Blei, Andrew Y Ng, and Michael I Jordan. 2003. Latent dirichlet allocation. *Journal of machine Learning research*.

Léon Bottou. 2010. Large-scale machine learning with stochastic gradient descent. In *Proceedings of the 2010 International Conference on Computational Statistics*.

Nathanael Chambers and Dan Jurafsky. 2008. Jointly combining implicit constraints improves temporal ordering. In *Proceedings of the 2008 Conference on Empirical Methods in Natural Language Processing*.

Ciprian Chelba, Tomas Mikolov, Mike Schuster, Qi Ge, Thorsten Brants, Phillipp Koehn, and Tony Robinson. 2013. One billion word benchmark for measuring progress in statistical language modeling. *arXiv preprint arXiv:1312.3005*.

Nancy Chinchor and Patricia Robinson. 1997. Muc-7 named entity task definition. In *Proceedings of the 7th Conference on Message Understanding*.

Ryan Cotterell and Kevin Duh. 2017. Low-resource named entity recognition with cross-lingual, character-level neural conditional random fields. In *Proceedings of the Eighth International Joint Conference on Natural Language Processing*.

Quang Xuan Do, Wei Lu, and Dan Roth. 2012. Joint inference for event timeline construction. In *Proceedings of the 2012 Joint Conference on Empirical Methods in Natural Language Processing and Computational Natural Language Learning*.

R. Florian, H. Hassan, A. Ittycheriah, H. Jing, N. Kambhatla, X. Luo, N. Nicolov, and S. Roukos. 2004. A statistical model for multilingual entity detection and tracking. In *Proceedings of the Human Language Technology Conference of the North American Chapter of the Association for Computational Linguistics (HLT-NAACL 2004)*.

Dan Gillick, Cliff Brunk, Oriol Vinyals, and Amarnag Subramanya. 2015. Multilingual language processing from bytes. *arXiv preprint arXiv:1512.00103*.

Alan Graves, Navdeep Jaitly, and Abdel-rahman Mohamed. 2013. Hybrid speech recognition with deep bidirectional lstm. In *Proceedings of the 2013 IEEE Workshop on Automatic Speech Recognition and Understanding*.

Ulf Hermjakob, Qiang Li, Daniel Marcu, Jonathan May, Sebastian J. Mielke, Nima Pourdamghani,

Michael Pust, Xing Shi, Kevin Knight, Tomer Levinboim, Kenton Murray, David Chiang, Boliang Zhang, Xiaoman Pan, Di Lu, Ying Lin, and Heng Ji. 2017. Incident-driven machine translation and name tagging for low-resource languages. *Machine Translation*, pages 1–31.

Lifu Huang, Taylor Cassidy, Xiaocheng Feng, Heng Ji, Clare R Voss, Jiawei Han, and Avirup Sil. 2016. Liberal event extraction and event schema induction. In *Proceedings of the 54th Annual Meeting of the Association for Computational Linguistics*.

Lifu Huang, Kyunghyun Cho, Boliang Zhang, Heng Ji, and Kevin Knight. 2018. Multi-lingual common semantic space construction via cluster-consistent word embedding. *arXiv preprint arXiv:1804.07875*.

Zhiheng Huang, Wei Xu, and Kai Yu. 2015. Bidirectional lstm-crf models for sequence tagging. *arXiv preprint arXiv:1508.01991*.

Heng Ji and Ralph Grishman. 2008. Refining event extraction through cross-document inference. *Proceedings of the 2008 Annual Meeting of the Association for Computational Linguistics*.

Yangfeng Ji and Noah Smith. 2017. Neural discourse structure for text categorization. *Proceedings of the 2017 Annual Meeting of the Association for Computational Linguistics*.

Yoon Kim. 2014. Convolutional neural networks for sentence classification. *Proceedings of the 2014 Conference on Empirical Methods in Natural Language Processing*.

Guillaume Lample, Miguel Ballesteros, Sandeep Subramanian, Kazuya Kawakami, and Chris Dyer. 2016. Neural architectures for named entity recognition. In *Proceedings of 2016 Annual Conference of the North American Chapter of the Association for Computational Linguistics*.

Qi Li, Heng Ji, and Liang Huang. 2013. Joint event extraction via structured prediction with global features. In *Proceedings of the 51st Annual Meeting of the Association for Computational Linguistics*.

Shasha Liao and Ralph Grishman. 2010. Using document level cross-event inference to improve event extraction. In *Proceedings of the 48th Annual Meeting of the Association for Computational Linguistics*.

Liyuan Liu, Jingbo Shang, Frank Xu, Xiang Ren, Huan Gui, Jian Peng, and Jiawei Han. 2017. Empower sequence labeling with task-aware neural language model.

Shulin Liu, Yubo Chen, Shizhu He, Kang Liu, and Jun Zhao. 2016. Leveraging framenet to improve automatic event detection. In *Proceedings of the 54th Annual Meeting of the Association for Computational Linguistics*.

Gang Luo, Xiaojiang Huang, Chin-Yew Lin, and Zaiqing Nie. 2015. Joint entity recognition and disambiguation. In *Proceedings of the 2015 Conference on Empirical Methods in Natural Language Processing*.

Xuezhe Ma and Eduard Hovy. 2016a. End-to-end sequence labeling via bi-directional lstm-cnns-crf.

Xuezhe Ma and Eduard Hovy. 2016b. End-to-end sequence labeling via bi-directional lstm-cnns-crf. In *Proceedings of the 54th Annual Meeting of the Association for Computational Linguistics*.

David McClosky and Christopher D Manning. 2012. Learning constraints for consistent timeline extraction. In *Proceedings of the 2012 Joint Conference on Empirical Methods in Natural Language Processing and Computational Natural Language Learning*.

Andrei Mikheev. 2000. Document centered approach to text normalization. In *Proceedings of the 23rd annual international ACM SIGIR conference on Research and development in information retrieval*, pages 136–143. ACM.

Andrei Mikheev, Claire Grover, and Marc Moens. 1998. Description of the ltg system used for muc-7. In *Seventh Message Understanding Conference (MUC-7): Proceedings of a Conference Held in Fairfax, Virginia, April 29-May 1, 1998*.

Karthik Narasimhan, Adam Yala, and Regina Barzilay. 2016. Improving information extraction by acquiring external evidence with reinforcement learning. *arXiv preprint arXiv:1603.07954*.

Matthew E Peters, Waleed Ammar, Chandra Bhagavatula, and Russell Power. 2017. Semi-supervised sequence tagging with bidirectional language models.

Matthew E Peters, Mark Neumann, Mohit Iyyer, Matt Gardner, Christopher Clark, Kenton Lee, and Luke Zettlemoyer. 2018. Deep contextualized word representations. *arXiv preprint arXiv:1802.05365*.

Nils Reimers and Iryna Gurevych. 2017. Optimal hyperparameters for deep lstm-networks for sequence labeling tasks. *arXiv preprint arXiv:1707.06799*.

Motoki Sato, Hiroyuki Shindo, Ikuya Yamada, and Yuji Matsumoto. 2017. Segment-level neural conditional random fields for named entity recognition. In *Proceedings of the Eighth International Joint Conference on Natural Language Processing*.

Erik F Tjong Kim Sang and Fien De Meulder. 2003. Introduction to the conll-2003 shared task: Language-independent named entity recognition. In *Proceedings of the 2003 Annual Conference of the North American Chapter of the Association for Computational Linguistics*.

Yadollah Yaghoobzadeh and Hinrich Schütze. 2016. Corpus-level fine-grained entity typing using contextual information. *arXiv preprint arXiv:1606.07901*.

Bishan Yang and Tom Mitchell. 2016. Joint extraction of events and entities within a document context. *arXiv preprint arXiv:1609.03632*.

Zhilin Yang, Ruslan Salakhutdinov, and William W Cohen. 2017. Transfer learning for sequence tagging with hierarchical recurrent networks. *arXiv preprint arXiv:1703.06345*.

David Yarowsky. 2003. Unsupervised word sense disambiguation rivaling supervised methods. In *Proc. ACL1995*.

Boliang Zhang, Di Lu, Xiaoman Pan, Ying Lin, Halidanmu Abudukelimu, Heng Ji, and Kevin Knight. 2017. Embracing non-traditional linguistic resources for low-resource language name tagging. In *Proceedings of the Eighth International Joint Conference on Natural Language Processing (Volume 1: Long Papers)*.

Boliang Zhang, Xiaoman Pan, Tianlu Wang, Ashish Vaswani, Heng Ji, Kevin Knight, and Daniel Marcu. 2016. Name tagging for low-resource incident languages based on expectation-driven learning. In *Proceedings of the 2016 Conference of the North American Chapter of the Association for Computational Linguistics: Human Language Technologies*.

Pervasive Attention: 2D Convolutional Neural Networks
for Sequence-to-Sequence Prediction

Maha Elbayad[1,2]   **Laurent Besacier**[1]   **Jakob Verbeek**[2]

Univ. Grenoble Alpes, CNRS, Grenoble INP, Inria, LIG, LJK, F-38000 Grenoble France

[1] `firstname.lastname@univ-grenoble-alpes.fr`
[2] `firstname.lastname@inria.fr`

Abstract

Current state-of-the-art machine translation systems are based on encoder-decoder architectures, that first encode the input sequence, and then generate an output sequence based on the input encoding. Both are interfaced with an attention mechanism that recombines a fixed encoding of the source tokens based on the decoder state. We propose an alternative approach which instead relies on a single 2D convolutional neural network across both sequences. Each layer of our network recodes source tokens on the basis of the output sequence produced so far. Attention-like properties are therefore pervasive throughout the network. Our model yields excellent results, outperforming state-of-the-art encoder-decoder systems, while being conceptually simpler and having fewer parameters.

1 Introduction

Deep neural networks have made a profound impact on natural language processing technology in general, and machine translation in particular (Blunsom, 2013; Sutskever et al., 2014; Cho et al., 2014; Jean et al., 2015; LeCun et al., 2015). Machine translation (MT) can be seen as a sequence-to-sequence prediction problem, where the source and target sequences are of different and variable length. Current state-of-the-art approaches are based on encoder-decoder architectures (Blunsom, 2013; Sutskever et al., 2014; Cho et al., 2014; Bahdanau et al., 2015). The encoder "reads" the variable-length source sequence and maps it into a vector representation. The decoder takes this vector as input and "writes" the target sequence, updating its state each step with the most recent word that it generated. The basic encoder-decoder model is generally equipped with an attention model (Bahdanau et al., 2015), which repetitively re-accesses the source sequence during the decoding process. Given the current state of the decoder,

a probability distribution over the elements in the source sequence is computed, which is then used to select or aggregate features of these elements into a single "context" vector that is used by the decoder. Rather than relying on the global representation of the source sequence, the attention mechanism allows the decoder to "look back" into the source sequence and focus on salient positions. Besides this inductive bias, the attention mechanism bypasses the problem of vanishing gradients that most recurrent architectures encounter.

However, the current attention mechanisms have limited modeling abilities and are generally a simple weighted sum of the source representations (Bahdanau et al., 2015; Luong et al., 2015), where the weights are the result of a shallow matching between source and target elements. The attention module re-combines the same source token codes and is unable to re-encode or re-interpret the source sequence while decoding.

To address these limitations, we propose an alternative neural MT architecture, based on deep 2D convolutional neural networks (CNNs). The product space of the positions in source and target sequences defines the 2D grid over which the network is defined. The convolutional filters are masked to prohibit accessing information derived from future tokens in the target sequence, obtaining an autoregressive model akin to generative models for images and audio waveforms (Oord et al., 2016a,b). See Figure 1 for an illustration.

This approach allows us to learn deep feature hierarchies based on a stack of 2D convolutional layers, and benefit from parallel computation during training. Every layer of our network computes features of the the source tokens, based on the target sequence produced so far, and uses these to predict the next output token. Our model therefore has attention-like capabilities by construction, that are pervasive throughout the layers of the network,

97

Proceedings of the 22nd Conference on Computational Natural Language Learning (CoNLL 2018), pages 97–107
Brussels, Belgium, October 31 - November 1, 2018. ©2018 Association for Computational Linguistics

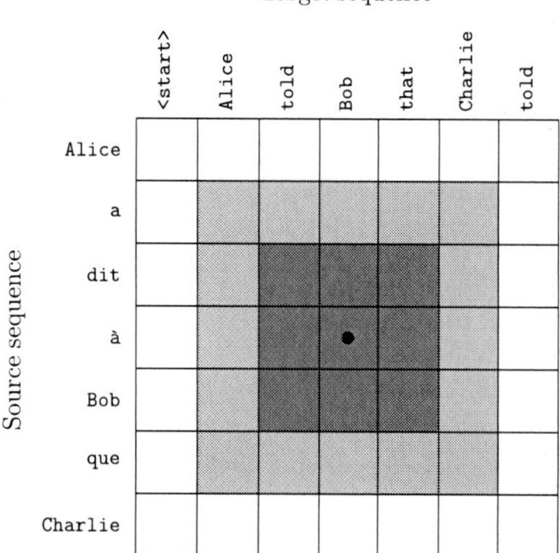

Figure 1: Convolutional layers in our model use masked 3×3 filters so that features are only computed from previous output symbols. Illustration of the receptive fields after one (dark blue) and two layers (light blue), together with the masked part of the field of view of a normal 3×3 filter (gray).

rather than using an "add-on" attention model.

We validate our model with experiments on the IWSLT 2014 German-to-English (De-En) and English-to-German(En-De) tasks. We improve on state-of-the-art encoder-decoder models with attention, while being conceptually simpler and having fewer parameters.

In the next section we will discuss related work, before presenting our approach in detail in Section 3. We present our experimental evaluation results in Section 4, and conclude in Section 5.

2 Related work

The predominant neural architectures in machine translation are recurrent encoder-decoder networks (Graves, 2012; Sutskever et al., 2014; Cho et al., 2014). The encoder is a recurrent neural network (RNN) based on gated recurrent units (Hochreiter and Schmidhuber, 1997; Cho et al., 2014) to map the input sequence into a vector representation. Often a bi-directional RNN (Schuster and Paliwal, 1997) is used, which consists of two RNNs that process the input in opposite directions, and the final states of both RNNs are concatenated as the input encoding. The decoder consists of a second RNN, which takes the input encoding, and sequentially samples the output sequence one to-

ken at a time whilst updating its state.

While best known for their use in visual recognition models, (Oord et al., 2016a; Salimans et al., 2017; Reed et al., 2017; Oord et al., 2016c). Recent works also introduced convolutional networks to natural language processing. The first convolutional apporaches to encoding variable-length sequences consist of stacking word vectors, applying 1D convolutions then aggregating with a max-pooling operator over time (Collobert and Weston, 2008; Kalchbrenner et al., 2014; Kim, 2014). For sequence generation, the works of Ranzato et al. (2016); Bahdanau et al. (2017); Gehring et al. (2017a) mix a convolutional encoder with an RNN decoder. The first entirely convolutional encoder-decoder models where introduced by Kalchbrenner et al. (2016b), but they did not improve over state-of-the-art recurrent architectures. Gehring et al. (2017b) outperformed deep LSTMs for machine translation 1D CNNs with gated linear units (Meng et al., 2015; Oord et al., 2016c; Dauphin et al., 2017) in both the encoder and decoder modules.

Such CNN-based models differ from their RNN-based counterparts in that temporal connections are placed between layers of the network, rather than within layers. See Figure 2 for a conceptual illustration. This apparently small difference in connectivity has two important consequences. First, it makes the field of view grow linearly across layers in the convolutional network, while it is unbounded within layers in the recurrent network. Second, while the activations in the RNN can only be computed in a sequential manner, they can be computed in parallel across the temporal dimension in the convolutional case.

In all the recurrent or convolutional models mentioned above, each of the input and output sequences are processed separately as a one-dimensional sequence by the encoder and decoder respectively. Attention mechanisms (Bahdanau et al., 2015; Luong et al., 2015; Xu et al., 2015) were introduced as an interface between the encoder and decoder modules. During encoding, the attention model finds which hidden states from the source code are the most salient for generating the next target token. This is achieved by evaluating a "context vector" which, in its most basic form, is a weighted average of the source features. The weights of the summation are predicted by a small neural network that scores these features condi-

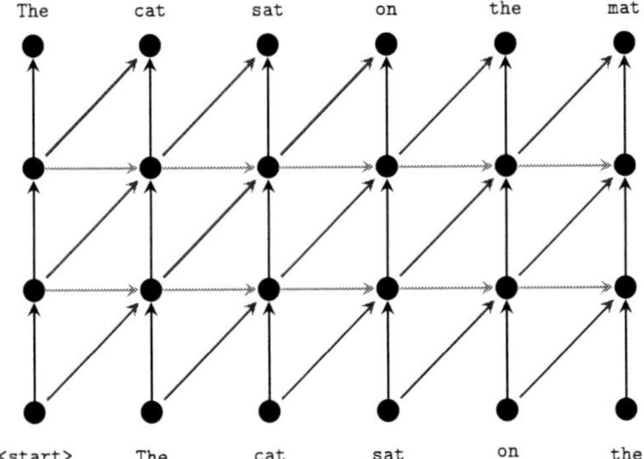

Figure 2: Illustration of decoder network topology with two hidden layers, nodes at bottom and top represent input and output respectively. Horizontal connections are used for RNNs, diagonal connections for convolutional networks. Vertical connections are used in both cases. Parameters are shared across time-steps (horizontally), but not across layers (vertically).

tioning on the current decoder state.

Vaswani et al. (2017) propose an architecture relying entirely on attention. Positional input coding together with self-attention (Parikh et al., 2016; Lin et al., 2017) replaces recurrent and convolutional layers. Huang et al. (2018) use an attention-like gating mechanism to alleviate an assumption of monotonic alignment in the phrase-based translation model of Wang et al. (2017). Deng et al. (2018) treat the sentence alignment as a latent variable which they infer using a variational inference network during training to optimize a variational lower-bound on the log-likelihood.

Beyond uni-dimensional encoding/decoding. Kalchbrenner et al. (2016a) proposed a 2D LSTM model similar to our 2D CNN for machine translation. Like our model, a 2D grid is defined across the input and output sequences, as in Figure 1. In their model, each cell takes input from its left and bottom neighbor. In a second LSTM stream, each cell takes input from its left and top neighbor, as well as from the corresponding cell in the first stream. They also observed that such a structure implements an implicit form of attention, by producing an input encoding that depends on the output sequence produced so far.

Wu et al. (2017) used a CNN over the 2D source-target representation as in our work, but only as a discriminator in an adversarial training setup. They do not use masked convolutions, since their CNN is used to predict if a given source-target pair is a human or machine translation. A standard encoder-decoder model with attention is used to generate translations.

3 Translation by 2D Convolution

In this section we present our 2D CNN translation model in detail.

Input source-target tensor. Given the source and target pair (s, t) of lengths $|s|$ and $|t|$ respectively, we first embed the tokens in d_s and d_t dimensional spaces via look-up tables. The word embeddings $\{x_1, \ldots, x_{|s|}\}$ and $\{y_1, \ldots, y_{|t|}\}$ are then concatenated to form a 3D tensor $X \in \mathbb{R}^{|t| \times |s| \times f_0}$, with $f_0 = d_t + d_s$, where

$$X_{ij} = [y_i \ x_j]. \tag{1}$$

This joint unigram encoding is the input to our convolutional network.

Convolutional layers. We use the DenseNet (Huang et al., 2017) convolutional architecture, which is the state of the art for image classification tasks. Layers are densely connected, meaning that each layer takes as input the activations of all the preceding layers, rather than just the last one, to produce its g feature maps. The parameter g is called the "growth rate" as it is the number of appended channels to the network's output at each layer. The long-distance connections in the network improve gradient flow to early network layers during training, which is beneficial for deeper networks.

Each layer first batch-normalizes (Ioffe and Szegedy, 2015) its input and apply a ReLU (Nair and Hinton, 2010) non-linearity. To reduce the computation cost, each layer first computes $4g$ channels using a 1×1 convolution from the $f_0 + (l-1)g$ input channels to layer $l \in \{1, \ldots, L\}$. This is followed by a second batch-normalization and ReLU non-linearity. The second convolution has $(k \times \lceil \frac{k}{2} \rceil)$ kernels, *i.e.* masked as illustrated in Figure 1, and generates the g output features maps to which we apply dropout (Srivastava et al., 2014). The architecture of the densely connected network is illustrated in Figure 3.

We optionally use gated linear units (Dauphin et al., 2017) in both convolutions, these double the number of output channels, and we use half of them to gate the other half.

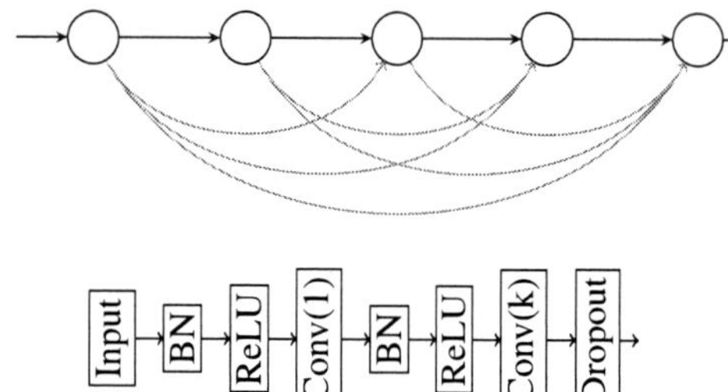

Figure 3: Architecture of the DenseNet at block level (top), and within each block (bottom).

Target sequence prediction. Starting from the initial f_0 feature maps, each layer $l \in \{1, \dots, L\}$ of our DenseNet produces a tensor H^l of size $|t| \times |s| \times f_l$, where f_l is the number of output channels of that layer. To compute a distribution over the tokens in the output vocabulary, we need to collapse the second dimension of the tensor, which is given by the variable length of the input sequence, to retrieve a unique encoding for each target position.

The simplest aggregation approach is to apply max-pooling over the input sequence to obtain a tensor $H^{\text{pool}} \in \mathbb{R}^{|t| \times f_L}$, *i.e.*

$$H^{\text{pool}}_{id} = \max_{j \in \{1, \dots, |s|\}} H^L_{ijd}. \tag{2}$$

Alternatively, we can use average-pooling over the input sequence:

$$H^{\text{pool}}_{id} = \frac{1}{\sqrt{|s|}} \sum_{j \in \{1, \dots, |s|\}} H^L_{ijd}. \tag{3}$$

The scaling with the inverse square-root of the source length acts as a variance stabilization term, which we find to be more effective in practice than a simple averaging.

The pooled features are then transformed to predictions over the output vocabulary $\mathcal{V}$, by linearly mapping them with a matrix $E \in \mathbb{R}^{|\mathcal{V}| \times f_L}$ to the vocabulary dimension $|\mathcal{V}|$, and then applying a soft-max. Thus the probability distribution over $\mathcal{V}$ for the i-th output token is obtained as

$$p_i = \text{SoftMax}(EH^{\text{pool}}_i). \tag{4}$$

Alternatively, we can use E to project to dimension d_t, and then multiply with the target word embedding matrix used to define the input tensor. This reduces the number of parameters and generally improves the performance.

Implicit sentence alignment. For a given output token position i, the max-pooling operator of Eq. (2) partitions the f_L channels by assigning them across the source tokens j. Let us define

$$B_{ij} = \{d \in \{1, \dots, f_L\} \mid j = \arg\max(H^L_{ijd})\}$$

as the channels assigned to source token j for output token i. The energy that enters into the soft-max to predict token $w \in \mathcal{V}$ for the i-th output position is given by

$$e_{iw} = \sum_{d \in \{1, \dots, f_L\}} E_{wd} H^{\text{pool}}_{id} \tag{5}$$

$$= \sum_{j \in \{1, \dots, |s|\}} \sum_{d \in B_{ij}} E_{wd} H^L_{ijd}. \tag{6}$$

The total contribution of the j-th input token is thus given by

$$\alpha_{ij} = \sum_{d \in B_{ij}} E_{wd} H^L_{ijd}, \tag{7}$$

where we dropped the dependence on w for simplicity. As we will show experimentally in the next section, visualizing the values α_{ij} for the ground-truth output tokens, we can recover an implicit sentence alignment used by the model.

Self attention. Besides pooling we can collapse the source dimension of the feature tensor with an attention mechanism. This mechanism will generate a tensor H^{att} that can be used instead of, or concatenated with, H^{Pool}.

We use the self-attention approach of Lin et al. (2017), which for output token i computes the attention vector $\rho_i \in \mathbb{R}^{|s|}$ from the activations H^L_i:

$$\rho_i = \text{SoftMax}\left(H^L_i w + b\mathbb{1}_{|s|}\right), \tag{8}$$

$$H^{\text{att}}_i = \sqrt{|s|}\rho_i^\top H^L_i, \tag{9}$$

where $w \in \mathbb{R}^{f_L}$ and $b \in \mathbb{R}$ are parameters of the attention mechanism. Scaling of attention vectors with the square-root of the source length was also used by Gehring et al. (2017b), and we found it effective here as well as in the average-pooling case.

4 Experimental evaluation

In this section, we present our experimental setup, followed by quantitative results, qualitative examples of implicit sentence alignments from our model, and a comparison to the state of the art.

4.1 Experimental setup

Data and pre-processing. We experiment with the IWSLT 2014 bilingual dataset (Cettolo et al., 2014), which contains transcripts of TED talks aligned at sentence level, and translate between German (De) and English (En) in both directions. Following the setup of (Edunov et al., 2018), sentences longer than 175 tokens and pairs with length ratio exceeding 1.5 were removed from the original data. There are 160+7K training sentence pairs, 7K of which are separated and used for validation/development. We report results on a test set of 6,578 pairs obtained by concatenating dev2010 and tst2010-2013. We tokenized and lowercased all data using the standard scripts from the Moses toolkit (Koehn et al., 2007).

For open-vocabulary translation, we segment sequences using joint byte pair encoding (Sennrich et al., 2016) with 14K merge operations on the concatenation of source and target languages. This results in a German and English vocabularies of around 12K and 9K types respectively.

Implementation details. Unless stated otherwise, we use DenseNets with masked convolutional filters of size 5×3, as given by the light blue area in Figure 1. To train our models, we use maximum likelihood estimation (MLE) with Adam ($\beta_1 = 0.9, \beta_2 = 0.999, \epsilon = 1e^{-8}$) starting with a learning rate of $5e^{-4}$ that we scale by a factor of 0.8 if no improvement ($\delta \leq 0.01$) is noticed on the validation loss after three evaluations, we evaluate every 8K updates.

After training all models up to 40 epochs, the best performing model on the validation set is used for decoding the test set. We use a beam-search of width 5 without any length or coverage penalty and measure translation quality using the BLEU metric (Papineni et al., 2002).

Baselines. For comparison with state-of-the-art architectures, we implemented a bidirectional LSTM encoder-decoder model with dot-product attention (Bahdanau et al., 2015; Luong et al., 2015) using PyTorch (Paszke et al., 2017), and used Facebook AI Research Sequence-to-Sequence Toolkit (Gehring et al., 2017b) to train the ConvS2S and Transformer (Vaswani et al., 2017) models on our data.

For the Bi-LSTM encoder-decoder, the encoder is a single layer bidirectional LSTM with input embeddings of size 128 and a hidden state of size

Model	BLEU	Flops$\times 10^5$	#params
Average	31.57 ± 0.11	3.63	7.18M
Max	33.70 ± 0.06	3.44	7.18M
Attn	32.07 ± 0.13	3.61	7.24M
Max, gated	33.66 ± 0.16	3.49	9.64M
[Max, Attn]	33.81 ± 0.03	3.51	7.24M

Table 1: Our model ($L = 24, g = 32, d_s = d_t = 128$) with different pooling operators and using gated convolutional units.

256 (128 in each direction). The decoder is a single layer LSTM with similar input size and a hidden size of 256, the target input embeddings are also used in the pre-softmax projection. For regularization, we apply a dropout of rate 0.2 to the inputs of both encoder and decoder and to the output of the decoder prior to softmax. As in (Bahdanau et al., 2015), we refer to this model as RNNsearch.

The ConvS2S model we trained has embeddings of dimension 256, a 16-layers encoder and 12-layers decoder. Each convolution uses 3×1 filters and is followed by a gated linear unit with a total of 2×256 channels. Residual connections link the input of a convolutional block to its output. We first trained the default architecture for this dataset as suggested in FairSeq (Gehring et al., 2017b), which has only 4 layers in the encoder and 3 in the decoder, but achieved better results with the deeper version described above. The model is trained with MLE using Nesterov accelerated gradient with a momentum of 0.99 and an initial learning rate of 0.25 decaying by a factor of 0.1 every epoch. ConvS2S is also regularized with a dropout rate of 0.2.

For the transformer model, use the settings of (Vaswani et al., 2017). We use token embeddings of dimension 512, and the encoder and decoder have 6 layers and 8 attention heads. For the inner layer in the per-position feed-forawrd network we use $d_{ff} = 2048$. For MLE training we use Adam ($\beta_1 = 0.9, \beta_2 = 0.98, \epsilon = 1e^{-8}$) (Kingma and Ba, 2015), and a learning rate starting from $1e^{-5}$ that is increased during 4,000 warm-up steps then used a learning rate of $5e^{-4}$ that follows an inverse-square-root schedule afterwards (Vaswani et al., 2017). Similar to previous models we set the dropout rate to 0.2.

4.2 Experimental results

Architecture evaluation. In this section we explore the impact of several parameters of our

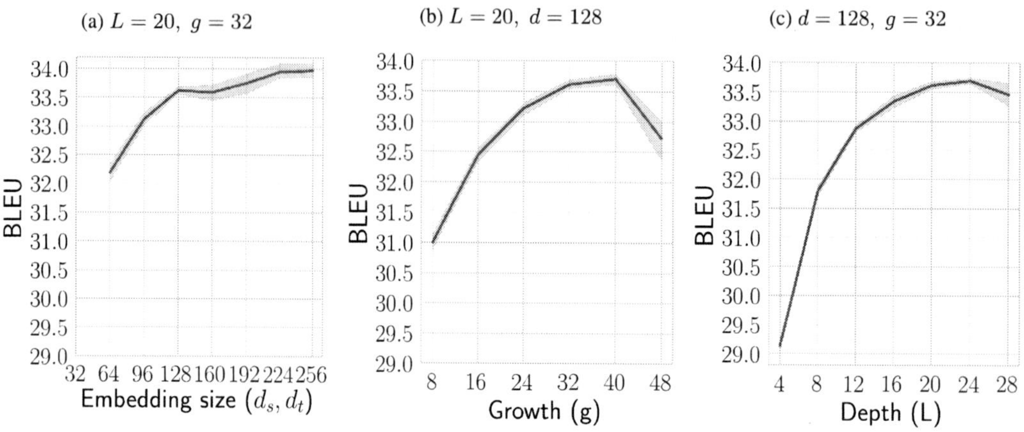

Figure 4: Impact of token embedding size, number of layers (L), and growth rate (g).

model: the token embedding dimension, depth, growth rate and filter sizes. We also evaluate different aggregation mechanisms across the source dimension: max-pooling, average-pooling, and attention.

In each chosen setting, we train five models with different initializations and report the mean and standard deviation of the BLEU scores. We also state the number of parameters of each model and the computational cost of training, estimated in a similar way as Vaswani et al. (2017), based on the wall clock time of training and the GPU single precision specs.

In Table 1 we see that using max-pooling instead average-pooling across the source dimension increases the performance with around 2 BLEU points. Scaling the average representation with $\sqrt{|s|}$ Eq. (3) helped improving the performance but it is still largely outperformed by the max-pooling. Adding gated linear units on top of each convolutional layer does not improve the BLEU scores, but increases the variance due to the additional parameters. Stand-alone self-attention *i.e.* weighted average-pooling is slightly better than uniform average-pooling but it is still outperformed by max-pooling. Concatenating the max-pooled features (Eq. (2)) with the representation obtained with self-attention (Eq. (9)) leads to a small but significant increase in performance, from 33.70 to 33.81. In the remainder of our experiments we only use max-pooling for simplicity, unless stated otherwise.

In Figure 4 we consider the effect of the token embedding size, the growth rate of the network, and its depth. The token embedding size together with the growth rate g control the number of features that are passed though the pooling operator along the source dimension, and that can be used used for token prediction. Using the same embedding size $d = d_t = d_s$ on both source and target, the total number of features for token prediction produced by the network is $f_L = 2d + gL$. In Figure 4 we see that for token embedding sizes between 128 to 256 lead to BLEU scores vary between 33.5 and 34. Smaller embedding sizes quickly degrade the performance to 32.2 for embeddings of size 64. The growth rate (g) has an important impact on performance, increasing it from 8 to 32 increases the BLEU scrore by more than 2.5 point. Beyond $g = 32$ performance saturates and we observe only a small improvement. For a good trade-off between performance and computational cost we choose $g = 32$ for the remaining experiments. The depth of the network also has an important impact on performance, increasing the BLEU score by about 2 points when increasing the depth from 8 to 24 layers. Beyond this point performance drops due to over-fitting, which means we should either increase the dropout rate or add another level of regularization before considering deeper networks. The receptive field of our model is controlled by its depth and the filter size. In Table 2, we note that narrower receptive fields are better than larger ones with less layers at equivalent complextities *e.g.* comparing $(k = 3, L = 20)$ to $(k = 5, L = 12)$, and $(k = 5, L = 16)$ with $(k = 7, L = 12)$.

Comparison to the state of the art. We compare our results to the state of the art in Ta-

k	L	BLEU	Flops$\times 10^5$	#params
3	16	32.99±0.08	2.47	4.32M
3	20	33.18±0.19	3.03	4.92M
5	8	31.79±0.09	0.63	3.88M
5	12	32.87±0.07	2.61	4.59M
5	16	33.34±0.12	3.55	5.37M
5	20	33.62±0.07	3.01	6.23M
5	24	33.70±0.06	3.44	7.18M
5	28	33.46±0.23	5.35	8.21M
7	12	32.58±0.12	2.76	5.76M

Table 2: Performance of our model ($g = 32, d_s = d_t = 128$) for different filter sizes k and depths L and filter sizes k.

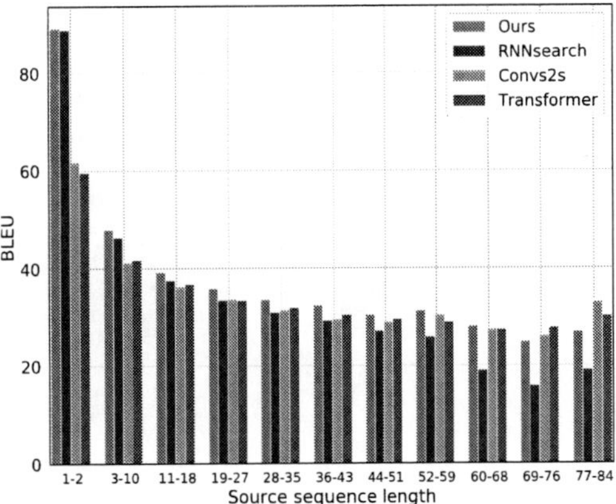

Figure 5: BLEU scores across sentence lengths.

ble 3 for both directions German-English (De-En) and English-German (En-De). We refer to our model as Pervasive Attention . Unless stated otherwise, the parameters of all models are trained using maximum likelihood estimation (MLE). For some models we additionally report results obtained with sequence level estimation (SLE, *e.g.* using reinforcement learning approaches), typically aiming directly to optimize the BLEU measure rather than the likelihood of correct translation.

First of all we find that all results obtained using byte-pair encodings (BPE) are superior to word-based results. Our model has about the same number of parameters as RNNsearch, yet improves performance by almost 3 BLEU points. It is also better than the recent work of Deng et al. (2018) on recurrent architectures with variational attention. Our model outperforms both the recent transformer approach of Vaswani et al. (2017) and the convolutional model of Gehring et al. (2017b) in both translation directions, while having about 3 to 8 times fewer parameters. Our model has an equivalent training cost to the transformer (as implemented in fairseq) while the convs2s implementation is well optimized with fast running 1d-convolutions leading to shorter training times.

Performance across sequence lengths. In Figure 5 we consider translation quality as a function of sentence length, and compare our model to RNNsearch, ConvS2S and Transformer. Our model gives the best results across all sentence lengths, except for the longest ones where ConvS2S and Transformer are better. Overall, our model combines the strong performance of RNNsearch on short sentences with good perfor-

mance of ConvS2S and Transformer on longer ones.

Implicit sentence alignments. Following the method described in Section 3, we illustrate in Figure 6 the implicit sentence alignments the max-pooling operator produces in our model. For reference we also show the alignment produced by our model using self-attention. We see that with both max-pooling and attention qualitatively similar implicit sentence alignments emerge.

Notice in the first example how the max-pool model, when writing *I've been working*, looks at *arbeite* but also at *seit* which indicates the past tense of the former. Also notice some cases of non-monotonic alignment. In the first example *for some time* occurs at the end of the English sentence, but *seit einiger zeit* appears earlier in the German source. For the second example there is non-monotonic alignment around the negation at the start of the sentence. The first example illustrates the ability of the model to translate proper names by breaking them down into BPE units. In the second example the German word *Karriereweg* is broken into the four BPE units *karri,er,e,weg*. The first and the fourth are mainly used to produce the English *a carreer*, while for the subsequent *path* the model looks at *weg*.

Finally, we can observe an interesting pattern in the alignment map for several phrases across the three examples. A rough lower triangular pattern is observed for the English phrases *for some time, and it's fantastic, and it's not, a little step, and in that direction*. In all these cases the phrase seems to be decoded as a unit, where features are first taken across the entire corresponding source

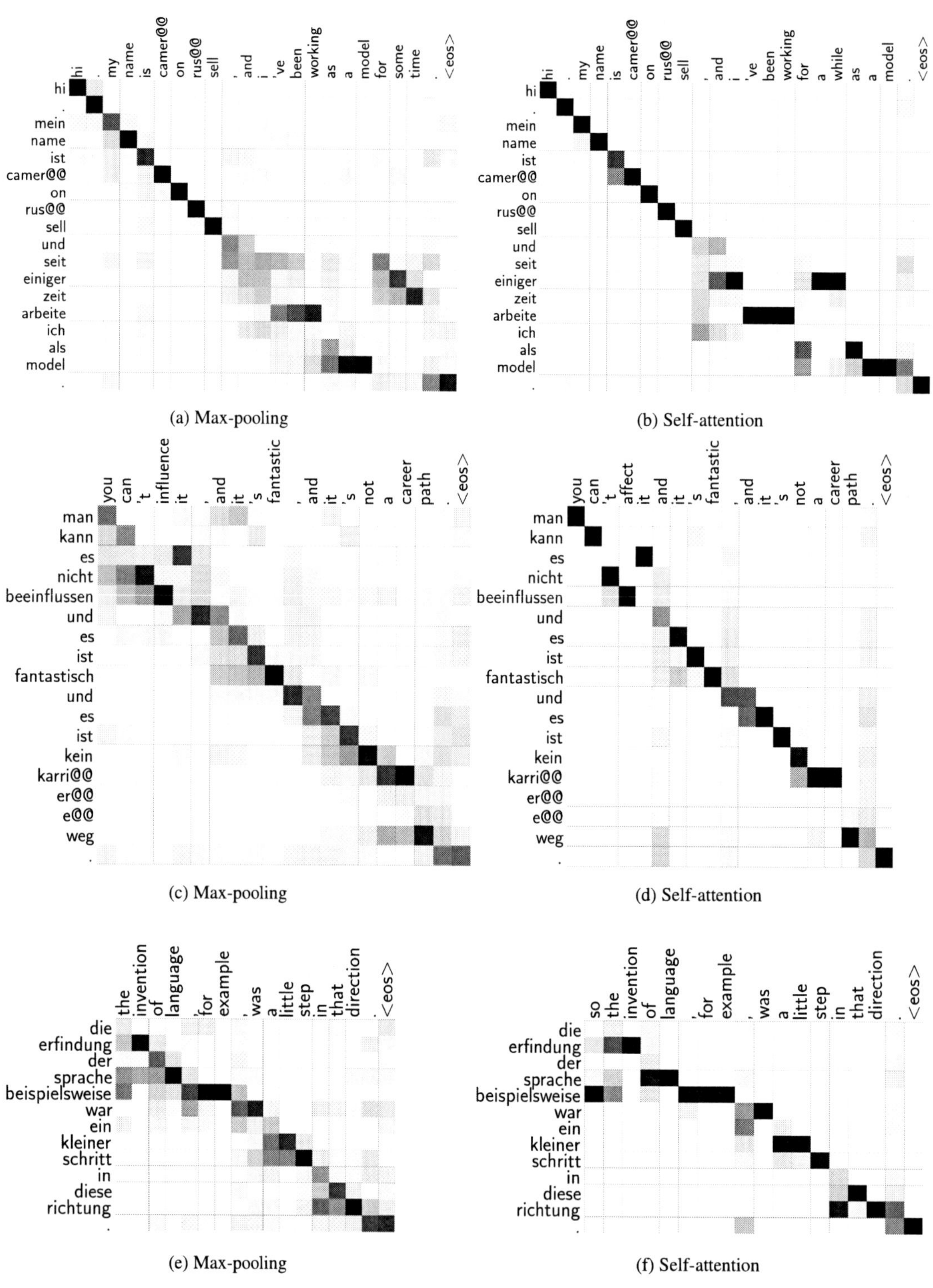

(a) Max-pooling   (b) Self-attention

(c) Max-pooling   (d) Self-attention

(e) Max-pooling   (f) Self-attention

Figure 6: Implicit BPE token-level alignments produced by our Pervasive Attention model. For the max-pooling aggregation we visualize α obtained with Eq. (7) and for self-attention the weights ρ of Eq. (8).

Word-based	De-En	Flops ($\times 10^5$)	# prms	En-De	# prms
Conv-LSTM (MLE) (Bahdanau et al., 2017)	27.56				
Bi-GRU (MLE+SLE) (Bahdanau et al., 2017)	28.53				
Conv-LSTM (deep+pos) (Gehring et al., 2017a)	30.4				
NPMT + language model (Huang et al., 2018)	30.08			25.36	
BPE-based					
RNNsearch* (Bahdanau et al., 2015)	31.02	1.79	6M	25.92	7M
Varational attention (Deng et al., 2018)	33.10				
Transformer** (Vaswani et al., 2017)	32.83	3.53	59M	27.68	61M
ConvS2S** (MLE) (Gehring et al., 2017b)	32.31	1.35	21M	26.73	22M
ConvS2S (MLE+SLE) (Edunov et al., 2018)	32.84				
Pervasive Attention (this paper)	33.81± 0.03	3.51	7M	27.77± 0.1	7M

Table 3: Comparison to state-of-the art results on IWSLT German-English translation. (*): results obtained using our implementation. (**): results obtained using FairSeq (Gehring et al., 2017b).

phrase, and progressively from the part of the source phrase that remains to be decoded.

5 Conclusion

We presented a novel neural machine translation architecture that departs from the encoder-decoder paradigm. Our model jointly encodes the source and target sequence into a deep feature hierarchy in which the source tokens are embedded in the context of a partial target sequence. Max-pooling over this joint-encoding along the source dimension is used to map the features to a prediction for the next target token. The model is implemented as 2D CNN based on DenseNet, with masked convolutions to ensure a proper autoregressive factorization of the conditional probabilities.

Since each layer of our model re-encodes the input tokens in the context of the target sequence generated so far, the model has attention-like properties in every layer of the network by construction. Adding an explicit self-attention module therefore has a very limited, but positive, effect. Nevertheless, the max-pooling operator in our model generates implicit sentence alignments that are qualitatively similar to the ones generated by attention mechanisms. We evaluate our model on the IWSLT'14 dataset, translation German to English and vice-versa. We obtain excellent BLEU scores that compare favorably with the state of the art, while using a conceptually simpler model with fewer parameters.

We hope that our alternative joint source-target encoding sparks interest in other alternatives to the encoder-decoder model. In the future, we plan to explore hybrid approaches in which the input to our joint encoding model is not provided by token-embedding vectors, but the output of 1D source and target embedding networks, *e.g.* (bi-)LSTM or 1D convolutional. We also want to explore how our model can be used to translate across multiple language pairs.

Our PyTorch-based implementation is available at `https://github.com/elbayadm/attn2d`.

References

D. Bahdanau, P. Brakel, K. Xu, A. Goyal, R. Lowe, J. Pineau, A. Courville, and Y. Bengio. 2017. An actor-critic algorithm for sequence prediction. In *ICLR*.

D. Bahdanau, K. Cho, and Y. Bengio. 2015. Neural machine translation by jointly learning to align and translate. In *ICLR*.

N. Kalchbrenner P. Blunsom. 2013. Recurrent continuous translation models. In *ACL*.

M. Cettolo, J. Niehues, S. Stüker, L. Bentivogli, and M. Federico. 2014. Report on the 11th IWSLT evaluation campaign. In *IWSLT*.

K. Cho, B. van Merrienboer, Ç. Gülçehre, D. Bahdanau, F. Bougares, H. Schwenk, and Y. Bengio. 2014. Learning phrase representations using RNN encoder-decoder for statistical machine translation. In *EMNLP*.

R. Collobert and J. Weston. 2008. A unified architecture for natural language processing: Deep neural networks with multitask learning. In *ICML*.

Y. Dauphin, A. Fan, M. Auli, and D. Grangier. 2017. Language modeling with gated convolutional networks. In *ICML*.

Y. Deng, Y. Kim, J. Chiu, D. Guo, and A. Rush. 2018. Latent alignment and variational attention. *arXiv preprint arXiv:1807.03756*.

S. Edunov, M. Ott, M. Auli, D. Grangier, and M. Ranzato. 2018. Classical structured prediction losses for sequence to sequence learning. In *NAACL*.

J. Gehring, M. Auli, D. Grangier, and Y. Dauphin. 2017a. A convolutional encoder model for neural machine translation. In *ACL*.

J. Gehring, M. Auli, D. Grangier, D. Yarats, and Y. Dauphin. 2017b. Convolutional sequence to sequence learning. In *ICML*.

A. Graves. 2012. Sequence transduction with recurrent neural networks. *arXiv preprint arXiv:1211.3711*.

S. Hochreiter and J. Schmidhuber. 1997. Long short-term memory. *Neural Computation*, 9(8):1735–1780.

G. Huang, Z. Liu, L. van der Maaten, and K. Weinberger. 2017. Densely connected convolutional networks. In *CVPR*.

P. Huang, C. Wang, S. Huang, D. Zhou, and L. Deng. 2018. Towards neural phrase-based machine translation. In *ICLR*.

S. Ioffe and C. Szegedy. 2015. Batch normalization: Accelerating deep network training by reducing internal covariate shift. In *ICML*.

S. Jean, K. Cho, R. Memisevic, and Y. Bengio. 2015. On using very large target vocabulary for neural machine translation. In *ACL*.

N. Kalchbrenner, I. Danihelka, and A. Graves. 2016a. Grid long short-term memory. In *ICLR*.

N. Kalchbrenner, L. Espeholt, K. Simonyan, A. van den Oord, A. Graves, and K. Kavukcuoglu. 2016b. Neural machine translation in linear time. *arXiv*, arXiv:1610.10099.

N. Kalchbrenner, E. Grefenstette, and P. Blunsom. 2014. A convolutional neural network for modelling sentences. In *ACL*.

Y. Kim. 2014. Convolutional neural networks for sentence classification. In *ACL*.

D. Kingma and J. Ba. 2015. Adam: A method for stochastic optimization. In *ICLR*.

P. Koehn, H. Hoang, A. Birch, C. Callison-Burch, M. Federico, N. Bertoldi, B. Cowan, W. Shen, C. Moran, R. Zens, C. Dyer, O. Bojar, A. Constantin, and E. Herbst. 2007. Moses: Open source toolkit for statistical machine translation. In *ACL*.

Y. LeCun, Y. Bengio, and G. Hinton. 2015. Deep learning. *Nature*, 52:436–444.

Z. Lin, M. Feng, C. dos Santos, M. Yu, B. Xiang, B. Zhou, and Y. Bengio. 2017. A structured self-attentive sentence embedding. In *ICLR*.

T. Luong, H. Pham, and C. Manning. 2015. Effective approaches to attention-based neural machine translation. In *EMNLP*.

F. Meng, Z. Lu, M. Wang, H. Li, W. Jiang, and Q. Liu. 2015. Encoding source language with convolutional neural network for machine translation. In *ACL*.

V. Nair and G. Hinton. 2010. Rectified linear units improve restricted Boltzmann machines. In *ICML*.

A. van den Oord, S. Dieleman, H. Zen, K. Simonyan, O. Vinyals, A. Graves, N. Kalchbrenner, A. Senior, and K. Kavukcuoglu. 2016a. Wavenet: a generative model for raw audio. In *ISCA Speech Syntesis Workshop*.

A. van den Oord, N. Kalchbrenner, and K. Kavukcuoglu. 2016b. Pixel recurrent neural networks. In *ICML*.

A. van den Oord, N. Kalchbrenner, O. Vinyals, L. Espeholt, A. Graves, and K. Kavukcuoglu. 2016c. Conditional image generation with PixelCNN decoders. In *NIPS*.

K. Papineni, S. Roukos, T. Ward, and W.-J. Zhu. 2002. BLEU: a method for automatic evaluation of machine translation. In *ACL*.

A. Parikh, O. Täckström, D. Das, and J. Uszkoreit. 2016. A decomposable attention model for natural language inference. In *EMNLP*.

A. Paszke, S. Gross, S. Chintala, G. Chanan, E. Yang, Z. DeVito, Z. Lin, A. Desmaison L. Antiga, and A. Lerer. 2017. Automatic differentiation in pytorch. In *NIPS-W*.

M. Ranzato, S. Chopra, M. Auli, and W. Zaremba. 2016. Sequence level training with recurrent neural networks. In *ICLR*.

S. Reed, A. van den Oord, N. Kalchbrenner, S. Gómez Colmenarejo, Z. Wang, D. Belov, and N. de Freitas. 2017. Parallel multiscale autoregressive density estimation. In *ICML*.

T. Salimans, A. Karpathy, X. Chen, and D. Kingma. 2017. PixelCNN++: Improving the PixelCNN with discretized logistic mixture likelihood and other modifications. In *ICLR*.

M. Schuster and K. Paliwal. 1997. Bidirectional recurrent neural networks. *Signal Processing*, 45(11):2673–2681.

R. Sennrich, B. Haddow, and A. Birch. 2016. Neural machine translation of rare words with subword units. In *ACL*.

N. Srivastava, G. Hinton, A. Krizhevsky, I. Sutskever, and R. Salakhutdinov. 2014. Dropout: A simple way to prevent neural networks from overfitting. *JMLR*.

I. Sutskever, O. Vinyals, and Q. Le. 2014. Sequence to sequence learning with neural networks. In *NIPS*.

A. Vaswani, N. Shazeer, N. Parmar, J. Uszkoreit, L. Jones, A. Gomez, L. Kaiser, and I. Polosukhin. 2017. Attention is all you need. In *NIPS*.

C. Wang, Y. Wang, P.-S. Huang, A. Mohamed, D. Zhou, and L. Deng. 2017. Sequence modeling via segmentations. In *ICML*.

L. Wu, Y. Xia, L. Zhao, F. Tian, T. Qin, J. Lai, and T.-Y. Liu. 2017. Adversarial neural machine translation. *arXiv*, arXiv:1704.06933.

K. Xu, J. Ba, R. Kiros, K. Cho, A. Courville, R. Salakhutdinov, R. Zemel, and Y. Bengio. 2015. Show, attend and tell: Neural image caption generation with visual attention. In *ICML*.

Comparing Attention-based Convolutional and Recurrent Neural Networks: Success and Limitations in Machine Reading Comprehension

Matthias Blohm, Glorianna Jagfeld, Ekta Sood, Xiang Yu, Ngoc Thang Vu
Institute for Natural Language Processing (IMS)
Universität Stuttgart, Germany
{blohmms,jagfelga,soodea,xiangyu,thangvu}
@ims.uni-stuttgart.de

Abstract

We propose a machine reading comprehension model based on the compare-aggregate framework with two-staged attention that achieves state-of-the-art results on the MovieQA question answering dataset. To investigate the limitations of our model as well as the behavioral difference between convolutional and recurrent neural networks, we generate adversarial examples to confuse the model and compare to human performance. Furthermore, we assess the generalizability of our model by analyzing its differences to human inference, drawing upon insights from cognitive science.

1 Introduction

Current state-of-the-art deep learning (DL) models outperform other techniques in many tasks including computer vision (Krizhevsky et al., 2012), speech recognition (Hinton et al., 2012) and more recently natural language processing (NLP) (Collobert et al., 2011). Neural-based NLP systems often use word embeddings (Bengio et al., 2003; Collobert and Weston, 2008; Mikolov et al., 2013) which are then fed into a convolutional neural network (CNN) (LeCun et al., 1990; Waibel et al., 1990) or a recurrent neural network (RNN) (Elman, 1990; Hochreiter and Schmidhuber, 1997) for further classification. These approaches proved to be successful for many NLP tasks (Mikolov et al., 2010; Kim, 2014; Hu et al., 2014; Bahdanau et al., 2014). Along with the success of DL in a wide range of applications, adversarial examples (Goodfellow et al., 2014) - that aim to confuse the system - have gained popularity in a wide range of research communities such as computer vision and NLP, since they can reveal the limitations in the generalizability of the models. As opposed to adversarial examples in computer vision, which are computed on continuous data and can thus easily be imperceptible if desired, adversarial attacks in NLP entail the necessity to perform discrete and perceptible changes to the data. Thus, attack methods for computer vision such as the Fast Gradient Sign Method (FGSM) (Goodfellow et al., 2014) cannot be directly applied to NLP.

Machine comprehension has recently received increased interest in the NLP community (Yang et al., 2015; Tapaswi et al., 2016; Rajpurkar et al., 2016; Chen et al., 2016). Neural network models perform reasonably well on many data sets with different question answering setups, e.g. multiple choice or answer generation (Wang and Jiang, 2016; Liu et al., 2017; Yu et al., 2018).

Among others, Wang and Jiang (2016) proposed the compare-aggregate framework, which uses an attention mechanism (Luong et al., 2015) to compare the question and candidate answers, and a CNN to aggregate information. However, there is still an ongoing debate whether CNNs or RNNs are more suitable to NLP (Yin et al., 2017), and the behavioral differences between them are still under research. Many papers reported remarkable gains when combining these two models in ensembles (Deng and Platt, 2014; Zhou et al., 2015; Vu et al., 2016), since they process information in different ways and thus are complimentary to each other.

Despite the seemingly high accuracies of many models on machine comprehension tasks, Jia and Liang (2017) argued that many questions in such datasets are easily solvable by superficial cues. They showed with adversarial examples that most models can be easily tricked by modifications on the data which do not confuse humans. Similarly, Sanchez et al. (2018) performed controlled experiments on the robustness of several Natural Language Inference models by altering hypernym, hyponym, and antonym relations in the data. Both

Proceedings of the 22nd Conference on Computational Natural Language Learning (CoNLL 2018), pages 108–118
Brussels, Belgium, October 31 - November 1, 2018. ©2018 Association for Computational Linguistics

studies revealed a major weakness of the models: They largely rely on pattern matching instead of human decision-making processes as required in the tasks, including heuristics (Gigerenzer and Gaissmaier, 2011) and elimination by aspects (Tversky, 1972).

In this paper, we implement two machine comprehension models based on the compare-aggregate framework with a hierarchical attention structure using CNNs and RNNs. First we show that we achieve state-of-the-art results on the MovieQA multiple choice question answering dataset (Tapaswi et al., 2016) outperforming other systems by a large margin.[1] Second, we investigate the different behavior of the two systems applying adversarial attacks in a systematic way. To our best knowledge, this is the first work exploring the difference between CNNs and RNNs by such an approach. Third, we present a detailed comparison between human and machine reading comprehension, giving insights when and why our systems fail. Therefore, these insights are important for future research towards enhancing machine comprehension systems loosely inspired by human processing. All code necessary to reproduce our experimental results is made available.[2]

2 Hierarchical Attention-based Compare-Aggregate Model

The basis for our model is the compare-aggregate model with attention (Wang and Jiang, 2016) that has been shown effective for reading comprehension. We extend the model in two aspects that lead to significant improvements.

Given a preprocessed matrix-representation of the question Q, a text (movie plot) P, and k answer candidates $A_1 \ldots A_k$, the main idea of Wang and Jiang (2016)'s compare-aggregate model is to compare P to Q and each A_j and then aggregate this information into a vector to derive a confidence score c_j for each answer candidate.

Wang and Jiang (2016) concatenate all plot sentences and do not leverage the inherent structuring of the text into sentences. Inspired by the recent success of hierarchical models in NLP (Sordoni et al., 2015; Yang et al., 2016; Liu et al., 2017) we extend the model to perform comparison and aggregation on the word and sentence level separately (see Figure 1). Specifically, we first apply the compare-aggregate model to each plot sentence P_i individually to obtain question and answer-weighted representations $T_{q_i}^w$, $T_{a_{ij}}^w$ for each sentence. We then run the aggregation operation on each sentence representation individually to obtain sentence vector representations $r_{p_{ij}}$. The sentence representations are concatenated to obtain a plot representation r_{p_j}, which enters the sentence level of comparison and aggregation that mirrors the word level architecture.

As a second modification of the base model, we implement an RNN-based aggregation function to replace the CNN-based aggregation originally proposed by Wang and Jiang (2016). In the following we detail the building blocks of our hierarchical attention-based compare-aggregate model as depicted in Figure 1.

Preprocessing We represent the words in the question q, the plot sentences p_i and the answer candidates a_j by pretrained embeddings to obtain matrices $\overline{Q}, \overline{P}, \overline{A_j}$. We project them to lower dimensional Q, P, A_j via the following operation:

$$X = \sigma \left(W^i \overline{X} + b^i \right) \odot \tanh \left(W^u \overline{X} + b^u \right) \quad (1)$$

Attention The attention operation weights the plot regarding the question or a candidate answer.

$$G = \text{softmax} \left(X^T P \right) \quad (2)$$
$$H = XG, \quad (3)$$

where X on the word level represents Q or an answer candidate A_j and on the sentence level r_q or r_{a_j}.[3]

Comparison The comparison operation performs an element-wise comparison of each h_l in H with its counterparts q_l/a_{j_l} on the word level and r_q/r_{a_j} on the sentence level, respectively. Wang and Jiang (2016) compared many comparison functions. Here we use only the SUBMULT function since it performed best for MovieQA:

$$t_l = \text{ReLU}(W \left[\begin{array}{c} (x_l - h_l) \odot (x_l - h_l) \\ x_l \odot h_l \end{array} \right] + b)$$

where $\odot$ denotes element-wise multiplication and x_l corresponds to entries of Q/A_j or r_q/r_{a_j}.

---

[1]See MovieQA leaderboard, `http://movieqa.cs.toronto.edu/leaderboard/`

[2]`https://github.com/DigitalPhonetics/reading-comprehension`

[3]Different from Wang and Jiang (2016) we use dot-product attention instead of general attention (Luong et al., 2015) because we found no benefit of the additional parameters of general attention in preliminary experiments.

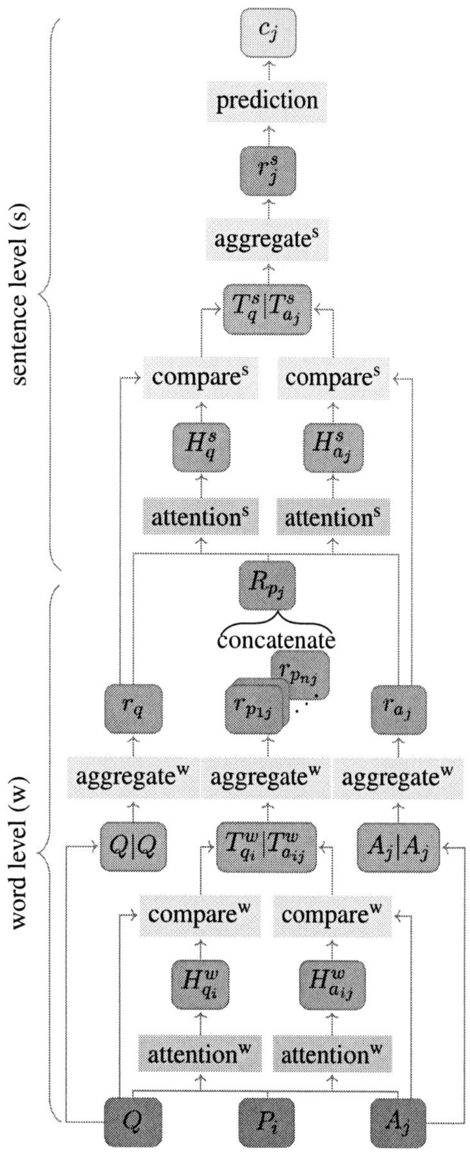

Figure 1: Hierarchical compare-aggregate model to compute the confidence score c_j of a preprocessed answer candidate A_j given question Q and plot $P = P_1 \ldots P_n$.

Aggregation The goal of the aggregation operation is to condense the information of a variable-length sequence into a single vector. Wang and Jiang (2016) implemented the aggregation operation as a single-layer CNN following Kim (2014). Specifically, they used a 1D convolution with filter sizes $\{1,3,5\}$, to capture unigrams, trigrams and 5-grams.

$$\text{aggregate}_{\text{CNN}} = \text{CNN}([z_1 \ldots z_m]) \quad (4)$$

where $[z_1 \ldots z_m]$ on the word level corresponds to the sequence of row vectors of $Q, T^w = T^w_{q_i} | T^w_{a_{ij}}, A_j$, and on the sentence level to that of $T^s = T^s_q | T^s_{a_j}$.

While CNNs are effective in modeling location-independent n-gram patterns, they cannot capture longer-range dependencies. Yet, we argue that it is important to also consider the context of the matched phrases. This motivates our proposed sequential aggregation function based on a single-layer unidirectional RNN with Long Short-Term Memory (LSTM) units (Hochreiter and Schmidhuber, 1997).

$$\text{aggregate}_{\text{RNN-LSTM}} = \text{RNN}([z_1 \ldots z_m]) \quad (5)$$

By performing 1-max pooling over the outputs of $\text{aggregate}_{\text{CNN}}$ or $\text{aggregate}_{\text{RNN-LSTM}}$[4] we obtain a single vector r (representing $r_q, r_{p_{ij}}, r_{a_j}$ on the word level, or r^s_j on the sentence level):

$$r = \text{max\_pool}(\text{aggregate}([z_1 \ldots z_m])) \quad (6)$$

We share the weights between the comparison and aggregation operations within the word and sentence level but not across levels.

Prediction We map each aggregated answer-specific plot representation r^s_j to a confidence score c_j by two dense layers with shared weights for all answer candidates and of which the first uses tanh activation and the second one no activation function. The confidence scores are normalized to form a probability distribution $p_1 \ldots p_k$ by a softmax operation.

3 Experimental Set-Up

The hyperparameters for our models are provided in §A.1 in the appendix.

3.1 Data

We evaluate our models on the MovieQA dataset (Tapaswi et al., 2016) that contains 14,944 multiple-choice questions on 408 movies collected by human annotators. The questions vary from simple *"who"* or *"when"* to more complex *"why"* or *"how"* question types. Each question is provided along with five candidate answers of which only one is correct.

While the dataset contains multiple sources of information about the movie contents such as

---

[4]Using only the last RNN output for $\text{aggregate}_{\text{RNN-LSTM}}$ did not provide convincing results.

videos, subtitles, and movie scripts, here we focus on answering the questions only from *plot synopses*. Plot synopses are summaries of the movies collected from Wikipedia that mostly describe the actions happening in the story. They were used as references for the question collection and so far yield the best results on the dataset according to the MovieQA leaderboard. Figure 2 shows a sample question together with its candidate answers and an excerpt of the corresponding movie plot which contains the necessary information to answer the question. The dataset is split into 9,848 training, 1,958 development and 3,138 test questions, respectively. Note that the test set accuracies can only be evaluated by submitting the predictions to the server.

Plot: ... Aragorn is crowned King of Gondor and taking Arwen as his queen before all present at his coronation bowing before Frodo and the other Hobbits. The Hobbits return to **the Shire** where Sam marries Rosie Cotton. ...

Question: Where does Sam marry Rosie?

Candidate Answers: 0) Grey Havens
1) Gondor 2) **The Shire** 3) Erebor 4) Mordor

Figure 2: *MovieQA* example question (Wang and Jiang, 2016).

4   Results

We train 11 models with different random initializations for both the CNN and RNN-LSTM aggregation function and form majority-vote ensembles of the nine models with the highest validation accuracy. Table 1 shows the accuracies of ensembles of our proposed model variations in comparison to the published results on the MovieQA validation and test set. To the best of our knowledge, the results of Wang and Jiang (2016) and Dzendzik et al. (2017) were achieved by single models, while the results of Liu et al. (2017) corresponds to an ensemble of multiple models.

All our hierarchical single and ensemble models outperform the previous state of the art on both the validation and test set. With a test accuracy of 85.12, the RNN-LSTM ensemble achieves a new state of the art that is more than five percentage points above the previous best result.

The hierarchical structure is crucial for the model's success. Adding it to the CNN that oper-

Systems	Val.	Test
Wang and Jiang (2016)	72.10	72.90
Liu et al. (2017)	79.00	79.99
Dzendzik et al. (2017)	-	80.02
Proposed models		
CNN word level only	76.51	-
CNN	79.62	-
CNN ensemble	82.58	82.73
RNN-LSTM	83.14	-
RNN-LSTM ensemble	84.37	**85.12**
CNN RNN-LSTM ensemble	**84.78**	84.70

Table 1: MovieQA accuracies for previously published results and our proposed single models (best out of 11) and ensembles (nine best out of 11).

ates only at word level[5] causes a pronounced improvement on the validation set.

Furthermore, the RNN-LSTM aggregation function is superior to aggregation via CNNs, improving the validation accuracy by 1.5 percentage points. While this improvement is statistically significant,[6] combining both aggregation functions by ensembling the nine best CNN and RNN-LSTM models each, yields a small but statistically insignificant improvement of 0.41 percentage points over the RNN-LSTM ensemble on the validation set. This might explain why the RNN-LSTM ensemble even outperforms the CNN RNN-LSTM ensemble on the test set by a small margin. The difference in test set performance between these two ensembles is likely not significant. We cannot test this as the test set is not released and only accuracy values can be obtained for model evaluation on the test set.

4.1   Impact of Sentence Attention

The sentence attention allows us to get more insight into the models' inner state. For example, it allows us to check whether the model actually focuses on relevant sentences in order to answer the questions. The MovieQA dataset provides human annotations of the minimal set of plot sentences required to answer a question. In average, 1.15/1.11 sentences in the training/validation set are marked as containing the clue to the answer. We leverage

---

[5]The CNN word level only model essentially corresponds to our reimplementation of Wang and Jiang (2016). The performance gain on the validation set might be due to using consistent random initializations for unknown words.

[6]McNemar test (McNemar, 1947), $p < 0.05$.

Systems	CNN	RNN-LSTM
All questions	71.45	71.31
- Correctly solved	80.86	79.35
- Incorrectly solved	35.73	34.49

Table 2: Percentage of questions in which the plot sentences containing the clues for the answer are ranked highest according to the model's sentence attention distribution (relative to its selected answer) on the validation set (averaged results of nine models).

Systems	Average	Ensemble
CNN	78.74	81.72
RNN-LSTM	81.53	83.76
CNN RNN-LSTM	81.14	84.27

Table 3: Adversarial accuracies on the validation set under the word-level black-box attack based on manual lexical substitutions in questions.

this information and compute the ranks of these relevant plot sentences according to the models' sentence attention distribution. We extract the plot sentence relevance scores after the sentence-level comparison operation as average of T_q^s and $T_{a_j}^s$, where a_j corresponds to the selected answer of the model. As Table 2 reveals, both model variants pay most attention to the relevant plot sentences for 70% of the cases. Identifying the relevant sentences is an important success factor: Relevant sentences are ranked highest only in 35% of the incorrectly solved questions.

5 Limitations

To help us identifying the models' weaknesses, we design a series of systematic adversarial attacks. These attacks are defined in different categories depending on the linguistic level (word vs. sentence level) and the knowledge of the adversaries (black-box vs. white-box). According to the taxonomy proposed by Yuan et al. (2017), black-box and white-box attacks differ in the access of the adversary to the trained neural network model. In black-box settings, the adversary acts as a standard user that has only access to the output of the model in form of labels or confidence scores. In contrast, the adversary in white-box settings has access to all the details of the models such as training data, network architectures and hyperparameters. In this work, the white-box adversary has access to the attention weights of the model at the word and sentence level. We apply all our attacks to the nine selected models (see §4) for each aggregation type.

5.1 Word-level Black-box Attack

Adversarial examples for image recognition are typically created by adding some imperceptible noise (Szegedy et al., 2014; Goodfellow et al., 2015), yet this is difficult to do for natural language because of its discrete nature. The closest analogue would be paraphrasing but high-quality paraphrases are difficult to obtain automatically: Recent attempts with a sophisticated paraphrase-generation system based on a large paraphrase database yielded about 20% contradicting adversarial examples (Iyyer et al., 2018).

Thus, we designed an adversarial black-box attack on the questions based on manual lexical substitution. We inspected the 106 most frequent words of the validation set questions and manually defined lexical substitutions of single words and multiword expressions of up to two tokens wherever applicable. We made sure that the lexical substitutions were meaning preserving and resulted in grammatical sentences in all contexts.[7] Our final set of 51 substitution rules resulted in a modification of 25% of the validation set questions.

As can be seen from Table 3, the models are quite robust against meaning-preserving lexical substitutions: The accuracy drops by less than one percentage point for all ensembles. Although the differences are small, the RNN-LSTM and CNN RNN-LSTM ensembles are even less affected by lexical substitutions than the CNN ensemble. By only modifying the questions, we have likely reduced their lexical overlap with the answer candidates and the plots. The robustness of the models against this attack can probably be attributed to the pretrained GloVe embeddings, which allow it to generalize for semantically equivalent lexical choices. Stronger attacks involving substitutions with more infrequent words that do not appear in the pretrained embeddings could show the limitation of the models in this respect. We leave the automatic generation of further-reaching adversarial examples based on paraphrases to future work.

---

[7]We only substituted with words contained in the pretrained GloVe embeddings used by the models to avoid introducing unknown words. Even though we did not restrict the substitutes to words from the training set vocabulary, it turned out that all selected words and multiword expressions were indeed contained in the training set vocabulary already, except for the synonym *buddy* for *friend*.

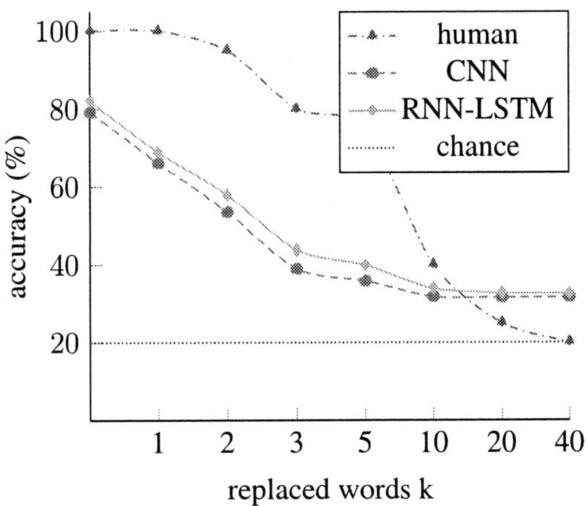

Figure 3: Adversarial accuracies on the validation set under the word-level white-box attack based on word exchange. k is the number of words that are modified in the plot sentence with most attention (average accuracies over nine models). Human evaluation is based on 20 randomly sampled questions with plots attacked for a single CNN model (single annotator, one of the authors of this paper).

5.2 Word-level White-box Attack

We performed a word-level white-box adversarial attack in which we used the models' internal attention distributions to explicitly target the plot words they base their decision on. More precisely, in this experiment we leveraged the models' sentence-level attention distribution to find the plot sentence it gave most weight to conditioned on the correct answer. In this sentence, the k words that received most attention were then exchanged by randomly chosen words from the MovieQA vocabulary.

As Figure 3 reveals, already modifying the single most important word in the most important sentence has a large effect on the average performance of both the CNN and RNN-LSTM models. For increasing k, the RNN-LSTM versions appeared to be a bit more robust against the attack, but for $k \geq 10$ the difference shrinks and the accuracy of both models drops to only about 30%. This experiment shows that manipulating the most relevant plot information by removing important words makes the model fail quickly, since it is no longer able to draw correct conclusions for the questions without the necessary plot context. Although the human annotator proved more robust against this attack for a small number of replaced words, increasing k beyond five showed the same drastic decline in performance.

Systems	Orig.	*AddC*	*AddQ*	*AddQA*
Without optimization				
CNN	76.87	76.67	76.66	76.33
RNN-LSTM	81.11	81.11	81.05	81.05
After two optimization epochs				
CNN	N/A	73.38	57.39	13.61
RNN-LSTM	N/A	79.94	68.05	23.22

Table 4: Adversarial accuracies on 200 random validation questions under the sentence-level black-box attacks (averaged results of nine models).

5.3 Sentence-level Black-box Attacks

In order to find out to which extent our models are susceptible to distracting information added to the plot, we adapt the *AddAny* attack by Jia and Liang (2017) originally designed for the SQuAD reading comprehension dataset. This adversarial attack consists of adding a distractor sentence s at the end of the plot, regardless of grammaticality. The word sequence $s = w_1 w_2 \ldots w_{10}$ is initialized by ten common English words. Then each word is greedily changed from a pool of 20 random common words (*AddC*) to minimize the model's confidence score for the correct answer. We refer the reader to Jia and Liang (2017) for the full details of this attack. Likewise we generate adversarial sentences using a pool of ten random common words for each w_i in conjunction with all question words (*AddQ*) or additionally the words from all incorrect answer candidates (*AddQA*). While these attacks do not take any particular measures to prevent the added sentence from contradicting the correct answer, this is very unlikely given the ungrammatical nature of the generated word sequences.

The first two rows in Table 4 show the effect of appending a random sentence to the plot.[8] The impact on performance is fairly small indicating the robustness of both models. However, after only two epochs of optimizing the selected words in the added sentence, the performance drops markedly under all variants of the sentence-level black-box attacks as displayed in the two bottom rows of Table 4. While composing the sentence of just common English words (*AddC*) does not affect the models too much, adding words from the question

---

[8]As this attack is computationally very expensive we only ran it on a random subset of 200 validation questions for two optimization epochs of the distractor sentence.

Evaluated systems	Attack optimized for	
	CNN	RNN-LSTM
CNN	13.61	21.50
RNN-LSTM	22.06	23.22

Table 5: *AddQA* attack results when testing models on adversarial examples optimized to fool another model (averaged results of nine models).

Systems	Average	Ensemble
CNN	31.59	32.07
RNN-LSTM	32.61	32.17

Table 6: Adversarial accuracies on the validation set under the sentence-level white-box attack based on removal of the plot sentence with highest attention (averaged results of nine models).

and incorrect answers (*AddQA*) is most detrimental and causes both models to perform at or even below chance level. The models' performance under *AddQ*, where the distractor sentence does not contain answer candidate words, is much higher than under *AddQA*. We observe that the models can be easily distracted by adding a single sequence of significant words, even though it bears no semantic relation to the rest of the plot. This suggests that both models heavily rely on the content of the provided answer candidates and might just perform matching of learned patterns to select the right answer.

Another observation is that the RNN-LSTM models outperform the CNN models by a large margin under all attacks. The stronger the attack, the larger is the performance gap, indicating that RNNs depend less on pattern matching and are less prone to this kind of attack. Figure 5 and 6 in the appendix provide an example of the sentence and word attention distributions of a CNN model before and after the *AddQA* attack.

To test the transferability of the adversarial examples across models, we test the CNN models on the adversarial examples optimized to fool the RNN models and vice versa. As Table 5 shows, the performance of both models is degraded to the same level independent of the model the attack was optimized for. This suggests that both models suffer from similar weaknesses.

A straightforward way to try to improve the models' robustness against adversarial attacks is to mix some adversarial examples into the training data. Jia and Liang (2017) evaluated this for the *AddAny* attack on SQuAD and found that training on a mix of adversarial and original samples indeed improves the performance with respect to this specific adversarial attack. Yet a slight change of the attack, e.g. adding the distracting sentence as first instead of last sentence, made the adversarially-trained models to fail almost as badly as without adversarial training. Therefore,

we argue that it is more promising to look for general improvements of the model than training on adversarial examples generated by a specific attack.

5.4 Sentence-level White-box Attack

Instead of modifying the words in the sentence we also attempted to attack the model by removing the whole plot sentence with the highest attention. In this experiment, we wanted to test (1) if the model really focuses on the most important sentence, so it would become more difficult to answer the question, and (2) if the model is able to pick up more subtle cues or perform answer elimination to still be able to infer the correct answer with some confidence. As can be seen from Table 6, the accuracy decreases dramatically for both models by removing only one plot sentence. This proves that the model indeed focuses on the correct sentence where the hint to answer a question is given. These results correspond to those of the white-box attack at word level with a large number k of modified words. For the remaining 30% of correctly answered questions we observed that sometimes the models still were able to answer correctly because of the context information provided in other plot sentences.

We also measured human performance under this attack on 20 randomly sampled questions on distinct plots, where the sentence containing the answer information was removed. A single annotator (one of the authors of this paper) achieved 55% accuracy on this task, which is way above chance level and the models' performance. The human reported to be able to answer nine questions with reasonable confidence by deducing from other information distributed across the plots; two answers were correct by guessing. Answering the questions under this attack took a lot of time and effort. This highlights the weakness of the model to give answers in more complex scenarios where the answer is less obvious.

6 Human vs. Machine Processing

In order to gain insights how to further improve machine reading comprehension, we performed a case study in which a human was asked to answer difficult questions that none of 11 CNN or RNN-LSTM models solved correctly. The human evaluator obtained the plots and the questions with the corresponding five answer candidates; having access to the information in the same manner as the models. There are clear motifs in the type of reasoning and logic required, inherent to human cognition. In this light, we aim at inferring the gap between the model's and human cognitive information processing to identify problems followed by potential solutions.

Since we were especially interested in getting insights on human strategies for the cases where our models failed, 50 difficult questions of the CNN models in the validation set were analyzed by a human evaluator. All of the questions were correctly answered by the human evaluator noticing several key postulates: textual entailment, choice by elimination, referential knowledge and their combination (Hummel and Holyoak, 2005).

Textual entailment is required to solve 60% of the questions, such as the question *"What do Matt, Steve, and Andrew record themselves doing weeks after their experience in the woods?"* with the relevant sentence *"Weeks later, Andrew, Matt, and Steve record themselves as they display telekinetic abilities, but begin bleeding from their noses when they overexert themselves"*. The human predicts the correct answer, *"Moving objects with their mind"*, based on world knowledge of the word *telekinetic*. A further example in this regard is the question *"Do the robbers take people in the bank as hostage?"* with the relevant sentence *"They seize control of a Manhattan bank and take the employees and patrons hostage."* The human picks the correct answer *"Yes, they do"*, as *people in the bank* is a hypernym of *employees* and *patrons* in this context. Lacking notion of these semantic relations, the model answers incorrectly.

The process of elimination and heuristics proved essential to solve 44% of the questions. One example is *"Where is New Penzance located?"* with the relevant sentence *"In September 1965, on a New England island called New Penzance, 12-year-old orphan Sam Shakusky is attending Camp Ivanhoe [...]"*. The human could not infer the answer *"Off the coast of North Carolina"* from reading the plot alone, as this region is not inherently known to be associated with New England, the location mentioned in the plot. However, by using the process of elimination and heuristics, the annotator was able to deduce the likely answer with the certainty that the other candidates are less likely correct. Additionally, with the ranking of keywords, humans can infer the correct answer in examples such as the question *"What kind of classes does Toula take up?"*, with the relevant sentence *"After some persuasion by his wife, Maria [...], Gus reluctantly permits Toula to begin taking computer classes at a local community college [...]"*. In this case, the human identified the keywords *classes* and *Toula*. The word *classes* obtains a higher ranking as it appears in three of the five possible answers. Ultimately, the correct prediction was made using ranking and the main keyword to find the correct answer, *"Computer classes"*.

Referential knowledge is presumed in 36% of the questions, e.g. in the question *"What does Stigman do with the money?"* with the relevant sentence *"After the heist, Stigman follows orders to betray Trench and escape with the money, managing to pull his gun right as Trench is about to pull his own"*. The human chooses the correct answer *"He takes it"*, however the models select either *"He splits it with Trench"* or *"He leaves it in the vault"*. When analyzing the plot, we can see that the two pronouns, *He* and *it*, are ambiguous to the models but clear to the human, leading to incorrect model predictions. The variance is due to the notion that humans have the ability to understand the referents from the plot. Another example where lack of referential knowledge effects the models' performances, but not the human, can be observed with the question *"What happens to any human who is encountered in Narnia?"* with the relevant sentence *"If a human is encountered they are to be brought to her"*. The human is able to select the correct answer, *"They are to be brought to the White Witch"*, even though the plot refers to the character by the pronoun *her*.

Furthermore, it is apparent that many questions expect a combination of various reasoning skills. The question *"What is Xavier's mutant ability?"* with the relevant sentence *"Present are Lehnsherr, now known as Magneto, and the telepathic Professor Charles Xavier, who privately discuss their differing views on the relationship between humans and mutants*", depicts this phenomena. The human reports that she utilized the keywords *Xavier*, *mutant* and *ability*, raking *Xavier* more predominantly. By identifying *Professor Charles Xavier* in the plot as referent of the most important keyword, she could eliminate the incorrect answers.

The human evaluator also conducted an extensive comparison of the baseline word-level models with the hierarchical CNN models. In particular, she looked at those questions where the performance of both model types differed most (in terms of the number of models out of 11 that solved the question correctly). There are 101 validation questions which the majority of hierarchical CNN models solved correctly but only a minority (at least six less) word-level models did so. These were compared to the 28 validation questions on which the word-level models outperformed the hierarchical ones.

No prevailing pattern could be identified for the few instances where the word-level models did better than the hierarchical ones. Yet, we found some evidence that the hierarchical models seem to do better for questions requiring matching longer answer candidates and handling lexical variation. An example for such a more complex question is "*What happens to Deon in the end?*". The relevant plot sentence is "*He then transfers the dying Deon's consciousness into a spare robot through the modified MOOSE helmet*", and the correct answer "*His consciousness is transferred into a robot*". All answer candidates consist of at least five words; the lexical overlap between the question and correct answer with the plot sentence is just {*into, a, robot*}. While only two baseline models identify the correct answer, all but one of the hierarchical models do so.

Additionally, among the 101 questions where the hierarchical models do far better than the word-level models there are only very few (18) questions where none of the word-level models predicted the correct answer. It seems to be the case that the hierarchical structure helps the model to gain confidence, causing more models to make the correct prediction. An example for this is the question "*What does Lucius tell Harry?*, where the relevant sentence is "*Lucius reveals that Harry only saw a dream of Sirius being tortured; it was a method to lure Harry into the Death Eaters' grasp, not an actual situation.*, and the correct answer is "*His vision of Sirius being tortured was a dream used to lure Harry to the Death* . The majority of the word-level models predicted an incorrect answer "*His vision of Sirius being tortured was true*, and only five of them selected the correct answer. In contrast, all hierarchical models solved this question correctly.

The same comparison was conducted between the hierarchical CNN and RNN-LSTM models. Although there are improvements, which indicate that sequential processing is better suited for QA tasks, the RNN-LSTM models exhibit the same fundamental drawbacks. They suffer from co-reference errors, lack the entailment ability, and are inefficient at keyword elimination. This observation reveals the fundamental weaknesses of our proposed network architecture and indicates directions for future improvements.

7   Conclusion

We proposed a machine reading comprehension model based on the compare-aggregate framework with a hierarchical attention structure that achieves state-of-the-art results on the MovieQA question answering dataset, greatly outperforming previous models. Then, we explored the limitations of our models and the behavioral difference between CNNs and RNN-LSTMs with adversarial examples generated at different linguistic levels (word vs. sentence level) and from different adversary's knowledge (black-box vs. white-box). In general, RNN-LSTM models outperformed CNN models, but our results for sentence-level black-box attacks indicate they might share the same weaknesses.

Finally, our intensive analysis on the differences between the model and human inference suggest that both models seem to learn matching patterns to select the right answer rather than performing plausible inferences as humans do. The results of these studies also imply that other human like processing mechanism such as referential relations, implicit real world knowledge, i.e., entailment, and answer by elimination via ranking plausibility (Hummel and Holyoak, 2005) should be integrated in the system to further advance machine reading comprehension.

References

Dzmitry Bahdanau, Kyunghyun Cho, and Yoshua Bengio. 2014. Neural machine translation by jointly learning to align and translate. *arXiv preprint arXiv:1409.0473*.

Yoshua Bengio, Réjean Ducharme, Pascal Vincent, and Christian Jauvin. 2003. A neural probabilistic language model. *Journal of machine learning research*, 3(Feb):1137–1155.

Danqi Chen, Jason Bolton, and Christopher D Manning. 2016. A thorough examination of the cnn/daily mail reading comprehension task. *arXiv preprint arXiv:1606.02858*.

Ronan Collobert and Jason Weston. 2008. A Unified Architecture for Natural Language Processing: Deep Neural Networks with Multitask Learning. In *Proceedings of the 25th International Conference on Machine Learning*, ICML '08, New York, New York, USA. ACM.

Ronan Collobert, Jason Weston, Léon Bottou, Michael Karlen, Koray Kavukcuoglu, and Pavel Kuksa. 2011. Natural language processing (almost) from scratch. *Journal of Machine Learning Research*, 12(Aug):2493–2537.

Li Deng and John C Platt. 2014. Ensemble deep learning for speech recognition. In *Fifteenth Annual Conference of the International Speech Communication Association*.

Daria Dzendzik, Carl Vogel, and Qun Liu. 2017. Who framed roger rabbit? multiple choice questions answering about movie plot.

Jeffrey L Elman. 1990. Finding Structure in Time. *Cognitive science*, 14(2).

Gerd Gigerenzer and Wolfgang Gaissmaier. 2011. Heuristic decision making. *Annual review of psychology*, 62:451–482.

Xavier Glorot and Yoshua Bengio. 2010. Understanding the difficulty of training deep feedforward neural networks. In *Proceedings of the Thirteenth International Conference on Artificial Intelligence and Statistics*, volume 9 of *Proceedings of Machine Learning Research*, pages 249–256, Chia Laguna Resort, Sardinia, Italy. PMLR.

Ian Goodfellow, Jonathon Shlens, and Christian Szegedy. 2015. Explaining and harnessing adversarial examples. In *International Conference on Learning Representations*.

Ian J Goodfellow, Jonathon Shlens, and Christian Szegedy. 2014. Explaining and harnessing adversarial examples. *arXiv preprint arXiv:1412.6572*.

Geoffrey Hinton, Li Deng, Dong Yu, George E Dahl, Abdel-rahman Mohamed, Navdeep Jaitly, Andrew Senior, Vincent Vanhoucke, Patrick Nguyen, Tara N Sainath, et al. 2012. Deep neural networks for acoustic modeling in speech recognition: The shared views of four research groups. *IEEE Signal Processing Magazine*, 29(6):82–97.

Sepp Hochreiter and Jürgen Schmidhuber. 1997. Long Short-Term Memory. *Neural Computation*, 9(8).

Baotian Hu, Zhengdong Lu, Hang Li, and Qingcai Chen. 2014. Convolutional neural network architectures for matching natural language sentences. In *Advances in neural information processing systems*, pages 2042–2050.

John E Hummel and Keith J Holyoak. 2005. Relational reasoning in a neurally plausible cognitive architecture: An overview of the lisa project. *Current Directions in Psychological Science*, 14(3):153–157.

Mohit Iyyer, John Wieting, Kevin Gimpel, and Luke Zettlemoyer. 2018. Adversarial example generation with syntactically controlled paraphrase networks. *arXiv preprint arXiv:1804.06059*.

Robin Jia and Percy Liang. 2017. Adversarial examples for evaluating reading comprehension systems. In *Proceedings of the 2017 Conference on Empirical Methods in Natural Language Processing*, pages 2021–2031.

Yoon Kim. 2014. Convolutional neural networks for sentence classification. In *Proceedings of the 2014 Conference on Empirical Methods in Natural Language Processing (EMNLP)*, pages 1746–1751.

Alex Krizhevsky, Ilya Sutskever, and Geoffrey E Hinton. 2012. Imagenet classification with deep convolutional neural networks. In *Advances in neural information processing systems*, pages 1097–1105.

Yann LeCun, Bernhard E Boser, John S Denker, Donnie Henderson, Richard E Howard, Wayne E Hubbard, and Lawrence D Jackel. 1990. Handwritten digit recognition with a back-propagation network. In *Advances in neural information processing systems*, pages 396–404.

Tzu-Chien Liu, Yu-Hsueh Wu, and Hung-yi Lee. 2017. Attention-based CNN matching net. *CoRR*, abs/1709.05036.

Thang Luong, Hieu Pham, and Christopher D. Manning. 2015. Effective approaches to attention-based neural machine translation. In *Proceedings of the 2015 Conference on Empirical Methods in Natural Language Processing, EMNLP 2015, Lisbon, Portugal, September 17-21, 2015*, pages 1412–1421.

Quinn McNemar. 1947. Note on the sampling error of the difference between correlated proportions or percentages. *Psychometrika*, 12(2):153–157.

Tomas Mikolov, Kai Chen, Greg Corrado, and Jeffrey Dean. 2013. Efficient Estimation of Word Representations in Vector Space. *CoRR*, abs/1301.3781.

Tomáš Mikolov, Martin Karafiát, Lukáš Burget, Jan Černocký, and Sanjeev Khudanpur. 2010. Recurrent neural network based language model. In *Eleventh Annual Conference of the International Speech Communication Association*.

Jeffrey Pennington, Richard Socher, and Christopher D. Manning. 2014. Glove: Global vectors for word representation. In *Empirical Methods in Natural Language Processing (EMNLP)*, pages 1532–1543.

Pranav Rajpurkar, Jian Zhang, Konstantin Lopyrev, and Percy Liang. 2016. Squad: 100,000+ questions for machine comprehension of text. In *Proceedings of the 2016 Conference on Empirical Methods in Natural Language Processing*, pages 2383–2392. Association for Computational Linguistics.

Ivan Sanchez, Jeff Mitchell, and Sebastian Riedel. 2018. Behavior analysis of nli models: Uncovering the influence of three factors on robustness. In *Proceedings of the 2018 Conference of the North American Chapter of the Association for Computational Linguistics: Human Language Technologies, Volume 1 (Long Papers)*, volume 1, pages 1975–1985.

Alessandro Sordoni, Yoshua Bengio, Hossein Vahabi, Christina Lioma, Jakob Grue Simonsen, and Jian-Yun Nie. 2015. A hierarchical recurrent encoder-decoder for generative context-aware query suggestion. In *Proceedings of the 24th ACM International on Conference on Information and Knowledge Management*, CIKM '15.

Christian Szegedy, Wojciech Zaremba, Ilya Sutskever, Joan Bruna, Dumitru Erhan, Ian Goodfellow, and Rob Fergus. 2014. Intriguing properties of neural networks. In *International Conference on Learning Representations*.

Makarand Tapaswi, Yukun Zhu, Rainer Stiefelhagen, Antonio Torralba, Raquel Urtasun, and Sanja Fidler. 2016. Movieqa: Understanding stories in movies through question-answering. In *Proceedings of the IEEE Conference on Computer Vision and Pattern Recognition*, pages 4631–4640.

Amos Tversky. 1972. Elimination by aspects: A theory of choice. *Psychological review*, 79(4):281.

Ngoc Thang Vu, Heike Adel, Pankaj Gupta, and Hinrich Schütze. 2016. Combining recurrent and convolutional neural networks for relation classification. In *Proceedings of NAACL HLT*.

Alexander Waibel, Toshiyuki Hanazawa, Geoffrey Hinton, Kiyohiro Shikano, and Kevin J Lang. 1990. Phoneme recognition using time-delay neural networks. In *Readings in speech recognition*, pages 393–404. Elsevier.

Shuohang Wang and Jing Jiang. 2016. A compare-aggregate model for matching text sequences. *CoRR*, abs/1611.01747.

Yi Yang, Wen-tau Yih, and Christopher Meek. 2015. Wikiqa: A challenge dataset for open-domain question answering. In *Proceedings of the 2015 Conference on Empirical Methods in Natural Language Processing*, pages 2013–2018.

Zichao Yang, Diyi Yang, Chris Dyer, Xiaodong He, Alexander J. Smola, and Eduard H. Hovy. 2016. Hierarchical Attention Networks for Document Classification. In *HLT-NAACL*.

Wenpeng Yin, Katharina Kann, Mo Yu, and Hinrich Schütze. 2017. Comparative study of cnn and rnn for natural language processing. *arXiv preprint arXiv:1702.01923*.

Adams Wei Yu, David Dohan, Quoc Le, Thang Luong, Rui Zhao, and Kai Chen. 2018. Fast and accurate reading comprehension by combining self-attention and convolution. In *International Conference on Learning Representations*.

Xiaoyong Yuan, Pan He, Qile Zhu, Rajendra Rana Bhat, and Xiaolin Li. 2017. Adversarial examples: Attacks and defenses for deep learning. *arXiv preprint arXiv:1712.07107*.

Chunting Zhou, Chonglin Sun, Zhiyuan Liu, and Francis Lau. 2015. A c-lstm neural network for text classification. *arXiv preprint arXiv:1511.08630*.

Uncovering Code-Mixed Challenges: A Framework for Linguistically Driven Question Generation and Neural based Question Answering

Deepak Gupta[‡], Pabitra Lenka[†*], Asif Ekbal[‡], Pushpak Bhattacharyya[‡]
[‡]Indian Institute of Technology Patna, India
[†]International Institute of Information Technology Bhubaneswar, India
[‡]{deepak.pcs16, asif, pb}@iitp.ac.in
[†]pabitra.lenka18@gmail.com

Abstract

Existing research on question answering (QA) and comprehension reading (RC) are mainly focused on the resource-rich language like English. In recent times, there has been a rapid growth of multi-lingual contents on the web, and this has posed several challenges to the existing QA systems. Code-mixing is one such challenge that makes the task even more complex. In this paper, we propose a linguistically motivated technique for code-mixed question generation (CMQG) and a neural network based architecture for code-mixed question answering (CMQA). For evaluation, we manually create the code-mixed questions for Hindi-English language pair. In order to show the effectiveness of our neural network based CMQA technique, we utilize two benchmark datasets, *viz.* SQuAD and MMQA. Experiments show that our proposed model achieves encouraging performance on CMQG and CMQA.

1 Introduction

The people who are multilingual in nature often switch back and forth between their native languages and the foreign (popular) languages to express themselves on the web. This is very common nowadays, particularly when people express their opinions (or making any communication) through various social media platforms. This phenomenon of embedding the morphemes, words, phrases, etc. of one language into another is popularly termed as code-mixing (CM) (Myers-Scotton, 1997, 2002). The recent study (Safran, 2015) has uncovered that users frequently use question patterns, namely 'how' (38%), 'why' (24%), 'where' (15%), 'what' (11%), and 'which' (12%) in their queries as opposed to a 'statement query'.

Presently, the search engines have become intelligent and are capable enough to provide precise answer to a natural language query/question[1].Several virtual assistants such as Siri, Cortana, Alexa, Google Assistant, etc are also equipped with these facilities. However, these search engines and virtual assistants are efficient only in handling the queries written in English. Let us consider the following two representations (English and code-mixed) of the same question.
(i) **Q:** *"Who is the foreign secretary of USA?"*
(ii) **Q:** *"USA **ke** foreign secretary **koun hai?"***
(Trans:"Who is the foreign secretary of USA?")
Search engines are able to provide the exact answer to the first question. It is to be noted that although both the questions are same, the search engine is unable to return the exact answer for the second question, which is code-mixed in nature. It rather returns the top-most relevant web pages.

In this paper, we propose a framework for code-mixed question generation (CMQG) as well as code-mixed question answering (CMQA) involving English and Hindi. Firstly, we propose a linguistically motivated technique for generating the code-mixed questions. We followed this approach as we did not have access to any labeled data for code-mixed question generation. Thereafter, we propose an effective framework based on deep neural network for Code-mixed Question Answering (CMQA). In our proposed CMQA technique, we use multiple attention based recurrent units to represent the code-mixed questions and the English passages. Finally, our answer-type focused network (attentive towards the answer-type of the question being asked) extracts the answer for a given code-mixed question. We summarize our contributions as follows:
(i). We propose a linguistically motivated unsuper-

---

[*]Work carried out during the internship at IIT Patna

[1]The capability of handling factoid questions is higher than the complex questions or descriptive questions.

Proceedings of the 22nd Conference on Computational Natural Language Learning (CoNLL 2018), pages 119–130
Brussels, Belgium, October 31 - November 1, 2018. ©2018 Association for Computational Linguistics

vised algorithm for Code-mixed Question Generation (CMQG). **(ii).** We propose a bilinear attention and answer-type focused neural framework to deal with CMQA. **(iii).** We create two CMQA datasets to further explore the research on CMQA. In addition to this, we manually create a code-mixed question dataset, and subsequently a code-mixed question classification dataset. **(iv)** We provide a state-of-the-art setup to extract answers from the English passages for the corresponding code-mixed questions. The source code of our proposed systems and the datasets can be found here[2].

2 Related Work

Code-mixing refers to the mixing of more than one language in the same sentence. Creating resources and tools capable of handling code-mixed languages is more challenging in comparison to the traditional language processing activities that are concerned with only one language. In recent times, researchers have started investigating methods for creating tools and resources for various Natural Language Processing (NLP) applications involving code-mixed languages. Some of the applications include language identification (Chittaranjan et al., 2014; Barman et al., 2014), part-of-speech (PoS) tagging (Vyas et al., 2014; Jamatia et al., 2015; Gupta et al., 2017), question classification (Raghavi et al., 2015), entity extraction (Gupta et al., 2018a, 2016b), sentiment analysis (Rudra et al., 2016; Gupta et al., 2016a) etc. Developing QA system in a code-mixed scenario is, itself, very novel in the sense that there have not been very significant attempts towards this direction, except the few such as (Chandu et al., 2017). Our literature survey shows that the existing methods of question generation (general) include both rules Heilman and Smith (2010); Ali et al. (2010) and machine learning (Serban et al., 2016; Wang et al., 2017a) techniques. A joint model of question generation and answering based on sequence-to-sequence neural network model is proposed in (Wang et al., 2017a).

In recent times, there have been several studies on deep learning based reading comprehension/ QA (Hermann et al., 2015; Cui et al., 2017; Shen et al., 2017; Wang et al., 2017b; Gupta et al., 2018c; Wang and Jiang, 2016; Berant et al., 2014; Maitra et al., 2018; Cheng et al., 2016; Trischler

et al., 2016). To the best of our knowledge, this is the very first attempt to automatically generate the code-mixed questions (i.e. question generation), as well as provide a robust solution by developing an end-to-end neural network model for CMQA.

3 Code-Mixed Question Generation

We focus on a code-mixed scenario involving two languages, *viz.* English and Hindi. Due to the scarcity of labeled data, we could not employ any sophisticated machine learning technique for question generation. Rather, we propose an unsupervised algorithm that automatically formulates the code-mixed questions. The algorithm makes use of several NLP components such as PoS tagger, transliteration and lexical translation. We construct Hindi-English code-mixed question from a given Hindi question. Let us consider the following three questions:

- **Q$_1$**: *What is the name of the baseball team in Seattle?*
- **Q$_2$**: सिएटल में बेसबॉल दल का नाम क्या है?
  (**Trans:** *What is the name of the baseball team in Seattle?*)
  (**Transliteration**: Seattle mai baseball dal ka naam kya hai?)
- **Q$_3$**:*Seattle mein baseball team ka naam kya hai?*
  (**Trans:** *What is the name of the baseball team in Seattle?*)

All the three questions are same but are asked in English, Hindi and the code-mixed English-Hindi languages. It can be seen that **Q$_2$** and **Q$_3$** are similar and share many *false cognates (Moss, 1992)* [(Seattle, सिएटल), (naam, नाम), (kya, क्या), (mai, में), (baseball, बेसबॉल)]. The question **Q$_3$** has the direct transliteration of the Hindi words (सिएटल $\rightarrow$ Seattle), (नाम $\rightarrow$ naam), (क्या $\rightarrow$ kya), (में $\rightarrow$ mai) and (बेसबॉल $\rightarrow$ baseball). There are some words (e.g. *'team'*) in **Q$_3$** which are the English lexical translations from Hindi. We perform a thorough study of Hindi sentences and their corresponding code-mixed Hindi-English sentences, and observe the following:

(1) Named entities (NEs) of type person (PER) remain same in both Hindi as well as the code-mixed English-Hindi (EN-HI) sentence. These NEs are only transliterated. E.g.
Hindi: महात्मा गांधी का जन्म कब हुआ था?
(**Trans:** When was <u>Mahatma Gandhi</u> born?)

Code-Mixed (EN-HI): *Mahatma Gandhi ka birth kab hua tha?*
The NE *Mahatma Gandhi* of type 'PER' is transliterated in code-mixed sentence.

(2) NEs of type location (LOC) and organization (ORG) present in a Hindi sentence are replaced with their best lexical translations in English. For example:
Hindi: लखनऊ दिल्ली से कितनी दूर है?
(**Trans:** How far is Lucknow is from Delhi?)
Code-Mixed (EN-HI): *Lucknow New Delhi se kitni dur hai?*
The 'PER' type NEs are only transliterated as the names do not have any variation in Hindi or English. For example, सचिन तेंदुलकर (**Trans:** Sachin Tendulkar) → 'Sachin Tendulkar'. It is just needed to be written in Roman script. However, same does not hold for 'LOC' and 'ORG'. For example, transliterating भारतीय अंतरिक्ष अनुसंधान संगठन (**Trans:** Indian Space Research Organisation) → 'Bharatiya Antriksh Anushandhan Sangathan' is incorrect.

(3) PoS tags such as singular or plural noun (NN), proper noun (NNP), spatio-temporal noun (NST) and adjective (JJ) present in a Hindi sentence are often replaced with their context aware lexical translation in English. For example:
Hindi: व्यक्तियों को उनकी रचनात्मकता के लिए कौन से अधिकार दिए जाते हैं?
(**Trans:** Which rights are given to individuals for their creativity?)
Code-Mixed (EN-HI): *Individuals ko unki creativity ke liye koun se rights diya jate hain?*

The underlined words in the Hindi sentence have noun (NN) PoS tags, therefore the corresponding words are replaced with their best lexical translations in their respective code-mixed sentence.

(4) The remaining words in the Hindi sentence are transliterated (in English) and a code-mixed EN-HI sentence is formed. For example, the remaining words of the previous Hindi sentence are transliterated (in underlines) and the code-mixed EN-HI sentence is formed.
Code-Mixed (EN-HI): *Individuals ko unki creativity ke liye koun se rights diye jate hain?*

The main challenge of automatic CMQG is to find the best lexical translation which suits the most in the given context of the particular question. Let us consider the various lexical translation choices $tr_i = \{tr_{(i,\,1)}, tr_{(i,\,2)}, \ldots, tr_{(i,\,l_i)}\}$ for the token (t_i), where l_i is the number of lexical translations available for the token t_i. The lexical translation disambiguation algorithm selects the most probable lexical translation of token t_i from a set of l_i possible translations. We generate a query by adding the previous token t_{i-1} and the next token t_{i+1} with the token of interest designated by t_i. The context within a query provides important clues for choosing the right transliteration of a given query word. For example, for a query $S =\{$शहर, पूर्व, स्कॉटलैंड$\}$ (**Trans:** {city, east, Scotland}), where the word 'पूर्व' is the word in interest for which the most probable lexical translation needs to be identified from the list $\{BC, East\}$. Here, based on the context, we can see that the choice of translation for the word 'पूर्व' is *'east'* since the combinations {*city, east*} and {*east, Scotland*} are more likely to co-occur in the corpus than {*city, BC*} and {*BC, Scotland*}. We follow the iterative disambiguation algorithm (Monz and Dorr, 2005) which judges a pair of items to gather partial evidences for the likelihood of a translation in a given context. An occurrence graph is constructed using the query term S and the translation set TR, such that the translation candidates of different query terms are connected with the associated Dice Co-efficient weight between them. At the same time, it is also ensured that there should not be any edge between the different translation candidates of the same query term. We initialize each translation candidate with equal likelihood of a translation. After initialization, the weight of each translation candidate is iteratively updated using the weights of the translation candidate linked to it and the weight of the link connecting them. At the end of the iteration the weight of each translation candidate is normalized to ensure that these all sum up to 1.

4   Proposed Approach for CMQA

Given a code-mixed question Q with tokens $\{q_1, q_2 \ldots, q_m\}$ and an English passage P having tokens $\{p_1, p_2 \ldots, p_n\}$, where m and n are the number of tokens in the question and the passage, respectively. The task is to identify answer A with tokens $\{p_i, p_{i+1} \ldots, p_j\}$ of length $j - i + 1$, where $1 \leq i \leq n$ and $i \leq j \leq n$.
Each model component is described below:

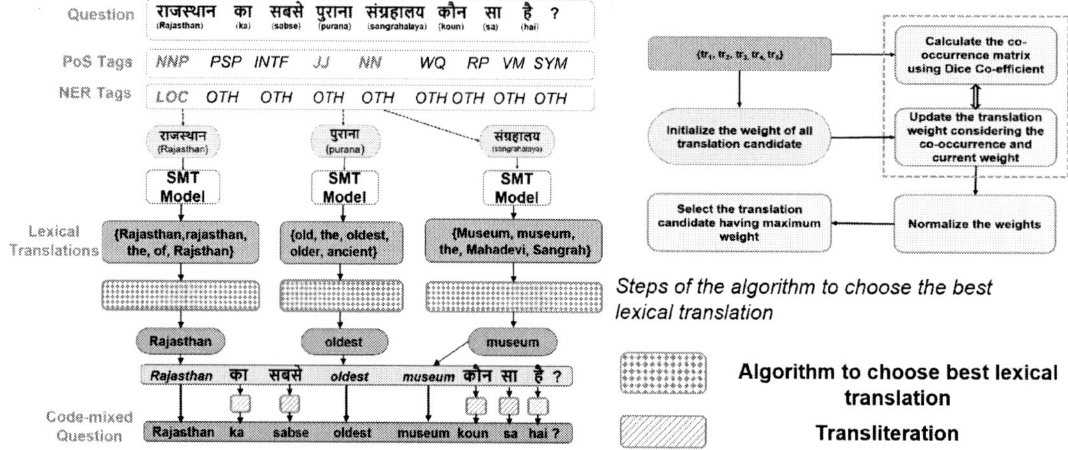

Figure 1: Illustrations of the proposed CMQG. The English transliterations are given in the bracket. The right part of the image shows the basic steps to select the best lexical translation. The red color tags in PoS and NER tags list denote the tags of the words that qualify to the next step.

4.1 Token and Sequence Encoding

From the given code-mixed question Q and passage P, we first obtain the respective token-level embeddings $\{x_t^Q\}_{t=1}^m$ and $\{x_t^P\}_{t=1}^n$ from the pre-trained word embedding matrix. Due to the code-mixed nature, our model faces the out-of-vocabulary (OOV) word issue. To tackle this, we adopt character-level embedding to represent each token of the question and passage. These are denoted by $\{c_t^Q\}_{t=1}^m$ and $\{c_t^P\}_{t=1}^n$ for question and passage, respectively. The character-level embeddings are generated by taking the final hidden states of a bi-directional gated recurrent units (Bi-GRU) (Chung et al., 2014) applied to the character embedding of the tokens. The final representations of each token u_t^Q and u_t^P of question and passage, respectively, are obtained through the Bi-GRU as follows:

$$u_t^Q = \text{Bi-GRU}(u_{t-1}^Q, [x_t^Q \oplus c_t^Q])$$
$$u_t^P = \text{Bi-GRU}(u_{t-1}^P, [x_t^P \oplus c_t^P]) \quad (1)$$

where, $\oplus$ is the concatenation operator. In order to encode the token sequence, we apply convolution followed by Bi-GRU operation as follows: First, the convolution operation is performed on the zero-padded sequence $\bar{u}^P$ over the passage sequence u^P, where $\bar{u}_t^P \in \mathbb{R}^d$. A set of k filters $F \in \mathbb{R}^{k \times l \times d}$, is applied to the sequence. We obtain the convoluted features c_t^P at given time t for $t = 1, 2, \ldots, n$ by the following formula.

$$c_t^P = tanh(F[\bar{u}_{t-\frac{l-1}{2}}^P \ldots \bar{u}_t^P \ldots \bar{u}_{t+\frac{l-1}{2}}^P]) \quad (2)$$

The feature vector $\bar{C}^P = [\bar{c}_1^P, \bar{c}_2^P \ldots \bar{c}_n^P]$ is generated by applying the max pooling on each element c_t^P of C^P. This sequence of convolution feature vector $\bar{C}^P$ is passed through a Bi-GRU network. The same convolution operations are also performed over the question sequence u^Q and the convolution feature vector $\bar{C}^Q$ is obtained. Similar to e.q. 1, we compute Bi-GRU outputs v_t^P (v_t^Q) by giving the inputs v_{t-1}^P (v_{t-1}^Q) and $\bar{c}_t^P$ ($\bar{c}_t^Q$). We represent the question and passage representation matrix by $V^Q \in \mathbb{R}^{m \times h}$ and $V^P \in \mathbb{R}^{n \times h}$, respectively, where h is the number of hidden units of the Bi-GRUs.

4.2 Question-aware Passage Encoding

When a single passage contains the answer of two or more than two different questions then the passage encoding obtained from the previous layer (c.f. section 4.1) will not be effective enough to provide the answer of each question. It is because the obtained passage encoding does not take into account the question information. In this layer first we compute an attention matrix $M \in \mathbb{R}^{n \times m}$ as follows:

$$M_{i, j} = 1/(1 + dist(V^P[i, :], V^Q[j, :])) \quad (3)$$

$M_{i, j}$ is the similarity score between the ith element of the passage encoding V^P and j^{th} element of the question encoding V^Q. The $dist(x, y)$ function is an euclidean distance[3] between x and y.

____
[3]We observe that e.q. 3 performs well, when $dist$ is an euclidean distance.

122

Thereafter, the normalization of element $M_{i,j}$ of matrix M is performed with respect to the $i^t h$ row.

$$\overline{M}_{i,\,j} = \frac{M_{i,\,j}}{\sum_{k=0}^{m} M_{i,\,k}} \tag{4}$$

Intuitively, it calculates the relevance of a word in the given passage with each word in the question. We compute the question vector $Q \in \mathbb{R}^{n \times h}$ corresponding to all the words in the passage as $Q = \overline{M} \times V^Q$. Each row t of the question vector Q denotes the encoding of the passage word t with respect to all the words in the question. The question aware passage encoding will be computed by the word-level concatenation of the passage encoding v_t^P and question vector of the tth row Q_t. More formally, the question aware passage encoding a_t of the word at time t will be $a_t = v_t^P \oplus Q_t$. Finally, we apply a Bi-GRU to encode the question aware information over time. It is computed as follows:

$$s_t = \text{Bi-GRU}(s_{t-1}, a_t) \tag{5}$$

We can represent the question aware passage encoding matrix as $S \in \mathbb{R}^{n \times h}$.

4.3 Bilinear Attention on Passage

Question aware passage encoding accounts the relevance of the words in a question with the given passage. If the answer spans more than one token (i.e. a multi-word tokens), it is important to compute the relevance between the constituents of the multi-word tokens. We calculate the bilinear attention matrix $B \in \mathbb{R}^{n \times n}$ on question aware passage encoding $S \in \mathbb{R}^{n \times h}$ as follows:

$$B = S \times \mathbf{W_b} \times S^T \tag{6}$$

where, $\mathbf{W_b} \in \mathbb{R}^{h \times h}$ is a bilinear weight matrix. Similar to e.q. 4, normalization is performed on B, and the normalized attention matrix is denoted as $\overline{B}$. The element $\overline{B}_{i,j}$ is the measure of relevance between the ith and j^{th} words of the passage. Similar to the question vector Q, we calculate the passage vector $R \in \mathbb{R}^{n \times h}$ as computed on $R = \overline{B} \times S$. The concatenation (word wise) of question dependent passage encoding vector s_t and passage vector r_t is performed to obtain $\overline{R}_t$ and form the matrix $\overline{R} \in \mathbb{R}^{n \times 2h}$. Similar to Wang et al. (2017b), we introduce a gating mechanism to control the impact of $\overline{R}$ and denote it as the $G \in \mathbb{R}^{n \in 2h}$. In order to identify the start and end indices of the answer from the passage, we employ two Bi-GRU with input as G. Similar to e.q. 1, output of the Bi-GRUs is computed as $P_s \in \mathbb{R}^{n \times h}$ and $P_e \in \mathbb{R}^{n \times h}$.

4.4 Answer-type Focused Answer Extraction

The answer-type of a question provides the clues to detect the correct answer from the passage. Consider a code-mixed question **Q:** *Kaun sa Portuguese player, Spanish club Real Madrid ke liye as a forward player khelta hai?* (**Trans:** *Which Portuguese player plays as a forward for Spanish club Real Madrid?*.) The answer-type of the question Q is 'person'. Even though the network has the capacity to capture this information up to a certain degree, it would be better if the model takes into account this information in advance while selecting the answer span. Li and Roth (2002) proposed a hierarchical question classification based on the answer-type of a question. Based on the coarse and fine classes of Li and Roth (2002), we train two separate answer-type detection networks on the Text REtrieval Conference (TREC) question classification dataset[4]. First, we translate[5] 5952 TREC English questions into Hindi and thereafter transform the Hindi questions into the code-mixed questions by using our proposed CMQG algorithm. We train the answer-type detection network with code-mixed questions and their associated labels using the technique as discussed in (Gupta et al., 2018b). The network learns the encoding of coarse ($C_{at} \in \mathbb{R}^h$) and fine class ($F_{at} \in \mathbb{R}^h$) of answer-types obtained from the answer-type detection network. The attention matrix M calculated in e.q. 3 undergoes the max-pooling over the columns to capture the most relevant parts of the question.

$$Q_p^j = \text{max-pool}(M[:,j]) \tag{7}$$

The max-pooled representation of question and answer-type representation are concatenated in the following way:

$$Q_f = Q_p.V^P \oplus C_{at} \oplus F_{at} \tag{8}$$

A feed-forward neural network with *tanh* activation function is used to obtain the final output $\overline{Q}_f \in \mathbb{R}^h$. The probability distribution of the beginning of answer A_s and the end of answer A_e is computed as:

$$\begin{aligned} prob(A_s) &= \text{softmax}(\overline{Q}_f \times P_s) \\ prob(A_e) &= \text{softmax}(\overline{Q}_f \times P_e) \end{aligned} \tag{9}$$

---

[4]http://cogcomp.org/Data/QA/QC/
[5]We use Google Translate because of its better performance on EN $\rightarrow$ HI translation.

# of CM Questions	5,535	# of Hindi Words	37,300
# of words	59,733	Average # of Hindi Words/Question	6.7389
Average Length of CM Questions	10.79	# of English Words	22,433
Code-Mixing Index (CMI) Score	37.14	Average # of English Words/Question	4.05

Table 1: Statistics of manually formulated CM questions

Datasets	Train	Dev	Test	Total
CM-SQuAD	16,632	2,080	2,080	20,792
CM-MMQA	2,746	341	341	3,428

Table 2: Detailed statistics (# of question-passage pairs) of the derived CMQA datasets

To train the network, we minimize the sum of the negative log probabilities of the ground truth start and end position by the predicted probability distributions.

5 Datasets and Experiments

In this section, we report the datasets and the experimental setups.

5.1 Datasets (CMQG)

For CMQG task, we require the input question to be in Hindi. We use the manually created Hindi questions obtained from the Hindi-English question answering dataset (Gupta et al., 2018b). We generate the code-mixed questions by our proposed approach (c.f. Section 3). In order to evaluate the performance of our proposed CMQG algorithm, we also manually formulate[6] the Hindi-English code-mixed questions. Details of this dataset are shown in Table 1. We compute the complexity of code-mixing using the metric, Code-mixing Index (CMI) score (Gambäck and Das, 2014). We name this code-mixed question dataset as 'HinglishQue'. We observe that our *HinglishQue* dataset has higher CMI score as compared to the FIRE[7] 2015 (CMI=11.65) and ICON[8] 2015 (5.73) CM corpus (Soumil Mandal and Das, 2018)[9]. This implies that our *HinglishQue* dataset is more complex and challenging in comparison to the other Hindi-English code mixing (CM) dataset. The CMI score of the system generated code-mixed questions is 37.22.

5.2 Datasets (CMQA)

(1) CM-SQuAD: We generate the CMQA dataset from the portion of SQuAD (Rajpurkar et al., 2016) dataset. We translate the English

questions into Hindi and use our approach of CMQG (c.f. Section 3) to transform the Hindi questions into the code-mixed questions. We manually verify the questions to ensure the quality. We use the corresponding English passage to find the answer pair of the code-mixed question. Detailed statistics of the dataset are shown in Table 2. We randomly split the dataset into training, development and test set.

(2) CM-MMQA: We experiment with a recently released multilingual QA dataset (Gupta et al., 2018b). It provides Hindi questions along with their English passages. Similar to the CM-SQuAD dataset, we create code-mixed questions and their respective answer pairs. Details of the dataset are shown in Table 2.

5.3 Experimental Setup for CMQG

The tokenization and PoS tagging are performed using the publicly available Hindi Shallow Parser[10]. The Polyglot[11] Named Entity Recognizer (NER) (Al-Rfou et al., 2015) is used for named entity recognition. The lexical translation set is obtained by the lexical translation table generated as an intermediate output of Statistical Machine Translation (SMT) training by Moses (Koehn et al., 2007) on publicly available[12] English-Hindi (EN-HI) parallel corpus (Bojar et al., 2014). We aggregate the output probability $p(e|h)$ and inverse probability $p(h|e)$ along with their associated words in both English (e) and Hindi (h) languages. We choose a threshold (5) to filter out the least probable translations. The co-occurrence weight (Dice Co-efficient) is calculated on the available[13] n-gram dataset consisting of unique $2, 86, 358$ bigrams and $3, 33, 333$ unigrams. For Devanagari (Hindi) to Roman (English) transliteration, we use the transliteration system[14] based on Ekbal et al. (2006). We evaluate

---

[6]The question formulators are the undergraduate and postgraduate students having good proficiencies in English and Hindi.

[7]http://fire.irsi.res.in/fire/2015/home

[8]http://ltrc.iiit.ac.in/icon2015/

[9]Please note that these two datasets are not related to QA

[10]http://ltrc.iiit.ac.in/showfile.php?filename=downloads/shallow_parser.php

[11]http://polyglot.readthedocs.io/en/latest/NamedEntityRecognition.html

[12]http://ufal.mff.cuni.cz/hindencorp

[13]http://norvig.com/ngrams/

[14]https://github.com/libindic/indic-trans

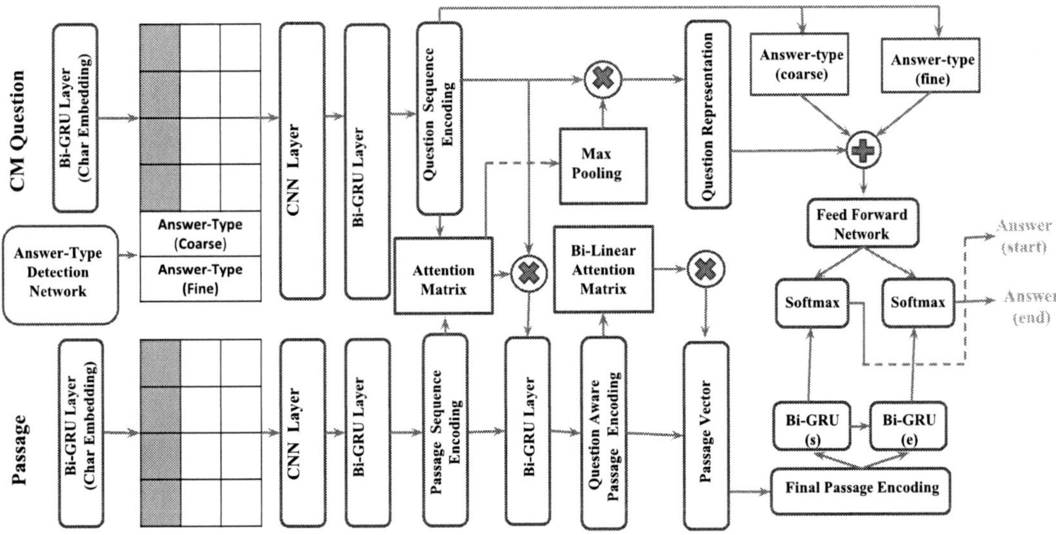

Figure 2: Proposed CMQA model architecture. The green color column denotes the character embeddings.

5.4 Experimental Setup for CMQA

CMQA datasets contain the words both in Roman script and English. For English, we use the *fastText* (Bojanowski et al., 2016) word embedding of dimension 300. We use the Hindi sentences from Bojar et al. (2014), and then transliterate it into the Roman script. These sentences are used to train the word embeddings of dimension 300 by the word embedding algorithm (Bojanowski et al., 2016). Finally, we align monolingual vectors of English and Roman words in an unified vector space using a linear transformation matrix learned by the approach as discussed in Smith et al. (2017). Other optimal hyper-parameters are set to: character embedding dimension=50, GRU hidden unit size=150, CNN filter size=150, filter size=3, 4, batch size=60, # of epochs=100, initial learning rate=0.001. Optimal values of the hyperparameters are decided based on the model performance on the development set of CM-SQuAD dataset. Adam optimizer (Kingma and Ba, 2014) is used to optimize the weights during training. For the evaluation of CMQA, we adopt the exact match (EM) and F1-score (Rajpurkar et al., 2016).

5.5 Baselines

5.5.1 Baselines (CMQG)

We portray the problem of code-mixed question generation with respect to sequence to sequence learning where the input sequence comprises of Hindi question and the output sequence is the code-mixed EN-HI question. A seq2seq with attention (Sutskever et al., 2014; Bahdanau et al., 2014) network is trained using the default parameters of Nematus (Sennrich et al., 2017). The training dataset of the pair of Hindi translated question and code-mixed questions from CM-SQuAD dataset (c.f. Section 5.2) is used for training the seq2seq network. We evaluate the network on the manually created CMQG dataset (c.f. Section 5.1).

5.5.2 Baselines (CMQA)

To compare the performance of our proposed CMQA model, we define the following baseline models.

1) IR based model: This baseline is our implementation of the *WebShodh* (Chandu et al., 2017) with improvements in some existing components. We replaced *WebShodh*'s support vector machine based (SVM) based question classification with our recurrent CNN based answer-type detection network (c.f. Section 4.4). In spite of searching the answer on the web (as *WebShodh* does), we search it within the passage. We choose the high-

Datasets →	CM-SQuAD (1)						CM-MMQA (2)			
	Dev		Test		Test (2)		Dev		Test	
Models	EM	F1	EM	F1	EM	F1	EM	F1	EM	F1
IR (Chandu et al., 2017)	5.82	9.51	5.02	8.92	-	-	5.52	9.66	6.10	10.64
BiDAF (Seo et al., 2016)	21.44	29.18	21.63	28.45	22.26	37.54	22.38	33.10	22.09	32.82
R-Net (Wang et al., 2017b)	24.17	31.12	23.76	30.74	24.47	39.15	24.27	37.33	23.72	36.86
Proposed Approach	**31.12**	**37.78**	**31.05**	**36.97**	**30.91**	**46.18**	**28.14**	**46.25**	**30.56**	**46.10**

Table 3: Performance comparison of the proposed CMQA algorithm with the IR-based and neural-based baselines. **Test (2)** refers the test set of CM-MMQA.

Models	Accuracy	Bleu	ROUGE-1	ROUGE-2	ROUGE-L
Seq2Seq	39.24	52.18	53.28	56.05	52.11
Proposed Algorithm	67.11	86.17	95.15	90.53	95.13

Table 4: Performance comparison of the proposed CMQG algorithm with *seq2seq* baseline.

est ranked answer as our final answer.

2) R-Net (Wang et al., 2017b): This is a deep neural network based comprehension reading (RC) model. We train the R-Net model with the hyperparameters as described in Wang et al. (2017b).

3) BiDAF (Seo et al., 2016): This is another state-of-the-art neural model for RC. We trained this model with the same hyperparameters as given in (Seo et al., 2016).

6 Results and Analysis

We demonstrate the evaluation results of our proposed CMQG algorithm on the *HinglishQue* dataset in Table 4. For evaluation, we employed three annotators who were instructed to assign the label (*same* or *different*) depending upon whether the system generated and manually created questions are similar or dissimilar. The agreement among the annotators was calculated by Cohen's Kappa (Cohen, 1960) coefficient, and it was found to be 92.45%. Evaluation of question generation

Model	CM-SQuAD		CM-MMQA	
Components	EM	F1	EM	F1
Proposed	31.12	37.78	28.14	46.25
(-) Convolution	29.46	36.14	26.19	43.76
(-) Bilinear Attention	26.42	33.31	25.36	41.29
(-) Answer-type Focused	28.41	35.14	26.69	42.37

Table 5: Effect of the various components of the CMQA model on the development set of CM-SQuAD and CM-MMQA dataset. **(-) X** denotes the model architecture after removal of '**X**'.

shows that our proposed CMQG algorithm performs better than the seq2seq based baseline. One reason could be the insufficient amount $(16, 632)$

of training instances and the out-of-vocabulary (only 62.35% words available in the vocab) issue. Performance improvement in our proposed model over the baseline is statistically significant as $p < 0.05$. In literature, we find only one study on English-Hindi code-mixed question classification i.e. Raghavi et al. (2015). They used only $1, 000$ code-mixed questions, and used Support Vector Machine (SVM) to classify the questions into coarse and fine-grained answer-types. They reported to achieve 63% and 45% accuracies for coarse and fine-grained answer-type detection, respectively under 5-fold cross validation setup. In contrast, we manually create $5, 535$ code-mixed questions and train a CNN model that shows 87.21% and 83.56% accuracies for coarse and fine answer types, respectively, for the 5-fold cross validation.

Results of CMQA for both the datasets are shown in Table 3. Performance of IR based baseline (Chandu et al., 2017) on both the datasets are poor. This may be because Chandu et al. (2017)'s system was mainly developed to answer pure factoid questions based only on the named entities denoting person, location and organization. However, the datasets used in this experiment have different types of answers beyond the basic factoid questions. We also perform a cross-domain experiment, where the test data of CM-MMQA is used to evaluate the system trained on CM-SQuAD. Performance improvements in our proposed model over the baselines are statistically significant as $p < 0.05$. Experiments show that the performance of CM-MMQA is better than CM-SQuAD. This might be due to the relatively smaller length passages in CM-MMQA, extracting answers from which are easier.

We perform ablation study to observe the effects of various components of the CMQA model. Results are shown in Table 5. The component convolution refers to the convolution operation per-

Sr. No.	Reference Questions	System Generated Questions
1	Maharaja Ranjit Singh ne Mandi par kab **occupy** kar liya tha?	Maharaja Ranjit Singh ne Mandi par kab *Czechoslovakia* kar liya tha?
2	Babur kaa **death** kab ho gaya tha?	Babur kaa *died* kab ho gaya tha?
3	**IMF** kaa primary purpose kya hai?	*Imef* kaa primary purpose kya hai?
4	**Demographics** kya hai?	*Population* kya hai?

Table 6: Some examples from the *HinglishQue* dataset depicting the errors occurred. The **correct** and *incorrect* words in the questions are denoted with **bold** and *italic* fonts, respectively.

formed before the Bi-GRUs in sequence encoding.

6.1 Error Analysis

We analyze the errors encountered by our CMQG and CMQA systems. The CMQG algorithm uses several NLP components such as PoS tagger, NE tagger, translation, transliteration etc. The errors occurred in these components propagate towards the final question generation. We list some of the major causes of errors with examples in Table 6. As in **(1)**, the algorithm could not find the correct lexical translation from the lexical table itself and therefore selected an irrelevant word 'Czechoslovakia' instead of 'occupy'. In **(2)** and **(4)**, the algorithm picked the words 'died' and 'population' instead of 'death' and 'demographics', respectively. It could be because the word 'died' and 'population' have higher n-gram frequencies compared to the words 'death' and 'demographics' in the n-gram corpus. In **(3)**, the system generated incorrect word ('imef') instead of 'IMF'. Here, the Hindi word 'आईएमएफ' is incorrectly tagged as 'Other' instead of 'Organization'. Thereafter, the transliteration system provides an incorrect transliteration ('imef') of the abbreviated Hindi word 'आईएमएफ' (**Trans**: IMF).

We observe that sometimes our CMQA system incorrectly predicts the answer words which are actually very close to some other word in the shared embedding space ((c.f. section 5.4), and hence gets high attention score in the bilinear attention module. For example, in this passage '...*India* was ruled by the **Bharata** clan and ...', the system predicted the answer 'India' instead of 'Bharata' (reference answer) because the word 'Bharata' is the transliteration form of भारत and भारत is the correct translation form of the word 'India'.

Our close analysis to the prediction of CM-SQuAD and CM-MMQA development data reveals that the systems suffer mostly due to the errors where the answer strings are relatively longer. The CM-MMQA dataset has some definitional questions (requires at least one-sentence long answer). We evaluate the performance on CM-MMQA dataset after removing those questions (92), and obtain the EM and F1 scores of 40.50% and 53.73%, respectively. These are much higher (28.14%, 46.25%) than the model where all the questions are considered. Due to ambiguity in selecting answers (between two candidate answers, location type answer) the system sometimes predicts incorrectly. We also observed some other types of errors which were mainly due to the context mismatch as well as long-distance dependence between the answer and the context words.

7 Conclusion

In this work, we have proposed a linguistically motivated unsupervised algorithm for CMQG and a neural framework for CMQA. We have proposed a bilinear attention and answer-type focused neural framework to deal with CMQA. We have evaluated the performance of CMQG on manually created code-mixed questions involving English and Hindi. For CMQA, we have created two CMQA datasets. Experiments show that our proposed models attain state-of-the-art performance. In the future, we would like to scale our work for other code-mixed languages.

8 Acknowledgment

Asif Ekbal acknowledges the Young Faculty Research Fellowship (YFRF), supported by Visvesvaraya PhD scheme for Electronics and IT, Ministry of Electronics and Information Technology (MeitY), Government of India, being implemented by Digital India Corporation (formerly Media Lab Asia). We would like to thank Sukanta Sen, IIT Patna for extending his support in machine translation experiment.

References

Rami Al-Rfou, Vivek Kulkarni, Bryan Perozzi, and Steven Skiena. 2015. Polyglot-NER: Massive Multilingual Named Entity Recognition. *Proceedings of the 2015 SIAM International Conference on Data Mining, Vancouver, British Columbia, Canada, April 30 - May 2, 2015.*

Husam Ali, Yllias Chali, and Sadid A Hasan. 2010. Automation of Question Generation From Sentences. In *Proceedings of QG2010: The Third Workshop on Question Generation*, pages 58–67.

Dzmitry Bahdanau, Kyunghyun Cho, and Yoshua Bengio. 2014. Neural Machine Translation by Jointly Learning to Align and Translate. *arXiv preprint arXiv:1409.0473.*

Utsab Barman, Amitava Das, Joachim Wagner, and Jennifer Foster. 2014. Code Mixing: A Challenge for Language Identification in the Language of Social Media. In *Proceedings of the First Workshop on Computational Approaches to Code Switching*, pages 13–23.

Jonathan Berant, Vivek Srikumar, Pei-Chun Chen, Abby Vander Linden, Brittany Harding, Brad Huang, Peter Clark, and Christopher D. Manning. 2014. Modeling Biological Processes for Reading Comprehension. In *Proceedings of the 2014 Conference on Empirical Methods in Natural Language Processing (EMNLP)*, pages 1499–1510, Doha, Qatar. Association for Computational Linguistics.

Piotr Bojanowski, Edouard Grave, Armand Joulin, and Tomas Mikolov. 2016. Enriching Word Vectors with Subword Information. *arXiv preprint arXiv:1607.04606.*

Ondřej Bojar, Vojtěch Diatka, Pavel Rychlý, Pavel Straňák, Vít Suchomel, Aleš Tamchyna, and Daniel Zeman. 2014. HindEnCorp - Hindi-English and Hindi-only Corpus for Machine Translation. In *Proceedings of the Ninth International Conference on Language Resources and Evaluation (LREC'14)*, Reykjavik, Iceland. European Language Resources Association (ELRA).

Khyathi Raghavi Chandu, Manoj Chinnakotla, Alan W Black, and Manish Shrivastava. 2017. WebShodh: A Code Mixed Factoid Question Answering System for Web. In *International Conference of the Cross-Language Evaluation Forum for European Languages*, pages 104–111. Springer.

Jianpeng Cheng, Li Dong, and Mirella Lapata. 2016. Long Short-Term Memory-Networks for Machine Reading. In *Proceedings of the 2016 Conference on Empirical Methods in Natural Language Processing*, pages 551–561, Austin, Texas. Association for Computational Linguistics.

Gokul Chittaranjan, Yogarshi Vyas, Kalika Bali, and Monojit Choudhury. 2014. Word-level Language Identification using CRF: Code-switching Shared Task Report of MSR India System. In *Proceedings of The First Workshop on Computational Approaches to Code Switching*, pages 73–79.

Junyoung Chung, Caglar Gulcehre, KyungHyun Cho, and Yoshua Bengio. 2014. Empirical Evaluation of Gated Recurrent Neural Networks on Sequence Modeling. *arXiv preprint arXiv:1412.3555.*

Jacob Cohen. 1960. A Coefficient of Agreement for Nominal Scales. *Educational and psychological measurement*, 20(1):37–46.

Yiming Cui, Zhipeng Chen, Si Wei, Shijin Wang, Ting Liu, and Guoping Hu. 2017. Attention-over-Attention Neural Networks for Reading Comprehension. In *Proceedings of the 55th Annual Meeting of the Association for Computational Linguistics (Volume 1: Long Papers)*, pages 593–602. Association for Computational Linguistics.

Asif Ekbal, Sudip Kumar Naskar, and Sivaji Bandyopadhyay. 2006. A Modified Joint Source-Channel Model for Transliteration. In *Proceedings of the COLING/ACL on Main conference poster sessions*, pages 191–198. Association for Computational Linguistics.

Björn Gambäck and Amitava Das. 2014. On Measuring the Complexity of Code-Mixing. In *Proceedings of the 11th International Conference on Natural Language Processing, Goa, India*, pages 1–7.

Deepak Gupta, Asif Ekbal, and Pushpak Bhattacharyya. 2018a. A Deep Neural Network based Approach for Entity Extraction in Code-Mixed Indian Social Media Text. In *Proceedings of the Eleventh International Conference on Language Resources and Evaluation (LREC 2018)*, Miyazaki, Japan. European Language Resources Association (ELRA).

Deepak Gupta, Surabhi Kumari, Asif Ekbal, and Pushpak Bhattacharyya. 2018b. MMQA: A Multi-domain Multi-lingual Question-Answering Framework for English and Hindi. In *Proceedings of the Eleventh International Conference on Language Resources and Evaluation (LREC 2018)*, Miyazaki, Japan. European Language Resources Association (ELRA).

Deepak Gupta, Ankit Lamba, Asif Ekbal, and Pushpak Bhattacharyya. 2016a. Opinion Mining in a Code-Mixed Environment: A Case Study with Government Portals. In *International Conference on Natural Language Processing*, pages 249–258. NLP Association of India.

Deepak Gupta, Rajkumar Pujari, Asif Ekbal, Pushpak Bhattacharyya, Anutosh Maitra, Tom Jain, and Shubhashis Sengupta. 2018c. Can Taxonomy Help? Improving Semantic Question Matching using Question Taxonomy. In *Proceedings of the 27th International Conference on Computational Linguistics,*

128

pages 499–513. Association for Computational Linguistics.

Deepak Gupta, Shubham Tripathi, Asif Ekbal, and Pushpak Bhattacharyya. 2016b. A Hybrid Approach for Entity Extraction in Code-Mixed Social Media Data. *MONEY*, 25:66.

Deepak Gupta, Shubham Tripathi, Asif Ekbal, and Pushpak Bhattacharyya. 2017. SMPOST: Parts of Speech Tagger for Code-Mixed Indic Social Media Text. *arXiv preprint arXiv:1702.00167*.

Michael Heilman and Noah A Smith. 2010. Good Question! Statistical Ranking for Question Generation. In *Human Language Technologies: The 2010 Annual Conference of the North American Chapter of the Association for Computational Linguistics*, pages 609–617. Association for Computational Linguistics.

Karl Moritz Hermann, Tomas Kocisky, Edward Grefenstette, Lasse Espeholt, Will Kay, Mustafa Suleyman, and Phil Blunsom. 2015. Teaching Machines to Read and Comprehend. In *Advances in Neural Information Processing Systems*, pages 1693–1701.

Anupam Jamatia, Björn Gambäck, and Amitava Das. 2015. Part-of-Speech Tagging for Code-Mixed English-Hindi Twitter and Facebook Chat Messages. In *Proceedings of the International Conference Recent Advances in Natural Language Processing*, pages 239–248.

Diederik P Kingma and Jimmy Ba. 2014. Adam: A Method for Stochastic Optimization. *arXiv preprint arXiv:1412.6980*.

Philipp Koehn, Hieu Hoang, Alexandra Birch, Chris Callison-Burch, Marcello Federico, Nicola Bertoldi, Brooke Cowan, Wade Shen, Christine Moran, Richard Zens, et al. 2007. Moses: Open Source Toolkit for Statistical Machine Translation. In *Proceedings of the 45th Annual Meeting of the ACL on Interactive Poster and Demonstration Sessions*, pages 177–180. Association for Computational Linguistics.

Xin Li and Dan Roth. 2002. Learning Question Classifiers. In *Proceedings of the 19th International Conference on Computational Linguistics, COLING 2002*, pages 1–7. Association for Computational Linguistics.

Chin-Yew Lin. 2004. ROUGE: A Package for Automatic Evaluation of Summaries. In *Text Summarization Branches Out: Proceedings of the ACL-04 workshop*, volume 8. Barcelona, Spain.

Anutosh Maitra, Shubhashis Sengupta, Deepak Gupta, Rajkumar Pujari, Asif Ekbal, Pushpak Bhattacharyya, Anutosh Maitra, Mukhopadhyay Abhisek, and Tom Jain. 2018. Semantic Question Matching in Data Constrained Environment. In *Proceedings of the 21st International Conference on Text, Speech and Dialogue (TSD-2018)*.

Christof Monz and Bonnie J Dorr. 2005. Iterative Translation Disambiguation for Cross-language Information Retrieval. In *Proceedings of the 28th Annual International ACM SIGIR Conference on Research and Development in Information Retrieval*, pages 520–527. ACM.

Gillian Moss. 1992. Cognate Recognition: Its Importance in the Teaching of ESP Reading Courses to Spanish Speakers. *English for specific purposes*, 11(2):141–158.

Carol Myers-Scotton. 1997. *Duelling Languages: Grammatical Structure in Codeswitching*. Oxford University Press.

Carol Myers-Scotton. 2002. *Contact Linguistics: Bilingual Encounters and Grammatical Outcomes*. Oxford University Press on Demand.

Kishore Papineni, Salim Roukos, Todd Ward, and Wei-Jing Zhu. 2002. BLEU: a Method for Automatic Evaluation of Machine Translation. In *Proceedings of the 40th Annual Meeting on Association for Computational Linguistics*, pages 311–318. Association for Computational Linguistics.

Khyathi Chandu Raghavi, Manoj Kumar Chinnakotla, and Manish Shrivastava. 2015. Answer ka type kya he? Learning to Classify Questions in Code-Mixed Language. In *Proceedings of the 24th International Conference on World Wide Web*, pages 853–858. ACM.

Pranav Rajpurkar, Jian Zhang, Konstantin Lopyrev, and Percy Liang. 2016. SQuAD: 100,000+ Questions for Machine Comprehension of Text. In *Proceedings of the 2016 Conference on Empirical Methods in Natural Language Processing*, pages 2383–2392. Association for Computational Linguistics.

Koustav Rudra, Shruti Rijhwani, Rafiya Begum, Kalika Bali, Monojit Choudhury, and Niloy Ganguly. 2016. Understanding Language Preference for Expression of Opinion and Sentiment: What do Hindi-English Speakers do on Twitter? In *Proceedings of the 2016 Conference on Empirical Methods in Natural Language Processing*, pages 1131–1141.

Nathan Safran. 2015. *Psychology of the Searcher: Patterns in How Searchers Formulate Queries*. Blue Nile Research.

Rico Sennrich, Orhan Firat, Kyunghyun Cho, Alexandra Birch, Barry Haddow, Julian Hitschler, Marcin Junczys-Dowmunt, Samuel Läubli, Antonio Valerio Miceli Barone, Jozef Mokry, and Maria Nadejde. 2017. Nematus: a Toolkit for Neural Machine Translation. In *Proceedings of the Software Demonstrations of the 15th Conference of the European Chapter of the Association for Computational Linguistics*, pages 65–68, Valencia, Spain. Association for Computational Linguistics.

Minjoon Seo, Aniruddha Kembhavi, Ali Farhadi, and Hannaneh Hajishirzi. 2016. Bidirectional Attention Flow for Machine Comprehension. *arXiv preprint arXiv:1611.01603*.

Iulian Vlad Serban, Alberto García-Durán, Caglar Gulcehre, Sungjin Ahn, Sarath Chandar, Aaron Courville, and Yoshua Bengio. 2016. Generating Factoid Questions With Recurrent Neural Networks: The 30M Factoid Question-Answer Corpus. In *Proceedings of the 54th Annual Meeting of the Association for Computational Linguistics (Volume 1: Long Papers)*, pages 588–598. Association for Computational Linguistics.

Yelong Shen, Po-Sen Huang, Jianfeng Gao, and Weizhu Chen. 2017. ReasoNet: Learning to Stop Reading in Machine Comprehension. In *Proceedings of the 23rd ACM SIGKDD International Conference on Knowledge Discovery and Data Mining*, pages 1047–1055. ACM.

Samuel L. Smith, David H. P. Turban, Steven Hamblin, and Nils Y. Hammerla. 2017. Offline Bilingual Word Vectors, Orthogonal Transformations and the Inverted Softmax. *CoRR*, abs/1702.03859.

Sainik Kumar Mahata Soumil Mandal and Dipankar Das. 2018. Preparing Bengali-English Code-Mixed Corpus for Sentiment Analysis of Indian Languages. In *Proceedings of the Eleventh International Conference on Language Resources and Evaluation (LREC 2018)*, Paris, France. European Language Resources Association (ELRA).

Ilya Sutskever, Oriol Vinyals, and Quoc V Le. 2014. Sequence to Sequence Learning with Neural Networks. In *Advances in Neural Information Processing Systems*, pages 3104–3112.

Adam Trischler, Zheng Ye, Xingdi Yuan, Philip Bachman, Alessandro Sordoni, and Kaheer Suleman. 2016. Natural Language Comprehension with the EpiReader. In *Proceedings of the 2016 Conference on Empirical Methods in Natural Language Processing*, pages 128–137, Austin, Texas. Association for Computational Linguistics.

Yogarshi Vyas, Spandana Gella, Jatin Sharma, Kalika Bali, and Monojit Choudhury. 2014. POS Tagging of English-Hindi Code-Mixed Social Media Content. In *Proceedings of the 2014 Conference on Empirical Methods in Natural Language Processing (EMNLP)*, pages 974–979.

Shuohang Wang and Jing Jiang. 2016. Machine Comprehension Using Match-LSTM and Answer Pointer. *CoRR*, abs/1608.07905.

Tong Wang, Xingdi Yuan, and Adam Trischler. 2017a. A Joint Model for Question Answering and Question Generation. *CoRR*, abs/1706.01450.

Wenhui Wang, Nan Yang, Furu Wei, Baobao Chang, and Ming Zhou. 2017b. Gated Self-Matching Networks for Reading Comprehension and Question Answering. In *Proceedings of the 55th Annual Meeting of the Association for Computational Linguistics (Volume 1: Long Papers)*, volume 1, pages 189–198.

Learning to Embed Semantic Correspondence
for Natural Language Understanding

Sangkeun Jung[1], Jinsik Lee[2], and Jiwon Kim[3]

[1,2,3]T-Brain, AI Research Center, SK telecom
[1]Dept. of Computer Science and Engineering, Chungnam National University
[1]hugmanskj@gmail.com
[2,3] {jinsik16.lee, jk}@sktbrain.com

Abstract

While learning embedding models has yielded fruitful results in several NLP subfields, most notably Word2Vec, embedding correspondence has relatively not been well explored especially in the context of natural language understanding (NLU), a task that typically extracts structured semantic knowledge from a text. A NLU embedding model can facilitate analyzing and understanding relationships between unstructured texts and their corresponding structured semantic knowledge, essential for both researchers and practitioners of NLU. Toward this end, we propose a framework that learns to embed semantic correspondence between text and its extracted semantic knowledge, called *semantic frame*. One key contributed technique is semantic frame reconstruction used to derive a one-to-one mapping between embedded vectors and their corresponding semantic frames. Embedding into semantically meaningful vectors and computing their distances in vector space provide a simple, but effective way to measure semantic similarities. With the proposed framework, we demonstrate three key areas where the embedding model can be effective: visualization, semantic search and re-ranking.

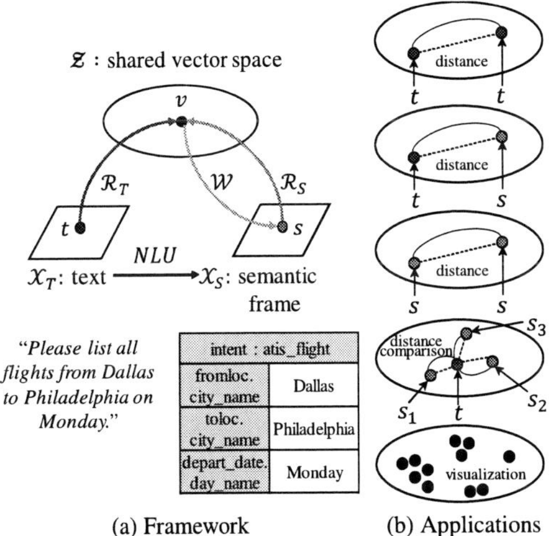

Figure 1: Semantic vector learning framework and applications. We assume a pair of corresponding text and semantic frame (t, s), which has semantically the same meaning in a raw text domain (χ_T), and a semantic frame domain (χ_S) can be encoded to a vector v in a shared embedding vector space $\mathcal{Z}$. $\mathcal{R}_T$ and $\mathcal{R}_S$ are two reader functions that encode raw and structured text to a semantic vector. $\mathcal{W}$ is a writing function that decodes a semantic vector to a symbolic semantic frame.

1 Introduction

The goal of NLU is to extract meaning from a natural language and infer the user intention. NLU typically involves two tasks: identifying user intent and extracting domain-specific entities, the second of which is often referred to as slot-filling (Mesnil et al., 2013; Jeong and Lee, 2006; Kim et al., 2016). Typically, the NLU task can be viewed as an extraction of structured text from a raw text. In NLU literature, the structured form of intent and filled slots is called a *semantic frame*.

In this study, we aim to learn the meaningful distributed semantic representation, rather than focusing on building the NLU system itself. Once we obtained a reliable and reasonable semantic representation in a vector form, we can devise many useful and new applications around the NLU (Figure 1). Because all the instances of text and semantic frame are placed on a single vector space, we can obtain the natural and direct distance measure between them. Using the distance measure, the similar text or semantic frame instances can

131

Proceedings of the 22nd Conference on Computational Natural Language Learning (CoNLL 2018), pages 131–140
Brussels, Belgium, October 31 - November 1, 2018. ©2018 Association for Computational Linguistics

be searched directly and interchangeably by the distance comparison. Moreover, re-ranking of multiple NLU results can be applied without further learning by comparing the distances between the text and the corresponding predicted semantic frame. Converting symbols to vectors makes it possible to do visualization naturally as well.

In this study, we assumed that the reasonable semantic vector representation satisfies the following properties.

- **Property - embedding correspondence**: Distributed representation of text should be the same as the distributed representation of the corresponding semantic frame.

- **Property - reconstruction**: Symbolic semantic frame should be recovered from the learned semantic vector.

We herein introduce a novel semantic vector learning framework called ESC (Embedding Semantic Correspondence learning), which satisfies the assumed properties.

The remainder of the paper is structured as follows: Section 2 describes the detailed structure of the framework. Section 3 introduces semantic vector applications in NLU. Section 4 describes the experimental settings and results. Section 5 discusses the related work. Finally, section 6 presents the conclusion.

2 ESC Framework

Our framework consists of ***text reader***, ***semantic frame reader***, and ***semantic frame writer***. The text reader embeds a sequence of tokens to a distributed vector representation. The semantic frame reader reads the structured texts and encodes each to a vector. v_t represents a vector semantic frame derived from the text reader, and v_s represents a vector semantic frame derived from the semantic frame reader. Finally, the semantic frame writer generates a symbolic semantic frame from a vector representation.

2.1 Text Reader

A text reader (Figure 2), implementing a neural sentence encoder, reads a sequence of input tokens and encodes each to a vector. In this study, we used long short-term memory (LSTM) (Hochreiter and Schmidhuber, 1997) for encoding input sequences. The encoding process can be defined as

$$\overrightarrow{h}_s = R_{text}(E_X(x_s), \overrightarrow{h}_{s-1})$$
$$v_t = sigmoid(\overrightarrow{h}_S)$$

where $s = \{1, 2, ..., S\}$ and $\overrightarrow{h}_s$ is the forward hidden states over the input sequence at time s; R_{text} is an RNN cell; and $E_X(x_s)$ is the token embedding function, which returns a distributed vector representation of token x at time s. The final RNN output $\overrightarrow{h}_S$ is taken as v_t, which is a semantic vector derived from the text.

2.2 Semantic Frame Reader

A semantic frame consists of structured tags such as the intent and slot-tag and slot-values. In this study, the intent tag is handled as a symbol, and the slot-tags and slot-values are handled as a sequence of symbols. For example, the sentence, "Please list all flights from Dallas to Philadelphia on Monday." is handled as

- intent tag : *atis_flight*

- slot-tag sequence :
  [*fromloc.city_name, toloc.city_name, depart_date.day_name*]

- slot-value sequence :
  [*Dallas, Philadelphia, Monday*].

The intent reader is a simple embedding function $v_{intent} = E_I(i)$, which returns a distributed vector representation of the intent tag i for a sentence.

Stacked LSTM layer is used to read the sequences of slot-tags and slot-values. $E_S(o)$ is a slot-tag embedding function with o as a token. $E_V(a)$ is an embedding function with a as a token. The embedding result $E_S(o_m)$ and $E_V(a_m)$ are concatenated at time-step m, and the merged vectors are fed to the stacked layer for each time-step (Figure 2). $v_{tag,value}$ - the reading result of sequence of slot-tags and values - is taken from the final output of RNN at time M. Finally, intent, slot-tag and value encoded vectors are merged to construct a distributed semantic frame representation as

$$v_s = sigmoid(W_{sf}([v_{intent}; v_{tag,value}]) + b_{sf})$$

where $[;]$ denotes the vector concatenation operator. The dimension of v_s is same as v_t. All embedding weights are randomly initialized and learned through the training process.

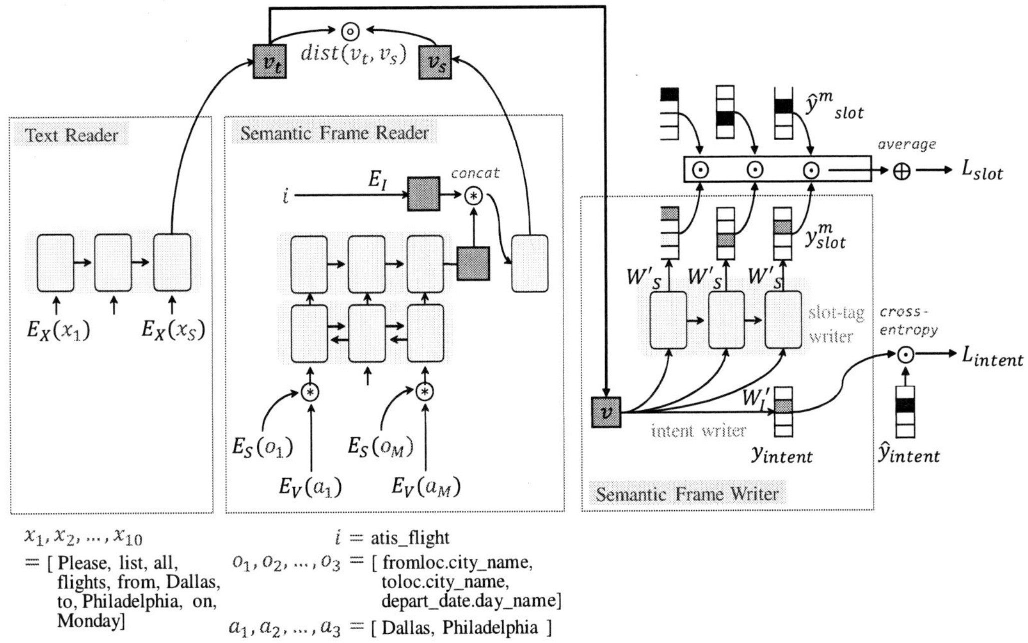

Figure 2: Text reader, semantic reader and semantic frame writer neural architecture. E_X is an embedding function for the input text token x. E_I, E_S, and E_V are the embedding functions for the intent tag, slot-tag and slot-value, respectively. $\circledast$ is a vector concatenation operation; $\odot$ is a cross-entropy; $\oplus$ is an average calculation; $\circledcirc$ represents the distance calculation. $\hat{y}_{intent}$ is a reference intent tag vector and $\hat{y}^m_{slot}$ is a reference slot tag vector at time m. M is the number of slots in a sentence (in the above example, $M = 3$).

2.3 Semantic Frame Writer and Loss Functions

One of the objectives of this study is to learn semantically the reasonable vector representations of text and a related semantic frame. Hence, we set the properties of the desirable semantic vector, and the loss functions are defined to satisfy the properties.

Loss for Property "embedding correspondence" Distance loss measures the dissimilarity between the encoded semantic vectors from the text reader and those from the semantic frame reader in the vector space. The loss is defined as

$$L_{dist} = dist(v_t, v_s)$$

where the $dist$ function can be any vector distance measure; however, in this study, we employed a Euclidean and a cosine distance (=1.0 - cosine similarity).

Loss for Property "reconstruction" Content loss provides a measure of how much semantic information the semantic frame vector contains. Without the content loss, v_t and v_s tend to quickly converge to zero vectors, implying the failure to learn the semantic representation. To measure the content keeping, symbolic semantic frame generations from semantic vector is performed, and the difference between the original semantic frame and the generated semantic frame is calculated.

Because the semantic frame's slot-value has a large vocabulary size to generate the slot values, a *reduced semantic frame* is devised to ease the generation problem. A reduced semantic frame is created by simply dropping the slot values from the corresponding semantic frame. For example, in Figure 2, slot values [*Dallas, Philadelphia, Monday*] are removed to create a reduced semantic frame. Content loss calculation is performed on this reduced semantic frame. Another advantage of employing reduced semantic frame is that the learned distributed semantic vectors have more abstract power because the learned semantic vectors are less sensitive to the lexical vocabulary.

For content loss, the intent and slot-tags' generation qualities are measured. The intent generation network can be simply defined using linear

Notation	Dim.	Description
E_X	50	Token embedding
E_S	50	Slot-tag embedding
E_V	50	Slot-value embedding
v_{intent}	50	Intent reader output
$v_{tag,value}$	200	Slot-tag and value reader output
v	200	Semantic vector

Table 1: Hyperparameters of the model.

projection as

$$y_{intent} = W_I' v + b_I$$

where v is the semantic vector, and y_{intent} is the output vector.

The slot-tag generation networks are defined as

$$\overrightarrow{q}_m = R_G(v, \overrightarrow{q}_{m-1})$$
$$y_{slot}^m = W_S' \overrightarrow{q}_m + b_S$$

where R_G is an RNN cell. The semantic vector v is copied and repeatedly fed into each RNN input. The outputs from the RNN are projected onto the slot tag space with W_S'.

Figure 2 shows the intent and slot tag generation networks and the corresponding loss calculation methods. The generational losses can be defined with the cross entropy between the generated tag vector and the reference tag vector as

$$L_{intent} = CrossEntropy(\hat{y}_{intent}, y_{intent})$$

$$L_{slot} = \frac{1}{M} \sum_{m=1}^{M} CrossEntropy(\hat{y}_{slot}^m, y_{slot}^m)$$

where M is the number of slots in a sentence.

With the combination of intent and slot losses, the *content loss($L_{content}$)* to reconstruct a semantic frame from a semantic vector v can be defined as follows:

$$L_{content} = L_{intent} + L_{slot}$$

Finally, the total loss value (L) for learning the semantic frame representation is defined with the **distance loss** and **content loss** as

$$L = L_{dist} + L_{content}$$

The hyperparameters of the proposed model are summarized in Table 1.

3 Applications

3.1 Multi-form Distance Measurement

Using the learned text- and semantic-frame reader, we can measure not only the instances from the same form (text or semantic frame form) but also from different forms. Let's denote a text as t and a semantic frame as s, and the text and semantic frame reader as $\mathcal{R}_T$ and $\mathcal{R}_S$, respectively. The distance measurements between them can be performed as follows:

- $dist(v_t^i, v_t^j)$:
$$t_i \rightarrow \mathcal{R}_T(t_i) = v_t^i$$
$$t_j \rightarrow \mathcal{R}_T(t_j) = v_t^j$$

- $dist(v_t^i, v_s^j)$:
$$t_i \rightarrow \mathcal{R}_T(t_i) = v_t^i$$
$$s_j \rightarrow \mathcal{R}_S(t_j) = v_s^j$$

- $dist(v_s^i, v_s^j)$:
$$s_i \rightarrow \mathcal{R}_S(s_i) = v_s^i$$
$$s_j \rightarrow \mathcal{R}_S(s_j) = v_s^j$$

3.2 Visualization

With vector semantic representation, we can visualize the instances (sentences) in an easier and more natural way. Once the symbolic text or semantic frame are converted to vector, vector visualization methods such as *t*-sne (Maaten and Hinton, 2008) can be used directly to check the relationship between instances or the distribution of the entire corpus.

3.3 Re-ranking Without Further Learning

Re-ranking the NLU results from multiple NLU modules is difficult but important if a robust NLU system is to be built. Typically, a choice is made by comparing the scores produced by each system. However, this technique is not always feasible because the scores are often in different scales, or are occasionally not provided at all (e.g., in the purely rule-based NLU systems). The vector form of the semantic frame provides a very clear and natural solution for the re-ranking problem.

Figure 3 shows the flow of the re-ranking algorithm with the proposed vector semantic representation. In this study, we reordered the NLU results from multiple NLU systems according to their corresponding distances of v_t to v_s. It is noteworthy that the proposed re-ranking algorithm does not require further learning for ranking such as ensemble learning or learning-to-rank techniques. Further, the proposed methods are applicable to any type of NLU system. Even purely rule-based systems can be satisfactorily compared to purely statistical systems.

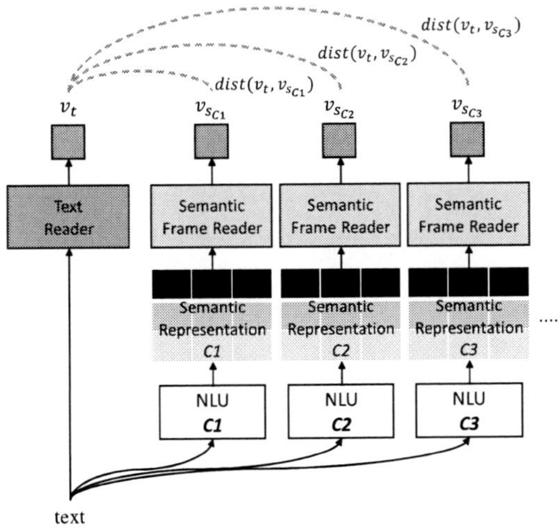

Figure 3: Re-ranking multiple NLU results using the semantic vector. The semantic vector from the text (v_t) functions as a pivot. We show three different NLU systems in this illustration.

4 Experiments

For training and testing purposes, we used the ATIS2 dataset (Price, 1990). The ATIS2 dataset consists of an annotated intent and slot corpus for an air travel information search task. ATIS2 data set comes with a commonly used training and test split. For tuning parameters, we further split the training set into 90% training and 10% development set.

4.1 Validity of Learned Semantic Vector with Visualization

The intuition behind the proposed method is that semantically similar instances will be grouped together if the semantic vector learning is performed successfully. Figure 4 supports that the intuition is correct. In the early stages of training, the instances are scattered randomly; however, as the training progresses, semantically similar instances gather closer to each other. We observed that the proposed framework groups and depicts the sentences based on the intent tag remarkably well.

4.2 Multi-form Distance Measurement

In our framework, the instances having different forms (text or semantic frame) can be compared directly on a semantic vector space. To demonstrate that multi-form distance measurement works well, the sentence and semantic frame search results with a sentence and a semantic

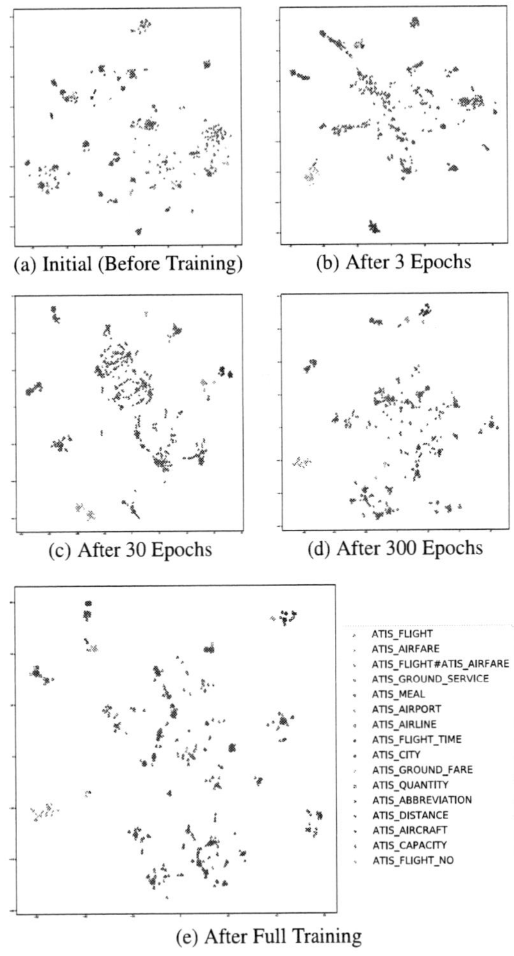

(a) Initial (Before Training)
(b) After 3 Epochs
(c) After 30 Epochs
(d) After 300 Epochs

(e) After Full Training

Figure 4: Visualization of semantic vectors through training process. The plotted points are v_t from the text reader by t-sne processing in the testing sentences. The different colors and shape combinations represent different intent tags.

frame query are shown in Table 2.

Table 2 shows that *text to text* search is very well done with the learned vector. The retrieved sentence patterns are similar to the given text, and the vocabulary presented is also similar. On the other hand, in the case of the *text to semantic frame* search, The sentence patterns are similar, but the content words such as city name are not similar. In fact, this is what we predicted, because the content loss for reconstruction property is measured on *reduced semantic frame* which does not include slot-values. In *semantic frame to text* search, we can find similar behaviors. Retrieved results have almost same intent tag and slot-tags, but have dif-

No.	Text		Semantic Frame	
			"Show Delta Airlines from Boston to Salt Lake"	
1	Show Delta Airlines flights from Boston to Salt Lake	1	**ATIS_FLIGHT**	
			airline_name	Delta Airlines
			fromloc.city_name	Boston
			toloc.city_name	Salt Lake
2	Show Delta Airlines flights from Boston to Salt Lake City	2	**ATIS_FLIGHT**	
			airline_name	American Airlines
			fromloc.city_name	Phoenix
			toloc.city_name	Milwaukee
3	List Delta flights from Seattle to Salt Lake City	3	**ATIS_FLIGHT**	
			airline_name	Delta Airlines
			fromloc.city_name	Montreal
			toloc.city_name	Orlando

(a) Text as Query

No.	Text		Semantic Frame	
			[ATIS_FLIGHT] flight_mod(last), depart_date.day_name(Wednesday), fromloc.city_name(Oakland), toloc.city_name(Salt Lake City)	
1	Get last flight from Oakland to Salt Lake City on Wednesday	1	**ATIS_FLIGHT**	
			flight_mod	last
			depart_date.day_name	Wednesday
			fromloc.city_name	Oakland
			toloc.city_name	Salt Lake City
2	Get last flight from Oakland to Salt Lake City on Wednesday or first flight from Oakland to Salt Lake City on Thursday	2	**ATIS_FLIGHT**	
			flight_mod	first
			depart_date.day_name	Thursday
			fromloc.city_name	Oakland
			toloc.city_name	Salt Lake City
3	Get first flight from Oakland to Salt Lake City on Thursday	3	**ATIS_FLIGHT**	
			flight_mod	last
			depart_date.day_name	Wednesday
			fromloc.city_name	Oakland
			toloc.city_name	Salt Lake City
			or	or
			flight_mod	first
			depart_date.day_name	Thursday
			fromloc.city_name	Oakland
			toloc.city_name	Salt Lake City

(b) Semantic Frame as Query

Table 2: Example of most similar instance search results in the test data according to the proposed framework. Top-3 text and semantic frame retrieved instances given a single query are shown in left and right side respectively.

ferent city or airport names which are corresponding to slot-values. If we could include the slot-value generation in the reconstruction loss with large data, a better multi-form semantic search result might be expected.

To measure the quantitative search performance, *precision at K* are reported in Table 3. Precision at K corresponds to the number of same sentence pattern instances in the top K results. From the search result, we can conclude that the learned semantic vectors keep sentence pattern (intent tag and slot-tags) information very well.

4.3 Re-ranking

We prepared 11 NLU systems for re-ranking. Nine intent-/slot-combined classifiers and two in-

K	Text Query			SF Query		
	I	S	J	I	S	J
1	98.30	63.15	62.93	99.43	70.75	70.52
3	99.09	72.45	72.00	99.55	77.78	77.44
5	99.09	75.17	74.72	99.77	78.80	78.68
10	99.09	76.98	76.42	99.77	80.39	80.27

Table 3: Same sentence pattern (intent and slot-tags should be matched) search performance (Precision @K). SF, I, S and J stand for semantic frame, intent, slot-tag and joint of intent and slot-tag.

Identifier	Combinations	
C1		CRF
C2	CNN	RNN
C3		RNN+CRF
C4		CRF
C5	MaxEnt	RNN
C6		RNN+CRF
C7		CRF
C8	SVM	RNN
C9		RNN+CRF
C10	Joint Liu (Liu and Lane, 2016)	
C11	Joint Tur (Hakkani-Tür et al., 2016)	

Table 4: Multiple NLU systems for re-ranking.

tent/slot joint classifiers were implemented. For the combined classifiers, three intent classifiers and three slot sequential classifiers were prepared and combined. For the joint classifiers, those of Liu and Lane (2016) and Hakkani-Tür et al. (2016) were each implemented. Here, we did not significantly tune the NLU systems, as the purpose of this paper is to learn the semantic vector, not to build the state-of-the-art NLU systems.

A maximum-entropy (MaxEnt)- and a support vector machine (SVM)-based intent classifier were implemented as a traditional sentence classification method. Both classifiers share the same feature set (1-gram, 2-gram, 3-gram, and 4-gram around each word). Also, a convolutional-neural network-based (CNN-based) (Kim, 2014) sentence classification method was implemented.

A conditional random field (CRF)-based sequential classifier was implemented as a traditional slot classifier. Also, an RNN- and an RNN+CRF-based sequential classifier were implemented as a deep learning method. Bidirectional LSTMs were used to build the simple RNN-based classifier. By placing a CRF layer on top of the bidirectional LSTM network (Lee, 2017), an RNN+CRF-based network was implemented. In addition, two joint NLU systems (Liu and Lane, 2016; Hakkani-Tür et al., 2016) are prepared by reusing their codes, which are publicly accessible[1][2][3].

Table 4 shows the summary of the NLU systems that we prepared and used for the re-ranking experiments.

Table 5 shows the performance of all the NLU

---

[1]https://github.com/yvchen/JointSLU.git

[2]https://github.com/DSKSD/RNN-for-Joint-NLU

[3]The reported performance of C10 and C11 in their paper were not reproduced with the open code.

NLU systems	Intent	Slot		
	acc.	prec.	rec.	f_m
C1	90.70	94.36	89.61	91.92
C2	90.70	92.33	92.46	92.40
C3	90.70	93.53	92.39	92.96
C4	94.10	94.36	89.61	91.92
C5	94.10	92.33	92.46	92.40
C6	94.10	93.53	92.39	92.96
C7	91.84	94.36	89.61	91.92
C8	91.84	92.33	92.46	92.40
C9	91.84	93.53	92.39	92.96
C10	96.03	93.68	92.64	93.16
C11	93.54	94.74	94.00	94.37
random	92.86	93.96	92.29	93.12
majority vote (baseline)	94.10	**95.63**	93.68	94.64
NLU score (baseline)	95.58	94.81	93.89	94.35
re-ranked (Euclidean)	**97.05**	93.74	91.96	92.84
re-ranked (cosine)	**97.05**	95.40	**94.11**	**94.75**
oracle	97.85	96.77	95.29	96.02

Table 5: NLU performance of multiple NLU systems and re-ranked results. Acc., prec., rec., and f_m stand for accuracy, precision, recall, and f-measure, respectively.

systems, the proposed re-ranking algorithm's performance, and the oracle performance. Typical choices in re-ranking NLU results are majority voting and score-based ranking. In the majority voting method, the semantic frame most predicted by the NLU systems is selected. The score of the NLU scoring method in Table 5 is the prediction probability. In the case of joint NLU classifiers (C10 and C11), the joint prediction probabilities are used for the score. In the case of combination NLU systems (C1 to C9), the product of the intent and slot prediction probabilities is used for the score.

The proposed distance-based re-ranking method using semantic vector shows superior selection performance at both intent and slot-filling tasks. It is noteworthy that the re-ranked intent prediction performance (acc. 97.05) is relatively close to the oracle intent performance (acc. 97.85), which is the upper bound. Compared to the baseline re-ranker (NLU score), the proposed re-ranker (cosine) achieves 33.25% and 7.07% relative error reduction for intent prediction and slot-filling task, respectively.

5   Related Work

The task of spoken NLU consists of intent classification and domain entity slot filling. Traditionally, both tasks are approached using statistical machine-learning methods (Schwartz et al., 1997; He and Young, 2005; Dietterich, 2002). Recently, with the advances in deep learning, RNN-based sequence encoding techniques have been used to detect the intent or utterance type (Ravuri and Stolcke, 2015), and RNN-based neural architectures have been employed for slot-filling tasks (Mesnil et al., 2013, 2015). The combinations of CRF and neural networks have also been explored by Xu and Sarikaya (2013).

Recent works have focused on enriching the representations for neural architectures to implement NLU. For example, Chen et al. focused on leveraging substructure embeddings for joint semantic frame parsing (Chen et al., 2016). Kim et al. utilized several semantic lexicons, such as WordNet, PPDB, and the Macmillan dictionary, to enrich the word embeddings, and later used them in the initial representation of words for intent detection (Kim et al., 2016).

Previous NLU works have used statistical modeling for the intent and slot-filling tasks, and input representation. None of the work performed has represented the text and semantic frame as a vector form simultaneously. To our best knowledge, this is the first presentation of a method for learning the distributed semantic vector for both text and semantic frame and it's applications in NLU research.

In general natural language processing literature, many *raw text to vector* studies to learn the vector representations of text have been performed. Mikolov et al. (2013); Pennington et al. (2014); Collobert et al. (2011) proposed word to vector techniques. Mueller and Thyagarajan (2016); Le and Mikolov (2014) introduced embedding methods at the sentence and document level. Some attempts have shown that in this embedding process, certain semantic information such as analogy, antonym, and gender can be obtained in the vector space.

Further, many *structured text to vector* techniques have been introduced recently. Preller (2014) introduced a logic formula embedding method while Bordes et al. (2013); Do et al. (2018) proposed translating symbolic structured knowledge such as Wordnet and freebase.

We herein introduce a novel semantic frame embedding method by simultaneously executing the *raw text to vector* and *structured text to vector* method in a single framework to learn semantic representations more directly. In this framework, the text and semantic frame are each projected onto a vector space, and the distance loss between the vectors is minimized to satisfy *embedding correspondence*. Our research goes a step further to guarantee that the learned vector indeed keep the semantic information by checking the *reconstruction* the symbolic semantic frame from the vector.

In learning the parameters by minimizing the vector distances, this work is similar to a Siamese constitutional neural network (Chopra et al., 2005; Mueller and Thyagarajan, 2016) or an autoencoder (Hinton and Salakhutdinov, 2006); however, the weights are not shared or transposed in this work.

6   Conclusion

In this study, we have proposed a new method to learn a correspondence embedding model for NLU. To learn a valid and meaningful distributed semantic representation, two properties - *embedding correspondence* and *reconstruction* - are considered. By minimizing the distance between the semantic vectors which are the outputs of text and semantic frame reader, the semantically equivalent vectors are placed very close in the vector space. In addition, reconstruction consistency from a semantic vector to symbol semantic frame was jointly enforced to prevent the method from learning trivial degenerate mappings (e.g. mapping all to zeros).

Through various experiments with ATIS2 dataset, we confirmed that the learned semantic vectors indeed contain semantic information. Semantic vector visualization and the results of similar text and semantic frame search showed that semantically similar instances are actually located near on the vector space. Also, using the learned semantic vector, re-ranking multiple NLU systems can be implemented without further learning by comparing semantic vector values of text and semantic frame.

Based on the results of the proposed research, various research directions can be considered in the future. A semantic operation or algebra on a vector space will be a very promising research topic. Furthermore, with enough training data and appropriate modification to our method, adding text reconstruction constraint can be pursed and generating text directly from a semantic vector would be possible, somewhat resembling problem settings of neural machine translation tasks.

References

Antoine Bordes, Nicolas Usunier, Alberto Garcia-Duran, Jason Weston, and Oksana Yakhnenko. 2013. Translating embeddings for modeling multi-relational data. In *Advances in neural information processing systems*, pages 2787–2795.

Yun-Nung Chen, Dilek Hakanni-Tür, Gokhan Tur, Asli Celikyilmaz, Jianfeng Guo, and Li Deng. 2016. Syntax or semantics? knowledge-guided joint semantic frame parsing. In *Spoken Language Technology Workshop (SLT), 2016 IEEE*, pages 348–355. IEEE.

Sumit Chopra, Raia Hadsell, and Yann LeCun. 2005. Learning a similarity metric discriminatively, with application to face verification. In *Computer Vision and Pattern Recognition, 2005. CVPR 2005. IEEE Computer Society Conference on*, volume 1, pages 539–546. IEEE.

Ronan Collobert, Jason Weston, Léon Bottou, Michael Karlen, Koray Kavukcuoglu, and Pavel Kuksa. 2011. Natural language processing (almost) from scratch. *Journal of Machine Learning Research*, 12(Aug):2493–2537.

Thomas Dietterich. 2002. Machine learning for sequential data: A review. *Structural, syntactic, and statistical pattern recognition*, pages 227–246.

Kien Do, Truyen Tran, and Svetha Venkatesh. 2018. Knowledge graph embedding with multiple relation projections. *arXiv preprint arXiv:1801.08641*.

Dilek Hakkani-Tür, Gökhan Tür, Asli Celikyilmaz, Yun-Nung Chen, Jianfeng Gao, Li Deng, and Ye-Yi Wang. 2016. Multi-domain joint semantic frame parsing using bi-directional rnn-lstm. In *Interspeech*, pages 715–719.

Yulan He and Steve Young. 2005. Semantic processing using the hidden vector state model. *Computer speech & language*, 19(1):85–106.

Geoffrey E Hinton and Ruslan R Salakhutdinov. 2006. Reducing the dimensionality of data with neural networks. *science*, 313(5786):504–507.

Sepp Hochreiter and Jürgen Schmidhuber. 1997. Long short-term memory. *Neural computation*, 9(8):1735–1780.

Minwoo Jeong and Gary Geunbae Lee. 2006. Jointly predicting dialog act and named entity for spoken language understanding. In *Spoken Language Technology Workshop, 2006. IEEE*, pages 66–69. IEEE.

Joo-Kyung Kim, Gokhan Tur, Asli Celikyilmaz, Bin Cao, and Ye-Yi Wang. 2016. Intent detection using semantically enriched word embeddings. In *Spoken Language Technology Workshop (SLT), 2016 IEEE*, pages 414–419. IEEE.

Yoon Kim. 2014. Convolutional neural networks for sentence classification. *arXiv preprint arXiv:1408.5882*.

Quoc Le and Tomas Mikolov. 2014. Distributed representations of sentences and documents. In *International Conference on Machine Learning*, pages 1188–1196.

Changki Lee. 2017. Lstm-crf models for named entity recognition. *IEICE Transactions on Information and Systems*, 100(4):882–887.

Bing Liu and Ian Lane. 2016. Attention-based recurrent neural network models for joint intent detection and slot filling. *arXiv preprint arXiv:1609.01454*.

Laurens van der Maaten and Geoffrey Hinton. 2008. Visualizing data using t-sne. *Journal of Machine Learning Research*, 9(Nov):2579–2605.

Grégoire Mesnil, Yann Dauphin, Kaisheng Yao, Yoshua Bengio, Li Deng, Dilek Hakkani-Tur, Xiaodong He, Larry Heck, Gokhan Tur, Dong Yu, et al. 2015. Using recurrent neural networks for slot filling in spoken language understanding. *IEEE/ACM Transactions on Audio, Speech and Language Processing (TASLP)*, 23(3):530–539.

Grégoire Mesnil, Xiaodong He, Li Deng, and Yoshua Bengio. 2013. Investigation of recurrent-neural-network architectures and learning methods for spoken language understanding. In *Interspeech*, pages 3771–3775.

Tomas Mikolov, Kai Chen, Greg Corrado, and Jeffrey Dean. 2013. Efficient estimation of word representations in vector space. *arXiv preprint arXiv:1301.3781*.

Jonas Mueller and Aditya Thyagarajan. 2016. Siamese recurrent architectures for learning sentence similarity. In *AAAI*, pages 2786–2792.

Jeffrey Pennington, Richard Socher, and Christopher Manning. 2014. Glove: Global vectors for word representation. In *Proceedings of the 2014 conference on empirical methods in natural language processing (EMNLP)*, pages 1532–1543.

Anne Preller. 2014. From logical to distributional models. *arXiv preprint arXiv:1412.8527*.

Patti J Price. 1990. Evaluation of spoken language systems: The atis domain. In *Speech and Natural Language: Proceedings of a Workshop Held at Hidden Valley, Pennsylvania, June 24-27, 1990*.

Suman V Ravuri and Andreas Stolcke. 2015. Recurrent neural network and lstm models for lexical utterance classification. In *INTERSPEECH*, pages 135–139.

Richard Schwartz, Scott Miller, David Stallard, and John Makhoul. 1997. Hidden understanding models for statistical sentence understanding. In *Acoustics, Speech, and Signal Processing, 1997. ICASSP-97., 1997 IEEE International Conference on*, volume 2, pages 1479–1482. IEEE.

Puyang Xu and Ruhi Sarikaya. 2013. Convolutional neural network based triangular crf for joint intent detection and slot filling. In *Automatic Speech Recognition and Understanding (ASRU), 2013 IEEE Workshop on*, pages 78–83. IEEE.

Commonsense Knowledge Base Completion and Generation

Itsumi Saito   Kyosuke Nishida   Hisako Asano   Junji Tomita
NTT Media Intelligence Laboratories
{saito.itsumi, nishida.kyosuke}@lab.ntt.co.jp,
{asano.hisako, tomita.junji}@lab.ntt.co.jp

Abstract

This study focuses on acquisition of commonsense knowledge. A previous study proposed a commonsense knowledge base completion (CKB completion) method that predicts a confidence score of triplet-style knowledge for improving the coverage of CKBs. To improve the accuracy of CKB completion and expand the size of CKBs, we formulate a new commonsense knowledge base generation task (CKB generation) and propose a joint learning method that incorporates both CKB completion and CKB generation. Experimental results show that the joint learning method improved completion accuracy and the generation model created reasonable knowledge. Our generation model could also be used to augment data and improve the accuracy of completion.

1 Introduction

Knowledge bases (KBs) are a kind of information network, and they have been applied to many natural language processing tasks such as question answering (Yang and Mitchell, 2017; Long et al., 2017) and dialog tasks (Young et al., 2018). In this paper, we focus on commonsense knowledge bases (CKBs). Commonsense knowledge is also referred to as background knowledge and is used in natural language application tasks that require reasoning based on implicit knowledge. For example, machine comprehension tasks that need commonsense reasoning have been proposed very recently (Lin et al., 2017; Ostermann et al., 2018). In particular, Wang et al. (2018) used commonsense knowledge provided by ConceptNet (Speer et al., 2017) to efficiently resolve ambiguities and infer implicit information.

Information in CKB is represented in RDF-style triples $\langle t_1, r, t_2 \rangle$, where t_1 and t_2 are arbitrary words or phrases, and $r \in R$ is a relation between t_1 and t_2. For example, $\langle \text{go to restaurant}, subevent, \text{order food} \rangle$ means "order food" happens as a subevent of "go to restaurant". Although researchers have developed techniques for acquiring CKB from raw text with patterns (Angeli and Manning, 2013), it has been pointed out that some sorts of knowledge are rarely expressed explicitly in textual corpora (Gordon and Van Durme, 2013). Therefore, researchers have developed curated CKB resources by manual annotation (Speer et al., 2017). While manually created knowledge has high precision, these resources suffer from lack of coverage.

Knowledge base completion methods are used to improve the coverage of existing general-purpose KBs, such as Freebase (Bollacker et al., 2008; Bordes et al., 2013; Lin et al., 2015). For example, given a node pair $\langle \text{Athens}, \text{Greece} \rangle$, a completion method predicts the missing relation "IsLocatedIn". Such KBs consist of well-connected entities; thus, the completion methods are mainly used to find missing links of the existing nodes. On the other hand, CKBs are very sparse because their nodes contain arbitrary phrases and it is difficult to define all phrases in advance. Therefore, it is important to consider CKB completion that can robustly take arbitrary phrases as input queries, even if they are not contained in the CKBs, to improve the coverage.

Li et al. (2016b) proposed an on-the-fly CKB completion model to improve the coverage of CKBs. They defined the CKB completion task as a binary classification distinguishing true knowledge from false knowledge for arbitrary triples. They proposed a simple neural network model that can embed arbitrary phrases on-the-fly and achieved reasonable accuracy for ConceptNet. Here, in order to acquire new knowledge by using a CKB completion model, we have to prepare triplet candidates as input for the completion

Proceedings of the 22nd Conference on Computational Natural Language Learning (CoNLL 2018), pages 141–150
Brussels, Belgium, October 31 - November 1, 2018. ©2018 Association for Computational Linguistics

model, because the model can only verify whether the triple is true or not. Li et al. (2016b) extracted such triplet candidates from the raw text of Wikipedia and also randomly selected from the phrase and relation set of ConceptNet. Extracts from raw text likely contain unseen phrases, i.e., ones which do not exist in the CKB, and these phrases are useful for expanding the node size of the CKB; however, they reported that the quality of triples acquired from Wikipedia were significantly lower than that of combination triples from ConceptNet, because patterns extracted from Wikipedia by using linguistic patterns are noisier than those from ConceptNet. For acquiring new knowledge with high quality, there are still problems with expanding new nodes and with the accuracy of CKB completion.

In this study, we focus on problems of increasing the node size of CKBs and increasing the connectivity of CKBs. We introduce a new commonsense knowledge base generation (CKB generation) task for generating new nodes. We also devise a model that jointly learns the completion and generation tasks. The generation task can generate an arbitrary phrase t_2 from an input query and relation pair $\langle t_1, r \rangle$. The joint learning of the two tasks improves the completion task and triples generated by the generation model can be used as additional training data for the completion model.

Our contributions are summarized as follows:

- We define a new task, called commonsense knowledge base generation, and propose a method for joint learning of knowledge base completion and knowledge base generation.

- Experimental results demonstrate that our method achieved state-of-the-art CKB completion results on both ConceptNet and Japanese commonsense knowledge datasets.

- Experimental results show that our CKB generation can generate reasonable knowledge and augmented data generated by the model can improve CKB completion.

2 Task Definition

Our study focuses on two tasks, CKB completion and CKB generation. We describe the settings of these tasks below.

Problem 1 (CKB completion). *Given a triple* $\langle t_1, r, t_2 \rangle$, *CKB completion provides a confidence score that distinguishes true triples from false ones. t_1 and t_2 are arbitrary phrases. r is a relation in a set R.*

Problem 2 (CKB generation). *Given a pair of* $t_1(t_2)$ *and* $r \in R$, *CKB generation generates* $t_2(t_1)$, *which has a relationship r with $t_1(t_2)$. t_1 and t_2 are arbitrary phrases.*

3 Proposed Method

The proposed method is illustrated in Figure 1. Our method consists of two models. It performs both the CKB completion task and CKB generation task. Two models share the parameters of a phrase encoder, word embeddings, and relation embeddings. We describe these models in detail in Sections 3.1 and 3.2.

3.1 CKB Completion Model

The basic structure of our CKB completion model is similar to that of Li et al. (2016b). The main difference between ours and theirs is that our method learns the CKB completion and generation tasks jointly. The completion model only considers the binary classification task, and therefore, it can be easily overfitted when there are not enough training data. By incorporating the generation model, the shared layers are trained for both binary classification and phrase generation. This is expected to be a good constraint to prevent overfitting.

Previous model Li et al. (2016b) defined a CKB completion model that estimates a confidence score of an arbitrary triple $\langle t_1, r, t_2 \rangle$. They used a simple neural network model to formulate $\text{score}(t_1, r, t_2) \in \mathbb{R}$.

$$\text{score}(t_1, r, t_2) = W_2 g(W_1 v_{in} + b_1) + b_2 \quad (1)$$

where $v_{in} = \text{concat}(v_{12}, v_r) \in \mathbb{R}^{d_v + d_r}$. $v_{12} \in \mathbb{R}^{d_v}$ is a phrase representation of concatenating t_1 and t_2. $v_r \in \mathbb{R}^{d_r}$ is a relation embedding for r. g is a nonlinear activation function. Note that we use ReLU for g.

Our model Our CKB completion model is based on Li et al.'s (2016b). However, the shared structure and the formulation of the phrase representations v_{12} are different. Li et al. (2016b) used the average of the word embeddings (called DNN AVG) and max pooling of LSTM (called DNN LSTM) for calculating v_{12}. On the other hand, we

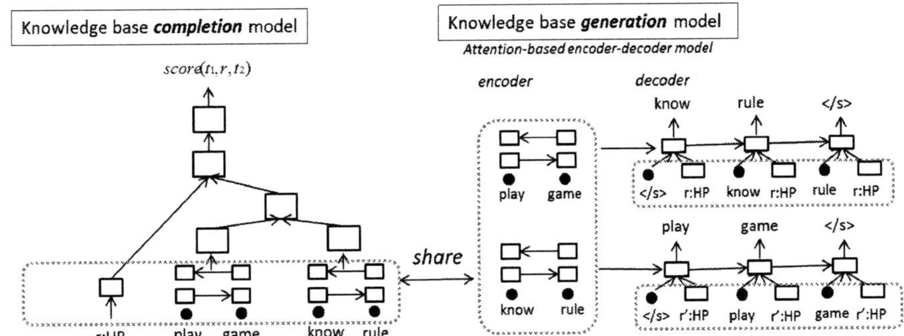

Figure 1: Architecture of proposed method. The CKB completion model estimates the score of $\langle t_1 =$ "play game", $r =$ "HasPrerequisite (HP)", $t_2 =$ "know rule"$\rangle$, and the CKB generation model generates t_2 from $\langle t_1, r \rangle$ and t_1 from $\langle t_2, r' \rangle$. r':HP denotes the reverse direction of "HasPrerequisite".

formulate the phrase embedding by using attention pooling of LSTM and a bilinear function.

$$h_j^i = \text{BiLSTM}(x_j^i, h_{j-1}^i)(i = 1, 2) \tag{2}$$

$$v_i = \sum_{j=1}^{J} \frac{\exp(e_j)}{\sum_{k=1}^{J} \exp(e_k)} h_j^i \tag{3}$$

$$e_k = u^\top \tanh(W h_k^i) \tag{4}$$

$$v_{12} = \text{Bilinear}(v_1, v_2) \tag{5}$$

$$v_{in} = \text{concat}(v_{12}, v_r) \tag{6}$$

where J is the word length of phrase t_i, u is a linear transformation vector for calculating the attention vector, x_j^i and h_j^i are the j th word embedding and hidden state of the LSTM for phrase t_i, and v_r is the relation embedding. Note that we calculated v_{12} for DNN AVG and DNN LSTM by concatenating v_1 and v_2. We used batch normalization (Ioffe and Szegedy, 2015) for v_{in} before passing through the next layer.

3.2 CKB Generation Model

We use an attentional encoder-decoder model to generate phrase knowledge. Here, we expected that the quality of the phrase representation would be increased by sharing the BiLSTM and embeddings between the CKB completion and CKB generation models.

For constructing the encoder-decoder model, we use relation information in addition to word sequences. Let $X = (x_1, x_2, ..., x_J)$ be the input word sequences and $Y = (y_1, y_2, ..., y_T)$ be the output word sequences. The conditional gen-

eration probability of Y is as follows:

$$p(Y|X, \theta) = \prod_{t=1}^{T} p(y_t|y_{<t}, c_t, r) \tag{7}$$

$$p(y_t|y_{<t}, c_t, r) = g(y_{t-1}, s_t, c_t, r) \tag{8}$$

$$s_t = \text{LSTM}(\text{concat}(v_{y_{t-1}}, v_r), s_{t-1}) \tag{9}$$

where θ is a set of model parameters, s_t is a hidden state of the decoder, and c_t is a context vector of input sequences that is weighted by the attention probability and calculated as

$$h_j = \text{BiLSTM}(x_j, h_{j-1}) \tag{10}$$

$$c_t = \sum_{j=1}^{J} \frac{\exp(e_t)}{\sum_{k=1}^{J} \exp(e_k)} h_j \tag{11}$$

$$e_k = v^\top \tanh(W_a s_t + W_e h_k) \tag{12}$$

Here, the BiLSTM, which is the encoder of the CKB generation model, is shared with that of the CKB completion model described in equation (2). As shown in equation (9), we use relation embedding v_r as additional input information. There are several related studies on incorporating additional label information in a decoder (Li et al., 2016a). Although the previous work used additional labels mainly for representing individuality or style information, we use this idea to represent relation information. We also use the technique of tying word vectors and word classifiers (Inan et al., 2016). The encoder BiLSTM is a single-layer bidirectional LSTM, and the decoder LSTM is a single-layer LSTM.

We use a triple $\langle t_1, r, t_2 \rangle$ for training the encoder-decoder model. We train our models to be dual directional. In the forward direction, the model predicts t_2 with the input $\langle t_1, r \rangle$, and in the backward direction, it predicts t_1 with the input $\langle t_2, r \rangle$. Here, since the relation r has a direction, we introduce a new relation r' for each r to train dual-directional CKB generation in one model. In the reverse direction, we replace the relation label r with r'; namely, the output is t_1, and the input is $\langle t_2, r' \rangle$. Therefore, in our CKB generation model, the vocabulary size of the relation is twice that of the original relation set.

4 Training

Loss Function We use the following loss function for training: $L(\theta) = L_\text{c} + \lambda L_\text{g}$, where θ is the set of model parameters, L_c is the loss function of our CKB completion model, and L_g is the loss function of our CKB generation model. We use binary cross entropy for L_c.

$$L_\text{c}(\tau, l) = -\frac{1}{N} \sum_{n=1}^{N} \{l \log \sigma(score(\tau)) \qquad (13)$$
$$+ (1-l)\log(1 - \sigma(score(\tau)))\},$$

where τ indicates the triple $\langle t_1, r, t_2 \rangle$, l is a binary variable that is 1 if the triple is a positive example (true triple) and 0 if the triple is a negative example (false triple), which we will explain in the next subsection. σ is a sigmoid function. We formulate the loss function for the encoder-decoder (CKB generation) model by using the cross entropy:

$$L_\text{g} = -\frac{1}{N} \sum_{n=1}^{N} \sum_{t=1}^{T^{(n)}} \log p(y_t^{(n)} | y_{<t}^{(n)}, c_t^{(n)}, r^{(n)}), \quad (14)$$

where N is the sample size, $T^{(n)}$ is the number of words in the output phrase, c_t is the context vector of the input sequence, and r is the relation label.

Negative sampling We generate negative examples automatically for training the CKB completion model by using random sampling. Specifically, we create three negative examples $\tau_{neg1} = \langle t_1^{neg}, r, t_2 \rangle$, $\tau_{neg2} = \langle t_1, r^{neg}, t_2 \rangle$, and $\tau_{neg3} = \langle t_1, r, t_2^{neg} \rangle$ for the positive triple τ by replacing each component. Here, t_1^{neg} and t_2^{neg} are sampled in mini-batches, while r^{neg} is sampled in all relation sets.

Generating augmentation data using CKB generation model For training the CKB completion and generation model, we need a large amount of data that covers a wide range of commonsense knowledge. Since our CKB generation model can

	ConceptNet	Ja-KB
train	100,000	192,714
validation1	1,200	13,778
validation2	1,200	-
test	2,400	13,778
size of relation	34	7
size of vocabulary	21,471	18,119
average word length	2.02	3.96

Table 1: Summary of data

make new triples, we use it to make the augmentation data. We use the original training data as seed data and generate new triples on the basis of it. More specifically, given a training triple $\langle t_1, r, t_2 \rangle$, we generate a new t_2^{gen} with the input $\langle t_1, r \rangle$ and new t_1^{gen} with the input $\langle t_2, r' \rangle$. This idea is inspired by a technique for improving NMT models (Sennrich et al., 2016). To filter out unreliable candidates, we use the CKB completion score as a threshold. We refer to the generated augmentation data as "auggen" in the experiment section.

5 Experimental Setup

5.1 Data

For the experiments with English, we used the ConceptNet 100K data released by Li et al. (2016b)[1]. The original ConceptNet is a large-scale and multi-lingual CKB. However, the evaluation set, which was created from a subset of the whole ConceptNet, consists of data only in English and contains many short phrases including single words. In order to evaluate the robustness of CKB completion models in terms of the language and long phrases, we created a new open-domain Japanese commonsense knowledge dataset, Ja-KB. The statistics of these data are listed in Table 1. There are more relation labels in ConceptNet than in Ja-KB, because we limited the relation types, which often contain nouns and verbs, when creating the Ja-KB data. The relation set of Ja-KB is Causes, MotivatedBy, Subevent, HasPrerequisite, ObstructedBy, Antonym, and Synonym. The average length of phrases in Ja-KB is longer than in ConceptNet because of the data creation process. The details of our dataset are described below:

To create the Ja-KB data, we used crowdsourcing like in Open Mind Common Sense (OMCS) (Singh et al., 2002). Since data annotated by

---

[1] http://ttic.uchicago.edu/ kgimpel/commonsense.html

crowd workers is usually noisy, we performed a two-step data collection process to eliminate noisy data. In the data creating step, a crowd worker created triples $\langle t_1, r, t_2 \rangle$ from the provided keywords. The keywords consisted of combinations of nouns and verbs that frequently appeared in Web texts.

Each crowd worker created an arbitrary phrase t_1 (or t_2) by using the provided keywords and then selected a relation $r \in R$ and created a corresponding phrase t_2 (or t_1). In the evaluation step, three workers chose a suitable $r \in R$ when they were given $\langle t_1, t_2 \rangle$, which were created by another worker. Since a worker does not know which relation r the creator selected in the creation step, we can measure the reliability of the created knowledge from the overlap of the selected relations. We used triples for which three or more workers selected the same relation label r. In our preliminary study, we found that the accuracy of CKB completion is lower when using low-reliability data.

We randomly selected the test and validation data among the data for which all workers chose the same label. The remaining data were used as training data. For the training data, we added the same number of triples as the evaluator selected same label for considering data reliability. For example, if three evaluators selected the same label for a triple, we added the three triples. For the test and validation data, we randomly sampled negative examples, as described in Section 4, whose size was the same as the number of positive examples according to (Li et al., 2016b). The details are described in the Supplementary Material.

5.2 Model Configurations

We set the dimensions of the hidden layer of the shared BiLSTM to 200, the word and relation embeddings to 200, and the intermediate hidden layer of the completion model to 1000. We set the batch size to 100, dropout rate to 0.2, and weight decay to 0.00001. For optimization, we used SGD and set the initial learning rate to 1.0. We set the reduction of the learning rate to 0.5 and adjusted the learning rate. We set λ of the loss function to 1.0. fastText (Bojanowski et al., 2016) and Wikipedia text were used to train the initial word embeddings. When generating the augmentation data, we set the threshold score of CKB completion to 0.95 for the ConceptNet data and 0.8 for the Ja-KB data. The additional data amounted to about 200,000 triples.

5.3 Baseline Method

CKB completion As baselines, we used the DNN AVG and DNN LSTM models (Li et al., 2016b) that were described in Section 3.1. To assess the effectiveness of joint learning, we compared our CKB completion model only (proposed w/o CKB generation) and the joint model (proposed w/ CKB generation). Moreover, we evaluated the effectiveness of simply adding augmentation data, as described in Section 4 to the training data (+auggen). We used the accuracy of binary classification as the evaluation measure. The threshold was determined by using the validation1 data to maximize the accuracy of binary classification for each method, as in (Li et al., 2016b).

CKB generation We used a simple attentional encoder-decoder model that does not use relation information as a baseline (base). We compared the proposed model with and without joint learning (proposed and proposed w/o CKBC). We also evaluated the effectiveness of simply adding augmentation data as described in Section 4 to the training data (+auggen).

6 Results

6.1 CKB completion

Does joint learning method improve the accuracy of CKB completion? Table 2 shows the accuracy of the CKB completion model. The bottom two lines show the best performances reported in (Li et al., 2016b). The results indicate that our method improved the accuracy of CKB completion compared with the previous method. Our method achieved 0.945 accuracy on the validation2 data. This result is close to human accuracy (about 0.95). By comparing the results of the single model (proposed w/o CKB generation) and joint model (proposed w/ CKB generation), we can see that the joint model improved the accuracy for both ConceptNet and Ja-KB. This indicates that the loss function of CKB generation works as a good constraint for the CKB completion model.

Does data augmentation from CKB generation improve the accuracy of CKB completion? Table 2 shows that augmentation data slightly improved the accuracy of both the ConceptNet test data and Ja-KB test data.

method	ConceptNet		Ja-KB
	valid2	test	test
base (DNN AVG)	0.923	0.929	0.904
base (DNN LSTM)	0.927	0.936	0.901
proposed w/o CKBG	0.927	0.932	0.907
proposed w/ CKBG	**0.945**	0.947	0.910
proposed w/ CKBG (+auggen)	0.944	**0.954**	**0.912**
Li et al (Li et al., 2016b)	0.913	0.920	-
human (Li et al., 2016b)	0.950	-	-

Table 2: Results of CKB completion. CKBG denotes CKB generation.

	ConceptNet	Ja-KB
base(DNN AVG)	0.66	0.58
proposed	0.74	0.62
proposed (+auggen)	0.72	0.61

Table 3: Accuracy of binary classification for manually annotated triples

Human evaluation for assessing the quality of CKB completion Since negative examples were randomly selected from the whole test set in the experiments described above (Table 2), it was easy to distinguish some of them as positive and negative examples. To evaluate the ability of CKB completion in a more difficult setting, we eliminated obviously-false triples and performed manual annotation with the remaining triples. Then we conducted a binary classification experiment with these annotated triples. The details are described below:

First, we prepared triple candidates by using the ConceptNet and Ja-KB datasets. We replaced one of the phrases of the existing triple with a similar phrase, where the similarity was calculated by using the average of the word embeddings. We made 100 replacement triples per triple. Next, we scored the prepared triples by using our CKB completion model and randomly sampled 500 triples whose CKB completion scores were larger than a threshold. Then, ten annotators gave subjective evaluation scores to all 500 triples. In this evaluation, the annotators rated the degree of agreement with each statement (triple) on 0-4 rating scale (0 = strongly disagree, 4 = strongly agree), where the annotator interpreted each triple as a statement by using the relation explanation. For example, $\langle dog, HasA, tail \rangle$ means "a dog has a tail". Finally, we sampled the top 100 triples which had small variance from the 500 annotated data and labeled those having average scores of 3 or over with 1 (positive examples; 57% and 55% of the top 100

triples of CN and Ja-KB, respectively) and those having average scores lower than 3 with 0 (negative examples; 43% and 45%).

Table 3 indicates the binary classification accuracy for the 100 sampled triples. While the proposed method improved accuracy, the accuracy of +auggen was slightly lower than it. This indicates that we have to select the augmentation data and the thresholds more carefully to improve the accuracy of difficult examples. Moreover, the overall score is lower than the result of Table 2. This indicates there is room for improving the CKB completion accuracy for difficult examples. To distinguish more difficult examples and improve the accuracy of knowledge acquisition, we have to develop a better negative sampling strategy for training.

6.2 CKB generation

It is difficult to evaluate the quality of the CKB generation model directly, since there are many correct phrase candidates in addition to phrases that appear in the test data. For that reason, we evaluated our CKB generation model from different viewpoints.

Can our CKB generation model generate reasonable phrases? To see whether the top-n phrases generated from each query in the test set included the reference phrase that corresponds to the query, we calculated the recall of the reference phrases as follows:

$$recall = N_{match}/N_{reference}, \qquad (15)$$

where N_{match} is the number of generated phrases that exactly match the reference phrases. Figure 2 shows the recall of the reference phrases for each CKB generation model. The results shown in the figure are averages over the test queries. Compared with the baseline system, our CKB generation model achieved higher recalls on both ConceptNet and Ja-KB. This indicates that considering relation information worked well.

The effectiveness of using augmentation data is also illustrated in Figure 2. For the Ja-KB data, recall improved as a result of adding augmentation data. Since the phrase length of the node in ConceptNet is shorter than in Ja-KB, it is easier to cover reference phrases for ConceptNet.

Can our CKB generation model generate new phrases? To evaluate the effectiveness of our

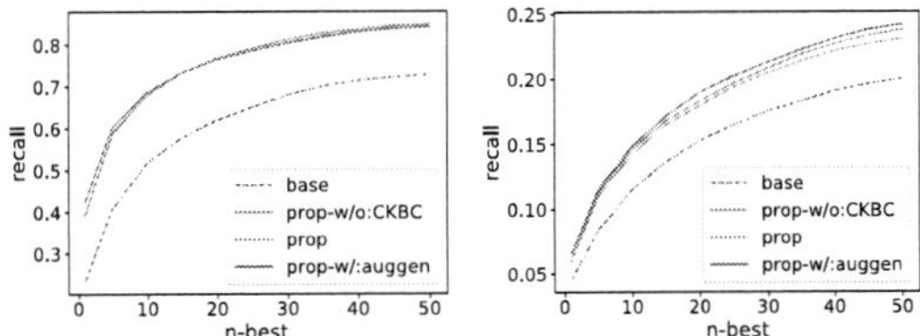

Figure 2: Recall of reference phrase (left: ConceptNet, right: Ja-KB)

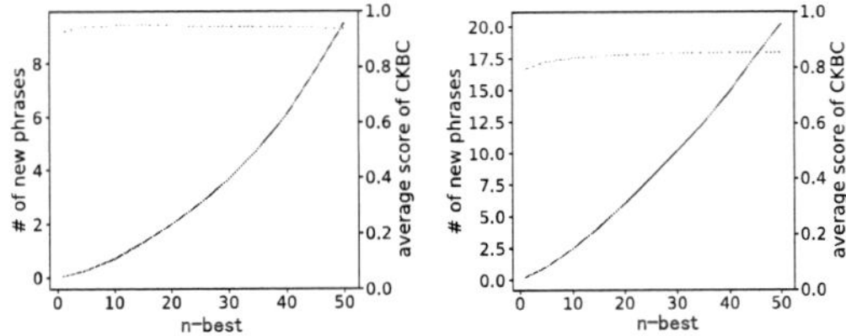

Figure 3: Average number of new phrases generated by CKBG (blue lines) and average score of CKBC of each triple (orange dashed lines). Left: ConceptNet, Right: Ja-KB.

generated triple $\langle t_1, r, t_2 \rangle$ input $\langle t_1, r \rangle$, output t_2	score-g	score-c
play game , HP , learn rule *	-3.57	0.985
play game , HP , have game **	-3.87	0.955
play game , HP , find someone to play **	-4.20	0.984
play game , HP , find friend *	-4.23	0.978
play game , HP , skill	-4.24	0.988
play game , UsedFor , entertainment	-2.21	0.950
play game , UsedFor , fun	-2.29	0.934
play game , UsedFor , have fun *	-2.64	0.920
play game , UsedFor , enjoyment	-3.13	0.976
play game , UsedFor , recreation *	-3.38	0.971

Table 4: Examples of phrases created using CKB generation model. The relation label "HP" represents HasPrerequisite. t_2 is the generated phrase, and the input is $\langle t_1, r \rangle$. * represents that the generated triple is new, and ** represents that the generated t_2 is new.

generation model at increasing the node size of a CKB, we determined whether our model could generate new phrases that are not included in the existing CKB. Figure 3 shows that the average number of such new phrases in the n-best outputs of our model that were generated from a query pair of a phrase and a relation in the test set of ConceptNet and Ja-KB. We can see from the figure that our model could make triples that contain new phrases by generating multiple phrases from a query pair. The figure also plots the average CKB completion score of each generated triple that contains new phrases; the results confirm that the generated triples had a high CKB completion score.

Generated examples Table 4 lists examples of phrases created by the generation model; score-g indicates the logarithmic probability of the generation model, and score-c indicates the score of the completion model. The upper row lists the top-five results with the input $\langle t_1, r \rangle$=(play game, HasPrerequisite). The lower row lists the top-five results with the input $\langle t_1, r \rangle$=(play game, Used-For). These results indicate that our CKB generation model can generate reasonable candidates including new triples that reflected relation information. More examples are shown in the Supplementary Material.

How high is the quality of knowledge acquired with our CKB generation? We performed subjective evaluations of the quality of the triples generated with our model. First, we generated two types of query pairs: ones generated from ConceptNet (CN_gen) and ones generated from Wikipedia (Wiki_gen). In CN_gen, we used all phrase and relation pairs $\langle t, r \rangle$ appearing in the test data. In Wiki_gen, we used triples extracted by using the POS tag sequence pattern for each relation according to Li et al. (2016b) and scored each triple with CKB completion scores. Then, we used $\langle t, r \rangle$ pairs of 10000 triples that had higher scores than a threshold as the input query pairs.

Next, we generated a phrase t_{gen} from $\langle t, r \rangle$ and made new triples $\langle t, r, t_{gen} \rangle$ with our CKB generation model. We sorted the generated triples according to the CKB completion score and selected the top-100 new triples for CN_gen and Wiki_gen. The annotators assigned a (semantic) quality score and grammatical score to each triple. We used a 0-4 degree agreement score (described in 6.1) for evaluating triple quality and a 0-2 score (0. Doesn't make sense. 1. There are some grammatical errors. 2. There are no grammatical errors.) for the evaluation of grammatical quality. We recruited ten annotators who were native speakers of each language.

We show the results in Table 5. The quality score of each triple of CN_gen was quite high. The quality score of Wiki_gen was lower than that of CN_gen. Since Wikipedia has lots of specific information, it is difficult to extract an input query that is useful for making commonsense knowledge. This tendency is similar to the results reported in Li et al. (Li et al., 2016b). The grammatical score was high for both CN_gen and Wiki_gen.

method	ConceptNet		Ja-KB	
	semantic	grammar	semantic	grammar
CN_gen	3.452	1.651	3.466	1.996
Wiki_gen	2.685	1.749	2.415	1.849

Table 5: Subjective evaluation of CKB generation model

This indicates that our CKB generation model can generate phrases that have almost no grammatical errors for high confidence triples for top ranked triples.

7 Related Work

Knowledge base completion for entity-relation triples There are many studies that embed graph structures such as TransE, TransR, HolE, and STransE (Bordes et al., 2013; Lin et al., 2015; Nickel et al., 2016; Nguyen et al., 2016). Their methods aim to learn low-dimensional representations for entities and relationships by using topological features. Although these methods are widely used, they rely on the connectivity of the existing KB and are only suitable for predicting relationships between existing, well-connected entities (Shi and Weninger, 2018). Therefore, it is difficult to get good representations for new nodes that have no connections with existing nodes.

Several studies have added text information to the graph embeddings (Zhong et al., 2015; Wang and Li, 2016; Xiao et al., 2017). These studies aim to incorporate richer information in the graph embedding. They combine a graph embedding model and a text embedding model into one. The text information they use is the description or definition statement of each node. For example, they would use the description "Barack Obama is the 44th and current President of United States" for the node "Barack Obama" and make better quality embeddings. Although these methods effectively incorporate text information, they assume that the descriptions of entities can be easily acquired. For example, they use the originally aligned descriptions (e.g., DBpedia, Freebase) or descriptions acquired by using a simple entity linking method. Moreover, the methods use topological information, and they are not designed for on-the-fly knowledge base completion.

Knowledge base completion for commonsense triples In commonsense knowledge base completion, the nodes of the KB consist of arbitrary phrases (word sequences), and there are a huge number of unique nodes. In such case, the KB graph becomes very sparse, and consequently, there is almost no merit to considering the topological features of the KBs. Moreover, on-the-fly KBC is needed because we have to handle new nodes as input. It is thus more important to formulate phrase and relation embeddings that can robustly represent arbitrary phrases. There are a few studies on CKB completion models. In particular, Li et al. (2016b) and Socher et al. (2013) proposed a simple KBC model for CKB. The formulations of CKB completion in the two studies are the same, and we evaluated Li et al. (2016b)'s method as a baseline.

Open Information Extraction Open Information Extraction (OpenIE) aims to extract triple knowledge from raw text. It finds triples that have specific predefined relations by using lexical and syntactic patterns (Mintz et al., 2009; Fader et al., 2011). Several neural-network-based relation extraction methods have been proposed (Lin et al., 2016; Zhang et al., 2017). These models construct classifiers to estimate the relation between two arbitrary entities. OpenIE models are trained with sentence-level annotation data or distant supervision, while our model is trained with triples in a knowledge base. Since openIE can extract new triples from raw text, it can be used to make augmentation data for the CKB completion model.

Knowledge generation There are several studies on the knowledge generation task that use neural network models. For example, Hu et al. (2017) proposed an event prediction model that uses a sequence-to-sequence model. Prakash et al. (2016) and Li et al. (2017) proposed a paraphrase generation model. These studies targeted only specific relationships and did not explicitly incorporate relations into the generation model. Our CKB generation model explicitly incorporates relation information into the decoder and can model multiple relationships in one model.

8 Conclusion

We proposed a new CKB generation task and joint learning method of CKB completion and generation. Experimental results with two commonsense datasets demonstrated that our model has two strengths: it improves the coverage of the knowledge bases. While conventional completion tasks are limited to verifying given triples, our generative model can create new knowledge including new phrases that are not in the knowledge bases. Second, our completion model can improve the verification accuracy. Two characteristics of our completion model contribute to this improvement: (i) the model shares the hidden layers, word embedding, and relation embedding with the generation model to acquire good phrase and relation representations, and (ii) it can be trained with the augmentation data created by the generation model.

In this study, we did not utilize raw text information such as from Wikipedia during training except for pre-trained word embeddings. We would like to extend our method so that it can incorporate raw text information. Moreover, we would like to develop a method that effectively utilizes this commonsense knowledge for other NLP tasks that need commonsense reasoning.

References

Gabor Angeli and Christopher Manning. 2013. Philosophers are mortal: Inferring the truth of unseen facts. In *Proceedings of the Seventeenth Conference on Computational Natural Language Learning*, pages 133–142.

Piotr Bojanowski, Edouard Grave, Armand Joulin, and Tomas Mikolov. 2016. Enriching word vectors with subword information. *arXiv preprint arXiv:1607.04606*.

Kurt Bollacker, Colin Evans, Praveen Paritosh, Tim Sturge, and Jamie Taylor. 2008. Freebase: A collaboratively created graph database for structuring human knowledge. In *Proceedings of the 2008 ACM SIGMOD International Conference on Management of Data*, SIGMOD '08, pages 1247–1250. ACM.

Antoine Bordes, Nicolas Usunier, Alberto Garcia-Durán, Jason Weston, and Oksana Yakhnenko. 2013. Translating embeddings for modeling multi-relational data. In *Proceedings of the 26th International Conference on NIPS*, pages 2787–2795.

Anthony Fader, Stephen Soderland, and Oren Etzioni. 2011. Identifying relations for open information extraction. In *Proceedings of the Conference on EMNLP*, pages 1535–1545.

Jonathan Gordon and Benjamin Van Durme. 2013. Reporting bias and knowledge acquisition. In *Proceedings of the 2013 Workshop on Automated Knowledge Base Construction*, AKBC '13, pages 25–30. ACM.

Linmei Hu, Juanzi Li, Liqiang Nie, Xiaoli Li, and Chao Shao. 2017. What happens next? future subevent prediction using contextual hierarchical LSTM. In *Proceedings of the Thirty-First AAAI Conference on Artificial Intelligence*, pages 3450–3456.

Hakan Inan, Khashayar Khosravi, and Richard Socher. 2016. Tying word vectors and word classifiers: A loss framework for language modeling. *CoRR*, abs/1611.01462.

Sergey Ioffe and Christian Szegedy. 2015. Batch normalization: Accelerating deep network training by reducing internal covariate shift. *CoRR*, abs/1502.03167.

Jiwei Li, Michel Galley, Chris Brockett, Georgios Spithourakis, Jianfeng Gao, and Bill Dolan. 2016a. A persona-based neural conversation model. In *Proceedings of the 54th Annual Meeting of the ACL*, pages 994–1003.

Xiang Li, Aynaz Taheri, Lifu Tu, and Kevin Gimpel. 2016b. Commonsense knowledge base completion. In *Proceedings of the 54th Annual Meeting of the ACL*, pages 1445–1455.

Zichao Li, Xin Jiang, Lifeng Shang, and Hang Li. 2017. Paraphrase generation with deep reinforcement learning. *CoRR*, abs/1711.00279.

Hongyu Lin, Le Sun, and Xianpei Han. 2017. Reasoning with heterogeneous knowledge for commonsense machine comprehension. In *Proceedings of the 2017 Conference on EMNLP*, pages 2032–2043.

Yankai Lin, Zhiyuan Liu, Maosong Sun, Yang Liu, and Xuan Zhu. 2015. Learning entity and relation embeddings for knowledge graph completion. In *Proceedings of the Twenty-Ninth AAAI Conference on Artificial Intelligence*, pages 2181–2187.

Yankai Lin, Shiqi Shen, Zhiyuan Liu, Huanbo Luan, and Maosong Sun. 2016. Neural relation extraction with selective attention over instances. In *Proceedings of the 54th Annual Meeting of the ACL*.

Teng Long, Emmanuel Bengio, Ryan Lowe, Jackie Chi Kit Cheung, and Doina Precup. 2017. World knowledge for reading comprehension: Rare entity prediction with hierarchical lstms using external descriptions. In *Proceedings of the 2017 Conference on EMNLP*, pages 825–834.

M. Mintz, S. Bills, R. Snow, and D. Jurafsky. 2009. Distant supervision for relation extraction without labeled data. In *Proceedings of the Joint Conference of the 47th Annual Meeting of the ACL and the 4th IJCNLP*, pages 1003–1011.

Dat Quoc Nguyen, Kairit Sirts, Lizhen Qu, and Mark Johnson. 2016. Stranse: a novel embedding model of entities and relationships in knowledge bases. In *Proceedings of the 2016 Conference of the NAACL: HLT*, pages 460–466.

Maximilian Nickel, Lorenzo Rosasco, and Tomaso Poggio. 2016. Holographic embeddings of knowledge graphs. In *Proceedings of the Thirtieth AAAI Conference on Artificial Intelligence*, pages 1955–1961.

Simon Ostermann, Ashutosh Modi, Michael Roth, Stefan Thater, and Manfred Pinkal. 2018. Mcscript: A novel dataset for assessing machine comprehension using script knowledge. *CoRR*, abs/1803.05223.

aaditya prakash, Sadid A. Hasan, Kathy Lee, Vivek Datla, Ashequl Qadir, Joey Liu, and Oladimeji Farri. 2016. Neural paraphrase generation with stacked residual lstm networks. In *Proceedings of COLING 2016*, pages 2923–2934.

Rico Sennrich, Barry Haddow, and Alexandra Birch. 2016. Improving neural machine translation models with monolingual data. In *Proceedings of the 54th Annual Meeting of the ACL*, pages 86–96.

Baoxu Shi and Tim Weninger. 2018. Open-world knowledge graph completion. *AAAI Conference on Artificial Intelligence*.

Push Singh, Thomas Lin, Erik T. Mueller, Grace Lim, Travell Perkins, and Wan Li Zhu. 2002. Open mind common sense: Knowledge acquisition from the general public. In *On the Move to Meaningful Internet Systems, 2002 - DOA/CoopIS/ODBASE 2002 Confederated International Conferences DOA, CoopIS and ODBASE 2002*, pages 1223–1237.

Richard Socher, Danqi Chen, Christopher D. Manning, and Andrew Y. Ng. 2013. Reasoning with neural tensor networks for knowledge base completion. In *Proceedings of the 26th International Conference on NIPS*, pages 926–934.

Robert Speer, Joshua Chin, and Catherine Havasi. 2017. Conceptnet 5.5: An open multilingual graph of general knowledge. In *Proceedings of the Thirty-First AAAI Conference on Artificial Intelligence*, pages 4444–4451.

Liang Wang, Meng Sun, Wei Zhao, Kewei Shen, and Jingming Liu. 2018. Yuanfudao at semeval-2018 task 11: Three-way attention and relational knowledge for commonsense machine comprehension. In *Proceedings of The 12th International Workshop on Semantic Evaluation, SemEval@NAACL-HLT*.

Zhigang Wang and Juanzi Li. 2016. Text-enhanced representation learning for knowledge graph. In *Proceedings of the Twenty-Fifth International Joint Conference on Artificial Intelligence*, pages 1293–1299.

Han Xiao, Minlie Huang, Lian Meng, and Xiaoyan Zhu. 2017. SSP: semantic space projection for knowledge graph embedding with text descriptions. In *Proceedings of the Thirty-First AAAI Conference on Artificial Intelligence*, pages 3104–3110.

Bishan Yang and Tom Mitchell. 2017. Leveraging knowledge bases in lstms for improving machine reading. In *Proceedings of the 55th Annual Meeting of the ACL*, pages 1436–1446.

Tom Young, Erik Cambria, Iti Chaturvedi, Hao Zhou, Subham Biswas, and Minlie Huang. 2018. Augmenting end-to-end dialogue systems with commonsense knowledge. In *Proceedings of the Thirty-Second AAAI Conference on Artificial Intelligence*.

Meishan Zhang, Yue Zhang, and Guohong Fu. 2017. End-to-end neural relation extraction with global optimization. In *Proceedings of the 2017 Conference on EMNLP*, pages 1730–1740.

Huaping Zhong, Jianwen Zhang, Zhen Wang, Hai Wan, and Zheng Chen. 2015. Aligning knowledge and text embeddings by entity descriptions. In *Proceedings of the 2015 Conference on EMNLP*, pages 267–272.

Active Learning for Interactive Neural Machine Translation of Data Streams

Álvaro Peris and **Francisco Casacuberta**
Pattern Recognition and Human Language Technology Research Center
Universitat Politècnica de València, València, Spain
{lvapeab, fcn}@prhlt.upv.es

Abstract

We study the application of active learning techniques to the translation of unbounded data streams via interactive neural machine translation. The main idea is to select, from an unbounded stream of source sentences, those worth to be supervised by a human agent. The user will interactively translate those samples. Once validated, these data is useful for adapting the neural machine translation model.

We propose two novel methods for selecting the samples to be validated. We exploit the information from the attention mechanism of a neural machine translation system. Our experiments show that the inclusion of active learning techniques into this pipeline allows to reduce the effort required during the process, while increasing the quality of the translation system. Moreover, it enables to balance the human effort required for achieving a certain translation quality. Moreover, our neural system outperforms classical approaches by a large margin.

1 Introduction

The translation industry is a high-demand field. Large amounts of data must be translated on a regular basis. Machine translation (MT) techniques greatly boost the productivity of the translation agencies (Arenas, 2008). However, despite the recent advances achieved in this field, MT systems are still far to be perfect and make errors. The correction of such errors is usually done in a post-processing step, called post-editing. This requires a great effort, as it needs from expert human supervisors.

The requirements of the translation industry have increased in the last years. We live in a global world, in which large amounts of data must be periodically translated. This is the case of the European Parliament, whose proceedings must be reg-ularly translated; or the Project Syndicate[1] platform, which translates editorials from newspapers to several languages. In these scenarios, the sentences to be translated can be seen as unbounded streams of data (Levenberg et al., 2010).

When dealing with such massive volumes of data, it is prohibitively expensive to manually revise all the translations. Therefore, it is mandatory to spare human effort, at the expense of some translation quality. Hence, when facing this situation, we have a twofold objective: on the one hand, we aim to obtain translations with the highest quality possible. On the other hand, we are constrained by the amount of human effort spent in the supervision and correction process of the translations proposed by an MT system.

The active learning (AL) framework is well-suited for these objectives. The application of AL techniques to MT involve to ask a human oracle to supervise a fraction of the incoming data (Bloodgood and Callison-Burch, 2010). Once the human has revised these samples, they are used for improving the MT system, via incremental learning. Therefore, a key element of AL is the so-called sampling strategy, which determines the sentences that should be corrected by the human.

Aiming to reduce the human effort required during post-editing, other alternative frameworks have been study. A successful one is the interactive-predictive machine translation (IMT) paradigm (Foster et al., 1997; Barrachina et al., 2009). In IMT, human and MT system jointly collaborate for obtaining high-quality translations, while reducing the human effort spent in this process.

In this work, we explore the application of NMT to the translation of unbounded data streams. We apply AL techniques for selecting the instances to

---

[1]www.project-syndicate.org

Proceedings of the 22nd Conference on Computational Natural Language Learning (CoNLL 2018), pages 151–160
Brussels, Belgium, October 31 - November 1, 2018. ©2018 Association for Computational Linguistics

be revised by a human oracle. The correction process is done by means of an interactive-predictive NMT (INMT) system, which aims to reduce the human effort of this process. The supervised samples will be used for the NMT system to incrementally improve its models. To the best of our knowledge, this is the first work that introduces an INMT system into the scenario involving the translation of unbounded data. Our main contributions are:

- We study the application of AL on an INMT framework when dealing with large data streams. We introduce two sampling strategies for obtaining the most useful samples to be supervised by the human. We compare these techniques with other classical, well-performing strategies.

- We conduct extensive experiments, analyzing the different sampling strategies and studying the amount of effort required for obtaining a certain translation quality.

- The results show that AL succeeds at improving the translation pipeline. The translation systems featuring AL have better quality and require less human effort in the IMT process than static systems. Moreover, the application of the AL framework allows to obtain a balance between translation quality and effort required for achieving such quality. This balance can be easily tuned, according to the needs of the users.

- We open-source our code[2] and use publicly-available corpora, fostering further research on this area.

2   Related work

The translation of large data streams is a problem that has been thoroughly studied. Most works aim to continuously modify the MT system as more data become available. These modifications are usually performed in an incremental way (Levenberg et al., 2010; Denkowski et al., 2014; Turchi et al., 2017), learning from user post-edits. This incremental learning has also been applied to IMT, either to phrase-based statistical machine translation (SMT) systems (Nepveu et al., 2004; Ortiz-Martínez, 2016) or NMT (Peris and Casacuberta, 2018b).

---

[2]The source code can be found at: `https://github.com/lvapeab/nmt-keras/tree/interactive_NMT`.

The translation of large volumes of data is a scenario very appropriate for the AL framework (Cohn et al., 1994; Olsson, 2009; Settles, 2009). The application of AL to SMT has been studied for pool-based (Haffari et al., 2009; Bloodgood and Callison-Burch, 2010) and stream-based (González-Rubio et al., 2011) setups. Later works (González-Rubio et al., 2012; González-Rubio and Casacuberta, 2014), combined AL together with IMT, showing that AL can effectively reduce the human effort required for achieving a certain translation quality.

All these works were based on SMT systems. However, the recently introduced NMT paradigm (Sutskever et al., 2014; Bahdanau et al., 2015) has irrupted as the current state-of-the-art for MT (Bojar et al., 2017). Several works aimed at building more productive NMT systems. Related to our work, studies on interactive NMT systems (Knowles and Koehn, 2016; Peris et al., 2017; Hokamp and Liu, 2017) proved the efficacy of this framework. A body of work has been done aiming to build adaptive NMT systems, which continuously learn from human corrections (Turchi et al., 2017; Peris and Casacuberta, 2018b). Recently, Lam et al. (2018) applied AL techniques to an INMT system, for deciding whether the user should revise a partial hypothesis or not. However, to our knowledge, a study on the use of AL for NMT in a scenario of translation of unbounded data streams is still missing.

3   Neural machine translation

NMT is a particular case of sequence-to-sequence learning: given a sequence of words from the source language, the goal is to generate another sequence of words in the target language. This is usually done by means of an encoder–decoder architecture (Sutskever et al., 2014; Vaswani et al., 2017). In this work, we use a recurrent encoder–decoder system with long short-term memory (LSTM) units (Hochreiter and Schmidhuber, 1997) and an attention mechanism (Bahdanau et al., 2015).

Each element from the input sequence is projected into a continuous space by means of an embedding matrix. The sequence of embeddings is then processed by a bidirectional (Schuster and Paliwal, 1997) LSTM network, that concatenates the hidden states from forward and backward layers and produces a sequence of annotations.

The decoder is a conditional LSTM (cLSTM) network (Peris and Casacuberta, 2018b). A cLSTM network is composed of several LSTM transition blocks with an attention mechanism in between. We use two LSTM blocks.

The output of the decoder is combined together with the attended representation of the input sentence and with the word embedding of the word previously generated in a deep output layer (Pascanu et al., 2014). Finally, a softmax layer computes a probability distribution over the target language vocabulary.

The model is jointly trained by means of stochastic gradient descent (SGD) (Robbins and Monro, 1951), aiming to minimize the cross-entropy over a bilingual training corpus. SGD is usually applied to mini-batches of data; but it can be also applied sample-to-sample, allowing the training of the NMT system in an incremental way (Turchi et al., 2017).

For decoding, the model uses a beam search method (Sutskever et al., 2014) for obtaining the most probable target sentence $\hat{\mathbf{y}}$, given a source sentence $\mathbf{x}$:

$$\hat{\mathbf{y}} = \arg\max_{\mathbf{y}} \ p(\mathbf{y} \mid \mathbf{x}) \qquad (1)$$

3.1 Interactive machine translation

As previously discussed, MT systems are not perfect. Their outputs must be corrected by a human agent in a post-editing stage, in order to achieve high-quality translations.

The IMT framework constitutes a more efficient alternative to the regular post-editing. In a nutshell, IMT consists in an iterative process in which, at each iteration, the user introduces a correction to the system hypothesis. The system takes into account the correction and provides an alternative hypothesis, considering the feedback from the user.

In this work, we use a prefix-based IMT protocol: the user corrects the left-most wrong character of the hypothesis. With this action, the user has also validated a correct prefix. Then, the system must complete the provided prefix, generating a suitable suffix. Fig. 1 shows an example of the prefix-based IMT protocol.

More formally, the expression for computing the most probable suffix ($\hat{\mathbf{y}}_s$) is:

$$\hat{\mathbf{y}}_s = \arg\max_{\mathbf{y}_s} \ p(\mathbf{y}_s \mid \mathbf{x}, \mathbf{y}_p) \qquad (2)$$

Source (x):		They are lost forever .
Target (ŷ):		Ils sont perdus à jamais .
IT-0	**MT**	Ils sont perdus pour toujours .
IT-1	User	*Ils sont perdus* [à] *pour toujours .*
	MT	*Ils sont perdus à* jamais .
IT-2	User	*Ils sont perdus à jamais .*

Figure 1: IMT session to translate a sentence from English to French. **IT-** is the number of iterations of the process. The **MT** row shows the MT hypothesis in the current iteration. In the **User** row is the feedback introduced by the user: the corrected character (boxed). We color in green the prefix that the user inherently validated with the character correction.

where $\mathbf{y}_p$ is the validated prefix provided by the user and $\mathbf{x}$ is the source sentence. Note that this expression is similar to Eq. (1). The difference is that now, the search space is the set of suffixes that complete $\mathbf{y}_p$.

For NMT systems, Eq. (2) is implemented as a beam search, constrained by the prefix provided by the user (Peris et al., 2017; Peris and Casacuberta, 2018b).

4 Active learning in machine translation

When dealing with potentially unbounded datasets, it becomes prohibitively expensive to manually supervise all the translations. Aiming to address this problem, in the AL framework, a sampling strategy selects a subset of sentences worth to be supervised by the user. Once corrected, the MT system adapts its models with these samples.

Therefore, the AL protocol applied to unbounded data streams is as follows (González-Rubio et al., 2012): first, we retrieve from the data stream $\mathcal{S}$ a block $\mathcal{B}$ of consecutive sentences, with the function getBlockFromStream($\mathcal{S}$). According to the sampling($\mathcal{B}, \varepsilon$) function, we select from $\mathcal{B}$ a subset $\mathcal{V}$ of ε instances, worth to be supervised by the user. See Section 5 for deeper insights on the sampling functions used in this work. These sampled sentences are interactively translated together with the user (Section 3.1). This process is done in the function INMT($\theta, \mathbf{x}, \mathbf{y}$). Once the user translates via INMT a source sentence $\mathbf{x}$, a correct translation $\hat{\mathbf{y}}$ is obtained. Then, we use the pair $(\mathbf{x}, \hat{\mathbf{y}})$ to retrain the parameters

---

Algorithm 1: Active learning for unbounded data streams with interactive neural machine translation.

input : θ (NMT model)
$\mathcal{S}$ (stream of source sentences)
ε (effort level desired)
auxiliar : $\mathcal{B}$ (block of source sentences)
$\mathcal{V} \subseteq \mathcal{B}$ (sentences to be supervised by the user

1 **begin**
2   **repeat**
3      $\mathcal{B} = \texttt{getBlockFromStream}(\mathcal{S})$;
4      $\mathcal{V} = \texttt{sampling}(\mathcal{B}, \varepsilon)$;
5   **foreach** $\mathbf{x} \in \mathcal{B}$ **do**
6        $\mathbf{y} = \texttt{translate}(\theta, \mathbf{x})$;
7   **if** $\mathbf{x} \in \mathcal{V}$ **then**
8          $\hat{\mathbf{y}} = \texttt{INMT}(\theta, \mathbf{x}, \mathbf{y})$;
9          $\theta = \texttt{update}(\theta, (\mathbf{x}, \hat{\mathbf{y}}))$;
10          $\texttt{output}(\hat{\mathbf{y}})$;
11   **else**
12          $\texttt{output}(\mathbf{y})$;
13   **end**
14   **end**
15   **until** $\mathcal{S} \neq \emptyset$;
16 **end**

θ from the NMT model, via SGD. This is done with the function $\texttt{update}(\theta, (\mathbf{x}, \hat{\mathbf{y}}))$. Therefore, the NMT system is incrementally adapted with new data. The sentences considered unworthy to be supervised are automatically translated according to according Eq. (1), with the function $\texttt{translate}(\theta, \mathbf{x})$. Once we finish the translation of the current block $\mathcal{B}$, we start the process again. Algorithm 1 details the full procedure.

5 Sentence sampling strategies

One of the key elements of AL is to have a meaningful strategy for obtaining the most useful samples to be supervised by the human agent. This requires an evaluation of the informativeness of unlabeled samples. The sampling strategies used in this work belong to two major frameworks: uncertainty sampling (Lewis and Catlett, 1994) and query-by-committee (Seung et al., 1992).

As baseline, we use a random sampling strategy: sentences are randomly selected from the data stream $\mathcal{S}$. Although simple, this strategy usually works well in practice. In the rest of this section, we describe the sampling strategies used in

this work.

5.1 Uncertainty sampling

The idea behind this family of methods is to select those instances for which the model has the least confidence to be properly translated. Therefore, all techniques compute, for each sample, an uncertainty score. The selected sentences will be those with the highest scores.

Quality estimation sampling

A common and effective way for measuring the uncertainty of a MT system is to use confidence estimation (Gandrabur and Foster, 2003; Blatz et al., 2004; Ueffing and Ney, 2007). The idea is to estimate the quality of a translation according to confidence scores of the words.

More specifically, given a source sentence $\mathbf{x} = x_1, \ldots, x_J$ and a translation hypothesis $\mathbf{y} = y_1, \ldots, y_I$, a word confidence score (C_w) as computed as (Ueffing and Ney, 2005):

$$C_w(\mathbf{x}, y_i) = \max_{0 \leq j \leq J} p(y_i | x_j) \qquad (3)$$

where $p(y_i | x_j)$ is the alignment probability of y_i and x_j, given by an IBM Model 2 (Brown et al., 1993). x_0 denotes the empty source word. The choice of the IBM Model 2 is twofold: on the one hand, it is a very fast method, which only requires to query in a dictionary. We are in an interactive framework, therefore speed becomes a crucial requirement. On the other hand, its performance is close to more complex methods (Blatz et al., 2004; Dyer et al., 2013).

Following González-Rubio et al. (2012), the uncertainty score for the quality estimation sampling is defined as:

$$C_{\text{qe}}(\mathbf{x}, \mathbf{y}) = 1 - \frac{|\{y_i \in \mathbf{y} | C_w(\mathbf{x}, y_i) > \tau_w\}|}{|\mathbf{y}|} \qquad (4)$$

where τ_w is a word confidence threshold, adjusted according to a development corpus. $|\cdot|$ denotes the size of a sequence or set.

Coverage sampling

One of the main issues suffered by NMT systems is the lack of coverage: the NMT system may not translate all words from a source sentence. This results in over-translation or under-translation problems (Tu et al., 2016).

We propose to use the translation coverage as a measure of the uncertainty suffered by the NMT system when translating a sentence. Therefore, we modify the coverage penalty proposed by Wu et al. (2016), for obtaining a coverage-based uncertainty score:

$$C_{\text{cov}}(\mathbf{x}, \mathbf{y}) = \frac{\sum_{j=1}^{|\mathbf{x}|} \log \left(\min(\sum_{i=1}^{|\mathbf{y}|} \alpha_{i,j}, 1) \right)}{|\mathbf{x}|} \tag{5}$$

where $\alpha_{i,j}$ is attention probability of the i-th target word and the j-th source word.

Attention distraction sampling

When generating a target word, an attentional NMT system should attend on meaningful parts of the source sentence. If the system is translating an uncertain sample, its attention mechanism will be *distracted*. That means, dispersed throughout the source sequence. A sample with a great distraction will feature an attention probability distribution with heavy tails (e.g. a uniform distribution). Therefore, for the attention distraction sampling strategy, the sentences to select will be those with highest attention distraction.

For computing a distraction score, we compute the kurtosis of the weights given by the attention model for each target word y_i:

$$\text{Kurt}(y_i) = \frac{\frac{1}{|\mathbf{x}|} \sum_{j=1}^{|\mathbf{x}|} (\alpha_{i,j} - \frac{1}{|\mathbf{x}|})^4}{\left(\frac{1}{|\mathbf{x}|} \sum_{j=1}^{|\mathbf{x}|} (\alpha_{i,j} - \frac{1}{|\mathbf{x}|})^2 \right)^2} \tag{6}$$

being, as above, $\alpha_{i,j}$ the weight assigned by the attention model to the j-th source word when decoding the i-th target word. Note that, by construction of the attention model, $\frac{1}{|\mathbf{x}|}$ is equivalent to the mean of the attention weights of the word y_i.

Since we want to obtain samples with heavy tails, we average the minus kurtosis values for all words in the target sentence, obtaining the attention distraction score C_{ad}:

$$C_{\text{ad}}(\mathbf{x}, \mathbf{y}) = \frac{\sum_{i=1}^{|\mathbf{y}|} -\text{Kurt}(y_i)}{|\mathbf{y}|} \tag{7}$$

5.2 Query-by-committee

This framework maintains a committee of models, each one able to vote for the sentences to be selected. The query-by-committee (QBC) method selects the samples with the largest disagreement among the members of the committee. The level of disagreement of a sample $\mathbf{x}$ measured according

to the vote-entropy function (Dagan and Engelson, 1995):

$$C_{\text{qbc}}(\mathbf{x}) = -\frac{\#V(\mathbf{x})}{|\mathcal{C}|} + \log \frac{\#V(\mathbf{x})}{|\mathcal{C}|} \tag{8}$$

where $\#V(\mathbf{x})$ is the number of members of the committee that voted $\mathbf{x}$ to be worth to be supervised and $|\mathcal{C}|$ is the number of members of the committee. If $\#V(\mathbf{x})$ is zero, we set the value of $C_{\text{qbc}}(\mathbf{x})$ to $-\infty$.

Our committee was composed by the four uncertainty sampling strategies, namely quality estimation, coverage, attention distraction and random sampling. The inclusion of the latter into the committee can be seen as a way of introducing some noise, aiming to prevent overfitting.

6 Experimental framework

In order to assess the effectiveness of AL for INMT, we conducted a similar experimentation than the latter works in AL for IMT (González-Rubio and Casacuberta, 2014): we started from a NMT system trained on a general corpus and followed Algorithm 1. This means that the sampling strategy selected those instances to be supervised by the human agent, who interactively translated them. Next, the NMT system was updated in an incremental way with the selected samples.

Due to the prohibitive cost that an experimentation with real users conveys, in our experiments, the users were simulated. We used the references from our corpus as the sentences the users would like to obtain.

6.1 Evaluation

An IMT scenario with AL requires to assess two different criteria: translation quality of the system and human effort spent during the process.

For evaluating the quality of the translations, we used the BLEU (bilingual evaluation understudy) (Papineni et al., 2002) score. BLEU computes an average mean of the precision of the n-grams (up to order 4) from the hypothesis that appear in the reference sentence. It also has a brevity penalty for short translations.

For estimating the human effort, we simulated the actions that the human user would perform when using the IMT system. Therefore, at each iteration the user must search in the hypothesis the next error, and position the mouse pointer on it.

Once the pointer is positioned, the user would introduce the correct character. These actions correspond to a *mouse-action* and a *keystroke*, respectively.

Therefore, we use a commonly-used metric that accounts for both types of interaction: the keystroke mouse-action ratio (KSMR) (Barrachina et al., 2009). It is defined as the number of keystrokes plus the number of mouse-actions required for obtaining the desired sentence, divided by the number of characters of such sentence. We add a final mouse-action, accounting for action of accepting the translation hypothesis. Although keystrokes and mouse-actions are different and require a different amount of effort (Macklovitch et al., 2005), KSMR makes an approximation and assumes that both actions require a similar effort.

6.2 Corpora

To ensure a fair comparison with the latter works of AL applied to IMT (González-Rubio and Casacuberta, 2014), we used the same datasets: our training data was the Europarl corpus (Koehn, 2005), with the development set provided at the 2006 workshop on machine translation (Koehn and Monz, 2006). As test set, we used the News Commentary corpus (Callison-Burch et al., 2007). This test set is suitable to our problem at hand because i. it contains data from different domains (politics, economics and science), which represent challenging out-of-domain samples, but account for a real-life situation in a translation agency; and ii. it is large enough to properly simulate long-term evolution of unbounded data streams. All data are publicly available. We conducted the experimentation in the Spanish to English language direction. Table 1 shows the main figures of our data.

Table 1: Corpora main figures, in terms of number of sentences ($|S|$), number of running words ($|W|$) and vocabulary size ($|V|$). k and M stand for thousands and millions of elements, respectively.

Corpus	Usage		$|S|$	$|W|$	$|V|$
Europarl	Train	En	2M	46M	106k
		Es		48M	160k
	Dev.	En	2k	58k	6.1k
		Es		61k	7.7k
News Commentary	Test	En	51k	1.2M	35k
		Es		1.5M	49k

6.3 NMT systems and AL setup

Our NMT system was built using NMT-Keras (Peris and Casacuberta, 2018a) and featured a bidirectional LSTM encoder and a decoder with cLSTM units. Following Britz et al. (2017), we set the dimension of the LSTM, embeddings and attention model to 512. We applied batch normalizing transform (Ioffe and Szegedy, 2015) and Gaussian noise during training (Graves, 2011). The L_2 norm of the gradients was clipped to 5, for avoiding the exploiting gradient effect (Pascanu et al., 2012). We applied joint byte pair encoding (BPE) (Sennrich et al., 2016) to all corpora. For training the system, we used Adam (Kingma and Ba, 2014), with a learning rate of 0.0002 and a batch size of 50. We early-stopped the training according to the BLEU on our development set. For decoding, we used a beam of 6.

We incrementally update the system (Line 9 in Algorithm 1), with vanilla SGD, with a learning rate of 0.0005. We chose this configuration according to an exploration on the validation set.

The rest of hyperparameters were set according to previous works. The blocks retrieved from the data stream contained 500 samples (according to González-Rubio et al. (2012), the performance is similar regardless the block size). For the quality estimation method, the IBM Model 2 was obtained with `fast_align` (Dyer et al., 2013) and τ_w was set to 0.4 (González-Rubio et al., 2010).

7 Results and discussion

A system with AL involves two main facets to evaluate: the improvement on the quality of the system and the amount of human effort required for achieving such quality. In this section, we compare and study our AL framework for all our sampling strategies: quality estimation sampling (QES), coverage sampling (CovS), attention distraction sampling (ADS), random sampling (RS) and query-by-committee (QBC).

7.1 Active learning evaluation

First, we evaluated the effectiveness of the application of AL in the NMT system, in terms of translation quality. Fig. 2 shows the BLEU of the initial hypotheses proposed by the NMT system (Line 6 in Algorithm 1), as a function of the percentage of sentences supervised by the user (ε in Algorithm 1). That means, the percentage of sentences used to adapt the system. The BLEU of a static system without AL was 34.6. Applying AL, we obtained improvements up to 4.1 points of BLEU.

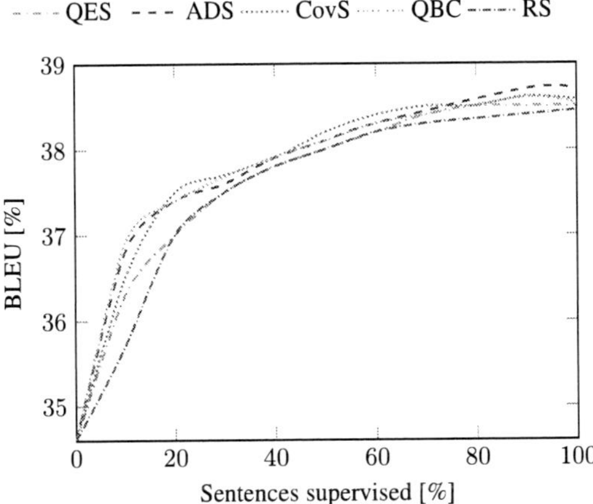

Figure 2: BLEU of the initial hypotheses proposed by the the NMT system as a function of the amount of data used to adapt it. The percentage of sentences supervised refers to the value of ε with respect to the block size.

As expected, the addition of the new knowledge had a larger impact when applied to a non-adapted system. Once the system becomes more specialized, a larger amount of data was required to further improve.

The sampling strategies helped the system to learn faster. Taking RS as a baseline, the learning curves of the other techniques were better, especially when using few (up to a 30%) data for fine-tuning the system. The strategies that achieved a fastest adaptation were those involving the attention mechanism (ADS, CovS and QBC). This indicates that the system is learning from the most useful data. The QES and RS required more supervised data for achieving the comparable BLEU results. When supervising high percentages of the data, we observed BLEU differences. This is due to the ordering in which the selected sentences were presented to the learner. The sampling strategies performed a sort of curriculum learning (Bengio et al., 2009).

7.2 Introducing the human into the loop

From point of view a user, it is important to assess not only the quality of the MT system, but also the effort spent to obtain such quality. Fig. 3 relates both, showing the amount of effort required for obtaining a certain translation quality. We compared the results of system with AL against the same NMT system without AL and with two other SMT systems, with and without AL, from González-Rubio and Casacuberta (2014).

Results in Fig. 3 show consistent positive results of the AL framework. In all cases, AL reduced the human effort required for achieving a certain translation quality. Compared to a static NMT system, approximately a 25% of the human effort can be spent using AL techniques.

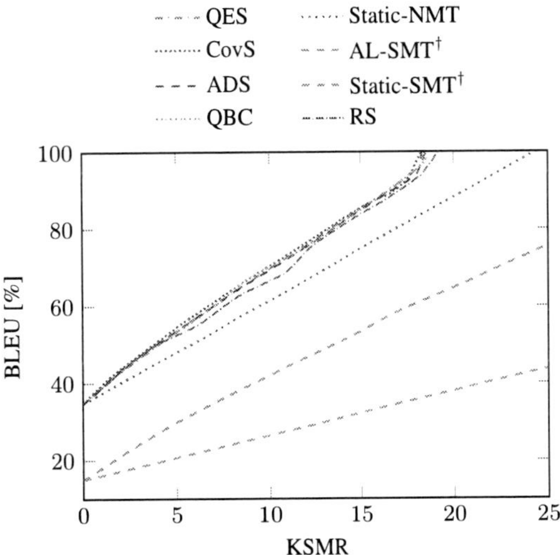

Figure 3: Translation quality (BLEU) as a function of the human effort (KSMR) required. Static-NMT relates to the same NMT system without AL. † denotes systems from González-Rubio and Casacuberta (2014): Static-SMT is a SMT system without AL and AL-SMT is the coverage augmentation SMT system.

Regarding the different sampling strategies, all of them behaviored similarly. They provided consistent and stable improvements, regardless the level of effort desired (ε). This indicates that, although the BLEU of the system may vary (Fig. 2), this had small impact on the effort required for correcting the samples. All sampling strategies outperformed the random baseline, which had a more unstable behavior.

Compared to classical SMT systems, NMT performed surprisingly well. Even the NMT system without AL largely outperformed the best AL-SMT system. This is due to several reasons: on the one hand, the initial NMT system was much better than the original SMT system (34.6 vs. 14.9 BLEU points). Part of this large difference were presumably due to the BPE used in NMT: the data stream contained sentences from different domains, but they can be effectively encoded into known sequences via BPE. The SMT system was unable to handle well such unseen sentences. On the other hand, INMT systems usually respond much better to the human feedback than interactive SMT systems (Knowles and Koehn, 2016; Peris et al., 2017). Therefore, the differences between SMT and NMT were enlarged even more.

Finally, it should be noted that all our sampling strategies can be computed speedily. They involve analysis of the NMT attention weights, which are computed as a byproduct of the decoding process; or queries to a dictionary (in the case of QES). The update of NMT system is also fast, taking approximately 0.1 seconds. This makes AL suitable for a real-time scenario.

8 Conclusions and future work

We studied the application of AL methods to INMT systems. The idea was to supervise the most useful samples from a potentially unbounded data stream, while automatically translating the rest of samples. We developed two novel sampling strategies, able to outperform other well-established methods, such as QES, in terms of translation quality of the final system.

We evaluated the capabilities and usefulness of the AL framework by simulating real-life scenario, involving the aforementioned large data streams. AL was able to enhance the performance of the NMT system in terms of BLEU. Moreover, we obtained consistent reductions of approximately a 25% of the effort required for reaching a desired translation quality. Finally, it is worth noting that NMT outperformed classical SMT systems by a large margin.

We want to explore several lines of work in a future. First, we intend to apply our method to other datasets, involving linguistically diverse language pairs and low-resource scenarios, in order to observe whether the results obtained in this work hold. We also aim to devise more effective sampling strategies. To take into account the cognitive effort or time required for interactively translating a sentence seem promising objective functions. Moreover, these sampling strategies can be used as a data selection technique. It would be interesting to assess their performance on this task. We also want to study the addition of reinforcement or bandit learning into our framework. Recent works (Nguyen et al., 2017; Lam et al., 2018) already showed the usefulness of these learning paradigms, which are orthogonal to our work. Finally, we intend to assess the effectiveness of our proposals with real users in a near future.

Acknowledgments

The research leading this work received funding from grants PROMETEO/2018/004 and CoMUN-HaT - TIN2015-70924-C2-1-R. We also acknowledge NVIDIA Corporation for the donation of GPUs used in this work.

References

Ana Guerberof Arenas. 2008. Productivity and quality in the post-editing of outputs from translation memories and machine translation. *Localisation Focus*, 7(1):11–21.

Dzmitry Bahdanau, Kyunghyun Cho, and Yoshua Bengio. 2015. Neural machine translation by jointly learning to align and translate. *arXiv:1409.0473*.

Sergio Barrachina, Oliver Bender, Francisco Casacuberta, Jorge Civera, Elsa Cubel, Shahram Khadivi, Antonio Lagarda, Hermann Ney, Jesús Tomás, Enrique Vidal, and Juan-Miguel Vilar. 2009. Statistical approaches to computer-assisted translation. *Computational Linguistics*, 35(1):3–28.

Yoshua Bengio, Jérôme Louradour, Ronan Collobert, and Jason Weston. 2009. Curriculum learning. In *Proceedings of the 26th annual international conference on machine learning*, pages 41–48.

John Blatz, Erin Fitzgerald, George Foster, Simona Gandrabur, Cyril Goutte, Alex Kulesza, Alberto Sanchis, and Nicola Ueffing. 2004. Confidence estimation for machine translation. In *Proceedings of the international conference on Computational Linguistics*, pages 315–321.

Michael Bloodgood and Chris Callison-Burch. 2010. Bucking the trend: Large-scale cost-focused active learning for statistical machine translation. In *Proceedings of the 48th Annual Meeting of the Association for Computational Linguistics*, pages 854–864.

Ondřej Bojar, Christian Buck, Rajen Chatterjee, Christian Federmann, Yvette Graham, Barry Haddow, Matthias Huck, Antonio Jimeno Yepes, Philipp Koehn, and Julia Kreutzer, editors. 2017. *Proceedings of the Second Conference on Machine Translation*.

Denny Britz, Anna Goldie, Thang Luong, and Quoc Le. 2017. Massive exploration of neural machine translation architectures. *arXiv:1703.03906*.

Peter F. Brown, Vincent J. Della Pietra, Stephen A. Della Pietra, and Robert L. Mercer. 1993. The mathematics of statistical machine translation: Parameter estimation. *Computational Linguistics*, 19(2):263–311.

Chris Callison-Burch, Cameron Fordyce, Philipp Koehn, Christof Monz, and Josh Schroeder. 2007. (Meta-) evaluation of machine translation. In *Proceedings of the Workshop on Statistical Machine Translation*, pages 136–158.

David Cohn, Les Atlas, and Richard Ladner. 1994. Improving generalization with active learning. *Machine learning*, 15(2):201–221.

Ido Dagan and Sean P Engelson. 1995. Committee-based sampling for training probabilistic classifiers. In *Machine Learning Proceedings 1995*, pages 150–157.

Michael Denkowski, Chris Dyer, and Alon Lavie. 2014. Learning from post-editing: Online model adaptation for statistical machine translation. In *Proceedings of the 14th Conference of the European Chapter of the Association for Computational Linguistics*, pages 395–404.

Chris Dyer, Victor Chahuneau, and Noah A Smith. 2013. A simple, fast, and effective reparameterization of IBM Model 2. In *Proceedings of the 2013 Conference of the North American Chapter of the Association for Computational Linguistics: Human Language Technologies*, pages 644–648.

George Foster, Pierre Isabelle, and Pierre Plamondon. 1997. Target-text mediated interactive machine translation. *Machine Translation*, 12:175–194.

Simona Gandrabur and George Foster. 2003. Confidence estimation for text prediction. In *Proceedings of the Conference on Computational Natural Language Learning*, pages 315–321.

Jesús González-Rubio and Francisco Casacuberta. 2014. Cost-sensitive active learning for computer-assisted translation. *Pattern Recognition Letters*, 37:124–134.

Jesús González-Rubio, Daniel Ortiz-Martínez, and Francisco Casacuberta. 2010. Balancing user effort and translation error in interactive machine translation via confidence measures. In *Proceedings of the Annual Meeting of the Association for Computational Linguistics*, pages 173–177.

Jesús González-Rubio, Daniel Ortiz-Martínez, and Francisco Casacuberta. 2011. An active learning scenario for interactive machine translation. In *Proceedings of the 13th international conference on multimodal interfaces*, pages 197–200.

Jesús González-Rubio, Daniel Ortiz-Martínez, and Francisco Casacuberta. 2012. Active learning for interactive machine translation. In *Proceedings of the Conference of the European Chapter of the Association for Computational Linguistics*, pages 245–254.

Alex Graves. 2011. Practical variational inference for neural networks. In *Advances in Neural Information Processing Systems*, pages 2348–2356.

Gholamreza Haffari, Maxim Roy, and Anoop Sarkar. 2009. Active learning for statistical phrase-based machine translation. In *Proceedings of Human Language Technologies: The 2009 Annual Conference of the North American Chapter of the Association for Computational Linguistics*, pages 415–423.

Sepp Hochreiter and Jürgen Schmidhuber. 1997. Long short-term memory. *Neural Computation*, 9(8):1735–1780.

Chris Hokamp and Qun Liu. 2017. Lexically constrained decoding for sequence generation using grid beam search. *arXiv:1704.07138*.

Sergey Ioffe and Christian Szegedy. 2015. Batch normalization: Accelerating deep network training by reducing internal covariate shift. *arXiv:1502.03167*.

Diederik Kingma and Jimmy Ba. 2014. Adam: A method for stochastic optimization. *arXiv:1412.6980*.

Rebecca Knowles and Philipp Koehn. 2016. Neural interactive translation prediction. In *Proceedings of the Association for Machine Translation in the Americas*, pages 107–120.

Philipp Koehn. 2005. Europarl: A parallel corpus for statistical machine translation. In *Proceedings of the Machine Translation Summit*, pages 79–86.

Philipp Koehn and Christof Monz, editors. 2006. *Proceedings on the Workshop on Statistical Machine Translation*. Association for Computational Linguistics.

Tsz Kin Lam, Julia Kreutzer, and Stefan Riezler. 2018. A reinforcement learning approach to interactive-predictive neural machine translation. In *Proceedings of the European Association for Machine Translation conference*, pages 169–178.

Abby Levenberg, Chris Callison-Burch, and Miles Osborne. 2010. Stream-based translation models for statistical machine translation. In *Human Language Technologies: The 2010 Annual Conference of the North American Chapter of the Association for Computational Linguistics*, pages 394–402.

David D Lewis and Jason Catlett. 1994. Heterogeneous uncertainty sampling for supervised learning. In *Machine Learning Proceedings 1994*, pages 148–156.

Elliot Macklovitch, Nam-Trung Nguyen, and Roberto Silva. 2005. User evaluation report. Technical report. Transtype2 (ISR-2001-32091).

Laurent Nepveu, Guy Lapalme, Philippe Langlais, and George Foster. 2004. Adaptive language and translation models for interactive machine translation. In *Proceedings of the Conference on Empirical Method in Natural Language Processing*, pages 190–197.

Khanh Nguyen, Hal Daumé III, and Jordan Boyd-Graber. 2017. Reinforcement learning for bandit neural machine translation with simulated human feedback. In *Proceedings of the Conference on Empirical Methods in Natural Language Processing*, pages 1464–1474.

Fredrik Olsson. 2009. A literature survey of active machine learning in the context of natural language processing. Technical report.

Daniel Ortiz-Martínez. 2016. Online learning for statistical machine translation. *Computational Linguistics*, 42(1):121–161.

Kishore Papineni, Salim Roukos, Todd Ward, and Wei-Jing Zhu. 2002. BLEU: a method for automatic evaluation of machine translation. In *Proceedings of the Annual Meeting of the Association for Computational Linguistics*, pages 311–318.

Razvan Pascanu, Caglar Gulcehre, Kyunghyun Cho, and Yoshua Bengio. 2014. How to construct deep recurrent neural networks. *arXiv:1312.6026*.

Razvan Pascanu, Tomas Mikolov, and Yoshua Bengio. 2012. On the difficulty of training recurrent neural networks. *arXiv:1211.5063*.

Álvaro Peris and Francisco Casacuberta. 2018a. NMT-Keras: a very flexible toolkit with a focus on interactive NMT and online learning. *The Prague Bulletin of Mathematical Linguistics*, 111:113–124.

Álvaro Peris and Francisco Casacuberta. 2018b. Online learning for effort reduction in interactive neural machine translation. *arXiv:1802.03594*.

Álvaro Peris, Miguel Domingo, and Francisco Casacuberta. 2017. Interactive neural machine translation. *Computer Speech & Language*, 45:201–220.

Herbert Robbins and Sutton Monro. 1951. A stochastic approximation method. *The Annals of Mathematical Statistics*, pages 400–407.

Mike Schuster and Kuldip K. Paliwal. 1997. Bidirectional recurrent neural networks. *IEEE Transactions on Signal Processing*, 45(11):2673–2681.

Rico Sennrich, Barry Haddow, and Alexandra Birch. 2016. Improving neural machine translation models with monolingual data. In *Proceedings of the Annual Meeting of the Association for Computational Linguistics*, pages 86–96.

B. Settles. 2009. Active learning literature survey. Computer Sciences Technical Report 1648, University of Wisconsin–Madison.

H Sebastian Seung, Manfred Opper, and Haim Sompolinsky. 1992. Query by committee. In *Proceedings of the fifth annual workshop on Computational learning theory*, pages 287–294.

Ilya Sutskever, Oriol Vinyals, and Quoc V. Le. 2014. Sequence to sequence learning with neural networks. In *Proceedings of the Advances in Neural Information Processing Systems*, volume 27, pages 3104–3112.

Zhaopeng Tu, Zhengdong Lu, Yang Liu, Xiaohua Liu, and Hang Li. 2016. Modeling coverage for neural machine translation. In *Proceedings of the Annual Meeting of the Association for Computational Linguistics*, volume 1, pages 76–85.

Marco Turchi, Matteo Negri, M Amin Farajian, and Marcello Federico. 2017. Continuous learning from human post-edits for neural machine translation. *The Prague Bulletin of Mathematical Linguistics*, 108(1):233–244.

Nicola Ueffing and Hermann Ney. 2005. Application of word-level confidence measures in interactive statistical machine translation. In *Proceedings of the European Association for Machine Translation conference*, pages 262–270.

Nicola Ueffing and Hermann Ney. 2007. Word-level confidence estimation for machine translation. *Computational Linguistics*, 33:9–40.

Ashish Vaswani, Noam Shazeer, Niki Parmar, Jakob Uszkoreit, Llion Jones, Aidan N Gomez, Lukasz Kaiser, and Illia Polosukhin. 2017. Attention is all you need. *arXiv:1706.03762*.

Y. Wu, M. Schuster, Z. Chen, Q. V. Le, M. Norouzi, W. Macherey, M. Krikun, Y. Cao, Q. Gao, K. Macherey, J. Klingner, A. Shah, M. Johnson, X. Liu, Ł. Kaiser, S. Gouws, Y. Kato, T. Kudo, H. Kazawa, K. Stevens, G. Kurian, N. Patil, W. Wang, C. Young, J. Smith, J. Riesa, A. Rudnick, O. Vinyals, G. Corrado, M. Hughes, and J. Dean. 2016. Google's Neural Machine Translation System: Bridging the Gap between Human and Machine Translation. *arXiv:1609.08144*.

Churn Intent Detection in Multilingual Chatbot Conversations and Social Media

Christian Abbet[†‡]**, Meryem M'hamdi**[†‡]**, Athanasios Giannakopoulos**[*]**,**
Robert West[†]**, Andreea Hossmann**[*]**, Michael Baeriswyl**[*] **and Claudiu Musat**[*]

[‡] Equal Contribution
[*]Data, Analytics & AI — Swisscom AG
{firstName.lastName}@swisscom.com
[†] Ecole Polytechnique Fédérale de Lausanne (EPFL)
{firstName.lastName}@epfl.ch

Abstract

We propose a new method to detect when users express the intent to leave a service, also known as churn. While previous work focuses solely on social media, we show that this intent can be detected in chatbot conversations. As companies increasingly rely on chatbots, they need an overview of potentially churny users. To this end, we crowdsource and publish a dataset of churn intent expressions in chatbot interactions in German and English. We show that classifiers trained on social media data can detect the same intent in the context of chatbots.

We introduce a classification architecture that outperforms existing work on churn intent detection in social media. Moreover, we show that, using bilingual word embeddings, a system trained on combined English and German data outperforms monolingual approaches. As the only existing dataset is in English, we crowdsource and publish a novel dataset of German tweets. We thus underline the universal aspect of the problem, as examples of churn intent in English help us identify churn in German tweets and chatbot conversations.

1 Introduction

Identifying customers who intend to terminate their relation with a company is commonly known as *churn detection*. This is very important for companies if we consider that attracting new customers is a time and cost-intensive task. Therefore, it is often preferable for companies to focus on the existing customers in order to prevent losing them instead of trying to acquire new ones.

Traditionally, churn detection is based on tracking the user behavior and correlating it with the decision to churn. The analysis of the user behavior typically includes metadata such as the subscription information, network usage or customer transactions (Qian et al., 2007; Dave et al., 2013).

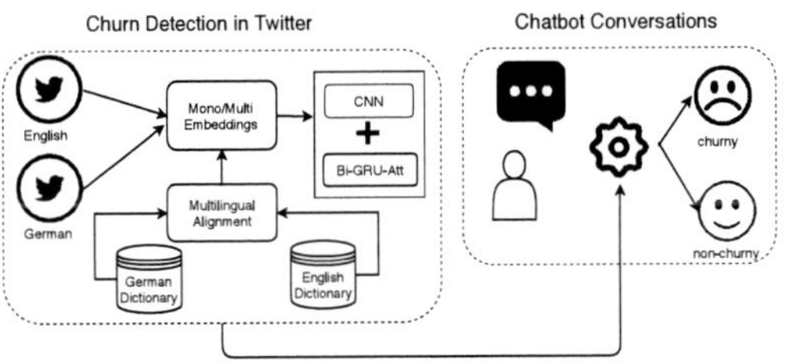

Figure 1: Overview of Overall Pipeline.

The behavior-based techniques thus require a significant amount of data that are not easily available. In addition, there is a cold start problem with novel systems which may not have access to the background required for this type of analysis.

The current trend for detecting churn intent is to focus on textual user statements. This intent is sufficient evidence for the likely following churn decision of a user. Moreover, it is an actionable insight, as it allows companies to allocate resources to prevent the likely customer churn decision. Textual churn detection is only based on the current interaction between the user and the service provider. As a result, no a priori knowledge of the customer background is needed, thus bypassing the cold start problem.

A text-based analysis of the intent to churn is even more relevant today in the context of the chatbot explosion (Hill et al., 2015; Fadhil and Gabrielli, 2017; Xu et al., 2017; Argal et al., 2018). Chatbots are becoming one of the main means of textual communication with the evolution of automation processes.

This chatbot explosion aims at converting the usual human-to-human interaction into a human-to-machine one, which however comes at a high cost. Concretely, companies have no longer a full grasp on their users' level of discontent, since the customer contact is handled by chatbots. Adding a

Proceedings of the 22nd Conference on Computational Natural Language Learning (CoNLL 2018), pages 161–170
Brussels, Belgium, October 31 - November 1, 2018. ©2018 Association for Computational Linguistics

churn detection functionality to bots allows companies to spot cases where the discontent reaches a high level, and the user expresses an intent to churn. This, in turn, becomes an actionable insight, as the bot can decide if human intervention is needed and route the conversation to a human agent.

Churn detection is hard, as it requires discriminating between the intent to *switch to* and *switch from* a service. For instance in the tweet *"@MARKE das klingt gut zu den genannten Konditionen würde ich dann doch gern wechseln :)"* which translates as *"@BRAND the conditions sound good to me. I would like to switch :)"*, the intention is not churny for the brand this tweet is addressed to. However in *"@MARKE Internet langsamer als gedrosseltes. bin deshalb zu eurer konkurrenz gewechselt"* which translates as *"@BRAND Internet slower than throttled. So I switched to your competitor"* the intention is churny.

In this paper, we claim that (i) we can transfer knowledge about churn intent detection from social media to chatbot conversations and (ii) churn intent detection can work in a multilingual way for both social media and chatbot conversations. We visualize the approach we adopt in Fig. 1.

We start by creating churn intent detectors, that are based on a neural architecture, that exploits convolutional, recurrent and attention layers. We compare the performance of our model with the existing state-of-the-art for churn detection in English microblogs (Mourad Gridach, 2017) and validate that our classifier achieves top-notch performance in this task.

We also contribute by providing datasets in English and German for churn detection to the research community. First, we collect and annotate a dataset with German tweets that refer to any German telecommunication brand (e.g., Vodafone and O2). This dataset complements the already existing microblog based dataset released from Hadi Amiri (2015). Secondly, we create our own chatbot platform which helps us in building and annotating the first datasets in German and English for chatbot conversations. We later use these datasets as evaluation sets in order to prove our claim that we can successfully transfer knowledge from data extracted from social media to chatbot conversations.

In addition, we contribute by showing that expressions of churn intent are language-independent. The intuition is that if we train a classifier to detect churny intents in a language, this knowledge can help identify churn intents in a second language. To make the computation lighter, we do not use translation but rely on multilingual embeddings. Multilingual embeddings extend monolingual ones with the objective of mapping similar words from different languages closely together in a unified space.

We perform experiments and show that models trained on data coming from both languages are more accurate than language-specific ones. This is true for both the social media and the chatbot corpora. As a result, we demonstrate not only that churn intent models generalize across media, but also across languages. Our findings have a major implication. Concretely, we prove that knowing how a customer, writing in English, expresses discontent with a telecommunications company in the US helps the system detect the churn intent in simulated chatbot conversations written in German about a German operator.

We summarize our contributions as follows:

- we present a neural-based model that achieve state-of-the-art model results for churn detection (Section 3.1).
- we create a first multilingual approach for churn intent detection using multilingual embeddings (Section 3.2).
- we show that churn detection patterns can be learned from social media content and successfully applied to chatbot conversations (Section 3.3).
- we publish a novel dataset for churn detection in German tweets (Section 4.2).
- and finally, we create the first German and English datasets for churn intent detection in chatbot conversations (Section 4.3).

The paper continues with an outline of related work in Section 2. Section 3 describes our text classifier and our approach for multilingual word embeddings. The dataset construction is detailed in Section 4. We describe our experiments in Section 5 and finally conclude in Section 6.

2 Related Work

This work is an intersection of (i) churn detection in social media, (ii) multilingual churn detection and (iii) churn detection in chatbots Therefore we present the related work for each domain separately. As there are no direct applications of multilingual embeddings and knowledge transfer from social media to churn detection in chatbot conversations, we include other applications that inspired our work.

2.1 Churn in Social Media

The first approach of performing churn detection relies on user metadata. Metadata are information about the customer activity for a particular service. Qian et al. (2007) propose a method based on customer transactions over time to detect churn whereas Dave et al. (2013) focus on user's session duration. Such techniques have proven to be efficient but rely on the fact that we possess a large amount of data regarding the user behavior, a fact which is rarely true.

The second approach focuses on textual interactions such as in social media. Here, no a priori knowledge of the customer actions is required since churn detection is solely based on textual interactions between the user and the company. Hadi Amiri (2015) distributed a labeled English dataset of tweets (hereafter denoted as EN_T) about telecommunication brands and provided a baseline for churn detection in social media.

Hadi Amiri (2016); Mourad Gridach (2017) worked on EN_T. Hadi Amiri (2016) focused on the extraction of additional features from tweets. They gathered information about the context of the tweet (e.g. number of replies). This contextual information was passed through a pre-trained RNN to generate new features and improve classification performance. Unfortunately, this technique depends on the availability of additional data which is not always present and therefore does not scale well. On the contrary, Mourad Gridach (2017) focused only on tweets and achieved the best-known performance on textual churn detection. They did so by performing text classification using a Convolutional Neural Networks (CNN) (Lecun and Y., 1995) enriched with rule-based features. Even though this approach has proven to improve the score significantly, it directly limits the model to English applications.

2.2 Transfer from Social Media to Chatbots

Previous work on churn intent detection is centered on social media while chatbots are slowly replacing human-to-human interaction and becoming the main way of communication between customers and brands. Due to the novel aspect of the topic, there are no publicly available datasets related to churn detection in chatbot conversations, and therefore no previous work on that field exists. Lee et al. (2018) propose multiple sentiment-based reply models for chatbot conversation. They trained their models on a Twitter sentiment analysis corpus (Pak and Paroubek, 2010) which is composed of 15M data points with labeled sentiment. However, to the best of our knowledge, there is no work that uses churn detection in the context of chatbot conversations.

2.3 Multilingual Aspect

Multilingual word embeddings have been applied in the context of tasks like Cross-Lingual Document Classification (CLDC) as in (Klementiev et al., 2012). The authors evaluate the quality of multilingual embeddings they induced using parallel data to classify unlabeled documents in a target language using only labeled documents in a source language. However, a comparison between the performance using monolingual versus multilingual data is missing. We try to address this problem in our research.

Other downstream tasks which benefited from multilingual embeddings include Cross Language Sentiment Classification (CLSC) as in (Huiwei Zhou and Huang, 2015). They train the bilingual embeddings jointly using the task data and its translation and show that the multilingual approach outperforms the monolingual experiments. This gain in performance encouraged us to try this approach to churn detection. To the best of our knowledge, there is no prior work leveraging multilingual embeddings for this task.

3 Methodology

Social media includes a wide range of platforms, however, we choose to use Twitter. We do so for the following reasons. First, we would like to take advantage of the free and widely used Twitter API. Secondly, we would like to compile and annotate a German dataset for churn detection in order to complement the already existing dataset of Hadi Amiri (2015). Twitter helps to this end with its flexible policy for data distribution which allows us to release our novel dataset effortlessly.

Churn intent detection can be seen as a classification task where the input is a text, and the output is one of two classes (churn and non churn). Here, we adapt a new architecture, tailored to the nature of tweets (e.g., short text length) and also low data availability.

In addition, the churn intent detection problem is not tied to a single language or domain of application. We analyze the synergies between churn intents in multiple languages and how multilingual embeddings can help us solve the problem at hand. For chatbot applications, the intuition is that a model trained on the social media domain might be helpful in finding churn expressions in the context of chatbots.

3.1 Text Classification Architecture

Our churn detection architecture is a text classifier based on cascaded collaborative layers where different feature extractors and aggregators complement each other. More precisely, we employ a combination of a CNN and a bidirectional Gated Recurrent Unit (BiGRU) to make use of both spatial and temporal dependencies in the data (Sainath et al., 2015; Chen et al., 2017). On top of that, an attention mechanism (Bahdanau et al., 2014) is employed in order to recognize which BiGRU outputs have higher weights of importance.

While CNN acts as n-grams feature extractors, GRU cells are used to take word order into consideration. This is crucially important as the word order can play an important role to understand the context and detect something as churny or non-churny. We use GRU since it is a lightweight and more computationally efficient version of Long Short-Term Memory (LSTM) networks that preserves a comparable performance without using a memory unit (Chung et al., 2014). BiGRU is used instead of unidirectional GRU to preserve information from the past and future.

The overall view of the architecture is depicted in Fig. 2. Each sentence can be represented as an $n \times m$ input matrix, where n is the maximum number of words over all sentences (padding is performed to the length of the longest tweet) and m is the number of features (i.e., dimensionality of word embeddings). We apply dropout directly to the embedding matrix to reduce overfitting. For each sentence matrix, we apply f convolution filters of kernel size k which result in f vectors of size $n - k + 1$. We then feed the extracted features to a BiGRU which traverses the sentence in both the forward and backward directions. In the end, we apply a *softmax* activation function to get the final prediction.

3.2 Multilingual Churn Intent Detection

We introduce the task of cross-lingual churn detection by aiming at detecting churn in any language. More specifically, we train and test one single robust model by concatenating data coming from English and German using multilingual embeddings. We rely on the assumption that using multilingual embeddings — as a mechanism to represent words coming from different languages into the same low dimensional vector space — can capture the semantic and syntactic similarities between the languages which help with transfer learning between them. In a sense, languages which are resource rich in churn detection can help those which lack the features needed to build a strong classifier by their own. Our aim with this multilingual approach is to bridge the gap between English and German and improve the performance of German for which data is not as strongly labeled.

We build our multilingual embeddings which map words from different languages into one joint vector space by learning translation of embeddings in the source space into the target space. We set German as the source space and English as the target space. We then learn the transformation matrix that aligns German to English. In other words, this approach fine-tunes German embeddings by applying a linear transformation that maps them into the English space. Due to the presence of compound words and high availability of training data, the embedding space for English allows for a richer representation of the semantics of individual words. The availability of multiple bilingual dictionaries, where English is one of the languages, motivates us to choose English as a target language.

For that purpose, we adopt an offline approach to guarantee a fair comparison between monolingual and multilingual churn detection. We do so to show clearly the added value of the multilingual approach where both monolingual and multilingual embeddings are initially trained using the same monolingual constraints.

According to Smith et al. (2017), this transformation matrix can be learned analytically using the product of the left and right singular vectors obtained from SVD of the product of the source and target dictionary vectors X_D and Y_D. Concretely, $W_{DE \rightarrow EN} = U \cdot V$ such that $X_D \cdot Y_D = U \cdot \Sigma \cdot V$ which was proven to have the same quality

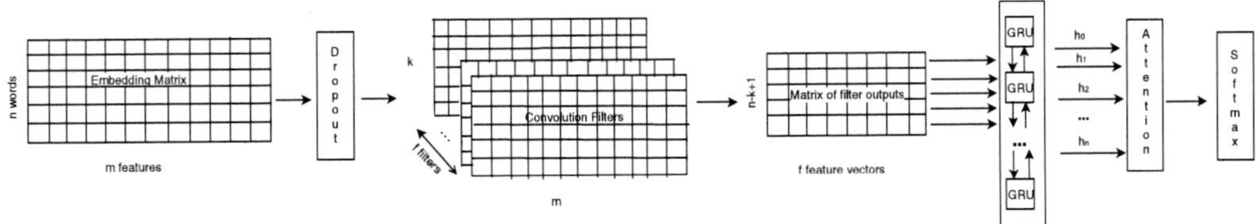

Figure 2: Architecture of CNN-GRU with Attention.

as those obtained via iterative optimization. The product of U and V is the closed form solution that optimizes the transformation from the source to the target spaces Smith et al. (2017).

3.3 Transfer from Social Media to Chatbots

We make the assumption that tweets and chatbot conversations are similar to a certain extent. Even if the language is mostly different, we believe that the parts that are relevant to churn detection stay the same. In other words, if a model trained on tweets gives promising results on chatbot conversations, then it confirms that there is an underlying churn intent pattern that can be generalized across mediums. Still, differences exist between the way costumers express themselves through social media and chatbot conversations. Social media, and especially Twitter, tend to carry specific structures that might prevent our model from detecting churn in chatbot conversations. To this end, we work towards removing domain specific features of the text in order to be able to transfer knowledge from Twitter to chatbots successfully. Therefore, we first remove patterns such as RT, # and @ that are Twitter-specific. Moreover, users usually start their message with the mention of the brand such as "@**X** *I want to switch to* @**Y***!*" where **X** is the targeted brand and **Y** any potential competitor. However, this is rarely true for chatbot conversations. We can generalize these examples by removing the mention of the source brand to obtain "*I want to switch to* @**Y***!*" where the targeted brand is implicitly known and therefore is more likely to represent a typical chatbot entry.

4 Churn Intent Datasets

In this work, we use pairs of datasets from two different languages (English and German) with the certainty that churn detection is a universal problem and therefore does not depend on the language. Each pair is composed of a Twitter and a chatbot conversations dataset denoted as Lang_T

Twitter English Data (EN_T)		
brand	**churn**	**non churn**
Verizon	447	1543
AT&T	402	1389
T-Mobile	95	978

Table 1: Distribution of English tweets along the different brands.

and Lang_C respectively. Lang is a 2-letter abbreviation of the source language. As a result, we discuss the creation of 4 different datasets, namely EN_T, EN_C, DE_T and DE_C [1].

4.1 English Twitter Dataset (EN_T)

The dataset is introduced by Hadi Amiri (2015) and is composed of English tweets that show mentions of Verizon, AT&T, and T-Mobile (telecommunication brands). Each tweet is associated with a source brand (name of the company that is targeted by the tweet) and a label (1 or 0 whether the content is churny or not). Table 1 tabulates the exact distribution of the data as a function of the source brand where **churn** is the number of churny tweets associated to the brand and **non churn** the number of non-churny ones. Overall, the dataset contains 4339[2] labeled tweets and is highly imbalanced regarding the distribution of churny/non-churny tweets.

4.2 German Twitter Dataset (DE_T)

Since there is no existing dataset for churn detection except for English, we create a novel German dataset. As a first step, we crawl all mentions on Twitter of multiple telecommunication brands that are active in German-speaking countries for a period of six months. The result is a large Twitter dataset, $\text{DE}_{T_{FULL}}$, containing more than 160000 tweets. However, labeling such a large corpus

---

[1] The created datasets are publicly available at https://github.com/swisscom/churn-intent-DE

[2] We only keep those with annotation confidence above 0.7 as in (Hadi Amiri, 2015).

Filters	
DE	**Translation EN**
zur konkurrenz	to the competitor
tschüss	goodbye
vertrag beende	end contract
anbieter wechs	change provider
zurückkommen zu	return to
verlassen	quit
wechseln	switch to

Table 2: Non-exhaustive list of word filters used to detect potential churny tweets in German.

Twitter German Data (DE_T)		
brand	**churn**	**non churn**
O2	247	905
Vodafone	203	1061
Telekom	121	1397
Others	40	365

Table 3: Distribution of German tweets along the different brands.

is extremely time intensive and would result in a waste of resources since the density of churny tweets is extremely low. A solution to reduce the size of $DE_{T_{FULL}}$ is to apply filters composed of predefined keywords to isolate potential churny tweets and generate a sub-dataset of candidates, $DE_{T_{FILTER}}$, as depicted in Fig. 3. Those keywords are manually selected and are assumed to be linked with or carry churny content. A non-exhaustive list of used keywords is displayed in Table 2.

The final result is German Twitter dataset as $DE_T = DE_{T_{FILTER}} + DE_{T_{BOOT}}$.

The complete distribution of the labels of DE_T is displayed in Table 3 for comparison purposes with EN_T. Here, three main companies emerged from our dataset, namely O2, Vodafone and Telekom (all other brands are grouped in the table as *Others*). It is interesting to note that the size and distribution of the labels of the German dataset is comparable to the English one which allows fair performance comparison across languages.

4.3 Chatbot Conversations ($EN_C + DE_C$)

Our ultimate goal is to detect churn intent in chatbot conversations. However, no English nor German labeled chatbot conversations are available for this purpose. To overcome this problem, we create our own chatbot platform to gather data and build our German (DE_C) and English (EN_C) chatbot conversations. Our platform consists of a basic interface where the user can enter text that is processed by the chatbot as depicted in Fig. 4.

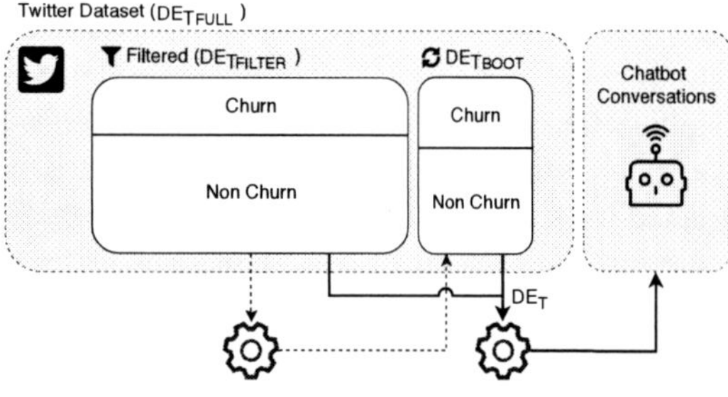

Figure 3: Creation of DE_T and transition to chatbots.

The resulting subset, $DE_{T_{FILTER}}$, is given to annotation through a platform specifically created for this purpose. All tweets are annotated by at least two annotators. We keep in our dataset only the entries where both annotators agree on the label. We train the first version of our model with the newly labeled subset and then apply it to our initial dataset $DE_{T_{FULL}}$. By selecting only predictions with high confidence, we can generate an additional subset, $DE_{T_{BOOT}}$, of potential churny tweets. This new subset has the advantage of not being biased by the predefined filter keywords as opposed to $DE_{T_{FILTER}}$. Therefore, we can reduce the overall bias of our dataset by labeling $DE_{T_{BOOT}}$ and concatenating it to $DE_{T_{FILTER}}$.

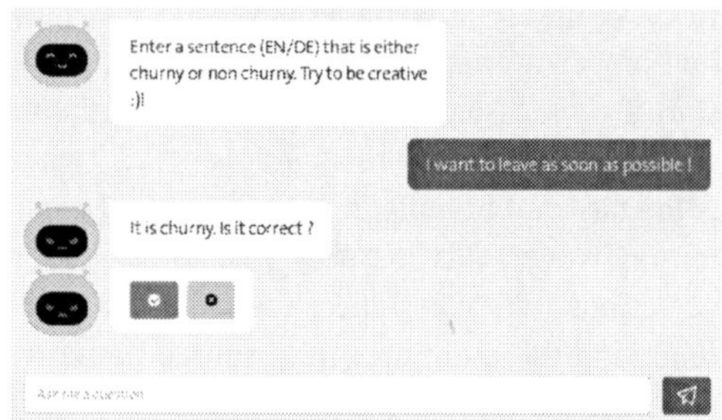

Figure 4: Annotation process using our platform.

We want the user to enter customer service related examples and their ground truth (churn or non-churn) to create our dataset. However, creating and labeling data is a tedious task for the user and might lower the quality of our text-label pairs. Therefore, we choose to present the chatbot interface as a game to make it more user-friendly.

Chatbot Conversation Data		
Lang	**churn**	**non churn**
EN	119	188
DE	116	218

Table 4: Distribution of labels in chatbot conversations for both languages (EN/DE).

Firstly, the user is asked to enter a sentence that is either churny or non churny. Then, the chatbot predicts the output using a model trained on social media and informs the user about the prediction. Finally, the user can approve or disapprove the prediction of the chatbot using buttons. In both cases, we get the ground truth of the text and are able of expanding our database and even giving feedback to the user accordingly. A second annotator is then responsible for double-checking the labeled data coming from the chatbot. We keep only the data points where the two annotators agree. Note that we append the results to the databases (EN_C + DE_C) as a function of the detected language of the input text.

We end up with two novel datasets for churn detection in chatbot conversations. Table 4 presents the distribution of the labels in both languages. The two columns indicate the number of churny and non-churny examples in each dataset respectively.

5   Evaluation

For textual churn detection, we design and report on the performance of three experiments:

- Training on EN_T and testing on EN_T using English monolingual embeddings.
- Training on DE_T and testing on DE_T using German monolingual embeddings.
- Training on $(EN+DE)_T$ and testing on EN_T and DE_T using multilingual embeddings.

For all experiments, a consistent model with the same hyper-parameters is used to ensure a fair comparison. We employ 256 filters with a kernel size of 2 for the convolutional layer. In addition, we set the number of GRU units to 128 and apply a dropout with a rate of 0.3. Finally, we use the *Adam* optimizer with its default parameters. To allow a fair comparison, 10-fold cross validation is used as in (Hadi Amiri, 2015). This ensures that the results are less affected by the train/test split and all models are trained until convergence for each fold. In the end, the mean and standard deviation of macro precision, recall and F1-score are computed over the maximum of each fold. We execute all experiments 20 times, test them under statistical dependence and reject with a threshold of $\alpha = 5\%$.

For chatbot conversations, we directly evaluate the best model trained on datasets from social media on chatbot conversation data. We report the performance for the following three experiments in Section 5.3:

- Best model trained on EN_T and tested on EN_C using English embeddings.
- Best model trained on DE_T and tested on DE_C using German embeddings.
- Best model trained on $(EN+DE)_T$ and tested on EN_C and DE_C using multilingual embeddings.

5.1   Embeddings and Data Augmentation

We use pre-trained 300-dimensional word embeddings for English and German from fastText (Piotr Bojanowski and Mikolov, 2017). The same distributional vectors used in monolingual experiments are employed in building multilingual embeddings. We learn the alignment based on a train part of a ground truth bilingual dictionary consisting of 5000 German-English pairs (Conneau et al., 2017). We then apply dimensionality reduction on top of SVD by deleting the last few rows corresponding to a value threshold of 1 in the diagonal vector. The threshold value is chosen to maximize the performance on the test part of the bilingual dictionary pairs used for learning the alignment from DE to EN.

We also replace all brands with either "target" or "competitor" to improve vocabulary coverage. "Target" refers to the brand concerned by the churny content and "competitor" to all other brands mentioned in the text. Finally, it is important to notice that if a tweet is churny for a specific brand, it is not churny for the other cited brands. For example, *"@X I want switch to @Y!"* is churny for brand **X** but not for **Y**. We can, therefore, generate more examples where **Y** is replaced as "target". We use this procedure for each fold to augment the training set.

5.2   Social Media Results

Table 5 contains the results for churn detection in social media. The first row shows the results for training and testing on EN_T data which allows us to compare our score to state-of-the-art

Twitter Data					
Model	**Train**	**Test**	**F1-Score (%)**	**Precision (%)**	**Recall (%)**
Churn teacher	EN_T	EN_T	83.85	82.56	85.18
CNN-GRU-Att	EN_T	EN_T	84.23 ± 3.14	87.70 ± 3.21	81.22 ± 4.08
CNN-GRU-Att	$(EN+DE)_T$	EN_T	85.88 ± 2.36	85.85 ± 2.49	85.94 ± 2.56
CNN-GRU-Att	DE_T	DE_T	66.69 ± 3.30	63.90 ± 5.80	70.44 ± 5.32
CNN-GRU-Att	$(EN+DE)_T$	DE_T	78.09 ± 2.43	78.62 ± 2.05	77.72 ± 3.09

Table 5: Performance comparison of our model on English against the current state-of-the-art (Mourad Gridach, 2017). *EN* and *DE* are scores for language dependent models using monolingual embeddings, whereas *EN+DE* is for system trained on both languages at the same time using multilingual word embeddings. The indices T stands for Twitter.

Chatbot conversations					
Model	**Train**	**Test**	**F1-Score (%)**	**Precision (%)**	**Recall (%)**
CNN-GRU-Att	EN_T	EN_C	82.10	78.99	85.45
CNN-GRU-Att	$(EN+DE)_T$	EN_C	84.43	84.75	84.18
CNN-GRU-Att	DE_T	DE_C	74.25	74.14	74.32
CNN-GRU-Att	$(EN+DE)_T$	DE_C	73.58	73.45	73.72

Table 6: Results on chatbot conversations. *EN* and *DE* are scores for language dependent models using monolingual embeddings. *EN+DE* are for system trained on both languages at the same time using multilingual word embeddings. We distinguish Twitter from chatbot dataset using respectively the indices T and C.

results. We outperform the previous performance from Mourad Gridach (2017) and reach 85.88% using multilingual word embeddings. Note that the standard deviation over the 10-fold cross validation is not provided by Mourad Gridach (2017). However, an increase of 2.03% of the mean still represents an important improvement over the state-of-the-art. As a result, we prove that our novel architecture provides an efficient way to detect churn in social media.

We notice a significant improvement in the performance of Twitter data when both English and German tweets are aggregated and used for training with multilingual embeddings. The advantage of our multilingual model is promising especially for German with an increase of 7.8% in F1-score. English also benefits with a slight increase of 1.65%. The better quality of the English word embeddings makes it easier for our model to identify the churn patterns, compared to German. This explains the gap between the gain in performance for German compared to English, although we used two corpora comparable in size for both languages.

To gain more insights into why the multilingual approach improves the test performance in German, it is worth reconsidering the example introduced earlier: *"@MARKE das klingt gut zu den genannten Konditionen würde ich dann doch gern wechseln :)"*. This example is predicted as churny using German monolingual model, while it is not churny according to the multilingual model. This can be explained by the fact that the German model could only rely on the presence of *switch* keyword, while the multilingual approach can learn more complex patterns that are present in both languages. There is a similar example in English: *"I want to switch to @BRAND already"* that portrays more or less the same pattern.

5.3 Chatbot Results

Table 6 shows that for chatbot conversations we obtain results comparable to Twitter. This proves that our model is able of capturing the structure of the churny tweets in both languages and generalize it to other applications (e.g., chatbot conversations).

Moreover, we observe that the performance of churn detection in English chatbot conversations also benefits from the multilingual approach. Concretely, the model trained on $(EN+DE)_T$ and tested on EN_C outperforms its monolingual counterpart trained on EN_T and tested on EN_C with an increase 2.34% in F1-score. On the other hand, performance for German exhibits a marginal drop compared to its monolingual counterpart. This can be due to the small number of conversation examples and their lack of variability which makes them more similar in structure to the training tweets. Therefore, even a monolingual model would work well in this case.

A final observation is that the recall is usually higher than the precision on chatbot conversations. This is noteworthy in our application since it is more important to reduce the number of false negative in churn prediction. Indeed, it is better for companies to falsely detect churn intent (in case of false positives) than missing actual customers (in case of false negatives).

6 Conclusion

Preventing customers from leaving a service is an essential topic for companies, as acquiring new customers is a time and cost-intensive procedure. While previous work solely focuses on user behavior over time or social media, here, we propose a novel approach for churn intent detection in chatbot conversations.

In this paper, we work towards multilingual churn intent detection in chatbot conversation with knowledge transfer from Twitter datasets. First, we release a novel dataset of German tweets for churn intent detection to complement the existing English one. Moreover, we create and distribute a dataset for churn intent detection in chatbot conversations for both English and German. We present a model based on a neural architecture that outruns the state-of-the-art performance on churn intent detection in social media.

Our experiments show that our model can generalize churn intent patterns learned from social media and successfully apply them to chatbot conversations, proving that we can transfer churn detection knowledge from Twitter to chatbots. In addition, we prove that our model, trained using multilingual word embeddings, surpasses monolingual approaches. This result highlights the universal facet of the problem, as examples of churn intent in English help us in identifying churn about German telecommunication brands in German tweets and chatbot conversations.

References

Ashay Argal, Siddharth Gupta, Ajay Modi, Pratik Pandey, Simon Shim, and Chang Choo. 2018. Intelligent travel chatbot for predictive recommendation in echo platform. In *Computing and Communication Workshop and Conference (CCWC), 2018 IEEE 8th Annual*, pages 176–183. IEEE.

Dzmitry Bahdanau, Kyunghyun Cho, and Yoshua Bengio. 2014. Neural machine translation by jointly learning to align and translate. *CoRR*, abs/1409.0473.

Tao Chen, Ruifeng Xu, Yulan He, and Xuan Wang. 2017. Improving sentiment analysis via sentence type classification using bilstm-crf and cnn. *Expert Systems with Applications*, 72:221–230.

Junyoung Chung, Caglar Gulcehre, KyungHyun Cho, and Yoshua Bengio. 2014. Empirical evaluation of gated recurrent neural networks on sequence modeling. *arXiv preprint arXiv:1412.3555*.

Alexis Conneau, Guillaume Lample, Marc'Aurelio Ranzato, Ludovic Denoyer, and Hervé Jégoi. 2017. Word translation without parallel data. *arXiv preprint arXiv:1710.04087*.

Kushal S. Dave, Vishal Vaingankar, Sumanth Kolar, and Vasudeva Varma. 2013. *Timespent Based Models for Predicting User Retention*. WWW '13. ACM, New York, NY, USA.

Ahmed Fadhil and Silvia Gabrielli. 2017. Addressing challenges in promoting healthy lifestyles: The ai-chatbot approach.

Hal Daume III Hadi Amiri. 2015. Target-dependent churn classification in microblogs. *AAAI*, pages 2361–2367.

Hal Daume III Hadi Amiri. 2016. Short text representation for detecting churn in microblogs. *AAAI*, pages 2566–2572.

Jennifer Hill, W Randolph Ford, and Ingrid G Farreras. 2015. Real conversations with artificial intelligence: A comparison between human–human online conversations and human–chatbot conversations. *Computers in Human Behavior*, 49:245–250.

Fulin Shi Huiwei Zhou, Long Chen and Degen Huang. 2015. Learning bilingual sentiment word embeddings for cross-language sentiment classification. In *Proceedings of the 53rd Annual Meeting of the Association for Computational Linguistics and the 7th International Conference on Natural Language Processing*, pages 26–31, Beijing, China.

Alexandre Klementiev, Ivan Titov, and Binod Bhattarai. 2012. Inducing crosslingual distributed representations of words. In *Proceedings of COLING 2012: Technical Papers*, pages 1459–1474, Mumbai, India.

Yann Lecun and Bengio Y. 1995. Convolutional networks for images, speech, and time-series.

Chih-Wei Lee, Yau-Shian Wang, Tsung-Yuan Hsu, Kuan-Yu Chen, Hung-yi Lee, and Lin-shan Lee. 2018. Scalable sentiment for sequence-to-sequence chatbot response with performance analysis.

Hala Mulki Mourad Gridach, Hatem Haddad. 2017. Churn identification in microblogs using convolutional neural networks with structured logical knowledge. *Proceedings of the 3rd Workshop on Noisy User-generated Text*, pages 21–30.

Alexander Pak and Patrick Paroubek. 2010. Twitter as a corpus for sentiment analysis and opinion mining. In *LREc*, volume 10.

Armand Joulin Piotr Bojanowski, Edouard Grave and Tomas Mikolov. 2017. Enriching word vectors with subword information. In *Transactions of the Association for Computational Linguistics*, pages 135–146.

Qian, Wei Jiang, and Kwok-Leung Tsui. 2007. Churn detection via customer profile modelling. *International Journal of Production Research*, 44(14):2913–2933.

T. N. Sainath, O. Vinyals, A. Senior, and H. Sak. 2015. Convolutional, long short-term memory, fully connected deep neural networks. In *2015 IEEE International Conference on Acoustics, Speech and Signal Processing (ICASSP)*, pages 4580–4584.

Samuel L. Smith, David H. P. Turban, Steven Hamblin, and Nils Y. Hammerla. 2017. Offline bilingual word vectors, orthogonal transformations and the inverted softmax. *CoRR*, abs/1702.03859.

Anbang Xu, Zhe Liu, Yufan Guo, Vibha Sinha, and Rama Akkiraju. 2017. A new chatbot for customer service on social media. In *Proceedings of the 2017 CHI Conference on Human Factors in Computing Systems*, pages 3506–3510. ACM.

Learning text representations for 500K classification tasks on Named Entity Disambiguation

Ander Barrena and **Aitor Soroa** and **Eneko Agirre**
IXA NLP Group
UPV/EHU University of the Basque Country
Donostia, Basque Country
`ander.barrena,a.soroa,e.agirre@ehu.eus`

Abstract

Named Entity Disambiguation algorithms typically learn a single model for all target entities. In this paper we present a word expert model and train separate deep learning models for each target entity string, yielding 500K classification tasks. This gives us the opportunity to benchmark popular text representation alternatives on this massive dataset. In order to face scarce training data we propose a simple data-augmentation technique and transfer-learning. We show that bag-of-word-embeddings are better than LSTMs for tasks with scarce training data, while the situation is reversed when having larger amounts. Transferring an LSTM which is learned on all datasets is the most effective context representation option for the word experts in all frequency bands. The experiments show that our system trained on out-of-domain Wikipedia data surpasses comparable NED systems which have been trained on in-domain training data.

1 Introduction

Named Entity Disambiguation (NED), also known as Entity Linking or Entity Resolution, is a task where entity mentions in running text need to be linked to its entity entry in a Knowledge Base (KB), such as Wikidata, Wikipedia or other derived resources like DBpedia (Bunescu and Pasca, 2006; McNamee and Dang, 2009; Hoffart et al., 2011). This task is challenging, as some entity mentions like "London" can refer to a number of places, people, fictional characters, brands, movies, books or songs.

Given a mention in context, NED methods (Cucerzan, 2007; Han and Sun, 2011; Ratinov et al., 2011; Lazic et al., 2015) typically rely on three models: (1) a mention model which collects possible entities which can be referred to by the mention string (aliases or surface forms), possibly weighted according to prior probabilities; (2) a context model which measures to which extent the entities fit well in the context of the mention, using textual features; (3) a coherence model which prefers entities that are related to the other entities in the document. The first and second models are *local* in that they only require a short context of occurrence and disambiguate each mention in the document separately. The third model is *global*, in that all mentions are disambiguated simultaneously (Ratinov et al., 2011). Recent work has shown that local models can be improved adding a global coherence model (Ratinov et al., 2011; Globerson et al., 2016). In this work we focus on a local model, and a global model could improve the results further.

All local and global systems mentioned above, as well as the current state-of-the-art systems (Lazic et al., 2015; Globerson et al., 2016; Yamada et al., 2016; Ganea and Hofmann, 2017), rely on single models for each of the above, that is, they have a single mention model, context model and coherence model for all entities, e.g. the 500K ambiguous entity mentions occurring more than 10 times in Wikipedia. While this has the advantage of reusing the parameters across mentions, it also makes the problem unnecessarily complex.

In this paper we propose to break the task of NED into 500K classification tasks, one for each target mention, as opposed to building a single model for all 500K mentions. The advantage of this approach is that each of the 500K classification tasks is simpler, as the classifier needs to focus on learning a good context model for a single mention and a limited set of entities (those returned by the mention model). On the negative side, training instances for mentions follow a long tail distribution, with some mentions having a huge number of examples, but with the vast majority

Proceedings of the 22nd Conference on Computational Natural Language Learning (CoNLL 2018), pages 171–180
Brussels, Belgium, October 31 - November 1, 2018. ©2018 Association for Computational Linguistics

of mentions having very limited training data, e.g. 10 occurrences linking to an entity in Wikipedia. Our results will show that data-augmentation and transfer learning allow us to overcome the sparseness problem, yielding the best results among local systems, very close to the best local/global combined systems. Contrary to systems trained on in-domain data (Cucerzan, 2012; Chisholm and Hachey, 2015; Globerson et al., 2016; Yamada et al., 2016; Sil et al., 2018), ours is trained on Wikipedia and tested out-of-domain.

From another perspective, a set of 500K classification problems provides a great experimental framework for testing text representation and classification algorithms. More specifically, deep learning methods provide end-to-end algorithms to learn both representations and classifiers jointly (LeCun et al., 2015). In fact, learning text representations models has become a center topic in natural language understanding, as it allows to transfer representation models across tasks (Conneau and Kiela, 2018; Peters et al., 2018; Wang et al., 2018). In this paper, we explore several popular text representation options, as well as data-augmentation (Zhang and LeCun, 2015) and transfer learning (Bengio, 2012). All training examples and models in this paper, as well as the pytorch code to reproduce results is availabe [1].

This paper is structured as follows. We first present our models. Section 3 presents the experiments, followed by related work and conclusions.

2 Deep Learning models for NED

In this section we describe the deep learning models proposed in this work. We first present our use of Wikipedia to produce the candidate model and the training instances, followed by the deep learning models. We will mention options and hyperparameters as we explain each component. Unless explicitly stated we used default values. The rest were selected and tuned solely on development data from Wikipedia itself, with no access to other datasets (cf. Section 3).

2.1 Pre-processing and Resources

We used the English Wikipedia[2] as the only resource for training the models. On the one hand, Wikipedia articles define the target set of entities.

On the other hand, Wikipedia editors have manually added hyperlinks to articles, where the anchor text corresponds to the mention, and the url corresponds to the entity.

We first built a candidate model as a dictionary that links each text anchor to possible entities, using the method presented in (Spitkovsky and Chang, 2012; Barrena et al., 2016). Let M be the set of all unique mention strings m, E the set of all target entities e, and $E_m = \{e_1, \ldots, e_m\}$ the set of entities that can be referred by mention m. We kept the 30 most frequent candidates for each mention for the sake of efficiency. We report the sizes of E and M below.

We then extracted annotated examples by scanning through the page contents for hyperlinks that link anchors (the mentions) to the corresponding Wikipedia pages (the entities). For each such hyperlink, we build a context $\mathbf{c}$ by first tokenizing and removing the stop words, and then extracting a window of 20 words to the left and 20 words to the right from the anchor. We thus construct a set of N_m labeled instances $\{\mathbf{c}_i, y_i\}$, where $y_i \in E_m$, for each m. We did not apply any kind of lemmatization or stemming to the training contexts.

2.2 Word Expert models

In the word expert approach we train one classifier for each possible ambiguous mention. We are thus interested in learning a classifier that assigns a target mention $m \in M$ appearing in a context $\mathbf{c}$ to one of its possible entity candidates $E_m = \{e_1, \ldots, e_m\}$ based on the set of N_m training instances $\{\mathbf{c}_i, y_i\}$, where $y_i \in E_m$. From the approximately $1M$ ambiguous mentions in Wikipedia only $523K$ occur more than 10 times as anchors in Wikipedia, and we thus limit M to 523 mentions and learn $523K$ classifiers.

Given the textual context of a mention, $\mathbf{c}_i$, the text representations model will output a vector representation h. We tried different alternatives for representing context, as described below. Given the vector h, we define the classifier as a neural network consisting of a number of fully connected layers, followed by a softmax layer with as many output dimension as the number of candidates of the target mention E_m. The whole network (representation model and classifier) is trained end-to-end using cross-entropy loss.

In order to tune the hyper-parameters, we split the examples into training (90%) and development

---

[1] https://github.com/anderbarrena/
500kNED

[2] We chose the 2014 snapshot, which gives good results in the contemporary evaluation datasets.

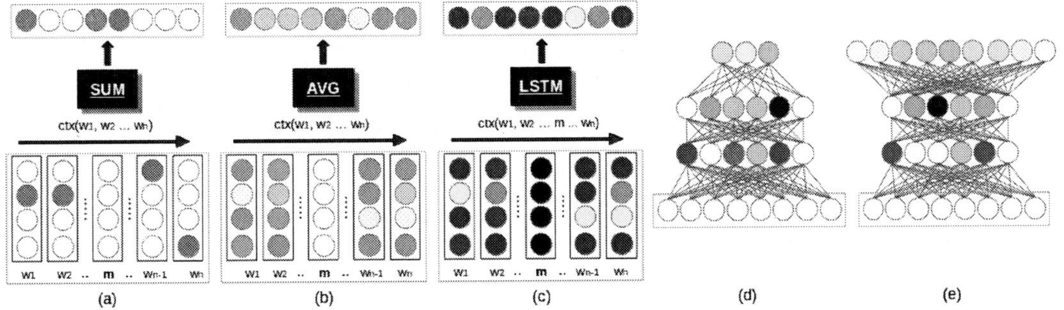

Figure 1: Deep learning models for NED. On the left side, context models: (a) Sparse BoW, (b) Continuous BoW, (c) LSTM. On the right side the classification models: (d) word expert model, (e) single model. The transfer model first learns an LSTM on the single model, then reuses the LSTM to learn each of the word expert models.

(10%). We tried different configurations of the classifier, such as the number of fully connected layers or the activation function. Two layers of ReLUs performed best in the development set. The rest of parameters were set by default: 256 hidden units, adam optimizer with an initial learning rate of $1.0e - 3$ and batches of 256 instances. Training stops when the accuracy in the development set drops for 10 consecutive epochs or when a maximum of 300 epochs is reached. We select the model that obtained the best accuracy in the development set before stopping. The same parameters and model were used for all word experts.

We now describe the how to represent context.

Sparse bag-of-words (BoW): In this model, depicted in Figure 1 (a), the context is represented as the addition of the one-hot vector for each word, with as many dimensions as the vocabulary size. The target mention is assigned a zero vector, akin to ignoring it. The vocabulary is large, comprising more than 200K different words, which slowed down learning. Alternatively, we also clustered the words in the vocabulary. In this case, we use those clusters to represent the words in the one-hot vector, yielding a bag of clusters representation. We used the *word2vec*[3] toolkit to build the clusters from English Wikipedia text. The corpus was lower-cased and tokenized. We found that using 3K cluster size does best in development.[4] As the results on development for the models using words were below those of clusters we will report only results for clusters.

Continuous bag-of-words (CBoW): In this case, see Figure 1 (b), context is represented with the

centroid of pre-trained word embeddings, where the mention is represented by a vector of zeros. The embeddings were trained over the English Wikipedia using word2vec (Mikolov et al., 2013). The corpus was first lower-cased, and we used a window size of 20, 10 negative samples and 7 iterations. The embeddings have a dimensionality of 300. We also tested a number of pre-trained embeddings, but we did not obtain better results, perhaps because our embeddings were trained on Wikipedia, which is also the training corpus for the NED system. When combined with the classifiers, we kept the embeddings fixed.

Recurrent Neural Network (LSTM): As a third alternative, we considered a recurrent neural network based on LSTMs (Hochreiter and Schmidhuber, 1997) to exploit the dependencies among the word sequence that forms the input context (Figure 1, (c)). We use a single LSTM to encode the input contexts as follows. We first replace the target mention with a special symbol which has a manually assigned constant embedding, and then feed the sequence into the LSTM. The last hidden vector is taken to represent the context. The LSTMs have 512 hidden units and 300 dimensional word embeddings, which are initialized with the embeddings vectors used in the continuous BoW model described above. The LSTM layers have a dropout layer, with 0.2 dropout probability.

We explored GRUs, stacking LSTMs, temporal average and max pooling among hidden states, but did not improve results on development.

2.3 Single model

One of the main problems of word experts is that they need a large number of manually annotated

---

[3] https://code.google.com/archive/p/word2vec/

[4] We tried 100,300,800,1K,3K,8K and 10K cluster sizes.

examples for each possible mention, which makes it unsuitable for less frequent mentions. As an alternative, we also trained a single model. Given the set of all training instances N_m for all possible mentions $m \in M$, we train a classifier that, for each context $\mathbf{c}_i$ produces the correct entity $e_i \in E$. This classifier has a large number of classes $|E|$. We discarded entities with less than 50 mentions, and gather up to 5K random instances for the rest. Note that clipping the instance number to 5K effectively downsamples those entities that are highly frequent. All in all, we gather a training corpus of 53M annotated examples for 248K target entities in this single model.

We adopted the recurrent model presented in the previous section. In this case, we also replace the target mention with a special symbol which has a manually assigned constant embedding vector, we feed it into the LSTM, and use the last hidden vector h as the context representation. The classifier follows the same architecture as the word expert model. In this case the LSTM has 2048 hidden units, producing a 512-dimensional context representation and 300 dimensional word embeddings, which are again initialized with the pretrained embeddings in the previous section keeping them fixed. The final softmax layer has 248K dimensions, the number of candidate entities. We checked other hidden-unit sizes with no better results. In order to improve results, we filter out the candidates which are not in dictionary.

Regarding the training details, we use the Adam optimization algorithm with an initial learning rate of $1.0e^{-4}$, and a dropout value of 0.2. In this case, we used a 1% sample of Wikipedia instances as a validation set, and we stop early, whenever the accuracy in this validation set does not improve for 3 consecutive epochs. Training the model takes around 16 hours per epoch in a single GPU, taking at most 18 iterations.

2.4 Transfer learning

As an alternative to learning a single model, we can use the text representation layer of the aforementioned single model in the word expert model. That is, after training the single model with the whole Wikipedia, we use the learned model of the LSTM as the text representation layer of the word expert models. This way, we reuse the LSTM which was learned alongside the single model instead of learning a separate LSTM layer for each

word expert (see Section 2.2). When training the word experts, we keep the LSTM layer fixed.

2.5 Data augmentation

As mentioned above, some mentions only have as few as 10 training instances. In order to have a larger number of training instances, we augment the training set for target mention m with the contexts of other mentions that occur as anchors of one of the e_i candidates m ($e_i \in E_m$). Using this strategy, we randomly select up to $250K$ examples as training instances for each mention. Although augmenting the training set has the advantage of providing more training instances, it also has the drawback of distorting the number of examples for each entity. For instance, in the case of the mention *EU* most of the examples in Wikipedia refer to the European Union (around 2800) and only a few to Europe (the continent, 716). When augmenting the training set with examples for the entities, we add more examples for Europe (around 44000) than for European Union (around 13000), changing the ratio of labels in the training data significantly. In order to counter-balance this effect, we tried to combine the priors from the original data with the output of the classifier trained with the augmented dataset. Alternatively, we combined both original and augmented classifiers, yielding better results in development. We thus train two classifiers for each mention, one using the original training set $P(e|\mathbf{c})_{orig}$, and one using the augmented dataset $P(e|\mathbf{c})_{aug}$. Finaly, we combine their scores to produce the combined output $P(e|\mathbf{c})$:

$$P(e|\mathbf{c}) = P(e|\mathbf{c})_{orig}P(e|\mathbf{c})_{aug} \qquad (1)$$

3 Experiments

We developed and evaluated our model in standard datasets for easier comparison to the state of the art. The main dataset is the Aida CoNLL dataset which is composed of news documents from the Reuters corpus. It comprises three parts: *Aidatrain* training set, *Aidatesta* development set and *Aidatestb* test set. We also include the three earliest Text Analysis Conference (TAC) datasest, that focus on highly ambiguous mentions from news, web and discussion forums: *Tac2010*, *Tac2011* and *Tac2012*. As we are interested in building a robust model based on Wikipedia alone, we ignore the training data accompanying each dataset. We

	testa	testb	tac2010	tac2011	tac2012
mentions	5917	5616	2250	2250	2229
inKB mentions	4792	4485	1020	1124	1177
uniq mentions	2600	2441	750	1315	781
uniq inKB mentions	1850	1685	386	628	509
inKB mentions in dict	1841	1675	382	597	499

Table 1: Statistics of the datasets (see text for details).

use *Aidatesta* for model selection only (i.e. the parameters were tuned on a subset of Wikipedia, cf. Section 2), and *Aidatestb*, *Tac2010*, *Tac2011* and *Tac2012* for out-of-domain test.

Note that we used *Aidatesta* only to select the best models, given that all hyperparameters where tuned over Wikipedia itself. Table 1 shows the statistics for all datasets. From all mentions, only a subset of them actually refers to an entity in the KB provided by the dataset authors ("inKB mentions" row). Our dictionary covers most but not all of those KB entities ("uniq inKB mentions in dict" row). Some of the mentions in the datasets are resolved as NIL, for cases where the mention refers to an entity which is not in the KB. The simplest method to return NIL is to first resolve over all Wikipedia entities, and if the selected entity is not in the KB then to return NIL. We focus the evaluation in the mentions linked to an entity in the respective KB, and use the so-called *inKB accuracy* as the evaluation measure, which is defined as the fraction of correctly disambiguated mentions divided by the total number of mentions which are linked to the KB. We perform 3 runs for each reported result, reporting mean accuracy and standard deviation values. We also include MFS baselines in the results: given a mention, the baseline is computed assigning the entity in the dictionary with highest prior probabilities.

During testing, given a mention, we search the document and try to find the longest string that a) contains the mention and b) matches an entry in the dictionary. Next, we replace every mention string with that longer string in the document.[5] We also apply the *'One entity per Document'* hypothesis, averaging the results of the occurrences for the same mention in the same document (Barrena et al., 2014).

3.1 Development results

Table 2 shows the performance of each of the context representation models and data augmentation options in *Aidatesta*. The MFS baseline obtains 71.91, which is a good point of comparison to benchmark our candidate model (the dictionary) with respect to other systems. All our models improve over the MFS baseline by a large margin. As mentioned in Section 2.5, we have three classifiers for each mention. $P(e|\mathbf{c})_{orig}$ uses the original training set, $P(e|\mathbf{c})_{aug}$ uses the augmented training set, and $P(e|\mathbf{c})$ combines both. The table shows that the results of the original and augmented classifiers are more or less comparable, while the combination consistently yields the best results for all context representations options.

Regarding the representation models, we can observe that the sparse Bag-of-word model yields worse results than the continuous Bag-of-words. The LSTMs learned separately do not improve over continuous BoW, while the LSTM transferred from the single model obtains the best results. In addition to the results in the table, the single model obtains an accuracy of 45.95, well below the rest.

These results confirm our intuitions. Regarding the single model vs. word experts, the classifier has a much easier task in the second case, as the number of classes to predict is much smaller for each classifier. Regarding the performance of the word expert LSTMs, our hypothesis was that, given the long tail distribution of the number of training instances, the per-mention LSTMs of many mentions would not have enough training instances to learn effective representations. We checked this hypothesis plotting the results for each method according to the number of training instances. Figure 2 shows the inKB accuracy for mentions bucketed according to the number of training instances[6]. Continuous BoW overpeforms LSTMs on mentions with a small number of

---

[5] Mentions that are named as a DBPedia entity classified as location are not expanded.

[6] We set 10 buckets with an equal number of mentions in each bucket

	Sparse BoW	**CBoW**	**LSTM**	**Transfer**
$P(e\|c)_{orig}$	79.65±0.06	82.48±0.48	80.35±0.05	84.70±0.06
$P(e\|c)_{aug}$	79.54±0.26	81.74±0.21	80.66±0.26	82.39±0.42
$P(e\|c)$	83.28±0.17	86.19±0.19	84.35±0.30	**86.87±0.14**

Table 2: Development results (Aidatesta) as inKB accuracy and standard deviation for Sparse BoW, Continuous BoW, LSTM and transferred LSTMs. Each row corresponds to the original training data, augmented training data, and combination.

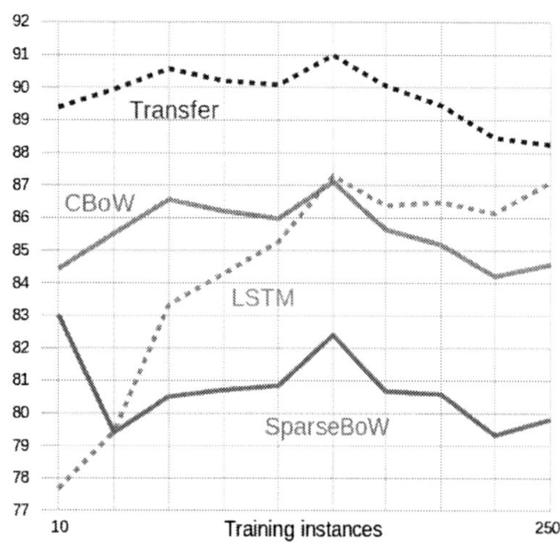

Figure 2: Development results (Aidatesta) as inKB accuracy according to number of training instances.

Method	testb
Local models	
(Lazic et al., 2015) sup.	79.7
Sparse BoW	86.72±0.23
Continuous BoW	89.39±0.44
LSTM	88.44±0.26
Transfer LSTM	**91.19±0.07**
(Lazic et al., 2015)† semi-sup.	86.4 †
(Yamada et al., 2016)*	87.2*
(Ganea and Hofmann, 2017)*	88.8*
Local & Global models	
(Chisholm and Hachey, 2015)*	88.7*
(Globerson et al., 2016)*	91.0*
(Yamada et al., 2016)*	91.5*
(Ganea and Hofmann, 2017)*	92.2*

Table 3: Test results on *Aidatestb* as inKB accuracy. * for systems trained on in-domain data. † for systems using semi-supervised methods.

training instances, while the situation is reversed for mentions with a large number of training instances. The graph also shows that the transferred LSTM yields better results for all frequencies, and that the Sparse BoW model underperforms the rest of models consistently. As an aside, we observed that for the words which have more than 200.000 training instances, both the per-mention LSTM and the transferred LSTM yield similar results.

3.2 Final results

In this section we compare our system with the state-of-the-art in Named Entity Disambiguation. Given the vast number of NED systems, we only report the results of the most relevant high performing systems only. Note that, contrary to us, many high-performing systems use in-domain training data (Ganea and Hofmann, 2017; Globerson et al., 2016), and/or external candidates and link counts when building the dictionary (Lazic et al., 2015; Globerson et al., 2016; Yamada et al., 2016).

Table 3 shows the inKB results on *Aidatestb*, the most popular evaluation dataset. The results show that all our models improve over locals out-of-domain systems trained solely on Wikipedia, but, most notably, also over in-domain systems which were trained on *Aidatrain* (marked with *) and the semi-supervised system (marked with †), which uses large numbers of un-annotated data. As expected, the relative performance of our systems is the same as in development.

All the systems included in Table 3 (except Lazic et al., 2015) use the "means" tables of YAGO as candidates, as this was the entity inventory used by the developers of the dataset (Hoffart et al., 2011). In our case, as we link mention to Wikipedia entities, we just ignore those entities not belonging to the YAGO "means" table. In order to provide head-to-head comparison, the results of our best system when not using the YAGO information is 89.93, more than three points better.

Table 4 shows the inKB accuracy results on the three TAC datasets. In this case, the dataset is accompanied by a KB which is a subset of the Wikipedia 2008 snapshot. Following standard procedure (Globerson et al., 2016), we fil-

Method	tac10	tac11	tac12
Local models			
(Lazic et al., 2015) sup.	—	74.5	68.7
Sparse BoW	85.82	80.25	63.12
Continuous BoW	86.96	81.55	67.49
LSTM	86.73	81.44	67.32
Transfer LSTM	87.32	84.41	72.58
(Lazic et al., 2015)† semi-sup.	—	79.3†	74.2†
(Chang et al., 2016)*	84.5*	—	—
(Yamada et al., 2016)*	84.6*	—	—
Local & Global models			
(Cucerzan, 2012)*	—	—	72.0*
(Chisholm and Hachey, 2015)*	80.7*	—	—
(Globerson et al., 2016)*	87.2*	84.3*	82.4*
(Yamada et al., 2016)*	85.2*		

Table 4: Test results on TAC datasets as inKB accuracy. * for systems trained on in-domain data. † for systems using semi-supervised methods.

ter out entities not listed in the KB before evaluating the results. The table shows that the relative performance of our systems is stable. Our best system outperforms the results of the local system trained on Wikipedia on both Tac2011 and Tac2012 (10 and 3 points). Regarding the comparison with other local systems (in-domain and semi-supervised), our results are the best, including global methods. The only exception is on the TAC2012 dataset, where the mentions were short and known to be specially challenging. In fact, the winner of the task (Cucerzan, 2012) performed an especial effort on finding longer correferent mentions in the document. In the case of (Lazic et al., 2015; Globerson et al., 2016), they use a coreference resolver, which could explain their better results on this dataset.

Note that in this section we do not report results of systems which use the candidate dictionary of (Pershina et al., 2015). As observed by (Globerson et al., 2016), among others, that candidate dictionary has been manually pruned and extended to contain the gold standard entity, yielding a dictionary that has a 100% upperbound and very limited ambiguity. This makes the results of systems using this dictionary look much better than those using automatically constructed candidate models. We thus miss results from some papers (Pershina et al., 2015; Sil et al., 2018), and report the results using automatically constructed dictionaries for the rest (e.g. Globerson et al., 2016).

4 Related Work

In this section we will briefly review NED systems and text representation literature. Hachey et al.

(2012) present a detailed overview of all possible components, but in this section we will focus on the most relevant high performing systems. Please see (Ling et al., 2015) for a more detailed review of past research.

4.1 NED systems

Among local systems that are trained on Wikipedia alone, (Lazic et al., 2015) was the best performing one to date. Their system is based on probabilistic estimation, with a rich pre-processing pipeline, including dependency parsing, common noun phrase identificacion and coreference resolution. They present the results for both a supervised version, and a graph-based semi-supervised extension which improves results. We think that the results of our method could be improved using richer pre-processing, specially the use of coreference to find longer coreferent mentions, which reduces the ambiguity of the mention and improve results.

Among global models, (Chisholm and Hachey, 2015) use a learning to rank algorithm which combines local and global features, trained on in-domain corpora (*Aidatrain* and *Tac2010 train*, respectively). They improve the results significantly by extending the information extracted from Wikipedia with a web crawl.

In (Yamada et al., 2016), the authors jointly learn word and entity embeddings using Wikipedia. The similarity of word and entity embeddings are used as features to train a Gradient Boosted Regression Trees on in-domain data. They report both local and global results, with a clear improvement when adding a global component.

Ganea and Hofmann (2017) also present a local and global algorithm. In their local algorithm, they combine word and entity embeddings with an attention mechanism trained on in-domain data. The global component is Loopy Belief Propagation, which optimizes the global sequence coherence initialized by the local algorithm. They report the best results among both local and global algorithms in *Aidatestb*, but, unfortunately they don not provide results on the TAC datasets. Given that their global algorithm yields an improvement of 3 points, and that our local method exploits complementary information, we would like to combine both in future work.

Globerson et al. (2016) add a global component to Plato (Lazic et al., 2015), whose weights are used to initialize a multi-focal attention mechanism. The global model is trained and optimized on in-domain training datasets. They report the best performance for *TAC* datasets to date, and very good results on *Aida*. Their very strong results on TAC 2012 (together with those of Lazic et al., 2015) seem to be due to the use coreference in the candidate model, as this dataset includes shorter target mentions than the rest.

More recently, Sil et al. (2018) introduce a deep neural cross-lingual entity linking system using a combination of CNN, LSTM and NTNs, with strong results. Their method performs similar to ours on TAC2010, but using the manually curated dictionary of (Pershina et al., 2015), which, as stated before, greatly simplifies the task (c.f. Section 3.2).

All NED systems mentioned above build a single model for all possible target mentions. The only word expert approach that we are aware of is briefly mentioned in (Chang et al., 2016). This paper compares NED and word sense disambiguation, and builds a bag of words logistic regression classifier for each mention. Their results on the *TAC2010* dataset is 84.5, below our results.

4.2 Text representation

Text representation for deep learning is a hot topic on natural language processing (LeCun et al., 2015), and several evaluation frameworks have been proposed (Conneau and Kiela, 2018; Wang et al., 2018). Our 500K classification tasks can be seen as an additional large-scale testbed for text representation proposals.

In a setting similar to ours, (Yuan et al., 2016; Peters et al., 2018) propose to train a language model based on LSTMs and then use it for word sense disambiguation. Instead of using the context representations to learn a classifier directly as we do, they use label propagation in representation space. In our case, instead of using a language model, we train the text representation model on a more closely related task, i.e., that of disambiguating all possible entities.

While bags of pre-trained word embeddings and LSTMs are the most popular approaches for text representation, many alternatives exist. For instance, ELMo (Peters et al., 2018) obtains word embeddings that include contextual information, and then combine them using bag-of-words or

other alternative. Alternatively, universal sentence encoding models that are useful in many tasks are being proposed (Arora et al., 2017; Logeswaran and Lee, 2018; Subramanian et al., 2018; Cer et al., 2018). We think that, in supervised classification tasks such as ours, the transferred LSTM already captures well contextual information and that the performance bottleneck might lie on the classifier. If that is the case, stronger context representation models might not make much of a difference. We plan to explore this in future work.

5 Conclusions and Future Work

In this paper we propose to break the task of NED into 500K classification tasks, one for each target mention, as opposed to building a single model for all 500K mentions. The advantage of this word expert approach is that each of the 500K classification tasks is simpler. On the negative side, scarcity of training data is made worse. We show that this problem can be effectively alleviated with data-augmentation and specially with transfer learning.

A set of 500K classification problems provides a great experimental framework for testing text representation and classification algorithms. Given the scarce data available, learning a classifier directly on a bag-of-words or LSTM representation yields weak results. Bringing in pre-trained embeddings improves results, but the key to strong performance is to learn a single model for all entities using an LSTM and then transfer the LSTM to each of the word experts.

Our model is a local system using Wikipedia information alone, yielding the best results among local systems, comparable to systems trained on in-domain data and incorporating global coherence models. All training examples and models in this paper, as well as the pytorch code to reproduce results is availabe [7].

For the future, the performance of our system can be easily improved combining it with a global method such as (Ganea and Hofmann, 2017). There are also specific improvements that can be done, such as using correference (Lazic et al., 2015) or additional information from web crawls (Chisholm and Hachey, 2015). Regarding the use of in-domain training, we think that our out-of-domain results reflect the most realistic scenario, as in-domain training data is rare in practice.

---

[7] https://github.com/anderbarrena/
500kNED

Regarding text representation, we tested some straightforward alternatives. Recent work has proposed stronger options which could improve the results of our word experts further.

Acknowledgments

This research was partially supported by the Spanish MINECO (TUNER TIN2015-65308-C5-1-R, MUSTER PCIN-2015-226, cofunded by EU FEDER), the UPV/EHU (excellence research group), and the NVIDIA GPU grant program.

References

Sanjeev Arora, Yingyu Liang, and Tengyu Ma. 2017. A simple but tough-to-beat baseline for sentence embeddings. In *International Conference on Learning Representations*.

Ander Barrena, Eneko Agirre, Bernardo Cabaleiro, Anselmo Peñas, and Aitor Soroa. 2014. "one entity per discourse" and "one entity per collocation" improve named-entity disambiguation. In *Proceedings of COLING 2014, the 25th International Conference on Computational Linguistics: Technical Papers*, pages 2260–2269, Dublin, Ireland. Dublin City University and Association for Computational Linguistics.

Ander Barrena, Aitor Soroa, and Eneko Agirre. 2016. Alleviating poor context with background knowledge for named entity disambiguation. In *Proceedings of the 54th Annual Meeting of the Association for Computational Linguistics (Volume 1: Long Papers)*, pages 1903–1912, Berlin, Germany. Association for Computational Linguistics.

Yoshua Bengio. 2012. Deep learning of representations for unsupervised and transfer learning. In *Proceedings of ICML Workshop on Unsupervised and Transfer Learning*, pages 17–36.

R. C. Bunescu and M. Pasca. 2006. Using encyclopedic knowledge for named entity disambiguation. In *Proceesings of the 11th Conference of the European Chapter of the Association for Computational Linguistics (EACL)*, pages 9–16, Trento, Italy. The Association for Computer Linguistics.

D. Cer, Y. Yang, S.-y. Kong, N. Hua, N. Limtiaco, R. St. John, N. Constant, M. Guajardo-Cespedes, S. Yuan, C. Tar, Y.-H. Sung, B. Strope, and R. Kurzweil. 2018. Universal Sentence Encoder. *ArXiv e-prints*.

Angel Chang, Valentin I. Spitkovsky, Christopher D. Manning, and Eneko Agirre. 2016. A comparison of named-entity disambiguation and word sense disambiguation. In *Proceedings of the Tenth International Conference on Language Resources and Evaluation (LREC 2016)*, Paris, France. European Language Resources Association (ELRA).

Andrew Chisholm and Ben Hachey. 2015. Entity disambiguation with web links. *Transactions of the Association for Computational Linguistics*, 3:145–156.

A. Conneau and D. Kiela. 2018. SentEval: An Evaluation Toolkit for Universal Sentence Representations. *ArXiv e-prints*.

S. Cucerzan. 2007. Large-Scale Named Entity Disambiguation Based on Wikipedia Data. In *Proceedings of the 2007 Joint Conference on Empirical Methods in Natural Language Processing and Computational Natural Language Learning (EMNLP-CoNLL)*, pages 708–716, Prague, Czech Republic.

Silviu Cucerzan. 2012. Msr system for entity linking at tac 2012. In *Text Analysis Conference - Knowledge Base Population 2012 TAC-KBP 2012*.

Octavian-Eugen Ganea and Thomas Hofmann. 2017. Deep joint entity disambiguation with local neural attention. In *Proceedings of the 2017 Conference on Empirical Methods in Natural Language Processing*, pages 2619–2629, Copenhagen, Denmark. Association for Computational Linguistics.

Amir Globerson, Nevena Lazic, Soumen Chakrabarti, Amarnag Subramanya, Michael Ringaard, and Fernando Pereira. 2016. Collective entity resolution with multi-focal attention. In *Proceedings of the 54th Annual Meeting of the Association for Computational Linguistics (Volume 1: Long Papers)*, pages 621–631, Berlin, Germany. Association for Computational Linguistics.

B. Hachey, W. Radford, J. Nothman, M. Honnibal, and J.R. Curran. 2012. Evaluating Entity Linking with Wikipedia. *Artificial Intelligence*, 194:130–150.

X. Han and L. Sun. 2011. A generative entity-mention model for linking entities with knowledge base. In *Proceedings of the 49th Annual Meeting of the Association for Computational Linguistics: Human Language Technologies - Volume 1*, HLT '11, pages 945–954, Stroudsburg, PA, USA. Association for Computational Linguistics.

Sepp Hochreiter and Jürgen Schmidhuber. 1997. Long short-term memory. *Neural computation*, 9(8):1735–1780.

J. Hoffart, M.A. Yosef, I. Bordino, H. Fürstenau, M. Pinkal, M. Spaniol, B. Taneva, S. Thater, and G. Weikum. 2011. Robust Disambiguation of Named Entities in Text. In *Proceedings of the Conference on Empirical Methods in Natural Language Processing*, EMNLP '11, pages 782–792, Stroudsburg, PA, USA. Association for Computational Linguistics.

Nevena Lazic, Amarnag Subramanya, Michael Ringgaard, and Fernando Pereira. 2015. Plato: A selective context model for entity resolution. *Transactions of the Association for Computational Linguistics*, 3:503–515.

Yann LeCun, Yoshua Bengio, and Geoffrey Hinton. 2015. Deep learning. *Nature*, 521(7553):436.

Xiao Ling, Sameer Singh, and Daniel S Weld. 2015. Design challenges for entity linking. *Transactions of the Association for Computational Linguistics*, 3:315–328.

Lajanugen Logeswaran and Honglak Lee. 2018. An efficient framework for learning sentence representations. In *International Conference on Learning Representations*.

Paul McNamee and Hoa Dang. 2009. Overview of the TAC 2009 Knowledge Base Population track. In *TAC*.

Tomas Mikolov, Kai Chen, Greg Corrado, and Jeffrey Dean. 2013. Efficient estimation of word representations in vector space. *arXiv preprint arXiv:1301.3781*.

Maria Pershina, Yifan He, and Ralph Grishman. 2015. Personalized page rank for named entity disambiguation. In *Proceedings of the 2015 Conference of the North American Chapter of the Association for Computational Linguistics: Human Language Technologies*, pages 238–243, Denver, Colorado. Association for Computational Linguistics.

Matthew E. Peters, Mark Neumann, Mohit Iyyer, Matt Gardner, Christopher Clark, Kenton Lee, and Luke Zettlemoyer. 2018. Deep contextualized word representations. In *Proc. of NAACL*.

L.A. Ratinov, D. Roth, D. Downey, and M. Anderson. 2011. Local and Global Algorithms for Disambiguation to Wikipedia. In *The 49th Annual Meeting of the Association for Computational Linguistics: Human Language Technologies, Proceedings of the Conference, 19-24 June, 2011, Portland, Oregon, USA*, pages 1375–1384. The Association for Computer Linguistics.

Avirup Sil, Gourab Kundu, Radu Florian, and Wael Hamza. 2018. Neural cross-lingual entity linking. In *AAAI2018*.

Valentin I Spitkovsky and Angel X Chang. 2012. A cross-lingual dictionary for english wikipedia concepts. In *LREC*, pages 3168–3175.

S. Subramanian, A. Trischler, Y. Bengio, and C. J Pal. 2018. Learning General Purpose Distributed Sentence Representations via Large Scale Multi-task Learning. *ArXiv e-prints*.

A. Wang, A. Singh, J. Michael, F. Hill, O. Levy, and S. R. Bowman. 2018. GLUE: A Multi-Task Benchmark and Analysis Platform for Natural Language Understanding. *ArXiv e-prints*.

Ikuya Yamada, Hiroyuki Shindo, Hideaki Takeda, and Yoshiyasu Takefuji. 2016. Joint learning of the embedding of words and entities for named entity disambiguation. In *Proceedings of The 20th SIGNLL Conference on Computational Natural Language Learning*, pages 250–259, Berlin, Germany. Association for Computational Linguistics.

Dayu Yuan, Julian Richardson, Ryan Doherty, Colin Evans, and Eric Altendorf. 2016. Semi-supervised word sense disambiguation with neural models. In *COLING 2016, 26th International Conference on Computational Linguistics, Proceedings of the Conference: Technical Papers, December 11-16, 2016, Osaka, Japan*, pages 1374–1385.

Xiang Zhang and Yann LeCun. 2015. Text understanding from scratch. *arXiv preprint arXiv:1502.01710*.

Hierarchical Attention Based Position-aware Network
for Aspect-level Sentiment Analysis

Lishuang Li, Yang Liu and **AnQiao Zhou**
School of Computer Science and Technology, Dalian University of Technology
lilishuang314@163.com

Abstract

Aspect-level sentiment analysis aims to identify the sentiment of a specific target in its context. Previous works have proved that the interactions between aspects and the contexts are important. On this basis, we also propose a succinct hierarchical attention based mechanism to fuse the information of targets and the contextual words. In addition, most existing methods ignore the position information of the aspect when encoding the sentence. In this paper, we argue that the position-aware representations are beneficial to this task. Therefore, we propose a hierarchical attention based position-aware network (HAPN), which introduces position embeddings to learn the position-aware representations of sentences and further generate the target-specific representations of contextual words. The experimental results on SemEval 2014 dataset show that our approach outperforms the state-of-the-art methods.

1 Introduction

Aspect-level sentiment analysis is a fine-grained task in sentiment analysis, which aims to identify the sentiment polarity (i.e., negative, neutral, or positive) of a specific opinion target expressed in a comment/review by a reviewer. For example, given a sentence "The *price* is reasonable although the *service* is poor", the sentiment polarity for aspects *"price"* and *"service"* are positive and negative respectively.

Traditional methods for aspect-level sentiment analysis mainly focus on designing a set of features (such as bag-of-words, sentiment lexicons, and linguistic features) to train a classifier for sentiment classification (Kiritchenko et al., 2014; Wagner et al., 2014; Vo and Zhang, 2015). However, such kind of feature engineering work often relies on human ingenuity, which is a time-consuming process and lacks generalization. In recent years, more and more neural network based models have been proposed and obtained the state-of-the-art results (Wang et al., 2016; Tang et al., 2016a;2016b; Chen et al,. 2017; Ma et al., 2017; Tay et al., 2017; Zheng et al., 2018; Huang et al., 2018).

As previous research (Jiang et al., 2011) reveals that 40% of sentiment classification errors are caused by not considering targets in sentiment classification, recent works tend to focus on fusing the information of the targets and the contexts. Wang et al. (2016) and Tang et al. (2016a) both concatenated the aspect embeddings and embeddings of each word as inputs to a LSTM based model so as to introduce the information of the target into the model. Tay et al. (2017) adopted circular convolution and circular correlation to model the similarity between aspect and contextual words. Ma et al. (2017) and Zheng et al. (2018) both employed a bidirectional attention operation to achieve the representations of targets and contextual words determined by each other. Huang et al. (2018) introduced an attention-over-attention based network to model the aspects and contexts in a joint way and explicitly capture the interaction between aspects and the context.

As described above, the existing studies show that the interactions between aspects and the context are important to the aspect-level sentiment analysis. Leveraging this idea, we also propose a succinct hierarchical attention based mechanism to fuse the information of targets and the contextual words, which aims to generate the target-specific representations of each word.

In addition, most of the above methods ignore the position information of the aspect when

Proceedings of the 22nd Conference on Computational Natural Language Learning (CoNLL 2018), pages 181–189
Brussels, Belgium, October 31 - November 1, 2018. ©2018 Association for Computational Linguistics

encoding the sentence. We argue that the position of a candidate aspect is important for the sentence modelling. For instance, consider the sentence "I bought a mobile phone, its *camera* is wonderful but the *battery life* is a bit short". For the candidate aspect *"battery life"*, *"wonderful"* and *"short"* are both likely to be considered as its adjunct word. In this case, if we encode the position information into the representation of each word effectively, we would have more confidence in concluding that the *"short"* is the adjunct word of *"battery life"* and predict the sentiment as negative. Then, the next problem is how to introduce the position information. In some previous works (Tang et al., 2016b; Chen et al,. 2017), they weighted the representation of each word according to the position, and the words close to the aspect could be paid more attention. However, this operation is not always reasonable and sometimes the adjunct word may be far away from the target word. Thus, we introduce position embeddings when modelling the sentence and further generate the position-aware representations. In other words, the position information is considered as a kind of features and embedded into position embeddings. The model will learn to exploit both of the semantic information and the position clues.

Based on the analysis above, in this paper, we propose a hierarchical attention based position-aware network (HAPN) for aspect-level sentiment classification. A position-aware encoding layer is introduced for modelling the sentence to achieve the position-aware abstract representation of each word. On this basis, a succinct fusion mechanism is further proposed to fuse the information of aspects and the contexts, achieving the final sentence representation. Finally, we feed the achieved sentence representation into a softmax layer to predict the sentiment polarity.

We evaluate our approach on SemEval 2014 dataset (Pontiki et al., 2014), containing reviews of restaurant domain and laptop domain. The experimental results demonstrate that the proposed approach is effective for aspect-level sentiment classification, and it outperforms state-of-the-art approaches with remarkable gains. We make our source code public at `https://github.com/DUT-LiuYang/Aspect-Sentiment-Analysis`.

2 Related Work

Many approaches have been proposed to address the problem of aspect-level sentiment analysis. Traditional approaches to this task normally exploited a diverse set of strategies to convert classification clues (i.e., sentiment lexicons, bag-of-word) into feature vectors (Kiritchenko et al., 2014; Wagner et al., 2014; Vo and Zhang, 2015). Although these methods have achieved comparable performance, their models highly depend on the effectiveness of the handcraft features which are labor intensive and lack generalization.

Therefore, many neural network based models have been proposed in recent years. And most current state-of-the-art works in aspect-based sentiment analysis pay more attention to fusing the information of the targets and contextual words. Wang et al., (2016) proposed an attention based LSTM which introduced the aspect clues by concatenating the aspect embeddings and the word representations. Tang et al. (2016a) developed two target-dependent LSTM to model the left and right contexts with target, where the target information was automatically taken into account. Tay et al. (2017) proposed an attention based LSTM which learned to attend based on associative relationships between sentence words and aspect by adopting circular convolution and circular correlation. Ma et al. (2017) proposed an interactive attention network which interactively learned attentions in the contexts and targets. Similarly, Zheng et al. (2018) introduced a rotatory attention mechanism to achieve the representations of the targets, the left context and the right context, which were determined by each other. Huang et al. (2018) introduced an attention-over-attention network modeled the aspects and sentences in a joint way, which jointly learned the representations for aspects and sentences and automatically focused on the important parts in sentences. In addition, other current researches focus on capturing more accurate information by adopting multiple attentions. Tang et al. (2016b) designed a deep memory network which consisted of multiple computational layers, each of which was an attention model over an external memory. Chen et al. (2017) proposed a recurrent attention based network which introduced multiple attention mechanisms.

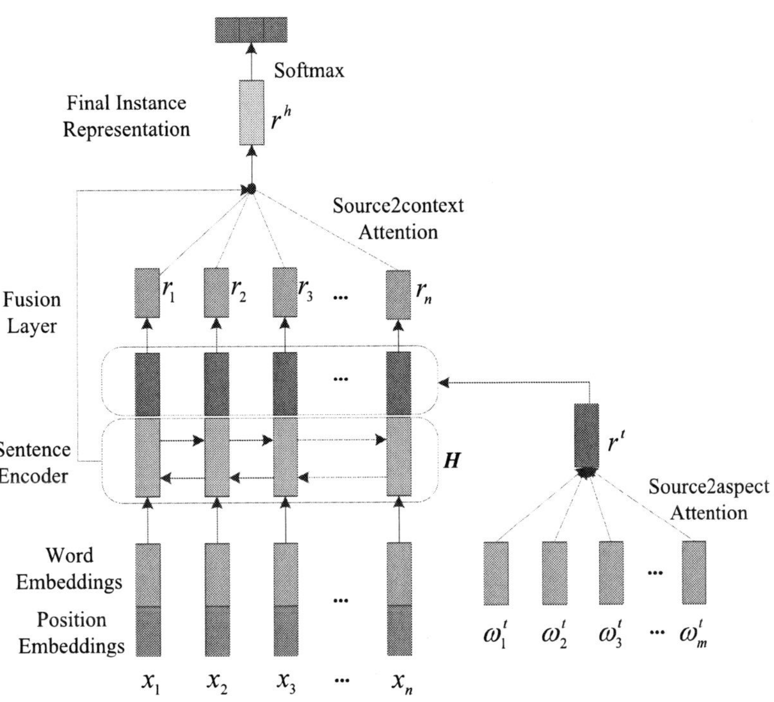

Figure 1: The architecture of the proposed model.

Compared with the above models, we introduce position embeddings when modelling the sentence to generate position-aware representations; on this basis, we propose a hierarchical attention based fusion mechanism to fuse the clues of aspects and the contexts.

3 Model

In our approach, each target along with the sentence where the target is located constitutes an instance. We suppose that a sentence consists of n words $\boldsymbol{w} = \{w_1, w_2, \cdots, w_n\}$ and a target has m words $\boldsymbol{w}^t = \{w_1^t, w_2^t, \cdots, w_m^t\}$. $\boldsymbol{w}^t$ is a subsequence of $\boldsymbol{w}$. The goal of our model is to predict the sentiment polarity of the sentence over the target.

As shown in Figure 1, our model primarily includes four parts: input embeddings, Bi-GRU based encoding layer, hierarchical attention based fusion layer and the output layer.

3.1 Input Embedding

The embedding layer has two parts: the word embeddings and the position embeddings. Let $W_w \in \mathbb{R}^{d_w \times v_w}$ be a word embedding lookup table generated by an unsupervised method such as GloVe (Pennington et al., 2014) or CBOW

(Mikolov et al., 2013), where d_w is the dimension of the word embeddings and v_w is the size of word vocabulary. As described in Section 1, we also introduce position embeddings, which have been widely used in CNN based models, as a part of the inputs to the model. Similar as the word embedding layer, the position embedding layer is a $W_p \in \mathbb{R}^{d_p \times v_p}$, where d_p is the dimension of the position embeddings and v_p is the number of possible relevant positions between each word and the target. The position embedding lookup table is initialized randomly and tuned in the training phase.

3.2 Bi-GRU Based Sentence Encoder

In this paper, we apply a Bi-GRU (Cho et al., 2014) to learn a more abstract representation of the sentence. In the following, we describe our encoding layer in detail.

In the encoding phase, we first transform each token w_i in the sentence into a real-valued vector x_i using the concatenation of the following vectors:

- The pre-trained word embeddings ω_i of w_i.

- The position embeddings of w_i: the relevant position between the i-th word and the target is defined as the relative offset with respect to the target and calculated by the follow equation:

$$\begin{cases} i - k & i < k \\ i - k - m & n \geq i > k + m \\ 0 & k + m \geq i \geq k \end{cases} \quad (1)$$

where k is the index of the first word of target, m is the length of the target, n is the length of the sentence, and *none* is the special marks assigned to the token padded. The position embedding vector is obtained by looking up the randomly initialized embeddings table according to the relevant position.

Hence a sequence of words can be represented as $X = \{x_1, x_2, ..., x_n\}$. We then run two parallel GRU layers: forward GRU layer and backward GRU layer. We run the forward GRU to generate the hidden representation $(\vec{h}_1, \vec{h}_2, ..., \vec{h}_n)$ and run the backward GRU to get the hidden representation $(\overleftarrow{h}_1, \overleftarrow{h}_2, ..., \overleftarrow{h}_n)$. Eventually, we obtain the new representation $H = (h_1, h_2, ..., h_n)$ by concatenating the hidden vectors in $(\vec{h}_1, \vec{h}_2, ..., \vec{h}_n)$ and $(\overleftarrow{h}_1, \overleftarrow{h}_2, ..., \overleftarrow{h}_n)$: $h_i = [\vec{h}_i, \overleftarrow{h}_i]$. Note that $h_i \in \mathbb{R}^{2d_h}$ essentially encapsulates the context information over the whole sentence (from 1 to n) with a greater focus on position i, where d_h is the dimension of hidden states. Due to the introduction of the position embeddings, h_i is considered to be position-aware.

3.3 Hierarchical Attention Based Fusion Layer

In this subsection, we illustrate the proposed succinct mechanism to fuse the information of targets and the contextual words. In detail, a source2aspect attention is first employed to capture the most important clues in the target words and the representation of the aspect is obtained. Subsequently, an aspect-specific representation of each word is generated based on the aspect representation and the encoded position-aware representation. A source2context attention is then used to capture the most indicative sentiment words in the context and generate the weighted sum embeddings as the final sentence representation.

Source2aspect Attention: Due to the fact that substantial numbers of aspects contain at least two words (Zheng et al., 2018), we introduce a source2aspect mechanism to generate the representation of the aspect. The source2* attention is inspired by the related research of self-attention network (Shen et al., 2017). First, we introduce a score function by taking the word embeddings of each word in target as inputs.

$$f_t\left(\omega_i^t\right) = tanh\left(W_t \cdot \omega_i^t\right) \quad (2)$$

where $W_t \in \mathbb{R}^{d_w}$ is a weight vector and *tanh* is a non-linear function. The score f_t is then used as a weight denoting the importance of a word in the target. On this basis, the normalized importance weight of i-th word in the target α_i^t is computed as follows:

$$\alpha_i^t = \frac{exp\left(f_t(\omega_i^t)\right)}{\sum_{j=1}^{m} exp\left(f_t\left(\omega_j^t\right)\right)} \quad (3)$$

At last, a weighted combination of word embeddings is considered as the representation for the target:

$$r^t = \sum_{i=1}^{m} \alpha_i^t \cdot \omega_i^t \quad (4)$$

Information Fusion: After achieving the target representation, we then further make use of the achieved representation to construct the target-specific representation of each word in the sentence by the following equation:

$$r_i = W_s \cdot [h_i, r^t] \quad (5)$$

where $W_s \in \mathbb{R}^{(2d_h + d_w) \times d_w}$ is a weight matrix. r_i denotes the target-specific representation of the i-th word w_i in the sentence.

Source2context Attention: Then, the target-specific representation of each word is used to learn attentions and further generate the final sentence representation. The attention is defined as the following equations:

$$f_s([r_i, h_i]) = tanh(W_c \cdot [r_i, h_i]) \quad (6)$$

$$\alpha_i = \frac{exp(f_s([r_i, h_i]))}{\sum_{j=1}^{n} exp(f_s([r_i, h_i]))} \quad (7)$$

where $W_c \in \mathbb{R}^{2d_h + d_w}$ is a weight vector and α_i denotes the importance of the i-th word in the sentence.

At last, a weighted combination of position-aware hidden states is computed:

$$r^h = \sum_{i=1}^{n} \alpha_i \cdot h_i \quad (8)$$

which is considered as the final representation of the current instance.

Dataset	Positive		Neutral		Negative	
	Train	Test	Train	Test	Train	Test
Restaurant	2164	728	633	196	805	196
Laptop	987	341	460	169	866	128

Table 1: Statistics of SemEval 2014 Dataset.

3.4 Output and Model Training

Hence, we can get the final representation r^h of the current instance after the last three subsections. Then we feed it into a softmax layer to predict the target sentiment.

Given all of our (suppose N) training samples $\left(x^{(i)}; y^{(i)}\right)$, we can then define the loss function as the negative log-likelihood:

$$\mathcal{L}(\theta) = -\sum_{j=1}^{N} log\ p\left(y^{(j)} \mid x^{(j)}, \theta\right) \quad (9)$$

In order to compute the network parameter θ, we minimize the average negative log-likelihood $\mathcal{L}(\theta)$ via RMSprop proposed by Tieleman and Hinton (2012) over shuffled mini-batches. We also adopt the dropout regularization (Zaremba et al., 2014) and early stopping to ease overfitting.

4 Experiments

4.1 Experiment Settings

We conduct experiments on SemEval 2014 Task 4 to validate the effectiveness of our model, as shown in Table 1. The SemEval 2014 dataset contains reviews of restaurant and laptop domains, which are widely used in previous works. The evaluation metric is classification accuracy.

We use 300-dimension word vectors pre-trained by GloVe (Pennington et al., 2014) (whose vocabulary size is 1.9M) for our experiments, as previous works did (Tang et al., 2016b; Chen et al., 2017; Zheng et al., 2018). All out-of-vocabulary words are initialized as zero vectors, and all biases are set to zero. The dimensions of hidden states and fused embeddings are set to 300. The dimension of position embeddings is set to 50. Keras is used for implementing our neural network model. In model training, we set the learning rate to 0.001, the batch size to 64, and dropout rate to 0.5. The paired t-test is used for the significance testing.

4.2 Compared Methods

In order to evaluate the performance of proposed model, we select the following state-of-the-art methods for comparison:

- **Majority** assigns the sentiment polarity with most frequent occurrences in the training set to each sample in test set.
- **Bi-LSTM** and **Bi-GRU** adopt a Bi-LSTM and a Bi-GRU network to model the sentence and use the hidden state of the final word for prediction respectively.
- **TD-LSTM** adopts two LSTMs to model the left context with target and the right context with target respectively (Tang et al., 2016a); It takes the hidden states of LSTM at last time-step to represent the sentence for prediction.
- **MemNet** (Tang et al., 2016b) applies attention multiple times on the word embeddings, and the output of last attention is fed to softmax for prediction.
- **IAN** (Ma et al., 2017) interactively learns attentions in the contexts and targets, and generates the representations for targets and contexts separately.
- **RAM** (Chen et al., 2017) is a multilayer architecture where each layer consists of attention-based aggregation of word features and a GRU cell to learn the sentence representation.
- **LCR-Rot** (Zheng et al., 2018) employs three Bi-LSTMs to model the left context, the target and the right context. Then they propose a rotatory attention mechanism which models the relation between target and left/right contexts.
- **AOA-LSTM** (Huang et al., 2018) introduces an attention-over-attention (AOA) based network to model aspects and sentences in a joint way and explicitly capture the interaction between aspects and context sentences.

4.3 System Performance Comparision

Table 2 shows the performance comparison of our method with the state-of-the-art methods on the same test dataset. From the table, we make the following observations:

(1) As shown in the table, we can clearly observe that the **Majority** method is the worst, which means the majority sentiment polarity occupies 65.0% and 53.45% of all samples on the *Restaurant* and *Laptop* corpus respectively. In addition to MemNet, all the other models are RNN based models and better than the **Majority** method. This indicates that RNN based models can obtain better representations of sentence automatically

Dataset	Restaurant (%)	Laptop (%)
Majority	65.00	53.45
Bi-LSTM	78.57	70.53
Bi-GRU	80.27	73.35
TD-LSTM	75.63*	68.13*
MemNet	79.98	70.33
IAN	78.60	72.10
RAM	80.23	74.49
LCR-Rot	81.34	75.24
AOA-LSTM	81.20	74.50
HAPN	*82.23*	*77.27*

Table 2: Comparison with baselines on SemEval 2014 dataset. The results with * are retrieved from MemNet paper.

without manual feature engineering and improve the performance in this task.

(2) The **TD-LSTM** model, which has been shown to be better than LSTM (Tang et al., 2016a), gets the worst performance of all RNN based models and the accuracy achieved by **TD-LSTM** is 2.94% and 2.4% lower than those by **Bi-LSTM** on the two datasets respectively. This results show that introducing target clues only by splitting the sentence according to the position of target is inadequate and bidirectional RNN based model can achieve better performance than unidirectional model in this task. Another noticeable observation is that **Bi-GRU** achieves 80.27% and 73.35% accuracies which are 1.7% and 2.82% higher than those of **Bi-LSTM** on the *Restaurant* and *Laptop* dataset respectively. It indicates that Bi-GRU is more suitable to this task than Bi-LSTM.

(3) Compared with the state-of-the-art methods, our model achieves the best performance, which illustrates the effectiveness of the proposed approach. Our method achieves accuracies of 82.23% as well as 77.27% on the *Restaurant* and *Laptop* dataset respectively, which are 0.89% and 2.03% higher than the current best method. We will give a detailed analysis in the following subsections.

4.4 Effects of Position Embeddings

In order to verify the efficiency and advantage of position embeddings, we design the following models:

Bi-GRU employs the standard Bi-GRU to encode the sentence and predict the sentiment polarity.

Dataset	Restaurant (%)	Laptop (%)
Bi-GRU	80.27	73.35
Bi-GRU-PW	79.55	71.94
Bi-GRU-PE	*80.89*	*76.02*

Table 3: The performance of models with different strategies to introduce position information.

Dataset	Restaurant (%)	Laptop (%)
HAPN	*82.23*	*77.27*
No-fusion	81.88	76.49

Table 4: The performance of models with or without fusion operation.

Bi-GRU-PW first weights the word embeddings of each word in the sentence based on the distance from the target, as did in (Tang et al., 2016b; Chen et al,. 2017). Then the weighted representations are fed into the Bi-GRU.

Bi-GRU-PE concatenates the word embeddings and the position embeddings of each word as inputs to the Bi-GRU when modelling the sentence.

In Table 3, we report the performance of the three models. It can be observed that **Bi-GRU-PE** performs better than **Bi-GRU** significantly. After introducing the position embeddings, the accuracy has an increase of 0.62% and 2.67% on two datasets. This indicates that exploiting the position clues effectively can improve the performance of models in this task. In addition, another observation is that **Bi-GRU-PW** performs even worse than **Bi-GRU**. The accuracy achieved by **Bi-GRU-PW** is 0.72% as well as 1.41% lower than that by **Bi-GRU** on the *Restaurant* and *Laptop* dataset respectively. To an extent, the results verify that weighting the word representations according to the distance to the aspect is ineffective in this task.

4.5 Effects of the Information Fusion

To verify the efficiency of the information fusion, we further design the following model for comparison:

No-fusion is a simplified version of **HAPN**, where we directly concatenate the target representation and the position-aware representation of each word as the inputs to the source2context attention.

In Table 4, we report the performance comparison of **HAPN** and **No-fusion**. From the Table, we can observe that **HAPN** performs better

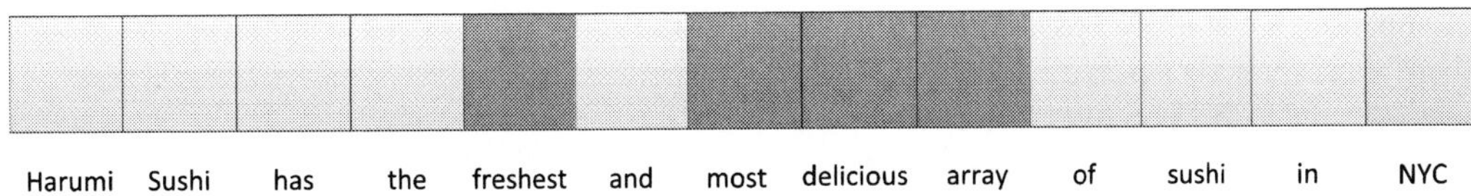

Figure 2: Attention visualizations of an example sentence.

than **No-fusion**. **HAPN** achieves improvement of 0.35% and 0.78% on accuracy respectively on the two dataset. It indicates that the fusion operation we propose has potentials in automatically generating target-specific representations and improves the performance.

4.6 Effects of The Hierarchical Attention

This subsection evalutes the effectiveness of the hierarchical attention mechanism. To achieve this goal, we deactivate the two attention respectively from the proposed model.

Firstly, to verify the efficiency of the Source2aspect attention, we design the following model for comparison:

No-S2A-attention is a simplified version of **HAPN**, where the Source2aspect attention is replaced with averaging the initial word embeddings to represent the target phrase.

Table 5 presents the performance comparison of **HAPN** and **No-S2A-attention**. From Table 5, we can see that **No-S2A-attention** achieve the accuracies of 81.34% as well as 76.49% on the Restaurant and Laptop dataset respectively, which are 0.89% and 0.78% lower than the proposed model. This indicates that the Source2aspect attention in our model is effective to this task.

Secondly, as described in the privious sections, the Source2context attention in the paper aims at weighted summing the position-aware hidden states based on the target-specific representations generated by the information fusion operation. From Figure 1, it could be observed that: (1) The information fusion operation is only used to calculate the Source2context attention value. (2) The output of Source2aspect attention is only used for information fusion.

Dataset	Restaurant (%)	Laptop (%)
HAPN	*82.23*	*77.27*
No- S2A-Attention	81.34	76.49

Table 5: The performance of models with or without Source2aspect attention.

Therefore, we remove the fusion operation and Source2aspect attention while removing the Source2context attention. And the achieved model is "Bi-GRU-PE" reported in the Table 3, achieving the accuracies of 80.89% and 76.02% on the two datasets respectively, which are 1.34% and 1.25% lower than the proposed model. This indicates that the Source2context attention is necessary in the proposed model.

4.7 Case Study

In this section, we use a review sentence "Harumi Sushi has the freshest and most delicious *array of sushi* in NYC" and the target *"array of sushi"* from the Restaurant dataset as a case study. We apply our HAPN to model the sentence and the target, and obtain the correct sentiment polarity: *positive*. In Figure 2, we give the visualization of the attention weights (Source2context) on this sentence computed by HAPN.

The meaning of the example sentence in the case study is that the *"array of sushi"* is good. Obviously, the words *"freshest"* and *"most delicious"* play an important role in judging the sentiment polarity of *"array of sushi"*. From Figure 2, we can observe that those words are paid much attention as we expect. And it is worth noting that the word *"freshest"* obtains as much attention as *"delicious"*, although *"freshest"* is much farther from the target than *"delicious"*. This shows that our model doesn't reduce a word's weight only according to the long distance from the target. This may be because that our HAPN embeds the position information and can consider the influence of position in combination with semantic information instead of simply weighting.

5 Discussion

Experimental results show that our proposed method has better performance than state-of-the-art approaches. The detailed analysis for improvement is as follows:

(1) Position embeddings

As discussed in Section 1, position information is important when modelling the sentence. When there are several aspects in a sentence, it is easy to pay attention to the adjectives of another aspect by error. In this case, the relevant position between a word and the target can help to understand the structure of sentences. We introduce position embeddings as a part of inputs when modelling the sentence. Therefore, we can achieve the position-aware representations of each word and the model will learn to exploit both the semantic information and the position clues of each word. As shown in Table 3, the introduction of position embeddings bring a performance improvement of 0.62% and 2.67% on two datasets respectively, which illustrates the effectiveness of the position embeddings.

(2) Hierarchical attention based fusion operation

Compared with the traditional sentiment analysis task, the aspect-level sentiment analysis is more fine-grained and need the information of specific target. As described in Section 3.3, we introduce a hierarchical attention based fusion layer to generate the target-specific representation of each word. By exploiting the specific representations to further compute the attention value and generate the final sentence representation, the model can obtain more target clues. As shown in Table 4 and Table 5, the experimental results show that the hierarchical attention based information fusion operation can bring performance improvement to this task.

(3) Bi-GRU based encoder

In this paper, we employ a Bi-GRU based encoder to model the sentence. GRU has been shown to achieve comparable performance with less parameters than LSTM (Chung et al., 2014; Jozefowicz et al., 2015). And we run two parallel GRUs to obtain richer semantic information and position clues. The experimental results in Table 2 also show that Bi-GRU can achieve better performance in this task.

6   Conclusions

In this paper, we propose a hierarchical attention based position-aware network for aspect-level sentiment analysis. This architecture introduces position embeddings as a part of inputs to further generate position-aware representations. Furthermore, we propose a succinct hierarchical attention based mechanism to fuse the information of targets and the contextual words, and achieve the final sentence representation. Experimental results show that our approach achieves state-of-the-art performance on the Semeval 2014 dataset.

Acknowledgments

This paper is supported by the National Natural Science Foundation of China under NO.61672126. We thank anonymous reviewers for their valuable comments.

References

Peng Chen, Zhongqian Sun, Lidong Bing, and Wei Yang. 2017. Recurrent attention network on memory for aspect sentiment analysis. In *Proceedings of EMNLP*, pages 463-472.

Kyunghyun Cho, Bart van Merrienboer, Caglar Gulcehre, Dzmitry Bahdanau, Fethi Bougares, Holger Schwenk and Yoshua Bengio. 2014. Learning phrase representations using rnn encoder-decoder for statistical machine translation. *Computer Science*.

Junyoung Chung, Caglar Gulcehre, KyungHyun Cho, and Yoshua Bengio. 2014. Empirical evaluation of gated recurrent neural networks on sequence modeling. *arXiv preprint arXiv:1412.3555*.

Binxuan Huang, Yanglan Ou and Kathleen M. Carley. 2018. Aspect Level Sentiment Classification with Attention-over-Attention Neural Networks. *arxiv preprint arXiv:1804.06536*.

Long Jiang, Mo Yu, Ming Zhou, Xiaohua Liu, and Tiejun Zhao. 2011. Target-dependent twitter sentiment classification. In *Proceedings of ACL: Human Language Technologies-Volume1*, pages 151-160.

Rafal Jozefowicz, Wojciech Zaremba, and Ilya Sutskever. 2015. An empirical exploration of recurrent network architectures. In *ICML*, pages 2342-2350.

Svetlana Kiritchenko, Xiaodan Zhu, Colin Cherry, and Saif Mohammad. 2014. Nrc-canada-2014: Detecting aspects and sentiment in customer reviews. In *Proceedings of SemEval*, pages 437-442

Dehong Ma, Sujian Li, Xiaodong Zhang, and Houfeng Wang. 2017. Interactive attention networks for aspect-level sentiment classification. In *Proceedings of IJCAI*, pages 4068-4074.

Tomas Mikolov, Ilya Sutskever, Kai Chen, Greg S Corrado, and Jeff Dean. 2013. Distributed representations of words and phrases and their compositionality. In *Advances in Neural Information Processing Systems*, pages 3111-3119.

Jeffrey Pennington, Richard Socher, and Christopher D. Manning. 2014. Glove: Global vectors for word representation. In *Proceedings of EMNLP*, pages 1532-1543.

Maria Pontiki, Dimitrios Galanis, John Pavlopoulos, Haris Papageorgiou, Ion Androutsopoulos, and Suresh Manandhar. 2014. Semeval-2014 task 4: Aspect based sentiment analysis. In *SemEval@COLING*, pages 27-35, Stroudsburg, PA, USA. Association for Computational Linguistics.

Tao Shen, Tianyi Zhou, Guodong Long, Jing Jiang, Shirui Pan, and Chengqi Zhang. 2017. DiSAN: Directional Self-Attention Network for RNN/CNN-Free Language Understanding. *arXiv preprint arXiv: 1709.04696.*

Duyu Tang, Bing Qin, Xiaocheng Feng, and Ting Liu. 2016a. Effective lstms for target-dependent sentiment classification. In *Proceedings of COLING*, pages 3298-3307.

Duyu Tang, Bing Qin, and Ting Liu. 2016b. Aspect level sentiment classification with deep memory network. In *Proceedings of EMNLP*, pages 214-224.

Yi Tay, Anh Tuan Luu, and Siu Cheung Hui. 2017. Learning to attend via word-aspect associative fusion for aspect-based sentiment analysis. *arXiv preprint arXiv:1712.05403.*

Tijmen Tieleman and Geoffrey Hinton. 2012. Lecture 6.5-rmsprop. In COURSERA: *Neural networks for machine learning.*

Duy-Tin Vo and Yue Zhang. 2015. Target-dependent twitter sentiment classification with rich automatic features. In *Proceedings of IJCAI*, pages 1347-1353.

Joachim Wagner, Piyush Arora, Santiago Cortes, Utsab Barman, Dasha Bogdanova, Jennifer Foster, and Lamia Tounsi. 2014. Dcu: Aspect-based polarity classification for semeval task 4. In *Proceedings of SemEval*, pages 223-229.

Yequan Wang, Minlie Huang, xiaoyan zhu, and Li Zhao. 2016. Attention-based lstm for aspect-level sentiment classification. In *Proceedings of EMNLP*, pages 606-615.

Wojciech Zaremba, Ilya Sutskever, and Oriol Vinyals. 2014. Recurrent neural network regularization. *preprint arXiv: 1409.2329.*

Shiliang Zheng and Rui Xia. 2018. Left-Center-Right Separated Neural Network for Aspect-based Sentiment Analysis with Rotatory Attention. *arxiv preprint arXiv:1802.00892.*

Bidirectional Generative Adversarial Networks for Neural Machine Translation

Zhirui Zhang[†*], **Shujie Liu**[§], **Mu Li**[¶], **Ming Zhou**[§], **Enhong Chen**[†]
[†]University of Science and Technology of China, Hefei, China
[§]Microsoft Research Asia
[†]zrustc11@gmail.com [†]cheneh@ustc.edu.cn
[§]{shujliu,mingzhou}@microsoft.com [¶]limugx@outlook.com

Abstract

Generative Adversarial Network (GAN) has been proposed to tackle the exposure bias problem of Neural Machine Translation (NMT). However, the discriminator typically results in the instability of the GAN training due to the inadequate training problem: the search space is so huge that sampled translations are not sufficient for discriminator training. To address this issue and stabilize the GAN training, in this paper, we propose a novel Bidirectional Generative Adversarial Network for Neural Machine Translation (BGAN-NMT), which aims to introduce a generator model to act as the discriminator, whereby the discriminator naturally considers the entire translation space so that the inadequate training problem can be alleviated. To satisfy this property, generator and discriminator are both designed to model the joint probability of sentence pairs, with the difference that, the generator decomposes the joint probability with a source language model and a source-to-target translation model, while the discriminator is formulated as a target language model and a target-to-source translation model. To further leverage the symmetry of them, an auxiliary GAN is introduced and adopts generator and discriminator models of original one as its own discriminator and generator respectively. Two GANs are alternately trained to update the parameters. Experiment results on German-English and Chinese-English translation tasks demonstrate that our method not only stabilizes GAN training but also achieves significant improvements over baseline systems.

1 Introduction

The past several years have witnessed the rapid development of Neural Machine Translation (NMT)

(Cho et al., 2014; Sutskever et al., 2014; Bahdanau et al., 2014), from catching up with Statistical Machine Translation (SMT) (Koehn et al., 2003; Chiang, 2007) to outperforming it by significant margins on many languages (Sennrich et al., 2016; Gehring et al., 2017; Vaswani et al., 2017; Hassan et al., 2018). The most common approach to training NMT is to maximize the conditional log-probability of the correct translation given the source sentence. However, as argued in Bengio et al. (2015), the Maximum Likelihood Estimation (MLE) principle suffers from so-called exposure bias in the inference stage: the model predicts next token conditional on its previously predicted ones that may be never observed in the training data. To address this problem, much recent work attempts to reduce the inconsistency between training and inference, such as adopting sequence-level objectives and directly maximizing BLEU scores (Bengio et al., 2015; Ranzato et al., 2015; Shen et al., 2016; Wiseman and Rush, 2016).

Generative Adversarial Network (GAN) (Goodfellow et al., 2014) is another promising framework for alleviating exposure bias problem and recently shows remarkable promise in NMT (Yang et al., 2017; Wu et al., 2017). Formally, GAN consists of two "adversarial" models: a generator and a discriminator. In machine translation, NMT model is used as the generator that produces translation candidates given a source sentence, and another neural network is introduced to serve as the discriminator, which takes sentence pairs as input and distinguishes whether a given sentence pair is real or generated. Adversarial training between the two models involves optimizing a min-max objective, in which, the discriminator learns to distinguish whether a given data instance is real or fake, and the generator learns to confuse the discriminator by generating high-quality translation candidates. Since the generated data is based on

---

*This work was done when the first author was the intern at Microsoft Research Asia.

Proceedings of the 22nd Conference on Computational Natural Language Learning (CoNLL 2018), pages 190–199
Brussels, Belgium, October 31 - November 1, 2018. ©2018 Association for Computational Linguistics

discrete symbols (words), we usually adopt policy gradient method (Yu et al., 2017) to update model parameters of the generator. Specifically, given a bunch of translation candidates sampled from the generator, confidence scores calculated by the discriminator are employed as rewards to update the generator.

However, in this training process, the discriminator typically suffers from inadequate training problem, leading to the instability of GAN training. In practice, sampling large translation candidates is time-consuming for NMT system, so we only use a few samples to train the discriminator. For a given source sentence, there is usually only one positive example (real target sentence). If the sampled negative examples are also few, the discriminator will easily overfit to the data. This is the inadequate training problem for the discriminator. In such a case, rewards calculated by the discriminator could be biased, especially for unobserved samples. These biased rewards will provide a wrong signal to the generator and make it update incorrectly, resulting in performance degradation of the generator. Since such issue can occur repeatedly throughout the entire training process, GAN training becomes unstable and the performance of generator will drop drastically.

On the other hand, the generator has well-designed properties that benefit the discriminator, since it models the probability distribution over the entire translation space so that the generator does not overfit to observed samples, while prior knowledge for unobserved samples is naturally considered. At the same time, the generator also exhibits a certain ability to identify whether a given data instance is good enough. For example, target-to-source translation model serves as the discriminator to improve source-to-target translation model (He et al., 2016; Tu et al., 2017). Inspired by this, we propose a novel Bidirectional Generative Adversarial Network for Neural Machine Translation (aka BGAN-NMT), which employs a generator model to perform the role of the discriminator so as to handle inadequate training problem and stabilize GAN training. To satisfy this property, both generator and discriminator of original GAN are designed to model the joint probability of sentence pairs, with the difference that, the generator model A is decomposed into a source language model and a source-to-target translation model, while the discriminator model

B is formulated as a target language model and a target-to-source translation model. Intuitively, we can also leverage A to act as the discriminator to improve B, and then improved B reversely serves as a better discriminator to guide the training of A. To make use of this symmetry, we bring in an auxiliary GAN that adopts generator and discriminator models of original one as its own discriminator and generator respectively. Then we design a joint training algorithm to alternately utilize these two GANs to update the source-to-target and target-to-source translation models.

Our experiments are conducted on German-English and Chinese-English translation data sets. Experimental results demonstrate that our BGAN-NMT not only achieves the stability of GAN training but also significantly improves translation performance over baseline systems.

2　Background

2.1　Neural Machine Translation

Attention-based NMT model (Bahdanau et al., 2014) is adopted as the source-to-target and target-to-source translation models used in our BGAN-NMT. The attention-based NMT system is implemented as an encoder-decoder framework with recurrent neural networks (RNN), which can be Gated Recurrent Unit (GRU) (Cho et al., 2014) or Long Short-Term Memory (LSTM) (Hochreiter and Schmidhuber, 1997) networks in practice.

2.1.1　Encoder-Decoder Framework

The encoder reads the source sentence $x = (x_1, x_2, \ldots, x_T)$ and transforms it into a sequence of hidden states $h = (h_1, h_2, \ldots, h_T)$ using a bi-directional RNN. The decoder uses another RNN to generate the translation $y = (y_1, y_2, \ldots, y_{T'})$ based on the hidden states h. At each time stamp i, the conditional probability of each word y_i from a target vocabulary V_y is computed with

$$p(y_i|y_{<i}, h) = g(y_{i-1}, z_i, c_i), \tag{1}$$

where z_i is the i_{th} hidden state of the decoder, which is calculated conditioned on the previous hidden state z_{i-1}, previous word y_{i-1} and the source context vector c_i:

$$z_i = \text{RNN}(z_{i-1}, y_{i-1}, c_i), \tag{2}$$

The source context vector c_i is a weighted sum of the hidden states $(h_1, h_2, \ldots, h_T)$ with the coefficients $\alpha_1, \alpha_2, \dots, \alpha_T$ calculated with

$$\alpha_t = \frac{\exp\left(a(h_t, z_{i-1})\right)}{\sum_k \exp\left(a(h_k, z_{i-1})\right)} \quad (3)$$

where a is a feed-forward neural network with a single hidden layer.

2.1.2 MLE Training

NMT systems are usually trained to maximize the conditional log-probability of the correct translation given a source sentence with respect to the parameters θ of the model:

$$\theta^* = \arg\max_\theta \sum_{n=1}^{N} \sum_{i=1}^{|y^n|} \log p(y_i^n | y_{<i}^n, x^n) \quad (4)$$

where N is size of the training corpus, and $|y^n|$ is the length of the target sentence y^n. However, MLE training suffers from exposure bias problem: in training stage, the history of any target word is correct and has been observed in the training data, while during testing, the model predicts next token conditioned on its previously predicted ones that may be never observed in the training data. To solve this problem, reinforcement learning methods are used to sample translation candidates, based on which, rewards are calculated and utilized to update the parameters. GAN follows the same way to solve exposure bias problem and rewards are computed by the discriminator.

2.2 Generative Adversarial Network

As a new paradigm of training generative models, GAN (Goodfellow et al., 2014) has been successfully applied in computer vision tasks (Radford et al., 2015; Arjovsky et al., 2017). Conceptually, GAN consists of two "adversarial" models: a generator G that captures the data distribution, and a discriminator D that estimates the probability that a sample is sampled from the training data rather than from G. When GAN is used for NMT, NMT model is employed as G, and CNN-based or RNN-based neural networks serve as D (Yang et al., 2017; Wu et al., 2017). During adversarial training, G and D play a two-player minmax game with the following value function $V(D, G)$:

$$\min_G \max_D V(D, G) = \mathrm{E}_{(x,y)\sim P_d(x,y)} \left[\log D(x, y)\right]$$
$$+ \mathrm{E}_{(x,y')\sim P_G(x,y)} \left[\log(1 - D(x, y'))\right] \quad (5)$$

where (x, y) is a sentence pair, P_d represents the data distribution and P_G denotes the generator distribution. With this objective function, the discriminator learns to distinguish whether sentence pair is real (sampled from bilingual corpus) or fake (generated by G), and the generator tries to confuse the discriminator by generating high-quality translation samples.

In practice, policy gradient method (Yu et al., 2017) is usually used to calculate gradients for the generator due to discrete symbols (words). To update the generator model, translation candidates are firstly sampled, for which rewards are calculated using the discriminator. With these rewards, we can compute gradients and run back-propagation to update the generator. In such a training process, real target sentence and sampled translation candidates are used as positive and negative examples of discriminator training respectively. Due to the computation cost, we cannot generate many negative examples, so that the discriminator is easy to overfit. The overfitted discriminator will give biased signals to the generator and make it update incorrectly, leading to the instability of the generator training. Wu et al. (2017) found that combining adversarial training objective with MLE can significantly improve the stability of generator training, which is also reported in language model and neural dialogue generation (Lamb et al., 2016; Li et al., 2017). Actually, although this method leverages real translation signal to guide the generator and alleviate the effect of overfitted discriminator, it cannot deal with the inadequate training problem of the discriminator, which essentially plays a more important role in GAN training.

3 Bidirectional Generative Adversarial Network

In GAN for NMT, the generator does not suffer from the inadequate training problem, because the generator is proposed to model probability distribution over the entire translation space (maximizing probability of one translation candidate means minimizing probabilities of the others). At the same time, the generator exhibits a certain ability to discriminate good sentence pairs, for example, target-to-source translation model is used to score samples generated from source-to-target translation model. Thus, introducing a generator model to perform the role of the discriminator is expected

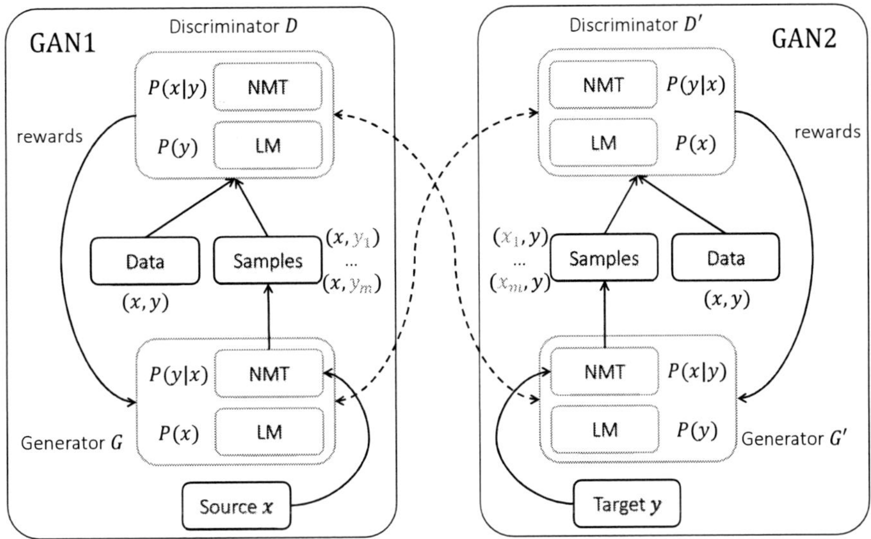

Figure 1: The architecture of BGAN-NMT consisting of two GANs. The dotted line represents that $GAN2$ adopts both generator and discriminator models of $GAN1$ but interchanges their roles.

to address the inadequate training problem and stabilize GAN training. Based on these observations, we design a Bidirectional Generative Adversarial Network for Neural Machine Translation, named as BGAN-NMT.

As illustrated in Figure 1, the overall architecture of BGAN-NMT consists of an original GAN ($GAN1$) and an auxiliary GAN ($GAN2$). Both generator and discriminator of original GAN are defined to model the joint probability of sentence pairs $P(x, y)$. Formally, $P(x, y)$ can be decomposed in two equivalent ways: $P(x, y) = P(x)P(y|x)$ and $P(x, y) = P(y)P(x|y)$, and they are used as generator G and discriminator D for $GAN1$ respectively. Further, the generator model can be decomposed into a source language model and a source-to-target translation model, while the discriminator can be formulated as a target language model and a target-to-source translation model. Auxiliary GAN ($GAN2$) employs G and D of $GAN1$ as its own discriminator D' and generator G' to better exploit the symmetry between G and D. The following of this section details the objective function and joint training algorithm for BGAN-NMT.

3.1 Training Objective

As G and D are defined as $P(x)P(y|x)$ and $P(y)P(x|y)$ respectively, the adversarial training objective $V(D, G)$ of $GAN1$ in Equation 5 can be

rewritten as

$$
\min_G \max_D V(D, G) = \mathrm{E}_{(x,y) \sim P_d(x,y)} \left[\log P(x|y)P(y) \right] \\
+ \mathrm{E}_{x \sim P_d(x), y' \sim P(y|x)} \left[\log(1 - P(x|y')P(y')) \right] \tag{6}
$$

which means, given a source sentence x, source-to-target translation model $P(y|x)$ tries to generate high quality translation y' to fool the discriminator $P(x|y)P(y)$, while target-to-source translation model $P(x|y)$ and language model $P(y)$ learn to distinguish translation candidates from real sentence pairs. In our implementations, two language models $P(x)$ and $P(y)$ are fixed to reduce training complexity.

For discriminator D, D is trained with the ground-truth sentence pair (x, y) and the generated sample (x, y') from G, respectively as positive and negative examples. Formally, the objective function of D is to maximize $V(D, G)$:

$$
L_D = \mathrm{E}_{(x,y) \sim P_d(x,y)} \left[\log P(x|y)P(y) \right] \\
+ \mathrm{E}_{x \sim P_d(x), y' \sim P(y|x)} \left[\log \left(1 - P(x|y')P(y') \right) \right] \tag{7}
$$

Since $P(y)$ is fixed, the gradient of parameter θ_D for the target-to-source translation model $P(x|y)$ is calculated as:

$$
\frac{\partial L_D}{\partial \theta_D} = \mathrm{E}_{(x,y) \sim P_d(x,y)} \left[\frac{\partial \log P(x|y)}{\partial \theta_D} \right] \\
+ \mathrm{E}_{x \sim P_d(x), y' \sim P(y|x)} \\
\left[\left(1 - \frac{1}{1 - P(x|y')P(y')} \right) \frac{\partial \log P(x|y')}{\partial \theta_D} \right] \tag{8}
$$

193

in which $\frac{\partial \log P(x|y)}{\partial \theta_D}$ is the gradient specified with standard sequence-to-sequence NMT network.

For generator G, following Goodfellow (2016), the objective of training G is to maximize the expected rewards (probability of D) instead of directly minimizing $V(D, G)$:

$$L_G = \mathrm{E}_{x \sim P_d(x), y' \sim P(y|x)} \left[P(x|y')P(y') \right] \quad (9)$$

Since the output of the generator G is a sequence of discrete symbols (words), policy gradient is used to update the parameters, and then the gradient of parameter θ_G for source-to-target translation model $P(y|x)$ can be calculated as:

$$\frac{\partial L_G}{\partial \theta_G} = \mathrm{E}_{x \sim P_d(x), y' \sim P(y|x)} \left[P(x|y')P(y') \frac{\partial \log P(y'|x)}{\partial \theta_G} \right] \quad (10)$$

By exchanging generator and discriminator models of $GAN1$, we introduce $GAN2$, in which the original G is used as the discriminator D' and original D serves as the generator G'. Similarly, the adversarial training objective $V(D', G')$ of $GAN2$ is defined as:

$$\min_{G'} \max_{D'} V(D', G') = \mathrm{E}_{(x,y) \sim P_d(x,y)} \left[\log P(y|x)P(x)\right]$$
$$+ \mathrm{E}_{y \sim P_d(y), x' \sim P(x|y)} \left[\log(1 - P(y|x')P(x'))\right] \quad (11)$$

According to this adversarial training objective, the objective functions of D' and G' are defined as following:

$$L_{D'} = \mathrm{E}_{(x,y) \sim P_d(x,y)} \left[\log P(y|x)P(x)\right]$$
$$+ \mathrm{E}_{y \sim P_d(y), x' \sim P(x|y)} \left[\log(1 - P(y|x')P(x'))\right] \quad (12)$$

$$L_{G'} = \mathrm{E}_{y \sim P_d(y), x' \sim P(x|y)} \left[P(y|x')P(x')\right] \quad (13)$$

where the gradients of parameters $\theta_{D'} = \theta_G$ for $P(y|x)$ and $\theta_{G'} = \theta_D$ for $P(x|y)$ can be respectively calculated as:

$$\frac{\partial L_{D'}}{\partial \theta_G} = \mathrm{E}_{(x,y) \sim P_d(x,y)} \left[\frac{\partial \log P(y|x)}{\partial \theta_G}\right]$$
$$+ \mathrm{E}_{y \sim P_d(y), x' \sim P(x|y)} \quad (14)$$
$$[(1 - \frac{1}{1 - P(y|x')P(x')}) \frac{\partial \log P(y|x')}{\partial \theta_G}]$$

$$\frac{\partial L_{G'}}{\partial \theta_D} = \mathrm{E}_{y \sim P_d(y), x' \sim P(x|y)} [P(y|x')P(x') \frac{\partial \log P(x'|y)}{\partial \theta_D}] \quad (15)$$

3.2 Joint Training Algorithm

In our approach, G and D actually act as discriminator systems for each other in a joint training process: the generator G can be improved with the discriminator D in $GAN1$, and then the enhanced G serves as a better discriminator to guide

---

Algorithm 1: Joint Training Algorithm for BGAN-NMT

Input : Bilingual corpus $T = \{(x, y)\}_{n=1}^N$;
Pre-trained source-side language model $P(x)$;
Pre-trained target-side language model $P(y)$;
Output: Well-trained models $P(y|x)$ and $P(x|y)$

1 Pre-train $P(y|x)$ and $P(x|y)$ on T with MLE principle ;
2 **for** *number of training iterations* **do**
3   **for** k *steps* **do**
4   Get m samples $\{(x, y)\}_{i=1}^m$ from T ;
5   Generate m samples $\{(x, y')\}_{i=1}^m$ using $P(y|x)$ given source sentences of $\{(x, y)\}_{i=1}^m$;
6   Update the parameter θ_D with Equation 8 ;
7   Generate m samples $\{(x', y)\}_{i=1}^m$ using $P(x|y)$ given target sentences of $\{(x, y)\}_{i=1}^m$;
8   Update the parameter θ_G with Equation 14 ;
9   **end**
10   Get m samples $\{(x, y)\}_{i=1}^m$ from T ;
11   Generate m samples $\{(x, y')\}_{i=1}^m$ using $P(y|x)$ given source sentences of $\{(x, y)\}_{i=1}^m$;
12   Update the parameter θ_G with Equation 10 ;
13   Generate m samples $\{(x', y)\}_{i=1}^m$ using $P(x|y)$ given target sentences of $\{(x, y)\}_{i=1}^m$;
14   Update the parameter θ_D with Equation 15 ;
15 **end**

---

the training of D in $GAN2$. This training process can be iteratively carried out to obtain further improvements because after each iteration both G and D are expected to be improved with adversarial training. To simultaneously optimize these two models, we design a joint training algorithm to learn the parameters (θ_G and θ_D) shared in two GANs of BGAN-NMT ($GAN1$ and $GAN2$).

As shown in Algorithm 1, the whole algorithm is mainly divided into two steps. Firstly, given parallel corpora $T = \{(x, y)\}_{n=1}^N$, we pre-train $P(y|x)$ and $P(x|y)$ with MLE principle, while source and target language models $P(x)$ and $P(y)$ are pre-trained with corresponding sentences of bilingual data. Next, based on these pre-trained models, we implement the two player minmax game using an iterative approach, in which, we alternate between k (equals to 5 in our experiments) steps of optimizing all discriminators (D and D') and one step of optimizing all generators (G and G'). The iterative training continues until the performance of a development data set is not increased.

4 Experiments

4.1 Setup

To examine the effectiveness of our proposed approach, we conduct experiments on translation tasks with two language pairs: German-English (De-En for in short) and Chinese-English (Zh-En for in short). In all experiments, BLEU (Papineni et al., 2002) is adopted as the automatic metric for translation quality evaluation and computed using Moses *multi-bleu.perl* script.

4.1.1 Dataset

For German-English translation task, following previous work (Ranzato et al., 2015; Bahdanau et al., 2016), we select data from German-English machine translation track of IWSLT2014 evaluation tasks, which consists of sentence-aligned subtitles of TED and TEDx talks. We closely follow the pre-processing as described in Ranzato et al. (2015). The training corpus contains 153k sentence pairs with 2.83M English words and 2.68M German words. The validation set comprises of 6,969 sentence pairs taken from the training data, and the test set is a combination of dev2010, dev2012, tst2010, tst2011 and tst2012 with total number of 6,750 sentence pairs.

For Chinese-English translation task, training data consists of a set of LDC datasets[1], which has around 2.6M sentence pairs with 65.1M Chinese words and 67.1M English words respectively. Any sentence longer than 80 words is removed from training data. NIST OpenMT 2006 evaluation set is used as the validation set, and NIST 2005, 2008, 2012 datasets as test sets. We limit the vocabulary to contain up to 50K most frequent words on both source and target sides, and convert remaining words into the <unk> token.

4.1.2 Model Architecture

RNNSearch model proposed by Bahdanau et al. (2014) is leveraged to be the translation model, but it should be noted that our BGAN-NMT is independent of the NMT network structure. We use a single layer GRU for encoder and decoder. For Zh-En, the size of word embedding (for both source and target words) is 256 and the size of hidden layer is set to 1024. For De-En, in order to compare with previous work (Ranzato et al., 2015; Bahdanau et al., 2016), the size of word embedding and GRU hidden state are both set to 256. In addition, $P(x)$ and $P(y)$ are designed as a single-layer GRU language model, which is pre-trained

---

[1] LDC2002E17, LDC2002E18, LDC2003E07, LDC2003E14, LDC2005E83, LDC2005T06, LDC2005T10, LDC2006E17, LDC2006E26, LDC2006E34, LDC2006E85, LDC2006E92, LDC2006T06, LDC2004T08, LDC2005T10

Methods	Baseline	Model
MIXER (Ranzato et al., 2015)	20.10	21.81
MRT (Shen et al., 2016)	-	25.84
BSO (Wiseman and Rush, 2016)	24.03	26.36
Adversarial-NMT (Wu et al., 2017)	-	27.94
A-C (Bahdanau et al., 2016)	27.56	28.53
Softmax-Q (Ma et al., 2017)	27.66	28.77
Adversarial-NMT*	27.63	28.03
BGAN-NMT	27.63	**29.17**

Table 1: Comparison with previous work on IWSLT2014 German-English translation task. The "Baseline" means the performance of pre-trained model used to warmly start training.

to compute the marginal probability of a sentence, and the size of word embedding and GRU hidden state are the same as RNNSearch model.

4.1.3 Training Details

For the training of BGAN-NMT, parameters are firstly initialized using a normal distribution with a mean of 0 and a variance of $\sqrt{6/(d_{row} + d_{col})}$, where d_{row} and d_{col} are the number of rows and columns in the structure (Glorot and Bengio, 2010). Then we pre-train NMT and language models with MLE principle to convergence, and select the best model according to the performances on the validation set, where BLEU scores and the perplexity are adopted as evaluation metrics for NMT and language models respectively. Both generator and discriminator models in BGAN-NMT are warmly started with those pre-trained models, and optimized using the vanilla SGD algorithm with mini-batch 32 for De-En and 128 for Zh-En. We re-normalize gradients if their norm exceeds 2.0. The initial learning rate is set as 0.2 for De-En and 0.02 for Zh-En, and it is halved when BLEU scores on the validation set do not increase for 20,000 batches. To generate the synthetic bilingual data, beam search strategy with beam size 4 is adopted for both De-En and Zh-En. At test time, beam search is employed to find the best translation with beam size 8 and translation probabilities normalized by the length of the candidate translations. Follow Luong et al. (2015), <unk> is replaced with the corresponding target word in a post processing step.

4.2 Results on German-English Translation

For German-English translation task, in addition to the baseline system which is used to warmly start our BGAN-NMT training, we also include

System	NIST2006	NIST2005	NIST2008	NIST2012	Average
HPSMT	32.46	32.42	25.23	26.20	29.08
RNNSearch	38.61	38.31	30.04	28.48	33.86
Adversarial-NMT*	39.79	38.81	31.86	30.19	35.16
BGAN-NMT	**40.74**	**39.20**	**33.55**	**31.30**	**36.19**

Table 2: Case-insensitive BLEU scores (%) on Chinese-English translation. The "Average" denotes the average results of all datasets.

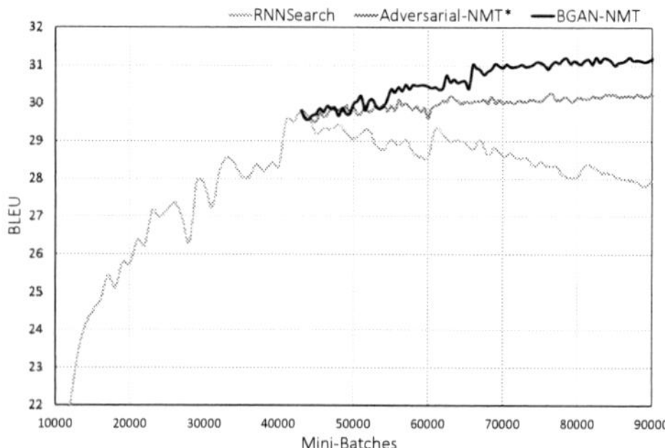

Figure 2: The BLEU score changes on IWSLT2014 German-English validation set for RNNSearch, Adversarial-NMT* and BGAN-NMT as training progresses.

results of other existing NMT systems, including MIXER (Ranzato et al., 2015), MRT (Shen et al., 2016)[2], BSO (Wiseman and Rush, 2016), Adversarial-NMT (Wu et al., 2017), A-C (Bahdanau et al., 2016) and Softmax-Q (Ma et al., 2017). Besides, following Wu et al. (2017), we also implement Adversarial-NMT* system which combines adversarial training objective with MLE. All the results are reported based on case-sensitive BLEU.

From Table 1, we can see that our BGAN-NMT achieves significant improvements over the baseline RNNSearch system. It demonstrates that GAN framework can alleviate exposure bias problem and improve the robustness of NMT systems. Our BGAN-NMT also obtains satisfactory translation quality against other existing NMT systems. In particular, our BGAN-NMT outperforms Adversarial-NMT* by 1.14 BLEU points. Adversarial-NMT* adopts MLE to stabilize the training of generator but gains limited improvement due to the inadequate training problem of the discriminator, while our BGAN-NMT can effectively handle this issue and obtain significant improvement.

To better analyze training process of the different methods, we compare the BLEU score changes on IWSLT2014 German-English validation set for RNNSearch, Adversarial-NMT* and BGAN-NMT during the entire training. As illustrated in Figure 2, initialized with the best RNNSearch model, Adversarial-NMT* and BGAN-NMT can continually improve the translation performance. In addition, our BGAN-NMT steadily performs much better than Adversarial-NMT* in the whole training process. It confirms that our proposed approach not only stabilizes GAN training but also achieves better results.

4.3 Results on Chinese-English Translation

We also conduct experiments on Chinese-English translation task with strong SMT and NMT baselines: HPSMT, RNNSearch and Adversarial-NMT*. HPSMT is an in-house implementation of the hierarchical phrase-based MT system (Chiang, 2007), where a 4-gram language model is trained using the modified Kneser-Ney smoothing algorithm over the target data from bilingual data.

Table 2 shows the evaluation results of different models on NIST datasets. All the results are reported based on case-insensitive BLEU. We can observe that RNNSearch significantly outperforms HPSMT by 4.78 BLEU points on average, and BGAN-NMT can further improve the performances, with 2.33 BLEU points on average. Additionally, our BGAN-NMT gains better performances than Adversarial-NMT* with 1.03 BLEU points on average. These experimental results confirm the effectiveness of our proposed approach, similar as shown in the German-English translation task.

4.4 Effect on Long Sentences

Longer source sentence implies longer translation that more easily suffers from exposure bias problem. In this subsection, we group source sentence of similar length together and calculate the

---

[2]The result of MRT method is taken from Wu et al. (2017)

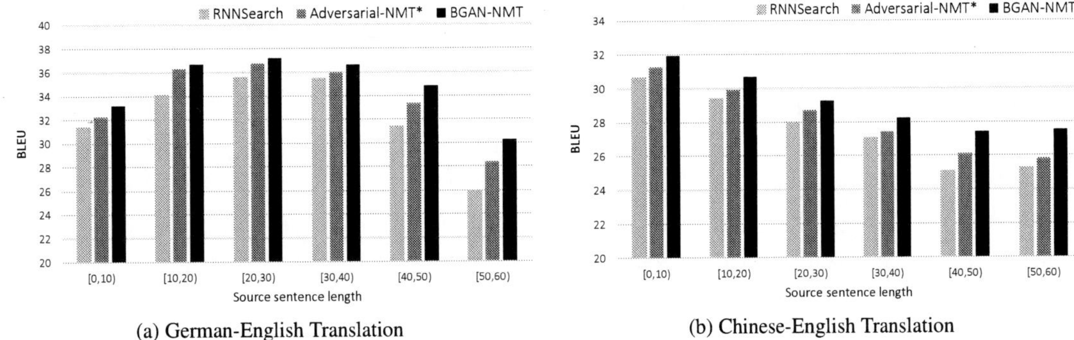

(a) German-English Translation (b) Chinese-English Translation

Figure 3: Performance of the generated translations with respect to the length of source sentences on different datasets. For Chinese-English, we merge all NIST datasets in this experiment. For German-English, we only use test datasets.

BLEU score for each group. As shown in Figure 3, we can view that our approach outperforms RNNSearch and Adversarial-NMT* in all length segments, especially achieving notable improvements on long sentences. These results further demonstrate that our approach can better handle this problem and yield higher quality translations.

4.5 Effect of Discriminative Loss

We also perform an ablation experiment in order to quantify the effect of the discriminative loss on our models. As shown in Table 3, the discriminative loss can bring 0.58 and 0.73 BLEU score improvements on English-German and Chinese-English dataset respectively. This result proves that the discriminative loss can improve the discriminative ability of bidirectional NMT models, which can give more accurate rewards for the generator training in GAN framework.

5 Related Work

As a new paradigm of machine translation, NMT typically suffers from the exposure bias problem due to MLE training. To handle this issue, many methods have been proposed, including designing new training objectives (Shen et al., 2016; Wiseman and Rush, 2016) and adopting reinforcement learning approaches (Ranzato et al., 2015; Bahdanau et al., 2016). Shen et al. (2016) proposed to directly minimize expected loss (maximize the expected BLEU) with Minimum Risk Training (MRT). Wiseman and Rush (2016) adopted a beam-search optimization algorithm to reduce inconsistency between training and inference. Besides, Ranzato et al. (2015) proposed a mixture training method to perform a gradual transition

Model	DE-EN	ZH-EN
BGAN-NMT	29.17	36.19
-Discriminative Loss	28.59	35.46

Table 3: Translation performance of BGAN-NMT without discriminative loss on German-English (DE-EN) and Chinese-English (ZH-EN) translations. The BLEU score for Chinese-English translation is the average results of all datasets we used in the experiment.

from maximum likelihood learning into optimizing BLEU scores using reinforcement algorithm. Bahdanau et al. (2016) designed an actor-critic algorithm for sequence prediction, in which the NMT system is the actor, and a critic network is proposed to predict the value of output tokens. Recently, Yang et al. (2017) and Wu et al. (2017) proposed to leverage GAN framework to deal with the exposure bias problem, in which NMT model is employed as the generator, and CNN-based or RNN-based model is used as the discriminator. Different from their work, both generator and discriminator in our approach are designed to model the joint probability of sentence pairs and then we design an auxiliary GAN to take advantage of the symmetry of them.

Another similar research in NMT is to leverage bidirectional dependency to improve translation quality. Tu et al. (2017) designed a re-constructor module for NMT in order to make the target representation contain the complete source information which can reconstruct back to the source sentence. Cheng et al. (2016) and He et al. (2016) proposed to reconstruct monolingual data by auto-encoder, in which bidirectional translation models form a closed loop and are jointly updated. Recently, this similar idea is used in unsupervised machine translation tasks(Artetxe et al., 2017; Lample et al., 2018).

6 Conclusion

In this paper, we have presented a Bidirectional Generative Adversarial Network for Neural Machine Translation, consisting of an original GAN and an auxiliary GAN. Both generator and discriminator in original GAN are designed to model the joint probability of sentence pairs. Auxiliary GAN adopts generator and discriminator models of original one but exchanges their roles to full utilize the symmetry of them. Then these two GANs are alternately updated using joint training algorithm. Experimental results on German-English and Chinese-English translation tasks demonstrate that our proposed approach not only stabilizes GAN training but also leads to significant improvements. In the future, we plan to extend this method to other sequence-to-sequence NLP tasks.

Acknowledgments

We appreciate Dongdong Zhang, Shuangzhi Wu, Wenhu Chen and Guanlin Li for the fruitful discussions. We also thank the anonymous reviewers for their careful reading of our paper and insightful comments.

References

Martín Arjovsky, Soumith Chintala, and Léon Bottou. 2017. Wasserstein gan. *CoRR*, abs/1701.07875.

Mikel Artetxe, Gorka Labaka, Eneko Agirre, and Kyunghyun Cho. 2017. Unsupervised neural machine translation. *CoRR*, abs/1710.11041.

Dzmitry Bahdanau, Philemon Brakel, Kelvin Xu, Anirudh Goyal, Ryan Lowe, Joelle Pineau, Aaron C. Courville, and Yoshua Bengio. 2016. An actor-critic algorithm for sequence prediction. *CoRR*, abs/1607.07086.

Dzmitry Bahdanau, Kyunghyun Cho, and Yoshua Bengio. 2014. Neural machine translation by jointly learning to align and translate. *CoRR*, abs/1409.0473.

Samy Bengio, Oriol Vinyals, Navdeep Jaitly, and Noam Shazeer. 2015. Scheduled sampling for sequence prediction with recurrent neural networks. In *NIPS*.

Yong Cheng, Wei Xu, Zhongjun He, Wei He, Hua Wu, Maosong Sun, and Yang Liu. 2016. Semi-supervised learning for neural machine translation. In *ACL*.

David Chiang. 2007. Hierarchical phrase-based translation. *Computational Linguistics*, 33:201–228.

Kyunghyun Cho, Bart van Merrienboer, Çaglar Gulçehre, Dzmitry Bahdanau, Fethi Bougares, Holger Schwenk, and Yoshua Bengio. 2014. Learning phrase representations using rnn encoder-decoder for statistical machine translation. In *EMNLP*.

Jonas Gehring, Michael Auli, David Grangier, Denis Yarats, and Yann Dauphin. 2017. Convolutional sequence to sequence learning. In *ICML*.

Xavier Glorot and Yoshua Bengio. 2010. Understanding the difficulty of training deep feedforward neural networks. In *AISTATS*.

Ian J. Goodfellow. 2016. Nips 2016 tutorial: Generative adversarial networks. *CoRR*, abs/1701.00160.

Ian J. Goodfellow, Jean Pouget-Abadie, Mehdi Mirza, Bing Xu, David Warde-Farley, Sherjil Ozair, Aaron C. Courville, and Yoshua Bengio. 2014. Generative adversarial nets. In *NIPS*.

Hany Hassan, Anthony Aue, Chang Chen, Vishal Chowdhary, Jonathan Clark, Christian Federmann, Xuedong Huang, Marcin Junczys-Dowmunt, William Lewis, Mu Li, Shujie Liu, Tie-Yan Liu, Renqian Luo, Arul Menezes, Tao Qin, Frank Seide, Xu Tan, Fei Tian, Lijun Wu, Shuangzhi Wu, Yingce Xia, Dongdong Zhang, Zhirui Zhang, and Ming Zhou. 2018. Achieving human parity on automatic chinese to english news translation. *CoRR*, abs/1803.05567.

Di He, Yingce Xia, Tao Qin, Liwei Wang, Nenghai Yu, Tie-Yan Liu, and Wei-Ying Ma. 2016. Dual learning for machine translation. In *NIPS*.

Sepp Hochreiter and Jurgen Schmidhuber. 1997. Long short-term memory. *Neural computation*.

Philipp Koehn, Franz Josef Och, and Daniel Marcu. 2003. Statistical phrase-based translation. In *HLT-NAACL*.

Alex Lamb, Anirudh Goyal, Ying Zhang, Saizheng Zhang, Aaron C. Courville, and Yoshua Bengio. 2016. Professor forcing: A new algorithm for training recurrent networks. In *NIPS*.

Guillaume Lample, Myle Ott, Alexis Conneau, Ludovic Denoyer, and Marc'Aurelio Ranzato. 2018. Phrase-based & neural unsupervised machine translation. *CoRR*, abs/1804.07755.

Jiwei Li, Will Monroe, Tianlin Shi, Alan Ritter, and Daniel Jurafsky. 2017. Adversarial learning for neural dialogue generation. In *EMNLP*.

Thang Luong, Ilya Sutskever, Quoc V. Le, Oriol Vinyals, and Wojciech Zaremba. 2015. Addressing the rare word problem in neural machine translation. In *ACL*.

Xuezhe Ma, Pengcheng Yin, Jingzhou Liu, Graham Neubig, and Eduard H. Hovy. 2017. Softmax q-distribution estimation for structured prediction: A theoretical interpretation for raml. *CoRR*, abs/1705.07136.

Kishore Papineni, Salim E. Roucos, Todd Ward, and Wei-Jing Zhu. 2002. Bleu: a method for automatic evaluation of machine translation. In *ACL*.

Alec Radford, Luke Metz, and Soumith Chintala. 2015. Unsupervised representation learning with deep convolutional generative adversarial networks. *arXiv preprint arXiv:1511.06434*.

Marc'Aurelio Ranzato, Sumit Chopra, Michael Auli, and Wojciech Zaremba. 2015. Sequence level training with recurrent neural networks. *CoRR*, abs/1511.06732.

Rico Sennrich, Barry Haddow, and Alexandra Birch. 2016. Improving neural machine translation models with monolingual data. In *ACL*.

Shiqi Shen, Yong Cheng, Zhongjun He, Wei He, Hua Wu, Maosong Sun, and Yang Liu. 2016. Minimum risk training for neural machine translation. In *ACL*.

Ilya Sutskever, Oriol Vinyals, and Quoc V. Le. 2014. Sequence to sequence learning with neural networks. In *NIPS*.

Zhaopeng Tu, Yang Liu, Lifeng Shang, Xiaohua Liu, and Hang Li. 2017. Neural machine translation with reconstruction. In *AAAI*.

Ashish Vaswani, Noam Shazeer, Niki Parmar, Jakob Uszkoreit, Llion Jones, Aidan N. Gomez, Lukasz Kaiser, and Illia Polosukhin. 2017. Attention is all you need. In *NIPS*.

Sam Wiseman and Alexander M. Rush. 2016. Sequence-to-sequence learning as beam-search optimization. In *EMNLP*.

Lijun Wu, Yingce Xia, Li Zhao, Fei Tian, Tao Qin, Jian-Huang Lai, and Tie-Yan Liu. 2017. Adversarial neural machine translation. *CoRR*, abs/1704.06933.

Zhen Yang, Wei Chen, Feng Wang, and Bo Xu. 2017. Improving neural machine translation with conditional sequence generative adversarial nets. *CoRR*, abs/1703.04887.

Lantao Yu, Weinan Zhang, Jun Wang, and Yong Yu. 2017. Seqgan: Sequence generative adversarial nets with policy gradient. In *AAAI*.

Latent Entities Extraction:
How to Extract Entities that Do Not Appear in the Text?

Eylon Shoshan[1], Kira Radinsky[1,2]
{eylonsho999, kirar}@cs.technion.ac.il

[1]Department of Computer Science, Technion - Israel Institute of Technology, Haifa, Israel
[2]eBay Research, Israel

Abstract

Named-entity Recognition (NER) is an important task in the NLP field , and is widely used to solve many challenges. However, in many scenarios, not all of the entities are explicitly mentioned in the text. Sometimes they could be inferred from the context or from other indicative words. Consider the following sentence: *"CMA can easily hydrolyze into free acetic acid."* Although water is not mentioned explicitly, one can infer that H2O is an entity involved in the process. In this work, we present the problem of *Latent Entities Extraction* (LEE). We present several methods for determining whether entities are discussed in a text, even though, potentially, they are not explicitly written. Specifically, we design a neural model that handles extraction of multiple entities jointly. We show that our model, along with multi-task learning approach and a novel task grouping algorithm, reaches high performance in identifying latent entities. Our experiments are conducted on a large biological dataset from the biochemical field. The dataset contains text descriptions of biological processes, and for each process, all of the involved entities in the process are labeled, including implicitly mentioned ones. We believe LEE is a task that will significantly improve many NER and subsequent applications and improve text understanding and inference.

1 Introduction

Named entity recognition (NER) is an important building block in many natural-language-processing algorithms and applications. For example, representing texts as a knowledge graph, where nodes are extracted entities, has been proved to be effective for question answering (Berant and Clark, 2014) as well as for summarization tasks (Ganesan et al., 2010). Other applications, such as semantic annotation (Marrero et al., 2013) require recognition of entities in the text as well.

Babych and Hartley (2003) have also shown that identifying named entities correctly, has an effect both on the global syntactic and lexical structure, additionally to the local and immediate context.

NER today focuses on extracting existing entities in the text. However, many texts, contain "hidden" entities, which are not mentioned explicitly in the text, but might be inferred from the context. For example, special verbs could help a human reader infer the discussed entity implicitly. Consider the following textual passage of a biochemical reaction:

> *"At the plasma membrane, phosphatidylcholine is **hydrolyzed**, removing one of its acyl groups, to 1-acyl lysophosphatidylcholine by membrane-associated phospholipase b1. "*

The words *water* or *H2O* are not mentioned. Nonetheless, one could easily infer that water is involved in the process, since the word hydrolyzed refers to water. Therefore, water is a latent entity in this case. Other contexts, do not involve only indicating verbs. Consider the following sentence:

> *"The conversion of Testosterone to Estradiol is catalyzed by Aromatase associated with the endoplasmic reticulum membrane."*

Here, *Oxygen* is a latent entity. Aromatase is an enzyme that belongs to the Monooxygenases family. This family is characterized by requiring Oxygen when performing catalyzation.

Latent entities do not only play a prominent role in biochemical and medical fields, but are also common in other domains. For example, consider the following snippet as published in business section, New York Times magazine in January 2017:

> *"The free app, which Facebook owns, is offering another vehicle to advertisers,*

Proceedings of the 22nd Conference on Computational Natural Language Learning (CoNLL 2018), pages 200–210
Brussels, Belgium, October 31 - November 1, 2018. ©2018 Association for Computational Linguistics

*who since late 2015 have been buying
space on its original photo feed."*

To an average human reader who is familiar with contemporary norms and trends, it is quite clear that *Instagram* app is discussed in the textual passage above. However, it is not explicitly written, thus it is practically a latent entity.

Identifying latent entities in texts, and gaining the ability to infer them from a context, will significantly enrich our ability to comprehend and perform inference over complex texts.

In this work, we formulate the novel problem of Latent-Entities Extraction (LEE). We study several deep and non-deep models for this task, that learn to extract latent entities from texts and overcome the fact that these are not mentioned explicitly. Specifically, we study a model that combines a neural recurrent network (Bi-GRUs) and multi-task learning, showing that joint prediction of correlated entities could refine the performance. We present a novel algorithm for task grouping in the multi-task learning setting for LEE. The algorithm chooses which latent entities to learn together. We show this approach reaches the best performance for LEE.

The contribution of our works is threefold: (1) We formulate a novel task of LEE, where the goal is to extract entities which are implicitly mentioned in the text. (2) We present a large labeled biological dataset to study LEE. (3) We present several algorithms for this task. Specifically, we find that learning multiple latent entities in a multi-task learning setting, while selecting the correct entities to learn together, reaches the best results for LEE. We share our code and data with the community to enable the community to develop additional algorithms for LEE: `https://github.com/EylonSho/LatentEntitiesExtraction`

2 Related Work

Entities Recognition Named-entity recognition (NER) aims at identifying different types of entities, such as people names, companies, locations, organizations, etc. within a given text. Such deduced information is necessary for many application, e.g. summarization tasks (Ganesan et al., 2010), data mining (Chen et al., 2004), and translation (Babych and Hartley, 2003).

This problem has been widely researched. Several benchmark data sets such as CoNLL-2003 (Tjong Kim Sang and De Meulder, 2003) and OntoNotes 5.0 (Hovy et al., 2006; Pradhan et al., 2013) were published. Traditional approaches label each token in texts as part of named-entity, and achieve high performance (Ratinov and Roth, 2009; Passos et al., 2014; Chiu and Nichols, 2016).

However, these approaches are relying on the assumption that entities are necessarily mentioned in the text. To the best of our knowledge, the problem of latent entities extraction, where entities could potentially not be mentioned in the text at all, is yet to be researched.

Multi-Task Learning Multitask learning (Caruana, 1998) was extensively used across many NLP fields, including neural speech translation (Anastasopoulos and Chiang, 2018), neural machine translation (Domhan and Hieber, 2017), and summarization tasks (Isonuma et al., 2017). In this work we study several approaches for LEE, including multi-task learning. We observe that the vanilla approach of multi-task learning is reaching limited results in our setting (Section 6). Previous work (Liu and Pan, 2017; Zhong et al., 2016; Jeong and Jun, 2018) have suggested that multi-task learning should be applied on related tasks. We present an extension to the multi-task learning setting by performing clustering to related tasks to improve performance.

3 The Reactome Dataset

It is quite common to have implicit entities in texts in the biomedical field. *Reactome* (Croft et al.) is a large publicly-available biological dataset of human biological pathways and reactions. The data consists of 9,333 biochemical reaction diagrams and their textual description. Each reaction is labeled by experts regarding its reactants and products. We consider each reactant or product of a reaction as an entity. If an entity is not mentioned in the textual description, it will be considered as a *latent entity*. In more than 90% of the reactions, there are 3–5 involved entities. We have performed an exploration to find latent frequency, i.e., how many times the entity was found as latent, among all of its occurrences in the dataset. We identify that 97.53% of the texts contain at least one latent entity and that 80.65% of the entities are latent at least 10% of the times. The analysis results for several entities are shown in Table 1. We observe an interesting phenomena – several entities, such as ATP, mostly appear as a latent en-

Entity	Times Not Mentioned	Total Occurrences	Latent Frequency (%)
ATP	1177	1448	81.28
ADP	1221	1326	92.08
H2O	949	1087	87.30
PI	249	492	50.61
H+	296	487	60.78
O2	159	275	57.82
NADPH	145	254	57.09
NADP+	175	253	69.17
COA-SH	123	191	64.40
PPI	105	190	55.26
ADOMET	120	181	66.30
GTP	40	181	22.10
GDP	60	179	33.52
ADOHCY	155	169	91.72
UB	0	157	0.00
CO2	75	145	51.72
NAD+	56	134	41.79
AMP	53	128	41.41
NADH	46	112	41.07
NA+	23	94	24.47
2OG	33	93	35.48
L-GLU	66	82	80.49
AC-COA	43	75	57.33

Table 1: Latent frequency of top common entities

tity in the descriptions, i.e., most of the times they are not mentioned explicitly in the text.

4 One-vs-all Algorithms for LEE

Given a single entity which frequently tends to be latent, we need to classify whether it is involved within a given text. We train a classifier per entity using multiple techniques. We then apply the classifier on each text passage that may discuss several latent entities, and output their prediction in a one-vs-all approach.

We present several models which predict whether a given entity is implicitly (or explicitly) involved in a textual paragraph. We construct a classifier per entity which detects the entity in texts, and overcomes the cases where it is latent. We devise a few simple yet relatively powerful algorithms presented in Sections 4.1 – 4.5.

4.1 Bag-of-words (TF-IDF)

To tackle the LEE problem, we try to leverage the context to infer latent entities. We transform a text to a TF-IDF vector representation (applied on bi-grams). Using these vectors we train several supervised classification models. We did not observe a significant difference between the models, and present results for Support Vector Machine (SVM) model (Cortes and Vapnik, 1995) that have shown the highest performance on a validation set. The models are trained to predict whether a given entity is involved or not. As can be observed in Table 1, most of the entities are latent enough, thus this data set is appropriate to the LEE task.

4.2 Weighted Document Embedding

One of the state-of-the-art approaches for modeling text was presenting by Arora et al. (2017). We leverage pre-trained word embedding vectors (Chiu et al., 2016) to generate an embedding for a text which might contain implicit entities. Based on these embeddings, a supervised classifier per entity is trained as before, i.e., we create a classifier per entity to predict whether it is implicitly mentioned in the text.

4.3 Element-Wise Document Embedding

We study several additional methods of representing a document using several word embedding compositions (De Boom et al., 2016). We leverage pre-trained word embedding vectors, that were trained on Pubmed data (Chiu et al., 2016), and suggest the following composition techniques: (1) We compute the element-wise maximum vector of each word from the text, denoted as v_{max}; (2) We compute the element-wise minimum vector of word embedding, denoted as v_{min}. (3) We compute the element-wise mean vector, denoted as v_{avg}.

We concatenate these three vectors into the final document representation: $v = [v_{max}; v_{min}; v_{avg}]$. This is the feature vector which is fed as an input to the SVM classifier, built for each entity separately.

4.4 Combined Document Embedding

In this approach, we attempt to combine several ways of representing a document into a single representation. We concatenate the feature vectors for each document as generated in sections 4.2, 4.3. A classification model is then trained similarly to the previous sections and applied on the new representation.

4.5 Deep Document Embedding

Instead of disregarding word order as in the previous approaches (Sections 4.2 – 4.4), we leverage pre-trained word embedding vectors that were trained on Pubmed data (Chiu et al., 2016), and learn an unsupervised deep model to produce a document embedding. We experiment with several deep models, including Bi-LSTM and Bi-GRU unit: each textual description is translated to sequence of pre-trained embeddings. That sequence is fed into a Bi-Directional Long Short Term Memory (Bi-LSTM) (Hochreiter and Schmidhuber, 1997; Schuster and Paliwal, 1997) or Bi-GRU (Cho et al., 2014), and based on the final cell state, we perform a binary prediction whether the given entity is implicitly mentioned or not.

5 Multi-Task-Learning Algorithms for LEE

Given a predefined list of entities, we wish to classify whether *one entity or more* from that list, are involved in a given text passage. We train a single multi-task-learning classifier that outputs the set of latent entities relevant to the text. Intuitively, the model might capture correlation of entities that tend to be involved (or not) together, and therefore their latent behavior might be similar. For each entity which is listed in a predefined list, the model will output a probability as an estimation for its likelihood to be involved in a given text.

5.1 Multi-Task-Learning Model Architecture

Figure 1 illustrates the general design of our architecture: an embedding layer, a Bi-GRU components that are fed by the embedding, and ultimately a prediction layer containing as many outputs as the total number of latent entities to be extracted.

Embedding The embedding layer first embeds a sequence of words into a sequence of embedding vectors of 200 dimension.

Bidirectional GRU The output vectors from the last layer are fed into a RNN unit to capture context out of the text. This unit is capable of analyzing context that is spanned over sub-sequences in texts. This is done when the RNN component is sequentially fed by the embedding vectors $\{v_t\}$, and iteratively compute a hidden state vector $\{h_t\}$ based on the previous hidden state and the current input embedding vector, using some function f. Moreover, the output of this unit $\{o_t\}$ in each timestamp t, is computed based on the current hidden state using a function g.

Specifically we use a GRU unit as a RNN as presented by Cho et al. (2014). Hidden state's dimension is set to 200, with sigmoid as an activation function. Additionally, we use the bidirectional version (Schuster and Paliwal, 1997) of GRU.

We also apply natural dropout (Srivastava et al., 2014) of 0.5 on the input embedding vectors. Another refinement is dropout that is applied on the recurrent neural network hidden layers, as Gal and Ghahramani (2016) have suggested. This recurrent dropout is set to 0.25.

Classifier The outputs of the Bi-GRU unit, of the first and last cell, are considered during classification phase. The classifier unit is a fully connected layer with a sigmoid activation layer with k outputs, where k is the number of all tasks, i.e., entities being predicted.

Loss Function We define a loss function to address the multi-task learning approach. Currently, we present a loss function for multi-task prediction that joins all of the entities together into a single prediction unit. Denote m as the number of training samples, and k as the number of latent entities that are intended to be extracted. We define the following loss function:

$$L(y, \hat{y}) =$$
$$-\frac{1}{m} \sum_{i=1}^{m} \sum_{j=1}^{k} \left(y_j^{(i)} \log \hat{y}_j^{(i)} + \left(1 - y_j^{(i)}\right) \log \left(1 - \hat{y}_j^{(i)}\right) \right)$$

where y and $\hat{y}$ are the labeled and predicted values, respectively. Practically, we aggregate the log-losses over all of the training samples and latent entities, and then averaging to get the final loss.

Note that we address all of the entities as they were related in here, since the loss is calculated based on them all with no exceptions.

Training Model optimization was carried out using standard backpropagation and an Adam optimizer (Kingma and Ba, 2014). We have trained our model with 300 epochs and a batch size of 128. Backpropagation is allowed through all layers, except the embedding layer, which is set using pre-trained embeddings.

Word Embedding Initialization We use pre-trained word embedding to represent each text passage. Note that fine-tuning as well as learning embedding from scratch are not practical due to data scarcity, hence we directly use *word2vec*

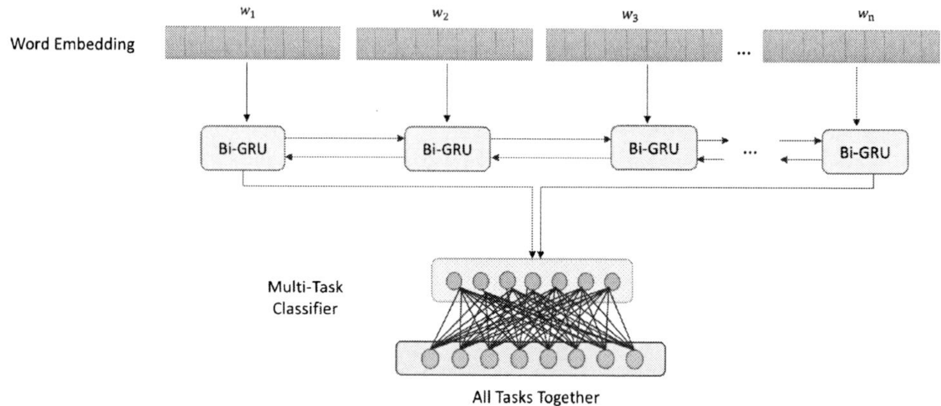

Figure 1: The multi-task model architecture for latent entities extraction. Word embeddings are fed to several Bi-GRU units which are connected via a multi-task learning approach to numerous outputs, each representing a different latent entity prediction

trained vectors[1]. These were trained over large corpora, the PubMed archive of the biochemical, biological and medical field by Chiu et al. (2016). We fit this choice to the nature of our data set, Reactome, which is consisted of biochemical reactions and biological processes.

5.2 Task-Grouping Model Architecture

The common approach in multi-task learning is handle all tasks altogether (Evgeniou and Pontil, 2004; Rai and Daume III, 2010). Therefore, a possible approach could possibly suggest that all of the entities should be predicted together as a single multi-task classification process. However, this method is based on the assumption that all entities are necessarily related to one another (as presented in section 5.1).

Several studies have shown that separation of tasks into disjoint groups could boost classification performance. Intuitively, multi-task learning among tasks that are mutually related reduces noise in prediction (Liu and Pan, 2017; Zhong et al., 2016; Jeong and Jun, 2018). We present an algorithm that divides all of the tasks, i.e., all entities predictions, into task groups according to their inherent relatedness. Capturing these connections is performed using a co-occurrence matrix that we compute based on training-set information and behavior. Conceptually, latent entities that are labeled many times together in processes would be considered as related, thus grouped together in a joint multi-task classification unit.

Our tasks are divided into groups based on a co-occurrence matrix M which is computed as follows:

$$M_{ij} = \frac{\# \text{ mutual occurrences of } e_i, e_j}{\# \text{ occurrences of } e_i}$$

where e_i is the i-th latent entity that should be predicted. Additionally, note the elements of M are normalized. Figure 2 presents an example of such a co-occurrence matrix for 5 sampled entities.

After generating the co-occurrence matrix, we leverage it to select task groups. We denote α as a minimum threshold in order to group a pairwise of tasks together ($0 \leq \alpha \leq 1$). Then, two prediction tasks (a pair of entities) e_i and e_j will be grouped together if $M_{ij} > \alpha$ or $M_{ji} > \alpha$. Later, we would like to avoid from multi-task group that contains one task only. Therefore, if any singletons remain, we attach each one of them to its most related entity's group, according to the same co-occurrence distribution. This reunion phase comes with the exception of $\alpha/2$ as a minimum threshold rather than α as was done previously.

Clusters of tasks are computed according to $\alpha = 0.65$. This value is chosen empirically such that groups are divided fairly, in terms of size, both subjectively and objectively.

This process induces a division of the tasks to T disjoint groups of tasks, where each group is consisted of k_r prediction tasks (a task per latent entity), where $r \in \{1, 2, \ldots, T\}$. Note that each group is potentially of different size, i.e., k_r is not

---

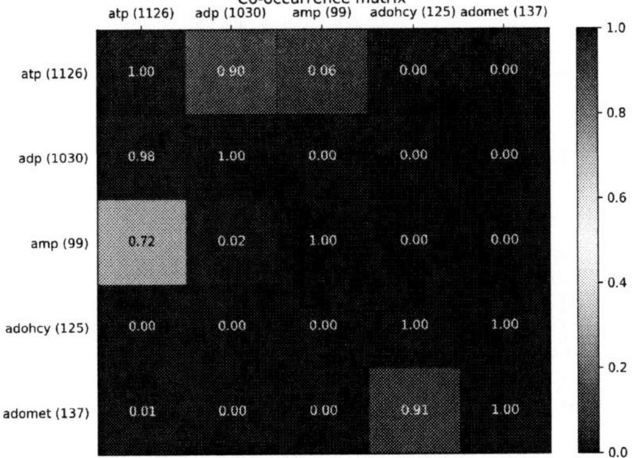

Figure 2: An example of co-occurrence matrix which describes the relatedness of entities to one another. Numbers in parentheses next to entities' names are an indication for their frequency in the training-set. As follows from the distribution, ATP and ADP are high correlated. AMP also tends to co-exist with ATP (not reciprocally though). Similarly, ADOHCY and ADOMET are quite related to one another.

fixed. Ultimately, these groups are going to represent as the multi-task units of classification in our model.

Figure 3 illustrates the design of our architecture along with the task-grouping layer. It contains an embedding layer, a Bi-GRU components that are fed by the embedding, and ultimately T multi-task classification units, one per task group.

Classifier Similarly to the classifier in Section 5.1, the first and last cell of the GRU are connected to several disjoint groups of prediction tasks. These outputs represent the features for several multi-task classifier units, one such unit per a group of tasks. For the r-th ($r \in \{1, 2, ..., T\}$) task group, we define a classifier unit as a fully connected layer with a sigmoid activation layer with k_r outputs, where k_r is the size of the r-th task group.

Loss Function As opposed to the loss function previously presented, here we would like to preserve relatedness among prediction tasks when they are actually related only. Therefore, we use task grouping feature to recognize T disjoint sets of entities as prediction task groups. For each task group, we force the preservation of entities' known correlation using a unique loss function that is designated for the classifier of that specific group. Denote m as the number of training samples, and k_r as the number of entities that are grouped in the r-th task-group ($r \in \{1, 2, \ldots, T\}$). The need for latent entities from the same task group to retain their relatedness, will be forced using the following loss function:

$$L(y, \hat{y}) =$$
$$-\frac{1}{m} \sum_{i=1}^{m} \sum_{j=1}^{k_r} \left(y_j^{(i)} \log \hat{y}_j^{(i)} + \left(1 - y_j^{(i)}\right) \log \left(1 - \hat{y}_j^{(i)}\right) \right)$$

where y and $\hat{y}$ are the labeled and predicted values, respectively. Whereas the concept is similar to the presented loss function in the vanilla multi-task approach, now each task group classifier has a customized loss function that learns the behavior of its relevant entities it is responsible of.

Note that the penalty for each predicted value is equal while in the same task group, whereas, between different task-groups the loss value may be different. In that way, we refine the classification per each task-group, and thus per each latent entity.

6 Experimental Results

In this section, we evaluate the algorithms for LEE. We first show the performance of the algorithms for a single entity extraction, focusing on the ATP entity. We then present results for the general task of LEE, extracting multiple entities from a text. We then conclude this section by a few qualitative examples illustrating the feature importance considered for the LEE task over several texts.

6.1 Single Latent Entity Extraction

We start by exploring the performance of the different classifiers for the task of identifying a single latent entity. As a representative test-case we consider the extraction of the *ATP* entity. The entity is considered of high importance to many biological processes. Additionally, it has the highest frequency in the dataset, i.e., there are many data examples (biochemical reactions) where ATP is involved in. In more than 81% of its existences in reactions, it is not explicitly mentioned in the text, which practically makes it to a pure latent entity.

The results of all the algorithms for the prediction of the latent entity ATP are shown in Table 2. We emphasize that here, training, validating and testing were all performed on pure latent samples,

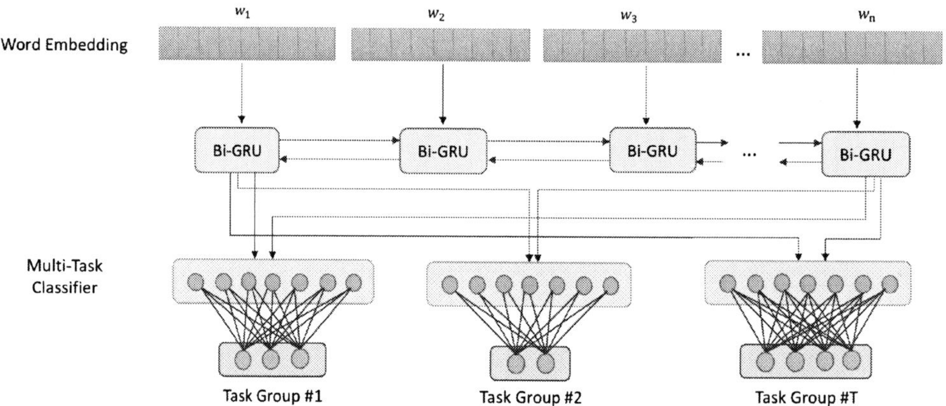

Figure 3: Multi-Task model architecture for latent entities extraction, based on task grouping approach. Word embeddings are fed to several Bi-GRU units which are connected via a multi-task learning approach to numerous groups of tasks, each representing a different group of related latent entities sharing a similar loss.

i.e., texts that did contain the examined entity were filtered out. The last row stands for the multi-task approach with grouping, where ADP was selected to be in the same prediction task group along with ATP (ADP is known to be high correlated with ATP as also can be deduced from Figure 2). The improved empirical results in that experiment suggest that using multi-task learning for related tasks could be beneficial for the performance.

6.2 Multiple Latent Entities Extraction

In this section, we consider the full problem of LEE of extracting multiple entities jointly. The results are presented in Table 4.

We measure the performance in two metrics: *micro-average* and *macro-average*. Whereas micro method is considered to be a measurement for the quality of all the predictions altogether, macro stands for the performance of predictions per each task. Note that the average is calculated over the number of latent entities to extract.

Among the one-vs-all possible methods (Section 4), the most successful method, in terms of macro metric, is the bag-of-words & SVM model (section 4.1). At first sight, it could be surprising that such a simple approach outperforms more sophisticated methods, and mainly the deep-learning techniques. We speculate that this is an outcome of the data-set imbalance. That imbalance holds in the sense that different entities could occur in different frequencies in data examples. For example, there are quite many training examples of

ATP and ADP (both are involved in more than 14% of the reactions), while other entities may be significantly less frequent (e.g. Oxygen, NADPH, NADP+ and more occurs in less than 3% of the reactions). Therefore, many classes of entities have very little training examples. This does not allow deep-learning models to train well, and therefore the macro score of SVM methods tends to be higher. The reason the SVM with BOW performs better than the more semantic embeddings (Section 4.2–4.4) with SVM might also be due to the low amount of training examples that cause the contribution of semantics to be limited for the LEE task in this dataset.

The vanilla multi-task approach as described in Section 5.1, performs well according to micro-averaging metric, but fails in terms of macro measurement.

Ultimately, our proposed multi-task GRU based model with task-grouping (Section 5.2), outperforms all other baselines in both metrics: micro and macro. Thus, not only generally extracting entities with high performance, but also preserving fairness among different prediction tasks. We conclude that selecting the tasks to learn together in the a multi-task approach is critical for the LEE task.

Further, we present Area Under the Curve (AUC) scores of performance per entity, for top frequent entities in the dataset in Table 3. The results are shown for the two best performing classifiers (bag-of-words embedding with SVM classi-

Model	Precision	Recall	F1
Bag-of-Words (TF-IDF) & SVM (Section 4.1)	0.803	0.873	0.837
Weighted-average Embedding & SVM (Section 4.2)	0.770	0.746	0.758
Element-wise Document Embedding & SVM (Section 4.3)	0.817	0.817	0.817
Combined Document Embedding & SVM (Section 4.4)	0.823	0.810	0.816
Pre-Trained PubMed Word Embedding & Bi-LSTM (Section 4.5)	0.888	0.867	0.877
Pre-Trained PubMed Word Embedding & Bi-GRU (Section 4.5)	0.899	0.836	0.866
Multitask - Embedding based Bi-GRU (Section 5.1)	0.869	**0.883**	0.876
Multitask - Embedding based Bi-LSTM (Section 5.1)	0.869	**0.883**	0.876
Multitask with Grouping - Embedding based Bi-LSTM (Section 5.2)	0.909	0.859	**0.884**
Multitask with Grouping - Embedding based Bi-GRU (Section 5.2)	**0.914**	0.828	0.869

Table 2: Extraction of ATP as a latent entity. Statistically significant results are shown in bold.

Entity	Bag-of-Words AUC	Grouped-MTL AUC
ATP	0.906	**0.938**
ADP	0.910	**0.965**
H2O	0.864	**0.928**
PI	0.872	**0.937**
H+	**0.924**	0.889
O2	0.904	**0.928**
NADPH	0.917	**0.998**
NADP+	0.918	**0.972**
COA-SH	0.960	**0.998**

Table 3: AUC scores for bag-of-words vectors & SVM baseline performance compared to the multi-task learner with task-grouping. The results are shown for top frequent entities in the data set. Statistically significant results are shown in bold.

fication and multi task with grouping).

6.3 Multi-Task Approach Contribution in Multiple Latent Entity Extraction

It should be noted that multi-task learning approach is much more effective in the multiple latent entity extraction (Table 4) compared to the single latent entity extraction case (Table 2). Specifically, multi-task learning approach along with task-grouping performs much better than the other baselines. Naturally, the wins are significant in terms of macro-metric, as our loss-function (as defined in Section 5.2) is aimed for macro optimization. However, we notice that the method also improves performance in terms of micro-metric. To motivate this, consider an example of a sentence with water as a latent entity. Let us assume water is not appearing many times in the corpora, but appears many times in the data with Oxygen. As water is not appearing in many sentences it would be hard to learn indicative features in a sentence to predict it. However, in many cases it is possible to infer Oxygen. The prior of having an Oxygen as latent entity in the sentence can be considered as an indicative feature that also helps to predict water as a latent entity. As those entities do not appear many times in the corpus, learning the indicative features for a multi-task learner is hard. However, when only grouping relevant entities, we then overcome this issue and scores are improved.

Table 2 provides results on the extraction of the ATP entity only, which is the most common latent entity in the Reactome dataset. Since there are many training examples for this entity in the corpus (most frequent latent entity), it is possible to learn indicative features even in non-multitask models, which therefore perform well. Thus, there is a small difference between multitask and non-multitask approaches in Table 2. On the other hand, in Table 4 we examine the performance over the top-40 frequent entities, including very frequent entities (such ATP and ADP), and less frequent (such Oxygen, NADPH, NADP+ and water) as well. This leads to the results over all entities both frequent and infrequent to be much better in multitask learning settings with task-grouping specifically.

6.4 Qualitative Examples

To help understand the LEE problem, we present several examples of prominent words that contribute to the prediction of a latent entity. We leverage LIME algorithm (Ribeiro et al., 2016) to explain the multi task learning algorithm and present feature importance for ATP and NADPH in Figure 4.

The model inferred that words such as *phosphorylation* or *phosphorylates* are good indicators for the existence of ATP. Phosphorylation is the process through which a phosphate group, which is usually provided by ATP, is transferred from one

Model	micro			macro		
	Prec.	**Rec.**	**F1**	**Prec.**	**Rec.**	**F1**
Bag-of-Words (TF-IDF) & SVM (Section 4.1)	0.784	0.746	0.795	0.785	0.750	0.754
Weighted-average Embedding & SVM (Section 4.2)	0.682	0.649	0.665	0.636	0.565	0.580
Element-wise Document Embedding & SVM (Section 4.3)	0.740	0.728	0.734	0.696	0.647	0.648
Combined Document Embedding & SVM (Section 4.4)	0.743	0.729	0.736	0.707	0.651	0.656
Pre-Trained PubMed Word Embedding & Bi-LSTM (Section 4.5)	0.817	0.773	0.794	0.707	0.645	0.664
Pre-Trained PubMed Word Embedding & Bi-GRU (Section 4.5)	0.798	0.817	0.808	0.707	0.690	0.687
Multitask - Embedding based Bi-GRU (Section 5.1)	0.798	0.820	0.809	0.671	0.664	0.662
Multitask & Task-Grouping - Embedding based Bi-GRU (Section 5.2)	**0.822**	**0.849**	**0.835**	**0.809**	**0.839**	**0.811**

Table 4: Results of multiple latent entities extraction of top 40 frequent entities. Left side is *micro* metric based, while the right side is according to *macro* metric. Statistically significant results are shown in bold.

molecule to a protein.

To infer NADPH, the algorithm gives a high importance to the words P450 and reductase. Cytochrome P450 are proteins that use a variety of molecules as substrates in enzymatic reactions. They usually serve as oxidase enzymes in electron transfer chains. One of the common system they are involved in are microsomal P450 systems, where electrons are transferred from NADPH via cytochrome P450 reductase.

Weight	Feature
0.0939	phosphorylation
0.0741	phosphorylates
0.0534	kinase
0.0449	phosphorylate
0.0273	autophosphorylation
0.0214	synthetase
0.0184	serine
0.0181	activation loop
0.0181	binds
0.0170	phosphorylated

(a) ATP Extraction Top Features

Weight	Feature
0.0609	p450
0.0369	reductase
0.0357	atral trans
0.0341	cytochrome
0.0319	oxidation
0.0308	arachidonic
0.0307	associated endoplasmic
0.0302	estradiol
0.0294	nadp
0.0289	p450s

(b) NADPH Extraction Top Features

Figure 4: An example of prominent words when inferring latent entities.

7 Conclusions

In this paper, we presented a new task of latent entities extraction from text, which gives a new insight over the original named-entity recognition task. Specifically, we focus on how to extract an entity when it is not explicitly mentioned in the text, but rather implicitly mentioned in the context.

We developed several methods to detect existence of such entities in texts, and present a large labeled dataset for exploring the LEE task, and perform an extensive evaluation of our methods. We explore one-vs-all methods with several methods to embed the text and a multi-task learning approach that attempts to predict several entities at once. We observe that learning *highly-relevant* entities together when during LEE prediction substantially boosts detection performance. We present several explanations of the classification, as they are taken into account behind the scenes of the best-performing classifier for LEE.

For future work, we consider learning the LEE in an end-to-end fashion, learning to weight which tasks to group together to improve LEE.

We believe the LEE task would spur additional research in the field to improve NER when entities are implicitly mentioned and help better comprehend complex texts.

References

Antonios Anastasopoulos and David Chiang. 2018. Tied multitask learning for neural speech translation. *CoRR*, abs/1802.06655.

Sanjeev Arora, Yingyu Liang, and Tengyu Ma. 2017. A simple but tough-to-beat baseline for sentence embeddings.

Bogdan Babych and Anthony Hartley. 2003. Improving machine translation quality with automatic named entity recognition. In *Proceedings of the 7th International EAMT workshop on MT and other Language Technology Tools, Improving MT through other Language Technology Tools: Resources and Tools for Building MT*, pages 1–8. Association for Computational Linguistics.

Jonathan Berant and Peter Clark. 2014. Modeling Biological Processes for Reading Comprehension. *Proceedings of the 2014 Conference on Empirical Methods in Natural Language Processing (EMNLP)*, pages 1499–1510.

Rich Caruana. 1998. Multitask learning. In *Learning to learn*, pages 95–133. Springer.

Hsinchun Chen, Wingyan Chung, Jennifer Jie Xu, Gang Wang, Yi Qin, and Michael Chau. 2004. Crime data mining: a general framework and some examples. *computer*, 37(4):50–56.

Billy Chiu, Gamal Crichton, Anna Korhonen, and Sampo Pyysalo. 2016. How to Train Good Word Embeddings for Biomedical NLP. pages 166–174.

Jason Chiu and Eric Nichols. 2016. Named entity recognition with bidirectional lstm-cnns. *Transactions of the Association for Computational Linguistics*, 4:357–370.

Kyunghyun Cho, Bart van Merriënboer, Çalar Gülçehre, Dzmitry Bahdanau, Fethi Bougares, Holger Schwenk, and Yoshua Bengio. 2014. Learning phrase representations using rnn encoder–decoder for statistical machine translation. In *Proceedings of the 2014 Conference on Empirical Methods in Natural Language Processing (EMNLP)*, pages 1724–1734, Doha, Qatar. Association for Computational Linguistics.

Corinna Cortes and Vladimir Vapnik. 1995. Support-vector networks. *Machine learning*, 20(3):273–297.

David Croft, Gavin O 'kelly, Guanming Wu, Robin Haw, Marc Gillespie, Lisa Matthews, Michael Caudy, Phani Garapati, Gopal Gopinath, Bijay Jassal, Steven Jupe, Irina Kalatskaya, Shahana Mahajan, Bruce May, Nelson Ndegwa, Esther Schmidt, Veronica Shamovsky, Christina Yung, Ewan Birney, Henning Hermjakob, Peter D 'eustachio, and Lincoln Stein. Reactome: a database of reactions, pathways and biological processes.

Cedric De Boom, Steven Van Canneyt, Thomas Demeester, and Bart Dhoedt. 2016. Representation learning for very short texts using weighted word embedding aggregation. *Pattern Recognition Letters*, 80(C):150–156.

Tobias Domhan and Felix Hieber. 2017. Using target-side monolingual data for neural machine translation through multi-task learning. In *Proceedings of the 2017 Conference on Empirical Methods in Natural Language Processing*, pages 1500–1505.

Theodoros Evgeniou and Massimiliano Pontil. 2004. Regularized multi–task learning. In *Proceedings of the tenth ACM SIGKDD international conference on Knowledge discovery and data mining*, pages 109–117. ACM.

Yarin Gal and Zoubin Ghahramani. 2016. A theoretically grounded application of dropout in recurrent neural networks. In *Advances in neural information processing systems*, pages 1019–1027.

Kavita Ganesan, ChengXiang Zhai, and Jiawei Han. 2010. Opinosis: A graph-based approach to abstractive summarization of highly redundant opinions. pages 340–348.

Sepp Hochreiter and Jürgen Schmidhuber. 1997. Long short-term memory. *Neural computation*, 9(8):1735–1780.

Eduard Hovy, Mitchell Marcus, Martha Palmer, Lance Ramshaw, and Ralph Weischedel. 2006. Ontonotes: the 90% solution. In *Proceedings of the human language technology conference of the NAACL, Companion Volume: Short Papers*, pages 57–60. Association for Computational Linguistics.

Masaru Isonuma, Toru Fujino, Junichiro Mori, Yutaka Matsuo, and Ichiro Sakata. 2017. Extractive summarization using multi-task learning with document classification. In *Proceedings of the 2017 Conference on Empirical Methods in Natural Language Processing*, pages 2101–2110.

Jun-Yong Jeong and Chi-Hyuck Jun. 2018. Variable selection and task grouping for multi-task learning. *arXiv preprint arXiv:1802.04676*.

Diederik P. Kingma and Jimmy Ba. 2014. Adam: A method for stochastic optimization. *CoRR*, abs/1412.6980.

Sulin Liu and Sinno Jialin Pan. 2017. Adaptive group sparse multi-task learning via trace lasso. In *Proceedings of the 26th International Joint Conference on Artificial Intelligence*, pages 2358–2364. AAAI Press.

Mónica Marrero, Julián Urbano, Sonia Sánchez-Cuadrado, Jorge Morato, and Juan Miguel Gómez-Berbís. 2013. Named entity recognition: fallacies, challenges and opportunities. *Computer Standards & Interfaces*, 35(5):482–489.

Alexandre Passos, Vineet Kumar, and Andrew D McCallum. 2014. Lexicon infused phrase embeddings for named entity resolution. In *CoNLL*.

Sameer Pradhan, Alessandro Moschitti, Nianwen Xue, Hwee Tou Ng, Anders Björkelund, Olga Uryupina, Yuchen Zhang, and Zhi Zhong. 2013. Towards robust linguistic analysis using ontonotes. In *Proceedings of the Seventeenth Conference on Computational Natural Language Learning*, pages 143–152.

Piyush Rai and Hal Daume III. 2010. Infinite predictor subspace models for multitask learning. In *Proceedings of the Thirteenth International Conference on Artificial Intelligence and Statistics*, pages 613–620.

Lev Ratinov and Dan Roth. 2009. Design challenges and misconceptions in named entity recognition. In *Proceedings of the Thirteenth Conference on Computational Natural Language Learning*, pages 147–155. Association for Computational Linguistics.

Marco Tulio Ribeiro, Sameer Singh, and Carlos Guestrin. 2016. Why should i trust you?: Explaining the predictions of any classifier. In *Proceedings of the 22nd ACM SIGKDD International Conference on Knowledge Discovery and Data Mining*, pages 1135–1144. ACM.

Mike Schuster and Kuldip K Paliwal. 1997. Bidirectional recurrent neural networks. *IEEE Transactions on Signal Processing*, 45(11):2673–2681.

Nitish Srivastava, Geoffrey Hinton, Alex Krizhevsky, Ilya Sutskever, and Ruslan Salakhutdinov. 2014. Dropout: A simple way to prevent neural networks from overfitting. *The Journal of Machine Learning Research*, 15(1):1929–1958.

Erik F Tjong Kim Sang and Fien De Meulder. 2003. Introduction to the conll-2003 shared task: Language-independent named entity recognition. In *Proceedings of the seventh conference on Natural language learning at HLT-NAACL 2003-Volume 4*, pages 142–147. Association for Computational Linguistics.

Shi Zhong, Jian Pu, Yu-Gang Jiang, Rui Feng, and Xiangyang Xue. 2016. Flexible multi-task learning with latent task grouping. *Neurocomputing*, 189:179–188.

Generalizing Procrustes Analysis for Better Bilingual Dictionary Induction

Yova Kementchedjhieva[◇]   Sebastian Ruder[♠♣]   Ryan Cotterell[♡]   Anders Søgaard[◇]
[◇]University of Copenhagen, Copenhagen, Denmark
[♠]Insight Research Centre, National University of Ireland, Galway, Ireland
[♣]Aylien Ltd., Dublin, Ireland
[♡]University of Cambridge, Cambridge, UK
`{yova|soegaard}@di.ku.dk`, `sebastian@ruder.io`, `ryan.cotterell@gmail.com`,

Abstract

Most recent approaches to bilingual dictionary induction find a linear alignment between the word vector spaces of two languages. We show that projecting the two languages onto a third, latent space, rather than directly onto each other, while equivalent in terms of expressivity, makes it easier to learn approximate alignments. Our modified approach also allows for supporting languages to be included in the alignment process, to obtain an even better performance in low resource settings.

1 Introduction

Several papers recently demonstrated the potential of very weakly supervised or entirely unsupervised approaches to bilingual dictionary induction (BDI) (Barone, 2016; Artetxe et al., 2017; Zhang et al., 2017; Conneau et al., 2018; Søgaard et al., 2018), the task of identifying translational equivalents across two languages. These approaches cast BDI as a problem of aligning monolingual word embeddings. Pairs of monolingual word vector spaces can be aligned without any explicit cross-lingual supervision, solely based on their distributional properties (for an adversarial approach, see Conneau et al. (2018)). Alternatively, weak supervision can be provided in the form of numerals (Artetxe et al., 2017) or identically spelled words (Søgaard et al., 2018). Successful unsupervised or weakly supervised alignment of word vector spaces would remove much of the data bottleneck for machine translation and push horizons for cross-lingual learning (Ruder et al., 2018).

In addition to an unsupervised approach to aligning monolingual word embedding spaces with adversarial training, Conneau et al. (2018) present a supervised alignment algorithm that assumes a gold-standard seed dictionary and performs Procrustes Analysis (Schönemann, 1966).

Søgaard et al. (2018) show that this approach, weakly supervised with a dictionary seed of *cross-lingual homographs*, i.e. words with identical spelling across source and target language, is superior to the completely unsupervised approach. We therefore focus on weakly-supervised Procrustes Analysis (PA) for BDI here.

The implementation of PA in Conneau et al. (2018) yields notable improvements over earlier work on BDI, even though it learns a simple linear transform of the source language space into the target language space. Seminal work in supervised alignment of word vector spaces indeed reported superior performance with linear models as compared to non-linear neural approaches (Mikolov et al., 2013). The relative success of the simple linear approach can be explained in terms of isomorphism across monolingual semantic spaces,[1] an idea that receives support from cognitive science (Youn et al., 1999). Word vector spaces are not *perfectly* isomorphic, however, as shown by Søgaard et al. (2018), who use a Laplacian graph similarity metric to measure this property. In this work, we show that projecting both source and target vector spaces into a *third* space (Faruqui and Dyer, 2014), using a variant of PA known as Generalized Procrustes Analysis (Gower, 1975), makes it easier to learn the alignment between two word vector spaces, as compared to the single linear transform used in Conneau et al. (2018).

Contributions We show that Generalized Procrustes Analysis (GPA) (Gower, 1975), a method that maps two vector spaces into a third, latent space, is superior to PA for BDI, e.g., improving the state-of-the-art on the widely used English-Italian dataset (Dinu et al., 2015) from a P@1 score of 66.2% to 67.6%. We compare GPA to PA

---

[1]Two vector spaces are isomorphic if there is an invertible linear transformation from one to the other.

Proceedings of the 22nd Conference on Computational Natural Language Learning (CoNLL 2018), pages 211–220
Brussels, Belgium, October 31 - November 1, 2018. ©2018 Association for Computational Linguistics

on aligning English with five languages representing different language families (Arabic, German, Spanish, Finnish, and Russian), showing that GPA consistently outperforms PA. GPA also allows for the use of additional support languages, aligning three or more languages at a time, which can boost performance even further. We present experiments with multi-source GPA on an additional five low-resource languages from the same language families (Hebrew, Afrikaans, Occitan, Estonian, and Bosnian), using their bigger counterpart as a support language. Our code is publicly available.[2]

2 Procrustes Analysis

Procrustes Analysis is a graph matching algorithm, used in most mapping-based approaches to BDI (Ruder et al., 2018). Given two graphs, E and F, Procrustes finds the linear transformation T that minimizes the following objective:

$$\arg\min_{T} \ ||TE - F||^2 \tag{1}$$

thus minimizing the trace between each two corresponding rows of the transformed space TE and F. We build E and F based on a seed dictionary of N entries, such that each pair of corresponding rows in E and F, (e_n, f_n) for $n = 1, \ldots, N$ consists of the embeddings of a translational pair of words. In order to preserve the monolingual quality of the transformed embeddings, it is beneficial to use an orthogonal matrix T for cross-lingual mapping purposes (Xing et al., 2015; Artetxe et al., 2017). Conveniently, the orthogonal Procrustes problem has an analytical solution, based on Singular Value Decomposition (SVD):

$$\begin{aligned} F^{\top}E &= U\Sigma V^{\top} \\ T &= VU^{\top} \end{aligned} \tag{2}$$

3 Generalized Procrustes Analysis

Generalized Procrustes Analysis (Gower, 1975) is a natural extension of PA that aligns k vector spaces at a time. Given embedding spaces $E_1, \ldots, E_k$, GPA minimizes the following objective:

$$\arg\min_{\{T_1,\ldots,T_k\}} \sum_{i<j}^{k} ||T_iE_i - T_jE_j)||^2 \tag{3}$$

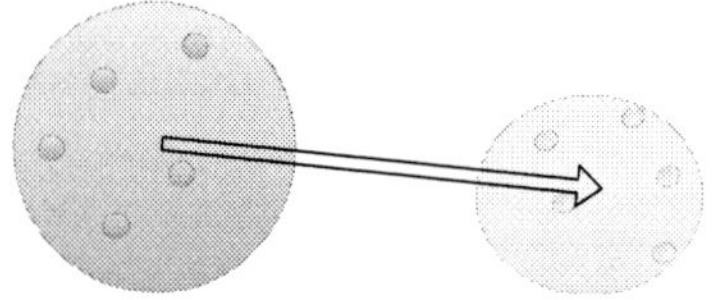

(a) Procrustes Analysis

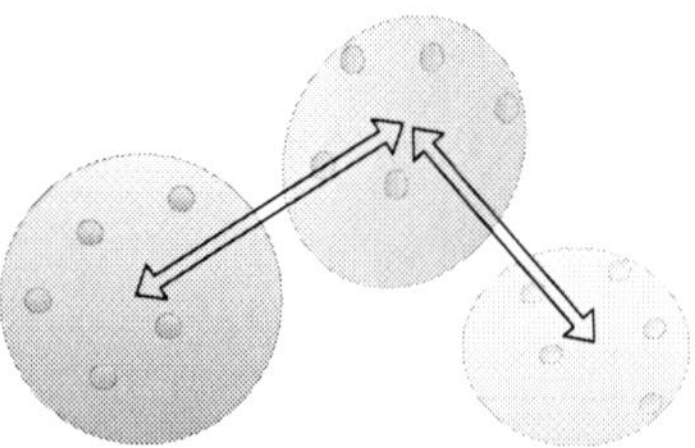

(b) Generalized Procrustes Analysis

Figure 1: Visualization of the difference between PA, which maps the source space directly onto the target space, and GPA, which aligns both source and target spaces with a third, latent space, constructed by averaging over the two language spaces.

For an analytical solution to GPA, we compute the average of the embedding matrices $E_{1\ldots k}$ after transformation by $T_{1\ldots k}$:

$$G = k^{-1} \sum_{i=1}^{k} E_i T_i \tag{4}$$

thus obtaining a latent space, G, which captures properties of each of $E_{1\ldots k}$, and potentially additional properties emerging from the combination of the spaces. On the very first iteration, prior to having any estimates of $T_{1\ldots k}$, we set $G = E_i$ for a random i. The new values of $T_{1\ldots k}$ are then obtained as:

$$\begin{aligned} G^{\top}E_i &= U\Sigma V^{\top} \\ T_i &= VU^{\top} \text{ for } i \text{ in } 1\ldots k \end{aligned} \tag{5}$$

Since G is dependent on $T_{1\ldots k}$ (see Eq.4), the solution of GPA cannot be obtained in a single step (as is the case with PA), but rather requires that we loop over subsequent updates of G (Eq.4) and $T_{1\ldots k}$ (Eq.5) for a fixed number of steps or until satisfactory convergence. We observed little improvement when performing more than 100 updates, so we fixed that as the number of updates.

Notice that for $k = 2$ and with the orthogonality constraint in place, the objective for Generalized Procrustes Analysis (Eq. 3) reduces to that for

212

High-resource	AR	DE	ES	FI	RU
	575k	2,183k	1,412k	437k	1,474k
Low-resource	HE	AF	OC	ET	BS
	224k	49k	84k	175k	77k

Table 1: Statistics for Wikipedia corpora.

simple Procrustes (Eq. 1):

$$\arg \min_{\{T_1, T_2\}} ||T_1 E_1 - T_2 E_2||^2$$
$$= \arg \min_{T} ||T E_1 - E_2||^2 \qquad (6)$$
$$\text{where } T = T_1 T_2^T$$

Here T itself is also orthogonal. Yet, the solution found with GPA may differ from the one found with simple Procrustes: the former maps E_1 and E_2 onto a third space, G, which is the average of the two spaces, instead of mapping E_1 directly onto E_2. To understand the consequences of this difference, consider a single step of the GPA algorithm where after updating G according to Eq.4 we are recomputing T_1 using SVD. Due to the fact that G is partly based on E_1, these two spaces are bound to be more similar to each other than E_1 and E_2 are.[3] Finding a good mapping between E_1 and G, i.e. a good setting of T_1, should therefore be easier than finding a good mapping from E_1 to E_2 directly. In this sense, by mapping E_1 onto G, rather than onto E_2 (as PA would do), we are solving an easier problem and reducing the chance of a poor solution.

4 Experiments

In our experiments, we generally use the same hyper-parameters as used in Conneau et al. (2018), unless otherwise stated. When extracting dictionaries for the bootstrapping procedure, we use cross-domain local scaling (CSLS, see Conneau et al. (2018) for details) as a metric for ranking candidate translation pairs, and we only use the ones that rank higher than 15,000. We do not put any restrictions on the initial seed dictionaries, based on cross-lingual homographs: those vary considerably in size, from 17,012 for Hebrew to 85,912 for Spanish. Instead of doing a single training epoch, however, we run PA and GPA with early stopping, until five epochs of no improvement in the validation criterion as used in Conneau

et al. (2018), i.e. the average cosine similarity between the top 10,000 most frequent words in the source language and their candidate translations as induced with CSLS. Our metric is Precision at $k \times 100$ (P@k), i.e. percentage of correct translations retrieved among the k nearest neighbor of the source words in the test set (Conneau et al., 2018). Unless stated otherwise, experiments were carried out using the publicly available pre-trained fastText embeddings, trained on Wikipedia data,[4] and bilingual dictionaries—consisting of 5000 and 1500 unique word pairs for training and testing, respectively—provided by Conneau et al. (2018)[5].

4.1 Comparison of PA and GPA

High resource setting We first present a direct comparison of PA and GPA on BDI from English to five fairly high-resource languages: Arabic, Finnish, German, Russian, and Spanish. The Wikipedia corpus sizes for these languages are reported in Table 1. **Results** are listed in Table 2. GPA improves over PA consistently for all five languages. Most notably, for Finnish it scores 2.5% higher than PA.

Common benchmarks For a more extensive comparison with previous work, we include results on English–{Finnish, German, Italian} dictionaries used in Conneau et al. (2018) and Artetxe et al. (2018)—the second best approach to BDI known to us, which also uses Procrustes Analysis. We conduct experiments using three forms of supervision: gold-standard seed dictionaries of 5000 word pairs, cross-lingual homographs, and numerals. We use train and test bilingual dictionaries from Dinu et al. (2015) for English-Italian and from Artetxe et al. (2017) for English-{Finnish, German}. Following Conneau et al. (2018), we report results with a set of CBOW embeddings trained on the WaCky corpus (Barone, 2016), and with Wikipedia embeddings.

Results are reported in Table 3. We observe that GPA outperforms PA consistently on Italian and German with the WaCky embeddings, and on all languages with the Wikipedia embeddings. Notice that once more, Finnish benefits the most from a switch to GPA in the Wikipedia embeddings setting, but it is also the only language to suffer from

---

[3]A theoretical exception being the case there E_1 and E_2 are identical.

[4]`https://github.com/facebookresearch/fastText`

[5]`https://github.com/facebookresearch/MUSE`

	AR		DE		ES		FI		RU		Ave	
	$k=1$	$k=10$	$k=1$	$k=10$	$k=1$	$k=10$	$k=1$	$k=10$	$k=1$	$k=10$	$k=1$	$k=10$
PA	34.73	61.87	73.67	91.73	81.67	92.93	45.33	75.53	47.00	79.00	56.48	80.21
GPA	**35.33**	**64.27**	**74.40**	**91.93**	**81.93**	**93.53**	**47.87**	**76.87**	**48.27**	**79.13**	**57.56**	**81.15**

Table 2: Bilingual dictionary induction performance, measured in P@k, of PA and GPA across five language pairs.

	IT			DE			FI		
	5000	Identical	Numerals	5000	Identical	Numerals	5000	Identical	Numerals
					WACKY				
Artetxe et al. (2018)	45.27*	38.33	39.40*	44.27*	40.73	40.27*	32.94*	27.39	26.47*
PA	44.90	45.47	01.13	47.26	47.20	45.93	**33.50**	**31.46**	01.05
GPA	**45.33**	**45.80**	**45.93**	**48.46**	**47.60**	**47.60**	31.39	31.04	**28.93**
					WIKIPEDIA				
PA	66.24	66.39	-	65.33	64.77	-	36.77	35.40	-
GPA	**67.60**	**67.14**	-	**66.21**	**65.81**	-	**38.14**	**37.87**	-

Table 3: Results on standard benchmarks, measured in P@1. * Results as reported in the original paper. **Notes:** Conneau et al. (2018) report 63.7 on Italian with Wikipedia embeddings; results with different embedding sets are not comparable due to a non-zero out-of-vocabulary rate on the test set for Wikipedia embeddings; Wikipedia embeddings are trained on corpora with removed numerals, so supervision from numerals cannot be applied.

that switch in the WaCky setup.

Interestingly, PA fails to learn a good alignment for Italian and Finnish when supervised with numerals, while GPA performs comparably with numerals as with other forms of supervision. Conneau et al. (2018) point out that improvement from subsequent iterations of PA is generally negligible, which we also found to be the case. We also found that while PA learned a slightly poorer alignment than GPA, it did so faster. With our criterion for early stopping, PA converged in 5 to 10 epochs, while GPA did so within 10 to 15 epochs[6] . In the case of Italian and Finnish alignment supervised by numerals, PA converged in 8 and 5 epochs, respectively, but clearly got stuck in local minima. GPA took considerably longer to converge: 27 and 74 epochs, respectively, but also managed to find a reasonable alignment between the language spaces. This points to an important difference in the learning properties of PA and GPA—unlike PA, GPA has a two-fold objective of opposing forces: it is simultaneously aligning each embedding space to two others, thus pulling it in different directions. This characteristic helps GPA avoid particularly adverse local minima.

4.2 Multi-support GPA

In these experiments, we perform GPA with $k = 3$, including a third, linguistically-related supporting language in the alignment process. To best evaluate the benefits of the multi-support setup, we use as targets five low-resource languages: Afrikaans, Bosnian, Estonian, Hebrew and Occitan (see statistics in Table 1)[7]. Three-way dictionaries, both the initial one (consisting of cross-lingual homographs) and subsequent ones, are obtained by assuming transitivity between two-way dictionaries: if two pairs of words, e^m–e^n and e^m–e^l, are deemed translational pairs, then we consider e^n–e^m–e^l a translational triple.

We report **results** in Table 4 with multi-support GPA in two settings: a three-way alignment trained for 10 epochs (MGPA), and a three-way alignment trained for 10 epochs, followed by 5 epochs of two-way fine-tuning (MGPA+). We observe that at least one of our new methods always improves over PA. GPA always outperforms PA and it also outperforms the multi-support settings on three out of five languages. Yet, results for Hebrew and especially for Occitan, are best in a

---

[6]Notice that one epoch with both PA and GPA takes less than half a minute, so the slower convergence of GPA is in no way prohibitive.

[7]Occitan dictionaries were not available from the MUSE project, so we extracted a test dictionary of 911 unique word pairs from an English-Occitan lexicon available at `http://www.occitania.online.fr/aqui.comenca.occitania/en-oc.html`.

	AF		BS		ET		HE		OC		Ave	
	$k=1$	$k=10$	$k=1$	$k=10$	$k=1$	$k=10$	$k=1$	$k=10$	$k=1$	$k=10$	$k=1$	$k=10$
PA	28.87	50.53	22.40	48.40	30.00	57.93	37.53	67.27	17.12	33.26	27.18	51.48
GPA	**29.93**	**50.67**	**24.20**	**50.20**	**31.87**	**60.07**	38.93	**68.93**	17.12	34.91	28.41	52.96
MGPA	28.93	49.20	21.00	48.60	30.73	59.53	37.53	66.47	**23.82**	**40.18**	28.40	52.80
MGPA$^+$	28.80	49.20	23.46	48.87	31.27	59.80	**40.40**	68.80	22.83	38.53	**29.35**	**53.04**

Table 4: Results for low-resource languages with PA, GPA and two multi-support settings.

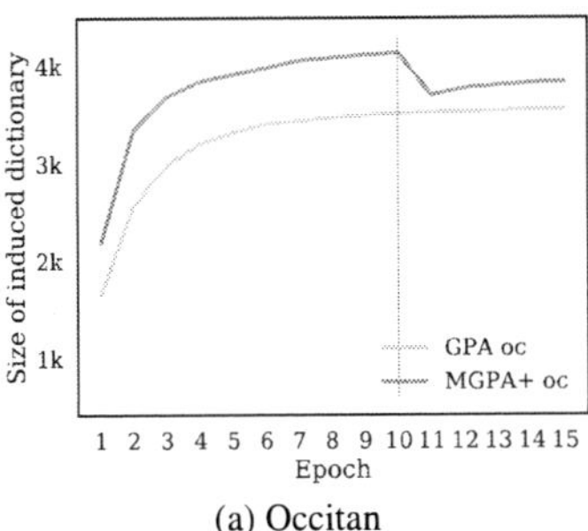

(a) Occitan

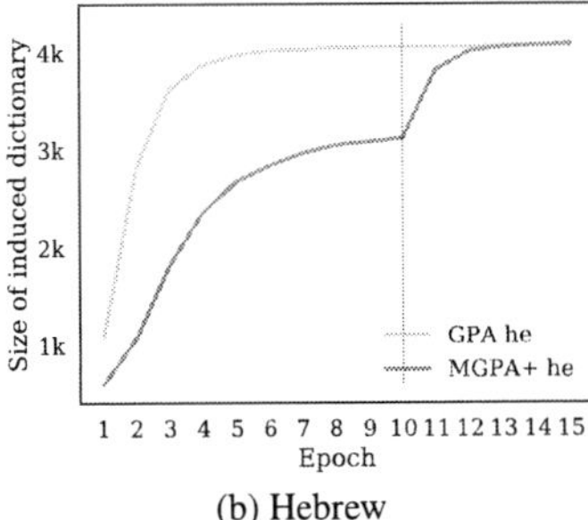

(b) Hebrew

Figure 2: Progression of dictionary size during GPA and MGPA+ training. The dotted line marks the boundary between MGPA and fine-tuning.

multi-support setting—we thus mostly focus on these two languages in the following subsections.

MGPA has variable performance: for four languages precision suffers from the addition of a third language, e.g. compare 38.93 for Hebrew with GPA to 37.53 with MGPA; for Occitan, however, the most challenging target language in our experiments, MGPA beats all other approaches by a large margin: 17.12 with GPA versus 23.81 with MGPA. This pattern relates to the effect a supporting language has on the size of the induced seed dictionary. Figure 2 visualizes the progression of dictionary size during training with and without a supporting language for Occitan and Hebrew. The portion of the purple curves to the left of the dotted line corresponds to MGPA: notice how the curves are swapped between the two plots. Spanish *actually* provides support for the

English-Occitan alignment, by contributing to an increasingly larger seed dictionary—this provides better anchoring for the learned alignment. Having Arabic as support for English-Hebrew alignment, on the other hand, causes a considerable reduction in the size of the seed dictionaries, giving GPA less anchor points and thus damaging the learned alignment. The variable effect of a supporting language on dictionary size, and consequently on alignment precision, relates to the quality of alignment of the support language with English and with the target language: referring back to Table 2, English-Spanish, for example, scores at 81.93, while English-Arabic precision is 35.33. Notice that despite our linguistically-motivated choice to pair related low- and high-resource languages for multi-support training, it is not necessarily the case that those should align especially well, as that would also depend on practical factors, such as embeddings quality and training corpora similarity (Søgaard et al., 2018).

MGPA+ applies two-way fine-tuning on top of MGPA. This leads to a drop in precision for Occitan, due to the removed support of Spanish and the consequent reduction in size of the induced dictionary (observe the fall of the purple curve after the dotted line in Figure 2 (a)). Meanwhile, precision for Hebrew is highest with MGPA+ out of all methods included. While Arabic itself is not a good support language, its presence in the three-way MGPA alignment seems to have resulted in a good initialization for the English-Hebrew two-way fine-tuning, thus helping the model reach an even better minimum along the loss curve.

5 Discussion: Why it works

If word vector spaces were completely isomorphic, the introduction of a third (or fourth) space, and the application of GPA, would lead to the same alignment as the alignment learned by PA, projecting the source language E into the target space F. This follows from the transitivity of isomorphism: if E is isomorphic to G and G is isomorphic to F, then E is isomorphic to F, via the isomorphism obtained by composing the isomorphisms from E to G and from G to F. So why do we observe improvements?

Søgaard et al. (2018) have shown that word vector spaces are often relatively far from being isomorphic, and approximate isomorphism is not transitive. What we observe therefore appears to be an instance of the Poincaré Paradox (Poincaré, 1902). While GPA is not more expressive than PA, it may still be easier to align each monolingual space to an intermediate space, as the latter constitutes a more similar target (albeit a non-isomorphic one); for example, the loss landscape of aligning a source and target language word embedding with an average of the two may be much smoother than when aligning source directly with target. Our work is in this way similar in spirit to Raiko et al. (2012), who use simple linear transforms to make learning of non-linear problems easier.

5.1 Error Analysis

Table 5 lists example translational pairs as induced from alignments between English and Bosnian, learned with PA, GPA and MGPA+. For interpretability, we query the system with words in Bosnian and seek their nearest neighbors in the English embedding space. P@1 over the Bosnian-English test set of Conneau et al. (2018) is 31.33, 34.80, and 34.47 for PA, GPA and MGPA+, respectively. The examples are grouped in three blocks, based on success and failure of PA and GPA alignments to retrieve a valid translation.

It appears that a lot of the difference in performance between PA and GPA concerns **morphologically related words**, e.g. *campaign* v. *campaigning, dialogue* v. *dialogues, merger* v. *merging* etc. These word pairs are naturally confusing to a BDI system, due to their related meaning and possibly identical syntactic properties (e.g. *merger* and *merging* can both be nouns). Another common mistake we observed in mismatches between PA and GPA predictions, was the wrong choice between two **antonyms**, e.g. *stable* v. *unstable* and *visible* v. *unnoticeable*. Distributional word representations are known to suffer from limitations with respect to capturing opposition of meaning (Mohammad et al., 2013), so it is not surprising that both PA- and GPA-learned alignments can

fail in making this distinction. While it is not the case that GPA always outperforms PA on a query-to-query basis in these rather challenging cases, on average GPA appears to learn an alignment more robust to subtle morphological and semantic differences between neighboring words. Still, there are cases where PA and GPA both choose the wrong morphological variant of an otherwise correctly identified target word, e.g. *transformation* v. *transformations*.

Notice that many of the queries for which both algorithms fail, do result in a **nearly synonymous word** being predicted, e.g. *participant* for *attendee, earns* for *gets, footage* for *video*, etc. This serves to show that the learned alignments are generally good, but they are not sufficiently precise. This issue can have two sources: a suboptimal method for learning the alignment and/or a ceiling effect on how good of an alignment can be obtained, within the space of orthogonal linear transformations.

5.2 Procrustes fit

To explore the latter issue and to further compare the capabilities of PA and GPA, we perform a *Procrustes fit* test, where we learn alignments in a fully supervised fashion, using the test dictionaries of Conneau et al. (2018)[8] for both training *and* evaluation[9]. In the ideal case, i.e. if the subspaces defined by the words in the seed dictionaries are perfectly alignable, this setup should result in precision of 100%.

We found the difference between the fit with PA and GPA to be negligible, 0.20 on average across all 10 languages (5 low-resource and 5 high-source languages). It is not surprising that PA and GPA results in almost equivalent fits—the two algorithms both rely on linear transformations, i.e. they are equal in expressivity. As pointed out earlier, the superiority of GPA over PA stems from its more robust learning procedure, not from higher expressivity. Figure 3 thus only visualizes the Procrustes fit as obtained with GPA.

The Procrustes fit of all languages is indeed lower than 100%, showing that there is a **ceiling on the linear alignability** between the source and target spaces. We attribute this ceiling ef-

---

[8]For Occitan, we use our own test dictionary.

[9]In this experiment, we only run a single epoch of each alignment algorithm, as that is guaranteed to give us the best Procrustes fit for the particular set of training word pairs we would then evaluate on.

	QUERY	GOLD	PA	GPA	MGPA+
PA ✗, GPA ✓	variraju	vary	varies	vary	varies
	kanjon	canyon	headwaters	canyon	headwaters
	dijalog	dialogue	dialogues	dialogue	dialogue
	izjava	statement	deniable	statement	statements
	plazme	plasma	conduction	plasma	microspheres
	raunari	computers	minicomputers	computers	mainframes
	aparat	apparatus	duplex	apparatus	apparatus
	sazvijea	constellations	asterisms	constellations	constellations
	uspostavljanje	establishing	reestablishing	establishing	establishing
	industrijska	industrial	industry	industrial	industrial
	stabilna	stable	unstable	stable	stable
	disertaciju	dissertation	habilitation	dissertation	thesis
	protivnici	opponents	opposing	opponents	opponents
	pozitivni	positive	negative	positive	positive
	instalacija	installation	installations	installation	installation
	duhana	tobacco	liquors	tobacco	tobacco
PA ✓, GPA ✗	hor	choir	choir	musicum	choir
	crijevo	intestine	intestine	intestines	intestine
	vidljiva	visible	visible	unnoticeable	visible
	temelja	foundations	foundations	superstructures	pillars
	kolonijalne	colonial	colonial	colonialists	colonialists
	spajanje	merger	merger	merging	merging
	suha	dry	dry	humid	dry
	janez	janez	janez	mariza	janez
	kampanju	campaign	campaign	campaigning	campaign
	migracije	migration	migration	migrations	migrations
	sobu	room	room	bathroom	bathroom
	predgrau	suburb	suburb	outskirts	suburb
	specijalno	specially	specially	specialist	specially
	hiv	hiv	hiv	meningococcal	hiv
	otkrije	discover	discover	discovers	discover
	proizlazi	arises	arises	differentiates	deriving
	tajno	secretly	secretly	confidentially	secretly
PA ✗, GPA ✗	odred	squad	reconnoitre	stragglers	skirmished
	uesnik	attendee	participant	participant	participant
	saznao	learned	confided	confided	confided
	dobiva	gets	earns	earns	earns
	harris	harris	guinn	zachary	zachary
	snimke	videos	footage	footages	footage
	usne	lips	ear	ear	toes
	ukinuta	lifted	abolished	abolished	abolished
	objave	posts	publish	publish	publish
	obiljeje	landmark	commemorates	commemorates	commemorates
	molim	please	appologize	thank	kindly
	vrste	solid	concretes	concretes	concretes
	intel	intel	genesys	motorola	transputer
	transformacije	transformations	transformation	transformation	transformation

Table 5: Example translations from Bosnian into English.

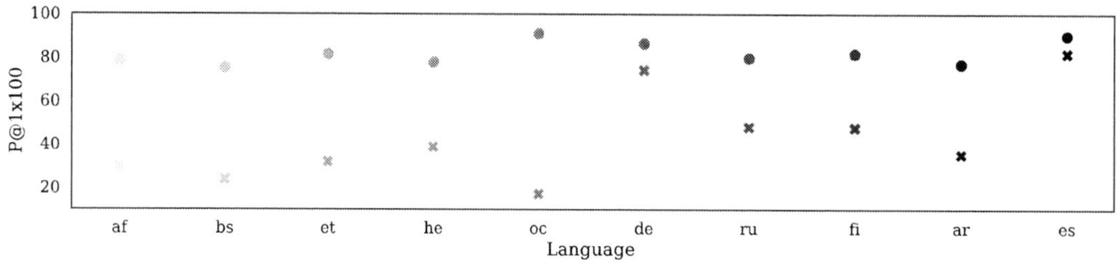

Figure 3: Procrustes fit test. Circles mark the results from fitting and evaluating GPA on the test dictionaries to measure the *Procrustes fit*. xs mark the weakly-supervised results reported in Tables 2 and 4.

fect to variable degrees of linguistic difference between source and target language and possibly to differences in the contents of cross-lingual Wikipedias (recall that the embeddings we use are trained on Wikipedia corpora). An apparent correlation emerges between the Procrustes fit and precision scores for weakly-supervised GPA, i.e. between the circles and the xs in the plot. The only language that does not conform here is Occitan, which has the highest Procrustes fit and the lowest GPA precision out of all languages, but this result has an important caveat: our dictionary for Occitan comes from a different source and is much smaller than all the other dictionaries.

For some of the high-resource languages, weakly-supervised GPA takes us rather close to the best possible fit: e.g. for Spanish GPA scores 81.93%, and the Procrustes fit is 90.07%. While low-resource languages do not necessarily have lower Procrustes fits than high-resource ones (compare Estonian and Finnish, for example), the gap between the Procrustes fit and GPA precision is on average much higher within low-resource languages than within high-resource ones (52.46^{10} compared to 25.47, respectively). This finding is in line with the common understanding that the quality of distributional word vectors depends on the amount of data available—we can infer from these results that suboptimal embeddings results in suboptimal cross-lingual alignments.

5.3 Multilinguality

Finally, we note that there may be specific advantages to including support languages for which large monolingual corpora exist, as those should, theoretically, be easier to align with English (also a high-resource language): variance in vector di-

rectionality, as studied in Mimno and Thompson (2017), increases with corpus size, so we would expect embedding spaces learned from corpora comparable in size, to also be more similar in shape.

6 Related work

Bilingual embeddings Many diverse cross-lingual word embedding models have been proposed (Ruder et al., 2018). The most popular kind learns a linear transformation from source to target language space (Mikolov et al., 2013). In most recent work, this mapping is constrained to be orthogonal and solved using Procrustes Analysis (Xing et al., 2015; Artetxe et al., 2017, 2018; Conneau et al., 2018; Lu et al., 2015). The approach most similar to ours, Faruqui and Dyer (2014), uses canonical correlation analysis (CCA) to project both source and target language spaces into a third, joint space. In this setup, similarly to GPA, the third space is iteratively updated, such that at timestep t, it is a product of the two language spaces as transformed by the mapping learned at timestep $t - 1$. The objective that drives the updates of the mapping matrices is to maximize the correlation between the projected embeddings of translational equivalents (where the latter are taken from a gold-standard seed dictionary). In their analysis of the transformed embedding spaces, Faruqui and Dyer (2014) focus on the improved quality of monolingual embedding spaces themselves and do not perform evaluation of the task of BDI. They find that the transformed monolingual spaces better encode the difference between synonyms and antonyms: in the original monolingual English space, synonyms and antonyms of *beautiful* are all mapped close to each other in a mixed fashion; in the transformed space the synonyms of *beautiful* are mapped in a clus-

---

[10]Even if we leave Occitan out as an outlier, this number is still rather high: 47.10.

ter around the query word and its antonyms are mapped in a separate cluster. This finding is in line with our observation that GPA-learned alignments are more precise in distinguishing between synonyms and antonyms.

Multilingual embeddings Several approaches extend existing methods to space alignments between more than two languages (Ammar et al., 2016; Ruder et al., 2018). Smith et al. (2017) project all vocabularies into the English space. In some cases, multilingual training has been shown to lead to improvements over bilingually trained embedding spaces (Vulić et al., 2017), similar to our findings.

7 Conclusion

Generalized Procrustes Analysis yields benefits over simple Procrustes Analysis for Bilingual Dictionary Induction, due to its smoother loss landscape. In line with earlier research, benefits from the introduction of a common latent space seem to relate to a better distinction of synonyms and antonyms, and of syntactically-related words. GPA also offers the possibility to include multilingual support for inducing a larger seed dictionary during training, which better anchors the English to target language alignment in low-resource scenarios.

Acknowledgements

Sebastian is supported by Irish Research Council Grant Number EBPPG/2014/30 and Science Foundation Ireland Grant Number SFI/12/RC/2289, co-funded by the European Regional Development Fund.

References

Waleed Ammar, George Mulcaire, Yulia Tsvetkov, Guillaume Lample, Chris Dyer, and Noah A. Smith. 2016. Massively Multilingual Word Embeddings.

Mikel Artetxe, Gorka Labaka, and Eneko Agirre. 2017. Learning bilingual word embeddings with (almost) no bilingual data. In *Proceedings of the 55th Annual Meeting of the Association for Computational Linguistics*, pages 451–462.

Mikel Artetxe, Gorka Labaka, and Eneko Agirre. 2018. Generalizing and Improving Bilingual Word Embedding Mappings with a Multi-Step Framework of Linear Transformations. In *Proceedings of AAAI 2018*.

Antonio Valerio Miceli Barone. 2016. Towards cross-lingual distributed representations without parallel text trained with adversarial autoencoders. *Proceedings of the 1st Workshop on Representation Learning for NLP*, pages 121–126.

Alexis Conneau, Guillaume Lample, Marc'Aurelio Ranzato, Ludovic Denoyer, and Hervé Jégou. 2018. Word Translation Without Parallel Data. In *Proceedings of ICLR 2018*.

Georgiana Dinu, Angeliki Lazaridou, and Marco Baroni. 2015. Improving Zero-Shot Learning by Mitigating the Hubness Problem. *ICLR 2015 Workshop track*, pages 1–10.

Manaal Faruqui and Chris Dyer. 2014. Improving Vector Space Word Representations Using Multilingual Correlation. *Proceedings of the 14th Conference of the European Chapter of the Association for Computational Linguistics*, pages 462 – 471.

John C Gower. 1975. Generalized procrustes analysis. *Psychometrika*, 40(1):33–51.

Ang Lu, Weiran Wang, Mohit Bansal, Kevin Gimpel, and Karen Livescu. 2015. Deep Multilingual Correlation for Improved Word Embeddings. In *HLT-NAACL*.

Tomas Mikolov, Quoc V. Le, and Ilya Sutskever. 2013. Exploiting Similarities among Languages for Machine Translation.

David Mimno and Laure Thompson. 2017. The strange geometry of skip-gram with negative sampling. In *Proceedings of EMNLP*.

Saif M. Mohammad, Bonnie J. Dorr, Graeme Hirst, and Peter D. Turney. 2013. Computing lexical contrast. *Computational Linguistics*, 39(3):555–590.

Henri Poincaré. 1902. *La Science et l' Hypothese*. Flammario, Paris, France.

Tapani Raiko, Harri Valpola, and Yann LeCun. 2012. Deep learning made easier by linear transformations in perceptrons. In *AISTATS*.

Sebastian Ruder, Ivan Vulić, and Anders Søgaard. 2018. A Survey of Cross-lingual Word Embedding Models. *Journal of Artificial Intelligence Research*.

Peter H Schönemann. 1966. A generalized solution of the orthogonal procrustes problem. *Psychometrika*, 31(1):1–10.

Samuel L. Smith, David H. P. Turban, Steven Hamblin, and Nils Y. Hammerla. 2017. Bilingual word vectors, orthogonal transformations and the inverted softmax. In *Proceedings of ICLR*.

Anders Søgaard, Sebastian Ruder, and Ivan Vulić. 2018. On the Limitations of Unsupervised Bilingual Dictionary Induction. In *Proceedings of ACL 2018*.

Ivan Vulić, Nikola Mrkšić, and Anna Korhonen. 2017. Cross-Lingual Induction and Transfer of Verb Classes Based on Word Vector Space Specialisation. In *Proceedings of the 2017 Conference on Empirical Methods in Natural Language Processing*.

Chao Xing, Chao Liu, Dong Wang, and Yiye Lin. 2015. Normalized Word Embedding and Orthogonal Transform for Bilingual Word Translation. *NAACL-2015*, pages 1005–1010.

Hyejin Youn, Logan Sutton, Eric Smith, Cristopher Moore, Jon F. Wilkins, Ian Maddieson, William Croft, and Tanmoy Bhattacharya. 1999. On the universal structure of human lexical semantics. In *NIPS*.

Meng Zhang, Yang Liu, Huanbo Luan, and Maosong Sun. 2017. Adversarial Training for Unsupervised Bilingual Lexicon Induction. In *Proceedings of ACL*.

Simple Unsupervised Keyphrase Extraction using Sentence Embeddings

Kamil Bennani-Smires[1], Claudiu Musat[1], Andreaa Hossmann[1],
Michael Baeriswyl[1], Martin Jaggi[2]
[1]Data, Analytics & AI, Swisscom AG
`firstname.lastname@swisscom.com`
[2]Machine Learning and Optimization Laboratory, EPFL
`martin.jaggi@epfl.ch`

Abstract

Keyphrase extraction is the task of automatically selecting a small set of phrases that best describe a given free text document. Supervised keyphrase extraction requires large amounts of labeled training data and generalizes very poorly outside the domain of the training data. At the same time, unsupervised systems have poor accuracy, and often do not generalize well, as they require the input document to belong to a larger corpus also given as input. Addressing these drawbacks, in this paper, we tackle keyphrase extraction from single documents with EmbedRank: a novel unsupervised method, that leverages sentence embeddings. EmbedRank achieves higher F-scores than graph-based state of the art systems on standard datasets and is suitable for real-time processing of large amounts of Web data. With EmbedRank, we also explicitly increase coverage and diversity among the selected keyphrases by introducing an embedding-based maximal marginal relevance (MMR) for new phrases. A user study including over 200 votes showed that, although reducing the phrases' semantic overlap leads to no gains in F-score, our high diversity selection is preferred by humans.

1 Introduction

Document keywords and keyphrases enable faster and more accurate search in large text collections, serve as condensed document summaries, and are used for various other applications, such as categorization of documents. In particular, keyphrase extraction is a crucial component when gleaning real-time insights from large amounts of Web and social media data. In this case, the extraction must be *fast* and the keyphrases must be *disjoint*. Most existing systems are slow and plagued by overgeneration, i.e. extracting redundant keyphrases. Here, we address both these problems with a new unsupervised algorithm.

Unsupervised keyphrase extraction has a series of advantages over supervised methods. Supervised keyphrase extraction always requires the existence of a (large) annotated corpus of both documents and their manually selected keyphrases to train on - a very strong requirement in most cases. Supervised methods also perform poorly outside of the domain represented by the training corpus - a big issue, considering that the domain of new documents may not be known at all. Unsupervised keyphrase extraction addresses such information-constrained situations in one of two ways: (a) by relying on in-corpus statistical information (e.g., the inverse document frequency of the words), and the current document; (b) by only using information extracted from the current document.

We propose EmbedRank - an unsupervised method to automatically extract keyphrases from a document, that is both simple and *only requires the current document itself*, rather than an entire corpus that this document may be linked to. Our method relies on notable new developments in text representation learning (Le et al., 2014; Kiros et al., 2015; Pagliardini et al., 2017), where documents or word sequences of arbitrary length are embedded into the same continuous vector space. This opens the way to computing semantic relatedness among text fragments by using the induced similarity measures in that feature space. Using these semantic text representations, we guarantee the two most challenging properties of keyphrases: *informativeness* obtained by the distance between the embedding of a candidate phrase and that of the full document; *diversity* expressed by the distances among candidate phrases themselves.

In a traditional F-score evaluation, EmbedRank clearly **outperforms the current state of the art** (i.e. complex graph-based methods (Mihalcea and Tarau, 2004; Wan and Xiao, 2008; Rui Wang, Wei Liu, 2015)) on two out of three common datasets

Proceedings of the 22nd Conference on Computational Natural Language Learning (CoNLL 2018), pages 221–229
Brussels, Belgium, October 31 - November 1, 2018. ©2018 Association for Computational Linguistics

for keyphrase extraction. We also evaluated the impact of **ensuring diversity** by conducting a user study, since this aspect cannot be captured by the F-score evaluation. The study showed that users highly prefer keyphrases with the diversity property. Finally, to the best of our knowledge, we are the first to present an unsupervised method based on phrase and document embeddings for keyphrase extraction, as opposed to standard individual word embeddings.

The paper is organized as follows. Related work on keyphrase extraction and sentence embeddings is presented in Section 2. In Section 3 we present how our method works. An enhancement of the method allowing us to gain a control over the redundancy of the extracted keyphrases is then described in Section 4. Section 5 contains the different experiments that we performed and Section 6 outlines the importance of Embedrank in real-world examples.

2   Related Work

A comprehensive, albeit slightly dated survey on keyphrase extraction is available (Hasan and Ng, 2011). Here, we focus on unsupervised methods, as they are superior in many ways (domain independence, no training data) and represent the state of the art in performance. As EmbedRank relies heavily on (sentence) embeddings, we also discuss the state of the art in this area.

2.1   Unsupervised Keyphrase Extraction

Unsupervised keyphrase extraction comes in two flavors: corpus-dependent (Wan and Xiao, 2008) and corpus-independent.

Corpus-independent methods, including our proposed method, require no other inputs than the one document from which to extract keyphrases. Most such existing methods are graph-based, with the notable exceptions of KeyCluster (Liu et al., 2009) and TopicRank (Bougouin et al., 2013). In graph-based keyphrase extraction, first introduced with TextRank (Mihalcea and Tarau, 2004), the target document is a graph, in which nodes represent words and edges represent the co-occurrence of the two endpoints inside some window. The edges may be weighted, like in SingleRank (Wan and Xiao, 2008), using the number of co-occurrences as weights. The words (or nodes) are scored using some node ranking metric, such as degree centrality or PageRank (Page,

1998). Scores of individual words are then aggregated into scores of multi-word phrases. Finally, sequences of consecutive words which respect a certain sequence of part-of-speech tags are considered as candidate phrases and ranked by their scores. Recently, WordAttractionRank (Rui Wang, Wei Liu, 2015) followed an approach similar to SingleRank, with the difference of using a new weighting scheme for edges between two words, to incorporate the distance between their word embedding representation. Florescu and Caragea (2017) use node weights, favoring words appearing earlier in the text.

Scoring a candidate phrase as the aggregation of its words score (Mihalcea and Tarau, 2004; Wan and Xiao, 2008; Florescu and Caragea, 2017) can lead to over-generation errors. This happens as several candidate phrases can obtain a high score because one of their consitutent words has a high score. This behavior leads to uninformative keyphrase with one important word present but lacking informativeness as a whole. In addition focusing on individual words hurts the diversity of the results.

2.1.1   Diversifying results

Ensuring diversity is important in the presentation of results to users in the information retrieval literature. Examples include MMR (Goldstein, 1998), IA-Select (Agrawal et al., 2009) or Max-Sum Diversification (Borodin et al., 2012). We used MMR in this work because of its simplicity in terms of both implementation and, more importantly, interpretation.

The following methods directly integrate a diversity factor in the way they are selecting keyphrases. Departing from the popular graph approach, KeyCluster (Liu et al., 2009) introduces a clustering-based approach. The words present in the target document are clustered and, for each cluster, one word is selected as an "exemplar term". Candidate phrases are filtered as before, using the sequence of part-of-speech tags and, finally, candidates which contain at least one exemplar term are returned as the keyphrases.

TopicRank (Bougouin et al., 2013) combines the graph and clustering-based approaches. Candidate phrases are first clustered, then a graph where each node represents a cluster is created. TopicRank clusters phrases based on the percentage of shared words, resulting in e.g., *"fantastic teacher"* and *"great instructor"* not being clustered together, despite expressing the same idea. In the follow-up work using multipartite graphs (Boudin, 2018), the authors encode topical information within a multipartite graph structure.

In contrast, EmbedRank represents both the document and candidate phrases as vectors in a high-dimensional space, leveraging novel semantic document embedding methods beyond simple averaging of word vectors. In the resulting vector space, we can thus compute meaningful distances between a candidate phrase and the document (for informativeness), as well as the semantic distance between candidates (for diversity).

2.2 Word and Sentence Embeddings

Word embeddings (Mikolov et al., 2013) marked a very impactful advancement in representing words as vectors in a continuous vector space. Representing words with vectors in moderate dimensions solves several major drawbacks of the classic bag-of-words representation, including the lack of semantic relatedness between words and the very high dimensionality (size of the vocabulary).

Different methods are needed for representing entire sentences or documents. Skip-Thought (Kiros et al., 2015) provides sentence embeddings trained to predict neighboring sentences. Paragraph Vector (Le et al., 2014) finds paragraph embeddings using an unordered list of paragraphs. The method can be generalized to also work on sentences or entire documents, turning paragraph vectors into more generic document vectors (Lau and Baldwin, 2016).

Sent2Vec (Pagliardini et al., 2017) uses word n-gram features to produce sentence embeddings. It produces word and n-gram vectors specifically trained to be additively combined into a sentence vector, as opposed to general word-vectors. Sent2Vec features much faster inference than Paragraph Vector (Le et al., 2014) or Skip-Thought (Kiros et al., 2015). Similarly to recent word and document embeddings, Sent2Vec reflects semantic relatedness between phrases when using standard similarity measures on the corresponding vectors. This property is at the core of our method, as we show it outperforms competing embedding methods for keyphrase extraction.

3 EmbedRank: From Embeddings to Keyphrases

In this and the next section, we introduce and describe our novel keyphrase extraction method, EmbedRank [1]. The method consists of three main steps, as follows: (1) We extract candidate phrases from the text, based on part-of-speech sequences. More precisely, we keep only those phrases that consist of zero or more adjectives followed by one or multiple nouns (Wan and Xiao, 2008). (2) We use sentence embeddings to represent (**embed**), both the candidate phrases and the document itself in the same high-dimensional vector space (Sec. 3.1). (3) We **rank** the candidate phrases to select the output keyphrases (Sec. 3.2). In addition, in the next section, we show how to improve the ranking step, by providing a way to tune the diversity of the extracted keyphrases.

3.1 Embedding the Phrases and the Document

State-of-the-art text embeddings (word, sentence, document) capture semantic relatedness via the distances between the corresponding vector representations within the shared vector space. We use this property to rank the candidate phrases extracted in the previous step, by measuring their distance to the original document. Thus, semantic relatedness between a candidate phrase and its document becomes a proxy for informativeness of the phrase.

Concretely, this second step of our keyphrase extraction method consists of:

(a) Computing the *document embedding*. This includes a noise reduction procedure, where we keep only the adjectives and nouns contained in the input document.

(b) Computing the *embedding of each candidate phrase* separately, again with the same algorithm.

To determine the impact the document embedding method may have on the final outcome, we evaluate keyphrases obtained using both the popular Doc2Vec (Lau and Baldwin, 2016) (denoted EmbedRank d2v) and ones based on the newer Sent2vec (Pagliardini et al., 2017) (denoted Em-

---

[1] https://github.com/swisscom/ai-research-keyphrase-extraction

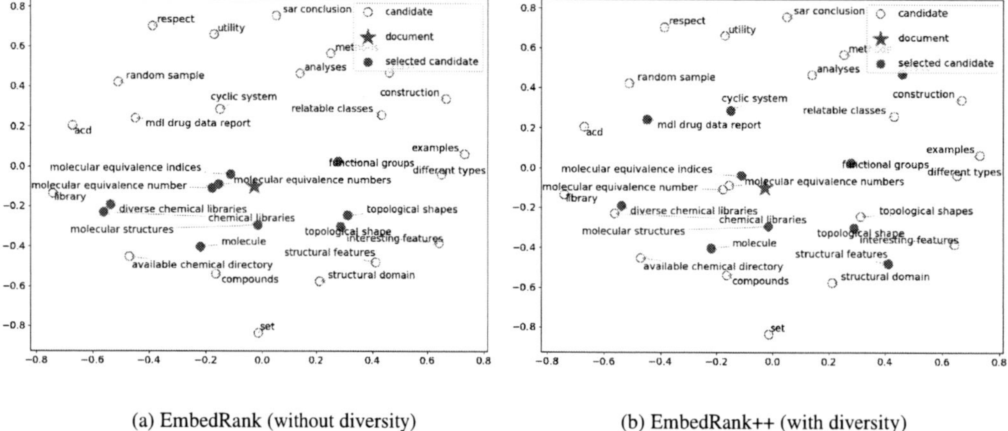

(a) EmbedRank (without diversity)   (b) EmbedRank++ (with diversity)

Figure 1: Embedding space[2] of a scientific abstract entitled *"Using molecular equivalence numbers to visually explore structural features that distinguish chemical libraries"*

bedRank s2v). Both embedding methods **allow us to embed arbitrary-length sequences of words**. To embed both phrases and documents, we employ publicly available pre-trained models of Sent2Vec[3] and Doc2vec[4]. The pre-computed Sent2vec embeddings based on words and n-grams vectors have $Z = Z_s = 700$ dimensions, while for Doc2vec $Z = Z_d = 300$. All embeddings are trained on the large English Wikipedia corpus.[5] EmbedRank s2v is very fast, since Sent2vec infers a document embedding from the pre-trained model, by averaging the pre-computed representations of the text's components (words and n-grams), in a single linear pass through the text. EmbedRank d2v is slower, as Doc2vec uses the embedding network to infer a vector for the whole document. Both methods provide vectors comparable in the same semantic space, no matter if the input "document" is a word, a phrase, a sentence or an entire document.

After this step, we have one Z-dimensional vector representing our document and a Z-dimensional vector for each of our candidate phrases, all sharing the same reference space. Figure 1 shows a concrete example, using Em-

bedRank s2v, from one of the datasets we used for evaluation (scientific abstracts). As can be seen by comparing document titles and candidate phrases, our initial assumption holds in this example: the closer a phrase is to the document vector, the more informative that phrase is for the document. Therefore, it is sensible to use the cosine similarity between the embedding of the candidate phrase and the document embedding as a measure of informativeness.

3.2 Selecting the Top Candidates

Based on the above, we select the top keyphrases out of the initial set, by ranking the candidate phrases according to their cosine distance to the document embedding. In Figure 1, this results in ten highlighted keyphrases, which are clearly in line with the document's title.

Nevertheless, it is notable that there can be significant redundancy in the set of top keyphrases. For example, *"molecular equivalence numbers"* and *"molecular equivalence indices"* are both selected as separate keyphrases, despite expressing the same meaning. This problem can be elegantly solved by once again using our phrase embeddings and their cosine similarity as a proxy for semantic relatedness. We describe our proposed solution to this in the next section.

Summarizing this section, we have proposed an unsupervised step-by-step method to extract *informative keyphrases* from a single document by using sentence embeddings.

---

[2]Visualization based on multidimensional scaling with cosine distance on the original $Z = Z_s = 700$ dimensional embeddings.

[3]https://github.com/epfml/sent2vec

[4]https://github.com/jhlau/doc2vec

[5]The generality of this corpus, as well as the unsupervised embedding method itself ensure that the computed text representations are general-purpose, thus domain-independent.

224

Dataset	Documents	Avg tok	Avg cand	Keyphrases	Avg kp	Missing kp in doc	Missing kp in cand	Missing due to cand
Inspec	500	134.63	26.39	4903	9.81	21.52%	39.85%	18.34%
DUC	308	850.02	138.47	2479	8.05	2.18%	12.38%	10.21%
NUS	209	8448.55	765.56	2272	10.87	14.39%	30.85%	16.46%

Table 1: The three datasets we use. Columns are: number of documents; average number of tokens per document; average number of unique candidates per document; total number of unique keyphrases; average number of unique keyphrases per document; percentage of keyphrases not present in the documents; percentage of keyphrases not present in the candidates; percentage of keyphrases present in the document, but not in the candidates. These statistics were computed after stemming the candidates, the keyphrases and the document.

4 EmbedRank++: Increasing Keyphrase Diversity with MMR

By returning the N candidate phrases closest to the document embedding, EmbedRank only accounts for the phrase informativeness property, leading to redundant keyphrases. In scenarios where users directly see the extracted keyphrases (e.g. text summarization, tagging for search), this is problematic: redundant keyphrases adversely impact the user's experience. This can deteriorate to the point in which providing keyphrases becomes completely useless.

Moreover, if we extract a fixed number of top keyphrases, redundancy hinders the diversification of the extracted keyphrases. In the document from Figure 1, the extracted keyphrases include {*topological shape, topological shapes*} and {*molecular equivalence number, molecular equivalence numbers, molecular equivalence indices*}. That is, four out of the ten keyphrase "slots" are taken by redundant phrases.

This resembles search result diversification (Drosou and Pitoura, 2010), where a search engine balance query-document relevance and document diversity. One of the simplest and most effective solutions to this is the Maximal Marginal Relevance (MMR) (Goldstein, 1998) metric, which combines in a controllable way the concepts of relevance and diversity. We show how to adapt MMR to keyphrase extraction, in order to combine keyphrase informativeness with dissimilarity among selected keyphrases.

The original MMR from information retrieval and text summarization is based on the set of all initially retrieved documents, R, for a given input query Q, and on an initially empty set S representing documents that are selected as good answers for Q. S is iteratively populated by computing MMR as described in (1), where D_i and D_j are retrieved documents, and Sim_1 and Sim_2 are similarity functions.

$$\text{MMR} := \arg\max_{D_i \in R \setminus S} \left[\lambda \cdot Sim_1(D_i, Q) - (1 - \lambda) \max_{D_j \in S} Sim_2(D_i, D_j) \right] \quad (1)$$

When $\lambda = 1$ MMR computes a standard, relevance-ranked list, while when $\lambda = 0$ it computes a maximal diversity ranking of the documents in R. To use MMR here, we adapt the original equation as:

$$\text{MMR} := \arg\max_{C_i \in C \setminus K} \left[\lambda \cdot \widetilde{cos}_{sim}(C_i, \text{doc}) - (1 - \lambda) \max_{C_j \in K} \widetilde{cos}_{sim}(C_i, C_j) \right], \quad (2)$$

where C is the set of candidate keyphrases, K is the set of extracted keyphrases, doc is the full document embedding, C_i and C_j are the embeddings of candidate phrases i and j, respectively. Finally, $\widetilde{cos}_{sim}$ is a normalized cosine similarity (Mori and Sasaki, 2003), described by the following equations. This ensures that, when $\lambda = 0.5$, the relevance and diversity parts of the equation have equal importance.

$$\widetilde{cos}_{sim}(C_i, \text{doc}) = 0.5 + \frac{ncos_{sim}(C_i, \text{doc}) - \overline{ncos_{sim}(C, \text{doc})}}{\sigma(ncos_{sim}(C, \text{doc}))}. \quad (3a)$$

$$ncos_{sim}(C_i, \text{doc}) = \frac{cos_{sim}(C_i, \text{doc}) - \min_{C_j \in C} cos_{sim}(C_j, \text{doc})}{\max_{C_j \in C} cos_{sim}(C_j, \text{doc})} \quad (3b)$$

We apply an analogous transformation for the similarities between candidate phrases.

Summarizing, the method in the previous section is equivalent to using MMR for keyphrase extraction from Equation (2) with $\lambda = 1$. The generalized version of the algorithm, EmbedRank++, remains the same, except for the last step, where we instead use Equation (2) to perform the final selection of the N candidates, therefore returning simultaneously relevant and diverse keyphrases, tuned by the trade-off parameter λ.

5   Experiments and results

In this section we show that EmbedRank outperforms the graph-based state-of-the-art schemes on the most common datasets, when using traditional F-score evaluation. In addition, we report on the results of a sizable user study showing that, although EmbedRank++ achieves slightly lower F-scores than EmbedRank, users prefer the semantically diverse keyphrases it returns to those computed by the other method.

5.1   Datasets

Table 1 describes three common datasets for keyphrase extraction.

The **Inspec** dataset (Hulth, 2003) consists of 2 000 short documents from scientific journal abstracts. To compare with previous work (Mihalcea and Tarau, 2004; Hasan and Ng, 2010; Bougouin et al., 2013; Wan and Xiao, 2008), we evaluated our methods on the test dataset (500 documents).

DUC 2001 (Wan and Xiao, 2008) consists of 308 medium length newspaper articles from TREC-9. The documents originate from several newspapers and are organized in 30 topics. For keyphrase extraction, we used exclusively the text contained in the first <TEXT> tags of the original documents (we do not use titles and other metadata).

NUS (Nguyen and Kan, 2007) consists of 211 long documents (full scientific conference papers), of between 4 and 12 pages. Each document has several sets of keyphrases: one created by the authors and, potentially, several others created by annotators. Following Hasan and Ng (2010), we evaluate on the union of all sets of assigned keyphrases (author and annotator(s)). The dataset is very similar to the SemEval dataset which is also often used for keyphrase extraction. Since our results on SemEval are very similar to NUS, we omit them due to space constraints.

As shown in Table 1, not all assigned keyphrases are present in the documents (missing kp in doc). It is thus impossible to achieve a recall of 100%. We show in the next subsection that our method beats the state of the art on short scientific documents and clearly outperforms it on medium length news articles.

5.2   Performance Comparison

We compare EmbedRank s2v and d2v (no diversity) to five state-of-the-art, corpus-independent methods[6]: TextRank (Mihalcea and Tarau, 2004), SingleRank (Wan and Xiao, 2008), WordAttractionRank (Rui Wang, Wei Liu, 2015), TopicRank[7] (Bougouin et al., 2013) and Multipartite (Boudin, 2018).

For TextRank and SingleRank, we set the window size to 2 and to 10 respectively, i.e. the values used in the respective papers. We used the same PoS tagged text for all methods. For both underlying d2v and s2v document embedding methods, we use their standard settings as described in Section 3. We followed the common practice to stem - with the Porter Stemmer (Porter, 1980) - the extracted and assigned keyphrases when computing the number of true positives.

As shown in Table 2, EmbedRank outperforms competing methods on two of the three datasets in terms of precision, recall, and Macro F_1 score. In the context of typical Web-oriented use cases, most data comes as either very short documents (e.g. tweets) or medium ones (e.g. news articles). The expected performance for Web applications is thus closer to the one observed on the Inspec and DUC2001 datasets, rather than on NUS.

However, on long documents, Multipartite outperforms all other methods. The most plausible explanation is that Multipartite, like TopicRank incorporates positional information about the candidates. Using this feature leads to an important gain on long documents – not using it can lead to a 90% relative drop in F-score for TopicRank. We verify this intuition in the context of EmbedRank by naively multiplying the distance of a candidate to the document by the candidate's normalized offset position. We thus confirm the "positional bias" hypothesis, with EmbedRank$_{positional}$ matching the TopicRank scores on long documents and approaching the Multipartite ones. The Multipartite

---

[6]TextRank, SingleRank, WordAttractionRank were implemented using the graph-tool library `https://graph-tool.skewed.de`. We reset the co-occurence window on new sentence.

[7]`https://github.com/boudinfl/pke`

N	Method	Inspec			DUC			NUS		
		P	R	F_1	P	R	F_1	P	R	F_1
5	TextRank	24.87	10.46	14.72	19.83	12.28	15.17	5.00	2.36	3.21
	SingleRank	38.18	23.26	28.91	30.31	19.50	23.73	4.06	1.90	2.58
	TopicRank	33.25	19.94	24.93	27.80	18.28	22.05	16.94	8.99	11.75
	Multipartite	34.61	20.54	25.78	29.49	19.42	23.41	**19.23**	**10.18**	**13.31**
	WordAttractionRank	38.55	23.55	29.24	30.83	19.79	24.11	4.09	1.96	2.65
	EmbedRank d2v	**41.49**	**25.40**	**31.51**	30.87	19.66	24.02	3.88	1.68	2.35
	EmbedRank s2v	39.63	23.98	29.88	**34.84**	**22.26**	**27.16**	5.53	2.44	3.39
	EmbedRank++ s2v ($\lambda = 0.5$)	37.44	22.28	27.94	24.75	16.20	19.58	2.78	1.24	1.72
	EmbedRank$_{positional}$ s2v	38.84	23.77	29.49	39.53	25.23	30.80	15.07	7.80	10.28
10	TextRank	22.99	11.44	15.28	13.93	16.83	15.24	6.54	6.59	6.56
	SingleRank	34.29	39.04	36.51	24.74	30.97	27.51	5.22	5.04	5.13
	TopicRank	27.43	30.8	29.02	21.49	27.26	24.04	13.68	13.94	13.81
	Multipartite	28.07	32.24	30.01	22.50	28.85	25.28	**16.51**	**17.36**	**16.92**
	WordAttractionRank	34.10	38.94	36.36	25.06	31.41	27.88	5.15	5.12	5.14
	EmbedRank d2v	**35.75**	**40.40**	**37.94**	25.38	31.53	28.12	3.95	3.28	3.58
	EmbedRank s2v	34.97	39.49	37.09	**28.82**	**35.58**	**31.85**	5.69	5.18	5.42
	EmbedRank++ s2v ($\lambda = 0.5$)	30.31	34.29	32.18	18.27	23.34	20.50	1.91	1.69	1.79
	EmbedRank$_{positional}$ s2v	32.46	36.61	34.41	32.23	39.95	35.68	13.50	13.36	13.43
15	TextRank	22.80	11.50	15.29	11.25	19.21	14.19	6.14	9.16	7.35
	SingleRank	30.91	48.92	37.88	21.20	38.77	27.41	5.42	8.24	6.54
	TopicRank	24.51	37.45	29.62	17.78	32.92	23.09	11.04	16.47	13.22
	Multipartite	25.38	41.32	31.44	19.72	36.87	25.7	**14.13**	**21.86**	**17.16**
	WordAttractionRank	30.74	48.62	37.66	21.82	40.05	28.25	5.11	7.41	6.05
	EmbedRank d2v	31.06	48.80	37.96	22.37	40.48	28.82	4.33	5.89	4.99
	EmbedRank s2v	**31.48**	**49.23**	**38.40**	**24.49**	**44.20**	**31.52**	5.34	7.06	6.08
	EmbedRank++ s2v ($\lambda = 0.5$)	27.24	43.25	33.43	14.86	27.64	19.33	1.59	2.06	1.80
	EmbedRank$_{positional}$ s2v	29.44	46.25	35.98	27.38	49.73	35.31	12.27	17.63	14.47

Table 2: Comparison of our method with state of the art on the three datasets. Precision (P), Recall (R), and F-score (F_1) at 5, 10, 15 are reported. Two variations of EmbedRank with $\lambda = 1$ are presented: s2v uses Sent2Vec embeddings, while d2v uses Doc2Vec.

results underline the importance of explicitly representing topics for long documents. This does not hold for short and medium documents, where the semantic information is successfully captured by the topology of the embedding space.

EmbedRank$_{positional}$ also outperforms on medium-length documents but, as the assumption that the keyphrases appear in a decreasing order of importance is very strong for the general case, we gray out the results, to stress the importance of the more generic EmbedRank variants.

The results also show that the choice of document embeddings has a high impact on the keyphrase quality. Compared to EmbedRank d2v, EmbedRank s2v is significantly better for DUC2001 and NUS, regardless of how many phrases are extracted. On Inspec however, changing the embeddings from doc2vec to sent2vec made almost no difference. A possible explanation is that, given the small size of the original text, the extracted keyphrases have a high likelihood of being single words, thus removing the advantage of having better embeddings for word groups. In all other cases, the results show a clear accuracy gain of Sent2Vec over Doc2Vec, adding to the practical advantage of improved inference speed for very large datasets.

5.3 Keyphrase Diversity and Human Preference

In this section, we add EmbedRank++ to the evaluation using the same three datasets. We fixed λ to 0.5 in the adapted MMR equation (2), to ensure equal importance to informativeness and diversity. As shown in Figure 1b, EmbedRank++ reduces the redundancy we faced with EmbedRank. However, EmbedRank++ surprisingly results in a decrease of the F-score, as shown in Table 2.

We conducted a user study where we asked people to choose between two sets of extracted

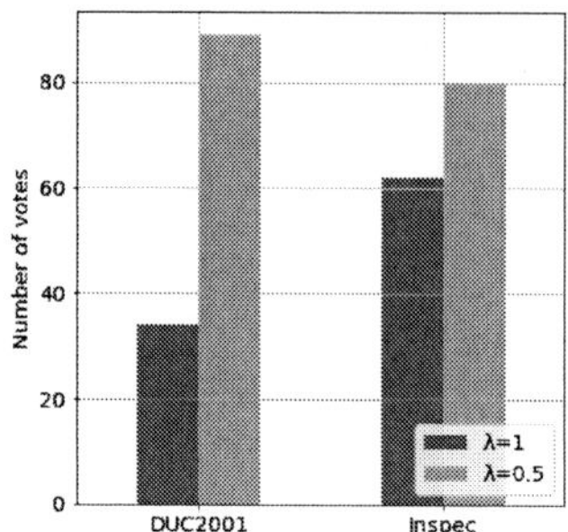

Figure 2: User study among 20 documents from Inspec and 20 documents from DUC2001. Users were asked to choose their preferred set of keyphrases between the one extracted with EmbedRank++ ($\lambda = 0.5$) and the one extracted with EmbedRank ($\lambda = 1$).

keyphrases: one generated with EmbedRank ($\lambda = 1$) and another with EmbedRank++ ($\lambda = 0.5$). We set N to the number of assigned keyphrases for each document. During the study, we provided the annotators with the original text, and ask them to choose between the two sets.

For this user study, we randomly selected 20 documents from the Inspec and 20 documents from the DUC2001 dataset, collected 214 binary user preference votes. The long scientific papers (NUS) were included in the study, as the full papers were considered too long and too difficult for non-experts to comprehend and summarize.

As shown in Figure 2, users largely prefer the keyphrase extracted with EmbedRank++ ($\lambda = 0.5$). This is a major finding, as it is in contradiction with the F-scores given in Table 2. If the result is confirmed by future tests, it casts a shadow on using solely F-score as an evaluation measure for keyphrase quality. A similar issue was shown to be present in Information Retrieval test collections (Tonon et al., 2015), and calls for research on new evaluation methodologies. We acknowledge that the presented study is a preliminary one and does not support a strong claim about the usefulness of the F-score for the given problem. It does however show that people dislike redundancy in summaries and that the $\lambda < 1$ parameter in EmbedRank is a promising way of reducing it.

Our intuition behind this novel result is that the EmbedRank method ($\lambda = 1$), as well as WordAttractionRank, SingleRank and TextRank can suffer from an accumulation of redundant keyphrases in which a true positive is present. By restrict-

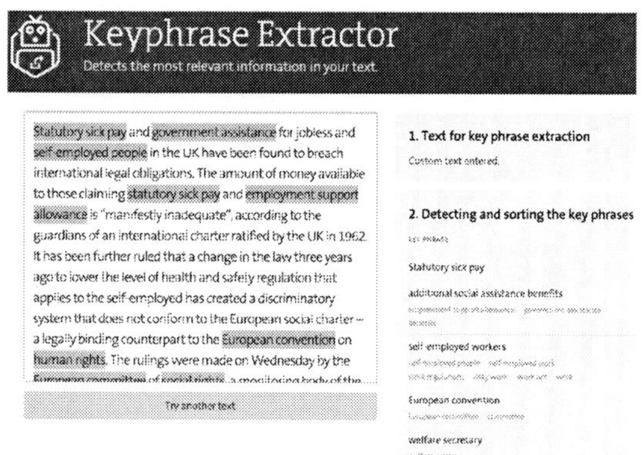

Figure 3: Keyphrase Grouping in news articles

ing the redundancy with EmbedRank++, we can select a keyphrase that is not present in the gold keyphrases, but expresses the same idea. The current F-score evaluation penalizes us as if we had chosen an unrelated keyphrase.

6 Discussion

The usefulness of the corpus-free approach is in that we can extract keyphrases in any environment, for instance for news articles. In Figure 3 we show the keyphrases extracted from a sample article. The EmbedRank keyphrase extraction is fast, enabling real time computation and visualization. The disjoint nature of the EmbedRank keyphrases make them highly readable, creating a succinct summary of the original article.

By performing the analysis at phrase instead of word level, EmbedRank opens the possibility of grouping candidates with keyphrases before presenting them to the user. Phrases within a group have similar embeddings, like *additional social assistance benefits, employment support allowance* and *government assistance benefits*. Multiple strategies can be employed to select the most visible phrase - for instance the one with the highest score or the longest one. This grouping counters the over-generation problem.

7 Conclusion

In this paper we presented EmbedRank and EmbedRank++, two simple and scalable methods for keyphrase extraction from a single document, that leverage sentence embeddings. Both methods are entirely unsupervised, corpus-independent, and they only require the current document itself, rather than the entire corpus to which it belongs (that might not exist at all). They both depart from traditional methods for keyphrase extraction based on graph representations of the input text, and fully embrace sentence embeddings and their ability to model informativeness and diversity.

EmbedRank can be implemented on top of any underlying document embeddings, provided that these embeddings can encode documents of arbitrary length. We compared the results obtained with Doc2Vec and Sent2Vec, the latter one being much faster at inference time, which is important in a Web-scale setting. We showed that on short and medium length documents, EmbedRank based on Sent2Vec consistently improves the state of the art. Additionally, thanks to a fairly large user study that we run, we showed that users appreciate diversity of keyphrases, and we raised questions on the reliability of evaluations of keyphrase extraction systems based on F-score.

References

Rakesh Agrawal, Sreenivas Gollapudi, Alan Halverson, and Samuel Ieong. 2009. Diversifying search results. In *Proceedings of the Second ACM International Conference on Web Search and Data Mining*, WSDM '09, pages 5–14, New York, NY, USA. ACM.

Allan Borodin, Hyun Chul Lee, and Yuli Ye. 2012. Max-sum diversification, monotone submodular functions and dynamic updates. In *Proceedings of the 31st ACM SIGMOD-SIGACT-SIGAI Symposium on Principles of Database Systems*, PODS '12, pages 155–166, New York, NY, USA. ACM.

Florian Boudin. 2018. Unsupervised keyphrase extraction with multipartite graphs. *CoRR*, abs/1803.08721.

Adrien Bougouin, Florian Boudin, and Béatrice Daille. 2013. TopicRank : Graph-Based Topic Ranking for Keyphrase Extraction. *Proc. IJCNLP 2013*, (October):543–551.

Marina Drosou and Evaggelia Pitoura. 2010. Search result diversification. *SIGMOD Rec.*, 39(1):41–47.

Corina Florescu and Cornelia Caragea. 2017. A position-biased pagerank algorithm for keyphrase extraction. In *AAAI Student Abstracts*, pages 4923–4924.

Jade Goldstein. 1998. The Use of MMR , Diversity-Based Reranking for Reordering Documents and Producing Summaries. pages 335–336.

Kazi Saidul Hasan and Vincent Ng. 2010. Conundrums in Unsupervised Keyphrase Extraction : Making Sense of the State-of-the-Art.

Kazi Saidul Hasan and Vincent Ng. 2011. Automatic Keyphrase Extraction: A Survey of the State of the Art. *Association for Computational Linguistics Conference (ACL)*, pages 1262–1273.

Anette Hulth. 2003. Improved automatic keyword extraction given more linguistic knowledge. In *Proceedings of the 2003 Conference on Empirical Methods in Natural Language Processing*, EMNLP '03, pages 216–223, Stroudsburg, PA, USA. Association for Computational Linguistics.

Ryan Kiros, Yukun Zhu, Ruslan Salakhutdinov, Richard S Zemel, Antonio Torralba, Raquel Urtasun, and Sanja Fidler. 2015. Skip-Thought Vectors. (786):1–11.

Jey Han Lau and Timothy Baldwin. 2016. An empirical evaluation of doc2vec with practical insights into document embedding generation. *ACL 2016*, page 78.

Quoc Le, Tomas Mikolov, and Tmikolov Google Com. 2014. Distributed Representations of Sentences and Documents. *ICML*, 32.

Zhiyuan Liu, Peng Li, Yabin Zheng, and Maosong Sun. 2009. Clustering to Find Exemplar Terms for Keyphrase Extraction. *Language*, 1:257–266.

Rada Mihalcea and Paul Tarau. 2004. TextRank: Bringing Order into Texts. *Proceedings of EMNLP*, 85:404–411.

Tomas Mikolov, Greg Corrado, Kai Chen, and Jeffrey Dean. 2013. Efficient Estimation of Word Representations in Vector Space. pages 1–12.

Tatsunori Mori and Takuro Sasaki. 2003. Information Gain Ratio meets Maximal Marginal Relevance.

Thuy Dung Nguyen and Min-yen Kan. 2007. Keyphrase Extraction in Scientific Publications.

L Page. 1998. The PageRank Citation Ranking: Bringing Order to the Web.

Matteo Pagliardini, Prakhar Gupta, and Martin Jaggi. 2017. Unsupervised Learning of Sentence Embeddings using Compositional n-Gram Features.

Martin F. Porter. 1980. An algorithm for suffix stripping. *Program*, 14(3):130–137.

Chris McDonald Rui Wang, Wei Liu. 2015. Corpus-independent Generic Keyphrase Extraction Using Word Embedding Vectors.

Alberto Tonon, Gianluca Demartini, and Philippe Cudré-Mauroux. 2015. Pooling-based continuous evaluation of information retrieval systems. *Inf. Retr. Journal*, 18(5):445–472.

Xiaojun Wan and Jianguo Xiao. 2008. Single Document Keyphrase Extraction Using Neighborhood Knowledge. pages 855–860.

A Temporally Sensitive Submodularity Framework for Timeline Summarization

Sebastian Martschat[*]
Knowledge Architecture & Innovation
BASF SE
67056 Ludwigshafen am Rhein, Germany
`sebastian.martschat@basf.com`

Katja Markert
Institute of Computational Linguistics
Heidelberg University
69120 Heidelberg, Germany
`markert@cl.uni-heidelberg.de`

Abstract

Timeline summarization (TLS) creates an overview of long-running events via dated daily summaries for the most important dates. TLS differs from standard multi-document summarization (MDS) in the importance of date selection, interdependencies between summaries of different dates and by having very short summaries compared to the number of corpus documents. However, we show that MDS optimization models using submodular functions can be adapted to yield well-performing TLS models by designing objective functions and constraints that model the temporal dimension inherent in TLS. Importantly, these adaptations retain the elegance and advantages of the original MDS models (clear separation of features and inference, performance guarantees and scalability, little need for supervision) that current TLS-specific models lack. An open-source implementation of the framework and all models described in this paper is available online.[1]

1 Introduction

There is an abundance of reports on events, crises and disasters. *Timelines* (see Table 1) summarize and date these reports in an ordered overview. *Automatic Timeline Summarization* (TLS) constructs such timelines from corpora that contain articles about the corresponding event.

In contrast to standard *multi-document summarization* (MDS), in TLS we need to explicitly model the temporal dimension of the task, specifically we need to select the most important dates for a long-running event and summarize each of these dates. In addition, TLS deals with a much larger number of documents to summarize,

---

2011-03-16
Security forces break up a gathering in Marjeh Square in Damascus of 150 protesters holding pictures of imprisoned relatives. Witnesses say 30 people are arrested.
2011-03-24
President Bashar al-Assad orders the formation of a committee to study how to raise living standards and lift the law covering emergency rule, in place for 48 years.
2011-03-29
Government resigns.

Table 1: Excerpt from a Syrian War Reuters timeline.

enhancing scalability and redundancy problems. These differences have significant consequences for constraints, objectives, compression rates and scalability (see Section 2.2).

Due to these differences, most work on TLS has been separate from the MDS community.[2] Instead, approaches to TLS start from scratch, optimizing task-specific heuristic criteria (Chieu and Lee, 2004; Yan et al., 2011b; Wang et al., 2016, inter alia), often with manually determined parameters (Chieu and Lee, 2004; Yan et al., 2011b) or needing supervision (Wang et al., 2016). As features and architectures are rarely reused or indeed separated from each other, it is difficult to assess reported improvements. Moreover, none of these approaches give performance guarantees for the task, which are possible in MDS models based on function optimization (McDonald, 2007; Lin and Bilmes, 2011) that yield state-of-the art models for MDS (Hong et al., 2014; Hirao et al., 2017).

In this paper we take a step back from the differences between MDS and TLS and consider the following question: *Can MDS optimization models be expanded to yield scalable, well-performing TLS models that take into account the temporal properties of TLS, while keeping MDS advantages*

---

[*]Work conducted while the author was a researcher at the Institute of Computational Linguistics, Heidelberg University.

[1]`http://smartschat.de/software`

[2]The TLS systems in (Yan et al., 2011b; Tran et al., 2013a) are compared to some simple MDS systems as baselines, but not to state-of-the art ones.

Proceedings of the 22nd Conference on Computational Natural Language Learning (CoNLL 2018), pages 230–240
Brussels, Belgium, October 31 - November 1, 2018. ©2018 Association for Computational Linguistics

such as modularity and performance guarantees?
In particular, we make the following contributions:

- We adapt the submodular function model of Lin and Bilmes (2011) to TLS (Section 3). This framework is scalable and modular, allowing a "plug-and-play" approach for different submodular functions. It needs little supervision or parameter tuning. We show that even this straightforward MDS adaptation equals or outperforms two strong TLS baselines on two corpora for most metrics.

- We modify the MDS-based objective function by adding temporal criteria that take date selection and interdependencies between daily summaries into account (Section 4).

- We then add more complex temporal constraints, going beyond the simple cardinality constraints in MDS (Section 5). These new constraints specify the uniformity of the timeline daily summaries and date distribution. We also give the first performance guarantees for TLS using these constraints.

- We propose a TLS evaluation framework, in which we study the effect of temporal objective functions and constraints. We show performance improvements of our temporalizations (Section 6). We also present the first oracle upper bounds for the problem and study the impact that timeline properties, such as compression rates, have on performance.

2 Timeline Summarization

Given a query (such as *Syrian war*) TLS needs to (i) extract the most important events for the query and their corresponding dates and (ii) obtain concise daily summaries for each selected date (Allan et al., 2001; Chieu and Lee, 2004; Yan et al., 2011b; Tran et al., 2015a; Wang et al., 2016).

2.1 Task Definition and Notation

A *timeline* is a sequence $(d_1, v_1), \ldots, (d_k, v_k)$ where the d_i are dates and the v_i are summaries for the dates d_i. Given are a query q and an associated corpus C that contains documents relevant to the query. The task of *timeline summarization* is to generate a timeline t based on C. The number of dates in t as well as the length of the daily summaries are typically controlled by the user.

We denote with U the set of sentences in C. We assume that each sentence in U is dated (either by a date expression appearing in the sentence or by

the publication date of the article it appears in). For a sentence s we write $d(s)$ for the date of s.

2.2 Relation to MDS

In MDS, we also need to generate a (length-limited) summary of texts in a corpus C (with an optional query q used to retrieve the corpus). In the traditional DUC multi-document summarization tasks[3], most tasks are either not event-based at all or concentrate on one single event. In contrast, in TLS, the corpus describes an event that consists of several subevents that happen on different days.

This difference has substantial effects. In MDS, criteria (such as coverage and diversity) and length constraints apply on a global level. In TLS, the whole summary is naturally divided into per-day summaries. Criteria and constraints apply on a global level as well as on a per-day level.

Even for the small number of DUC tasks that do focus on longer-running events, several differences to TLS still hold. First, the temporal dimension in the DUC gold standard summaries and system outputs is playing a minor role, with few explicit datings of events and a non-temporal structure of the output, leading again to the above-mentioned differences in constraints and criteria. The ROUGE evaluation measures used in MDS (Lin, 2004) also do not take into account temporality and do not explicitly penalize wrong datings. Second, corpora in TLS typically contain thousands of documents per query (Tran et al., 2013b, 2015a). This is magnitudes larger than the corpora usually considered for MDS (Over and Yen, 2004). This leads to a low compression rate[4] and requires approaches to be scalable.

3 Casting TLS as MDS

In the introduction, we identified several issues in existing TLS research, including lack of modularity, insufficient separation between features and model, and the lack of performance guarantees. Global constrained optimization frameworks used in MDS (McDonald, 2007; Lin and Bilmes, 2011) do separate constraints, features and inference and allow for optimal solutions or solutions with performance guarantees. They also can be used in an unsupervised manner. We now cast TLS as MDS, employing constraints and criteria used for stan-

---

[3] https://duc.nist.gov/
[4] *Compression rate* is the length of the summary divided by the length of the source (Radev et al., 2004).

dard MDS (Lin and Bilmes, 2011). While this ignores the temporal dimension of TLS, it will give us a baseline and a starting point for systematically incorporating temporal information.

3.1 Problem Statement and Inference

We can understand summarization as an optimization of an objective function that evaluates sets of sentences over constraints. Hence, let U be a set of sentences in a corpus and let $f: 2^U \to \mathbb{R}_{\geq 0}$ be a function that measures the quality of a summary. Let $\mathcal{I} \subseteq \{X \mid X \in 2^U\}$ be a set of constraints[5]. We then consider the optimization problem

$$S^* = \underset{S \subseteq U, S \in \mathcal{I}}{\arg\max} f(S). \qquad (1)$$

Solving Equation 1 exactly does not scale well (McDonald, 2007) and is therefore inappropriate for the large-scale data used in TLS. The greedy Algorithm 1 that iteratively constructs an output solves the equation approximately (also used in McDonald (2007) and Lin and Bilmes (2011)).

Algorithm 1 Greedy algorithm.

Input: A set of sentences U, a function f, a set of constraints $\mathcal{I}$
    function GREEDY(U, f, $\mathcal{I}$)
        Set $S = \emptyset$, $K = U$
        while $K \neq \emptyset$ **do**
            $s = \arg\max_{t \in K} f(S \cup \{t\}) - f(S)$
            if $S \cup \{s\} \in \mathcal{I}$ **then**
                $S = S \cup \{s\}$
            $K = K \setminus \{s\}$
Output: A summary S

3.2 Monotonicity and Submodularity

The results obtained by GREEDY can be arbitrarily bad. However, there are performance guarantees if the objective function f and the constraints $\mathcal{I}$ are "sufficiently nice" (Calinescu et al., 2011). Many results rely on objective functions that are *monotone* and *submodular*. A function f is monotone if $A \subseteq B$ implies that $f(A) \leq f(B)$. A function f is submodular if it possesses a "diminishing returns property", i.e. if for $A \subseteq B \subset U$ and $v \in U \setminus B$ we have $f(A \cup \{v\}) - f(A) \geq f(B \cup \{v\}) - f(B)$.

From now on we assume that the function f is of the form $f \equiv \sum_{i=1}^{m} f_i$ with monotone submod-

---

[5]An example are length constraints, which can be expressed as $\mathcal{I} = \{X \mid |X| \leq m, X \in 2^U\}$ for some m.

ular $f_i: U \to [0, 1]$ ($i \in \{1, \ldots, m\}$). We normalize all f_i to $[0, 1]$. By closure properties of monotonicity and submodularity, f is also submodular.

3.3 MDS Constraints

Constraints help to define a summary's structure, and the performance guarantee of the greedy algorithm depends on them. In MDS, typical constraints are upper bounds in the number of sentences or words, corresponding to cardinality ($|S| \leq m$) or knapsack constraints ($\sum_{s \in S} |\text{words}(s)| \leq m$) for some upper bound m. When optimizing a submodular monotone function under such constraints, GREEDY has a performance guarantee of ≈ 0.63 and ≈ 0.39 respectively (Calinescu et al., 2011; Lin and Bilmes, 2011). That is, for cardinality constraints, the output is at least 0.63 as good as the optimal solution in terms of objective function value.

3.4 MDS Objective Functions

In MDS, approaches typically try to maximize coverage and diversity. In its simplest form, Lin and Bilmes (2011) model coverage as

$$f_{\text{Cov}}(S) = \sum_{s \in S} \sum_{v \in U} \text{sim}(s, v), \qquad (2)$$

where sim: $U \times U \to \mathbb{R}_{\geq 0}$ is a sentence similarity function, e.g. cosine of word vectors.

Lin and Bilmes (2011) model diversity via

$$f_{\text{Div}}(S) = \sum_{i=1}^{k} \sqrt{\sum_{s \in P_i \cap S} r(s)} \qquad (3)$$

where $P_1, \ldots, P_k$ is a partition of U (e.g. obtained by semantic clustering) and $r: U \to \mathbb{R}_{\geq 0}$ is a singleton reward function. We get diminished reward for adding additional sentences from one cluster.

3.5 Application to TLS

Applying this MDS model to TLS as-is may not be adequate. For example, since the length constraints only limit the total number of sentences, some days in the timeline could be overrepresented. Furthermore, if objective functions ignore temporal information, we may not be able to extract sentences that describe very important events lasting only for short time periods. Instead, natural units for TLS are both the whole timeline as well as individual dates, so criteria and constraints for TLS should accommodate both units.

4 Temporalizing Objective Functions

We now systematically add temporal information to the objective function by (i) temporalizing coverage functions, (ii) temporalizing diversity functions, and (iii) adding date selection functions. We prove the monotonicity and submodularity of all functions in the supplementary material.

4.1 Temporalizing Coverage

MDS coverage functions (Equation 2) ignore temporal information, computing coverage on a corpus-wide level. We temporalize them by modifying the similarity computation. This is a minimal but fundamental modification. Previous work in TLS noted that coverage for candidate summaries for a day d should look mainly at the temporally local neighborhood, i.e. at sentences whose dates are close to d (Chieu and Lee, 2004; Yan et al., 2011b). We investigate two variants of this idea. The first uses a hard cutoff (Chieu and Lee, 2004), restricting similarity computations to sentences that are at most p days apart:

$$\mathrm{sim}_p(s,t) = \begin{cases} \mathrm{sim}(s,t) & |d(s) - d(t)| \le p \\ 0 & |d(s) - d(t)| > p \end{cases} \quad (4)$$

The second uses a soft variant (Yan et al., 2011b). Let $g \colon \mathbb{N} \to \mathbb{R}_{>0}$ be monotone with $g(0) = 1$. We set $\mathrm{sim}^g(s,t) = \mathrm{sim}(s,t)/g(|d(s) - d(t)|)$. Thus, all date differences are penalized, and greater date differences are penalized more.

4.2 Temporalizing Diversity

As with coverage, standard MDS diversity functions (Equation 3) ignore temporal information. If the singleton reward r in f_{Div} relies on sim, as is the case with many implementations, then temporalizing sim implicitly temporalizes diversity. We now go beyond such an implicit temporalization.

In TLS, we want to apply diversity on a temporal basis: we do not want to concentrate the summary on very few, albeit important dates, but we want date (and subevent) diversity. f_{Div}, however, typically uses only a semantic criterion to obtain a partition, e.g. by k-means clustering of sentence vector representations (Lin and Bilmes, 2011). This may wrongly conflate events, such as two unrelated protests on different dates. We can instead employ a temporal partition. The simplest method is to partition the sentences by their date, i.e. for a temporalized diversity function

f_{TempDiv} we have the same form as in Equation 3, but P_i contains all sentences with date d_i, where $d_1, \ldots, d_k$ are all sentence dates.

4.3 Date Selection Criteria

An important part of TLS is *date selection*. Dedicated algorithms for date selection use frequency and patterns in date referencing to determine date importance (Tran et al., 2015b). Most date importance measures can be integrated into the objective function to allow for joint date selection and summary generation.[6] One well-performing date selection baseline is to measure for each date how many sentences refer to it. This objective can be described by the monotone submodular function

$$f_{\mathrm{DateRef}}(S) = \sum_{d \in d(S)} |\{u \in U \mid u \text{ refers to } d\}| \,.$$

4.4 Combining Criteria

We combine coverage, diversity and date importance via unweighted sums for our final objective functions. An alternative would be to combine them via weighted sums learned from training data (Lin and Bilmes, 2011, 2012) but since there are only few datasets available for training and testing TLS algorithms we choose the unweighted sum to estimate as few parameters as possible from data.

5 Temporalizing Constraints

The MDS knapsack/cardinality constraints are too simple for TLS as an overall sentence limit does not constrain a timeline to have daily summaries of roughly similar length or enforce other uniformity properties. We introduce constraints going beyond simple cardinality, and prove performance guarantees of GREEDY under such constraints.

5.1 Definition of Constraints

Typically, we have two requirements on the timeline: the total number of days should not exceed a given number ℓ and the length of the daily summary (in sentences) should not exceed a given number k (for every day). Let d be the function that assigns each sentence its date. For a set $S \subseteq U$, the requirements can be formalized as

$$|\{d(s) \mid s \in S\}| \le \ell \quad (5)$$

and, for all $s \in S$,

$$|\{s' \mid s' \in S, \, d(s') = d(s)\}| \le k. \quad (6)$$

---

[6]Our framework can also be extended to accommodate pipelined date selection. We leave this to future work.

5.2 Performance Guarantees

While the constraints expressed by Equations 5 and 6 are more complex than constraints used in MDS, they have a property in common: if a set S fulfills the constraints (i.e. $S \in \mathcal{I}$), then also any subset $T \subseteq S$ fulfills the constraints (i.e. $T \in \mathcal{I}$). In combinatorics, such constraints are called *independence systems* (Calinescu et al., 2011).

Definition 1. *Let V be some set and $\mathcal{I} \subset 2^V$ be a collection of subsets of V. The tuple $(V, \mathcal{I})$ is called an* independence system *if (i) $\emptyset \in \mathcal{I}$ and (ii) $B \in \mathcal{I}$ and $A \subseteq B$ implies $A \in \mathcal{I}$.*

Optimization theory shows that GREEDY also has performance guarantees when generalizing cardinality/knapsack constraints to "sufficiently nice" independence systems. Based on these results, we prove Lemma 1 (see the suppl. material):

Lemma 1. *Let $\mathcal{I}$ be the set of subsets of U that fulfill Equations 5 and 6. Then* GREEDY *has a performance guarantee of $1/(k+1)$.*

The lemma implies that for small k that is typical in TLS (e.g. $k = 2$), we obtain a good approximation with reasonable constraints. However, our performance guarantees are still weaker than for MDS (for example, 0.33 for $k = 2$ compared to 0.63 in MDS). The reason for this is that our constraints are more complex, going beyond the simple well-studied cardinality and knapsack constraints. We also observe that this is a worst-case bound: in practice the performance of the algorithm may approach the exact solution (as Lin and Bilmes (2010) show for MDS). However, such an analysis is out of scope for our paper, since computing the exact solution is intractable in TLS.[7]

6 Experiments

We evaluate the performance of modeling TLS as MDS and the effect of various temporalizations.

6.1 Data and Preprocessing

We run experiments on *timeline17* (Tran et al., 2013b) and *crisis* (Tran et al., 2015a). Both data sets consist of (i) journalist-generated timelines on events such as the Syrian War as well as (ii) corresponding corpora of news articles on the topic scraped via Google News. They are publically

Name	Topics	TLs	Docs	Sentences	
				Total	Filtered
timeline17	9	19	4,622	273,432	56,449
crisis	4	22	18,246	689,165	121,803

Table 2: Data set statistics.

No	Start	End	Dates	Avg. Daily Summ. Length
1	2010-04-20	2010-05-02	13	4
2	2010-04-20	2012-11-15	16	2
3	2010-04-20	2010-10-15	12	2
4	2010-04-20	2010-09-19	48	2
5	2010-04-20	2011-01-06	102	3

Table 3: Properties for the *BP oil spill* timelines in *timeline17*. The corpus contains documents for 218 dates from 2010-04-01 to 2011-01-31.

available[8] and have been used in previous work (Wang et al., 2016).[9] Table 2 shows an overview.

In the data sets, even timelines for the same topic have considerable variation. Table 3 shows properties for the five *BP oil spill* timelines in *timeline17*. There is substantial variation in range, granularity and average daily summary length.

Following previous work (Chieu and Lee, 2004; Yan et al., 2011b), we filter sentences in the corpus using keywords. For each topic we manually define a set of keywords. If any of the keywords appears in a sentence, the sentence is retained.

We identify temporal expressions with Heidel-Time (Strötgen and Gertz, 2013). If a sentence s contains a time expression that can be mapped to a day d via HeidelTime we set the date of s to d (if there are multiple expressions we take the first one). Otherwise, we set the date of s to the publication date of the article which contains s.[10]

6.2 Evaluation Metrics

Automatic evaluation of TLS is done by ROUGE (Lin, 2004). We report ROUGE-1 and ROUGE-2 F_1 scores for the *concat*, *agreement* and *align+ m:1* metrics for TLS we presented in Martschat and Markert (2017). These metrics perform evaluation by concatenating all daily summaries, evaluating only matching days and evaluating aligned

---

[7]McDonald (2007) and Lin and Bilmes (2010) already report scalability issues for obtaining exact solutions for MDS, which is of smaller scale and has simpler constraints than our task.

[8]http://www.l3s.de/~gtran/timeline/

[9]The datasets used in Chieu and Lee (2004) or Nguyen et al. (2014) are not available.

[10]This procedure is in line with previous TLS work (Chieu and Lee, 2004). The focus of the current paper is not on further improving date assignment.

dates based on date and content similarity, respectively. We evaluate date selection using F_1 score.

6.3 Experimental Settings

TLS has no established settings. Ideally, reference and predicted timelines should be given the same compression parameters, such as overall length or number of days.[11] Since there is considerable variation in timeline parameters (Table 3), we evaluate against each reference timeline individually, providing systems with the parameters they need via extraction from the reference timeline, including range and needed length constraints. We set m to the number of sentences in the reference timeline, ℓ to the number of dates in the timeline, and k to the average length of the daily summaries.

Most previous work uses different or unreported settings, which makes comparison difficult. For instance, Tran et al. (2013b) do not report how they obtain timeline length. Wang et al. (2015, 2016) create a constant-length summary for each day that has an article in the corpus, thereby comparing reference timelines with few days with predicted timelines that have summaries for each day.

6.4 Baselines

Past work on *crisis* generated summaries from headlines (Wang et al., 2016) or only used manual evaluation (Tran et al., 2015a). Past work on *timeline17* evaluates with ROUGE (Tran et al., 2013b; Wang et al., 2016) but suffers from the fact that parameters for presented systems, baselines and reference timelines differ or are not reported (see above). Therefore, we reimplement two baselines that were competitive in previous work (Yan et al., 2011b; Wang et al., 2015, 2016).

Chieu. Our first baseline is CHIEU, the unsupervised approach of Chieu and Lee (2004). It operates in two stages. First, it ranks sentences based on similarity: for each sentence s, similarities to all sentences in a 10-day window around the date of s are summed up[12]. This yields a ranked list of sentences, sorted by highest to lowest summed up similarities. Using this list, a timeline containing one-sentence daily summaries is constructed

as follows: iterating through the ranked sentence list, a sentence is added to the timeline depending on the *extent* of the sentences already in the timeline. Extent of a sentence s is defined as the smallest window of days such that the total similarity of s to sentences in this window reaches at least 80% of the similarity to the sentences in the full 10-day window. If the candidate sentence does not fall into the extent of any sentence already in the timeline, it is added to the timeline.

As we can see, the model and parameters such as daily summary length are intertwined in this approach. We therefore reimplement CHIEU exactly instead of giving it reference timeline parameters. As we describe below, we use the same sentence similarity function as Chieu and Lee (2004).

Regression. Our second baseline is REG, a supervised linear regression model (Tran et al., 2013b; Wang et al., 2015). We represent each sentence with features describing its length, number of named entities, unigram features, and averaged/summed tf-idf scores. During training, for each sentence, standard ROUGE-1 F_1 w.r.t. the reference summary of the sentence's date is computed. The model is trained to predict this score.[13] During prediction, sentences are selected greedily according to predicted F_1 score, respecting temporal constraints defined by the reference timeline.

6.5 Model Parameters

For all submodular models and for CHIEU we use sparse inverse-date-frequency sentence representations (Chieu and Lee, 2004)[14]. This yields a vector representation v_s for each sentence s. We set $\text{sim}(s, t) = \cos(v_s, v_t)$. We did not tune any further parameters but re-used settings from previous work. For modifications to sim when temporalizing coverage and diversity (Section 4), we use a cutoff of 10 (as Chieu and Lee (2004)), and consider $g(x) = \sqrt{x+1}$ for reweighting. We choose the square root since it quickly provides strong penalizations for date differences but then saturates. Following Lin and Bilmes (2011), we set singleton reward for f_{Div} to $r(s) = \sum_{u \in U} \text{sim}(s, u)$ and obtain the partition $P_1, \ldots, P_k$ by k-means clustering with $k = 0.2 \cdot |U|$. We obtain a temporalization f_{TempDiv} of diversity by considering a partition of sentences induced by their dates (see Section 4).

---

[11]This would mirror settings in MDS, where reference and predicted summary have the same length constraint.

[12]This corresponds to the *Interest* ranking proposed by Chieu and Lee (2004). We do not use the more complex *Burstiness* measure since *Interest* was found to perform at least as well in previous work when evaluated with ROUGE-based measures (Wang et al., 2015, p.c.)

[13]We use per-topic cross-validation (Tran et al., 2013b).

[14]In preliminary experiments, results using such sparse representations were higher than results using dense vectors.

6.6 Results

Results are displayed in Table 4. The numbers are averaged over all timelines in the respective corpus. We test for significant differences using an approximate randomization test (Noreen, 1989) with a p-value of 0.05.

Baselines. Overall, performance on *crisis* is much lower than on *timeline17*. This is because (i) the corpora in *crisis* contain articles for more days over a larger time span and (ii) average percentage of article publication dates for which a summary in a corresponding reference timeline exists is 11% for *timeline17* and 3% for *crisis*. This makes date selection more difficult. On *crisis*, CHIEU outperforms REG except for date selection. On *timeline17*, REG outperforms CHIEU for four out of seven metrics. Timelines in *crisis* contain fewer dates and shorter daily summaries than timelines in *timeline17*, which aligns well with CHIEU's redundancy post-processing.

TLS as MDS. The model AsMDS uses standard length constraints from MDS and an objective function combining non-temporalized f_{Cov} and f_{Div}. It allows us to evaluate how well standard MDS ports to TLS. Except for *concat* and *date selection* on *crisis*, this model outperforms both baselines, while providing the advantages of modularity, non-supervision and feature/inference separation discussed throughout the paper.

Temporalizing Constraints. The model TLSCONSTRAINTS uses the temporal constraints described in Section 5, but has the same objective function as AsMDS. Compared to AsMDS, there are improvements on all metrics on *timeline17* and similar performance on *crisis*.

Temporalizing Criteria. We temporalize AsMDS objective functions (Section 4) via modifications of the similarity function (cutoffs/reweightings), replacing diversity by temporal diversity f_{TempDiv}, and adding date selection f_{DateRef}. Constraints are kept non-temporal. If modifications improve over AsMDS we also check for cumulative improvements. Modifying similarity is not effective, results drop or stay roughly the same according to most metrics. The other modifications improve performance w.r.t. most metrics, especially for date selection.

Temporalizing Constraints and Criteria. Lastly, we evaluate the joint contribution of temporalized constraints and criteria.[15] Modifications to the similarity function have a positive effect, especially reweighting. f_{DateRef} provides information about date importance not encoded in the constraints, improving results on *crisis*.

Oracle Results. Previous research in MDS computed oracle upper bounds (e.g. Hirao et al. (2017)). To estimate TLS difficulty and our limitations, we provide the first oracle upper bound for TLS: For each sentence s, we compute ROUGE-1 F_1 g_s w.r.t. the reference summary for the sentence's date. We then run GREEDY for $f_{\text{Oracle}}(S) = \sum_{s \in S} g_s$, employing the same constraints as TLSCONSTRAINTS (see Table 7).

Scores of the models are most similar to oracle results for the temporally insensitive *concat* metric, with gaps comparable to gaps in MDS (Hirao et al., 2017). The biggest gap is in *date selection* F_1. This also leads to higher differences in the scores of temporally sensitive metrics, highlighting the importance of temporal information.

6.7 Analysis

We now investigate where and how temporal information helps compared to AsMDS. We have already identified two potential weaknesses of modeling TLS as MDS: the low compression rate (Section 2) and the likely case that AsMDS overrepresents certain dates in a timeline (Section 3). We now analyze the behavior of AsMDS w.r.t. these points and discuss the effect of temporal information. To avoid clutter, we restrict analysis to *timeline17* and report only *align+ m:1* ROUGE-1 F_1.

Effect of Compression Rate. We hypothesize that difficulty increases as compression rate decreases. We measure compression rate in two ways. We first adopt the definition from MDS and define *corpus compression rate* as the number of sentences in a reference timeline divided by the number of sentences in the (unfiltered) corresponding corpus. Second, we define a TLS-specific notion called *spread* as the number of dates in the reference timeline divided by the maximum possible number of dates given its start and end date. For example, the timeline from Table 1 in the introduction has spread 3/14. We see that timelines with lowest compression rate/spread are indeed the hardest (Table 5). Temporal information leads to improvements in all categories.

---

[15] We do not evaluate f_{TempDiv}, since the temporal constraints already capture temporal diversity.

Model	concat		agree		align+ m:1		Date Sel.
	R1	R2	R1	R2	R1	R2	F_1
timeline17							
Baselines							
CHIEU	0.296	0.072	0.039	0.016	0.066	0.019	0.251
REG	0.336	0.065	0.063	0.014	0.074	0.016	0.491
Non-temporal Submodular Models							
AsMDS	$0.351^\dagger$	0.088^*	$0.071^\dagger$	0.019	$0.086^\dagger$	0.022	$0.452^\dagger$
Temporalizing Constraints							
TLSCONSTRAINTS	$0.368^\dagger$	$0.090^{\dagger*}$	$0.082^{\dagger*}$	0.022	$0.098^{\dagger*}$	0.025^*	$0.482^\dagger$
Temporalizing Criteria							
AsMDS+cutoff	0.338^x	0.083^*	$0.065^\dagger$	0.021	0.077	0.024	$0.393^{\dagger*x}$
AsMDS+reweighting	0.329^x	0.081^x	$0.063^\dagger$	0.019	0.075^x	0.022	$0.390^{\dagger*x}$
AsMDS+f_{DateRef}	$0.357^\dagger$	$\mathbf{0.092}^{\dagger*x}$	$0.082^{\dagger*x}$	0.022^*	$0.095^{\dagger*x}$	0.025^*	$0.529^{\dagger x}$
AsMDS+f_{TempDiv}	0.347	0.088^*	$0.088^{\dagger*x}$	$0.026^{\dagger*}$	$0.103^{\dagger*x}$	$0.029^{\dagger*x}$	$0.526^{\dagger x}$
AsMDS+f_{TempDiv}+f_{DateRef}	0.347	0.090^*	$\mathbf{0.092}^{\dagger*x}$	$\mathbf{0.027}^{\dagger*x}$	$0.105^{\dagger*x}$	$\mathbf{0.030}^{\dagger*x}$	$\mathbf{0.544}^{\dagger*x}$
Temporalizing Constraints and Criteria							
TLSCONSTRAINTS+cutoff	$0.366^\dagger$	0.085^*	$0.091^{\dagger*x}$	0.023^*	$0.105^{\dagger*x}$	0.026^*	$0.505^{\dagger x}$
TLSCONSTRAINTS+reweighting	$\mathbf{0.371}^\dagger$	$0.088^{\dagger*}$	$0.091^{\dagger*x}$	$0.026^{\dagger*x}$	$\mathbf{0.106}^{\dagger*x}$	$0.028^{\dagger*x}$	$0.506^{\dagger x}$
TLSCONSTRAINTS+f_{DateRef}	$\mathbf{0.371}^{\dagger*x}$	$0.090^{\dagger*}$	$0.089^{\dagger*x}$	0.023^*	$0.103^{\dagger*x}$	0.026^*	$0.517^{\dagger x}$
TLSCONSTRAINTS+f_{DateRef}+reweighting	$0.370^{\dagger*}$	$0.091^{\dagger*}$	$0.090^{\dagger*x}$	0.024^*	$0.104^{\dagger*x}$	0.027^*	$0.515^{\dagger x}$
crisis							
Baselines							
CHIEU	**0.374**	0.070	0.029	0.008	0.052	0.012	0.142
REG	0.271	0.034	0.014	0.001	0.028	0.003	0.189
Non-temporal Submodular Models							
AsMDS	$0.309^{\dagger*}$	0.064^*	0.037^*	0.009^*	0.060^*	0.014^*	$0.183^\dagger$
Temporalizing Constraints							
TLSCONSTRAINTS	$0.339^{\dagger*x}$	0.066^*	0.035^*	0.008^*	0.058^*	0.012^*	$0.180^\dagger$
Temporalizing Criteria							
AsMDS+cutoff	$0.283^{\dagger x}$	$0.061^{\dagger*}$	0.036^*	0.011^*	0.050^*	0.014^*	0.186
AsMDS+reweighting	$0.294^{\dagger*}$	$0.061^{\dagger*}$	0.039^*	0.011^*	0.056^*	0.015^*	$0.212^{\dagger*}$
AsMDS+f_{DateRef}	$0.314^{\dagger*}$	0.067^*	$0.042^{\dagger*}$	0.009^*	$0.065^{\dagger*x}$	0.014^*	$0.248^{\dagger*x}$
AsMDS+f_{TempDiv}	$0.311^\dagger$	0.062^*	0.034^*	0.007^*	0.058^*	0.012^{*x}	$0.196^{\dagger*}$
AsMDS+f_{TempDiv}+f_{DateRef}	$0.311^{\dagger*}$	0.064^*	$0.039^{\dagger*}$	0.008^*	$0.063^{\dagger*}$	0.012^*	$0.233^{\dagger*x}$
Temporalizing Constraints and Criteria							
TLSCONSTRAINTS+cutoff	$0.323^{\dagger*x}$	0.068^*	$0.046^{\dagger*}$	0.011^*	$0.066^{\dagger*}$	0.015^*	$0.242^{\dagger x}$
TLSCONSTRAINTS+reweighting	$0.332^{\dagger*x}$	0.071^{*x}	$0.044^{\dagger*}$	0.009^*	$0.068^{\dagger*}$	0.014^*	$0.237^{\dagger x}$
TLSCONSTRAINTS+f_{DateRef}	$0.333^{\dagger*x}$	0.069^{*x}	$0.045^{\dagger*x}$	0.009^*	$0.067^{\dagger*x}$	0.013^*	$0.248^{\dagger*x}$
TLSCONSTRAINTS+f_{DateRef}+reweighting	$0.333^{\dagger*x}$	$\mathbf{0.072}^{*x}$	$\mathbf{0.054}^{\dagger*x}$	$\mathbf{0.012}^{\dagger*}$	$\mathbf{0.075}^{\dagger*x}$	$\mathbf{0.016}^*$	$\mathbf{0.281}^{\dagger*x}$

Table 4: Results. Highest values per column/dataset are boldfaced. For the submodular models, † denotes sign. difference to CHIEU, * to REG, ^{x} to AsMDS.

(Over)representation of Dates. We hypothesized that AsMDS may overrepresent certain dates. We test this hypothesis by measuring the length (in sentences) of the longest daily summary in a timeline, and computing mean and median over all timelines (Table 6). The numbers confirm the hypothesis: When modeling TLS as MDS, some daily summaries tend to be very long. By construction of the constraints employed, the effect does not occur or is much weaker for CHIEU, REG and TLSCONSTRAINTS. Temporal objective functions (as in AsMDS+f_{TempDiv}+f_{DateRef}) also weaken the effect substantially.

7 Related Work

The earliest work on TLS is Allan et al. (2001), who introduce the concepts of usefulness (conceptually similar to coverage) and novelty (similar to diversity), using a simple multiplicative combination. However, both concepts are not temporalized. The notion of usefulness is developed further as "interest" by Chieu and Lee (2004), which we use as one of our baselines. Chieu and Lee (2004) compute interest/coverage in a static local date-based window, instead of using global optimization as we do. They handle redundancy only during post-processing s.t. the interplay between coverage and diversity is not adequately modeled. Further optimization criteria are intro-

Name	Compression rate r			Spread s		
	$r \in [0, 0.001]$	$r \in (0.001, 0.01]$	$r \in (0.01, 0.1]$	$s \in [0, 1/3]$	$s \in (1/3, 2/3]$	$s \in (2/3, 1]$
CHIEU	0.06	0.08	0.07	0.06	0.08	0.04
REG	0.04	0.09	0.07	0.05	0.11	0.11
AsMDS	0.05	0.10	0.09	0.07	0.10	0.10
TLSCONSTRAINTS	0.08	0.10	0.10	0.08	0.12	0.14
AsMDS+f_{TempDiv}+f_{DateRef}	0.09	0.11	0.12	0.09	0.13	0.13

Table 5: Results (*align+ m:1* ROUGE-1 F_1) by *compression rate* and *spread* on timeline 17.

Name	Max. Length	
	Mean	Median
Reference	5.6 ± 2.7	5
CHIEU	1.0 ± 0.0	1
REGRESSION	2.3 ± 1.7	2
AsMDS	23.7 ± 41.2	8
TLSCONSTRAINTS	2.3 ± 1.7	2
AsMDS+f_{TempDiv}+f_{DateRef}	3.8 ± 5.3	1

Table 6: Length of longest daily summary, mean and median over all timelines on *timeline 18*.

	concat		agree		align+ m:1		Date
Corpus	R1	R2	R1	R2	R1	R2	F_1
tl17	0.50	0.18	0.30	0.14	0.30	0.14	0.87
crisis	0.49	0.16	0.34	0.14	0.35	0.14	0.95

Table 7: Oracle results optimizing per-day R1 F_1.

duced by Yan et al. (2011b,a) and Nguyen et al. (2014), but their frameworks suffer from a lack of modularity or from an unclear separation of features and architecture. Wang et al. (2015) devise a local submodular model for predicting daily summaries in TLS, but they do not model the whole timeline generation as submodular function optimization under suitable constraints.

Wang et al. (2016) tackle only the task of generating daily summaries without date selection using a supervised framework, greedily optimizing per-day predicted ROUGE scores, using images and text. In contrast, Kessler et al. (2012) and Tran et al. (2015b) only tackle date selection but do not generate any summaries. We consider the full task, including date selection and summary generation.

TLS is related to standard MDS. We discussed differences in Section 2. Our framework is inspired by Lin and Bilmes (2011) who cast MDS as optimization of submodular functions under cardinality and knapsack constraints. We go beyond their work by modeling temporally-sensitive objective functions as well as more complex constraints encountered in TLS.

A related task is TREC *real-time summarization* (RTS) (Lin et al., 2016).[16] In contrast to TLS, this task requires *online* summarization by presenting the input as a stream of documents and emphasizes novelty detection and lack of latency. In addition, RTS focuses on social media and has a very fine-grained temporal granularity. TLS also has an emphasis on date selection and dating for algorithms and evaluation which is not present in RTS as the social media messages are dated a priori.

8 Conclusions

We show that submodular optimization models for MDS can yield well-performing models for TLS, despite the differences between the tasks. Therefore we can port advantages such as modularity and separation between features and inference, which current TLS models lack. In addition, we temporalize these MDS-based models to take into account TLS-specific properties, such as timeline uniformity constraints, importance of date selection and temporally sensitive objectives. These temporalizations increase performance without losing the mentioned advantages. We prove that the ensuing functions are still submodular and that the more complex constraints still retain performance guarantees for a greedy algorithm, ensuring scalability.

Acknowledgments

We thank the anonymous reviewers and our colleague Josef Ruppenhofer for feedback on earlier drafts of this paper.

References

James Allan, Rahul Gupta, and Vikas Khandelwal. 2001. Temporal summaries of new topics. In *Proceedings of the 24th Annual International ACM SIGIR Conference on Research and Development in*

---

[16] Predecessors of this task were the *update* and *temporal summarization tasks* (Aslam et al., 2015)

Information Retrieval, New Orleans, Louis., 9–12 September 2001, pages 49–56.

Javed A. Aslam, Fernando Diaz, Matthew Ekstrand-Abueg, Richard McCreadie, Virgil Pavlu, and Testuya Sakai. 2015. TREC 2015 temporal summarization track overview. In *Proceedings of the Twenty-Fourth Text REtrieval Conference*, Gaithersburg, Md., 17–20 November 2015.

Gruia Calinescu, Chandra Chekuri, Martin Pál, and Jan Vondrák. 2011. Maximizing a monotone submodular function subject to a matroid constraint. *SIAM Journal on Computing*, 40(6):1740–1766.

Hai Leong Chieu and Yoong Keok Lee. 2004. Query based event extraction along a timeline. In *Proceedings of the 27th Annual International ACM SIGIR Conference on Research and Development in Information Retrieval*, New York, N.Y., 25–29 July 2004, pages 425–432.

Tsutomu Hirao, Masaaki Nishino, Jun Suzuki, and Masaaki Nagata. 2017. Enumeration of extractive oracle summaries. In *Proceedings of the 15th Conference of the European Chapter of the Association for Computational Linguistics, volume 1: Long Papers*, Valencia, Spain, 3–7 April 2017, pages 386–396.

Kai Hong, John M. Conroy, Benoit Favre, Alex Kulesza, Hui Lin, and Ani Nenkova. 2014. A repository of state of the art and competitive baseline summaries for generic news summarization. In *Proceedings of the 9th International Conference on Language Resources and Evaluation*, Reykjavik, Iceland, 26–31 May 2014, pages 1608–1616.

Remy Kessler, Xavier Tannier, Carloine Hagège, Véronique Moriceau, and André Bittar. 2012. Finding salient dates for building thematic timelines. In *Proceedings of the 50th Annual Meeting of the Association for Computational Linguistics (Volume 1: Long Papers)*, Jeju Island, Korea, 8–14 July 2012, pages 730–739.

Chin-Yew Lin. 2004. ROUGE: A package for automatic evaluation of summaries. In *Proceedings of the Text Summarization Branches Out Workshop at ACL '04*, Barcelona, Spain, 25–26 July 2004, pages 74–81.

Hui Lin and Jeff Bilmes. 2010. Multi-document summarization via budgeted maximization of submodular functions. In *Proceedings of Human Language Technologies 2010: The Conference of the North American Chapter of the Association for Computational Linguistics*, Los Angeles, Cal., 2–4 June 2010, pages 912–920.

Hui Lin and Jeff Bilmes. 2011. A class of submodular functions for document summarization. In *Proceedings of the 49th Annual Meeting of the Association for Computational Linguistics (Volume 1: Long Papers)*, Portland, Oreg., 19–24 June 2011, pages 510–520.

Hui Lin and Jeff Bilmes. 2012. Learning mixtures of submodular shells with application to document summarization. In *Proceedings of the 28th Conference on Uncertainty in Artificial Intelligence*, Catalina Island, CA, USA, 14–18 July 2012, pages 479–490.

Jimmy Lin, Adam Roegiest, Luchen Tan, Richard McCreadie, Ellen Voorhees, and Fernando Diaz. 2016. Overview of the TREC 2016 real-time summarization track. In *Proceedings of the Twenty-Fifth Text REtrieval Conference, 2016*.

Sebastian Martschat and Katja Markert. 2017. Improving ROUGE for timeline summarization. In *Proceedings of the 15th Conference of the European Chapter of the Association for Computational Linguistics, volume 2: Short Papers*, Valencia, Spain, 3–7 April 2017, pages 285–290.

Ryan McDonald. 2007. A study of global inference algorithms in multi-document summarization. In *Proceedings of the European Conference on Information Retrieval*, Rome, Italy, 2-5 April 2007, pages 557–564.

Kiem-Hieu Nguyen, Xavier Tannier, and Véronique Moriceau. 2014. Ranking multidocument event descriptions for building thematic timelines. In *Proceedings of the 25th International Conference on Computational Linguistics*, Dublin, Ireland, 23–29 August 2014, pages 1208–1217.

Eric W. Noreen. 1989. *Computer-Intensive Methods for Testing Hypotheses. An Introduction.* Wiley, New York.

Paul Over and James Yen. 2004. An introduction to DUC 2004: Intrinsic evaluation of generic news text summarization systems. In *Proceedings of the 2004 Document Understanding Conference held at the Human Language Technology Conference of the North American Chapter of the Association for Computational Linguistics*, Boston, Mass., 6–7 May 2004, pages 1–21.

Dragomir R. Radev, Hongyan Jing, Małgorzata Styś, and Daniel Tam. 2004. Centroid-based summarization of multiple documents. *Information Processing and Management*, 40:919–938.

Jannik Strötgen and Michael Gertz. 2013. Multilingual and cross-domain temporal tagging. *Language Resources and Evaluation*, 47(2):269–298.

Giang Tran, Mohammad Alrifai, and Eelco Herder. 2015a. Timeline summarization from relevant headlines. In *Proceedings of the 37th European Conference on Information Retrieval*, Vienna, Austria, 29 March – 2 April 2015, pages 245–256.

Giang Tran, Mohammad Alrifai, and Dat Quoc Nguyen. 2013a. Predicting relevant news events for timeline summaries. In *Proceedings of the 22nd World Wide Web Conference*, Rio de Janeiro, Brasil, 13–17 May, 2013, pages 91–92.

Giang Tran, Eelco Herder, and Katja Markert. 2015b. Joint graphical models for date selection in timeline summarization. In *Proceedings of the 53rd Annual Meeting of the Association for Computational Linguistics (Volume 1: Long Papers)*, Beijing, China, 26–31 July 2015, pages 1598–1607.

Giang Tran, Tuan Tran, Nam-Khanh Tran, Mohammad Alrifai, and Nattiya Kanhabua. 2013b. Leveraging learning to rank in an optimization framework for timeline summarization. In *Proceedings of the SIGIR 2013 Workshop on Time-aware Information Access (TAIA-13)*, Dubling, Ireland, 1 August 2013.

Lu Wang, Claire Cardie, and Galen Marchetti. 2015. Socially-informed timeline generation for complex events. In *Proceedings of the 2015 Conference of the North American Chapter of the Association for Computational Linguistics: Human Language Technologies*, Denver, Col., 31 May – 5 June 2015, pages 1055–1065.

William Yang Wang, Yashar Mehdad, Dragomir R. Radev, and Amanda Stent. 2016. A low-rank approximation approach to learning joint embeddings of news stories and images for timeline summarization. In *Proceedings of the 2016 Conference of the North American Chapter of the Association for Computational Linguistics: Human Language Technologies*, San Diego, Cal., 12 – 17 June 2016, pages 58–68.

Rui Yan, Liang Kong, Congrui Huang, Xiajun Wan, Xiaoming Li, and Yan Zhang. 2011a. Timeline generation through evolutionary trans-temporal summarization. In *Proceedings of the 2011 Conference on Empirical Methods in Natural Language Processing*, Edinburgh, Scotland, U.K., 27–29 July 2011, pages 433–443.

Rui Yan, Xiaojun Wan, Jahna Otterbacher, Liang Kong, Xiaming Li, and Yan Zhang. 2011b. Evolutionary timeline summarization: a balanced optimization framework via iterative substitution. In *Proceedings of the 34th Annual International ACM SIGIR Conference on Research and Development in Information Retrieval*, Beijing, China, 25–29 July 2011, pages 745–754.

Chinese Poetry Generation with a Salient-Clue Mechanism

Xiaoyuan Yi[1,2,3], **Ruoyu Li**[5], **Maosong Sun**[1,2,4*]

[1]Department of Computer Science and Technology, Tsinghua University
[2]Institute for Artificial Intelligence, Tsinghua University
[3]State Key Lab on Intelligent Technology and Systems, Tsinghua University
[4]Beijing Advanced Innovation Center for Imaging Technology, Capital Normal University
[5]6ESTATES PTE LTD, Singapore

yi-xy16@mails.tsinghua.edu.cn, liruoyu@6estates.com,
sms@mail.tsinghua.edu.cn

Abstract

As a precious part of the human cultural heritage, Chinese poetry has influenced people for generations. Automatic poetry composition is a challenge for AI. In recent years, significant progress has been made in this area benefiting from the development of neural networks. However, the coherence in meaning, theme or even artistic conception for a generated poem as a whole still remains a big problem. In this paper, we propose a novel Salient-Clue mechanism for Chinese poetry generation. Different from previous work which tried to exploit all the context information, our model selects the most salient characters automatically from each so-far generated line to gradually form a salient clue, which is utilized to guide successive poem generation process so as to eliminate interruptions and improve coherence. Besides, our model can be flexibly extended to control the generated poem in different aspects, for example, poetry style, which further enhances the coherence. Experimental results show that our model is very effective, outperforming three strong baselines.

1 Introduction

As a fascinating literary form starting from the Pre-Qin Period, Chinese poetry has influenced people for generations and thus influenced Chinese culture and history in thousands of years. Poets often write poems to record interesting events and express their feelings. In fact, the ability to create high-quality poetry has become an indicator of knowledge, wisdom and elegance of a person in China.

Generally, a Chinese poem should meet two kinds of requirements. One is from the perspective of *form*: it must obey some structural and phonological rules strictly. For example (as shown in Figure 1), quatrain (*Jueju* in Chinese), one of the most popular types of Chinese poetry, contains

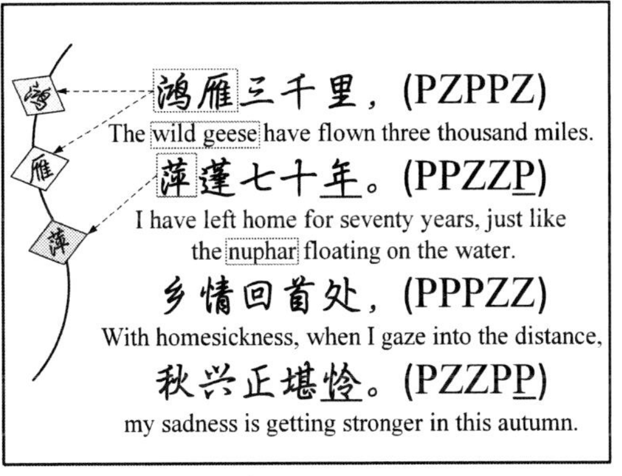

Figure 1: A *Wujue* generated by our model. The tone of each character is given in parentheses, where P and Z represent Ping (level tone) and Ze (oblique tone) respectively. Rhyming characters are underlined. The left part is an artistic illustration of the salient clue.

four lines with each consisting of five or seven characters (called *Wujue* and *Qijue* respectively); characters with particular tone must be in particular positions to make the poem cadenced and full of rhythmic beauty; and, the last character of the first (optional), second and fourth lines must rhyme. The other one is from the perspective of *content*, concerning: (1) if each line of the poem is adequate syntactically and semantically; (2) if the association between two adjacent lines is reasonable; and (3) if the poem as a whole is coherent in meaning, theme or even in artistic conception. Obviously, the second requirement is much more complicated and difficult than the first one.

In this paper, we investigate on automatic Chinese poetry generation, with emphasis on quatrains. We believe the *form* requirement is comparatively easy for a computer to deal with by some constraint checking. For the *content* requirement, point (1) and (2) can be also handled well owing to the use of powerful sequence-to-sequence neural networks (Sutskever et al., 2014), which are capable of producing well-formed tar-

---

*Corresponding author: sms@mail.tsinghua.edu.cn.

Proceedings of the 22nd Conference on Computational Natural Language Learning (CoNLL 2018), pages 241–250
Brussels, Belgium, October 31 - November 1, 2018. ©2018 Association for Computational Linguistics

get sentence given a source sentence. A challenging problem which remains unresolved for researchers is the point (3), where inter-lines associations are 'global' throughout a poem, rather than 'local' in point (2). The relevant experience tells us this is a major reason for the distinct gap between computer-generated poems and those written by poets. In fact, most previous models don't tackle this problem well and will produce incoherences and inconsistencies in generated poems.

Inter-lines coherence is the main concern of this paper. Intuitively, there should be a clear clue to keep the theme of a poem consistent. However, setting a fixed pattern of the clue in advance, e.g, pre-determining keywords for each line, may lose the flexibility and imagination, which are essential for poetry. When writing a poem, human poets will focus on some salient parts of the context to ignore distractions and create relevant content. During this process, poets gradually build a salient clue (or framework) of the poem (Zhang, 2015), allowing not only coherence but also some flexibility.

Inspired by this, we propose a novel Salient-Clue Mechanism for poetry generation. Different from previous models which tried to exploit all the context, our model chooses a few salient characters out of each previously generated line, forming a vital clue for generating succeeding lines, so as to maintain the coherence of the whole poem to the maximum extent. In addition, owing to the flexible structure of our model, extra useful information (e.g., the user intent and poetry style) can be incorporated with the salient clue to control the generation process, further enhancing coherence.

Contributions of this work are as follows:

- To the best of our knowledge, we first propose to utilize the salient partial context to guide the poetry generation process.

- We extend our model to combine user intent and control the style of generated poems, which further enhance coherence.

- Experimental results show that our model outperforms three strong baselines.

2 Related Work

The research on automatic poetry generation has lasted for decades. The early approaches are based on rules and templates, such as the ASPERA system (Gervás, 2001) and Haiku system (Wu et al.,

2009). Genetic algorithms are exploited to improve the quality of generated poems (Manurung, 2003; Levy, 2001). Other approaches are also tried, for instance, Yan et al. (2013) adopt the automatic summarization method. Following the work that successfully applies the Statistical Machine Translation approach (SMT) to the task of Chinese classical couplets generation (Jiang and Zhou, 2008), He et al. (2012) further extend SMT to Chinese classical poetry generation.

In recent years, a big change in research paradigm occurred in this field, that is, the adoption of neural network-based approaches, which have shown great advantages in both English poetry (Hopkins and Kiela, 2017; Ghazvininejad et al., 2017) and Chinese poetry generation, as well as other generation tasks. Context coherence is essential for text generation. In some related tasks, researchers have taken a step towards this goal, for example, the discourse Neural Machine Translation (NMT) (Tiedemann and Scherrer, 2017; Maruf and Haffari, 2017; Jean et al., 2017). For poetry generation, some neural models have also recognized the importance of poem coherence. The fundamental issue here is how to define and use the context of a poem properly.

Zhang and Lapata (2014) first propose to generate Chinese poems incrementally with Recurrent Neural Network (RNN), which packs the full context into a single vector by a Convolutional Sentence Model. To enhance coherence, their model needs to be interpolated with two SMT features, as the authors state. Yan (2016) generates Chinese quatrains using two RNNs with an iterative polishing schema, which tries to refine the poem generated in one pass for several times. Yi et al. (2017) utilize neural Encoder-Decoder with attention mechanism (Bahdanau et al., 2015) and trains different models to generate lines in different positions of a poem. Wang et al. (2016) propose a two-stage Chinese classical poetry generation method which at first plans the sub-keywords of the poem, then generates each line sequentially with the allocated sub-keyword. However, the beforehand extracted planning patterns bring some explicit constraints, which may take a risk of losing some degree of flexibility as discussed in Section 1.

These neural network-based approaches are very promising, but there is still large room for exploration. For instance, whether packing the full context into a single vector really represents the 'full' context as well as expected? Can we do better to represent the inter-lines context more properly in pursuing better coherence of the entire generated poem? Our work tries to respond to these questions.

3 Model Design

We begin by formalizing our problem. Suppose a poem P consists of n lines, $P = L_1 L_2 \ldots L_n$. Given previous i-1 lines $L_{1:i-1}$, we need to generate the i-th line which is coherent with the context in theme and meaning. Since our model and most baselines are based on a powerful framework first proposed in NMT, that is, the Bidirectional LSTM (Schuster and Paliwal, 1997; Hochreiter and Schmidhuber, 1997) Encoder-Decoder with attention mechanism (Bahdanau et al., 2015), we first denote X a line in Encoder, $X = (x_1 x_2 \ldots x_T)$, and Y a generated line in Decoder, $Y = (y_1 y_2 \ldots y_T)$. T is the length of a line. h_t and h_t' represent the Encoder and Decoder hidden states respectively. $emb(y_{t-1})$ is the word embedding of y_{t-1}. The probability distribution of each character to be generated in the i-th line is calculated by:[1]

$$h_t' = LSTM(h_{t-1}', emb(y_{t-1}), c_t), \tag{1}$$

$$p(y_t|y_{1:t-1}, L_{1:i-1}) = g(h_t', emb(y_{t-1}), c_t, v), \tag{2}$$

where g is a normalization function, softmax with a maxout layer (Goodfellow et al., 2013) in this paper. $y_{1:t-1}$ means $y_1, \ldots, y_{t-1}$ (similar to $L_{1:i-1}$). c_t is the local context vector in attention mechanism. v is a global context vector. To avoid confusion, in the remainder of this paper when it comes to the word 'context', we all mean the global context, that is, so-far generated lines $L_{1:i-1}$.

Now the key point lies in how to represent and utilize the context for the sake of better coherence. Before presenting the proposed method, we first introduce two basic formalisms of utilizing full context.

3.1 Basic Models

nLto1L

We call the first formalism **nLto1L**, where poetry generation is regarded as a process similar to machine translation. The difference is that the pair in

---

[1] For brevity, we omit biases and use h_t to represent the combined state of bidirectional LSTM Encoder.

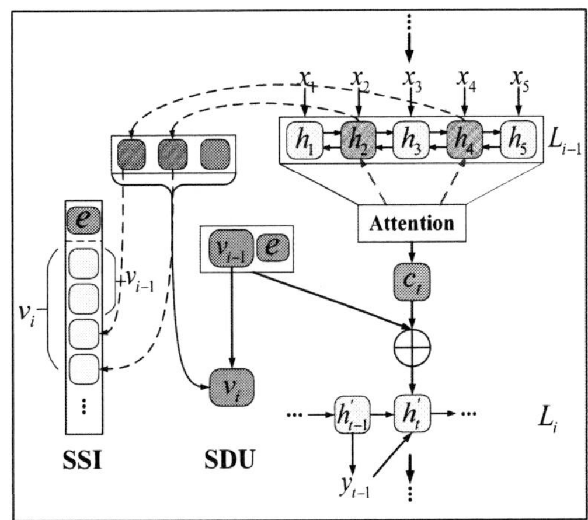

Figure 2: A graphical illustration of the proposed Salient-Clue mechanism. v_i is the salient-clue vector and e is the extension vector. We design two strategies for updating the salient clue. SDU: v_i is kept at the same size; SSI: the size of v_i increases during the generation process.

the parallel corpus for NMT models, is changed to the pair of <preceding lines in a poem, a line in a poem> here, which is semantically related rather than semantically equivalent.

The 'n' in nLto1L means at most n preceding lines are concatenated as a long sequence and used simultaneously in Encoder, corresponding to the preceding-lines-in-poem part in the pair, to generate a line in Decoder. In this case, the context is captured by c_t without extra v. (Wang et al., 2016) and (Yi et al., 2017) both belong to this formalism.

The nLto1L formalism is effective, but it has two drawbacks. For one thing, as 'n' increases in nLto1L, more global context can be exploited explicitly by attention, but the number of training pairs decreases, which hurts the generalization performance. For instance, from each quatrain, only one 3Lto1L pair (but two 2Lto1L pairs) can be extracted. For another, when the input sequence is too long, the performance of NMT models will still degrade, even with an attention mechanism (Shen et al., 2016). We find this problem more prominent in poetry generation, since attention may fail to capture all important parts of the context. Our preliminary experiment shows that, regarding generating the fourth line, both for Yi's model and Wang's model, more than 70% of the top three attention values fall into just the third line area and thus neglect other lines, which validates our assumption.

243

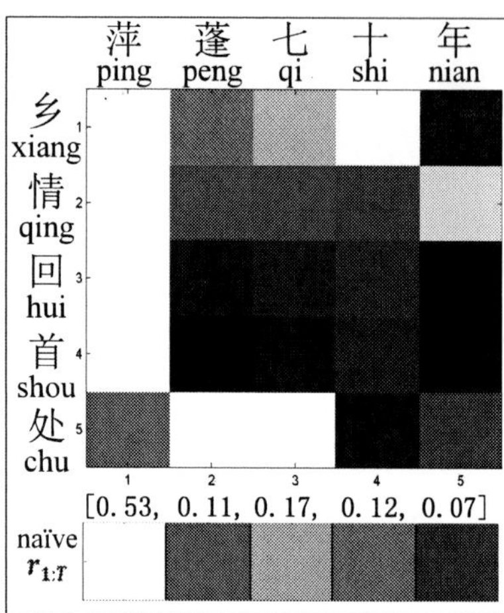

Figure 3: An example of calculating the saliency score of each character (in the x-axis) from the attention matrix (0:black, 1:white), in the naive Salient-Clue. The scores are normalized to interval [0,1] here.

Packing Full Context

Another formalism is to pack the full context into a single vector v, which is used to generate successive lines (Zhang and Lapata, 2014; Yan, 2016). Usually, v is updated by the vector of each generated line in a poem. This formalism is not as powerful as we expected. There is still much room for improvement. A single vector doesn't have enough capacity to store all context. Moreover, meaningful words and noises (e.g., stop words) are mixed in one vector, which results in the implicit and indiscriminate utilization of the context.

3.2 The Proposed Salient-Clue Mechanism

As discussed, using the full context directly cannot necessarily lead to the best performance. It becomes clear that we still need to develop a new mechanism to exploit the context in a proper way. Our design philosophy is ignoring the uninformative parts (e.g., stop words) and using some salient characters in context to represent the full context and form a salient clue, which is used to guide the generation process. Following this idea, we propose our Salient-Clue Model.

Naive Salient-Clue

As illustrated in Figure 2, to generate L_i, our model uses standard attention mechanism to exploit L_{i-1} so as to capture short-distance relevance. And it utilizes a salient-clue vector, v_i, to exploit long-distance context. After generating L_i, our model selects up to K (K is 2 for *Wujue* and

Algorithm 1 Saliency Selection Algorithm

Inputs: The saliency scores of characters in the preceding line, $r_{1:T}$; K; ·

Outputs: The number of finally selected salient characters, N; The indices of selected characters in the preceding line, $m_{1:N}$;

1: Calculate the mean value of $r_{1:T}$, avg;
2: Calculate the standard deviation of $r_{1:T}$, std;
3: Get sorted indices $i_{1:T}$ in descending order of $r_{1:T}$;
4: $k = 1$; $val = avg + 0.5 * std$;
5: **while** $(r_{i_k} \geq val)$ and $(k \leq K)$ **do**
6: $\quad m_k = i_k$; $val = val * 0.618$ (the golden ratio); $k = k + 1$;
7: **end while**
8: $N = k - 1$;
9: **return** $N, m_{1:N}$;

3 for *Qijue* in this work) most salient characters from L_{i-1} according to the attention values, and uses their corresponding Encoder hidden states to update the salient clue vector v_i. Thanks to the bidirectional LSTM, even if we only focus on part of the context characters, the information of those unselected won't be lost completely.

Concretely, let A denote the attention alignment matrix in the attention mechanism (Bahdanau et al., 2015) between the preceding line L_{i-1} and the current generated line L_i. We calculate the **saliency score** of j-th character in L_i, r_j, by:

$$r_j = \frac{\sum_{i=1}^{T} A_{ij}}{\sum_{j'=1}^{T} \sum_{i=1}^{T} A_{ij'}}, \quad (3)$$

where A_{ij} is the element in i-th row and j-th column of A. Figure 3 depicts an example. The most salient character is *"ping"* (nuphar, a kind of plant, a symbol of loneliness) and the second one is *"qi"* (seven), according to their saliency scores r(*ping*) = 0.53 and r(*qi*) = 0.17.

The character *"ping"* is very informative for the generated poem but *"qi"* isn't, as signaled by the sharp distinction between their saliency scores. So we design the **Saliency Selection Algorithm 1** to further filter out characters with quite low saliency scores, like *"qi"* here. We define this algorithm as a function $SSal(r_{1:T}, K)$, which takes the saliency scores and the maximum number of selected characters as inputs and outputs the number of finally selected characters and their indices.

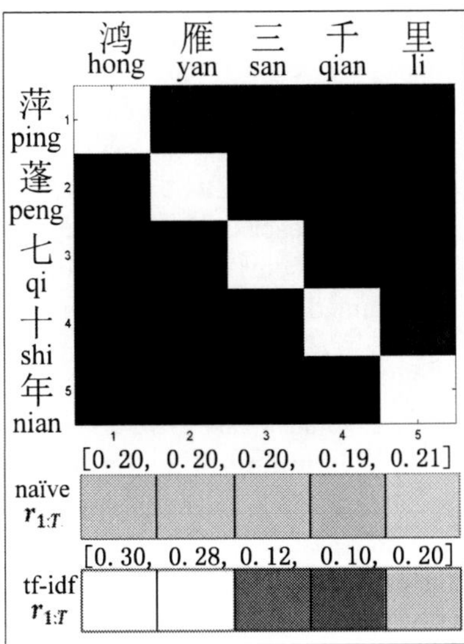

Figure 4: The comparison of saliency scores obtained by the naive model and the tf-idf weighting improved model: an example.

Then we update the salient-clue vector v_i as follows:

$$N, m_{1:N} = SSal(r_{1:T}, K), \tag{4}$$

$$s = \frac{\sum_{k=1}^{N} r_{m_k} * h_{m_k}}{\sum_{k'}^{N} r_{m_{k'}}}, \tag{5}$$

$$v_i = \sigma(v_{i-1}, s), v_0 = \vec{0}, \tag{6}$$

where σ is a non-linear layer. v_{i-1} is used to predict next character to be generated by formula (2). Please note that in formula (4), N may be smaller than K since we want to further ignore relatively less salient characters even though they are already in the list of the K most salient ones.

By the generation process presented above, each generated line is guided by the salient clue and therefore is coherent with it. Meanwhile, informative parts of each generated line are selected and maintained in the salient clue. As a result, the salient clue vector always keeps a coherent information flow, playing a role of a dynamically and incrementally built framework (skeleton) for the generated poem.

TF-IDF Weighted Attention

Observe an example in Figure 4. The scores $r_{1:T}$ given by the Naive Salient-Clue are very close to each other, not distinguishable in saliency. To cope with this, we further take into account the importance of characters both in the preceding line and the current generated line, by the traditional tf-idf scheme in Information Retrieval:

$$r_j = [(\mathbf{w}_{out} * A) \odot \mathbf{w}_{in}]_j, \tag{7}$$

where $\odot$ is element-wise multiplication and $[\cdot]_j$ is the j-th element in a vector. $\mathbf{w}_{in} \in \mathbb{R}^{1*T}$ is the tf-idf vector of preceding (input) line and the i-th element of it is the tf-idf value of i-th character. Similarly, $\mathbf{w}_{out}$ is the tf-idf vector of the current generated (output) line. Elements in $\mathbf{w}_{in}$ and $\mathbf{w}_{out}$ are normalized to [0,1].

As shown in Figure 4, by tf-idf weighting, two informative characters *"hong yan"* (wild goose, a symbol of autumn) are selected correctly, which leads to the generation of word *"qiu xing"* (sadness in autumn) in the fourth line in Figure 1.

Two Strategies for Salient-Clue

As shown in Figure 2, we use two strategies to form and utilize the salient-clue vector v_i. The first is called **Saliency Dynamic Update (SDU)** by formula (5) and (6), which means that hidden states of selected salient characters are packed into v_i. Thus v_i is kept at the same size and is updated dynamically after each line is generated.

The second one is the concatenation of these hidden states:

$$v_i = [v_{i-1}; h_{m_1}; ...; h_{m_N}], \tag{8}$$

where $[;]$ means vector concatenation. The size of v_i will increase in the generation process. We call this **Saliency Sensitive Identity (SSI)**, because the identity of each hidden state is kept independent, without being merged as one.

3.3 Extensions of Salient-Clue

Above we design different methods to select the salient partial context. Since the proposed model is quite flexible, aside from the selected characters, other information can be also utilized to form the salient clue, so as to further improve coherence. In this paper, we tried and evaluated two extensions: user intent and poetry style. This extra information is vectorized as an extension vector e and then concatenated to the salient clue vector:

$$p(y_t|y_{1:t-1}, L_{1:i-1}) =$$
$$g(h'_t, emb(y_{t-1}), c_t, [v_{i-1}; e]). \tag{9}$$

Intent Salient-Clue. The poem is generated with a user intent keyword. Taking user intent into

	Models	*Wujue*	*Qijue*
Different	Planning	0.460	0.554
	iPoet	0.502	0.591
Models	seq2seqPG	0.466	0.620
	SC	**0.532**	**0.669**
Different	naive-TopK-SDU	0.442	0.608
	naive-SSal-SDU	0.471	0.610
Strategies	tfidf-SSal-SDU	**0.533**	0.648
	tfidf-SSal-SSI	0.530	0.667
of SC	tfidf-SSal-SSI-intent	0.532	**0.669**

Table 1: BLEU evaluation results. The scores are calculated by the multi-bleu.perl script.

account can prevent later generated lines diverging from earlier generated ones in a poem. In detail, we feed the keyword into Encoder, then vector e is calculated by a non-linear transformation of the average of their hidden states.

Style Salient-Clue. The style of generated poems can also benefit coherence. Here we simply use a style embedding as the vector e, which provides a high-level indicator of style and is learned during the training process. It is noteworthy that Zhang et al. (2017) achieve style transfer with the help of an external memory, which stores hundreds of poems (thus thousands of hidden states). By contrast, our Style extension is simpler but still achieves comparable performance.

4 Experiments and Evaluations

4.1 Data and Setups

Our corpus contains 165,800 poems (half *Wujue* and half *Qijue*). We use 4,000 of them for validation, 4,000 for testing and other ones for training. From each poem, a keyword is extracted by tf-idf.

The sizes of word embedding, hidden state, saline-clue vector, intent vector and style embedding are set to 256, 512, 512, 128 and 64 respectively. For SSI, to reduce the model size, we map each hidden state to a 100-d vector by a non-linear transformation. Encoder and Decoder share the same word embedding. All different strategies of Salient-Clue are used both in training and generation. The optimization objective is standard cross entropy errors of the predicted character distribution and the actual one. Adam (Kingma and Ba, 2015) with shuffled mini-batches (batch size 64) is used. Then we use beam search (beam size 20) to generate each poem, with a keyword as input. For fairness, all baselines use the same configuration.

For Style Salient-Clue model, we first use LDA (Blei et al., 2003) to train the whole corpus (with 15 topics). We select three main styles in Chinese poetry: Pastoral, Battlefield and Romantic and find the corresponding topics manually. Then all poems are labeled by LDA inference. We select 5,000 poems for each style, together with other 5,000 non-style poems (20,000 in total), to fine-tune a pre-trained normal Salient-Clue model.

4.2 Models for Comparisons

We compare: **iPoet** (Yan, 2016), **seq2seqPG** (Yi et al., 2017), **Planning** (Wang et al., 2016), **SC** (our model, tfidf-SSal-SSI-intent, which is the best configure under BLEU evaluation), **Style-SC** (the style extension of our model) and **Human** (poems created by human poets). We choose these three previous models as our baselines, because they all achieve satisfactory performance and the authors have done thorough comparisons with other models, such as RNNPG (Zhang and Lapata, 2014) and SMT (He et al., 2012), and prove that their models outperform baselines. Besides, the three models can be classified into the two formalisms in Section 3.1.

4.3 Evaluation Design

To demonstrate the effectiveness of our model, we conduct four evaluations:

BLEU Evaluation. Following (He et al., 2012; Zhang and Lapata, 2014; Yan, 2016), we use BLEU (Papineni et al., 2002) to evaluate our model. BLEU isn't a perfect metric for generated poems, but in the scenario of pursuing better coherence, it still makes sense to some extent. Because higher BLEU scores indicate that the model can generate more n-grams of ground-truth, which certainly have better coherence.

Human Evaluation. Following (Manurung, 2003; Zhang and Lapata, 2014), we design five criteria: **Fluency** (are the lines fluent and well-formed?), **Coherence** (is the theme of the whole quatrain consistent?), **Meaningfulness** (does the poem convey some certain messages?), **Poeticness** (does the poem have some poetic features?), **Entirety** (the reader's general impression on the poem). Each criterion needs to be scored in a 5-point scale ranging from 1 to 5.

We select 20 typical keywords and generate two quatrains (one *Wujue* and one *Qijue*) for each keyword using these models. For Human, we select quatrains containing the given keywords. Therefore, we obtain 240 quatrains (20*6*2) in total.

Models	Fluency		Coherence		Meaningfulness		Poeticness		Entirety	
	Wujue	*Qijue*	*Wujue*	*Qijue*	*Wujue*	*Qijue*	*Wujue*	*Qijue*	*Wujue*	*Qijue*
Planning	2.56	2.84	2.50	2.64	2.49	2.64	2.59	2.88	2.39	2.66
iPoet	3.13	3.45	2.89	2.91	2.60	2.80	2.79	3.05	2.54	2.85
seq2seqPG	3.54	3.65	3.31	3.16	3.15	3.01	3.26	3.29	3.06	3.08
SC	4.01**	4.04**	3.85**	3.86**	3.55**	3.63**	**3.74****	**3.69***	3.63**	**3.70****
Style-SC	**4.03****	**4.16****	**3.90****	**4.01****	**3.68****	**3.75****	3.61*	3.68*	**3.65****	**3.70****
Human	4.09	4.43	3.90	4.33+	3.94	4.35++	3.83	4.24++	3.81	4.24++

Table 2: Human evaluation results. Diacritics * ($p < 0.05$) and ** ($p < 0.01$) indicates SC models significantly outperform the three baselines; + ($p < 0.05$) and ++ ($p < 0.01$) indicates Human is significantly better than all the five models. The Intraclass Correlation Coefficient of the four groups of scores is 0.596, which indicates an acceptable inter-annotator agreement.

We invite 12 experts on Chinese poetry to evaluate these quatrains, who are Chinese literature students or members of a poetry association. Experts are divided into four groups and required to focus on the quality as objectively as possible, even if they recognize the human-authored ones. Each group completes the evaluation of all poems and we use the average scores.

Style-SC is not suitable for BLEU, because we can't expect LDA to predict a correct style label by a short keyword. Thus Style-SC is only tested under Human Evaluation. We label each keyword with an appropriate style manually, which is used to guide the generation.

Style Control Evaluation. Poetry style is usually coupled with content. Not all keywords are compatible with every style. Therefore we select ten normal keywords without obvious style (e.g., moon and wind). We use SC to generate one poem and use Style-SC to generate three poems with the three specified styles. The experts are asked to identify the style of each poem from four options (Unknown, Battlefield, Romantic and Pastoral).

Saliency Selection Evaluation. The main idea of our method is to select the salient partial context to guide successive generation. To evaluate the reasonableness of selected characters, we randomly select 20 *Wujue*s and 20 *Qijue*s from the test set. Then three experts are asked to select up to K salient characters from each line. When experts have different opinions, they stop and discuss until reaching an agreement. **Jaccard similarity** is used to measure the overlap of human-selected characters and the model-selected ones.

4.4 Evaluation Results and Discussion

As shown in Table 1, our SC outperforms other models under BLEU evaluation. We also compare different strategies of SC. As we expected, tfidf-SC models outperform the naive ones, because

tf-idf values lower the weights of uninformative characters. We also compare our SSal 1 with TopK (just select top K salient characters) and SSal gets better results. Please note that, from naive-TopK-SDU to tfidf-SSal-SDU, BLEU scores are getting higher without any increase of model size (Table 4). SSI is better on *Qijue*, but performs slightly worse than SDU on *Wujue*. We use SSI for Human evaluation here, but SDU is more suitable for longer poetry, e.g., Chinese Song Iambics. Besides, the intent extension makes a little bit of improvement, not as prominent as we expected. We think the reason may lie in that the keyword selected by tf-idf can't accurately represent the user intent. Generally, the results show both for packing and concatenation formalisms, the proper utilization of partial salient context (SDU and SSI) can be better than the improper utilization of full context (Packing Full Context and nLto1L).

Table 2 gives human evaluation results. SC and Style-SC achieve better results than other models and get close to Human, though there is still a gap. Especially on Coherence, our Style-SC gets the same score as Human for *Wujue*. Moreover, Style-SC makes a considerable improvement on Coherence compared to SC (+0.05 for *Wujue* and +0.15 for *Qijue*), which demonstrates that consistent style can actually enhance the coherence, though it's not easy to predict an appropriate style automatically. Interestingly, Style-SC outperforms SC on most criteria, except for Poeticness. We believe this is mainly because that style control forces the model to always generate some style-related words, which limits the imagination and thus hurts the Poeticness.

Besides, as we can see, seq2seqPG outperforms other two baselines, but at the expense that it is three times the model size of iPoet (Table 4). Surprisingly, Planning gets the worst re-

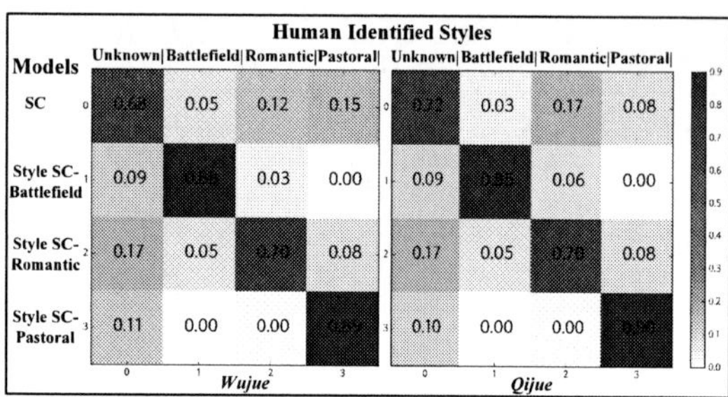

Figure 5: Style control evaluation results. The values are ratios that generated poems are identified as different styles by human experts.

Models	Wujue	Qijue
Random	0.271	0.247
tf-idf	0.417	0.378
naive-TopK SC	0.347	0.415
naive-SSal SC	0.431	0.441
tfidf-SSal SC	**0.525**	**0.461**

Table 3: Saliency selection results. Random: randomly select K characters for three times and use the average Jaccard values. tf-idf: directly select K characters in terms of tf-idf, without SC.

sults. This is because that Planning uses a neural language model to generate the planned sub-keywords, which performs poorly on our corpus and thus hurts fluency and coherence.

Figure 5 gives style control evaluation results. Incorporating one style vector with the salient-clue, our Style-SC achieves comparable performance with (Zhang et al., 2017). The good results partially lie in that we only use those non-style keywords, such as moon, wind, water and so on, for this experiment. Empirically, transferring from a keyword with obvious style to arbitrary style is intractable, e.g., from the word 'army' to Pastoral style, which may need more complicated model design. Even so, our results still show that rough style control is not as difficult as we thought.

Table 3 shows the effectiveness of our salient character selection methods. tfidf-SSal achieves about 50% overlap of human-selected salient characters, which is notably higher than Random and tf-idf. With only attention values, naive-TopK performs worse than tf-idf on *Wujue*. Combining tf-idf and SSal makes notable improvement.

Models	Innovation	Param	Speed
Planning	**0.039**	15.1	2.49
iPoet	0.044	**11.0**	1.76
seq2seqPG	0.047	37.1	1.85
SC Model	0.041	13.6	**1.57**
naive-TopK-SDU	0.058	13.7	1.49
naive-SSal-SDU	0.056	13.7	1.51
tfidf-SSal-SDU	0.042	13.7	1.52
tfidf-SSal-SSI	0.043	**13.1**	**1.48**
tfidf-SSal-SSI-intent	**0.041**	13.6	1.57

Table 4: Extra comparisons of different models. Innovation, Param (million parameters) and Speed (seconds per poem) are compared. The generation speed is tested on an Intel CORE i5 4-core CPU.

4.5 Extra Comparisons and Case Study

Besides the metrics above, we also compare innovation, model size and generation speed of different models. The innovation is measured by Jaccard similarity of generated poems (3,000 for each model). Intuitively, the basic requirement for innovation is that poems generated with different keywords should be different with each other.

As shown in Table 4, SC makes a good balance on quality, innovation, generation speed and model size. The iPoet has the smallest size, but the generation is slow, since it may polish the poem for several times, costing more time than other one-pass-generation models. For SC, the use of tf-idf significantly improves innovation. Due to planned sub-keywords, Planning achieves the best innovation but the worst quality, which shows pursuing innovation takes the risk of abruptness and incoherence.

Figure 6 shows two *Wujue*s generated by seq2seqPG and SC respectively, with the same input "Yangzhou City". A word "moon" is generated by seq2seqPG in the first line, which determines the time (at night) of the whole poem. However, in the fourth line, seq2seqPG still generates an inconsistent word "sunset". For the poem generated by SC, the word "autumn" in the second line is selected for successive generation. As a result, a word "fallen leaves" is generated in the fourth line. Furthermore, in the second line, except for "autumn", other four uninformative characters, which have quite low saliency scores, are filtered out by **SSal** 1 as shown at the bottom of Figure 6.

5 Conclusion and Future Work

In this paper, we address the problem of the context coherence in poetry generation. How to prop-

seq2seqPG

一夜扬州月， The moon in Yangzhou city makes me depressed,
凄凉万里心。 since I am far away from it.
故乡无限意， The missing for my hometown is endless.
惆怅暮云阴。 It seem the cloud is also sad at sunset.

SC

忆昔扬州月， I recall the past moon in Yangzhou city.
于今又一秋。 Now, another autumn has come.
故人何处是， Where can I find my old friends?
落叶满汀洲。 Maybe on the shoal covered with fallen leaves

	于	今	又	一	秋
salience	at	now	again	one	autumn
scores:	[0.084,	0.120,	0.121,	0.058,	0.616]

Figure 6: Two *Wujue*s generated with the same input. Green boxes and arrows show consistencies, and the red ones show inconsistencies. Automatically selected charcters by SC are underlined.

erly treat the global context is a key factor to consider. We propose a Salient-Clue mechanism[2]. Our model selects highly salient characters in preceding generated lines to form a representation of the so-far context, which can be considered as a dynamically and incrementally built framework, then uses it to guide the successive generation. Both automatic and human evaluations demonstrate that our model can effectively improve the global coherence of meaning, theme and artistic conception of generated poems. This implies the proper treatment of a partial context could be better than the improper treatment of the full context.

Furthermore, our model can be flexibly combined with different auxiliary information and we show the utilization of style and user intent can further enhance coherence.

There still exists a gap between our model and human poets, which indicates that there are lots to do in the future. Though we experimented on Chinese corpus, the proposed model is genre-free. We also plan to extend our model to generate other types of poetry, such as Chinese Regulated Verse and English sonnet. Besides, we also want to design some explicit supervisory signals or utilize external knowledge to improve the saliency selection algorithm.

Acknowledgments

We would like to thank Cheng Yang, Jiannan Liang, Zhipeng Guo, Huimin Chen, Wenhao Li and anonymous reviewers for their insightful comments. This research is funded by Major Project of the National Social Science Foundation of China (No. 13&ZD190). It is also partially supported by the NExT++ project, the National Research Foundation, Prime Ministers Office, Singapore under its IRC@Singapore Funding Initiative.

---

[2]Based on this work, we build an online poetry generation system, **Jiuge**: https://jiuge.thunlp.cn.

References

Dzmitry Bahdanau, KyungHyun Cho, and Yoshua Bengio. 2015. Neural machine translation by jointly learning to align and translate. In *Proceedings of the 2015 International Conference on Learning Representations*, San Diego, CA.

David Blei, Andrew Ng, and Michael Jordan. 2003. Latent dirichlet allocation. *machine Learning research*, (3):993–1022.

Pablo Gervás. 2001. *An Expert System for the Composition of Formal Spanish Poetry*. Springer London.

Marjan Ghazvininejad, Xing Shi, Jay Priyadarshi, and Kevin Knight. 2017. Hafez: an interactive poetry generation system. In *Proceedings of ACL 2017, System Demonstrations*, pages 43–48. Association for Computational Linguistics.

Ian J. Goodfellow, David Warde-Farley, Mehdi Mirza, Aaron Courville, and Yoshua Bengio. 2013. Maxout networks. In *Proceedings of the 30th International Conference on Machine Learning*, pages 1319–1327, Atlanta, USA.

Jing He, Ming Zhou, and Long Jiang. 2012. Generating chinese classical poems with statistical machine translation models. In *Proceedings of the 26th AAAI Conference on Artificial Intelligence*, pages 1650–1656, Toronto, Canada.

Sepp Hochreiter and Juärgen Schmidhuber. 1997. Long short-term memory. *Neural computation*, 9(8):1735–1780.

Jack Hopkins and Douwe Kiela. 2017. Automatically generating rhythmic verse with neural networks. In *Proceedings of the 55th Annual Meeting of the Association for Computational Linguistics (Volume 1: Long Papers)*, pages 168–178. Association for Computational Linguistics.

Sebastien Jean, Stanislas Lauly, Orhan Firat, and Kyunghyun Cho. 2017. Does neural machine translation benefit from larger context? *arXiv preprint arXiv:1704.05135*.

Long Jiang and Ming Zhou. 2008. Generating chinese couplets using a statistical mt approach. In *Proceedings of the 22nd International Conference on Computational Linguistics*, pages 377–384, Manchester, UK.

Diederik P. Kingma and Jimmy Lei Ba. 2015. Adam: A method for stochastic optimization.

Robert P. Levy. 2001. A computational model of poetic creativity with neural network as measure of adaptive fitness. In *Proceedings of the ICCBR-01 Workshop on Creative Systems*.

Hisar Maruli Manurung. 2003. *An evolutionary algorithm approach to poetry generation*. Ph.D. thesis, University of Edinburgh.

Sameen Maruf and Gholamreza Haffari. 2017. Document context neural machine translation with memory networks. *arXiv preprint arXiv:1711.03688*.

Kishore Papineni, Salim Roukos, Todd Ward, and Wei-Jing Zhu. 2002. Bleu: a method for automatic evaluation of machine translation. In *Proceedings of the 40th Annual Meeting of the Association for Computational Linguistics*.

Mike Schuster and Kuldip K Paliwal. 1997. Bidirectional recurrent neural networks. *IEEE Transactions on Signal Processing*, 45(11):2673–2681.

Shiqi Shen, Yong Cheng, Zhongjun He, Wei He, Hua Wu, Maosong Sun, and Yang Liu. 2016. Minimum risk training for neural machine translation. In *Proceedings of the 54th Annual Meeting of the Association for Computational Linguistics (Volume 1: Long Papers)*, pages 1683–1692. Association for Computational Linguistics.

Ilya Sutskever, Oriol Vinyals, and Quoc V. Le. 2014. Sequence to sequence learning with neural networks. In *In Advances in Neural Information Processing Systems 2014*, Montreal, Canada.

Jörg Tiedemann and Yves Scherrer. 2017. Neural machine translation with extended context. In *Proceedings of the Third Workshop on Discourse in Machine Translation*, pages 82–92, Copenhagen, Denmark.

Zhe Wang, Wei He, Hua Wu nad Haiyang Wu, Wei Li, Haifeng Wang, and Enhong Chen. 2016. Chinese poetry generation with planning based neural network. In *Proceedings of COLING 2016, the 26th International Conference on Computational Linguistics:Technical Papers*, pages 1051–1060, Osaka, Japan.

Xiaofeng Wu, Naoko Tosa, and Ryohei Nakatsu. 2009. New hitch haiku: An interactive renku poem composition supporting tool applied for sightseeing navigation system. In *Proceedings of the 8th International Conference on Entertainment Computing*, pages 191–196, Paris, France.

Rui Yan. 2016. i,poet:automatic poetry composition through recurrent neural networks with iterative polishing schema. In *Proceedings of the Twenty-Fifth International Joint Conference on Artificial Intelligence*, pages 2238–2244, New York, USA.

Rui Yan, Han Jiang, Mirella Lapata, Shou-De Lin, Xueqiang Lv, and Xiaoming Li. 2013. I, poet:automatic chinese poetry composition through a generative summarization framework under constrained optimization. In *Proceedings of the 23rd International Joint Conference on Artificial Intelligence*, pages 2197–2203, Beijing, China.

Xiaoyuan Yi, Ruoyu Li, and Maosong Sun. 2017. Generating chinese plassical poems with rnn encoder-decoder. In *Proceedings of the Sixteenth Chinese Computational Linguistics*, pages 211–223, Nanjing, China.

Jiyuan Zhang, Yang Feng, Dong Wang, Yang Wang, Andrew Abel, Shiyue Zhang, and Andi Zhang. 2017. Flexible and creative chinese poetry generation using neural memory. In *Proceedings of the 55th Annual Meeting of the Association for Computational Linguistics (Volume 1: Long Papers)*, pages 1364–1373. Association for Computational Linguistics.

Xingxing Zhang and Mirella Lapata. 2014. Chinese poetry generation with recurrent neural networks. In *Proceedings of the 2014 Conference on Empirical Methods in Natural Language Processing*, pages 670–680, Doha, Qatar.

Yingzhong Zhang. 2015. *How to Create Chinese Classical Poetry*. The Commercial Press.

Multi-modal Sequence Fusion via Recursive Attention
for Emotion Recognition

Rory Beard[1,*]   **Ritwik Das**[2,*]   **Raymond W. M. Ng**[1,*]   **P. G. Keerthana Gopalakrishnan**[2]
Luka Eerens[2]   **Pawel Swietojanski**[1]   **Ondrej Miksik**[1]
[1]Emotech Labs   [2]Carnegie Mellon University

Abstract

Natural human communication is nuanced and inherently multi-modal. Humans possess specialised sensoria for processing vocal, visual, and linguistic, and para-linguistic information, but form an intricately fused percept of the multi-modal data stream to provide a holistic representation. Analysis of emotional content in face-to-face communication is a cognitive task to which humans are particularly attuned, given its sociological importance, and poses a difficult challenge for machine emulation due to the subtlety and expressive variability of cross-modal cues.

Inspired by the empirical success of recent so-called *End-To-End Memory Networks* (Sukhbaatar et al., 2015), we propose an approach based on recursive multi-attention with a shared external memory updated over multiple gated iterations of analysis. We evaluate our model across several large multi-modal datasets and show that global contextualised memory with gated memory update can effectively achieve emotion recognition.

1 Introduction

Multi-modal sequential data pose interesting challenges for learning machines that seek to derive representations. This constitutes an increasingly relevant sub-field of multi-view learning (Ngiam et al., 2011; Baltrusaitis et al., 2017). Examples of such modalities include visual, audio and textual data. Uni-modal observations are typically complementary to each other and hence they can reveal a fuller and more context-rich picture with better generalisation ability when used together. Through its complementary perspective, each view can unburden sub-modules specific to another modality of some of its modelling onus, which might otherwise learn implicit hidden

causes that are over-fitted to training data idiosyncrasies in order to explain the training labels.

On the other hand, multi-modal data introduces many difficulties to model designing and training due to the distinct inherent dynamics of each modality. For instance, combining modalities with different temporal resolution is an open problem. Other challenges include deciding where and how modalities are combined, leveraging the weak discriminative power of training label and the presence of variability and noise or dealing with complex situations such as modelling the emotion of sarcasm, where cues among modalities contradict.

In this paper, we address multi-modal sequence fusion for automatic emotion recognition. We believe, that a strong model should enable:

(i) *Specialisation of modality-specific submodules* exploiting the inherent properties of its data stream, tapping into the mode-specific dynamics and characteristic patterns.

(ii) *Weak (soft) data alignment* dividing heterogeneous sequences into segments with co-occuring events across modalities without alignment to a common time axis. This overcomes limitations of *hard alignments* which often introduce spurious modelling assumptions and data inefficiencies (*e.g.* re-sampling) which must be performed again from scratch if views are added or removed.

(iii) *Information exchange* for both view-specific information and statistical strength for learning shared representations.

(iv) *Scalability* of the approach to many modalities using (a) parallelisable computation over modalities, and (b) a parameter set size growing (at most) linearly with the number of modalities.

In the present work, we detail a *recursively attentive* modelling approach. Our model fulfills the desiderata above and performs multiple sweeps of globally-contextualised analysis so that one modality-specific representation cues the at-

---

* Equal contribution.

251

Proceedings of the 22nd Conference on Computational Natural Language Learning (CoNLL 2018), pages 251–259
Brussels, Belgium, October 31 - November 1, 2018. ©2018 Association for Computational Linguistics

tention of the next and vice-versa. We evaluate our approach on three large-scale multi-modal datasets to verify its suitability.

2 Related work

2.1 Multi-modal analysis

Most approaches to multi-modal analysis (Ngiam et al., 2011) focus on designing feature representations, co-learning mechanisms to transfer information between modalities, and fusion techniques to perform a prediction or classification. These models typically perform either "early" (input data are concatenated and pushed through a common model) or "late" (outputs of the last layer are combined together through linear or non-linear weighting) fusion. In contrast, our model does not fall into any of these categories directly as it is "iterative" in the sense that there are multiple fusions per decision, with an evolving belief state – the memory. In addition to that, our model is also "active" since feature extraction from one modality can influence the nature of the feature extraction from another modality in the next time step via the shared memory.

For instance, Kim et al. (2013) used low-level hand crafted features such as pitch, energy and mel-frequency filter banks (MFBs) capturing prosodic and spectral acoustic information and Facial Animation Parameters (FAP) describing the movement of face using distances between facial landmarks. In contrast, our model allows for an end-to-end training of feature representation.

Zhang et al. (2017) learnt motion cues in videos using 3D-CNNs from both spatial and temporal dimensions. They performed deep multi-modal fusion using a deep belief network that learnt non-linear relations across modalities and then used a linear SVM to classify emotions. Similarly, Vielzeuf et al. (2017) explored VGG-LSTM and 3DCNN-LSTM architectures and introduced a weighted score to prioritise the most relevant windows during learning. In our approach, exchange of information between different modalities is not limited to the last layer of the model, but due to memory component, each modality can influence every other in the following time steps.

Co-training and co-regularisation approaches of multi-view learning (Xu et al., 2013; Sindhwani and Niyogi, 2005) seek to leverage unlabelled data via a semi-supervised loss that encodes a consensus and complementarity principles. The for-

mer encodes the assertion that predictions made be each view-specific learner should largely agree, and the latter encodes the assumption that each view contains useful information that is hidden from others, until exchange of information is allowed to occur.

2.2 Memory Networks

End-To-End Memory Networks (Sukhbaatar et al., 2015) represent a fully differentiable alternative to the strong supervision-dependent *Memory Networks* (Weston, 2017). To bolster attention-based recurrent approaches to language modelling and question answering, they introduced a mechanism performing multiple hops of updates to a "memory" representation to provide context for next sweep of attention computation.

Dynamic Memory Networks (DMN) (Xiong et al., 2016) integrate an attention mechanism with a memory module and multi-modal bilinear pooling to combine features across views and predict attention over images for visual question answering task. Nam et al. (2017) iterated on this design to allow the memory update mechanism to reason over previous dual-attention outputs, instead of forgetting this information, in the subsequent sweep. The present work extends the multi-attention framework to leverage neural-based information flow control by dynamically routing it with neural gating mechanisms.

The very recent work (Zadeh et al., 2018a) also approaches multi-view learning with recourse to a system of recurrent encoders and attention mediated by global memory fusion. However, fusion takes place at the encoder cell level, requires hard alignment, and is performed online in one sweep so it cannot be informed by upstream context. The analysis window of the global memory is limited to the current and previous cell memories of each LSTM encoder, whereas our approach abstracts the shared memory update dynamics away from the ties of the encoding dynamics. Therefore our approach enables post-fusion and retrospective re-analysis of the entire cell memory history of all encoders at each analysis iteration.

3 Recursive Recurrent Neural Networks

Our approach is tailored to videos of single speakers, each divided into segments that roughly span one uttered sentence. We treat each segment as an independent datum constituting an individual multi-modal event with its own annotation, such that there is no temporal dependence across any two segments. In the following exposition, each of the various mechanisms we describe (encoding, attention, fusion, and memory update) act on each segment in isolation of all others. We will use the terms "view" and "modality" interchangeably.

We refer to our recursively attentive analysis model as a *Recursive Recurrent Neural Network* (RRNN) since it resembles an RNN, but the hidden state and the next cell input are coupled in a recursion. At each step of the cell update there is no new incoming information; rather the *same* original inputs are re-weighted by a new attention query to form the new cell inputs (see discussion in Section 3.5 for more details).

3.1 Independent recurrent encoding

The major modelling assumption herein, is that a single, independent recurrent encoding of each segment of each modality is sufficient to capture a range of semantic representations that can be tapped by several shared external memory queries. Each memory query is formed in a separate stage of an iterated analysis over the recurrent codes. Concretely, modality-specific attention-weighted summaries $(\mathbf{a}^{(\tau)}, \mathbf{v}^{(\tau)}, \mathbf{t}^{(\tau)})$ at analysis iteration τ contribute to the update of a shared dense memory/context vector $\mathbf{m}^{(\tau)}$, which in turn serves as a differentiable attention query at iteration $\tau + 1$ (*cf.* Fig. 1). This provides a recursive mechanism for sharing information within and across sequences, so the recurrent representations of one view can be revisited in light of cross-modal cues gleaned from previous sweeps of other views. This is an efficient alternative to re-encoding each view on every sweep, and is more modular and generalisable than routing information across views at the recurrent cell level.

For each multi-modal sequence segment $\mathbf{x}^n = \{\mathbf{x}_a^n, \mathbf{x}_v^n, \mathbf{x}_t^n\}$, a view-specific encoding is realised via a set of independent bi-directional LSTMs (Hochreiter and Schmidhuber, 1997), run over segments $n \in [1, N]$:

$$\mathbf{h}_s^{fwd}[n, k_s] = LSTM(\mathbf{x}_s^n[k_s], \mathbf{h}_s^{fwd}[n, k_s - 1]) \tag{1}$$

$$\mathbf{h}_s^{bwd}[n, k_s] = LSTM(\mathbf{x}_s^n[k_s], \mathbf{h}_s^{bwd}[n, k_s + 1]) \tag{2}$$

$$\mathbf{h}_s[n, k_s] = [\mathbf{h}_s^{fwd}[n, k_s]; \mathbf{h}_s^{bwd}[n, k_s]] \tag{3}$$

Here, $s \in \{a, v, t\}$ denotes respectively audio, vi-

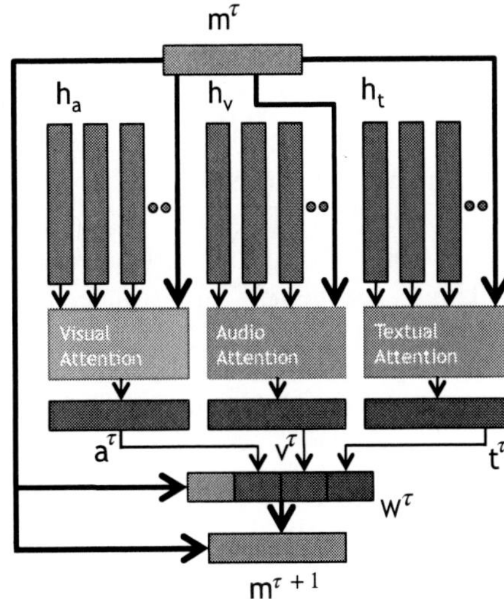

Figure 1: Schematic overview of the proposed neural architecture. Shared memory m^τ is updated with with the contextualised embeddings from a^τ, v^τ and t^τ.

sual and textual modalities, and $k_s \in \{1, ..., K_s\}$ are view-specific state indices.

The number of recurrent steps is view-specific (*i.e.* $K_a \neq K_v \neq K_t$) and is governed by the feature representation and sampling rate for the given view, *e.g.* number of word (embeddings) in a the text contained within a time-stamped segment. This is in contrast to Zadeh et al. (2018a), where the information in different views was grounded to a common time axis or the number of steps in an early stage, either via up-sampling or down-sampling. Thus the extracted representations in our approach preserve the inherent time-scales of each modality and avoid the need for hard alignment, satisfying desiderata (i) and (ii) outlined in Section 1. Note that the input sequences $\mathbf{x}_s^{(n)}$ may refer to either raw or pre-processed data (see Section 4 for details). In the remainder, we drop the segment id n to reduce notational clutter.

3.2 Globally-contextualised attention

We used a view-specific attention-based weighting mechanism to compute a contextualised embedding $\mathbf{c}_s$ for a view s. Encoder output $\mathbf{h}_s$ is stacked along time to form matrices $\mathbf{H}_s \in \mathbb{R}^{(D \times K_s)}$. A shared dense memory $\mathbf{m}^{(\tau=0)}$ is initialised by summing the time-average of the $\mathbf{H}_s$ across three modalities. $\mathbf{M}^{(\tau)}$ is then constructed by repeating the shared memory, $\mathbf{m}^{(\tau)}$, K_s times such that it has the same size as the corresponding context $\mathbf{H}_s$, *i.e.* $\mathbf{H}_s, \mathbf{M} \in \mathbb{R}^{(D \times K_s)}$. An alignment function then scores how well $\mathbf{H}_s$ and $\mathbf{M}^{(\tau)}$ are matched

$$\tilde{\alpha}_s^{(\tau)} = \mathrm{align}(\mathbf{H}_s, \mathbf{M}^{(\tau)}). \tag{4}$$

The alignment mechanism entails a feedforward neural network with $\mathbf{H}_s$ and $\mathbf{M}^{(\tau)}$ as inputs. A softmax is applied on the network output to derive the attention strength α. This architecture resembles that in Bahdanau et al. (2014); concretely

$$\mathbf{R}^{(\tau)} = \tanh\big(\mathbf{W}_{s1}^{(\tau)}\mathbf{H}_s\big) \odot \tanh\big(\mathbf{W}_{s2}^{(\tau)}\mathbf{M}^{(\tau)}\big), \tag{5}$$

$$\tilde{\alpha}_s^{(\tau)} = \mathbf{w}_{s3}^{(\tau)\mathrm{T}}\mathbf{R}^{(\tau)}, \tag{6}$$

$$\alpha_s^{(\tau)}[k_s] = \frac{\tilde{\alpha}_s^{(\tau)}[k_s]}{\sum_l \tilde{\alpha}_s^{(\tau)}[l]}. \tag{7}$$

In Eq. (5), $\mathbf{W}_s^{(\tau)}$ (where $s \in \{s1, s2\}$) are square or fat matrices in the first layer of the alignment network, containing parameters governing the *self-influence* within view s and influence from the shared memory $\mathbf{M}$. For the majority of our experiments, we used the multiplicative method of Nam et al. (2017) to combine the two activation terms, but similar results were also obtained with the concatenative approach of Bahdanau et al. (2014). In eq. (6), $\mathbf{w}_{s3}^{(\tau)\mathrm{T}}$ is a vector projecting an un-normalised attention weight $\mathbf{R}$ onto an alignment vector $\tilde{\alpha}$, which has the same dimensions as K_s. Finally, eq. (7) applies the softmax operation along the time step k_s.

Parameters $\mathbf{W}_{s1}, \mathbf{W}_{s2}, \mathbf{w}_{s3}$ for deriving attention strength α_s are in general distinct parameters for each memory update step, τ. However, they could also be tied across steps. In the standard attention schemes, attention weight α_s is a vector spanning across K_s. Note, that $\mathbf{w}_{s3}^{(\tau)}$ in eq. (6) could be replaced by a matrix-form $\mathbf{W}_{s3}^{(\tau)}$ to produce a *multi-head attention* weight (Vaswani et al., 2017). Alternatively, the transposition of network inputs can be performed such that attention scales each dimension, D, instead of each time step k. This can be seen as a variant of *key-value attention* (Daniluk et al., 2017), where the values differ from their keys by a linear transformation with weights governed by the alignment scores.

Each globally-contextualised view representation $\mathbf{c}_s$ is defined as the convex combination of the view-specific encoder outputs weighted by attention strength

$$\mathbf{c}_s^{(\tau+1)} = \sum_k \alpha_s^{(\tau)}[k_s]\mathbf{h}_s[k_s]. \tag{8}$$

3.3 Shared memory update

The previous section described how the current shared memory state is used to modulate the attention-based re-analysis of the (encoded) inputs. Here we detail how the outcome of the re-analysis is used to update the shared memory state.

In contrast to the memory update employed in Nam et al. (2017), our approach includes a set of coupled gating mechanisms outlined below, and depicted schematically in Fig. 2:

$$\mathbf{g}_w^{(\tau)} = \sigma\big(\mathbf{W}_{wm}\mathbf{m}^{(\tau-1)} + \mathbf{W}_{ww}\mathbf{w}^{(\tau)} + \mathbf{b}_w\big) \tag{9}$$

$$\mathbf{g}_c^{(\tau)} = \sigma\big(\mathbf{W}_{cm}\mathbf{m}^{(\tau-1)} + \mathbf{W}_{cw}\mathbf{w}^{(\tau)} + \mathbf{b}_c\big) \tag{10}$$

$$\mathbf{g}_s^{(\tau)} = \sigma\big(\mathbf{W}_{sm}\mathbf{m}^{(\tau-1)} + \mathbf{W}_{ss}\mathbf{c}_s^{(\tau)} + \mathbf{b}_s\big)$$
$$\forall s \in \{a, v, t\} \tag{11}$$

$$\mathbf{u}^{(\tau)} = \tanh\big(\mathbf{W}_{um}\mathbf{m}^{(\tau-1)} +$$
$$\mathbf{W}_{uw}\mathbf{g}_w^{(\tau)} \odot \mathbf{w}^{(\tau)} + \mathbf{b}_u\big) \tag{12}$$

$$\mathbf{m}^{(\tau)} = \big(1 - \mathbf{g}_c^{(\tau)}\big) \odot \mathbf{m}^{(\tau-1)} + \mathbf{g}_c^{(\tau)} \odot \mathbf{u}^{(\tau)}, \tag{13}$$

where $\mathbf{w}^{(\tau)} = [\mathbf{a}^{(\tau)}; \mathbf{v}^{(\tau)}; \mathbf{t}^{(\tau)}]$, $\mathbf{m}^{(0)} = \mathbf{0}$ and $\sigma()$ denotes an element-wise sigmoid non-linearity. The function of the view context gate defined in eq. (9) and invoked in eq. (12), is to block *corrupted* or *uninformative* view segments from influencing the proposed shared memory update content, $\mathbf{u}^{(\tau)}$. The attention mechanism, outlined in eq. (5)-(7), cannot fulfill this task alone since the full attention divided over a view segment must sum to 1 even if no part of that segment is pertinent/salient. The utility of this gating will be empirically demonstrated in noise-injection experiments in Section 5.

The new memory content $\mathbf{u}^{(\tau)}$ is written to the memory state according to eq. (12), subject to the action of the memory update gate defined in eq. (10). This update gate determines how much of the past global information should be passed on to contextualise subsequent stages of re-analysis. If parameters $\mathbf{W}_{s1}, \mathbf{W}_{s2}, \mathbf{w}_{s3}$ are untied across each re-analysis step, this update gate additionally accommodates short-cut or "highway" routing (Srivastava et al., 2015) of regression error gradients from the end of the multi-hop procedure back through the parameters of the earlier attention sweeps.

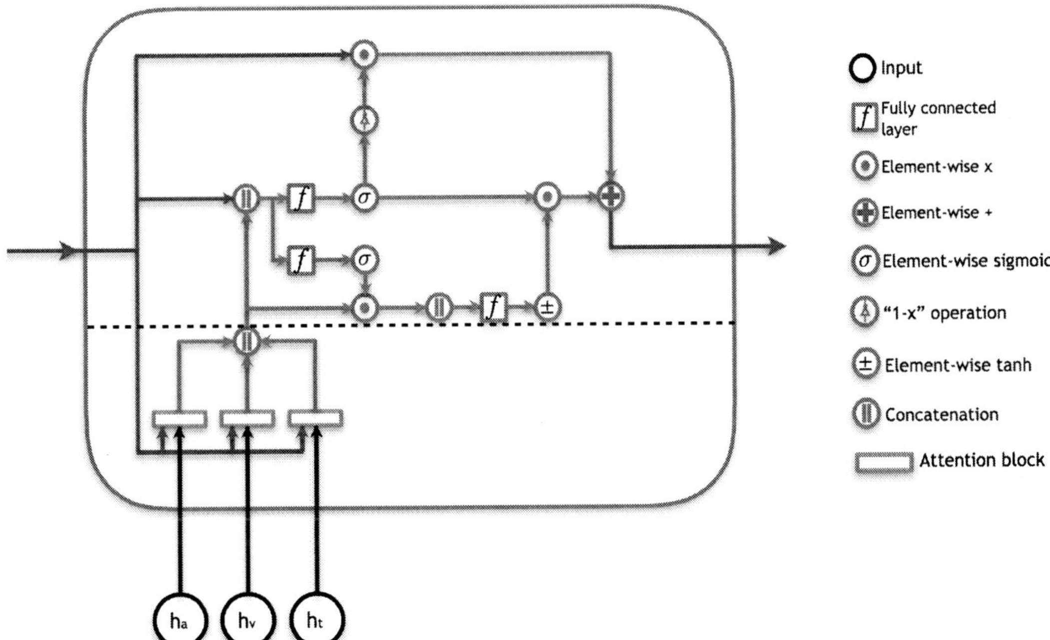

Figure 2: A detailed schematic of the proposed RRNN cell (left) and its legend (right). The routing above the dashed black line resembles that of a (non-recursive) GRU cell, where the concatenated attention output constitutes the cell's input. In this case, the cell's input at time τ is available only once the cell's state at time $\tau - 1$ has been computed. When the static representations $\{\mathbf{h}_a, \mathbf{h}_v, \mathbf{h}_t\}$ are instead viewed as the cell's input, then the cell forms a recursive RNN, which subsumes the attention mechanism as a cell sub-component.

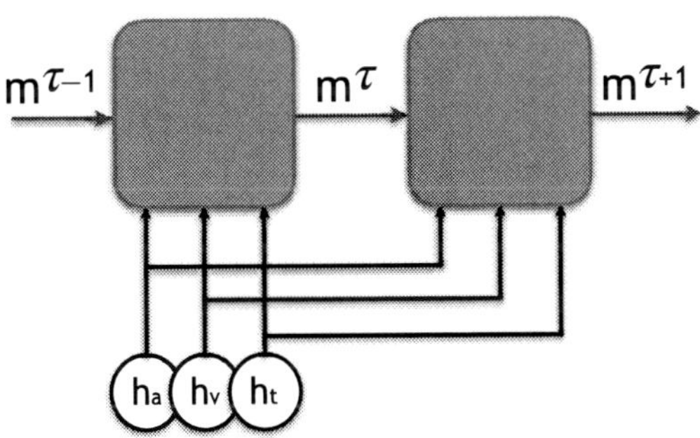

Figure 3: Two consecutive cells of a Recursive Recurrent Neural Network. Note that the cells share a common input, in contrast with a typical RNN which has a separate input to each cell.

3.4 Final Projection

After τ iterations of fusion and re-analysis, the resulting memory state $\mathbf{m}^{(\tau)}$ is passed through a final fully-connected layer to yield the output corresponding to a particular task (regression predictions or logits in case of classification). In our experiments we found that increasing τ yields meaningful performance gains (up to $\tau = 3$).

3.5 Recursive RNN: another perspective

The proposed gated memory update corresponds to maintaining an external recurrent cell memory that is recurrent in the consecutive analysis hops, τ, rather than the actual time-steps of the given modality, k_s. This allows the relevant memories of older hops to persist for use in the subsequent analysis hops.

The memory update equations (9)-(13) strongly resemble the GRU cell update (Cho et al., 2014); we treat concatenated view context vectors as the GRUs inputs, one at each analysis hop, τ. When viewed as a recurrent encoding of inputs $\{\mathbf{h}_s\}$, we refer to this architecture as a *recursive recurrent neural net* (RRNN), due to the recursive relationship between the cell's recurrent state and the attention-based re-weighting of the inputs. From this perspective, the attention mechanism forms a sub-component of the RRNN cell.

The key distinction from a typical GRU cell is that the *reset* or *relevance* gate $\mathbf{g}_w$ in a GRU typically gates the recurrent state ($\mathbf{m}^{(\tau)}$ in our case), whereas we use it to gate the input, allowing for uninformative view contexts to be excluded from the memory update. Gating the recurrent state is essential for avoiding vanishing gradients over long sequences, which is not such a concern for our recursion lengths of ≈ 3. One could of course reinstate the gating of the recurrent state, should recursions grow to more appreciable lengths.

A further distinction is that here the GRU "inputs" (view contexts $\{\mathbf{a}^{(\tau)}, \mathbf{v}^{(\tau)}, \mathbf{t}^{(\tau)}\}$ in our case) are computed online as the memory state recurs, unlike the standard case where they are data or pre-extracted features available before the RNN begins to operate. Figure 3 depicts 2 consecutive RRNN cells, illustrating the recycling of the same cell inputs. Figure 2 shows the details of a single cell, which subsumes the globally-contextualised attention mechanism detailed in Section 3.2.

4 Experimental setup

Datasets. We evaluated our approach on CREMA-D (Cao et al., 2014), RAVDESS (Livingstone and Russo, 2012) and CMU-MOSEI (Zadeh et al., 2018b) datasets for multimodal emotion analysis. The first two datasets provide audio and visual modalities while CMU-MOSEI adds also text transcriptions. The CREMA-D dataset contains $\sim$7400 clips of 91 actors covering 6 emotions. The RAVDESS is a speech and song database comprising of $\sim$7300 files of 24 actors covering 8 emotional classes (including two canonical classes for "neutral" and "calm"). The CMU-MOSEI dataset consists of $\sim$3300 long clips segmented into $\sim$23000 short clips. In addition to audio and visual data, it contains also text transcriptions allowing evaluation of tri-modal models.

These datasets are annotated by a continuous-valued vector corresponding to multi-class emotion labels. The ground-truth labels were generated by multiple human transcribers with score normalisation and agreement analysis. For further details, refer to respective references.

Test conditions and baselines. Since each dataset consists of different emotion classification schema, we trained and evaluated all models separately for each of them. The training was performed in an end-to-end manner with $L2$ loss defined over multi-class emotion labels.

To establish a baseline, we evaluated a naive classifier predicting the test-set empirical mean intensities (with MSE loss function) for each output regression dimension. Similar baselines were obtained for other loss functions by training a model with just one parameter per output dimension on that loss, where the model has an access to the training labels but not the training inputs.

Evaluation. For CREMA-D and RAVDESS, we report the accuracy scores as these datasets contain labels for multiclass classification task.

For CMU-MOSEI, we report the result of the 6-way emotion recognition. Recursive models as described in Sec. 3 predicted the 6-dimensional emotion vectors. Their values represent the emotion intensity of the six emotion classes and are continuous-valued. Following Zadeh et al. (2018b), these predictions were evaluated against the reference emotions using the criteria of mean square error (MSE) and mean absolute error (MAE), summing across 6 classes. In addition, an acceptance threshold 0.1 was set for each dimension/emotion, and weighted accuracy (Tong et al., 2017) was computed.

Complementary views across modality. All experiments in this paper use independent recurrent encoding (Sec. 3.1). The encoding scheme differs for every modality. COVAREP (Degottex et al., 2014) was used for the audio modality. OpenFace (Amos et al., 2016) and FACET (iMotion, 2017) were used for visual one and Glove (Pennington et al., 2014) was used for encoding the text features.

Independent recurrent encoding used bi-directional view-specific encoders with 2×128 dimensional outputs on CREMA-D and RAVDESS and 2×512 on CMU-MOSEI. The complementary effects of multiple views from different modalities would be illustrated by controlling the available input views to different systems.

Attention. Global contextualised attention (GCA) was implemented for the emotion recognition systems. Global and view-specific memory were projected to the alignment space (Eq. (5)). The attention weights were computed (Eq. (6)-Eq. (7)) and the contextual view representation was derived (Eq. (8)). For more details, refer to Sec. 3.2. The encoder-decoder used a 128 dimensional (or 512 for CMU-MOSEI) fully-connected layer. A final linear layer mapped the decoder output to multi-class targets.

GCA was compared to standard "early" and "late" fusion strategies. In early fusion, encoders

Model	Modality	Accuracy
Human performance	Audio	40.9
COVAREP Features + LSTM Decoder	Audio	41.5
OpenFace Features + LSTM Decoder	Vision	52.5
Human performance	Vision	58.2
Human performance	Vision+Audio	63.6
(OpenFace features + LSTM) + (COVAREP Features + LSTM) + Dual Attention	Vision+Audio	65.0

Table 1: Results on the CREMA-D dataset across 8 emotions

Modality	Feature	Encoder	Attention	Accuracy
Audio	COVAREP	LSTM	Nil	41.25
Vision	OpenFace	LSTM	Nil	52.08
Audio + Vision	COVAREP, OpenFace	LSTM	GCA	58.33

Table 2: Results on the RAVDESS dataset across 8 emotions for normal speech mode

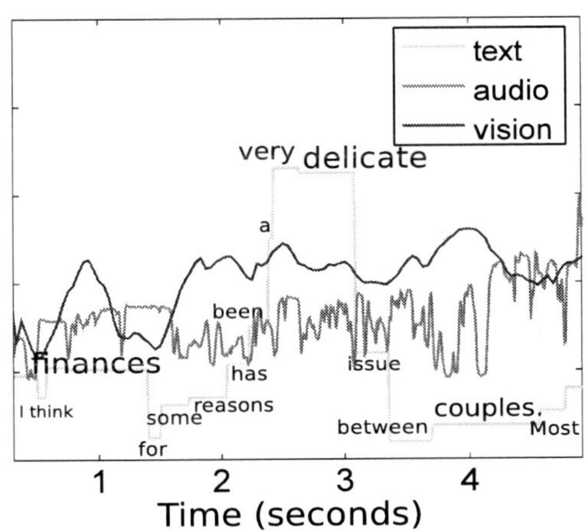

Figure 4: Visualisation of view-specific attention across time. Attention in the text modality focuses on the words "very" and "delicate" as cues for emotion recogntion. Also, the difference in oscillation rates between the audio and visual modalities is noted.

outputs across all views are resampled to their highest temporal resolution (*i.e.* audio, at 100Hz), and resulting (aligned) outputs are concatenated across views. We used similar encoder-decoder structure to one described in Sec 3.2 (Fig. 1), except that the three parallel blocks for modalities were reduced to one. In late fusion, the final-step encoder outputs from all modalities were independently processed by 1-layer feed-forward networks (Sec 3.4) and view-specific multi-class targets were combined using linear weighting.

Memory updates and ablation study. GCA was enhanced with the extra gating functions (*cf.* Eq. (9)-(13), Sec. 3.3) . The extended system was compared with the GCA system on CMU-MOSEI data. To this end, we perform an ablation study using the test data corrupted by additive Gaussian white noise added to the visual modality.

5 Results

Table 1 and 2 show the results of emotion recognition on the CREMA-D and RAVDESS dataset respectively. Audio, visual and the joint use of bi-modal information were compared using identification accuracy. Models trained on the visual modality consistently outperformed models that use solely audio data. Highest accuracy was achieved when the audio and visual modality were jointly modelled, giving 65% and 58.33% on the two datasets. Interestingly, the joint bi-modal system outperformed human performance on CREMA-D (Cao et al., 2014) by 1.4%.

On CMU-MOSEI, the errors between the reference and hypothesis six-dimensional emotion vectors were computed and the results were shown in Table 3.

The use of visual modality resulted in the lowest mean square error (MSE). Meanwhile, when evaluated by mean absolute error (MAE) and weighted accuracy (WA), text modality gave the best performance. Basic techniques in combining information among modalities was not very effective, as indicated by the neglible gain in early and late fusion model.

Globally contextualised attention (GCA) gave an MSE of 0.4696. Gating on global and view-specific memory updates led to further improvements to 0.4691. The improvement in terms of MAE is even more significant (from 0.9412 to 0.8705).

Figure 4 visualises the attention weights in different modalities on a CMU-MOSEI test sentence. The x-axis denotes time t and y-axis is the magnitude of attention $\alpha_s(t)$ in different views $s \in \{a, v, t\}$. The transcribed text was added alongside the attention profile of the textual modality to align the attention weights with the recording. It can be seen that the GCA emotion recognition

Modality	Feature	Encoder	Attention/Fusion	Corruption	MSE	MAE	WA
Text (T)	Word-vec	LSTM	Nil	Nil	0.6326	0.9830	0.5485
Audio (A)	COVAREP	LSTM	Nil	Nil	0.6049	1.0562	0.5249
Vision (V)	FACET	LSTM	Nil	Nil	0.5026	0.9909	0.5476
T+A+V	COVAREP, FACET, Word-vec	LSTM	Early fusion	Nil	0.5319	0.7694	0.5188
T+A+V	COVAREP, FACET, Word-vec	LSTM	Late fusion	Nil	0.5047	0.9825	0.5889
T+A+V	COVAREP, FACET, Word-vec	LSTM	GCA	Nil	0.4696	0.9412	0.6163
T+A+V	COVAREP, FACET, Word-vec	LSTM	GCA	Vision	0.5034	0.9920	0.6068
T+A+V	COVAREP, FACET, Word-vec	LSTM	GCA + Gating	Nil	0.4691	0.8705	0.5765
T+A+V	COVAREP, FACET, Wrod-vec	LSTM	GCA + Gating	Vision	0.4742	0.8857	0.5688

Table 3: Results on CMU-MOSEI dataset

system was trained to attend dynamically to features of varying importance across the time, unlike systems performing early or late fusion. Attention weights of text modality show a clear jump for the words "very" and "delicate". The word "very", combined with an adjective, is often a strong cue to sentiment analysis, resulting in a spike in attention. The subject in this clip was speaking mostly in a neutral tone, with a nod and slight frowning towards the beginning of the sentence. This may correspond to the first peak in the attention trajectory of visual data. The weight of audio modality exhibited a higher oscillation rate compared to the counterpart on visual data. COVAREP features had $4\times$ higher temporal frequency than FACET.

Finally, we verified contribution of the gating system to the GCA using the corrupted visual data. When the GCA system is used without the gating mechanism, corrupted data results in increased MSE (from 0.4696 to 0.5034) and MAE (from 0.9412 to 0.9920). This is in contrast to the full system with gating (GCA + Gating in Table 3). The system cancels the effects of additive visual noise, which is evidenced by the small gap in MSE (0.4691 vs 0.4742) and MAE (0.8705 vs 0.8857) between clean and noisy data.

6 Conclusion

We have presented an approach for combining sequential, heterogeneous data. An external memory state is updated recursively, using globally-contextualised attention over a set of recurrent view-specific state histories. Our model was tested on the challenging tasks of emotion recognition from audio, visual, and textual data on three large-scale datasets. The complementary effect of joint modelling of emotions using multi-modal data was consistently shown across experiments with multiple datasets. Importantly this approach eschews hard alignment of the data streams, allowing view-specific encoders to respect the inherent dynamics of its input sequence. Encoder state histories are fused into cross-modal features via an attention mechanism that is modulated by a shared, external memory. The control of information flow in this fusion is further enhanced by using a GRU-like gating mechanism, which can persist shared memory through multiple iterations while blocking corrupted or uninformative view-specific features. In future study, it would be interesting to investigate more structured fusion operations such as sparse tensor multilinear maps (Ben-younes et al., 2017).

References

Brandon Amos, Bartosz Ludwiczuk, and Mahadev Satyanarayanan. 2016. Openface: A general-purpose face recognition library with mobile applications. Technical report, CMU-CS-16-118, CMU School of Computer Science.

Dzmitry Bahdanau, Kyunghyun Cho, and Yoshua Bengio. 2014. Neural machine translation by jointly learning to align and translate. *CoRR*, abs/1409.0473.

Tadas Baltrusaitis, Chaitanya Ahuja, and Louis-Philippe Morency. 2017. Multimodal machine learning: A survey and taxonomy. *CoRR*, abs/1705.09406.

Hedi Ben-younes, Rémi Cadène, Matthieu Cord, and Nicolas Thome. 2017. MUTAN: multimodal tucker fusion for visual question answering. *CoRR*, abs/1705.06676.

Houwei Cao, David G. Cooper, and Michael K. Keutmann. 2014. CREMA-D: Crowd-sourced emotional multimodal actors dataset. *IEEE Transactions on Affective Computing*.

Kyunghyun Cho, Bart van Merriënboer, Çalar Gülçehre, Dzmitry Bahdanau, Fethi Bougares, Holger Schwenk, and Yoshua Bengio. 2014. Learning phrase representations using rnn encoder–decoder for statistical machine translation. In *EMNLP*.

Michal Daniluk, Tim Rocktäschel, Johannes Welbl, and Sebastian Riedel. 2017. Frustratingly short attention spans in neural language modeling. *CoRR*, abs/1702.04521.

Gilles Degottex, John Kane, Thomas Drugman, Tuomo Raitio, and Stefan Scherer. 2014. COVAREP – a collaborative voice analysis repository for speech technologies. In *ICASSP*.

S. Hochreiter and J. Schmidhuber. 1997. Long short-term memory. In *Neural Computation*.

iMotion. 2017. Facial expression analysis.

Yelin Kim, Honglak Lee, and Emily Mower Provost. 2013. Deep learning for robust feature generation in audiovisual emotion recognition. In *ICASSP*.

S. R. Livingstone and F. A. Russo. 2012. The ryerson audio-visual database of emotional speech and song (RAVDESS): A dynamic, multimodal set of facial and vocal expressions in north american english. *PloS one*.

Hyeonseob Nam, Jung-Woo Ha, and Jeonghee Kim. 2017. Dual attention networks for multimodal reasoning and matching. *CVPR*.

Jiquan Ngiam, Aditya Khosla, Mingyu Kim, Juhan Nam, Honglak Lee, and Andrew Y. Ng. 2011. Multimodal deep learning. In *ICML*.

Jeffrey Pennington, Richard Socher, and Christopher D. Manning. 2014. Glove: Global vectors for word representation. *EMNLP*.

Vikas Sindhwani and Partha Niyogi. 2005. A co-regularized approach to semi-supervised learning with multiple views. In *Proceedings of the ICML Workshop on Learning with Multiple Views*.

Rupesh Kumar Srivastava, Klaus Greff, and Jürgen Schmidhuber. 2015. Training very deep networks. In *NIPS*.

Sainbayar Sukhbaatar, arthur szlam, Jason Weston, and Rob Fergus. 2015. End-to-end memory networks. In *NIPS*.

Edmund Tong, Amir Zadeh, Cara Jones, and Louis-Philippe Morency. 2017. Combining human trafficking with multimodal deep models. *ACL*.

Ashish Vaswani, Noam Shazeer, Niki Parmar, Jakob Uszkoreit, Llion Jones, Aidan N. Gomez, and Lukasz Kaiser. 2017. Attention is all you need. *NIPS*.

Valentin Vielzeuf, Stéphane Pateux, and Frédéric Jurie. 2017. Temporal multimodal fusion for video emotion classification in the wild. *CoRR*, abs/1709.07200.

Jason Weston. 2017. Memory networks for recommendation. In *RecSys*.

Caiming Xiong, Stephen Merity, and Richard Socher. 2016. Dynamic memory networks for visual and textual question answering. In *ICML*.

Chang Xu, Dacheng Tao, and Chao Xu. 2013. A survey on multi-view learning. *CoRR*, abs/1304.5634.

Amir Zadeh, Paul Pu Liang, Navonil Mazumder, Soujanya Poria, Erik Cambria, and Louis-Philippe Morency. 2018a. Memory fusion network for multi-view sequential learning. *CoRR*, abs/1802.00927.

Amir Zadeh, Paul Pu Liang, Jonathan Vanbriesen, Soujanya Poria, Emdund Tong, Erik Cambria, Minghai Chen, and Louis-Philippe Morency. 2018b. Multimodal language analysis in the wild: CMU-MOSEI dataset and interpretable dynamic fusion graph. In *ACL*.

Shiqing Zhang, Shiliang Zhang, Tiejun Huang, Wen Gao, and Qi Tian. 2017. Learning Affective Features with a Hybrid Deep Model for Audio-Visual Emotion Recognition. *IEEE Transactions on Circuits and Systems for Video Technology*.

Using sparse semantic embeddings learned from multimodal text and image data to model human conceptual knowledge

Steven Derby[1]   **Paul Miller**[1]   **Brian Murphy**[1,2]   **Barry Devereux**[1]

[1] Queen's University Belfast, Belfast, United Kingdom
[2] BrainWaveBank Ltd., Belfast, United Kingdom
`{sderby02, p.miller, brian.murphy, b.devereux}@qub.ac.uk`

Abstract

Distributional models provide a convenient way to model semantics using dense embedding spaces derived from unsupervised learning algorithms. However, the dimensions of dense embedding spaces are not designed to resemble human semantic knowledge. Moreover, embeddings are often built from a single source of information (typically text data), even though neurocognitive research suggests that semantics is deeply linked to both language and perception. In this paper, we combine multimodal information from both text and image-based representations derived from state-of-the-art distributional models to produce sparse, interpretable vectors using *Joint Non-Negative Sparse Embedding*. Through in-depth analyses comparing these sparse models to human-derived behavioural and neuroimaging data, we demonstrate their ability to predict interpretable linguistic descriptions of human ground-truth semantic knowledge.

1 Introduction

Distributional Semantic Models (DSMs) are used to represent semantic information about concepts in a high-dimensional vector space, where each concept is represented as a point in the space such that concepts with more similar meanings are closer together. Unsupervised learning algorithms are regularly employed to produce these models, where learning depends on statistical regularities in the distribution of words, exploiting a theory in linguistics called the *distributional hypothesis*. Recent developments in deep learning have resulted in weakly-supervised prediction-based methods, where, for example, a neural network is trained to predict words from surrounding contexts, and the network parameters are interpreted as vectors of the distributional model (Mikolov et al., 2013). Like their counterparts in machine vision, neural network algorithms for DSMs automate feature extraction from highly complex

data without prior feature selection (Krizhevsky et al., 2012; Mikolov et al., 2013; Karpathy and Li, 2015; Antol et al., 2015). Such deep learning techniques have led to state-of-the-art performance in many domains, though this is often at the expense of the interpretability and cognitive plausibility of the learned features (Murphy et al., 2012; Zeiler and Fergus, 2013). Furthermore, these compact, dense embeddings are structurally dissimilar to the way in which humans conceptualise the meanings of words (McRae et al., 2005). One way of drawing interpretability from highly latent data is by transforming it into a sparse representation (Faruqui et al., 2015; Senel et al., 2017). Moreover, the design of distributional models has been for the most part unimodal, typically relying on text corpora, even though studies in psychology have shown that human semantic processing is deeply linked with visual perception.

In cognitive neuroscience, research demonstrates that representations of high-level concepts corresponding to the meanings of nouns and visual objects are widely distributed and overlapping across the cortex (Haxby et al., 2001; Devereux et al., 2013), which has opened up research into exploiting machine learning for neurosemantic prediction tasks using distributed semantic models (Mitchell et al., 2008; Huth et al., 2016; Clarke et al., 2015; Devereux et al., 2018). Such research has helped with both the construction and evaluation of semantic distributional embeddings in computer science (Devereux et al., 2010; Søgaard, 2016). In this paper, we utilise a matrix factorisation algorithm known as *Non-Negative Sparse Embedding* (NNSE) (Murphy et al., 2012), and an extension known as *Joint Non-Negative Sparse Embedding* (JNNSE) (Fyshe et al., 2014) to produce joint sparse multimodal distributions from text and image data. Furthermore, we show that this joint multimodal semantic embedding approach offers a more faithful and parsimonious description of se-

Proceedings of the 22nd Conference on Computational Natural Language Learning (CoNLL 2018), pages 260–270
Brussels, Belgium, October 31 - November 1, 2018. ©2018 Association for Computational Linguistics

mantics as exhibited in human cognitive knowledge and neurocognitive processing, when compared with dense embeddings learned from the same data.

2 Related Work

Much of the research aimed at the sparse decomposition of dense vector spaces is closely associated with the work of Hoyer (2002), who proposed a *Non-Negative Matrix Factorization technique* (NMF) known as *Non-Negative Sparse Coding* (NNSC) which produces a sparse representation of the original compact matrix. With the use of new optimisation techniques (Mairal et al., 2010), Murphy et al. (2012) later implemented a variation of this approach that forces an L1 penalty on the new sparse matrix, yielding *Non-Negative Sparse Embedding* (NNSE). The purpose of the NNSE algorithm is to generate an embedding that attains the desirable qualities of effectiveness and interpretability (Murphy et al. (2012)). Building upon this approach, Fyshe et al. (2014) extended NNSE to incorporate other sources of semantic information using an extension of NNSE known as *Joint Non-Negative Sparse Embedding* (JNNSE). Their experiments made use of neuroimaging data as an additional source of semantic information, and recent work has seen a push for the incorporation of a broader range of semantic knowledge into DSMs, including semantic knowledge derived from visual image information.

Bruni et al. (2014) combined embeddings from text and co-occurrence statistics from data via mining techniques derived from pictures using a procedure known as Visual Bag-of-Words (VBOW). Later this approach was extended by Kiela and Bottou (2014) who incorporated the penultimate layer of modified Convolutional Neural Networks (CNN) to forge a more grounded, semantically faithful model that improved on the state-of-the-art. Lazaridou et al. (2015) extend the architecture of the skip-gram model associated with Word2Vec (Mikolov et al., 2013) to incorporate a measure of visual semantic information by forcing the network to learn linguistic and visual-based features. Instead of performing a context-based prediction task, Ngiam et al. (2011) combine multimodal information from both audio and image-based information using a stacked autoencoder to reconstruct both modalities with a shared representation layer in the middle of the network.

Modality	Source Embeddings	#D	#S
Text	GloVe	1000	200
Text	Word2Vec	1000	200
Image	CNN-Mean	6144	1000
Image	CNN-Max	6144	1000
Both	CNN-Mean + GloVe	7144	200
Both	CNN-Max + GloVe	7144	200
Both	CNN-Mean + Word2Vec	7144	200
Both	CNN-Max + Word2Vec	7144	200

Table 1: List of all dense (D) and sparse (S) models used in this paper, and the number of dimensions (#) in each model.

Silberer et al. (2017) similarly combine information from multiple modalities from both visual and linguistic data sources by using a stacked autoencoder to reconstruct both types of information separately with a shared representation layer, and a softmax layer connected to the representation layer used to predict the concept characterised by these representations. Rather than trying to construct each modality separately, Collell et al. (2017) make use of a simple perceptron and a neural network to reconstruct the visual modality from pretrained linguistic representations.

Criticism towards traditional distributional models and the benchmarks used to evaluate them (Batchkarov et al., 2016) are now compelling more researchers to consider evaluation techniques that analyse how well distributional models encode different aspects of grounded meaning (Lucy and Gauthier, 2017; Collell and Moens, 2016; Gladkova and Drozd, 2016). In particular, one aspect of cognitive plausibility that is lacking in dense representations is in their interpretability, something that could be solved using sparsity (Faruqui et al., 2015; Senel et al., 2017). In this paper, we combine both text and image-based data in conjunction with matrix factorisation strategies to build sparse and multimodal distributional models, with the goal of demonstrating that these models are more interpretable with respect to human semantic knowledge about concepts. In particular, we show that these models attain a structural composition and semantic representation that is closer to the way humans represent concepts, evaluated using human similarity judgements, human semantic feature knowledge, and neuroimaging data.

3 Multimodal Representation

In total, we used sixteen distributional semantic models, eight of which are dense and eight of which are their sparse counterparts. These models are summarized in Table 1, which describes the eight sources of semantic information (two text-based, two image-based, and four multimodal image+text-based) used to construct both the dense and sparse embedding models. Construction of the eight dense models largely followed Kiela and Bottou (2014), with eight corresponding sparse models later constructed using JNNSE.

3.1 Text-based models

We implemented two state-of-the-art text-based embedding models, Word2Vec and GloVe, to act as initialisers for our sparse models, following a similar approach to Faruqui et al. (2015). Both text-based models were trained on 4.5 gigabytes of preprocessed Wikipedia data, with fixed context windows of size 5 and 1000 embedding dimensions. The Wikipedia preprocessing was standard and included removal of Wikipedia markup, stop words and non-words, as well as lemmatisation (implemented using standard *NLTK* tools). After model training, the embeddings for each word were normalised to mean zero and unit length, using the L2 norm. Vector normalisation was carried out to ensure magnitudes of the text-based vectors were in line with the image-based vectors, which are normalised by default.

GloVe. Global Vector for Word Representation (Pennington et al., 2014) is an unsupervised learning algorithm that captures fine-grained semantic information using co-occurrence statistics. It achieves this by constructing real vector embeddings using bilinear logistic regression with non-zero word co-occurrences in the training corpus within a specific context. Our model was trained using a learning rate of 0.05 over 100 epochs.

Word2Vec. Word2Vec (Mikolov et al., 2013) uses shallow neural networks with negative sampling techniques, which are trained to predict either the word from the context or the context from the word using a fixed window of words as the context. In particular, we choose the CBOW version (predict the word using the context) of this model which was trained using the *gensim* package with the minimum word count threshold set to 0 (i.e., a vector representation was created for all words in the corpus).

3.2 Image models

We make use of the image embeddings constructed by Kiela and Bottou (2014). In their paper, the AlexNet (Krizhevsky et al., 2012) CNN was extended from 1000 output units to 1512 outputs, using the additional 512 object label categories chosen by Oquab et al. (2014) and retrained using transfer learning (Oquab et al., 2014). This new network was trained using the 2012 version of the *ImageNet Large Scale Visual Recognition Challenge* (ILSVRC) competition dataset with extra images from 512 other categories, which was then later used to gather embeddings for the ESP game image dataset (Von Ahn and Dabbish, 2004). After training, the network was sliced to remove the final fully-connected softmax layer, in order to retrieve the activation vectors for each image on the penultimate layer. There are systematic differences in the kinds of images that appear in the ImageNet and ESP game training sets. The ImageNet dataset (Deng et al., 2009) consists of 12.5 million images over 22K different object categories, with each image typically corresponding to a single labelled object (i.e. images do not tend to be cluttered with several objects). In contrast, the ESP game dataset consists of 100000 images with many labelled objects present in each image.

To retrieve activation vectors for object categories from the ESP dataset, Kiela and Bottou (2014) used a fair proportional sampling technique: for each object category label, 1000 images were sampled according to the WordNet (Miller, 1995) subtree for that concept. If sampling up to 1000 images was not possible, then the subtree of the concepts hypernym parent node was further sampled until 1000 images were retrieved. The activation vector for each of these images was then obtained from the truncated CNN. To retrieve the final embedding vectors for each object label from the sampled activation vectors, Kiela and Bottou (2014) combined the 1000 activation vectors for each label using two techniques, described below.

CNN-Max. Each word embedding was produced by taking the elementwise maximum value over all 1000 CNN activation vectors obtained for the sampled images with the same label word.

CNN-Mean. Each word embedding was produced by taking the elementwise average of all 1000 activation vectors associated with the same label word.

All image embeddings are of size 6144, corresponding to the size of the penultimate layer of the CNN. The embeddings used in our paper correspond to the ESP game labels (which uses a larger number of images, more natural images, and more labels than ImageNet), and all embeddings are normalised to mean zero and L2 unit length before downstream analysis.

3.3 Multimodal models

Again following Kiela and Bottou (2014), we produce four new dense models from combinations of text and image embeddings by simply concatenating the embedding vectors of each model corresponding to each word to create new multimodal text+image embeddings:

$$Vec_{multi} = \alpha \times Vec_{text} \, || \, (1 - \alpha) \times Vec_{image} \tag{1}$$

Here, α is a mixing parameter that determines the relative contribution of each modality to the combined semantic space. We set $\alpha = 0.5$, so that text and image sources contribute equally to the combined embeddings.

4 Sparse matrix factorization

Following Faruqui et al. (2015), we use the dense text and image model embeddings as initialisers for corresponding sparse embedding spaces. The embedding vectors are concatenated into an embedding matrix for each model, with the number of rows corresponding to the number of words in their respective lexicons, and the number of columns corresponding to the embedding dimensionality.

To produce the new sparse representations, we use the NNSE matrix factorisation technique [1] (Murphy et al. (2012)) which maps a dense word-feature matrix X to a non-negative sparse matrix A with an identical lexicon. Let $X \in \mathbb{R}^{w \times k}$ be an embedding matrix, where w is the number of words, and k is the embedding dimension size. NNSE factorises X into two matrices, a dictionary transformation matrix $D \in \mathbb{R}^{p \times k}$ and the sparse matrix $A \in \mathbb{R}^{w \times p}$ by minimising the objective function:

$$arg \min_{D,A} \sum_{i=1}^{w} ||X_{i,:} - A_{i,:} \times D||^2 + \lambda||A_{i,:}||_1 \tag{2}$$

[1] Non-Negative Sparse Embedding code was kindly provided by Partha Talukdar.

subject to the constraints

$$D_{i,:} D_{i,:}^T \leq 1, \forall 1 \leq i \leq p$$
$$A_{i,j} \geq 0, \forall 1 \leq i \leq w, \forall 1 \leq j \leq p$$

which ensure sparse and non-trivial solutions for A (Murphy et al. (2012)).

NNSE has been extended as a method to combine multiple dense word-feature matrices $X \in \mathbb{R}^{w_x \times k}$ and $Y \in \mathbb{R}^{w_y \times n}$ into a single non-negative sparse matix, an extension called Joint Non-Negative Sparse Embedding (JNNSE; Fyshe et al. (2014)). Although JNNSE can be used with feature matrices with different lexicons, in this paper we take only the w rows of the two matrices that correspond to the intersection of words used to build the two embedding models and a set of 2234 unique concept words taken from the four similarity evaluation datasets discussed in the next section. JNNSE gives a new joint sparse feature matrix $A \in \mathbb{R}^{w \times p}$ by minimising the objective function:

$$arg \min_{D^{(x)},D^{(y)},A} \sum_{i=1}^{w} ||X_{i,:} - A_{i,:} \times D^{(x)}||^2 \tag{3}$$
$$+ \sum_{i=1}^{w} ||Y_{i,:} - A_{i,:} \times D^{(y)}||^2 + \lambda||A_{i,:}||_1$$

where

$$D_{i,:}^{(x)} D_{i,:}^{(x)T} \leq 1, \forall 1 \leq i \leq p$$
$$D_{i,:}^{(y)} D_{i,:}^{(y)T} \leq 1, \forall 1 \leq i \leq p$$
$$A_{i,j} \geq 0, \forall 1 \leq i \leq w, \forall 1 \leq j \leq p$$

For the NNSE factorization of each of the four initial dense unimodal text and image models (GloVe, Word2Vec, CNN-Mean and CNN-Max), the sparsity parameter λ was set to 0.05 and each model's dimensionality (p) was reduced down from its original size by a factor of approximately 5; the text embedding size was reduced to 200 and both image model embedding sizes were reduced to 1000 (see Table 1).

To create sparse multimodal models corresponding to the concatenated multimodal dense models, four new models were produced using Equation 3. These models were constructed by combining all combinations of pruned image and text-based models through JNNSE to produce sparse embeddings of size 200 from their original dimensions of 6144 and 1000 respectively. The

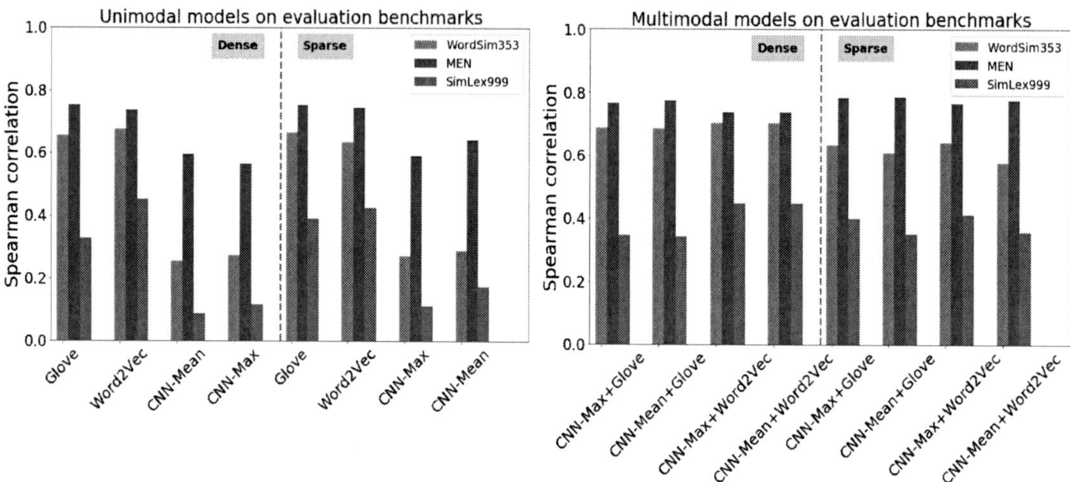

Figure 1: Results for the dense and sparse embeddings for the three semantic similarity benchmarks, for the eight unimodal models (left panel) and the eight multimodal image+text models (right panel).

sparsity parameter λ was set to 0.025. Though all sparse embedding matrices are calculated over a smaller lexicon and have a much smaller embedding size compared to the original dense embeddings, in the next section, we investigate how these models still produce competitive results on semantic evaluation benchmarks, including neurocognitive data.

5 Experiments

The aim of our experiments is to compare the quality of the dense and sparse unimodal and multimodal embedding models, with a focus on their ability to explain human-derived semantic data. We use several qualitatively different analyses of how well the models explain human-derived measures of semantic representation and processing. In the results that follow, we first demonstrate that sparse multimodal models are competitive with larger dense embedding models on standard semantic similarity evaluation benchmarks. We then investigate whether the underlying representations of the sparse, multimodal models are more easily interpreted in terms of human semantic property knowledge about familiar concepts, by evaluating the models' ability to predict predicates describing property knowledge found in human property norm data. Finally, we evaluate the models' ability to predict human brain activation data.

5.1 Semantic similarity benchmarks

A widely used evaluation technique for distributional models is the comparison with human se-

mantic similarity rating benchmarks. We evaluate our models on three popular datasets which each reflect slightly different intuitions about semantic similarity.

WordSim353 (Finkelstein et al., 2001) consists of 353 word pairs with human ratings indicating how related the two concepts in each pair are. The definition of similarity is left quite ambiguous for the human annotators, and words which share any kind of association tend to receive high scores.

MEN (Bruni et al., 2012) consists of 3000 word pairs with human ratings of how semantically related each pair of concepts are. Pairs with high scores tend to be linked more by semantic relatedness than by similarity; for example, the words "coffee" and "cup" are semantically related (even though a cup is not similar to coffee). Semantic relatedness often corresponds to meronym or holonym concept pairings (e.g. "finger" - "hand").

SimLex999. (Hill et al., 2015) is a comprehensive and modern benchmark consisting of 999 pairs of words with human ratings of semantic similarity. Semantic similarity tends to reflect words with shared hypernym relations between concept pairs (e.g. "coffee" & "tea" are more similar than "coffee" & "cup").

In evaluating against the benchmarks, we use the intersection of the words occurring in the benchmarks and the words used in creating our embeddings. Not all words used in the similarity benchmarks appear in our word embedding mod-

Model	Encyclopedic	Functional	Taxonomic	Visual	Other Perceptual	Overall
CNN-Mean	23.479	28.309	45.756	31.256	26.467	29.244
CNN-Max	22.878	28.765	50.140	32.843	27.508	30.202
GloVe	30.870	37.176	61.517	35.909	38.385	36.984
Word2Vec	27.494	30.372	55.455	32.298	32.800	32.363
GloVe NNSE	31.171	34.645	59.497	35.066	36.738	35.880
Word2Vec NNSE	29.662	34.320	55.073	35.302	33.261	34.956
CNN-Max NNSE	15.320	17.138	26.263	19.646	17.453	18.279
CNN-Mean NNSE	15.996	18.297	27.330	20.954	18.376	19.339
CNN-Max + GloVe	30.669	37.404	63.887	35.790	36.077	36.760
CNN-Mean + GloVe	31.560	38.441	64.459	36.675	36.625	37.637
CNN-Max + Word2Vec	22.114	24.653	51.471	27.566	27.332	27.088
CNN-Mean + Word2Vec	22.057	24.780	51.926	27.527	27.407	27.124
CNN-Max + GloVe JNNSE	32.481	38.787	63.669	39.848	36.245	39.080
CNN-Mean + GloVe JNNSE	31.104	38.009	64.866	40.267	35.998	38.784
CNN-Max + Word2Vec JNNSE	32.718	38.601	61.493	39.663	36.496	38.901
CNN-Mean + Word2Vec JNNSE	31.084	36.939	57.659	38.145	33.436	37.057

Table 2: Average cross-validation F1 $\times 100$ scores for each model. The blue highlighting indicates the model that scores the highest on each property class.

els, although the overlap is quite high[2]. Evaluations in the next section are based on the subsets of word-pairs for which we have embedding vectors for each word.

5.2 Semantic Similarity Results

Figure 1 shows the results for all 16 models on the three evaluation datasets. Even with their significant dimensionality reduction and forced sparsity regularisation, the sparse (NNSE) unimodal text and image-based models perform comparatively with their original dense counterparts, with better results for the sparse unimodal models on several of the benchmarks. The JNNSE models perform comparably to their dense counterparts, with performance on MEN slightly improved, performance on WordSem353 marginally worse, and performance on SimLex999 approximately the same (in spite of the JNNSE models having less than $1/35$ times the number dimensions of their sparse counterparts)[3]. Finally, the combined text+image multimodal embeddings are better than unimodal models overall at fitting the similarity rating data. The results on these con-

ventional benchmarks suggest redundancy in the dense embedding representations, with the sparse embeddings providing a parsimonious representation of semantics that retains information about semantic similarity. Moreover, multimodal models combining both linguistic and perceptual experience better account for human similarity judgements.

5.3 Property norm prediction

Following Collell and Moens (2016) and Lucy and Gauthier (2017), we make use of a dataset of human-derived property norms for a set of concepts and analyse how well our distributional models can predict human-elicited property knowledge for words. We use the CSLB property norms (Devereux et al. (2014)), a dataset of semantic features for a set of 541 noun concepts, elicited by participants in a large-scale property norming study. (For example, for "apple", properties include *is-a-fruit*, *is-red*, *grows-on-trees*, *has-seeds*, *is-round*, etc.). For each embedding model, we train an $L2$ regularised logistic regression classifier for each property that predicts whether the property is true for a given concept.

The human-elicited property$\times$concept matrix is sparse; most properties are not true of most concepts. For the logistic regression model trained for each semantic property, we therefore balance positive and negative training items by weighting coefficients inversely proportional to the frequency of the two classes. Properties which are true of less

---

[2]Atleast 83% for SimLex999, 81% WordSim353 and 94% for MEN.

[3]In order to ensure that the dense models were not disadvantaged by having more dimensions, we also trained dense text models with 200 dimensions and found that these did not perform better than the 1000-dimensional models. Furthermore, we applied SVD to each of the 1000-dimensional dense models to reduce the number of dimensions to 200 but again found the results to be worse than the results for both the 1000-dimensional dense models and the sparse models.

than five concepts (across the set of concepts appearing in both the CSLB norms and our embedding models) were removed, to ensure sufficient positive and negative training cases across concepts. To evaluate the logistic regression models' ability to predict human property knowledge for held-out concepts, we used 5-fold cross-validation with stratified sampling to ensure that at least one positive case occurred in each test set. Using the embedding dimensions as training data, we train on the 4 folds and test on the final fold, and evaluate the logistic regression classifier by taking the average F1 score over all the test folds. For subsequent analysis of the fitted regression models for each property, the semantic properties were partitioned into the five general classes given in Devereux et al. (2014). These property classes were *visual* (e.g. *is-green*; *is-round*), *functional* (e.g. *is-eaten*; *used-for-cutting*), *taxonomic* (e.g. *is-a-fruit*; *is-a-tool*), encyclopedic (*has-vitimans*; *uses-fuel*), and *other-perceptual* (e.g. *is-tasty*; *is-loud*). We hypothesised that properties of different types would differ in how accurately they could be predicted from the different embedding models, given the different sources of information available in the models (for example, visual properties may be more predictable from models trained with image data; see also Collell and Moens (2016)).

Table 2 shows the average F1 scores overall properties and over each of the five property categories. Since the dense and sparse models trained on the same source data (text, images, or text+images) encode similar information, they perform similarly on the task of predicting human semantic property knowledge. However, sparse multimodal models (the last four rows of the table) are the top scoring models for four of the five property categories, and over the full set of properties (last column of Table 2) the top three models are all sparse and multimodal. These results indicate that sparse multimodal embeddings are superior to their single modality and dense counterparts in their ability to predict interpretable semantic properties corresponding to elements of human conceptual knowledge.

5.4 Interpretating embedding dimensions in terms of semantic properties

Information about a specific semantic property can be stored latently over the dimensions of a semantic embedding model, such that the semantic property can be reliably decoded given an embedding vector, as tested in the previous section. However, a stronger test of how closely an embedding model relates to human-elicited conceptual knowledge is to investigate whether the embedding dimensions encode interpretable, human-like semantic properties directly. In other words, does an embedding model learn a set of basis vectors for the semantic space that corresponds to verbalisable, human semantic properties like *is-round*, *is-a-fruit*, and so on? To address this question, we evaluated how the dense and sparse embeddings differ in their degree of correspondence to the property norms by analysing the fitted parameters of our property prediction logistic regression classifiers. For each embedding model and semantic property, we average the fitted parameters in the logistic regression models across cross-validation iterations and extract the 20 parameters with the highest average magnitude. For each property, we store these 20 parameters in a vector sorted by decreasing magnitude. If a particular semantic property is decodable directly from only one (or very few) embedding dimensions, then the magnitude of the first element (or few elements) of the sorted parameter vector will be very high. Over all properties, we then apply element-wise averaging of the sorted parameter vectors. Figure 2 shows the magnitudes of these 20 averaged parameters for the dense and sparse multimodal GloVe+CNN-Mean models[4]. As we can see, the dense model has a more uniform distribution, indicating that the information is highly diffuse over the dimensions of the dense embedding space. Conversely, the top few parameters for the sparse model have very high magnitude, indicating that, on average, information about semantic properties tend to be strongly associated with a small number of dimensions in the sparse space.

As a further test of how well dimensions of embedding models correspond to human semantic knowledge, we calculated pairwise correlations, across concepts, between embedding dimensions and properties. For a given semantic property, we can test which of two embedding models best encode that semantic property in a single dimension – an embedding model that more directly matches the property norm data will tend to have a dimension that correlates more strongly with that

---

[4]The results are similar for all other pairs of sparse and dense models.

	GloVe	Word2Vec	CNN-Max	CNN-Mean	CNN-Max + GloVe	CNN-Mean + GloVe	CNN-Max + Word2Vec	CNN-Mean + Word2Vec
fMRI (S)	0.654	0.652	0.641	0.647	0.662	**0.686**	0.649	0.671
fMRI (D)	0.670	0.676	0.654	0.651	0.673	0.677	0.676	0.676
MEG (S)	0.664	0.669	0.651	0.641	0.671	0.668	0.675	0.665
MEG (D)	0.680	0.664	0.654	0.643	**0.684**	**0.684**	0.664	0.664

Table 3: Results of all sparse (S) and dense (D) models on 2 vs. 2 tests against the fMRI and MEG neuroimaging data, averaged over participants.

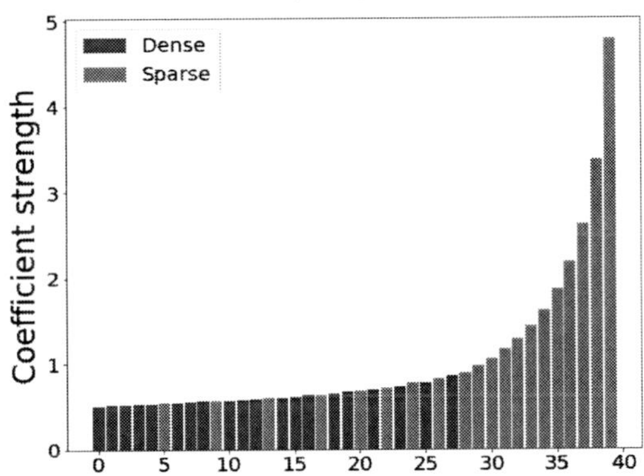

Figure 2: The ranking of the top 20 model coefficients for the logistic regression classifiers trained on each feature, for the dense GloVe + CNN-Mean model (blue bars), and the joint sparse GloVe + CNN-Mean model (red bars).

property than *any* dimension of a model that encodes information about that property more latently. For this analysis, we first filtered the set of concepts in the dense models to include only the concepts in the CSLB norms, and recalculated the (J)NNSE sparse models over these concepts only. We tuned the sparsity parameter so that the sparsity of the sparse embedding models closely matched the sparsity of CSLB concept-property matrix (97% sparse), and kept the dimensionality of the sparse embeddings the same as our original sparse models. Let v_P be the values for a property P for each concept in the CSLB norms, and let M_d and M_s represent the set of embedding columns for a dense model and its sparse counterpart respectively. Then for each property P, we evaluate the inequality

$$max_{c \in M_d}(\rho(c, v_P)) < max_{c \in M_s}(\rho(c, v_P))$$

where ρ is the Spearman correlation. We count the proportion of times the inequality is true across all properties in the norms, repeat this for each of the eight dense models and their sparse counterparts,

and calculate the average. The results show that the sparse models have the most correlated dimension 63.2% of the time. In order to ensure that the dense models were not disadvantaged by having more dimensions (and to test that the sparsity constraint rather than dimensionality reduction was the reason for the superior performance of the sparse models), we used SVD on all dense models to reduce the dimensions down to the same size as their sparse counterparts and reran the test. Here the results show that the sparse models have the most correlated dimension 81.1% of the time, indicating that the sparse models do learn semantics-encoding dimensions from the dense models that more closely correspond to human-derived property knowledge.

5.5 Evaluation on brain data

For our final set of analysis, we tested how closely each of the eight dense and eight sparse models relate to neurocognitive processing in the human brain. We used BrainBench (Xu et al., 2016), an evaluation benchmark for semantic models that allows us to evaluate each model's ability to predict patterns of activation in neuroimaging data. The BrainBench dataset includes brain activation data recorded using two complementary neuroimaging modalities: **fMRI** (which measures cerebral blood oxygenation and which has relatively good spatial resolution but poor temporal resolution) and **MEG** (which measures aggregate magnetic field changes induced by neural activity and which has good temporal resolution but poorer spatial resolution). The neuroimaging data in both modalities are taken from nine participants that viewed pictures of 60 different concepts.

The first step is to transform the embedding matrices and the brain activation data into a format that more readily facilitates comparison of these two very different kinds of data. For each distributional model, we calculated the pairwise correlation between concepts to produce the 60×60

	GloVe	Word2Vec	CNN-Max	CNN-Mean	CNN-Max + GloVe	CNN-Mean + GloVe	CNN-Max + Word2Vec	CNN-Mean + Word2Vec
fMRI (D)	0.162	0.164	0.145	0.151	0.150	0.152	0.152	0.155
fMRI (S)	0.138	0.136	0.140	0.144	0.139	0.140	0.154	**0.168**
MEG (D)	0.163	0.161	0.163	0.158	0.162	0.158	**0.168**	0.162
MEG (S)	**0.168**	0.152	0.149	0.149	0.152	0.157	0.145	0.147

Table 4: Average RSA results (Spearman's ρ) for all sparse (S) and dense (D) models.

similarity matrix M where each element $M_{i,j}$ in the matrix is the correlation between the embedding vectors of the distributional model for the i-th and j-th concepts. In Brainbench, the brain data is already preprocessed and transformed into such a representation for both the fMRI and MEG neuroimaging modalities, giving a 60×60 similarity matrix for each participant for both modalities. The next step for BrainBench evaluation is to perform a "2 vs. 2" test between each distributional model and the brain data. Let M_D and M_B be the similarity matrices associated with a distributional semantic model and a participant's brain data respectively. Let r be the Pearson correlation function, then a 2 vs. 2 test is a positive case for any two pairs of concepts w_1 and w_2 if

$$r(M_D(w_1), M_B(w_1)) + r(M_D(w_2), M_B(w_2))$$
$$> r(M_D(w_1), M_B(w_2)) + r(M_D(w_2), M_B(w_1))$$

where $M_D(w_1)$ and $M_D(w_2)$ denote the rows of values corresponding to the concepts w_1 and w_2 respectively, omitting the columns that correspond to the correlation between w_1 and w_2. This 2 vs. 2 test is performed on all pairs of the 60 concepts, to obtain the proportion of positive cases for the pair M_D and M_B. The distributional models are evaluated against all brain-based representations and averaged by imaging modality. The results for both sparse and dense models are displayed in Table 3. For the fMRI data, the model with the highest average 2 vs. 2 test score is the sparse multimodal GloVe+CNN-Max embedding, whilst on the MEG data the highest scoring model is a tie between the dense multimodal GloVe+CNN-Max embedding and the dense multimodal GloVe+CNN-Mean embedding. The results demonstrate that semantic distributional models that encode a range of different information are better at making statistically significant predictions on brain data. In general, the multimodal models do better than the unimodal text and image models at fitting the brain data.

Finally, we computed the direct correlation be-tween the representations M_D and M_B, using the technique of *Representational Semantic Analsysis* (RSA) (Kriegeskorte et al., 2008) commonly employed in cognitive neuroscience. Given that M_D and M_B have the same number of words and word indexing (words associated with certain rows and columns are shared across representations), we take the Spearman's correlation between the flattened upper triangular similarity matrices of these two representations for each pair of DSM and brain dataset[5].

For a given distributional model, we average all Spearman correlation values across the nine participants for each imaging modality; the results are presented in Table 4. The results show that sparse models give the closest representation to both fMRI and MEG data, with the multimodal sparse word2vec+CNN-Mean model best fitting the fMRI data, and the sparse GloVe model best fitting the MEG data. These results indicate that semantic model sparsity is an important property reflected in neurocognitive semantic representations.

6 Conclusion

In this paper, we have demonstrated the representational potential of sparse multimodal distributional models using several qualitatively different and complimentary evaluation tasks that are derived from human data: semantic similarity ratings, conceptual property knowledge, and neuroimaging data. We show that both sparse and multimodal embeddings achieve a more faithful representation of human semantics than dense models constructed from a single information source.

---

[5]Usually RSA is performed on a new matrix produced by subtracting an $N \times N$ matrix of all 1's from these concept matrices M_D and M_B, where N is the number of shared concepts. Such a representation is known as a *Representational Dissimilarity Matrix* (RDM), although here we follow Xu et al. (2016) and use similarities.

7   Acknowledgements

We would like to thank Partha Talukdar for generously providing us with the code for the Non-Negative Sparse Embedding algorithm. We would also like to thank Alona Fyshe for providing the Joint Non-Negative Sparse Embedding code.

References

Stanislaw Antol, Aishwarya Agrawal, Jiasen Lu, Margaret Mitchell, Dhruv Batra, C Lawrence Zitnick, and Devi Parikh. 2015. Vqa: Visual question answering. In *Proceedings of the IEEE International Conference on Computer Vision*, pages 2425–2433.

Miroslav Batchkarov, Thomas Kober, Jeremy Reffin, Julie Weeds, and David Weir. 2016. A critique of word similarity as a method for evaluating distributional semantic models.

Elia Bruni, Gemma Boleda, Marco Baroni, and Nam-Khanh Tran. 2012. Distributional semantics in technicolor. In *Proceedings of the 50th Annual Meeting of the Association for Computational Linguistics: Long Papers-Volume 1*, pages 136–145. Association for Computational Linguistics.

Elia Bruni, Nam-Khanh Tran, and Marco Baroni. 2014. Multimodal distributional semantics. *Journal of Artificial Intelligence Research*, 49:1–47.

Alex Clarke, Barry J. Devereux, Billi Randall, and Lorraine K. Tyler. 2015. Predicting the time course of individual objects with meg. *Cerebral Cortex*, 25(10):3602–3612.

Guillem Collell and Marie-Francine Moens. 2016. Is an image worth more than a thousand words? on the fine-grain semantic differences between visual and linguistic representations. In *Proceedings of COLING 2016, the 26th International Conference on Computational Linguistics: Technical Papers*, pages 2807–2817. The COLING 2016 Organizing Committee.

Guillem Collell, Ted Zhang, and Marie-Francine Moens. 2017. Imagined visual representations as multimodal embeddings. In *AAAI*, pages 4378–4384.

Jia Deng, Wei Dong, Richard Socher, Li-Jia Li, Kai Li, and Li Fei-Fei. 2009. Imagenet: A large-scale hierarchical image database. In *Computer Vision and Pattern Recognition, 2009. CVPR 2009. IEEE Conference on*, pages 248–255. IEEE.

Barry Devereux, Colin Kelly, and Anna Korhonen. 2010. Using fmri activation to conceptual stimuli to evaluate methods for extracting conceptual representations from corpora. In *Proceedings of the NAACL HLT 2010 First Workshop on Computational Neurolinguistics*, pages 70–78. Association for Computational Linguistics.

Barry J Devereux, Alex Clarke, Andreas Marouchos, and Lorraine K Tyler. 2013. Representational similarity analysis reveals commonalities and differences in the semantic processing of words and objects. *Journal of Neuroscience*, 33(48):18906–18916.

Barry J Devereux, Alex Clarke, and Lorraine K Tyler. 2018. Integrated deep visual and semantic attractor neural networks predict fmri pattern-information along the ventral object processing pathway. *Scientific Reports*, 8:10636.

Barry J Devereux, Lorraine K Tyler, Jeroen Geertzen, and Billi Randall. 2014. The centre for speech, language and the brain (cslb) concept property norms. *Behavior research methods*, 46(4):1119–1127.

Manaal Faruqui, Yulia Tsvetkov, Dani Yogatama, Chris Dyer, and Noah Smith. 2015. Sparse overcomplete word vector representations. *arXiv preprint arXiv:1506.02004*.

Lev Finkelstein, Evgeniy Gabrilovich, Yossi Matias, Ehud Rivlin, Zach Solan, Gadi Wolfman, and Eytan Ruppin. 2001. Placing search in context: The concept revisited. In *Proceedings of the 10th international conference on World Wide Web*, pages 406–414. ACM.

Alona Fyshe, Partha P Talukdar, Brian Murphy, and Tom M Mitchell. 2014. Interpretable semantic vectors from a joint model of brain-and text-based meaning. In *Proceedings of the conference. Association for Computational Linguistics. Meeting*, volume 2014, page 489. NIH Public Access.

Anna Gladkova and Aleksandr Drozd. 2016. Intrinsic evaluations of word embeddings: What can we do better? In *RepEval@ACL*.

James V Haxby, M Ida Gobbini, Maura L Furey, Alumit Ishai, Jennifer L Schouten, and Pietro Pietrini. 2001. Distributed and overlapping representations of faces and objects in ventral temporal cortex. *Science*, 293(5539):2425–2430.

Felix Hill, Roi Reichart, and Anna Korhonen. 2015. Simlex-999: Evaluating semantic models with (genuine) similarity estimation. *Computational Linguistics*, 41(4):665–695.

Patrik O Hoyer. 2002. Non-negative sparse coding. In *Neural Networks for Signal Processing, 2002. Proceedings of the 2002 12th IEEE Workshop on*, pages 557–565. IEEE.

Alexander G Huth, Wendy A de Heer, Thomas L Griffiths, Frédéric E Theunissen, and Jack L Gallant. 2016. Natural speech reveals the semantic maps that tile human cerebral cortex. *Nature*, 532(7600):453–458.

Andrej Karpathy and Fei-Fei Li. 2015. Deep visual-semantic alignments for generating image descriptions. In *Proceedings of the IEEE conference on computer vision and pattern recognition*, pages 3128–3137.

Douwe Kiela and Léon Bottou. 2014. Learning image embeddings using convolutional neural networks for improved multi-modal semantics. In *Proceedings of the 2014 Conference on Empirical Methods in Natural Language Processing (EMNLP)*, pages 36–45.

Nikolaus Kriegeskorte, Marieke Mur, and Peter A Bandettini. 2008. Representational similarity analysis-connecting the branches of systems neuroscience. *Frontiers in systems neuroscience*, 2:4.

Alex Krizhevsky, Ilya Sutskever, and Geoffrey E Hinton. 2012. Imagenet classification with deep convolutional neural networks. In *Advances in neural information processing systems*, pages 1097–1105.

Angeliki Lazaridou, Nghia The Pham, and Marco Baroni. 2015. Combining language and vision with a multimodal skip-gram model. *arXiv preprint arXiv:1501.02598*.

Li Lucy and Jon Gauthier. 2017. Are distributional representations ready for the real world? evaluating word vectors for grounded perceptual meaning. *arXiv preprint arXiv:1705.11168*.

Julien Mairal, Francis Bach, Jean Ponce, and Guillermo Sapiro. 2010. Online learning for matrix factorization and sparse coding. *Journal of Machine Learning Research*, 11(Jan):19–60.

Ken McRae, George S Cree, Mark S Seidenberg, and Chris McNorgan. 2005. Semantic feature production norms for a large set of living and nonliving things. *Behavior research methods*, 37(4):547–559.

Tomas Mikolov, Ilya Sutskever, Kai Chen, Greg S Corrado, and Jeff Dean. 2013. Distributed representations of words and phrases and their compositionality. In *Advances in neural information processing systems*, pages 3111–3119.

George A Miller. 1995. Wordnet: a lexical database for english. *Communications of the ACM*, 38(11):39–41.

Tom M Mitchell, Svetlana V Shinkareva, Andrew Carlson, Kai-Min Chang, Vicente L Malave, Robert A Mason, and Marcel Adam Just. 2008. Predicting human brain activity associated with the meanings of nouns. *science*, 320(5880):1191–1195.

Brian Murphy, Partha Talukdar, and Tom Mitchell. 2012. Learning effective and interpretable semantic models using non-negative sparse embedding. *Proceedings of COLING 2012*, pages 1933–1950.

Jiquan Ngiam, Aditya Khosla, Mingyu Kim, Juhan Nam, Honglak Lee, and Andrew Y Ng. 2011. Multimodal deep learning. In *Proceedings of the 28th international conference on machine learning (ICML-11)*, pages 689–696.

Maxime Oquab, Leon Bottou, Ivan Laptev, and Josef Sivic. 2014. Learning and transferring mid-level image representations using convolutional neural networks. In *Computer Vision and Pattern Recognition (CVPR), 2014 IEEE Conference on*, pages 1717–1724. IEEE.

Jeffrey Pennington, Richard Socher, and Christopher Manning. 2014. Glove: Global vectors for word representation. In *Proceedings of the 2014 conference on empirical methods in natural language processing (EMNLP)*, pages 1532–1543.

Lutfi Kerem Senel, Ihsan Utlu, Veysel Yucesoy, Aykut Koc, and Tolga Cukur. 2017. Semantic structure and interpretability of word embeddings. *arXiv preprint arXiv:1711.00331*.

Carina Silberer, Vittorio Ferrari, and Mirella Lapata. 2017. Visually grounded meaning representations. *IEEE transactions on pattern analysis and machine intelligence*, 39(11):2284–2297.

Anders Søgaard. 2016. Evaluating word embeddings with fmri and eye-tracking. In *Proceedings of the 1st Workshop on Evaluating Vector-Space Representations for NLP*, pages 116–121.

Luis Von Ahn and Laura Dabbish. 2004. Labeling images with a computer game. In *Proceedings of the SIGCHI conference on Human factors in computing systems*, pages 319–326. ACM.

Haoyan Xu, Brian Murphy, and Alona Fyshe. 2016. Brainbench: A brain-image test suite for distributional semantic models. In *Proceedings of the 2016 Conference on Empirical Methods in Natural Language Processing*, pages 2017–2021.

Matthew D. Zeiler and Rob Fergus. 2013. Visualizing and understanding convolutional networks. *CoRR*, abs/1311.2901.

Similarity dependent Chinese Restaurant Process for Cognate Identification in Multilingual Wordlists

Taraka Rama
Department of Informatics
University of Oslo, Norway
`tarakark@ifi.uio.no`

Abstract

We present and evaluate two similarity dependent Chinese Restaurant Process (sd-CRP) algorithms at the task of automated cognate detection. The sd-CRP clustering algorithms do not require any predefined threshold for detecting cognate sets in a multilingual word list. We evaluate the performance of the algorithms on six language families (more than 750 languages) and find that both the sd-CRP variants performs as well as InfoMap and better than UPGMA at the task of inferring cognate clusters. The algorithms presented in this paper are family agnostic and can be applied to any linguistically under-studied language family.

1 Introduction

Cognates are related words across languages that have descended from a common ancestral language. Identification of cognates is an important step in historical linguistics while establishing genetic relations between languages that are hypothesized to have descended from a single language that existed in the past. For instance, English *hound* and German *Hund* "dog" are cognates that go back to the Proto-Germanic stage. Cognate identification requires great amount of scholarly effort and is available for some language families such as Indo-European, Dravidian, Austronesian, and Uralic which have a long tradition of comparative linguistic research that involves decades (Dravidian family) to centuries (Indo-European family) of scholarly effort. Automatic detection of cognates with high accuracy is very much desired for reducing the effort required in analyzing understudied language families of the world.

Typically, expert annotated cognate sets are employed to infer phylogenetic trees showing language relationships that can be used to test hypotheses about temporal and spatial evolution of language families (Bouckaert et al., 2012; Chang et al., 2015), linguistic reconstruction of ancestral states on a tree (Jäger and List, 2017), or lexical reconstruction (Bouchard-Côté et al., 2013). Rama et al. (2018) showed that cognates inferred from automated methods of cognate detection can be used to infer high quality phylogenetic trees. The authors noted that there is a need for more research towards developing highly accurate cognate identification methods that can be applied to the data of not so well-studied language families which will be of assistance to historical linguists to automate parts if not the whole of the comparative method.

The last decades have seen a large amount of computational effort towards automatizing the process of cognate identification since the work of Covington (1996) and Kondrak (2002). The computational effort involved devising new sequence alignment algorithms (Kondrak, 2005, 2009), novel sound transition matrices which are linguistically guided (Kondrak, 2001; List, 2012b) or data-driven (Jäger, 2013; Rama et al., 2013, 2017; List, 2012a), and machine learning approaches (Hauer and Kondrak, 2011; Rama, 2015, 2016; Jäger et al., 2017) to identify cognates within multilingual word lists (see table 1; Swadesh, 1952) belonging to different language families and dictionaries (St Arnaud et al., 2017).

Most of the above cognate identification methods involve a workflow consisting of computation of distances between all the word pairs that have the same meaning using a machine learning algorithm or a sequence alignment algorithm; and, then clustering the pairwise distance matrix using a clustering algorithm such as InfoMap (Rosvall and Bergstrom, 2008) or UPGMA (Unweighted Pair Group Method with Arithmetic Mean; Sokal and Michener, 1958).

Both InfoMap and UPGMA require a predefined threshold that is either set heuristically or through tuned to obtain to obtain optimal perfor-

Proceedings of the 22nd Conference on Computational Natural Language Learning (CoNLL 2018), pages 271–281
Brussels, Belgium, October 31 - November 1, 2018. ©2018 Association for Computational Linguistics

Language	ALL	AND	...
English	ol[1]	End[1]	...
German	al3[1]	unt[1]	...
French	tu[2]	e[2]	...
Spanish	to8o[2]	i[2]	...
Swedish	ala[1]	ok[3]	...

Table 1: Excerpt of the Indo-European word list (from our dataset) in ASJP code for five languages belonging to Germanic (English, German, and Swedish) and Romance (Spanish and French) sub-families. Cognates are indicated with the same superscript.

mance at identifying cognate clusters on a held-out expert annotated cognate dataset(s). The clustering threshold is a single number that is tuned for all the meanings and not separately for each of the meanings. A single global threshold can lead to poor performance since the number of cognate sets vary a lot across meanings for different language families. For instance, the Indo-European dataset has cognate cluster sizes ranging from 37 for meaning *because* to 1 for meaning *name*.

On the other hand, a non-parametric clustering method such as Chinese Restaurant Process (CRP; Gershman and Blei 2012) can form clusters directly from the data without the need for tuning the threshold. CRP has found application in different NLP tasks such as morphological segmentation (Goldwater et al., 2006), language modeling (Goldwater et al., 2011), machine translation (Ravi and Knight, 2011), part-of-speech induction (Blunsom and Cohn, 2011; Sirts et al., 2014), and language decipherment (Snyder et al., 2010).

In this paper, we present two clustering algorithms inspired from similarity dependent Chinese Restaurant Process for the purpose of inferring cognate clusters. Our CRP based clustering algorithms take a word pair similarity matrix as input and infer cognate clusters automatically without needing any threshold. The sd-CRP algorithms have a hyperparameter α that allows us to form new clusters. We compare the performance of the CRP algorithms on six different language families and find that the CRP algorithms better than UPGMA and yields better or competing performance against InfoMap. We sample α so that the algorithms are robust to the initial value of α.

The paper is organized as follows. We describe related work in section 2. In section 3, we describe the word similarity features used to train the SVM model. We describe sd-CRP, UPGMA, and InfoMap algorithms in section 4. We describe the evaluation metrics and datasets in section 5. We present the results of our experiments in section 6. We discuss the results by analyzing the effect of features on SVM model, initial α values, and missing data on the performance of clustering in section 7. Finally, we conclude and present directions for future work in section 8.

2 Related work

Most of the automated cognate identification work mentioned in the previous section employed either UPGMA or InfoMap algorithms. Hauer and Kondrak (2011) were the first to apply UPGMA clustering algorithm to infer cognate sets from Swadesh lists. The authors trained a SVM classifier based on string similarity features to calculate word distances between all word pairs for a meaning. The pair-wise distance matrix is supplied to UPGMA with a predefined threshold for inferring word clusters. The UPGMA algorithm is simple and yields reasonable results across various language families (List, 2012a). However, UPGMA clustering algorithm is dependent on the threshold that needs to be tuned to obtain optimal performance (List et al., 2017b).

The cognate identification work of Hall and Klein (2011) and Bouchard-Côté et al. (2013) requires the phylogenetic tree of the language family to be known beforehand which is an unrealistic assumption for large number of world's language families. In another work, List et al. (2016) employ a weighted variant of Levenshtein distance known as SCA (see section 3) for calculating similarity between two words. Then, they apply a community detection algorithm known as InfoMap for the purpose of discovering partial cognate sets in multiple groups of Sino-Tibetan language family. The authors find that the InfoMap algorithm works better than UPGMA when tuned for threshold. In this paper, we compare the CRP clustering algorithms against InfoMap and the similarity variant of UPGMA algorithm described in section 4.3.

3 Word similarity model

In this section, we present the word similarity features used to train our SVM model at the binary task of classifying if a word pair is cognate or non-cognate.

String similarity features We use length normalized edit distance, number of common bigrams, common prefix length, individual word lengths, and absolute difference between the word lengths as features for training a SVM classifier (Hauer and Kondrak, 2011). We refer to this feature set as HK.

Point-wise Mutual Information (PMI) We include PMI weighted Needleman-Wunsch (Needleman and Wunsch, 1970) word similarity score (Jäger, 2013) as an additional feature for training the SVM classifier. The (unweighted or vanilla) Needleman-Wunsch algorithm is the similarity counterpart of the Levenshtein distance. The vanilla Needleman-Wunsch algorithm assigns equal negative weight to a common sound correspondence such as /s/ $\sim$ /h/ and a highly improbable sound correspondence such as /p/ $\sim$ /r/. The PMI weighted sound pair matrix inferred in Jäger (2013) assigns a positive weight to common sound correspondences and a negative weight to the latter ones. The PMI weight for two sounds i and j is defined as $\log \frac{p(i,j)}{q(i) \cdot q(j)}$ where, $p(i,j)$ is the relative frequency of i, j occurring at the same position in the aligned word pairs and $q(.)$ is the relative frequency of a sound in the whole word list. The similarity score for a word pair is computed using PMI-weighted Needleman-Wunsch algorithm. We transform the word similarity score using sigmoid function to yield a score between 0 and 1.0.

SCA We experimented with SCA (Sound Class Based Phonetic Alignment) word distance score (List et al., 2016) as an additional feature in our SVM model and found that inclusion of this feature improves the performance of cognate clustering systems. The SCA distance score is computed using the LingPy library (List et al., 2017a).

All the above features are widely used in cognate identification papers cited in sections 1 and 2. All the string similarity features are computed on words represented in ASJP code consisting of symbols on standard QWERTY keyboard. The ASJP code consists of 41 symbols that is used to represent common sounds of the world's languages. As such it collapses some distinctions between similar sounds such as using a single 'r' symbol for all the rhotic sounds. In this paper, we used LingPy library to convert IPA symbols to ASJP symbols. Our SVM model is implemented using scikit-learn (Buitinck et al., 2013). The trained SVM model is then used to predict the confidence scores for all the word pairs having the same meaning.

4 Clustering algorithms

In this section, we motivate and describe the two sd-CRP algorithms followed by InfoMap and UP-GMA clustering algorithms.

4.1 Motivation for CRP

In the traditional CRP, the probability that a new customer i sits at a table already filled with customers is proportional to the number of customers sitting at the table. The probability that the new customer sits at a new table is proportional to α. Blei and Frazier (2011) extended the traditional CRP model to a distance-dependent CRP model (dd-CRP) where customer i sits with a different customer j with a probability proportional to $f(d_{ij})$ where f is a decay function and d_{ij} is the distance between customers i and j. The new customer can sit by itself with a probability proportional to α. The dd-CRP formulation forms clusters through connections between the customers. This property to form clusters depending on the data is directly relevant for inferring cognate clusters from a word pair distance matrix.

In a later paper, Socher et al. (2011) introduced a similarity dependent CRP (sd-CRP) algorithm that can handle arbitrary similarities between two customers. Socher et al. (2011) showed that their sd-CRP variant performs better than dd-CRP when clustering MNIST digits dataset and Newsgroup articles. A customer is a word in the context of cognate identification. We describe the two variants of sd-CRP – ns-CRP and sb-CRP – that work directly with a similarity matrix S in the next section.

4.2 sd-CRP algorithms

Given a word similarity matrix $S \in \mathbb{R}^{N \times N}$ and α, the CRP algorithm clusters N elements into K clusters where $1 <= K <= N$.

4.2.1 ns-CRP

The algorithm starts by placing each word into its own cluster. At each step, the algorithm assign a word w_i to the cluster C that has the highest net similarity with w_i which gives the name to the algorithm. We define net similarity as

---

Algorithm 1 ns-CRP

Input: S, α
Ouput: Cluster assignments

1. Initialize each word into its own cluster and set α to 0.1.
2. Repeat until convergence:
   - For each word w_i
     - Remove w_i from its cluster.
     - Compute the net similarity s_{ik} between w_i to all words in a cluster k.
     - If $\arg\max\limits_{k} s_{ik} < \alpha S(w_i, w_i)$ assign w_i to a new cluster.
     - Else, assign w_i to the cluster k where $k = \arg\max\limits_{k} s_{ik}$.
   - Sample α using a Metropolis-Hastings step

$\sum_{j=1}^{|C|} S(w_i, w_j)$. We call the algorithm ns-CRP after the net similarity criterion used to perform cluster assignments. w_i is assigned to a new cluster if $\alpha S(w_i, w_i)$ is greater than any of the similarities with the existing clusters. Any empty clusters remaining at the end of an iteration are removed. The cluster inference procedure is summarized in Algorithm 1.

Algorithm 2 sb-CRP

Input: S, α
Ouput: Cluster assignments

1. Initialize each word to its own cluster and set α to 0.1.
2. Repeat until convergence:
   - For each word w_i
     - Remove the outgoing link from w_i.
     - Compute the net similarity s_{ik} between w_i and the words in the set returned by SitBehind(w_k).
     - If $\arg\max\limits_{k} s_{ik} < \alpha S(w_i, w_i)$ assign w_i to a new cluster.
     - Else, link w_i to a word w_k where $k = \arg\max\limits_{k} s_{ik}$.
   - Sample α using a Metropolis-Hastings step

4.2.2 sb-CRP

The sd-CRP variant of Socher et al. (2011) forms a directed link from word w_i to a different word w_{-i} based on the SITBEHIND function. We call this variant of sd-CRP algorithm as sb-CRP after SitBehind function. The function SitBehind(w_i) is recursive in nature and returns the set of words from which there is a path to w_i including itself. A directed link between w_i to itself indicates that there is no path from w_i to any other word and

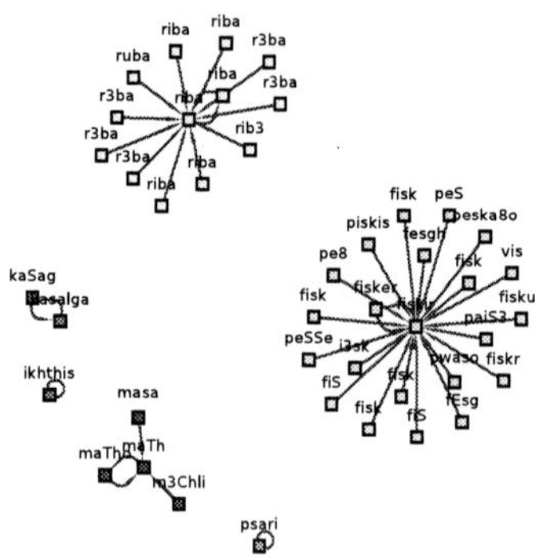

Figure 1: sb-CRP clustering for meaning *fish*. Vertices (words) with the same color are cognates.

that w_i is in its own cluster. The probability of forming a directed link from w_i and w_j is proportional to the sum of the similarity between w_i and all the words in the set returned by SitBehind(w_j). The weight for linking w_i to itself is computed as $\alpha S(w_i, w_i)$. The sb-CRP is summarized in Algorithm 2.

We present the result of application of sb-CRP algorithm to meaning *fish* in figure 1. The algorithm places the words correctly in their own clusters. The algorithm forms singleton clusters by forming self-loops. For instance, the algorithm links Ancient Greek `ikhthis` to itself thus, placing the word in its own cluster. When two words belonging to Bihari and Oriya are highly similar `maTh` $\sim$ `maTho` then, the algorithm links both the words to each other forming a cycle.

4.2.3 Underlying objective

Given K clusters out of which n are non-singleton, algorithm 1 maximizes the following objective where k is the cluster index.

$$\sum_{k=1}^{n} \sum_{(i,j)\in k} S(w_i, w_j) - \sum_{k=n+1, i\in k}^{K} \alpha S(w_i, w_i) \quad (1)$$

In the initial step, the objective in equation 1 is $-\alpha \sum_i S(w_i, w_i)$ which increases until there is no change in the cluster reassignments. The objective for algorithm 2 is similar to equation 1 and only differs in the positive part due to SitBehind function. We use the above objective to sample α which is explained below. We observe that the objective function given in equation 1 is similar to the CRP extension to K-Means (DP-Means) proposed by Kulis and Jordan (2011) who show that the DP-means algorithm converges to a local optimum.

4.2.4 Sampling α

We sample α using a Metropolis-Hastings step. We will assume an exponential prior for α with rate parameter 10. We assume an exponential prior since α should be greater than zero and the support for the exponential distribution is $\mathbb{R}^+$. α is sampled through a Metropolis-Hastings step at the end of each iteration. We use an asymmetric multiplier proposal $q(\alpha^*|\alpha) = \alpha \cdot e^{\varepsilon(u-0.5)}$ where $u(\in [0,1])$ is a uniform random number to propose a new α^*. The Hastings ratio for a multiplier proposal is $\varepsilon(u - 0.5)$ where $\varepsilon (= 1)$ is the tuning parameter that controls the range of proposed α^* (Lakner et al., 2008). Since we sample α on fixed cluster assignments, the likelihood ratio is equal to $\frac{\alpha^*}{\alpha}$. The prior ratio is equal to $\frac{\exp(\alpha^*)}{\exp(\alpha)}$.

In this paper, we run both the sd-CRP algorithms by setting the initial value of α to 0.1 and running the algorithms for 100 iterations. We found that the algorithm converges within the first ten iterations (see section 7.4). The algorithms take less than three hours to run for the Austronesian language family. We report the final iteration's B-cubed F-scores and ARI scores (see section 5.2) for each dataset.

4.3 Other Clustering algorithms

UPGMA The variant of St Arnaud et al. (2017) applied a ReLU transformation ($max(0, s)$) to the pairwise similarity matrix S such that the matrix consists only of positive similarity scores. In the initial step, each word is placed in its own cluster. The mutual score between two clusters is computed as the average of the similarity scores between all the word pairs. In each step, the algorithm merges two clusters with the highest pairwise score. The merging process is only stopped when no two clusters have positive average similarity score.

InfoMap is an information-theoretic based clustering algorithm that uses random walks to detect clusters in a network (Rosvall and Bergstrom, 2008). We transform the similarity matrix into a distance matrix by applying a sigmoid transformation then subtracting the matrix values from 1.0. Then, we apply a pre-defined threshold to form a disconnected graph. Finally, we supply the disconnected graph as input to the InfoMap algorithm

to infer clusters. We also experimented with the threshold during cross-validation experiments on the training dataset and found that a threshold of 0.57 yielded slightly higher performance than a threshold of 0.5.

5 Materials and Evaluation

In this section, we describe the datasets and cluster evaluation metrics.

5.1 Datasets

Training dataset Wichmann and Holman (2013) and List (2014) compiled cognacy annotated multilingual word lists for subsets of families from various scholarly sources such as comparative handbooks and historical linguistics' articles. The detailed references to all the datasets are given in Jäger et al. (2017). Below, we provide the number of languages/number of meanings in each language group in parantheses.

- Afrasian (21/40), Kadai (12/40), Kamasau (8/36), Lolo-Burmese (15/40), Mayan (30/100), Miao-Yao (6/36), Mixe-Zoque (10/100), Mon-Khmer (16/100), Bai dialects (9/110), Chinese dialects (18/180), Japanese (10/200), ObUgrian (21/110; Hungarian excluded from Ugric sub-family).

We extracted a total of 48,389 cognate pairs (positive) and 51,452 non-cognate pairs (negative) for training our SVM model.

Test datasets We test our clustering algorithms on word lists belonging to four language families given in table 2.

Dataset	Meanings	Languages	Source
Austronesian	210	395	Gray et al. (2009)
Austro-Asiatic	200	122	Sidwell (2015)
Indo-European	208	52	Bouckaert et al. (2012)
Central Asian dialects	183	88	Mennecier et al. (2016)

Table 2: The second, third, and fourth columns show the number of number of meanings, languages, and the source of each dataset respectively.

5.2 Evaluation

We use B-cubed F-score (Amigó et al., 2009) and Adjusted Rand Index (Hubert and Arabie, 1985) to evaluate the quality of the inferred clusters.

B-cubed F-scores are defined for each individual item (word) as follows. The precision for an item is defined as the ratio between the number of cognates in its cluster to the total number of items

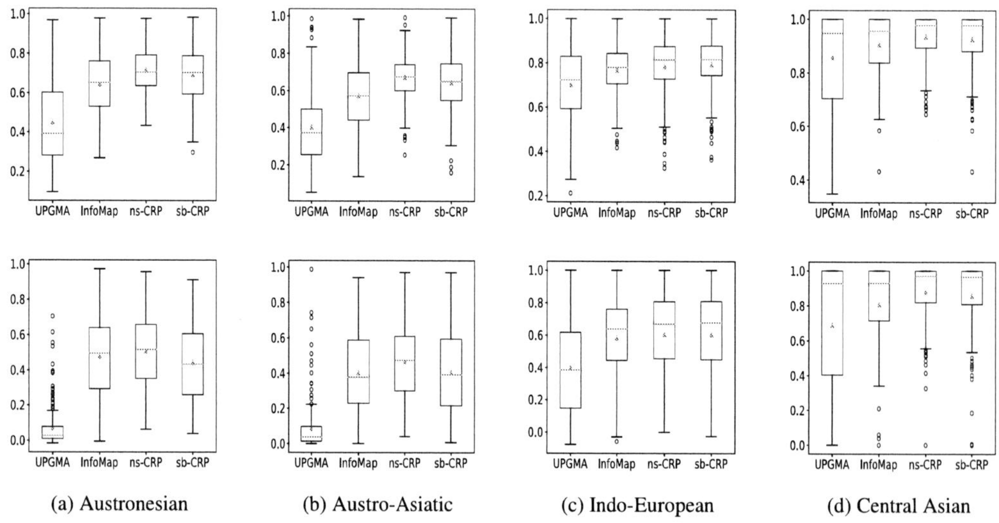

Figure 2: The B-cubed F-scores are shown in the top row. The bottom row shows the ARI scores for each of the datasets. The horizontal bar shows the median score and the mean of the scores is shown by ▲.

in its cluster. The recall for an item is defined as the ratio between the number of cognates in its cluster to the total number of expert labeled cognates. Finally, the B-cubed F-score for a meaning is computed as the harmonic mean of the items' average precision and recall. The B-cubed F-score for the whole dataset is computed as the average of the B-cubed F-scores across all the meanings.

Adjusted Rand Index (ARI) is a chance corrected version of rand index (Hubert and Arabie, 1985). The ARI scores are in the range of -1 to $+1$. A score of 0 indicates that the obtained clusters are randomly labelled whereas a score $+1$ indicates perfect match between the two clusters. The ARI score is zero whenever the gold standard groups all the words belonging to the same meaning slot (e.g. words for meaning *name* are cognate across the daughter Indo-European languages) as one cluster, whereas the B-cubed F-score is not zero in such a case.

6 Results

6.1 F-scores and ARI

We visualize the B-cubed F-scores and ARI scores in figure 2. The spread of the F-scores and ARI scores suggest that InfoMap and sd-CRP variants are better than UPGMA in the case of all the datasets except for the Central Asian dataset. The box plots for InfoMap are similar to the box plots of sd-CRP variants across all the language fami-

lies. InfoMap and sd-CRP variants have shorter width boxes than those of UPGMA across all the families. All the algorithms show the lowest performance in terms of both F-scores and ARI scores on the Austro-Asiatic dataset. Based on mean F-scores and ARI scores across all the four language families, we determine the ns-CRP algorithm to be the winner.

6.2 Size of inferred clusters

Method	Austro-Asiatic	Austronesian	Central Asian	Indo-European
UPGMA	0.194	0.186	0.722	0.659
InfoMap	0.438	0.617	0.8	0.753
ns-CRP	0.609	0.77	0.833	0.816
sb-CRP	0.564	0.716	0.833	0.817

Table 3: Pearson's R between number of predicted clusters and number of clusters in the gold standard data. The best correlation for each language family is shaded in light gray.

Apart from evaluating the cluster quality using B-cubed F-scores and ARI scores, we compare the number of inferred clusters by each algorithm against the number of clusters given in the gold standard data using Pearson's R. We present the results of Pearson's correlation in table 3. The Pearson's correlation between the number of predicted clusters and the number of gold clusters shows that the sd-CRP variants are successful at retrieving the right number of clusters when compared to UPGMA. InfoMap comes close to both sd-CRP variants' performance only in the case of the Central Asian languages dataset. The ns-CRP algorithm is the winner at being the best predictor of cluster sizes since it predicts clusters of sizes close to those given in the gold standard in the case of Austro-Asiatic and Austronesian datasets and shows same performance as sb-CRP in the case of the Central Asian dialects dataset.

7 Discussion

In this section, we discuss the effect of feature selection and initial value of α on the performance of sd-CRP algorithms. We verify the effect of missing data on all the clustering algorithms and present the results. Finally, we analyze the working of sd-CRP algorithms.

7.1 Feature ablation

To ascertain which word similarity features contribute the most to the performance of the ns-CRP algorithm, we trained three simpler SVM models and evaluated the quality of the inferred clusters using these models. The first model HK uses only orthographic features. The second model uses the PMI word similarity as an additional feature to the HK model. The third model uses SCA word similarity as an additional feature to the HK model. The results presented in previous section showed that ns-CRP performs the worst on Austronesian and Austro-Asiatic datasets.

Therefore, we present the cluster evaluation results only for these two datasets in table 4. The HK model yields high F-scores for both the datasets. Addition of PMI or SCA as an additional feature always improves both F-scores and ARI scores. In fact, including both PMI and SCA as features yields the best results even if the improvement is marginal in the case of the Austro-Asiatic dataset. We note that we observe similar trends for the rest of the datasets. We do not present the results for other datasets due to space constraints. Finally, the ablation experiments suggest that including both data-driven PMI and linguistically guided SCA as features gives the best results at cognate clustering.

7.2 Effect of lexical coverage

In this subsection, we investigate the effect of missing data on the clustering algorithms. In the case of the Austronesian dataset, less than 50% of the languages have word forms attested in 70% of

System	F-score	ARI
	Austronesian	
HK	0.675 ± 0.111	0.416 ± 0.189
HK+PMI	0.706 ± 0.126	0.489 ± 0.20
HK+SCA	0.683 ± 0.111	0.443 ± 0.193
HK+PMI+SCA	0.715 ± 0.111	0.509 ± 0.193
	Austro-Asiatic	
HK	0.638 ± 0.117	0.389 ± 0.185
HK+PMI	0.651 ± 0.139	0.435 ± 0.219
HK+SCA	0.666 ± 0.117	0.441 ± 0.197
HK+PMI+SCA	0.672 ± 0.127	0.467 ± 0.213

Table 4: Results of feature ablation experiments on Austronesian and Austro-Asiatic datasets.

the meanings. The situation is slightly better in the case of Austro-Asiatic with more than 80% of the languages having meanings attested in 70% of the meanings.

In a separate paper, Rama et al. (2018) presented pruned datasets for five different language families – Pama-Nyungan and Sino-Tibetan in addition to Austronesian, Austro-Asiatic, and Indo-European – consisting of only those languages that show the highest mutual lexical coverage. For each dataset, the authors pruned any language which has less than 75% mutual attestations with the rest of the languages. We attempted to prune the Central Asian dataset but found that we could only exclude a single dialect which has less than 50% attestation. Therefore, we did not include the Central Asian dataset in our experiments. The statistics of the pruned datasets is given in table 5.

Family	Meanings	Languages
Austronesian	210	45
Austro-Asiatic	200	58
Indo-European	208	42
Pama-Nyungan	183	67
Sino-Tibetan	110	64

Table 5: The dataset shows the number of meanings and languages in the pruned datasets.

The results of this experiment are visualized in figure 3. The sd-CRP algorithms perform better than UPGMA and InfoMap in the case of Pama-Nyungan and Austro-Asiatic datasets. There

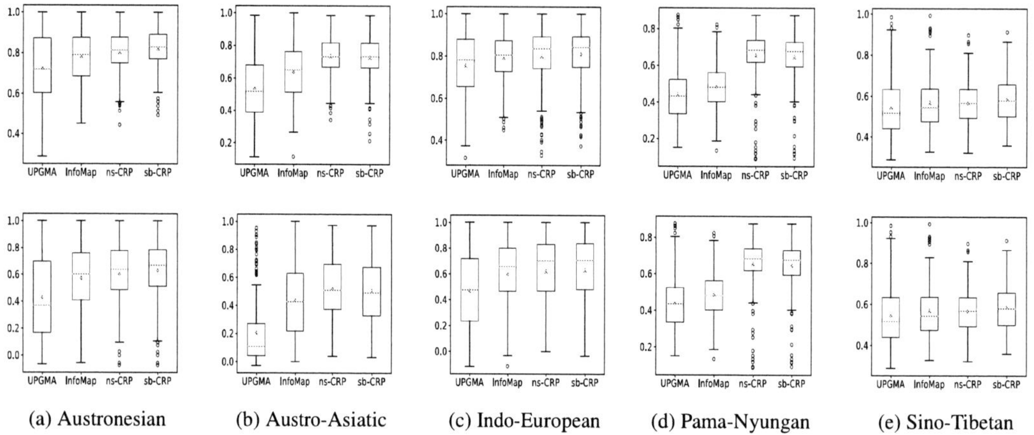

(a) Austronesian	(b) Austro-Asiatic	(c) Indo-European	(d) Pama-Nyungan	(e) Sino-Tibetan

Figure 3: The top row shows the B-cubed F-scores and the bottom row shows the ARI scores for pruned datasets of five language families.

seems to be no difference in the performance of all the algorithms in the case of the Sino-Tibetan dataset. There is no difference between sd-CRP and InfoMap algorithms in the case of the Austronesian dataset. Although the mean B-cubed F-scores indicate that there is no difference between the algorithms in the case of the Indo-European dataset, the spread of the box plots suggests that non-UPGMA algorithms perform better than UP-GMA. The B-cubed F-scores are not decisive in the case of the Indo-European dataset, whereas the ARI score clearly shows that non-UPGMA perform better than UPGMA. In conclusion, both the sd-CRP algorithms perform at least as good or better than InfoMap algorithm in the case of pruned datasets.

7.3 Effect of initial alpha

Family	F-score	ARI
Austro-Asiatic	0.735 ± 0.119	0.524 ± 0.217
Austronesian	0.805 ± 0.109	0.609 ± 0.242
Indo-European	0.8 ± 0.135	0.62 ± 0.278
Pama-Nyungan	0.655 ± 0.141	0.354 ± 0.174
Sino-Tibetan	0.569 ± 0.114	0.276 ± 0.17

Table 6: The mean and standard deviation of the F-scores and ARI scores for $\alpha = 0.001$ on pruned datasets.

In this experiment, we test the sensitivity of ns-CRP algorithm to the initial α by initializing α to 0.001, 0.01, and 1.0. We hypothesize that our sampling step makes the algorithm robust to the initial value of α. We run the ns-CRP clustering algorithm for 100 iterations for different starting values of α on each of the pruned datasets. The results of the experiment are given in table 6 for $\alpha = 0.001$. The B-cubed F-scores and ARI scores are quite similar for other initial values of α, and therefore we do not present those results to avoid repetition. These results suggest that the ns-CRP algorithm is not sensitive to the value of initial α.

7.4 Convergence of ns-CRP

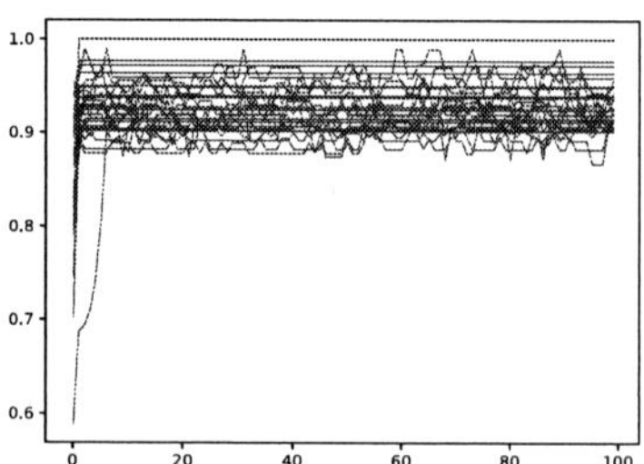

Figure 4: Plot showing the convergence of the sd-CRP algorithm for 30 meanings from the Indo-European dataset.

Here, we investigate the stability of the ns-CRP algorithm by plotting the B-cubed F-scores against the number of iterations for 30 random meanings from the Indo-European dataset in figure 4. The plot shows that the ns-CRP algorithm quickly moves from an initial configuration with low F-score to a configuration that has high F-scores within the first 20 iterations. We observe similar behaviour of ns-CRP in the case of other language families. In conclusion, the plot shows that the quality of the clusters inferred by the ns-CRP algorithm achieves a high F-score. Moreover, the cluster quality does not change drastically after reaching a local optimum.

7.5 Analysis of sd-CRP algorithms

In this subsection, we analyze the difference in the behaviours of sd-CRP algorithms. If w_i and w_j are cognate and w_j and w_k are cognate, then all the three words are cognate with each other which follows from the definition of cognacy. The sb-CRP algorithm captures this cognacy relation through the SitBehind function. During cluster formation, w_i only has to connect to a word that might have no other words other than itself sitting behind it. We hypothesize that the sb-CRP algorithm would be more efficient at identifying partial cognates where only part of the lexical material is cognate with another word. An example of a partial cognate is the meaning of *meat* in *sweetmeat* which is cognate with Swedish *mat* 'food' (Campbell, 2004). In contrast, the ns-CRP algorithm is stricter than sb-CRP algorithm in that a word is assigned to the cluster with which it has the highest net similarity. If a word has net similarity of zero with all the existing clusters, then, the word would form its own cluster since $\alpha S(w_i, w_i)$ is always positive.

8 Conclusion

We presented and compared the performance of two similarity dependent Chinese Restaurant process algorithms at the task of automated cognate detection for six different language families. The sensitivity experiments suggested that the sd-CRP algorithms is not sensitive to initial α and missing data. The feature ablation experiments suggest that the inclusion of PMI and SCA features improve the performance of the sd-CRP algorithms. We conclude that the sd-CRP algorithms perform better than the existing clustering algorithms across multiple settings.

As future work, we plan to include language relatedness as features into SVM training and also train the SVM classifier in an unsupervised fashion using the sd-CRP algorithms.

Acknowledgments

The author thanks the anonymous reviewers for the comments which helped improved the paper. The author is supported by BIGMED project (a Norwegian Research Council LightHouse grant, see bigmed.no). The algorithms were designed when the author took part in the ERC Advanced Grant 324246 EVOLAEMP project led by Gerhard Jäger. All these sources of support are gratefully acknowledged.

References

Enrique Amigó, Julio Gonzalo, Javier Artiles, and Felisa Verdejo. 2009. A comparison of extrinsic clustering evaluation metrics based on formal constraints. *Information retrieval*, 12(4):461–486.

David M Blei and Peter I Frazier. 2011. Distance dependent chinese restaurant processes. *Journal of Machine Learning Research*, 12(Aug):2461–2488.

Phil Blunsom and Trevor Cohn. 2011. A hierarchical pitman-yor process hmm for unsupervised part of speech induction. In *Proceedings of the 49th Annual Meeting of the Association for Computational Linguistics: Human Language Technologies-Volume 1*, pages 865–874. Association for Computational Linguistics.

Alexandre Bouchard-Côté, David Hall, Thomas L. Griffiths, and Dan Klein. 2013. Automated reconstruction of ancient languages using probabilistic models of sound change. *Proceedings of the National Academy of Sciences*, 110(11):4224–4229.

Remco Bouckaert, Philippe Lemey, Michael Dunn, Simon J. Greenhill, Alexander V. Alekseyenko, Alexei J. Drummond, Russell D. Gray, Marc A. Suchard, and Quentin D. Atkinson. 2012. Mapping the origins and expansion of the Indo-European language family. *Science*, 337(6097):957–960.

Lars Buitinck, Gilles Louppe, Mathieu Blondel, Fabian Pedregosa, Andreas Mueller, Olivier Grisel, Vlad Niculae, Peter Prettenhofer, Alexandre Gramfort, Jaques Grobler, Robert Layton, Jake VanderPlas, Arnaud Joly, Brian Holt, and Gaël Varoquaux. 2013. API design for machine learning software: experiences from the scikit-learn project. In *ECML PKDD Workshop: Languages for Data Mining and Machine Learning*, pages 108–122.

Lyle Campbell. 2004. *Historical Linguistics: An Introduction*. Edinburgh University Press, Edinburgh.

Will Chang, Chundra Cathcart, David Hall, and Andrew Garrett. 2015. Ancestry-constrained phylogenetic analysis supports the Indo-European steppe hypothesis. *Language*, 91(1):194–244.

Michael A. Covington. 1996. An algorithm to align words for historical comparison. *Computational Linguistics*, 22(4):481–496.

Samuel J Gershman and David M Blei. 2012. A tutorial on bayesian nonparametric models. *Journal of Mathematical Psychology*, 56(1):1–12.

Sharon Goldwater, Thomas L Griffiths, and Mark Johnson. 2006. Contextual dependencies in unsupervised word segmentation. In *Proceedings of the 21st International Conference on Computational Linguistics and the 44th annual meeting of the Association for Computational Linguistics*, pages 673–680. Association for Computational Linguistics.

Sharon Goldwater, Thomas L Griffiths, and Mark Johnson. 2011. Producing power-law distributions and damping word frequencies with two-stage language models. *Journal of Machine Learning Research*, 12(Jul):2335–2382.

Russell D Gray, Alexei J Drummond, and Simon J Greenhill. 2009. Language phylogenies reveal expansion pulses and pauses in pacific settlement. *science*, 323(5913):479–483.

David Hall and Dan Klein. 2011. Large-scale cognate recovery. In *Proceedings of the Conference on Empirical Methods in Natural Language Processing*, pages 344–354. Association for Computational Linguistics.

Bradley Hauer and Grzegorz Kondrak. 2011. Clustering semantically equivalent words into cognate sets in multilingual lists. In *Proceedings of 5th International Joint Conference on Natural Language Processing*, pages 865–873, Chiang Mai, Thailand. Asian Federation of Natural Language Processing.

Lawrence Hubert and Phipps Arabie. 1985. Comparing partitions. *Journal of classification*, 2(1):193–218.

Gerhard Jäger. 2013. Phylogenetic inference from word lists using weighted alignment with empirically determined weights. *Language Dynamics and Change*, 3(2):245–291.

Gerhard Jäger and Johann-Mattis List. 2017. Using ancestral state reconstruction methods for onomasiological reconstruction in multilingual word lists. *Forthcoming, Language Dynamics and Change*.

Gerhard Jäger, Johann-Mattis List, and Pavel Sofroniev. 2017. Using support vector machines and state-of-the-art algorithms for phonetic alignment to identify cognates in multi-lingual wordlists. In *Proceedings of the 15th Conference of the European Chapter of the Association for Computational Linguistics: Volume 1, Long Papers*, pages 1205–1216. Association for Computational Linguistics.

Grzegorz Kondrak. 2001. Identifying cognates by phonetic and semantic similarity. In *North American Chapter Of The Association For Computational Linguistics*, pages 1–8. Association for Computational Linguistics Morristown, NJ, USA.

Grzegorz Kondrak. 2002. *Algorithms for language reconstruction*. Ph.D. thesis, University of Toronto, Ontario, Canada.

Grzegorz Kondrak. 2005. Cognates and word alignment in bitexts. In *Proceedings of the Tenth Machine Translation Summit (MT Summit X)*, pages 305–312.

Grzegorz Kondrak. 2009. Identification of cognates and recurrent sound correspondences in word lists. *Traitement Automatique des Langues et Langues Anciennes*, 50(2):201–235.

Brian Kulis and Michael I Jordan. 2011. Revisiting k-means: New algorithms via Bayesian nonparametrics. *arXiv preprint arXiv:1111.0352*.

Clemens Lakner, Paul Van Der Mark, John P Huelsenbeck, Bret Larget, and Fredrik Ronquist. 2008. Efficiency of Markov chain Monte Carlo tree proposals in Bayesian phylogenetics. *Systematic biology*, 57(1):86–103.

Johann-Mattis List. 2012a. LexStat: Automatic detection of cognates in multilingual wordlists. In *Proceedings of the EACL 2012 Joint Workshop of LINGVIS & UNCLH*, pages 117–125, Avignon, France. Association for Computational Linguistics.

Johann-Mattis List. 2012b. SCA: phonetic alignment based on sound classes. In *New Directions in Logic, Language and Computation*, pages 32–51. Springer.

Johann-Mattis List. 2014. *Sequence comparison in historical linguistics*. Düsseldorf University Press, Düsseldorf.

Johann-Mattis List, Simon Greenhill, and Robert Forkel. 2017a. Lingpy. a python library for quantitative tasks in historical linguistics.

Johann-Mattis List, Simon J. Greenhill, and Russell D. Gray. 2017b. The potential of automatic word comparison for historical linguistics. *PLOS ONE*, 12(1):1–18.

Johann-Mattis List, Philippe Lopez, and Eric Bapteste. 2016. Using sequence similarity networks to identify partial cognates in multilingual wordlists. In *Proceedings of the 54th Annual Meeting of the Association for Computational Linguistics (Volume 2: Short Papers)*, pages 599–605, Berlin, Germany. Association for Computational Linguistics.

Philippe Mennecier, John Nerbonne, Evelyne Heyer, and Franz Manni. 2016. A central asian language survey. *Language Dynamics and Change*, 6(1):57–98.

Saul B. Needleman and Christian D. Wunsch. 1970. A general method applicable to the search for similarities in the amino acid sequence of two proteins. *Journal of Molecular Biology*, 48(3):443–453.

Taraka Rama. 2015. Automatic cognate identification with gap-weighted string subsequences. In *Proceedings of the 2015 Conference of the North American Chapter of the Association for Computational Linguistics: Human Language Technologies.*, pages 1227–1231.

Taraka Rama. 2016. Siamese convolutional networks for cognate identification. In *Proceedings of COLING 2016, the 26th International Conference on Computational Linguistics: Technical Papers*, pages 1018–1027.

Taraka Rama, Prasant Kolachina, and Sudheer Kolachina. 2013. Two methods for automatic identification of cognates. *QITL*, 5:76.

Taraka Rama, Johann-Mattis List, Johannes Wahle, and Gerhard Jäger. 2018. Are automatic methods for cognate detection good enough for phylogenetic reconstruction in historical linguistics? In *Proceedings of the 2018 Conference of the North American Chapter of the Association for Computational Linguistics: Human Language Technologies, Volume 2 (Short Papers)*, volume 2, pages 393–400.

Taraka Rama, Johannes Wahle, Pavel Sofroniev, and Gerhard Jäger. 2017. Fast and unsupervised methods for multilingual cognate clustering. *arXiv preprint arXiv:1702.04938*.

Sujith Ravi and Kevin Knight. 2011. Deciphering foreign language. In *Proceedings of the 49th Annual Meeting of the Association for Computational Linguistics: Human Language Technologies-Volume 1*, pages 12–21. Association for Computational Linguistics.

Martin Rosvall and Carl T Bergstrom. 2008. Maps of random walks on complex networks reveal community structure. *Proceedings of the National Academy of Sciences*, 105(4):1118–1123.

Paul Sidwell. 2015. Austroasiatic lexical data set for phylogenetic analyses 2015 version.

Kairit Sirts, Jacob Eisenstein, Micha Elsner, and Sharon Goldwater. 2014. Pos induction with distributional and morphological information using a distance-dependent chinese restaurant process. In *ACL (2)*, pages 265–271.

Benjamin Snyder, Regina Barzilay, and Kevin Knight. 2010. A statistical model for lost language decipherment. In *Proceedings of the 48th Annual Meeting of the Association for Computational Linguistics*, pages 1048–1057. Association for Computational Linguistics.

Richard Socher, Andrew L Maas, and Christopher D Manning. 2011. Spectral chinese restaurant processes: Nonparametric clustering based on similarities. In *AISTATS*, pages 698–706.

Robert R Sokal and Charles D Michener. 1958. A statistical method for evaluating systematic relationships. *University of Kansas Science Bulletin*, 38:1409–1438.

Adam St Arnaud, David Beck, and Grzegorz Kondrak. 2017. Identifying cognate sets across dictionaries of related languages. In *Proceedings of the 2017 Conference on Empirical Methods in Natural Language Processing*, pages 2509–2518.

Morris Swadesh. 1952. Lexico-statistic dating of prehistoric ethnic contacts: with special reference to North American Indians and Eskimos. *Proceedings of the American philosophical society*, 96(4):452–463.

Søren Wichmann and Eric W Holman. 2013. Languages with longer words have more lexical change. In *Approaches to Measuring Linguistic Differences*, pages 249–281. Mouton de Gruyter.

A Supplemental Material

The code and data used in this paper are uploaded as a zip file along with this paper. In addition, they are available for download at: `https://github.com/PhyloStar/sd-CRP-cognates`

Uncovering divergent linguistic information in word embeddings with lessons for intrinsic and extrinsic evaluation

Mikel Artetxe, Gorka Labaka, Iñigo Lopez-Gazpio, Eneko Agirre
IXA NLP Group
University of the Basque Country (UPV/EHU)
{mikel.artetxe,gorka.labaka,inigo.lopez,e.agirre}@ehu.eus

Abstract

Following the recent success of word embeddings, it has been argued that there is no such thing as an ideal representation for words, as different models tend to capture divergent and often mutually incompatible aspects like semantics/syntax and similarity/relatedness. In this paper, we show that each embedding model captures more information than directly apparent. A linear transformation that adjusts the similarity order of the model without any external resource can tailor it to achieve better results in those aspects, providing a new perspective on how embeddings encode divergent linguistic information. In addition, we explore the relation between intrinsic and extrinsic evaluation, as the effect of our transformations in downstream tasks is higher for unsupervised systems than for supervised ones.

1 Introduction

Word embeddings have recently become a central topic in natural language processing. Several unsupervised methods have been proposed to efficiently train dense vector representations of words (Mikolov et al., 2013; Pennington et al., 2014; Bojanowski et al., 2017) and successfully applied in a variety of tasks like parsing (Bansal et al., 2014), topic modeling (Batmanghelich et al., 2016) and document classification (Taddy, 2015).

While there is still an active research line to better understand these models from a theoretical perspective (Levy and Goldberg, 2014c; Arora et al., 2016; Gittens et al., 2017), the fundamental idea behind all of them is to assign a similar vector representation to similar words. For that purpose, most embedding models build upon co-occurrence statistics from large monolingual corpora, following the distributional hypothesis that similar words tend to occur in similar contexts (Harris, 1954).

Nevertheless, the above argument does not formalize what "similar words" means, and it is not entirely clear what kind of relationships an embedding model should capture in practice. For instance, some authors distinguish between genuine similarity[1] (as in *car - automobile*) and relatedness[2] (as in *car - road*) (Budanitsky and Hirst, 2006; Hill et al., 2015). From another perspective, word similarity could focus on semantics (as in *sing - chant*) or syntax (as in *sing - singing*) (Mikolov et al., 2013). We refer to these two aspects as the two axes of similarity with two ends each: the semantics/syntax axis and the similarity/relatedness axis.

In this paper, we propose a new method to tailor any given set of embeddings towards a specific end in these axes. Our method is inspired by the work on first order and second order co-occurrences (Schütze, 1998), generalized as a continuous parameter of a linear transformation applied to the embeddings that we call *similarity order*. While there have been several proposals to learn specialized word embeddings (Levy and Goldberg, 2014a; Kiela et al., 2015; Bojanowski et al., 2017), previous work explicitly altered the training objective and often relied on external resources like knowledge bases, whereas the proposed method is applied as a post-processing of any pre-trained embedding model and does not require any additional resource. As such, our work shows that standard embedding models are able to encode divergent linguistic information but have limits on how this information is surfaced, and analyzes the implications that this has in both intrinsic evaluation and downstream tasks. This paper makes the following contributions:

1. We propose a linear transformation with a free parameter that adjusts the perfor-

---

[1] Also referred to as *functional similarity* or just *similarity*.
[2] Also referred to as *associative similarity*, *topical similarity* or *domain similarity*.

Proceedings of the 22nd Conference on Computational Natural Language Learning (CoNLL 2018), pages 282–291
Brussels, Belgium, October 31 - November 1, 2018. ©2018 Association for Computational Linguistics

mance of word embeddings in the similarity/relatedness and semantics/syntax axes, as measured in word analogy and similarity datasets.

2. We show that the performance of embeddings as used currently is limited by the impossibility of simultaneously surfacing divergent information (e.g. the aforementioned axes). Our method uncovers the fact that embeddings capture more information than what is immediately obvious.

3. We show that standard intrinsic evaluation offers a static and incomplete picture, and complementing it with the proposed method can offer a better understanding of what information an embedding model truly encodes.

4. We show that the effect of our method also carries out to downstream tasks, but its effect is larger in unsupervised systems directly using embedding similarities than in supervised systems using embeddings as input features, as the latter have enough expressive power to learn the optimal transformation themselves.

All in all, our work sheds light in how word embeddings represent divergent linguistic information, analyzes the role that this plays in intrinsic evaluation and downstream tasks, and opens new opportunities for improvement.

The remaining of this paper is organized as follows. We describe our proposed post-processing in Section 2. Section 3 and 4 then present the results in intrinsic and extrinsic evaluation, respectively. Section 5 discusses the implications of our work on embedding evaluation and their integration in downstream tasks. Section 6 presents the related work, and Section 7 concludes the paper.

2 Proposed post-processing

Let X be the matrix of word embeddings in a given language, so that X_{i*} is the embedding of the ith word in the vocabulary. Such embeddings are meant to capture the meaning of their corresponding words in such a way that the dot product $sim(i,j) = X_{i*} \cdot X_{j*}$ gives some measure of the similarity between the ith and the jth word[3]. Based on this, we can define the similarity matrix $M(X) = XX^T$ so that $sim(i,j) = M(X)_{ij}$.

Inspired by first order and second order co-occurrences (Schütze, 1998), one can also define a second order similarity measure on top of this (first order) similarity. In second order similarity, the similarity of two words is not assessed in terms of how similar they directly are, but in terms of how their similarity with third words agrees. For instance, even if i and j are not directly similar, they might both be similar to a third word k, which would make them more similar in second order similarity, and one could similarly define third, fourth or nth order similarity. The idea that we try to exploit next is that some of these similarity orders can be better at capturing different aspects of language as discussed in Section 1.

More formally, we define the second order similarity matrix $M_2(X) = XX^TXX^T$, so that $sim_2(i,j) = M_2(X)_{ij}$. Note that $M_2(X) = M(M(X))$, so second order similarity can be seen as the similarity of the similarities across all words, which is in line with the intuitive definition given above. More generally, we could define the nth order similarity matrix as $M_n(X) = (XX^T)^n$, so that $sim_n(i,j) = M_n(X)_{ij}$. We next show that, instead of changing the similarity measure, one can change the word embeddings themselves through a linear transformation so they directly capture this second or nth order similarity.

Let $X^TX = Q\Lambda Q^T$ be the eigendecomposition of X^TX, so that Λ is a positive diagonal matrix whose entries are the eigenvalues of X^TX and Q is an orthogonal matrix with their respective eigenvectors as columns[4]. We define the linear transformation matrix $W = Q\sqrt{\Lambda}$ and apply it to the original embeddings X, obtaining the transformed embeddings $X' = XW$. As it can be trivially seen, $M(X') = M_2(X)$, that is, such transformed embeddings capture the second order similarity as defined for the original embeddings.

More generally, we can define $W_\alpha = Q\Lambda^\alpha$, where α is a parameter of the transformation that adjusts the desired similarity order. Following the above definitions, such transformation would lead to first order similarity as defined for the original embeddings when $\alpha = 0$, second order similarity when $\alpha = 0.5$ and, in general, nth order similarity when $\alpha = (n-1)/2$, that is, $M(XW_0) = M(X)$, $M(XW_{0.5}) = M_2(X)$ and $M(XW_{(n-1)/2}) = M_n(X)$.

---

[3] Note that the cosine similarity is the dot product of two length normalized vectors.

[4] Note that these constraints hold because X^TX is a real symmetric matrix by definition.

Note that the proposed transformation is relative in nature (i.e. it does not make any assumption on the similarity order captured by the embeddings it is applied to) and, as such, negative values of α can also be used to reduce the similarity order. For instance, let X be the second order transformed embeddings of some original embeddings Z, so $X = ZW_{0.5}$, where $W_{0.5}$ was computed over Z. It can be easily verified that $W_{-0.25}$, as computed over X, would recover back the original embeddings, that is, $M(XW_{-0.25}) = M(Z)$. In other words, assuming that the embeddings X capture some second order similarity, it is possible to transform them so that they capture the corresponding first order similarity, and one can easily generalize this to higher order similarities by simply using smaller values of α.

All in all, this means that the parameter α can be used to either increase or decrease the similarity order that we want our embeddings to capture. Moreover, even if the similarity order is intuitively defined as a discrete value, the parameter α is continuous, meaning that the transformation can be smoothly adjusted to the desired level.

3 Intrinsic evaluation

In order to better understand the effect of the proposed post-processing in the two similarity axes introduced in Section 1, we adopt the widely used word analogy and word similarity tasks, which offer specific benchmarks for semantics/syntax and similarity/relatedness, respectively.

More concretely, **word analogy** measures the accuracy in answering questions like "what is the word that is similar to *France* in the same sense as *Berlin* is similar to *Germany*?" (semantic analogy) or "what is the word that is similar to *small* in the same sense as *biggest* is similar to *big*?" (syntactic analogy) using simple word vector arithmetic (Mikolov et al., 2013). The analogy resolution method is commonly formalized in terms of vector additions and subtractions. Levy and Goldberg (2014b) showed that this was equivalent to searching for a word that maximizes a linear combination of three pairwise word similarities, so the proposed post-processing has a direct effect on it. For these experiments, we use the dataset published as part of word2vec[5], which consists of 8,869 semantic and 10,675 syntactic questions of this type

(Mikolov et al., 2013).

On the other hand, **word similarity** measures the correlation[6] between the similarity scores produced by a model and a gold standard created by human annotators for a given set of word pairs. As discussed before, there is not a single definition of what human similarity scores should capture, which has lead to a distinction between genuine similarity datasets and relatedness datasets. In order to better understand the effect of our post-processing in each case, we conduct our experiments in SimLex-999 (Hill et al., 2015), a genuine similarity dataset that consists of 999 word pairs, and MEN (Bruni et al., 2012), a relatedness dataset that consists of 3,000 word pairs[7].

So as to make our evaluation more robust, we run the above experiments for three popular **embedding methods**, using large pre-trained models released by their respective authors as follows:

Word2vec (Mikolov et al., 2013) is the original implementation of the CBOW and skip-gram architectures that popularized neural word embeddings. We use the pre-trained model published in the project homepage[8], which was trained on about 100 billion words of the Google News dataset and consists of 300-dimensional vectors for 3 million words and phrases.

Glove (Pennington et al., 2014) is a global log-bilinear regression model to train word embeddings designed to explicitly enforce the model properties needed to solve word analogies. We use the largest pre-trained model published by the authors[9], which was trained on 840 billion words of the Common Crawl corpus and contains 300-dimensional vectors for 2.2 million words.

Fasttext (Bojanowski et al., 2017) is an extension of the skip-gram model implemented by word2vec that enriches the embeddings with subword information using bags of character n-grams. We use the largest pre-trained model published in the project website[10], which was trained on 600 billion tokens of the Common Crawl corpus and con-

---

[6]Following common practice, we report Spearman.

[7]These datasets were selected because the instructions used to elicit human scores are clearly geared towards genuine similarity and relatedness, respectively, and because they have been already used in similar studies (Kiela et al., 2015)

[8]https://code.google.com/archive/p/word2vec/

[9]http://nlp.stanford.edu/data/glove.840B.300d.zip

[10]https://fasttext.cc/docs/en/english-vectors.html

---

[5]https://github.com/tmikolov/word2vec/blob/master/questions-words.txt

		Word analogy		Word similarity	
		Semantic	Syntactic	Similarity (SimLex-999)	Relatedness (MEN)
word2vec	Original	76.49	74.87	44.21	76.96
	Best	81.00 $\alpha = -0.65$	74.96 $\alpha = 0.10$	47.81 $\alpha = -0.70$	78.09 $\alpha = -0.30$
glove	Original	83.17	76.19	40.70	80.06
	Best	86.73 $\alpha = -0.85$	76.51 $\alpha = -0.10$	51.54 $\alpha = -0.85$	84.00 $\alpha = -0.45$
fasttext	Original	89.76	82.44	50.48	83.55
	Best	90.85 $\alpha = -0.45$	84.45 $\alpha = 0.25$	51.55 $\alpha = -0.25$	84.06 $\alpha = -0.15$

Table 1: Results in intrinsic evaluation for the original embeddings and the best post-processed model with the corresponding value of α. The evaluation measure is accuracy for word analogy and Spearman correlation for word similarity.

tains 300-dimensional vectors for 2 million words.

Given that the above models were trained in very large corpora and have an unusually large **vocabulary**, we decide to restrict its size to the most frequent 200,000 words in each case, leaving the few resulting out-of-vocabularies outside evaluation. In all the cases, we test the proposed post-processing for all the values of the **parameter** α in the $[-1, 1]$ range in increments of 0.05. As the goal of this paper is not to set the state-of-the-art but to perform an empirical exploration, we report results across all parameter values on test data.

3.1 Results on word analogy

Table 1 shows the results of the original embeddings ($\alpha = 0$) and those of the best α, while Figure 1 shows the relative error reduction with respect to the original embeddings for all α values[11]. As it can be seen, the proposed post-processing brings big improvements in word analogy, with a relative error reduction of about 20% in semantic analogies for word2vec and glove and a relative error reduction of about 10% in both semantic and syntactic analogies for fasttext.

The graphs in Figure 1 clearly reflect that, within certain limits, smaller values of α (i.e. lower similarity orders) tend to favor semantic analogies, whereas larger values (i.e. higher similarity orders) tend to favor syntactic analogies. In this regard, both objectives seem mutually incompatible, in that every improvement in one type of analogy comes at a cost of a degradation in the other type. This suggests that standard embedding

models already encode enough information to perform better than they do in word analogy resolution, yet this potential performance is limited by the impossibility to optimize for both semantic and syntactic analogies at the same time.

Apart from that, the results also show that, while the general trend is the same for all embedding models, their axes seem to be centered at different points. This is clearly reflected in the optimal values of α for semantic and syntactic analogies (-0.65 and 0.10 for word2vec, -0.85 and -0.10 for glove, and -0.45 and 0.25 for fasttext): the distance between them is very similar in all cases (either 0.70 or 0.75), yet they are centered at different points. This suggests that different embedding models capture a different similarity order and, therefore, obtain a different balance between semantic and syntactic information in the original setting ($\alpha = 0$), yet our method is able to adjust it to the desired level in a post-processing step.

3.2 Results on word similarity

As the results in Table 1 and Figure 2 show, the proposed post-processing can bring big improvements in word similarity as well, although there are important differences among the different embedding models tested. This way, we achieve an improvement of about 11 and 4 points for SimLex-999 and MEN in the case of glove, and only 1 and 0.5 points in the case of fasttext, while word2vec is somewhat in between with 3.5 and 1 points.

Following the discussion in Section 3.1, this behavior seems clearly connected with the differences in the default similarity order captured by different embedding models. In fact, the optimal

---

[11] We choose to show relative error reduction in order to have all curves in the same scale for easier illustration.

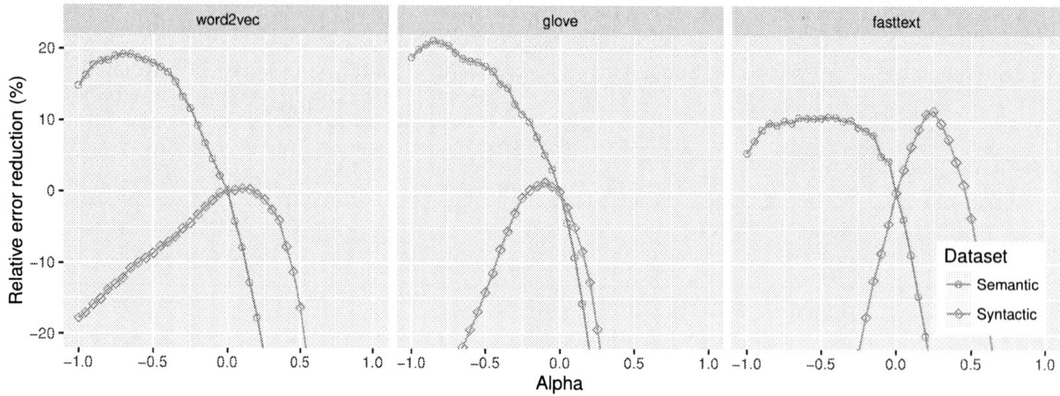

Figure 1: Results in word analogy as the relative error reduction with respect to the original embeddings (α=0) for different values of α.

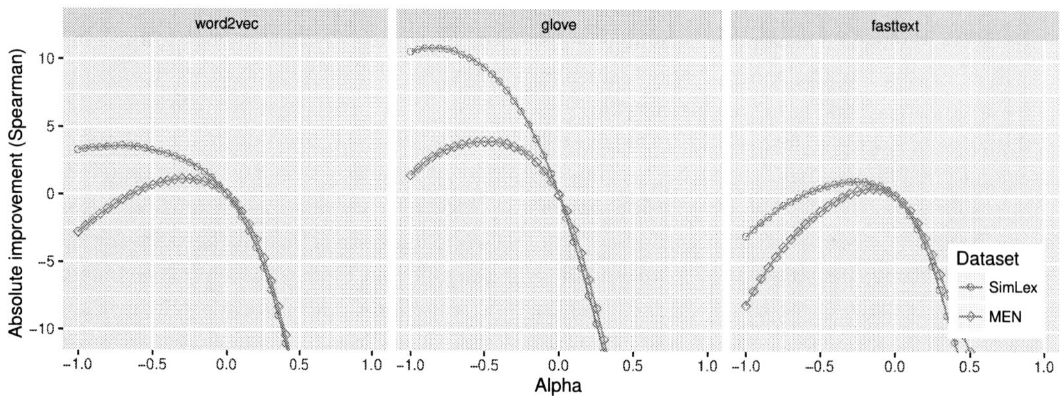

Figure 2: Results in word similarity as the absolute improvement in Spearman correlation with respect to the original embeddings (α=0) for different α. SimLex for genuine similarity, MEN for relatedness.

values of α reflect the same trend observed for word analogy, with glove having the smallest values with -0.85 and -0.45, followed by word2vec with -0.70 and -0.30, and fasttext with -0.25 and -0.15. Moreover, the effect of this phenomenon is more dramatic in this case: fasttext achieves significantly better results than glove for the original embeddings (a difference of nearly 10 and 3.5 points for SimLex-999 and MEN, respectively), but this proves to be an illusion after adjusting the similarity order with our post-processing, as both models get practically the same results with differences below 0.1 points.

At the same time, although less pronounced than with semantic/syntactic analogies[12], the results show clear differences in the optimal configurations for genuine similarity (SimLex-999) and

relatedness (MEN), with smaller values of α (i.e. lower similarity levels) favoring the former.

4   Extrinsic evaluation

In order to better understand the effect of the proposed post-processing in downstream systems, we adopt the STS Benchmark dataset on semantic textual similarity (Cer et al., 2017)[13]. This task is akin to word similarity, but instead of assessing the similarity of individual word pairs, it is the similarity of entire sentence pairs as scored by the model that is compared against the gold standard produced by human annotators[14]. This evaluation is attractive for our purposes because, while the state-of-the-art systems are supervised and based on elaborated deep learning or feature engineer-

---

[12]Agreeing with the fact that relatedness subsumes similarity (Budanitsky and Hirst, 2006)

[13]http://ixa2.si.ehu.es/stswiki/index.php/STSbenchmark

[14]Following common practice, we report Pearson.

		Centroid	DAM
word2vec	Original	65.77	72.65
	Best	66.43 $\alpha = -0.30$	73.08 $\alpha = 0.10$
glove	Original	64.54	74.89
	Best	68.96 $\alpha = -0.50$	76.36 $\alpha = -0.70$
fasttext	Original	69.84	77.33
	Best	70.74 $\alpha = -0.20$	77.33 $\alpha = 0.00$

Table 2: Results in semantic textual similarity as measured by Pearson correlation for the original embeddings and the best post-processed model with the corresponding value of α. The DAM scores are averaged across 10 runs.

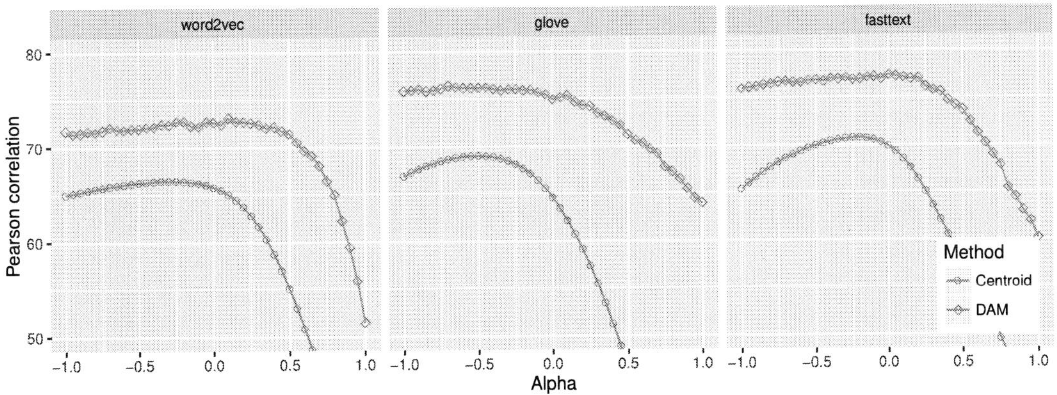

Figure 3: Results in semantic textual similarity for different values of α. The DAM scores are averaged across 10 runs.

ing approaches, simpler embedding-based unsupervised models are also highly competitive, making it easier to analyze the effect of the proposed post-processing when integrating the embeddings in a larger model. This way, we test two such systems in our experiments: a simple embedding-based model that computes the cosine similarity between the centroids of each sentence after discarding stopwords, and the Decomposable Attention Model (DAM) proposed by Parikh et al. (2016) and minimally adapted for the task[15]. The centroid model is thus a simple but very competitive baseline system where the proposed post-processing has a direct effect, whereas DAM is a prototypical deep learning model that uses fixed pre-trained embeddings as input features, producing results that are almost at par with the state-of-the-art in the task.

As the results in Table 2 and Figure 3 show, the centroid method is much more sensitive to the proposed post-processing than DAM. More concretely, negative values of α are beneficial for the centroid method up to certain point, bringing an improvement of nearly 4.5 points for glove, and the results clearly start degrading after that ceiling. In contrast, DAM is almost unaffected by negative values of α. Positive values do have a clear negative effect in both cases, but the centroid method is much more severely affected than DAM. For instance, for glove, the performance of the centroid method drops 18.19 points when $\alpha = 0.50$, in contrast with only 3.69 points for DAM.

This behavior can be theoretically explained by the fact that the proposed post-processing consists in a linear transformation. More concretely, DAM also applies a linear transformation to the input embeddings and, given that the product of two linear transformations is just another linear transformation, its global optimum is unaffected by the linear transformation previously applied by our method. Note, moreover, that the same rationale applies to the majority of machine learning systems that use pre-trained embeddings as input features, including both linear and deep learning models. While there are many practical aspects

---

[15] https://github.com/lgazpio/DAM_STS

that can interfere with this theoretical reasoning (e.g. regularization, the optional length normalization of embeddings, the resulting difficulty of the optimization problem...), and explain the variations observed in our experiments, this shows that typical downstream systems are able to adjust the similarity order themselves.

5 Discussion

Our experiments reveal that standard word embeddings encode more information than what is immediately obvious, yet their potential performance is limited by the impossibility of optimally surfacing divergent linguistic information at the same time. This can be clearly seen in the word analogy experiments in Section 3.1, where we are able to achieve significant improvements over the original embeddings, yet every improvement in semantic analogies comes at the cost of a degradation in syntactic analogies and vice versa. At the same time, our work shows that the effect of this phenomenon is different for unsupervised systems that directly use embedding similarities and supervised systems that use pre-trained embeddings as features, as the latter have enough expressive power to learn the optimal balance themselves.

We argue that our work thus offers a new perspective on how embeddings encode divergent linguistic information and its relation with intrinsic and extrinsic evaluation as follows:

- Standard intrinsic evaluation offers a static and incomplete picture of the information encoded by different embedding models. This can be clearly seen in the word similarity experiments in Section 3.2, where fasttext achieves significantly better results than glove for the original embeddings, yet the results for their best post-processed embeddings are at par. As a consequence, if one simply looks at the results of the original embeddings, they might wrongly conclude that fasttext is vastly superior to glove at encoding semantic similarity information, but this proves to be a mere illusion after applying our post-processing. As such, intrinsic evaluation combined with our post-processing provides a more complete and dynamic picture of the information that is truly encoded by different embedding models.

- Supervised systems that use pre-trained em-

beddings as features have enough expressive power to learn the optimal similarity order for the task in question. While there are practical aspects that interfere with this theoretical consideration, our experiments confirm that the proposed post-processing has a considerably smaller effect in a prototypical deep learning system. This reinforces the previous point that standard intrinsic evaluation offers an incomplete picture, as it is severely influenced by an aspect that has a much smaller effect in typical downstream systems. For that reason, using our proposed post-processing to complement intrinsic evaluation offers a better assessment of how each embedding model might perform in a downstream task.

- Related to the previous point, while our work shows that the default similarity order captured by embeddings has a relatively small effect in larger learning systems as they are typically used, this is not necessarily the best possible integration strategy. If one believes that a certain similarity order is likely to better suit a particular downstream task, it would be possible to design integration strategies that encourage it to be so during training, and we believe that this is a very interesting research direction to explore in the future. For instance, one could design regularization methods that penalize large deviations from this predefined similarity order.

6 Related work

There have been several proposals to learn word embeddings that are specialized in certain linguistic aspects. For instance, Kiela et al. (2015) use a joint-learning approach and two variants of retrofitting (Faruqui et al., 2015a) to specialize word embeddings for either similarity or relatedness. At the same time, Levy and Goldberg (2014a) propose a modification of skip-gram that uses a dependency-based context instead of a sliding windows, which produces embeddings that are more tailored towards genuine similarity than relatedness. Bansal et al. (2014) follow a similar approach to train specialized embeddings that are used as features for dependency parsing. Finally, Mitchell and Steedman (2015) exploit morphology and word order information to learn embeddings that decompose into orthogonal semantic and syntactic subspaces. Note, however, that all these previous methods alter the training objective of specific embedding models and often require additional resources like knowledge bases and syntactic annotations, while the proposed method is a simple post-processing that can be applied to any embedding model and does not require any additional resource.

Other authors have also proposed post-processing methods for word embeddings with different motivations. For instance, Faruqui et al. (2015b) transform word embeddings into more interpretable sparse representations, obtaining improvements in several benchmark tasks. Rothe et al. (2016) propose an orthogonal transformation to concentrate the information relevant for a task in a lower dimensional subspace, and Rothe and Schütze (2016) extend this work to decompose embeddings into four subspaces specifically capturing polarity, concreteness, frequency and part-of-speech information. Finally, Labutov and Lipson (2013) perform unconstrained optimization with proper regularization to specialize embeddings in a supervised task.

The proposed method is also connected to a similar parameter found in traditional count-based distributional models as introduced by Caron (2001) and further analyzed by Bullinaria and Levy (2012) and Turney (2012). More concretely, these models work by factorizing some co-occurrence matrix using singular value decomposition, so given the co-occurrence matrix $M = USV^T$, the word vectors will correspond to the first n dimensions of $W = US^\alpha$, where the parameter α plays a similar role as in our method. Note, however, that our proposal is more general and can be applied to any set of word vectors in a post-processing step, including neural embedding models that have superseded these traditional count-based models as we in fact do in this paper.

Finally, there are others authors that have also pointed limitations in the intrinsic evaluation of word embeddings. For instance, Faruqui et al. (2016) and Batchkarov et al. (2016) argue that word similarity has many problems like the subjectivity and difficulty of the task, the lack of statistical significance and the inability to account for polysemy, warning that results should be interpreted with care. Chiu et al. (2016) analyze the correlation between results on word similarity benchmarks and sequence labeling tasks, and conclude that most intrinsic evaluations are poor predictors of downstream performance. In relation to that, our work explains how embeddings encode divergent linguistic information and the different effect this has in intrinsic evaluation and downstream tasks, showing that the proposed post-processing can be easily used together with any intrinsic evaluation benchmark to get a more complete picture of the representations learned.

7 Conclusions and future work

In this paper, we propose a simple post-processing to tailor word embeddings in the semantics/syntax and similarity/relatedness axes without the need of additional resources. By measuring the effect of our post-processing in word analogy and word similarity, we show that standard embedding models are able to encode more information than what is immediately obvious, yet their potential performance is limited by the impossibility of optimally surfacing divergent linguistic information. We analyze the different role that this phenomenon plays in intrinsic and extrinsic evaluation, concluding that intrinsic evaluation offers a static picture that can be complemented with the proposed post-processing, and prompting for better integration strategies for downstream tasks. We release our implementation at `https://github.com/artetxem/uncovec`, which allows to easily reproduce our experiments for any given set of embeddings.

In the future, we would like to explore better integration strategies for machine learning systems that use pre-trained embeddings as features, so that downstream systems can better benefit from previously adjusting the embeddings in the semantics/syntax and similarity/relatedness axes. At the same time, we would like to extend our analysis to more specialized embedding models (Kiela et al., 2015; Levy and Goldberg, 2014a) to get a more complete picture of what information they capture.

Acknowledgments

This research was partially supported by the Spanish MINECO (TUNER TIN2015-65308-C5-1-R, MUSTER PCIN-2015-226 and TADEEP TIN2015-70214-P, cofunded by EU FEDER), the UPV/EHU (excellence research group), and the NVIDIA GPU grant program. Mikel Artetxe and Iñigo Lopez-Gazpio enjoy a doctoral grant from the Spanish MECD.

References

Sanjeev Arora, Yuanzhi Li, Yingyu Liang, Tengyu Ma, and Andrej Risteski. 2016. A latent variable model approach to pmi-based word embeddings. *Transactions of the Association for Computational Linguistics*, 4:385–399.

Mohit Bansal, Kevin Gimpel, and Karen Livescu. 2014. Tailoring continuous word representations for dependency parsing. In *Proceedings of the 52nd Annual Meeting of the Association for Computational Linguistics (Volume 2: Short Papers)*, pages 809–815, Baltimore, Maryland. Association for Computational Linguistics.

Miroslav Batchkarov, Thomas Kober, Jeremy Reffin, Julie Weeds, and David Weir. 2016. A critique of word similarity as a method for evaluating distributional semantic models. In *Proceedings of the 1st Workshop on Evaluating Vector-Space Representations for NLP*, pages 7–12, Berlin, Germany. Association for Computational Linguistics.

Kayhan Batmanghelich, Ardavan Saeedi, Karthik Narasimhan, and Sam Gershman. 2016. Nonparametric spherical topic modeling with word embeddings. In *Proceedings of the 54th Annual Meeting of the Association for Computational Linguistics (Volume 2: Short Papers)*, pages 537–542, Berlin, Germany. Association for Computational Linguistics.

Piotr Bojanowski, Edouard Grave, Armand Joulin, and Tomas Mikolov. 2017. Enriching word vectors with subword information. *Transactions of the Association for Computational Linguistics*, 5:135–146.

Elia Bruni, Gemma Boleda, Marco Baroni, and Nam Khanh Tran. 2012. Distributional semantics in technicolor. In *Proceedings of the 50th Annual Meeting of the Association for Computational Linguistics (Volume 1: Long Papers)*, pages 136–145, Jeju Island, Korea. Association for Computational Linguistics.

Alexander Budanitsky and Graeme Hirst. 2006. Evaluating wordnet-based measures of lexical semantic relatedness. *Computational Linguistics*, 32(1):13–47.

John A. Bullinaria and Joseph P. Levy. 2012. Extracting semantic representations from word co-occurrence statistics: stop-lists, stemming, and svd. *Behavior Research Methods*, 44(3):890–907.

John Caron. 2001. Computational information retrieval. chapter Experiments with LSA Scoring: Optimal Rank and Basis, pages 157–169. Society for Industrial and Applied Mathematics.

Daniel Cer, Mona Diab, Eneko Agirre, Inigo Lopez-Gazpio, and Lucia Specia. 2017. Semeval-2017 task 1: Semantic textual similarity multilingual and crosslingual focused evaluation. In *Proceedings of the 11th International Workshop on Semantic Evaluation (SemEval-2017)*, pages 1–14, Vancouver, Canada. Association for Computational Linguistics.

Billy Chiu, Anna Korhonen, and Sampo Pyysalo. 2016. Intrinsic evaluation of word vectors fails to predict extrinsic performance. In *Proceedings of the 1st Workshop on Evaluating Vector-Space Representations for NLP*, pages 1–6, Berlin, Germany. Association for Computational Linguistics.

Manaal Faruqui, Jesse Dodge, Sujay Kumar Jauhar, Chris Dyer, Eduard Hovy, and Noah A. Smith. 2015a. Retrofitting word vectors to semantic lexicons. In *Proceedings of the 2015 Conference of the North American Chapter of the Association for Computational Linguistics: Human Language Technologies*, pages 1606–1615, Denver, Colorado. Association for Computational Linguistics.

Manaal Faruqui, Yulia Tsvetkov, Pushpendre Rastogi, and Chris Dyer. 2016. Problems with evaluation of word embeddings using word similarity tasks. In *Proceedings of the 1st Workshop on Evaluating Vector-Space Representations for NLP*, pages 30–35, Berlin, Germany. Association for Computational Linguistics.

Manaal Faruqui, Yulia Tsvetkov, Dani Yogatama, Chris Dyer, and Noah A. Smith. 2015b. Sparse overcomplete word vector representations. In *Proceedings of the 53rd Annual Meeting of the Association for Computational Linguistics and the 7th International Joint Conference on Natural Language Processing (Volume 1: Long Papers)*, pages 1491–1500, Beijing, China. Association for Computational Linguistics.

Alex Gittens, Dimitris Achlioptas, and Michael W. Mahoney. 2017. Skip-gram - zipf + uniform = vector additivity. In *Proceedings of the 55th Annual Meeting of the Association for Computational Linguistics (Volume 1: Long Papers)*, pages 69–76, Vancouver, Canada. Association for Computational Linguistics.

Zellig S Harris. 1954. Distributional structure. *Word*, 10(2-3):146–162.

Felix Hill, Roi Reichart, and Anna Korhonen. 2015. Simlex-999: Evaluating semantic models with (genuine) similarity estimation. *Computational Linguistics*, 41(4):665–695.

Douwe Kiela, Felix Hill, and Stephen Clark. 2015. Specializing word embeddings for similarity or relatedness. In *Proceedings of the 2015 Conference on Empirical Methods in Natural Language Processing*, pages 2044–2048, Lisbon, Portugal. Association for Computational Linguistics.

Igor Labutov and Hod Lipson. 2013. Re-embedding words. In *Proceedings of the 51st Annual Meeting of the Association for Computational Linguistics (Volume 2: Short Papers)*, pages 489–493, Sofia, Bulgaria. Association for Computational Linguistics.

Omer Levy and Yoav Goldberg. 2014a. Dependency-based word embeddings. In *Proceedings of the 52nd Annual Meeting of the Association for Computational Linguistics (Volume 2: Short Papers)*, pages 302–308. Association for Computational Linguistics.

Omer Levy and Yoav Goldberg. 2014b. Linguistic regularities in sparse and explicit word representations. In *Proceedings of the Eighteenth Conference on Computational Natural Language Learning*, pages 171–180. Association for Computational Linguistics.

Omer Levy and Yoav Goldberg. 2014c. Neural word embedding as implicit matrix factorization. In *Advances in Neural Information Processing Systems 27*, pages 2177–2185.

Tomas Mikolov, Ilya Sutskever, Kai Chen, Greg S Corrado, and Jeff Dean. 2013. Distributed representations of words and phrases and their compositionality. In *Advances in Neural Information Processing Systems 26*, pages 3111–3119.

Jeff Mitchell and Mark Steedman. 2015. Orthogonality of syntax and semantics within distributional spaces. In *Proceedings of the 53rd Annual Meeting of the Association for Computational Linguistics and the 7th International Joint Conference on Natural Language Processing (Volume 1: Long Papers)*, pages 1301–1310. Association for Computational Linguistics.

Ankur Parikh, Oscar Täckström, Dipanjan Das, and Jakob Uszkoreit. 2016. A decomposable attention model for natural language inference. In *Proceedings of the 2016 Conference on Empirical Methods in Natural Language Processing*, pages 2249–2255, Austin, Texas. Association for Computational Linguistics.

Jeffrey Pennington, Richard Socher, and Christopher Manning. 2014. Glove: Global vectors for word representation. In *Proceedings of the 2014 Conference on Empirical Methods in Natural Language Processing (EMNLP)*, pages 1532–1543, Doha, Qatar. Association for Computational Linguistics.

Sascha Rothe, Sebastian Ebert, and Hinrich Schütze. 2016. Ultradense word embeddings by orthogonal transformation. In *Proceedings of the 2016 Conference of the North American Chapter of the Association for Computational Linguistics: Human Language Technologies*, pages 767–777, San Diego, California. Association for Computational Linguistics.

Sascha Rothe and Hinrich Schütze. 2016. Word embedding calculus in meaningful ultradense subspaces. In *Proceedings of the 54th Annual Meeting of the Association for Computational Linguistics (Volume 2: Short Papers)*, pages 512–517, Berlin, Germany. Association for Computational Linguistics.

Hinrich Schütze. 1998. Automatic word sense discrimination. *Computational Linguistics Special Issue on Word Sense Disambiguation*, 24(1).

Matt Taddy. 2015. Document classification by inversion of distributed language representations. In *Proceedings of the 53rd Annual Meeting of the Association for Computational Linguistics and the 7th International Joint Conference on Natural Language Processing (Volume 2: Short Papers)*, pages 45–49, Beijing, China. Association for Computational Linguistics.

Peter D. Turney. 2012. Domain and function: A dual-space model of semantic relations and compositions. *Journal of Artificial Intelligence Research*, 44(1):533–585.

Comparing Models of Associative Meaning: An Empirical Investigation of Reference in Simple Language Games

Judy Hanwen Shen   **Matthias Hofer**   **Bjarke Felbo**   **Roger Levy**

Massachusetts Institute of Technology

77 Massachusetts Avenue

Cambridge, MA 02139

{judyshen, mhofer, felbo, rplevy}@mit.edu

Abstract

Simple reference games (Wittgenstein, 1953) are of central theoretical and empirical importance in the study of situated language use. Although language provides rich, compositional truth-conditional semantics to facilitate reference, speakers and listeners may sometimes lack the overall lexical and cognitive resources to guarantee successful reference through these means alone. However, language also has rich associational structures that can serve as a further resource for achieving successful reference. Here we investigate this use of associational information in a setting where *only* associational information is available: a simplified version of the popular game Codenames. Using optimal experiment design techniques, we compare a range of models varying in the type of associative information deployed and in level of pragmatic sophistication against human behavior. In this setting we find that listeners' behavior reflects direct bigram collocational associations more strongly than word-embedding or semantic knowledge graph-based associations and that there is little evidence for pragmatically sophisticated behavior by either speakers or listeners of the type that might be predicted by recursive-reasoning models such as the Rational Speech Acts theory. These results shed light on the nature of the lexical resources that speakers and listeners can bring to bear in achieving reference through associative meaning alone.

1   Introduction

In his 1953 book *Philosophical Investigations*, Wittgenstein makes the argument for studying simple reference games to learn about the nature of language (Wittgenstein, 1953). Various applications of this idea in different fields, including linguistics (Pietarinen, 2007), cognitive science (Frank and Goodman, 2012), artificial intelligence (Lazaridou et al., 2016), and behavior-based robotics (Steels, 1997) have validated this fundamental insight and demonstrated the theoretical and empirical importance of studying language learning and use in simplified contexts. Here we describe a novel framework that uses a simple reference game to study the *semantic resources* speakers and listeners use to facilitate reference. In particular, placing strong constraints on word choice and modes of interaction allows us to better isolate specific aspects that contribute towards the complexity of natural language semantics. Language provides a multitude of different resources for its users to cooperatively achieve reference. In particular, language provides truth-conditional semantic structures. These information structures are characterized in terms of their logical truth conditions and can be precisely stated using formal logic. Across many cases, however, successful reference cannot be guaranteed through these means alone. Another possible source of semantic information are *associative resources* (e.g. the meaning associations of 'nurse' with 'female nurse' rather than 'male nurse'). The question of how to best formally characterize these rich associative structures to adequately account for our linguistic abilities is still largely unresolved.

We compare the performance of different models in accounting for human behavior in a simple reference game, a modified version of the popular board game *Codenames*. Crucially, in this setting, only associational information is available. To allow us to additionally address questions about possible pragmatic effects when playing the game, our models are formulated in the context of the Rational Speech Act (RSA) framework (Frank and Goodman, 2012). The candidate models of human semantic reasoning we consider involve different types of associative resources and different degrees of pragmatic sophistication by speaker and

Proceedings of the 22nd Conference on Computational Natural Language Learning (CoNLL 2018), pages 292–301

Brussels, Belgium, October 31 - November 1, 2018. ©2018 Association for Computational Linguistics

listener. The models correspond to qualitatively different sources of information, including collocations, distributional similarity across contexts, topic similarity, or common-sense conceptual relatedness.

In the closest predecessor to our work, Xu and Kemp (2010) used observational data from the television game *Password*, where the goal is to guess a target word on an associated cue word freely generated, to model whether speaker and listener alignment based on their differential reliance on forward vs backward word associations (estimated using the experimental norms of Nelson et al., 2004). They found that similar mixtures of forward and backward associations best explained both speaker and hearer behaviors, suggesting game participants are well calibrated and cooperative with another, but did not investigate the nature of the lexical knowledge accounting for the associations underlying participant behavior.

In this paper, we construct a simplified reference game involving word associations where constrained sets of potential reference clues words and reference target words are provided. We construct a variety of different semantic association measures and conduct a series of experiments to test which source of information humans use. Furthermore, we combine these measures with the RSA framework to derive predictions about pragmatic behavior on the task.

2 Experimental methods

We create a simplified version of the board game Codenames (Chvátil, 2015) where the objective is for a speaker to select a clue word that allows a listener to correctly identify a set of target words. Subjects play one scenario per turn. A scenario consists of a set of *codenames* drawn from a list of 50 common nouns, two of which are *targets* while the remaining nouns are *non-targets*. While both listeners and speakers always see the set of codenames, only the speaker knows which nouns are targets and non-targets (see Figure 1A, the listener views three identical black and white cards). We refer to any combination of two nouns as a *noun pair*. Each scenario also contains a set of *clues* drawn from 100 descriptive adjectives. Throughout the paper, we will interchangeably refer to codenames as nouns and to clues as adjectives. A *configuration* is a scenario that additionally includes an *index*, either indicating the target noun

pair (speaker configuration) or the adjective that was provided to the listener (listener configuration). Thus, while scenarios are just lists of adjectives and nouns, there are $\binom{\#codenames}{2}$ possible speaker configurations and $\#clues$ possible listener configurations. Speakers and listeners participated in separate versions of the experiment, but were told that they would be teamed up with another player to increase engagement with the task. Subjects were either in the speaker role or in the listener role. On each trial, depending on their role, they were either given a speaker configuration or a listener configuration, that is, a scenario plus corresponding index. The speaker's task is to select a single adjective to best communicate the target noun pair without including any non-target nouns. For the listener task, participants are given an adjective and asked to select the two nouns that the adjective most likely refers to. To quantify the difficulty of a particular configuration for participants, we additionally asked them to rate how confident they were in their answer on a scale from 1 (least confident) to 5 (most confident). We conducted four experiments for which we recruited a total of 1460 subjects on Amazon's Mechanical Turk platform. Each subject completed 20 different configurations, lasting approximately $7 - 10$ minutes and were paid a fixed amount of \$0.60 for their participation. We make all data and analysis code available [1].

2.1 Modeling word choice

Following previous work on linguistic reasoning as Bayesian inference, subjects' choices for a given configuration are modeled using the Rational Speech Acts (RSA) model. In the model, a pragmatic listener L_1 reasons recursively about a pragmatic speaker S_1 that in turn reasons about a literal listener L_0. Referents are noun pairs, p, and utterances are adjectives, a. We assume a uniform prior over possible adjectives and over possible noun pairs. Communication costs are set to 0. Assuming that adjectives are chosen in proportion to the degree of semantic association between a noun pair and an adjective, denoted as $s_{p,a}$, we obtain the set of simplified equations shown in Table 1. Experiments 1-3 in the following sections will use $P_{L_0}(p|a)$ and $P_{S_0}(p|a)$ while Experiment 4 compares the two aforementioned literal agents

[1] `https://github.com/heyyjudes/`
`codenames-language-game/`

Listener	Speaker
$P_{L_0}(p\|a) \propto s_{p,a}$	$P_{S_0}(a\|p) \propto s_{p,a}$
$P_{S_1}(a\|p) \propto [P_{L_0}(p\|a)]^\alpha$	$P_{L_1}(p\|a) \propto [P_{S_0}(a\|p)]^\alpha$
$P_{L_1}(p\|a) \propto P_{S_1}(a\|p)$	$P_{S_1}(a\|p) \propto P_{L_1}(p\|a)$

Table 1: RSA equations for constructing literal and pragmatic models from semantic metrics.

with the pragmatic versions using $P_{L_1}(p|a)$ and $P_{S_1}(p|a)$.

2.2 Modeling semantic association strength

Our primary interest is understanding how people reason about the semantic relatedness of arbitrary noun–adjective pairings, formally expressed as different semantic association metrics $s_{p,a}$. Unlike in previous applications of RSA, where an utterance is either true of a particular referent or not, the relation between nouns and adjectives in the present setting is one of *associative strength*: an adjective can fit a noun to different degrees (Perea and Rosa, 2002).[2] Here we consider four different types of models to quantify the semantic relatedness $s_{n,a}$ between a noun n and an adjective a. This measure is extended to cover noun pairs $p = \{n_1, n_2\}$ by product aggregation: $s_{p,a} = s_{n_1,a} \cdot s_{n_2,a}$.

2.2.1 Bigram semantic association

The first metric we consider is derived from the bigram co-occurrence counts of noun–adjective pairs $z_{n,a}$, describing how relevant an adjective $a \in A$ is for a noun $n \in N$. We create one set of these relationships using Google Ngram probabilities averaged across the years 1990 to 2000 (Michel et al., 2011). A comparison set is obtained from a real-world corpus containing 30B messages from Twitter. The semantic association is computed as:

$$s_{n,a} = \frac{P(a|n)}{P(a)} \qquad (1)$$

Eqn. 1 captures how often an adjective occurs with a noun while normalizing for the frequency of the adjectives.

2.2.2 Vector embedding cosine distance

Global Vectors for Word Representation (GloVe) (Pennington et al., 2014) and skip-gram model trained vectors (Word2Vec) provide vector representations for words that encompass semantic and linguistic similarity. We examine the Twitter GloVe set ($d = 200$), the Wiki-GigaWord GloVe set of ($d = 200$) (Pennington et al., 2014), and Google News Word2Vec vectors ($d = 300$) (Mikolov et al., 2013). To calculate noun–adjective similarities, we compute cosine distance between each noun–adjective pair's vector embeddings.

2.2.3 ConceptNet5 similarity

ConceptNet combines knowledge from a variety of sources, including Wiktionary [3], Verbosity (Von Ahn et al., 2006), and WordNet (Miller, 1995), to create a comprehensive network of common-sense relationships with crowd-sourced human ratings (Speer and Havasi, 2013). Knowledge about words is represented as a semantic graph and relatedness of concepts are edges in this graph. We use these relatedness scores to construct noun–adjective associations.

2.2.4 Topic Modeling (LDA)

Topic models assume that words in a document are generated from a mixture of topics, defined as probability distributions over the lexicon. We train a Latent Dirichlet Allocation (LDA) model (Blei, Ng & Jordan, 2002) on the RCV1 news corpus (Rose et al., 2002, 804k documents). A noun–adjective similarity metric was obtained by computing the Euclidean distance between each word's respective distribution over topics z.

2.3 Quantile normalization and correlations between metrics

Across these seven different semantic association metrics, distributions of scores varies from Gaussian (GloVe, Word2Vec, ConceptNet5) to exponential (Bigram). To standardize scores across the set of 50 nouns and 100 adjectives, we used quantile normalization into a standard uniform distribution. Since metrics derived from similar model classes (e.g. vector representations) were highly correlated (Figure 1), we picked a subset of association metrics that derive from qualitatively different model classes with the constraint of being trained on similar corpora (e.g. news

---

[2] The adjective 'dirty', for instance, is more strongly associated with the noun 'pig' than with the noun 'slate'. In contrast, 'slate' is more strongly associated with the adjective's antonym 'clean', likely owing the widespread collocation 'clean slate'.

[3] en.wiktionary.org

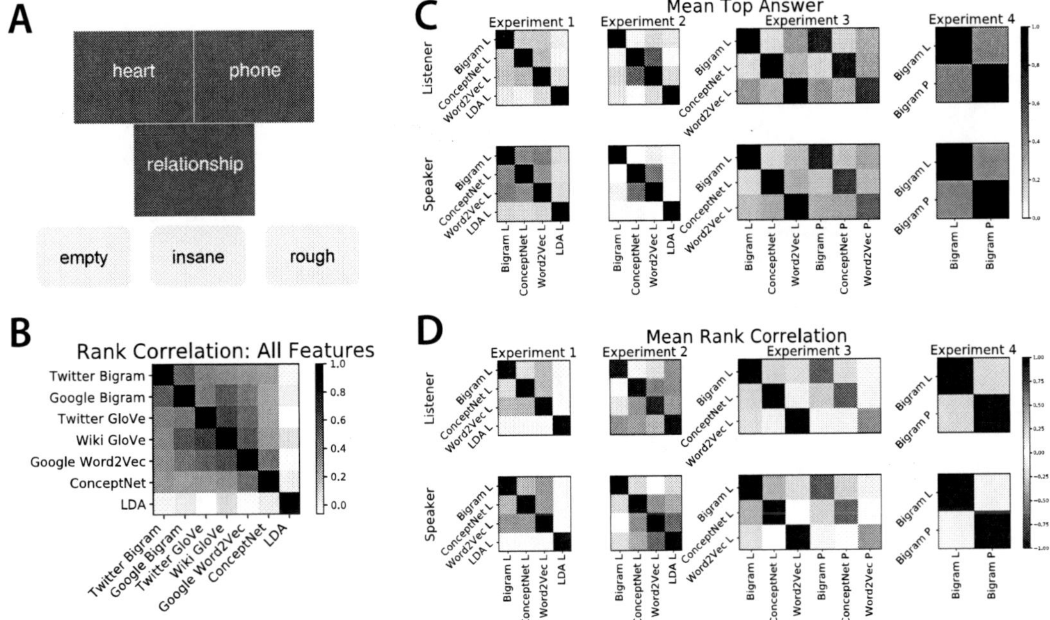

Figure 1: **A.** Example of an experimental display in the speaker condition. The choice is between three adjectives (gray) to best communicate the (blue) target words while avoiding the (red) non-target words. **B.** Rank correlation between semantic association scores on the entire set of 5,000 noun–adjective pairs that all experiments draw from. **C.** Each cell shows the mean top answer matches between model pairs for the configurations used in a particular experiment (speaker and listener side). **D.** Here each cell shows the mean Spearman's correlation coefficient between model pairs for the configurations used in a particular experiment (speaker and listener side).

and books) whenever possible. This resulted in a choice of four measures, *Bigram* (Googe Ngram), *Word2Vec* (Google News), *ConceptNet* (Concept-Net5), and *LDA*, as candidate semantic models of human word choices.[4] Unless otherwise noted, we will use 'Bigram' and 'Word2Vec' to refer to those metrics based on Google Ngram and Google News, respectively.

2.4 Optimal Experimental Design

Despite focusing on a relatively small set of nouns and adjectives, the space of possible experimental configurations is still too large to allow exhaustive search. Furthermore, the model rank correlations displayed in Figure 1 suggest that naively picking configurations could result in strongly correlated predictions. To generate experimental configurations that are highly informative with respect to discriminating between different semantic association metrics, we employed Bayesian optimal ex-

---

[4]LDA was excluded in the final two rounds of experiments. With the current training regime, its success in fitting human responses was substantially smaller than the other three semantic association measures we chose.

perimental design (OED) techniques (Cavagnaro et al., 2010).

$$d^* = \arg\max_{c \in D} U(c) \qquad (2)$$

$$U(c) = \sum_y u(y, c) P(y|c) \qquad (3)$$

Assuming that a particular response y is recorded (a choice of noun pair or adjective), the utility of an experimental configuration c, $u(y, c)$, is proportional to the mutual information between the distributions over models M before and after obtaining datum y. Since response y has not yet been observed, we compute the expectation of $u(y, c)$ with respect to y to obtain the desired (global) utility of the configuration $U(c)$. Assuming a uniform prior distribution over models M, the equations simplify in the following way. Optimal designs were computed using Monte Carlo methods for sampling-based stochastic optimization (Müller, 2005).

Figure 2 illustrates a representative example configuration obtained using OED. We can see

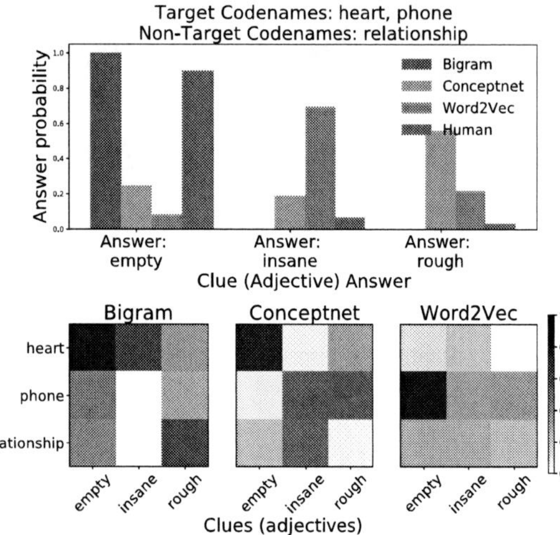

Figure 2: This example speaker configuration shows how different clues are preferred by different models: 'empty' most often co-occurs with 'heart' and 'phone' and is thus favored by the Bigram model. ConceptNet assigns a high association score to 'heart' and 'empty' but the adjective 'rough' fits the noun pair better overall when using product aggregation. Similarly, since 'insane' appears most often in the context windows for both 'heart' and 'phone', it is the top prediction for Word2Vec. We also show human data for the configuration, which shows a strong preference for the adjective preferred by the Bigram model.

that model predictions diverge strongly, with each semantic measure predicting a different response and little distributional overlap. The accompanying matrices illustrate how the different models arrive at those predictions.

2.5 Scoring

To evaluate how well a particular model accounts for human responses we use two performance scores: For each configuration, we count when a model's top prediction matches the most frequent response given by participants and refer to this score as *top answer*. When normalized by the total number of responses, chance performance is at $1/\#$answers. To additionally take into account information beyond the most probable answer, we computed the Spearman's *rank correlation* coefficient between model predictions, sorted by probability, and subjects' choices, sorted by frequency. Chance performance is zero for this measure.

	Top answer		Rank correlation	
	Mean	SEM	Mean	SEM
Listener				
Bigram	**0.416**	± 0.056	**0.384**	± 0.037
ConceptNet	0.208	± 0.046	0.196	± 0.046
Word2Vec	0.247	± 0.055	0.253	± 0.037
LDA	0.052	± 0.050	-0.053	± 0.045
Speaker				
Bigram	**0.418**	± 0.055	**0.516**	± 0.033
ConceptNet	0.405	± 0.055	0.346	± 0.045
Word2Vec	0.278	± 0.050	0.279	± 0.043
LDA	0.089	± 0.032	0.055	± 0.045

Table 2: Comparison of semantic association measures in matching human responses in Experiment 1 (No OED). Chance performance is 0.1 (listener) and 0.125 (speaker) for top answer and 0 for rank correlation.

3 Results

3.1 Experiment 1: Comparing semantic metrics using heuristic designs

In this experiment, configurations on each trial consisted of five nouns and eight adjectives. Subjects completed the task either in the speaker or in the listener condition. OED was not used for this first experiment, instead words were chosen according to heuristic criteria, detailed in the supplementary material. We did not collect confidence scores for this experiment. Using the literal speaker and listener equations from Table 1 in combination with different semantic association metrics, we derived probabilistic predictions for each configuration. Predictions were scored against human responses using the two performance scores outlined above. We also explored fits of pragmatic versions of the models to the data but found that they were qualitatively similar.[5]

Table 2 shows that, while all models except LDA perform above chance, the Bigram metric performs best on both the listener task and the speaker task. While the difference on the listener side is large, differences between Bigram and ConceptNet on the speaker side are substantially smaller. To gain insights into why the results for Bigram and ConceptNet were so similar we directly evaluated the models' predictions against each other, quantifying how often they make the same top prediction (1C), or how rank correlated their predictions are on average (1C). The bottom left matrix in Figure 1C shows that the measure's

---

[5]Full pragmatic model fits for all experiments are reported in the supplementary material.

similarity on top answer and rank correlation on the speaker task might in part stem from their overlapping predictions. This highlights a basic design issue: The experimental designs we picked might not allow us to fully distinguish the different models by capitalizing on the differences they make in their predictions.

3.2 Experiment 2: Comparing semantic metrics using OED

To remedy this shortcoming and obtain better discriminability on the speaker side, we utilized optimal experiment design techniques (Section 2.4) to overcome the limitations associated with Experiment 1. The procedure was run for the four designated models (Bigram, Word2Vec, ConceptNet and LDA), separately for the listener and the speaker side, for $100,000$ sampling iterations. We reduced the number of nouns and adjectives to three and four, respectively, significantly decreasing search complexity. Since some high utility configurations differed only by one or two words, and some words generally occurred much more frequently than others, we eliminated configurations that differed from higher utility configurations in less than two words and by limiting the total occurrence of a word across configurations to 20. This reduced the top 500 configurations for each down to 119 speaker and 137 listener configurations. Results from prior experiments show that the difficulty of a configuration, which is not explicitly operationalized and incorporated into our search process, may significantly impact response quality. To ensure that the selected configurations generate meaningful responses from human participants, we ran a preliminary experiment on the filtered configurations and only admitted those configurations to the main experiment whose confidence rating was above mean (58 speaker and 67 listener configurations).

Model fits were again calculated using the literal speaker and listener equations in section 2.1. Table 3 summarizes how well the four semantic association measures fit human responses. For the listener task, the Bigram association metric scores marginally higher than Word2Vec in top answer but strongly outperforms other models in rank correlation. While ConceptNet (top answer) and Word2Vec (rank correlation) win on the speaker side, surprisingly, Bigram performs considerably worse than in experiment 1. In terms of task diffi-

	Top answer		Rank correlation	
	Mean	SEM	Mean	SEM
Listener				
Bigram	**0.561**	± 0.092	**0.618**	± 0.044
ConceptNet	0.424	± 0.080	0.164	± 0.092
Word2Vec	0.545	± 0.091	0.408	± 0.084
LDA	0.106	± 0.040	-0.461	± 0.074
Speaker				
Bigram	0.130	± 0.044	-0.006	± 0.068
ConceptNet	**0.564**	± 0.098	0.170	± 0.076
Word2Vec	0.491	± 0.092	**0.200**	± 0.077
LDA	0.091	± 0.040	-0.083	± 0.069

Table 3: Comparison of semantic association measures to human data from Experiment 2 (separate speaker and listener OED). Chance performance is 0.33 (listener) and 0.25 (speaker) for top answer and 0 for rank correlation.

culty, speakers judged the task to be more difficult than listeners ($t = 8.27$, $p < 0.001$).

The surprisingly low performance of the Bigram model could be due to data sparsity that was systematically exploited by OED. On average, 45% of the Bigram values for the noun–adjective associations used in the experiment, which are used to compute model predictions, were effectively zero (i.e. zero counts are quantile normalized to $1e^{-7}$). This level of sparsity is much higher than both the total set of Bigram associations (17%) as well as in subsequent speaker configurations (30%). In contrast, on the listener side, the percentage of values with near zero probability is similar between this set of configurations and those in later experiments. To further explore the data sparsity hypothesis, we computed model fits using bigram associations derived from the Twitter corpus, where only 5% of speaker configurations are sparse. This raises the fit of the Bigram model to human data to 0.37, even though the Twitter and Google Bigram features are highly correlated.

Irrespective of how much of the bad performance of the bigram model could be explained away by data sparsity, the basic asymmetry between Bigram's performance across the two experimental conditions seems to hold. One likely confound in assessing speaker and listener resources is that we searched for high utility configurations independently, and that this difference in material is driving the difference in performance. This hypothesis was directly addressed in the next experiment.

	Top answer		Rank Correlation	
	Mean	SEM	Mean	SEM
Listener				
Bigram	**0.586**	± 0.072	**0.496**	± 0.056
ConceptNet	0.207	± 0.043	-0.050	± 0.063
Word2Vec	0.441	± 0.063	0.242	± 0.064
Speaker				
Bigram	**0.505**	± 0.047	**0.280**	± 0.062
ConceptNet	0.290	± 0.051	-0.061	± 0.066
Word2Vec	0.383	± 0.059	0.041	± 0.069

Table 4: Comparison of semantic association measures to human data from Experiment 3 (joint speaker-listener OED). Chance performance is 0.33 (listener and speaker) for top answer and 0 for rank correlation.

	Top answer		Rank Correlation	
	Mean	SEM	Mean	SEM
Listener (Bigram)				
Literal	**0.744**	± 0.079	**0.551**	± 0.053
Pra. $\alpha = 0.1$	0.470	± 0.046	0.159	± 0.063
Pra. $\alpha = 1.0$	0.521	± 0.046	0.184	± 0.065
Pra. $\alpha = 5.0$	0.547	± 0.046	0.242	± 0.065
Speaker (Bigram)				
Literal	**0.652**	± 0.074	**0.378**	± 0.057
Pra. $\alpha = 0.1$	0.478	± 0.046	0.069	± 0.068
Pra. $\alpha = 1.0$	0.496	± 0.046	0.105	± 0.066
Pra. $\alpha = 5.0$	0.496	± 0.046	0.144	± 0.066

Table 5: Comparison of pragmatic RSA models in predicting human responses in Experiment 4. Chance performance is 0.33 (listener and speaker) for top answer and 0 for rank correlation.

3.3 Experiment 3: Comparing listeners and speakers on the same scenarios

To further investigate potential asymmetries between the speaker and the listener condition, we modified the design optimization procedure to jointly optimize the geometric mean of all speaker and listener configurations for the same scenario. Our intention was to collect data for all possible configurations of a scenario so that we could have listeners and speakers engage with the identical words. We then applied the same filtering procedure to reduce our set to 120 scenarios (760 unique configurations). Here we restrict ourselves to three adjectives, matching the number of choices on the speaker side and minimizing differences in task difficulty. Due to its weak performance in the previous experiments, we eliminated LDA from the comparison set for subsequent experiments.

Table 4 summarizes how well the remaining three semantic association measures fit human responses. In contrast to Experiment 2, and in line with the results from Experiment 1, we find that Bigram associations perform best in both the listener and speaker condition. This difference is more pronounced for the Rank correlation measure, where other models perform at chance with the exception of Word2Vec in the listener task. Based on this result, it appears likely that the difference in Experiment 2 was driven by choice of scenario configurations. When adding the constraint of finding scenarios that are jointly informative in discriminating between models on the speaker side and on the listener side, Bigram robustly outperforms other semantic association measures. While reducing the number of adjectives from 4 to 3 did not result in a significant de-crease in difficulty, as measured by mean confidence, the difference in difficulty between speaker and listener task ($t = 9.38$, $p < 0.0001$) still remains significant.

3.4 Experiment 4: Comparing literal and pragmatic models

Since correlation matrices from the stimuli in Experiment 3 (Figure 1), which was only optimized to elicit differences between the semantic association metrics, shows that the literal models' predictions are highly correlated with their pragmatic counterparts, we ran another design optimization iteration to find configurations for which literal and pragmatic models strongly disagree. We restricted ourselves to the Bigram semantic association metric because it was the highest performing model in nine out of twelve cases (across the speaker/listener sides of three experiments, on two performance scores). Again, we jointly optimized over speaker and listener configurations, using the literal version of the model and the corresponding pragmatic model with $\alpha = 1$ from applying the RSA equations in Table 2.1. After filtering for overlap and limiting word co-occurrence as in the previous experiments, we select the highest 60 utility scenarios later reduced to 40 by highest mean confidence. In the experiment, we again tested each scenario in all its six configurations.

Table 5 summarizes the top answer and rank correlation scores for literal and pragmatic models of various degrees of pragmatic behavior ($\alpha = [0.1, 1.0, 5.0]$). We do not see strongly scalar inferential behavior of the type predicted by RSA when applied to our setting. The literal model outperforms all pragmatic models by a large mar-

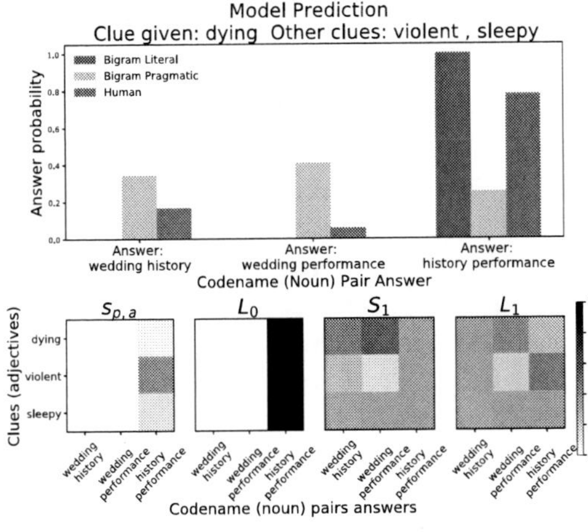

Figure 3: Representative model predictions and RSA probability matrices ($\alpha = 1$) from a configuration that illustrates the consequences of repeated re-normalization on model predictions.

gin across both performance scores and experimental conditions. As before, speakers judged the task to be more difficult than listeners ($t = 6.56$, $p < 0.0001$).

This stark difference between pragmatic and literal models is surprising. Figure 3 illustrates a common pattern that helps to better interpret this behavior. The literal model's predictions are more categorical and best reflect the probabilities from the original association values after aggregation. Through the recursive reasoning from RSA, small differences in raw probabilities, which might be non-obvious to humans, are magnified to sway top pragmatic model prediction. For example, 'history' and 'performance' are initially the best choice for the given adjective 'dying' (see top row of matrices in Figure 3), the pair is an even better choice for the adjective 'violent'. The non-obvious advantage that 'dying' has over 'violent' for the pair 'wedding' and 'performance' is becomes dominant in the S_1 normalization where this pair becomes the best pair for the clue 'dying'.[6]

3.5 Evaluating Human Performance

For experiments 1, 3, and 4, where we obtained data on matching speaker and listener scenarios,

---

[6]We replicated the findings with ConceptNet to find the same pattern of pragmatic reasoning over-emphasizing small differences between semantic measures which leads to poor pragmatic model performance.

	Avg. Success	Random Success
Exp. 1	0.321 ± 0.0273	0.100
Exp. 3	0.427 ± 0.0257	0.333
Exp. 4	0.393 ± 0.0264	0.333

Table 6: Summary of average success on speakers and listeners in human data.

we can quantify the average one-shot success that would hold if a randomly selected speaker and listener were drawn from our experimental population and played together. For a given scenario G, adjective clue a, speaker noun pair configuration c, listener choice L, and speaker choice S, the average success probability:

$$\sum_{a \in S} P(L = c|a, G)P(S = a|G) \qquad (4)$$

where we use relative frequency to estimate the first term from our listener data and the second term from our speaker data. This average success is summarized in table 6. This shows that even though OED (section 2.4) may create scenarios of a wide range of difficulties, our results as seen in Tables 4 and 5 show that our models still predict human behavior well in these difficult scenarios.

4 Discussion

In a series of experiments, we investigated how associative information is recruited to resolve reference in language games when truth-conditional information is not available. Experiments 1-3 compared different computational models of semantics. We found that subjects' word choices were predominantly best described using a simple bigram model, derived from Google Ngrams. Experiment 4 contrasted a literal and several pragmatic versions of the winning Bigram model and found that the literal version best fit human answers. Furthermore, despite providing speakers and listeners with the same number of alternatives to choose from, speakers consistently judged their side of the game to be harder.

While employing optimal experimental design techniques was generally helpful, especially in deriving configurations for contrasting literal and pragmatic models, the method worked to our disadvantage in experiment 2, where data sparsity in the Bigram model was exacerbated. This illustrates that, despite its strength in finding good configurations, the method might be especially prone to exploiting cases of data sparsity (where models strongly predict that a noun–adjective pair does not go together) that lead to a suboptimal choice of configurations. In future extensions of this work, taking into account uncertainty in the estimates semantic associations within the OED process could address these concerns.

With the exception of Experiment 2, our data indicate that both speaker and listener behavior are both best predicted by bigram statistics. Experiment 4 further shows that both speaker and listener behavior are best accounted for by models without a recursive pragmatic inference component. These results are consistent with the conclusion of Xu and Kemp (2010) that speakers and listeners are well *calibrated* to one another, bringing to bear the same lexical resource and applying it using similar principles.

Although our experiments do not provide support for RSA as a good model of pragmatic behavior for the scenarios that most sharply distinguish level-0 and level-1 RSA models, this does not rule out the possibility that participants are not engaged in any pragmatic behavior at all. In our Experiment 4, optimal experiment design drew us to cases where pragmatic agents can transform a 'least-bad' fit between a clue and target word pair to a 'best' fit, through repeated renormalization of speaker and listener probability distributions. This transformation may simply be a more arbitrary overriding of direct associative fit than humans are prepared to consider. Furthermore, there may be other types of pragmatic behavior that humans engage in for this task that we did not represent in our model space.

It is possible that, since participants in our experiments spent $20 - 30$ seconds on each question, their responses are based on first instinct while pragmatic decisions may require careful, more time-consuming reasoning. We only collected confidence ratings from participants and did not ask for their reasoning behind the answers given, thus limiting the interpretability of our findings. Another limitation is that the use of pragmatic devices in the current setup might require people to have repeated interactions so that they can align their resources more effectively. One interesting future direction of study that would make use of an interactive game design could investigate how people coordinate their reference strategies across repeated interactions.

There are scenarios that none of the models predict correctly. This could suggest other sources of semantic information that we did not incorporate in our study. Besides competing hypotheses about the nature of the semantic knowledge deployed during the task, we suggest that the metrics could alternatively describe complementary sources of information people might draw on when playing the game. Another direction of future work could focus on combining a mixture of different semantic models in explaining human choices and should focus on factors that will likely bring out pragmatic reasoning in participants.

5 Conclusion

We model speaker and listener behavior through a simplified version of the game *Codenames* and do not find strong evidence for the sophisticated pragmatic behavior of the type predicted by RSA-like models (Experiment 4). This suggests that there are limits on *strong* scalar inference in one-shot associative settings. Furthermore, we find that bigram lexical statistics (Google Bigrams) were the strongest predictors of human behavior in our task, especially for listeners. This finding suggests that direct co-occurrence statistics are particularly salient in associative settings such as ours. This result may be a consequence of our restricting codenames and clues to be nouns and adjectives respectively or may hold more generally. Finally, our data suggest a potential discrepancy between the information sources relied upon by speakers and listeners: In some experiments (Experiment 2), different models performed best on the speaker and on the listener side where we would intuitively expect that successful communication requires that speakers and listeners semantic knowledge be aligned. In addition, even when controlling for the number of choices per trial, mean answer confidence in the listener condition is significantly higher, suggesting that the speaker task is intrinsically harder. Future research further exploring inference in language game settings could investigate repeated rounds of interaction, or even one-shot interaction in richer referential domains.

Acknowledgments

This work was supported by NSF grants BCS-1456081 and BCS-1551866 to RPL. We'd like to thank Iyad Rahwan and the Scalable Cooperation group for their valuable input and support.

References

Daniel R Cavagnaro, Jay I Myung, Mark A Pitt, and Janne V Kujala. 2010. Adaptive design optimization: A mutual information-based approach to model discrimination in cognitive science. *Neural Computation*, 22(4):887–905.

Vladimír Chvátil. 2015. Codenames.

Michael C Frank and Noah D Goodman. 2012. Predicting pragmatic reasoning in language games. *Science*, 336(6084):998–998.

Angeliki Lazaridou, Alexander Peysakhovich, and Marco Baroni. 2016. Multi-agent cooperation and the emergence of (natural) language. *arXiv preprint arXiv:1612.07182*.

Jean-Baptiste Michel, Yuan Kui Shen, Aviva Presser Aiden, Adrian Veres, Matthew K Gray, Joseph P Pickett, Dale Hoiberg, Dan Clancy, Peter Norvig, Jon Orwant, Steven Pinker, Martin A. Nowak, and Erez Lieberman Aiden. 2011. Quantitative analysis of culture using millions of digitized books. *Science*, 331(6014):176–182.

Tomas Mikolov, Ilya Sutskever, Kai Chen, Greg S Corrado, and Jeff Dean. 2013. Distributed representations of words and phrases and their compositionality. In *Advances in Neural Information Processing Systems*, pages 3111–3119.

George A Miller. 1995. Wordnet: a lexical database for English. *Communications of the ACM*, 38(11):39–41.

Peter Müller. 2005. Simulation based optimal design. *Handbook of Statistics*, 25:509–518.

Douglas L Nelson, Cathy L McEvoy, and Thomas A Schreiber. 2004. The university of south florida free association, rhyme, and word fragment norms. *Behavior Research Methods, Instruments, & Computers*, 36(3):402–407.

Jeffrey Pennington, Richard Socher, and Christopher Manning. 2014. GloVe: Global vectors for word representation. In *Proceedings of the 2014 Conference on Empirical Methods in Natural Language Processing (EMNLP)*, pages 1532–1543.

Manuel Perea and Eva Rosa. 2002. The effects of associative and semantic priming in the lexical decision task. *Psychological Research*, 66(3):180–194.

Ahti-Veikko Pietarinen. 2007. *Game theory and linguistic meaning*. Brill.

Tony Rose, Mark Stevenson, and Miles Whitehead. 2002. The Reuters corpus volume 1: from yesterday's news to tomorrow's language resources. In *LREC*, volume 2, pages 827–832. Las Palmas.

Robert Speer and Catherine Havasi. 2013. Conceptnet 5: A large semantic network for relational knowledge. In *The Peoples Web Meets NLP*, pages 161–176. Springer.

Luc Steels. 1997. The synthetic modeling of language origins. *Evolution of Communication*, 1(1):1–34.

Luis Von Ahn, Mihir Kedia, and Manuel Blum. 2006. Verbosity: a game for collecting common-sense facts. In *Proceedings of the CHI Conference on Human Factors in Computing Systems*, pages 75–78. ACM.

Ludwig Wittgenstein. 1953. *Philosophical Investigations*. London: Macmillan.

Yang Xu and Charles Kemp. 2010. Inference and communication in the game of Password. In J. D. Lafferty, C. K. I. Williams, J. Shawe-Taylor, R. S. Zemel, and A. Culotta, editors, *Advances in Neural Information Processing Systems 23*, pages 2514–2522. Curran Associates, Inc.

Sequence classification with human attention

Maria Barrett[1]   **Joachim Bingel**[2]
Nora Hollenstein[3]   **Marek Rei**[4]   **Anders Søgaard**[2]
[1]Department of Nordic Studies and Linguistics, University of Copenhagen, Denmark
[2]Department of Computer Science, University of Copenhagen, Denmark
[3]Department of Computer Science, ETH Zurich, Switzerland
[4]Department of Computer Science and Technology, University of Cambridge, United Kingdom
`barrett@hum.ku.dk`   `{bingel, soegaard}@di.ku.dk`
`noraho@ethz.ch`   `marek.rei@cl.cam.ac.uk`

Abstract

Learning attention functions requires large volumes of data, but many NLP tasks simulate human behavior, and in this paper, we show that human attention really does provide a good inductive bias on many attention functions in NLP. Specifically, we use estimated human attention derived from eye-tracking corpora to regularize attention functions in recurrent neural networks. We show substantial improvements across a range of tasks, including sentiment analysis, grammatical error detection, and detection of abusive language.

1 Introduction

When humans read a text, they do not attend to *all* its words (Carpenter and Just, 1983; Rayner and Duffy, 1988). For example, humans are likely to omit many function words and other words that are predictable in context and focus on less predictable content words. Moreover, when they fixate on a word, the duration of that fixation depends on a number of linguistic factors (Clifton et al., 2007; Demberg and Keller, 2008).

Since learning good attention functions for recurrent neural networks requires large volumes of data (Zoph et al., 2016; Britz et al., 2017), and errors in attention are known to propagate to classification decisions (Alkhouli et al., 2016), we explore the idea of using human attention, as estimated from eye-tracking corpora, as an inductive bias on such attention functions. Penalizing attention functions for departing from human attention may enable us to learn better attention functions when data is limited.

Eye-trackers provide millisecond-accurate records on where humans look when they are reading, and they are becoming cheaper and more easily available by the day (San Agustin et al., 2009). In this paper, we use publicly available eye-tracking corpora, i.e., texts augmented with eye-tracking measures such as fixation duration times, and large eye-tracking corpora have appeared increasingly over the past years. Some studies suggest that the relevance of text can be inferred from the gaze pattern of the reader (Salojärvi et al., 2003) – even on word-level (Loboda et al., 2011).

Contributions We present a recurrent neural architecture with attention for sequence classification tasks. The architecture jointly learns its parameters and an attention function, but can alternate between supervision signals from labeled sequences (with no explicit supervision of the attention function) and from attention trajectories. This enables us to use per-word fixation durations from eye-tracking corpora to regularize attention functions for sequence classification tasks. We show such regularization leads to significant improvements across a range of tasks, including sentiment analysis, detection of abusive language, and grammatical error detection. Our implementation is made available at `https://github.com/coastalcph/Sequence_classification_with_human_attention`.

2 Method

We present a recurrent neural architecture that jointly learns the recurrent parameters and the attention function, but can alternate between supervision signals from labeled sequences and from attention trajectories in eye-tracking corpora. The input will be a set of labeled sequences (sentences paired with discrete category labels) and a set of sequences, in which each token is associated with a scalar value representing the attention human readers devoted to this token on average.

The two input datasets, i.e., the target task train-

Proceedings of the 22nd Conference on Computational Natural Language Learning (CoNLL 2018), pages 302–312
Brussels, Belgium, October 31 - November 1, 2018. ©2018 Association for Computational Linguistics

ing data of sentences paired with discrete categories, and the eye-tracking corpus, need not (and will not in our experiments) overlap in any way. Our experimental protocol, in other words, does not require in-task eye-tracking recordings, but simply leverages information from existing, available corpora.

Behind our approach lies the simple observation that we can correlate the token-level attention devoted by a recurrent neural network, even if trained on sentence-level signals, with any measure defined at the token level. In other words, we can compare the attention devoted by a recurrent neural network to various measures, including token-level annotation (Rei and Søgaard, 2018) and eye-tracking measures. The latter is particularly interesting as it is typically considered a measurement of *human* attention.

We go beyond this: Not only can we compare machine attention with human attention, we can also constrain or inform machine attention by human attention in various ways. In this paper, we explore this idea, proposing a particular architecture and training method that, in effect, uses human attention to *regularize* machine attention.

Our training method is similar to a standard approach to training multi-task architectures (Dong et al., 2015; Søgaard and Goldberg, 2016; Bingel and Søgaard, 2017), sometimes referred to as the *alternating* training approach (Luong et al., 2016): We randomly select a data point from our training data or the eye-tracking corpus with some (potentially equal) probability. If the data point is sampled from our training data, we predict a discrete category and use the computed loss to update our parameters. If the data point is sampled from the eye-tracking corpus, we still run the recurrent network to produce a category, but this time we only monitor the attention weights assigned to the input tokens. We then compute the minimum squared error between the normalized eye-tracking measure and the normalized attention score. In other words, in multi-task learning, we optimize each task for a fixed number of parameter updates (or mini-batches) before switching to the next task (Dong et al., 2015); in our case, we optimize for a target task (for a fixed number of updates), then improve our attention function based on human attention (for a fixed number of updates), then return to optimizing for the target task and continue iterating.

2.1 Model

Our architecture is a bidirectional LSTM (Hochreiter and Schmidhuber, 1997) that encodes word representations x_i into forward and backward representations, and into combined hidden states h_i (of slightly lower dimensionality) at every timestep. In fact, our model is a hierarchical model whose word representations are concatenations of the output of character-level LSTMs and word embeddings, following Plank et al. (2016), but we ignore the character-level part of our architecture in the equations below:

$$\overrightarrow{h_i} = LSTM(x_i, \overrightarrow{h_{i-1}}) \tag{1}$$

$$\overleftarrow{h_i} = LSTM(x_i, \overleftarrow{h_{i+1}}) \tag{2}$$

$$\widetilde{h_i} = [\overrightarrow{h_i}; \overleftarrow{h_i}] \tag{3}$$

$$h_i = \tanh(W_h \widetilde{h_i} + b_h) \tag{4}$$

The final (reduced) hidden state is sometimes used as a sentence representation s, but we instead use attention to compute s by multiplying dynamically predicted attention weights with the hidden states for each time step. The final sentence predictions y are then computed by passing s through two more hidden layers:

$$s = \sum_i \widetilde{a}_i h_i \tag{5}$$

$$y = \sigma(W_y \tanh(W_{\tilde{y}} s + b_{\tilde{y}}) + b_y) \tag{6}$$

From the hidden states, we directly predict token-level raw attention scores a_i:

$$e_i = \tanh(W_e h_i + b_e) \tag{7}$$

$$a_i = W_a e_i + b_a \tag{8}$$

We normalize these predictions to attention weights $\widetilde{a}_i$:

$$\widetilde{a}_i = \frac{a_i}{\sum_k a_k} \tag{9}$$

Our model thus combines two distinct objectives: one at the sentence level and one at the token level. The sentence-level objective is to minimize the squared error between output activations and true sentence labels $\widehat{y}$.

$$L_{sent} = \sum_j (y^{(j)} - \widehat{y}^{(j)})^2 \tag{10}$$

The token-level objective, similarly, is to minimize the squared error for the attention not aligning with our human attention metric.

$$L_{tok} = \sum_{j} \sum_{t} (a^{(j)(t)} - \widehat{a}^{(j)(t)})^2 \qquad (11)$$

These are finally combined to a weighted sum, using λ (between 0 and 1) to trade off loss functions at the sentence and token levels.

$$L = L_{sent} + \lambda L_{tok} \qquad (12)$$

Note again that our architecture does not require the target task data to come with eye-tracking information. We instead learn jointly to predict sentence categories and to attend to the tokens humans tend to focus on for longer. This requires a training schedule that determines when to optimize for the sentence-level classification objective, and when to optimize the machine attention at the token level. We therefore define an epoch to comprise a fixed number of batches, and sample every batch of training examples either from the target task data or from the eye-tracking corpus, as determined by a coin flip, the bias of which is tuned as a hyperparameter. Specifically, we define an epoch to consist of n batches, where n is the number of training sentences in the target task data divided by the batch size. This coin is potentially weighted with data being drawn from the auxiliary task with some probability or a decreasing probability of $\frac{1}{E+1}$, where E is the current epoch; see Section 4 for hyper-parameters.

3   Data

As mentioned in the above, our architecture requires no overlap between the eye-tracking corpus and the training data for the target task. We therefore rely on publicly available eye-tracking corpora. For sentiment analysis, grammatical error detection, and hate speech detection, we use publicly available research datasets that have been used previously in the literature. All datasets were lower-cased.

3.1   Eye-tracking corpora

For our experiments, we concatenate two publicly available eye-tracking corpora, the Dundee Corpus (Kennedy et al., 2003) and the reading parts of the ZuCo Corpus (Hollenstein et al., 2018), described below. Both corpora contain eye-tracking measurements from several subjects reading the same text. For every token, we compute the mean duration of all fixations to this token as our measure of human attention, following previous work (Barrett et al., 2016a; Gonzalez-Garduno and Søgaard, 2018).

Dundee   The English part of the Dundee corpus (Kennedy et al., 2003) comprises 2,368 sentences and more than 50,000 tokens. The texts were read by ten skilled, adult, native speakers. The texts are 20 newspaper articles from *The Independent*. The reading was self-paced and as close to natural, contextualized reading as possible for a laboratory data collection. The apparatus was a Dr Bouis Oculometer Eyetracker with a 1000 Hz monocular (right) sampling. At most five lines were shown per screen while subjects were reading.

ZuCo   The ZuCo corpus (Hollenstein et al., 2018) is a combined eye-tracking and EEG dataset. It contains approximately 1,000 individual English sentences read by 12 adult, native speakers. Eye movements were recorded with the infrared video-based eye tracker *EyeLink 1000 Plus* at a sampling rate of 500 Hz. The sentences were presented at the same position on the screen, one at a time. Longer sentences spanned multiple lines. The subjects used a control pad to switch to the next sentence and to answer the control questions, which allowed for natural reading speed. The corpus contains both natural reading and reading in a task-solving context. For compatibility with the Dundee corpus, we only use the subset of the data, where humans were encouraged to read more naturally. This subset contains 700 sentences. This part of the Zuco corpus contains positive, negative or neutral sentences from the Stanford Sentiment Treebank (Socher et al., 2013) for passive reading, to analyze the elicitation of emotions and opinions during reading. As a control condition, the subjects sometimes had to rate the quality of the described movies; in approximately 10% of the cases. The Zuco corpus also contains instances where subjects were presented with Wikipedia sentences that contained semantic relations such as *employer*, *award* and *job_title* (Culotta et al., 2006). The control condition for this tasks consisted of multiple-choice questions about the content of the previous sentence; again, approximately 10% of all sentences were followed by a question.

TASK	TRAINS SET		DEV. SET		TEST SET	
	DOMAIN	n SENT	DOMAIN	n SENT	DOMAIN	n SENT
Sentiment	SEMEVAL TWITTER	7,177	SEMEVAL TWITTER	1,205	SEMEVAL TWITTER	2,870
Sentiment					SEMEVAL SMS	2,094
Grammatical error	FCE	28,731	FCE	2,222	FCE	2,720
Abusive language	WASEEM (2016)	5,529	WASEEM (2016)	690	WASEEM (2016)	690
Abusive language	WASEEM AND HOVY (2016)	11,225	WASEEM AND HOVY (2016)	1,403	WASEEM AND HOVY (2016)	1,403

Table 1: Overview of the tasks and datasets used.

Preprocessing of eye-tracking data Mean fixation duration (MEAN FIX DUR) is extracted from the Dundee Corpus. For Zuco, we divide total reading time per word token with the number of fixations to obtain mean fixation duration. The mean fixation duration is selected empirically among gaze duration (sum of all fixations in the first pass reading of the a word) and total fixation duration, and n fixations. Then we average these numbers for all readers of the corpus to get a more robust average processing time. Eye-tracking is known to correlate with word frequency (Rayner and Duffy, 1988). We include a frequency baseline on the eye tracking text, BNC INV FREQ. The word frequencies comes from the British National Corpus (BNC) frequency lists (Kilgarriff, 1995). We use log-transformed frequency per million. Before normalizing, we take the additive inverse of the frequency, such that rare words get a high value, making it comparable to gaze.

MEAN FIX DUR and BNC INV FREQ are min-max-normalized to a value in the range 0-1. MEAN FIX DUR is normalized separately for the two eye tracking corpora. We expect the experimental bias – especially the fact that ZuCo contains reading of isolated sentences and Dundee contains longer texts – to influence the reading and therefore separate normalization should preserve the signal within each corpus better.

3.2 Sentiment classification

Table 1 presents an overview of all train, development and test sets used in this paper.

Our first task is sentence-level sentiment classification. We note that many sentiment analysis datasets contain document-level labels or include more fine-grained annotation of text spans, say phrases or words. For compatibility with our other tasks, we focus on sentence-level sentiment analysis. We use the SemEval-2013 Twitter dataset (Wilson et al., 2013; Rosenthal et al., 2015) for training and development. For test, we use a same-domain test set, the SemEval-2013 Twitter test

set (SEMEVAL TWITTER POS | NEG), and an out-of-domain test set, SemEval-2013 SMS test set (SEMEVAL SMS POS | NEG). The SemEval-2013 sentiment classification task was a three-way classification task with positive, negative and neutral classes. We reduce the task to binary tasks detecting negative sentences vs. non-negative and vice versa for the positive class. Therefore the dataset size is the same for POS and NEG experiments.

3.3 Grammatical error detection

Our second task is grammatical error detection. We use the First Certificate in English error detection dataset (FCE) (Yannakoudakis et al., 2011). This dataset contains essays written by English learners during language examinations, where any grammatical errors have been manually annotated by experts. Rei and Yannakoudakis (2016) converted the dataset for a sequence labeling task and we use their splits for training, development and testing. Similarly to Rei and Søgaard (2018), we perform sentence-level binary classification of sentences that need some editing vs. grammatically correct sentences. We do not use the token-level labels for training our model.

3.4 Hate speech detection

Our third and final task is detection of abusive language; or more specifically, hate speech detection. We use the datasets of Waseem (2016) and Waseem and Hovy (2016). The former contains 6,909 tweets; the latter 14,031 tweets. They are manually annotated for sexism and racism. In this study, sexism and racism are conflated into one category in both datasets. Both datasets are split in train, development and test splits consisting of 80%, 10% and 10% of the tweets respectively.

4 Experiments

Models In our experiments, we compare three models: (a) a baseline model with automatically learned attention, (b) our model with an attention

	BL			BNC INV FREQ			MEAN FIX DUR		
TASK	P	R	F_1	P	R	F_1	P	R	F_1
SEMEVAL SMS NEG	43.55	45.41	43.77	45.82	48.65	45.24	47.15	46.98	**45.77**
SEMEVAL SMS POS	65.79	50.81	57.08	65.92	51.04	57.45	65.46	52.95	**58.50**
SEMEVAL TWITTER NEG	57.39	26.87	35.70	62.50	28.66	37.78	60.52	30.67	**40.23**
SEMEVAL TWITTER POS	77.96	53.88	63.63	79.66	54.66	64.78	78.77	55.35	**64.96**
FCE	79.01	89.33	83.84	79.18	89.26	83.89	79.03	90.28	**84.28**
WASEEM (2016)	76.42	62.07	68.29	77.20	61.71	68.54	77.20	63.06	**69.30**
WASEEM AND HOVY (2016)	76.23	72.23	74.16	76.33	74.70	75.48	76.95	74.43	**75.61**
MEAN	68.05	57.23	60.92	69.52	58.38	61.88	69.30	59.10	**62.67**

Table 2: Sentence classification results. P(recision), R(ecall) and F_1. Averages over 10 random seeds. The best average F_1 score per task is shown in bold.

function regularized by information about human attention, and finally, (c) a second baseline using frequency information as a proxy for human attention and using the same regularization scheme as in our human attention model.

Hyperparameters Basic hyper-parameters such as number of hidden layers, layer size, and activation functions were following the settings of Rei and Søgaard (2018). The dimensionality of our word embedding layer was set to size 300, and we use publicly available pre-trained Glove word embeddings (Pennington et al., 2014) that we fine-tune during training. The dimensionality of the character embedding layer was set to 100. The recurrent layers in the character-level component have dimensionality 100; the word-level recurrent layers dimensionality 300. The dimensionality of our feed-forward layer, leading to reduced combined representations h_i, is 200, and the attention layer has dimensionality 100.

Three hyper-parameters, however, we tune for each architecture and for each task, by measuring sentence-level F_1-scores on the development sets. These are: (a) learning rate, (b) λ in Equation (12), i.e., controlling the relative importance of the attention regularization, and (c) the probability of sampling data from the eye-tracking corpus during training.

For all tasks and all conditions (baseline, frequency-informed baseline, and our human attention model), we perform a grid search over learning rates [.01 .1 1.], L_{att} weight λ values [.2 .4 .6 .8 1.], and probability of sampling from the eye-tracking corpus [.125 .25 .5 1., decreasing] – where *decreasing* means that the probability of

sampling from the eye-tracking corpus initially is 0.5, but drops linearly for each epoch ($\frac{1}{E+1}$; see 2.1. We apply the models with the best average F_1 scores over three random seeds on the validation data, to our test sets.

Initialization Our models are randomly initialized. This leads to some variance in performance across different runs. We therefore report averages over 10 runs in our experiments below.

5 Results

Our performance metric across all our experiments is the sentence-level F_1 score. We report precision, recall and F_1 scores for all tasks in Table 2.

Our main finding is that our human attention model, based on regularization from mean fixation durations in publicly available eye-tracking corpora, consistently outperforms the recurrent architecture with learned attention functions. The improvements over both baseline and BNC frequency are significant ($p < 0.01$) using bootstrapping (Calmettes et al., 2012) over all tasks, with one seed. The mean error reduction over the baseline is 4.5%.

Unsurprisingly, knowing that human attention helps guide our recurrent architecture, the frequency-informed baseline is also better than the non-informed baseline across the board, but the human attention model is still significantly better across all tasks ($p < 0.01$). For all tasks except negative sentiment, we note that generally, most of the improvements over the learned attention baseline for the gaze-informed models, are due to improvements in recall. Precision is not worse, but we do not see any larger improvements on precision either. For the negative SEMEVAL tasks, we also see larger improvements for precision.

The observation that improvements are primarily due to increased recall, aligns well with the hypothesis that human attention serves as an efficient regularization, preventing overfitting to surface statistical regularities that can lead the network to rely on features that are not there at test time (Globerson and Roweis, 2006), at the expense of target class precision.

6 Analysis

We illustrate the differences between our baseline models and the model with gaze-informed attention by the attention weights of an example sentence. Though it is a single, cherry-picked example, it is representative of the general trends we observe in the data, when manually inspecting attention patterns. Table 3 presents a coarse visualization of the attention weights of six different models, namely our baseline architecture and the architecture with gaze-informed attention, trained on three different tasks: hate speech detection, negative sentiment classification, and error detection. The sentence is a positive hate speech example from the Waseem and Hovy (2016) development set. The words with more attention than the sentence average are bold-faced.

First note that the baseline models only attend to one or two coherent text parts. This pattern was very consistent across all the sentences we examined. This pattern was not observed with gaze-informed attention.

Our second observation is that the baseline models are more likely to attend to stop words than gaze-informed attention. This suggests that gaze-informed attention has learned to simulate human attention to some degree. We also see many differences between the jointly learned task-specific, gaze-informed attention functions.

The gaze-informed hate speech classifier, for example, places considerable attention on *BUT*, which in this case is a passive-aggressive hate speech indicator. It also gives weight to *double standards* and *certain rules*.

The gaze-informed sentiment classifier, on the other hand, focuses more on *sorry I am not sexist* which, in isolation, reads like an apologetic disclaimer. This model also gives weight to *double standards* and *certain rules*

The gaze-informed grammatical error detection

model gives attention to *standards*, which is ungrammatical, because of the morphological number disagreement with its determiner *a*; it also gives attention to *certain rules*, which is disagreeing, again in number, with *there's*. It also gives attention to the non-word *fem*.

Overall, this, in combination with our results in Table 3, suggests that the regularization effect from human attention enables our architecture to learn to better attend to the most relevant aspects of sentences for the target tasks. In other words, human attention provides the inductive bias that makes learning possible.

7 Discussion and related work

Gaze in NLP It has previously been shown that several NLP tasks benefit from gaze information, including part-of-speech tagging (Barrett and Søgaard, 2015b; Barrett et al., 2016a), prediction of multiword expressions (Rohanian et al., 2017) and sentiment analysis (Mishra et al., 2017b).

Gaze information and other measures from psycholinguistics have been used in different ways in NLP. Some authors have used discretized, single features (Pate and Goldwater, 2011, 2013; Plank, 2016; Klerke et al., 2016), whereas others have used multidimensional, continuous values (Barrett et al., 2016a; Bingel et al., 2016). We follow Gonzalez-Garduno and Søgaard (2018) in using a single, continuous feature. We did not experiment with other representations, however. Specifically, we only considered the signal from token-level, normalized mean fixation durations.

Fixation duration is a feature that carries an enormous amount of information about the text and the language understanding process. Carpenter and Just (1983) show that readers are more likely to fixate on open-class words that are not predictable from context, and Kliegl et al. (2004) show that a higher cognitive load results in longer fixation durations. Fixations before skipped words are shorter before short or high-frequency words and longer before long or low-frequency words in comparison with control fixations (Kliegl and Engbert, 2005). Many of these findings suggest correlations with syntactic information, and many authors have confirmed that gaze information is useful to discriminate between syntactic phenomena (Demberg and Keller, 2008; Barrett and Søgaard, 2015a,b).

Gaze data has also been used in the context of

FCE		SemEval Twitter NEG		Waseem and Hovy (2016)	
BL	MFD	BL	MFD	BL	MFD
@CharlesClassiqk:	**@CharlesClassiqk:**	**@CharlesClassiqk:**	**@CharlesClaqqqqqqqssiqk:**	@CharlesClassiqk:	@CharlesClassiqk:
sorry	**sorry**	**sorry**	**sorry**	sorry	sorry
I'm	I'm	**I'm**	**I'm**	I'm	I'm
not	not	**not**	**not**	not	not
sexist	sexist	**sexist**	sexist	sexist	sexist
BUT	BUT	BUT	BUT	BUT	**BUT**
there	**there**	there	there	there	**there**
is	is	is	is	is	is
a	a	a	a	a	a
double	**double**	double	**double**	double	**double**
standards	**standards**	standards	**standards**	standards	**standards**
there's	**there's**	there's	there's	**there's**	**there's**
certain	**certain**	certain	**certain**	certain	certain
rules	rules	rules	**rules**	**rules**	**rules**
for	for	for	for	**for**	**for**
dudes	dudes	dudes	dudes	**dudes**	dudes
and	and	and	and	**and**	and
there's	**there's**	there's	there's	**there's**	**there's**
certain	certain	certain	**certain**	certain	certain
rules	**rules**	rules	**rules**	rules	rules
for	for	for	for	**for**	for
femâĂę	**femâĂę**	femâĂę	femâĂę	**femâĂę**	femâĂę

Table 3: One sentence marked as containing sexism from Waseem and Hovy (2016) development set. Using trained baseline (BL) and gaze model (MFD) for three tasks: error detection, sentiment classification, and hate speech detection. Words with more attention than sentence average are boldfaced.

sentiment analysis before (Mishra et al., 2017b,a). Mishra et al. (2017b) augmented a sentiment analysis system with eye-tracking features, including first fixation durations and fixation counts. They show that fixations not only have an impact in detecting sentiment, but also improve sarcasm detection. They train a convolutional neural network that learns features from both gaze and text and uses them to classify the input text (Mishra et al., 2017a). On a related note, Raudonis et al. (2013) developed a emotion recognition system from visual stimulus (not text) and showed that features such as pupil size and motion speed are relevant to accurately detect emotions from eye-tracking data. Wang et al. (2017) use variables shown to correlate with human attention, e.g. surprisal, to guide the attention for sentence representations.

Gaze has also been used in the context of grammaticality (Klerke et al., 2015a,b), as well as in readability assessment (Gonzalez-Garduno and Søgaard, 2018).

Gaze has either been used as features (Barrett and Søgaard, 2015a; Barrett et al., 2016b) or as a direct supervision signal in multi-task learning scenarios (Klerke et al., 2016; Gonzalez-Garduno and Søgaard, 2018). We are, to the best of our knowledge, the first to use gaze to inform attention functions in recurrent neural networks.

Human-inspired attention functions Ibraheem et al. (2017), however, uses optimal attention to simulate human attention in an interactive machine translation scenario, and Britz et al. (2017) limit attention to a local context, inspired by findings in studies of human reading. Rei and Søgaard (2018) use auxiliary data to regularize attention functions in recurrent neural networks; not from psycholinguistics data, but using small amounts of task-specific, token-level annotations. While their motivation is very different from ours, technically our models are very related. In a different context, Das et al. (2017) investigated whether humans attend to the same regions as neural networks solving visual question answering problems. Lindsey (2017) also used human-inspired, unsupervised attention in a computer vision context.

Other work on multi-purpose attention functions While our work is the first to use gaze data to guide attention in a recurrent architectures, there has recently been some work on sharing attention functions across tasks. Firat et al. (2016), for example, share attention functions between languages in the context of multi-way neural machine translation.

Sentiment analysis While sentiment analysis is most often considered a supervised learning problem, several authors have leveraged other signals than annotated data to learn sentiment analysis models that generalize better. Felbo et al. (2017), for example, use emoji prediction to pretrain their sentiment analysis models. Mishra et al. (2018) use several auxiliary tasks, including gaze prediction, for document-level sentiment analysis. There is a lot of previous work, also, leveraging information across different sentiment analysis datasets, e.g., Liu et al. (2016).

Error detection In grammatical error detection, Rei (2017) used an unsupervised auxiliary language modeling task, which is similar in spirit to our second baseline, using frequency information as auxiliary data. Rei and Yannakoudakis (2017) go beyond this and evaluate the usefulness of many auxiliary tasks, primarily syntactic ones. They also use frequency information as an auxiliary task.

Hate speech detection In hate speech detection, many signals beyond the text are often leveraged (see Schmidt and Wiegand (2017) for an overview of the literature). Interestingly, many authors have used signals from sentiment analysis, e.g., Gitari et al. (2015), motivated by the correlation between hate speech and negative sentiment. This correlation may also explain why we see the biggest improvements with gaze-informed attention on those two tasks.

Human inductive bias Finally, our work relates to other work on providing better inductive biases for learning human-related tasks by observing humans (Tamuz et al., 2011; Wilson et al., 2015). We believe this is a truly exciting line of research that can help us push research horizons in many ways.

8 Conclusion

We have shown that human attention provides a useful inductive bias on machine attention in recurrent neural networks for sequence classification problems. We present an architecture that enables us to leverage human attention signals from general, publicly available eye-tracking corpora, to induce better, more robust task-specific NLP models. We evaluate our architecture and show improvements across three NLP tasks, namely sentiment analysis, grammatical error detection, and detection of abusive language. We observe that not only does human attention help models distribute their attention in a generally useful way; human attention also seems to act like a regularizer providing more robust performance across domains, and it enables better learning of task-specific attention functions through joint learning.

References

Tamer Alkhouli, Gabriel Bretschner, Jan-Thorsten Peter, Mohammed Hethnawi, Andreas Guta, and Hermann Ney. 2016. Alignment-based neural machine translation. In *Proceedings of the First Conference on Machine Translation*, pages 54–65.

Maria Barrett, Joachim Bingel, Frank Keller, and Anders Søgaard. 2016a. Weakly supervised part-of-speech tagging using eye-tracking data. In *Proceedings of the 54th Annual Meeting of the Association for Computational Linguistics (ACL)*, volume 2, pages 579–584.

Maria Barrett, Frank Keller, and Anders Søgaard. 2016b. Cross-lingual transfer of correlations between parts of speech and gaze features. In *Proceedings of the 26th International Conference on Computational Linguistics (COLING)*, pages 1330–1339.

Maria Barrett and Anders Søgaard. 2015a. Reading behavior predicts syntactic categories. In *Proceedings of the nineteenth conference on computational natural language learning (CoNLL)*, pages 345–249.

Maria Barrett and Anders Søgaard. 2015b. Using reading behavior to predict grammatical functions. In *Workshop on Cognitive Aspects of Computational Language Learning (CogACLL)*, pages 1–5.

Joachim Bingel, Maria Barrett, and Anders Søgaard. 2016. Extracting token-level signals of syntactic processing from fMRI-with an application to POS induction. In *Proceedings of the 54th Annual Meeting of the Association for Computational Linguistics (ACL)*, volume 1, pages 747–755.

Joachim Bingel and Anders Søgaard. 2017. Identifying beneficial task relations for multi-task learning in deep neural networks. In *Proceedings of the 15th Conference of the European Chapter of the Association for Computational Linguistics (EACL)*, volume 2, pages 164–169.

Denny Britz, Melody Y. Guan, and Minh-Thang Luong. 2017. Efficient attention using a fixed-size memory representation. In *Proceedings of the 2017 Conference on Empirical Methods in Natural Language Processing (EMNLP)*, pages 392–400.

Guillaume Calmettes, Gordon B Drummond, and Sarah L Vowler. 2012. Making do with what we have: use your bootstraps. *The Journal of physiology*, 590(15):3403–3406.

Patricia A Carpenter and Marcel Adam Just. 1983. What your eyes do while your mind is reading. *Eye movements in reading: Perceptual and language processes*, pages 275–307.

Charles Clifton, Adrian Staub, and Keith Rayner. 2007. Eye movements in reading words and sentences. In *Eye Movements: A Window on Mind and Brain*, pages 341–371. Elsevier, Amsterdam, The Netherlands.

Aron Culotta, Andrew McCallum, and Jonathan Betz. 2006. Integrating probabilistic extraction models and data mining to discover relations and patterns in text. In *Proceedings of the main conference on Human Language Technology Conference of the North American Chapter of the Association of Computational Linguistics*, pages 296–303. Association for Computational Linguistics.

Abhishek Das, Harsh Agrawal, Lawrence Zitnick, Devi Parikh, and Dhruv Batra. 2017. Human attention in visual question answering: Do humans and deep networks look at the same regions? *Computer Vision and Image Understanding*, 163:90–100.

Vera Demberg and Frank Keller. 2008. Data from eye-tracking corpora as evidence for theories of syntactic processing complexity. *Cognition*, 109(2):193–210.

Daxiang Dong, Hua Wu, Wei He, Dianhai Yu, and Haifeng Wang. 2015. Multi-task learning for multiple language translation. In *Proceedings of the 53rd Annual Meeting of the Association for Computational Linguistics and the 7th International Joint Conference on Natural Language Processing (Volume 1: Long Papers)*, volume 1, pages 1723–1732.

Bjarke Felbo, Alan Mislove, Anders Søgaard, Iyan Rahwan, and Sune. Lehmann. 2017. Using millions of emoji occurrences to pretrain any-domain models for detecting emotion, sentiment, and sarcasm. In *Proceedings of the 2017 Conference on Empirical Methods in Natural Language Processing*, pages 1615–1625.

Orhan Firat, Kyunghyun Cho, and Yoshua Bengio. 2016. Multi-way, multilingual neural machine translation with a shared attention mechanism. In *Proceedings of 14th Annual Conference of the North American Chapter of the Association for Computational Linguistics (NAACL)*, pages 866–875.

Njagi Dennis Gitari, Zhang Zuping, Hanyurwimfura Damien, and Jun Long. 2015. A lexicon-based approach for hate speech detection. *International Journal of Multimedia and Ubiquitous Engineering*, 10(4):215–230.

Amir Globerson and Sam Roweis. 2006. Nightmare at test time: robust learning by feature deletion. In *Proceedings of the 23rd International Conference on Machine Learning (ICML)*, pages 353–360.

Ana Gonzalez-Garduno and Anders Søgaard. 2018. Learning to predict readability using eye-movement data from natives and learners. In *Proceedings of the Thirty-Second Association for the Advancement of Artificial Intelligence Conference (AAAI)*.

Sepp Hochreiter and Jürgen Schmidhuber. 1997. Long short-term memory. *Neural computation*, 9(8):1735–1780.

Nora Hollenstein, Jonathan Rotsztejn, Marius Troendle, Andreas Pedroni, Ce Zhang, and Nicolas Langer. 2018. ZuCo: A simultaneous EEG and eye-tracking resource for natural sentence reading. *Scientific data, Under Review*.

Samee Ibraheem, Nicholas Altieri, and John DeNero. 2017. Learning an interactive attention policy for neural machine translation. In *MTSummit*.

Alan Kennedy, Robin Hill, and Joël Pynte. 2003. The dundee corpus. In *Proceedings of the 12th European conference on eye movement*.

Adam Kilgarriff. 1995. BNC database and word frequency lists. *Retrieved Dec. 2017*.

Sigrid Klerke, Héctor Martínez Alonso, and Anders Søgaard. 2015a. Looking hard: Eye tracking for detecting grammaticality of automatically compressed sentences. In *Proceedings of the 20th Nordic Conference of Computational Linguistics (NODALIDA 2015)*, pages 97–105.

Sigrid Klerke, Sheila Castilho, Maria Barrett, and Anders Søgaard. 2015b. Reading metrics for estimating task efficiency with MT output. In *Proceedings of the Sixth Workshop on Cognitive Aspects of Computational Language Learning (CogACLL)*, pages 6–13.

Sigrid Klerke, Yoav Goldberg, and Anders Søgaard. 2016. Improving sentence compression by learning to predict gaze. In *Proceedings of 14th Annual Conference of the North American Chapter of the Association for Computational Linguistics (NAACL)*, pages 1528–1533.

Reinhold Kliegl and Ralf Engbert. 2005. Fixation durations before word skipping in reading. *Psychonomic Bulletin & Review*, 12(1):132–138.

Reinhold Kliegl, Ellen Grabner, Martin Rolfs, and Ralf Engbert. 2004. Length, frequency, and predictability effects of words on eye movements in reading. *European Journal of Cognitive Psychology*, 16(1-2):262–284.

Jack Lindsey. 2017. Pre-training attention mechanisms. In *NIPS Workshop on Cognitive Informed Artificial Intelligence*.

Pengfei Liu, Xipeng Qiu, and Xuanjing Huang. 2016. Deep multi-task learning with shared memory. In *Proceedings of the 2016 Conference on Empirical Methods in Natural Language Processing*, pages 118–127.

Tomasz D Loboda, Peter Brusilovsky, and Jöerg Brunstein. 2011. Inferring word relevance from eye-movements of readers. In *Proceedings of the 16th international conference on intelligent user interfaces*, pages 175–184. ACM.

Minh-Thang Luong, Quoc V. Le, Ilya Sutskever, Oriol Vinyals, and Lukasz Kaiser. 2016. Multi-task sequence-to-sequence learning. In *International Conference on Learning Representations (ICLR)*.

Abhijit Mishra, Kuntal Dey, and Pushpak Bhattacharyya. 2017a. Learning cognitive features from gaze data for sentiment and sarcasm classification using convolutional neural network. In *Proceedings of the 55th Annual Meeting of the Association for Computational Linguistics (Volume 1: Long Papers)*, volume 1, pages 377–387.

Abhijit Mishra, Diptesh Kanojia, Seema Nagar, Kuntal Dey, and Pushpak Bhattacharyya. 2017b. Leveraging cognitive features for sentiment analysis. In *Proceedings of the 20th SIGNLL Conference on Computational Natural Language Learning (CoNLL)*, pages 156–166.

Abhijit Mishra, Srikanth Tamilselvam, Riddhiman Dasgupta, Seema Nagar, and Kuntal Dey. 2018. Cognition-cognizant sentiment analysis with multitask subjectivity summarization based on annotators' gaze behavior. In *Proceedings of the Thirty-Second AAAI Conference on Artificial Intelligence (AAAI)*.

John K Pate and Sharon Goldwater. 2011. Unsupervised syntactic chunking with acoustic cues: computational models for prosodic bootstrapping. In *Proceedings of the 2nd Workshop on Cognitive Modeling and Computational Linguistics*, pages 20–29.

John K Pate and Sharon Goldwater. 2013. Unsupervised dependency parsing with acoustic cues. *Transactions of the Association for Computational Linguistics (TACL)*, 1:63–74.

Jeffrey Pennington, Richard Socher, and Christopher Manning. 2014. Glove: Global vectors for word representation. In *Proceedings of the 2014 conference on empirical methods in natural language processing (EMNLP)*, pages 1532–1543.

Barbara Plank. 2016. Keystroke dynamics as signal for shallow syntactic parsing. In *Proceedings of the 25th International Conference on Computational Linguistics (COLING)*, pages 609–618.

Barbara Plank, Yoav Goldberg, and Anders Søgaard. 2016. Multilingual part-of-speech tagging with bidirectional long short-term memory models and auxiliary loss. In *Proceedings of the 54th Annual Meeting of the Association for Computational Linguistics (ACL)*, pages 412–418.

Vidas Raudonis, Gintaras Dervinis, Andrius Vilkauskas, Agne Paulauskaite-Taraseviciene, and Gintare Kersulyte-Raudone. 2013. Evaluation of human emotion from eye motions. *Evaluation*, 4(8).

Keith Rayner and Susan A. Duffy. 1988. On-line comprehension processes and eye movements in reading. In *Reading research: Advances in theory and practice*, pages 13–66, New York, NY, USA. Academic Press.

Marek Rei. 2017. Semi-supervised multitask learning for sequence labeling. In *Proceedings of the 55th Annual Meeting of the Association for Computational Linguistics (ACL)*, volume 1, pages 2121–2130.

Marek Rei and Anders Søgaard. 2018. Zero-shot sequence labeling: Transferring knowledge from sentences to tokens. *Proceedings of the 16th Annual Conference of the North American Chapter of the Association for Computational Linguistics: Human Language Technologies (NAACL 2018)*, pages 293–302.

Marek Rei and Helen Yannakoudakis. 2016. Compositional sequence labeling models for error detection in learner writing. *Proceedings of the 54th Annual Meeting of the Association for Computational Linguistics (ACL)*, pages 1181–1191.

Marek Rei and Helen Yannakoudakis. 2017. Auxiliary objectives for neural error detection models. In *Proceedings of the 12th Workshop on Innovative Use of NLP for Building Educational Applications*, pages 33–43.

Omid Rohanian, Shiva Taslimipoor, Victoria Yaneva, and Le An Ha. 2017. Using gaze data to predict multiword expressions. In *Proceedings of the International Conference Recent Advances in Natural Language Processing (RANLP)*, pages 601–609.

Sara Rosenthal, Preslav Nakov, Svetlana Kiritchenko, Saif Mohammad, Alan Ritter, and Veselin Stoyanov. 2015. Semeval-2015 Task 10: Sentiment analysis in Twitter. In *Proceedings of the 9th international workshop on semantic evaluation (SemEval 2015)*, pages 451–463.

Jarkko Salojärvi, Ilpo Kojo, Jaana Simola, and Samuel Kaski. 2003. Can relevance be inferred from eye movements in information retrieval. In *Proceedings of WSOM*, volume 3, pages 261–266.

Javier San Agustin, Henrik Skovsgaard, John Paulin Hansen, and Dan Witzner Hansen. 2009. Low-cost gaze interaction: ready to deliver the promises. In *CHI'09 Extended Abstracts on Human Factors in Computing Systems*, pages 4453–4458. ACM.

Anna Schmidt and Michael Wiegand. 2017. A survey on hate speech detection using natural language processing. In *Proceedings of the Fifth International Workshop on Natural Language Processing for Social Media*, pages 1–10.

Richard Socher, Alex Perelygin, Jean Wu, Jason Chuang, Christopher D Manning, Andrew Ng, and Christopher Potts. 2013. Recursive deep models for semantic compositionality over a sentiment tree-bank. In *Proceedings of the 2013 conference on empirical methods in natural language processing*, pages 1631–1642.

Anders Søgaard and Yoav Goldberg. 2016. Deep multi-task learning with low level tasks supervised at lower layers. In *Proceedings of the 54th Annual Meeting of the Association for Computational Linguistics*, volume 2, pages 231–235.

Omer Tamuz, Ce Liu, Serge Belongie, Ohad Shamir, and Adam Tauman Kalai. 2011. Adaptively learning the crowd kernel. In *Proceedings of the 28th International Conference on Machine Learning (ICML)*, pages 673–680.

Shaonan Wang, Jiajun Zhang, and Chengqing Zong. 2017. Learning sentence representation with guidance of human attention. *Proceedings of the Twenty-Sixth International Joint Conference on Artificial Intelligence*, pages 4137–4143.

Zeerak Waseem. 2016. Are you a racist or am i seeing things? Annotator influence on hate speech detection on Twitter. In *Proceedings of the first workshop on NLP and computational social science*, pages 138–142.

Zeerak Waseem and Dirk Hovy. 2016. Hateful symbols or hateful people? Predictive features for hate speech detection on Twitter. In *Proceedings of the NAACL student research workshop*, pages 88–93.

Andrew Wilson, Christoph Dann, Chris Lucas, and Eric Xing. 2015. The human kernel. In *Advances in neural information processing systems (NIPS)*, pages 2854–2862.

Theresa Wilson, Zornitsa Kozareva, Preslav Nakov, Sara Rosenthal, Veselin Stoyanov, and Alan Ritter. 2013. Sentiment analysis in Twitter. In *Proceedings of the Seventh International Workshop on Semantic*, pages 312–320.

Helen Yannakoudakis, Ted Briscoe, and Ben Medlock. 2011. A new dataset and method for automatically grading esol texts. In *Proceedings of the 49th Annual Meeting of the Association for Computational Linguistics (ACL)*, volume 1, pages 180–189. Association for Computational Linguistics.

Barret Zoph, Deniz Yuret, Jonathan May, and Kevin Knight. 2016. Transfer learning for low-resource neural machine translation. In *Proceedings of the 2016 Conference on Empirical Methods in Natural Language Processing (EMNLP)*, pages 1568–1575.

Sentence-Level Fluency Evaluation:
References Help, But Can Be Spared!

Katharina Kann[*]
Center for Data Science
New York University
New York, USA
`kann@nyu.edu`

Sascha Rothe
Google Research
Zurich, Switzerland
`rothe@google.com`

Katja Filippova
Google Research
Berlin, Germany
`katjaf@google.com`

Abstract

Motivated by recent findings on the probabilistic modeling of acceptability judgments,
we propose syntactic log-odds ratio (SLOR),
a normalized language model score, as a metric for referenceless fluency evaluation of natural language generation output at the sentence
level. We further introduce WPSLOR, a novel
WordPiece-based version, which harnesses a
more compact language model. Even though
word-overlap metrics like ROUGE are computed with the help of hand-written references,
our referenceless methods obtain a significantly higher correlation with human fluency
scores on a benchmark dataset of compressed
sentences. Finally, we present ROUGE-LM, a
reference-based metric which is a natural extension of WPSLOR to the case of available
references. We show that ROUGE-LM yields
a significantly higher correlation with human
judgments than all baseline metrics, including
WPSLOR on its own.

1 Introduction

Producing sentences which are perceived as natural by a human addressee—a property which we
will denote as *fluency*[1] throughout this paper —is
a crucial goal of all natural language generation
(NLG) systems: it makes interactions more natural, avoids misunderstandings and, overall, leads
to higher user satisfaction and user trust (Martindale and Carpuat, 2018). Thus, fluency evaluation
is important, e.g., during system development, or

If access to a synonym dictionary is likely to be of use, then this package may be of service.	3
Participants are invited to submit a set pair do domain name that is already taken along with alternative.	1.6
Even $15 was The HSUS.	1

Table 1: Example compressions from our dataset with
their fluency scores; scores in $[1, 3]$, higher is better.

for filtering unacceptable generations at application time. However, fluency evaluation of NLG
systems constitutes a hard challenge: systems are
often not limited to reusing words from the input,
but can generate in an *abstractive* way. Hence, it
is not guaranteed that a correct output will match
any of a finite number of given references. This
results in difficulties for current reference-based
evaluation, especially of fluency, causing word-
overlap metrics like ROUGE (Lin and Och, 2004)
to correlate only weakly with human judgments
(Toutanova et al., 2016). As a result, fluency evaluation of NLG is often done manually, which is
costly and time-consuming.

Evaluating sentences on their fluency, on the
other hand, is a linguistic ability of humans which
has been the subject of a decade-long debate
in cognitive science. In particular, the question
has been raised whether the grammatical knowledge that underlies this ability is probabilistic or
categorical in nature (Chomsky, 1957; Manning,
2003; Sprouse, 2007). Within this context, Lau
et al. (2017) have recently shown that neural lan-

---

[*]This research was carried out while the first author was
interning at Google.

[1]Alternative names include *naturalness*, *grammaticality*
or *readability*. Note that the exact definitions of all those
terms vary slightly throughout the literature.

Proceedings of the 22nd Conference on Computational Natural Language Learning (CoNLL 2018), pages 313–323
Brussels, Belgium, October 31 - November 1, 2018. ©2018 Association for Computational Linguistics

guage models (LMs) can be used for modeling human ratings of acceptability. Namely, they found SLOR (Pauls and Klein, 2012)—sentence log-probability which is normalized by unigram log-probability and sentence length—to correlate well with acceptability judgments at the sentence level.

However, to the best of our knowledge, these insights have so far gone disregarded by the natural language processing (NLP) community. In this paper, we investigate the practical implications of Lau et al. (2017)'s findings for fluency evaluation of NLG, using the task of automatic compression (Knight and Marcu, 2000; McDonald, 2006) as an example (cf. Table 1). Specifically, we test our hypothesis that SLOR should be a suitable metric for evaluation of compression fluency which (i) does not rely on references; (ii) can naturally be applied at the sentence level (in contrast to the system level); and (iii) does not need human fluency annotations of any kind. In particular the first aspect, i.e., SLOR not needing references, makes it a promising candidate for automatic evaluation. Getting rid of human references has practical importance in a variety of settings, e.g., if references are unavailable due to a lack of resources for annotation, or if obtaining references is impracticable. The latter would be the case, for instance, when filtering system outputs at application time.

We further introduce WPSLOR, a novel, Word-Piece (Wu et al., 2016)-based version of SLOR, which drastically reduces model size and training time. Our experiments show that both approaches correlate better with human judgments than traditional word-overlap metrics, even though the latter do rely on reference compressions. Finally, investigating the case of available references and how to incorporate them, we combine WPSLOR and ROUGE to ROUGE-LM, a novel reference-based metric, and increase the correlation with human fluency ratings even further.

Contributions. To summarize, we make the following contributions:

1. We empirically show that SLOR is a good referenceless metric for the evaluation of NLG fluency at the sentence level.

2. We introduce WPSLOR, a WordPiece-based version of SLOR, which disposes of a more compact LM without a significant loss of performance.

3. We propose ROUGE-LM, a reference-based metric, which achieves a significantly higher correlation with human fluency judgments than all other metrics in our experiments.

2   On Acceptability

Acceptability judgments, i.e., speakers' judgments of the well-formedness of sentences, have been the basis of much linguistics research (Chomsky, 1964; Schütze, 1996): a speakers intuition about a sentence is used to draw conclusions about a language's rules. Commonly, "acceptability" is used synonymously with "grammaticality", and speakers are in practice asked for grammaticality judgments or acceptability judgments interchangeably. Strictly speaking, however, a sentence can be unacceptable, even though it is grammatical – a popular example is Chomsky's phrase "Colorless green ideas sleep furiously." (Chomsky, 1957) In turn, acceptable sentences can be ungrammatical, e.g., in an informal context or in poems (Newmeyer, 1983).

Scientists—linguists, cognitive scientists, psychologists, and NLP researcher alike—disagree about how to represent human linguistic abilities. One subject of debates are acceptability judgments: while, for many, acceptability is a binary condition on membership in a set of well-formed sentences (Chomsky, 1957), others assume that it is gradient in nature (Heilman et al., 2014; Toutanova et al., 2016). Tackling this research question, Lau et al. (2017) aimed at modeling human acceptability judgments automatically, with the goal to gain insight into the nature of human perception of acceptability. In particular, they tried to answer the question: Do humans judge acceptability on a gradient scale? Their experiments showed a strong correlation between human judgments and normalized sentence log-probabilities under a variety of LMs for artificial data they had created by translating and back-translating sentences with neural models. While they tried different types of LMs, best results were obtained for neural models, namely recurrent neural networks (RNNs).

In this work, we investigate if approaches which have proven successful for modeling acceptability can be applied to the NLP problem of automatic fluency evaluation.

3 Method

In this section, we first describe SLOR and the intuition behind this score. Then, we introduce WordPieces, before explaining how we combine the two.

3.1 SLOR

SLOR assigns to a sentence S a score which consists of its log-probability under a given LM, normalized by unigram log-probability and length:

$$\text{SLOR}(S) = \frac{1}{|S|}(\ln(p_M(S)) \tag{1}$$
$$- \ln(p_u(S)))$$

where $p_M(S)$ is the probability assigned to the sentence under the LM. The unigram probability $p_u(S)$ of the sentence is calculated as

$$p_u(S) = \prod_{t \in S} p(t) \tag{2}$$

with $p(t)$ being the unconditional probability of a token t, i.e., given no context.

The intuition behind subtracting unigram log-probabilities is that a token which is rare on its own (in contrast to being rare at a given position in the sentence) should not bring down the sentence's rating. The normalization by sentence length is necessary in order to not prefer shorter sentences over equally fluent longer ones.[2] Consider, for instance, the following pair of sentences:

(i) He is a citizen of France.

(ii) He is a citizen of Tuvalu.

Given that both sentences are of equal length and assuming that France appears more often in a given LM training set than Tuvalu, the length-normalized log-probability of sentence (i) under the LM would most likely be higher than that of sentence (ii). However, since both sentences are equally fluent, we expect taking each token's unigram probability into account to lead to a more suitable score for our purposes.

We calculate the probability of a sentence with a long-short term memory (LSTM, Hochreiter and Schmidhuber (1997)) LM, i.e., a special type of RNN LM, which has been trained on a large corpus. More details on LSTM LMs

	ILP	NAMAS	SEQ2SEQ	T3
fluency	2.22	1.30	1.51	1.40

Table 2: Average fluency ratings for each compression system in the dataset by Toutanova et al. (2016).

can be found, e.g., in Sundermeyer et al. (2012). The unigram probabilities for SLOR are estimated using the same corpus.

3.2 WordPieces

Sub-word units like WordPieces (Wu et al., 2016) are getting increasingly important in NLP. They constitute a compromise between characters and words: On the one hand, they yield a smaller vocabulary, which reduces model size and training time, and improve handling of rare words, since those are partitioned into more frequent segments. On the other hand, they contain more information than characters.

WordPiece models are estimated using a data-driven approach which maximizes the LM likelihood of the training corpus as described in Wu et al. (2016) and Schuster and Nakajima (2012).

3.3 WPSLOR

We propose a novel version of SLOR, by incorporating a LM which is trained on a corpus which has been split by a WordPiece[3] model. This leads to a smaller vocabulary, resulting in a LM with less parameters, which is faster to train (around 12h compared to roughly 5 days for the word-based version in our experiments). We will refer to the word-based SLOR as WordSLOR and to our newly proposed WordPiece-based version as WPSLOR.

4 Experiment

Now, we present our main experiment, in which we assess the performances of WordSLOR and WPSLOR as fluency evaluation metrics.

4.1 Dataset

We experiment on the compression dataset by Toutanova et al. (2016). It contains single sentences and two-sentence paragraphs from the Open American National Corpus (OANC), which belong to 4 genres: *newswire, letters, journal,* and *non-fiction*. Gold references are manually created and the outputs of 4 compression systems (ILP (extractive), NAMAS (abstractive),

---

[2]Note that the sentence log-probability which is normalized by sentence length corresponds to the negative cross-entropy.

[3]https://github.com/google/sentencepiece

SEQ2SEQ (extractive), and T3 (abstractive); cf. Toutanova et al. (2016) for details) for the test data are provided. Each example has 3 to 5 independent human ratings for content and fluency. We are interested in the latter, which is rated on an ordinal scale from 1 (disfluent) through 3 (fluent). We experiment on the 2955 system outputs for the test split.

Average fluency scores per system are shown in Table 2. As can be seen, ILP produces the best output. In contrast, NAMAS is the worst system for fluency. In order to be able to judge the reliability of the human annotations, we follow the procedure suggested by Pavlick and Tetreault (2016) and used by Toutanova et al. (2016), and compute the quadratic weighted κ (Cohen, 1968) for the human fluency scores of the system-generated compressions as 0.337.

4.2 LM Hyperparameters and Training

We train our LSTM LMs on the English Gigaword corpus (Parker et al., 2011), which consists of news data.

The hyperparameters of all LMs are tuned using perplexity on a held-out part of Gigaword, since we expect LM perplexity and final evaluation performance of WordSLOR and, respectively, WPSLOR to correlate. Our best networks consist of two layers with 512 hidden units each, and are trained for $2,000,000$ steps with a minibatch size of 128. For optimization, we employ ADAM (Kingma and Ba, 2014).

4.3 Baseline Metrics

ROUGE-L. Our first baseline is ROUGE-L (Lin and Och, 2004), since it is the most commonly used metric for compression tasks. ROUGE-L measures the similarity of two sentences based on their longest common subsequence. Generated and reference compressions are tokenized and lowercased. For multiple references, we only make use of the one with the highest score for each example.

N-gram-overlap metrics. We compare to the best n-gram-overlap metrics from Toutanova et al. (2016); combinations of linguistic units (bi-grams (LR2) and tri-grams (LR3)) and scoring measures (recall (R) and F-score (F)). With multiple references, we consider the union of the sets of n-grams. Again, generated and reference compressions are tokenized and lowercased.

Negative cross-entropy. We further compare to the negative LM cross-entropy, i.e., the log-probability which is only normalized by sentence length. The score of a sentence S is calculated as

$$\text{NCE}(S) = \tfrac{1}{|S|} \ln(p_M(S)) \qquad (3)$$

with $p_M(S)$ being the probability assigned to the sentence by a LM. We employ the same LMs as for SLOR, i.e., LMs trained on words (WordNCE) and WordPieces (WPNCE).

Perplexity. Our next baseline is perplexity, which corresponds to the exponentiated cross-entropy:

$$\text{PPL}(S) = \exp(-\text{NCE}(S)) \qquad (4)$$

About BLEU. Due to its popularity, we also performed initial experiments with BLEU (Papineni et al., 2002). Its correlation with human scores was so low that we do not consider it in our final experiments.

4.4 Correlation and Evaluation Scores

Pearson correlation. Following earlier work (Toutanova et al., 2016), we evaluate our metrics using Pearson correlation with human judgments. It is defined as the covariance divided by the product of the standard deviations:

$$\rho_{X,Y} = \frac{\text{cov}(X,Y)}{\sigma_X \sigma_Y} \qquad (5)$$

Mean squared error. Pearson cannot accurately judge a metric's performance for sentences of very similar quality, i.e., in the extreme case of rating outputs of identical quality, the correlation is either not defined or 0, caused by noise of the evaluation model. Thus, we additionally evaluate using mean squared error (MSE), which is defined as the squares of residuals after a linear transformation, divided by the sample size:

$$\text{MSE}_{X,Y} = \min_f \frac{1}{|X|} \sum_{i=1}^{|X|} (f(x_i) - y_i)^2 \qquad (6)$$

with f being a linear function. Note that, since MSE is invariant to linear transformations of X but not of Y, it is a non-symmetric quasi-metric. We apply it with Y being the human ratings. An additional advantage as compared to Pearson is that it has an interpretable meaning: the expected error made by a given metric as compared to the human rating.

metric	refs	Pearson	MSE
WordSLOR	**0**	**0.454**	**0.261**
WPSLOR	**0**	0.437	0.267
WordNCE	**0**	0.403*	0.276*
WPNCE	**0**	0.413*	0.273*
WordPPL	**0**	0.325*	0.295*
WPPPL	**0**	0.344*	0.290*
ROUGE-L-mult	$3-5$	0.429*	0.269
LR3-F-mult	$3-5$	0.405*	0.275*
LR2-F-mult	$3-5$	0.375*	0.283*
LR3-R-mult	$3-5$	0.412*	0.273*
ROUGE-L-single	1	0.406*	0.275*

Table 3: Pearson correlation (higher is better) and MSE (lower is better) for all metrics; best results in bold; *refs*=number of references used to compute the metric.

4.5 Results and Discussion

As shown in Table 3, WordSLOR and WPSLOR correlate best with human judgments: Word-SLOR (respectively WPSLOR) has a 0.025 (respectively 0.008) higher Pearson correlation than the best word-overlap metric ROUGE-L-mult, even though the latter requires multiple reference compressions. Furthermore, if we consider with ROUGE-L-single a setting with a single given reference, the distance to WordSLOR increases to 0.048 for Pearson correlation. Note that, since having a single reference is very common, this result is highly relevant for practical applications. Considering MSE, the top two metrics are still WordSLOR and WPSLOR, with a 0.008 and, respectively, 0.002 lower error than the third best metric, ROUGE-L-mult.

Comparing WordSLOR and WPSLOR, we find no significant differences: 0.017 for Pearson and 0.006 for MSE. However, WPSLOR uses a more compact LM and, hence, has a shorter training time, since the vocabulary is smaller ($16,000$ vs. $128,000$ tokens).

Next, we find that WordNCE and WPNCE perform roughly on par with word-overlap metrics. This is interesting, since they, in contrast to traditional metrics, do not require reference compressions. However, their correlation with human fluency judgments is strictly lower than that of their respective SLOR counterparts. The difference between WordSLOR and WordNCE is bigger than that between WPSLOR and WPNCE. This might be due to accounting for differences in frequencies being more important for words than for Word-Pieces. Both WordPPL and WPPPL clearly underperform as compared to all other metrics in our experiments.

The traditional word-overlap metrics all perform similarly. ROUGE-L-mult and LR2-F-mult are best and worst, respectively.

4.6 Analysis I: Fluency Evaluation per Compression System

The results per compression system (cf. Table 4) look different from the correlations in Table 3: Pearson and MSE are both lower. This is due to the outputs of each given system being of comparable quality. Therefore, the datapoints are similar and, thus, easier to fit for the linear function used for MSE. Pearson, in contrast, is lower due to its invariance to linear transformations of both variables. Note that this effect is smallest for ILP, which has uniformly distributed targets ($\mathrm{Var}(Y) = 0.35$ vs. $\mathrm{Var}(Y) = 0.17$ for SEQ2SEQ).

Comparing the metrics, the two SLOR approaches perform best for SEQ2SEQ and T3. In particular, they outperform the best word-overlap metric baseline by 0.244 and 0.097 Pearson correlation as well as 0.012 and 0.012 MSE, respectively. Since T3 is an abstractive system, we can conclude that WordSLOR and WPSLOR are applicable even for systems that are not limited to make use of a fixed repertoire of words.

For ILP and NAMAS, word-overlap metrics obtain best results. The differences in performance, however, are with a maximum difference of 0.072 for Pearson and ILP much smaller than for SEQ2SEQ. Thus, while the differences are significant, word-overlap metrics do not outperform our SLOR approaches by a wide margin. Recall, additionally, that word-overlap metrics rely on references being available, while our proposed approaches do not require this.

4.7 Analysis II: Fluency Evaluation per Domain

Looking next at the correlations for all models but different domains (cf. Table 5), we first observe that the results across domains are similar, i.e., we do not observe the same effect as in Subsection 4.6. This is due to the distributions of scores being uniform ($\mathrm{Var}(Y) \in [0.28, 0.36]$).

*Significantly worse than best (bold) result with $p < 0.05$; one-tailed; Fisher-Z-transformation for Pearson, two sample t-test for MSE.

	refs	Pearson				MSE			
		ILP	**NAMAS**	**S2S**	**T3**	**ILP**	**NAMAS**	**S2S**	**T3**
# samples		679	762	767	747	679	762	767	747
WordSLOR	**0**	0.363*	0.340*	**0.257**	0.343	0.307*	0.104	**0.161**	0.174
WPSLOR	**0**	0.417*	0.312*	0.201*	**0.360**	0.292*	0.106*	0.166	**0.172**
WordNCE	**0**	0.311*	0.270*	0.128*	0.342	0.319*	0.109*	0.170*	0.174
WPNCE	**0**	0.302*	0.258*	0.124*	0.357	0.322*	0.110*	0.170*	**0.172**
ROUGE-L-mult	3 − 5	0.471	**0.392**	0.013*	0.256*	0.275	**0.100**	0.173*	0.184*
LR3-F-mult	3 − 5	**0.489**	0.266*	0.007*	0.234*	**0.269**	0.109*	0.173*	0.187*
LR2-F-mult	3 − 5	0.484	0.213*	-0.013*	0.236*	0.271	0.112*	0.173*	0.186*
LR3-R-mult	3 − 5	0.473	0.246*	-0.002*	0.232*	0.275*	0.111*	0.173*	0.187*
ROUGE-L-single	1	0.363*	0.308*	0.008*	0.263*	0.307*	0.107*	0.173*	0.184*

Table 4: Pearson correlation (higher is better) and MSE (lower is better), reported by compression system; best results in bold; *refs*=number of references used to compute the metric.

Next, we focus on an important question: How much does the performance of our SLOR-based metrics depend on the domain, given that the respective LMs are trained on Gigaword, which consists of news data?

Comparing the evaluation performance for individual metrics, we observe that, except for *letters*, WordSLOR and WPSLOR perform best across all domains: they outperform the best word-overlap metric by at least 0.019 and at most 0.051 Pearson correlation, and at least 0.004 and at most 0.014 MSE. The biggest difference in correlation is achieved for the *journal* domain. Thus, clearly even LMs which have been trained on out-of-domain data obtain competitive performance for fluency evaluation. However, a domain-specific LM might additionally improve the metrics' correlation with human judgments. We leave a more detailed analysis of the importance of the training data's domain for future work.

5 Incorporation of Given References

ROUGE was shown to correlate well with ratings of a generated text's content or meaning at the sentence level (Toutanova et al., 2016). We further expect content and fluency ratings to be correlated. In fact, sometimes it is difficult to distinguish which one is problematic: to illustrate this, we show some extreme examples—compressions which got the highest fluency rating and the lowest possible content rating by at least one rater, but the lowest fluency score and the highest content score by another—in Table 6. We, thus, hypothesize that ROUGE should contain information about fluency which is complementary to SLOR, and want to make use of references for fluency evaluation, if available. In this section, we experiment with two *reference-based* metrics – one trainable one, and one that can be used without fluency annotations, i.e., in the same settings as pure word-overlap metrics.

5.1 Experimental Setup

First, we assume a setting in which we have the following available: (i) system outputs whose fluency is to be evaluated, (ii) reference generations for evaluating system outputs, (iii) a small set of system outputs with references, which has been annotated for fluency by human raters, and (iv) a large unlabeled corpus for training a LM. Note that available fluency annotations are often uncommon in real-world scenarios; the reason we use them is that they allow for a proof of concept. In this setting, we train scikit's (Pedregosa et al., 2011) support vector regression model (SVR) with the default parameters on predicting fluency, given WPSLOR and ROUGE-L-mult. We use 500 of our total 2955 examples for each of training and development, and the remaining 1955 for testing.

Second, we simulate a setting in which we have only access to (i) system outputs which should be evaluated on fluency, (ii) reference compressions, and (iii) large amounts of unlabeled text. In particular, we assume to not have fluency ratings for system outputs, which makes training a regression model impossible. Note that this is the standard setting in which word-overlap metrics are applied. Under these conditions, we propose to normalize both given scores by mean and variance, and to simply add them up. We call this new reference-

	refs	Pearson				MSE			
		letters	journal	news	non-fi	letters	journal	news	non-fi
# samples		640	999	344	972	640	999	344	972
WordSLOR	0	0.452	**0.453**	**0.403**	**0.484**	0.258	**0.250**	**0.234**	**0.278**
WPSLOR	0	0.435*	0.415*	0.389	0.483	0.263	0.260	0.237	0.278
WordNCE	0	0.395*	0.412*	0.342*	0.425*	0.273*	0.261*	0.247	0.297*
WPNCE	0	0.424*	0.398*	0.363	0.460	0.266*	0.265*	0.243	0.286
ROUGE-L-mult	3 − 5	**0.487**	0.382*	0.384	0.451*	**0.247**	0.269*	0.238	0.289
LR3-F-mult	3 − 5	0.404*	0.402*	0.278*	0.439*	0.271*	0.264*	0.258*	0.293
LR2-F-mult	3 − 5	0.390*	0.363*	0.292*	0.395*	0.275*	0.273*	0.256*	0.306*
LR3-R-mult	3 − 5	0.420*	0.395*	0.272*	0.453	0.267*	0.266*	0.259*	0.288
ROUGE-L-single	1	0.453	0.347*	0.335*	0.450*	0.258*	0.277*	0.248	0.289

Table 5: Pearson correlation (higher is better) and MSE (lower is better), reported by domain of the original sentence or paragraph; best results in bold; *refs*=number of references used to compute the metric.

model	generated compression
ILP	Objectives designed to lead incarcerated youth to an understanding of grief and loss related influences on their behavior.
ILP	In Forster's A Passage to India is created.
SEQ2SEQ	Jogged my thoughts back to Muscat Ramble.
SEQ2SEQ	Between Sagres and Lagos, pleasant beach with fishing boats, and a market.
T3	Your support of the Annual Fund maintaining the core values in GSAS the ethics.

Table 6: Sentences for which raters were unsure if they were perceived as problematic due to fluency or content issues, together with the model which generated them.

	metric	refs	train?	Pearson	MSE
1	**SVR**: ROUGE+WPSLOR	3 − 5	yes	**0.594**	**0.217**
2	**ROUGE-LM**	3 − 5	no	0.496	0.252
3	ROUGE-L-mult	3 − 5	no	0.430	0.273
4	WPSLOR	0	no	0.439	0.270

Table 7: Combinations; all differences except for 3 and 4 are statistically significant; *refs*=number of references used to compute the metric; ROUGE=ROUGE-L-mult; best results in bold.

based metric ROUGE-LM. In order to make this second experiment comparable to the SVR-based one, we use the same 1955 test examples.

5.2 Results and Discussion

Results are shown in Table 7. First, we can see that using SVR (line 1) to combine ROUGE-L-mult and WPSLOR outperforms both individual scores (lines 3-4) by a large margin. This serves as a proof of concept: the information contained in the two approaches is indeed complementary.

Next, we consider the setting where only references and no annotated examples are available. In contrast to SVR (line 1), ROUGE-LM (line 2) has only the same requirements as conventional word-overlap metrics (besides a large corpus for training the LM, which is easy to obtain for most languages). Thus, it can be used in the same settings as other word-overlap metrics. Since ROUGE-LM—an uninformed combination—performs significantly better than both ROUGE-L-mult and WPSLOR on their own, it should be the metric of choice for evaluating fluency with given references.

6 Related Work

6.1 Fluency Evaluation

Fluency evaluation is related to grammatical error detection (Atwell, 1987; Wagner et al., 2007; Schmaltz et al., 2016; Liu and Liu, 2017) and grammatical error correction (Islam and Inkpen, 2011; Ng et al., 2013, 2014; Bryant and Ng, 2015; Yuan and Briscoe, 2016). However, it differs from those in several aspects; most importantly, it is concerned with the degree to which errors matter to humans.

Work on automatic fluency evaluation in NLP

has been rare. Heilman et al. (2014) predicted the fluency (which they called *grammaticality*) of sentences written by English language learners. In contrast to ours, their approach is supervised. Stent et al. (2005) and Cahill (2009) found only low correlation between automatic metrics and fluency ratings for system-generated English paraphrases and the output of a German surface realiser, respectively. Explicit fluency evaluation of NLG, including compression and the related task of summarization, has mostly been performed manually. Vadlapudi and Katragadda (2010) used LMs for the evaluation of summarization fluency, but their models were based on part-of-speech tags, which we do not require, and they were non-neural. Further, they evaluated longer texts, not single sentences like we do. Toutanova et al. (2016) compared 80 word-overlap metrics for evaluating the content and fluency of compressions, finding only low correlation with the latter. However, they did not propose an alternative evaluation. We aim at closing this gap.

6.2 Compression Evaluation

Automatic compression evaluation has mostly had a strong focus on content. Hence, word-overlap metrics like ROUGE (Lin and Och, 2004) have been widely used for compression evaluation. However, they have certain shortcomings, e.g., they correlate best for extractive compression, while we, in contrast, are interested in an approach which generalizes to abstractive systems. Alternatives include success rate (Jing, 2000), simple accuracy (Bangalore et al., 2000), which is based on the edit distance between the generation and the reference, or word accuracy (Hori and Furui, 2004), the equivalent for multiple references.

6.3 Criticism of Common Metrics for NLG

In the sense that we promote an explicit evaluation of fluency, our work is in line with previous criticism of evaluating NLG tasks with a single score produced by word-overlap metrics.

The need for better evaluation for machine translation (MT) was expressed, e.g., by Callison-Burch et al. (2006), who doubted the meaningfulness of BLEU, and claimed that a higher BLEU score was neither a necessary precondition nor a proof of improved translation quality. Similarly, Song et al. (2013) discussed BLEU being unreliable at the sentence or sub-sentence level (in contrast to the system-level), or for only one single

reference. This was supported by Isabelle et al. (2017), who proposed a so-called challenge set approach as an alternative. Graham et al. (2016) performed a large-scale evaluation of human-targeted metrics for machine translation, which can be seen as a compromise between human evaluation and fully automatic metrics. They also found fully automatic metrics to correlate only weakly or moderately with human judgments. Bojar et al. (2016a) further confirmed that automatic MT evaluation methods do not perform well with a single reference. The need of better metrics for MT has been addressed since 2008 in the WMT metrics shared task (Bojar et al., 2016b, 2017).

For unsupervised dialogue generation, Liu et al. (2016) obtained close to no correlation with human judgements for BLEU, ROUGE and METEOR. They contributed this in a large part to the unrestrictedness of dialogue answers, which makes it hard to match given references. They emphasized that the community should move away from these metrics for dialogue generation tasks, and develop metrics that correlate more strongly with human judgments. Elliott and Keller (2014) reported the same for BLEU and image caption generation. Dušek et al. (2017) suggested an RNN to evaluate NLG at the utterance level, given only the input meaning representation.

7 Future Work

The work presented in this paper brings up multiple interesting next steps for future research.

First, in Subsection 4.7, we investigated the performances of WordSLOR and WPSLOR in dependence of the domain of the considered text. We concluded that an application was possible even for unrelated domains. However, we did not experiment with alternative LMs, which leaves the following questions unresolved: (i) Would training LMs on specific domains improve WordSLOR's and WPSLOR's correlation with human fluency judgments, i.e., to what degree are the properties of the training data important? (ii) How does the size of the training corpus influence performance? Ultimately, this research could lead to answering the following question: Is it better to train a LM on a small, in-domain corpus or on a large corpus from another domain?

Second, we showed that, in certain settings, Pearson correlation does not give reliable insight into a metric's performance. Since in general evaluation of *evaluation metrics* is hard, an important topic for future research would be the investigation of better ways to do so, or to study under which conditions a metric's performance can be assessed best.

Last but not least, a straight-forward continuation of our research would encompass the investigation of SLOR as a fluency metric for other NLG tasks or languages. While the results for compression strongly suggest a general applicability to a wider range of NLP tasks, this has yet to be confirmed empirically. As far as other languages are concerned, the question what influence a given language's grammar has would be an interesting research topic.

8 Conclusion

We empirically confirmed the effectiveness of SLOR, a LM score which accounts for the effects of sentence length and individual unigram probabilities, as a metric for fluency evaluation of the NLG task of automatic compression at the sentence level. We further introduced WP-SLOR, an adaptation of SLOR to WordPieces, which reduced both model size and training time at a similar evaluation performance. Our experiments showed that our proposed referenceless metrics correlate significantly better with fluency ratings for the outputs of compression systems than traditional word-overlap metrics on a benchmark dataset. Additionally, they can be applied even in settings where no references are available, or would be costly to obtain. Finally, for given references, we proposed the reference-based metric ROUGE-LM, which consists of a combination of WPSLOR and ROUGE. Thus, we were able to obtain an even more accurate fluency evaluation.

Acknowledgments

We would like to thank Sebastian Ebert and Samuel Bowman for their detailed and helpful feedback.

References

Eric Steven Atwell. 1987. How to detect grammatical errors in a text without parsing it. In *EACL*.

Srinivas Bangalore, Owen Rambow, and Steve Whittaker. 2000. Evaluation metrics for generation. In *INLP*.

Ondrej Bojar, Christian Federmann, Barry Haddow, Philipp Koehn, Matt Post, and Lucia Specia. 2016a. Ten years of WMT evaluation campaigns: Lessons learnt. In *Translation Evaluation: From Fragmented Tools and Data Sets to an Integrated Ecosystem*.

Ondřej Bojar, Yvette Graham, and Amir Kamran. 2017. Results of the WMT17 metrics shared task. In *WMT*.

Ondřej Bojar, Yvette Graham, Amir Kamran, and Miloš Stanojević. 2016b. Results of the WMT16 metrics shared task. In *WMT*.

Christopher Bryant and Hwee Tou Ng. 2015. How far are we from fully automatic high quality grammatical error correction? In *ACL-IJCNLP*.

Aoife Cahill. 2009. Correlating human and automatic evaluation of a german surface realiser. In *ACL-IJCNLP*.

Chris Callison-Burch, Miles Osborne, and Philipp Koehn. 2006. Re-evaluating the role of BLEU in machine translation research. In *EACL*.

Noam Chomsky. 1957. *Syntactic structures*. Walter de Gruyter.

Noam Chomsky. 1964. *Aspects of the Theory of Syntax*. MIT Press.

Jacob Cohen. 1968. Weighted kappa: Nominal scale agreement provision for scaled disagreement or partial credit. *Psychological bulletin*, 70(4):213.

Ondřej Dušek, Jekaterina Novikova, and Verena Rieser. 2017. Referenceless quality estimation for natural language generation. *arXiv:1708.01759*.

Desmond Elliott and Frank Keller. 2014. Comparing automatic evaluation measures for image description. In *ACL*.

Yvette Graham, Timothy Baldwin, Meghan Dowling, Maria Eskevich, Teresa Lynn, and Lamia Tounsi. 2016. Is all that glitters in machine translation quality estimation really gold? In *COLING*.

Michael Heilman, Aoife Cahill, Nitin Madnani, Melissa Lopez, Matthew Mulholland, and Joel Tetreault. 2014. Predicting grammaticality on an ordinal scale. In *ACL*.

Sepp Hochreiter and Jürgen Schmidhuber. 1997. Long short-term memory. *Neural computation*, 9(8):1735–1780.

Chiori Hori and Sadaoki Furui. 2004. Speech summarization: An approach through word extraction and a method for evaluation. *IEICE Transactions on Information and Systems*, 87(1):15–25.

Pierre Isabelle, Colin Cherry, and George Foster. 2017. A challenge set approach to evaluating machine translation. In *EMNLP*.

Aminul Islam and Diana Inkpen. 2011. Correcting different types of errors in texts. In *CAIAC*.

Hongyan Jing. 2000. Sentence reduction for automatic text summarization. In *ANLP*.

Diederik Kingma and Jimmy Ba. 2014. Adam: A method for stochastic optimization. *arXiv:1412.6980*.

Kevin Knight and Daniel Marcu. 2000. Statistics-based summarization – step one: Sentence compression. In *AAAI*.

Jey Han Lau, Alexander Clark, and Shalom Lappin. 2017. Grammaticality, acceptability, and probability: A probabilistic view of linguistic knowledge. *Cognitive Science*, 41(5):1202–1241.

Chin-Yew Lin and Franz Josef Och. 2004. Automatic evaluation of machine translation quality using longest common subsequence and skip-bigram statistics. In *ACL*.

Chia-Wei Liu, Ryan Lowe, Iulian Serban, Mike Noseworthy, Laurent Charlin, and Joelle Pineau. 2016. How NOT to evaluate your dialogue system: An empirical study of unsupervised evaluation metrics for dialogue response generation. In *EMNLP*.

Zhuo-Ran Liu and Yang Liu. 2017. Exploiting unlabeled data for neural grammatical error detection. *Journal of Computer Science and Technology*, 32(4):758–767.

Christopher D Manning. 2003. Probabilistic syntax. *Probabilistic linguistics*.

Marianna J Martindale and Marine Carpuat. 2018. Fluency over adequacy: A pilot study in measuring user trust in imperfect MT. *arXiv:1802.06041*.

Ryan McDonald. 2006. Discriminative sentence compression with soft syntactic evidence. In *EACL*.

Frederick J Newmeyer. 1983. *Grammatical theory: Its limits and its possibilities*. University of Chicago Press.

Hwee Tou Ng, Siew Mei Wu, Ted Briscoe, Christian Hadiwinoto, Raymond Hendy Susanto, and Christopher Bryant. 2014. The CoNLL-2014 shared task on grammatical error correction. In *CoNLL*.

Hwee Tou Ng, Siew Mei Wu, Yuanbin Wu, Christian Hadiwinoto, and Joel Tetreault. 2013. The CoNLL-2013 shared task on grammatical error correction. In *CoNLL*.

Kishore Papineni, Salim Roukos, Todd Ward, and Wei-Jing Zhu. 2002. BLEU: a method for automatic evaluation of machine translation. In *ACL*.

Robert Parker, David Graff, Junbo Kong, Ke Chen, and Kazuaki Maeda. 2011. English Gigaword fifth edition, Linguistic Data Consortium.

Adam Pauls and Dan Klein. 2012. Large-scale syntactic language modeling with treelets. In *ACL*.

Ellie Pavlick and Joel Tetreault. 2016. An empirical analysis of formality in online communication. *TACL*, 4:61–74.

Fabian Pedregosa, Gaël Varoquaux, Alexandre Gramfort, Vincent Michel, Bertrand Thirion, Olivier Grisel, Mathieu Blondel, Peter Prettenhofer, Ron Weiss, Vincent Dubourg, Jake VanderPlas, Alexandre Passos, David Cournapeau, Matthieu Brucher, Matthieu Perrot, and Edouard Duchesnay. 2011. Scikit-learn: Machine learning in Python. *Journal of Machine Learning Research*, 12:2825–2830.

Allen Schmaltz, Yoon Kim, Alexander M Rush, and Stuart M Shieber. 2016. Sentence-level grammatical error identification as sequence-to-sequence correction. *arXiv:1604.04677*.

M Schuster and K Nakajima. 2012. Japanese and Korean voice search. In *ICASSP*.

Carson T Schütze. 1996. *The empirical base of linguistics: Grammaticality judgments and linguistic methodology*. University of Chicago Press.

Xingyi Song, Trevor Cohn, and Lucia Specia. 2013. BLEU deconstructed: Designing a better MT evaluation metric. *International Journal of Computational Linguistics and Applications*, 4(2):29–44.

Jon Sprouse. 2007. Continuous acceptability, categorical grammaticality, and experimental syntax. *Biolinguistics*, 1:123–134.

Amanda Stent, Matthew Marge, and Mohit Singhai. 2005. Evaluating evaluation methods for generation in the presence of variation. In *CICLing*.

Martin Sundermeyer, Ralf Schlüter, and Hermann Ney. 2012. Lstm neural networks for language modeling. In *ISCA*.

Kristina Toutanova, Chris Brockett, Ke M Tran, and Saleema Amershi. 2016. A dataset and evaluation metrics for abstractive compression of sentences and short paragraphs. In *EMNLP*.

Ravikiran Vadlapudi and Rahul Katragadda. 2010. On automated evaluation of readability of summaries: Capturing grammaticality, focus, structure and coherence. In *NAACL-HLT SRW*.

Joachim Wagner, Jennifer Foster, and Josef van Genabith. 2007. A comparative evaluation of deep and shallow approaches to the automatic detection of common grammatical errors. In *EMNLP-CoNLL*.

Yonghui Wu, Mike Schuster, Zhifeng Chen, Quoc V Le, Mohammad Norouzi, Wolfgang Macherey, Maxim Krikun, Yuan Cao, Qin Gao, Klaus Macherey, et al. 2016. Google's neural machine translation system: Bridging the gap between human and machine translation. *arXiv:1609.08144*.

Zheng Yuan and Ted Briscoe. 2016. Grammatical error correction using neural machine translation. In *NAACL-HLT*.

Predefined Sparseness in Recurrent Sequence Models

Thomas Demeester, Johannes Deleu, Fréderic Godin, Chris Develder
Ghent University - imec
Ghent, Belgium
`firstname.lastname@ugent.be`

Abstract

Inducing sparseness while training neural networks has been shown to yield models with a lower memory footprint but similar effectiveness to dense models. However, sparseness is typically induced starting from a dense model, and thus this advantage does not hold during training. We propose techniques to enforce sparseness upfront in recurrent sequence models for NLP applications, to also benefit training. First, in language modeling, we show how to increase hidden state sizes in recurrent layers without increasing the number of parameters, leading to more expressive models. Second, for sequence labeling, we show that word embeddings with predefined sparseness lead to similar performance as dense embeddings, at a fraction of the number of trainable parameters.

1 Introduction

Many supervised learning problems today are solved with deep neural networks exploiting large-scale labeled data. The computational and memory demands associated with the large amount of parameters of deep models can be alleviated by using *sparse* models. Applying sparseness can be seen as a form of regularization, as it leads to a reduced amount of model parameters[1], for given layer widths or representation sizes. Current successful approaches gradually induce sparseness during training, starting from densely initialized networks, as detailed in Section 2. However, we propose that models can also be built with *predefined sparseness*, i.e., such models are already sparse by design and do not require sparseness inducing training schemes.

The main benefit of such an approach is memory efficiency, even at the start of training. Especially in the area of natural language processing, in

line with the hypothesis by Yang et al. (2017) that natural language is "high-rank", it may be useful to train larger sparse representations, even when facing memory restrictions. For example, in order to train word representations for a large vocabulary using limited computational resources, predefined sparseness would allow training larger embeddings more effectively compared to strategies inducing sparseness from dense models.

The contributions of this paper are (i) a predefined sparseness model for recurrent neural networks, (ii) as well as for word embeddings, and (iii) proof-of-concept experiments on part-of-speech tagging and language modeling, including an analysis of the memorization capacity of dense vs. sparse networks. An overview of related work is given in the next Section 2. We subsequently present predefined sparseness in recurrent layers (Section 3), as well as embedding layers (Section 4), each illustrated by experimental results. This is followed by an empirical investigation of the memorization capacity of language models with predefined sparseness (Section 5). Section 6 summarizes the results, and points out potential areas of follow-up research.

The code for running the presented experiments is publically available.[2]

2 Related Work

A substantial body of work has explored the benefits of using sparse neural networks. In deep convolutional networks, common approaches include sparseness regularization, e.g., using decomposition (Liu et al., 2015) or variational dropout (Molchanov et al., 2017)), pruning of connections (Han et al., 2016, 2015; Guo et al., 2016) and low rank approximations (Jaderberg et al., 2014; Tai et al., 2016). Regularization and pruning often

---

[1] The sparseness focused on in this work, occurs on the level of trainable parameters, i.e., we do not consider data sparsity.

[2] https://github.com/tdmeeste/SparseSeqModels

Proceedings of the 22nd Conference on Computational Natural Language Learning (CoNLL 2018), pages 324–333
Brussels, Belgium, October 31 - November 1, 2018. ©2018 Association for Computational Linguistics

lead to mostly random connectivity, and therefore to irregular memory accesses, with little practical effect in terms of hardware speedup. Low rank approximations are structured and thus do achieve speedups, with as notable examples the works of Wen et al. (2016) and Lebedev and Lempitsky (2016).

Whereas above-cited papers specifically explored convolutional networks, our work focuses on recurrent neural networks (RNNs). Similar ideas have been applied there, e.g., see Lu et al. (2016) for a systematic study of various new compact architectures for RNNs, including low-rank models, parameter sharing mechanisms and structured matrices. Also pruning approaches have been shown to be effective for RNNs, e.g., by Narang et al. (2017). Notably, in the area of audio synthesis, Kalchbrenner et al. (2018) showed that large sparse networks perform better than small dense networks. Their sparse models were obtained by pruning, and importantly, a significant speedup was achieved through an efficient implementation.

For the domain of natural language processing (NLP), recent work by Wang et al. (2016) provides an overview of sparse learning approaches, and in particular noted that "application of sparse coding in language processing is far from extensive, when compared to speech processing". Our current work attempts to further fill that gap. In contrast to aforementioned approaches (that either rely on inducing sparseness starting from a denser model, or rather indirectly try to impose sparseness by enforcing constraints), we explore ways to predefine sparseness.

In the future, we aim to design models where predefined sparseness will allow using very large representation sizes at a limited computational cost. This could be interesting for training models on very large datasets (Chelba et al., 2013; Shazeer et al., 2017), or for more complex applications such as joint or multi-task prediction scenarios (Miwa and Bansal, 2016; Bekoulis et al., 2018; Hashimoto et al., 2017).

3 Predefined Sparseness in RNNs

Our first objective is designing a recurrent network cell with fewer trainable parameters than a standard cell, with given input dimension i and hidden state size h. In Section 3.1, we describe one way to do this, while still allowing the use of fast RNN libraries in practice. This is illustrated for the task of language modeling in Section 3.2.

3.1 Sparse RNN Composed of Dense RNNs

The weight matrices in RNN cells can be divided into input-to-hidden matrices $\mathbf{W}_{hi} \in \mathbb{R}^{h \times i}$ and hidden-to-hidden matrices $\mathbf{W}_{hh} \in \mathbb{R}^{h \times h}$ (assuming here the output dimension corresponds to the hidden state size h), adopting the terminology used in (Goodfellow et al., 2016). A *sparse* RNN cell can be obtained by introducing sparseness in $\mathbf{W}_{hh}$ and $\mathbf{W}_{hi}$. Note that our experiments make use of the Long Short-Term Memory (LSTM) cell (Hochreiter and Schmidhuber, 1997), but our discussion should hold for any type of recurrent network cell. For example, an LSTM contains 4 matrices $\mathbf{W}_{hh}$ and $\mathbf{W}_{hi}$, whereas the Gated Recurrent Unit (GRU) (Chung et al., 2014) only has 3.

We first propose to organize the hidden dimensions in several disjoint groups, i.e, N segments with lengths s_n $(n = 1, \ldots, N)$, with $\sum_n s_n = h$. We therefore reduce $\mathbf{W}_{hh}$ to a block-diagonal matrix. For example, a uniform segmentation would reduce the number of trainable parameters in $\mathbf{W}_{hh}$ to a fraction $1/N$. Figure 1 illustrates an example $\mathbf{W}_{hh}$ for $N = 3$. One would expect that this simplification has a significant regularizing effect, given that the number of possible interactions between hidden dimensions is strongly reduced. However, our experiments (see Section 3.2) show that a larger sparse model may still be more expressive than its dense counterpart with the same number of parameters. Yet, Merity et al. (2017) showed that applying weight dropping (i.e., DropConnect, Wan et al. (2013)) in an LSTM's $\mathbf{W}_{hh}$ matrices has a stronger positive effect on language models than other ways to regularize them. Sparsifying $\mathbf{W}_{hh}$ upfront can hence be seen as a similar way to avoid the model's 'over-expressiveness' in its recurrent weights.

As a second way to sparsify the RNN cell, we propose to not provide all hidden dimensions with explicit access to each input dimension. In each row of $\mathbf{W}_{hi}$ we limit the number of trainable parameters to a fraction $\gamma \in \left]0, 1\right]$. Practically, we choose to organize the γi trainable parameters in each row within a window that gradually moves from the first to the last input dimension, when advancing in the hidden (i.e., row) dimension. Furthermore, we segment the hidden dimension of $\mathbf{W}_{hi}$ according to the segmentation of $\mathbf{W}_{hh}$, and

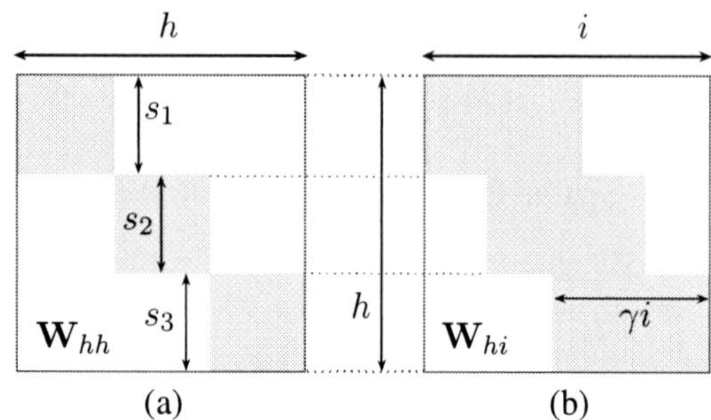

Figure 1: Predefined sparseness in hidden-to-hidden ($\mathbf{W}_{hh}$) and input-to-hidden ($\mathbf{W}_{hi}$) matrices in RNNs. Trainable parameters (yellow) vs. zeros (white).

move the window of γi trainable parameters discretely per segment, as illustrated in Fig. 1(b).

Because of the proposed practical arrangement of sparse and dense blocks in $\mathbf{W}_{hh}$ and $\mathbf{W}_{hi}$, the sparse RNN cell is equivalent to a composition of smaller dense RNN's operating in parallel on (partly) overlapping input data segments, with concatenation of the individual hidden states at the output. This will be illustrated at the end of Section 5. As a result, fast libraries like CuDNN (Chetlur et al., 2014) can be used directly. Further research is required to investigate the potential benefit in terms of speed and total cell capacity, of physically distributing computations for the individual dense recurrent cells.

Note that this is only possible because of the initial requirement that the output dimensions are divided into disjoint segments. Whereas inputs can be shared entirely between different components, joining overlapping segments in the h dimension would need to be done within the cell, before applying the gating and output non-linearities. This would make the proposed model less interesting for practical use.

We point out two special cases: (i) dense $\mathbf{W}_{hi}$ matrices ($\gamma = 1$) lead to N parallel RNNs that share the inputs but with separate contributions to the output, and (ii) organizing $\mathbf{W}_{hi}$ as a block matrix (e.g., $\gamma = 1/N$ for N same-length segments), leads to N isolated parallel RNNs. In the latter case, the reduction in trainable parameters is highest, for a given number of segments, but there is no more influence from any input dimension in a given segment to output dimensions in non-corresponding segments. We recommend option (i) as the most rational way to apply our ideas: the sparse RNN output is a concatenation of individual outputs of a number of RNN components connected in parallel, all sharing the entire input.

3.2 Language Modeling with Sparse RNNs

We apply predefined sparse RNNs to language modeling. Our baseline approach is the AWD-LSTM model introduced by Merity et al. (2017). The recurrent unit consists of a three-layer stacked LSTM (Long Short-Term Memory network (Hochreiter and Schmidhuber, 1997)), with 400-dimensional inputs and outputs, and intermediate hidden state sizes of 1150. Since the vocabulary contains only 10k words, most trainable parameters are in the recurrent layer (20M out of a total of 24M). In order to cleanly measure the impact of predefined sparseness in the recurrent layer, we maintain the original word embedding layer dimensions, and sparsify the recurrent layer.[3] In this example, we experiment with increasing dimensions in the recurrent layer while maintaining the number of trainable parameters, whereas in Section 4.2 we increase sparseness while maintaining dimensions.

Specifically, each LSTM layer is made sparse in such a way that the hidden dimension 1150 is increased by a factor 1.5 (chosen *ad hoc*) to 1725, but the embedding dimensions and total number of parameters remain the same (within error margins from rounding to integer dimensions for the dense blocks). We use uniform segments. The number of parameters for the middle LSTM layer can be calculated as:[4]

$$\text{\# params. LSTM layer 2}$$
$$= 4(h_d\, i_d + h_d^2 + 2h_d) \qquad \text{(dense)}$$
$$= 4N\left(\frac{h_s}{N}\gamma i_s + \frac{h_s^2}{N^2} + 2\frac{h_s}{N}\right) \quad \text{(sparse)}$$

in which the first expression represents the general case (e.g., the *dense* case has input and state sizes $i_d = h_d = 1150$), and the second part is the *sparse* case composed of N parallel LSTMs

---

[3]Alternative models could be designed for comparison, with modifications in both the embedding and output layer. Straightforward ideas include an ensemble of smaller independent models, or a mixture-of-softmaxes output layer to combine hidden states of the parallel LSTM components, inspired by (Yang et al., 2017).

[4]This follows from an LSTM's 4 $\mathbf{W}_{hh}$ and 4 $\mathbf{W}_{hi}$ matrices, as well as bias vectors. However, depending on the implementation the equations may differ slightly in the contribution from the bias terms. We assume the standard Pytorch implementation (Paszke et al., 2017).

	finetune	test perplexity
(Merity et al., 2017)	no	58.8
baseline	no	58.8 ± 0.3
sparse LSTM	no	$\mathbf{57.9 \pm 0.3}$
(Merity et al., 2017)	yes	57.3
baseline	yes	$\mathbf{56.6 \pm 0.2}$
sparse LSTM	yes	57.0 ± 0.2

Table 1: Language modeling for PTB (mean $\pm$ stdev).

with input size γi_s, and state size h_s/N (with $i_s = h_s = 1725$). *Dense* and *sparse* variants have the same number of parameters for $N = 3$ and $\gamma = 0.555$. These values are obtained by identifying both expressions. Note that the equality in model parameters for the dense and sparse case holds only approximately due to rounding errors in (γi_s) and (h_s/N).

Figure 1 displays $\mathbf{W}_{hh}$ and $\mathbf{W}_{hi}$ for the middle layer, which has close to 11M parameters out of the total of 24M in the whole model. A dense model with hidden size $h = 1725$ would require 46M parameters, with 24M in the middle LSTM alone.

Given the strong hyperparameter dependence of the AWD-LSTM model, and the known issues in objectively evaluating language models (Melis et al., 2017), we decided to keep all hyperparameters (i.e., dropout rates and optimization scheme) as in the implementation from Merity et al. (2017)[5], including the weight dropping with $p = 0.5$ in the sparse $\mathbf{W}_{hh}$ matrices. Table 1 shows the test perplexity on a processed version (Mikolov et al., 2010) of the Penn Treebank (PTB) (Marcus et al., 1993), both with and without the 'finetune' step[6], displaying mean and standard deviation over 5 different runs. Without finetuning, the sparse model consistently performs around 1 perplexity point better, whereas after finetuning, the original remains slightly better, although less consistently so over different random seeds. We observed that the sparse model overfits more strongly than the baseline, especially during the finetune step. We hypothesize that the

regularization effect of *a priori* limiting interactions between dimensions does not compensate for the increased expressiveness of the model due to the larger hidden state size. Further experimentation, with tuned hyperparameters, is needed to determine the actual benefits of predefined sparseness, in terms of model size, resulting perplexity, and sensitivity to the choice of hyperparameters.

4 Sparse Word Embeddings

Given a vocabulary with V words, we want to construct vector representations of length k for each word such that the total number of parameters needed (i.e., non-zero entries), is smaller than kV. We introduce one way to do this based on word frequencies (Section 4.1), and present part-of-speech tagging experiments (Section 4.2).

4.1 Word-Frequency based Embedding Size

Predefined sparseness in word embeddings amounts to deciding which positions in the word embedding matrix $\mathbf{E} \in \mathbb{R}^{V \times k}$ should be fixed to zero, prior to training. We define the fraction of trainable entries in $\mathbf{E}$ as the embedding density δ_E. We hypothesize that rare words can be represented with fewer parameters than frequent words, since they only appear in very specific contexts. This will be investigated experimentally in Section 4.2. Word occurrence frequencies have a typical Zipfian nature (Manning et al., 2008), with many rare and few highly frequent terms. Thus, representing the long tail of rare terms with short embeddings should greatly reduce memory requirements.

In the case of a low desired embedding density δ_E, we want to save on the rare words, in terms of assigning trainable parameters, and focus on the fewer more popular words. An exponential decay in the number of words that are assigned longer representations is one possible way to implement this. In other words, we propose to have the number of words that receive a trainable parameter at dimension j decrease with a factor α^j ($\alpha \in\ ]0, 1]$). For a given fraction δ_E, the parameter α can be determined from requiring the total number of non-zero embedding parameters to amount to a given fraction δ_E of all parameters:

$$\text{\# embedding params.} = \sum_{j=0}^{k-1} \alpha^j V = \delta_E\, k V$$

and numerically solving for α.

[5]Our implementation extends `https://github.com/salesforce/awd-lstm-lm`.

[6]The 'finetune' step indicates hot-starting the Averaged Stochastic Gradient Descent optimization once more, after convergence in the initial optimization step (Merity et al., 2017).

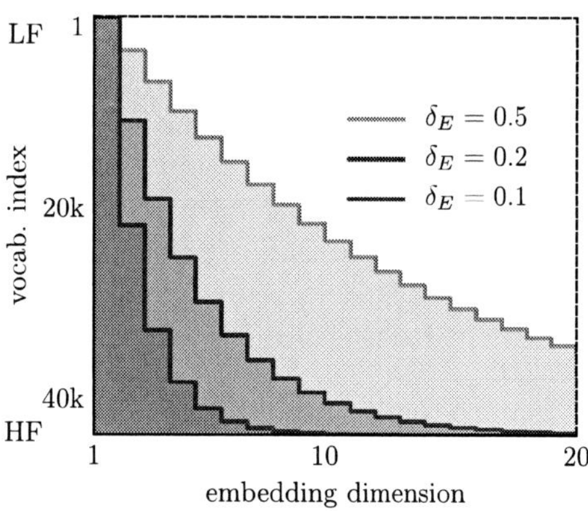

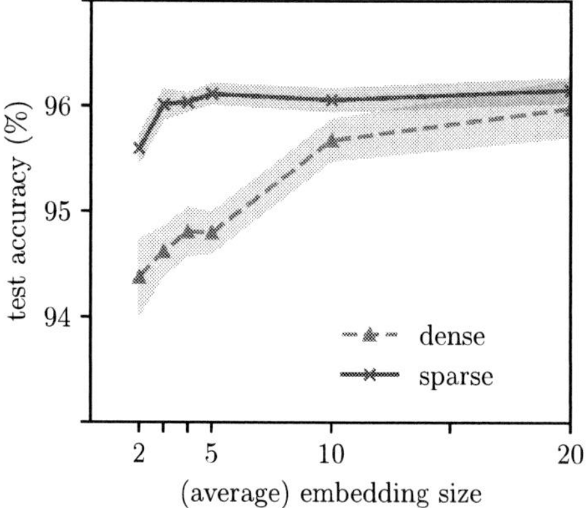

Figure 2: Visualization of sparse embedding matrices for different densities δ_E (with $k = 20$). Colored region: non-zero entries. Rows represent word indices, sorted from least frequent (LF) to highly frequent (HF).

Figure 3: POS tagging accuracy on PTB data: dense (red) vs. sparse (green). X-axis: embedding size k for the dense case, and average embedding size (or 20 δ_E) for the sparse case. Shaded bands indicate *stdev* over 4 randomly seeded runs.

Figure 2 gives examples of embedding matrices with varying δ_E. For a vocabulary of 44k terms and maximum embedding length $k = 20$, the density $\delta_E = 0.2$ leads to 25% of the words with embedding length 1 (corresponding $\alpha = 0.75$), only 7.6% with length of 10 or higher, and with the maximum length 20 for only the 192 most frequent terms. The particular configurations shown in Fig. 2 are used for the experiments in Section 4.2.

In order to set a minimum embedding length for the rarest words, as well as for computational efficiency, we note that this strategy can also be applied on M bins of embedding dimensions, rather than per individual dimensions. The width of the first bin then indicates the minimum embedding length. Say bin m has width κ_m (for $m = 0, \ldots, M - 1$, and $\sum_m \kappa_m = k$). The multiplicative decay factor α can then be obtained by solving

$$\delta_E = \frac{1}{k} \sum_{m=0}^{M-1} \kappa_m \alpha^m, \tag{1}$$

while numerically compensating for rounding errors in the number $V \alpha^m$ of words that are assigned trainable parameters in the mth bin.

4.2 Part-of-Speech Tagging Experiments

We now study the impact of sparseness in word embeddings, for a basic POS tagging model, and report results on the PTB Wall Street Journal data. We embed 43,815 terms in 20-dimensional space,

as input for a BiLSTM layer with hidden state size 10 for both forward and backward directions. The concatenated hidden states go into a fully connected layer with tanh non-linearity (down to dimension 10), followed by a *softmax* classification layer with 49 outputs (i.e., the number of POS tags). The total number of parameters is 880k, of which 876k in the embedding layer. Although character-based models are known to outperform pure word embedding based models (Ling et al., 2015), we wanted to investigate the effect of sparseness in word embeddings, rather than creating more competitive but larger or complex models, risking a smaller resolution in the effect of changing individual building blocks. To this end we also limited the dimensions, and hence the expressiveness, of the recurrent layer.[7] Our model is similar to but smaller than the 'word lookup' baseline by Ling et al. (2015).

Figure 3 compares the accuracy for variable densities δ_E (for $k = 20$) vs. different embedding sizes (with $\delta_E = 1$). For easily comparing sparse and dense models with the same number of embedding parameters, we scale δ_E, the x-axis for the sparse case, to the average embedding size of $20 \delta_E$.

---

[7]With LSTM state sizes of 50, the careful tuning of dropout parameters gave an accuracy of 94.7% when reducing the embedding size to $k = 2$, a small gap compared to 96.8% for embedding size 50. The effect of larger sparse embeddings was therefore much smaller in absolute value than the one visualized in Fig. 3, because of the much more expressive recurrent layer.

Training models with shorter dense embeddings appeared more difficult. In order to make a fair comparison, we therefore tuned the models over a range of regularization hyperparameters, provided in Table 2.

We observe that the sparse embedding layer allows lowering the number of parameters in $\mathbf{E}$ down to a fraction of 15% of the original amount, with little impact on the effectiveness, provided $\mathbf{E}$ is sparsified rather than reduced in size. The reason for that is that with sparse 20-dimensional embeddings, the BiLSTM still receives 20-dimensional inputs, from which a significant subset only transmits signals from a small set of frequent terms. In the case of smaller dense embeddings, information from all terms is uniformly present over fewer dimensions, and needs to be processed with fewer parameters at the encoder input.

Finally, we verify the validity of our hypothesis from Section 4.1 that frequent terms need to be embedded with more parameters than rare words. Indeed, one could argue in favor of the opposite strategy. It would be computationally more efficient if the terms most often encountered had the smallest representation. Also, stop words are the most frequent ones but are said to carry little information content. However, Table 3 confirms our initial hypothesis. Applying the introduced strategy to sparsify embeddings on randomly ordered words ('no sorting') leads to a significant decrease in accuracy compared to the proposed sorting strategy ('up'). When the most frequent words are encoded with the shortest embeddings ('down' in the table), the accuracy goes down even further.

5   Learning To Recite

From the language modeling experiments in Section 3.2, we hypothesized that an RNN layer becomes more expressive, when the dense layer is replaced by a larger layer with predefined sparseness and the same number of model parameters. In this section, we design an experiment to further investigate this claim. One way of quantifying an RNN's capacity is in measuring how much information it can memorize. We name our experimental setup *learning to recite*: we investigate to what extent dense vs. sparse models are able to learn an entire corpus by heart in order to recite it afterwards. We note that this toy problem could have interesting applications, such as the design of neu-

ral network components that keep entire texts or even knowledge bases available for later retrieval, encoded in the component's weight matrices.[8]

5.1   Experimental Results

The initial model for our *learning to recite* experiment is the baseline language model used in Section 3.2 (Merity et al., 2017), with the PTB data. We set all regularization parameters to zero, to focus on memorizing the training data. During training, we measure the ability of the model to correctly predict the next token at every position in the training data, by selecting the token with highest predicted probability. When the model reaches an accuracy of 100%, it is able to recite the entire training corpus. We propose the following optimization setup (tuned and tested on dense models with different sizes): minibatch SGD (batch size 20, momentum 0.9, and best initial learning rate among 5 or 10). An exponentially decaying learning rate factor (0.97 every epoch) appeared more suitable for memorization than other learning rate scheduling strategies, and we report the highest accuracy in 150 epochs.

We compare the original model (in terms of network dimensions) with versions that have less parameters, by either reducing the RNN hidden state size h or by sparsifying the RNN, and similarly for the embedding layer. For making the embedding matrix sparse, $M = 10$ equal-sized segments are used (as in eq. 1). Table 4 lists the results. The dense model with the original dimensions has 24M parameters to memorize a sequence of in total 'only' 930k tokens, and is able to do so. When the model's embedding size and intermediate hidden state size are halved, the number of parameters drops to 7M, and the resulting model now makes 67 mistakes out of 10k predictions. If h is kept, but the recurrent layers are made sparse to yield the same number of parameters, only 5 mistakes are made for every 10k predictions. Making the embedding layer sparse as well introduces new errors. If the dimensions are further reduced to a third the original size, the memorization capacity goes down strongly, with less than 4M trainable parameters. In this case, sparsifying both the recurrent and embedding layer yields the best result, whereas the dense model works better than

---

[8]It is likely that recurrent networks are not the best choice for this purpose, but here we only wanted to measure the LSTM-based model's capacity to memorize with and without predefined sparseness.

hyperparameter	value(s)
optimizer	Adam (Kingma and Ba, 2015)
learning rate	0.001
epochs	50
word level embedding dropout †	[0.0, 0.1, 0.2]
variational embedding dropout †	[0.0, 0.1, 0.2, 0.4]
DropConnect on $\mathbf{W}_{hh}$ †	[0.0, 0.2, 0.4]
batch size	20

Table 2: Hyperparameters for POS tagging model (†as introduced in (Merity et al., 2017)). A list indicates tuning over the given values was performed.

	$\delta_E = 1.0$	$\delta_E = 0.25$	$\delta_E = 0.1$
# params. ($\mathbf{E}$; all)	876k; 880k	219k; 222k	88k ; 91k
up		$\mathbf{96.1 \pm 0.1}$	$\mathbf{95.6 \pm 0.1}$
no sorting	96.0 ± 0.3	94.3 ± 0.4	93.0 ± 0.3
down		89.8 ± 2.2	90.6 ± 0.5

Table 3: Impact of vocabulary sorting on POS accuracy with sparse embeddings: up vs. down (most frequent words get longest vs. shortest embeddings, resp.) or not sorted, for different embedding densities δ_E.

	embeddings size k,	density δ_E	hidden state size h	# parameters	memorization accuracy (%)
dense model (orig. dims.)	400	1	1150	24.22M	**100.0**
dense model (see Fig. 4(a))	200	1	575	7.07M	99.33
sparse RNN (see Fig. 4(b))	200	1	1150	7.07M	**99.95**
sparse RNN + sparse emb.	400	1/2	1150	7.07M	99.74
dense model	133	1	383	3.59M	81.48
sparse RNN	133	1	1150	3.59M	76.37
sparse RNN + sparse emb.	400	1/3	1150	3.59M	**89.98**

Table 4: PTB train set memorization accuracies for dense models vs. models with predefined sparseness in recurrent and embedding layers with comparable number of parameters.

the model with sparse RNNs only. A possible explanation for that is the strong sparseness in the RNNs. For example, in the middle layer only 1 out of 10 recurrent connections is non-zero. In this case, increasing the size of the word embeddings (at least, for the frequent terms) could provide an alternative for the model to memorize parts of the data, or maybe it makes the optimization process more robust.

5.2 Visualization

Finally, we provide an illustration of the high-level composition of the recurrent layers in two of the models used for this experiment. Figure 4(a) sketches the stacked 3-layer LSTM network from the 'dense RNN' model (see Table 4) with $k = 200$ and $h = 575$. As already mentioned, our proposed sparse LSTMs are equivalent to a well-chosen composition of smaller dense LSTM components with overlapping inputs and disjoint outputs. This composition is shown in Fig. 4(b) for the model 'sparse RNN' (see Table 4), which in every layer has the same number of parameters as the dense model with reduced dimensions.

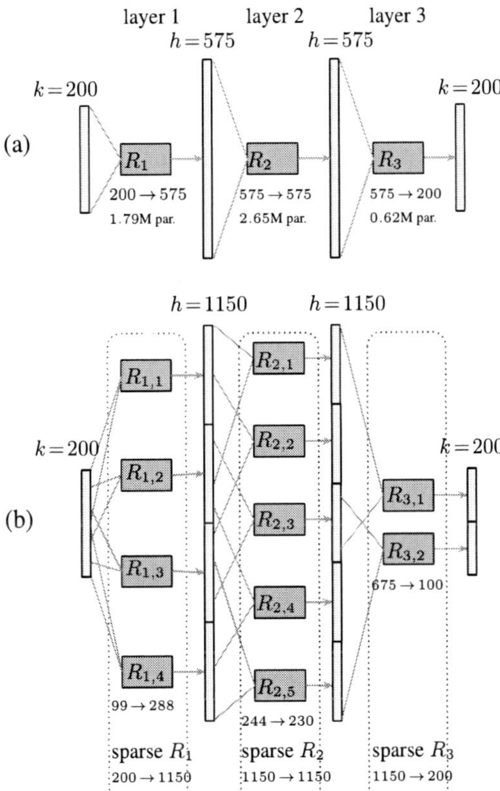

Figure 4: Schematic overview of 3-layer stacked (a) dense vs. (b) sparse LSTMs with the same number of parameters (indicated with 'par.'). Sparse layers are effectively composed of smaller dense LSTMs. '$R_{i,j}$' indicates component j within layer i, and '$675 \rightarrow 100$' indicates an LSTM compoment with input size 675 and output size 100.

6 Conclusion and Future Work

This paper introduces strategies to design word embedding layers and recurrent networks with predefined sparseness. Effective sparse word representations can be constructed by encoding less frequent terms with smaller embeddings and vice versa. A sparse recurrent neural network layer can be constructed by applying multiple smaller recurrent cells in parallel, with partly overlapping inputs and concatenated outputs.

The presented ideas can be applied to build models with larger representation sizes for a given number of parameters, as illustrated with a language modeling example. Alternatively, they can be used to reduce the number of parameters for given representation sizes, as investigated with a part-of-speech tagging model.

We introduced ideas on predefined sparseness in sequence models, as well as proof-of-concept experiments, and analysed the memorization capacity of sparse networks in the 'learning to recite' toy problem.

More elaborate experimentation is required to investigate the benefits of predefined sparseness on more competitive tasks and datasets in NLP. For example, language modeling results on the Penn Treebank rely on heavy regularization due to the small corpus. Follow-up work could therefore investigate to what extent language models for large corpora can be trained with limited computational resources, based on predefined sparseness. Other ideas for future work include the use of predefined sparseness for pretraining word embeddings, or other neural network components besides recurrent models, as well as their use in alternative applications such as sequence-to-sequence tasks or in multi-task scenarios.

Acknowledgments

We thank the anonymous reviewers for their time and effort, and the valuable feedback.

References

Giannis Bekoulis, Johannes Deleu, Thomas Demeester, and Chris Develder. 2018. Joint entity recognition and relation extraction as a multi-head selection problem. *Expert Systems with Applications*, 114:34–45.

Ciprian Chelba, Tomas Mikolov, Mike Schuster, Qi Ge, Thorsten Brants, Phillipp Koehn, and Tony Robinson. 2013. One billion word benchmark for measuring progress in statistical language modeling. Technical report, Google.

Sharan Chetlur, Cliff Woolley, Philippe Vandermersch, Jonathan Cohen, John Tran, Bryan Catanzaro, and Evan Shelhamer. 2014. cuDNN: Efficient primitives for deep learning. *arXiv:1410.0759*.

Junyoung Chung, Çalar Gülçehre, Kyunghyun Cho, and Yoshua Bengio. 2014. Empirical evaluation of gated recurrent neural networks on sequence modeling. *arXiv:1412.3555*. Deep Learning workshop at NIPS 2014.

Ian Goodfellow, Yoshua Bengio, and Aaron Courville. 2016. *Deep Learning*. MIT Press. http://www.deeplearningbook.org.

Yiwen Guo, Anbang Yao, and Yurong Chen. 2016. Dynamic network surgery for efficient DNNs. In *Proc. 30th International Conference on Neural Information Processing Systems (NIPS 2016)*, NIPS'16, pages 1387–1395.

Song Han, Huizi Mao, and William J. Dally. 2016. Deep compression: Compressing deep neural networks with pruning, trained quantization and Huffman coding. In *Proc. 4th International Conference on Learning Representations (ICLR 2016)*.

Song Han, Jeff Pool, John Tran, and William J. Dally. 2015. Learning Both Weights and Connections for Efficient Neural Networks. In *Proc. 28th International Conference on Neural Information Processing Systems (NIPS 2015)*, NIPS'15, pages 1135–1143.

Kazuma Hashimoto, Caiming Xiong, Yoshimasa Tsuruoka, and Richard Socher. 2017. A joint many-task model: Growing a neural network for multiple nlp tasks. In *Proc. Conference on Empirical Methods in Natural Language Processing (EMNLP)*, pages 1923–1933.

Sepp Hochreiter and Jürgen Schmidhuber. 1997. Long short-term memory. *Neural computation*, 9(8):1735–1780.

Max Jaderberg, Andrea Vedaldi, and Andrew Zisserman. 2014. Speeding up convolutional neural networks with low rank expansions. In *Proc. 27th British Machine Vision Conference (BMVC 2014)*. ArXiv: 1405.3866.

Nal Kalchbrenner, Erich Elsen, Karen Simonyan, Seb Noury, Norman Casagrande, Edward Lockhart, Florian Stimberg, Aäron van den Oord, Sander Dieleman, and Koray Kavukcuoglu. 2018. Efficient neural audio synthesis. ArXiv: 1802.08435.

Diederik Kingma and Jimmy Ba. 2015. Adam: A method for stochastic optimization. In *International Conference on Learning Representations*, San Diego, USA.

V. Lebedev and V. Lempitsky. 2016. Fast ConvNets using group-wise brain damage. In *Proc. 29th IEEE Conference on Computer Vision and Pattern Recognition (CVPR 2016)*, pages 2554–2564.

Wang Ling, Chris Dyer, Alan W Black, Isabel Trancoso, Ramon Fermandez, Silvio Amir, Luis Marujo, and Tiago Luis. 2015. Finding function in form: Compositional character models for open vocabulary word representation. In *Proceedings of the 2015 Conference on Empirical Methods in Natural Language Processing*, pages 1520–1530, Lisbon, Portugal. Association for Computational Linguistics.

Baoyuan Liu, Min Wang, H. Foroosh, M. Tappen, and M. Penksy. 2015. Sparse convolutional neural networks. In *Proc. 28th IEEE Conference on Computer Vision and Pattern Recognition (CVPR 2015)*, pages 806–814.

Zhiyun Lu, Vikas Sindhwani, and Tara N. Sainath. 2016. Learning compact recurrent neural networks. In *Proc. 41st IEEE International Conference on Acoustics, Speech and Signal Processing (ICASSP 2016)*.

Christopher D. Manning, Prabhakar Raghavan, and Hinrich Schütze. 2008. *Introduction to Information Retrieval*. Cambridge University Press, New York, NY, USA.

Mitchell P. Marcus, Beatrice Santorini, and Mary Ann Marcinkiewicz. 1993. Building a large annotated corpus of english: The penn treebank. *Computational Linguistics*, 19(2):313–330.

Gbor Melis, Chris Dyer, and Phil Blunsom. 2017. On the state of the art of evaluation in neural language models. In *Proc. 6th International Conference on Learning Representations (ICLR 2017)*.

Stephen Merity, Nitish Shirish Keskar, and Richard Socher. 2017. Regularizing and optimizing LSTM language models. *arXiv:1708.02182*.

Tomas Mikolov, Martin Karafit, Luks Burget, Jan Cernock, and Sanjeev Khudanpur. 2010. Recurrent neural network based language model. In *INTERSPEECH*, pages 1045–1048. ISCA.

Makoto Miwa and Mohit Bansal. 2016. End-to-end relation extraction using LSTMs on sequences and tree structures. In *Proc. 54th Annual Meeting of the Association for Computational Linguistics*, pages 1105–1116.

Dmitry Molchanov, Arsenii Ashukha, and Dmitry Vetrov. 2017. Variational dropout sparsifies deep neural networks. In *Proc. 35th International Conference on Machine Learning (ICML 2017)*. ArXiv: 1701.05369.

Sharan Narang, Erich Elsen, Gregory Diamos, and Shubho Sengupta. 2017. Exploring sparsity in recurrent neural networks. In *Proc. 5th International Conference on Learning Representations (ICLR 2017)*.

Adam Paszke, Sam Gross, Soumith Chintala, Gregory Chanan, Edward Yang, Zachary DeVito, Zeming Lin, Alban Desmaison, Luca Antiga, and Adam Lerer. 2017. Automatic differentiation in pytorch. In *Proceedings of the Workshop on The future of gradient-based machine learning software and techniques, co-located with the 31st Annual Conference on Neural Information Processing Systems (NIPS 2017)*.

Noam Shazeer, Azalia Mirhoseini, Krzysztof Maziarz, Andy Davis, Quoc Le, Geoffrey Hinton, and Jeff Dean. 2017. Outrageously large neural networks: The sparsely-gated mixture-of-experts layer. In *Proc. International Conference on Learning Representations (ICLR)*.

Cheng Tai, Tong Xiao, Yi Zhang, Xiaogang Wang, and Weinan E. 2016. Convolutional neural networks with low-rank regularization. In *Proc. 4th International Conference on Learning Representations (ICLR 2016)*. ArXiv: 1511.06067.

Li Wan, Matthew Zeiler, Sixin Zhang, Yann LeCun, and Rob Fergus. 2013. Regularization of neural networks using dropconnect. In *Proc. 30th International Conference on International Conference on Machine Learning (ICML 2013)*, pages III–1058–III–1066, Atlanta, GA, USA.

Dong Wang, Qiang Zhou, and Amir Hussain. 2016. Deep and sparse learning in speech and language processing: An overview. In *Proc. 8th International Conference on (BICS2016)*, pages 171–183. Springer, Cham.

Wei Wen, Chunpeng Wu, Yandan Wang, Yiran Chen, and Hai Li. 2016. Learning structured sparsity in deep neural networks. In *Proc. 30th International Conference on Neural Information Processing Systems (NIPS 2016)*, NIPS'16, pages 2082–2090, USA.

Zhilin Yang, Zihang Dai, Ruslan Salakhutdinov, and William W. Cohen. 2017. Breaking the softmax bottleneck: A high-rank rnn language model. ArXiv: 1711.03953.

Learning to Actively Learn Neural Machine Translation

Ming Liu   **Wray Buntine**   **Gholamreza Haffari**
Faculty of Information Technology, Monash University
{ming.m.liu, wray.buntine, gholamreza.haffari} @ monash.edu

Abstract

Traditional active learning (AL) methods for machine translation (MT) rely on heuristics. However, these heuristics are limited when the characteristics of the MT problem change due to e.g. the language pair or the amount of the initial bitext. In this paper, we present a framework to *learn* sentence selection *strategies* for neural MT. We train the AL query strategy using a high-resource language-pair based on AL simulations, and then transfer it to the low-resource language-pair of interest. The learned query strategy capitalizes on the shared characteristics between the language pairs to make an effective use of the AL budget. Our experiments on three language-pairs confirms that our method is more effective than strong heuristic-based methods in various conditions, including cold-start and warm-start as well as small and extremely small data conditions.

1 Introduction

Parallel training bitext plays a key role in the quality neural machine translation (NMT). Learning high-quality NMT models in bilingually low-resource scenarios is one of the key challenges, as NMT's quality degrades severely in such setting (Koehn and Knowles, 2017).

Recently, the importance of learning NMT models in scarce parallel bitext scenarios has gained attention. Unsupervised approaches try to learn NMT models without the need for parallel bitext (Artetxe et al., 2017; Lample et al., 2017a). Dual learning/backtranslation tries to start off from a small amount of bilingual text, and leverage monolingual text in the source and target language (Sennrich et al., 2015a; He et al., 2016). Zero/few shot approach attempts to transfer NMT learned from rich bilingual settings to low-resource settings (Johnson et al., 2016; Gu et al., 2018).

In this paper, we approach this problem from the active learning (AL) perspective. Assuming the availability of an annotation budget and a pool of monolingual source text as well as a small training bitext, the goal is to select the *most useful* source sentences and query their translation from an oracle up to the annotation budget. The queried sentences need to be selected carefully to get the value for the budget, i.e. get the highest improvements in the translation quality of the re-trained model. The AL approach is orthogonal to the aforementioned approaches to bilingually low-resource NMT, and can be potentially combined with them.

We present a framework to *learn* the sentence selection *policy* most suitable and effective for the NMT task at hand. This is in contrast to the majority of work in AL-MT where hard-coded heuristics are used for query selection (Haffari and Sarkar, 2009; Bloodgood and Callison-Burch, 2010). More concretely, we learn the query policy based on a high-resource language-pair sharing similar characteristics with the low-resource language-pair of interest. After trained, the policy is applied to the language-pair of interest capitalising on the learned signals for effective query selection. We make use of imitation learning (IL) to train the query policy. Previous work has shown that the IL approach leads to more effective policy learning (Liu et al., 2018), compared to reinforcement learning (RL) (Fang et al., 2017) . Our proposed method effectively trains AL policies for *batch* queries needed for NMT, as opposed to the previous work on single query selection.

We conduct experiments on three language pairs Finnish-English, German-English, and Czech-English. Simulating low resource scenarios, we consider various settings, including cold-start and warm-start as well as small and extremely small data conditions. The experiments

Proceedings of the 22nd Conference on Computational Natural Language Learning (CoNLL 2018), pages 334–344
Brussels, Belgium, October 31 - November 1, 2018. ©2018 Association for Computational Linguistics

show the effectiveness and superiority of our policy query compared to strong baselines.

2 Learning to Actively Learn MT

Active learning is an iterative process: Firstly, a model is built using some initially available data. Then, the most worthwhile data points are selected from the unlabelled set for annotation by the oracle. The underlying model is then re-trained using the expanded labeled data. This process is then repeated until the budget is exhausted. The main challenge is how to identify and select the most beneficial unlabelled data points during the AL iterations.

The AL strategy can be learned by attempting to actively learn on tasks sampled from a distribution over the tasks (Bachman et al., 2017). We *simulate* the AL scenario on *instances* of a low-resource MT problem created using the bitext of the resource-rich language pair, where the translation of some part of the bitext is kept hidden. This allows to have an *automatic* oracle to reveal the translations of the queried sentences, resulting in an efficient way to quickly evaluate an AL strategy. Once the AL strategy is learned on simulations, it is then applied to real AL scenarios. The more related are the low-resource language-pair in the real scenario to those used to train the AL strategy, the more effective the AL strategy would be.

We are interested to train a translation model m_ϕ which maps an input sentence from a source language $x \in \mathcal{X}$ to its translation $y \in \mathcal{Y}_x$ in a target language, where $\mathcal{Y}_x$ is the set of candidate translations for the input x and ϕ is the parameter vector of the translation model. Let $D = \{(x, y)\}$ be a support set of parallel corpus, which is randomly partitioned into parallel bitext D^{lab}, monolingual text D^{unl}, and evaluation D^{evl} datasets. Repeated random partitioning creates multiple instances of the AL problem.

3 Hierarchical MDP Formulation

A crucial difference of our setting to the previous work (Fang et al., 2017; Liu et al., 2018) is that the AL *agent* receives the reward from the oracle only after taking a *sequence* of actions, i.e. selection of an AL batch which may correspond to multiple training minibatches for the underlying NMT model. This fulfils the requirements for effective training of NMT, as minibatch updates are more effective than those of single sentence pairs.

Furthermore, it is presumably more efficient and practical to query the translation of an untranslated batch from a human translator, rather than one sentence in each AL round.

At each time step t of an AL problem, the algorithm interacts with the oracle and queries the labels of a *batch* selected from the pool D_t^{unl} to form b_t. As the result of this *sequence of actions* to select sentences in b_t, the AL algorithm receives a reward BLEU(m_ϕ, D^{evl}) which is the BLEU score on D^{evl} based on the retrained NMT model using the batch $m_\phi^{b_t}$.

Formally, this results in a hierarchical Markov decision process (HMDP) for batch sentence selection in AL. A state $s_t := \langle D_t^{lab}, D_t^{unl}, b_t, \phi_t \rangle$ of the HMDP in the time step t consist of the bitext D_t^{lab}, the monotext D_t^{unl}, the current text batch b_t, and the parameters of the currently trained NMT model ϕ_t. The high-level MDP consists of a *goal* set $\mathcal{G} := \{retrain, halt_{HI}\}$, where setting a goal $g_t \in \mathcal{G}$ corresponds to either halting the AL process, or giving the execution to the low-level MDP to collect a new batch of bitext b_t, re-training the underlying NMT model to get the update parameters ϕ_{t+1}, receiving the reward $R_{HI}(s_t, a_t, s_{t+1}) :=$ BLEU$(m_{\phi_{t+1}}, D^{evl})$, and updating the new state as $s_{t+1} = \langle D_t^{lab} \cup b_t, D_t^{unl}, \emptyset, \phi_{t+1} \rangle$. The $halt_{HI}$ goal is set in case the full AL annotation budget is exhausted, otherwise the re-train goal is set in the next time step.

The low-level MDP consists of primitive actions $a_t \in D_t^{unl} \cup \{halt_{LO}\}$ corresponding to either selecting of the monolingual sentences in D_t^{unl}, or halting the low-level policy and giving the execution back to the high-level MDP. The halt action is performed in case the maximum amount of source text is chosen for the current AL round, when the oracle is asked for the translation of the source sentences in the monolingual batch, which is then replaced by the resulting bitext. The sentence selection action, on the other hand, forms the next state by adding the chosen monolingual sentence to the batch and removing it from the pool of monolingual sentences. The underlying NMT model is not trained as a result of taking an action in the low-level policy, and the reward function is constant zero.

A trajectory in our HMDP consists of $\sigma :=$ $(s_1, g_1, \tau_1, r_1, s_2, ..., s_H, g_H, r_H, s_{H+1})$ which is the concatenation of interleaved high-level trajectory $\tau_{HI} := (s_1, g_1, r_1, s_2, .., s_{H+1})$ and low-level

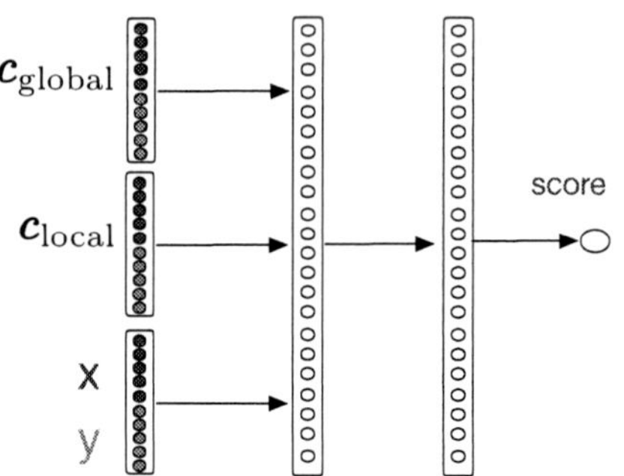

Figure 1: The policy network.

trajectories $\tau := (s_1, a_1, s_2, a_2, ..., s_T, a_T, s_{T+1})$. Clearly, the intermediate goals set by the top-level MDP into the σ are $retrain$, and only the last goal g_H is $halt_{\text{HI}}$, where H is determined by checking whether the total AL budget $\mathcal{B}_{\text{HI}}$ is exhausted. Likewise, the intermediate actions in τ_h are sentence selection, and only the last action a_T is $halt_{\text{LO}}$, where T is determined by checking whether the round-AL budget $\mathcal{B}_{\text{LO}}$ is exhausted.

We aim to find the optimal AL *policy* prescribing which datapoint needs to be queried in a given state to get the most benefit. The optimal policy is found by maximising the expected long-term reward, where the expectation is over the choice of the synthesised AL problems and other sources of randomness, i.e. partioing of D into D^{lab}, D^{unl}, and D^{evl}. Following Bachman et al. (2017), we maximise the sum of the rewards after each AL *round* to encourage the *anytime* behaviour, i.e. the model should perform well after each batch query.

4   Deep Imitation learning for AL-NMT

The question remains of how to train the policy network to maximize the reward, i.e. the generalisation performance of the underlying NMT model. As the policy for the high-level MDP is fixed, we only need to learn the optimal policy for the low-level MDP. We formulate learning the AL policy as an imitation learning problem. More concretely, the policy is trained using an *algorithmic expert*, which can generate a *reasonable* AL trajectories (batches) for each AL state in the high-level MDP. The algorithmic expert's trajectories, i.e. sequences of AL states paired with the expert's actions in the low-level MDP, are then used to train the policy network. As such, the policy network is a classifier, conditioned on a context summarising both global and local histories, to choose the best sentence (action) among the candidates. After the

AL policy is trained based on AL simulations, it is then transferred to the real AL scenario.

For simplicity of presentation, the training algorithms are presented using a fixed number of AL iterations for the high-level and low-level MDPs. This corresponds to AL with the sentence-based budget. However, extending them for AL with token-based budget is straightforward, and we experiment with both versions in §5.

Policy Network's Architecture   The policy scoring network is a fully-connected network with two hidden layers (see Figure 1). The input involves the representation for three elements: (i) global context which includes all previous AL batches, (ii) local context which summarises the previous sentences selected for the current AL batch, and (iii) the candidate sentence paired with its translation generated by the currently trained NMT model.

For each source sentence x paired with its translation y, we denote the representation by rep(x, y). We construct it by simply concatenating the representations of the source and target sentences, each of which is built by summing the embeddings of its words. We found this simple method to work well, compared to more complicated methods, e.g. taking the last hidden state of the decoder in the underlying NMT model. The global context (c_{global}) and local contexts (c_{local}) are constructed by summing the representation of the previously selected batches and sentence-pairs, respectively.

IL-based Training Algorithm   The IL-based training method is presented in Algorithm 1. The policy network is initialised randomly, and trained based $\mathcal{T}$ simulated AL problems (lines 3–20), by portioning the available large bilingual corpus into three sets: (i) D^{lab} as the growing training bitex, (ii) D^{unl} as the pool of untranslated sentences where we pretend the translations are not given, and (iii) D^{evl} as the evaluation set used by our algorithmic expert.

For each simulated AL problem, Algorithm 1 executes T_{HI} iterations (lines 7–19) to collect AL batches for training the underlying NMT model *and* the policy network. An AL batch is obtained either from the policy network (line 15) or from the algorithmic expert (lines 10-13), depending on tossing a coin (line 9). The latter also includes adding the selected batch, the candidate batches, and the relevant state information to the *replay*

Algorithm 1 Learning AL-NMT Policy

Input: Parallel corpus D, I_{width} the width of the constructed search lattices, the coin parameter α, the number of sampled AL batches K

Output: policy π

1:   $M \leftarrow \emptyset$ $\triangleright$ Replay Memory
2:   Initialise π with a random policy
3:   **for** $\mathcal{T}$ training iterations **do**
4:      $D^{lab}, D^{evl}, D^{unl} \leftarrow \text{randomPartition}(D)$
5:      $\phi \leftarrow \text{trainModel}(D^{lab})$
6:      $c_{\text{global}} \leftarrow \mathbf{0}$
7:      **for** $t \leftarrow 1$ to T_{HI} **do** $\triangleright$ MDP$_{\text{HI}}$
8:         $\mathcal{S} \leftarrow \text{searchLattice}(D^{unl}, I_{\text{width}})$
9:         **if** $\text{coinToss}(\alpha) = \text{Head}$ **then**
10:           $\mathbf{B} \leftarrow \{\text{samplePath}(\mathcal{S}, \phi, c_{\text{global}}, \pi, \beta)\}_1^K$
11:           $\mathbf{B} \leftarrow \mathbf{B} + \text{samplePath}(\mathcal{S}, \phi, c_{\text{global}}, \pi, 0)$
12:           $\mathbf{b} \leftarrow \arg\max_{\mathbf{b}' \in \mathbf{B}} \text{BLEU}(m_{\phi}^{\mathbf{b}'}, D^{evl})$ $\triangleright$ expert
13:           $M \leftarrow M \cup \{(c_{\text{global}}, \phi, \mathbf{B}, \mathbf{b})\}$
14:         **else**
15:           $\mathbf{b} \leftarrow \text{samplePath}(\mathcal{S}, \phi, c_{\text{global}}, \pi, 0)$ $\triangleright$ policy
16:         $D^{lab} \leftarrow D^{lab} + \mathbf{b}$
17:         $D^{unl} \leftarrow D^{unl} - \{\mathbf{x} \text{ s.t. } (\mathbf{x}, \mathbf{y}) \in \mathbf{b}\}$
18:         $\phi \leftarrow \text{retrainModel}(\phi, D^{lab})$
19:         $c_{\text{global}} \leftarrow c_{\text{global}} \oplus \text{rep}(\mathbf{b})$
20:      $\pi \leftarrow \text{updatePolicy}(\pi, M, \phi)$
21:   **return** π

Algorithm 2 samplePath (selecting an AL batch)

Input: Search lattice $\mathcal{S}$, global context c_{global}, policy π, perturbation probability β

Output: Selected AL batch $\mathbf{b}$

1:   $\mathbf{b} \leftarrow \emptyset$
2:   $c_{\text{local}} \leftarrow \mathbf{0}$
3:   **for** $t \leftarrow 1$ to T_{LO} **do** $\triangleright$ MDP$_{\text{LO}}$
4:      **if** $\text{coinToss}(\beta) = \text{Head}$ **then**
5:         $\mathbf{x}_t \leftarrow \pi_0(\mathcal{S}[t])$ $\triangleright$ perturbation policy
6:      **else**
7:         $\mathbf{x}_t \leftarrow \arg\max_{\mathbf{x} \in \mathcal{S}[t]} \pi(c_{\text{global}}, c_{\text{local}}, \mathbf{x})$
8:      $\mathbf{y}_t \leftarrow \text{oracle}(\mathbf{x}_t)$ $\triangleright$ getting the gold translation
9:      $c_{\text{local}} \leftarrow c_{\text{local}} \oplus \text{rep}(\mathbf{x}_t, \mathbf{y}_t)$
10:     $\mathbf{b} \leftarrow \mathbf{b} + (\mathbf{x}_t, \mathbf{y}_t)$
11:   **return** $\mathbf{b}$

---

memory M, based on which the policy will be retrained. The selected batch is then used to retrain the underlying NMT model, update the training bilingual corpus and pool of monotext, and update the global context vector (lines 16–19).

The mixture of the policy network and algorithmic expert in batch collection on simulated AL problems is inspired by Dataset Aggregation DAGGER (Ross and Bagnell, 2014). This makes sure that the collected states-actions pairs in the replay memory include situations encountered beyond executing only the algorithmic expert. This informs the trained AL policy how to act reasonably in new situations encountered in the test time, where only the network policy is in charge and the expert does not exist.

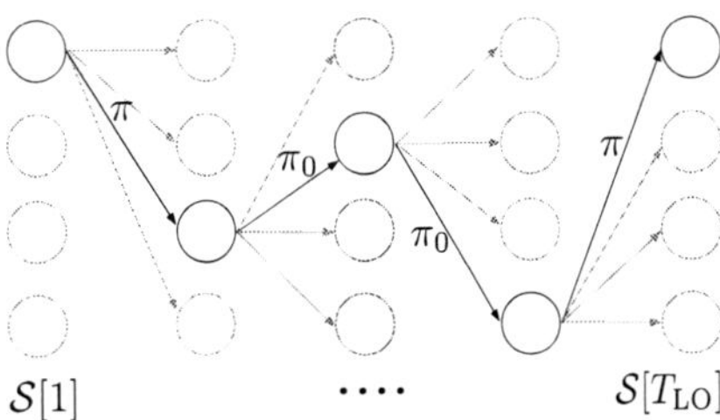

Figure 2: The search lattice and the selection of a batch based on the perturbed policy. Each circle denotes a sentence from the pool of monotext. The number of sentences at each time step, denoted by $\mathcal{S}[t]$, is I_{width}. The black sentences are selected in this AL batch.

Algorithmic Expert   At a given AL state, the algorithmic expert selects a reasonable batch from the pool, D^{unl} via:

$$\arg\max_{\mathbf{b} \in B} \text{BLEU}(m_{\phi}^{\mathbf{b}}, D^{evl}) \tag{1}$$

where $m_{\phi}^{\mathbf{b}}$ denotes the underlying NMT model ϕ further retrained by incorporating the batch $\mathbf{b}$, and B denotes the possible batches from D^{unl} (Liu et al., 2018). However, the number of possible batches is exponential in the size D^{unl}, hence the above optimisation procedure would be very slow even for a moderately-sized pool.

We construct a *search lattice* $\mathcal{S}$ from which the candidate batches in B are sampled (see Figure 2). The search lattice is constructed by sampling a fixed number of candidate sentences I_{width} from D^{unl} for each position in a batch, whose size is T_{LO}. A candidate AL batch is then be selected using Algorithm 2. It executes a mixture of the current AL policy π and a perturbation policy π_0 (e.g. random sentence selection or any other heuristic) in the lower-level MDP to sample a batch. After several such batches are sampled to form B, the best one is selected according to eqn 1.

We have carefully designed the search space to be able to incorporate the current policy's recommended batch and sampled deviations from it in B. This is inspired by the LOLS (Locally Optimal Learning to Search) algorithm (Chang et al., 2015), to invest efforts in the neighbourhood of the current policy and improve it. Moreover, having to deal with only I_{width} number of sentences at each selection stage makes the batch formation algorithm based on the policy fast and efficient.

Re-training the Policy Network   To train our policy network, we turn sentence preference scores to probabilities over the candidate batches,

Algorithm 3 Policy Transfer

Input: Bitext D^{lab}, monotext D^{unl}, pre-trained policy π
Output: NMT model ϕ
1: Initialise ϕ with D^{lab}
2: $c_{\text{global}} \leftarrow \mathbf{0}$
3: **for** $t \leftarrow 1$ to T_{HI} **do**
4:     $\mathcal{S} \leftarrow \text{searchLattice}(D^{unl}, I_{\text{width}})$
5:     $\boldsymbol{b} \leftarrow \text{samplePath}(\mathcal{S}, \phi, c_{\text{global}}, \pi, 0)$
6:     $D^{lab} \leftarrow D^{lab} + \boldsymbol{b}$
7:     $D^{unl} \leftarrow D^{unl} - \{\boldsymbol{x} \text{ s.t. } (\boldsymbol{x}, \boldsymbol{y}) \in \boldsymbol{b}\}$
8:     $\phi \leftarrow \text{retrainModel}(\phi, D^{lab})$
9:     $c_{\text{global}} \leftarrow c_{\text{global}} \oplus \text{rep}(\boldsymbol{b})$
10: **return** ϕ

---

and optimise the parameters to maximise the log-likelihood objective (Liu et al., 2018).

More specifically, let $(c_{\text{global}}, \boldsymbol{B}, \boldsymbol{b})$ be a training tuple in the replay memory. We define the probability of the correct action/batch as

$$Pr(\boldsymbol{b}|\boldsymbol{B}, c_{\text{global}}) := \frac{\text{score}(\boldsymbol{b}, c_{\text{global}})}{\sum_{\boldsymbol{b}' \in \boldsymbol{B}} \text{score}(\boldsymbol{b}', c_{\text{global}})}.$$

The preference score for a batch is the sum of its sentences' preference scores,

$$\text{score}(\boldsymbol{b}, c_{\text{global}}) := \sum_{t=1}^{|\boldsymbol{b}|} \pi\left(c_{\text{global}}, c_{\text{local}<t}, \text{rep}(\boldsymbol{x}_t, \boldsymbol{y}_t)\right)$$

where $c_{\text{local}<t}$ denotes the local context up to the sentence t in the batch.

To form the log-likelihood, we use recent tuples and randomly sample several older ones from the replay memory. We then use stochastic gradient descent (SGD) to maximise the training objective, where the gradient of the network parameters are calculated using the backpropagation algorithm.

Transfering the Policy We now apply the policy learnt on the source language pair to AL in the target task (see Algorithm 3). To enable transferring the policy to a new language pair, we make use of pre-trained multilingual word embeddings. In our experiments, we either use the pre-trained word embeddings from Ammar et al. (2016) or build it based on the available bitext and monotext in the source and target language (c.f. §5.2). To retrain our NMT model, we make parameter updates based on the mini-batches from the AL batch as well as sampled mini-batches from the previous iterations.

5 Experiment

Datasets Our experiments use the following language pairs in the news domain based on WMT2018: English-Czech (EN-CS), English-German (EN-DE), English-Finnish (EN-FI). For AL evaluation, we randomly sample 500K sentence pairs from the parallel corpora in WMT2018 for each of the three language pairs, and take 100K as the initially available bitext and the rest of 400K as the pool of untranslated sentences, pretending the translation is not available. During the AL iterations, the translation is revealed for the queried source sentences in order to retrain the underlying NMT model.

For pre-processing the text, we normalise the punctuations and tokenise using `moses`[1] scripts. The trained models are evaluated using BLEU on tokenised and cased sensitive test data from `newstest 2017`.

NMT Model Our baseline model consists of a 2-layer bi-directional LSTM encoder with an embeddings size of 512 and a hidden size of 512. The 1-layer LSTM decoder with 512 hidden units uses an attention network with 128 hidden units. We use a multiplicative-style attention attention architecture (Luong et al., 2015). The model is optimized using Adam (Kingma and Ba, 2014) with a learning rate of 0.0001, where the dropout rate is set to 0.3. We set the mini-batch size to 200 and the maximum sentence length to 50. We train the base NMT models for 5 epochs on the initially available bitext, as the perplexity on the dev set do not improve beyond more training epochs. After getting new translated text in each AL iteration, we further sample $\times 5$ more bilingual sentences from the previously available bitext, and make one pass over this data to re-train the underlying NMT model. For decoding, we use beam-search with the beam size of 3.

Selection Strategies We compare our policy-based sentence selection for NMT-AL with the following heuristics:

- **Random** We randomly select monolingual sentences up to the AL budget.

- **Length-based** We use shortest/longest monolingual sentences up to the AL budget.

- **Total Token Entropy (TTE)** We sort monolingual sentences based on their TTE which has been shown to be a strong AL heuristic (Settles and Craven, 2008) for

---

[1] http://www.statmt.org/moses

System	EN→DE	EN→FI	EN→DE	EN→CS	EN→CS	EN→FI
Base NMT (100K)	13.2	10.3	13.2	8.1	8.1	10.3
AL with 135K token budget						
Random	13.9	11.2	13.9	8.3	8.3	11.2
Shortest	14.5	11.5	14.5	**8.6**	8.6	11.5
Longest	14.1	11.3	14.1	8.2	8.2	11.3
TTE	14.2	11.3	14.2	8.5	8.5	11.3
Token Policy	**15.5**	**12.8**	**14.8**	8.5	**9.0**	**12.5**
AL with 677K token budget						
Random	15.9	13.5	15.9	**9.2**	9.2	13.5
Shortest	15.8	13.7	15.8	8.9	8.9	13.7
Longest	15.6	13.5	15.6	8.5	8.5	13.5
TTE	15.6	13.7	15.6	8.6	8.6	13.7
Token Policy	**16.6**	**14.1**	**16.3**	9.2	**10.3**	**13.9**
FULL bitext (500K)	20.5	18.3	20.5	12.1	12.1	18.3

Table 1: BLEU scores on tests sets with different selection strategies, the budget is at token level with annotation for 135.45k tokens and 677.25k tokens respectively.

sequence-prediction tasks. Given a monolingual sentence x, we compute the TTE as $\sum_{i=1}^{|\hat{y}|} \text{Entropy}[P_i(.|\hat{y}_{<i}, x, \phi)]$ where $\hat{y}$ is the decoded translation based on the current underlying NMT model ϕ, and $P_i(.|\hat{y}_{<i}, x, \phi)$ is the distribution over the vocabulary words for the position i of the translation given the source sentence and the previously generated words. We also experimented with the normalised version of this measure, i.e. dividing TTE by $|\hat{y}|$, and found that their difference is negligible. So we only report TTE results.

5.1 Translating from English

Setting We train the AL policy on a language-pair treating it as high-resource, and apply it to another language-pair treated as low-resource. To transfer the policies across languages, we make use of pre-trained multilingual word embeddings learned from monolingual text and bilingual dictionaries (Ammar et al., 2016). Furthermore, we use these cross-lingual word embeddings to initialise the embedding table of the NMT in the low-resource language-pair. The source and target vocabularies for the NMT model in the low-resource scenario are constructed using the initially available 100K bitext, and are expanded during the AL iterations as more translated text becomes available.

Results Table 1 shows the results. The experiments are performed with two limits on token annotation budget: 135k and 677k corresponding to select roughly 10K and 50K sentences in to-

System	EN→DE	EN→FI
Base NMT (100K)	13.2	10.3
AL with 10K sentence budget		
Random	14.2	11.3
Shortest	13.9	11.0
Longest	14.7	**11.8**
TTE	14.3	11.2
Sent $\pi_{\text{EN}\to\text{CS}}$	14.5	11.5
Token $\pi_{\text{EN}\to\text{CS}}$	**15.3**	**11.8**
AL with 50K sentence budget		
Random	16.1	13.5
Shortest	15.5	12.9
Longest	**17.2**	**14.2**
TTE	16.6	13.5
Sent $\pi_{\text{EN}\to\text{CS}}$	16.3	14.0
Token $\pi_{\text{EN}\to\text{CS}}$	17.0	14.1

Table 2: BLEU scores on tests sets for different language pairs with different selection strategies, the budget is at sentence level with annotation for 10k sentences and 50k sentences respectively.

tal in AL[2], respectively. The number of AL iterations is 50, hence the token annotation budget for each round is 2.7K and 13.5K. As we can see our policy-based AL method is very effective, and outperforms the strong AL baselines in all cases except, when transferring the policy trained on EN $\to$ FI to EN $\to$ CS where it is on-par with the best baseline.

Sentence vs Token Budget In our results in Table 1, we have taken the number of tokens in the selected sentences as a proxy for the annotation cost. Another option to measure the annotation cost is the number of selected sentences, which admittedly is not the best proxy. Nonetheless, one

---

[2]These token limit budgets are calculated using random selection of 10K and 50K sentences multiple times, and taking the average of the tokens across the sampled sets.

AL method	100K initial bitext		10K initial bitext	
	cold-start	warm-start	cold-start	warm-start
Base NMT	10.6/11.8	13.9/14.7	2.3/2.5	5.4/5.8
Random	12.9/13.3	15.1/16.2	5.5/5.6	9.3/9.6
Shortest	13.0/13.5	15.9/16.4	5.9/6.1	9.1/9.3
Longest	12.5/12.9	15.3/15.8	5.7/5.9	9.8/10.2
TTE	12.8/13.2	15.8/16.1	5.9/6.2	9.8/10.1
$\pi_{CS \to EN}$	13.9/**14.2**	16.8/**17.3**	6.3/**6.5**	10.5/**10.9**
$\pi_{FI \to EN}$	13.5/14.0	16.5/16.9	6.1/6.4	10.2/10.3
$\pi_{EN \to CS}$	13.3/13.6	16.4/16.5	5.1/5.7	10.3/10.5
$\pi_{EN \to FI}$	13.2/13.5	15.9/16.3	5.1/5.6	9.8/10.2
Ensemble				
$\pi_{CS,FI \to EN}$	14.1/**14.3**	16.8/**17.5**	6.3/**6.5**	10.5/**10.9**
$\pi_{EN \to CS,FI}$	13.6/13.8	16.5/16.9	5.8/5.9	10.3/10.5
Full Model (500K)	20.5/20.6	22.3/22.5	-	-

Table 3: BLEU scores on tests sets using different selection strategies. The token level annotation budget is 677K.

may be interested to see how different AL methods compare against each other based on this cost measure.

Table 2 show the results based on the sentence-based annotation cost. We train a policy on EN → CS, and apply it to EN → DE and EN → FI translation tasks. In addition to the token-based AL policy from Table 1, we *train* another policy based on the sentence budget. The token-based policy is competitive in EN → DE, where the longest sentence heuristic achieves the best performance, presumably due to the enormous training signal obtained by translation of long sentences. The token-based policy is on par with longest sentence heuristic in EN → FI for both 10K and 100K AL budgets to outperform the other methods.

5.2 Translating into English

Setting We investigate the performance of the AL methods on DE → EN based on the policies trained on the other language pairs. In addition to 100K training data condition, we assess the effectiveness of the AL methods in an extremely low-resource condition consisting of only 10K bilingual sentences as the initial bitext.

In addition to the source word embedding table that we initialised in the previous section's experiments using the cross lingual word embeddings, we are able further to initialise *all* of the other NMT parameters for DE → EN translation. This includes the target word embedding table and the decoder softmax, as the target language is the same (EN) in the language-pairs used for both policy training and policy testing. We refer to this setting as *warm-start*, as opposed to *cold-start* in which we only initialised the source embedding table with the cross-lingual embeddings. For the warm-start experiments, we transfer the NMT trained on 500K CS-EN bitext, based on which the policy is trained. We use byte-pair encoding (BPE) (Sennrich et al., 2015b) with 30K operations to bpe the EN side. For the source side, we use words in order to use the cross-lingual word embeddings. All parameters of the transferred NMT are frozen, except the ones corresponding to the bidirectional RNN encoder and the source word embedding table.

To make this experimental condition as realistic as possible, we learn the cross-lingual word embedding for DE using large amounts of monolingual text and the initially available bitext, assuming a multilingual word embedding already exists for the languages used in the policy training phase. More concretely, we sample 5M DE text from WMT2018 data[3], and train monolingual word embeddings as part of a skip-gram language model using `fastText`.[4] We then create a bilingual EN-DE word dictionary based on the initially available bitext (either 100K or 10K) using word alignments generated by `fast_align`.[5] The bilingual dictionary is used to project the monolingual DE word embedding space into that of EN,

---

[3]We make sure that it does not include the DE sentences in the 400K pool used in the AL experiments.

[4]https://github.com/facebookresearch/fastText

[5]https://github.com/clab/fast_align

hence aligning the spaces through the following orthogonal projection:

$$\arg\max_{\boldsymbol{Q}} \sum_{i=1}^{m} \boldsymbol{e}[y_i]^T \cdot \boldsymbol{Q} \cdot \boldsymbol{e}[x_i] \quad \text{s.t.} \quad \boldsymbol{Q}^T \cdot \boldsymbol{Q} = \boldsymbol{I}$$

where $\{(y_i, x_i)\}_{i=1}^{m}$ is the bilingual dictionary consisting of pairs of DE-EN words[6], $\boldsymbol{e}[y_i]$ and $\boldsymbol{e}[x_i]$ are the embeddings of the DE and EN words, and $\boldsymbol{Q}$ is the orthogonal transformation matrix aligning the two embedding spaces. We solve the above optimisation problem using SVD as in Smith et al. (2017). The cross-lingual word embedding for a DE word y is then $\boldsymbol{e}[y]^T \cdot \boldsymbol{Q}$. We build two such cross-lingual embeddings based on the two bilingual dictionaries constructed from the 10K and 100K bitext, in order to use in their corresponding experiments.

Results Table 3 presents the results, on two conditions of 100K and 10K initial bilingual sentences. For each of these data conditions, we experiments with both cold-start and warm-start settings using the pre-trained multilingual word embeddings from Ammar et al. (2016) or those we have trained with the available bitext plus additional monotext. Firstly, the warm start strategy to transfer the NMT system from CS $\rightarrow$ EN to DE $\rightarrow$ EN has been very effective, particularly on extremely low bilingual condition of 10K sentence pairs. It is worth noting that our multilingual word embeddings are very effective, even-though they are trained using small bitext. Secondly, our policy-based AL methods are more effective than the baseline methods and lead to up to +1 BLEU score improvements.

We further take the ensemble of multiple trained policies to build a new AL query strategy. In the ensemble, we rank sentences based on each of the policies. Then we produce a final ranking by combining these rankings. Specifically, we sum the ranking of each sentence according to each policy to get a rank score, and re-rank the sentences according to their rank score. Table 3 shows that ensembling is helpful, but does not produce significant improvements compared to the best policy.

5.3 Analysis

Distribution of word frequency TTE is a competitive heuristic-based strategy, as shown in the

---

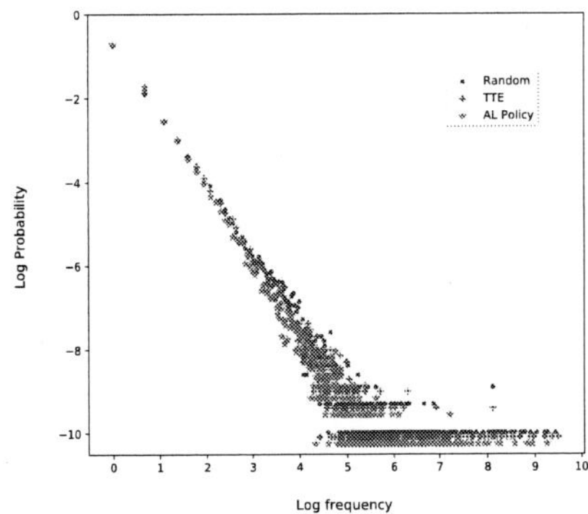

Figure 3: On the task of DE→EN, the plot shows the log fraction of words vs the log frequency from the selected data returned by different strategies, in which we have a 677K token budget and do warm start with 100K initial bitext. The AL policy here is $\pi_{CS \rightarrow EN}$.

above experiments. We compare the word frequency distributions of the selected source text returned by Random, TTE against our AL policy. The policy we use here is $\pi_{CS \rightarrow EN}$ and applied on the task of DE→EN, which is conducted in the warm-start scenario with 100K initial bitext and 677K token budget.

Fig. 3 is the log-log plot of the fraction of vocabulary words (y axis) having a particular frequency (x axis). Our AL policy is less likely to select high-frequency words than other two methods when it is given a fixed token budget.

Weighted combination of heuristics In order to get the intuition of which of the heuristics our AL policy resorts to, we again use policy $\pi_{CS \rightarrow EN}$ and apply on the task of DE→EN, which is conducted in the warm-start scenario with 100K initial bitext and 677K token budget. Meanwhile, we get the preference scores for the sentences from the monolingual set. Then, we fit a linear regression model based on the sentences and their scores, in which the response variable is the preference score and the predictor variables are extracted features or heuristics based on the sentences. The extracted features are $(length, TTE, f_0, f_1, f_2, f_{3+})$, where f_i is the fraction of words in the sentence that appear i times in the bitext. Table 4 shows the the coeffients of these heuristics, their standard errors (SE) and t values. We can see that our AL policy considers length and TTE in parallel as they have a close range of coefficients, the policy also prefers low frequency than high frequency words.

---

[6]One can incorporate human curated bilingual lexicons to the automatically curated dictionaries as well.

heuristics	coefficient	SE	t value
length	0.0328	0.0105	3.1238
TTE	0.0357	0.0147	2.4285
f_0	0.0223	0.0132	1.6893
f_1	0.0105	0.0092	1.1413
f_2	0.0052	0.0023	2.260
f_{3+}	-0.0043	0.0006	-7.1667

Table 4: The table gives an estimation of the resorted heuristics.

6 Related Work

For statistical MT (SMT), active learning is well explored, e.g. see Haffari and Sarkar (2009); Haffari et al. (2009), where several heuristics for query sentence selection have been proposed, including the entropy over the potential translations (uncertainty sampling), query by committee, and a similarity-based sentence selection method. However, active learning is largely under-explored for NMT. The goal of this paper is to provide an approach to learn an active learning strategy for NMT based on a Hierarchical Markov Decision Process (HMDP) formulation of the pool-based AL (Bachman et al., 2017; Liu et al., 2018).

Expoliting monolingual data for nmt Monolingual data play a key role in neural machine translation systems, previous work have considered training a seperate language model on the target side (Jean et al., 2014; Gulcehre et al., 2015; Domhan and Hieber, 2017). Rather than using explicit language model, Cheng et al. (2016) introduced an auto-encoder-based approach, in which the source-to-target and target-to-source translation models act as encoder and decoder respectively. Moreover, back translation approaches (Sennrich et al., 2015a; Zhang et al., 2018; Hoang et al., 2018) show efficient use of monolingual data to improve neural machine translation. Dual learning (He et al., 2016) extends back translation by using a deep RL approach. More recently, unsupervised approaches (Lample et al., 2017b; Artetxe et al., 2017) and phrase-based NMT (Lample et al., 2018) learn how to translate when having access to only a large amount of monolingual corpora, these models also extend the use of back translation and cross-lingual word embeddings are provided as the latent semantic space for sentences from monolingual corpora in different languages.

Meta-AL learning Several meta-AL approaches have been proposed to learn the AL selection strategy automaticclay from data. These methods rely on deep reinforcement learning framework (Yue et al., 2012; Wirth et al., 2017) or bandit algorithms (Nguyen et al., 2017). Bachman et al. (2017) introduced a policy gradient based method which jointly learns data representation, selection heuristic as well as the model prediction function. Fang et al. (2017) designed an active learning algorithm based on a deep Q-network, in which the action corresponds to binary annotation decisions applied to a stream of data. Woodward and Finn (2017) extended one shot learning to active learning and combined reinforcement learning with a deep recurrent model to make labeling decisions. As far as we know, we are the first one to develop the Meta-AL method to make use of monolingual data for neural machine translation, the method we proposed in this paper can be applied at mini-batch level and conducted in cross lingual settings.

7 Conclusion

We have introduced an effective approach for learning active learning policies for NMT, where the learner needs to make batch queries. We have provides a hierarchical MDP formulation of the problem, and proposed a policy network structure capturing the context in both MDP levels. Our policy training method uses imitation learning and a search lattice to carefully collect AL trajectories for further improvement of the current policy. We have provided experimental results on three language pairs, where the policies are transferred across languages using multilingual word embeddings. Our experiments confirms that our method is more effective than strong heuristic-based methods in various conditions, including cold-start and warm-start as well as small and extremely small data conditions.

Acknowledgments

We would like to thank the feedback from anonymous reviewers. This work was supported by computational resources from the Multi-modal Australian ScienceS Imaging and Visualisation Environment (MASSIVE) at Monash University, and partly by an NVIDIA GPU grant.

References

Waleed Ammar, George Mulcaire, Yulia Tsvetkov, Guillaume Lample, Chris Dyer, and Noah A Smith. 2016. Massively multilingual word embeddings. *arXiv preprint arXiv:1602.01925*.

Mikel Artetxe, Gorka Labaka, Eneko Agirre, and Kyunghyun Cho. 2017. Unsupervised neural machine translation. *arXiv preprint arXiv:1710.11041*.

Philip Bachman, Alessandro Sordoni, and Adam Trischler. 2017. Learning algorithms for active learning. In *Proceedings of the 34th International Conference on Machine Learning*, volume 70 of *Proceedings of Machine Learning Research*, pages 301–310, International Convention Centre, Sydney, Australia. PMLR.

Michael Bloodgood and Chris Callison-Burch. 2010. Bucking the trend: Large-scale cost-focused active learning for statistical machine translation. In *Proceedings of the 48th Annual Meeting of the Association for Computational Linguistics*, pages 854–864.

Kai-Wei Chang, Akshay Krishnamurthy, Alekh Agarwal, Hal Daumé, III, and John Langford. 2015. Learning to search better than your teacher. In *Proceedings of the 32Nd International Conference on International Conference on Machine Learning*, pages 2058–2066.

Yong Cheng, Wei Xu, Zhongjun He, Wei He, Hua Wu, Maosong Sun, and Yang Liu. 2016. Semi-supervised learning for neural machine translation. *arXiv preprint arXiv:1606.04596*.

Tobias Domhan and Felix Hieber. 2017. Using target-side monolingual data for neural machine translation through multi-task learning. In *Proceedings of the 2017 Conference on Empirical Methods in Natural Language Processing*, pages 1500–1505.

Meng Fang, Yuan Li, and Trevor Cohn. 2017. Learning how to active learn: A deep reinforcement learning approach. *arXiv preprint arXiv:1708.02383*.

Jiatao Gu, Hany Hassan, Jacob Devlin, and Victor OK Li. 2018. Universal neural machine translation for extremely low resource languages. *arXiv preprint arXiv:1802.05368*.

Caglar Gulcehre, Orhan Firat, Kelvin Xu, Kyunghyun Cho, Loic Barrault, Huei-Chi Lin, Fethi Bougares, Holger Schwenk, and Yoshua Bengio. 2015. On using monolingual corpora in neural machine translation. *arXiv preprint arXiv:1503.03535*.

Gholamreza Haffari, Maxim Roy, and Anoop Sarkar. 2009. Active learning for statistical phrase-based machine translation. In *Proceedings of Human Language Technologies: The 2009 Annual Conference of the North American Chapter of the Association for Computational Linguistics*, pages 415–423. Association for Computational Linguistics.

Gholamreza Haffari and Anoop Sarkar. 2009. Active learning for multilingual statistical machine translation. In *Proceedings of the Joint Conference of the 47th Annual Meeting of the ACL*, pages 181–189.

Di He, Yingce Xia, Tao Qin, Liwei Wang, Nenghai Yu, Tieyan Liu, and Wei-Ying Ma. 2016. Dual learning for machine translation. In *Advances in Neural Information Processing Systems*, pages 820–828.

Vu Cong Duy Hoang, Philipp Koehn, Gholamreza Haffari, and Trevor Cohn. 2018. Iterative back-translation for neural machine translation. In *Proceedings of the 2nd Workshop on Neural Machine Translation and Generation*, pages 18–24.

Sébastien Jean, Kyunghyun Cho, Roland Memisevic, and Yoshua Bengio. 2014. On using very large target vocabulary for neural machine translation. *arXiv preprint arXiv:1412.2007*.

Melvin Johnson, Mike Schuster, Quoc V. Le, Maxim Krikun, Yonghui Wu, Zhifeng Chen, Nikhil Thorat, Fernanda Vigas, Martin Wattenberg, G.s Corrado, Macduff Hughes, and Jeffrey Dean. 2016. Google's multilingual neural machine translation system: Enabling zero-shot translation.

Diederik P Kingma and Jimmy Ba. 2014. Adam: A method for stochastic optimization. *arXiv preprint arXiv:1412.6980*.

Philipp Koehn and Rebecca Knowles. 2017. Six challenges for neural machine translation. In *Proceedings of the First Workshop on Neural Machine Translation*, pages 28–39. Association for Computational Linguistics.

Guillaume Lample, Alexis Conneau, Ludovic Denoyer, and Marc'Aurelio Ranzato. 2017a. Unsupervised machine translation using monolingual corpora only. *arXiv preprint arXiv:1711.00043*.

Guillaume Lample, Ludovic Denoyer, and Marc'Aurelio Ranzato. 2017b. Unsupervised machine translation using monolingual corpora only. *arXiv preprint arXiv:1711.00043*.

Guillaume Lample, Myle Ott, Alexis Conneau, Ludovic Denoyer, and Marc'Aurelio Ranzato. 2018. Phrase-based & neural unsupervised machine translation. *arXiv preprint arXiv:1804.07755*.

Ming Liu, Wray Buntine, and Gholamreza Haffari. 2018. Learning how to actively learn: A deep imitation learning approach. In *Proceedings of the Annual Meeting of the Association for Computational Linguistics*.

Minh-Thang Luong, Hieu Pham, and Christopher D Manning. 2015. Effective approaches to attention-based neural machine translation. *arXiv preprint arXiv:1508.04025*.

Khanh Nguyen, Hal Daumé III, and Jordan Boyd-Graber. 2017. Reinforcement learning for bandit neural machine translation with simulated human feedback. *arXiv preprint arXiv:1707.07402*.

Stephane Ross and J Andrew Bagnell. 2014. Reinforcement and imitation learning via interactive no-regret learning. *arXiv preprint arXiv:1406.5979*.

Rico Sennrich, Barry Haddow, and Alexandra Birch. 2015a. Improving neural machine translation models with monolingual data. *arXiv preprint arXiv:1511.06709*.

Rico Sennrich, Barry Haddow, and Alexandra Birch. 2015b. Neural machine translation of rare words with subword units. *arXiv preprint arXiv:1508.07909*.

Burr Settles and Mark Craven. 2008. An analysis of active learning strategies for sequence labeling tasks. In *Proceedings of the conference on empirical methods in natural language processing*, pages 1070–1079. Association for Computational Linguistics.

Samuel L. Smith, David H. P. Turban, Steven Hamblin, and Nils Y. Hammerla. 2017. Offline bilingual word vectors, orthogonal transformations and the inverted softmax. *arXiv preprint arXiv:1702.03859*.

Christian Wirth, Riad Akrour, Gerhard Neumann, and Johannes Fürnkranz. 2017. A survey of preference-based reinforcement learning methods. *Journal of Machine Learning Research*, 18(136):1–46.

Mark Woodward and Chelsea Finn. 2017. Active one-shot learning. *arXiv preprint arXiv:1702.06559*.

Yisong Yue, Josef Broder, Robert Kleinberg, and Thorsten Joachims. 2012. The k-armed dueling bandits problem. *J. Comput. Syst. Sci.*, 78(5):1538–1556.

Zhirui Zhang, Shujie Liu, Mu Li, Ming Zhou, and Enhong Chen. 2018. Joint training for neural machine translation models with monolingual data. *arXiv preprint arXiv:1803.00353*.

Upcycle Your OCR: Reusing OCRs for Post-OCR Text Correction in Romanised Sanskrit

**Amrith Krishna[#], Bodhisattwa Prasad Majumder[*], Rajesh Shreedhar Bhat[**],
and Pawan Goyal[#]**

[#]Dept. of Computer Science and Engineering, IIT Kharagpur,
[*]Dept. of Computer Science, University of California, San Diego
[**]Walmart Labs, India

`amrith@iitkgp.ac.in`, `bmajumde@eng.ucsd.edu`,
`rajeshbhatpesit@gmail.com`, `pawang@cse.iitkgp.ernet.in`

Abstract

We propose a post-OCR text correction approach for digitising texts in Romanised Sanskrit. Owing to the lack of resources our approach uses OCR models trained for other languages written in Roman. Currently, there exists no dataset available for Romanised Sanskrit OCR. So, we bootstrap a dataset of 430 images, scanned in two different settings and their corresponding ground truth. For training, we synthetically generate training images for both the settings. We find that the use of copying mechanism (Gu et al., 2016) yields a percentage increase of 7.69 in Character Recognition Rate (CRR) than the current state of the art model in solving monotone sequence-to-sequence tasks (Schnober et al., 2016). We find that our system is robust in combating OCR-prone errors, as it obtains a CRR of 87.01% from an OCR output with CRR of 35.76% for one of the dataset settings. A human judgement survey performed on the models shows that our proposed model results in predictions which are faster to comprehend and faster to improve for a human than the other systems[1].

1 Introduction

Sanskrit used to be the 'lingua franca' for the scientific and philosophical discourse in ancient India with literature that spans more than 3 millennia. Sanskrit primarily had an oral tradition, and the script used for writing Sanskrit varied widely across the time spans and regions. With the advent of printing press, Devanagari emerged as the prominent script for representing Sanskrit. With standardisation of Romanisation using IAST in 1894 (Monier-Williams, 1899), printing in Sanskrit was extended to roman scripts as well. There

has been a surge in digitising printed Sanskrit manuscripts written in Roman such as the ones currently digitised by the 'Krishna Path' project[2].

In this work, we propose a model for post-OCR text correction for Sanskrit written in Roman. Post-OCR text correction, which can be seen as a special case of spelling correction (Schnober et al., 2016), is the task of correcting errors that tend to appear in the output of the OCR in the process of converting an image to text. The errors incurred from OCR can be quite high due to numerous factors including typefaces, paper quality, scan quality, etc. The text can often be eroded, can contain noises and the paper can be bleached or tainted as well (Schnober et al., 2016). Figure 1 shows the sample images we have collected for the task. Hence it is beneficial to perform a post-processing on the OCR output to obtain an improved text.

(a) Bhagavad Gītā

(b) Sahaśranāma

Figure 1: Sample images from our test set with different stylistic parameters

In the case of Indic OCRs, there have been considerable efforts in collection and annotation of data pertaining to Indic Scripts (Kumar and Jawahar, 2007; Bhaskarabhatla et al., 2004; Govindaraju and Setlur, 2009; Krishnan et al., 2014). Earlier attempts on Indian scripts were primarily based on handcrafted templates (Govindan and Shivaprasad, 1990; Chaudhuri and Pal, 1997) or features (Arora et al., 2010; Pal et al., 2009) which extensively used the script and language-specific

---

[1]The data and the codes for our system are available here - `https://github.com/majumderb/sanskrit-ocr`

[2]`http://www.krishnapath.org/library/`

Proceedings of the 22nd Conference on Computational Natural Language Learning (CoNLL 2018), pages 345–355
Brussels, Belgium, October 31 - November 1, 2018. ©2018 Association for Computational Linguistics

information (Krishnan et al., 2014). Sequential labelling approaches were later proposed that take the word level inputs and make character level predictions (Shaw et al., 2008; Hellwig, 2015). The word based sequence labelling approaches were further extended to use neural architectures, especially using RNNs and its variants such as LSTMs and GRUs (Sankaran and Jawahar, 2012; Krishnan et al., 2014; Saluja et al.; Adiga et al., 2018; Mathew et al., 2016). But, OCR is putative in exhibiting few long-range dependencies (Schnober et al., 2016). Singh and Jawahar (2015) find that extending the neural models to process the text at the sentence level (or a textline) leads to improvement in the performance of the OCR systems. This was further corroborated by Saluja et al. where the authors found that using words within a context window of 5 for a given input word worked particularly well for the Post-OCR text correction in Sanskrit. In the case of providing a text line as input, we are essentially providing more context about the input in comparison to the word level models and the RNN (or LSTM) cells are powerful enough to capture the long-term dependencies. Particularly for Indian languages, this decision is beyond a question of performance. In Sanskrit, the word boundaries are often obscured due to phonetic transformations at the word boundaries known as Sandhi. Word segmentation of Sanskrit constructions is a matter of research on its own (Krishna et al., 2016a; Reddy et al., 2018). However, none of the existing systems are equipped for incorrect spellings and hence these systems may be brittle (Belinkov and Bisk, 2018) when it comes to handling spelling variations in the input. Hence, in our case, we assume an unsegmented sequence as our input and then we perform our Post-OCR text correction on the text. We hypothesise that this will improve the segmentation process and other downstream tasks for Sanskrit in a typical NLP pipeline.

Our major contributions are:

1. Contrary to what is observed in Schnober et al. (2016), an encoder-decoder model, when equipped with copying mechanism (Gu et al., 2016), can outperform a traditional sequence labelling model in a monotone sequence labelling task. Our model outperforms Schnober et al. (2016) in the Post-OCR text correction for Romanised Sanskrit task by 7.69 % in terms of CRR.

2. By making use of digitised Sanskrit texts, we generate images as synthetic training data for our models. We systematically incorporate various distortions to those images so as to emulate the settings of the original images.

3. Through a human judgement experiment, we asked the participants to correct the mistakes from a predicted output from the competing systems. We find that participants were able to correct predictions from our system more frequently and the corrections were done much faster than the CRF model by Schnober et al. (2016). We observe that predictions from our model score high on acceptability (Lau et al., 2015) than other methods as well.

2   Model Architecture

In principle, the output from any OCR which recognises Romanised Sanskrit can be used as the input to our model. Currently, there exist limited options for recognising Romanised Sanskrit texts from scanned documents. Possibly, the commercial OCR offering by Google as part of their proprietary cloud vision API and SanskritOCR[3] might be the only two viable options. SanskritOCR provides an online interface to the Tesseract OCR, an open source multilingual OCR (Smith, 2007; Smith et al., 2009; Smith, 1987), trained specifically for recognising Romanised Sanskrit. Additionally, we trained an offline version of Tesseract to recognise the graphemes in the Romanised Sanskrit alphabet. In both the models we find that many scanned images, especially similar to the one shown in Figure 1b, were not recognised by the system. We hypothesise this to be due to lack of enough font styles available in our collection, in spite of using a site with the richest collection of Sanskrit fonts[4]. This leaves the Google OCR as the only option.

Considering the fact that working with a commercial offering from Google OCR may not be an affordable option for various digitisation projects, we chose to use Tesseract with models trained for other languages written in Roman script. All the Latin or Roman scripts in the pre-trained models

---

[3] https://sri.auroville.org/projects/sanskrit-ocr/. It provides interface to tesseract and Google OCR as well.

[4] More details about the training procedure in §1 of the supplementary material

of Tesseract are trained on 400,000 text-lines spanning about 4500 fonts[5].

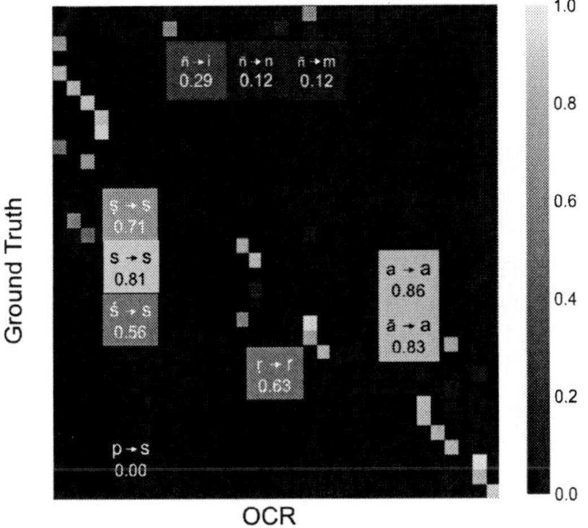

Figure 2: Heatmap of occurrences of majorly confusing character pairs between Ground Truth and OCR

Use of OCR with pre-trained models for other languages French alphabet has the highest grapheme overlap with that of the Sanskrit alphabet (37 of 50), while all other languages have one less grapheme common with Sanskrit. Hence, we arbitrarily take 5 of the languages in addition to French and perform our analysis. Table 1 shows the character recognition rate (CRR) for OCR using alphabets of different languages, when performed on a dataset of 430 scanned images (§3.1). The table also shows the count of error types made by the OCR after alignment (Jiampojamarn et al., 2007; D'hondt et al., 2016). All the languages have a near similar CRR with English and French leading the list. Based on our observations on the OCR performance, we select English for our further experiments.

Upcycling such a pre-trained model brings its own challenges. For instance, the missing 14 Sanskrit graphemes[6] in English are naturally mispredicted to other graphemes. This leads to ambiguity as the correct and the mispredicted characters now share the same target. Figure 2 shows the heat-map for such mis-predictions when we used the OCR on the set of 430 scanned images. Here, we zoom the relevant cases and show the

row-normalised proportion of predictions[7].

2.1 System Descriptions

We formalise the task as a monotone seq2seq model. We use an encoder-decoder framework that takes in a character sequence as input and the model finds embeddings at a sub-word level both at the encoder and decoder side. Here the OCR output forms input to the model. Keeping the task in mind we make two design decisions for the model. One is the use of copying mechanism (Gu et al., 2016) and other is the use of Byte Pair Encoding (BPE) (Sennrich et al., 2016) to learn a new vocabulary for the model.

CopyNet (Gu et al., 2016): Since it is possible that there will be reasonable overlap between the input and output strings, we use the copying mechanism as mentioned in CopyNet (Gu et al., 2016). The model essentially learns two probability distributions, one for generating an entry at the decoder and the other for copying the entry from the encoder. The final prediction is based on the sum of both the probabilities for the class. Given an input sequence $X = (x_1, ..., x_N)$ we define $\mathcal{X}$, for all the *unique* entries in the input sequence. We also define the vocabulary $\mathcal{V} = \{v_1, ..., v_N\}$. Let the out-of-vocabulary (OOV) words be represented with UNK. The probability of the generate mode g and copy mode c are given by

$$p(y_t, \mathsf{g}|\cdot) = \begin{cases} \frac{1}{Z}e^{\psi_g(y_t)}, & y_t \in \mathcal{V} \\ 0, & y_t \in \mathcal{X} - \mathcal{V} \\ \frac{1}{Z}e^{\psi_g(\text{UNK})} & y_t \notin \mathcal{V} \cup \mathcal{X} \end{cases}$$

$$p(y_t, \mathsf{c}|\cdot) = \begin{cases} \frac{1}{Z}\sum_{j:x_j=y_t} e^{\psi_c(x_j)}, & y_t \in \mathcal{X} \\ 0 & \text{otherwise} \end{cases}$$

where $\psi_g(\cdot)$ and $\psi_c(\cdot)$ are score functions for generate-mode (g) and copy-mode (c), respectively, and Z is the normalization term shared by the two modes, $Z = \sum_{v \in \mathcal{V} \cup \{\text{UNK}\}} e^{\psi_g(v)} + \sum_{x \in \mathcal{X}} e^{\psi_c(x)}$. The scoring function for both the modes, respectively, are

$$\psi_g(y_t = v_i) = v_i^\top W_o s_t, \quad v_i \in \mathcal{V} \cup \text{UNK}$$

$$\psi_c(y_t = x_j) = \sigma\left(\mathbf{h}_j^\top \mathbf{W}_c\right) s_t, \quad x_j \in \mathcal{X}$$

where $\mathbf{W}_c \in \mathbb{R}^{d_h \times d_s}$, and σ is a non-linear activation function (Gu et al., 2016).

---

[5] https://github.com/tesseract-ocr/tesseract/wiki/TrainingTesseract-4.00

[6] Detailed in §2 of the Supplementary Material

[7] A more detailed figure with all the cases are available in the supplementary material in §3.

Language	Bhagavad Gītā				Sahaśranāma				Combined
	CRR	Ins	Del	Sub	CRR	Ins	Del	Sub	CRR
English	84.92	23	63	1868	64.06	73	696	1596	80.08
French	84.90	21	102	1710	63.91	91	702	1670	80.04
Finnish	82.61	15	141	1902	61.31	80	730	1821	78.81
Italian	83.45	20	73	1821	62.19	84	690	1673	79.03
Irish	84.52	12	78	1810	63.81	72	709	1841	79.93
German	84.40	33	72	1821	63.79	87	723	1874	79.12

Table 1: OCR performances for different languages with overall CRR, total Insertion, Deletion and Substitution errors.

BPE (Sennrich et al., 2016) : Sanskrit is a morphologically rich language. A noun in Sanskrit can have 72 different inflections and a verb may have more than 90 inflections. Additionally, Sanskrit corpora generally express a compound rich vocabulary (Krishna et al., 2016b). Hence, in a typical Sanskrit corpus, the majority of the tokens appear less than 5 times (§3.1). These are generally considered to be rare words in a corpus (Sennrich et al., 2016). However, corpora dominated by rare words are difficult to handle for a statistical model like ours. To combat the sparsity of the data, we convert the tokens into sub-word n-grams using Byte Pair Encoding (BPE) (Sennrich et al., 2016). Methods such as wordpiece (Schuster and Nakajima, 2012) as well as Sennrich et al. (2016) are means of obtaining a new vocabulary for a given corpus. Every sequence in the corpus is then re-written as a sequence of tokens in terms of the sub-word units which forms the type in the new vocabulary so obtained. These methods essentially use a data-driven approach to maximise the language-model likelihood of the training data, given an evolving word definition (Wu et al., 2016).

We explicitly set the minimum count for a token in the new vocabulary to appear in the corpora as 30. We learn a new vocabulary of size 82 with 22 of them having a length 1 and the rest with a length 2. The IAST standardisation of the Romanised Sanskrit contains 50 graphemes in Sanskrit alphabet. About 12 of the graphemes are represented using 2 character roman character combinations. Now, in the vocabulary learnt using BPE, 7 of the graphemes were not present. Hence, we add them in addition to the 82 entries learnt as vocabulary. This makes the total vocabulary to be 89. By using the new vocabulary, it is guaranteed that there will be no Out Of Vocabulary (OOV) words in our model.

We use 3 stacked layers of LSTM at the encoder and the decoder with the same settings as in Bah-danau et al. (2015). To enable copying, we share the embeddings of the source and the target vocabulary. By eliminating OOV, we make sure that copying always happens by virtue of the evidence from the training data and not by the presence of an OOV word.

3 Experiments

3.1 Dataset

Sanskrit is a low-resource language. It is extremely scarce to obtain datasets with scanned images and the corresponding aligned texts for Romanised Sanskrit. We obtain 430 scanned images as shown in Figure 1 and manually annotate the corresponding text. We use this as our test dataset, henceforth to be referred to as *OCRTest*. For training, we synthetically generate images from digitised Sanskrit texts and use them as our training set and development set. The images for training, *OCRTrain*, were generated by synthetically adding distortions to those images to match the settings of the real scanned documents.

OCRTest contains 430 images from 1) scanned copy of Vishnu Sahaśranāma[8] and 2) scanned copy of Bhagavad Gītā, a sample of each is shown in Figure 1a and 1b. 140 out of these 430 are from Sahaśranāma and the remaining are from Bhagavad Gītā.

OCRTrain: Similar to Ul-Hasan and Breuel (2013), we synthetically generate the images, which are then fed to the OCR, to obtain our training data. We use the digitised text from Śrīmad Bhāgavatam[9] for generating the synthetic images. The text contains about 14,094 verses in total, divided into 50,971 text-lines. The dataset is divided into 80-20 split as training set and development set, respectively. The corpus contains a vocabulary of 52,882 word types. 48,249 of the word types

---

[8] http://kirtimukha.com/
[9] https://www.vedabase.com/en/sb

348

in the vocabulary appear less than or equal to 5 times, of which 32,411 appear exactly once. This is primarily due to the inflectional nature of Sanskrit. We find similar trends in the vocabulary of Rāmāyaṇa[10] and Digital Corpus of Sanskrit (Hellwig, 2010-2016) as well.

3.2 Synthetic Generation of training set

Using the text-lines from Bhāgavatam, we generate synthetic images using ImageMagick[11]. The images were generated with a quality of 60 Dots Per Inch (DPI). The number of pixels along the height for each textline was kept constant at 65 pixels. We add several distortions to the synthetically generated images so as to visually match with the same settings as that of *OCRTest*. Previously, Ul-Hasan and Breuel (2013) used the approach of synthetically generating training data for multilingual OCR solution of theirs.

Table 2 shows the different parameters, namely, gamma correction, noise addition, use of structural kernel for erosion and perspective distortion, that we apply sequentially on the images so as to distort and degrade the images (Chen et al., 2014). We use grid search for the parameter estimation for these processes, where those parameters and the range of values experimented with are provided in Table 2. Finally, we filter 7 (out of 38,400 combinations) different configurations based on the distribution of Character Recognition Rate (CRR) across the images compared with that of the *OCRTest* using KL-divergence. Among these seven configurations, four are closer to the settings for Bhagavad Gītā and the remaining three for Sahaśranāma. Figure 3 shows the two different settings (closer to each of the source textbook) for the string *"ajo durmarṣanaḥ śāstā viśrutātmā surārihā"*, along with their corresponding parameter settings and KL-Divergence. Our training set contains images from all the 7 settings for each of the textline in OCRTrain[12].

Evaluation Metrics We use three different metrics for evaluating all our models. We use Character Recognition Rate (CRR) and Word Recognition Rate (WRR) averaged over each of the sentences in the 430 lines in the test dataset (Sankaran

ajo durmarṣaṇaḥ śāstā viśrutātmā surārihā

**GM 8; E 3x3; HPD 0.45;
KL-divergence = 0.0610 with Gītā**

ajo durmarṣaṇaḥ śāstā viśrutātmā surārihā

**GM 32; E 4x4; HPD 0.5;
KL-divergence = 0.1392 with Sahaśranāma**

Figure 3: Samples of synthetically generated images. The parameter settings for the distortions are mentioned below the corresponding image.

and Jawahar, 2012). CRR is the fraction of characters recognised correctly against the total number of characters in a line, whereas WRR is the fraction of words correctly recognised against the total number of words in a line. Additionally, we use a sentence level metric, called the acceptability score. The measure indicates the extent to which a sentence is permissible or acceptable to the speakers of the language (Lau et al., 2015). From Lau et al. (2015), we use the *NormLP* formulation for the task, as it is found to have a high correlation with the human judgements in evaluating acceptability. NormLP is calculated by obtaining the likelihood of a predicted sentence as per the model, and then normalising it by the likelihood of the string as per a unigram language model trained on a corpus with gold standard sentences. A negative sign is then given to the score. The higher the score, the more acceptable the sentence is.

3.3 Baselines

Character Tagger - Sequence Labelling using BiLSTMs This is a sequence labelling model which uses BiLSTM cells and input is a character sequence (Saluja et al.). We use categorical cross-entropy as the loss function and softmax as the activation function. For dropout, we employ spatial dropout in our architecture. The model consists of 3 layers with each layer having 128 cells. Embeddings of size 100 are randomly initialised and the learnt representations are stored in a character look-up table similar to Lample et al. (2016). In addition to every phoneme in Sanskrit as a class, we add an additional class 'no change' which signifies that the character remains as is. We also experimented with a variant where the final layer is a CRF layer (Lafferty et al., 2001). We henceforth refer to both the systems as *BiLSTM* and *BiLSTM-CRF*, respectively.

Pruned CRFs (Schnober et al., 2016): They

---

[10]https://sanskritdocuments.org/sites/valmikiramayan/

[11]https://www.imagemagick.org/script/index.php

[12]Samples of all the 7 seven configurations are shown in the supplementary material in §4

Process	Parameters	Range		Step size
Gamma Correction (GM)	gamma (γ)	4	64	4
Salt & Pepper Noise (SPN) (with 50% salt and 50% pepper)	percentage of pixels corrupted	0.1%	1%	0.1
Gaussian Noise (GN) (mean = 0)	standard deviation	2.5	3.5	0.25
Erosion (E) (one iteration)	kernel size (m $\times$ m)	2	5	1
Horizontal perspective distortion (HPD)	image width by image height	0.3	1	0.05

Table 2: Image pre-processing steps and parameters

are higher order CRF models (Ishikawa, 2011) that approximate the CRF objective function using coarse-to-fine decoding. Schnober et al. (2016) adapt the sequence labeling model as a seq2seq model that can handle variable length input-output pairs. Schnober et al. (2016) show that none of the neural seq2seq models considered in their work were able to outperform the Pruned CRF with order-5. The features to the model are consecutive characters within a window of size w in either of the directions of the current position at which a prediction is made. The model is designed to handle 1-to-zero and 1-to-many matches, facilitated by the use of alignment prior to training. We consider all the three settings reported in Schnober et al. (2016) and report the results for the best setting. The order-5 model which uses 6-grams within a window of 6 performs the best. Henceforth, this model is referred to as *PCRF-seq2seq* (also referred to as PCRF interchangeably).

Encoder-Decoder Models: For the seq2seq model (Sutskever et al., 2014), we use 3 stacked layers of LSTM each at the encoder and the decoder. Each layer is of 128 dimensions and weighted cross-entropy is used as the loss. We also add residual connections among the layers in a stack (Wu et al., 2016). To further capture the entire input context for making each prediction at the output, we make use of attention (Bahdanau et al., 2015), specifically Luong's attention mechanism (Luong et al., 2015). We experiment with two variants where *EncDec+Char* uses character level embeddings and *EncDec+BPE* uses embeddings with BPE.

CopyNet+BPE: The model discussed in §2. We use CopyNet+BPE and CopyNet interchangeably throughout the paper.

3.4 Results

Table 3 shows the results for all the competing systems based on the predictions from *OCRTest*. CopyNet performs the best among the competing

systems across all the three metrics and on both the source texts. For the Gītā dataset, the models CopyNet and PCRF-Seq2Seq report similar performances. However, Sahasranāma is a noisier dataset, and we find that CopyNet outperforms all other models by a huge margin. The WRR for the system is double that of the next best system (EncDec) on this dataset.

System performances for various input lengths: From Figure 4a, it can be observed that the performance in terms of CRR for CopyNet and PCRF is robust across all the lengths on strings from Gītā and never goes below 90%. For Sahasranāma, as shown in Figure 4b, CopyNet outperforms PCRF across inputs of all the lengths except for one setting. But, in the case of WRR, CopyNet is the best performing model across all the lengths as shown in Figure 4d.

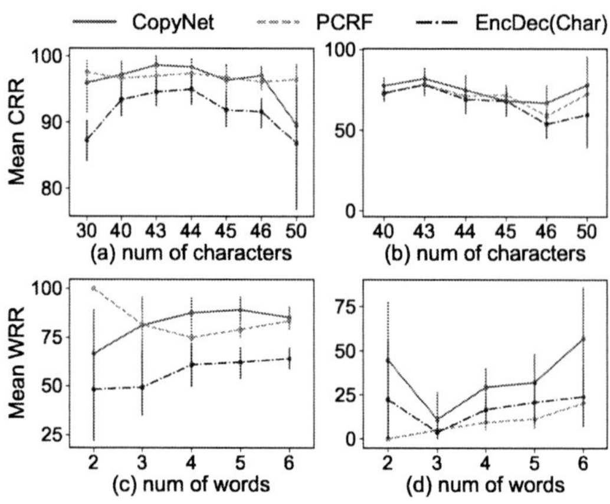

Figure 4: (a) and (b) show CRR for Gītā and Sahasranāma respectively, for the competing systems. (c) and (d) shows WRR for Gītā and Sahasranāma, respectively. All the entries with insufficient data-points were merged to the nearest smaller number.

Error type analysis In Table 5, we analyse the reduction in specific error types for PCRF

Model	Bhagavad Gītā			Sahaśranāma			Combined		
	CRR	WRR	Norm LP	CRR	WRR	Norm LP	CRR	WRR	Norm LP
OCR	84.81%	64.40%	–	35.76%	0.65%	–	77.88%	23.84%	–
BiLSTM	93.79%	68.60%	-0.553	61.31%	7.28%	-1.292	85.23%	45.60%	-0.852
BiLSTM-CRF	94.68%	68.60%	-0.548	65.31%	7.28%	-1.281	85.82%	45.60%	-0.847
PCRF-seq2seq	**96.87%**	70.56%	-0.227	81.77%	9.34%	-1.216	87.94%	57.17%	-0.803
EncDec+Char	91.48%	68.00%	-0.542	63.63%	15.74%	-1.321	82.51%	47.37%	-0.865
EncDec+BPE	90.92%	68.00%	-0.496	61.53%	15.74%	-1.384	83.14%	45.98%	-0.842
CopyNet+BPE	**97.01%**	**75.21%**	**-0.165**	**87.01%**	**33.47%**	**-0.856**	**89.65%**	**68.71%**	**-0.551**

Table 3: Performance in terms of CRR, WRR and Norm LP (acceptability) for all the competing models

	CRR	WRR
Bhagavad Gītā	96.80%	71.23%
Sahaśranāma	82.81%	26.01%
Combined	87.88%	60.91%

Table 4: Performance in terms of CRR, WRR for Google OCR

Model	Bhagavad Gītā			Sahaśranāma			System errors		
	Ins	Del	Sub	Ins	Del	Sub	Ins	Del	Sub
OCR	23	63	1868	73	696	1596	–	–	–
PCRF	22	57	641	72	663	932	0	73	209
CopyNet	22	**45**	629	72	**576**	561	10	5	52

Table 5: Insertion, Deletion and Substitution errors for OCR, PCRF and CopyNet modes for both the datasets. The system errors are extra errors added by the respective systems.

and CopyNet after the alignment of the predicted string with that of the ground truth in terms of insertion, deletion and substitution. We also report the system induced errors, where a correct component at the input (OCR output) is mispredicted to a wrong output by the model. CopyNet outperforms PCRF in correcting the errors and it also introduces lesser number of errors of its own. Both CopyNet and PCRF (Schnober et al., 2016) are seq2seq models and can handle varying length input and output. Both the systems perform well in handling substitution errors, the type which dominated the strings in *OCRTest*, though neither of the systems was able to correct the insertion errors. Insertion can be seen as a special case of 1-to-many insertion matches, which both systems are ideally capable of handling. We see that for Sahaśranāma, CopyNet corrects about 17.24 % of the deletion errors as against <5% of the deletion errors corrected by PCRF.

Since there exist 14 graphemes in Sanskrit alphabet which are not present in the English alphabet, all 14 of them get substituted to a different grapheme by the OCR. While most of them get substituted to an orthographically similar character such as ā → a and ḥ → h, we find that ñ → i does not fit the scheme, as shown in Figure 2. In the majority of the cases, CopyNet predicts them to the correct grapheme. But PCRF still fails to correct the OCR induced confusion for ñ → i in the majority of the instances. Additionally, we find that PCRF introduces its own errors, for instance it often mispredicts p → s. Figure 5 shows the over-

all variations in both the systems as compared to Figure 2 for OCR induced errors.

Copy or generate? For the 14 graphemes, missing at the encoder (input) but present at the decoder side during training, those predictions have to happen with high values of generate probability in general. We find that not only the average generate probability for such instances is high but also the copy probability is extremely low. For the remaining cases, we find that both generate and copy probability are higher. But it needs to be noted that the prediction is made generally by summing of both the distributions and the distributions are not complementary to each other. A similar trend can be observed in Figure 6 as well. For example in the case of a → ā, only the generate probability is high. But, for a → a, both the copy and generate probability scores are high.

Effect of BPE and alphabet in the vocabulary We further investigate the effect of our vocabulary which is the union of the alphabet in Romanised Sanskrit and what is learnt using BPE. We train the model with only the alphabet as vocabulary and find the CRR and WRR for the combined test sentences to be 86.1% and 66.09%, respectively. When using the original BPE vocabulary, we find that there is a slight increase in the performance than the current vocabulary with a CRR and WRR of 89.53% and 68.11%, respectively[13]. We also find that the current setting performs better than

---

[13]Please refer to §5 of the Supplementary material for the performance table

copy	0.89	0.34			copy	0.9	0.12	0.19
gen	0.87	0.92			gen	0.87	0.97	0.98
	a to a	a to ā				s to s	s to ṣ	s to ś

0.4	0.5	0.6	0.7	0.8	0.9		0.15	0.30	0.45	0.60	0.75	0.90
		(a)							(b)			

Figure 7: mean copy and generate scores for different predictions from (a) 'a' and (b) 's'.

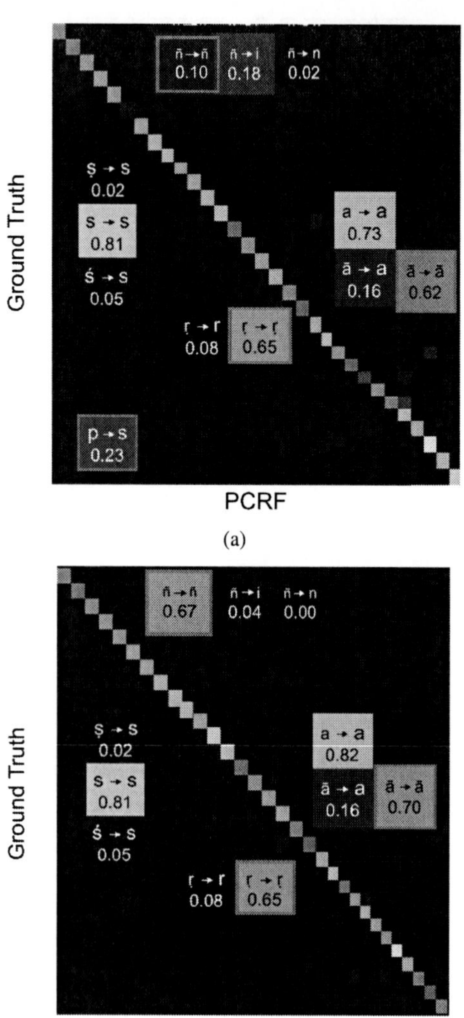

Figure 5: Heatmap for occurrences of majorly confusing character pairs between Ground Truth and predictions of (a) PCRF model (b) CopyNet model

copy	0.14	0.11	0.12	0.2	0.15	0.18
gen	0.79	0.56	0.6	0.72	0.59	0.72
	ā	ū	ṃ	ṇ	ñ	ī

0.15	0.30	0.45	0.60	0.75

Figure 6: Heatmap of mean copy score (copy) and mean generate score (gen), respectively for 6 (of 14) graphemes not present in the English alphabet.

a model that takes word level input. The word level model shows a drop in the performance with a CRR and WRR of 86.42% and 66.54%, respectively.

Performance comparison to Google OCR: Google OCR is probably the only available OCR that can handle Romanised Sanskrit. We could not find the architecture of the OCR or whether the service employs post-OCR text correction. We empirically compare the performance of Google OCR on *OCRTest* with our model. Table 4 shows the results for Google OCR. Overall we find that CopyNet outperforms Google OCR across all the metrics. We find that Google OCR reports a similar CRR for Gītā with that of ours, but still reports a lower WRR than ours. The system performs better than PCRF in all the metrics other than CRR for Gītā.

Image quality: Our training set was generated with a quality of 60 DPI for the images. We generate images corresponding to strings in *OCRTrain* with DPI of 50 to 300 in step sizes of 50 for a sample of 500 images. We use noise settings as shown in Figure 3. The OCR output of the said strings remained as is with that of the one generated with a DPI of 60. This experiment can be seen as a proxy in evaluating the robustness of the OCR to various scanning qualities of input. Our choice of DPI as 60 was based on the lowest setting we observed in digitisation attempts in Sanskrit texts.

Effect of adding distortions to the synthetically generated images: Table 3 shows the system performance after training our model on data generated as per the procedure mentioned in Section 3.2. Here, we make an implicit assumption that we can have access to a sample of textline images annotated with the corresponding text from the manuscript for which the Post-OCR text correction needs to be performed. This also mandates retraining the model for every new manuscript. We attempted for a more generalised version of our model, by using training data where the image generation settings are not inspired from the target manuscript for which the task needs to be performed. Using the settings from (Chen et al., 2014) for inducing noise, we generated 10 random noise configurations. Here the step sizes were fixed at values such that each parameter, except erosion (E), can assume 5 values each uniformly spread across the corresponding ranges considered. From a total of 2500 ($5{\times}5{\times}5{\times}5{\times}4$) configuration options, 10 random settings were chosen. Every textline was generated with each of the 10 different settings. The resulting model using CopyNet produced a CRR of 89.02% (96.99% for Gītā and 85.62% for Sahaśranāma) on the test set, which is close to the reported CRR of 89.65 in Table 3. The noise ranges chosen are used directly from (Chen et al., 2014) and are not influenced by the test data in hand.

We also experimented with a setting where no noise was added to the synthetically generated images and the images were fed to the OCR. We obtained a CRR of 80.12% from OCR, where the errors arose mostly from the missing graphemes in the alphabet getting mispredicted to a different grapheme. CopyNet after training with the text so generated reported a CRR of 86.81% (96.01% for Gītā, 75.78% for Sahaśranāma) on the test data.

Human judgement survey: In this survey[14], we evaluate how often a human can recognise the correct construction by viewing only the prediction from one of the systems. We also evaluate how fast a human can correct them. We selected 15 constructions from Sahaśranāma, and obtained the system outputs from the OCR, CopyNet and PCRF for each of these. The average length of a sentence is 41.73 characters, all ranging between 23 and 47 characters. A respondent is shown a system prediction (system identity anonymised) and is asked to type the corrected string without referring to any sources. A respondent gets 15 different strings altogether, 5 each from each of the three systems. We consider responses from 9 participants where all of them at least have an undergraduate degree in Sanskrit linguistics. Altogether from 3 sets of questionnaires, we have 45 strings (3 outputs for a given string). Every string obtained 3 impressions. We find that a participant on an average could identify 4.44 sentences out of 5 from the CopyNet, while it was only 3.56 for PCRF and 3.11 for the OCR output. The average time taken to complete the correction of a string was 81.4 seconds, 106.6 seconds and 127.6 seconds for CopyNet, PCRF and OCR, respectively.

---

¹⁴More details at §6 of Supplementary material

4 Conclusion

In this work, we proposed an OCR based solution for digitising Romanised Sanskrit. Our work acts as a Post-OCR text correction approach and is devoid of any OCR-specific feature engineering. We find that the use of copying mechanism in encoder-decoder performs significantly better than other seq2seq models for the task. Our model outperforms the commercially available Google OCR on the Sahaśranāma texts. From our experiments, we find that CopyNet performs stably even for OCR outputs with a CRR as low as 36%. Our immediate research direction will be to rectify insertion errors which currently are not properly handled. Also, there are 135 languages which directly share the Roman alphabet but only 35 of them have OCR system available. Our approach can be easily extended to provide a post-processed OCR for those languages.

Acknowledgements

We are grateful to Amba Kulkarni, Arnab Bhattacharya, Ganesh Ramakrishnan, Rohit Saluja, Devaraj Adiga and Hrishikesh Terdalkar for helpful comments and discussions related to Indic OCRs. We would like to thank Madhusoodan Pai, Sanjeev Panchal, Ganesh Iyer and his students for helping us with the human judgement survey. We thank the anonymous reviewers for their constructive and helpful comments, which greatly improved the paper.

References

Devaraj Adiga, Rohit Saluja, Vaibhav Agrawal, Ganesh Ramakrishnan, Parag Chaudhuri, K Ramasubramaniam, and Malhar Kulkarni. 2018. Improving the learnability of classifiers for sanskrit ocr corrections. In *The 17th World Sanskrit Conference, Vancouver, Canada.* IASS.

Sandhya Arora, Debotosh Bhattacharjee, Mita Nasipuri, Dipak Kumar Basu, and Mahantapas Kundu. 2010. Recognition of non-compound handwritten devnagari characters using a combination of mlp and minimum edit distance. *International Journal of Industrial Electronics and Electrical Engineering.*

Dzmitry Bahdanau, KyungHyun Cho, and Yoshua Bengio. 2015. Neural machine translation by jointly learning to align and translate. In *Proceedings of the Third International Conference on Learning Representation (ICLR)*, San Diego, CA, USA.

Yonatan Belinkov and Yonatan Bisk. 2018. Synthetic and natural noise both break neural machine translation. In *The Sixth International Conference on Learning Representations (ICLR)*, New Orleans, USA.

Ajay S Bhaskarabhatla, Sriganesh Madhvanath, MNSSKP Kumar, A Balasubramanian, and CV Jawahar. 2004. Representation and annotation of online handwritten data. In *Ninth International Workshop on Frontiers in Handwriting Recognition*, pages 136–141, Tokyo, Japan. IEEE.

BB Chaudhuri and U Pal. 1997. An ocr system to read two indian language scripts: Bangla and devnagari (hindi). In *Proceedings of the Fourth International Conference on Document Analysis and Recognition*, volume 2, pages 1011–1015, Ulm, Germany. IEEE.

Guang Chen, Jianchao Yang, Hailin Jin, Jonathan Brandt, Eli Shechtman, Aseem Agarwala, and Tony X Han. 2014. Large-scale visual font recognition. In *Proceedings of the IEEE Conference on Computer Vision and Pattern Recognition*, pages 3598–3605.

Eva D'hondt, Cyril Grouin, and Brigitte Grau. 2016. Low-resource ocr error detection and correction in french clinical texts. In *Proceedings of the Seventh International Workshop on Health Text Mining and Information Analysis*, pages 61–68, Auxtin, TX. Association for Computational Linguistics.

VK Govindan and AP Shivaprasad. 1990. Character recognitiona review. *Pattern recognition*, 23(7):671–683.

Venu Govindaraju and Srirangaraj Setlur. 2009. *Guide to OCR for Indic Scripts*. Springer.

Jiatao Gu, Zhengdong Lu, Hang Li, and Victor O.K. Li. 2016. Incorporating copying mechanism in sequence-to-sequence learning. In *Proceedings of the 54th Annual Meeting of the Association for Computational Linguistics (Volume 1: Long Papers)*, pages 1631–1640, Berlin, Germany. Association for Computational Linguistics.

Oliver Hellwig. 2010-2016. *DCS - The Digital Corpus of Sanskrit*. Berlin.

Oliver Hellwig. 2015. ind. senz–ocr software for hindi, marathi, tamil, and sanskrit.

Hiroshi Ishikawa. 2011. Transformation of general binary mrf minimization to the first-order case. *IEEE transactions on pattern analysis and machine intelligence*, 33(6):1234–1249.

Sittichai Jiampojamarn, Grzegorz Kondrak, and Tarek Sherif. 2007. Applying many-to-many alignments and hidden markov models to letter-to-phoneme conversion. In *Human Language Technologies 2007: The Conference of the North American Chapter of the Association for Computational Linguistics;*

Proceedings of the Main Conference, pages 372–379, Rochester, New York. Association for Computational Linguistics.

Amrith Krishna, Bishal Santra, Pavankumar Satuluri, Sasi Prasanth Bandaru, Bhumi Faldu, Yajuvendra Singh, and Pawan Goyal. 2016a. Word segmentation in sanskrit using path constrained random walks. In *Proceedings of COLING 2016, the 26th International Conference on Computational Linguistics: Technical Papers*, pages 494–504, Osaka, Japan. The COLING 2016 Organizing Committee.

Amrith Krishna, Pavankumar Satuluri, Shubham Sharma, Apurv Kumar, and Pawan Goyal. 2016b. Compound type identification in sanskrit: What roles do the corpus and grammar play? In *Proceedings of the 6th Workshop on South and Southeast Asian Natural Language Processing (WS-SANLP2016)*, pages 1–10, Osaka, Japan. The COLING 2016 Organizing Committee.

Praveen Krishnan, Naveen Sankaran, Ajeet Kumar Singh, and CV Jawahar. 2014. Towards a robust ocr system for indic scripts. In *Eleventh IAPR International Workshop on Document Analysis Systems (DAS)*, pages 141–145, Tours, France. IEEE.

Anand Kumar and CV Jawahar. 2007. Content-level annotation of large collection of printed document images. In *Ninth International Conference on Document Analysis and Recognition (ICDAR)*, volume 2, pages 799–803, Parana, Brazil. IEEE.

John Lafferty, Andrew McCallum, and Fernando CN Pereira. 2001. Conditional random fields: Probabilistic models for segmenting and labeling sequence data. In *Proceedings of the 18th International Conference on Machine Learning (ICML)*, volume 951, pages 282–289, Williamstown, MA, USA.

Guillaume Lample, Miguel Ballesteros, Sandeep Subramanian, Kazuya Kawakami, and Chris Dyer. 2016. Neural architectures for named entity recognition. In *Proceedings of the 2016 Conference of the North American Chapter of the Association for Computational Linguistics: Human Language Technologies*, pages 260–270, San Diego, California. Association for Computational Linguistics.

Jey Han Lau, Alexander Clark, and Shalom Lappin. 2015. Unsupervised prediction of acceptability judgements. In *Proceedings of the 53rd Annual Meeting of the Association for Computational Linguistics and the 7th International Joint Conference on Natural Language Processing (Volume 1: Long Papers)*, pages 1618–1628, Beijing, China. Association for Computational Linguistics.

Thang Luong, Hieu Pham, and Christopher D. Manning. 2015. Effective approaches to attention-based neural machine translation. In *Proceedings of the*

2015 Conference on Empirical Methods in Natural Language Processing*, pages 1412–1421, Lisbon, Portugal. Association for Computational Linguistics.

Minesh Mathew, Ajeet Kumar Singh, and CV Jawahar. 2016. Multilingual ocr for indic scripts. In *Document Analysis Systems (DAS), 2016 12th IAPR Workshop on*, pages 186–191. IEEE.

Monier Monier-Williams. 1899. A sanskrit-english dictionary.

Umapada Pal, Tetsushi Wakabayashi, and Fumitaka Kimura. 2009. Comparative study of devnagari handwritten character recognition using different feature and classifiers. In *Tenth International Conference on Document Analysis and Recognition (ICDAR)*, pages 1111–1115. IEEE.

Vikas Reddy, Amrith Krishna, Vishnu Dutt Sharma, Prateek Gupta, MR Vineeth, and Pawan Goyal. 2018. Building a word segmenter for sanskrit overnight. In *Eleventh Language Resources and Evaluation Conference (LREC)*, Miyazaki, Japan.

Rohit Saluja, Devaraj Adiga, Parag Chaudhuri, Ganesh Ramakrishnan, and Mark Carman. Error detection and corrections in indic ocr using lstms. In *14th IAPR International Conference on Document Analysis and Recognition (ICDAR)*.

Naveen Sankaran and CV Jawahar. 2012. Recognition of printed devanagari text using blstm neural network. In *21st International Conference on Pattern Recognition (ICPR)*, pages 322–325, Tsukuba Science City, JAPAN. IEEE.

Carsten Schnober, Steffen Eger, Erik-Lân Do Dinh, and Iryna Gurevych. 2016. Still not there? comparing traditional sequence-to-sequence models to encoder-decoder neural networks on monotone string translation tasks. In *Proceedings of COLING 2016, the 26th International Conference on Computational Linguistics: Technical Papers*, pages 1703–1714.

M. Schuster and K. Nakajima. 2012. Japanese and korean voice search. In *IEEE International Conference on Acoustics, Speech and Signal Processing (ICASSP)*, pages 5149–5152, Kyoto, Japan.

Rico Sennrich, Barry Haddow, and Alexandra Birch. 2016. Neural machine translation of rare words with subword units. In *Proceedings of the 54th Annual Meeting of the Association for Computational Linguistics (Volume 1: Long Papers)*, pages 1715–1725, Berlin, Germany. Association for Computational Linguistics.

Bikash Shaw, Swapan Kumar Parui, and Malayappan Shridhar. 2008. Offline handwritten devanagari word recognition: A holistic approach based on directional chain code feature and hmm. In *International Conference on Information Technology (ICIT)*, pages 203–208, Bhubaneswar, India. IEEE.

Ajeet Kumar Singh and CV Jawahar. 2015. Can rnns reliably separate script and language at word and line level? In *13th International Conference on Document Analysis and Recognition (ICDAR)*, pages 976–980. IEEE.

Ray Smith. 2007. An overview of the tesseract ocr engine. In *Ninth International Conference on Document Analysis and Recognition, (ICDAR)*, volume 2, pages 629–633. IEEE.

Ray Smith, Daria Antonova, and Dar-Shyang Lee. 2009. Adapting the tesseract open source ocr engine for multilingual ocr. In *Proceedings of the International Workshop on Multilingual OCR*, page 1. ACM.

Raymond W Smith. 1987. *The Extraction and Recognition of Text from Multimedia Document Images*. Ph.D. thesis, University of Bristol.

Ilya Sutskever, Oriol Vinyals, and Quoc V Le. 2014. Sequence to sequence learning with neural networks. In *Advances in neural information processing systems*, pages 3104–3112.

Adnan Ul-Hasan and Thomas M. Breuel. 2013. Can we build language-independent ocr using lstm networks? In *Proceedings of the 4th International Workshop on Multilingual OCR*, MOCR '13, pages 9:1–9:5, New York, NY, USA. ACM.

Yonghui Wu, Mike Schuster, Zhifeng Chen, Quoc V. Le, Mohammad Norouzi, Wolfgang Macherey, Maxim Krikun, Yuan Cao, Qin Gao, Klaus Macherey, Jeff Klingner, Apurva Shah, Melvin Johnson, Xiaobing Liu, ukasz Kaiser, Stephan Gouws, Yoshikiyo Kato, Taku Kudo, Hideto Kazawa, Keith Stevens, George Kurian, Nishant Patil, Wei Wang, Cliff Young, Jason Smith, Jason Riesa, Alex Rudnick, Oriol Vinyals, Greg Corrado, Macduff Hughes, and Jeffrey Dean. 2016. Google's neural machine translation system: Bridging the gap between human and machine translation. *CoRR*, abs/1609.08144.

Weakly-supervised Neural Semantic Parsing with a Generative Ranker

Jianpeng Cheng and **Mirella Lapata**
Institute for Language, Cognition and Computation
School of Informatics, University of Edinburgh
10 Crichton Street, Edinburgh EH8 9AB
jianpeng.cheng@ed.ac.uk   mlap@inf.ed.ac.uk

Abstract

Weakly-supervised semantic parsers are trained on utterance-denotation pairs, treating logical forms as latent. The task is challenging due to the large search space and spuriousness of logical forms. In this paper we introduce a neural parser-ranker system for weakly-supervised semantic parsing. The parser generates candidate tree-structured logical forms from utterances using clues of denotations. These candidates are then ranked based on two criterion: their likelihood of executing to the correct denotation, and their agreement with the utterance semantics. We present a scheduled training procedure to balance the contribution of the two objectives. Furthermore, we propose to use a neurally encoded lexicon to inject prior domain knowledge to the model. Experiments on three Freebase datasets demonstrate the effectiveness of our semantic parser, achieving results within the state-of-the-art range.

1 Introduction

Semantic parsing is the task of converting natural language utterances into machine-understandable meaning representations or logical forms. The task has attracted much attention in the literature due to a wide range of applications ranging from question answering (Kwiatkowski et al., 2011; Liang et al., 2011) to relation extraction (Krishnamurthy and Mitchell, 2012), goal-oriented dialog (Wen et al., 2015), and instruction understanding (Chen and Mooney, 2011; Matuszek et al., 2012; Artzi and Zettlemoyer, 2013).

In a typical semantic parsing scenario, a logical form is executed against a knowledge base to produce an outcome (e.g., an answer) known as denotation. Conventional semantic parsers are trained on collections of utterances paired with annotated logical forms (Zelle and Mooney, 1996; Zettlemoyer and Collins, 2005; Wong and Mooney,

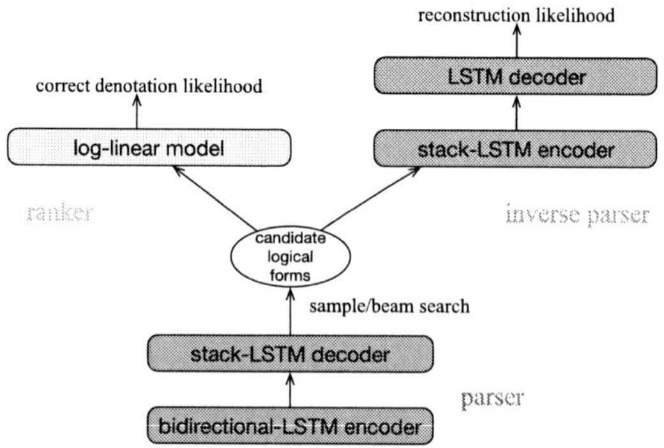

Figure 1: Overview of the weakly-supervised neural semantic parsing system.

2006; Kwiatkowksi et al., 2010). However, the labeling of logical forms is labor-intensive and challenging to elicit at a large scale. As a result, alternative forms of supervision have been proposed to alleviate the annotation bottleneck faced by semantic parsing systems. One direction is to train a semantic parser in a weakly-supervised setting based on utterance-denotation pairs (Clarke et al., 2010; Kwiatkowski et al., 2013; Krishnamurthy and Mitchell, 2012; Cai and Yates, 2013), since such data are relatively easy to obtain via crowd-sourcing (Berant et al., 2013a).

However, the unavailability of logical forms in the weakly-supervised setting, renders model training more difficult. A fundamental challenge in learning semantic parsers from denotations is finding *consistent* logical forms, i.e., those which execute to the correct denotation. This search space can be very large, growing exponentially as compositionality increases. Moreover, consistent logical forms unavoidably introduce a certain degree of *spuriousness* — some of them will accidentally execute to the correct denotation without reflecting the meaning of the utterance. These spurious logical forms are misleading supervision sig-

Proceedings of the 22nd Conference on Computational Natural Language Learning (CoNLL 2018), pages 356–367
Brussels, Belgium, October 31 - November 1, 2018. ©2018 Association for Computational Linguistics

nals for the semantic parser.

In this work we introduce a weakly-supervised neural semantic parsing system which aims to handle both challenges. Our system, shown in Figure 1, mainly consists of a sequence-to-tree parser which generates candidate logical forms for a given utterance. These logical forms are subsequently ranked by two components: a log-linear model scores the likelihood of each logical form executing to the correct denotation, and an inverse neural parser measures the degree to which the logical form represents the meaning of the utterance. We present a scheduled training scheme which balances the contribution of the two components and objectives. To further boost performance, we propose to neurally encode a lexicon, as a means of injecting prior domain knowledge to the neural parameters.

We evaluate our system on three Freebase datasets which consist of utterance denotation pairs: WEBQUESTIONS (Berant et al., 2013a), GRAPHQUESTIONS (Su et al., 2016), and SPADES (Bisk et al., 2016). Experimental results across datasets show that our weakly-supervised semantic parser achieves state-of-the-art performance.

2 The Neural Parser-Ranker

Conventional weakly-supervised semantic parsers (Liang, 2016) consist of two major components: a parser, which is chart-based and non-parameterized, recursively builds derivations for each utterance span using dynamic programming. A learner, which is a log-linear model, defines features useful for scoring and ranking the set of candidate derivations, based on the correctness of execution results. As mentioned in Liang (2016), the chart-based parser brings a disadvantage since it does not support incremental contextual interpretation. The dynamic programming algorithm requires that features of a span are defined over sub-derivations in that span.

In contrast to a chart-based parser, a parameterized neural semantic parser decodes logical forms with global utterance features. However, training a weakly-supervised neural parser is challenging since there is no access to gold-standard logical forms for backpropagation. Besides, it should be noted that a neural decoder is conditionally generative: decoding is performed greedily conditioned on the utterance and the generation history—it makes no use of global logical form features. In this section, we introduce a parser-ranker framework which combines the best of conventional and neural approaches in the context of weakly-supervised semantic parsing.

2.1 Parser

Our work follows Cheng et al. (2017b, 2018) in using LISP-style functional queries as the logical formulation. Advantageously, functional queries are recursive, tree-structured and can naturally encode logical form derivations (i.e., functions and their application order). For example, the utterance "*who is obama's eldest daughter*" is simply represented with the function-argument structure `argmax(daughterOf(Obama), ageOf)`. Table 1 displays the functions we use in this work; a more detailed specifications can be found in the appendix.

To generate logical forms, our system adopts a variant of the neural sequence-to-tree model proposed in Cheng et al. (2017b). During generation, the prediction space is restricted by the grammar of the logical language (e.g., the type and the number of arguments required by a function) in order to ensure that output logical forms are well-formed and executable. The parser consists of a bidirectional LSTM (Hochreiter and Schmidhuber, 1997) encoder and a stack-LSTM (Dyer et al., 2015) decoder, introduced as follows.

Bidirectional-LSTM Encoder The bidirectional LSTM encodes a variable-length utterance $x = (x_1, \cdots, x_n)$ into a list of token representations $[h_1, \cdots, h_n]$, where each representation is the concatenation of the corresponding forward and backward LSTM states.

Stack-LSTM Decoder After the utterance is encoded, the logical form is generated with a stack-LSTM decoder. The output of the decoder consists of functions which generate the logical form as a derivation tree in depth-first order. There are three classes of functions:

- *Class-1* functions generate non-terminal tree nodes. In our formulation, non-terminal nodes include language-dependent functions such as `count` and `argmax`, as described in the first four rows of Table 1. A special non-terminal node is the relation placeholder `relation`.

- *Class-2* functions generate terminal tree nodes. In our formulation, terminal nodes in-

Function	Utility	Example
`findAll`	returns the entity set of a given type	*find all mountains* `findAll(mountain)`

`filter=`
`filter<`
`filter>`
	filters an entity set with constraints	*all mountains in Europe*
		`filter=(findAll(mountain),`
		`mountain_location, Europe)`

`count`	computes the cardinality of an entity set	*how many mountains are there* `count(findAll(mountain))`

`argmax`
`argmin`
	finds the subset of an entity set whose certain property is maximum (or minimum)	*the highest mountain*
		`argmax(findAll(mountain),`
		`mountain_altitude)`

`relation`	denotes a KB relation; in generation, `relation` acts as placeholder for all relations	*height of mountain* `mountain_altitude`
`entity`	denotes a KB entity; in generation, `entity` acts as placeholder for all entities	*Himalaya* `Himalaya`

Table 1: List of functions supported by our functional query language, their utility, and examples.

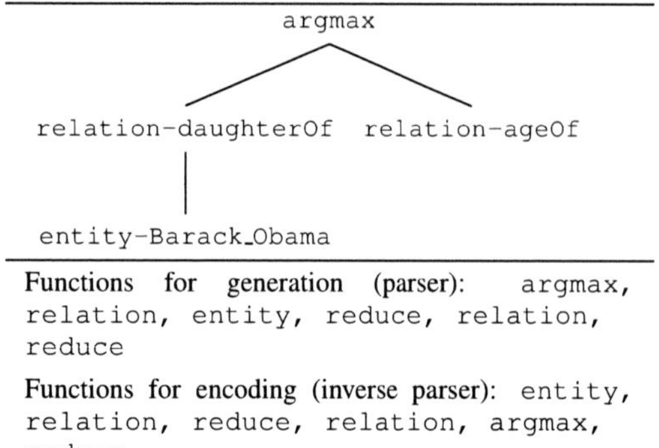

Functions for generation (parser): `argmax, relation, entity, reduce, relation, reduce`

Functions for encoding (inverse parser): `entity, relation, reduce, relation, argmax, reduce`

Figure 2: Derivation tree for the utterance "*who is obama's eldest daughter*" (top), and corresponding functions for generation and encoding (bottom).

clude the relation placeholder `relation` and the entity placeholder `entity`.

- *Class-3* function `reduce` completes a subtree. Since generation is performed in depth-first order, the parser needs to identify when the generation of a subtree completes, i.e., when a function has seen all its required arguments.

The functions used to generate the example logical form `argmax(daughterOf(Obama), ageOf)` are shown in Figure 2. The stack-LSTM makes two types of updates based on the functions it predicts:

- *Update-1*: when a *Class-1* or *Class-2* function is called, a non-terminal or terminal token l_t will be generated, At this point, the stack-LSTM state, denoted by g_t, is updated from its older state g_{t-1} as in an ordinary LSTM:

$$g_t = \text{LSTM}(l_t, g_{t-1}) \quad (1)$$

The new state is additionally pushed onto the stack marking whether it corresponds to a non-terminal or terminal.

- *Update-2*: when the `reduce` function is called (*Class-3*), the states of the stack-LSTM are recursively popped from the stack until a non-terminal is encountered. This non-terminal state is popped as well, after which the stack-LSTM reaches an intermediate state denoted by $g_{t-1:t}$. At this point, we compute the representation of the completed subtree z_t as:

$$z_t = W_z \cdot [p_z : c_z] \quad (2)$$

where p_z denotes the parent (non-terminal) embedding of the subtree, and c_z denotes the average embedding of the children (terminals or already-completed subtrees). W_z is the weight matrix. Finally, z_t serves as input for updating $g_{t-1:t}$ to g_t:

$$g_t = \text{LSTM}(z_t, g_{t-1:t}) \quad (3)$$

Prediction At each time step of the decoding, the parser first predicts a subsequent function f_{t+1} conditioned on the decoder state g_t and the encoder states $h_1 \cdots h_n$. We apply standard soft attention (Bahdanau et al., 2015) between g_t and the encoder states $h_1 \cdots h_n$ to compute a feature representation $\bar{h}_t$:

$$u_t^i = V \tanh(W_h h_i + W_g g_t) \quad (4)$$

$$a_t^i = \text{softmax}(u_t^i) \quad (5)$$

$$\bar{h}_t = \sum_{i=1}^{n} a_t^i h_i \quad (6)$$

where V, W_h, and W_g are all weight parameters. The prediction of the function f_{t+1} is computed with a softmax classifier, which takes the concatenated features $\bar{h}_t$ and g_t as input:

$$f_{t+1} \sim \text{softmax}(W_y \tanh(W_f[\bar{h}_t, g_t])) \quad (7)$$

where W_y and W_f are weight parameters. When f_{t+1} is a language-dependent function (first four rows in Table 1, e.g., `argmax`), it is directly used as a non-terminal token l_{t+1} to construct the logical form. However, when f_{t+1} is a `relation` or `entity` placeholder, we further predict the specific relation or entity l_{t+1} with another set of neural parameters:

$$l_{t+1} \sim \text{softmax}(W_{y'} \tanh(W_l[\bar{h}_t, g_t])) \quad (8)$$

where $W_{y'}$ and $W_{l'}$ are weight matrices.

Note that in the weakly supervised setting, the parser decodes a list of candidate logical forms Y with beam search, instead of outputting the most likely logical form y. During training, candidate logical forms are executed against a knowledge base to find those which are consistent (denoted by $Y_c(x)$) and lead to the correct denotation. Then, the parser is trained to maximize the total log likelihood of these consistent logical forms:

$$\sum_{y \in Y_c(x)} \log p(y|x) = \\ \sum_{y \in Y_c(x)} \log p(f_1, \cdots, f_k, l_1, \cdots, l_o|x) \quad (9)$$

where k denotes the number of functions used to generate the logical form, and o (smaller than k) denotes the number of tree nodes in the logical form.

2.2 Ranker

It is impractical to rely solely on a neural decoder to find the most likely logical form at run time in the weakly-supervised setting. One reason is that although the decoder utilizes global utterance features for generation, it cannot leverage global features of the logical form since a logical form is conditionally generated following a specific tree-traversal order. To this end, we follow previous work (Berant et al., 2013b) and introduce a ranker to the system. The role of the ranker is to score the candidate logical forms generated by the parser; at test time, the logical form receiving the highest score will be used for execution. The ranker

is a discriminative log-linear model over logical form y given utterance x:

$$\log_\theta p(y|x) = \frac{\exp(\phi(x, y)^T \theta)}{\sum_{y' \in Y(x)} \exp(\phi(x, y')^T \theta)} \quad (10)$$

where $Y(x)$ is the set of candidate logical forms; ϕ is the feature function that maps an utterance-logical form pair onto a feature vector; and θ denotes the weight parameters of the model.

Since the training data consists only of utterance-denotation pairs, the ranker is trained to maximize the log-likelihood of the correct answer z by treating logical forms as a latent variable:

$$\log p(z|x) = \log \sum_{y \in Y_c(x)} p(y|x)p(z|x, y) \quad (11)$$

where $Y_c(x)$ denotes the subset of candidate logical forms which execute to the correct answer; and $p(z|x, y)$ equates to 1 in this case.

Training of the neural parser-ranker system involves the following steps. Given an input utterance, the parser first generates a list of candidate logical forms via beam search. The logical forms are then executed and those which yield the correct denotation are marked as consistent. The parser is trained to optimize the total likelihood of consistent logical forms (Equation (9)), while the ranker is trained to optimize the marginal likelihood of denotations (Equation (11)). The search space can be further reduced by performing entity linking which restricts the number of logical forms to those containing only a small set of entities.

3 Handling Spurious Logical Forms

The neural parser-ranker system relies on beam search to find consistent logical forms that execute to the correct answer. These logical forms are then used as surrogate annotations and provide supervision to update the parser's parameters. However, some of these logical forms will be misleading training signals for the neural semantic parser on account of being spurious: they coincidentally execute to the correct answer without matching the utterance semantics.

In this section we propose a method of removing spurious logical forms by validating how well they match the utterance meaning. The intuition is that a meaning-preserving logical form should be able to reconstruct the original utterance with high likelihood. However, since spurious logical forms are not annotated either, a direct maximum likelihood solution does not exist. To this end, we propose a generative model for measuring the *reconstruction* likelihood.

The model assumes utterance x is generated from the corresponding logical form y, and only the utterance is observable. The objective is therefore to maximize the log marginal likelihood of x:

$$\log p(x) = \log \sum_y p(x, y) \qquad (12)$$

We adopt neural variational inference (Mnih and Gregor, 2014) to solve the above objective, which is equivalent to maximizing an evidence lower bound:

$$\log p(x) = \log \frac{q(y|x)p(x|y)p(y)}{q(y|x)} \qquad (13)$$

$$\geq \mathbb{E}_{q(y|x)} \log p(x|y) + \mathbb{E}_{q(y|x)} \log \frac{p(y)}{q(y|x)}$$

Since our semantic parser always outputs well-formed logical forms, we assume a uniform constant prior $p(y)$. The above objective can be thus reduced to:

$$\mathbb{E}_{q(y|x)} \log p(x|y) - \mathbb{E}_{q(y|x)} \log q(y|x) = \mathcal{L}(x) \quad (14)$$

where the first term computes the reconstruction likelihood $p(x|y)$; and the second term is the entropy of the approximated posterior $q(y|x)$ for regularization. Specifically, we use the semantic parser to compute the approximated posterior $q(y|x)$.[1] The reconstruction likelihood $p(x|y)$ is computed with an inverse parser which recovers utterance x from its logical form y. We use $p(x|y)$ to measure how well the logical form reflects the utterance meaning; details of the inverse parser are described as follows.

Stack-LSTM Encoder To reconstruct utterance x, logical form y is first encoded with a stack-LSTM encoder. To do that, we deterministically convert the logical form into a sequence of *Class-1* to *Class-3* functions, which correspond to the creation of tree nodes and subtrees. Slightly different from the top-down generation process, the functions here are obtained in a bottom-up order to facilitate encoding. Functions used to encode the example logical form `argmax(daughterOf(Obama),` `ageOf)` are shown in Figure 2.

The stack-LSTM sequentially processes the functions and updates its states based on the class of each function, following the same principle (*Update-1* and *Update-2*) described in Section 2.1. We save a list of terminal, non-terminal and subtree representations $[g_1, \cdots, g_s]$, where each representation is the stack-LSTM state at the corresponding time step of encoding. The list essentially contains the representation of every tree node and the representation of every subtree (the total number of representations is denoted by s).

LSTM Decoder Utterance x is reconstructed with a standard LSTM decoder attending to tree nodes and subtree representations. At each time step, the decoder applies attention between decoder state r_t and tree fragment representations $[g_1, \cdots, g_s]$:

$$v_t^i = V' \tanh(W_{g'} g_i + W_r r_t) \qquad (15)$$

$$b_t^i = \text{softmax}(v_t^i) \qquad (16)$$

$$\bar{g}_t = \sum_{i=1}^{s} b_t^i g_i \qquad (17)$$

and predicts the probability of the next word as:

$$x'_{t+1} \sim \text{softmax}(W_{x'} \tanh(W_{f'}[\bar{g}_t, r_t])) \quad (18)$$

where Ws and V' are all weight parameters.

Gradients The training objective of the generative model is given in Equation (14). The parameters of the neural network include those of the original semantic parser (denoted by θ) and the inverse parser (denoted by ϕ). The gradient of Equation (14) with respect to ϕ is:

$$\frac{\partial \mathcal{L}(x)}{\partial \phi} = \mathbb{E}_{q(y|x)} \frac{\partial \log p(x|y)}{\partial \phi} \qquad (19)$$

and the gradient with respect to θ is:

$$\frac{\partial \mathcal{L}(x)}{\partial \theta} = \mathbb{E}_{q(y|x)}[(\log p(x|y) - \log q(y|x))$$

$$\times \frac{\partial \log q(y|x)}{\partial \theta}] \qquad (20)$$

Both gradients involve expectations which we estimate with Monte Carlo method, by sampling logical forms from the distribution $q(y|x)$. Recall that in the parser-ranker framework these samples are obtained via beam search.

---

[1] In Section 2.1, we used a different notation for the output distribution of the semantic parser as $p(y|x)$.

4   Scheduled Training

Together with the inverse parser for removing spurious logical forms, the proposed system consists of three components: a parser which generates logical forms from an utterance, a ranker which measures the likelihood of a logical form executing to the *correct denotation*, and an inverse parser which measures the degree to which logical forms are *meaning-preserving* using reconstruction likelihood. Our semantic parser is trained following a scheduled training procedure, balancing the two objectives.

- *Phase 1*: at the beginning of training when all model parameters are far from optimal, we train only the parser and the ranker as described in Section 2; the parser generates a list of candidate logical forms, we find those which are consistent and update both the parser and the ranker.

- *Phase 2*: we turn on the inverse parser and update all three components in one epoch. However, the reconstruction loss is only used to update the inverse parser and we prevent it from back-propagating to the semantic parser. This is because at this stage of training the parameters of the inverse parser are sub-optimal and we cannot obtain an accurate approximation of the reconstruction loss.

- *Phase 3*: finally, we allow the reconstruction loss to back-propagate to the parser, and all three components are updated as normal. Both training objectives are enabled, the system maximizes the likelihood of consistent logical forms and the reconstruction likelihood.

5   Neural Lexicon Encoding

In this section we further discuss how the semantic parser presented so far can be enhanced with a lexicon. A lexicon is essentially a coarse mapping between natural language phrases and knowledge base relations and entities, and has been widely used in conventional chart-based parsers (Berant et al., 2013a; Reddy et al., 2014). Here, we show how a lexicon (either hard-coded or statistically-learned (Krishnamurthy, 2016)) can be used to benefit a neural semantic parser.

The central idea is that relations or entities can be viewed as a single-node tree-structured logical form. For example, based on the lexicon, the natural language phrase *"is influenced by"* can be parsed to the logical form `influence.influence_node.influenced_by`. We can therefore pretrain the semantic parser (and the inverse parser) with these basic utterance-logical form pairs which act as important prior knowledge for initializing the distributions $q(y|x)$ and $p(x|y)$. With pre-trained word embeddings capturing linguistic regularities on the natural language side, we also expect the approach to help the neural model generalize to unseen natural language phrases quickly. For example, by encoding the mapping between the natural language phrase *"locate in"* and the Freebase predicate `fb:location.location.containedby`, the parser can potentially link the new phrase *"located at"* to the same predicate. We experimentally assess whether the neural lexicon enhances the performance of our semantic parser.

6   Experiments

In this section we evaluate the performance our semantic parser. We introduce the various datasets used in our experiments, training settings, model variants used for comparison, and finally present and analyze our results.

6.1   Datasets

We evaluated our model on three Freebase datasets: WEBQUESTIONS (Berant et al., 2013a), GRAPHQUESTIONS (Su et al., 2016) and SPADES (Bisk et al., 2016). WEBQUESTIONS contains 5,810 real questions asked by people on the web paired by answers. GRAPHQUESTIONS contains 5,166 question-answer pairs which were created by showing 500 Freebase graph queries to Amazon Mechanical Turk workers and asking them to paraphrase them into natural language. SPADES contains 93,319 question-answer pairs which were created by randomly replacing entities in declarative sentences with a blank symbol.

6.2   Training

Across training regimes, the dimensions of word vector, logical form token vector, and LSTM hidden states (for the semantic parser and the inverse parser) are 50, 50, and 150, respectively. Word embeddings were initialized with Glove embeddings (Pennington et al., 2014). All other embeddings were randomly initialized. We used one

LSTM layer in the forward and backward directions. Dropout was used before the softmax activation (Equations (7), (8), and (18)). The dropout rate was set to 0.5. Momentum SGD (Sutskever et al., 2013) was used as the optimization method to update the parameters of the model.

As mentioned earlier, we use entity linking to reduce the beam search space. Entity mentions in SPADES are automatically annotated with Freebase entities (Gabrilovich et al., 2013). For WEBQUESTIONS and GRAPHQUESTIONS we perform entity linking following the procedure described in Reddy et al. (2016). We identify potential entity spans using seven handcrafted part-of-speech patterns and associate them with Freebase entities obtained from the Freebase/KG API.[2] We use a structured perceptron trained on the entities found in WEBQUESTIONS and GRAPHQUESTIONS to select the top 10 non-overlapping entity disambiguation possibilities. We treat each possibility as a candidate entity and construct candidate utterances with a beam search of size 300.

Key features of the log-linear ranker introduced in Section 2 include the entity score returned by the entity linking system, the likelihood score of the relation in the logical form predicted by the parser, the likelihood score of the the logical form predicted by the parser, the embedding similarity between the relation in the logical form and the utterance, the similarity between the relation and the question words in the utterance, and the answer type as indicated by the last word in the Freebase relation (Xu et al., 2016). All features are normalized across candidate logical forms. For all datasets we use average F1 (Berant et al., 2013a) as our evaluation metric.

6.3 Model Variants

We experiment with three variants of our model. We primarily consider the neural parser-ranker system (denoted by NPR) described in Section 2 which is trained to maximize the likelihood of consistent logical forms. We then compare it to a system augmented with a generative ranker (denoted by GRANKER), introducing the second objective of maximizing the reconstruction likelihood. Finally, we examine the impact of neural lexicon encoding when it is used for the generative ranker, and also when it is used for the entire system.

[2]http://developers.google.com/freebase/

Models	F1
Berant et al. (2013a)	35.7
Berant and Liang (2014)	39.9
Berant and Liang (2015)	49.7
Reddy et al. (2016)	50.3
Yao and Van Durme (2014)	33.0
Bast and Haussmann (2015)	49.4
Bordes et al. (2014)	39.2
Dong et al. (2015)	40.8
Yih et al. (2015)	52.5
Xu et al. (2016)	53.3
Cheng et al. (2017b)	49.4
NPR	50.1
+ GRANKER	50.2
+ lexicon encoding on GRANKER	51.7
+ lexicon encoding on parser and GRANKER	52.5

Table 2: WEBQUESTIONS results.

6.4 Results

Experimental results on WEBQUESTIONS are shown in Table 2. We compare the performance of NPR with previous work, including conventional chart-based semantic parsing models (e.g., Berant et al. (2013a); first block in Table 2), information extraction models (e.g., Yao and Van Durme (2014); second block in Table 2), and more recent neural question-answering models (e.g., Dong et al. (2015); third block in Table 2). Most neural models do not generate logical forms but instead build a differentiable network to solve a specific task such as question-answering. An exception is the neural sequence-to-tree model of Cheng et al. (2017b), which we extend to build the vanilla NPR model. A key difference of NPR is that it employs soft attention instead of hard attention, which is Cheng et al. (2017b) use to rationalize predictions.

As shown in Table 2, the basic NPR system outperforms most previous chart-based semantic parsers. Our results suggest that neural networks are powerful tools for generating candidate logical forms in a weakly-supervised setting, due to their ability of encoding and utilizing sentential context and generation history. Compared to Cheng et al. (2017b), our system also performs better. We believe the reason is that it employs soft attention instead of hard attention. Soft attention makes the parser fully differentiable and optimization easier. The addition of the inverse parser (+GRANKER) to the basic NPR model yields marginal gains while

Models	F1
SEMPRE (Berant et al., 2013a)	10.80
PARASEMPRE (Berant and Liang, 2014)	12.79
JACANA (Yao and Van Durme, 2014)	5.08
SCANNER (Cheng et al., 2017b)	17.02
UDEPLAMBDA (Reddy et al., 2017)	17.70
NPR	17.30
+ GRANKER	17.33
+ lexicon encoding on GRANKER	17.67
+ lexicon encoding on parser and GRANKER	18.22

Table 3: GRAPHQUESTIONS results.

Models	F1
Unsupervised CCG (Bisk et al., 2016)	24.8
Semi-supervised CCG (Bisk et al., 2016)	28.4
Supervised CCG (Bisk et al., 2016)	30.9
Rule-based system (Bisk et al., 2016)	31.4
Sequence-to-tree (Cheng et al., 2017b)	31.5
Memory networks (Das et al., 2017)	39.9
NPR	32.4
+ GRANKER	33.1
+ lexicon encoding on GRANKER	35.5
+ lexicon encoding on parser and GRANKER	37.6

Table 4: SPADES results.

the addition of the neural lexicon encoding to the inverse parser brings performance improvements over NPR and GRANKER. We hypothesize that this is because the inverse parser adopts an unsupervised training objective, which benefits substantially from prior domain-specific knowledge used to initialize its parameters. When neural lexicon encoding is incorporated in the semantic parser as well, system performance can be further improved. In fact, our final system (last row in Table 2) outperforms all previous models except that of Xu et al. (2016), which uses external Wikipedia resources to prune out erroneous candidate answers.

Tables 3 and 4 present our results on GRAPHQUESTIONS and SPADES, respectively. Comparison systems for GRAPHQUESTIONS include two chart-based semantic parsers (Berant et al., 2013a; Berant and Liang, 2014), an information extraction model (Yao and Van Durme, 2014), a neural sequence-to-tree model with hard attention (Cheng et al., 2017b) and a model based on universal dependency to logical form conversion (Reddy et al., 2017). On SPADES we compare with the method of Bisk et al. (2016) which parses an utterance into a syntactic representation which is subsequently grounded to Freebase; and also with Das et al. (2017) who employ memory networks and external text resources. Results on both datasets follow similar trends as in WEBQUESTIONS. The best performing NPR variant achieves state-of-the-art results on GRAPHQUESTIONS and it comes close to the best model on SPADES without using any external resources.

One of the claims put forward in this paper is that the extended NPR model reduces the impact of spurious logical forms during training. Table 5 highlights examples of spurious logical forms which are not semantically correct but are nevertheless assigned higher scores in the vanilla NPR (red colour). These logical forms become less likely in the extended NPR, while the scores of more semantically faithful representations (blue colour) are boosted.

6.5 Discussion

The vanilla NPR model is optimized with consistent logical forms which lead to correct denotations. Although it achieves competitive results compared to chart-based parsers, the training of this model can be misled by spurious logical forms. The introduction of the inverse parser aims to alleviate the problem by scoring how a logical form reflects the utterance semantics. Although the inverse parser is not directly used to rank logical forms at test time, the training objective it adopts encourages the parser to generate meaning-preserving logical forms with higher likelihood. These probabilities are used as features in the log-linear ranker, and therefore the inverse parser affects the ranking results, albeit implicitly.

However, we should point out that the unsupervised training objective is relatively difficult to optimize, since there are no constraints to regularize the latent logical forms. This motivates us to develop a scheduled training procedure; as our results show, when trained properly the inverse parser and the unsupervised objective bring performance gains. Moreover, the neural lexicon encoding method we applied essentially produces synthetic data to further regularize the latent space.

7   Related Work

Various types of supervision have been explored to train semantic parsers. Early semantic parsers

which baseball teams were coached by dave eiland
`baseball.batting_statistics.player:baseball.batting_statistics.team(ent.m.0c0x6v)`
`baseball.historical_coaching_tenure.baseball_coach:baseball.historical_coaching_tenure.baseball_team(ent.m.0c0x6v)`
who are coca-cola's endorsers
`food.nutrition_fact.food:food.nutrition_fact.nutrient(ent.m.01yvs)`
`business.product_endorsement.product:business..product_endorsement.endorser(ent.m.01yvs)`
what are the aircraft models that are comparable to airbus 380
`aviation.aviation_incident_aircraft_relationship.flight_destination:aviation.aviation_incident_aircraft_relationship.aircraft_model(ent.m.0qn2v)`
`aviation.comparable_aircraft_relationship(ent.m.018r12)`

Table 5: Comparison between logical forms preferred by NPR before and after the addition of the inverse parser. Spurious logical forms (red color) receive higher scores than semantically-correct ones (blue color). The scores of these spurious logical forms decrease when they are explicitly handled.

have used annotated training data consisting of sentences and their corresponding logical forms (Kate and Mooney, 2006; Kate et al., 2005; Lu et al., 2008; Kwiatkowksi et al., 2010). In order to scale semantic parsing to open-domain problems, weakly-supervised semantic parsers are trained on utterance-denotation pairs (Liang et al., 2011; Krishnamurthy and Mitchell, 2012; Berant et al., 2013b; Choi et al., 2015; Krishnamurthy and Mitchell, 2015; Pasupat and Liang, 2016; Gardner and Krishnamurthy, 2017; Reddy et al., 2017). Most previous work employs a chart-based parser to produce logical forms from a grammar which combines domain-general aspects with lexicons.

Recently, neural semantic parsing has attracted a great deal of attention. Previous work has mostly adopted fully-supervised, sequence-to-sequence models to generate logical form strings from natural language utterances (Dong and Lapata, 2016; Jia and Liang, 2016; Kočiský et al., 2016). Other work explores the use of reinforcement learning to train neural semantic parsers from question-answer pairs (Liang et al., 2016) or from user feedback (Iyer et al., 2017). More closely related to our work, Goldman et al. (2018) adopt a neural semantic parser and a discriminative ranker to solve a visual reasoning challenge. They attempt to alleviate the search space and spuriousness challenges with abstractive examples. Yin et al. (2018) adopt a tree-based variational autoencoder for semi-supervised semantic parsing. Neural variational inference has also been used in other NLP tasks including relation discovery (Marcheggiani and Titov, 2016), sentence compression (Miao and Blunsom, 2016), and parsing (Cheng et al., 2017a).

8 Conclusions

In this work we proposed a weakly-supervised neural semantic parsing system trained on utterance-denotation pairs. The system employs a neural sequence-to-tree parser to generate logical forms for a natural language utterance. The logical forms are subsequently ranked with two components and objectives: a log-linear model which scores the likelihood of correct execution, and a generative neural inverse parser which measures whether logical forms are meaning preserving. We proposed a scheduled training procedure to balance the two objectives, and a neural lexicon encoding method to initialize model parameters with prior knowledge. Experiments on three semantic parsing datasets demonstrate the effectiveness of our system. In the future, we would like to train our parser with other forms of supervision such as feedback from users (He et al., 2016; Iyer et al., 2017) or textual evidence (Yin et al., 2018).

Acknowledgments This research is supported by a Google PhD Fellowship and an AdeptMind Scolar Fellowship to the first author. We also gratefully acknowledge the financial support of the European Research Council (award number 681760; Lapata).

References

Yoav Artzi and Luke Zettlemoyer. 2013. Weakly supervised learning of semantic parsers for mapping instructions to actions. *Transactions of the Association for Computational Linguistics*, 1(1):49–62.

Dzmitry Bahdanau, Kyunghyun Cho, and Yoshua Bengio. 2015. Neural machine translation by jointly learning to align and translate. In *Proceedings of ICLR 2015*, San Diego, California.

Hannah Bast and Elmar Haussmann. 2015. More accurate question answering on freebase. In *Proceedings of the 24th ACM International on Conference on Information and Knowledge Management*, pages 1431–1440. ACM.

Jonathan Berant, Andrew Chou, Roy Frostig, and Percy Liang. 2013a. Semantic parsing on Freebase from question-answer pairs. In *Proceedings of the 2013 Conference on Empirical Methods in Natural Language Processing*, pages 1533–1544, Seattle, Washington.

Jonathan Berant, Andrew Chou, Roy Frostig, and Percy Liang. 2013b. Semantic parsing on Freebase from question-answer pairs. In *Proceedings of the 2013 Conference on Empirical Methods in Natural Language Processing*, pages 1533–1544, Seattle, Washington, USA.

Jonathan Berant and Percy Liang. 2014. Semantic parsing via paraphrasing. In *Proceedings of the 52nd Annual Meeting of the Association for Computational Linguistics (Volume 1: Long Papers)*, pages 1415–1425, Baltimore, Maryland.

Jonathan Berant and Percy Liang. 2015. Imitation learning of agenda-based semantic parsers. *Transactions of the Association for Computational Linguistics*, 3:545–558.

Yonatan Bisk, Siva Reddy, John Blitzer, Julia Hockenmaier, and Mark Steedman. 2016. Evaluating induced CCG parsers on grounded semantic parsing. In *Proceedings of the 2016 Conference on Empirical Methods in Natural Language Processing*, pages 2022–2027, Austin, Texas.

Antoine Bordes, Sumit Chopra, and Jason Weston. 2014. Question answering with subgraph embeddings. In *Proceedings of the 2014 Conference on Empirical Methods in Natural Language Processing (EMNLP)*, pages 615–620, Doha, Qatar.

Qingqing Cai and Alexander Yates. 2013. Large-scale semantic parsing via schema matching and lexicon extension. In *Proceedings of the 51st Annual Meeting of the Association for Computational Linguistics (Volume 1: Long Papers)*, pages 423–433, Sofia, Bulgaria.

David L Chen and Raymond J Mooney. 2011. Learning to interpret natural language navigation instructions from observations. In *Proceedings of the 25th AAAI Conference on Artificial IntelligenceAAAI*, volume 2, pages 859–865, San Francisco, California.

Jianpeng Cheng, Adam Lopez, and Mirella Lapata. 2017a. A generative parser with a discriminative recognition algorithm. In *Proceedings of the 55th Annual Meeting of the Association for Computational Linguistics (Volume 2: Short Papers)*, pages 118–124, Vancouver, Canada.

Jianpeng Cheng, Siva Reddy, Vijay Saraswat, and Mirella Lapata. 2017b. Learning structured natural language representations for semantic parsing. In *Proceedings of the 55th Annual Meeting of the Association for Computational Linguistics (Volume 1: Long Papers)*, pages 44–55, Vancouver, Canada.

Jianpeng Cheng, Siva Reddy, Vijay Saraswat, and Mirella Lapata. 2018. Learning an executable neural semantic parser. *Computational Linguistics*.

Eunsol Choi, Tom Kwiatkowski, and Luke Zettlemoyer. 2015. Scalable semantic parsing with partial ontologies. In *Proceedings of the 53rd Annual Meeting of the Association for Computational Linguistics and the 7th International Joint Conference on Natural Language Processing (Volume 1: Long Papers)*, pages 1311–1320, Beijing, China.

James Clarke, Dan Goldwasser, Ming-Wei Chang, and Dan Roth. 2010. Driving semantic parsing from the world's response. In *Proceedings of the 14th Conference on Computational Natural Language Learning*, pages 18–27, Uppsala, Sweden.

Rajarshi Das, Manzil Zaheer, Siva Reddy, and Andrew McCallum. 2017. Question answering on knowledge bases and text using universal schema and memory networks. In *Proceedings of the 55th Annual Meeting of the Association for Computational Linguistics (Volume 2: Short Papers)*, volume 2, pages 358–365.

Li Dong and Mirella Lapata. 2016. Language to logical form with neural attention. In *Proceedings of the 54th Annual Meeting of the Association for Computational Linguistics (Volume 1: Long Papers)*, pages 33–43, Berlin, Germany.

Li Dong, Furu Wei, Ming Zhou, and Ke Xu. 2015. Question answering over Freebase with multi-column convolutional neural networks. In *Proceedings of the 53rd Annual Meeting of the Association for Computational Linguistics and the 7th International Joint Conference on Natural Language Processing (Volume 1: Long Papers)*, pages 260–269, Beijing, China.

Chris Dyer, Miguel Ballesteros, Wang Ling, Austin Matthews, and Noah A. Smith. 2015. Transition-based dependency parsing with stack long short-term memory. In *Proceedings of the 53rd Annual Meeting of the Association for Computational Linguistics and the 7th International Joint Conference on Natural Language Processing (Volume 1: Long Papers)*, pages 334–343, Beijing, China.

Evgeniy Gabrilovich, Michael Ringgaard, and Amarnag Subramanya. 2013. FACC1: Freebase annotation of ClueWeb corpora, version 1 (release date 2013-06-26, format version 1, correction level 0).

Matt Gardner and Jayant Krishnamurthy. 2017. Open-Vocabulary Semantic Parsing with both Distributional Statistics and Formal Knowledge. In *Proceedings of the 31st AAAI Conference on Artificial Intelligence*, pages 3195–3201, San Francisco, California.

Omer Goldman, Veronica Latcinnik, Ehud Nave, Amir Globerson, and Jonathan Berant. 2018. Weakly supervised semantic parsing with abstract examples. In *Proceedings of the 56th Annual Meeting of the Association for Computational Linguistics (Volume 1: Long Papers)*, pages 1809–1819, Melbourne, Australia.

Luheng He, Julian Michael, Mike Lewis, and Luke Zettlemoyer. 2016. Human-in-the-loop parsing. In *Proceedings of the 2016 Conference on Empirical Methods in Natural Language Processing*, pages 2337–2342, Austin, Texas.

Sepp Hochreiter and Jürgen Schmidhuber. 1997. Long short-term memory. *Neural computation*, 9(8):1735–1780.

Srinivasan Iyer, Ioannis Konstas, Alvin Cheung, Jayant Krishnamurthy, and Luke Zettlemoyer. 2017. Learning a neural semantic parser from user feedback. In *Proceedings of the 55th Annual Meeting of the Association for Computational Linguistics (Volume 1: Long Papers)*, pages 963–973, Vancouver, Canada.

Robin Jia and Percy Liang. 2016. Data recombination for neural semantic parsing. In *Proceedings of the 54th Annual Meeting of the Association for Computational Linguistics (Volume 1: Long Papers)*, pages 12–22, Berlin, Germany.

Rohit J Kate and Raymond J Mooney. 2006. Using string-kernels for learning semantic parsers. In *Proceedings of the 21st International Conference on Computational Linguistics and the 44th annual meeting of the Association for Computational Linguistics*, pages 913–920, Sydney, Australia.

Rohit J. Kate, Yuk Wah Wong, and Raymond J. Mooney. 2005. Learning to Transform Natural to Formal Languages. In *Proceedings for the 20th National Conference on Artificial Intelligence*, pages 1062–1068, Pittsburgh, Pennsylvania.

Tomáš Kočiský, Gábor Melis, Edward Grefenstette, Chris Dyer, Wang Ling, Phil Blunsom, and Karl Moritz Hermann. 2016. Semantic parsing with semi-supervised sequential autoencoders. In *Proceedings of the 2016 Conference on Empirical Methods in Natural Language Processing*, pages 1078–1087, Austin, Texas.

Jayant Krishnamurthy. 2016. Probabilistic models for learning a semantic parser lexicon. In *Proceedings of the 2016 Conference of the North American Chapter of the Association for Computational Linguistics: Human Language Technologies*, pages 606–616.

Jayant Krishnamurthy and Tom Mitchell. 2012. Weakly supervised training of semantic parsers. In *Proceedings of the 2012 Joint Conference on Empirical Methods in Natural Language Processing and Computational Natural Language Learning*, pages 754–765, Jeju Island, Korea.

Jayant Krishnamurthy and Tom M Mitchell. 2015. Learning a compositional semantics for freebase with an open predicate vocabulary. *Transactions of the Association for Computational Linguistics*, 3:257–270.

Tom Kwiatkowksi, Luke Zettlemoyer, Sharon Goldwater, and Mark Steedman. 2010. Inducing probabilistic CCG grammars from logical form with higher-order unification. In *Proceedings of the 2010 Conference on Empirical Methods in Natural Language Processing*, pages 1223–1233, Cambridge, MA.

Tom Kwiatkowski, Eunsol Choi, Yoav Artzi, and Luke Zettlemoyer. 2013. Scaling semantic parsers with on-the-fly ontology matching. In *Proceedings of the 2013 Conference on Empirical Methods in Natural Language Processing*, pages 1545–1556, Seattle, Washington, USA.

Tom Kwiatkowski, Luke Zettlemoyer, Sharon Goldwater, and Mark Steedman. 2011. Lexical generalization in CCG grammar induction for semantic parsing. In *Proceedings of the 2011 Conference on Empirical Methods in Natural Language Processing*, pages 1512–1523, Edinburgh, Scotland.

Chen Liang, Jonathan Berant, Quoc Le, Kenneth D Forbus, and Ni Lao. 2016. Neural symbolic machines: Learning semantic parsers on Freebase with weak supervision. *arXiv preprint arXiv:1611.00020*.

Percy Liang. 2016. Learning executable semantic parsers for natural language understanding. *Communications of the ACM*, 59(9):68–76.

Percy Liang, Michael Jordan, and Dan Klein. 2011. Learning dependency-based compositional semantics. In *Proceedings of the 49th Annual Meeting of the Association for Computational Linguistics: Human Language Technologies*, pages 590–599, Portland, Oregon.

Wei Lu, Hwee Tou Ng, Wee Sun Lee, and Luke S Zettlemoyer. 2008. A generative model for parsing natural language to meaning representations. In *Proceedings of the Conference on Empirical Methods in Natural Language Processing*, pages 783–792, Honolulu, Hawaii.

Diego Marcheggiani and Ivan Titov. 2016. Discrete-state variational autoencoders for joint discovery and factorization of relations. *Transactions of the Association for Computational Linguistics*, 4:231–244.

Cynthia Matuszek, Nicholas FitzGerald, Luke Zettlemoyer, Liefeng Bo, and Dieter Fox. 2012. A joint model of language and perception for grounded attribute learning. In *Proceedings of the 29th International Conference on Machine Learning (ICML-12)*, pages 1671–1678, Edinburgh, Scotland.

Yishu Miao and Phil Blunsom. 2016. Language as a latent variable: Discrete generative models for sentence compression. In *Proceedings of the 2016 Conference on Empirical Methods in Natural Language Processing*, pages 319–328, Austin, Texas.

Andriy Mnih and Karol Gregor. 2014. Neural variational inference and learning in belief networks. In *Proceedings of the 31st International Conference on Machine Learning*, pages 1791–1799, Bejing, China.

Panupong Pasupat and Percy Liang. 2016. Inferring logical forms from denotations. In *Proceedings of the 54th Annual Meeting of the Association for Computational Linguistics (Volume 1: Long Papers)*, volume 1, pages 23–32, Berlin, Germany.

Jeffrey Pennington, Richard Socher, and Christopher Manning. 2014. Glove: Global vectors for word representation. In *Proceedings of the 2014 Conference on Empirical Methods in Natural Language Processing (EMNLP)*, pages 1532–1543, Doha, Qatar.

Siva Reddy, Mirella Lapata, and Mark Steedman. 2014. Large-scale semantic parsing without question-answer pairs. *Transactions of the Association for Computational Linguistics*, 2:377–392.

Siva Reddy, Oscar Täckström, Michael Collins, Tom Kwiatkowski, Dipanjan Das, Mark Steedman, and Mirella Lapata. 2016. Transforming dependency structures to logical forms for semantic parsing. *Transactions of the Association for Computational Linguistics*, 4:127–140.

Siva Reddy, Oscar Täckström, Slav Petrov, Mark Steedman, and Mirella Lapata. 2017. Universal semantic parsing. In *Proceedings of the 2017 Conference on Empirical Methods in Natural Language Processing*, pages 89–101, Copenhagen, Denmark.

Yu Su, Huan Sun, Brian Sadler, Mudhakar Srivatsa, Izzeddin Gur, Zenghui Yan, and Xifeng Yan. 2016. On generating characteristic-rich question sets for qa evaluation. In *Proceedings of the 2016 Conference on Empirical Methods in Natural Language Processing*, pages 562–572, Austin, Texas.

Ilya Sutskever, James Martens, George Dahl, and Geoffrey Hinton. 2013. On the importance of initialization and momentum in deep learning. In *Proceedings of the 30th International Conference on Machine Learning*, pages 1139–1147, Atlanta, Georgia.

Tsung-Hsien Wen, Milica Gasic, Nikola Mrkšić, Pei-Hao Su, David Vandyke, and Steve Young. 2015. Semantically conditioned LSTM-based natural language generation for spoken dialogue systems. In *Proceedings of the 2015 Conference on Empirical Methods in Natural Language Processing*, pages 1711–1721, Lisbon, Portugal.

Yuk Wah Wong and Raymond Mooney. 2006. Learning for semantic parsing with statistical machine translation. In *Proceedings of the Human Language Technology Conference of the NAACL, Main Conference*, pages 439–446, New York City, USA.

Kun Xu, Siva Reddy, Yansong Feng, Songfang Huang, and Dongyan Zhao. 2016. Question answering on Freebase via relation extraction and textual evidence. In *Proceedings of the 54th Annual Meeting of the Association for Computational Linguistics (Volume 1: Long Papers)*, pages 2326–2336, Berlin, Germany.

Xuchen Yao and Benjamin Van Durme. 2014. Information extraction over structured data: Question answering with Freebase. In *Proceedings of the 52nd Annual Meeting of the Association for Computational Linguistics (Volume 1: Long Papers)*, pages 956–966, Baltimore, Maryland.

Wen-tau Yih, Ming-Wei Chang, Xiaodong He, and Jianfeng Gao. 2015. Semantic parsing via staged query graph generation: Question answering with knowledge base. In *Proceedings of the 53rd Annual Meeting of the Association for Computational Linguistics and the 7th International Joint Conference on Natural Language Processing (Volume 1: Long Papers)*, pages 1321–1331, Beijing, China.

Pengcheng Yin, Chunting Zhou, Junxian He, and Graham Neubig. 2018. StructVAE: Tree-structured latent variable models for semi-supervised semantic parsing. In *Proceedings of the 56th Annual Meeting of the Association for Computational Linguistics (Volume 1: Long Papers)*, pages 754–765, Melbourne, Australia.

John M. Zelle and Raymond J. Mooney. 1996. Learning to parse database queries using inductive logic programming. In *Proceedings of the 13th National Conference on Artificial Intelligence*, pages 1050–1055, Portland, Oregon.

Luke S. Zettlemoyer and Michael Collins. 2005. Learning to Map Sentences to Logical Form: Structured Classification with Probabilistic Categorial Grammars. In *Proceedings of 21st Conference in Uncertainilty in Artificial Intelligence*, pages 658–666, Edinburgh, Scotland.

Modeling Composite Labels for Neural Morphological Tagging

Alexander Tkachenko
Institute of Computer Science
University of Tartu
Tartu, Estonia
aleksandr.tkatsenko@ut.ee

Kairit Sirts
Institute of Computer Science
University of Tartu
Tartu, Estonia
kairit.sirts@ut.ee

Abstract

Neural morphological tagging has been regarded as an extension to POS tagging task, treating each morphological tag as a monolithic label and ignoring its internal structure. We propose to view morphological tags as composite labels and explicitly model their internal structure in a neural sequence tagger. For this, we explore three different neural architectures and compare their performance with both CRF and simple neural multiclass baselines. We evaluate our models on 49 languages and show that the neural architecture that models the morphological labels as sequences of morphological category values performs significantly better than both baselines establishing state-of-the-art results in morphological tagging for most languages.[1]

1 Introduction

The common approach to morphological tagging combines the set of word's morphological features into a single monolithic tag and then, similar to POS tagging, employs multiclass sequence classification models such as CRFs (Müller et al., 2013) or recurrent neural networks (Labeau et al., 2015; Heigold et al., 2017). This approach, however, has a number of limitations. Firstly, it ignores the intrinsic compositional structure of the labels and treats two labels that differ only in the value of a single morphological category as completely independent; compare for instance labels [POS=NOUN,CASE=NOM,NUM=SG] and [POS=NOUN,CASE=NOM,NUM=PL] that only differ in the value of the NUM category. Secondly, it introduces a data sparsity issue as the less frequent labels can have only few occurrences in the

training data. Thirdly, it excludes the ability to predict labels not present in the training set which can be an issue for languages such as Turkish where the number of morphological tags is theoretically unlimited (Yuret and Türe, 2006).

To address these problems we propose to treat morphological tags as composite labels and explicitly model their internal structure. We hypothesise that by doing that, we are able to alleviate the sparsity problems, especially for languages with very large tagsets such as Turkish, Czech or Finnish, and at the same time also improve the accuracy over a baseline using monolithic labels. We explore three different neural architectures to model the compositionality of morphological labels. In the first architecture, we model all morphological categories (including POS tag) as independent multiclass classifiers conditioned on the same contextual word representation. The second architecture organises these multiclass classifiers into a hierarchy—the POS tag is predicted first and the values of morphological categories are predicted conditioned on the value of the predicted POS. The third architecture models the label as a sequence of morphological category-value pairs. All our models share the same neural encoder architecture based on bidirectional LSTMs to construct contextual representations for words (Lample et al., 2016).

We evaluate all our models on 49 UD version 2.1 languages. Experimental results show that our sequential model outperforms other neural counterparts establishing state-of-the-art results in morphological tagging for most languages. We also confirm that all neural models perform significantly better than a competitive CRF baseline. In short, our contributions can be summarised as follows:

1) We propose to model the compositional internal structure of complex morphological la-

---

[1]The source code is available at
https://github.com/AleksTk/seq-morph-tagger

Proceedings of the 22nd Conference on Computational Natural Language Learning (CoNLL 2018), pages 368–379
Brussels, Belgium, October 31 - November 1, 2018. ©2018 Association for Computational Linguistics

bels for morphological tagging in a neural sequence tagging framework;

2) We explore several neural architectures for modeling the composite morphological labels;

3) We find that tag representation based on the sequence learning model achieves state-of-the art performance on many languages.

4) We present state-of-the-art morphological tagging results on 49 languages on the UDv2.1 corpora.

2 Related Work

Most previous work on modeling the internal structure of complex morphological labels has occurred in the context of morphological disambiguation—a task where the goal is to select the correct analysis from a limited set of candidates provided by a morphological analyser. The most common strategy to cope with a large number of complex labels has been to predict all morphological features of a word using several independent classifiers whose predictions are later combined using some scoring mechanism (Hajič and Hladká, 1998; Hajič, 2000; Smith et al., 2005; Yuret and Türe, 2006; Zalmout and Habash, 2017; Kirov et al., 2017). Inoue et al. (2017) combined these classifiers into a multitask neural model sharing the same encoder, and predicted both POS tag and morphological category values given the same contextual representation computed by a bidirectional LSTM. They showed that the multitask learning setting outperforms the combination of several independent classifiers on tagging Arabic. In this paper, we experiment with the same architecture, termed as multiclass multilabel model, on many languages. Additionally, we extend this approach and explore a hierarchical architecture where morphological features directly depend on the POS tag.

Another previously adopted approach involves modeling complex morphological labels as sequences of morphological feature values (Hakkani-Tur et al., 2000; Schmid and Laws, 2008). In neural networks, this idea can be implemented with recurrent sequence modeling. Indeed, one of our proposed models generates morphological tags with an LSTM network. Similar idea has been applied for the morphological reinflection task (Kann and Schütze, 2016; Faruqui et al., 2016) where the sequential model is used to generate the spellings of inflected forms given the lemma and the morphological label of the desired form. In morphological

tagging, however, we generate the morphological labels themselves.

Another direction of research on modeling the structure of complex morphological labels involves structured prediction models (Müller et al., 2013; Müller and Schütze, 2015; Malaviya et al., 2018; Lee et al., 2011). Lee et al. (2011) introduced a factor graph model that jointly infers morphological features and syntactic structures. Müller et al. (2013) proposed a higher-order CRF model which handles large morphological tagsets by decomposing the full label into POS tag and morphology part. Malaviya et al. (2018) proposed a factorial CRF to model pairwise dependencies between individual features within morphological labels and also between labels over time steps for cross-lingual transfer. Recently, neural morphological taggers have been compared to the CRF-based approach (Heigold et al., 2017; Yu et al., 2017). While Heigold et al. (2017) found that their neural model with bidirectional LSTM encoder surpasses the CRF baseline, the results of Yu et al. (2017) are mixed with the convolutional encoder being slightly better or on par with the CRF but the LSTM encoder being worse than the CRF baseline.

Most previous work on neural POS and morphological tagging has shared the general idea of using bidirectional LSTM for computing contextual features for words (Ling et al., 2015; Huang et al., 2015; Labeau et al., 2015; Ma and Hovy, 2016; Heigold et al., 2017). The focus of the previous work has been mostly on modeling the inputs by exploring different character-level representations for words (Heigold et al., 2016; Santos and Zadrozny, 2014; Ma and Hovy, 2016; Inoue et al., 2017; Ling et al., 2015; Rei et al., 2016). We adopt the general encoder architecture from these works, constructing word representations from characters and using another bidirectional LSTM to encode the context vectors. In contrast to these previous works, our focus is on modeling the compositional structure of the complex morphological labels.

The morphologically annotated Universal Dependencies (UD) corpora (Nivre et al., 2017) offer a great opportunity for experimenting on many languages. Some previous work have reported results on several UD languages (Yu et al., 2017; Heigold et al., 2017). Morphological tagging results on many UD languages have been also reported for parsing systems that predict POS and morphological tags as preprocessing (Andor et al., 2016; Straka et al., 2016; Straka and Straková, 2017). Since UD treebanks have been in constant development, these results have been obtained on different UD versions and thus are not necessarily directly comparable. We conduct experiments on all UDv2.1 languages and we aim to provide a baseline for future work in neural morphological tagging.

3 Neural Models

We explore three different neural architectures for modeling morphological labels: multiclass multilabel model that predicts each category value separately, hierarchical multiclass multilabel model where the values of morphological features depend on the value of the POS, and a sequence model that generates morphological labels as sequences of feature-value pairs.

3.1 Notation

Given a sentence $w_1, \ldots, w_n$ consisting of n words, we want to predict the sequence $t_1, \ldots, t_n$ of morphological labels for that sentence. Each label $t_i = \{f_{i0}, f_{i1}, \ldots, f_{im}\}$ consists of a POS tag ($f_{i0} \equiv$ POS) and a sequence of m category values. For each word w_i, the encoder computes a contextual vector h_i, which captures information about the word and its left and right context.

3.2 Decoder Models

Multiclass Multilabel model (MCML) This model formulates the morphological tagging as a multiclass multilabel classification problem. For each morphological category, a separate multiclass classifier is trained to predict the value of that category (Figure 1 (a)). Because not all categories are always present for each POS (e.g., a noun does not have a *tense* category), we extend the morphological label of each word by adding all features that are missing from the annotated label and assign them a special value that marks the category as "off". Formally, the model can be described as:

$$p(t|h)_{\text{MCML}} = \prod_{j=0}^{M} p(f_j|h), \quad (1)$$

where M is the total number of morphological categories (such as case, number, tense, etc.) observed in the training corpus. The probability of each feature value is computed with a softmax function:

$$p(f_j|h)_{\text{MCML}} = \text{softmax}(W_j h + b_j),$$

where W_j and b_j are the parameter matrix and bias vector for the jth morphological feature ($j = 0, \ldots, M$). The final morphological label for a word is obtained by concatenating predictions for individual categories while filtering out off-valued categories.

Hierarchical Multiclass Multilabel model (HMCML) This is a hierarchical version of the MCML architecture that models the values of morphological categories as directly dependent on the POS tag (Figure 1 (b)):

$$p(t|h)_{\text{HMCML}} = p(\text{POS}|h) \prod_{j=1}^{M} p(f_j|\text{POS}, h) \quad (2)$$

The probability of the POS is computed from the context vector h using the respective parameters:

$$p(\text{POS}|h) = \text{softmax}(W_{\text{POS}} h + b_{\text{POS}})$$

The POS-dependent context vector l is obtained by concatenating the context vector h with the unnormalised log probabilities of the POS:

$$l = [h; W_{\text{POS}} h + b_{\text{POS}}]$$

The probabilities of the morphological features are computed using the POS-dependent context vector:

$$p(f_j|\text{POS}, h) = \text{softmax}(W_j l + b_j) \quad j = 1, \ldots, M$$

Sequence model (SEQ) The SEQ model predicts complex morphological labels as sequences of category values. This approach is inspired from neural sequence-to-sequence models commonly used for machine translation (Cho et al., 2014; Sutskever et al., 2014). For each word in a sentence, the decoder uses a unidirectional LSTM network (Figure 1 (c)) to generate a sequence of morphological category-value pairs based on the context vector h and the previous predictions. The probability of a morphological label t is under this model:

$$p(t|h)_{\text{SEQ}} = \prod_{j=0}^{m} p(f_j|f_0, \ldots, f_{j-1}, h) \quad (3)$$

Decoding starts by passing the start-of-sequence symbol as input. At each time step, the decoder computes the label context vector g_j based on the previously predicted category value, previous label context vector and the word's context vector.

$$g_j = \text{LSTM}([f_{j-1}; h], g_{j-1})$$

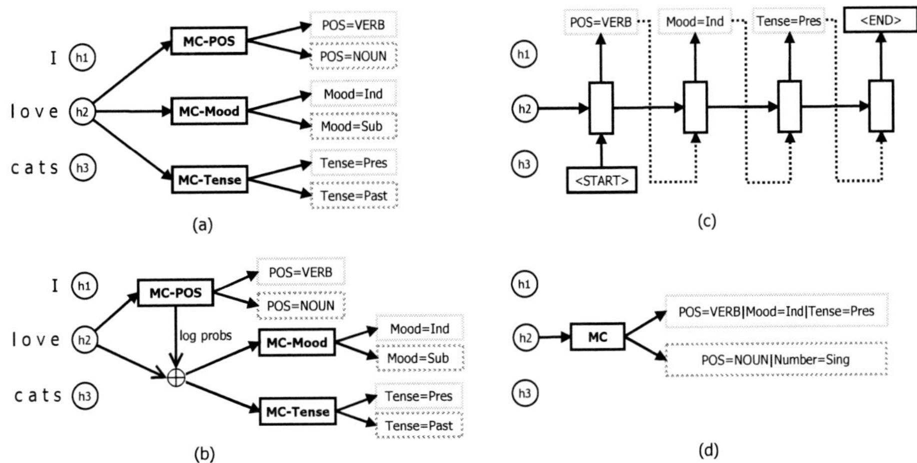

Figure 1: Neural architectures for modeling complex morphological labels: a) Multiclass Multilabel model (MCML), b) Hierarchical Multiclass Multilabel model (HMCML), c) Sequence model (SEQ) and d) Multiclass baseline model (MC). Correct labels are shown with a green border, incorrect labels have a red dotted border.

The probability of each morphological feature-value pair is then computed with a softmax.

$$p(f_j|g_j)_{\text{SEQ}} = \text{softmax}(W_{\text{SEQ}}g_j + b_{\text{SEQ}})$$

At training time, we feed correct labels as inputs while at inference time, we greedily emit the best prediction from the set of all possible feature-value pairs. The decoding terminates once the end-of-sequence symbol is produced.

3.3 Encoder

We adopt a standard sequence tagging encoder architecture for all our models. It consists of a bidirectional LSTM network that maps words in a sentence into context vectors using character and word-level embeddings. Character-level word embeddings are constructed with a bidirectional LSTM network and they capture useful information about words' morphology and shape. Word level embeddings are initialised with pre-trained embeddings and fine-tuned during training. The character and word-level embeddings are concatenated and passed as inputs to the bidirectional LSTM encoder. The resulting hidden states h_i capture contextual information for each word in a sentence. Similar encoder architectures have been applied recently with notable success to morphological tagging (Heigold et al., 2017; Yu et al., 2017) as well as several other sequence tagging tasks (Lample et al., 2016; Chiu and Nichols, 2016; Ling et al., 2015).

4 Experimental Setup

This section details the experimental setup. We describe the data, then we introduce the baseline models and finally we report the hyperparameters of the models.

4.1 Data

We run experiments on the Universal Dependencies version 2.1 (Nivre et al., 2017). We excluded corpora that did not include train/dev/test split, word form information[2], or morphological features[3]. Additionally, we excluded corpora for which pre-trained word embeddings were not available.[4] The resulting dataset contains 69 corpora covering 49 different languages. Tagsets were constructed by concatenating the POS and morphological annotations of the treebanks. Table 1 gives corpus statistics. We present type and token counts for both training and test sets. For training set, we also show the average and maximum number of tags per word type and the size of the morphological tagset. For the test set, we report the proportion of out-of-vocabulary (OOV) words as well as the number of OOV tag tokens and types.

In the encoder, we use fastText word embeddings (Bojanowski et al., 2017) pre-trained on Wikipedia.[5] Although these embeddings are uncased, our model still captures case information by

---

[2]French-FTB and Arabic-NYUAD
[3]Japanese
[4]Ancient Greek and Coptic
[5]https://github.com/facebookresearch/fastText

Dataset	Train set						Test set				
	Tokens	Types	Tags per word Avg	Max	% Emb	# Tags	Tokens	Types	% OOV	OOV Tags Tokens	OOV Tags Types
Afrikaans	33894	5080	1.1	4	62.7	61	10065	2476	13.8	3	3
Arabic	254340	33225	1.8	10	90.1	349	32128	8754	9.8	6	6
Basque	72974	19222	1.4	13	53.8	884	24374	8896	17.8	71	61
Belarusian	5217	2303	1.4	6	74.6	346	1382	708	39.7	48	32
Bulgarian	124336	25047	1.1	7	65.7	432	15724	5974	12.3	4	3
Catalan	418494	31544	1.2	8	62.0	267	58017	9832	5.2	3	3
Chinese	98608	17610	1.3	6	65.8	31	12012	4055	12.5	1	1
Croatian	169283	34968	1.6	19	66.0	1105	13228	5513	14.1	13	13
Czech	1175374	125358	1.7	25	59.7	2630	174252	37727	7.0	127	94
Czech-CAC	473622	66272	1.7	21	72.4	1746	10900	4499	12.6	17	17
Czech-CLTT	27005	4336	1.5	21	73.3	418	4126	1169	17.2	39	30
Czech-FicTree	134059	25943	1.4	58	72.9	1464	16761	5691	12.8	46	43
Danish	80378	16330	1.2	5	62.3	157	10023	3424	15.3	3	2
Dutch	186046	26665	1.2	6	59.8	62	11046	3054	13.7	23	1
Dutch-LassySmall	81243	14622	1.1	5	54.7	60	10080	3573	7.4	0	0
English	204607	19672	1.4	10	58.3	117	25097	5630	9.1	3	3
English-LinES	50095	7436	1.2	4	79.8	17	15623	3530	10.3	0	0
English-ParTUT	43545	6963	1.3	8	74.7	133	3412	1136	9.3	3	3
Estonian	85567	23055	1.3	7	58.0	662	10618	4928	18.6	28	24
Finnish	162827	49210	1.1	9	59.4	2052	21070	9112	23.7	144	119
Finnish-FTB	127845	39755	1.2	8	59.3	1762	16311	8011	23.0	83	76
French	366371	42268	1.2	10	53.5	228	10298	3284	5.8	1	1
French-ParTUT	24922	3815	1.3	10	87.3	197	2693	831	11.2	2	2
French-Sequoia	51924	8463	1.2	5	73.2	200	10360	3023	8.9	0	0
Galician	86676	13236	1.1	4	73.5	27	32390	7169	9.9	3	2
Galician-TreeGal	5262	1873	1.3	9	77.7	173	10900	3182	26.8	81	41
German	268145	49472	2.3	38	25.3	684	16537	5406	11.7	28	26
Gothic	35024	6787	1.4	12	1.5	623	10182	2827	12.4	28	23
Greek	43440	9049	1.3	15	74.4	349	10922	3370	16.4	9	6
Hebrew	169360	29638	1.3	8	87.8	521	15134	5115	16.1	7	6
Hindi	281057	16974	2.4	55	79.3	939	35430	5335	4.6	23	23
Hungarian	20166	7767	1.4	5	75.7	580	10448	4558	37.1	108	85
Indonesian	97531	19223	1.2	6	45.3	21	11780	4354	13.8	0	0
Irish	3183	1257	1.5	8	62.3	236	10138	3245	36.1	276	113
Italian	288750	28915	1.2	11	70.1	278	11153	3533	5.6	0	0
Italian-ParTUT	52390	8323	1.1	6	82.0	205	3929	1318	9.1	1	1
Italian-PoSTWITA	53725	12363	1.2	9	48.7	201	6778	2550	17.3	6	4
Kazakh	547	343	1.2	2	73.2	72	10142	4559	71.9	2371	371
Korean	52328	27714	1.1	4	68.8	11	10926	7060	37.5	0	0
Latin	8018	3854	1.4	7	64.6	347	10954	4996	45.8	153	76
Latin-ITTB	270403	12526	1.5	13	63.1	985	10561	1642	2.2	14	12
Latin-PROIEL	147044	22258	1.4	21	50.6	993	12152	4331	9.8	15	13
Latvian	62397	17745	1.3	30	64.0	742	14490	5467	23.9	46	36
Lithuanian	3210	1522	1.2	3	73.2	297	1060	625	54.7	72	57
Marathi	3253	969	1.6	70	78.1	261	448	199	26.3	19	15
Norwegian-Bokmaal	243887	30072	1.2	6	61.8	203	29966	6616	11.3	4	3
Norwegian-Nynorsk	245330	29133	1.3	8	50.0	184	24773	5963	11.1	3	2
Old_Church_Slavonic	37432	7745	1.4	11	2.2	859	10031	3243	14.1	87	66
Persian	122180	13859	1.1	5	89.7	162	16122	3945	8.5	3	2
Polish	63070	21230	1.5	12	72.3	991	10906	5107	24.2	30	26
Portuguese	222070	27396	1.4	35	61.9	375	10942	3417	8.2	3	3
Portuguese-BR	273176	29944	1.2	8	58.5	22	33638	8047	6.8	0	0
Romanian	185113	30970	1.2	6	69.3	451	16324	5755	10.4	7	6
Russian	75964	25708	1.5	15	66.6	693	11548	5717	26.4	31	23
Russian-SynTagRus	871082	107891	1.4	12	74.7	723	117470	29078	9.5	14	14
Serbian	65764	14713	1.4	12	59.4	539	10891	4038	16.2	8	8
Slovak	80575	21104	1.4	39	63.7	1199	13028	6049	35.8	72	58
Slovenian	112530	29390	1.4	7	67.2	1101	14077	5856	19.9	20	19
Slovenian-SST	9487	2672	1.4	5	90.5	500	10000	2812	21.6	202	132
Spanish	389703	46979	1.4	12	56.7	399	12267	4114	7.4	3	3
Spanish-AnCora	446145	38456	1.2	8	68.3	295	52801	10615	5.6	4	2
Swedish	66645	12911	1.2	8	70.3	202	20377	5127	14.9	12	8
Swedish-LinES	48325	9659	1.2	6	77.3	168	15029	4150	15.0	875	16
Tamil	6849	3040	1.1	4	78.7	201	2183	1132	44.3	20	15
Telugu	5082	1743	1.1	4	0.3	14	721	387	25.0	0	0
Turkish	39169	14576	1.2	9	67.5	972	10256	5139	26.4	87	82
Ukrainian	75054	23970	1.4	23	72.6	1197	14939	6337	27.2	72	60
Urdu	108690	9547	2.7	52	73.9	1001	14806	2949	6.4	27	21
Vietnamese	20285	3625	1.2	4	33.7	15	11955	2684	17.1	1	1

Table 1: Descriptive statistics for all UDv2.1 datasets. For training sets we report the number of word tokens and types, the average (Avg) and maximum (Max) tags per word type, the proportion of word types for which pre-trained embeddings were available (% Emb) and the size of the morphological tagset (# Tags). For the test sets, we also give the total number of tokens and types, the proportion of OOV words (% OOV) and the number of OOV tag tokens and types.

means of character-level embeddings. In Table 1, we also report for each language the proportion of word types for which the pre-trained embeddings are available.

4.2 Baseline Models

We use two models as baseline: the CRF-based MARMOT (Müller et al., 2013) and the regular neural multiclass classifier.

MarMoT (MMT) MARMOT[6] is a CRF-based morphological tagger which has been shown to achieve competitive performance across several languages (Müller et al., 2013). MARMOT approximates the CRF objective using a pruning strategy which enables training higher-order models and handling large tagsets. In particular, the tagger first predicts the POS part of the label and based on that, constrains the set of possible morphological labels. Following the results of Müller et al. (2013), we train second-order models. We tuned the regularization type and weight on German development set and based on that, we use L2 regularization with weight 0.01 in all our experiments.

Neural Multiclass classifier (MC) As the second baseline, we employ the standard multiclass classifier used by both Heigold et al. (2017) and Yu et al. (2017). The proposed model consists of an LSTM-based encoder, identical to the one described above in section 3.3, and a softmax classifier over the full tagset. The tagset sizes for each corpora are shown in Table 1. During preliminary experiments, we also added CRF layer on top of softmax, but as this made the decoding process considerably slower without any visible improvement in accuracy, we did not adopt CRF decoding here. The multiclass model is shown in Figure 1 (d).

The inherent limitation of both baseline models is their inability to predict tags that are not present in the training corpus. Although the number of such tags in our data set is not large, it is nevertheless non-zero for most languages.

4.3 Training and Parametrisation

Since tuning model hyperparameters for each of the 69 datasets individually is computationally demanding, we optimise parameters on Finnish—a morphologically complex language with a reasonable dataset size—and apply the resulting values to

---

⁶`http://cistern.cis.lmu.de/marmot/`

	SEQ	OTHER NN
Encoder		
Word embedding size	300	300
Character embedding size	100	100
Character LSTM hidden layer size	150	150
Word embedding dropout	0.5	0.5
LSTM layers	1	1
LSTM hidden state size	400	400
LSTM input dropout	0.5	0.5
LSTM state dropout	0.3	0.3
LSTM output dropout	0.5	0.5
Decoder		
LSTM hidden state size	800	800
Tag embedding size	150	–
Training		
Initial learning rate	1.0	1.0
Batch size	5	20
Maximum epochs	400	400
Learning rate decay factor	–	0.98

Table 2: Hyperparameters for neural models.

other languages. We first tuned the character embedding size and character-LSTM hidden layer size of the encoder on the SEQ model and reused the obtained values with all other models. We tuned the batch size, the learning rate and the decay factor for the SEQ and MC models separately since these models are architecturally quite different. For the MCML and HMCML models we reuse the values obtained for the MC model. The remaining hyperparameter values are fixed. Table 2 lists the hyperparameters for all models.

We train all neural models using stochastic gradient descent for up to 400 epochs and stop early if there has been no improvement on development set within 50 epochs. For all models except SEQ, we decay the learning rate by a factor of 0.98 after every 2500 batch updates. We initialise biases with zeros and parameter matrices using Xavier uniform initialiser (Glorot and Bengio, 2010).

Words in training sets with no pre-trained embeddings are initialised with random embeddings. At test time, words with no pre-trained embedding are assigned a special UNK-embedding. We train the UNK-embedding by randomly substituting the singletons in a batch with the UNK-embedding with a probability of 0.5.

5 Results

Table 3 presents the experimental results. We report tagging accuracy for all word tokens and also for OOV tokens only. A full morphological tag is considered correct if both its POS and all morphological features are correctly predicted.

Dataset	Full tag (all words)					Full tag (OOV words)					POS (all words)				
	MMT	Mc	McMl	HMcMl	Seq	MMT	Mc	McMl	HMcMl	Seq	MMT	Mc	McMl	HMcMl	Seq
Afrikaans	94.17	95.17	94.46	94.65	**95.45**	79.77	84.67	81.93	82.72	**84.88**	96.47	97.40	97.62	97.48	**97.66**
Arabic	90.96	93.39	93.25	93.23	**93.84**	81.25	86.06	85.24	85.14	**87.14**	95.22	96.01	96.18	96.20	**96.22**
Basque	87.15	89.92	89.96	90.15	**90.33**	63.67	**72.65**	71.61	71.86	71.95	93.87	95.25	**96.00**	96.00	95.89
Belarusian	73.66	71.35	72.29	75.54	**78.15**	48.18	46.35	47.81	52.92	**59.12**	90.38	86.54	91.53	**93.42**	93.20
Bulgarian	95.90	97.03	96.76	96.76	**97.04**	82.62	**88.74**	86.66	86.72	88.22	98.04	98.64	98.76	**98.82**	98.79
Catalan	96.60	97.52	97.39	97.36	**97.59**	89.21	91.95	91.75	91.35	**92.28**	98.05	98.63	98.68	98.65	**98.70**
Chinese	90.91	92.97	92.79	92.47	**93.27**	77.90	82.24	81.71	81.17	**82.91**	91.89	93.84	93.70	93.44	**94.11**
Croatian	84.99	88.66	88.96	88.96	**89.24**	66.11	74.87	75.89	**76.48**	76.37	96.47	97.25	**97.54**	97.41	97.45
Czech	93.00	**95.81**	95.06	95.05	95.39	73.07	**82.92**	80.81	80.53	79.70	98.56	98.95	**99.00**	98.99	98.88
Czech-CAC	90.46	**95.19**	94.74	94.72	95.14	69.39	**82.25**	80.13	79.91	81.59	98.65	99.06	99.17	**99.28**	99.05
Czech-CLTT	89.21	89.63	90.45	91.01	**91.37**	73.00	77.78	78.48	78.20	**80.03**	98.01	97.99	98.91	**99.05**	98.67
Czech-FicTree	91.24	93.93	94.54	94.48	**94.64**	75.32	83.96	84.48	83.87	**85.46**	97.55	98.14	**98.57**	98.51	98.38
Danish	93.90	95.73	95.26	95.46	**95.97**	78.74	85.24	83.03	83.68	**85.96**	95.79	97.26	97.30	97.44	**97.51**
Dutch	91.84	94.62	93.70	93.81	**94.73**	70.49	**81.23**	77.65	77.52	80.57	94.39	96.23	96.22	96.11	**96.35**
Dutch-LassySmall	97.09	97.05	97.33	97.29	**97.54**	80.73	83.96	83.15	82.35	**84.10**	97.82	97.83	**98.41**	98.36	98.26
English	93.03	**94.92**	94.40	94.36	94.80	76.22	**85.43**	83.33	83.38	84.69	94.54	**96.13**	96.09	95.96	96.06
English-LinES	95.03	**96.52**	96.36	96.39	96.36	83.72	**90.34**	89.41	90.09	89.23	95.03	**96.52**	96.36	96.39	96.36
English-ParTUT	92.32	93.76	93.17	93.17	**94.17**	70.22	76.49	73.35	73.67	**81.82**	93.87	95.43	**96.10**	96.07	95.87
Estonian	91.40	93.28	93.17	93.25	**93.30**	79.25	84.78	84.42	84.32	**85.13**	95.54	96.61	96.74	**96.85**	96.68
Finnish	91.41	93.13	93.18	93.29	**93.41**	78.35	84.05	**84.79**	84.71	84.71	95.68	96.55	97.02	**97.05**	96.79
Finnish-FTB	90.59	93.91	**94.13**	93.88	91.93	76.06	84.65	**85.50**	85.24	80.85	93.36	95.73	**96.28**	96.19	94.56
French	95.68	96.36	95.97	96.17	**96.39**	82.67	87.02	86.36	85.19	**87.85**	96.93	97.48	97.43	**97.50**	97.49
French-ParTUT	92.91	93.50	93.28	92.94	**93.95**	71.10	**73.42**	70.10	70.10	72.43	95.77	96.10	**96.77**	96.73	96.77
French-Sequoia	95.99	96.66	96.51	96.31	**96.91**	76.99	**83.64**	80.82	80.39	82.23	97.68	98.06	**98.33**	98.17	98.32
Galician	96.97	97.65	97.72	97.70	**97.76**	84.94	88.66	88.98	88.85	**89.01**	97.10	97.80	97.87	97.84	**97.90**
Galician-TreeGal	86.31	83.83	85.00	85.31	**86.61**	68.40	66.77	67.83	68.28	**71.80**	90.13	88.36	91.99	**92.00**	91.48
German	80.81	87.98	87.11	87.16	**88.32**	63.12	**78.53**	75.00	76.14	78.37	92.60	94.47	94.56	**94.62**	94.35
Gothic	87.09	86.49	86.25	86.86	**87.99**	**69.70**	65.59	60.84	62.03	65.27	95.47	94.48	95.45	**96.02**	95.59
Greek	91.00	92.63	93.85	93.58	**94.14**	73.17	78.42	80.55	79.32	**81.89**	96.74	97.21	**97.80**	97.74	97.73
Hebrew	93.19	95.05	94.73	94.60	**95.09**	81.05	87.90	86.87	86.63	**88.02**	96.15	**97.59**	97.59	97.53	97.56
Hindi	89.00	**91.78**	91.47	91.34	91.75	62.35	**72.37**	69.99	68.77	71.70	96.20	97.00	**97.32**	97.22	97.03
Hungarian	71.47	80.96	82.89	82.45	**84.12**	49.42	67.14	70.08	68.87	**72.01**	92.78	93.94	95.30	95.31	**95.44**
Indonesian	93.56	**93.79**	93.73	93.74	93.65	88.22	88.04	**88.53**	88.16	87.67	93.57	93.81	93.81	**93.85**	93.69
Irish	**67.99**	60.73	62.02	61.95	65.81	**35.48**	28.05	29.50	28.70	34.50	83.62	79.10	84.01	**84.22**	83.63
Italian	97.06	97.53	97.31	97.31	**97.61**	86.61	**88.87**	86.61	86.29	88.71	97.74	98.16	98.19	**98.32**	98.26
Italian-ParTUT	96.13	**97.12**	96.79	96.84	97.12	80.22	**90.81**	86.35	85.79	88.30	97.28	97.86	**98.14**	98.12	98.12
Italian-PoSTWITA	91.92	**93.79**	93.23	93.36	93.69	75.85	**82.34**	80.20	80.80	81.83	93.54	95.32	**95.72**	95.68	95.16
Kazakh	**37.19**	31.63	28.84	28.70	34.35	**20.97**	13.52	10.45	10.38	17.84	52.73	48.94	52.38	**54.74**	54.57
Korean	93.98	95.82	95.55	95.49	**95.87**	90.48	**93.51**	93.12	92.90	93.33	93.98	95.82	95.55	95.50	**95.87**
Latin	64.94	64.10	65.35	65.88	**67.45**	41.05	42.54	42.58	43.30	**46.99**	80.73	80.97	84.84	**85.57**	84.81
Latin-ITTB	92.98	95.18	**95.60**	95.57	95.27	68.26	74.78	**75.65**	74.35	72.61	97.30	98.12	98.30	**98.34**	98.17
Latin-PROIEL	88.37	**90.64**	90.20	90.13	89.66	68.43	**78.39**	74.46	73.20	71.69	95.78	96.68	**96.80**	96.72	95.94
Latvian	85.59	87.67	87.14	87.14	**87.79**	67.91	73.59	71.94	71.94	**73.88**	92.80	94.38	94.87	**94.88**	94.55
Lithuanian	65.00	58.02	64.91	63.58	**67.92**	44.66	36.72	43.79	43.10	**51.03**	73.87	70.00	81.60	79.25	**81.70**
Marathi	66.07	68.75	64.06	64.96	**70.09**	39.83	**49.15**	33.05	36.44	44.92	82.14	82.81	84.15	**84.82**	84.60
Norwegian-Bokmaal	94.99	96.37	96.13	95.94	**96.54**	80.14	84.53	83.11	82.54	**84.68**	97.33	98.24	98.39	98.26	**98.44**
Norwegian-Nynorsk	94.65	**96.25**	95.69	95.69	96.07	81.32	**85.30**	81.93	82.11	83.82	97.08	98.12	**98.22**	98.14	98.08
Old_Church_Slavonic	87.58	86.96	87.01	86.87	**87.96**	60.31	**60.59**	57.49	57.13	58.83	94.98	94.40	95.38	**95.61**	94.94
Persian	95.84	96.75	96.38	96.38	**96.79**	79.36	**86.09**	84.04	83.67	85.43	96.39	97.13	97.11	97.10	**97.30**
Polish	86.04	90.46	**90.99**	90.78	90.99	69.13	**81.21**	79.36	79.81	80.87	96.65	97.73	**98.25**	98.11	98.04
Portuguese	94.21	95.59	95.34	95.59	**95.75**	79.48	86.66	86.66	**86.77**	86.43	97.21	97.72	**98.06**	97.95	98.04
Portuguese-BR	97.59	98.20	98.20	98.14	**98.21**	92.30	95.20	**95.56**	95.03	95.16	97.60	98.20	98.21	98.16	**98.22**
Romanian	96.30	97.00	96.72	96.61	**97.16**	85.15	89.51	88.10	87.92	**89.75**	97.18	97.61	97.74	**97.78**	97.77
Russian	85.99	90.21	90.73	90.93	**91.05**	66.91	77.85	78.24	78.90	**79.26**	95.42	96.43	96.72	**96.84**	96.50
Russian-SynTagRus	94.44	**96.78**	96.48	96.58	96.67	78.91	**88.50**	87.21	87.48	86.98	98.51	98.84	98.92	98.93	**98.94**
Serbian	91.17	93.25	93.32	93.58	**93.93**	77.32	83.22	82.20	82.48	**83.50**	97.47	97.89	**98.25**	98.17	98.19
Slovak	81.72	87.50	88.16	**88.54**	88.46	68.42	78.66	78.98	79.24	**79.69**	94.62	95.85	**96.49**	96.34	96.46
Slovenian	89.39	94.32	94.05	93.98	**94.62**	73.14	86.34	83.94	83.58	**86.41**	97.07	98.15	98.29	98.39	**98.42**
Slovenian-SST	78.71	75.75	79.18	80.02	**80.44**	45.45	44.06	48.40	49.88	**52.24**	88.44	87.54	92.04	**92.38**	90.99
Spanish	94.33	**95.05**	94.82	94.81	94.90	77.34	**82.95**	82.29	82.18	81.52	95.88	96.89	96.95	**96.98**	96.83
Spanish-AnCora	97.13	**97.67**	97.54	97.58	97.63	90.26	93.22	93.09	93.19	**93.36**	98.25	98.64	98.75	**98.78**	98.68
Swedish	94.28	95.41	95.07	95.25	**95.65**	82.72	86.11	84.20	84.07	**86.37**	96.38	97.49	97.69	**97.72**	97.66
Swedish-LinES	85.24	86.38	85.99	85.98	**86.47**	64.01	**68.33**	66.28	65.79	67.26	95.00	96.17	**96.69**	96.65	96.25
Tamil	81.40	82.18	83.05	81.26	**85.75**	67.87	71.90	72.42	70.56	**75.83**	86.39	87.49	**91.07**	90.24	90.75
Telugu	**92.23**	90.43	89.04	89.32	91.26	**80.00**	75.56	70.00	71.67	78.33	**92.23**	90.43	89.04	89.32	91.26
Turkish	86.09	89.47	90.69	90.51	**90.70**	63.97	74.85	**79.83**	79.02	79.13	92.86	94.67	**95.54**	95.51	95.19
Ukrainian	85.33	88.98	89.94	**89.96**	89.31	61.19	78.89	79.24	79.34	**79.36**	95.97	96.40	**97.23**	97.06	97.03
Urdu	77.37	80.09	79.52	78.54	**80.66**	54.99	64.54	60.30	61.68	**65.07**	92.56	93.29	**93.87**	93.71	93.81
Vietnamese	86.13	**88.66**	88.51	88.22	88.44	55.19	**70.81**	70.46	69.29	68.70	86.15	**88.67**	88.58	88.34	88.46
Average (>100K)	92.18	**94.37**	94.12	94.07	94.37	76.65	**84.03**	82.67	82.47	83.42	96.49	97.37	**97.52**	97.50	97.40
Average (50K-100K)	91.27	93.36	93.36	93.40	**93.66**	76.96	**83.46**	82.39	82.43	83.40	95.39	96.43	**96.71**	96.67	96.65
Average (20K-50K)	87.56	89.42	89.69	89.66	**90.43**	66.35	72.55	71.76	71.47	**73.84**	94.37	95.13	95.83	**95.86**	95.69
Average (<20K)	71.35	68.68	69.37	69.65	**72.78**	49.19	47.46	46.58	47.52	**53.26**	82.07	80.22	84.27	84.60	**84.70**
Overall average	88.18	89.58	89.61	89.64	**90.42**	71.12	76.74	75.62	75.64	**77.52**	93.76	94.27	95.11	**95.14**	95.08

Table 3: Morphological tagging accuracies on UDv2.1 test sets for MarMot (MMT) and Mc baselines as well as for McML, HMcML and Seq compositional models. The left section shows the full Pos+Morph tag results, the middle section gives accuracies for OOV words only, the right-most section shows the POS tagging accuracy. The best result in each section for each language is in bold. The languages are color-coded according to the training set size, lighter color denotes larger training set: cyan (<20K), violet (20K-50K), magenta (50K-100K), pink (>100K).

Feature	SEQ	MC	#	Feature	SEQ	MC	#
POS	**91.03**	90.20	69	NumType	**89.68**	87.82	54
Number	**94.02**	93.05	63	Polarity	**93.83**	92.86	54
VerbForm	**91.29**	89.86	61	Degree	**87.44**	84.12	48
Person	**89.02**	87.52	60	Poss	**94.52**	93.60	44
Tense	**92.96**	91.31	59	Voice	**88.40**	82.85	42
PronType	**89.83**	88.81	58	Definite	**95.26**	94.10	37
Mood	**87.34**	85.40	58	Aspect	**89.76**	87.71	29
Gender	**89.31**	87.78	55	Animacy	**86.22**	83.73	19
Case	**88.90**	87.04	55	Polite	75.76	**80.48**	10

Table 4: Performance of SEQ and MC models on individual features reported as macro-averaged F1-scores.

First of all, we can confirm the results of Heigold et al. (2017) that the performance of neural morphological tagging indeed exceeds the results of a CRF-based model. In fact, all our neural models perform significantly better than MARMOT ($p < 0.001$).[7]

The best neural model on average is the SEQ model, which is significantly better from both the MC baseline as well as the other two compositional models, whereby the improvement is especially well-pronounced on smaller datasets. We do not observe any significant differences between MCML and HMCML models neither on all words nor OOV evaluation setting.

We also present POS tagging results in the rightmost section of Table 3. Here again, all neural models are better than CRF which is in line with the results presented by Plank et al. (2016). For POS tags, the HMCML is the best on average. It is also significantly better than the neural MC baseline, however, the differences with the MCML and SEQ models are insignificant.

In addition to full-tag accuracies, we assess the performance on individual features. Table 4 reports macro-averaged F1-cores for the SEQ and the MC models on universal features. Results indicate that the SEQ model systematically outperforms the MC model on most features.

6 Analysis and Discussion

OOV label accuracy Our models are able to predict labels that were not seen in the training data. Figure 2 presents the accuracy of test tokens with OOV labels obtained with our best performing SEQ model plotted against the number of OOV label types. The datasets with zero accuracy are omitted. The main observation is that although the OOV label accuracy is zero for some languages, it is above zero on ca. half of the datasets—a result that would be impossible with MARMOT or MC baselines.

---

[7] As indicated by Wilcoxon signed-rank test.

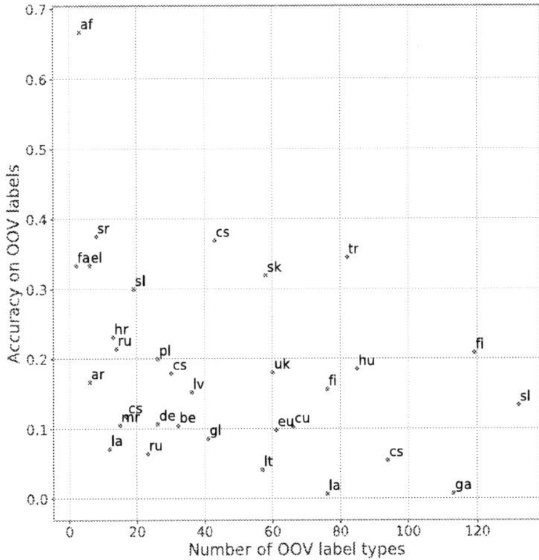

Figure 2: OOV label accuracies of the SEQ model.

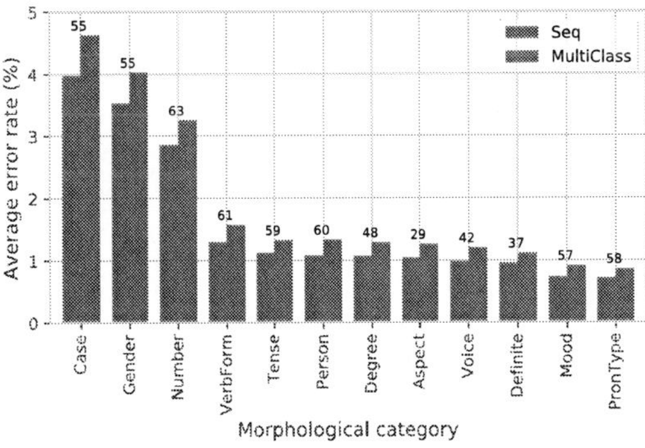

Figure 3: Average error rates of distinct morphological categories for SEQ and MC models.

Error Analysis Figure 3 shows the largest error rates for distinct morphological categories for both SEQ and MC models averaged over all languages. We observe that the error patterns are similar for both models but the error rates of the SEQ model are consistently lower as expected.

Stability Analysis To assess the stability of our predictions, we picked five languages from different families and with different corpus size, and performed five independent train/test runs for each language. Table 5 summarises the results of these experiments and demonstrates a reasonably small variance for all languages. For all languages, except for Finnish, the worst accuracy of the SEQ model was better than the best accuracy of the MC model, confirming our results that in those languages, the SEQ model is consistently better than the MC baseline.

Dataset	SEQ	MC
Finnish	93.24 ± 0.12	93.20 ± 0.07
German	88.45 ± 0.21	87.74 ± 0.17
Hungarian	84.51 ± 0.54	80.68 ± 0.48
Russian	91.08 ± 0.18	90.13 ± 0.15
Turkish	90.29 ± 0.24	89.16 ± 0.27

Table 5: Mean accuracy with standard deviation over five independent runs for SEQ and MC models.

Hyperparameter Tuning It is possible that the hyperparameters tuned on Finnish are not optimal for other languages and thus, tuning hyperparameters for each language individually would lead to different conclusions than currently drawn. To shed some light on this issue, we tuned hyperparameters for the SEQ and MC models on the same subset of five languages. We first independently optimised the dropout rates on word embeddings, encoder's LSTM inputs and outputs, as well as the number of LSTM layers. We then performed a grid search to find the optimal initial learning rate, the learning rate decay factor and the decay step. Value ranges for the tuned parameters are given in Table 6.

Parameter	Values
Word embedding dropout	$\{0, 0.1, \ldots, 0.5\}$
LSTM input dropout	$\{0, 0.1, \ldots, 0.5\}$
LSTM input dropout	$\{0, 0.1, \ldots, 0.5\}$
Number of LSTM layers	$\{1, 2\}$
Initial learning rate	$\{0.01, 0.1, 1, 2\}$
Learning rate decay factor	$\{0.97, 0.98, 0.99, 1\}$
Decay step	$\{1250, 2500, 5000\}$

Table 6: The grid values for hyperparameter tuning.

Table 7 reports accuracies for the tuned models compared to the mean accuracies reported in Table 5. As expected, both tuned models demonstrate superior performance on all languages, except for German with the SEQ model. Hyperparameter tuning has a greater overall effect on the MC model, which suggests that it is more sensitive to the choice of parameters than the SEQ model. Still, the tuned SEQ model performs better or at least as good as the MC model on all languages.

Comparison with Previous Work Since UD datasets have been in rapid development and different UD versions do not match, direct comparison of our results to previously published results is difficult. Still, we show the results taken from Heigold et al. (2017), which were obtained on UDv1.3, to provide a very rough comparison. In addition, we compare our SEQ model with a neural tagger presented by Dozat et al. (2017), which is similar to

Dataset	SEQ	Gain	MC	Gain
Finnish	93.44	+0.20	93.43	+0.23
German	88.35	−0.10	88.14	+0.40
Hungarian	85.56	+1.05	82.29	+1.61
Russian	91.44	+0.36	90.74	+0.61
Turkish	90.56	+0.27	89.32	+0.16

Table 7: Accuracies of the tuned SEQ and MC models compared to the mean accuracies in Table 5.

Dataset	SEQ	Dozat	Heigold
Arabic	**93.84**	92.85	93.78
Bulgarian	97.04	**97.25**	95.14
Czech	**95.39**	95.22	96.32
English	94.80	**94.81**	93.32
Estonian	93.30	**93.90**	94.25
Finnish	93.41	**93.73**	93.52
French	**96.39**	95.90	94.91
Hindi	91.75	**92.36**	90.84
Hungarian	**84.12**	82.84	77.59
Romanian	97.16	**97.20**	94.12
Russian-SynTagRus	**96.67**	96.20	96.45
Turkish	**90.70**	90.22	89.12
Average	**93.71**	93.54	92.45

Table 8: Accuracies for the SEQ model, Dozat et al. (2017) and Heigold et al. (2017).

our MC model, but employs a more sophisticated encoder. We train this model on UDv2.1 on the same set of languages used by Heigold et al. (2017).

Table 8 reports evaluation results for the three models. The SEQ model and Dozat's tagger demonstrate comparable performance. This suggests that the SEQ model can be further improved by adopting a more advanced encoder from Dozat et al. (2017).

7   Conclusion

We hypothesised that explicitly modeling the internal structure of complex labels for morphological tagging improves the overall tagging accuracy over the baseline with monolithic tags. To test this hypothesis, we experimented with three approaches to model composite morphological tags in a neural sequence tagging framework. Experimental results on 49 languages demonstrated the advantage of modeling morphological labels as sequences of category values, whereas the superiority of this model is especially pronounced on smaller datasets. Furthermore, we showed that, in contrast to baselines, our models are capable of predicting labels that were not seen during training.

Acknowledgments

This work was supported by the Estonian Research Council (grants no. 2056, 1226 and IUT34-4).

References

Daniel Andor, Chris Alberti, David Weiss, Aliaksei Severyn, Alessandro Presta, Kuzman Ganchev, Slav Petrov, and Michael Collins. 2016. Globally normalized transition-based neural networks. In *Proceedings of the 54th Annual Meeting of the Association for Computational Linguistics*, volume 1 (Long Papers), pages 2442–2452. Association for Computational Linguistics.

Piotr Bojanowski, Edouard Grave, Armand Joulin, and Tomas Mikolov. 2017. Enriching word vectors with subword information. *Transactions of the Association of Computational Linguistics*, 5:135–146.

Jason Chiu and Eric Nichols. 2016. Named entity recognition with bidirectional lstm-cnns. *Transactions of the Association of Computational Linguistics*, 4:357–370.

Kyunghyun Cho, Bart van Merrienboer, Dzmitry Bahdanau, and Yoshua Bengio. 2014. On the properties of neural machine translation: Encoder–decoder approaches. In *Proceedings of the Eighth Workshop on Syntax, Semantics and Structure in Statistical Translation*, pages 103–111. Association for Computational Linguistics.

Timothy Dozat, Peng Qi, and Christopher D Manning. 2017. Proceedings of the conll 2017 shared task: Multilingual parsing from raw text to universal dependencies. In *CoNLL 2017 Shared Task." Proceedings of the CoNLL 2017 Shared Task: Multilingual Parsing from Raw Text to Universal Dependencies*, pages 20–30.

Manaal Faruqui, Yulia Tsvetkov, Graham Neubig, and Chris Dyer. 2016. Morphological inflection generation using character sequence to sequence learning. In *Proceedings of the 2016 Conference of the North American Chapter of the Association for Computational Linguistics: Human Language Technologies*, pages 634–643.

Xavier Glorot and Yoshua Bengio. 2010. Understanding the difficulty of training deep feedforward neural networks. In *Proceedings of the thirteenth International Conference on Artificial Intelligence and Statistics*, pages 249–256.

Jan Hajič. 2000. Morphological tagging: Data vs. dictionaries. In *Proceedings of the 1st Conference of the North American Chapter of the Association of Computational Linguistics*, pages 94–101. Association for Computational Linguistics.

Jan Hajič and Barbora Hladká. 1998. Tagging inflective languages: Prediction of morphological categories for a rich, structured tagset. In *Proceedings of the 36th Annual Meeting of the Association for Computational Linguistics and 17th International Conference on Computational Linguistics*, volume 1, pages 483–490. Association for Computational Linguistics.

Diiek Z Hakkani-Tur, Kemal Oflazer, and Gokhan Tur. 2000. Statistical morphological disambiguation for agglutinative languages. In *Proceedings of the 18th International Conference on Computational Linguistics*, volume 1.

Georg Heigold, Josef van Genabith, and Günter Neumann. 2016. Scaling character-based morphological tagging to fourteen languages. In *2016 IEEE International Conference on Big Data*, pages 3895–3902. IEEE.

Georg Heigold, Guenter Neumann, and Josef van Genabith. 2017. An extensive empirical evaluation of character-based morphological tagging for 14 languages. In *Proceedings of the 15th Conference of the European Chapter of the Association for Computational Linguistics*, volume 1 (Long Papers), pages 505–513.

Zhiheng Huang, Wei Xu, and Kai Yu. 2015. Bidirectional lstm-crf models for sequence tagging. *arXiv preprint arXiv:1508.01991*.

Go Inoue, Hiroyuki Shindo, and Yuji Matsumoto. 2017. Joint prediction of morphosyntactic categories for fine-grained arabic part-of-speech tagging exploiting tag dictionary information. In *Proceedings of the 21st Conference on Computational Natural Language Learning*, pages 421–431.

Katharina Kann and Hinrich Schütze. 2016. Single-model encoder-decoder with explicit morphological representation for reinflection. In *Proceedings of the 54th Annual Meeting of the Association for Computational Linguistics*, volume 2, pages 555–560. Association for Computational Linguistics.

Christo Kirov, John Sylak-Glassman, Rebecca Knowles, Ryan Cotterell, and Matt Post. 2017. A rich morphological tagger for english: Exploring the cross-linguistic tradeoff between morphology and syntax. In *Proceedings of the 15th Conference of the European Chapter of the Association for Computational Linguistics*, volume 2, pages 112–117.

Matthieu Labeau, Kevin Löser, and Alexandre Allauzen. 2015. Non-lexical neural architecture for fine-grained pos tagging. In *Proceedings of the 2015 Conference on Empirical Methods in Natural Language Processing*, pages 232–237.

Guillaume Lample, Miguel Ballesteros, Kazuya Kawakami, Sandeep Subramanian, and Chris Dyer. 2016. Neural architectures for named entity recognition. In *Proceedings of the 2016 Conference of the North American Chapter of the Association for Computational Linguistics: Human Language Technologies*.

John Lee, Jason Naradowsky, and David A Smith. 2011. A discriminative model for joint morphological disambiguation and dependency parsing. In *Proceedings of the 49th Annual Meeting of the Association for Computational Linguistics: Human Language Technologies-Volume 1*, pages 885–894. Association for Computational Linguistics.

Wang Ling, Chris Dyer, Alan W Black, Isabel Trancoso, Ramon Fermandez, Silvio Amir, Luis Marujo, and Tiago Luis. 2015. Finding function in form: Compositional character models for open vocabulary word representation. In *Proceedings of the 2015 Conference on Empirical Methods in Natural Language Processing*, pages 1520–1530. Association for Computational Linguistics.

Xuezhe Ma and Eduard Hovy. 2016. End-to-end sequence labeling via bi-directional lstm-cnns-crf. In *Proceedings of the 54th Annual Meeting of the Association for Computational Linguistics*, volume 1, pages 1064–1074. Association for Computational Linguistics.

Chaitanya Malaviya, Matthew R. Gormley, and Graham Neubig. 2018. Neural factor graph models for cross-lingual morphological tagging. In *Proceedings of the 56th Annual Meeting of the Association for Computational Linguistics (Volume 1: Long Papers)*, pages 2653–2663. Association for Computational Linguistics.

Thomas Müller, Helmut Schmid, and Hinrich Schütze. 2013. Efficient higher-order crfs for morphological tagging. In *Proceedings of the 2013 Conference on Empirical Methods in Natural Language Processing*, pages 322–332.

Thomas Müller and Hinrich Schütze. 2015. Robust morphological tagging with word representations. In *Proceedings of the 2015 Conference of the North American Chapter of the Association for Computational Linguistics: Human Language Technologies*, pages 526–536.

Joakim Nivre, Željko Agić, Lars Ahrenberg, Lene Antonsen, Maria Jesus Aranzabe, Masayuki Asahara, Luma Ateyah, Mohammed Attia, Aitziber Atutxa, Liesbeth Augustinus, Elena Badmaeva, Miguel Ballesteros, Esha Banerjee, Sebastian Bank, Verginica Barbu Mititelu, John Bauer, Kepa Bengoetxea, Riyaz Ahmad Bhat, Eckhard Bick, Victoria Bobicev, Carl Börstell, Cristina Bosco, Gosse Bouma, Sam Bowman, Aljoscha Burchardt, Marie Candito, Gauthier Caron, Gülşen Cebiroğlu Eryiğit, Giuseppe G. A. Celano, Savas Cetin, Fabricio Chalub, Jinho Choi, Silvie Cinková, Çağrı Çöltekin, Miriam Connor, Elizabeth Davidson, Marie-Catherine de Marneffe, Valeria de Paiva, Arantza Diaz de Ilarraza, Peter Dirix, Kaja Dobrovoljc, Timothy Dozat, Kira Droganova, Puneet Dwivedi, Marhaba Eli, Ali Elkahky, Tomaž Erjavec, Richárd Farkas, Hector Fernandez Alcalde, Jennifer Foster, Cláudia Freitas, Katarína Gajdošová, Daniel Galbraith, Marcos Garcia, Moa Gärdenfors, Kim Gerdes, Filip Ginter, Iakes Goenaga, Koldo Gojenola, Memduh Gökırmak, Yoav Goldberg, Xavier Gómez Guinovart, Berta Gonzáles Saavedra, Matias Grioni, Normunds Grūzītis, Bruno Guillaume, Nizar Habash, Jan Hajič, Jan Hajič jr., Linh Hà Mỹ, Kim Harris, Dag Haug, Barbora Hladká, Jaroslava Hlaváčová, Florinel Hociung, Petter Hohle, Radu Ion, Elena Irimia, Tomáš Jelínek, Anders Johannsen, Fredrik Jørgensen, Hüner Kaşıkara, Hiroshi Kanayama, Jenna Kanerva, Tolga Kayadelen, Václava Kettnerová, Jesse Kirchner, Natalia Kotsyba, Simon Krek, Veronika Laippala, Lorenzo Lambertino, Tatiana Lando, John Lee, PhƆ Lê Hồng, Alessandro Lenci, Saran Lertpradit, Herman Leung, Cheuk Ying Li, Josie Li, Keying Li, Nikola Ljubešić, Olga Loginova, Olga Lyashevskaya, Teresa Lynn, Vivien Macketanz, Aibek Makazhanov, Michael Mandl, Christopher Manning, Cătălina Mărănduc, David Mareček, Katrin Marheinecke, Héctor Martínez Alonso, André Martins, Jan Mašek, Yuji Matsumoto, Ryan McDonald, Gustavo Mendonça, Niko Miekka, Anna Missilä, Cătălin Mititelu, Yusuke Miyao, Simonetta Montemagni, Amir More, Laura Moreno Romero, Shinsuke Mori, Bohdan Moskalevskyi, Kadri Muischnek, Kaili Müürisep, Pinkey Nainwani, Anna Nedoluzhko, Gunta Nešpore-Bērzkalne, Lương Nguyễn Thị, Huyền Nguyễn Thị Minh, Vitaly Nikolaev, Hanna Nurmi, Stina Ojala, Petya Osenova, Robert Östling, Lilja Øvrelid, Elena Pascual, Marco Passarotti, Cenel-Augusto Perez, Guy Perrier, Slav Petrov, Jussi Piitulainen, Emily Pitler, Barbara Plank, Martin Popel, Lauma Pretkalniņa, Prokopis Prokopidis, Tiina Puolakainen, Sampo Pyysalo, Alexandre Rademaker, Loganathan Ramasamy, Taraka Rama, Vinit Ravishankar, Livy Real, Siva Reddy, Georg Rehm, Larissa Rinaldi, Laura Rituma, Mykhailo Romanenko, Rudolf Rosa, Davide Rovati, Benoît Sagot, Shadi Saleh, Tanja Samardžić, Manuela Sanguinetti, Baiba Saulīte, Sebastian Schuster, Djamé Seddah, Wolfgang Seeker, Mojgan Seraji, Mo Shen, Atsuko Shimada, Dmitry Sichinava, Natalia Silveira, Maria Simi, Radu Simionescu, Katalin Simkó, Mária Šimková, Kiril Simov, Aaron Smith, Antonio Stella, Milan Straka, Jana Strnadová, Alane Suhr, Umut Sulubacak, Zsolt Szántó, Dima Taji, Takaaki Tanaka, Trond Trosterud, Anna Trukhina, Reut Tsarfaty, Francis Tyers, Sumire Uematsu, Zdeňka Urešová, Larraitz Uria, Hans Uszkoreit, Sowmya Vajjala, Daniel van Niekerk, Gertjan van Noord, Viktor Varga, Eric Villemonte de la Clergerie, Veronika Vincze, Lars Wallin, Jonathan North Washington, Mats Wirén, Tak-sum Wong, Zhuoran Yu, Zdeněk Žabokrtský, Amir Zeldes, Daniel Zeman, and Hanzhi Zhu. 2017. Universal dependencies 2.1. LINDAT/CLARIN digital library at the Institute of Formal and Applied Linguistics (ÚFAL), Faculty of Mathematics and Physics, Charles University.

Barbara Plank, Anders Søgaard, and Yoav Goldberg. 2016. Multilingual part-of-speech tagging with bidirectional long short-term memory models and auxiliary loss. In *Proceedings of the 54th Annual Meeting of the Association for Computational Linguistics*, page 412. Association for Computational Linguistics.

Marek Rei, Gamal Crichton, and Sampo Pyysalo. 2016. Attending to characters in neural sequence labeling models. In *Proceedings of the 26th International Conference on Computational Linguistics: Technical Papers*, pages 309–318.

Cicero D Santos and Bianca Zadrozny. 2014. Learning character-level representations for part-of-speech tagging. In *Proceedings of the 31st International Conference on Machine Learning*, pages 1818–1826.

Helmut Schmid and Florian Laws. 2008. Estimation of conditional probabilities with decision trees and an application to fine-grained pos tagging. In *Proceedings of the 22nd International Conference on Computational Linguistics*, volume 1, pages 777–784. Association for Computational Linguistics.

Noah A Smith, David A Smith, and Roy W Tromble. 2005. Context-based morphological disambiguation with random fields. In *Proceedings of the 2005 Conference on Human Language Technology and Empirical Methods in Natural Language Processing*, pages 475–482. Association for Computational Linguistics.

Milan Straka, Jan Hajic, and Jana Straková. 2016. Udpipe: Trainable pipeline for processing conll-u files performing tokenization, morphological analysis, pos tagging and parsing. In *Proceedings of the Tenth International Conference on Language Resources and Evaluation*.

Milan Straka and Jana Straková. 2017. Tokenizing, pos tagging, lemmatizing and parsing ud 2.0 with udpipe. *Proceedings of the CoNLL 2017 Shared Task: Multilingual Parsing from Raw Text to Universal Dependencies*, pages 88–99.

Ilya Sutskever, Oriol Vinyals, and Quoc V Le. 2014. Sequence to sequence learning with neural networks. In *Advances in Neural Information Processing Systems*, pages 3104–3112.

Xiang Yu, Agnieszka Falenska, and Ngoc Thang Vu. 2017. A general-purpose tagger with convolutional neural networks. In *Proceedings of the First Workshop on Subword and Character Level Models in NLP*, pages 124–129.

Deniz Yuret and Ferhan Türe. 2006. Learning morphological disambiguation rules for turkish. In *Proceedings of the main conference on Human Language Technology Conference of the North American Chapter of the Association of Computational Linguistics*, pages 328–334. Association for Computational Linguistics.

Nasser Zalmout and Nizar Habash. 2017. Don't throw those morphological analyzers away just yet: Neural morphological disambiguation for arabic. In *Proceedings of the 2017 Conference on Empirical Methods in Natural Language Processing*, pages 704–713.

Evolutionary Data Measures: Understanding the Difficulty of Text Classification Tasks

Edward Collins
Wluper Ltd.
London, United Kingdom
ed@wluper.com

Nikolai Rozanov
Wluper Ltd.
London, United Kingdom
nikolai@wluper.com

Bingbing Zhang
Wluper Ltd.
London, United Kingdom
bingbing@wluper.com

Abstract

Classification tasks are usually analysed and improved through new model architectures or hyperparameter optimisation but the underlying properties of datasets are discovered on an ad-hoc basis as errors occur. However, understanding the properties of the data is crucial in perfecting models. In this paper we analyse exactly which characteristics of a dataset best determine how difficult that dataset is for the task of text classification. We then propose an intuitive measure of difficulty for text classification datasets which is simple and fast to calculate. We show that this measure generalises to unseen data by comparing it to state-of-the-art datasets and results. This measure can be used to analyse the precise source of errors in a dataset and allows fast estimation of how difficult a dataset is to learn. We searched for this measure by training 12 classical and neural network based models on 78 real-world datasets, then use a genetic algorithm to discover the best measure of difficulty. Our difficulty-calculating code[1] and datasets[2] are publicly available.

1 Introduction

If a machine learning (ML) model is trained on a dataset then the same machine learning model on the same dataset but with more granular labels will frequently have lower performance scores than the original model (see results in Zhang et al. (2015); Socher et al. (2013a); Yogatama et al. (2017); Joulin et al. (2016); Xiao and Cho (2016); Conneau et al. (2017)). Adding more granularity to labels makes the dataset harder to learn - it increases the dataset's difficulty. It is obvious that some datasets are more difficult for learning models than others, but is it possible to quantify this

difficulty? In order to do so, it would be necessary to understand exactly what characteristics of a dataset are good indicators of how well models will perform on it so that these could be combined into a single measure of difficulty.

Such a difficulty measure would be useful as an analysis tool and as a performance estimator. As an analysis tool, it would highlight precisely what is causing difficulty in a dataset, reducing the time practitioners need spend analysing their data. As a performance estimator, when practitioners approach new datasets they would be able to use this measure to predict how well models are likely to perform on the dataset.

The complexity of datasets for ML has been previously examined (Ho and Basu, 2002; Mansilla and Ho, 2004; Bernadó-Mansilla and Ho, 2005; Maci et al., 2008), but these works focused on analysing feature space data $\in \mathbb{R}^n$. These methods do not easily apply to natural language, because they would require the language be embedded into feature space in some way, for example with a word embedding model which introduces a dependency on the model used. We extend previous notions of difficulty to English language text classification, an important component of natural language processing (NLP) applicable to tasks such as sentiment analysis, news categorisation and automatic summarisation (Socher et al., 2013a; Antonellis et al., 2006; Collins et al., 2017). All of our recommended calculations depend only on counting the words in a dataset.

1.1 Related Work

One source of difficulty in a dataset is mislabelled items of data (noise). Brodley and Friedl (1999) showed that filtering noise could produce large gains in model performance, potentially yielding larger improvements than hyperparameter optimisation (Smith et al., 2014). We ignored noise in

---

Proceedings of the 22nd Conference on Computational Natural Language Learning (CoNLL 2018), pages 380–391
Brussels, Belgium, October 31 - November 1, 2018. ©2018 Association for Computational Linguistics

this work because it can be reduced with proper data cleaning and is not a part of the true signal of the dataset. We identified four other areas of potential difficulty which we attempt to measure:

Class Interference. Text classification tasks to predict the 1 - 5 star rating of a review are more difficult than predicting whether a review is positive or negative (Zhang et al., 2015; Socher et al., 2013a; Yogatama et al., 2017; Joulin et al., 2016; Xiao and Cho, 2016; Conneau et al., 2017), as reviews given four stars share many features with those given five stars. Gupta et al. (2014) describe how as the number of classes in a dataset increases, so does the potential for "confusability" where it becomes difficult to tell classes apart, therefore making a dataset more difficult. Previous work has mostly focused on this confusability - or class interference - as a source of difficulty in machine learning tasks (Bernadó-Mansilla and Ho, 2005; Ho and Basu, 2000, 2002; Elizondo et al., 2009; Mansilla and Ho, 2004), a common technique being to compute a minimum spanning tree on the data and count the number of edges which link different classes.

Class Diversity. Class diversity provides information about the composition of a dataset by measuring the relative abundances of different classes (Shannon, 2001). Intuitively, it gives a measure of how well a model could do on a dataset without examining any data items and always predicting the most abundant class. Datasets with a single overwhelming class are easy to achieve high accuracies on by always predicting the most abundant class. A measure of diversity is one feature used by Bingel and Søgaard (2017) to identify datasets which would benefit from multi-task learning.

Class Balance. Unbalanced classes are a known problem in machine learning (Chawla et al., 2004, 2002), particularly if classes are not easily separable (Japkowicz, 2000). Underrepresented classes are more difficult to learn because models are not exposed to them as often.

Data Complexity. Humans find some pieces of text more difficult to comprehend than others. How difficult a piece of text is to read can be calculated automatically using measures such as those proposed by Mc Laughlin (1969); Senter and Smith (1967); Kincaid et al. (1975). If a piece of text is more difficult for a human to read and understand, the same may be true for an ML model.

2   Method

We used 78 text classification datasets and trained 12 different ML algorithms on each of the datasets for a total of 936 models trained. The highest achieved macro F1 score (Powers, 2011), on the test set for each model was recorded. Macro F1 score is used because it is valid under imbalanced classes. We then calculated 48 different statistics which attempt to measure our four hypothesised areas of difficulty for each dataset. We then needed to discover which statistic or combination thereof correlated with model F1 scores.

We wanted the discovered difficulty measure to be useful as an analysis tool, so we enforced a restriction that the difficulty measure should be composed only by summation, without weighting the constituent statistics. This meant that each difficulty measure could be used as an analysis tool by examining its components and comparing them to the mean across all datasets.

Each difficulty measure was represented as a binary vector of length 48 - one bit for each statistic - each bit being 1 if that statistic was used in the difficulty measure. We therefore had 2^{48} possible different difficulty measures that may have correlated with model score and needed to search this space efficiently.

Genetic algorithms are biologically inspired search algorithms and are good at searching large spaces efficiently (Whitley, 1994). They maintain a population of candidate difficulty measures and combine them based on their "fitness" - how well they correlate with model scores - so that each "parent" can pass on pieces of information about the search space (Jiao and Wang, 2000). Using a genetic algorithm, we efficiently discovered which of the possible combinations of statistics correlated with model performance.

2.1   Datasets

We gathered 27 real-world text classification datasets from public sources, summarised in Table 1; full descriptions are in Appendix A.

We created 51 more datasets by taking two or more of the original 27 datasets and combining all of the data points from each into one dataset. The label for each data item was the name of the dataset which the text originally came from. We combined similar datasets in this way, for example

Dataset Name	Num. Class.	Train Size	Valid Size	Test Size
AG's News (Zhang et al., 2015)	4	108000	12000	7600
Airline Twitter Sentiment (FigureEight, 2018)	3	12444	-	2196
ATIS (Price, 1990)	26	9956	-	893
Corporate Messaging (FigureEight, 2018)	4	2650	-	468
ClassicLit	4	40489	5784	11569
DBPedia (wiki.dbpedia.org, 2015)	14	50400	5600	7000
Deflategate (FigureEight, 2018)	5	8250	1178	2358
Disaster Tweets (FigureEight, 2018)	2	7597	1085	2172
Economic News Relevance (FigureEight, 2018)	2	5593	799	1599
Grammar and Product Reviews (Datafiniti, 2018)	5	49730	7105	14209
Hate Speech (Davidson et al., 2017)	3	17348	2478	4957
Large Movie Review Corpus (Maas et al., 2011)	2	35000	5000	10000
London Restaurant Reviews (TripAdvisor[3])	5	12056	1722	3445
New Year's Tweets (FigureEight, 2018)	10	3507	501	1003
New Year's Tweets (FigureEight, 2018)	115	3507	501	1003
Paper Sent. Classification (archive.ics.uci.edu, 2018)	5	2181	311	625
Political Social Media (FigureEight, 2018)	9	3500	500	1000
Question Classification (Li and Roth, 2002)	6	4906	546	500
Review Sentiments (Kotzias et al., 2015)	2	2100	300	600
Self Driving Car Sentiment (FigureEight, 2018)	6	6082	-	1074
SMS Spam Collection (Almeida and Hidalgo, 2011)	2	3901	558	1115
SNIPS Intent Classification (Coucke, 2017)	7	13784	-	700
Stanford Sentiment Treebank (Socher et al., 2013a)	3	236076	1100	2210
Stanford Sentiment Treebank (Socher et al., 2013a)	2	117220	872	1821
Text Emotion (FigureEight, 2018)	13	34000	-	6000
Yelp Reviews (Yelp.com, 2018)	5	29250	3250	2500
YouTube Spam (Alberto et al., 2015)	2	1363	194	391

Table 1: The 27 different publicly available datasets we gathered with references.

two different datasets of tweets, so that the classes would not be trivially distinguishable - there is no dataset to classify text as either a tweet or Shakespeare for example as this would be too easy for models. The full list of combined datasets is in Appendix A.2.

Our datasets focus on short text classification by limiting each data item to 100 words. We demonstrate that the difficulty measure we discover with this setup generalises to longer text classification in Section 3.1. All datasets were lowercase with no punctuation. For datasets with no validation set, 15% of the training set was randomly sampled as a validation set at runtime.

2.2 Dataset Statistics

We calculated 12 distinct statistics with different n-gram sizes to produce 48 statistics of each dataset. These statistics are designed to increase in value as difficulty increases. The 12 statistics are described here and a listing of the full 48 is in Appendix B in Table 5. We used n-gram sizes from unigrams up to 5-grams and recorded the average of each statistic over all n-gram sizes. All probability distributions were count-based - the probability of a particular n-gram / class / character was the count of occurrences of that particular entity

divided by the total count of all entities.

2.2.1 Class Diversity

We recorded the Shannon Diversity Index and its normalised variant the Shannon Equitability (Shannon, 2001) using the count-based probability distribution of classes described above.

2.2.2 Class Balance

We propose a simple measure of class imbalance:

$$Imbal = \sum_{c=1}^{C} \left| \frac{1}{C} - \frac{n_c}{T_{DATA}} \right| \qquad (1)$$

C is the total number of classes, n_c is the count of items in class c and T_{DATA} is the total number of data points. This statistic is 0 if there are an equal number of data points in every class and the upper bound is $2\left(1 - \frac{1}{C}\right)$ and is achieved when one class has all the data points - a proof is given in Appendix B.2.

2.2.3 Class Interference

Per-class probability distributions were calculated by splitting the dataset into subsets based on the class of each data point and then computing count-based probability distributions as described above for each subset.

Hellinger Similarity One minus both the average and minimum Hellinger Distance (Le Cam and Yang, 2012) between each pair of classes. Hellinger Distance is 0 if two probability distributions are identical so we subtract this from 1 to give a higher score when two classes are similar giving the Hellinger Similarity. One minus the minimum Hellinger Distance is the maximum Hellinger Similarity between classes.

Top N-Gram Interference Average Jaccard similarity (Jaccard, 1912) between the set of the top 10 most frequent n-grams from each class. N-grams entirely composed of stopwords were ignored.

Mutual Information Average mutual information (Cover and Thomas, 2012) score between the set of the top 10 most frequent n-grams from each class. N-grams entirely composed of stopwords were ignored.

2.2.4 Data Complexity

Distinct n-grams : Total n-grams Count of distinct n-grams in a dataset divided by the total number of n-grams. Score of 1 indicates that each n-gram occurs once in the dataset.

Inverse Flesch Reading Ease The Flesch Reading Ease (FRE) formula grades text from 100 to 0, 100 indicating most readable and 0 indicating difficult to read (Kincaid et al., 1975). We take the reciprocal of this measure.

N-Gram and Character Diversity Using the Shannon Index and Equitability described by Shannon (2001) we calculate the diversity and equitability of n-grams and characters. Probability distributions are count-based as described at the start of this section.

2.3 Models

To ensure that any discovered measures did not depend on which model was used (i.e. that they were model agnostic), we trained 12 models on every dataset. The models are summarised in Table 2. Hyperparameters were not optimised and were identical across all datasets. Specific implementation details of the models are described in Appendix C. Models were evaluated using the macro F1-Score. These models used three different representations of text to learn from to ensure that the discovered difficulty measure did not depend on the representation. These are:

Word Embeddings Our neural network models excluding the Convolutional Neural Network (CNN) used 128-dimensional FastText (Bojanowski et al., 2016) embeddings trained on the One Billion Word corpus (Chelba et al., 2013) which provided an open vocabulary across the datasets.

Term Frequency Inverse Document Frequency (tf-idf) Our classical machine learning models represented each data item as a tf-idf vector (Ramos et al., 2003). This vector has one entry for each word in the vocab and if a word occurs in a data item, then that position in the vector is the word's tf-idf score.

Characters Our CNN, inspired by Zhang et al. (2015), sees only the characters of each data item. Each character is assigned an ID and the list of IDs is fed into the network.

2.4 Genetic Algorithm

The genetic algorithm maintains a *population* of candidate difficulty measures, each being a binary vector of length 48 (see start of Method section). At each time step, it will evaluate each member of the population using a *fitness function*. It will then select pairs of parents based on their fitness, and perform *crossover* and *mutation* on each pair to produce a new child difficulty measure, which is added to the next population. This process is iterated until the fitness in the population no longer improves.

Population The genetic algorithm is non-randomly initialised with the 48 statistics described in Section 2.2 - each one is a difficulty measure composed of a single statistic. 400 pairs of parents are sampled with replacement from each population, so populations after this first time step will consist of 200 candidate measures. The probability of a measure being selected as a parent is proportional to its fitness.

Fitness Function The fitness function of each difficulty measure is based on the Pearson correlation (Benesty et al., 2009). Firstly, the Pearson correlation between the difficulty measure and the model test set score is calculated for each individual model. The Harmonic mean of the correlations of each model is then taken, yielding the fitness of that difficulty measure. Harmonic mean is used because it is dominated by its lowest constituents,

Word Embedding Based	tf-idf Based	Character Based
LSTM-RNN	Adaboost	3 layer CNN
GRU-RNN	Gaussian Naive Bayes (GNB)	-
Bidirectional LSTM-RNN	5-Nearest Neighbors	-
Bidirectional GRU-RNN	(Multinomial) Logistic Regression	-
Multilayer Perceptron (MLP)	Random Forest	-
-	Support Vector Machine	-

Table 2: Models summary organised by which input type they use.

so if it is high then correlation must be high for every model.

Crossover and Mutation To produce a new difficulty measure from two parents, the constituent statistics of each parent are randomly intermingled, allowing each parent to pass on information about the search space. This is done in the following way: for each of the 48 statistics, one of the two parents is randomly selected and if the parent uses that statistic, the child also does. This produces a child which has features of both parents. To introduce more stochasticity to the process and ensure that the algorithm does not get trapped in a local minima of fitness, the child is mutated. Mutation is performed by randomly adding or taking away each of the 48 statistics with probability 0.01. After this process, the child difficulty measure is added to the new population.

Training The process of calculating fitness, selecting parents and creating child difficulty measures is iterated until there has been no improvement in fitness for 15 generations. Due to the stochasticity in the process, we run the whole evolution 50 times. We run 11 different variants of this evolution, leaving out different statistics of the dataset each time to test which are most important in finding a good difficulty measure, in total running 550 evolutions. Training time is fast, averaging 79 seconds per evolution with a standard deviation of 25 seconds, determined over 50 runs of the algorithm on a single CPU.

3 Results and Discussion

The four hypothesized areas of difficulty - Class Diversity, Balance and Interference and Data Complexity - combined give a model agnostic measure of difficulty. All runs of the genetic algorithm produced different combinations of statistics which had strong negative correlation with model scores on the 78 datasets. The mean correlation was -0.8795 and the standard deviation

was 0.0046. Of the measures found through evolution we present two of particular interest:

1. **D1:** *Distinct Unigrams : Total Unigrams + Class Imbalance + Class Diversity + Top 5-Gram Interference + Maximum Unigram Hellinger Similarity + Unigram Mutual Info.* This measure achieves the highest correlation of all measures at -0.8845.

2. **D2:** *Distinct Unigrams : Total Unigrams + Class Imbalance + Class Diversity + Maximum Unigram Hellinger Similarity + Unigram Mutual Info.* This measure is the shortest measure which achieves a higher correlation than the mean, at -0.8814. This measure is plotted against model F1 scores in Figure 1.

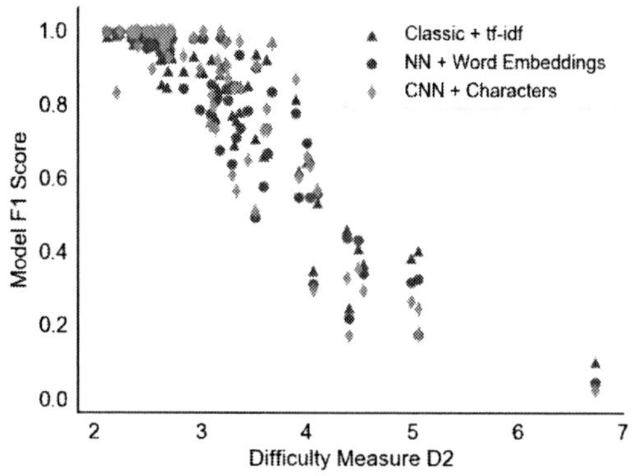

Figure 1: Model F1 scores against difficulty measure D2 for each of the three input types.

We perform detailed analysis on difficulty measure D2 because it relies only on the words of the dataset and requires just five statistics. This simplicity makes it interpretable and fast to calculate. All difficulty measures which achieved a correlation better than -0.88 are listed in Appendix D, where Figure 3 also visualises how often each metric was selected.

Model	AG	Sogou	Yelp P.	Yelp F.	DBP	Yah A.	Amz. P.	Amz. F.	Corr.
D2	3.29	3.77	3.59	4.42	3.50	4.51	3.29	4.32	-
char-CNN (Zhang et al., 2015)	87.2	95.1	94.7	62	98.3	71.2l	95.1	59.6	-0.86
Bag of Words (Zhang et al., 2015)	88.8	92.9	92.2	57.9	96.6	68.9	90.4	54.6	-0.87
Discrim. LSTM (Yogatama et al., 2017)	92.1	94.9	92.6	59.6	98.7	73.7	-	-	-0.87
Genertv. LSTM (Yogatama et al., 2017)	90.6	90.3	88.2	52.7	95.4	69.3	-	-	-0.88
Kneser-Ney Bayes (Yogatama et al., 2017)	89.3	94.6	81.8	41.7	95.4	69.3	-	-	-0.79
FastText Lin. Class. (Joulin et al., 2016)	91.5	93.9	93.8	60.4	98.1	72	91.2	55.8	-0.86
Char CRNN (Xiao and Cho, 2016)	91.4	95.2	94.5	61.8	98.6	71.7	94.1	59.2	-0.88
VDCNN (Conneau et al., 2017)	91.3	96.8	95.7	64.7	98.7	73.4	95.7	63	-0.88
Harmonic Mean									**-0.86**

Table 3: Difficulty measure D2 compared to recent results from papers on large-scale text classification. The correlation column reports the correlation between difficulty measure D2 and the model scores for that row.

3.1 Does it Generalise?

A difficulty measure is useful as an analysis and performance estimation tool if it is model agnostic and provides an accurate difficulty estimate on unseen datasets.

When running the evolution, the F1 scores of our character-level CNN were not observed by the genetic algorithm. If the discovered difficulty measure still correlated with the CNN's scores despite never having seen them during evolution, it is more likely to be model agnostic. The CNN has a different model architecture to the other models and has a different input type which encodes no prior knowledge (as word embeddings do) or contextual information about the dataset (as tf-idf does). D1 has a correlation of -0.9010 with the CNN and D2 has a correlation of -0.8974 which suggests that both of our presented measures do not depend on what model was used.

One of the limitations of our method was that our models never saw text that was longer than 100 words and were never trained on any very large datasets (i.e. >1 million data points). We also performed no hyperparameter optimisation and did not use state-of-the-art models. To test whether our measure generalises to large datasets with text longer than 100 words, we compared it to some recent state-of-the-art results in text classification using the eight datasets described by Zhang et al. (2015). These results are presented in Table 3 and highlight several important findings.

The Difficulty Measure Generalises to Very Large Datasets and Long Data Items. The smallest of the eight datasets described by Zhang et al. (2015) has 120 000 data points and the largest has 3.6 million. As D2 still has a strong negative correlation with model score on these datasets, it seems to generalise to large datasets. Furthermore, these large datasets do not have an upper limit of data item length (the mean data item length in Yahoo Answers is 520 words), yet D2 still has strong negative correlation with model score, showing that it does not depend on data item length.

The Difficulty Measure is Model and Input Type Agnostic. The state-of-the-art models presented in Table 3 have undergone hyperparameter optimisation and use different input types including per-word learned embeddings (Yogatama et al., 2017), n-grams, characters and n-gram embeddings (Joulin et al., 2016). As D2 still has a strong negative correlation with these models' scores, we can conclude that it has accurately measured the difficulty of a dataset in a way that is useful regardless of which model is used.

The Difficulty Measure Lacks Precision. The average score achieved on the Yahoo Answers dataset is 69.9% and its difficulty is 4.51. The average score achieved on Yelp Full is 56.8%, 13.1% less than Yahoo Answers and its difficulty is 4.42. In ML terms, a difference of 13% is significant yet our difficulty measure assigns a higher difficulty to the easier dataset. However, Yahoo Answers, Yelp Full and Amazon Full, the only three of Zhang et al. (2015)'s datasets for which the state-of-the-art is less than 90%, all have difficulty scores > 4, whereas the five datasets with scores $> 90\%$ all have difficulty scores between 3 and 4. This indicates that the difficulty measure in its current incarnation may be more effective at assigning a class of difficulty to datasets, rather than a regression-like value.

3.2 Difficulty Measure as an Analysis Tool

Statistic	Mean	Sigma
Distinct Words : Total Words	0.0666	0.0528
Class Imbalance	0.503	0.365
Class Diversity	0.905	0.759
Max. Unigram Hellinger Similarity	0.554	0.165
Top Unigram Mutual Info	1.23	0.430

Table 4: Means and standard deviations of the constituent statistics of difficulty measure D2 across the 78 datasets from this paper and the eight datasets from Zhang et al. (2015).

As our difficulty measure has no dependence on learned weightings or complex combinations of statistics - only addition - it can be used to analyse the sources of difficulty in a dataset directly. To demonstrate, consider the following dataset:

Stanford Sentiment Treebank Binary Classification (SST_2) (Socher et al., 2013b) SST is a dataset of movie reviews for which the task is to classify the sentiment of each review. The current state-of-the-art accuracy is 91.8% (Radford et al., 2017).

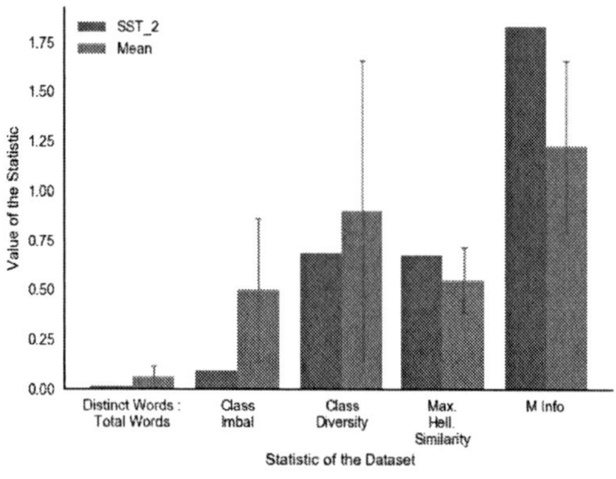

Figure 2: Constituents of difficulty measure D2 for SST, compared to the mean across all datasets.

Figure 2 shows the values of the constituent statistics of difficulty measure D2 for SST and the mean values across all datasets. The mean (right bar)

also includes an error bar showing the standard deviation of statistic values. The exact values of the means and standard deviations for each statistic in measure D2 are shown in Table 4.

Figure 2 shows that for SST_2 the Mutual Information is more than one standard deviation higher than the mean. A high mutual information score indicates that reviews have both positive and negative features. For example, consider this review: *"de niro and mcdormand give solid performances but their screen time is sabotaged by the story s inability to create interest"* which is labelled "positive". There is a positive feature referring to the actors' performances and a negative one referring to the plot. A solution to this would be to treat the classification as a multi-label problem where each item can have more than one class, although this would require that the data be relabelled by hand. An alternate solution would be to split reviews like this into two separate ones: one with the positive component and one with the negative.

Furthermore, Figure 2 shows that the Max. Hellinger Similarity is higher than average for SST_2, indicating that the two classes use similar words. Sarcastic reviews use positive words to convey a negative sentiment (Maynard and Greenwood, 2014) and could contribute to this higher value, as could mislabelled items of data. Both of these things portray one class with features of the other - sarcasm by using positive words with a negative tone and noise because positive examples are labelled as negative and vice versa. This kind of difficulty can be most effectively reduced by filtering noise (Smith et al., 2014).

To show that our analysis with this difficulty measure was accurately observing the difficulty in SST, we randomly sampled and analysed 100 misclassified data points from SST's test set out of 150 total misclassified. Of these 100, 48 were reviews with both strong positive and negative features and would be difficult for a human to classify, 22 were sarcastic and 8 were mislabelled. The remaining 22 could be easily classified by a human and are misclassified due to errors in the model rather than the data items themselves being difficult to interpret. These findings show that our difficulty measure correctly determined the source of difficulty in SST because 78% of the errors are implied by our difficulty measure and the remaining 22% are due to errors in the model itself, not difficulty in the dataset.

3.3 The Important Areas of Difficulty

We hypothesized that the difficulty of a dataset would be determined by four areas not including noise: Class Diversity, Class Balance, Class Interference and Text Complexity. We performed multiple runs of the genetic algorithm, leaving statistics out each time to test which were most important in finding a good difficulty measure which resulted in the following findings:

No Single Characteristic Describes Difficulty
When the Class Diversity statistic was left out of evolution, the highest achieved correlation was -0.806, 9% lower than D1 and D2. However, on its own Class Diversity had a correlation of -0.644 with model performance. Clearly, Class Diversity is necessary but not sufficient to estimate dataset difficulty. Furthermore, when all measures of Class Diversity and Balance were excluded, the highest achieved correlation was -0.733 and when all measures of Class Interference were excluded the best correlation was -0.727. These three expected areas of difficulty - Class Diversity, Balance and Interference - must all be measured to get an accurate estimate of difficulty because excluding any of them significantly damages the correlation that can be found. Correlations for each individual statistic are in Table 6, in Appendix D.

Data Complexity Has Little Affect on Difficulty Excluding all measures of Data Complexity from evolution yielded an average correlation of -0.869, only 1% lower than the average when all statistics were included. Furthermore, the only measure of Data Complexity present in D1 and D2 is Distinct Words : Total Words which has a mean value of 0.067 and therefore contributes very little to the difficulty measure. This shows that while Data Complexity is necessary to achieve top correlation, its significance is minimal in comparison to the other areas of difficulty.

3.4 Error Analysis

3.4.1 Overpowering Class Diversity

When a dataset has a large number of balanced classes, then Class Diversity dominates the measure. This means that the difficulty measure is not a useful performance estimator for such datasets.

To illustrate this, we created several fake datasets with 1000, 100, 50 and 25 classes. Each dataset had 1000 copies of the same randomly generated string in each class. It was easy for mod-els to overfit and score a 100% F1 score on these fake datasets.

For the 1000-class fake data, Class Diversity is 6.91, which by our difficulty measure would indicate that the dataset is extremely difficult. However, all models easily achieve a 100% F1 score. By testing on these fake datasets, we found that the limit for the number of classes before Class Diversity dominates the difficulty measure and renders it inaccurate is approximately 25. Any datasets with more than 25 classes with an approximately equal number of items per class will be predicted as difficult regardless of whether they actually are because of this diversity measure.

Datasets with more than 25 *unbalanced* classes are still measured accurately. For example, the ATIS dataset (Price, 1990) has 26 classes but because some of them have only 1 or 2 data items, it is not dominated by Class Diversity. Even when the difficulty measure is dominated by Class Diversity, examining the components of the difficulty measure independently would still be useful as an analysis tool.

3.4.2 Exclusion of Useful Statistics

One of our datasets of New Year's Resolution Tweets has 115 classes but only 3507 data points (FigureEight, 2018). An ML practitioner knows from the number of classes and data points alone that this is likely to be a difficult dataset for an ML model.

Our genetic algorithm, based on an unweighted, linear sum, cannot take statistics like data size into account currently because they do not have a convenient range of values; the number of data points in a dataset can vary from several hundred to several million. However, the information is still useful to practitioners in diagnosing the difficulty of a dataset.

Given that the difficulty measure lacks precision and may be better suited to classification than regression as discussed in Section 3.1, cannot take account of statistics without a convenient range of values and that the difficulty measure must be interpretable, we suggest that future work could look at combining statistics with a white-box, non-linear algorithm like a decision tree. As opposed to summation, such a combination could take account of statistics with different value ranges and perform either classification or regression while remaining interpretable.

3.5 How to Reduce the Difficulty Measure

Here we present some general guidelines on how the four areas of difficulty can be reduced.

Class Diversity can only be sensibly reduced by lowering the number of classes, for example by grouping classes under superclasses. In academic settings where this is not possible, hierarchical learning allows grouping of classes but will produce granular labels at the lowest level (Kowsari et al., 2017). Ensuring a large quantity of data in each class will also help models to better learn the features of each class.

Class Interference is influenced by the amount of noise in the data and linguistic phenomena like sarcasm. It can also be affected by the way the data is labelled, for example as shown in Section 3.2 where SST has data points with both positive and negative features but only a single label. Filtering noise, restructuring or relabelling ambiguous data points and detecting phenomena like sarcasm will help to reduce class interference. Easily confused classes can also be grouped under one superclass if practitioners are willing to sacrifice granularity to gain performance.

Class Imbalance can be addressed with data augmentation such as thesaurus based methods (Zhang et al., 2015) or word embedding perturbation (Zhang and Yang, 2018). Under- and over-sampling can also be utilised (Chawla et al., 2002) or more data gathered. Another option is transfer learning where knowledge from high data domains can be transferred to those with little data (Jaech et al., 2016).

Data Complexity can be managed with large amounts of data. This need not necessarily be labelled - unsupervised pre-training can help models understand the form of complex data before attempting to use it (Halevy et al., 2009). Curriculum learning may also have a similar effect to pre-training (Bengio et al., 2009).

3.6 Other Applications of the Measure

Model Selection Once the difficulty of a dataset has been calculated, a practitioner can use this to decide whether they need a complex or simple model to learn the data.

Performance Checking and Prediction Practitioners will be able to compare the results their models get to the scores of other models on datasets of an equivalent difficulty. If their models achieve lower results than what is expected according to the difficulty measure, then this could indicate a problem with the model.

4 Conclusion

When their models do not achieve good results, ML practitioners could potentially calculate thousands of statistics to see what aspects of their datasets are stopping their models from learning. Given this, how do practitioners tell which statistics are the most useful to calculate? Which ones will tell them the most? What changes could they make which will produce the biggest increase in model performance?

In this work, we have presented two measures of text classification dataset difficulty which can be used as analysis tools and performance estimators. We have shown that these measures generalise to unseen datasets. Our recommended measure can be calculated simply by counting the words and labels of a dataset and is formed by adding five different, unweighted statistics together. As the difficulty measure is an unweighted sum, its components can be examined individually to analyse the sources of difficulty in a dataset.

There are two main benefits to this difficulty measure. Firstly, it will reduce the time that practitioners need to spend analysing their data in order to improve model scores. As we have demonstrated which statistics are most indicative of dataset difficulty, practitioners need only calculate these to discover the sources of difficulty in their data. Secondly, the difficulty measure can be used as a performance estimator. When practitioners approach new tasks they need only calculate these simple statistics in order to estimate how well models are likely to perform.

Furthermore, this work has shown that for text classification the areas of Class Diversity, Balance and Interference are essential to measure in order to understand difficulty. Data Complexity is also important, but to a lesser extent.

Future work should firstly experiment with non-linear but interpretable methods of combining statistics into a difficulty measure such as decision trees. Furthermore, it should apply this difficulty measure to other NLP tasks that may require deeper linguistic knowledge than text classification, such as named entity recognition and parsing. Such tasks may require more advanced features than simple word counts as were used in this work.

References

Túlio C Alberto, Johannes V Lochter, and Tiago A Almeida. 2015. Tubespam: Comment spam filtering on youtube. In *Machine Learning and Applications (ICMLA), 2015 IEEE 14th International Conference on*, pages 138–143. IEEE. [Online; accessed 22-Feb-2018].

Tiago A. Almeida and Jos Mara Gmez Hidalgo. 2011. Sms spam collection v. 1. [Online; accessed 25-Feb-2018].

Ioannis Antonellis, Christos Bouras, and Vassilis Poulopoulos. 2006. Personalized news categorization through scalable text classification. In *Asia-Pacific Web Conference*, pages 391–401. Springer.

archive.ics.uci.edu. 2018. Sentence classification data set. `https://archive.ics.uci.edu/ml/datasets/Sentence+Classification`. [Online; accessed 20-Feb-2018].

Jacob Benesty, Jingdong Chen, Yiteng Huang, and Israel Cohen. 2009. Pearson correlation coefficient. In *Noise reduction in speech processing*, pages 1–4. Springer.

Yoshua Bengio, Jérôme Louradour, Ronan Collobert, and Jason Weston. 2009. Curriculum learning. In *Proceedings of the 26th annual international conference on machine learning*, pages 41–48. ACM.

Ester Bernadó-Mansilla and Tin Kam Ho. 2005. Domain of competence of xcs classifier system in complexity measurement space. *IEEE Transactions on Evolutionary Computation*, 9(1):82–104.

Joachim Bingel and Anders Søgaard. 2017. Identifying beneficial task relations for multi-task learning in deep neural networks. *arXiv preprint arXiv:1702.08303*.

Piotr Bojanowski, Edouard Grave, Armand Joulin, and Tomas Mikolov. 2016. Enriching word vectors with subword information. *arXiv preprint arXiv:1607.04606*.

Carla E Brodley and Mark A Friedl. 1999. Identifying mislabeled training data. *Journal of artificial intelligence research*, 11:131–167.

Nitesh V Chawla, Kevin W Bowyer, Lawrence O Hall, and W Philip Kegelmeyer. 2002. Smote: synthetic minority over-sampling technique. *Journal of artificial intelligence research*, 16:321–357.

Nitesh V Chawla, Nathalie Japkowicz, and Aleksander Kotcz. 2004. Special issue on learning from imbalanced data sets. *ACM Sigkdd Explorations Newsletter*, 6(1):1–6.

Ciprian Chelba, Tomas Mikolov, Mike Schuster, Qi Ge, Thorsten Brants, Phillipp Koehn, and Tony Robinson. 2013. One billion word benchmark for measuring progress in statistical language modeling. *arXiv preprint arXiv:1312.3005*.

Kyunghyun Cho, Bart Van Merriënboer, Caglar Gulcehre, Dzmitry Bahdanau, Fethi Bougares, Holger Schwenk, and Yoshua Bengio. 2014. Learning phrase representations using rnn encoder-decoder for statistical machine translation. *arXiv preprint arXiv:1406.1078*.

Ed Collins, Isabelle Augenstein, and Sebastian Riedel. 2017. A supervised approach to extractive summarisation of scientific papers. In *Proceedings of the 21st Conference on Computational Natural Language Learning (CoNLL 2017)*, pages 195–205.

Alexis Conneau, Holger Schwenk, Loïc Barrault, and Yann Lecun. 2017. Very deep convolutional networks for text classification. In *Proceedings of the 15th Conference of the European Chapter of the Association for Computational Linguistics: Volume 1, Long Papers*, volume 1, pages 1107–1116.

Alice Coucke. 2017. Benchmarking natural language understanding systems: Google, facebook, microsoft, amazon, and snips. [Online; accessed 7-Feb-2018].

Thomas M Cover and Joy A Thomas. 2012. *Elements of information theory*. John Wiley & Sons.

Datafiniti. 2018. Grammar and online product reviews. [Online; accessed 26-Feb-2018].

Thomas Davidson, Dana Warmsley, Michael Macy, and Ingmar Weber. 2017. Automated hate speech detection and the problem of offensive language. *arXiv preprint arXiv:1703.04009*.

D. A. Elizondo, R. Birkenhead, M. Gamez, N. Garcia, and E. Alfaro. 2009. Estimation of classification complexity. In *2009 International Joint Conference on Neural Networks*, pages 764–770.

FigureEight. 2018. Data for everyone. `https://www.figure-eight.com/data-for-everyone/`. [Online; accessed 25-Feb-2018].

Maya R Gupta, Samy Bengio, and Jason Weston. 2014. Training highly multiclass classifiers. *The Journal of Machine Learning Research*, 15(1):1461–1492.

Alon Halevy, Peter Norvig, and Fernando Pereira. 2009. The unreasonable effectiveness of data. *IEEE Intelligent Systems*, 24(2):8–12.

Trevor Hastie, Saharon Rosset, Ji Zhu, and Hui Zou. 2009. Multi-class adaboost. *Statistics and its Interface*, 2(3):349–360.

Tin Kam Ho and M. Basu. 2000. Measuring the complexity of classification problems. In *Proceedings 15th International Conference on Pattern Recognition. ICPR-2000*, volume 2, pages 43–47 vol.2.

Tin Kam Ho and M. Basu. 2002. Complexity measures of supervised classification problems. *IEEE Transactions on Pattern Analysis and Machine Intelligence*, 24(3):289–300.

Sepp Hochreiter and Jürgen Schmidhuber. 1997. Long short-term memory. *Neural computation*, 9(8):1735–1780.

Jin-Hyuk Hong and Sung-Bae Cho. 2008. A probabilistic multi-class strategy of one-vs.-rest support vector machines for cancer classification. *Neurocomputing*, 71(16-18):3275–3281.

Paul Jaccard. 1912. The distribution of the flora in the alpine zone. *New phytologist*, 11(2):37–50.

Aaron Jaech, Larry Heck, and Mari Ostendorf. 2016. Domain adaptation of recurrent neural networks for natural language understanding. *arXiv preprint arXiv:1604.00117*.

Nathalie Japkowicz. 2000. The class imbalance problem: Significance and strategies. In *Proc. of the Intl Conf. on Artificial Intelligence*.

Licheng Jiao and Lei Wang. 2000. A novel genetic algorithm based on immunity. *IEEE Transactions on Systems, Man, and Cybernetics-part A: systems and humans*, 30(5):552–561.

Armand Joulin, Edouard Grave, Piotr Bojanowski, and Tomas Mikolov. 2016. Bag of tricks for efficient text classification. *arXiv preprint arXiv:1607.01759*.

Mikael Kågebäck, Olof Mogren, Nina Tahmasebi, and Devdatt Dubhashi. 2014. Extractive summarization using continuous vector space models. In *Proceedings of the 2nd Workshop on Continuous Vector Space Models and their Compositionality (CVSC)*, pages 31–39.

J Peter Kincaid, Robert P Fishburne Jr, Richard L Rogers, and Brad S Chissom. 1975. Derivation of new readability formulas (automated readability index, fog count and flesch reading ease formula) for navy enlisted personnel. Technical report, Naval Technical Training Command Millington TN Research Branch.

Diederik P Kingma and Jimmy Ba. 2014. Adam: A method for stochastic optimization. *arXiv preprint arXiv:1412.6980*.

Dimitrios Kotzias, Misha Denil, Nando De Freitas, and Padhraic Smyth. 2015. From group to individual labels using deep features. In *Proceedings of the 21th ACM SIGKDD International Conference on Knowledge Discovery and Data Mining*, pages 597–606. ACM.

Kamran Kowsari, Donald E Brown, Mojtaba Heidarysafa, Kiana Jafari Meimandi, Matthew S Gerber, and Laura E Barnes. 2017. Hdltex: Hierarchical deep learning for text classification. In *Machine Learning and Applications (ICMLA), 2017 16th IEEE International Conference on*, pages 364–371. IEEE.

Lucien Le Cam and Grace Lo Yang. 2012. *Asymptotics in statistics: some basic concepts*. Springer Science & Business Media.

Xin Li and Dan Roth. 2002. Learning question classifiers. In *Proceedings of the 19th international conference on Computational linguistics-Volume 1*, pages 1–7. Association for Computational Linguistics.

Andrew L Maas, Raymond E Daly, Peter T Pham, Dan Huang, Andrew Y Ng, and Christopher Potts. 2011. Learning word vectors for sentiment analysis. In *Proceedings of the 49th annual meeting of the association for computational linguistics: Human language technologies-volume 1*, pages 142–150. Association for Computational Linguistics.

N. Maci, A. Orriols-Puig, and E. Bernad-Mansilla. 2008. Genetic-based synthetic data sets for the analysis of classifiers behavior. In *2008 Eighth International Conference on Hybrid Intelligent Systems*, pages 507–512.

E. B. Mansilla and Tin Kam Ho. 2004. On classifier domains of competence. In *Proceedings of the 17th International Conference on Pattern Recognition, 2004. ICPR 2004.*, volume 1, pages 136–139 Vol.1.

Diana Maynard and Mark A Greenwood. 2014. Who cares about sarcastic tweets? investigating the impact of sarcasm on sentiment analysis. In *Lrec*, pages 4238–4243.

G Harry Mc Laughlin. 1969. Smog grading-a new readability formula. *Journal of reading*, 12(8):639–646.

David Martin Powers. 2011. Evaluation: from precision, recall and f-measure to roc, informedness, markedness and correlation.

Patti J Price. 1990. Evaluation of spoken language systems: The atis domain. In *Speech and Natural Language: Proceedings of a Workshop Held at Hidden Valley, Pennsylvania, June 24-27, 1990*.

Alec Radford, Rafal Jozefowicz, and Ilya Sutskever. 2017. Learning to generate reviews and discovering sentiment. *arXiv preprint arXiv:1704.01444*.

Juan Ramos et al. 2003. Using tf-idf to determine word relevance in document queries. In *Proceedings of the first instructional conference on machine learning*, volume 242, pages 133–142.

Jason D Rennie, Lawrence Shih, Jaime Teevan, and David R Karger. 2003. Tackling the poor assumptions of naive bayes text classifiers. In *Proceedings of the 20th international conference on machine learning (ICML-03)*, pages 616–623.

Mike Schuster and Kuldip K Paliwal. 1997. Bidirectional recurrent neural networks. *IEEE Transactions on Signal Processing*, 45(11):2673–2681.

RJ Senter and Edgar A Smith. 1967. Automated readability index. Technical report, CINCINNATI UNIV OH.

Claude Elwood Shannon. 2001. A mathematical theory of communication. *ACM SIGMOBILE Mobile Computing and Communications Review*, 5(1):3–55.

Michael R Smith, Tony Martinez, and Christophe Giraud-Carrier. 2014. The potential benefits of filtering versus hyper-parameter optimization. *arXiv preprint arXiv:1403.3342*.

Richard Socher, Alex Perelygin, Jean Wu, Jason Chuang, Christopher D Manning, Andrew Ng, and Christopher Potts. 2013a. Recursive deep models for semantic compositionality over a sentiment treebank. In *Proceedings of the 2013 conference on empirical methods in natural language processing*, pages 1631–1642.

Richard Socher, Alex Perelygin, Jean Wu, Jason Chuang, Christopher D Manning, Andrew Ng, and Christopher Potts. 2013b. Recursive deep models for semantic compositionality over a sentiment treebank. In *Proceedings of the 2013 conference on empirical methods in natural language processing*, pages 1631–1642.

Darrell Whitley. 1994. A genetic algorithm tutorial. *Statistics and computing*, 4(2):65–85.

wiki.dbpedia.org. 2015. Data set 2.0. `http://wiki.dbpedia.org/data-set-20`. [Online; accessed 21-Feb-2018].

Yijun Xiao and Kyunghyun Cho. 2016. Efficient character-level document classification by combining convolution and recurrent layers. *arXiv preprint arXiv:1602.00367*.

Yelp.com. 2018. Yelp dataset challenge. `http://www.yelp.com/dataset_challenge`. [Online; accessed 23-Feb-2018].

Dani Yogatama, Chris Dyer, Wang Ling, and Phil Blunsom. 2017. Generative and discriminative text classification with recurrent neural networks. *arXiv preprint arXiv:1703.01898*.

Dongxu Zhang and Zhichao Yang. 2018. Word embedding perturbation for sentence classification. *arXiv preprint arXiv:1804.08166*.

Xiang Zhang, Junbo Zhao, and Yann LeCun. 2015. Character-level convolutional networks for text classification. In *Advances in neural information processing systems*, pages 649–657.

Vectorial semantic spaces do not encode human judgments of intervention similarity

Paola Merlo and **Francesco Ackermann**
Department of Linguistics
University of Geneva
5 Rue de Candolle, CH-1211 Genève 4
paola.merlo@unige.ch, francesco.ackermann@unige.ch

Abstract

Despite their practical success and impressive performances, neural-network-based and distributed semantics techniques have often been criticized as they remain fundamentally opaque and difficult to interpret. In a vein similar to recent pieces of work investigating the linguistic abilities of these representations, we study another core, defining property of language: the property of long-distance dependencies. Human languages exhibit the ability to interpret discontinuous elements distant from each other in the string as if they were adjacent. This ability is blocked if a similar, but extraneous, element intervenes between the discontinuous components. We present results that show, under exhaustive and precise conditions, that one kind of word embeddings and the similarity spaces they define do not encode the properties of intervention similarity in long-distance dependencies, and that therefore they fail to represent this core linguistic notion.

1 Introduction

Despite their practical success and impressive performances, neural-network-based and distributed semantics techniques have often been criticized as they remain fundamentally opaque and difficult to interpret.

To cast light on what linguistic information is learnt and encoded in these representations, several pieces of work have recently studied core properties of language in syntax (Linzen et al., 2016; Bernardy and Lappin, 2017; Gulordava et al., 2018; Linzen and Leonard, 2018; van Schijndel and Linzen, 2018), semantics (Herbelot and Ganesalingam, 2013; Erk, 2016), morphology (Cotterell and Schütze, 2015). In a similar vein, we study another core, defining property of human languages: the property of long-distance dependencies.

Human languages exhibit the ability to interpret discontinuous elements distant from each other in the string as if they were adjacent.[1] Sentence (1a) is a question about the object of the verb *buy*, whose canonical position is shown in angle brackets, thus connecting the first and last element in the sentence.[2] Sentence (2a) is a relative clause where the object of the verb *wash* is also the semantic object of the verb *show*, connecting two distant elements. Sentence (3a) is also a relative clause where the word *étudiant* (student) is the semantic object of the verb *endort* (put to sleep).

(1a) What do you wonder **John** bought <what> ?

(2a) Show me the elephant that **the lion** is washing <the elephant>.

(3a) Jules sourit aux étudiants que l'orateur endort < étudiants> sérieusement depuis le début.

  'Jules smiles to the students who the speaker is putting seriously to sleep from the beginning.'

Long-distance dependencies are not all equally acceptable. The precise description of the facts involving long-distance dependencies is complex, and is one of the major topics of research in current linguistic theory, with many competing proposals

---

[1] To clarify the perhaps confusing terminology: the term long-distance dependencies is a technical term that refers to discontinuous constructions where two elements in the string receive the same interpretation. Long-distance dependency constructions are *wh*-questions, relative clauses, right-node raising, among others (Rimell et al., 2009; Nivre et al., 2010; Merlo, 2015). Not all long-distance are actually long, for example subject-oriented relative clauses, and not all long dependencies are long-distance dependencies, for example, long subject-verb agreement as studied in Linzen et al. (2016); Bernardy and Lappin (2017); Gulordava et al. (2018) is usually not considered a long-distance dependency.

[2] The unpronounced element(s) in the long-distance relation are indicated by < >.

Proceedings of the 22nd Conference on Computational Natural Language Learning (CoNLL 2018), pages 392–401
Brussels, Belgium, October 31 - November 1, 2018. ©2018 Association for Computational Linguistics

(Rizzi, 1990; Gibson, 1998). We will adopt an intuitive and simple explanation, called intervention theory, some aspects of which will be explained in more detail below (Rizzi, 1990, 2004). In a nutshell, a long-distance dependency between two elements in a sentence is difficult or even impossible if a similar element intervenes. For example, sentence (1a) is acceptable while (2a) causes trouble for children (Friedmann et al., 2009) and (3a) triggers agreement errors, because in (1a) there is no sufficiently *similar* intervener (*John* is animate and is not a question word while *what* introduces a question and is not animate), while in (2) and (3) there is (*lion* is animate like *elephant* and *étudiants* (students) is animate like *orateur* (speaker)).

We present results that show, under precise conditions, that one kind of word embeddings and the similarity spaces they define do not encode the notion of intervention similarity involved in long-distance dependencies, but probably only semantic associations.

2 Long-distance phenomena and word embeddings

All languages allow some form of long-distance dependencies under restrictive conditions: for example, (1a) is allowed, but (1b) is not allowed (sentences like (1b) are called weak islands, we keep this terminology),[3] (2a) is hard for children, while (2b) is not, and neither of them is hard for adults, (3a), repeated here as (3b) often triggers agreement mistakes, as shown.

(1b) * What do you wonder **who** bought <what>?

(2b) Show me the elephant that <the elephant> is washing the lion.

(3b) Jules sourit aux étudiants que l'orateur <**étudiants**> endort/*endorment <étudiants> sérieusement depuis le début.

'Jules smiles to the students who the speaker is/*were putting seriously to sleep from the beginning.'

Core to the explanation of these facts is the notion of *intervener*. An intervener is an element that is *similar* to the two elements that are in a long-distance relation, and structurally intervenes

---

³As always, * means ungrammatical.

a. What do you wonder who bought?
b. Which book do you wonder who bought?
c. Which book do you wonder which linguist bought?
Figure 1: Weak islands (< means better). Acceptability judgments: c < b < a.

between the two, blocking the relation. In our examples, potential interveners are shown in bold.[4]

This explains why (1a) is ok, since there is a potential intervener, but *John* and *what* are not similar, but (1b) is not ok, since there is an intervener, and *who* and *what* are similar, as they are both *wh*-words. Sentence (2a) is hard for children as *the lion* intervenes between the two positions that give meaning to *the elephant*, but sentence (2b) is not, because nothing intervenes. Sentence (3b) triggers agreement mistakes because the intermediate position of *étudiants* intervenes between the word and the verb, causing interference.

Detailed investigations have shown that long-distance dependencies exhibit gradations of acceptability depending on which features are involved (Rizzi, 2004; Grillo, 2008; Friedmann et al., 2009). For example, all other things being equal, in complex question environments (weak islands), we have the gradation of judgments shown in Figure 1, where long-distance dependency involving a lexically restricted *wh*-phrase (*which book* or *which linguist*) is more acceptable than extraction of a bare *wh*-element (*who* or *wha*t), which is not very good. Experiments on weak islands and relative clauses also show that number triggers intervention effects (Belletti et al., 2012; Bentea, 2016). Thus, results from theoretical linguistics, acquisition and sentence processing point to a definition of intervener based on

---

⁴Notice that here and in all the following, intervention is defined structurally and not linearly. Linear intervention that does not structurally hierarchically dominate (technically c-command) does not matter as shown by the contrast *When do you wonder who won?/You wonder who won at five* compared to *When did the uncertainty about who won dissolve?/The uncertainty about who won dissolved at five.* (Rizzi, 2013) Also, intervention can be visible in the string, like in (1) and (2), or understood, as in (3). The intermediate step in relating the two elements of the long-distance dependency in (3) is postulated on theoretical grounds (see for example (Chomsky, 2001), and receives confirmation by participial agreement in languages like French (Kayne, 1989), or the agreement mistakes in the article we use here (Franck et al., 2015). See also Gibson and Warren (2004) for experimental evidence for the role of intermediate steps in long-distance dependencies.

syntactically-relevant features.[5] The status of a lexical-semantic feature such as *animacy* remains more controversial; some results argue in favor of an ameliorative effect (Brandt et al., 2009), some suggest animacy has no effect (Adani, 2012). Some recent studies show a clear effect of animacy as an intervention feature in *wh*-islands (Franck et al., 2015; Villata and Franck, 2016).

We are going to focus on those features for which relevant data is available, and there's reason to think they could be captured in lexical (semantic) vectors because they are properties of words (in contrast to the more discourse-oriented features, such as +Top.) In particular, we focus on *lexical restriction, number* and *animacy* in the definition of intervention similarity.

Sophisticated definition of lexical proximity in feature spaces, called *word embeddings*, have been defined recently in computational linguistics. These embeddings are the vectorial representation of the meaning of a word, defined as the usage of a word in its context (Wittgenstein, 1953 [2001]; Harris, 1954; Firth, 1957). Tasks that confirm this interpretation are association, analogy, lexical similarity, entailment (Mikolov et al., 2013a,b; Pennington et al., 2014; Bojanowski et al., 2016; Henderson and Popa, 2016).

We can, therefore, investigate whether the similarity spaces defined by word embeddings capture the notion of intervention similarity at work in long-distance dependencies. If they do, this means that they encode this core linguistic notion; if they don't this means that word embeddings semantic spaces capture association-based similarities based on world knowledge and textual co-occurrence, but not this more syntax-internal notion of intervention similarity.

3 The question

We investigate whether the popular notion of *word embeddings* and the notion of *vector space similarity* built on it are sensitive to the linguistic properties that are used to describe long-distance phenomena. These properties are the explanatory variables of the observed grammaticality judg-

ments derived by intuitive or experimental acceptability judgments. If word embeddings encode the linguistic properties that explain grammaticality judgment in long-distance dependencies, then they should also be effective predictors of the grammaticality of these same sentences.

More precisely, let C and C' be the two elements linked by a long-distance dependency in sentence F. Let I be the intervener. Let $S(C, I)$ be a similarity score indicating how similar I is to C.[6] Let G_F be a score representing the grammaticality of F, as measured numerically by psycholinguistic controlled experiments. Intervention locality theory tells us that high $S(C, I)$ yields ungrammaticality. Then $S(C, I)$ is correlated to G_F.

We can encode this theory in vectorial space. Let w_C be the word embedding of C and w_I the word embedding of I. Let $s(w_C, w_I)$ be the similarity score S measured as a distance in vectorial space. Then $s(w_C, w_I)$ is correlated to G_F, if the similarity notion encoded in word embeddings is the similarity notion that has been shown to be active in long-distance dependencies. If instead word embeddings do not encode an intervention-sensitive notion of similarity, we should find no correlation.

For example, consider the weak island examples in Figure 2. Clearly, both the pair *(class, student)* and the pair *(professor, student)* are close in a semantic space that simply measures semantic field and association-based similarity. If however, word embeddings learn intervention-relevant notions of similarity, then *(professor, student)* should be more similar, since they are both animate, compared to *(class, student)*, a pair with a mismatch in animacy.

Note that it is crucial here to compute word embeddings in a way that does not encode grammatical, and especially syntactic, information in some other way, to control for effects of syntactic similarity. This could yield positive results for the wrong reasons. This is why we use syntax-lean vectors, as explained below, and not the more dynamic word embeddings calculated in the process of training a neural parser, for example, or a language model (Linzen et al., 2016; Bernardy and Lappin, 2017; Gulordava et al., 2018).

---

[5]Villata (2017, 8) summarizes that the relevant features have been identified as being morphosyntactic features that have the potential to trigger movement, such as [+Q], for *wh*-elements, [+R(el)], for the head of the relative clause, [+Top], for the elements in a topic position, [+Foc], for the focalized elements, and the [+N] feature associated with lexically restricted *wh*-elements (e.g., *which NP*).

[6]C and C' are fundamentally the same, so we will consider only C here.

Weak islands, ANIMACY MISMATCH

Quel cours te demandes-tu **quel étudiant** a apprécié?
[+Q,+N,-A]   [+Q,+N,+A]

Which class do you wonder which student appreciated?

Weak islands, ANIMACY MATCH

Quel professeur te demandes-tu **quel étudiant** a apprécié?
[+Q,+N,+A]   [+Q,+N,+A]

Which professor do you wonder which student appreciated?

Object relatives, NUMBER MATCH

Jules sourit à l' **étudiant** que l' **orateur** <étudiant>$_2$ endort <étudiant>$_1$ sérieusement depuis le début.

Jules smiles to the student who the speaker is putting seriously to sleep from the beginning.

Object relatives, NUMBER MISMATCH

Jules sourit aux **étudiants** que l' **orateur** <étudiants>$_2$ endorment <étudiants>$_1$ sérieusement depuis le début.

Jules smiles to the students who the speaker is putting seriously to sleep from the beginning.

Figure 2: The linguistic constructions and experimental materials

4 The experiments

In what follows, we describe the multiple steps necessary to construct the materials of our experiments. To verify our hypothesis, we need two sets of materials: the experimental measures reflecting the grammaticality of a sentence and the word embeddings to calculate a vector space of similarities. We describe these in turn. We refer to the sentences in Figure 2 as examples.

4.1 Materials

For grammaticality measures, we use the carefully controlled stimuli of three psycholinguistics experiments, kindly provided to us by S. Villata and J. Franck (Franck et al., 2015; Villata and Franck, 2016). The language studied is French. Subjects were not the same across the tasks. Stimuli are exemplified in Figure 2.

From Franck et al. (2015) we only consider the first experiment, comprising 24 experimental items crossing structure (object relative clauses vs. complement clauses) and the number of the object (singular vs. plural).[7]

The experimental data is constituted by on-line reading times (milliseconds). Interference is examined on the agreement of the verb in the subordinate clause. We use the reading time corresponding to the critical region, the verb following the intervener word, *endort* or *endorment* in our examples in Figure 2, as was done in the analysis of results in the original experiments. The results show a speed-up effect of number in number mismatches configurations.

From Villata and Franck (2016), we consider both experiments, both manipulating *wh*-islands. Experiment 1 manipulated the lexical restriction of the *wh*-elements (both bare vs. both lexically restricted), and the match in animacy between the extracted wh-element and the intervening *wh*-element (animacy match, where both are animate vs. animacy mismatch, where the extracted *wh*-element is inanimate and the intervening *wh*-element is animate). All verbs required animate subjects. Experiment 2 manipulated the lexical restriction of the wh-elements (both bare vs. both lexically restricted), and the reversibility of thematic roles (reversible vs. non-reversible). All *wh*-elements were animate.

The data collected are acceptability judgments collected off-line from several subjects, on a seven-point Likert scale.[8] The results show a clear effect of animacy match and reversibility of thematic role match for lexically restricted phrases and less so for bare *wh*-phrases.

Notice that these stimuli ensure that the effects, or, more importantly, null effects, that we might find are not limited to a single type of construction and lexical relation, since we test two very different sets of constructions. In the same spirit of testing for a wide set of effects, in one case, we look at effects expressed as offline acceptability, and in the other at online reading times.

4.2 Methods

Calculating the word and phrase vectors The pairs of words or phrases indicated in bold in the examples in Figure 2 were used to collect the vector-based similarity space.

For each of these words we recover a word embedding. We use French word embeddings, from

---

[7]All subject head nouns (e.g. *orateur*) were singular. Subjects and objects were all animate. An adverb followed by a locative phrase were added after the verb in order to measure potential spillover effects. All test sentences were grammatical with respect to subject-verb agreement. Each sentence was followed by a yes/no comprehension question that probed participants interpretation of the thematic relations in the sentence. Instructions encouraged both rapid reading and correctness in answering the questions (48 fillers, 72 subject).

[8]Subjects (42) were instructed that there were no time constraints. The stimulus set consisted of 32 experimental items that gave rise to 128 sentences and 132 fillers.

Facebook Research. These publicly available vectors have been obtained on a 5-word window, for 300 resulting dimensions, on Wikipedia data using the skip-gram model described in Bojanowski et al. (2016).[9] Every word is represented as an n-grams of characters, for n training between 3 and 6. Each n-gram is represented by a vector and the sum of these vectors forms the vector representing the given word. This technique has been conceived to account for morphological similarities between words. Taking into consideration the fact that words may share morphological properties can improve the quality of the embeddings, and is important in a language like French, that has rich nominal and verbal inflectional morphology. The quality of a sample of these embedding vectors were checked by the two authors, proficient in French, by verifying that the words that are proposed as similar are consistent with intuition. Figure 3 shows the most similar words for two of the words whose word embeddings we calculated.

As shown in the examples in Figure 2, we need to measure the vector-based distance between phrases. Once the word vectors of individual words such as *quel* and *professeur*, are calculated, we calculate the embeddings of the noun phrases in which the single words combine, such as *quel professeur*. The vectorial representation of noun phrases is calculated by a composition operation. We used a simple vectorial sum. Since word embeddings are representations of lexical properties, we also report below results using only the bare head word of the noun phrase.

Calculating the similarity Once these vectors are calculated, we still have several options of which operator to use to calculate the distance between the vectors representing the two phrases C and I.

The similarity operators Beside the lexical specification of the vectors and their composition, the operator used to measure similarity also provides a dimension of experimental variation. The cosine is a well-known and efficient measure of vector similarity. It is based on a rescaling of the dot product of the vectors and it is a symmetric measure. It has been shown to capture associative and analogical semantic similarity in vector space

POLICIER (policeman)	ETUDIANT (student)
cambrioleur (burglar)	enseignant (teacher)
kidnappeur (kidnapper)	professeur (professor)
chauffeur (driver)	chercheur (researcher)
criminel (offender)	doctorant (doctoral student)
détective (detective)	camarade (fellow)

Figure 3: Five most similar words for word *policier* and *étudiant*.

(Mikolov et al., 2013a,b; Pennington et al., 2014; Bojanowski et al., 2016).

Once the distance between the vectors is calculated, in the final step, we correlate the calculated word embedding similarities with the psycholinguistic acceptability judgments.[10]

5   Results and discussion

Recall that in weak islands (see Figure 2), the expected outcome is an inverse proportionality between the two variables: the higher the semantic similarity, the stronger the interference, and consequently, the lower the average acceptability score of the sentence. In the case of object relative clauses (see Figure 2), we expected to observe a direct proportionality between the two variables: the higher the semantic similarity, the stronger the interference, and consequently the longer the average reading time devoted to the verb in the relative clause.

Results with the cosine operator Figures 4a and 4b show the (lack of) correlations between $s(w_C, w_I)$ and the grammaticality judgments of the experiments on weak islands, both with bare nouns and composed noun phrases. Figures 5a and 5b show the (lack of) correlations between $s(w_C, w_I)$ and the reaction times of the critical region, the verb, both with bare nouns and composed noun phrases, in object relative clauses. Regression values are shown in Table 1.

Results clearly show no correlations in all conditions. This is converging evidence that word embeddings do not represent the intervention notion of similarity, but they encode similarities based on associations and world knowledge. More explicitly, take the two examples of weak islands in Figure 2. Human judgments differentiate clearly the two sentences, the first being more acceptable than the second. In the first sentence, **Quel cours te demandes-tu quel étudiant** a apprécié? (*Which*

---

[9]`https://github.com/facebookresearch/fastText/blob/master/pretrained-vectors.md`

[10]The list of words and the detailed experimental results are given in the supplementary materials.

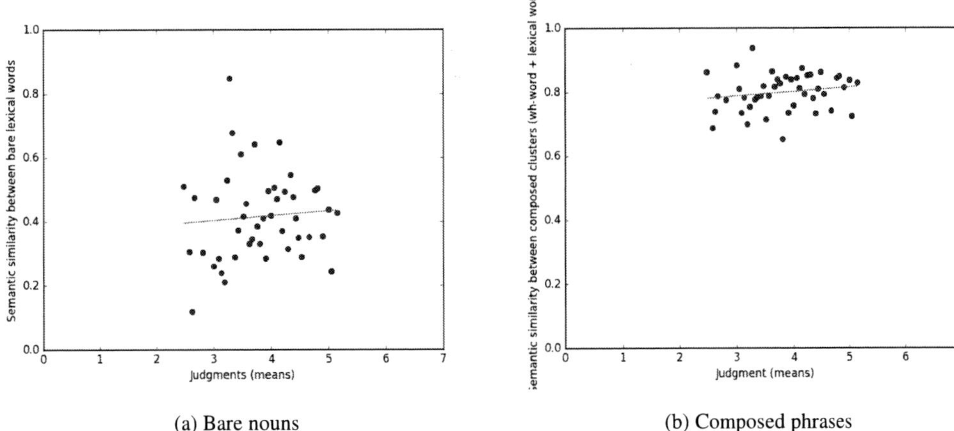

(a) Bare nouns   (b) Composed phrases

Figure 4: Weak islands, cosine operator.

Op	Conf	Args	m	r	p
ss	WI	b1, b2	0.02	0.08	0.61
ss	WI	whp1, whp2	0.01	0.17	0.26
ss	OR	b1, b2	-5.83×10^{-5}	-0.19	0.40
ss	OR	(b1,v),(b2,v)	2.42×10^{-5}	0.08	0.72
as	WI	b1, b2	-0.97	-0.12	0.43
as	OR	b1, b2	-4×10^{-3}	-0.22	0.33

Table 1: Regressions (m), correlations (Pearson r) and p-values. ss=semantic similarity (cosine); as=asymmetric similarity (lexical entailment); WI=weak island; OR=object relative clauses; b1/2=bare noun 1/2; whp1/2=*wh*-phrase 1/2; v=verb.

class do you wonder which student appreciated?), the two target words, in bold, do not match in animacy, hence the intervener does not block the long-distance relation as strongly as in the second sentence, **Quel professeur** te demandes-tu **quel étudiant** a apprécié? (*Which professor do you wonder which student appreciated?*), where they do. People are sensitive to this difference, even if *cours, professor* and *étudiant* are all words belonging to the same semantic field and closely connected by semantic association. The word embeddings we have tested here fail to capture this difference.

Analysis of results The lack of correlation prompts a more detailed analysis of the results. In particular, notice that in the experimental work a binary (not continuous) distinction – animate vs. inanimate, plural vs. singular – was manipulated and correlated to the acceptability and re-

action times. We are, instead, requiring a correlation between similarity and acceptability in the animacy case and similarity and number in the reaction times. That is, we are imposing a stricter correspondence, which requires the level of similarity to continuously vary with all the experimental results. We verify then if weaker forms of correlation give us more positive results.

First of all, we can require the similarity measure to make only a binary distinction. For the experiment manipulating *animacy* in *wh*-islands, we do find the expected inverse correlation between mean similarity and mean acceptability depending on the value of the animacy factor. [11] For the experiment manipulating *number* in relative clauses, instead, we do not find the expected direct correlation between mean similarity and mean reading time depending on the value of the number factor.[12]

Another less stringent way of looking for correspondences is to take the manipulated binary factor into account, and verify if there is a partial correlation. In both cases, the correlation is weak.[13]

---

[11] Animate relative head (match condition): mean similarity=0.394, mean acceptability=3.65; inanimate relative head (mismatch condition): mean similarity=0.293, mean acceptability=4.00).

[12] Singular relative head (match condition): mean similarity=0.678, mean reading time=962.96; plural relative head (mismatch condition): mean similarity=0.705, mean reading time=896.03). Notice in fact, that the lack of correspondence could be even more basic, as the average similarity score for the number match condition is lower than for the number mismatch condition.

[13] A multiple regression of accuracy on animacy and similarity yields *accuracy= 0.46 anim=inanimate + 0.83 similarity + 3.33* with correlation coefficient 0.229; a multiple regression of reading times on number and similarity yields *reading times= 72.48 num=plural + 203.53 similar-*

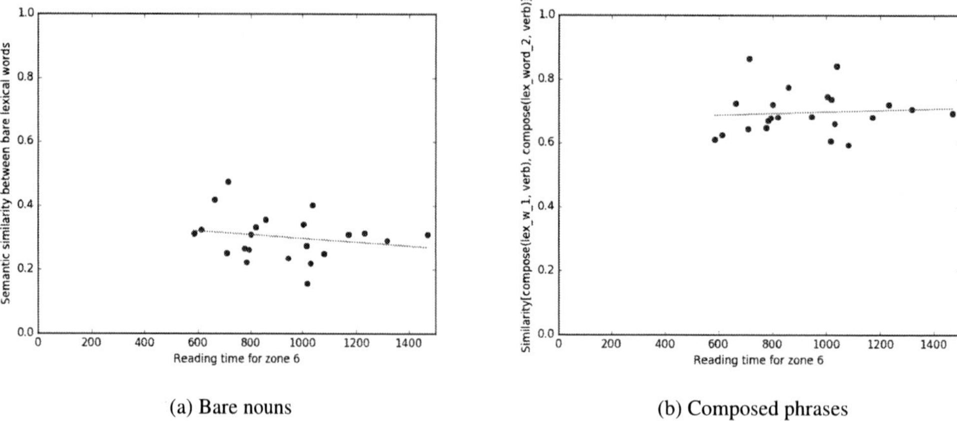

(a) Bare nouns   (b) Composed phrases

Figure 5: Object relative clauses, cosine operator.

Results with asymmetric operator It could also be pointed out that while the null results were confirmed across construction types (weak islands and object relatives), experimental methodologies (off-line grammaticality judgments and on-line reading times), only the cosine operator was used to calculate similarity. The two vectors that are being compared, w_C and w_I, correspond, linguistically to C and I above. It has been shown that, from a linguistic point of view, the grammaticality judgments differ depending on whether the feature set of C is properly included or properly includes I. If the features of C are a superset of the features of I, sentences are judged more acceptable (Rizzi, 2004). Independently of the exact details of the linguistic explanation, these fine-grained differences in grammaticality judgments suggest that it might be more appropriate to calculate similarity with an asymmetric operator.

The asymmetric measure we use here has been developed to capture the notion of entailment. It captures the idea that the values in a distributed semantic vector do not represent presence or absence of a property (true or false), but knowledge or lack of knowledge about a property of the referent entity of the noun whose meaning the vector represents: A entails B iff when I know A I know everything about B. This operator has been shown to learn the notion of hyponymy better than other methods (Henderson and Popa, 2016). [14]

Since this operator has so far only been applied to English, we need to develop the training and development sets for French. For our experiments,

we translated all the word pairs from English to French.[15] We kept the same configurations of the training sets of word pairs, as described in the experiments by Henderson and Popa. The system uses these pairs coupled with the gold answer (1 if the entailment is true, 0 if it is not) to train on hyponymy-hypernymy relations. The data used for training are noun-noun word pairs that include positive hyponymy pairs, negative pairs consisting of different hyponymy pairs reversed, pairs in other semantic relations, and some random pairs.

We modify the operator (we use *unk dup*, $\oslash$), so that it does not to give us a binary decision (x entails y yes/no), but so that it outputs a real value, indicating how much x entails y, or rather how much x is asymmetrically similar to y.

With this operator, we produce the results shown in Figures 6a and 6b, for bare noun phrases.[16] Figure 6a shows the (lack of) correlations between $s(w_C, w_I)$ and the grammaticality judgments of the experiments on weak islands. Figure 6b shows the (lack of) correlations between

projected in a different space.

$$\log(P(y{\Rightarrow}x)) \approx$$
$$(\sigma(-(y{-}1)) \cdot \log \sigma(-(x{-}1))$$
$$+ \sigma(-(-y{-}1)) \cdot \log \sigma(-(-x{-}1)))/d \quad (1)$$

The first dot product stands for the true-versus-unknown interpretation of the vectors and the second dot product represents the false-versus-unknown interpretation. σ is the logistic sigmoid function $\frac{1}{1+\exp(-x)}$, and the log and σ functions are applied componentwise.

[15]We use WordReference online multilingual dictionary, available at www.wordreference.com.

[16]Given the null results discussed below, we do not test another configuration, where we would have used the entailment operator on the composed noun phrase stimuli.

---

ity + 752.45, with correlation coefficient: -0.499.

[14] The operators are calculated by the following formula, where y, x are word embeddings vectors with length d, being

398

$s(w_C, w_I)$ and the reaction times of the critical region in object relative clauses. Regression values are shown in Table 1.

These results also confirm a lack of correlation. The convergence of these results is important as null effects are always hard to confirm and explain, and care must be taken to show that alternative explanations are not possible. In this case, all experiments, across constructions (weak island and object relative clauses), across type of noun phrase (bare or composed), across measurement method of the experimental dependent variable (off-line grammaticality judgments and on-line reaction times), and across operators (symmetric and asymmetric) show a consistent lack of correlation between measurements collected in experiments that manipulated the similarity of the elements, and the notion of similarity encoded in word embeddings.

This consistent lack of effect allows us to conclude that while current word embeddings, i.e. dictionaries in a multi-dimensional vectorial space, clearly encode a notion of similarity, as shown by many experiments on analogical tasks and textual and lexical similarity, they do not however encode the notion of similarity that has been shown in many human experiments to be at work and to be definitional in long-distance dependencies. They do not encode therefore this core notion of intervention similarity.

6 Related work

This work is situated in a rich body of computational research that attempts to establish the boundaries of what distributed semantic representations and neural networks can learn. These studies have concentrated on structural grammatical competence, exemplified by long-distance agreement, a task thought to require hierarchical, and not only linear, information. The first study, (Linzen et al., 2016), has tested recursive neural network (RNN) language models and found that RNNs can learn to predict English subject-verb agreement, if provided with explicit supervision. In a follow up paper, Bernardy and Lappin (2017) find that RNNs are better at long-distance agreement if they can use large vocabularies to form rich lexical representations to learn structural patterns. This finding suggests that RNNs learn syntactic patterns through rich lexical embeddings, based both on semantic and syntactic

evidence. Gulordava et al. (2018) revisit previous work, and extend the work on long-distance agreement to four languages of different linguistic properties (Italian, English, Hebrew, Russian). They use the technique of developing counterfactual data, typical of theoretical and experimental work and already used for parsing in Gulordava and Merlo (2016) and train the system on nonsensical sentences. Their model makes accurate predictions and compares well with humans, thereby suggesting that the networks learn deeper grammatical competence.

On the linguistic and psycholinguistic side, this work contributes to the investigation of the formal encoding of long-distance dependencies, following the theoretical lines laid in the first formulation of intervention theory of long-distance dependencies (Rizzi, 1990), made gradual and more fine-grained in subsequent work (Rizzi, 2004), and verified experimentally in both sentence processing and acquisition (Franck et al., 2015; Villata and Franck, 2016; Friedmann et al., 2009).

7 Conclusions

Human languages exhibit the ability to interpret discontinuous elements distant from each other in the string as if they were adjacent, but this long-distance relation can be disrupted by a similar intervening element. Speakers report lower acceptability and longer reading times. In this paper, we have presented results that show that the similarity spaces defined by one kind of word embeddings do not encode this notion of intervention similarity in long-distance dependencies.

Future work requires investigating more directly the grammatical aspects of the nature of the similar and dissimilar words in the embeddings and extend the experimentation to other kinds of vector spaces, a much larger dataset, and replication in more constructions and more languages.

8 Acknowledgments

We thank Julie Franck and Sandra Villata for sharing the data they have collected in their experiments, and James Henderson and Diana Nicoleta Popa for sharing with us their hyponymy detection script.

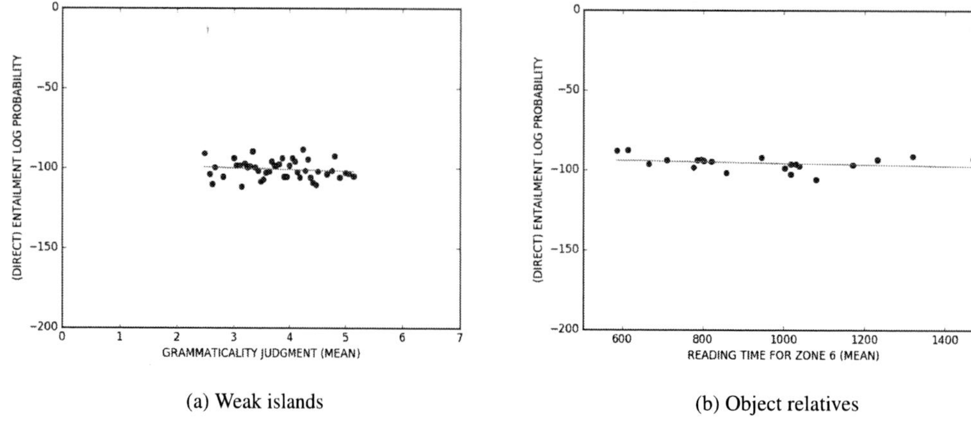

(a) Weak islands   (b) Object relatives

Figure 6: Asymmetric operator.

References

Flavia Adani. 2012. Some notes on the acquisition of relative clauses: new data and open questions. In *ENJOY LINGUISTICS! Papers offered to Luigi Rizzi on the occasion of his 60th birthday*, pages 6–13. CISCLPress.

Adriana Belletti, Naama Friedmann, Dominique Brunato, and Luigi Rizzi. 2012. Does gender make a difference? Comparing the effect of gender on children's comprehension of relative clauses in Hebrew and Italian. *Lingua*, 122(10):1053–1069.

Anamaria Bentea. 2016. *Intervention effects in language acquisition: the comprehension of A-bar dependencies in French and Romanian*. Ph.D. thesis, University of Geneva.

Jean-Philippe Bernardy and Shalom Lappin. 2017. Using deep neural networks to learn syntactic agreement. *Linguistic Issues in Language Technology*, 15(2):1–15.

Piotr Bojanowski, Edouard Grave, Armand Joulin, and Tomas Mikolov. 2016. Enriching word vectors with subword information. *CoRR*, abs/1607.04606.

Silke Brandt, Evan Kidd, Elena Lieven, and Michael Tomasello. 2009. The discourse bases of relativization: An investigation of young German and English-speaking children's comprehension of relative clauses. *Cognitive Linguistics*, 20(3):539–570.

Noam Chomsky. 2001. Derivation by phase. In Michael Kenstowicz, editor, *Ken Hale: A Life in Language*, pages 1–52. MIT Press, Cambridge,MA.

Ryan Cotterell and Hinrich Schütze. 2015. Morphological word-embeddings. In *Proceedings of the 2015 Conference of the North American Chapter of the Association for Computational Linguistics: Human Language Technologies*, pages 1287–1292, Denver, Colorado. Association for Computational Linguistics.

Katrin Erk. 2016. What do you know about an alligator when you know the company it keeps? *Semantics and Pragmatics*, 9(17):1–63.

John Rupert Firth. 1957. A synopsis of linguistic theory 1930-1955. In *Studies in linguistic analysis*, pages 1–32. Blackwell, Oxford.

Julie Franck, S. Colonna S., and Luigi Rizzi. 2015. Task-dependency and structure dependency in number interference effects in sentence comprehension. *Frontiers in Psychology*, 6.

Naama Friedmann, Adriana Belletti, and Luigi Rizzi. 2009. Relativized relatives: Types of intervention in the acquisition of A-bar dependencies. *Lingua*, 119(1):67 – 88.

Edward Gibson. 1998. Linguistic complexity: Locality of syntactic dependencies. *Cognition*, 68:1–76.

Edward Gibson and Tessa Warren. 2004. Reading time evidence for intermediate linguistic structure in long-distance dependencies. *Syntax*, pages 55–78.

Nino Grillo. 2008. *Generalized minimality: Syntactic underspecification in Broca's aphasia*. Ph.D. thesis, University of Utrecht.

Kristina Gulordava, Piotr Bojanowski, Edouard Grave, Tal Linzen, and Marco Baroni. 2018. Colorless green recurrent networks dream hierarchically. In *Proceedings of the 2018 Conference of the North American Chapter of the Association for Computational Linguistics: Human Language Technologies, Volume 1 (Long Papers)*, pages 1195–1205. Association for Computational Linguistics.

Kristina Gulordava and Paola Merlo. 2016. Multilingual dependency parsing evaluation: a large-scale analysis of word order properties using artificial data. *Transactions of the Association for Computational Linguistics*.

Zellig Harris. 1954. Distributional structure. *Word*, 10(23):146–162.

James Henderson and Diana Popa. 2016. A vector space for distributional semantics for entailment. In *Proceedings of the 54th Annual Meeting of the Association for Computational Linguistics (Volume 1: Long Papers)*, pages 2052–2062, Berlin, Germany. Association for Computational Linguistics.

Aurélie Herbelot and Mohan Ganesalingam. 2013. Measuring semantic content in distributional vectors. In *Proceedings of the 51st Annual Meeting of the Association for Computational Linguistics (Volume 2: Short Papers)*, pages 440–445, Sofia, Bulgaria. Association for Computational Linguistics.

Richard Kayne. 1989. Romance clitics,verb movement and PRO. *Linguistic Inquiry*, 22(4):647–686.

Tal Linzen, Emmanuel Dupoux, and Yoav Goldberg. 2016. Assessing the ability of LSTMs to learn syntax-sensitive dependencies. *Transactions of the Association for Computational Linguistics*, 4:521–535.

Tal Linzen and Brian Leonard. 2018. Distinct patterns of syntactic agreement errors in recurrent networks and humans. In *Proceedings of the 40th Annual Conference of the Cognitive Science Society*.

Paola Merlo. 2015. Evaluation of two-level dependency representations of argument structure in long-distance dependencies. In *Proceedings of the Third International Conference on Dependency Linguistics (Depling 2015)*, pages 221–230.

Tomas Mikolov, Kai Chen, Greg Corrado, and Jeffrey Dean. 2013a. Efficient estimation of word representations in vector space. *CoRR*, abs/1301.3781.

Tomas Mikolov, Ilya Sutskever, Kai Chen, Gregory S. Corrado, and Jeffrey Dean. 2013b. Distributed representations of words and phrases and their compositionality. In *Advances in Neural Information Processing Systems 26: 27th Annual Conference on Neural Information Processing Systems 2013. Proceedings of a meeting held December 5-8, 2013, Lake Tahoe, Nevada, United States.*, pages 3111–3119.

Joakim Nivre, Laura Rimell, Ryan McDonald, and Carlos Gómez Rodríguez. 2010. Evaluation of dependency parsers on unbounded dependencies. In *Proceedings of the 23rd International Conference on Computational Linguistics (Coling 2010)*, pages 833–841, Beijing, China.

Jeffrey Pennington, Richard Socher, and Christopher Manning. 2014. Glove: Global vectors for word representation. In *Proceedings of the 2014 Conference on Empirical Methods in Natural Language Processing (EMNLP)*, pages 1532–1543, Doha, Qatar. Association for Computational Linguistics.

Laura Rimell, Stephen Clark, and Mark Steedman. 2009. Unbounded dependency recovery for parser evaluation. In *Proceedings of the 2009 Conference on Empirical Methods in Natural Language Processing*, pages 813–821, Singapore. Association for Computational Linguistics.

Luigi Rizzi. 1990. *Relativized Minimality*. MIT Press, Cambridge, MA.

Luigi Rizzi. 2004. Locality and left periphery. In Adriana Belletti, editor, *The cartography of syntactic structures*, number 3 in Structures and beyond, pages 223–251. Oxford University Press, New York.

Luigi Rizzi. 2013. Locality. *Lingua*, 130(1):69 – 86.

Marten van Schijndel and Tal Linzen. 2018. Modeling garden path effects without explicit hierarchical syntax. In *Proceedings of the 40th Annual Conference of the Cognitive Science Society*.

Sandra Villata. 2017. *Intervention effects in sentence processing*. Ph.D. thesis, Universite de Geneve. Https://archive-ouverte.unige.ch/unige:101927.

Sandra Villata and Julie Franck. 2016. Semantic similarity effects on weak islands acceptability. In *41st Incontro di Grammatica Generativa Conference*, Perugia, Italy. Https://archive-ouverte.unige.ch/unige:82418.

Ludwig Wittgenstein. (1953) [2001]. *Philosophical Investigations*. Blackwell Publishing.

Lessons learned in multilingual grounded language learning

Ákos Kádár
Tilburg University
a.kadar@uvt.nl

Desmond Elliott*
University of Copenhagen
de@di.ku.dk

Marc-Alexandre Côté
Microsoft Research Montreal
macote@microsoft.com

Grzegorz Chrupała
Tilburg University
g.chrupala@uvt.nl

Afra Alishahi
Tilburg University
a.alishahi@uvt.nl

Abstract

Recent work has shown how to learn better visual-semantic embeddings by leveraging image descriptions in more than one language. Here, we investigate in detail which conditions affect the performance of this type of grounded language learning model. We show that multilingual training improves over bilingual training, and that low-resource languages benefit from training with higher-resource languages. We demonstrate that a multilingual model can be trained equally well on either translations or comparable sentence pairs, and that annotating the same set of images in multiple language enables further improvements via an additional caption-caption ranking objective.

1 Introduction

Multimodal representation learning is largely motivated by evidence of perceptual grounding in human concept acquisition and representation (Barsalou et al., 2003). It has been shown that visually grounded word and sentence-representations (Kiela et al., 2014; Baroni, 2016; Elliott and Kádár, 2017; Kiela et al., 2017; Yoo et al., 2017) improve performance on the downstream tasks of paraphrase identification, semantic entailment, and multimodal machine translation (Dolan et al., 2004; Marelli et al., 2014; Specia et al., 2016). Multilingual sentence representations have also been successfully applied to many-languages-to-one character-level machine translation (Chung et al., 2016) and multilingual dependency parsing (Ammar et al., 2016).

Recently, Gella et al. (2017) proposed to learn both bilingual and multimodal sentence representations using images paired with captions independently collected in English and German. Their results show that bilingual training improves image-sentence ranking performance over a monolingual

baseline, and it improves performance on semantic textual similarity benchmarks (Agirre et al., 2014, 2015). These findings suggest that it may be beneficial to consider another language as another *modality* in a monolingual grounded language learning model. In the grounded learning scenario, descriptions of an image in multiple languages can be considered as multiple views of the same or closely related data. These additional views can help overcome the problems of data sparsity, and have practical implications for efficiently collecting image-text datasets in different languages. In real-life applications, many tasks and domains can involve code switching (Barman et al., 2014), which is easier to deal with using a multilingual model. Furthermore, it is more convenient to maintain a single multilingual system than one system for each considered language. However, there is a need for a systematic exploration of the conditions under which it is useful to add additional views of the data. We investigate the impact of the following conditions on the performance of a multilingual grounded language learning model in sentence and image retrieval tasks:

Additional languages. Multilingual models have not been explored yet in a multimodal setting. We investigate the contribution of adding more than one language by performing bilingual experiments on English and German (Section 5) as well as adding French and Czech captioned images (Section 6).

Data alignment: We assess the performance of a multilingual models trained using either captions that are translations of each other, or captions that are independently collected in different languages for the same set of images. The two scenarios are illustrated in Figure 1. Additionally we consider the setup when non-overlapping sets of images and their

---

*Work carried out at the University of Edinburgh.

Proceedings of the 22nd Conference on Computational Natural Language Learning (CoNLL 2018), pages 402–412
Brussels, Belgium, October 31 - November 1, 2018. ©2018 Association for Computational Linguistics

En: A group of people are eating noodles.

De: Eine Gruppe von Leuten isst Nudeln.

Fr: Un groupe de gens mangent des nouilles.

Cs: Skupina lidí jedí nudle.

En: Several asian people eating around a table.

De: Drei Männer und zwei Frauen südostasiatischen Aussehens sitzen, aus Schälchen essend, an einem schwarzen, Tisch, auf dem sich u.a. auch Pappbecher und eine Tasche befinden, im Hintergrund sind weitere Personen und Tische.[1]

(a) A translation tuple   (b) A comparable pair

Figure 1: An example taken from the *Translation* and *Comparable* portions of the Multi30K dataset. The translation portion (a) contains professional translations of the English captions into German, French, and Czech. The comparable portion (b) consists of five independently crowdsourced English and German descriptions, given only the image. Note that the sentences in (b) convey different information from the English–German translation pair in (a).

captions are collected in different languages. Such disjoint settings have been explored in pivot-based multimodal representation learning (Funaki and Nakayama, 2015; Rajendran et al., 2015) or zero-shot multi-modal machine translation (Nakayama and Nishida, 2017). We compare translated vs. independently collected captions in Sections 5.2 and 6.1, and overlapping vs. disjoint images in Section 5.3.

High-to-low resource transfer: In Section 6.2 we investigate whether low-resource languages benefit from jointly training on larger data sets from higher-resource languages. This type of transfer has previously been shown to be effective in machine translation (e.g., Zoph et al., 2016).

Training objective: In addition to learning to map images to sentences, we study the effect of also learning relationships between captions of the same image in different languages Gella et al. (2017). We assess the contribution of such a caption–caption ranking objective throughout our experiments.

Our results show that multilingual joint train-

ing improves upon bilingual joint training, and that grounded sentence representations for a low-resource language can be substantially improved with data from different high-resource languages. Our results suggest that independently-collected captions are more useful than translated captions, for the task of learning multilingual multimodal sentence embeddings. Finally, we recommend to collect captions for the same set of images in multiple languages, due to the benefits of the additional caption–caption ranking objective function.

2 Related work

Learning visually grounded word-representations has been an active area of research in the fields of multi-modal semantics and cross-situational word-learning. Such perceptually-grounded word representations have been shown to lead to higher correlation with human judgements on word-similarity benchmarks such as WordSim353 (Finkelstein et al., 2001) or SimLex999 (Hill et al., 2015) compared to uni-modal representations (Kádár et al.,

---

[1]Gloss: Three men and two women with a South-East Asian appearance eat out of bowls at a black table, on which there are, among other things, paper cups and a bag; in the background there are other people and tables.

2015; Bruni et al., 2014; Kiela and Bottou, 2014).

Grounded representations of sentences that are learned from image–caption data sets also improve performance on a number of sentence-level tasks (Kiela et al., 2017; Yoo et al., 2017) when used as additional features to skip-thought vectors (Kiros et al., 2015). The model architectures used for these studies have the same overall structure as our model and coincide with image–sentence retrieval systems (Kiros et al., 2014; Karpathy and Fei-Fei, 2015): a pre-trained CNN is fixed or fine-tuned as image feature extractor, followed by a learned transformation, while sentence representations are learned by a randomly initialized recurrent neural network. These models are trained to push the true image–caption pairs closer together, and the false image–caption pairs further from each other, in a joint embedding space.

In addition to learning grounded representations for image-sentence ranking, joint vision and language systems have been proposed to solve a wide range of tasks across modalities such as image captioning (Mao et al., 2014; Vinyals et al., 2015; Xu et al., 2015), visual question answering (Antol et al., 2015; Fukui et al., 2016; Jabri et al., 2016), text-to-image synthesis (Reed et al., 2016) and multimodal machine translation (Libovicky and Helcl, 2017; Elliott and Kádár, 2017).

Our work is also closely related to multilingual joint representation learning. In this scenario, a single model is trained to solve a task across multiple languages. Ammar et al. (2016) train a multilingual dependency parser on the Universal Dependencies treebank (Nivre et al., 2015) and show that on average the single multilingual model outperforms the monolingual baselines. Johnson et al. (2016) present a zero-shot neural machine translation model that is jointly trained on language pairs $A \leftrightarrow B$ and $B \leftrightarrow C$ and show that the model is capable of performing well on the unseen language pair $A \leftrightarrow C$. Lee et al. (2017) find that jointly training a many-languages-to-one translation model on unsegmented character sequences improves BLEU scores compared to monolingual training. They also show evidence that the model can handle intra-sentence code-switching. Peters et al. (2017) train a multilingual sequence-to-sequence translation architecture on grapheme-to-phoneme conversion using more than 300 languages. They report better performance when adding multiple languages, even those which are not present in the test data. Finally,

Require: p: task switching probability.
$\mathcal{D}_{c2i}$: datasets $D_1 \ldots D_k$ of image-caption pairs
$\quad < c, i >$ for all k languages.
$\mathcal{D}_{c2c}$: data set of all possible caption pairs
$\quad < c_a, c_b >$ for all k languages.
$\phi(c, \theta_\phi)$: caption encoder
$\psi(i, \theta_\phi)$: image encoder

while not stopping criterion **do**
$\quad T \sim \text{Bern}(p)$
$\quad$**if** $T = 1$ **then**
$\quad\quad D_n \sim \mathcal{D}_{c2i}$
$\quad\quad < c, i > \sim D_n$
$\quad\quad \mathbf{a} \leftarrow \phi(c, \theta_\phi)$
$\quad\quad \mathbf{b} \leftarrow \psi(i, \theta_\psi)$
$\quad$**else**
$\quad\quad < c_a, c_b > \sim D_{c2c}$
$\quad\quad \mathbf{a} \leftarrow \phi(c_a, \theta_\phi)$
$\quad\quad \mathbf{b} \leftarrow \phi(c_b, \theta_\phi)$
$\quad$**end if**
$\quad [\theta_\phi; \theta_\psi] \leftarrow \text{SGD}(\nabla_{[\theta_\phi; \theta_\psi]} \mathcal{J}(\mathbf{a}, \mathbf{b}))$
end while

Figure 2: Pseudo-code of the training procedure used to train our multilingual multi-task model.

massively multilingual language representations trained on over 900 languages have been shown to resemble language families (Östling and Tiedemann, 2016) and can successfully predict linguistic typology features (Malaviya et al., 2017).

In the vision and language domain, multilingual-multimodal sentence representation learning has been limited so far to two languages. The joint training of models on English and German data has been shown to outperform monolingual baselines on image-sentence ranking and semantic textual similarity tasks (Gella et al., 2017; Calixto et al., 2017). Recently Harwath et al. (2018) also showed the benefit of joint bilingual training in the domain of speech-to-image and image-to-speech retrieval using English and Hindi data.

3 Multilingual grounded learning

We train a standard model of grounded language learning which projects images and their textual descriptions into the same space (Kiros et al., 2014; Karpathy and Fei-Fei, 2015). The training procedure is illustrated by the pseudo-code in Figure 2. Images i are encoded by a fixed pre-trained CNN followed by a learned affine transformation

$\psi(i, \theta_\psi)$, and captions c are encoded by a randomly initialized RNN $\phi(c, \theta_\phi)$. The model learns to minimize the distance between pairs $<a, b>$ using a max-of-hinges ranking loss (Faghri et al., 2017):

$$\mathcal{J}(a, b) = \max_{<\hat{a}, b>} \left[\max(0, \alpha - s(a, b) + s(\hat{a}, b)) \right] +$$
$$\max_{<a, \hat{b}>} \left[\max(0, \alpha - s(a, b) + s(a, \hat{b})) \right]$$

where $< a, b >$ are the true pairs, and $< a, \hat{b} >$ and $< \hat{a}, b >$ are all possible contrastive pairs in the mini-batch. The pairs either consists of image-caption pairs $< i, c >$, where the model solves a caption-image **c2i** ranking task, or pairs of captions in multiple languages belonging to the same image $< c_a, c_b >$, where the model solves a caption-caption **c2c** ranking task (Gella et al., 2017). Our monolingual models are trained to minimize the caption-image ranking objective **c2i** on the training set. The multilingual models are trained to minimize the ranking loss for the set of all languages $\mathcal{L}$ in the collection: at each iteration the model is either updated for the **c2i** objective or the caption-caption **c2c** objective given either $< c^l, i >$ or a $< c_a^k, c_b^m >$ pair in languages $l, k, m, \ldots \in \mathcal{L}$. All models are trained by first selecting a task, either **c2i** or **c2c**. In the **c2i** case, a language is sampled at random followed by sampling a random batch; in the **c2c** case, all possible $< c_a, c_b >$ pairs across all languages are treated as a single data set. All of the model parameters are shared across all tasks and languages.

Implementation. We build our model on the PyTorch implementation of the VSE++ model (Faghri et al., 2017). Images are represented by the 2048D average-pool features extracted from the ResNet50 architecture (He et al., 2016) trained on ImageNet (Deng et al., 2009); this is followed by a trained linear layer $\mathbf{W}_I \in \mathbb{R}^{2048 \times 1024}$. Other implementation details follow (Faghri et al., 2017): sentences are represented as the final hidden state of a GRU (Chung et al., 2014) with 1024 units and 300 dimensional word-embeddings trained from scratch. We use a single word embedding matrix containing the union of all words in all considered languages. The similarity function s in the ranking loss is cosine similarity. We ℓ_2 normalize both the caption and image representations. The model is trained with the Adam optimizer (Kingma and Ba, 2014) using default parameters and learning-rate of 2e-4. We train the model with an early stopping crite-

	En	De	Fr	Cz
En	1.0	0.04	0.06	0.02
De	–	1.0	0.03	0.01
Fr	–	–	1.0	0.01
Cz	–	–	–	1.0

Table 1: Vocabulary overlap as measured by the Jaccard coefficient between the different languages on the translation portion of the Multi30K dataset.

rion, which is to maximise the sum of the image–sentence recall scores R@1, R@5, R@10 on the validation set with patience of 10 evaluations. In the monolingual setting the stopping criterion is evaluated at the end of each epoch, whereas in the multilingual setup it is evaluated every 500 iterations. The probability of switching between the **c2i** and **c2c** tasks is set to 0.5. Batches from all data sets are sampled by shuffling the full dataset, going through each batch and re-shuffling when exhausted. The sentence-pair dataset used to train the **c2c** ranking model for ℓ languages is generated as follows. For a given image i, a set of languages $1 \cdots \ell$, and a set of captions $C_1^i, \ldots, C_\ell^i$ associated with an image i, we generate the set of all possible combinations of size 2 from caption sets C^i and add the Cartesian product between all resulting pairs $C_m^i \times C_n^i$ in C^i to the training set.

4 Experimental setup[2]

Datasets. We train and evaluate our models on the *translation* and *comparable* portions of the Multi30K dataset (Elliott et al., 2016, 2017). The translation portion (a low-resource dataset) contains 29K images, each described in one English caption with German, French, and Czech translations. The comparable portion (a higher-resource dataset) contains the same 29K images paired with five English and five German descriptions collected independently. Figure 1 presents an example of the translation and comparable portions of the data. We used the preprocessed version of the dataset, in which the text is lowercased, punctuation is normalized, and the text is tokenized[3]. To reduce the vocabulary size of the joint models, we replace all words occurring fewer than four times with a spe-

---

[2]Code to reproduce our results is available at `https://github.com/kadarakos/mulisera`.
[3]`https://github.com/multi30k/dataset`

cial "UNK" symbol. Table 1 shows the overlap between the vocabularies of the *translation* portion of the Multi30K dataset. The total number of tokens across all four languages is 17,571, and taking the union of the tokens in these four languages results in vocabulary of 16,553 tokens – a 6% reduction in vocabulary size. On the *comparable* portion of the dataset, the total vocabulary between English and German contains 18,337 tokens, with a union of 17,667, which is a 4% reduction in vocabulary size.

Evaluation. We evaluate our models on the 1K images of the 2016 test set of Multi30K either using the 5K captions from the comparable data or the 1K translation pairs. We evaluate on image-to-text (I→ T) and text-to-image (T→ I) retrieval tasks. For most experiments we report Recall at 1 (R@1), 5 (R@5) and 10 (R@10) scores averaged over 10 randomly initialised models. However, in Section 6 we only report R@10 due to space limitations and because it has less variance than R@1 or R@5.

5 Bilingual Experiments

5.1 Reproducing Gella et al. (2017)

We start by attempting to reproduce the findings of Gella et al. (2017). In these experiments we train our multi-task learning model on the *comparable* portion of Multi30K. Our models re-implement their setups used for VSE (Monolingual) and bilingual models Pivot-Sym (Bilingual) and Parallel-Sym (Bilingual + c2c). The OE, Pivot-Asym and Parallel-Asym models are trained using the asymmetric similarity measure introduced for the order-embeddings (Vendrov et al., 2015). The main differences between our models and Gella et al. (2017) is that they use VGG-19 image features, whereas we use ResNet50 features, and we use the max-of-hinges loss instead of the more common sum-of-hinges loss.

Table 2 shows the results on the English comparable 2016 test set. Overall our scores are higher than Gella et al. (2017), which is most likely due to the different image features (Faghri et al. (2017) also report a large performance gain when they use the ResNet instead of the VGG image features). Nevertheless, our results show a similar trend to the symmetric cosine similarity models from Gella et al. (2017): our best results are achieved with bilingual joint training with the added c2c objective. Their models trained with an asymmetric similarity

measure show a different trend: the monolingual model is stronger than the bilingual model, and the c2c loss provides no clear improvement.

Table 3 presents the German results. Once again, our implementation outperforms Gella et al. (2017), and this is likely due to the different visual features and max-of-hinges loss. However, our Bilingual model with the additional c2c objective performs the best for German, whereas Gella et al. (2017) reports the overall best results for the monolingual baseline VSE. Their models that use the asymmetric similarity function are clearly better than the Monolingual OE model. In general, the results from Gella et al. (2017) indicate the benefits of bilingual joint training, however, they do not find a clear pattern between the model configurations across languages. In our implementation, we only focused on the symmetric cosine similarity function and found a systematic pattern across both languages: bilingual training improves results on all performance metrics for both languages, and the additional c2c objective always provides further improvements.

5.2 Translations vs. independent captions

We now study whether the model can be trained on either translation pairs or independently collected bilingual captions. Gella et al. (2017) only conducted experiments on independently collected captions. However, it is known that humans have equally strong preference for translated or independently collected captions of images (Frank et al., 2018), which has implications for the difficulty and cost of collecting training data. Our baseline is a Monolingual model trained on 29K single-captioned images in the *translation* portion of Multi30K. The Bi-translation model is trained on both German and English, with shared parameters. Table 4 shows that there is a substantial improvement in performance for both languages in the bilingual setting. However, the additional c2c loss degrades performance here. This could be because we only have one caption per image in each language and it is easier to find a relationship between these views of the translation pairs.

In the Bi-comparable setting, we randomly select an English and a German sentence for each image in the *comparable* portion of Multi30K. We only find a minor difference in performance between the Bi-translation and Bi-comparable models for English, but the German results are improved. Cru-

		I→T			T→I		
		R@1	R@5	R@10	R@1	R@5	R@10
Symmetric	VSE	31.6	60.4	72.7	23.3	53.6	**65.8**
	Pivot-Sym	31.6	61.2	73.8	23.5	53.4	**65.8**
	Parallel-Sym	**31.7**	**62.4**	**74.1**	**24.7**	**53.9**	65.7
Asymmetric	OE	**34.8**	**63.7**	74.8	25.8	**56.5**	67.8
	Pivot-Asym	33.8	62.8	**75.2**	26.2	56.4	**68.4**
	Parallel-Asym	31.5	61.4	74.7	**27.1**	56.2	66.9
	Monolingual	42.4	69.9	79.8	30.5	57.8	67.9
	Bilingual	42.7	70.7	80.1	30.6	58.1	68.3
	+ c2c	**43.8**	**71.8**	**81.4**	**32.3**	**59.9**	**70.2**

Table 2: English Image-to-text (I→T) and text-to-image (T→I) retrieval results on the *comparable* part of Multi30K, measured by Recall at 1, 5 at 10. `Typewriter` font shows performance of two sets of symmetric and asymmetric models from Gella et al. (2017).

		I→T			T→I		
		R@1	R@5	R@10	R@1	R@5	R@10
Symmetric	VSE	**29.3**	**58.1**	**71.8**	20.3	**47.2**	**60.1**
	Pivot-Sym	26.9	56.6	70.0	20.3	46.4	59.2
	Parallel-Sym	28.2	57.7	71.3	**20.9**	46.9	59.3
Asymmetric	OE	26.8	57.5	70.9	21.0	48.5	60.4
	Pivot-Asym	28.2	**61.9**	**73.4**	**22.5**	49.3	61.7
	Parallel-Asym	**30.2**	60.4	72.8	21.8	**50.5**	**62.3**
	Monolingual	34.2	63.0	74.0	23.9	49.5	60.5
	Bilingual	35.2	64.3	75.3	24.6	50.8	62.0
	+ c2c	**37.9**	**66.1**	**76.8**	**26.6**	**53.0**	**64.0**

Table 3: German Image-to-text (I→T) and text-to-image (T→I) retrieval results on the *comparable* part of Multi30K, measured by Recall at 1, 5 at 10. `Typewriter` font shows performance of two sets of symmetric and asymmetric models from Gella et al. (2017).

cially, it is still better than training on monolingual data. In the Bi-comparable setting, the c2c loss does not have a detrimental effect on model performance, unlike in the Bi-translation experiment. Overall we find that the *comparable* data leads to larger improvements in retrieval performance.

5.3 Overlapping vs. non-overlapping images

In a bilingual setting, we can improve an image-sentence ranking model by collecting more data in a second language. This can be achieved in two ways: by collecting captions in a new language for the same overlapping set of images, or by using a disjoint set of images and captions in a new language. We compare these two settings here.

In the Bi-overlap condition, we collect captions for the existing images in a new language, i.e. we use all of the English and German captions paired with a random selection of 50% of the images in *comparable* Multi30K. This results in a training

	English		German	
	I→T	T→I	I→T	T→I
Monolingual	56.3	40.1	39.5	20.9
Bi-translation	67.4	55.1	58.3	44.6
+ c2c	58.2	47.7	51.0	39.6
Bi-comparable	**67.9**	55.7	**62.0**	48.1
+ c2c	67.6	**56.0**	61.9	**49.1**

Table 4: R@10 retrieval results on the *comparable* part of Multi30K. Bi-translation is trained on 29K *translation pair* data; bi-comparable is trained by downsampling the *comparable* data to 29K.

	English		German	
	I→T	T→I	I→T	T→I
Full Monolingual	79.8	67.9	74.0	60.5
Half Monolingual	73.7	61.6	66.4	53.9
Bi-overlap	73.6	62.2	67.6	54.9
+ c2c	**76.0**	**65.9**	**71.2**	**59.1**
Bi-disjoint	73.1	62.1	67.9	54.9

Table 5: R@10 retrieval results on the *comparable* part of Multi30K. Full model trained on the 29K images of the *comparable* part, Half model on 14.5K images using random downsampling. For Bi-overlap, both English and German captions are used for 14.5K images. For Bi-disjoint, 14.5K images are used for English and the remaining 14.5K images for German.

dataset of 14.5K images with 145K bilingual captions. In the Bi-disjoint condition, we collect captions for new images in a new language, i.e. we use all of the English captions from a random selection of 50% of the images, and all of the German captions for the remaining 50% of the images. This results in a training dataset on 29K images with a total of 145K bilingual captions.

Table 5 shows the results of this experiment. The upper-bound is to train a Monolingual model on the full *comparable* corpus. For the lower bound, we train Half Monolingual models by randomly sampling half of the 29K images and their associated captions, giving 72.5K captions over 14.5K images. Unsurprisingly, the Half Monolingual models perform worse than the Full Monolingual models. In the Bi-overlap experiment, the German model is improved by collecting captions for the existing images in English. There is no difference in the performance of the English model, echoing the results from Section 5.1. The Bi-overlap model also benefits from the added c2c objective. Finally, the Bi-disjoint model performs as well as the Bi-overlap model without the c2c objective. (It was not possible to train the Bi-disjoint model with the additional c2c objective because there are no caption pairs for the same image.)

Overall, these results suggest that it is best to collect additional captions in the original language, but when adding a second language, it is better to collect extra captions for existing images and exploit the additional c2c ranking objective.

6 Multilingual experiments

We now turn out attention to multilingual learning using the English, German, French and Czech annotations in the *translation* portion of Multi30K. We only report the text-to-image (T→I) R@10 results due to space limitations.

We did not repeat the overlapping vs. non-overlapping experiments from Section 5.3 in a multilingual setting because this would introduce too much data sparsity. In order to conduct this experiment, we would have to downsample the already low-resource French and Czech captions by 50%, or even further for multi-way experiments.

6.1 Translation vs. independent captions

Table 6 shows the results of repeating the translations vs. comparable captions experiment from Section 5.2 with data in four languages. The Multi-translation models are trained on 29K images paired with a single caption in each language. These models perform better than their Monolingual counterparts, and the German, French, and Czech models are further improved with the c2c objective. The Multi-comparable models are trained by randomly sampling one English and one German caption from the *comparable* dataset, alongside the French and Czech translation pairs. These models perform as well as the Multi-translation models, and the c2c objective brings further improvements for all languages in this setting.

	En	De	Fr	Cz
Monolingual	50.4	39.5	47.0	42.0
Multi-translation	58.7	51.2	57.0	51.0
+ c2c	56.3	52.2	55.0	51.6
Multi-comparable	59.2	49.6	57.2	50.8
+ c2c	**61.8**	**52.7**	**59.2**	**55.2**

Table 6: The Monolingual and joint Multi-translation models trained on *translation pairs*, and the Multi-comparable trained on the downsampled *comparable* set with one caption per image.

These results clearly demonstrate the advantage of jointly training on more than two languages. Text-to-image retrieval performance increases by more than 11 R@10 points for each of the four languages in our experiment.

6.2 High-to-low resource transfer

We now examine whether the lower-resource French and Czech models benefit from training with the full complement of the higher-resource English and German comparable data. Therefore we train a joint model on the *translation* as well as *comparable* portions of Multi30K, and examine the performance on French and Czech.

Table 7 shows the results of this experiment. We find that the French and Czech models improve by 8.8 and 5.5 R@10 points respectively when they are only trained on the multilingual translation pairs (compared to the monolingual version), and by another 2.2 and 2.8 points if trained on the extra 155K English and German *comparable* descriptions. We also find that the additional c2c objective improves the Czech model by a further 4.8 R@10 points (this improvement is likely caused by training the model on 46 possible caption pairs). Our results show the impact of jointly training with the larger English and German resources, which demonstrates the benefits of high-to-low resource transfer.

6.3 Bilingual vs. multilingual

Finally, we investigate how useful it is to train on four languages instead of two. Figure 3 presents the image-to-text and text-to-image retrieval results of training Monolingual, Bilingual, or Multilingual models. The Monolingual and Bilingual models are trained on a random single-caption-image subsam-

	French	Czech
Monolingual	47.0	42.0
Multilingual	56.3	51.3
+ Comparable	58.9	52.4
+ c2c	**61.6**	**57.2**

Table 7: Multilingual is trained on all *translation pairs*, + Comparable adds the *comparable* data set.

ple of the *comparable* dataset with the additional c2c objective, as this configuration provided the overall best results in Sections 5.2 and 6.1. The Multilingual models are trained with the additional French and Czech *translation* data. As can be seen in Figure 3, the performance on both tasks and for both languages improves as we move from using data from one to two to four languages.

7 Conclusions

We learn multilingual multimodal sentence embeddings and show that multilingual joint training improves over bilingual joint training. We also demonstrate that low-resource languages can benefit from the additional data found in high-resource languages. Our experiments suggest that either translation pairs or independently-collected captions improve the performance of a multilingual model, and that the latter data setting provides further improvements through a caption–caption ranking objective. We also show that when collecting data in an additional language, it is better to collect captions for the existing images because we can exploit the caption–caption objective. Our results lead to several directions for future work. We would like to pin down the mechanism via which multilingual training contributes to improved performance for image-sentence ranking. Additionally, we only consider four languages and show the gain of multilingual over bilingual training only for the English-German language pair. In future work we will incorporate more languages from data sets such as the Chinese Flickr8K (Li et al., 2016) or Japanese COCO (Miyazaki and Shimizu, 2016).

Acknowledgements

Desmond Elliott was supported by an Amazon Research Award.

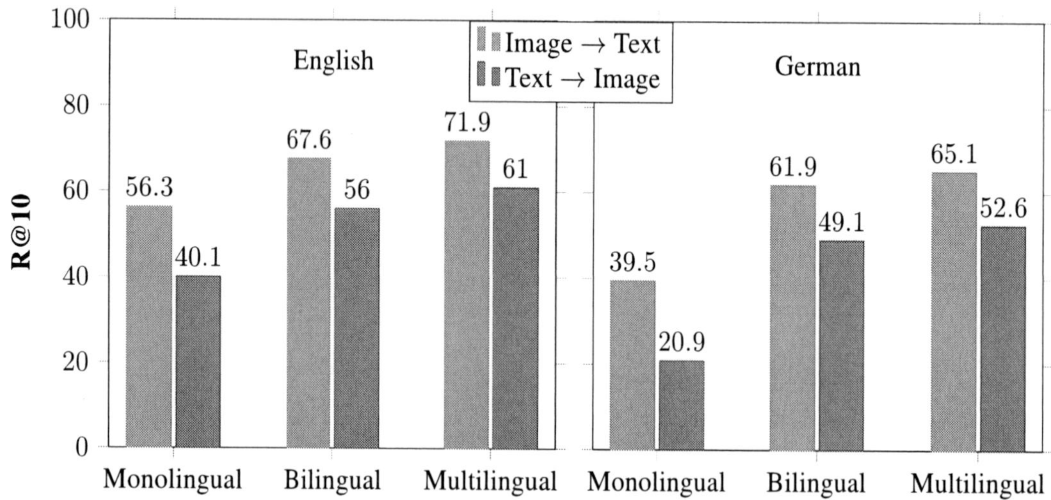

Figure 3: Comparing models from the Monolingual, Bilingual and Multilingual settings. The Monolingual and Bilingual models are trained on the downsampled English and German *comparable* sets with additional c2c objective. The Multilingual model uses the French and Czech *translation pairs* as additional data. The results are reported on the full 2016 test set of the *comparable* portion of Multi30K.

References

Agirre, E., Banea, C., Cardie, C., Cer, D., Diab, M., Gonzalez-Agirre, A., Guo, W., Lopez-Gazpio, I., Maritxalar, M., Mihalcea, R., et al. (2015). Semeval-2015 task 2: Semantic textual similarity, english, spanish and pilot on interpretability. In *Proceedings of the 9th international workshop on semantic evaluation (SemEval 2015)*, pages 252–263.

Agirre, E., Banea, C., Cardie, C., Cer, D., Diab, M., Gonzalez-Agirre, A., Guo, W., Mihalcea, R., Rigau, G., and Wiebe, J. (2014). Semeval-2014 task 10: Multilingual semantic textual similarity. In *Proceedings of the 8th international workshop on semantic evaluation (SemEval 2014)*, pages 81–91.

Ammar, W., Mulcaire, G., Ballesteros, M., Dyer, C., and Smith, N. A. (2016). Many languages, one parser. *arXiv preprint arXiv:1602.01595*.

Antol, S., Agrawal, A., Lu, J., Mitchell, M., Batra, D., Lawrence Zitnick, C., and Parikh, D. (2015). Vqa: Visual question answering. In *Proceedings of the IEEE International Conference on Computer Vision*, pages 2425–2433.

Barman, U., Das, A., Wagner, J., and Foster, J. (2014). Code mixing: A challenge for language identification in the language of social media. In *Proceedings of the first workshop on computational approaches to code switching*, pages 13–23.

Baroni, M. (2016). Grounding distributional semantics in the visual world. *Language and Linguistics Compass*, 10(1):3–13.

Barsalou, L. W., Simmons, W. K., Barbey, A. K., and Wilson, C. D. (2003). Grounding conceptual knowledge in modality-specific systems. *Trends in cognitive sciences*, 7(2):84–91.

Bruni, E., Tran, N.-K., and Baroni, M. (2014). Multimodal distributional semantics. *Journal of Artificial Intelligence Research*, 49:1–47.

Calixto, I., Liu, Q., and Campbell, N. (2017). Multilingual multi-modal embeddings for natural language processing. *arXiv preprint arXiv:1702.01101*.

Chung, J., Cho, K., and Bengio, Y. (2016). A character-level decoder without explicit segmentation for neural machine translation. *arXiv preprint arXiv:1603.06147*.

Chung, J., Gulcehre, C., Cho, K., and Bengio, Y. (2014). Empirical evaluation of gated recurrent neural networks on sequence modeling. *arXiv preprint arXiv:1412.3555*.

Deng, J., Dong, W., Socher, R., Li, L.-J., Li, K., and Fei-Fei, L. (2009). Imagenet: A large-scale hierarchical image database. In *Computer Vision and Pattern Recognition, 2009. CVPR 2009. IEEE Conference on*, pages 248–255. IEEE.

Dolan, B., Quirk, C., and Brockett, C. (2004). Unsupervised construction of large paraphrase corpora: Exploiting massively parallel news sources. In *Proceedings of the 20th international conference on Computational Linguistics*, page 350. Association for Computational Linguistics.

Elliott, D., Frank, S., Barrault, L., Bougares, F., and Specia, L. (2017). Findings of the second shared task on multimodal machine translation and multilingual image description. In *Proceedings of the Second Conference on Machine Translation, Volume 2: Shared Task Papers.*

Elliott, D., Frank, S., Sima'an, K., and Specia, L. (2016). Multi30k: Multilingual english-german image descriptions. *arXiv preprint arXiv:1605.00459.*

Elliott, D. and Kádár, A. (2017). Imagination improves multimodal translation. *arXiv preprint arXiv:1705.04350.*

Faghri, F., Fleet, D. J., Kiros, J. R., and Fidler, S. (2017). Vse++: Improved visual-semantic embeddings. *arXiv preprint arXiv:1707.05612.*

Finkelstein, L., Gabrilovich, E., Matias, Y., Rivlin, E., Solan, Z., Wolfman, G., and Ruppin, E. (2001). Placing search in context: The concept revisited. In *Proceedings of the 10th international conference on World Wide Web*, pages 406–414. ACM.

Frank, S., Elliott, D., and Specia, L. (2018). Assessing multilingual multimodal image description: Studies of native speaker preferences and translator choices. *Natural Language Engineering*, 24(3):393–413.

Fukui, A., Park, D. H., Yang, D., Rohrbach, A., Darrell, T., and Rohrbach, M. (2016). Multimodal compact bilinear pooling for visual question answering and visual grounding. *arXiv preprint arXiv:1606.01847.*

Funaki, R. and Nakayama, H. (2015). Image-mediated learning for zero-shot cross-lingual document retrieval. In *Proceedings of the 2015 Conference on Empirical Methods in Natural Language Processing*, pages 585–590.

Gella, S., Sennrich, R., Keller, F., and Lapata, M. (2017). Image pivoting for learning multilingual multimodal representations. *arXiv preprint arXiv:1707.07601.*

Harwath, D., Chuang, G., and Glass, J. (2018). Vision as an interlingua: Learning multilingual semantic embeddings of untranscribed speech. *arXiv preprint arXiv:1804.03052.*

He, K., Zhang, X., Ren, S., and Sun, J. (2016). Deep residual learning for image recognition. In *Proceedings of the IEEE conference on computer vision and pattern recognition*, pages 770–778.

Hill, F., Reichart, R., and Korhonen, A. (2015). Simlex-999: Evaluating semantic models with (genuine) similarity estimation. *Computational Linguistics*, 41(4):665–695.

Jabri, A., Joulin, A., and van der Maaten, L. (2016). Revisiting visual question answering baselines. In *European conference on computer vision*, pages 727–739. Springer.

Johnson, M., Schuster, M., Le, Q. V., Krikun, M., Wu, Y., Chen, Z., Thorat, N., Viégas, F., Wattenberg, M., Corrado, G., et al. (2016). Google's multilingual neural machine translation system: enabling zero-shot translation. *arXiv preprint arXiv:1611.04558.*

Kádár, Á., Alishahi, A., and Chrupała, G. (2015). Learning word meanings from images of natural scenes. *Traitement Automatique des Langues*, 55(3).

Karpathy, A. and Fei-Fei, L. (2015). Deep visual-semantic alignments for generating image descriptions. In *Proceedings of the IEEE conference on computer vision and pattern recognition*, pages 3128–3137.

Kiela, D. and Bottou, L. (2014). Learning image embeddings using convolutional neural networks for improved multi-modal semantics. In *Proceedings of the 2014 Conference on Empirical Methods in Natural Language Processing (EMNLP)*, pages 36–45.

Kiela, D., Conneau, A., Jabri, A., and Nickel, M. (2017). Learning visually grounded sentence representations. *arXiv preprint arXiv:1707.06320.*

Kiela, D., Hill, F., Korhonen, A., and Clark, S. (2014). Improving multi-modal representations using image dispersion: Why less is sometimes more. In *Proceedings of the 52nd Annual Meeting of the Association for Computational Linguistics (Volume 2: Short Papers)*, volume 2, pages 835–841.

Kingma, D. P. and Ba, J. (2014). Adam: A method for stochastic optimization. *arXiv preprint arXiv:1412.6980.*

Kiros, R., Salakhutdinov, R., and Zemel, R. S. (2014). Unifying visual-semantic embeddings with multimodal neural language models. *arXiv preprint arXiv:1411.2539.*

Kiros, R., Zhu, Y., Salakhutdinov, R. R., Zemel, R., Urtasun, R., Torralba, A., and Fidler, S. (2015). Skip-thought vectors. In *Advances in neural information processing systems*, pages 3294–3302.

Lee, J., Cho, K., and Hofmann, T. (2017). Fully character-level neural machine translation without explicit segmentation. *Transactions of the Association for Computational Linguistics*, 5:365–378.

Li, X., Lan, W., Dong, J., and Liu, H. (2016). Adding chinese captions to images. In *Proceedings of the 2016 ACM on International Conference on Multimedia Retrieval*, pages 271–275. ACM.

Libovicky, J. and Helcl, J. (2017). Attention strategies for multi-source sequence-to-sequence learning. In *Proceedings of the 55th Annual Meeting of the Association for Computational Linguistics (Volume 2: Short Papers)*, pages 196–202, Stroudsburg, PA, USA. Association for Computational Linguistics.

Malaviya, C., Neubig, G., and Littell, P. (2017). Learning language representations for typology prediction. *arXiv preprint arXiv:1707.09569.*

Mao, J., Xu, W., Yang, Y., Wang, J., Huang, Z., and Yuille, A. (2014). Deep captioning with multimodal recurrent neural networks (m-rnn). *arXiv preprint arXiv:1412.6632*.

Marelli, M., Menini, S., Baroni, M., Bentivogli, L., Bernardi, R., Zamparelli, R., et al. (2014). A sick cure for the evaluation of compositional distributional semantic models. In *LREC*, pages 216–223.

Miyazaki, T. and Shimizu, N. (2016). Cross-lingual image caption generation. In *Proceedings of the 54th Annual Meeting of the Association for Computational Linguistics (Volume 1: Long Papers)*, pages 1780–1790. Association for Computational Linguistics.

Nakayama, H. and Nishida, N. (2017). Zero-resource machine translation by multimodal encoder–decoder network with multimedia pivot. *Machine Translation*, 31(1-2):49–64.

Nivre, J., Agić, Ž., Aranzabe, M. J., Asahara, M., Atutxa, A., Ballesteros, M., Bauer, J., Bengoetxea, K., Bhat, R. A., Bosco, C., et al. (2015). Universal dependencies 1.2.

Östling, R. and Tiedemann, J. (2016). Continuous multilinguality with language vectors. *arXiv preprint arXiv:1612.07486*.

Peters, B., Dehdari, J., and van Genabith, J. (2017). Massively multilingual neural grapheme-to-phoneme conversion. In *Proceedings of the First Workshop on Building Linguistically Generalizable NLP Systems*, pages 19–26.

Rajendran, J., Khapra, M. M., Chandar, S., and Ravindran, B. (2015). Bridge correlational neural networks for multilingual multimodal representation learning. *arXiv preprint arXiv:1510.03519*.

Reed, S., Akata, Z., Yan, X., Logeswaran, L., Schiele, B., and Lee, H. (2016). Generative adversarial text to image synthesis. *arXiv preprint arXiv:1605.05396*.

Specia, L., Frank, S., Sima'an, K., and Elliott, D. (2016). A shared task on multimodal machine translation and crosslingual image description. In *Proceedings of the First Conference on Machine Translation*, pages 543–553, Berlin, Germany. Association for Computational Linguistics.

Vendrov, I., Kiros, R., Fidler, S., and Urtasun, R. (2015). Order-embeddings of images and language. *arXiv preprint arXiv:1511.06361*.

Vinyals, O., Toshev, A., Bengio, S., and Erhan, D. (2015). Show and tell: A neural image caption generator. In *Computer Vision and Pattern Recognition (CVPR), 2015 IEEE Conference on*, pages 3156–3164. IEEE.

Xu, K., Ba, J., Kiros, R., Cho, K., Courville, A., Salakhudinov, R., Zemel, R., and Bengio, Y. (2015). Show, attend and tell: Neural image caption generation with visual attention. In *International Conference on Machine Learning*, pages 2048–2057.

Yoo, K. M., Shin, Y., and Lee, S.-g. (2017). Improving visually grounded sentence representations with self-attention. *arXiv preprint arXiv:1712.00609*.

Zoph, B., Yuret, D., May, J., and Knight, K. (2016). Transfer learning for low-resource neural machine translation. *arXiv preprint arXiv:1604.02201*.

Unsupervised Sentence Compression using Denoising Auto-Encoders

Thibault Fevry[*]
Center for Data Science
New York University
Thibault.Fevry@nyu.edu

Jason Phang[*]
Center for Data Science
New York University
jasonphang@nyu.edu

Abstract

In sentence compression, the task of short-ening sentences while retaining the original meaning, models tend to be trained on large corpora containing pairs of verbose and compressed sentences. To remove the need for paired corpora, we emulate a summarization task and add noise to extend sentences and train a denoising auto-encoder to recover the original, constructing an end-to-end training regime without the need for any examples of compressed sentences. We conduct a human evaluation of our model on a standard text summarization dataset and show that it performs comparably to a supervised base-line based on grammatical correctness and retention of meaning. Despite being exposed to no target data, our unsupervised models learn to generate imperfect but reasonably readable sentence summaries. Although we underperform supervised models based on ROUGE scores, our models are competitive with a supervised baseline based on human evaluation for grammatical correctness and retention of meaning.

1 Introduction

Sentence compression is the task of condensing a longer sentence into a shorter one that still re-tains the meaning of the original. Past models for sentence compression have tended to rely heavily on strong linguistic priors such as syntactic rules or heuristics (Dorr et al., 2003; Cohn and Lap-ata, 2008). More recent work using deep learning involves models trained without strong linguistic priors, instead requiring large corpora consisting of pairs of longer and shorter sentences (Miao and Blunsom, 2016).

---

[*] Denotes equal contribution

Sentence compression can also be can be seen as a "scaled down version of the text summariza-tion problem" (Knight and Marcu, 2002). Within text summarization, two broad approaches exist: *extractive* approaches extract explicit tokens or phrases from the reference text, whereas *abstrac-tive* approaches involve a compressed paraphras-ing of the reference text, similar to the approach humans might take (Jing, 2000, 2002).

In the related domain of machine translation, a task that also involves learning a mapping from one string of tokens to another, state of the art models using deep learning techniques are trained on large parallel corpora. Recent promising work on unsupervised neural machine translation (Artetxe et al., 2017; Lample et al., 2017) has shown that with the right training regime, it is possible to train models for machine translation between two languages given only two unpaired monolingual corpora.

In this paper, we apply neural text summariza-tion techniques to the task of sentence compres-sion, focusing on on extractive summarization. However, we depart significantly from prior work by taking a fully unsupervised training approach. Beyond not using parallel corpora, we train our model using a single corpus. In contrast to un-supervised neural machine translation, which still uses two corpora, we do not have separate corpora of longer and shorter sentences.

We show that a simple denoising auto-encoder model, trained on removing and reordering words from a noised input sequence, can learn effec-tive sentence compression, generating shorter se-quences of reasonably grammatical text that retain the original meaning. While the models are still prone to both errors in grammar and meaning, we believe that this is a strong step toward reducing reliance on paired corpora.

We evaluate our model using both a stan-

Proceedings of the 22nd Conference on Computational Natural Language Learning (CoNLL 2018), pages 413–422
Brussels, Belgium, October 31 - November 1, 2018. ©2018 Association for Computational Linguistics

dard text-summarization benchmark as well as human evaluation of compressed sentences based on grammatical correctness and retention of meaning. Although our models do not capture the written style of the target summaries (headlines), they still produce reasonably readable and accurate compressed sentence summaries, without ever being exposed to any target sentence summaries. We find that our model underperforms based on ROUGE metrics, especially compared to supervised models, but performs competitively with supervised baselines in human evaluation. We further show that providing the model with a sentence embedding of the original sentence leads to better ROUGE scores but worse human evaluation scores. However, both unsupervised and supervised methods still fall short based on human evaluation, and effective sentence compression and summarization remains an open problem.

2 Related work

Early sentence compression approaches were extractive, focusing on deletion of uninformative words from sentences through learned rules (Knight and Marcu, 2002) or linguistically-motivated heuristics (Dorr et al., 2003). The first abstractive approaches also relied on learned syntactic transformations (Cohn and Lapata, 2008).

Recent work in automated text summarization has seen the application of sequence-to-sequence models to automatic summarization, including both extractive (Nallapati et al., 2017) and abstractive (Rush et al., 2015; Chopra et al., 2016; Nallapati et al., 2016; Paulus et al., 2017; Fan et al., 2017) approaches, as well as hybrids of both (See et al., 2017). Although these methods have achieved state-of-the-art results, they are constrained by their need for large amounts paired document-summary data.

Miao and Blunsom (2016) seek to overcome this shortcoming by training separate compressor and reconstruction models, allowing for training based on both paired (supervised) and unlabeled (unsupervised) data. For their compressor, they train a discrete variational auto-encoder for sentence compression and use the REINFORCE algorithm to allow end-to-end training. They further use a pre-trained language model as a prior for their compression model to induce their compressed output to be grammatical. However, their reported results are still based on models trained on at least 500k instances of paired data.

In machine translation, unsupervised methods for aligning word embeddings using only unmatched bilingual corpora, trained with only small seed dictionaries, (Mikolov et al., 2013; Lazaridou et al., 2015), adversarial training on similar corpora (Zhang et al., 2017; Conneau et al., 2017b) or even on distant corpora and languages (Artetxe et al., 2018) have enabled the development of unsupervised machine translation (Artetxe et al., 2017; Lample et al., 2017). However, it is not clear how to adapt these methods for summarization where the task is to shorten the reference rather than translate it. Wang and Lee (2018) train a generative adversarial network to encode references into a latent space and decode them in summaries using only unmatched document-summary pairs. However, in contrast with machine translation where monolingual data is plentiful and paired data scarce, summaries are paired with their respective documents when they exist, thus limiting the usefulness of such approaches. In contrast, our method requires no summary corpora.

Denoising auto-encoders (Vincent et al., 2008) have been successfully used in natural language processing for building sentence embeddings (Hill et al., 2016), training unsupervised translation models (Artetxe et al., 2017) or for natural language generation in narrow domains (Freitag and Roy, 2018). In all those instances, the added noise takes the form of random deletion of words and word swapping or shuffling. Although our noising mechanism relies on adding rather than removing words, we take some inspiration from these works.

Work in sentence simplification (see Shardlow (2014) for a survey) has some similarities with sentence compression, but it differs in that the key focus is on making sentences more easily understandable rather than shorter. Though word deletion is used, sentence simplification methods feature sentence splitting and word simplification which are not usually present in sentence compression. Furthermore, these methods often rely heavily on learned rules (e.g lexical simplification as in Biran et al. (2011)), integer linear programming and sentence parse trees which makes them starkly different from our deep learning-based approach. The exceptions that adopt end-to-end approaches, such as Filippova et al. (2015), are usually supervised and focus on word deletion.

3 Methods

3.1 Model

Our core model is based on a standard attentional encoder-decoder (Bahdanau et al., 2014), consisting of multiple layers bi-directional long short-term memory networks in both the encoder and decoder, with negative-log likelihood as our loss function. We detail below the training regime and model modifications to apply the denoising auto-encoding paradigm to sentence compression.

3.2 Additive Noising

Since we do not use paired sentence compression data with which to train our model in a supervised way, we simulate a supervised training regime by modifying a denoising auto-encoder (DAE) training regime to more closely resemble supervised sentence compression. Given a reference sentence, we extend and shuffle the input sentence, and then train our model to recover the original reference sentence. In doing so, the model has to exclude and reorder words, and hence learns to output shorter but grammatically correct sentences.

Additive Sampling We randomly sample additional sentences from our data set, and then subsample a number of words from each without replacement. We then append the newly sampled words to our reference sentence. In our experiments, we sample two additional sentences for each reference sentence, and the number of words sampled from each is dependent on the length of the original reference sentence. In practice, we aim to generate a noised sentence that extends the original sentence by 40% to 60%. To fit the fully unsupervised learning paradigm, we do not introduce any biases into our sampling of words in training our model. In particular, we excluded approaches that overweighted adjectives or speaker identification (e.g "said X on Tuesday") in noising.

Shuffling Next, we shuffle the resultant string of words. We experiment with two forms of shuffling: (i) a complete word (unigram) shuffle and (ii) bigram shuffling, where we only shuffle among the word bigrams, keeping pairs of adjacent words together.

This process is illustrated in Figure 1.

3.3 Length Countdown

To induce our model to output sequences of a desired length, we augment the RNN decoder in our model to take an additional *length countdown* input. In the context of text generation, RNN decoders can be formulated as follows:

$$h_t = \text{RNN}(h_{t-1}, x_t) \qquad (1)$$

where h_{t-1} is the hidden state at the previous step and x_t is an external input (often an embedding of the previously decoded token). Let T_{dec} be the desired length of our output sequence. We modify (1) with an additional input:

$$h_t = \text{RNN}(h_{t-1}, x_t, T_{\text{dec}} - t) \qquad (2)$$

The length countdown $T - t$ is a single scalar input that ticks down to 0 when the decoder reaches the desired length T, and goes negative after. In practice, $(x_t, T_{\text{dec}} - t)$ are concatenated into a single vector. We also experimented with adding a length penalty to our objective function to amplify the loss from predicting the end-of-sequence token <EOS> at the desired time step, but did not find that our models required this additional loss term to output sequences of the desired length.

Explicit length control has been used in previous summarization work. Fan et al. (2017) introduced a length marker token that induces the model to target an output of a desired length, coarsely divided into discrete bins. Kikuchi et al. (2016) examined several methods of introducing target output length information, and found that they were effective without negatively impacting summarization quality. We found more success with our models with a per time-step input compared to a token at the start of the sequence as in Fan et al. (2017).

3.4 Input Sentence Embedding

The model specified above is supplied only with an unordered set of words with which to construct a shorter sentence. However, there are typically many ways of ordering a given set of words into a grammatical sentence. In order to help our model better recover the original sentence, we also provide the model with an InferSent sentence embedding (Conneau et al., 2017a) of the original sentence, generated using a pre-trained InferSent model. The InferSent model is trained on NLI tasks, where, given a longer premise text and a

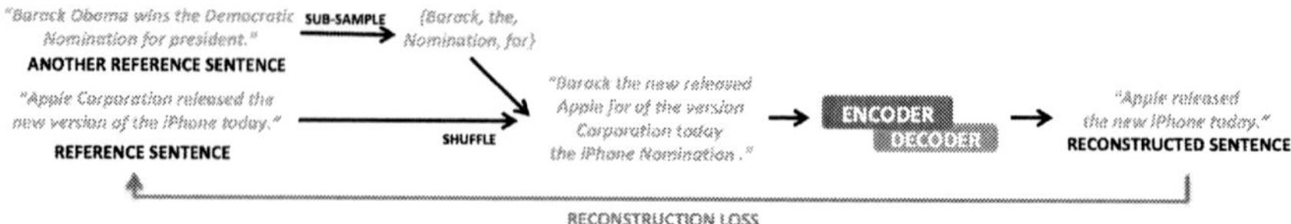

Figure 1: Illustration of Additive Noising. A reference sentence is noised with subsampled words from another sentence, and then shuffled. The denoising auto-encoder is trained to recover the original reference sentence. This simulates a text summarization training regimes without the need for parallel corpora.

shorter hypothesis text, the model is required to determine if the premise (i) entails, (ii) contradicts or (iii) is neutral to the hypothesis. The InferSent sentence embeddings are an intermediate output of the model, reflecting information captured from each text string. Conneau et al. show that InferSent sentence embeddings capture various aspects of the semantics of a string of text (Conneau et al., 2018), and should provide additional information to the model as to which ordering of words best match the meaning original sentence.

We incorporate the InferSent embeddings by modifying the hidden state passed between the encoder and the decoder. In typical RNN encoder-decoder architectures, the final hidden state of the encoder is used as the initial hidden state of the decoder. In other words, $h_0^{\text{dec}} = h_{T_{\text{enc}}}^{\text{enc}}$. We learn a fully connected layer f to be used as follows:

$$h_0^{\text{dec}} = f(h_{T_{\text{enc}}}^{\text{enc}}, s) \tag{3}$$

where s is the InferSent embedding of the input sentence. This transformation is only applied once on the hidden state shared from the encoder to the decoder. In the case of LSTMs, where there are both hidden states and cell states, we learn a fully connected mapping for each.

3.5 Numbered Out-of-Vocabulary (OOV) Embeddings

Many text summarization data sets are based on news articles and headlines, which often include names, proper nouns, and other rare words or tokens that may not appear in word embedding dictionaries. In addition, the output layer of most models are based on a softmax over all potential output tokens. This means that expanding the vocabulary to potentially include more rare words increases computation and memory costs in the final layer linearly. There are many approaches to tackle out-of-vocabulary (OOV) tokens (See et al., 2017; Nallapati et al., 2016), and we detail below our approach.

To address the frequent occurrences of OOV characters, we learn a fixed number of embeddings for numbered OOV tokens.[2] Given an input sequence, we first parse the sentence to identify OOV tokens and number them in order, while storing the map from numbered OOV tokens to words.[3] When embedding the respective tokens to be inputs to the RNN, we assign the corresponding embeddings for each numbered OOV token. We apply the same numbering system to the target, so the same word in the input and output will always be assigned the same numbered OOV token, and hence the same embedding. At inference, we replace any output numbered OOV tokens with their respective words. This allows us to output sentences using words not in our vocabulary.

This approach is similar to the pointer-generator model (See et al., 2017), but whereas See et al. compute attention weights over all tokens in the input to learn where to copy and have an explicit switch between copying (pointer) and output (generator), we learn embeddings for a fixed number of OOV tokens, and the embeddings are in the same latent space as our pre-trained word embeddings.

4 Experimental Setup

4.1 Data

For our text summarization task, We use the Annotated Gigaword (Napoles et al., 2012) in line with Rush et al. (2015). This data set is derived for news articles, and consists of pairs of the main sentences in the article (longer), and the headline (shorter). The former and latter are used as references and summaries respectively in the context of summarization tasks. We preprocess the data using the scripts made available by the authors, which produces about 3.8M training examples and 400K validation examples. We sample randomly

---

[2]We use a fixed number of 10 OOV tokens in our experiments.

[3]In the case of shuffling and noising, we number the OOV tokens before shuffling, and number any additional OOV tokens from the noised input sentence in a second pass.

10K examples for validation and 10K for testing from the validation set, similar to the procedure in Nallapati et al. (2016). Like Rush et al. (2015), we only extract the tokenized words of the first sentence, in contrast with Nallapati et al. (2016) who extract the first two sentences as well as part-of-speech and named-entities tags.

4.2 Training

In training, we only use the reference sentences from the Gigaword dataset. For all our models, we used GloVe word embeddings (Pennington et al., 2014). We freeze these embeddings during training. Our vocabulary is comprised of the 20000 most frequent words in the references, and we use the aforementioned numbered OOV embeddings for other unseen words. We similarly freeze the InferSent model for sentence embeddings. The encoder and decoder are both 3-layer LSTMs with 512 hidden units. We use a batch size of 128, and optimize our models using Adam (Kingma and Ba, 2014) with a initial learning rate of 0.0005, annealing it by 0.9 at every 10K mini-batches. We do not use dropout but use gradient clipping at 2. We train our models for 4 full epochs.

4.3 Inference

At inference, we supply our model with the unmodified reference sentences–hence no noising is applied. We use the length countdown to target outputs of half the length of the reference sentences. The application of sentence embeddings is unchanged from training.

4.4 Implementation

We implemented our models using Pytorch (Paszke et al., 2017), and will make our code publicly available at `https://github.com/zphang/usc_dae`.

5 Results

5.1 ROUGE Evaluation

In Table 1, we evaluate our models on ROUGE (Lin, 2004) F1 scores, where a higher score is better. We provide a comparison with a simple but strong baseline, *F8W* is simply first 8 words of the input, as is done in Wang and Lee (2018) and similarly to the *Prefix* baseline (first 75 bytes) of Rush et al. (2015), as well as the ROUGE of the whole text with the target. We provide scores of two supervised text-summarization

methods on Gigaword. One is our own baseline, consisting of a sequence-to-sequence attentional encoder-decoder trained on pairs of reference and target summary text, but incorporating the same length countdown mechanism as in our unsupervised models. The other is the *words-lvt2k-1sent* model of Nallapati et al. (2016). Although not their best model, it is most comparable to ours since it only uses the first sentence and does not extract *tf-idf* vectors nor named entities tags.

F8W and *All text* are strong baselines due to the tendency of news articles to contain specific terms that are rarely rephrased. We find that our models perform competitively with these baselines, although they pale in comparison to supervised methods, likely because they do not learn any style transfer and use only the reference's vocabulary and writing style. While our ROUGE-1 scores are in line with the baselines, our ROUGE-2 scores fall somewhat behind. Including InferSent sentence embeddings improves our ROUGE scores across the board. Our supervised baseline performance is close to that of Nallapati et al. (2016), with results lower in ROUGE-2 likely due to their use of beam search. Nevertheless, the supervised baseline is representative of the performance of a standard sequence-to-sequence attentional model on this task.

A direct comparison of ROUGE scores is not completely adequate for evaluating our model. Because of our training regime, our model primarily learned to generate shortened sentences that often still retain the style of the input sentences. Unlike other model setups, our model has never been exposed to any examples of summaries, and hence never adapts its output to match the style of the target summaries. In the case of Gigaword, the summaries are headlines from news articles, which are written in a particular linguistic style (e.g. dropping articles, having clauses rather than full sentences). ROUGE will thus penalize our model, that tends to output longer, full sentences. In addition, ROUGE is an imperfect metric for summarization as word/n-gram overlap does not fully capture summary relevancy and retention of meaning.[4] For this reason, we also conduct a separate human evaluation of our different models against

---

[4]See discussion in Nallapati et al. (2016), or in Paulus et al. (2017) where a reinforcement learning model trained on a Rouge-L objective alone achieves the best scores but "produces the least readable summaries among [their] experiments"

Example 1:
I: nearly ### of the released hostages remain in hospital , and more than ### of them are in very serious condition , russian medical authorities said sunday .
G: nearly ### people still hospitalized more than ### in critical condition
2-g shuf: more than ### hostages are in serious condition , russian medical authorities said .
2-g shuf + InferSent: nearly ### hostages of the nearly released in serious medical condition , said .

Example 2:
I: french president jacques chirac arrived here friday at the start of a <unk> during which he is expected to hold talks with romanian leaders on bucharest 's application to join nato .
G: chirac arrives in romania
2-g shuf: french president jacques chirac arrived here friday to hold talks with romanian leaders on nato .
2-g shuf + InferSent: french president jacques chirac arrived here friday at the start of talks to join nato .

Example 3:
I: swedish truck maker ab volvo on tuesday reported its third consecutive quarterly loss as sales plunged by one-third amid weak demand in the april-june period .
G: volvo posts $ ### million loss on falling sales
2-g shuf: swedish truck maker volvo ab on tuesday reported its third consecutive quarterly .
2-g shuf + InferSent: swedish truck maker ab volvo on tuesday reported its consecutive quarterly loss .

Example 4:
I: wall street stocks rallied friday as a weak report on us economic growth boosted hopes for an easier interest rate policy from the federal reserve and investors reacted to upbeat earnings news .
G: wall street shrugs off weak gdp pushes higher
2-g shuf: wall street stocks rallied friday as investors reacted to upbeat economic news and interest rate .
2-g shuf + InferSent: wall street stocks rallied friday as investors reacted to an economic growth report on hopes .

Figure 2: Examples of inputs, ground-truth summaries, and outputs from two of our models. **I** is input, **G** (gold) is the true summaries. Example 1 and 2 show our models summarizing pertinent information from the input. Example 3 demonstrates the ability to recover long ordered strings of tokens, even though the models are trained on shuffle data. Example 4 shows cases where the models output grammatical but semantically incorrect sentences.

a supervised baseline (Section 5.4).

5.2 ROUGE Ablation study

In Table 2, we report the results of an ablation study. We observe that all three components we vary, namely the use of attention, bigram shuffling, and incorporation of sentence embeddings, contribute positively to the performance of our model as measured by ROUGE. The model that incorporates all three obtains the highest ROUGE scores.

5.3 Impact of Length

To assess our models' ability to deal with sequences of text of different length, we measure the ROUGE scores on two bins of length of the input text, from 16 to 30 tokens and from 31 to 45. As expected, longer sentences pose a harder challenge to the model, with our model performing better on shorter than longer sentences. Across most sequence-based problems, models tend to perform better on shorter sequences. However, in the context of the text summarization or sentence compression, longer sentences not only contain more information that the model would need to selective remove, but also more information from which to identify the central theme of the sentence.

5.4 Human Evaluation

To qualitatively evaluate our model, we take inspiration from the methodology of Turner and Charniak (2005) to design our human evaluation. We asked 6 native English speakers to evaluate randomly chosen summaries from five models: our best models with and without InferSent sentence embeddings, a summary generated from a trained supervised model, and the ground truth summary. The sentences are evaluated based on two separate criteria: the grammaticality of the summary and how well it retained the information of the original sentence. In the former, only the summary is provided, whereas in the latter, the evaluator is shown both the original sentence as well as the summary. Each of these criteria were graded on a scale from 1 to 5. The examples are from the test set, with 50 examples randomly sampled for each evaluator and criterion.[5]

We report the average evaluation given by our 6 evaluators in Table 4. That the *Meaning* score for the ground truth is somewhat low (3.87) is not surprising. Within the Gigaword dataset, summaries (headlines) sometimes include information not within the reference (main line of the article). We observe that quantitative evaluation does not correlate well with human evaluation. Methods using InferSent embeddings improved our ROUGE scores but perform worse in human evaluation, which is in line with the summaries presented in 2. Notably, the model trained on shuffled bigrams and InferSent embeddings performed best within our ablation study, but the worst among the three models in human evaluation. Encouragingly, the model without InferSent embeddings performs competitively with the supervised baseline in both grammar and meaning scores, indicating that although it does not capture the style of headlines, it succeeds in generating grammatical sentences that

---

[5]The sampling is constrained to ensure each evaluator sees an equal number of summaries from each model, although evaluators are informed neither about the sampling process, nor how many or what models are involved.

| | ROUGE | | | |
Model	R-1	R-2	R-L	Avg. Length
Baselines:				
All text	**28.91**	**10.22**	**25.08**	31.3
F8W	26.90	9.65	25.19	8
Unsupervised (Ours):				
2-g shuf	27.72	7.55	23.43	15.4
2-g shuf + InferSent	**28.42**	**7.82**	**24.95**	15.6
Supervised abstractive:				
Seq2seq	**35.50**	15.54	32.45	15.4
(words-lvt2k-1sent) (Nallapati et al., 2016)	34.97	**17.17**	**32.70**	-

Table 1: Performance of Baseline, Unsupervised and Supervised Models. Our unsupervised models pale in comparison to supervised models, and perform in line with baselines. Simple baselines in text summarization benchmarks tend to be unusually strong. The unsupervised model incorporating sentence embeddings performs slightly better on ROUGE.

| | ROUGE | | |
Model	R-1	R-2	R-L
1-g shuf (w/o attn)	23.01	5.51	20.07
2-g shuf (w/o attn)	22.36	5.18	19.60
1-g shuf	27.22	7.63	23.55
2-g shuf	27.72	7.55	23.43
1-g shuf + InferSent	28.12	7.75	24.81
2-g shuf + InferSent	**28.42**	**7.82**	**24.95**

Table 2: Ablation study. We find that using attention, shuffling bigrams, and incorporating sentence embeddings all improve our ROUGE scores. All length countdowns settings are the same is in the main model.

| | ROUGE | | | |
Input Length	R-1	R-2	R-L	Avg. Length
16-30	30.79	9.20	27.73	12.6
31-45	26.89	6.76	23.04	17.7

Table 3: Effect of input sentence length on performance, using the 2-g shuf + InferSent model. Performance tends to be worse on longer input texts.

Model	Grammar	Meaning
2-g shuf	**3.53** (±**0.18**)	2.53 (±0.16)
1-g shuf + InferSent	2.82 (±0.17)	2.50 (±0.15)
2-g shuf + InferSent	2.87 (±0.16)	2.13 (±0.13)
Seq2seq (Supervised)	3.43 (±0.18)	**2.60** (±**0.17**)
Ground Truth	4.07 (±0.13)	3.87 (±0.16)

Table 4: Human Evaluation. Mean scores, with 1 standard error confidence bands in parentheses. Our best model performs competitively with a supervised baseline in both grammatical correctness and retuention of meaning. Models with sentence embeddings perform worse in human evaluation, despite obtaining better ROUGE scores.

roughly match the meaning in the reference. Some evaluators highlighted that it was problematic to rate meaning for ungrammatical sentences.

5.5 Output Analysis

We show in Figure 2 several examples of the inputs, ground-truths target summaries, and outputs from 2 of our models. We observe that the output sentences are generally well-conditioned though occasionally imperfectly grammatical. We also observe certain artifacts from training only on reference texts that are not reflected in ground-truth summaries. For example, every output sentence ends with a period, and several examples end with speaker identification clauses. In all instances, we observe that the model without InferSent outputs sentences are more readable and relevant, confirming human evaluation results in 4.

Example 1 shows that our model can extract the most pertinent information to generate a grammatical summary that captures the original meaning.

Example 2 shows an instance where our output accurately summarizes the input text despite low

ROUGE scores to the target (R-1 of 21.1 and R-2 of 11.8). In this case, both models capture the core meaning of the input.

Example 3 shows that although the models are provided completely shuffled words in training, at inference it is able to recover complex terms such as "swedish truck maker ab volvo". We note that this may be a bias in the data set (sentences in news often start with proper nouns preceded by qualifiers) and hence a simple strategy for the model to discover. This examples also shows common mistake of our models: in the output of model without InferSent, it drops an important word ("loss") right before the end of the sentence, causing it to fail to capture the original meaning.

Example 4 shows that on longer sentences, our models may sometimes fail to accurately capture meaning. In this case, for the model without InferSent, although the output is grammatical and meaningful, it captures a meaning different than that of the original input. Indeed, our model suggests that upbeat news cause the rally whereas the original sentence indicates that given poor economic news investors anticipate easier monetary policy and thus caused a stock rally.

5.6 Length Variation

Because the desired length of the output sequence is a user-defined input in the model, we can take an arbitrary sentence and use the model to output the corresponding compressed (or even expanded) sentence of any desired length. We show two examples in Figure 3, where we vary the desired length from 7 to the input length, using our best model based on human evaluation. We observe that for very short desired lengths, the model struggles to produce meaningful sentences, whereas for desired lengths close to the input length, the model nearly reconstructs the input sentence. Nevertheless, we observe that for many of the intermediate lengths, the model outputs sentences that are close in meaning to the input sentence, with different ways of rephrasing or shortening the input sentence in the interim. This suggests that when the ratio of the desired output sentence length to the input sentence length is close to that of the training regime, the model is able to perform better than when it has to generate sentences with other ratios.

Example 1:
I: three convicted serial killers have been hanged in tehran 's evin prison , the khorasan newspaper reported sunday .
L=9: three convicted serial killers have been hanged in .
L=11: three convicted serial killers have been hanged in prison sunday

L=13: three convicted serial killers have been hanged , a newspaper reported sunday .
L=15: three convicted serial killers have been hanged in tehran , a newspaper reported sunday .
L=17: three convicted serial killers have been hanged in tehran , the tehran 's newspaper reported sunday .
L=19: three convicted serial killers have been hanged in tehran 's prison , the newspaper tehran newspaper reported sunday .

Example 2:
I: a home-made bomb was found near a shopping center on indonesia 's ambon island , where ## people were wounded by an explosion at the weekend , state media said on monday .
L=9: a home-made bomb explosion wounded ## people monday .
L=11: a home-made bomb explosion wounded ## people on indonesia monday .
L=13: a home-made bomb explosion wounded ## people on indonesia 's ambon island .
L=15: a home-made bomb explosion wounded ## people at a shopping center on ambon monday .
L=17: a home-made bomb explosion wounded ## people at a shopping center on ambon island on monday .
L=19: a home-made bomb explosion wounded ## people at a shopping center near ambon on indonesia 's island state .
L=21: a home-made bomb explosion wounded ## people at a shopping center near ambon on indonesia 's ambon island on monday .
L=23: a home-made bomb was found on a shopping center near ambon , indonesia 's state on monday , state media said monday .
L=25: a home-made bomb was found on a shopping center near ambon , indonesia 's state media center where ## people were wounded by bomb .
L=27: a home-made bomb was found on a shopping center near ambon , indonesia 's state media center where ## people were wounded , media said monday .
L=29: a home-made bomb was found on a shopping center near ambon , indonesia 's state media on monday , where ## people were wounded by an explosion nearby .
L=31: a home-made bomb was found on a shopping center near ambon , indonesia 's state media on monday , where ## people were wounded by an explosion at the weekend .
L=33: a home-made bomb was found on a shopping center near ambon , indonesia 's state media on monday , where ## people were wounded by an explosion at the weekend on monday .

Figure 3: Summaries of varied desired lengths, using the 2-g shuf model. **L** is the desired output length provided to the model. Because the desired output length is a human-provided input, we can produce summaries of varying lengths, ranging from highly contracted to verbose.

6 Discussion

In our experiments, we found that denoising auto-encoders quickly learn to generate well-conditioned text, even from badly conditioned inputs. We were surprised by the ability of denoising auto-encoders to recover readable sentences even from completely shuffled and noised sets of words. We observed some cases where the denoising auto-encoders outputs sequences that are grammatical correct but nonsensical or semantically different from the input. However, the ability for denoising auto-encoders to subsample words to form grammatical sentences would significantly reduce the search space for candidate sentences, and we believe this could be useful for tasks involving sentence construction and reformulation.

Our attempts to better condition the denoising auto-encoders outputs on the original sentence using sentence embeddings had mixed results. Although the incorporation of InferSent embeddings improved our quantitative ROUGE scores, human evaluators scored outputs conditioned on InferSent embeddings markedly worse on both grammar and meaning retention. It is unclear whether this is due to InferSent embeddings failing to capture the most significant semantic information, or if our mechanism for incorporating the sentence embedding is suboptimal.

Lastly, we echo sentiments from previous authors that ROUGE remains an imperfect proxy for measuring the adequacy of summaries. We found that ROUGE scores can be fairly uncorrelated with human evaluation, and in general can be distorted by quirks of the data set or model outputs, particularly pertaining to length, formatting, and handling of special tokens. On the other hand, human evaluation can be more sensitive to comprehensibility and relevancy while being more robust to rewording and reasonable ambiguity. Based on our human evaluation, we find that both unsupervised and supervised methods still fall short of effective sentence compression and summarization.

7 Conclusion

We present a fully unsupervised approach to the task of sentence compression in the form of a denoising auto-encoder with additive noising and word shuffling. Our model achieves comparable scores in human evaluation to a supervised sequence-to-sequence attentional baseline in grammatical correctness and retention of meaning, but underperforms on ROUGE. Output analysis indicates that our model does not capture the particular style of the summaries in the Gigaword dataset, but nevertheless produces reasonably valid sentences that capture the meaning of the input. Although our models are still prone to making mistakes, they provide a strong baseline for future sentence compression and summarization work.

Acknowledgments

We would like to express our deepest gratitude to Sam Bowman for his thoughtful advice and feedback in the writing of this paper. We thank the NVIDIA Corporation for their support.

References

Mikel Artetxe, Gorka Labaka, and Eneko Agirre. 2018. A robust self-learning method for fully unsupervised cross-lingual mappings of word embeddings. *arXiv preprint 1805.06297*.

Mikel Artetxe, Gorka Labaka, Eneko Agirre, and Kyunghyun Cho. 2017. Unsupervised neural machine translation. *arXiv preprint 1710.11041*.

Dzmitry Bahdanau, Kyunghyun Cho, and Yoshua Bengio. 2014. Neural machine translation by jointly learning to align and translate. *CoRR*, abs/1409.0473.

Or Biran, Samuel Brody, and Noémie Elhadad. 2011. Putting it simply: a context-aware approach to lexical simplification. In *Proceedings of ACL*.

Sumit Chopra, Michael Auli, and Alexander M Rush. 2016. Abstractive sentence summarization with attentive recurrent neural networks. In *Proceedings of NAACL*.

Trevor Cohn and Mirella Lapata. 2008. Sentence compression beyond word deletion. In *Proceedings of ACL*, pages 137–144.

Alexis Conneau, Douwe Kiela, Holger Schwenk, Loïc Barrault, and Antoine Bordes. 2017a. Supervised learning of universal sentence representations from natural language inference data. *CoRR*, abs/1705.02364.

Alexis Conneau, German Kruszewski, Guillaume Lample, Loic Barrault, and Marco Baroni. 2018. What you can cram into a single vector: Probing sentence embeddings for linguistic properties. *arXiv e-prints*.

Alexis Conneau, Guillaume Lample, Marc'Aurelio Ranzato, Ludovic Denoyer, and Hervé Jégou. 2017b. Word translation without parallel data. *arXiv preprint 1710.04087*.

Bonnie Dorr, David Zajic, and Richard Schwartz. 2003. Hedge trimmer: A parse-and-trim approach to headline generation. In *Proceedings of NAACL*, pages 1–8.

Angela Fan, David Grangier, and Michael Auli. 2017. Controllable abstractive summarization. *arXiv preprint 1711.05217*.

Katja Filippova, Enrique Alfonseca, Carlos A Colmenares, Lukasz Kaiser, and Oriol Vinyals. 2015. Sentence compression by deletion with lstms. In *EMNLP*.

Markus Freitag and Scott Roy. 2018. Unsupervised natural language generation with denoising autoencoders. *arXiv preprint arXiv:1804.07899*.

Felix Hill, Kyunghyun Cho, and Anna Korhonen. 2016. Learning distributed representations of sentences from unlabelled data. *arXiv preprint 1602.03483*.

Hongyan Jing. 2000. Sentence reduction for automatic text summarization. In *Proceedings of ANLP*, pages 310–315.

Hongyan Jing. 2002. Using hidden markov modeling to decompose human-written summaries. *Computational linguistics*, 28(4):527–543.

Y. Kikuchi, G. Neubig, R. Sasano, H. Takamura, and M. Okumura. 2016. Controlling Output Length in Neural Encoder-Decoders. *ArXiv e-prints*.

Diederik P Kingma and Jimmy Ba. 2014. Adam: A method for stochastic optimization. *arXiv preprint 1412.6980*.

Kevin Knight and Daniel Marcu. 2002. Summarization beyond sentence extraction: A probabilistic approach to sentence compression. *Artificial Intelligence*, 139(1):91–107.

Guillaume Lample, Ludovic Denoyer, and Marc'Aurelio Ranzato. 2017. Unsupervised machine translation using monolingual corpora only. *arXiv preprint 1711.00043*.

Angeliki Lazaridou, Georgiana Dinu, and Marco Baroni. 2015. Hubness and pollution: Delving into cross-space mapping for zero-shot learning. In *Proceedings of ACL*.

Chin-Yew Lin. 2004. Rouge: A package for automatic evaluation of summaries. In *Proceedings of ACL*, page 10.

Yishu Miao and Phil Blunsom. 2016. Language as a latent variable: Discrete generative models for sentence compression. In *EMNLP*.

Tomas Mikolov, Quoc V Le, and Ilya Sutskever. 2013. Exploiting similarities among languages for machine translation. *arXiv preprint 1309.4168*.

Ramesh Nallapati, Feifei Zhai, and Bowen Zhou. 2017. Summarunner: A recurrent neural network based sequence model for extractive summarization of documents. In *AAAI*.

Ramesh Nallapati, Bowen Zhou, Cicero Nogueira dos Santos, Caglar Gulcehre, and Bing Xiang. 2016. Abstractive text summarization using sequence-to-sequence rnns and beyond. *arXiv preprint 1602.06023*.

Courtney Napoles, Matthew Gormley, and Benjamin Van Durme. 2012. Annotated gigaword. In *Proceedings of AKBC-WEKEX*, pages 95–100.

Adam Paszke, Sam Gross, Soumith Chintala, Gregory Chanan, Edward Yang, Zachary DeVito, Zeming Lin, Alban Desmaison, Luca Antiga, and Adam Lerer. 2017. Automatic differentiation in pytorch. In *NIPS*.

Romain Paulus, Caiming Xiong, and Richard Socher. 2017. A deep reinforced model for abstractive summarization. *arXiv preprint 1705.04304*.

Jeffrey Pennington, Richard Socher, and Christopher Manning. 2014. Glove: Global vectors for word representation. In *EMNLP*.

Alexander M Rush, Sumit Chopra, and Jason Weston. 2015. A neural attention model for abstractive sentence summarization.

Abigail See, Peter Liu, and Christopher Manning. 2017. Get to the point: Summarization with pointer-generator networks. *arXiv preprint 1704.04368*.

Matthew Shardlow. 2014. A survey of automated text simplification. *International Journal of Advanced Computer Science and Applications*, 4(1):58–70.

Jenine Turner and Eugene Charniak. 2005. Supervised and unsupervised learning for sentence compression. In *Proceedings of ACL*, pages 290–297.

Pascal Vincent, Hugo Larochelle, Yoshua Bengio, and Pierre-Antoine Manzagol. 2008. Extracting and composing robust features with denoising autoencoders. In *ICML*, pages 1096–1103.

Yau-Shian Wang and Hung-Yi Lee. 2018. Learning to encode text as human-readable summaries using generative adversarial networks.

Meng Zhang, Yang Liu, Huanbo Luan, and Maosong Sun. 2017. Adversarial training for unsupervised bilingual lexicon induction. In *Proceedings of ACL*.

Resources to Examine the Quality of Word Embedding Models Trained on n-Gram Data

Ábel Elekes   Adrian Englhardt   Martin Schäler   Klemens Böhm

Karlsruhe Institute of Technology (KIT), Karlsruhe, Germany

```
{abel.elekes, adrian.englhardt,
    martin.schaeler, klemens.boehm}@kit.edu
```


Abstract

Word embeddings are powerful tools that facilitate better analysis of natural language. However, their quality highly depends on the resource used for training. There are various approaches relying on n-gram corpora, such as the Google n-gram corpus. However, n-gram corpora only offer a small window into the full text – 5 words for the Google corpus at best. This gives way to the concern whether the extracted word semantics are of high quality. In this paper, we address this concern with two contributions. First, we provide a resource containing 120 word-embedding models – one of the largest collection of embedding models. Furthermore, the resource contains the n-gramed versions of all used corpora, as well as our scripts used for corpus generation, model generation and evaluation. Second, we define a set of meaningful experiments allowing to evaluate the aforementioned quality differences. We conduct these experiments using our resource to show its usage and significance. The evaluation results confirm that one generally can expect high quality for n-grams with $n \geq 3$.

1 Introduction

Motivation. Word embedding approaches like Word2Vec (Mikolov et al., 2013b) or Glove (Pennington et al., 2014) are powerful tools for the semantic analysis of natural language. One can train them on arbitrary text corpora. Each word in the corpus is mapped to a d-dimensional vector. These vectors feature the semantic similarity and analogy properties, as follows. Semantic similarity means that representations of words used in a similar context tend to be close to each other in the vector space. The analogy property can be described by the example that "man" is to "woman" like "king" to "queen" (Mikolov et al., 2013b,a; Jansen, 2017).

These properties have been applied in numerous approaches (Mitra and Craswell, 2017) like sentiment analysis (Tang et al., 2014), irony detection (Reyes et al., 2012), out-of-vocabulary word classification (Ma and Zhang, 2015), or semantic shift detection (Hamilton et al., 2016a; Martinez-Ortiz et al., 2016). One prerequisite when creating high-quality embedding models is a good training corpus. To this end, many approaches use the Google n-gram corpus (Hellrich and Hahn, 2016; Pyysalo et al., 2013; Kim et al., 2014; Martinez-Ortiz et al., 2016; Kulkarni et al., 2016, 2015; Hamilton et al., 2016b). It also is the largest currently available corpus with historic data and exists for several languages. It incorporates over 5 million books from the last centuries split into n-grams (Michel et al., 2015). n-grams are text segments separated into pieces consisting of n words each. The *fragmentation* of a corpus is the size of its n-grams. To illustrate, a corpus of 2-grams is highly fragmented, one of 5-grams is moderately fragmented.

n-gram counts over time can be published even if the underlying full text is subject to copyright protection. Next, this format reduces the data volume very much. So it is important to know how good models built on n-gram corpora are.

While the quality of word embedding models trained on full-text corpora is fairly well known (Lebret and Collobert, 2015; Baroni et al., 2014), an assessment of models built on fragmented corpora is missing (Hill et al., 2014). The resource advertised in this paper is a set of such models, which should help to shed some light on the issue, together with some experiments.

Difficulties. An obvious benefit of making these models available is the huge runtime necessary to build them. However, evaluating them is not straightforward, for various reasons. First, drawing *general* conclusions on the quality of em-

Proceedings of the 22nd Conference on Computational Natural Language Learning (CoNLL 2018), pages 423–432
Brussels, Belgium, October 31 - November 1, 2018. ©2018 Association for Computational Linguistics

bedding models only based on the performance of specific approaches, i.e., examining the extrinsic suitability of models, is error-prone (Gladkova and Drozd, 2016; Schnabel et al., 2015). Consequently, to come to general conclusions one needs to investigate *general properties* of the embedding models itself, i.e., examine their intrinsic suitability. Properties of this kind are semantic similarity and analogy. For both properties, one can use well-known test sets that serve as comprehensive baselines. Second, there are various parameters which influence how the model looks like. Using n-grams as training corpus gives way to two new parameters, fragmentation, as just discussed, and minimum count, i.e., the minimum occurrence count of an n-gram in order to be considered when building the model. The latter is often used to filter error-prone n-grams from a corpus, e.g., spelling errors. While the effect of the other parameters on the models is known (Lebret and Collobert, 2015; Baroni et al., 2014), the one of these new parameters is not. We have to define meaningful experiments to quantify and compare the effects. Third, the full text, such as the Google Books corpus, is not openly available as reference in many cases. Hence, we need to examine how to compare results from other corpora, where the full text is available, referring e.g., to well-known baselines as the Wikipedia corpus.

Contribution. The resource provided here is a systematic collection of word embedding models trained on n-gram corpora, accessible at our project website[1]. The collection consists of 120 word embedding models trained on the Wikipedia and 1 Billion words data set. Its training has required more than two months of computing time on a modern machine. To our knowledge, it currently is one of the most comprehensive collection of its type. In order to make this resource re-usable and our experiments repeatable, we also provide the n-grammed versions of the Wikipedia and 1-Billion word datasets, which we used for training and the tools to create n-gram corpora from arbitrary text as well.

In addition, we describe some experiments to examine how much model quality changes when the training corpus is not full-text, but n-grams. The experiments quantify how much fragmentation (i.e., values of n) and minimum count reduce the average quality of the corresponding word em-

___
[1] http://dbis.ipd.kit.edu/2568.php

bedding model, on common word similarity and analogical reasoning test sets.

To show the usefulness and significance of the experiments and to give general recommendations on which n-gram corpus to use as well as creating a baseline for comparison, we conduct the experiments on the full English Wikipedia dump and Chelba et al.'s 1-Billion word dataset. However, we recommend to conduct this examination for any corpus before using it as training resource, particularly if the corpus size differs from the ones of the baseline corpora by much:

1. What is the smallest number n for which an n-gram corpus is good training data for word embedding models?

2. How sensitive is the quality of the models to the fragmentation and the minimum count parameter?

3. What is the actual reason for any quality loss of models trained with high fragmentation or a high minimum count parameter?

Our results for the baseline test sets indicate that minimum count values exceeding a corpus-size-dependent threshold drastically reduce the quality of the models. Fragmentation in turn brings down the quality only if the fragments are very small. Based on this, one can conclude that n-gram corpora such as Google Books are valid training data for word embedding models.

2　Fundamentals and Notation

We first introduce word embedding models. Then we explain how to build word embedding models on n-gram corpora.

2.1　Background on Word Embedding Models

In the following, we review specific distributional models called word embedding models. Experiments have shown that word embedding models are superior to conventional distributional models (Baroni et al., 2014; Mikolov et al., 2013b). In this section, we briefly say how such models work, and which parameters influence their building process.

2.1.1　Building a Word Embedding Model

Word embedding models 'embed' words into a high-dimensional space, representing them as dense vectors of real numbers. Vectors close to each other according to a distance function, often the cosine distance, represent words that are semantically related. Formally, a word embedding model is a function F which takes a corpus C as input, generates a dictionary D and associates any word in the dictionary $w \in D$ with a d-dimensional vector $v \in \mathbb{R}^d$. The dimension size parameter d sets the dimensionality of the vectors. win is the window size parameter. It determines the context of a word. For example, a window size of 5 means that the context of a specific word is any other word in its sentence, and their distance is at most 5 words. The training is based on word-context pairs $w \times c \in D \times D^{2 \times \text{win}}$ extracted from the corpus. The parameter $epoch\_nr$ states how many times the training algorithm passes through the corpus. The model adds only words to the dictionary which are among the $dict\_size$ most frequent words of the corpus. Additionally, there are model specific parameters (θ) which change minor details in their algorithms. Having said this, one can define word embedding models as a function:

$$F(C, d, epoch\_nr, win, dict\_size, \theta) \in \mathbb{R}^d \quad (1)$$

There is related work that studies the impact of these parameters (Baroni et al., 2014; Hill et al., 2014; Elekes et al., 2017). Consequently, for all parameters mentioned except for the window size, we can rely on the results from the literature. This is because, as we outline shortly, win is highly relevant for building embedding models using n-gram corpora. Note that F has been defined to work on full text corpora so far, but not on n-grams. We explain how to adapt F in Section 2.3.

2.1.2 Realizations of Word Embedding Models

In this paper, we work with a well-known embedding model, Mikolov et al.'s Word2Vec model (Mikolov et al., 2013b). Word2Vec models use a neural-network based learning algorithm. They learn by maximizing the probability of predicting the word given the context (Continuous Bag of Words model, CBOW) (Mikolov et al., 2013c,b). Note that the results can be transferred to the skip-gram learning algorithm of Word2Vec as well as to Glove (Pennington et al., 2014; Levy and Goldberg, 2014). This is because very recent work has shown that the distribution of the cosine distances among the word vectors of all such models (after normalization) is highly similar (Elekes et al., 2017).

2.2 Generating Fragmented and Trimmed Corpora

To create fragmented n-gram corpora from raw text, we use a simple method described in the following. With a sliding window of size n passing through the whole raw text, we collect all the n-grams which appear in the corpus and store them in a dictionary, together with their match count. This means that we create datasets similar to the Google Books dataset, but from other raw text such as the Wikipedia dump. For every fragmented corpus, we create different versions of it, by trimming n-grams from the corpora with regard to different minimum count thresholds.

2.3 Building Word Embedding Models on N-grams

Distributional models conventionally are trained on full text corpora, by creating word-context pairs. It does not need to be a coherent text; it is sufficient if the sentences are meaningful. For n-gram corpora, this means the following. When creating the context of a word, we treat each n-gram as if it was a sentence.[2]

The word embedding models which we make available are trained on n-gram training corpora which are in the Google n-gram format. This format comprises 4 values: the n-gram, the match count, the book count and the year. For our purpose, only the first two values are relevant. When building a model with the n-gram versions, we deem every n-gram a sentence and use it as many times as it occurs in the raw text. We explain the impact of the window size and of the match count parameter in the following.

2.3.1 Window Size Parameter

The window size parameter win of the embedding model F depends on the fragmentation. For example, $win = 4$ is not meaningful when we work with 3-grams , because the maximum distance between two words in a 3-gram corpus is 2. The following Examples 1-3 illustrate how exactly the word-context pairs are generated on n-gram corpora depending on the size of the window.

Example 1. Let us look at the context of a specific word in a 5-gram corpus with $win = 4$. Let A B C D E F G H I be a segment of the raw text consisting of 9 words. In the raw text, the context

---

[2]Of course, if there is a punctuation mark in the n-gram ending a sentence, it splits the n-gram into several sentences.

of word E are words A, B, C, D, F, G, H, I. Now we create the 5-gram version of this segment and identify 5-grams which include word E. These are (A B C D E); (B C D E F); (C D E F G); (D E F G H) and (E F G H I). For word E on the 5-gram corpus, the contexts are words A, B, C, D; ...; words F, G, H, I. We can see that we have not lost any context words. But we also do not have all raw-text context words in one context, only fragmented into several ones.

Example 2. As extreme case, we consider a window size which is bigger than the size of the n-grams. In this setting, we naturally lose a lot of information. This is because distant words will not be in any n-gram at the same time. For example, look at the same text segment as in Example 1 with $win = 4$, but with a 3-gram variant of it. The raw-text context is the same as before for word E, but the fragmented contexts are words C, D; words D, F and words F, G.

Example 3. Another extreme case is when win is less than or equal to $\lfloor \frac{n-1}{2} \rfloor$. In this case at least one n-gram context will be the same as the full text context. This means that no information is lost. However, there also are fragmented contexts in the n-gram variant which can influence the training and, hence, model quality.

We point out that bigger window sizes do not necessarily induce higher accuracy on various test sets, as explained by Levy et al.(Levy et al., 2015).

2.3.2 Match Count Parameter

Another parameter to consider when building the models on the n-gram corpora is the match count of the n-grams. The intuition behind including only higher match-count n-grams in the training data is that they may be more valid segments of the raw text, as they appear several times in the same order. However, we naturally lose information by pruning low match-count n-grams. When we create the n-gram versions of our raw text corpora, we create different versions, by pruning the n-grams which do not appear in the corpus at least 2, 5, 10 times, respectively. These numbers are much smaller than the minimum count of 40 in the Google dataset. This is because the raw texts we use are much smaller than the Google Books dataset as well.

3 Experimental Setup

The experiments allow to to give general recommendations on which n-gram corpus to use to train word embedding models. In order to do this, we justify the selection of our text corpora and of the parameter values used. Finally, we explain the actual baseline test sets and say why this choice will yield general insights.

3.1 Raw Text Corpus Selection

In this study we work with two raw-text corpora. One is Chelba et al.'s 1-Billion word dataset (Chelba et al., 2013), the other one is a recent (November 1, 2016) Wikipedia dump, with the articles shuffled and sampled to contain approximately 1 billion words. Both corpora are good benchmark datasets for language modeling, with their huge size, large vocabulary and topical diversity (Chelba et al., 2013; Zesch and Gurevych, 2007). For both corpora we create their respective n-gram versions in the Google Books format, with n=2,3,5,8, cf. Section 2.3.

3.2 Baseline Test Sets

We see two properties of embedding models that makes them a worthwhile resource. First, word similarities, second, analogical reasoning. To illustrate, an analogical reasoning task is as follows: 'A is to B as C is to D', and the model has to guess Word D knowing the other three words. We have selected widely used word similarity and analogical reasoning baseline test sets for our evaluation.

3.2.1 Word Similarity

We use six test sets to evaluate word similarity. They contain word pairs with similarity scores, assigned by human annotators. The test sets are Finkelstein et al.'s WordSim353 (Finkelstein et al., 2001) partitioned into two test sets, WordSim Similarity and WordSim Relatedness (Zesch et al., 2008; Bruni et al., 2012); Bruni et al.'s MEN test set (Bruni et al., 2012); Hill et al.'s SimLex-999 test set (Hill et al., 2015); Rubenstein and Goodenough's RG-65 test set (Rubenstein and Goodenough, 1965); Radinsky et al.'s Mechanical Turk test set (Radinsky et al., 2011) and Luong et al.'s Rare Words test set (Luong et al., 2013). We evaluate the models with the conventional baseline evaluation method (Levy et al., 2015) (Baroni et al., 2014): We rank the word pairs of an evaluation test set by their similarity scores, based on cosine distance of the word vectors. Then we measure Spearman's correlation between this ranking and the one based on human annotators. This number is the score of the model on the test set.

3.2.2 Analogical Reasoning

We use two analogical reasoning test sets. The first one is MSR's analogy test set (Mikolov et al., 2013c), which contains 8000 syntactic analogy questions, such as "big is to biggest as good is to best". The other test set is Google's analogy test set (Mikolov et al., 2013b), which contains 19544 questions The models answer the questions with the following formula:

$$\text{argmax}_{d \in D \setminus \{a,b,c\}} \cos(d, b - a + c) \qquad (2)$$

Here $a, b, c, d \in D$ are the vectors of the corresponding word. The score of a model is the percentage of questions for which the result of the formula is the correct answer (d).

4 Experiment Questions

In order to make our experimental results more intuitive we attempt to explicitly answer the three following questions.

Question 1. What is the smallest number n for which an n-gram corpus is good for the training of embedding models?

Rationale behind Question 1. The size of any n-gram corpus highly increases with large n. Hence, it is important to know the smallest value that is expected to still yield good results.

Question 2. How does the minimum count parameter affect the quality of the models? How does this result compare to the effect caused by the fragmentation?

Rationale behind Question 2. Having answered the first question, we will be able to quantify the effect of the fragmentation. However, it is necessary to study the effect of the second parameter as well, in order to quantify the applicability of n-grams for embedding comprehensively. In other words, we want to compare the effects of both parameters; we will be able to give recommendations for both parameters.

Question 3. How does the quality loss of models trained on fragmented corpora of size n or with high minimum count parameter manifest itself in the embedding models?

Rationale behind Question 3. By answering Questions 1 and 2, we are able to quantify the effect of both parameters. We hypothesize that the parameters affect the quality of the models differently, and that we are able to observe this in the word vectors themselves. The rationale behind our hypothesis is that large minimum count values might eliminate various meaningful words from the vector space. Fragmentation in isolation however does not have the effect that a word is lost. Hence, a quality loss must manifest itself differently, which might be observable.

5 Experiment Results

We now turn to the questions just asked. We dedicate a subsection to each question. In the first two sections, we give an overview of the results using the Wikipedia corpus. The results for the 1-Billion word corpus are almost identical. For brevity, we do not show all results for this corpus.

5.1 Answering Question 1: Minimal Meaningful N-gram Size

We quantify the influence of the training-corpus fragmentation on the quality of the word-embedding models. We do not use a minimum count parameter in this section.

5.1.1 Results for the Wikipedia Corpus

Figure 1 shows the result for the models trained on the Wikipedia corpus.[3] The interpretation of the plots is as follows: We evaluate a specific model on every test set introduced in Section 3.2. We calculate the average scores for this model for both the similarity and analogy test sets. We do this for every trained model. We group the results by the window-size parameter of the models and plot the average values. So every plot shows the calculated average scores of such models which only differ in the fragmentation of their training corpus. As explained in Section 2.3.1, it is meaningless to train models on n-grammed corpora with window-size parameter $win < n$.

Figure 1 reveals that fragmentation does influence the quality of the models significantly. For the similarity test sets, fragmentation reduces the quality of the models for any value of the window-size parameter win almost linearly.

For the analogy test sets, the results are not as straightforward. Generally, the same observation holds as for the similarity test sets, namely that fragmentation reduces the quality of the models, however there are a few exceptions. It is true that the best models are trained on the 5 and 8-gram variants and the full text corpora for any window size. For models with smaller win however, the

---

[3]Note that we use different scales for the first and the second two subplots.

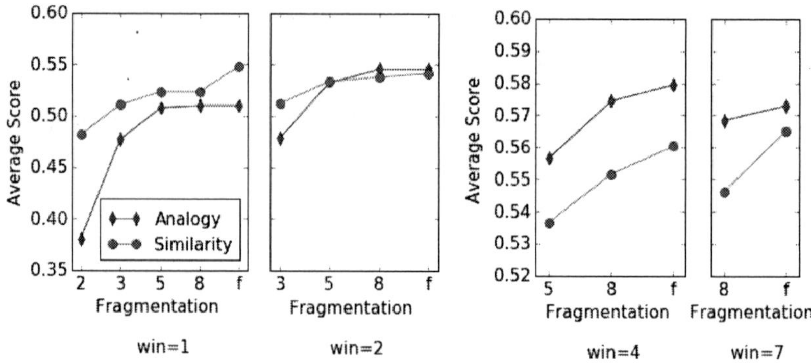

Figure 1: The average score of models trained on differently fragmented Wikipedia corpora on the analogy and similarity tasks

results do not always get better when the corpus is less fragmented. For example, the very best model for the MSR test set is trained on 8-grams, not the full text.

5.1.2 Generalization of Results

To generalize the results, we measure the overall average quality of the models trained on the differently fragmented corpora. Then we compare the results to ones computed on the full text. To this end, we calculate the averages of the previous results, grouped by training corpus fragmentation. To make the resulting numbers more intuitive, we do this in relative terms, compared to the results with the full text corpus. For example, on analogical reasoning tasks, the models trained on 3-grams are 7.5% worse than the models trained on full text with the same window size. Table 1 shows the results. The total column is the average of the similarity and analogy columns

Table 1: Average quality loss due to fragmentation compared to the full text on the Wikipedia corpus.

Wikipedia	total	similarity	analogy
2-gram	-20.2%	-14.4%	-26.0%
3-gram	-6.9%	-6.4%	-7.5%
5-gram	-2.8%	-3.6%	-1.9%
8-gram	-2.5%	-3.4%	-1.6%

5.1.3 Result Interpretation.

We conclude that embedding models built on fragmented corpora are worse than models based on full text, but the difference is not much. Embedding models trained on 2-gram corpora are 20.2% worse overall than models trained on full text, a significant drop. However, the 3-gram version is only 6.9% worse. The 5-gram version and the 8-gram version are almost tha same, they are only 2.8% and 2.5% worse, respectively. This answers Question 1, i.e., a 5-gram corpus is the most fragmented corpus which is almost as good as models trained on full text, and the 3-gram version is also not much worse. A general takeaway for other researchers when training embedding models on n-grams is that using at least 3-grams for training leads to good models and using at least 5-grams leads to almost identical models as training on full text.

5.1.4 Insight Confirmation Using a Different Text Corpus

So far, our results only rely on one corpus. To generalize, we verify our insights using another large corpus. We only list aggregated results to save space. We have calculated the numbers for all models trained on the 1-Billion word dataset and its fragmented versions. Table 2 shows that the numbers are generally very similar to the previous ones with Wikipedia. So the decline in quality most likely does not depend on the underlying text corpus, but on the fragmentation.

5.2 Answering Question 2: Effect of the Minimum Count Parameter

In the following, we aim at quantifying the influence of the minimum count parameter and investigate whether there is an interaction with the fragmentation. Our procedure is the same as in the prior section. First, we aggregate the raw results obtained from the Wikipedia corpus and *all* models built on it. Then we draw first conclusions and finally verify the insights using the second corpus.

Table 2: Average quality loss due to fragmentation compared to the full text on the 1-Billion word corpus.

1-Billion	total	similarity	analogy
2-gram	-19.3%	-15.0%	-23.6%
3-gram	-5.4%	-6.5%	-4.3%
5-gram	-1.8%	-2.9%	-0.8%
8-gram	-1.3%	-2.2%	-0.4%

Table 3: Average quality loss caused by the minimum count parameter parameter on Wikipedia.

Min. count	total	similarity	analogy
2	-23.6%	-19.2%	-28.0%
5	-56.5%	-47.9%	-65.1%
10	-72.3%	-64.0%	-78.6%

5.2.1 Results for the Wikipedia Corpus

Figure 2 shows the average quality of models trained on the same n-gram corpus with different minimum count parameter. The results indicate that an increase of this parameter usually leads to significantly worse models. However, there is one exception, where the minimum count parameter is 2 and the corpus is the 2-grammed version of Wikipedia. For this case the models actually gets slightly better on the analogy task using the minimum count threshold. The reason is that we do not lose too many 2-grams with the thresholding in this case, and those which we do lose may bias the model on the analogy tasks. However, on the similarity tasks the models get slightly worse, which means we lose meaningful training data as well. The reduction in quality is even more severe with n-gram corpora with a big value of n, such as 5 or 8-grams. This is because these corpora have fewer high match count n-grams than the more fragmented 2 or 3-gram corpora. Summing up, for corpora of a size such as the Wikipedia dump, any threshold for the minimum count of the n-grams significantly reduces the quality of the embedding models. One exception is when the corpus is highly fragmented with the smallest minimum count parameter.

5.2.2 Generalization of the Results

We generalize the aforementioned observations by computing the average quality loss for the models, just as in Section 5.1.2. The numbers in Table 3 are for the Wikipedia dataset. With the smallest minimum count threshold already, the models get significantly worse. For the 1-Billion word dataset, the results again differ only slightly. This again confirms our hypothesis that the quality differences are not corpus-dependent.

5.2.3 Implications for the Google N-gram Corpus

So far, the question how to transfer the results from the Wikipedia and the 1-Billion corpus to the Google n-gram corpus remains open. We aim to answer whether we lose any meaningful information in the Google 5-gram corpus, because of the, at first sight, large threshold value of 40. We assume that even for such comprehensive text corpora, including the Wikipedia or the 1-Billion corpus, all the extracted n-grams are contained in the Google n-gram data as well, despite its large threshold value. We verify this hypothesis by comparing the number of existing 5-grams in the Google n-gram corpus (1.4 Billion) with those in the full Wikipedia (1.25 Billion). A systematic analysis of the data reveals that more than 99% of the 5-grams included in the Wikipedia corpus is included in the Google corpus as well. The ones which are not usually are typos or contain words which have not been present in the language until 2008 (the last year in the Google dataset). This holds for all n-gram corpora. This means that we do not lose any relevant information if we train our models on the Google n-gram dataset, despite its high minimum count threshold value. So it is a suitable training corpus for word-embedding models.

5.2.4 Result Interpretation

To conclude, we can now answer Question 2. We see that the minimum count parameter reduces model quality. This conclusion depends on the size of the corpus . For smaller corpora, the effect will be even more pronounced. For such sizes of the training data we do not recommend to use any minimum count threshold when training embedding models. In combination with the results from Section 5.1, we conclude that the Google Books dataset is valid training data for embedding models. In general, one can expect good results using the 5-grams as training data, but anything above 2-grams could be used.

5.3 Answering Question 3: the Reason for the Quality Loss

Regarding Question 3, we start with an explanation why the increase of the minimum count pa-

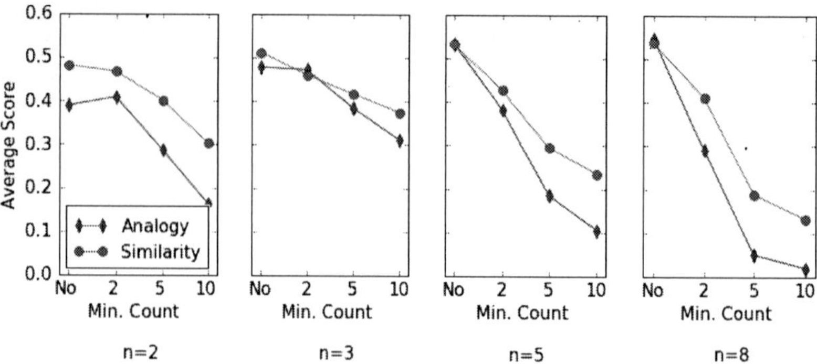

Figure 2: The average scores of models trained with different minimum count parameter on differently fragmented Wikipedia corpora on the Analogy and Similarity tasks

rameter decreases the quality of the embedding models. We have observed that in almost every case this has been a consequence of certain infrequent words of the evaluation test sets not occurring in sufficiently many n-grams. When analyzing the task specific results, we have seen that result quality on the rare words test set drops instantly even with the smallest threshold value. For other test sets on the other hand (WordSim353, RG-65 for instance) which include highly frequent words almost exclusively, results are not much worse. In summary, the reduced model quality generally is a consequence of the less frequent words not being trained sufficiently or even not at all. Therefore, they do not appear in the dictionaries of the model.

Table 4: Average movement in cosine distance of the word vectors with one extra iteration.

Corpus	2-gram	3-gram	5-gram	8-gram	Full text
Avg. movement	0.018	0.016	0.011	0.010	0.006

The fragmentation of the corpora causes a quality loss for a different reason. Every word of the evaluation test sets is included in the dictionary of every model, but fragmentation causes a mix-up of the word vectors, cf. Section 2.2. As explained in Example 1, each word is trained several times when fragmented corpora are used, and most of the time the context of the word, as considered by the algorithm during training, is not the full context. To quantify this effect, we have measured the average movement of a word vector when we iterate through the training data one extra time, after training the models. See Table 4; the numbers are average cosine distances. The lower the corpus quality is, the more the vectors move in the

additional iteration. The results seem to confirm our intuition that, with bad corpora, vectors move in suboptimal directions to a higher extent, ultimately resulting in worse models.

6 Conclusions

In this paper we present a resource and corresponding experiments which allow to answer which differences in quality one can expect when training word embedding models on fragmented corpora, such as the Google n-gram corpus, compared to full-text. The resource contains all models, corpora and scripts we have used. The resource contains one of the largest collection of systematically pre-trained embedding models currently openly available. It also contains the fragmented versions of both corpora used in this paper and our scripts used to conduct the experiments. We present experiments to give recommendations on which n-gram versions to use for word embedding model training. An in-depth evaluation using our presented comprehensive resource confirms that one generally can expect good quality for n-grams with $n \geq 3$. In addition, we show that the minimum count parameter is highly corpus size dependent and should not be used for corpora with size similar to or smaller than the Wikipedia dump. Finally, our results show that the fragmentation (i.e., small values for n) and the minimum count parameter introduce different kinds of error.

In summary, our results indicate that one can train high-quality embedding models with n-grams if some (mild) prerequisites hold. This is particularly true for the Google n-gram corpus, which is a good corpus to this end.

References

M. Baroni et al. 2014. Don't count, predict! A systematic comparison of context-counting vs. context-predicting semantic vectors. In *ACL*. ACL.

E. Bruni et al. 2012. Distributional semantics in technicolor. In *Proc. Annual Meeting of the Association for Computational Linguistics (ACL)*, pages 136–145. ACL.

C. Chelba et al. 2013. One billion word benchmark for measuring progress in statistical language modeling. *CoRR*, abs/1312.3005.

A. Elekes, M. Schäler, and K. Böhm. 2017. On the various semantics of similarity in word embedding models. In *JCDL*. IEEE.

L. Finkelstein et al. 2001. Placing search in context: The concept revisited. In *Proc. Int'l Conf. on World Wide Web (WWW)*, pages 406–414. ACM.

A. Gladkova and A. Drozd. 2016. Intrinsic evaluations of word embeddings: What can we do better? In *RepEval*. ACL.

W. Hamilton et al. 2016a. Cultural shift or linguistic drift? comparing two computational measures of semantic change. In *EMNLP*. ACL.

William L Hamilton, Jure Leskovec, and Dan Jurafsky. 2016b. Diachronic word embeddings reveal statistical laws of semantic change. *arXiv preprint arXiv:1605.09096*.

J. Hellrich and U. Hahn. 2016. An assessment of experimental protocols for tracing changes in word semantics relative to accuracy and reliability. In *LaTeCH*.

F. Hill, R. Reichart, and A. Korhonen. 2015. Simlex-999: Evaluating semantic models with genuine similarity estimation. *Computer Linguistics*, 41(4):665–695.

F. Hill et al. 2014. Not all neural embeddings are born equal. *CoRR*, abs/1410.0718.

S. Jansen. 2017. Word and phrase translation with word2vec. *CoRR*, abs/1705.03127.

Y. Kim et al. 2014. Temporal analysis of language through neural language models. *CoRR*, abs/1405.3515.

Vivek Kulkarni, Bryan Perozzi, and Steven Skiena. 2016. Freshman or fresher? quantifying the geographic variation of language in online social media. In *ICWSM*, pages 615–618.

Vivek Kulkarni et al. 2015. Statistically significant detection of linguistic change. In *24th International Conference on World Wide Web*, pages 625–635.

R. Lebret and R. Collobert. 2015. *Rehabilitation of Count-Based Models for Word Vector Representations*. Springer.

O. Levy and Y. Goldberg. 2014. Neural word embedding as implicit matrix factorization. In *NIPS*. MIT Press.

O. Levy, Y. Goldberg, and I. Dagan. 2015. Improving distributional similarity with lessons learned from word embeddings. *TACL*, 3.

T. Luong, R. Socher, and C. Manning. 2013. Better word representations with recursive neural networks for morphology. In *CoNLL*. ACL.

L. Ma and Y. Zhang. 2015. Using word2vec to process big text data. In *Proc. Int'l. Conf. on Big Data (Big Data)*, pages 2895–2897. IEEE.

C. Martinez-Ortiz et al. 2016. Design and implementation of shico: Visualising shifting concepts over time. In *HistoInformatics, DH*.

J.-B. Michel et al. 2015. Quantitative analysis of culture using millions of digitized books. *Science*, 331(6014):176–182.

T. Mikolov, Q. Le, and I. Sutskever. 2013a. Exploiting similarities among languages for machine translation. *CoRR*, abs/1309.4168.

T. Mikolov et al. 2013b. Distributed representations of words and phrases and their compositionality. In *NIPS*. Curran Associates Inc.

T. Mikolov et al. 2013c. Efficient estimation of word representations in vector space. *CoRR*, abs/1301.3781.

B. Mitra and N. Craswell. 2017. Neural text embeddings for information retrieval. In *WSDM*, pages 813–814. ACM.

J. Pennington et al. 2014. Glove: Global vectors for word representation. In *EMNLP*, pages 1532–1543. ACL.

S. Pyysalo et al. 2013. Distributional semantics resources for biomedical text processing. In *LBM*.

K. Radinsky et al. 2011. A word at a time: Computing word relatedness using temporal semantic analysis. In *WWW*, pages 337–346. ACM.

A. Reyes et al. 2012. From humor recognition to irony detection: The figurative language of social media. *DKE*.

Herbert Rubenstein and John B Goodenough. 1965. Contextual correlates of synonymy. *Communications of the ACM*, 8(10):627–633.

T. Schnabel et al. 2015. Evaluation methods for unsupervised word embeddings. In *EMNLP*.

Duyu Tang et al. 2014. Learning sentiment-specific word embedding for twitter sentiment classification. In *ACL*, volume 1, pages 1555–1565.

T. Zesch and I. Gurevych. 2007. Analysis of the wikipedia category graph for nlp applications. In *NAACL-HLT*, pages 1–8. ACL.

T. Zesch et al. 2008. Using wiktionary for computing semantic relatedness. In *AAAI*, pages 861–866. AAAI Press.

Linguistically-based Deep Unstructured Question Answering

Ahmad Aghaebrahimian
Charles University
Faculty of Mathematics and Physics
Institute of Formal and Applied Linguistics
Malostranske nam. 25, 11800 Praha 1, Czech Republic
ebrahimian@ufal.mff.cuni.cz

Abstract

In this paper, we propose a new linguistically-based approach to answering non-factoid open-domain questions from unstructured data. First, we elaborate on an architecture for textual encoding based on which we introduce a deep end-to-end neural model. This architecture benefits from a bilateral attention mechanism which helps the model to focus on a question and the answer sentence at the same time for phrasal answer extraction. Second, we feed the output of a constituency parser into the model directly and integrate linguistic constituents into the network to help it concentrate on chunks of an answer rather than on its single words for generating more natural output. By optimizing this architecture, we managed to obtain near-to-human-performance results and competitive to a state-of-the-art system on SQuAD and MS-MARCO datasets respectively.

1 Introduction

Reading, comprehending and reasoning over texts and answering a question about them (i.e. Question Answering) is a fundamental aspect of computational intelligence. Question Answering (QA), as a measure of intelligence, has been even suggested to replace Turing test (Clark and Etzioni, 2016).

The development of large datasets of QA in recent years (Hermann et al., 2015; Hill et al., 2015; Bordes et al., 2015; Rajpurkar et al., 2016) advanced the field especially for two significant branches of QA namely factoid (Aghaebrahimian and Jurčíček, 2016a,b) and non-factoid QA[1] (Rajpurkar et al., 2016). Non-factoid QA or QA over unstructured data is a somewhat new challenge in open-domain QA. A non-factoid QA system answers questions by reading and comprehending a context. The context in which we assume the answer is mentioned may have different granularities from a single sentence or paragraph to larger units of text. A QA system is supposed to extract a phrase answer from the provided paragraph or sentence depending on its granularity level.

The context for answering questions is usually extracted using an Information Retrieval (IR) technique. Then, a QA system should extract the best answer sentence. There are many studies about extracting answer sentences including but not limited to (He et al., 2015; He and Lin, 2016; Yih et al., 2013; Yu et al., 2016; Rao et al., 2016; Aghaebrahimian, 2017a).

Extracting the final or shortest possible answer from a set of candidate answer sentences is addressed in many studies as well (Zhang et al., 2017; Gong and Bowman, 2017; Shen et al., 2016; Weissenborn et al., 2017a). Instead of reasoning over and making inference on linguistic symbols (i.e., words or characters), almost all of these models use a neural architecture to encode contexts and questions into a vector representation and to reason over them.

A typical pattern in most of the current models is the use of a variant of uni- or bi-directional attention schemes (question to context and vice-versa) to encode the semantic content of questions' words with a focus on their context's words (Seo et al., 2016; Xiong et al., 2016; Weissenborn et al., 2017b; Chen et al., 2017; Wang et al., 2017). Compared to these models the novelty of our work is in explicitly conducting attention over both the context and the question for each candidate constituent[2] answer (every constituent

---

[1] While the answer to a non-factoid question is a chunk of one or more adjacent words, the answer to a factoid question is only an entity.

[2] Form now on and for the sake of brevity by constituents we mean linguistic constituents as they are referred to in Phrase Structure Grammar (Chomsky, 1957).

433

Proceedings of the 22nd Conference on Computational Natural Language Learning (CoNLL 2018), pages 433–443
Brussels, Belgium, October 31 - November 1, 2018. ©2018 Association for Computational Linguistics

Constituents Type	Training set	Development set
NP	59 %	62 %
ROOT	8 %	6 %
NNP	5 %	4 %
NN	4 %	2 %
JJ	3 %	1 %
VP	3 %	4 %
CD	3 %	2 %
PP	2 %	4 %
S	2 %	2 %
others	11 %(each < 2%)	13 %(each < 2%)

Table 1: The distribution of constituent types of answers in SQuAD training and development sets. For constituency parsing, we used the Standford CoreNLP tool (Manning et al., 2014). To see the full list of available constituency types in the dataset, please refer to Appendix A.

in the context). The fact that this is better than attending only to the question words is investigated and proved according to the results reported in Section 7.

Another observation is that a majority of recent studies are purely based on data science where one can barely see a linguistic intuition towards the problem. We show that a pure linguistic intuition could help neural reasoning and attention mechanisms to achieve quantitatively and qualitatively better results in QA.

By analyzing a human-generated QA dataset called SQuAD (Rajpurkar et al., 2016), we realized that people tend to answer questions in units called constituents (Table 1). We expect an answer to a question to be a valid constituent otherwise it would probably not be grammatical.

Constituents and Constituency relations are the bases of Phrase Structure Grammar first proposed by Noam Chomsky (Chomsky, 1957). Phrase Structure Grammar and many of its variants including Government and Binding theory (Chomsky, 1993) or Generalized and Head-driven Phrase Structure Grammar (Gazdar et al., 1994; Pollard and Sag, 1994) define hierarchical binary relations between the constituents of a text, and hence help to realize an exact and natural answer boundary for answer extraction.

Having these two points in mind and inspired by attentive pooling networks by Santos et al. (2016), we designed an attentive bilateral model and trained it on the constituents of questions and answers. We attempted to use some information from the parser, so to go beyond a simple word-based or vector-based representations. The results

obtained by the model are near to human performance on SQuAD dataset and competitive to a state-of-the-art system on MS-MARCO dataset. The contributions of our work are:

- A bilateral linguistically-based attention model for Question Answering

- Integrating linguistic constituents into a DNN architecture for the QA task.

In the next section, we review some of recent QA systems with a focus on unstructured QA. In Section 3, we briefly explain the constituency types. Then in Section 4, we discuss the details of our system architecture. In Section 5, we talk about the datasets and the way we prepared them for training. In Sections 6 and 7, we describe the training details and present the results of our experiments. Finally, we explain some ablation studies and error analysis in Section 8 before we conclude in Section 9.

2 Related work

In recent years, QA has been largely benefited from the development of Deep Neural Network (DNN) architectures largely in the form of Convolution Neural Networks (CNN) (LeCun et al., 1998) or Recurrent Neural Networks (RNN) (Elman, 1990). QA systems based on semantic parsing (Clarke et al., 2010; Kwiatkowski et al., 2010), IR-based systems (Yao and Durme, 2014), cloze-type (Kadlec et al., 2016; Hermann et al., 2015), factoid (Aghaebrahimian and Jurčíček, 2016b; Bordes et al., 2015) and non-factoid systems (Aghaebrahimian, 2017a; Rajpurkar et al., 2016) are some of the QA variants that have been improved by DNNs. Among all of these varieties, factoid and non-factoid are two most widely studied branches of QA systems.

In Factoid QA like air traffic information systems (ATIS) or dialogue systems, we answer the questions by extracting an entity from a structured database like relational databases or knowledge graphs. In contrast, in non-factoid systems, answers are extracted mostly from unstructured data like Wikipedia.

Unstructured QA in recent years has been studied with a few distinguishable different settings such as answer selection, answer trigging, and answers extraction. In answer selection (Aghaebrahimian, 2017a; Wang et al., 2016; Yu et al.,

2016) and answer trigging (Jurczyk et al., 2016) the goal is to find the best answer sentence given each question. These answer sentences may be non-existent in the provided context for answer triggering. In answer extraction (Shen and Klakow, 2006; Sultan et al., 2016), we extract a chunk of a sentence as the shortest possible answer.

Answer selection can be used as a measure of machine comprehension (Kadlec et al., 2016; Hermann et al., 2015). In this setting, a typical QA system reads a text and then answers either multiple-answer (cloze-type) or free-text questions. Cloze-type answers are limited to multiple distinct entities (usually 4 or 5) while a span of words answers free-text questions.

The performance of cloze-type systems is a good indication of machine comprehension. However, in QA systems for a real-life application like in dialogue systems or scientists' assistants, the answers, their boundaries and their types (e.g., proper noun, adjective or noun phrase) are not known in advance, and it makes this type of QA more challenging. In this setting, free-text QA or QA over unstructured data (Aghaebrahimian, 2017b; Rajpurkar et al., 2016; Cui et al., 2016) is advocated where answers are spans of multiple consecutive words in large repositories of textual data like Wikipedia.

Many successful studies have been performed for free-text (i.e., phrase) answer extraction from SQuAD since its release in 2016. Almost all of these models benefited from a form of DNN architecture and a majority of them integrated a kind of the attention mechanism. Some of these studies integrated attention to predicting the physical location of answers (Xiong et al., 2016; Cui et al., 2016; Hu et al., 2017; Seo et al., 2016). Others made an effort to find a match between queries and their contexts (Cui et al., 2016) or to compute a global distribution over the tokens in the context given a query (Wang and Jiang, 2016). Still, some other models integrated other mechanisms like memory networks (Pan et al., 2017) or reinforcement learning (Shen et al., 2016) to enhance their attention performance.

To add to these efforts, we intend to propose a new perspective on using attention and to enhance it by using linguistic constituents as a linguistically motivated feature.

3 Linguistic Constituents

There is hardly a universal agreement upon the definition of the term 'constituent'. In general, a constituent is an inseparable unit that can appear in different places of a sentence. Instead of defining what a constituent is, linguists define a set of experiments such as replacement or expansion to distinguish between constituents and non-constituents.

For instance, let's consider the sentence 'Plans for the relay were announced on April 26, 2007, in Beijing, China.' We can replace or expand some of its constituents and rephrase the sentence as 'on April 26, 2007, plans for the relay were announced , in Beijing, China.' or 'Plans for the great and important relay were announced on April 26, 2007, in Beijing, China.' while we are sure that these rephrases are not only both syntactically and semantically correct but also convey the same meaning as the original sentence. Some of the earliest works which tried to integrate more linguistic structures into QA are (Zhang et al., 2017; Xie and Eric, 2017). Using TreeLSTM, Zhang et al. (2017) tried to integrate linguistic structure into QA implicitly. At the prediction step, they used pointer network (Vinyals et al., 2017) to detect the beginning and the end of answer chunks. In contrast, (Xie and Eric, 2017) explicitly modeled candidate answers as sequences of constituents by encoding individual constituents using a chain of-trees LSTM (CT-LSTM) and tree-guided attention mechanism. However, their formulation of constituents is more complicated than ours and as we will see, a direct use of constituents as answer chunk is much less complicated and yields better results.

4 System Architecture

In this section, we describe how to represent questions, sentences and answers in vector space in Subsection 4.1 and then we train the vectors in Subsection 4.2 using a specific loss function and distance measure.

4.1 Representation Learning

Our goal is to extract constituent answers by loading their vector representations with the semantic content of their question and their containing answer sentence. To achieve this end, we integrated a bilateral attention mechanism into our model which lets us estimate a joint vector representation between answers when they are attending to questions' constituents and when they are attending to sentences' constituents.

To encode the semantic information in questions and sentences, we used a simple encoding unit (see Equations 1 to 6 and Figure 1). In this unit, $W_k \in \mathbb{R}^{|V|}$ are words in one-hot vector representations where k^{th} element of each vector is one and others are 0. V are all vocabularies in training questions and answers. $E \in \mathbb{R}^{|V| \times d_e}$ is the embedding matrix and d_e is the embedding dimension. The product of the multiplication in Equation 1 is the word embeddings in which each cell $W_{i,t}$ is the word in time step t in sample i. $W_{i,t}$ is the input of forward and backward RNN cells in Equations 2 and 4.

As RNN cell, we used Long Short-Term Memory architecture (LSTM) (Hochreiter and Schmidhuber, 1997). Pan et al. (2017) and Hu et al. (2017) show that bi-directional LSTM architectures provide more accurate representations of textual data. The common practice to form a bidirectional LSTM is to concatenate the last vectors in forward and backward LSTMs. Instead, we used a stepwise max pooling (SWMP) mechanism which takes the most important vectors from forward and backward LSTMs in Equations 3 and 5 and concatenate them in Equations 6.

$$W_{i,t} = E^{\top} W_k \tag{1}$$
$$\overrightarrow{enc}_{i,t} = LSTM(\overrightarrow{enc}_{i,t-1}, W_{i,t}) \tag{2}$$
$$\overrightarrow{enc}_i = SWMP(\overrightarrow{enc}_{i,t}) \tag{3}$$
$$\overleftarrow{enc}_{i,t} = LSTM(\overleftarrow{enc}_{i,t+1}, W_{i,t}) \tag{4}$$
$$\overleftarrow{enc}_i = SWMP(\overleftarrow{enc}_{i,t}) \tag{5}$$
$$enc_i = [\overrightarrow{enc}_i; \overleftarrow{enc}_i] \tag{6}$$

Using our encoding unit we encode questions and sentences and then concatenate the resulted vectors to generate a joint representation of questions and their answer sentences in Equation 7.

$$enc_i^{QS} = [enc_i^Q; enc_i^S] \tag{7}$$

In the next step, we need to encode the constituent answers. Our answer encoding unit has two modules, one with attention on questions enc_i^Q (equations 8-15) and the other with attention on sentences enc_i^S (equations 16-23). In both modules, we used an architecture similar to the one in the encoding unit with an additional attention unit.

In the answer encoding unit, again the input to LSTM cells are word embeddings generated by lookup table $W_{i,t}^A$. Two attention layers in this unit receive the output sequences of the forward and backward LSTM cells and focus once on questions and once on sentences. This is done using an attention mechanism similar to the one proposed by Santos et al. (2016).

In the end, the vectors generated by these two modules are concatenated in $h_i^{A_{QS}} = [h_i^{A_Q}; h_i^{A_S}]^3$ to form a general attentive representation of constituents with respect to their corresponding questions and sentences.

At training time, we try to learn the vector representations of questions, sentences, and their constituents jointly. However, we like to learn the vectors in a way that leads to a small distance between questions and their true constituents and a long distance between them and their false constituents. For this purpose, for each pair of question and sentence, we compute one true answer A_{QS}^+ and some false answer A_{QS}^- vectors.

We generated these vectors by passing a correct constituent A^+ and a random wrong constituent A^- through question-attentive (see equations 8-15) and sentence-attentive (see equations 16-23) modules and by concatenating the outputs.

4.2 Training

In this section, we train our model. Given a question and the constituents associated with its answer sentence, the model generates a score for each constituent. The score is an estimate of how similar the constituent to the gold answer is. Taking the argmax over the scores, the model returns the id of its true predicted constituent.

To train the model, we need to compute the distance between questions and their true constituents and to contrast it with the distance between questions and their false constituents.

There are various measures of distance or similarity between two vectors each with its own merits. Feng et al. (2015) did an exhaustive study on different distance measures for text classification and proposed some new measures including the Geometric mean of Euclidean and Sigmoid Dot product (GESD) (Formula 1) which outperformed other measures in their study.

We integrated GESD in our work to estimate

---

[3] All concatenations are performed on the last layer (i.e. data dimensions).

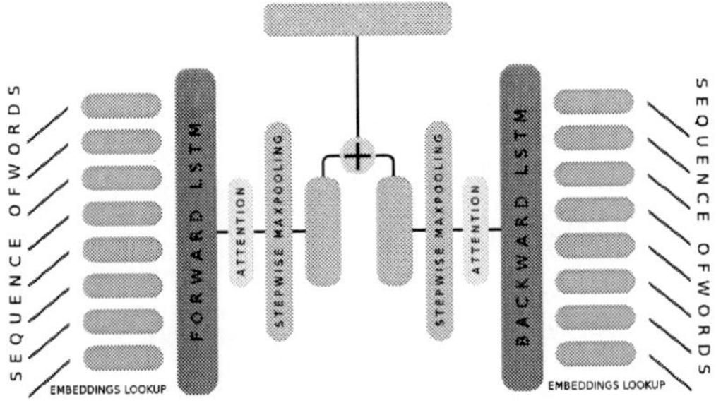

Figure 1: The encoding unit. The Embedding lookup uses pre-trained Glove word vectors (Pennington et al., 2014) and updates them through training. The output is the concatenation of max-pooled vectors of LSTM encoders.

$$W_{i,t}^A = E^\top W_k^A \tag{8}$$

$$\overrightarrow{h_{i,t}} = LSTM(\overrightarrow{h_{i,t-1}}, W_{i,t}^A) \tag{9}$$

$$\overrightarrow{h_{i,t}^{A_Q}} = ATT(\overrightarrow{h_{i,t}}, \mathbf{enc_i^Q}) \tag{10}$$

$$\overrightarrow{h_i^{A_Q}} = SWMP(\overrightarrow{h_{i,t}^{A_Q}}) \tag{11}$$

$$\overleftarrow{h_{i,t}^{A_Q}} = LSTM(\overleftarrow{h_{i,t+1}}, W_{i,t}^A) \tag{12}$$

$$\overleftarrow{h_{i,t}^{A_Q}} = ATT(\overleftarrow{h_{i,t}^{A_Q}}, \mathbf{enc_i^Q}) \tag{13}$$

$$\overleftarrow{h_i^{A_Q}} = SWMP(\overleftarrow{h_{i,t}^{A_Q}}) \tag{14}$$

$$h_i^{A_Q} = [\overrightarrow{h_i^{A_Q}}; \overleftarrow{h_i^{A_Q}}] \tag{15}$$

$$W_{i,t}^A = E^\top W_k^A \tag{16}$$

$$\overrightarrow{h_{i,t}} = LSTM(\overrightarrow{h_{i,t-1}}, W_{i,t}^A) \tag{17}$$

$$\overrightarrow{h_{i,t}^{A_S}} = ATT(\overrightarrow{h_{i,t}}, \mathbf{enc_i^S}) \tag{18}$$

$$\overrightarrow{h_i^{A_S}} = SWMP(\overrightarrow{h_{i,t}^{A_S}}) \tag{19}$$

$$\overleftarrow{h_{i,t}^{A_S}} = LSTM(\overleftarrow{h_{i,t+1}}, W_{i,t}^A) \tag{20}$$

$$\overleftarrow{h_{i,t}^{A_S}} = ATT(\overleftarrow{h_{i,t}^{A_S}}, \mathbf{enc_i^S}) \tag{21}$$

$$\overleftarrow{h_i^{A_S}} = SWMP(\overleftarrow{h_{i,t}^{A_S}}) \tag{22}$$

$$h_i^{A_S} = [\overrightarrow{h_i^{A_S}}; \overleftarrow{h_i^{A_S}}] \tag{23}$$

Figure 2: Question-aware (equations 16-23) and sentence-aware (equations 8-15) encoding

the distance between questions and their true and false constituents. GESD linearly combines two other measures called L2-norm and inner product. L2-norm is the forward-line semantic distance between two sentences and inner product measures the angle between two sentence vectors.

$$DIS(Q, A) = \frac{1}{1+exp(-(Q.A))} * \frac{1}{1+||Q-A||}$$

Formula 1: The distance between Question (Q) and Answer (A) vectors.

Now everything is ready to train the model. The overall system architecture is illustrated in Figure 3. We use Hinge loss function (Formula 2) to estimate the loss on each question-answer combination. Hinge function increases the loss with the distance between a question and its true constituents while decreases it with the distance between a question and its false constituents. In Equation 2, enc^{QS} is the joint vector representation of questions and their answer sentences, $h_i^{A_{QS}^-}$ is the vector of false answers, $h^{A_{QS}^+}$ is the vectors of true answers. Finally, m is the margin between positive and negative answers. It makes a trade-off between the mistakes in positive and negative classes.

$$\mathcal{L} = \sum_i \max(0, m + DIS(enc_i^{QS}, h_i^{A_{QS}^+}) - DIS(enc_i^{QS}, h_i^{A_{QS}^-}))$$

Formula 2: Hinge function. m is the margin, A_{QS}^- are false and A_{QS}^+ are true answers.

5 Datasets

The Stanford Question Answering Dataset (SQuAD) (Rajpurkar et al., 2016) is a dataset for sentence-level (i.e. answer selection) and word-level (i.e. answer extraction) QA. It includes 107,785 question-answer pairs synthesized by crowd workers on 536 Wikipedia articles. The dataset is randomly shuffled and divided into training (80%), development (10%) and test (10%) sets. Due to its large number of questions compared to previous datasets (Hirschman et al., 1999; Richardson et al., 2013), it is considered a good testbed for data-intensive QA methods. The answers in SQuAD are categorized into ten types including Person, Date, Location, etc (Rajpurkar et al., 2016). However, there are no statistics available on the constituent type of each answer.

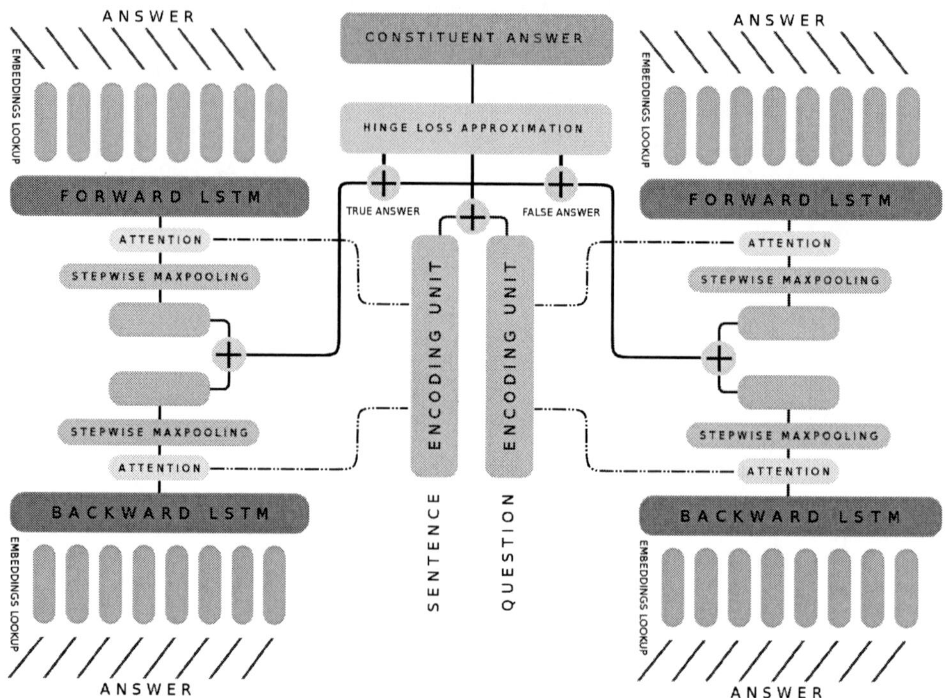

Figure 3: The system architecture. Two answer modules, one with attention on questions and the other on sentences, provide a joint representation containing all required information with respect to questions and sentences for making inference on true constituents.

To control the vocabulary size we needed to eliminate redundant numeric values, but at the same time, we wanted to parse the contents, and we needed to keep the semantic values of numeric tokens. Hence to preprocess the questions and sentences in the dataset, we removed all non-alphanumeric characters from all contents and then replaced numeric values with '9'. Then we used CoreNLP tool (Manning et al., 2014) to tokenize and to perform constituency parsing on the contents.

After extracting constituents from the tree of sentences and comparing them with gold answers, we realized that 72% of the answers are constituents. Other 21% of the answers had slight divergences from a constituent, like lacking or having a determiner or punctuation mark which were eventually going to be disregarded in the official evaluation script. The remaining 7% was a combination of two smaller constituents or a part of a larger one.

In the training set, to use constituents as answers, we replaced non-matching answers with the smallest and most similar constituents. Since at the evaluation time, we needed the gold answers and not their replaced constituents, we did not change the answers in the development set.

We extracted a total number of 48 different constituents types including both terminal and non-terminal ones from SQuAD. The percentage of each constituent type in training and development sets are presented in Table 1. The figures for development set are computed only based on exact match answers.

We used SQuAD's development set for testing the system and reporting the results. To prepare the dataset for training and evaluating our system we used a state-of-the-art answer sentence selection system (Aghaebrahimian, 2017a) to extract the best answer sentences. The system provides us the best sentence with 94.4 % accuracy given each question. After pre-processing the sentence as explained above, we extracted its constituents and trained the model using the correct constituents as true and other constituents as negative samples.

At test time, we used the same procedure to extract the constituents, but we used gold answers as they are without substituting non-matching answer-constituents. Then, we added other constituents as negative samples.

For evaluation purpose, we used SQuAD's official evaluation script which computes the exact match and the F1 score. The exact match is the percentage of predictions which exactly match the gold answer and the F1 (Macro-averaged) score is the average overlap between the prediction and ground truth answer while treating them both as bags of tokens, and computing their F1.

To experiment our model furthermore, we used MS-MARCO dataset (Nguyen et al., 2015). As a machine comprehension dataset, MS-MARCO has two fundamental differences with SQuAD. Every question in MS-MARCO has several passages from which the best answer should be retrieved. Moreover, the answers in MS-MARCO are not necessarily sub-spans of the provided contexts so that BLEU and ROUGE are used as the metrics in the official tool of MS-MARCO evaluation. During training we used the highest BLEU scored constituent as the answer and in the evaluation, we computed the BLEU and ROUGE scores of the constituents selected by the system. As the results in Table 7 show, our system obtained competitive results to another state-of-the-art system trained on the same dataset.

6 Experiment

To evaluate our new architecture and to see how integrating linguistic constituents affects its performance we set up two settings. We designed one setting for evaluating the effect of using constituents instead of words (constituent-base vs. word-base) and another to evaluate the effect of using attention mechanism on top of vector training modules (uni- vs. bi-attention). Therefore we conducted four experiments on both datasets or eight experiments in total.

In the constituent-base setting, we generated the training and test data as described in Section 5. In word-base however, we replaced constituents with the tokens in answer sentences for both train and test sets and trained our model to compute two scores for initial and final positions of answer chunks. In the constituent-base setting at test time, we directly used the predicted constituent as the final answer. In the word-base setting, however, we got the final answer using the highest-scored words for initial and final positions.

We also investigated the effect of bilateral attention on the model performance. In the bi-attention model, we used the model as described in Section 4. In the uni-attention model, we eliminated the attention on sentences and only used the module for attention on questions.

For training our model, we used 300-dimensional pre-trained Glove word vectors (Pennington et al., 2014) to generate the embedding matrix and kept the embedding matrix updated through training. We used 128-dimensional LSTMs for all recurrent networks and used 'Adam' with parameters learning rate=0.001, $\beta_1 = 0.9$, $\beta_2 = 0.999$ for optimization. We set batch size to 32 and dropout rate to 0.5 for all LSTMs and embedding layers. We performed the accuracy check only on the first best answer.

7 Result

The results of our experiments are summarized in Table 2. By contrasting the results of uni-/bi-attention and word/constituent-base models, we can see that the proposed bi-attention mechanism with linguistic constituents integrated into it makes a significant improvement on answer extraction. Another interesting observation is that the Exact Match metric benefits from restriction to constituents as answers. Concerning the MS-MARCO dataset, the results are competitive to a state-of-the-art system tested on the same dataset (Wang et al., 2017).

8 Ablation and Error Analysis

In this section, we analyze the SQuAD concerning answer distribution over different query types. Table 1 shows that the NP type constituents are the most prominent type among all other answers. However, to investigate the importance of other types in overall system performance, we performed an ablation study where we studied the influence of each constituent type on overall accuracy. The results are presented in Figure 4. We also studied how much the model succeeded in retrieving answers from each type. The results are presented in the same figure. This table also shows how often does the method succeed in cases where the correct answer is, in fact, a constituent span.

As seen in Figure 4, the answers are mostly singular noun phrases after which with a significant difference are proper nouns, verb phrases, and prepo-

	SQuAD Development set		MS-MARCO Evaluation set	
	Exact-match(%)	F1(%)	BLEU	ROUGE
Logistic Regression (Rajpurkar et al., 2016)	40.00 %	51.00 %	-	-
Uni-Attention Word-base (this work)	55.12 %	57.98 %	35.6	35.1
Bi-Attention Word-base (this work)	59.84 %	63.08 %	38.1	38.4
Uni-Attention Constituency-base (this work)	73.82 %	77.43 %	39.6	39.9
TreeLSTM (Zhang et al., 2017)	69.10 %	78.38 %	-	-
BIDAF (Seo et al., 2016)	72.6 %	80.7 %	-	-
CCNN (Xie and Eric, 2017)	74.1 %	82.6 %	-	-
R-net (Wang et al., 2017)	75.60 %	82.80 %	42.2	42.9
Bi-Attention Constituency-base (this work)	**80.72 %**	**83.25 %**	42.1	42.7
Human Performance (Rajpurkar et al., 2016)	82.30 %	91.22 %	-	-

Table 2: The performances of different models in the exact match and F1 metrics for SQuAD and BLEU and ROUGE for the MS-MARCO dataset.

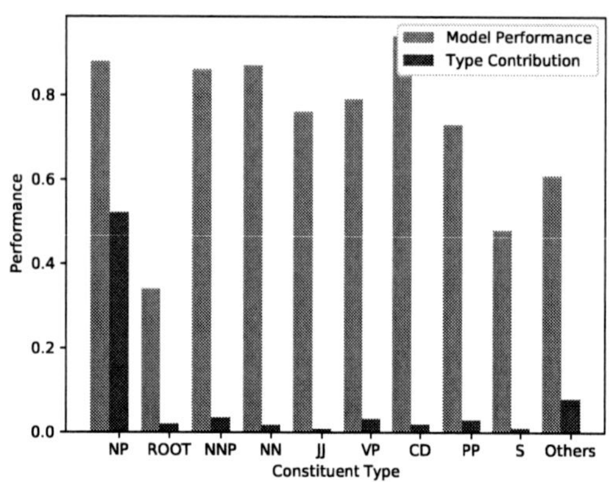

Figure 4: Blue lines are the contribution of each type in the overall system performance using the best model and at the convergence time. Red bars represent the performance of the model in retrieving each constituent type when the model is converged. Performance is expressed in the exact match metric (%). As a guide to how to read the chars, the first blue line for NP type says that 50% of all correctly extracted answers by the system are NP type-answers. The red line of the same type says that our system managed to retrieve about 87% of all NP-type answers in the dataset.

sitional phrases. We can also see how the model performed for each constituent. It seems that extracting cardinal numbers is much easier for the model than retrieving roots or full sentences.

An analysis of the errors shows that false answer sentence, non-constituent answers, parsing errors, overlapping constituents and unknown words are the primary reasons for the mistakes made by our system. The sentence selection process brought about six percent incorrect answers. The next primary reason for making mistakes is the constituents which contain other smaller constituents. While in all cases we extract the smallest constituent, in about three percent of overlapping constituents the more extended ones are the correct answer. Parsing errors where the constituents are not retrieved correctly and unknown words where the embeddings are not trained properly are responsible for other four percent of the errors. Finally, non-constituent answers led to around eight percent false answers in the system output.

9 Conclusion and Future Work

We described a new linguistically-based end-to-end DNN for Question Answering from unstructured data. This model is a neural formulation in which linguistic constituents are explicitly modeled. It operates an LSTM over the constituents and uses the resulting hidden states to attend both to question and to the encompassing context sentence, thereby enriching the constituents representation with both. The use of constituents instead of an arbitrary string of words in answers improves the system performance in three ways.

First, it increases the precision of the system. By looking at the small gap between the F1 and the exact match metrics in our system and compare it to the ones for the other systems, we can see that the ratio of exact-match answers in our system is higher than that of the other ones.

Second, it helps an answer to look more like a human-generated one. Considering prediction and ground truth as bags of tokens, the F1 (Macro-averaged) metric computes the average overlap between the prediction and ground truth answer. While a predicted answer may have a full overlap with the ground truth hence gains a high F1 score, due to the irrelevant words it contains, it poses an incoherent answer to users. The longer the gap between exact match and F1 measures, the more inappropriate words appear in answers. This is primarily an essential factor in the overall quality of dialogue QA systems where users expect to receive a natural and human-generated-like answer. Last but not least, imposing constraints on the candidate space, limit errors and make the system more efficient by decreasing the search space and weeding out non-relevant answers. In the future, we plan to integrate dependency relations into the model by designing a larger model and evaluating it on other QA datasets.

Acknowledgments

This research was partially funded by the Ministry of Education, Youth and Sports of the Czech Republic (project LM2015071), by Charles University SVV project number 260 453 and GAUK 207-10/250098 of Charles University in Prague.

References

Ahmad Aghaebrahimian. 2017a. Constrained deep answer sentence selection. In *Proceedings of the 20th International Conference on Text, Speech, and Dialogue (TSD)*.

Ahmad Aghaebrahimian. 2017b. Hybrid Deep Open-Domain Question Answering. In *Proceedings of the 8th Language and Technology Conference (LTC)*.

Ahmad Aghaebrahimian and Filip Jurčíček. 2016a. Constraint-Based Open-Domain Question Answering Using Knowledge Graph Search. In *Proceedings of the 19th International Conference on Text, Speech and Dialogue (TSD), LNAI 9924*.

Ahmad Aghaebrahimian and Filip Jurčíček. 2016b. Open-domain Factoid Question Answering via Knowledge Graph Search. In *Proceedings of the Workshop on Human-Computer Question Answering, The North American Chapter of the Association for Computational Linguistics (NAACL)*.

Antoine Bordes, Nicolas Usunier, Sumit Chopra, and Jason Weston. 2015. Large-scale simple question answering with memory networks. *arXiv preprint arXiv:1506.02075*.

Danqi Chen, Adam Fisch, Jason Weston, and Antoine Bordes. 2017. Reading wikipedia to answer open-domain questions. In *arXiv:1704.00051, 2017a*.

Noam Chomsky. 1957. *Syntactic structures*. The Hague, Paris: Mouton.

Noam Chomsky. 1993. *Lectures on Government and Binding: The Pisa Lectures*. Mouton de Gruyter.

Peter Clark and Oren Etzioni. 2016. My computer is an honor student but how intelligent is it? standardized tests as a measure of ai. *AI Magazine*.

James Clarke, Dan Goldwasser, Ming-Wei Chang, and Dan Roth. 2010. Driving semantic parsing from the worlds response. *In Proceedings of the Conference on Computational Natural Language Learning (CoNLL)*.

Yiming Cui, Zhipeng Chen, Si Wei, Shijin Wang, Ting Liu, and Guoping Hu. 2016. Attention-over-attention neural networks for reading comprehension. *arXiv:1607.04423*.

Jeffry L. Elman. 1990. Finding structure in time. *Cognitive Science*, 14(2):179–211.

Minwei Feng, Bing Xiang, Michael R. Glass, Lidan Wang, and Bowen Zhou. 2015. Applying deep learning to answer selection: a study and an open task. In *Proceedings of IEEE ASRU Workshop*.

Gerald Gazdar, Ewan H. Klein, Geoffrey K. Pullum, and Ivan A. Sag. 1994. *Generalized Phrase Structure Grammar*. Blackwell, Oxford.

Yichen Gong and Samuel R Bowman. 2017. Ruminating reader: Reasoning with gated multi-hop attention. *arXiv:1704.07415*.

Hua He, Kevin Gimpel, and Jimmy Lin. 2015. Multi-perspective sentence similarity modeling with convolutional neural networks. In *Proceedings of the Conference on Empirical Methods in Natural Language Processing(EMNLP)*.

Hua He and Jimmy Lin. 2016. Pairwise word interaction modeling with deep neural networks for semantic similarity measurement. In *Proceedings of The North American Chapter of the Association for Computational Linguistics (NAACL)*.

Karl Moritz Hermann, Tomas Kocisky, Edward Grefenstette, Lasse Espeholt, Will Kay, Mustafa Suleyman, and Phil Blunsom. 2015. Teaching machines to read and comprehend. In *Proceedings of Advances in Neural Information Processing Systems*.

Felix Hill, Antoine Bordes, Sumit Chopra, and Jason Weston. 2015. The goldilocks principle: Reading children's books with explicit memory representations. *arXiv :1511.02301*.

Lynette Hirschman, Marc Light, Eric Breck, and John D. Burger. 1999. Deep read: A reading comprehension system. In *Proceedings of Association for Computational Linguistics (ACL)*.

Sepp Hochreiter and Jurgen Schmidhuber. 1997. Long short-term memory. *Neural Comput.*, 9(8).

Minghao Hu, Yuxing Peng, and Xipeng Qiu. 2017. Reinforced mnemonic reader for machine comprehension. *arXiv:1705.02798*.

Tomasz Jurczyk, Michael Zhai, and Jinho D. Choi. 2016. Selqa: A new benchmark for selection- based question answering. In *Proceedings of the 28th International Conference on Tools with Artificial Intelligence*.

Rudolf Kadlec, Martin Schmid, Ondrej Bajgar, and Jan Kleindienst. 2016. Text understanding with the attention sum reader network. In *Proceedings of the Association for Computational Linguistics*.

Tom Kwiatkowski, Luke Zettlemoyer, Sharon Goldwater, and Mark Steedman. 2010. Inducing probabilistic ccg grammars from logical form with higher-order unification. In *Proceedings of the Conference on Empirical Methods in Natural Language Processing*.

Yann LeCun, Leon Bottou, Yoshua Bengio, and Patrick Haffner. 1998. Gradient-based learning applied to document recognition. In *Proceedings of the IEEE*.

Christopher D. Manning, Mihai Surdeanu, John Bauer, Jenny Finkel, Steven J. Bethard, and David McClosky. 2014. The Stanford CoreNLP natural language processing toolkit. In *proceedings of the Association for Computational Linguistics (ACL) System Demonstrations*.

Tri Nguyen, Mir Rosenberg, Xia Song, Jianfeng Gao, Saurabh Tiwary, Rangan Majumder, and Li Deng. 2015. Ms marco: A human generated machine reading comprehension dataset. *CoRR, abs/1611.09268*.

Boyuan Pan, Hao Li, Zhou Zhao, Bin Cao, Deng Cai, and Xiaofei He. 2017. Memen: Multi-layer embedding with memory networks for machine comprehension. *arXiv:1707.09098*.

Jeffrey Pennington, Richard Socher, and Christopher D. Manning. 2014. Glove: Global vectors for word representation. In *Procedings of the conference Empirical Methods in Natural Language Processing (EMNLP)*.

Carl Pollard and Ivan A. Sag. 1994. *Head-driven phrase structure grammar*. University of Chicago Press, Chicago.

Pranav Rajpurkar, Jian Zhang, Konstantin Lopyrev, and Percy Liang. 2016. Squad: 100,000+ questions for machine comprehension of text. *arXiv:1606.05250*.

Jinfeng Rao, Hua He, and Jimmy Lin. 2016. Noise-contrastive estimation for answer selection with deep neural networks. In *Proceedings of the 25th ACM International on Conference on Information and Knowledge Management*, CIKM '16.

Matthew Richardson, Burges, Christopher J.C., and Renshaw Erin. 2013. Mctest: A challenge dataset for the open-domain machine comprehension of text. In *Proceedings of Empirical Methods in Natural Language Processing(EMNLP)*.

Cicero dos Santos, Ming Tan, Bing Xiang, and Bowen Zhou. 2016. Attentive pooling networks. *arXiv:1602.03609v1*.

Minjoon Seo, Aniruddha Kembhavi, Ali Farhadi, and Hannaneh Hajishirzi. 2016. Bidirectional attention flow for machine comprehension. *arXiv:1611.01603*.

Dan Shen and Dietrich Klakow. 2006. Exploring correlation of dependency relation paths for answer extraction. In *Proceedings of the 21st International Conference on Computational Linguistics*.

Yelong Shen, Po-Sen Huang, Jianfeng Gao, and Weizhu Chen. 2016. Reasonet: Learning to stop reading in machine comprehension. In *Proceedings of the Workshop on Cognitive Computation: Integrating neural and symbolic approaches 2016 co-located with the 30th Annual Conference on Neural Information Processing Systems (NIPS 2016)*.

Md Arafat Sultan, Vittorio Castelli, and Radu Florian. 2016. A joint model for answer sentence ranking and answer extraction. In *Transactions of the Association for Computational Linguistics*.

Oriol Vinyals, Meire Fortunato, and Navdeep Jaitly. 2017. Pointer networks. In *Proceedings of NIPS*.

Shuohang Wang and Jing Jiang. 2016. Machine comprehension using match-lstm and answer pointer. *arXiv:1608.07905*.

Wenhui Wang, Nan Yang, Furu Wei, Baobao Chang, and Ming Zhou. 2017. Gated self-matching networks for reading comprehension and question answering. In *Proceedings of the Association for Computational Linguistics(ACL)*.

Zhiguo Wang, Haitao Mi, and Abraham Ittycheriah. 2016. Sentence similarity learning by lexical decomposition and composition. *arXiv:1602.07019*.

Dirk Weissenborn, Georg Wiese, and Laura Seiffe. 2017a. Fastqa: A simple and efficient neural architecture for question answering. *arXiv:1703.04816*.

Dirk Weissenborn, Georg Wiese, and Laura Seiffe. 2017b. Making neural qa as simple as possible but not simpler. In *Proceedings of the Computational Natural Language Learning (CoNLL)*.

Pengtao Xie and Xing Eric. 2017. A constituent-centric neural architecture for reading comprehension. In *Proceedings of the 55th Annual Meeting of the Association for Computational Linguistics*.

Caiming Xiong, Victor Zhong, and Richard Socher. 2016. Dynamic coattention networks for question answering. *arXiv:1611.01604*.

Xuchen Yao and Benjamin Van Durme. 2014. Information extraction over structured data: Question answering with freebase. *In Proceedings of Association for Computational Linguistics.*

Wen-tau Yih, Ming-Wei Chang, Christopher Meek, and Andrzej Pastusiak. 2013. Question answering using enhanced lexical semantic models. *In Proceedings of Association for Computational Linguistics(ACL).*

Lei Yu, Karl Moritz Hermann, Phil Blunsom, and Stephen Pulman. 2016. Deep learning for answer sentence selection. *Proceedings of the NIPS Deep Learning Workshop.*

Junbei Zhang, Xiaodan Zhu, Qian Chen, Lirong Dai, and Hui Jiang. 2017. Exploring question understanding and adaptation in neural-network-based question answering. *arXiv:1703.04617.*

A   Full Constituent types

Other constituent types include: NP, ROOT, NNP, NN, JJ, VP, CD, PP, S, NNS, ADJP, SBAR, NP-TMP, QP, ADVP, VBG, DT, VBN, IN, NNPS, VB, RB, VBD, VBZ, JJR, VBP, UCP, X, CC, FRAG, WHNP, JJS, NAC, NX, FW, TO, RBR, PDT, PRN, INTJ, PRT, WHPP, PRP, SINV, WHADJP, MD, RRC, WHADVP
For a description of each type please refer to (Manning et al., 2014)

DimSim: An Accurate Chinese Phonetic Similarity Algorithm based on Learned High Dimensional Encoding

Min Li
IBM Research
minli@us.ibm.com

Marina Danilevsky
IBM Research
mdanile@us.ibm.com

Sara Noeman
IBM
noemans@eg.ibm.com

Yunyao Li
IBM Research
yunyaoli@us.ibm.com

Abstract

Phonetic similarity algorithms identify words and phrases with similar pronunciation which are used in many natural language processing tasks. However, existing approaches are designed mainly for Indo-European languages and fail to capture the unique properties of Chinese pronunciation. In this paper, we propose a high dimensional encoded phonetic similarity algorithm for Chinese, DimSim. The encodings are learned from annotated data to separately map initial and final phonemes into n-dimensional coordinates. Pinyin phonetic similarities are then calculated by aggregating the similarities of initial, final and tone. DimSim demonstrates a $7.5X$ improvement on mean reciprocal rank over the state-of-the-art phonetic similarity approaches.

1 Introduction

Performing the mental gymnastics of transforming 'I'm hear' to 'I'm *here*,' or, 'I can't so buttons' to 'I can't *sew* buttons,' is familiar to anyone who has encountered autocorrected text messages, punny social media posts, or just friends with bad grammar. Although at first glance it may seem that phonetic similarity can only be quantified for audible words, this problem is often present in purely textual spaces, such as social media posts or text messages. Incorrect homophones and synophones, whether used in error or in jest, pose challenges for a wide range of NLP tasks, such as named entity identification, text normalization and spelling correction (Chung et al., 2011; Xia et al., 2006; Toutanova and Moore, 2002; Twiefel et al., 2014; Lee et al., 2013; Kessler, 2005). These tasks must therefore successfully transform incorrect words or phrases ('hear','so') to their phonetically similar correct counterparts ('here','sew'), which in turn requires a robust representation of phonetic similarity between word pairs. A reli-

Pinyin	initial	final	tone
xi1	x	i	1
fan4	f	an	4

Table 1: Example Pinyins.

偶(ou2,我wo2)稀饭(xi1fan4,喜欢xi2huan1)你。 I like you.
杯具(bei1ju4,悲剧bei1ju4)啊，为一个女孩纸(zhi2,子zi5)这么香菇(xiang1gu1,想哭 xiang2ku1)。 Sadly, I am heart broken for a girl.

Table 2: Microblogs using phonetic transcription.

able approach for generating phonetically similar words is equally crucial for Chinese text (Xia et al., 2006).

Unfortunately, most existing phonetic similarity algorithms such as Soundex (Archives and Administration, 2007) and Double Metaphone (DM) Philips (2000) are motivated by English and designed for Indo-European languages. Words are encoded to approximate phonetic presentations by ignoring vowels (except foremost ones), which is appropriate where phonetic transcription consists of a sequence of phonemes, such as for English. In contrast, the speech sound of a Chinese character is represented by a single syllable in Pinyin consisting of two or three parts: an *initial* (optional), a *final* or *compound finals*, and *tone* [1] (Table 1). As a result, phonetic similarity approaches designed for Indo-European languages often fall short when applied to Chinese text. Note that we use Pinyin as the phonetic representation because it is a widely accepted Romanization system (San, 2007; ISO, 2015) of Chinese syllables, used to teach pronunciation of standard Chinese. Table 2 shows two sentences from Chinese microblogs, containing informal words derived from phonetic transcription. The DM and Soundex encodings for

---

[1] Chinese has five tones, represented on a 1-5 scale.

Proceedings of the 22nd Conference on Computational Natural Language Learning (CoNLL 2018), pages 444–453
Brussels, Belgium, October 31 - November 1, 2018. ©2018 Association for Computational Linguistics

Words	DM	Soundex
稀xi1饭fan4	S:S,FN:FN	X000,F500
喜xi2欢huan1	S:S,HN:HN	X000,H500
泄xie4愤fen4	S:S,FN:FN	X000,F500

Table 3: DM and Soundex of Chinese words.

Figure 1: Grouping initials by phonetic similarity.

near-homonyms of 喜欢 from Table 2 are shown in Table 3. Since both DM and Soundex ignore vowels and tones, words with dissimilar pronunciations are incorrectly assigned to the same encoding (e.g. 稀饭 and 泄愤), while true near-homonyms are encoded much further apart (e.g. 稀饭 and 喜欢). On the other hand, additional candidates with similar phonetic distances such as 心xin1烦fan2，西xi1方fang1 for 稀饭 should be generated, for consumption by downstream applications such as text normalization.

The example highlights the importance of considering all Pinyin components and their characteristics when calculating Chinese phonetic similarity (Xia et al., 2006). One recent work (Yao, 2015) manually assigns a single numerical number to encode and derive phonetic similarity. However, this single-encoding approach is inaccurate since the phonetic distances between Pinyins are not captured well in a one dimensional space. Figure 1 illustrates the similarities between a subset of initials. Initial groups $"z, c"$, $"zh, ch"$, $"z, zh"$ and $"zh, ch"$ are all similar, which cannot be captured using a one dimensional representation (e.g., an encoding of $"zh=0,z=1,c=2,ch=3"$ fails to identify the $"zh, ch"$ pair as similar.) ALINE (Kondrak, 2003) is another illustration of the challenge of manually assigning numerical values in order to accurately represent the complex relative phonetic similarity relationships across various languages. Therefore, given the perceptual nature of the problem of phonetic similarity, it is critical to learn the distances based on as much empirical data as possible (Kessler, 2005), rather than using a manually encoded metric.

This paper presents DIMSIM, a learned n-dimensional phonetic encoding for Chinese along with a phonetic similarity algorithm, which uses the encoding to generate and rank phonetically

similar words. To address the complexity of relative phonetic similarities in Pinyin components, we propose a supervised learning approach to learn n dimensional encodings for finals and initials where n can be easily extended from one to two or higher dimensions. The learning model derives accurate encodings by jointly considering Pinyin linguistic characteristics, such as place of articulation and pronunciation methods, as well as high quality annotated training data sets. We compare DIMSIM to Double Metaphone(DM), Minimum edit distance(MED) and ALINE demonstrating that DIMSIM outperforms these algorithms by $7.5X$ on mean reciprocal rank, $1.4X$ on precision and $1.5X$ on recall on a real-world dataset. Our contributions are:

1. An encoding for Chinese Pinyin leveraging Chinese pronunciation characteristics.

2. A simple and effective phonetic similarity algorithm to generate and rank phonetically similar Chinese words.

3. An implementation and a comprehensive evaluation showing the effectiveness of DIMSIM over the state-of-the-art algorithms.

4. A package release of the implemented algorithm and a constructed dataset of Chinese words with phonetic corrections.[2]

2 Generating Phonetic Candidates

DIMSIM generates ranked candidate words with similar pronunciation to a seed word. Similarity is measured by a phonetic distance metric based on n-dimensional encodings, as introduced below.

2.1 Phonetic Comparison for Pinyin

An important characteristic of Pinyin is that the three components, initial, final and tone, can be independently phonetically compared. For example, the phonetic similarity of the finals $"ie"$ and $"ue"$ is identical in the Pinyin pairs $\{"xie2","xue2"\}$ and $\{"lie2","lue2"\}$, in spite of the varying initials. English, by contrast, does not have this characteristic. Consider as an example, the letter group "ough," which is pronounced quite differently in "rough," "through" and "though."

Note that depending on the initials, a final of same written form can represent different finals. For instance, $\ddot{u}$ is written as u after j, q and x; uo is written as o after b, p, m, f or w. There are a total

---

[2]https://github.com/System-T/DimSim.

of six rewritten rules in Pinyin (ISO, 2015). Since these rules are fixed, we preprocess the Pinyins according to these rules, transforming them into the original form for our internal representation (e.g., we represent *ju* as *jü* and *bo* as *buo*.)

2.2 Measuring Phonetic Similarity

DIMSIM represents a given word w as a list of characters $\{c_i | 1 \leq i \leq K\}$ where K is the number of characters and p_{c_i} denotes the Pinyin of i_{th} character. The initial, final, and tone components of p_{c_i} are denoted as $p_{c_i}^I$, $p_{c_i}^F$, and $p_{c_i}^T$, respectively.

Formally, the phonetic similarity S between the pronunciation of c_i and c_i' is computed using Manhattan distance as the sum of the distances between the three pairs of components, as follows:

$$\sum_{1 \leq i \leq K} S(c_i, c_i') = \sum_{1 \leq i \leq K} \{ S_p(p_{c_i}^I, p_{c_i'}^I) + S_p(p_{c_i}^F, p_{c_i'}^F) + S_T(p_{c_i}^T, p_{c_i'}^T) \} \tag{1}$$

Manhattan distance is an appropriate metric since the three components are independent. Any single change does not affect more than one component, and any change affecting several components is the result of multiple independent and additive changes. It follows that the similarity between two words is computed as the sum of the phonetic distances of characters. For example, the Pinyins of "童鞋" and "同学" are "*tong2xie2*" and "*tong2xue2*". The distance between "童(*tong2*)" and "同(*tong2*)" is zero; the distance between "鞋(*xie2*)" and "学(*xue2*)" is calculated as $S($ "鞋" , "学" $) = S_p(x, x) + S_p(ie, ue) + S_T(2, 2)$. Although the characters "鞋(*xie2*)" and "学(*xue2*)" are completely different, their Pinyins only differ in their finals.

2.3 Learning Pinyin Encodings

The next task is to compute encodings for initials, finals, and tones. While tonal similarity is easily handled (see Section 2.4), pairwise similarity for initials and finals is more complex. We adopt a supervised learning approach to obtain these encodings, using linguistic characteristics combined with a labeled dataset. The latter consists of word pairs, with specific pairs of initials or finals manually annotated for phonetic similarity. The set of annotated pairs between initials and finals are then used to learn the n-dimensional encodings of initials and finals, which will in turn be used for generating phonetically similar candidates.

	Labial	Alveolar	Retroflex	Alveolo-palatal	Velar
Plosive (u)	b	d			g
Plosive (a)	p	t			k
Nasal	m	n			
Affricate (u)		z	zh	j	
Affricate (a)		c	ch	q	
Fricative	f	s	sh	x	h
Liquid		l	r		
Semivowel			y and w		

(u) = unaspirated, (a) = aspirated

Figure 2: Table of Pinyin Initials.

2.3.1 Generating Similar Word Pairs

Phonetically similar word pairs are used to create annotations representing the phonetic similarity of initials, or finals. Chinese has 253 pairs of initials and 666 pairs of finals. Annotating examples of all these pairs is labor intensive and error-prone. Assuming twenty word pairs are provided as context per pair, the task quickly blows up to eighteen thousand annotations. However, we observe that the phonetic similarity of Pinyin is greatly impacted by the pronunciation methods and the place of articulation - this allows us to improve the accuracy and simplify the annotation task. Specifically, this is done by grouping Pinyin components into initial clusters and only annotating pairs within each cluster, and representative cluster pairs.

Figure 2 partitions initials into 12 clusters, consisting of "*bp*","*dt*","*gk*","*hf*","*nl*","*r*", "*jqx*", "*zcs*", "*zhchsh*", "*m*" ,"*y*" and "*w*", based on the pronunciation method and the place of articulation. "*f*" and "*h*" are grouped together as they are both fricative and sound very similar, especially for people from the southeast of China (Zhishihao, 2017). We then eliminate the comparison of pairs that are highly similar or highly dissimilar. For example, as the semivowel initials "*y*" and "*w*" are dissimilar to all other initials, we label every initial pair containing one of them with the lowest possible score. To compare between clusters, we randomly choose one initial from each cluster and generate just those comparison pairs. The number of pairs of initials decreases from 253 to 59.

We use a similar method for finals, partitioning them into six groups by the six basic vowels ("*a,o,e,i,u,ü*") (e.g., "*i,in,ing*" are clustered together.) We then use edit distance and common sequence length constraints to guide the pair generation; specifically, we compare a pair of finals if the edit distance between them is 1 or 2. Since the length of finals on average is two, an edit distance of three means a complete change to the final, resulting in pairs with the lowest similarity. To compare finals across clusters, since the edit distance between any such pair is at least two, we compare pairs only when the length of the common sequence is at least two (for example, "ian" and "uan"), and otherwise assign the lowest possible similarity to the pairs. This drops the number of comparison pairs of finals down to 113.

After generating the comparison pairs, we create word pairs whose Pinyins only differ in the these pairs. We identify and account for several confounding factors that may affect annotation: 1) the position of the character containing the initial or final being compared; 2) the word length; and 3) the combination of initials and finals. Since most Chinese words are of length two, we only generate word pairs of length two for this task. Providing word pairs of length greater than two would not make much difference to learned encodings as long as word pairs are representative.

For a given initial (or final) pair (p_1, p_2), such as (b, p), we first generate the all possible Pinyins with a component of p_1 such as *bao* and *bing*. For each Pinyin *py*, we retrieve all the words with length two in the dictionary which also have first or second character with the same *py*. Example words for *py*="*bao*" include 包bao1袱fu2. For each created word w, we change the initial (or final) from p_1 to p_2, retrieve the corresponding words from the dictionary and generate the word pairs to compare. One such example is (包bao1袱fu2, 泡pao4芙fu2). Finally, from the full list we randomly select five word pairs that vary the first character, and five word pairs that vary the second character.

We invite three native Chinese speakers to perform the annotations. For each word pair, the annotators give a label on a 7 point scale representing their agreement, where the labels range from 'Completely Disagree' (1) to 'Completely Agree' (7). We calculate Krippendorff's α (Hayes and Krippendorff, 2007) for the initials and finals annotations to be 0.69 and 0.54, representing the inter-annotator agreement. For each word pair, we use Equation 2 to calculate the distance θ with the average value ϕ of labels across the annotators. Equation 2 inverts the labels so that the output can be used as a distance metric (phonetically similar initials or finals are closer together), and scales the

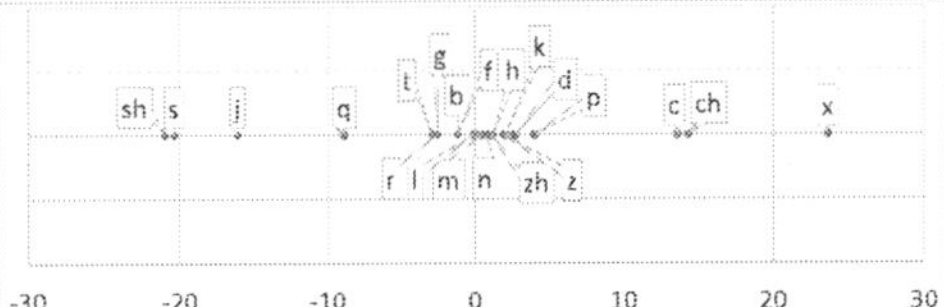

Figure 3: Learned initial encodings, n=1.

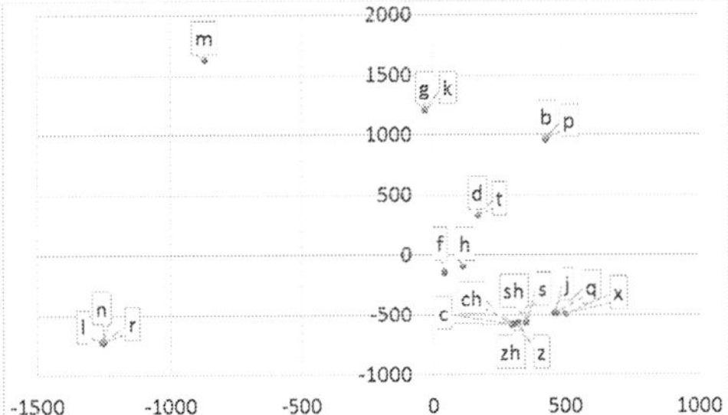

Figure 4: Learned initial encodings, n=2.

result to more accurately measure phonetic similarities. The parameters a and b are set 4 and 10^4 by default, but we also show that the performance of our method is not sensitive to the parameter settings (see Section 3.2).

$$\theta(\phi) = 1/a^\phi * b \qquad (2)$$

2.3.2 Learning Model

Once the average distances between pairs are computed from the annotated data sets, we define a constrained optimization to compute encodings of the initials and finals. The final goal is to map each initial (or final) to an n-dimensional point.

The distance S_p of a pair p of points $(x_1, x_2, ..., x_n), (y_1, y_2, ..., y_n)$ is calculated using Euclidean distance as shown in equation 3.

$$S_p = \sqrt{\sum_{1 \leq i \leq n} (x_i - y_i)^2} \qquad (3)$$

The model aims to minimize the sum of the absolute differences between the Euclidean distances of component pairs and the average distances obtained from the annotated training data across all pairs for initials (or finals) C. We also incorporate a penalty function, τ_p, for pairs deviating from the manually annotated distance θ so that more phonetically similar pairs are penalized more highly (we discuss τ further in Section 3.2). Equation 4 represents the cost function:

$$min \sum_{p \in C} |S_p^2 - \theta_p^2| * \tau_p \qquad (4)$$

One main advantage of our learning model is that it is generic and can easily extend to any n-dimensional space. Based on the structured of Table 2, we intuit that extending beyond one dimension will yield more accurate encodings. Figures 3 and 4 visualize the computed encodings of initials when setting n=1 and n=2 We see that when $n = 2$, the locations of initial coordinates align well with Table 2,. In particular, the twelve groups are clustered in a pattern that is defined in Section 2.3.1. For example, "bp,gk,jqx" are separated into different clusters. However, while Table 2 indicated the basic clusters for the initials, our learned model goes further than Table 2 by actually quantifying the inter- and intra-cluster similarities. Specifically, clusters "c, ch, j, q, x" are tighter than clusters "c, c, h" and "d, t", whereas the clusters "m" and "n, r, l" are well separated from other clusters. Interestingly, the learning algorithms organically discovers new clusters that are not reflected in Table 2; namely that "r,n" and "r,l" are pairs of phonetically similar initials.

When $n = 1$, the learned model collapses the coordinates into one dimension (Figure 3). We observe that the predefined clusters are not well aligned, and many clusters are mixed together (e.g., "bp,gk,nl,dt"), preventing DIMSIM from considering variations within a cluster to be more similar than variations between clusters. Visually comparing Figures 3 and 4 gives the intuition for why DIMSIM with $n = 2$ performs better than DIMSIM with $n = 1$, which is in turn reflected in our evaluation results. Section 3 presents the effects that varying the number of dimensions has on evaluation results.

2.4 Phonetic Tone Similarity

There are five tones in Chinese, represented by a *tone number scale* ranging from 1 to 5. It is simple to use tone numbers for tone encodings and the difference between the tones of two Pinyins as the raw measure of distance, ranging in value from 1 to 5 (e.g., $S_T(xue2, xue4) = 4 - 2 = 2$). One exception is that we encode tone 3 as the numerical value of 2.5 since tone 3 is more similar to tone 2 compared to tone 4 according to the relative pitch changes of the four tones (ISO, 2015). However, this measure must first be scaled to be comparable to the pairwise phonetic distances of initials and finals. There is an additional constraint: any pairwise difference in initials or finals must have

Input : $Word\ w, Threshold\ th, Dict\ dict$;
Output: $Words\ outws$;
begin

   $pys =$ `getPinyins` $(w,dict)$;
   $headPys =$
    `getSimPinyins`$(pys(0), th)$;
   $headWords =$
   `getWordswithHeadPy`$(headPys, dict)$;
   for $cw \in headWords$ **do**
     if $cw.size \neq w.size$ **then**
      | $continue$;
     end
     $sim =$ `getSimilarity` (cw,w);
     if $sim \leq th$ **then**
      | $outws.add(cw)$;
     end
   end
   `sortByAscSim` $(outws)$;
   $return\ outws$;
end

Algorithm 1: Generating phonetic candidates.

a greater negative effect on the phonetic similarity between characters than any difference in tones. For example, $S(xue1,lue1) < S(xue1,xue5)$ even though $xue1$ and $xue5$ are at opposite ends of the tone scale. We therefore scale S_T such that $Max(S_T) < Min(S_p)$.

2.5 Candidate Generation and Ranking

Having determined the phonetic encodings and the mechanism to compute the phonetic similarity using learned phonetic encodings, we now describe how to generate and rank similar candidates in Algorithm 1. Given a word w, a similarity threshold th, and a Chinese Pinyin dictionary $dict$, we retrieve the Pinyin py of w from $dict$. We derive a list of Pinyins Pys whose similarity to py falls within the threshold th. These are used to generate a list of words with the same Pinyin in Pys and the same number of characters as w. We calculate the similarity of each candidate word with w using Equation 1 and filter out candidates that fall outside the similarity threshold th. Thus, th is a parameter that affects the precision and recall of the generated candidates. A larger th generates more candidates, increasing recall while decreasing precision.[3] Finally, we output the candidates ranked in ascending order by similarity distance.

---

[3] We study the impact of varying th in Section 3.

3 Evaluation

We collect 350 words from social media (Wu, 2016), and annotate each with 1-3 phonetically similar words. We use a community-maintained free dictionary to map characters to Pinyins (CEDict, 2016). We compare DIMSIM with Double Metaphone (DM) (Philips, 2000), ALINE (Kondrak, 2003) and Minimum edit distance (MED) (Navarro, 2001) in terms of precision (P), recall (R), and average Mean Reciprocal Rank (MRR) (Voorhees and et al., 1999). We calculate recall automatically using the the full test set of word pairs (Wu, 2016). Since downstream applications will only consider a limited number of candidates in practice, we evaluate precision via a manual annotation task on the top-ranked candidates generated by each approach. DM considers word spelling, pronunciation and other miscellaneous characteristics to encode the word into a primary and a secondary code. DM as one of the baselines is known to perform poorly at ranking the candidates (Carstensen, 2005) since only two codes are used. We therefore use our method (Equation 1) to rank the DM-generated candidates, to create a second baseline, DM-rank.[4] The third baseline, ALINE, measures phonetic similarity based on manually coded multi-valued articulatory features weighted by their relative importance with respect to feature salience (again, manually determined). MED, the last baseline, computes similarity as the minimum-weight series of edit operations that transforms one sound component into another.

3.1 The Effectiveness of DIMSIM

Recall and MRR: We compare DIMSIM to DM, DM-rank, ALINE and MED. DIMSIM1 and DIM-SIM2 denotes DIMSIM encoding dimension $n = 1$ and $n = 2$, respectively. As shown in Figure 5, DIMSIM2 improves recall by factors of 1.5, 1.5, 1.3 and 1.2, and improves MRR by factors of 7.5, 1.4, 1.03 and 1.2 over DM, DM-Rank, ALINE and MED, respectively. DM performs relatively poorly, as it is designed for English, and does not accurately reflect Chinese pronunciation. Ranking DM candidates using the DIMSIM phonetic distance defined in Equation 1 improves its average MRR by a factor of 5.5. However, even DM-Rank is outperformed by the simple MED

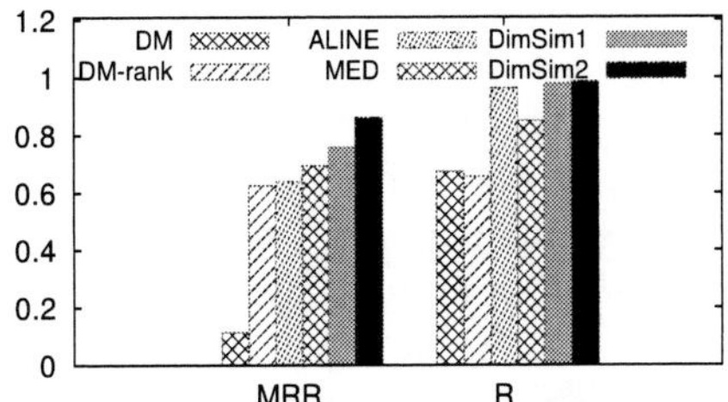

Figure 5: Recall and MRR.

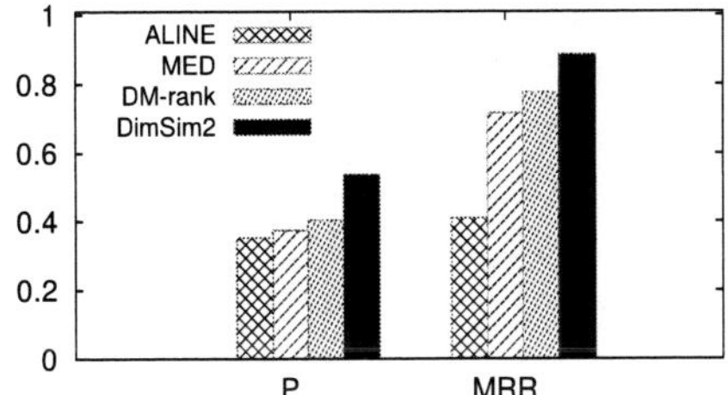

Figure 6: Precision and MRR.

baseline, demonstrating the inherent problem with DM's coarse encodings. While ALINE has a similar recall to DIMSIM, it performs worse on MRR than DIMSIM2 because it does not have a direct representation of compound vowels for Pinyin. It measures distance between compound vowels using phonetic features of basic vowels which leads to inaccuracy. In turn, MED struggles with representing accurate phonetic distances between initials, since most initials are of length 1, and the edit distance between any two characters of length 1 is identical. In contrast, DIMSIM encodes initials and finals separately, and thus even a 1-dimensional encoding (DIMSIM1) outperforms the other baselines. Finally, the intuition of Figures 3 and 4 is reflected in the data, as DIMSIM2 outperforms DIMSIM1 by 14% (MRR).

Precision and MRR: Here we evaluate the quality of the candidate ranking since in practice, downstream applications consider only a small number of possible candidates for every word. We ask two native Chinese speakers to annotate the quality of the generated candidates. Choosing 100 words randomly from the test set, we use DM-rank, MED, ALINE and DIMSIM2 to generate top-K candidates for each seed word ($K = 5$).[5] The annotators mark each candidate as phonetically similar to the seed word (1) or not (0), also marking the one candidate they believe to be the most similar-sounding (2), which may be any of

---

[4]We do not compare with Soundex as DM is accepted to be an improved phonetic similarity algorithm over Soundex.

[5]We do not evaluate DM and DIMSIM1 as they perform worse than DM-Rank and DIMSIM2, respectively.

the top-K candidates. We then compute precision and average MRR using the obtained annotations. We achieve inter-level agreement(ILA) of 0.75 for P and ILA of 0.84 for average MRR. DIMSIM once again outperforms MED and DM-Rank by up to $1.4X$ for precision and $1.24X$ for MRR. Since the only criteria for picking the best top-K candidate is phonetic similarity, this demonstrates that DIMSIM ranks the most phonetically similar candidates higher than the other baselines.

$\tau(\phi)$ \\ $\theta(\phi)$	$1/2^\phi$ $*10^2$	$1/4^\phi$ $*10^4$	$1/\phi^2$ $*10^2$	$1/\phi^4$ $*10^3$
None	F10	F20	F30	F40
2^ϕ	F11	F21	...	...
4^ϕ	F12	F22	..	..
ϕ^2	..	..	F33	F34
ϕ^4	..	..	F43	F44

Table 4: Variations of θ, τ.

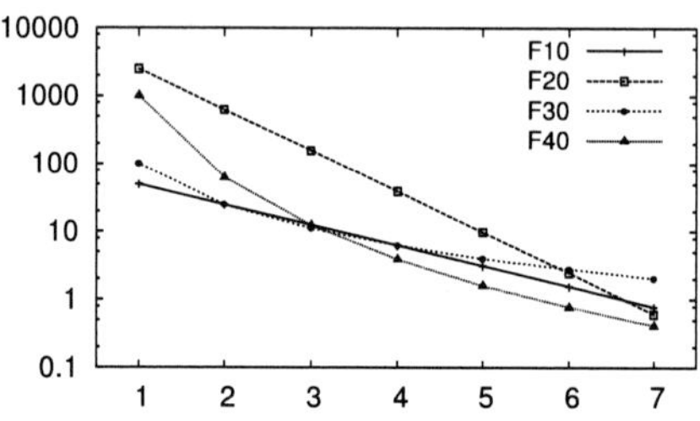

Figure 7: Distance by θ.

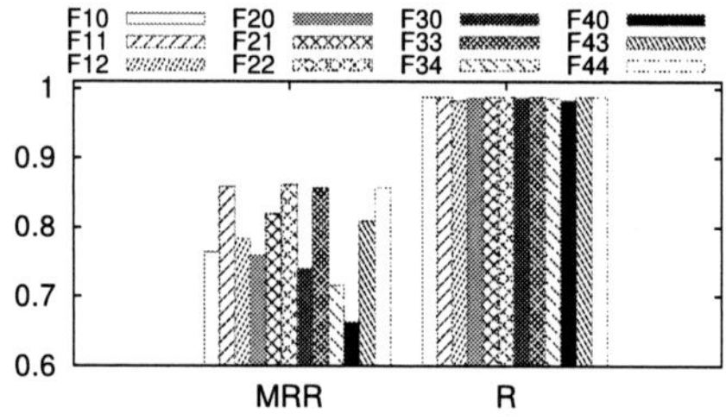

Figure 8: Impact of varying θ, τ.

3.2 Impact of Scoring and Penalty Functions

We study the sensitivity of DIMSIM to varying the scoring and penalty functions, using recall and average MRR for evaluation. Table 4 shows four different scoring functions θ and penalty functions τ (including the variation of not using a penalty

function) to convert the annotator scores ϕ to pairwise distances S, following Equation 4.

Figure 7 depicts the values of the four scoring functions θ as a function of the annotator scores on a log 10 scale, to demonstrate the effect of varying a and b, as well as using ϕ as the base or exponent. Figure 8 demonstrates how sensitive our model is to the different combinations of scoring and penalty functions. We see that although Recall is entirely insensitive to the variations, the performance of MRR is impacted. There is a clear preference for the variations on the "diagonal" of Table 4: F11, F22, F33, F44, but the near-identical performance of these variations demonstrates DIMSIM's robustness to the particular scoring and penalty functions used. Note that not using a penalty function impacts MRR significantly.

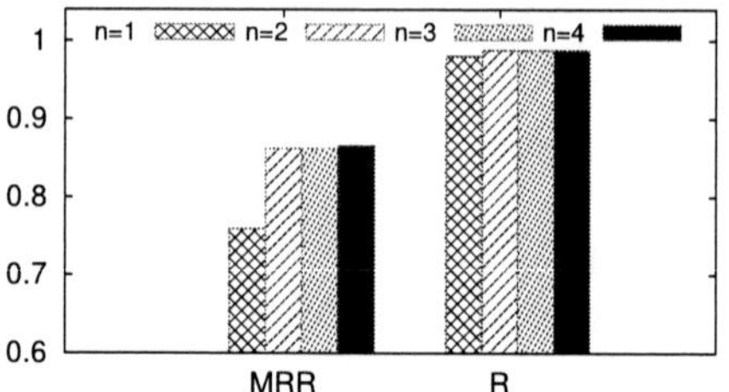

Figure 9: Impact of varying n.

3.3 Impact of the Encoding Dimensions

As demonstrated above, encoding initials and finals into a two-dimensional space is more effective than a one-dimensional space. Figure 9 presents the results of continuing to increase the number of dimensions, $n = [1, 4]$. We observe that recall is barely affected, with all variations able to successfully identify the targeted words 98% to 99% of the time. We also see that moving from n=1 to n=2 increases the average MRR by $1.14X$. However, further increasing the number of dimensions to n>2 no longer improves average MRR, indicating that learning a two-dimensional encoding is enough to capture the phonetic relationships between Pinyin components.

3.4 Impact of the Distance Threshold

We examine how the similarity distance threshold (th) impacts DIMSIM by varying th from 2 to 4096 (Figure 10) (using the scoring function F22). As th increases, recall increases from 0.75 to 0.99, converging when th reaches 2048. By increasing th DIMSIM matches more characters that are simi-

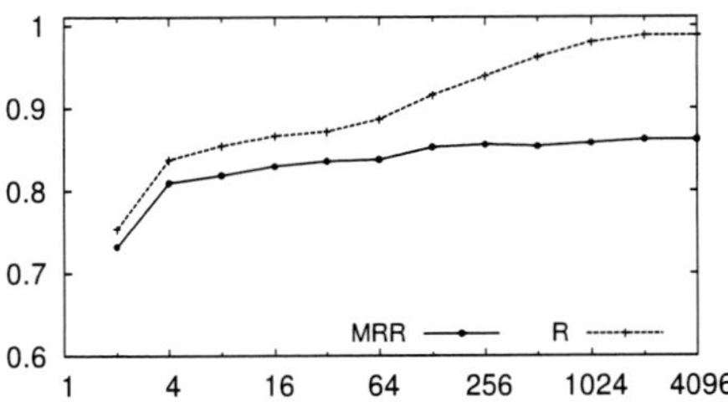

Figure 10: Impact of varying th.

lar to the first character of the given word, which in turn increases the number of candidates within the distance. Thus, the probability of including the labeled gold standard words in the results increases. MMR is less sensitive to th, converging when th reaches 128. However, the generated set of candidate words is reduced too much for $th < 128$, hurting the performance of MMR. To ensure both high recall and MRR we set $th = 2500$.

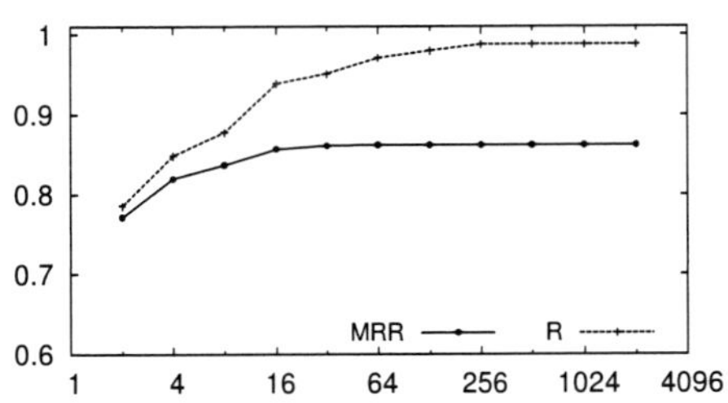

Figure 11: Varying candidate n_c.

3.5 Impact of Number of Candidates

While generating more candidates improves the recall, presenting too many candidates to a downstream application is not desirable. To find a balance, we study the impact of varying the upper limit of the number of generated candidates n_c from 2 to 2048 (Figure 11). We find that MRR converges at 64 candidates, while recall takes longer; however, setting the upper limit at 64 candidates already achieves almost 98% recall, suggesting it as a reasonable cutoff in practice. Unless otherwise mentioned, we set $n_c = 1,000$ for experiments, to isolate the impact of this parameter.

3.6 Error Analysis

We analyze and summarize three types of errors made by DIMSIM. The first occurs when targeted words are out of vocabulary(OOV). For instance, for the original word "药丸", the targed word is "要完" which is OOV. As is commonly the case in text normalization applications which convert informal language to well-formed terms, our method works as long as the targeted words are in the dictionary. This shortcoming is generally alleviated by adding new terms to the dictionary. Second, DIMSIM cannot derive phonetic candidates from dialects that are not encoded in our mapping table. For example, for "冻($dong4$)蒜($suan4$)", the targeted word "当($dang1$)选($xuan2$)" is obtained using the pronunciation of southern Fujian dialect. However, our approach can easily be extended to incorporate and capture such variants by learning mapping tables for each dialect and using them to generate corresponding candidates. Finally, we constrain DIMSIM to not identify candidates that differ in length from the seed word, as we observe that most transcriptions have the same word length - though some corner cases do occur.

4 Related Work

There is a plethora of work focusing on the phonetic similarities between words and characters (Archives and Administration, 2007; Mokotoff, 1997; Taft, 1970; Philips, 1990, 2000; Elsner et al., 2013). These algorithms encode words with similar pronunciation into the same code. For example, Soundex (Archives and Administration, 2007) converts words into fixed length code through a mapping table of initial groups to ordinal numbers. These algorithms fail to capture Chinese phonetic similarity since the conversion rules do not consider pronunciation properties of Pinyin. Linguists in the phonetic and phonology community have also proposed several phonetic comparison algorithms (Kessler, 2005; Mak and Barnard, 1996; Nerbonne and Heeringa, 1997; Ladefoged, 1969; Kondrak, 2003) for determining the similarity between speech forms. However, as features of articulatory phonetics are manually assigned, these algorithms fall short in capturing the perceptual essence of phonetic similarity through empirical data (Kessler, 2005). In contrast, DIMSIM achieves high accuracy by learning the encodings both from high quality training data sets and linguistic Pinyin features.

Several works in Named Entity translation (Lin and Chen, 2002; Lam et al., 2004; Kuo et al., 2007; Chung et al., 2011) focus on learning the phonetic similarity between English and Chinese automatically. These approaches first represent English and

451

Chinese words in basic phoneme units and apply edit distance algorithms to compute the similarity. Training frameworks are then used to learn the similarity. However, the phonetic similarity used in these systems cannot be applied to Chinese words since Pinyin has its own specific characteristics, which do not easily map to English, for determining phonetic similarity. Another main application of phonetic similarity algorithms is text normalization (Xia et al., 2006; Li et al., 2003; Han et al., 2012; Sonmez and Ozgur, 2014; Qian et al., 2015), where phonetic similarity is measured by a combination of initial and final similarities. However, the encodings used in these approaches are too coarse-grained, yielding low F1 measures. DIMSIM learns separate high dimensional encodings for initials and finals, and uses them to calculate and rank the distances between Pinyin representations of Chinese word pairs. Karl Stratos (Stratos, 2017) proposes a sub-character architecture to deal with the data sparsity problem in Korean language processing by breaking down each Korean character into a small set of primitive phonetic units. However, this work does not address the problem of the phonetic similarity and is thus orthogonal to DIMSIM.

5   Conclusion

Motivated by phonetic transcription as a widely observed phenomenon in Chinese social media and informal language, we have designed an accurate phonetic similarity algorithm. DIMSIM generates phonetically similar candidate words based on learned encodings that capture the pronunciation characteristics of Pinyin initial, final, and tone components. Using a real world dataset, we demonstrate that DIMSIM effectively improves MRR by $7.5X$, recall by $1.5X$ and precision by $1.4X$ over existing approaches.

The original motivation for this work was to improve the quality of downstream NLP tasks, such as named entity identification, text normalization and spelling correction. These tasks all share a dependency on reliable phonetic similarity as an intermediate step, especially for languages such as Chinese where incorrect homophones and synophones abound. We therefore plan to extend this line of work by applying DIMSIM to downstream applications, such as text normalization.

References

National Archives and Records Administration. 2007. The Soundex Indexing System. `https://www.archives.gov/research/census/soundex.html`.

Adam Carstensen. 2005. An Introduction to Double Metaphone and the Principles Behind Soundex. `http://www.b-eye-network.com/view/1596`.

CEDict. 2016. CC-CEDICT. `https://www.mdbg.net/chindict/chindict.php?page=cc-cedict`.

Jen-Ming Chung, Fu-Yuan Hsu, Cheng-Yu Lu, Hahn-Ming Lee, and Jan-Ming Ho. 2011. Automatic english-chinese name translation by using web-mining and phonetic similarity. In *IEEE International Conference on Information Reuse and Integration*, pages 283–287.

Micha Elsner, Sharon Goldwater, Naomi Feldman, and Frank Wood. 2013. A joint learning model of word segmentation, lexical acquisition, and phonetic variability. In *Proc. EMNLP*.

Bo Han, Paul Cook, and Timothy Baldwin. 2012. Automatically constructing a normalisation dictionary for microblogs. In *Proc. of the joint conference on EMNLP and CoNLL*, pages 421–432. ACL.

Andrew F. Hayes and Klaus Krippendorff. 2007. Answering the call for a standard reliability measure for coding data. *Communication Methods and Measures*, 1(1):77–89.

ISO. 2015. ISO 7098: Romanization of Chinese. `https://www.iso.org/standard/61420.html`.

Brett Kessler. 2005. Phonetic comparison algorithms. *Transactions of the Philological Society*, 103(2):243–260.

Grzegorz Kondrak. 2003. Phonetic alignment and similarity. *Computers and the Humanities*, 37(3):273–291.

Jin-Shea Kuo, Haizhou Li, and Ying-Kuei Yang. 2007. A phonetic similarity model for automatic extraction of transliteration pairs. *ACM Transactions on Asian Language Information Processing (TALIP)*, 6(2):6.

Peter Ladefoged. 1969. The measurement of phonetic similarity. In *Proceedings of the 1969 conference on Computational linguistics*, pages 1–14. Association for Computational Linguistics.

Wai Lam, Ruizhang Huang, and Pik-Shan Cheung. 2004. Learning phonetic similarity for matching named entity translations and mining new translations. In *Proc. ACM SIGIR*, pages 289–296.

Chia-ying Lee, Yu Zhang, and James R Glass. 2013. Joint learning of phonetic units and word pronunciations for asr. In *EMNLp*, pages 182–192.

Hong-lian Li, Wei He, and Bao-zong Yuan. 2003. An kind of chinese text strings' similarity and its application in speech recognition. *Journal of Chinese Information Processing*, 17(1):60–64.

Wei-Hao Lin and Hsin-Hsi Chen. 2002. Backward machine transliteration by learning phonetic similarity. In *Proc. CoNLL*, pages 1–7. ACL.

Brian Mak and Etienne Barnard. 1996. Phone clustering using the bhattacharyya distance. In *Spoken Language, 1996. ICSLP 96. Proceedings., Fourth International Conference on*, volume 4, pages 2005–2008. IEEE.

Gary Mokotoff. 1997. Soundexing and genealogy. *Avotaynu*.

Gonzalo Navarro. 2001. A guided tour to approximate string matching. *ACM computing surveys (CSUR)*, 33(1):31–88.

John Nerbonne and Wilbert Heeringa. 1997. Measuring dialect distance phonetically. In *Proceedings of the Third Meeting of the ACL Special Interest Group in Computational Phonology (SIGPHON-97)*.

Lawrence Philips. 1990. Hanging on the metaphone. *Computer Language*, 7(2):6.

Lawrence Philips. 2000. The double metaphone search algorithm. *C/C++ users journal*, 18(6):38–43.

Tao Qian, Yue Zhang, Meishan Zhang, Yafeng Ren, and Dong-Hong Ji. 2015. A transition-based model for joint segmentation, pos-tagging and normalization. In *EMNLP*, pages 1837–1846.

Duanmu San. 2007. *The Phonology of Standard Chinese*. Oxford University Press.

Cagil Sonmez and Arzucan Ozgur. 2014. A graph-based approach for contextual text normalization. In *EMNLP*, pages 313–324.

Karl Stratos. 2017. A sub-character architecture for korean language processing. In *Proceedings of the 2017 Conference on Empirical Methods in Natural Language Processing*, pages 721–726.

Robert L Taft. 1970. *Name search techniques*. 1. Bureau of Systems Development, New York State Identification and Intelligence System.

Kristina Toutanova and Robert C. Moore. 2002. Pronunciation modeling for improved spelling correction. In *Proc. ACL*, ACL '02, pages 144–151, Stroudsburg, PA, USA.

Johannes Twiefel, Timo Baumann, Stefan Heinrich, and Stefan Wermter. 2014. Improving domain-independent cloud-based speech recognition with domain-dependent phonetic post-processing. In *AAAI*, pages 1529–1536.

Ellen M Voorhees and et al. 1999. The trec-8 question answering track report. In *Trec*, volume 99, pages 77–82.

You Wu. 2016. Commonly used phonetic vocabulary. http://www.51wendang.com/doc/97585e99067d692a1bbaec92.

Yunqing Xia, Kam-Fai Wong, and Wenjie Li. 2006. A phonetic-based approach to chinese chat text normalization. In *Proc. ACL*, pages 993–1000.

Mabus Yao. 2015. An algorithm for Chinese Similarity based on phonetic grapheme coding. http://mabusyao.iteye.com/blog/2267661.

Zhishihao. 2017. Differentiating f and h. http://www.zhishihao.com/xue/show/51763.

Challenge or Empower:
Revisiting Argumentation Quality in a News Editorial Corpus

Roxanne El Baff   **Henning Wachsmuth** *   **Khalid Al-Khatib**   **Benno Stein**

Bauhaus-Universität Weimar, Weimar, Germany, <first>{.<last>}⁺@uni-weimar.de

* Paderborn University, Paderborn, Germany, henningw@upb.de

Abstract

News editorials are said to shape public opinion, which makes them a powerful tool and an important source of political argumentation. However, rarely do editorials change anyone's stance on an issue completely, nor do they tend to argue explicitly (but rather follow a subtle rhetorical strategy). So, what does argumentation quality mean for editorials then? We develop the notion that an effective editorial challenges readers with opposing stance, and at the same time empowers the arguing skills of readers that share the editorial's stance — or even challenges both sides. To study argumentation quality based on this notion, we introduce a new corpus with 1000 editorials from the New York Times, annotated for their perceived effect along with the annotators' political orientations. Analyzing the corpus, we find that annotators with different orientation disagree on the effect significantly. While only 1% of all editorials changed anyone's stance, more than 5% meet our notion. We conclude that our corpus serves as a suitable resource for studying the argumentation quality of news editorials.

1 Introduction

A news editorial is an article that argues in favor of a particular stance on a usually timely controversial issue, such as the relocation of the US embassy in Israel to Jerusalem. Usually, it reflects the political ideology of the newspaper, aiming to persuade readers of the respective stance. Such editorials are said to have the power to shape the opinion of the masses. Similarly, they can increase or decrease the gap between readers with opposing beliefs (van Dijk, 1995). As such, news editorials represent an important resource for research on argument mining (Mochales and Moens, 2011) and debating technologies (Rinott et al., 2015).

On the other hand, a single news editorial rarely changes the stance of a reader completely. More-

over, many editorials do not put an explicit focus on arguments. Rather, they follow a subtle rhetorical strategy combining emotional anecdotes with hidden claims and ethotic evidence, among others (Al-Khatib et al., 2017). So, if not persuasive arguments, what makes a news editorial effective or ineffective then? In other words: How can we measure its argumentation quality?

In this paper, we introduce a new corpus with 1000 news editorials from the New York Times where we consider argumentation quality from a dialectical perspective (van Eemeren and Grootendorst, 2004). While several quality dimensions are known in theory (Wachsmuth et al., 2017b), existing approaches rely on subjective assessments of absolute (Persing and Ng, 2015) or relative (Habernal and Gurevych, 2016) persuasiveness. In contrast, our corpus captures quality in terms of whether an editorial brings readers of opposing belief closer together or rather increases the gap between them. We argue that, thereby, we better account for the practically achieved persuasive effect, resulting in a qualitative media measurement analysis of editorials that intrigue our thoughts.

Persuasion, according to Halmari and Virtanen (2005), is an umbrella term for linguistic choices that aim at changing or affecting the behavior of others or at strengthening the existing beliefs of those who already agree, including the persuaders themselves. To study persuasion for editorials, four dimensions must be considered: (1) prior beliefs of readers, (2) prior beliefs and behaviors of authors, (3) effects of the text, and (4) linguistic choices. We account for these dimensions as follows.

Prior Beliefs of Readers Given the focus of news editorials on timely politics, we use the political typology quiz[1] developed by the Pew Research

---

[1]Typology quiz, http://www.people-press.org/quiz/political-typology/

Proceedings of the 22nd Conference on Computational Natural Language Learning (CoNLL 2018), pages 454–464

Brussels, Belgium, October 31 - November 1, 2018. ©2018 Association for Computational Linguistics

Center to measure the prior beliefs of readers. The underlying typology divides Americans into eight political groups, as detailed later on: four largely liberal and four largely conservative ones, along with a ninth group of the politically less engaged.

Prior Beliefs and Behaviors of Authors Each newspaper has its set of beliefs, reflected in particular stances on different controversial issues. To avoid newspaper-related side effects in the study of argumentation quality, we decided to control this dimension by annotating news editorials from one source only. In particular, we resort to the online portal of the New York Times for two practical reasons: (1) The political typology quiz is tailored to people from the United States. (2) A large source of news editorials and detailed metadata is already available (Sandhaus, 2008).

Effects of the Persuasive Text We tackle the outlined dialectical view of argumentation quality by asking annotators about how a given news editorial affected them: If you have a different stance than the editorial, did it *challenge* you, making you rethink your stance? Or, if you have the same stance, did it *empower* you, enabling you to better defend your stance? We postulate that high-quality argumentation challenges one side and empowers the other side at the same time, and we hypothesize that this notion allows distinguishing effective and ineffective editorials regardless of the annotators' stance. We analyze the corpus in order to investigate this hypothesis in comparison to classical approaches asking for persuasion.

Linguistic Choices Our goal is to provide a resource for studying the quality of editorial argumentation and their underlying rhetorical strategies. Accordingly, we leave an analysis of the linguistic features impacting quality to future research.

The contribution of this paper is three-fold:

- We propose a new notion of argumentation quality for news editorials based on how challenging and empowering an editorial is for readers with opposing stances.
- We create a freely available corpus[2] with quality assessments of 1000 news editorials, each annotated by three liberals and three conservatives. The annotators also reported free-text reasons for the effects they observed.

---

[2]Webis-Editorial-Quality-18 corpus, available at `http://www.webis.de/data`

- We analyze the corpus, finding that more than 5% of all editorials fulfill our notion of high quality, whereas only 1% really persuaded any annotator. As expected, annotators agree only when sharing similar prior beliefs.

2 Related Work

Computational argumentation has lately become popular in the natural language processing community. So far, most computational argumentation research deals with the mining of arguments from text (Mochales and Moens, 2011). Accordingly, many studied corpora capture argument structure, often for a specific text genre, such as persuasive essays (Stab and Gurevych, 2014), Wikipedia articles (Levy et al., 2014), or even pure arguments (Peldszus and Stede, 2015). These genres share that they make claims and reasons explicit, i.e., they argue rationally. In contrast, real-world argumentation related to politics often comprises more sophisticated mechanisms, bringing together logical arguments (Johnson and Blair, 2006) with rhetorical means (Aristotle, translated 2007) and dialectic (van Eemeren and Grootendorst, 2004). A typical genre of such kind is *news editorials*.

As outlined in Section 1, news editorials are opinionated articles that aim to persuade their readers of a stance towards some controversial issue, usually with implicit, hidden strategies (van Dijk, 1995). Editorials have been used for opinion mining and retrieval in some works (Yu and Hatzivassiloglou, 2003; Bal, 2009), partly towards analyzing argumentation (Bal and Dizier, 2010; Kiesel et al., 2015). To our knowledge, the only corpus of noteworthy size that exists for studying editorial argumentation explicitly is the one of Al-Khatib et al. (2016) who segmented 300 editorials into argumentative discourse units of different claim and evidence types.

Al-Khatib et al. (2017) trained classifiers on their corpus and applied them to 28,986 editorials from the New York Times Annotated Corpus (Sandhaus, 2008). They found topic-specific evidence type patterns, which appear to be related to persuasive strategies. However, editorial-level annotations are missing that actually connect the patterns to persuasiveness. For blog posts and forum discussions respectively, previous work has annotated persuasive acts (Anand et al., 2011) and the use of Aristotle's rhetorical means (Hidey et al., 2017). Still, this would not allow distinguishing effective from ineffective strategies. We fill this gap by presenting the first editorial corpus with persuasion-related annotations of *argumentation quality*. To obtain a larger corpus size, we rely on the editorials from Sandhaus (2008) rather than those from Al-Khatib et al. (2016). Potash et al. (2017) observe bias in existing corpora towards higher quality for longer arguments. To prevent such bias, we consider only editorials from a narrow length range.

Research on argumentation quality has recently been surveyed by Wachsmuth et al. (2017b). The authors developed a taxonomy with one main aspect each for logical (*cogency*), rhetorical (*effectiveness*), and dialectical quality (*reasonableness*), as well as several concrete quality dimensions. Effectiveness reflects to what extent an author persuades a reader, and reasonableness reflects an argument's contribution to agreement. As detailed in Section 3, the dimension we propose is meant to measure persuasive effectiveness, yet, from a dialectical perspective, which is more suitable for editorials. We hypothesize it to be related to the acceptability of arguments (Cabrio and Villata, 2012) and the helpfulness of argumentation (Liu et al., 2017).

While Louis and Nenkova (2013) study the general quality of news articles, our goal is to provide a basis for studying their argumentation quality more objectively. Some existing computational approaches to assessing argumentation quality rely on human persuasiveness ratings of essays (Persing and Ng, 2015; Wachsmuth et al., 2016) or debate portal arguments (Persing and Ng, 2017). The problem here is that persuasiveness is subjective by heart, underlined by the low inter-annotator agreement for effectiveness in the corpus of Wachsmuth et al. (2017b): effectiveness depends on the prior stance of the annotator.

Habernal and Gurevych (2016) compare the convincingness of arguments with only one stance on a given issue, which circumvents the problem, but does not help for actual persuasion. While Tan et al. (2016) analyze how people are persuaded by others with opposing stance, they restrict their view to good-faith discussions (where people are open to be persuaded) — a setting not common for political argumentation. Instead, we tackle subjectiveness by letting people with both stances on a discussed issue annotate quality.

Cano-Basave and He (2016) point out that persuasive argumentation is about both changing and reinforcing stance — a view that we follow. The

authors study the impact of persuasive language of political debates based on poll changes. Such a direct effect on different audiences is not accessible for most argumentative texts, including editorials. Persuasiveness does not only depend on a text itself, but also on the reader's beliefs and personality. Lukin et al. (2017) find that different types of arguments (rational vs. emotional) are effective depending on the "Big Five" personality traits (Goldberg, 1990). We captured our annotators' personality traits, too. However, we primarily focus on nine political profiles from left to right (Doherty et al., 2017) in order to represent prior stance. We are not aware of any previous work in computational argumentation considering such profiles so far.

3   A New Model of Argumentation Quality for News Editorials

We propose a model that quantifies the argumentation quality of an editorial at the discourse level. Two dimensions of persuasion are considered to this end: the *prior beliefs of the reader* and the *effect of the text*. Regarding the former, readers are profiled based on a political typology. Regarding the latter, we annotate an editorial's capability to either (1) challenge or to (2) reinforce a reader's stance; we also consider the magnitude of the effect. Based on the annotations, for which we consider a set of annotators belonging to at least two spectrums of beliefs (three annotators for each), the quality of an editorial can be assessed.

3.1   Prior Beliefs of a Reader

The existing beliefs of the reader of an editorial are a crucial factor when measuring the editorial's argumentation quality. Theoretically, it would be best to consider two reader groups for each editorial that have an opposite stance on the concrete issue discussed in the editorial. Practically, finding such readers for a considerable number of editorials is hardly feasible, because the reader's stance on the issue is not accessible beforehand.

As a proxy, we therefore decided to model the reader's prior beliefs by identifying the reader's political ideology. In particular, we profile the reader as being *liberal* or *conservative* based on the nine groups of the political typology developed by the PEW Research Center. The typology includes four groups that belong to the liberal ideology and four that belong to the conservative ideology:[3]

---

[3]The ninth rather small group is the *bystanders*, which we

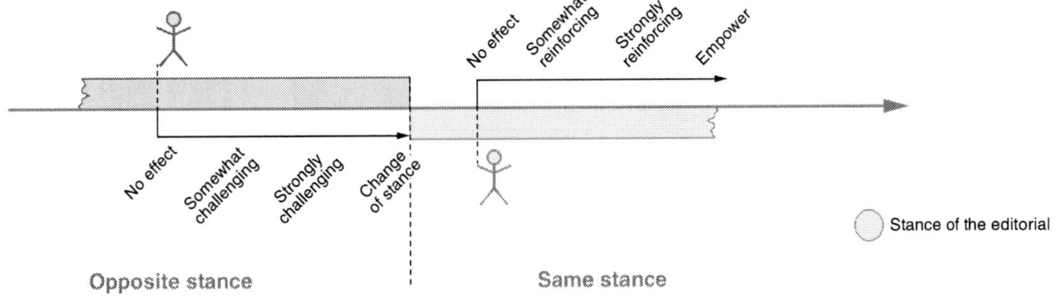

Figure 1: Illustration of potential effects of a news editorial on readers from two belief groups: Those whose prior stance matches the stance of the editorial on the discussed issue, and those whose prior stance opposes it.

Liberal Ideologies *solid liberals*, *opportunity democrats*, *disaffected democrats*, and *devout and diverse*.

Conservative Ideologies *core conservatives*, *country first conservatives*, *market skeptic republicans*, and *new era enterprisers*.

3.2 Effect of the Text

We measure the effect of a news editorial along two characteristics: how *challenging* and how *reinforcing* the editorial is. An editorial is challenging, if it makes the reader rethink his or her prior stance on the discussed issue, even though he or she may not change the stance in the end. On the other hand, an editorial is reinforcing, if it helps the reader in building or further corroborating his or her prior stance on the discussed topic. To capture the magnitude of the effect of the editorial's text, we consider the following labels:

- *Strongly challenging:* The editorial made the reader really rethink whether and why he/she thinks that his/her prior stance is right.

- *Somewhat challenging:* The editorial conveyed at least some information opposite to the reader's stance that was new and noteworthy for him/her.

- *No effect:* The reader did not find any new and noteworthy information opposing or supporting his/her prior stance.

- *Somewhat reinforcing:* The editorial conveyed at least some information supporting the reader's stance that was new and noteworthy for him/her.

- *Strongly reinforcing:* The editorial enabled the reader to argue really better for his/her stance.

The ultimate goal of a news editorial is to *change the stance* of readers with an opposite prior stance. An editorial may reach this effect in case it strongly challenges the reader. On the other hand, in case a reader already has the same stance as the editorial, then the ultimate goal of a news editorial is to *empower the reader* to argue better for his or her stance on the discussed issue. Analog to the previous case, an editorial may have this effect in case it strongly reinforces the stance of the reader. The potential effects on readers from opposing belief groups are visually illustrated in Figure 1.

3.3 Editorial Argumentation Quality

We argue that the argumentation quality of a news editorial is governed by two factors: (1) whether the news editorial increases or decreases the gap between readers with opposing beliefs (van Dijk, 1995) and (2) whether the news editorial presents new and/or persuasive argumentation.

Having the effect labels assigned by readers of opposing belief groups A and B, we follow the dialectical perspective outlined in Section 1 to interpret the argumentation quality of each possible combination *A & B* of labels as follows:

- *Challenging & Challenging:* The editorial challenges the stance of both groups. This suggests that it comprises new and noteworthy argumentation for understanding each other's stance. We see this as an indicator of high quality, since it helps bringing the two groups closer together.

- *Challenging & Reinforcing:* The editorial challenges the stance of one group and reinforces the stance of the other. This suggests

---

ignore, since it represents those people that are considered not involved in what is happening in politics. About 8% of the American population are supposed to be bystanders.

| | Group A | | |
	Challenging	*Reinforcing*	*No Effect*
Challenging	**High quality.** Brings groups closer together. New and persuasive argumentation.	**High quality.** Helps agreeing on one stance. New and persuasive argumentation.	**Medium quality.** Helps agreeing on one stance. Persuasive argumentation.
Reinforcing		**Medium quality.** New argumentation.	**Rather low quality.** Increase the gap between the groups. New argumentation.
No Effect			**Low quality.** Neither new nor persuasive.

Table 1: Interpretation of the combined effects and quality of a news editorial for two groups with opposing beliefs.

that it comprises new and persuasive argumentation in favor of one stance. We see this as an indicator of high quality, too, since it does not only help the two groups agree on the same stance, but also further supports that stance.

- *Challenging & No Effect:* The editorial challenges the stance of one group but does not affect the other. This suggests that it comprises persuasive but not fully new argumentation in favor of one stance. We see this as an indicator of medium quality, since it at least helps the two groups agree on the same stance.

- *Reinforcing & Reinforcing:* The editorial reinforces the stance of both groups. This suggests that it comprises new and noteworthy argumentation for clarifying the two possible stances. We see this as an indicator of medium quality, since it at least provides new insights into the discussed issue.

- *Reinforcing & No Effect:* The editorial reinforces the stance of one group but does not affect the other. This suggests that it comprises new but not fully persuasive argumentation in favor of one stance. We see this as an indicator of rather low quality, since it increases the gap between the two groups.

- *No Effect & No Effect:* The news editorial does not affect either group. This suggests that it comprises neither new nor persuasive argumentation. We see this as an indicator of low quality, since it makes the need for the editorial questionable.

Table 1 summarizes our interpretation of the effects and their quality for each combination.

4 Corpus Construction

Based on the model from Section 3, we conducted an annotation study to build a new corpus for studying the argumentation quality of news editorials. This section describes how editorials were acquired, sampled, and annotated. Furthermore, it presents an overview of the resulting corpus.

4.1 Editorial Acquisition and Sampling

As mentioned before, we decided to restrict our study to editorials from a single news portal (The New York Times), in order to exclude the portal impact on the quality assessment. Particularly, we used the New York Times Annotated Corpus (Sandhaus, 2008), which comprises around 1.8 million news articles written between 1987 and 2007. Each of these articles comes with 27 metadata tags capturing the article's type, topic, author, etc.

To identify news editorials, we used the tags *descriptor* and *taxonomic classifiers* with the values 'Opinion' and 'Editorial'. To maximize recency, we considered those written between 2005 and 2007 only. This resulted in 2556 editorials with a mean length of 492 words. To control the length, we left out short editorials (< 450 words) and long ones (> 650 words), ending up with 1022 editorials. We randomly selected five of these for the pilot study and 1000 for the main one.

4.2 Editorial Annotations

Carrying out the task of annotating all editorials in our corpus was divided into three phases: (1) the selection of annotators, (2) a pilot study, and (3) the main annotation. After discussing the annotation task, we explain the three phases in detail.

Annotation Task As shown in Table 2, we asked our annotators to assess the effect of each editorial's content along the five labels from Section 3 as well as a potential empowering or change of stance. Given an editorial, an annotator should first read its text carefully and then answer the question 'How did the news editorial affect you?' (question

#	Questions	Answers
1	How did the news editorial affect you?	a. It strongly challenged my stance b. It somewhat challenged my stance c. It neither challenged nor reinforced my stance d. It somewhat reinforced my stance e. It strongly reinforced my stance
1a	Did the editorial actually change your stance on the discussed issue (from pro to con, or vice versa)?	Yes / No
1e	Did the editorial empower you to better argue for your stance?	Yes / No
2	Explain your choice(s) (Keep it short)	*Free text*

Table 2: The questions that our annotators had to answer after reading each news editorial. Only in case option *a* was chosen for question 1, question 1a was asked. Accordingly, only in case option *e* was chosen for question 1, question 1e was asked. In any case, the annotator was asked to explain his or her answers (question 2).

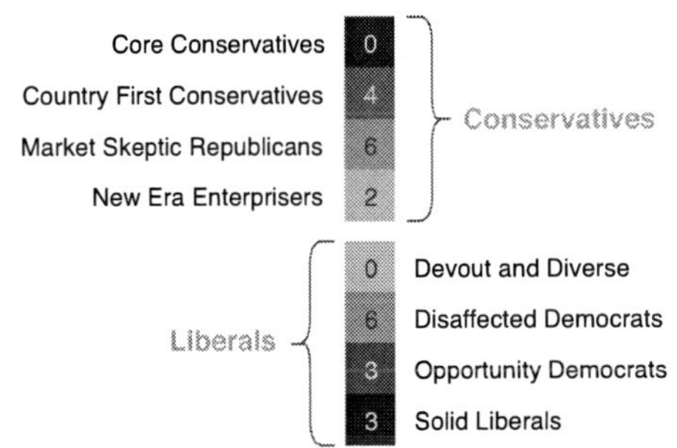

Figure 2: The distribution of the 24 selected annotators over the eight considered political ideologies.

1). The possible answers ranged from *strongly challenging* to *strongly reinforcing*. In case the answer was *strongly challenging*, we asked whether it actually changed his or her stance (question 1a). In case the answer was *strongly reinforcing*, we asked whether it actually empowered him or her to argue better about the topic (question 1e). Finally, the annotator should briefly explain the rationale of his or her choice(s) (question 2).

Selection of Annotators We recruited native English speakers from the United States with at least a bachelor's degree via *upwork.com*. We asked them to do the PEW political typology quiz and to report their results. 40 candidates were recruited until we had both 12 annotators with liberal ideology and 12 with conservative ideology. Figure 2 illustrates the distribution of annotators over the possible political ideologies. The annotators within each group, liberals or conservatives, were selected randomly.

Pilot study We conducted a pilot study with five randomly chosen news editorials in order to check whether our annotation guidelines were clear, consistent, and understood by the annotators. We randomly selected three liberals (one *solid liberal*

and two *disaffected democrats*) and three conservatives (one *core conservative, market skeptic republican*, and *new era enterpriser* each) to annotate all five editorials. We solicited the annotators to give a feedback about the guidelines and the process. All six annotators reported that the guidelines were easy to follow and easy to understand. Also, they gave some suggestions which we followed by rephrasing some questions in the guidelines.

Main Annotation We divided the sampled 1000 news editorials into four batches of size 250. Each batch was assigned to six annotators based on their political ideology (three liberals and three conservatives). As a result, we obtained 6000 different annotations. To prevent annotators from prejudging an editorial, we kept the source of the editorials as well as their titles hidden. Thereby, we focused on the editorial's content while leaving a study of the impact of its title to future work. As mentioned before, the editorials were somewhat outdated, hence, we asked the annotators to try to think back to when the discussed issue was current.

The annotation was done using a web application that we developed specifically for this purpose. Each annotator had to login with an assigned identification number and his or her result of the political typology quiz.

4.3 Corpus Overview

Table 3 shows statistics of the resulting corpus. The most frequently annotated effect was *somewhat reinforcing* followed by *no effect*. The rarest in turn was *strongly challenging* for both liberals and conservatives with only 143 out of 6000 annotations (i.e., 2.4%). Even more rare, in only 68 cases the reader actually changed his or her stance which is equivalent to about 1% of all annotations.

Political Orientation	Effect with Intensity					Effect without Intensity		
	Strongly challenging (change)	**Somewhat challenging**	**No effect**	**Somewhat reinforcing**	**Strongly reinforcing** (empower)	**Challenging**	**No effect**	**Reinforcing**
Liberals	71 (33)	269	708	1402	550 (509)	340	708	1952
Conservatives	72 (35)	275	1282	798	573 (461)	347	1282	1371
Overall	**143 (68)**	**544**	**1990**	**2200**	**1123 (970)**	**687**	**1990**	**3323**

Table 3: Counts of the annotated effects for the 1000 news editorials in our corpus depending on the annotators' political orientation, once with intensity (strongly vs. somewhat), once without. In parentheses: Annotators that changed stance or felt empowered. Each editorial was annotated by three liberal and three conservative annotators.

[...] Police officers firing 50 rounds early last Saturday killed Sean Bell, an unarmed man who was to have married his high school sweetheart later in the day. The mayor and the commissioner moved quickly to answer questions and to hear the concerns of the victim's family and the community. But their responsiveness will not bring back Sean Bell. The challenge here is far greater than good communications. The officers who killed Mr. Bell were part of a sting operation at a Queens nightclub suspected of narcotics, prostitution and weapons violations. According to published reports, the officers have said that as Mr. Bell and his friends left the club and headed toward their car, an undercover detective heard one of them say he was going to get a gun. They also reportedly said that when the men entered the car, the detective pulled his gun and identified himself, but the car suddenly gunned forward, hit him in the shin and then struck an unmarked police minivan. The officers then opened fire. The tragedy may simply involve two sets of very frightened men who reacted instinctively to what they thought was imminent danger. But only one of the sets was armed. There was no gun in the car, nor on the shooting victims, who sat helpless inside while five police officers began firing 50 rounds at them. [...]

Figure 3: An excerpt of the news editorial "50 Bullets and a Death in Queens". This editorial challenged the stance of annotators with conservative ideology and reinforced the stance of those with liberal ideology.

Weather is not primarily a moral affair. We do not deserve a long, slow patch of hot weather, like the one that sat on the city in early June, any more than we deserve the extraordinarily beautiful evenings that have come with these longest days of the year. Deserving has nothing to do with it. The weather comes, it goes, and sometimes it's occluded. The days of seeing the wrath of God in a prolonged drought or a heavy windstorm – believing that bad weather chastens our bad actions, in other words – are pretty much past. One sobering irony of global warming is the thought that it threatens to make weather moral again in a very different way. But these are thoughts too puzzling for the fine weather of these last few evenings, when it is almost impossible not to feel that this has come to us by right – as our due after a run of sticky days and as the best of what the month of June has to offer anyway. These are the nights for stoop sitting, not in long-suffering, as though we felt the curse of Cain on our shoulders, but like the young man and his dog I passed the other evening. Both sat quietly, watching the street. You could tell that what they were really doing was feeling the shape of the cool air around their bodies. It would have been a pleasure in itself, but it was all the more pleasurable for the memory of that hot spell. [...]

Figure 4: An excerpt of the news editorial "The Reward of Good Weather". This editorial neither affected the stance of annotators with conservative ideologies, nor the stance of those with liberal ideologies.

Exemplarily, Figure 3 shows an excerpt of an editorial on police brutality and misconduct from the corpus. This editorial challenged the stance of annotators with one ideology and reinforced the stance of those with the opposing ideology. Accordingly, it meets our conditions of being of high argumentation quality.

On the other hand, Figure 4 shows an excerpt of an editorial on global warming from the corpus. This editorial did not affect annotators of either ideology. As a result, it meets our conditions of being of low argumentation quality.

5 Analysis

This section provides insights into the annotations of our corpus. We first outline the reliability of the annotations in terms of inter-annotator agreement, and we compare the annotations of liberals and conservatives, highlighting the noteworthy differences. Then, we analyze the annotations regarding their argumentation quality according to our model.

5.1 Inter-Annotator Agreement

Table 4 lists agreement results for all annotators within each group (*liberals* and *conservatives*) as well as across both groups (*overall*).

The overall agreement is lower than the agreement within each group regarding the majority, full, and Krippendorff's α. For example, Krippendorff's α is 0.32 for liberals and 0.29 for conservatives, but only 0.16 overall. According to the Mann-Whitney test (Mann and Whitney, 1947), the difference be-

	Effect w/o Intensity			Effect vs. No Effect		
	Majority	**Full**	α	**Majority**	**Full**	α
Liberals	74%	33%	0.32	83%	48%	0.30
Conservatives	69%	20%	0.29	77%	31%	0.32
Overall	**64%**	**0%**	**0.16**	**72%**	**12%**	**0.17**

Table 4: Majority, full, and Krippendorff's α agreement for both political ideologies and overall for annotating *what* effect all news editorials in our corpus have (left side) and *whether* they have any effect (right side).

Quality	Group A	Group B	#	%
High	Challenging	Challenging	4	1%
	Challenging	Reinforcing	37	5%
Medium	Reinforcing	Reinforcing	338	44%
	Challenging	No Effect	19	2%
Low	Reinforcing	No Effect	296	38%
	No Effect	No Effect	76	10%
	Either group changed stance		1	0%
	Either group was empowered		151	20%

Table 5: Distribution of combined majority effects of the news editorials in our corpus on opposing belief groups, along with their quality according to our model. Editorials without majority agreement are ignored here.

tween the effects annotated by liberals and those annotated by conservatives is significant at $p < 0.05$.

In general, the liberal group agreed more than the conservative, with a majority agreement of 74% against 69%, full agreement of 33% against 20%, and an α of 0.32 against 0.29. One reason for this may be given by the varying ideology distributions within each group: As mentioned before, the PEW political typology ranges from far right to far left, and in Figure 2, we see that the annotators with liberal ideology are further from the middle than the conservative annotators. An annotator closer to the middle is likely to be less devoted than an annotator with a more extreme ideology (e.g., *solid liberals* or *core conservatives*).

The observed α agreement can be interpreted as "fair" for both liberals and conservatives, and as "slight" overall. We see two reasons for this limited agreement: (1) The task at hand is very subjective, and (2) the distribution of labels is skewed. For instance, *challenging* is chosen significantly less than *no effect* and *reinforcing*. Krippendorff's α has been shown to be often low in such cases (Di Eugenio and Glass, 2004). Indeed, the values are in line with those obtained for similar tasks in other studies (Wachsmuth et al., 2017a).

5.2 Editorial Argumentation Quality

Table 5 shows the distribution of news editorials over their combined effect on the two opposing belief groups, ignoring which group is liberal and which is conservative. According to our model, 6% of the editorials are of high quality, 46% of medium quality, and 48% of low quality.

Only one of the 1000 editorials changed the stance of either group with majority. According to a one-sided binomial test, the proportion of readers changing their stance after reading an editorial is significantly lower than 1% at $p < 0.001$. This speaks for our hypothesis that editorials do not serve to persuade readers in most cases. By con-

trast, 151 editorials empowered annotators of either groups to argue better about the discussed issue, which shows the importance and applicability of the 'empower' notion in our model.

296 editorials reinforced the stance of one group and did not affect the other group. From these, 244 reinforced the stance of liberal annotators, suggesting that their stance more often equals the stance of the editorials. This matches expectation, given that the New York Times is seen as a rather left news portal. According to a Fisher's exact test, the difference in choosing *reinforcing* between liberals and conservatives is significant at $p < 0.05$.

5.3 Personality Traits

Our model of argumentation quality is built by profiling readers based on their political ideologies, whereas Lukin et al. (2017) profiles the audience for the "Big Five" personality traits to see whether different personality types are more open to different types of arguments. Although we focus in this paper on the audience's political belief, we also expected useful insights from correlating the personality traits of our annotators to the editorials' effects. For this reason, we asked our annotators to take the personality test based on the "Big Five" (Goldberg, 1990).

Table 6 shows the counts of the personality traits of annotators based on their political orientations. Since our primary goal was to have annotators evenly distributed over their political orientations, we did not control the distribution based on personality traits.

We computed the correlations between the annotators' personality traits and their annotations regarding the effect of editorials. Table 7 shows Kendall's τ correlation coefficient between the

	"Big Five" Personality Traits														
	Agreeableness			Conscientiousness			Extraversion			Neuroticism			Openness		
	Low	Average	High	Low	Average	High	Low	Average	High	Low	Average	High	Low	Average	High
Liberals	3	2	7	2	6	4	4	3	5	8	2	2	3	2	7
Conservatives	5	0	7	4	3	5	8	2	2	2	3	7	4	6	2
Overall	**8**	**2**	**14**	**6**	**9**	**9**	**12**	**5**	**7**	**10**	**5**	**9**	**7**	**8**	**9**

Table 6: Counts of the annotators' "Big Five" personality trait values, depending on their political orientation.

Kendall's τ	"Big Five" Personality Traits				
	Agree.	Consc.	Extra.	Neuro.	Openn.
Liberals	0.02	0.04	*0.15	-0.06	0.06
Conservatives	0.14	-0.14	*0.23	0.02	*0.31
Overall	**0.10**	**-0.06**	**0.24**	**-0.11**	**0.22**

Table 7: Kendall's τ correlation between the annotators' "Big Five" personality traits and the effect of a news editorial depending on the annotators' political orientation. Values with * are discussed in Section 5.3.

"Big Five" (Goldberg, 1990) and the effect of an editorial on liberal and conservative annotators.

As discussed in Section 2, Lukin et al. (2017) found specific types of arguments to be persuasive for people with specific personality traits. Analogously, we found correlations between the effect of editorials and combinations of political ideology and personality traits of readers. For both liberals and conservatives, for instance, there is a positive correlation between their choices for editorial effect and the *extraversion* trait. This trait characterizes people who tend to be more dominant in social settings (Friedman et al., 2010). Similarly, for conservatives there is a positive correlation between their choices for editorial effect and the *openness* trait. This trait characterizes active imagination or high curiosity (Costa and McCrae, 1992).

5.4 Explanations

The annotators were asked to justify their answers, resulting in in a total of 6000 explanations. All explanations were manually inspected by us. Among others, we found that the majority of annotators selected *no effect* for two main reasons. One reason was that, as expected, an annotator already had a stance towards the discussed topic of the editorial, but he or she found the editorial rather ineffective. The second reason was that an annotator did not have a stance regarding the topic, but also expressed no interest in the topic.

6 Conclusion

This paper has presented a new model for the argumentation quality of news editorials. As its main dimensions the model combines the *reader's beliefs* and the *editorial effect*. While the reader's beliefs are defined in terms of the political orientation of a reader, the editorial effect is defined as an editorial's capability to either challenge readers with opposing stance or to empower readers with the same stance. This way, our model goes beyond approaches that aim at quantifying quality as an absolute value. Instead, we analyze how editorials increase or decrease the gap between readers with opposing beliefs (van Dijk, 1995).

To compute the determinants of our proposed model and to analyze its potential, we built a new corpus of 1000 editorials from the New York Times. Each editorial has been annotated regarding its perceived effect by three liberals and by three conservatives. Our analysis of the corpus provided first insights: As expected, readers with identical beliefs largely agree on the effect of editorials. In particular, we provide empirical evidence for the hypothesis that editorials rarely change the stance of readers. With our approach, we can quantify such effects more precisely.

We also observed that the ideology of the New York Times seems to be reflected in the annotated corpus: The editorials reinforced the stance of many annotators with liberal ideology, while they often had no effect on annotators with conservative ideology. In addition, we found correlations between the effects of editorials and the combination of political ideology and personality trait.

We consider the presented model and the new corpus as substantial resources for fostering research on computational argumentation. We ourselves plan to use these resources in future work, in particular, for developing computational approaches to assess argumentation quality.

References

Khalid Al-Khatib, Henning Wachsmuth, Matthias Hagen, and Benno Stein. 2017. Patterns of argumentation strategies across topics. In *Proceedings of the 2017 Conference on Empirical Methods in Natural Language Processing*, pages 1351–1357. Association for Computational Linguistics.

Khalid Al-Khatib, Henning Wachsmuth, Johannes Kiesel, Matthias Hagen, and Benno Stein. 2016. A news editorial corpus for mining argumentation strategies. In *Proceedings of COLING 2016, the 26th International Conference on Computational Linguistics: Technical Papers*, pages 3433–3443. The COLING 2016 Organizing Committee.

P. Anand, J. King, Jordan Boyd-Graber, E. Wagner, C. Martell, Douglas Oard, and Philip Resnik. 2011. Believe me — We can do this! Annotating persuasive acts in blog text. In *Workshops at the Twenty-Fifth AAAI Conference on Artificial Intelligence*.

Aristotle. translated 2007. *On Rhetoric: A Theory of Civic Discourse* (George A. Kennedy, Translator). Clarendon Aristotle series. Oxford University Press.

Bal Krishna Bal. 2009. Towards an analysis of opinions in news editorials: How positive was the year? (project abstract). In *Proceedings of the Eight International Conference on Computational Semantics*, pages 260–263. Association for Computational Linguistics.

Bal Krishna Bal and Patrick Saint Dizier. 2010. Towards building annotated resources for analyzing opinions and argumentation in news editorials. In *Proceedings of the Seventh conference on International Language Resources and Evaluation (LREC'10)*. European Languages Resources Association (ELRA).

Elena Cabrio and Serena Villata. 2012. Combining textual entailment and argumentation theory for supporting online debates interactions. In *Proceedings of the 50th Annual Meeting of the Association for Computational Linguistics (Volume 2: Short Papers)*, pages 208–212. Association for Computational Linguistics.

Amparo Elizabeth Cano-Basave and Yulan He. 2016. A study of the impact of persuasive argumentation in political debates. In *Proceedings of the 2016 Conference of the North American Chapter of the Association for Computational Linguistics: Human Language Technologies*, pages 1405–1413. Association for Computational Linguistics.

Paul T Costa and Robert R McCrae. 1992. Normal personality assessment in clinical practice: The neo personality inventory. *Psychological assessment*, 4(1):5.

Barbara Di Eugenio and Michael Glass. 2004. he Kappa Statistic: A Second Look. *Computational Linguistics*, 30(1):95–101.

Teun A. van Dijk. 1995. Opinions and Ideologies in Editorials. In *Proceedings of the 4th International Symposium of Critical Discourse Analysis, Language, Social Life and Critical Thought*, Athens.

Carrol Doherty, Jocelyn Kiley, and Bridget Johnson. 2017. Political typology reveals deep fissures on the right and left doherty.

Frans H. van Eemeren and Rob Grootendorst. 2004. *A Systematic Theory of Argumentation: The Pragma-Dialectical Approach*. Cambridge University Press, Cambridge, UK.

Howard S Friedman, Margaret L Kern, and Chandra A Reynolds. 2010. Personality and health, subjective well-being, and longevity. *Journal of Personality*, 78(1):179–216.

Lewis R. Goldberg. 1990. An alternative "description of personality": The Big-Five factor structure. *Journal of Personality and Social Psychology*, 59(6):1216–1229.

Ivan Habernal and Iryna Gurevych. 2016. Which argument is more convincing? Analyzing and predicting convincingness of web arguments using bidirectional LSTM. In *Proceedings of the 54th Annual Meeting of the Association for Computational Linguistics (Volume 1: Long Papers)*, pages 1589–1599. Association for Computational Linguistics.

H. Halmari and T. Virtanen. 2005. *Persuasion Across Genres: A linguistic approach*. Pragmatics & Beyond New Series. John Benjamins Publishing Company.

Christopher Hidey, Elena Musi, Alyssa Hwang, Smaranda Muresan, and Kathy McKeown. 2017. Analyzing the semantic types of claims and premises in an online persuasive forum. In *Proceedings of the 4th Workshop on Argument Mining*, pages 11–21.

Ralph H. Johnson and J. Anthony Blair. 2006. *Logical Self-defense*. International Debate Education Association.

Johannes Kiesel, Khalid Al Khatib, Matthias Hagen, and Benno Stein. 2015. A shared task on argumentation mining in newspaper editorials. In *Proceedings of the 2nd Workshop on Argumentation Mining*, pages 35–38. Association for Computational Linguistics.

Ran Levy, Yonatan Bilu, Daniel Hershcovich, Ehud Aharoni, and Noam Slonim. 2014. Context dependent claim detection. In *Proceedings of COLING 2014, the 25th International Conference on Computational Linguistics: Technical Papers*, pages 1489–1500. Dublin City University and Association for Computational Linguistics.

Haijing Liu, Yang Gao, Pin Lv, Mengxue Li, Shiqiang Geng, Minglan Li, and Hao Wang. 2017. Using argument-based features to predict and analyse review helpfulness. In *Proceedings of the 2017 Conference on Empirical Methods in Natural Language Processing*, pages 1358–1363. Association for Computational Linguistics.

Annie Louis and Ani Nenkova. 2013. What makes writing great? First experiments on article quality prediction in the science journalism domain. *Transactions of the Association for Computational Linguistics*, 1:341–352.

Stephanie Lukin, Pranav Anand, Marilyn Walker, and Steve Whittaker. 2017. Argument Strength is in the Eye of the Beholder: Audience Effects in Persuasion. In *Proceedings of the 15th Conference of the European Chapter of the Association for Computational Linguistics: Volume 1, Long Papers*, pages 742–753. Association for Computational Linguistics.

H. B. Mann and D. R. Whitney. 1947. On a test of whether one of two random variables is stochastically larger than the other. *Ann. Math. Statist.*, 18(1):50–60.

Raquel Mochales and Marie-Francine Moens. 2011. Argumentation mining. *Artificial Intelligence and Law*, 19(1):1–22.

Andreas Peldszus and Manfred Stede. 2015. Joint prediction in MST-style discourse parsing for argumentation mining. In *Proceedings of the 2015 Conference on Empirical Methods in Natural Language Processing*, pages 938–948. Association for Computational Linguistics.

Isaac Persing and Vincent Ng. 2015. Modeling argument strength in student essays. In *Proceedings of the 53rd Annual Meeting of the Association for Computational Linguistics and the 7th International Joint Conference on Natural Language Processing (Volume 1: Long Papers)*, pages 543–552. Association for Computational Linguistics.

Isaac Persing and Vincent Ng. 2017. Lightly-supervised modeling of argument persuasiveness. In *Proceedings of the Eighth International Joint Conference on Natural Language Processing (Volume 1: Long Papers)*, pages 594–604. Asian Federation of Natural Language Processing.

Peter Potash, Robin Bhattacharya, and Anna Rumshisky. 2017. Length, interchangeability, and external knowledge: Observations from predicting argument convincingness. In *Proceedings of the Eighth International Joint Conference on Natural Language Processing (Volume 1: Long Papers)*, pages 342–351. Asian Federation of Natural Language Processing.

Ruty Rinott, Lena Dankin, Carlos Alzate Perez, M. Mitesh Khapra, Ehud Aharoni, and Noam Slonim. 2015. Show me your evidence — An automatic method for context dependent evidence detection. In *Proceedings of the 2015 Conference on Empirical Methods in Natural Language Processing*, pages 440–450. Association for Computational Linguistics.

Evan Sandhaus. 2008. The New York Times Annotated Corpus. Corpus number LDC2008T19. In *Linguistic Data Consortium, Philadelphia*.

Christian Stab and Iryna Gurevych. 2014. Annotating argument components and relations in persuasive essays. In *Proceedings of COLING 2014, the 25th International Conference on Computational Linguistics: Technical Papers*, pages 1501–1510. Dublin City University and Association for Computational Linguistics.

Chenhao Tan, Vlad Niculae, Cristian Danescu-Niculescu-Mizil, and Lillian Lee. 2016. Winning arguments: Interaction dynamics and persuasion strategies in good-faith online discussions. In *Proceedings of the 25th International World Wide Web Conference*, pages 613–624.

Henning Wachsmuth, Khalid Al Khatib, and Benno Stein. 2016. Using argument mining to assess the argumentation quality of essays. In *Proceedings of COLING 2016, the 26th International Conference on Computational Linguistics: Technical Papers*, pages 1680–1691. The COLING 2016 Organizing Committee.

Henning Wachsmuth, Nona Naderi, Ivan Habernal, Yufang Hou, Graeme Hirst, Iryna Gurevych, and Benno Stein. 2017a. Argumentation quality assessment: Theory vs. practice. In *Proceedings of the 55th Annual Meeting of the Association for Computational Linguistics (Volume 2: Short Papers)*, pages 250–255. Association for Computational Linguistics.

Henning Wachsmuth, Nona Naderi, Yufang Hou, Yonatan Bilu, Vinodkumar Prabhakaran, Tim Alberdingk Thijm, Graeme Hirst, and Benno Stein. 2017b. Computational argumentation quality assessment in natural language. In *Proceedings of the 15th Conference of the European Chapter of the Association for Computational Linguistics: Volume 1, Long Papers*, pages 176–187. Association for Computational Linguistics.

Hong Yu and Vasileios Hatzivassiloglou. 2003. Towards answering opinion questions: Separating facts from opinions and identifying the polarity of opinion sentences. In *Proceedings of the 2003 Conference on Empirical Methods in Natural Language Processing*, pages 129–136. Association for Computational Linguistics.

Bringing Order to Neural Word Embeddings with Embeddings Augmented by Random Permutations (EARP)

Trevor Cohen
Biomedical and Health Informatics
University of Washington, Seattle
cohenta@uw.edu

Dominic Widdows
Grab, Inc.
Seattle, WA
dominic.widdows@grab.com

Abstract

Word order is clearly a vital part of human language, but it has been used comparatively lightly in distributional vector models. This paper presents a new method for incorporating word order information into word vector embedding models by combining the benefits of permutation-based order encoding with the more recent method of skip-gram with negative sampling. The new method introduced here is called Embeddings Augmented by Random Permutations (EARP). It operates by applying permutations to the coordinates of context vector representations during the process of training. Results show an 8% improvement in accuracy on the challenging Bigger Analogy Test Set, and smaller but consistent improvements on other analogy reference sets. These findings demonstrate the importance of order-based information in analogical retrieval tasks, and the utility of random permutations as a means to augment neural embeddings.

1 Introduction

The recognition of the utility of corpus-derived distributed representations of words for a broad range of Natural Language Processing (NLP) tasks (Collobert et al., 2011) has led to a resurgence of interest in methods of distributional semantics. In particular, the neural-probabilistic word representations produced by the Skip-gram and Continuous Bag-of-Words (CBOW) architectures (Mikolov et al., 2013a) implemented in the `word2vec` and `fastText` software packages have been extensively evaluated in recent years.

As was the case with preceding distributional models (see for example (Schütze, 1993; Lund and Burgess, 1996; Schütze, 1998; Karlgren and Sahlgren, 2001)), these architectures generate vector representations of words — or word embeddings — such that words with similar proximal neighboring terms within a corpus of text will have similar vector representations. As the relative position of these neighboring terms is generally not considered, distributional models of this nature are often (and sometimes derisively) referred to as *bag-of-words* models. While methods of encoding word order into neural-probabilistic representations have been evaluated, these methods generally require learning additional parameters, either for each position in the sliding window (Mnih and Kavukcuoglu, 2013), or for each context word-by-position pair (Trask et al., 2015; Ling et al., 2015).

In this paper we evaluate an alternative method of encoding the position of words within a sliding window into neural word embeddings using Embeddings Augmented by Random Permutations (EARP). EARP leverages random permutations of context vector representations (Sahlgren et al., 2008), a technique that has not been applied during the training of neural word embeddings previously. Unlike prior approaches to encoding position into neural word embeddings, it imposes no computational and negligible space requirements.

Results show that the word order information encoded through EARP leads to a nearly 8% improvement (from 29.17% to 37.07%) in the accuracy of analogy predictions in the Bigger Analogy Test Set of Gladkova et al (2016), with the improvement being largest (over 20%) in the category of analogies that exhibit derivational morphology (a case where the use of subword information also improves accuracy for all representations with and without order information). Smaller improvements in performance are evident on other analogy sets, and in downstream sequence labeling tasks. This makes EARP a strong contender for enriching word embeddings with order-based information, leading to greater accuracy on more challenging semantic processing tasks.

465

Proceedings of the 22nd Conference on Computational Natural Language Learning (CoNLL 2018), pages 465–475
Brussels, Belgium, October 31 - November 1, 2018. ©2018 Association for Computational Linguistics

2 Background

2.1 Distributed representations of words

Methods of distributional semantics learn representations of words from the contexts they occur in across large text corpora, such that words that occur in similar contexts will have similar representations (Turney and Pantel, 2010). Geometrically-motivated approaches to this problem often involve decomposition of a term-by-context matrix (Schütze, 1993; Landauer and Dumais, 1997; Pennington et al., 2014), resulting in word vectors of considerably lower dimensionality than the total number of contexts. Alternatively, reduced-dimensional representations can be generated online while processing individual units of text, without the need to represent a large term-by-context matrix explicitly. A seminal example of the latter approach is the Random Indexing (RI) method (Kanerva et al., 2000), which generates distributed representations of words by superposing randomly generated context vector representations.

Neural-probabilistic methods have shown utility as a means to generate semantic vector representations of words (Bengio et al., 2003). In particular, the Skip-gram and CBOW neural network architectures (Mikolov et al., 2013a) implemented within the `word2vec` and `fastText` software packages provide scalable approaches to online training of word vector representations that have been shown to perform well across a number of tasks (Mikolov et al., 2013a; Levy et al., 2015; Mikolov et al., 2017).

While the definition of what constitutes a context varies across models, a popular alternative is to use words in a sliding window centered on a focus term for this purpose. Consequently where decomposition is involved the matrix in question would be a term-by-term matrix. With online methods, each term has two vector representations — a *semantic vector* and a *context vector*, corresponding to the input and output weights for each word in neural-probabilistic approaches.

2.2 Order-based distributional models

In most word vector embedding models based on sliding windows, the relative position of words within this sliding window is ignored, but there have been prior efforts to encode this information. Before the popularization of neural word embeddings, a number of researchers developed and evaluated methods to encode word position

into distributed vector representations. The BEAGLE model (Jones et al., 2006) uses circular convolution — as described by Plate (1995) — as a *binding operator* to compose representations of n-grams from randomly instantiated context vector representations of individual terms. These composite representations are then added to the semantic vector representation for the central term in a sliding window. The cosine similarity between the resulting vectors is predictive of human performance in semantic priming experiments.

A limitation of this approach is that it involves a large number of operations per sliding window. For example, Jones and his colleagues (2006) employ eight superposition and nine convolution operations to represent a single sliding window of three terms (excluding the focus term). Sahlgren, Holst and Kanerva (2008) report a computationally simpler method of encoding word order in the context of RI. Like BEAGLE, this approach involves adding randomly instantiated context vectors for adjacent terms to the semantic vector of the central term in a sliding window. However, RI uses sparse context vectors, consisting of mostly zeroes with a small number non-zero components initialized at random. These vectors are assigned permutations indicating their position within a sliding window. For example, with $\prod_p$ representing the permutation assigned to a given position p and words to the right of the equation representing their context vectors, the sliding window "[fast is **fine** but accuracy] is everything" would result in the following update to $S(\text{fine})$, the semantic vector for the term "fine":

$$S(\text{fine}) \mathrel{+}= \prod_{-2} \overrightarrow{\text{fast}} + \prod_{-1} \overrightarrow{\text{is}} \\ + \prod_{+1} \overrightarrow{\text{but}} + \prod_{+2} \overrightarrow{\text{accuracy}}$$

Amongst the encoding schemes evaluated using this approach, using a pair of permutations to distinguish between words preceding the focus term and those following it resulted in the best performance on synonym test evaluations (Sahlgren et al., 2008). Furthermore, this approach was shown to outperform BEAGLE on a number of evaluations on account of its ability to scale up to larger amounts of input data (Recchia et al., 2010).

2.3 Encoding order into neural embeddings

Some recent work has evaluated the utility of encoding word order into neural word embeddings.

A straightforward way to accomplish this involves maintaining a separate set of parameters for each context word position, so that for a vocabulary of size v and p context window positions the number of output weights in the model is $v \times p \times d$ for embeddings of dimensionality d. This approach was applied by Ling and his colleagues (2015) to distinguish between terms occurring before and after the central term in a sliding window, with improvements in performance in downstream part-of-speech tagging and dependency parsing tasks.

Trask and his colleagues (2015) develop this idea further in a model they call a Partitioned Embedding Neural Network (PENN). In a PENN, both the input weights (word embeddings) and output weights (context embeddings) of the network have separate position-specific instantiations, so the total number of model parameters is $2v \times p \times d$. In addition to evaluating binary (before/after) context positions, the utility of training separate weights for each position within a sliding window was evaluated. Incorporating order in this way resulted in improvements in accuracy over `word2vec`'s CBOW implementation on proportional analogy problems, which were considerably enhanced by the incorporation of character-level embeddings.

A more space-efficient approach to encoding word order involves learning a vector V for each position p in the sliding window. These vectors are applied to rescale context vector representations using pointwise multiplication while constructing a weighted average of the context vectors for each term in the window (Mnih and Kavukcuoglu, 2013; Mikolov et al., 2017). Results reported using this approach are variable, with some authors reporting worse performance with position-dependent weights on a sentence completion task (Mnih and Kavukcuoglu, 2013), and others reporting improved performance on an analogy completion task (Mikolov et al., 2017).

3 Methods

3.1 Skipgram-with-negative-sampling

In the current work, we extend the skipgram-with-negative-sampling (SGNS) algorithm to encode positional information without additional computation. The Skip-gram model (Mikolov et al., 2013a) predicts $p(c|w)$: the probability of observing a context word, c, given an observed word, w. This can be accomplished by moving a slid-

ing window through a large text corpus, such that the observed word is at the center of the window, and the context words surround it. The architecture itself includes two sets of parameters for each unique word: The input weights of the network ($\vec{w}$), which represent observed words and are usually retained as semantic vectors after training, and the output weights of the network which represent context words ($\vec{c}$) and are usually discarded. The probability of observing a word in context is calculated by appying the sigmoid function to the scalar product between the input weights for the observed word, and the output weights for the context word, such that $p(c|w) = \sigma(\vec{w}.\vec{c})$. As maximizing this probability using the softmax over all possible context words would be computationally inconvenient, SGNS instead draws a small number of *negative samples* ($\neg c$) from the vocabulary to serve as counterexamples to each observed context term. With D representing observed term/context pairs, and D' representing randomly constructed counterexamples the SGNS optimization objective is as follows (Goldberg and Levy, 2014):

$$\sum_{(w,c)\in D} \log \sigma(\vec{w}.\vec{c}) + \sum_{(w,\neg c)\in D'} \log \sigma(-\vec{w}.\neg \vec{c})$$

3.2 Embeddings Augmented by Random Permutations (EARP)

Sliding window variants of RI are similar in some respects to the SGNS algorithm, in that training occurs through an online update step in which a vector representation for each context term is added to the semantic vector representation for a focus term (with SGNS this constitutes an update of the input weight vector for the focus term, weighted by the gradient and learning rate (for a derivation see (Rong, 2014)). Unlike SGNS, however, context vectors in RI are immutable and sparse. With SGNS, dense context vectors are altered during the training process, providing an enhanced capacity for inferred similarity. Nonetheless, the technique of permuting context vectors to indicate the position of a context term within a sliding window is readily adaptable to SGNS.

Our approach to encoding the position of context words involves assigning a randomly-generated permutation to each position within a sliding window. For example, with a sliding window of window radius 2 (considering two positions to the left and the right of a focus term), we assign a random permutation, $\prod_p$, to each element

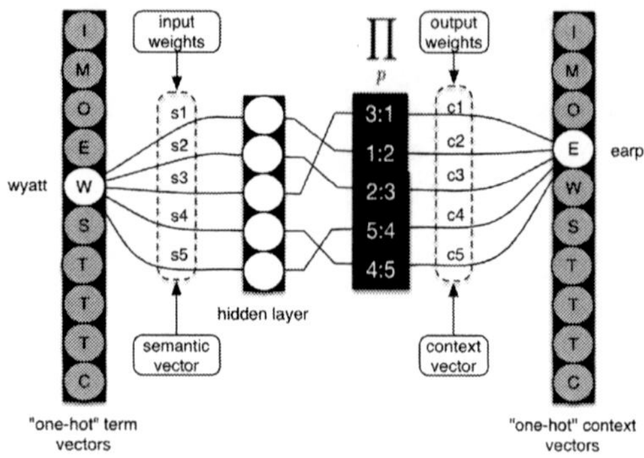

Figure 1: The Architecture of EARP

of the set of positions $\{-2; -1; +1; +2\}$. With $\prod_p$ indicating the application of a context-specific random permutation for position p, the optimization objective becomes:

$$\sum_{(w,c:p)\in D} \log \sigma(\vec{w} . \prod_p(\vec{c})) +$$

$$\sum_{(w,\neg c:p)\in D'} \log \sigma(-\vec{w} . \prod_p(\neg\vec{c}))$$

For example, upon observing the term "wyatt" in the context of the term "earp", the model would attempt to maximize $p(c|w) = \sigma(\overrightarrow{wyatt} . \prod_{+1}(\overrightarrow{earp}))$, with $\overrightarrow{wyatt}$ and $\overrightarrow{earp}$ as semantic and context vectors respectively. The underlying architecture is illustrated in Figure 1, using a simplified model generating 5-dimensional vector representations for a small vocabulary of 10 terms. The permutation $\prod_p$ can be implemented by "rewiring" the components of the input and output weights, without explicitly generating a permuted copy of the context vector concerned. In this way, $p(c|w)$ is estimated and maximized in place without imposing additional computational or space requirements, beyond those required to store the permutations. This is accomplished by changing the index values used to access components of $\overrightarrow{earp}$ when the scalar product is calculated, and when weights are updated. The inverse permutation (or reverse rewiring - connecting components 1:3 rather than 3:1) is applied to $\overrightarrow{wyatt}$ when updating $\overrightarrow{earp}$, and this procedure is used with both observed context terms and negative samples.

Within this general framework, we evaluate four word order encoding schemes, implemented by adapting the open source `Semantic Vectors`[1] package for distributional semantics research:

<hr>

[1] https://github.com/semanticvectors/semanticvectors

3.2.1 Directional ($EARP_{dir}$)

Directional encoding draws a distinction between terms that occur before or after the focus term in a sliding window. As such, only two permutations (and their inverse permutations) are employed: $\prod_{-1}$ for preceding terms, and $\prod_{+1}$ for all subseqent terms. Directional encoding with permutations has been shown to improve performance in synonym tests evaluations when applied in the context of RI (Sahlgren et al., 2008).

3.2.2 Positional ($EARP_{pos}$)

With positional encoding, a permutation is used to encode each space in the sliding window. As a randomly permuted vector is highly likely to be orthogonal or close-to-orthogonal to the vector from which it originated (Kanerva, 2009), this is likely to result in orthogonal encodings for the same context word in different positions. With RI, positional encoding degraded synonym test performance, but permitted a novel form of distributional query, in which permutation is used to retrieve words that occur in particular positions in relation to one another (Sahlgren et al., 2008). $EARP_{pos}$ facilitates queries of this form also: the nearest neighboring context vector to the permuted semantic vector $\prod_{-1}^{INV}(\overrightarrow{earp})$ is $\overrightarrow{wyatt}$ in both static-window subword-agnostic $EARP_{pos}$ spaces used in the experiments that follow.

3.2.3 Proximity-based ($EARP_{prox}$)

With proximity-based encoding, the positional encoding of a particular context term occurring in the first position in a sliding window will be somewhat similar to the encoding when this term occurs in the second position, and less similar (but still not orthogonal) to the encoding when it occurs in the third. This is accomplished by randomly generating an *index permutation* $\prod_{+1}$, randomly reassigning a half of its permutations to generate $\prod_{+2}$, and repeating this process iteratively until a permutation for every position in the window is obtained (for the current experiments, we assigned two index permutations $\prod_{+1}$ and $\prod_{-1}$, proceeding bidirectionally). As a low-dimensional example, if $\prod_{+1}$ were {4:1, 1:2, 2:3, 3:4}, $\prod_{+2}$ might be {4:3, 1:2, 2:1, 3:4}. The net result is that the similarity between the position-specific representations of a given context vector reflects the proximity between the positions concerned. While this method is reminiscent of interpolation between randomly generated vectors or matrices to encode character position within words (Cohen et al., 2013) and pixel position within images (Gallant and Culliton, 2016) respectively, the iterative application of permutations for this purpose is a novel approach to such positional binding.

3.3 Subword embeddings

The use of character n-grams as components of distributional semantic models was introduced by Schütze (1993), and has been shown to improve performance of neural-probabilistic models on analogical retrieval tasks (Bojanowski et al., 2017; Mikolov et al., 2017). It is intuitive that this should be the case as standard analogy evaluation reference sets include many analogical questions that require mapping from a morphological derivative of one word (e.g. fast:faster) to the same morphological derivative of another (e.g. high:higher).

Consequently, we also generated n-gram based variants of each of our models, by adapting the approach described in (Bojanowski et al., 2017) to our SGNS configuration. Specifically, we decomposed each word into character n-grams, after introducing characters indicating the start ($<$) and end ($>$) of a word. N-grams of size betweeen 3 and 6 characters (inclusive) were encoded, and in order to place an upper bound on memory requirements a hash function was used to map each observed n-gram to one of at the most two million vectors without constraints on collisions. The input vector V_i for a word with n included n-grams (including the word itself) was then generated as[2]

$$V_i = \frac{1}{n} \sum_{i=1}^{n} \overrightarrow{\text{ngram}_i}$$

During training, we used V_i as the input vector for EARP and SGNS, with updates propagating back to component word and n-gram vectors in proportion to their contribution to V_i.

3.4 Training data

All models were trained on the first January 2018 release of the English Wikipedia[3], to which we applied the pre-processing script distributed with the `fastText` package[4], resulting in a corpus of approximately 8.8 billion words.

3.5 Training procedure

All models used 500-dimensional vectors, and were trained for a single iteration across the corpus with five negative samples per context term. For each of the four models ($SGNS$, $EARP_{dir}$, $EARP_{pos}$, $EARP_{prox}$), embeddings were generated with sliding window radii r of 2 and 5 (in each direction), with and without subword embeddings. For all experiments, we excluded numbers, and terms occurring less than 150 times in the corpus. SGNS has a number of hyperparameters that are known to influence performance (Levy et al., 2015). We did not engage in tuning of these hyperparameters to improve performance of our models, but rather were guided by prior research in selecting hyper-parameter settings that are known to perform well with the SGNS baseline model.

Specifically, we used a subsampling threshold t of 10^{-5}. In some experiments (*EARP* and *SGNS*), we used dynamic sliding windows with uniform probability of a sliding window radius between one and r, in an effort to align our baseline model closely with other SGNS implementations. Stochastic reduction of the sliding window radius will result in distal words being ignored at times. With a dynamic sliding window, subsampled words are replaced by the next word in sequence. This increases the data available for training, but will result in relative position being distorted at times. Consequently, we also generated spaces with static fixed-width sliding windows (*EARPx*) for position-aware models.

After finding that `fastText` trained on Wikipedia performed better on analogy tests than prior results obtained with `word2vec` (Levy et al., 2015), we adopted a number of its hyperparameter settings. We set the probability of negative sampling for each term to $f^{\frac{1}{2}}$, where f is the number of term occurrences divided by the total token count. In addition we used an initial learning rate of .05, and subsampled terms with a probability of $1 - (\sqrt{\frac{t}{f}} + \frac{t}{f})^5$.[5]

---

[2]Words and n-grams are weighted equally, following (Bojanowski et al., 2017) and the `fastText` implementation

[3]`https://dumps.wikimedia.org/enwiki`

[4]`https://github.com/facebookresearch/fastText`

[5]While using this formula reliably improves performance on some of the analogy sets, it differs from both the formula described in Mikolov et al. (2013b), and the formula implemented in the canonical `word2vec` implementation of SGNS - see Levy et al. (2015) for details. It is also difficult to justify on theoretical grounds, as it returns values less than zero for some words that meet the subsampling threshold. Nevertheless, retaining it throughout our experiments seemed more principled than altering the `fastText` baseline in a manner that impaired its performance.

3.6 Evaluation

To evaluate the nature and utility of the additional information encoded by permutation-based variants, we utilized a set of analogical retrieval reference sets, including the MSR set (Mikolov et al., 2013c) consisting of 8,000 proportional analogy questions that are morphological in nature (e.g. *young:younger:quick:?*) and the Google analogy set (Mikolov et al., 2013a) which includes 8,869 semantic (and predominantly geographic, e.g. *brussels:belgium:dublin:?*) and 10,675 morphologically-oriented "syntactic" questions. We also included the Bigger Analogy Test Set (BATS) set (Gladkova et al., 2016), a more challenging set of 99,200 proportional analogy questions balanced across 40 linguistic types in four categories: Inflections (e.g. plurals, infinitives), Derivation (e.g. verb+er), Lexicography (e.g. hypernyms, synonyms) and Encyclopedia (e.g. country:capital, male:female). We obtained these sets from the distribution described in Finley et al (2017)[6], in which only the first correct answer to questions with multiple correct answers in BATS is retained, and used a parallelized implementation of the widely used vector offset method, in which for a given proportional analogy *a:b:c:d*, all word vectors in the space are rank-ordered in accordance with their cosine similarity to the vector $\overrightarrow{c + b - a}$. We report average accuracy, where a result is considered accurate if d is the top-ranked result aside from a, b and c.[7]

To evaluate the effects of encoding word order on the relative distance between terms, we used a series of widely used reference sets that mediate comparison between human and machine estimates of pairwise similarity and relatedness between term pairs. Specifically, we used Wordsim-353 (Finkelstein et al., 2001), split into subsets emphasizing similarity and relatedness (Agirre et al., 2009); MEN (Bruni et al., 2014) and Simlex-999 (Hill et al., 2015). For each of these sets, we estimated the Spearman correlation of the cosine similarity between vector representations of the words in a given pair, with the human ratings (averaged across raters) of similarity and/or relatedness provided in the reference standards.

Only those examples in which all relevant terms were represented in our vector spaces were considered. Consequently, our analogy test sets consisted of 6136; 19,420 and 88,108 examples for the MSR[8], Google and BATS sets respectively. With pairwise similarity, we retained 998; 335 and all 3,000 of the Simlex, Wordsim and MEN examples respectively. These numbers were identical across models, including `fastText` baselines.

In addition we evaluated the effects of incorporating word order with EARP on three standard sequence labeling tasks: part-of-speech tagging of the Wall Street Journal sections of the Penn Treebank (PTB) and the CoNLL'00 sentence chunking (Tjong Kim Sang and Buchholz, 2000) and CoNLL'03 named entity recognition (Tjong Kim Sang and De Meulder, 2003) shared tasks. As was the case with the pairwise similarity and relatedness evaluations, we conducted these evaluations using the `repEval2016` package [9] after converting all vectors to the `word2vec` binary format. This package provides implementations of the neural NLP architecture developed by Collobert and his colleagues (2011), which uses vectors for words within a five-word window as input, a single hidden layer of 300 units and an output Softmax layer. The implementation provided in `repEval2016` deviates by design from the original implementation by fixing word vectors during training in order to emphasize difference between models for the purpose of comparative evaluation, which tends to reduce performance (for further details, see (Chiu et al., 2016)). As spaces constructed with narrower sliding windows generally perform better on these tasks (Chiu et al., 2016), we conducted these experiments with models of window radius 2 only. To facilitate fair comparison, we added random vectors representing tokens available in the `fastText`-derived spaces only to all spaces, replacing the original vectors where these existed. This was important in this evaluation as only `fastText` retains vector representation for punctuation marks (these are eliminated by the `Semantic Vectors` tokenization procedure), resulting in a relatively large number of out-of-vocabulary terms and predictably reduced

---

[6] `https://github.com/gpfinley/analogies`

[7] For a finer-grained estimate of performance — which we considered particularly important in cases in BATS in which only the first of a set of correct answers was retained — we also calculated the mean reciprocal rank ($rank^{-1}$) (Voorhees et al., 1999) of d across all questions. As these results closely mirrored the accuracy results, we report accuracy only.

[8] The fraction of the MSR set retained is smaller, because 1000 of the examples in this set concern identifying possessives indicates by the presence of an apostrophe, and terms of this nature were eliminated by the pre-processing procedure.

[9] https://github.com/cambridgeltl/RepEval-2016

performance with the `Semantic Vectors` implementation of the same algorithm. With the random vectors added, out-of-vocabulary rates were equivalent across the two SGNS implementations, resulting in similar performance.

4 Results

4.1 Analogical retrieval

The results of our analogical retrieval experiments are shown in Table 1. With the single exception of the semantic component of the Google set, the best result on every set and subset was obtained by a variant of the $EARP_{prox}$ model, strongly suggesting that (1) information concerning relative position is of value for solving analogical retrieval problems; (2) encoding this information in a flexible manner that preserves the natural relationship of proximity between sliding window positions helps more than encoding only direction, or encoding window positions as disparate "slots".

On the syntactically-oriented subsets (Gsyn, Binf, Bder) adding subword information improves performance of baseline SGNS and EARP models, with subword-sensitive $EARPx_{prox}$ models showing improvements of between ~6% and ~21% in accuracy on these subtasks, as compared with the best performing baseline[10]. The results follow the same pattern at both sliding window radii, aside from a larger decrease in performance of $EARPx$ models on the semantic component of the Google set at radius 2, attributable to semantically useful information lost on account of subsampling without replacement. In general, better performance on syntactic subsets is obtained at radius 2 with subword-sensitive models, with semantic subsets showing the opposite trend.

While better performance on the total Google set has been reported with larger training corpora (Pennington et al., 2014; Mikolov et al., 2017), the best EARP results on the syntactic component of this set surpass those reported from order-insensitive models trained on more comprehensive corpora for multiple iterations. With this subset,

---

[10]To assess reproducibility, we repeated the window radius 2 experiments a further 4 times, with different stochastic initialization of network weights. Performance was remarkably consistent, with a standard error of the mean accuracy on the MSR, Google and BATS sets at or below .24% (.0024), .33% (.0033) and .12% (.0012) for all models. All differences in performance from the baseline (only $SGNS_{semVec}$ was repeated) were statistically significant by unpaired t-test, aside from the results of $EARP_{dir}$ and $EARP_{prox}$ on the Google set when no subwords were used.

the best $EARP_{prox}$ model obtained an accuracy of 76.74% after a single training iteration on a ~9 billion word Wikipedia-derived corpus. Pennington and his colleagues (2014) report a best accuracy of 69.3% after training Glove on a corpus of 42 billion words, and Mikolov and colleagues (2017) report an accuracy of 73% when training a subword-sensitive CBOW model for five iterations across a 630 billion word corpus derived from Common Crawl. The latter performance improved to 82% with pre-processing to tag phrases and position-dependent weighting – modifications that may improve EARP performance also, as would almost certainly be the case with multiple training iterations across a much larger corpus.

Regarding the performance of other order-sensitive approaches on this subset, Trask and his colleagues (2015) report a 1.41% to 3.07% increase in absolute accuracy over a standard CBOW baseline with PENN, and Mikolov and his colleagues (2017) report a 4% increase over a subword-sensitive CBOW model with incorporation of position-dependent weights[11]. By comparison, $EARPx_{prox}$ yields improvements of up to 4.27% over the best baseline when subwords are not considered, and 8.29% with subword-sensitive models (both at radius 5).

With the more challenging BATS analogies, Drozd and his colleagues (2016) report results for models trained on a 6 billion word corpus derived from the Wikipedia and several other resources, with best results with the vector offset method for BATS components of 61%, 11.2% (both SGNS), 10.9% and 31.5% (both Glove) for the Inflectional, Derivational, Lexicography and Encyclopedia components respectively. While not strictly comparable on account of our training on Wikipedia alone and acknowledging only one of a set of possible correct answers in some cases, our best results for these sets were 71.56%, 44.30%, 10.07% and 36.52% respectively, with a fourfold increase in performance on the derivational component. These results further support the hypothesis that order-related information is of value in several classes of proportional analogy problem.

4.2 Semantic similarity/relatedness

These improvements in analogy retrieval were not accompanied by better correlation with human es-

---

[11]CBOW baselines were around 10% higher than our SGNS baselines, attributable to differences in corpus size, composition and preprocessing; and perhaps architecture.

Radius 2	SW	BATS	MSR	Google	Gsem	Gsyn	Binf	Bder	Blex	Benc
$SGNS_{fastText}$		27.22	53.78	70.13	**77.30**	64.17	56.00	11.76	7.06	32.12
$SGNS_{semVec}$		27.46	53.72	69.53	**77.30**	63.07	56.28	11.65	7.25	32.66
$EARP_{dir}$		28.26	54.48	69.34	76.57	63.33	56.33	11.51	8.36	34.62
$EARP_{pos}$		28.80	54.38	67.71	71.85	64.28	57.22	12.75	8.47	34.70
$EARP_{prox}$		28.95	55.08	69.19	74.95	64.40	57.38	12.86	8.44	35.04
$EARPx_{pos}$		30.50	60.15	61.71	58.94	64.01	66.09	11.07	9.37	33.05
$EARPx_{prox}$		30.79	62.45	66.86	68.80	65.25	66.90	10.76	**9.46**	**33.56**
$SGNS_{fastText}$	✓	28.16	59.83	63.57	57.87	68.31	61.05	22.51	4.47	24.60
$SGNS_{semVec}$	✓	29.17	61.44	65.24	59.38	70.10	62.28	23.56	5.02	25.83
$EARP_{dir}$	✓	31.70	62.94	68.90	62.46	74.26	63.85	29.26	5.54	28.65
$EARP_{pos}$	✓	33.18	62.89	69.35	62.98	74.63	65.10	32.23	6.01	30.12
$EARP_{prox}$	✓	33.26	64.26	**70.82**	64.83	75.80	66.08	31.72	6.05	29.85
$EARPx_{pos}$	✓	36.89	68.90	61.12	44.05	75.29	71.32	44.14	6.81	27.62
$EARPx_{prox}$	✓	**37.07**	**69.07**	63.88	49.31	**75.98**	**71.56**	**44.30**	6.92	27.81

Radius 5	SW	BATS	MSR	Google	Gsem	Gsyn	Binf	Bder	Blex	Benc
$SGNS_{fastText}$		25.54	48.21	69.29	78.47	61.66	49.93	11.95	7.00	31.51
$SGNS_{semVec}$		25.76	46.90	68.75	**79.04**	60.20	49.42	11.84	6.87	33.08
$EARP_{dir}$		27.07	49.20	68.66	76.85	61.85	50.58	12.38	8.30	35.04
$EARP_{pos}$		26.14	45.39	61.29	65.53	57.76	49.82	12.41	7.71	32.80
$EARP_{prox}$		28.40	51.06	69.17	77.05	62.62	53.59	14.05	8.51	35.56
$EARPx_{pos}$		28.30	52.67	59.18	59.80	58.67	57.27	12.90	8.78	32.35
$EARPx_{prox}$		30.94	58.15	69.37	73.51	65.93	59.86	15.36	**10.07**	**36.52**
$SGNS_{fastText}$	✓	26.27	55.04	66.32	64.56	67.79	56.23	18.56	4.43	25.38
$SGNS_{semVec}$	✓	27.69	55.93	67.96	67.37	68.44	57.90	20.32	5.12	26.98
$EARP_{dir}$	✓	30.12	58.20	70.22	69.42	70.88	59.98	24.46	5.78	30.11
$EARP_{pos}$	✓	31.02	54.78	65.67	60.41	70.03	60.28	28.21	5.96	29.94
$EARP_{prox}$	✓	32.67	60.77	**72.23**	69.79	74.27	64.01	28.71	6.46	31.67
$EARPx_{pos}$	✓	34.75	61.08	63.83	54.41	71.66	66.02	36.32	7.51	30.33
$EARPx_{prox}$	✓	**36.67**	**67.44**	72.22	66.78	**76.74**	**69.16**	**38.72**	7.56	32.52

Table 1: Analogical retrieval results at radius 2 (top) and 5 (bottom). SW: subwords. Gsem/syn: "semantic" and "syntactic" components of Google set. Binf/der/lex/enc: inflectional, derivational, lexical and encyclopedia-derived components of the BATS. SGNS: `fastText` and `Semantic Vectors` (*semVec*) implementations of skipgram-with-negative-sampling. EARP: Embeddings Augmented by Random Permutations. EARPx: EARP with exact window positions. Best results are in **boldface**, and rows concerning baseline models are shaded.

timates of semantic similarity and relatedness. To the contrary with a window radius of 2, the best results on all sets and subsets were produced by SGNS baselines, with a best baseline Spearman Rho of .41 ($SGNS_{fastText}$), .72 ($SGNS_{semVec}$) and .77 ($SGNS_{semVec}$ + subwords) for SimLex-999, WS-353 and MEN respectively. Surprisingly, incorporating order-related information reduced performance on all of these sets, with best performance for SimLex-999, WS-353 and MEN of .40 ($EARPx_{prox}$), .71 ($EARP_{pos}$) and .76 ($EARP_{dir}$ + subwords) respectively; and worst performance of .37 ($EARP_{pos}$), .66 and .71 (both $EARPx_{prox}$) respectively. Other models fell between these ex-

tremes, with a similar pattern observed with window radius of 5. The differences in performance observed with these tasks are neither as stark nor as consistent as those with analogy tasks, with EARP performance falling between that of the two baseline models in several cases. Nonetheless, EARP models tend to correlate worse with human estimates of pairwise similarity and relatedness. This drop in performance may relate to how semantic information is dispersed with position-aware models - a neighboring word is encoded differently depending on position, which may obscure the semantically useful information that two other words both occur in proximity to it.

Task	CoNLL00	CoNLL03	PTB	CoNLL00	CoNLL03	PTB
$SGNS_{fastText}$	87.09	80.32	94.38	87.34	80.66	94.78
$SGNS_{semVec}$	87.11	77.93	95.59	87.57	80.33	95.96
$EARP_{dir}$	88.25	80.24	95.83	88.06	**80.96**	96.07
$EARP_{pos}$	88.71	80.10	95.74	88.55	80.84	95.89
$EARP_{prox}$	88.59	79.64	95.85	88.78	80.54	**96.09**
$EARPx_{pos}$	**89.05**	80.43	95.92	**89.52**	80.17	95.93
$EARPx_{prox}$	88.99	**80.77**	**96.02**	89.37	79.77	95.93
Subwords	-	-	-	✓	✓	✓

Table 2: Performance on Sequence Labeling Tasks. % accuracy shown for PTB, and % F-measure otherwise

4.3 Sequence labeling

Results of these experiments are shown in Table 2, and suggest an advantage for models encoding position in sequence labeling tasks. In particular, for the sentence chunking shared task (CoNLL00), the best results obtained with an order-aware model ($EARPx_{pos}$ + subwords) exceeds the best baseline result by around 2%, with smaller improvements in performance on the other two tasks, including a .43% improvement in accuracy for part-of-speech tagging (PTB, without subwords) that is comparable to the .37% improvement over a SGNS baseline reported on this dataset by Ling and his colleagues (2015) when using separate (rather than shared) position-dependent context weights.

4.4 Computational performance

All models were trained on a single multi-core machine. In general, `Semantic Vectors` takes slightly longer to run than `fastText`, which takes around an hour to generate models including building of the dictionary. With `Semantic Vectors`, models were generated in around 1h20 when the corpus was indexed at document level, which is desirable as this package uses `Lucene`[12] for tokenization and indexing. As the accuracy of `fastText` on analogy completion tasks dropped considerably when we attempted to train it on unsegmented documents, we adapted `Semantic Vectors` to treat each line of input as an individual document. As this approximately doubled the time required to generate each model, we would not recommend this other than for the purpose of comparative evaluation. Adding subword embeddings increased training time by three- to fourfold. Source code is available via GitHub[13], and

embeddings are publicly available at [14].

4.5 Limitations and future work

While this paper focused on encoding positional information, EARP is generalizable and could be used to encode other sorts of relational information also. An interesting direction for future work may involve using EARP to encode the nature of semantic and dependency relations, as has been done with RI previously (Cohen et al., 2009; Basile et al., 2011). As the main focus of the current paper was on comparative evaluation across models with identical hyper-parameters, we have yet to formally evaluate the extent to which hyper-parameter settings (such as dimensionality) may affect performance, and it seems likely that hyper-parameters that would further accentuate EARP performance remain to be identified.

4.6 Conclusion

This paper describes EARP, a novel method through which word order can be encoded into neural word embedding representations. Of note, this additional information is encoded without the need for additional computation, and space requirements are practically identical to those of baseline models. Upon evaluation, encoding word order results in substantive improvements in performance across multiple analogical retrieval reference sets, with best performance when order information is encoded using a novel permutation-based method of positional binding.

Acknowledgments

This work was supported by US National Library of Medicine grant (R01 LM011563), and conducted in part at the University of Texas School of Biomedical Informatics at Houston.

---

[12]https://lucene.apache.org/
[13]https://github.com/semanticvectors/semanticvectors

[14]https://doi.org/10.5281/zenodo.1345333

References

Eneko Agirre, Enrique Alfonseca, Keith Hall, Jana Kravalova, Marius Paşca, and Aitor Soroa. 2009. A study on similarity and relatedness using distributional and wordnet-based approaches. In *Proceedings of Human Language Technologies: The 2009 Annual Conference of the North American Chapter of the Association for Computational Linguistics*, pages 19–27. Association for Computational Linguistics.

Pierpaolo Basile, Annalina Caputo, and Giovanni Semeraro. 2011. Encoding syntactic dependencies by vector permutation. In *Proceedings of the GEMS 2011 Workshop on GEometrical Models of Natural Language Semantics*, pages 43–51. Association for Computational Linguistics.

Yoshua Bengio, Réjean Ducharme, Pascal Vincent, and Christian Jauvin. 2003. A neural probabilistic language model. *Journal of machine learning research*, 3(Feb):1137–1155.

Piotr Bojanowski, Edouard Grave, Armand Joulin, and Tomas Mikolov. 2017. Enriching word vectors with subword information. *Transactions of the Association of Computational Linguistics*, 5(1):135–146.

Elia Bruni, Nam-Khanh Tran, and Marco Baroni. 2014. Multimodal distributional semantics. *Journal of Artificial Intelligence Research*, 49:1–47.

Billy Chiu, Anna Korhonen, and Sampo Pyysalo. 2016. Intrinsic evaluation of word vectors fails to predict extrinsic performance. In *Proceedings of the 1st Workshop on Evaluating Vector-Space Representations for NLP*, pages 1–6.

Trevor Cohen, Roger W Schvaneveldt, and Thomas C Rindflesch. 2009. Predication-based semantic indexing: Permutations as a means to encode predications in semantic space. In *AMIA Annual Symposium Proceedings*, volume 2009, page 114. American Medical Informatics Association.

Trevor Cohen, Dominic Widdows, Manuel Wahle, and Roger Schvaneveldt. 2013. Orthogonality and orthography: introducing measured distance into semantic space. In *International Symposium on Quantum Interaction*, pages 34–46. Springer.

Ronan Collobert, Jason Weston, Léon Bottou, Michael Karlen, Koray Kavukcuoglu, and Pavel Kuksa. 2011. Natural language processing (almost) from scratch. *Journal of Machine Learning Research*, 12(Aug):2493–2537.

Aleksandr Drozd, Anna Gladkova, and Satoshi Matsuoka. 2016. Word embeddings, analogies, and machine learning: Beyond king-man+ woman= queen. In *Proceedings of COLING 2016, the 26th International Conference on Computational Linguistics: Technical Papers*, pages 3519–3530.

Lev Finkelstein, Evgeniy Gabrilovich, Yossi Matias, Ehud Rivlin, Zach Solan, Gadi Wolfman, and Eytan Ruppin. 2001. Placing search in context: The concept revisited. In *Proceedings of the 10th international conference on World Wide Web*, pages 406–414. ACM.

Gregory Finley, Stephanie Farmer, and Serguei Pakhomov. 2017. What analogies reveal about word vectors and their compositionality. In *Proceedings of the 6th Joint Conference on Lexical and Computational Semantics (* SEM 2017)*, pages 1–11.

Stephen I Gallant and Phil Culliton. 2016. Positional binding with distributed representations. In *Image, Vision and Computing (ICIVC), International Conference on*, pages 108–113. IEEE.

Anna Gladkova, Aleksandr Drozd, and Satoshi Matsuoka. 2016. Analogy-based detection of morphological and semantic relations with word embeddings: what works and what doesn't. In *Proceedings of the NAACL Student Research Workshop*, pages 8–15.

Yoav Goldberg and Omer Levy. 2014. word2vec explained: Deriving mikolov et al.'s negative-sampling word-embedding method. *arXiv preprint arXiv:1402.3722*.

Felix Hill, Roi Reichart, and Anna Korhonen. 2015. Simlex-999: Evaluating semantic models with (genuine) similarity estimation. *Computational Linguistics*, 41(4):665–695.

Michael N Jones, Walter Kintsch, and Douglas JK Mewhort. 2006. High-dimensional semantic space accounts of priming. *Journal of memory and language*, 55(4):534–552.

Pentii Kanerva, Jan Kristoferson, and Anders Holst. 2000. Random indexing of text samples for latent semantic analysis. In *Proceedings of the Annual Meeting of the Cognitive Science Society*, volume 22.

Pentti Kanerva. 2009. Hyperdimensional computing: An introduction to computing in distributed representation with high-dimensional random vectors. *Cognitive Computation*, 1(2):139–159.

Jussi Karlgren and Magnus Sahlgren. 2001. From words to understanding. *Foundations of Real-World Intelligence*, pages 294–308.

Thomas Landauer and Susan Dumais. 1997. A solution to Plato's problem: The latent semantic analysis theory of acquisition. *Psychological Review*, 104(2):211–240.

Omer Levy, Yoav Goldberg, and Ido Dagan. 2015. Improving distributional similarity with lessons learned from word embeddings. *Transactions of the Association for Computational Linguistics*, 3:211–225.

Wang Ling, Chris Dyer, Alan W Black, and Isabel Trancoso. 2015. Two/too simple adaptations of word2vec for syntax problems. In *Proceedings of the 2015 Conference of the North American Chapter of the Association for Computational Linguistics: Human Language Technologies*, pages 1299–1304.

Kevin Lund and Curt Burgess. 1996. Producing high-dimensional semantic spaces from lexical co-occurrence. *Behavior research methods, instruments, & computers*, 28(2):203–208.

Tomas Mikolov, Kai Chen, Greg Corrado, and Jeffrey Dean. 2013a. Efficient estimation of word representations in vector space. *arXiv preprint arXiv:1301.3781*.

Tomas Mikolov, Edouard Grave, Piotr Bojanowski, Christian Puhrsch, and Armand Joulin. 2017. Advances in pre-training distributed word representations. *arXiv preprint arXiv:1712.09405*.

Tomas Mikolov, Ilya Sutskever, Kai Chen, Greg S Corrado, and Jeff Dean. 2013b. Distributed representations of words and phrases and their compositionality. In *Advances in neural information processing systems*, pages 3111–3119.

Tomas Mikolov, Wen-tau Yih, and Geoffrey Zweig. 2013c. Linguistic regularities in continuous space word representations. In *Proceedings of the 2013 Conference of the North American Chapter of the Association for Computational Linguistics: Human Language Technologies*, pages 746–751.

Andriy Mnih and Koray Kavukcuoglu. 2013. Learning word embeddings efficiently with noise-contrastive estimation. In *Advances in neural information processing systems*, pages 2265–2273.

Jeffrey Pennington, Richard Socher, and Christopher Manning. 2014. Glove: Global vectors for word representation. In *Proceedings of the 2014 conference on empirical methods in natural language processing (EMNLP)*, pages 1532–1543.

Tony A Plate. 1995. Holographic reduced representations. *IEEE Transactions on Neural networks*, 6(3):623–641.

Gabriel Recchia, Michael Jones, Magnus Sahlgren, and Pentti Kanerva. 2010. Encoding sequential information in vector space models of semantics: Comparing holographic reduced representation and random permutation. In *Proceedings of the Annual Meeting of the Cognitive Science Society*, volume 32.

Xin Rong. 2014. word2vec parameter learning explained. *arXiv preprint arXiv:1411.2738*.

Magnus Sahlgren, Anders Holst, and Pentti Kanerva. 2008. Permutations as a means to encode order in word space.

Hinrich Schütze. 1993. Word space. In *Advances in neural information processing systems*, pages 895–902.

Hinrich Schütze. 1998. Automatic word sense discrimination. *Computational Linguistics*, 24(1):97–124.

Erik F Tjong Kim Sang and Sabine Buchholz. 2000. Introduction to the conll-2000 shared task: Chunking. In *Proceedings of the 2nd workshop on Learning language in logic and the 4th conference on Computational natural language learning-Volume 7*, pages 127–132. Association for Computational Linguistics.

Erik F Tjong Kim Sang and Fien De Meulder. 2003. Introduction to the conll-2003 shared task: Language-independent named entity recognition. In *Proceedings of the seventh conference on Natural language learning at HLT-NAACL 2003-Volume 4*, pages 142–147. Association for Computational Linguistics.

Andrew Trask, David Gilmore, and Matthew Russell. 2015. Modeling order in neural word embeddings at scale. In *Proceedings of the 32nd International Conference on International Conference on Machine Learning-Volume 37*, pages 2266–2275. JMLR. org.

Peter D Turney and Patrick Pantel. 2010. From frequency to meaning: Vector space models of semantics. *Journal of artificial intelligence research*, 37:141–188.

Ellen M Voorhees et al. 1999. The trec-8 question answering track report. In *Trec*, volume 99, pages 77–82.

Aggregated Semantic Matching for Short Text Entity Linking

Feng Nie[1*], Shuyan Zhou[2*], Jing Liu[3*], Jinpeng Wang[4], Chin-Yew Lin[4], Rong Pan[1*]

[1]Sun Yat-Sen University   [2]Harbin Institute of Technology   [3]Baidu Inc.   [4]Microsoft Research Asia

{fengniesysu, alexisxy0418}@gmail.com,
liujing46@baidu.com, {jinpwa, cyl}@microsoft.com, panr@sysu.edu.cn

Abstract

The task of entity linking aims to identify concepts mentioned in a text fragments and link them to a reference knowledge base. Entity linking in long text has been well studied in previous work. However, short text entity linking is more challenging since the texts are noisy and less coherent. To better utilize the local information provided in short texts, we propose a novel neural network framework, Aggregated Semantic Matching (ASM), in which two different aspects of semantic information between the local context and the candidate entity are captured via representation-based and interaction-based neural semantic matching models, and then two matching signals work jointly for disambiguation with a rank aggregation mechanism. Our evaluation shows that the proposed model outperforms the state-of-the-arts on public tweet datasets.

1 Introduction

The task of entity linking aims to link a mention that appears in a piece of text to an entry (i.e. entity) in a knowledge base. For example, as shown in Table 1, given a mention *Trump* in a tweet, it should be linked to the entity *Donald Trump*[1] in Wikipedia. Recent research has shown that entity linking can help better understand the text of a document (Schuhmacher and Ponzetto, 2014) and benefits several tasks, including named entity recognition (Luo et al.) and information retrieval (Xiong et al., 2017b). The research of entity linking mainly considers two types of documents: long text (e.g. news articles and web documents) and short text (e.g. tweets). In this paper, we focus on short text, particularly tweet entity linking.

---

*Correspondence author is Rong Pan. This work was done when the first and second author were interns and the third author was an employee at Microsoft Research Asia.

[1]https://en.wikipedia.org/wiki/Donald_Trump

Tweet
The vile #Trump humanity raises its gentle face in Canada ... chapeau to #Trudeau
Candidates
Donald Trump, Trump (card games), ...

Table 1: An illustration of short text entity linking, with mention *Trump* underlined.

One of the major challenges in entity linking task is ambiguity, where an entity mention could denote to multiple entities in a knowledge base. As shown in Table 1, the mention *Trump* can refer to U.S. president *Donald Trump* and also the card name *Trump (card games)*. Many of recent approaches for long text entity linking take the advantage of global context which captures the coherence among the mapped entities for a set of related mentions in a single document (Cucerzan, 2007; Han et al., 2011; Globerson et al., 2016; Heinzerling et al., 2017). However, short texts like tweets are often concise and less coherent, which lack the necessary information for the global methods. In the NEEL dataset (Weller et al., 2016), there are only 3.4 mentions in each tweet on average. Several studies (Liu et al., 2013; Huang et al., 2014) investigate collective tweet entity linking by pre-collecting and considering multiple tweets simultaneously. However, multiple texts are not always available for collection and the process is time-consuming. Thus, we argue that an efficient entity disambiguation which requires only a single short text (e.g., a tweet) and can well utilize local contexts is better suited in real word applications.

In this paper, we investigate entity disambiguation in a setting where only local information is available. Recent neural approaches have shown their superiority in capturing rich semantic sim-

Proceedings of the 22nd Conference on Computational Natural Language Learning (CoNLL 2018), pages 476–485
Brussels, Belgium, October 31 - November 1, 2018. ©2018 Association for Computational Linguistics

ilarities from mention contexts and entity contents. Sun et al. (2015); Francis-Landau et al. (2016) proposed using convolutional neural networks (CNN) with Siamese (symmetric) architecture to capture the similarity between texts. These approaches can be viewed as **representation**-focused semantic matching models. The representation-focused model first builds a representation for a single text (e.g., a context or an entity description) with a neural network, and then conducts matching between the abstract representation of two pieces of text. Even though such models capture distinguishable information from both mention and entity side, some concrete matching signals are lost (e.g., exact match), since the matching between two texts happens after their individual abstract representations have been obtained. To enhance the representation-focused models, inspired by recent advances in information retrieval (Lu and Li, 2013; Guo et al., 2016; Xiong et al., 2017a), we propose using **interaction**-focused approach to capture the concrete matching signals. The interaction-focused method tries to build local interactions (e.g., cosine similarity) between two pieces of text, and then uses neural networks to learn the final matching score based on the local interactions.

The representation- and interaction-focused approach capture abstract- and concrete-level matching signal respectively, they would be complement each other if designed appropriately. One straightforward way to combine multiple semantic matching signals is to apply a linear regression layer to learn a static weight for each matching signal(Francis-Landau et al., 2016). However, we observe that the importance of different signals can be different case by case. For example, as shown in Table 1, the context word *Canada* is the most important word for the disambiguation of *Trudeau*. In this case, the concrete-level matching signal is required. While for the tweet "*#StarWars #theForceAwakens #StarWarsForceAwakens @StarWars*", *@StarWars* is linked to the entity *Star Wars*[2]. In this case, the whole tweet describes the same topic "Star Wars", thus the abstract-level semantics matching signal is helpful. To address this issue, we propose using a rank aggregation method to dynamically combine multiple semantic matching signals for disambiguation.

In summary, we focus on entity disambiguation

by leveraging only the local information. Specifically, we propose using both representation-focused model and interaction-focused model for semantic matching and view them as complementary to each other. To overcome the issue of the static weights in linear regression, we apply rank aggregation to combine multiple semantic matching signals captured by two neural models on multiple text pairs. We conduct extensive experiments to examine the effectiveness of our proposed approach, ASM, on both NEEL dataset and MSR tweet entity linking (MSR-TEL for short) dataset.

2 Background

2.1 Notations

Given a tweet t, it contains a set of identified queries $Q = (q_1, ..., q_n)$. Each query q in a tweet t consists of m and ctx, where m denotes an entity mention and ctx denotes the context of the mention, i.e., a piece of text surrounding m in the tweet t. An entity is an unambiguous page (e.g., Donald Trump) in a referent Knowledge Base (KB). Each entity e consists of ttl and $desc$, where ttl denotes the title of e and $desc$ denotes the description of e (e.g., the article defining e).

2.2 An Overview of the Linking System

Typically, an entity linking system consists of three components: mention detection, candidate generation and entity disambiguation. In this section, we will briefly presents the existing solutions for the first two components. In next section, we will introduce our proposed aggregated semantic matching for entity disambiguation.

2.2.1 Mention Detection

Given a tweet t with a sequence of words $w_1, ..., w_n$, our goal is to identify the possible entity mentions in the tweet t. Specifically, every word w_i in tweet t requires a label to indicate that whether it is an entity mention word or not. Therefore, we view it as a traditional named entity recognition (NER) problem and use BIO tagging schema. Given the tweet t, we aim to assign labels $y = (y_1, ..., y_n)$ for each word in the tweet t.

$$y_i = \begin{cases} B & w_i \text{ is a begin word of a mention,} \\ I & w_i \text{ is a non-begin word of a mention,} \\ O & w_i \text{ is not a mention word.} \end{cases}$$

In our implementation, we apply an LSTM-CRF based NER tagging model which automatically

---

[2]https://en.wikipedia.org/wiki/Star_Wars

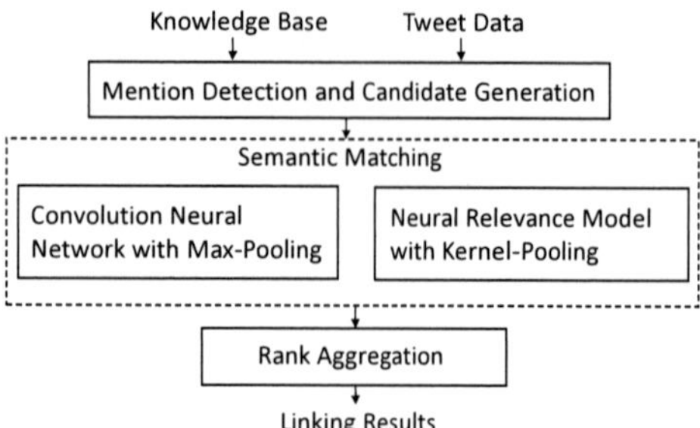

Figure 1: An overview of aggregated semantic matching for entity disambiguation.

learns contextual features for sequence tagging via recurrent neural networks (Lample et al., 2016).

2.2.2 Candidate Generation

Given a mention m, we use several heuristic rules to generate candidate entities similar to (Bunescu and Pasca, 2006; Huang et al., 2014; Sun et al., 2015). Specifically, given a mention m, we retrieve an entity as a candidate from KB, if it matches one of the following conditions: (a) the entity title exactly matches the mention, (b) the anchor text of the entity exactly matches the mention, (c) the title of the entity's redirected page exactly matches the mention Additionally, we add a special candidate **NIL** for each mention, which refers to a new entity out of KB. Given a mention, multiple candidates can be retrieved. Hence, we need to do entity disambiguation.

3 Aggregated Semantic Matching Model

We investigate entity disambiguation using only local information provided in short texts in this paper. Here, the local information includes a mention and its context in a tweet. Similar to (Francis-Landau et al., 2016), given a query q and an entity e, we consider semantic matching on the four text pairs for disambiguation: (1) the similarity $sim(m, ttl)$ between the mention and entity title, (2) the similarity $sim(m, desc)$ between the mention and entity description, (3) the similarity $sim(ctx, desc)$ between the context and entity description, (4) the similarity $sim(ctx, ttl)$ between the context and entity description. Fig. 1 illustrates an overview of our proposed Aggregated Semantic Matching for entity disambiguation. First, we use a representation-focused model and an interaction-focused neural model for semantic matching on four text pairs. Then, we introduce a pairwise rank aggregation to combine multiple semantic match-

ing signals captured by the two neural models on four text pairs.

3.1 Semantic Matching

Formally, given two texts T_1 and T_2, the semantic similarity of the two texts is measured as a score produced by a matching function based on the representation of each text:

$$match(T_1, T_2) = F(\Phi(T_1), \Phi(T_2)) \quad (1)$$

where Φ is a function to learn the text representation, and F is the matching function based on the interaction between the representations.

Existing neural semantic matching models can be categorized into two types: (a) the representation-focused model which takes a complex representation learning function and uses a relatively simple matching function, (b) the interaction-focused model which usually takes a simple representation learning function and uses a complex matching function. In the remaining of this section, we will present the details of a representation-focused model (M-CNN) and an interaction-focused model (K-NRM). We will also discuss the advantages of these two models in the entity linking task.

3.1.1 Convolution Neural Matching with Max Pooling (M-CNN)

Given two pieces of text $T_1 = \{w_1^1, ..., w_n^1\}$ and $T_2 = \{w_1^2, ..., w_m^2\}$, M-CNN aims to learn compositional and abstract representations (Φ) for T_1 and T_2 using a convolution neural network with a max pooling layer(Francis-Landau et al., 2016).

Figure 2a illustrates the architecture of M-CNN model. Given a sequence of words $w_1, ..., w_n$, we embed each word into a d dimensional vector, which yields a set of word vectors $v_1, ..., v_n$. We then map those word vectors into a fixed-size vector using a convolution network with a filter bank $M \in \mathbb{R}^{u \times d}$, where window size is l and u is the number of filters. The convolution feature matrix $H \in \mathbb{R}^{k \times (n-l+1)}$ is obtained by concatenating the convolution outputs $\overrightarrow{h}_i$:

$$\overrightarrow{h_j} = max\{0, Mv_{j:(j+l)}\}$$
$$H = [\overrightarrow{h}_1, ..., \overrightarrow{h}_{n-l+1}] \quad (2)$$

where $v_{j:j+l}$ is a concatenation of the given word vectors and the max is element-wise. In this way, we extract word-level n-gram features of T_1 and

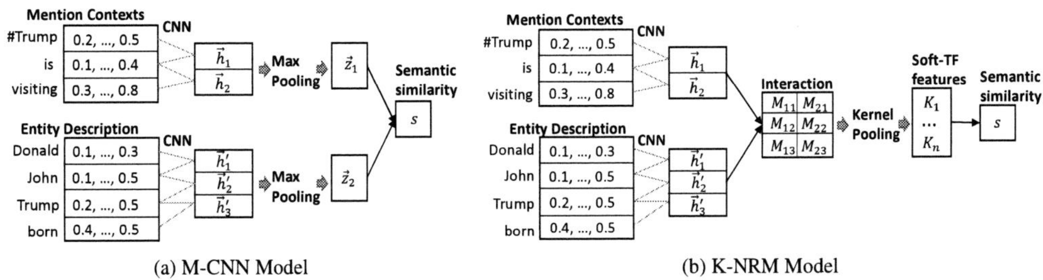

(a) M-CNN Model (b) K-NRM Model

Figure 2: The Architecture of models.

T_2 respectively. To capture the distinguishable information of T_1 and T_2, a max-pooling layer is applied and yields a fixed-length vector $\vec{z_1}$ and $\vec{z_2}$ for T_1 and T_2. The semantic similarity between T_1 and T_2 is measured using a cosine similarity $match(T_1, T_2) = cosine(\vec{z_1}, \vec{z_2})$.

In summary, M-CNN extracts distinguishable information representing the overall semantics (i.e. representations) of a string text by using a convolution neural network with max-pooling. However, the concrete matching signals (e.g., exact match) are lost, as the matching happens after their individual representation. We therefore introduce an interaction-focused model to better capture the concrete matching in the next section.

3.1.2 Neural Relevance Model with Kernel Pooling (K-NRM)

As shown in Fig. 2b, K-NRM captures the local interactions between T_1 and T_2 , and then uses a kernel-pooling layer (Xiong et al., 2017a) to softly count the frequencies of the local patterns. The final matching score is conducted based on the patterns. Therefore, the concrete matching information is captured.

Different from M-CNN, K-NRM builds the local interactions between T_1 and T_2 based on the word-level n-gram feature matrix calculated in Eq. 2. Formally, we construct a translation matrix M, where each element in M is the cosine similarity between an n-gram feature vector $\vec{h}^q_i$ in T_1 and an n-gram feature vector $\vec{h}^e_j$ in T_2, calculated as $M_{ij} = cosine(\vec{h}^q_i, \vec{h}^e_j)$.

Then, a scoring feature vector $\phi(M)$ is generated by a kernel-pooling technique.

$$\phi(M) = \sum_{i=1}^{n-l+1} \sqrt{\vec{K}(M_i)}$$

$$\vec{K}(M_i) = \{K_1(M_i), ..., K_K(M_i)\}$$

(3)

where $\vec{K}(M_i)$ applies K kernels to the i-th row of the translation matrix, and generates a $K-$dimensional scoring feature vector for the i-th n-gram feature in the query. The sqrt-sum of the scoring feature vectors of all n-gram features in query forms the scoring feature vector ϕ for the whole query, where the sqrt reduces the range of the value in each kernel vector. Note that the effect of $\vec{K}$ depends on the kernel used. We use the RBF kernel in this paper.

$$K_k(M_i) = \sum_j exp(\frac{-(M_{ij} - \mu_k)^2}{2\sigma^2})$$

(4)

The RBF kernel K_k calculates how pairwise similarities between n-gram feature vectors are distributed around its mean μ_k: the more similarities closed to its mean μ_k, the higher the output value is. The kernel functions act as 'soft-TF' bins, where μ defines the similarity level that 'soft-TF' focuses on and σ defines the range of its 'soft-TF' count. Then the semantic similarity is captured with a linear layer $match(T_1, T_2) = w^T \phi(M) + b$, where $\phi(M)$ is the scoring feature vector.

In summary, K-NRM captures the concrete matching signals based on word-level n-gram feature interactions between T_1 and T_2. In contrast, M-CNN captures the compositional and abstract meaning of a whole text. Thus, we produce the semantic matching signals using both models to capture different aspect of semantics that are useful for entity linking.

3.2 Normalization Scoring Layer

We compute 4 types of semantic similarities between the query q and the candidate entity e (e.g., $sim(m, tit)$, $sim(m, desc)$, $sim(ctx, tit)$, $sim(ctx, desc)$) with the above two semantic matching models. We obtain 8 semantic matching signals, denoted as $f_1(q, e), ..., f_8(q, e)$ in total. The normalized ranking score for each semantic matching signals $f_i(q, e)$ is calculated as

$$s_i(q, e, f) = \frac{exp(f_i(q, e))}{\sum_{e'} exp(f_i(q, e'))} \quad (5)$$

where e' stands for any of the candidate entities for the given mention m. We then produce 8 semantic matching scores for each candidate entity of m, denoted as $S_{q,e} = \{s_1, ..., s_8\}$.

3.3 Rank Aggregation

Given a query q, we obtain multiple semantic matching signals for each entity candidate after the last step. To take advantage of different semantic matching models on different text pairs, a straightforward approach is using a linear regression layer to combine multiple semantic matching signals (Francis-Landau et al., 2016). The linear combination learns a static weight for each matching signal. However, as we pointed out previously, the importance of different signals varies for different queries. In some cases, the abstract-level signals are important. While the concrete-level signals are more important in other cases. To address this issue, we introduce a pairwise rank aggregation method to aggregate multiple semantic matching signals.

In the area of information retrieval, rank aggregation is combining rankings from multiple retrieval systems and producing a better new ranking (Carterette and Petkova, 2006). In our problem, given a query q, we have one ranking of the entity candidates for each semantic matching signal. We aim to find the final ranking by aggregating multiple rankings. Specifically, given a ranking of entities for one semantic matching signal, $e_1 \succ e_2 \succ e_3 \ldots$, where $i \succ j$ means entity i is ranked above j, we extract all entity pairs (e_i, e_j) from the ranking and assume that if $e_i \succ e_j$, then e_i is preferred to e_j. We union all pairwise preferences generated from multiple rankings as a single set, from which the final ranking is learned. In this paper, we apply TrueSkill (Herbrich et al., 2006) which is a Bayesian skill rating model. We present a two-layer version of TrueSkill with no-draw.

TrueSkill assumes that the practical performance of each player in a game follows a normal distribution $N(\mu, \sigma^2)$, where μ means the skill level of the player and σ stands for the uncertainty of the estimated skill level. Basically, TrueSkill learns the skill levels of players by lever-

aging Bayes' theorem. Given the current estimated skill levels of two players (prior probability) and the outcome of a new game between them (likelihood), TrueSkill model updates its estimation of player skill levels (posterior probability). TrueSkill updates the skill level μ and the uncertainty σ intuitively: (a) if the outcome of a new competition is expected, i.e., the player with higher skill level wins the game, it will cause small updates in skill level μ and uncertainty σ; (b) if the outcome of a new competition is unexpected, i.e., the player with lower skill level wins the game, it will cause large updates in skill level μ and uncertainty σ. According to these intuitions, the equations to update the skill level μ and uncertainty σ are as follows:

$$\mu_{winner} = \mu_{winner} + \frac{\sigma_{winner}^2}{c} * v(\frac{t}{c}, \frac{\varepsilon}{c})$$

$$\mu_{loser} = \mu_{loser} - \frac{\sigma_{loser}^2}{c} * v(\frac{t}{c}, \frac{\varepsilon}{c})$$

$$\sigma_{winner}^2 = \sigma_{winner}^2 * [1 - \frac{\sigma_{winner}^2}{c^2} * w(\frac{t}{c}, \frac{\varepsilon}{c})]$$

$$\sigma_{loser}^2 = \sigma_{loser}^2 * [1 - \frac{\sigma_{loser}^2}{c^2} * w(\frac{t}{c}, \frac{\varepsilon}{c})]$$

$$(6)$$

where $t = \mu_{winner} - \mu_{loser}$ and $c^2 = 2\beta^2 + \sigma_{winner}^2 + \sigma_{loser}^2$. Here, ε is a parameter representing the probability of a draw in one game, and $v(t, \varepsilon)$ and $w(t, \varepsilon)$ are weighting factors for skill level μ and standard deviation σ respectively. β is a parameter representing the range of skills. In this paper, we set the initial values of the skill level μ and the standard deviation σ of each player the same as the default values used in (Herbrich et al., 2006). We use $\mu - 3\beta$ to rank entities following (Herbrich et al., 2006).

4 Experiments

In this section, we describe our experimental results on tweet entity linking. Particularly, we investigate the difference between two semantic matching models and the effectiveness of jointly combining these two semantic matching signals.

4.1 Datasets & Evaluation Metric

In our experiments, we evaluate our proposed model ASM on the following two datasets.

NEEL Weller et al. (2016). We use the dataset of Named Entity Extraction & Linking Challenge 2016. The training dataset consists of 6,025 tweets and includes 6,374 non-NIL queries and 2,291

NIL queries. The validation dataset consists of 100 tweets and includes 253 non-NIL queries and 85 NIL queries. The testing dataset consists of 300 tweets and includes 738 non-NIL queries and 284 NIL queries.

MSR-TEL Guo et al. (2013)[3]. This dataset consists of 428 tweets and 770 non-NIL queries. Since the NEEL test dataset has distribution bias problem, we add MSR-TEL as another dataset for the evaluation. In the NEEL testing dataset, 384 out of 1022 queries refer to three entities: 'Donald Trump', 'Star Wars' and 'Star Wars (The Force Awakens)'.

In this paper, we use accuracy as the major evaluation metric for entity disambiguation. Formally, we denote N as the number of queries and M as the number of correctly linked mentions given the gold mention (the top-ranked entity is the golden entity), $accuracy = \frac{M}{N}$. Besides, we use precision, recall and F1 measure to evaluate the end-to-end system. Formally, we denote N' as the number of mentions identified by a system and M' as the correctly linked mentions. Thus, $precision = \frac{M'}{N'}$, $recall = \frac{M'}{N}$ and $F1 = 2 * \frac{precision*recall}{precision+recall}$.

4.2 Data Preprocessing

Tweet data All tweets are normalized in the following way. First, we use the Twitter-aware tokenizer in NLTK[4] to tokenize words in a tweet. We convert each hyperlink in tweets to a special token *URL*. Since hashtags usually does not contain any space between words, we use a web service[5] to break hastags into tokens (e.g., the service will break '#TheForceAwakens' into 'the force awakens') by following (Guo et al., 2013). Regarding to usernames (@) in tweets, we replace them with their screen name (e.g., the screen name of the user '@jimmyfallon' is 'jimmy fallon').

Wikipedia data We use the Wikipedia Dump on December 2015 as the reference knowledge base. Since the most important information of an entity is usually at the beginning of its Wikipedia article, we utilize only the first 200 words in the article as its entity description. We use the default English word tokenizer in NLTK to do the tokenization for each Wikipedia article.

Word embedding We use the word2vec toolkit (Mikolov et al., 2013) to pre-train word embeddings on the whole English Wikipedia Dump. The dimensionality of the word embeddings is set to 400. Note that we do not update word embeddings during training.

4.3 Experimental Setup

In our main experiment, we compare our proposed approaches with the following baselines: (a) The officially ranked 1st and 2nd systems in NEEL 2016 challenge. We denote these two systems as `Rank1` and `Rank2`. (b) `TagMe`. Ferragina and Scaiella (2010) is an end-to-end linking system, which jointly performs mention detection and entity disambiguation. It focuses on short texts, including tweets. (c) `Cucerzan`. (Cucerzan, 2007) is a supervised entity disambiguation system that won TAC KBP competition in 2010. (d) `M-CNN`. To the best of our knowledge, (Francis-Landau et al., 2016) is the state-of-the-art neural disambiguation model. (e) `Ensemble`. The rank aggregated combination of two `M-CNN` models with different random seeds.

To fairly compare with the baselines of `Cucerzan` and `M-CNN`, we use the same mention detection and candidate generation for them and our approaches. We train an LSTM-CRF based tagger (Lample et al., 2016) for mention detection by using the NEEL training dataset. The precision, recall, and F1 of mention detection on NEEL testing dataset are 96.1%, 89.2%, 92.6% respectively. The precision, recall, and F1 of mention detection on MSR-TEL dataset are 80.3% 83.8% and 82% respectively. As we described in the previous section, we use the heuristic rules for candidate generation. The recall of candidate generation on NEEL and MSR-TEL is 88.7% and 92.5%.

When training our model, we use the stochastic gradient descent algorithm and the AdaDelta optimizer (Zeiler, 2012). The gradients are computed via back-propagation. The dimensionality of the hidden units in convolution neural network is set to 300. All the parameters are initialized with a uniform distribution $U(-0.01, 0.01)$. Since there is NIL entity in the dataset, we tune a NIL threshold for the prediction of NIL entities according to the validation dataset.

4.4 Main Results

The end-to-end performance of various approaches on the two datasets is shown in Table 2. Since there are no publicly available codes of

---

[3] Guo et al. (2013) only used a subset of this dataset for evaluation. Instead, we test on the full dataset.

[4] Natural Language Toolkit. http://www.nltk.org

[5] http://web-ngram.research.microsoft.com/info/break.html

Methods	NEEL			MSR-TEL[6]		
	Precision	Recall	F1	Precision	Recall	F1
Rank 1	-	-	50.1	-	-	-
Rank 2	-	-	39.6	-	-	-
TagMe	25.3	62.9	36.2	14.5	**69.2**	23.8
Cucerzan	65.4	57.9	61.4	62.6	63.3	62.9
M-CNN	69.5	64.9	67.1	61.6	62.3	62.1
+pre-train	69.7	65.1	67.3	64.5	65.2	64.8
Ensemble	69.7	65.1	67.3	63.5	64.2	63.8
+pre-train	70.2	65.5	67.8	64.9	65.6	65.2
ASM	70.6	65.9	68.2	64.2	64.9	64.5
+pre-train	**72.2**	**67.4**	**69.7**	**66.2**	66.9	**66.5**

Table 2: End-to-end performance of the systems on the two datasets

Methods	NEEL	MSR-TEL
Cucerzan	65.4	75.5
M-CNN	72.8	74.7
+pre-train	72.9	77.6
Ensemble	72.9	76.4
+pre-train	73.5	78.1
ASM	73.9	77.4
+pre-train	**75.5**	**79.4**

Table 3: The accuracy of entity disambiguation with golden mentions on the two datasets.

	(m, ttl)	(ctx, desc)	All Pairs
M-CNN	64.8	66.7	72.8
K-NRM	64.1	66.8	72.7
ASM	**65.1**	**69.7**	**73.9**

Table 4: The performance of two semantic matching models and their combinations on NEEL dataset.

Rank1 and Rank2, we give only the F1 scores of these two systems on NEEL dataset according to Weller et al. (2016). Note that the baseline systems Rank1, Rank2 and TagMe use different mention detection.

The systems of Rank1, Rank2, TagMe and Cucerzan are feature engineering based approaches. The systems of M-CNN and ASM are neural based approaches. From Table 2, we can observe that neural based approaches are superior to the feature engineering based approaches. Table 2 also shows that ASM outperforms the neural based method M-CNN. Our proposed method ASM also shows improvements over Ensemble, which indicates the necessity of combining representation- and interaction-focused models in entity disambiguation.

Moreover, we pre-train both M-CNN, Ensemble and ASM by using 0.5 million anchors in Wikipedia, and fine-tune the model parameters using non-NIL queries in NEEL training dataset. From Table 2, we can observe that the performance of neural models will be improved by using pre-training. The results in Table 2 show that our proposed ASM is still superior to M-CNN and Ensemble in the setting of pre-training.

Since entity disambiguation is our focus, we also give the disambiguation accuracy of different approaches by using the golden mentions in Table 3. Similarly, we observe that our proposed ASM outperforms baseline systems.

4.5 Model Analysis

In this section, we discuss several key observations based on the experimental results, and we mainly report the entity disambiguation *accuracy* when given the golden mentions.

4.5.1 Effect of Different Semantic Matching Methods

We empirically analyze the difference between the two semantic matching models (M-CNN and K-NRM) and show the benefits when combing the semantic matching signals from these two models.

---

[6]Note that the performance of all systems on MSR-TEL dataset might be under estimated, since not all mentions in each tweet were manually annotated. For example, a correctly identified mention given by a system, which was not manually annotated, will be judged as wrong. But we still give the comparisons of different approaches on MSR-TEL dataset.

	M-CNN win	M-CNN loss
K-NRM win	58.3%	6.3%
K-NRM loss	5.8%	29.6%

Table 5: The win-loss analysis of M-CNN and K-NRM on the pair (ctx, desc).

Query:	the vile #Trump humanity raises its gentle face in Canada ... chapeau to **#Trudeau**,URL
M-CNN:	Kevin Trudeau
K-NRM:	<u>Justin Trudeau</u>
Query:	RT @ MingNa : What is my plan to avoid spoiler about #theForceAwakens ? No Internet except to post my **@StarWars**
M-CNN:	<u>Star Wars</u>
K-NRM:	Comparison of Star Trek and Star Wars

Table 6: The top-1 results of M-CNN and K-NRM using (ctx,desc) pair for two queries. Mention is in **bold** and the golden answer is underlined.

Method	Without Pre-Train		With Pre-Train	
	NEEL	MSR-TEL	NEEL	MSR-TEL
Linear	73.1	75.7	73.8	78.1
ASM	**73.9**	**77.4**	**75.5**	**79.4**

Table 7: Comparison of rank aggregation and linear combination on two datasets.

We first compare the performance of two semantic matching models over the two text pairs: (a) *(m, ttl)* and (b) *(ctx, desc)*. These two pairs presents two extreme of the information used in the systems: *(m, ttl)* consumes the minimum amount of information from a query and an entity, while *(ctx, desc)* consumes the maximum amount of information from a query and an entity. From the first two columns in Table 4, we can observe that M-CNN performs comparably with K-NRM on the two text pairs. ASM that combines the two models obtains performance gains on the two individual text pairs. The third column in Table 4 also shows that ASM gives performance gains when using all text pairs. This indicates that M-CNN and K-NRM capture complementary information for entity disambiguation.

Moreover, we observe that the performance gains are different on the two pairs *(m, ttl)* and *(ctx, desc)*. The gain on *(ctx, desc)* is relatively larger. This indicates that M-CNN and K-NRM capture more different information when the text is long. Additionally, we show the win-loss analysis of the two semantic matching model for non-NIL queries on *(ctx, desc)* in Table 5. The 12.1% (=6.3% + 5.8%) difference between these two models confirms the necessity of combination.

To further investigate the difference between the two semantic matching models on short text, we did case study. Table 6 gives two examples. In the first example, the correct answer is 'Justin Trudeau' which contains the words of 'Canada' and 'trump' in its entity description. However, M-CNN fails to capture this concrete matching information, since the concrete information of text might be lost after the convolution layer and max-pooling layer. In contrast, K-NRM builds the n-gram level local interactions between texts, and thus successfully captures the concrete matching information (e.g. exact match) that results in a correct linking result. In the second example, both candidate entities 'Star Wars' and 'Comparison of Star Trek and Star Wars' contains the phrase 'Star Wars' for multiple times in their entity descriptions. In this case, K-NRM fails to distinguish the correct entity 'Star Wars' from the wrong entity 'Comparision of Star Trek and Star Wars', because it relies too much on the soft-TF information for matching. However, the soft-TF information in the descriptions of the two entities is similar. In contrast, M-CNN captures the whole meaning of the text and links the mention to the correct entity. A detailed analysis of n-grams extracted from the M-CNN is provided in the Appendix.

4.6 Effect of Rank Aggregation

Table 4 shows that the combination of multiple semantic matching signals yields the best performance. Table 7 compares two different combination of M-CNN and K-NRM models, the result shows that the rank aggregation method outperforms the linear combination. The rank aggregation method dynamically summarizes win-loss results for each signal and generates the final overall ranking by considering all win-loss results. The improvement of our method over the linear combination confirms that the importance of different semantic signals varies for different queries, and our method is more suitable for combining multiple semantic signals.

5 Related Work

Existing entity linking methods can roughly fall into two categories. Early work focus on local approaches, which identifies one mention each time, and each mention is disambiguated separately using hand-crafted features (Bunescu and Pasca, 2006; Ji and Grishman, 2008; Milne and Witten, 2008; Zheng et al., 2010). While recent work on entity linking has largely focus on global methods, which takes the mentions in the document as inputs and find their corresponding entities simultaneously by considering the coherency of entity assignments within a document. (Cucerzan, 2007; Hoffart et al., 2011; Globerson et al., 2016; Ganea and Hofmann, 2017).

Global models can tap into highly discriminative semantic signals (e.g. coreference and entity relatedness) that are unavailable to local methods, and have significantly outperformed the local approach on standard datasets(Globerson et al., 2016). However, global approaches are difficult to apply in domains where only short and noisy text is available (e.g. tweets). Many techniques have been proposed to short texts including tweets. Liu et al. (2013) and Huang et al. (2014) investigate the collective tweet entity linking by considering multiple tweets simultaneously. Meij et al. (2012) and Guo et al. (2013) perform joint detection and disambiguation of mentions for tweet entity linking using feature based learning methods.

Recently, some neural network methods have been applied to entity linking to model the local contextual information. He et al. (2013) investigate Stacked Denoising Auto-encoders to learn entity representation. Sun et al. (2015); Francis-Landau et al. (2016) apply convolutional neural networks for entity linking. Eshel et al. (2017) use recurrent neural networks to model the mention contexts. Nie et al. (2018) uses a co-attention mechanism to select informative contexts and entity description for entity disambiguation. However, none of these methods consider combining representation- and interaction-focused semantic matching methods to capture the semantic similarity for entity linking, and use rank aggregation method to combine multiple semantic signals.

6 Conclusion

We propose an aggregated semantic matching framework, ASM, for short text entity linking. The combination of the representation-focused semantic matching method and the interaction-focused semantic matching method capture both compositional and concrete matching signals (e.g. exact match). Moreover, the pairwise rank aggregation is applied to better combine multiple semantic signals. We have shown the effectiveness of ASM over two datasets through comprehensive experiments. In the future, we will try our model for long text entity linking.

7 Acknowledgement

We thank the anonymous reviewers for their helpful comments. We also thank Jin-Ge Yao, Zhirui Zhang, Shuangzhi Wu and Yin Lin for helpful conversations and comments on the work.

References

R Bunescu and M Pasca. 2006. Using encyclopedic knowledge for named entity disambiguation. In *EACL*, Trento, Italy.

Ben Carterette and Desislava Petkova. 2006. Learning a ranking from pairwise preferences. In *Proceedings of the 29th annual international ACM SIGIR conference on Research and development in information retrieval*, pages 629–630. ACM.

S Cucerzan. 2007. Large-scale named entity disambiguation based on wikipedia data. In *EMNLP-CoNLL*, volume 2007.

Yotam Eshel, Noam Cohen, and Kira Radinsky. 2017. Named entity disambiguation for noisy text. In *CoNLL*, volume 2017.

Paolo Ferragina and Ugo Scaiella. 2010. TAGME: on-the-fly annotation of short text fragments (by wikipedia entities). In *Proceedings of CIKM 2010*, pages 1625–1628.

Matthew Francis-Landau, Greg Durrett, and Dan Klein. 2016. Capturing semantic similarity for entity linking with convolutional neural networks. In *In Proceedings of NAACL-HLT 2016*, pages 1256–1261.

Octavian-Eugen Ganea and Thomas Hofmann. 2017. Deep joint entity disambiguation with local neural attention. In *Proceedings of the 2017 Conference on Empirical Methods in Natural Language Processing*.

Amir Globerson, Nevena Lazic, Soumen Chakrabarti, Amarnag Subramanya, Michael Ringgaard, and Fernando Pereira. 2016. Collective entity resolution with multi-focal attention. In *Proceedings of ACL 2016*.

Jiafeng Guo, Yixing Fan, Qingyao Ai, and W. Bruce Croft. 2016. A deep relevance matching model for ad-hoc retrieval. In *Proceedings of CIKM 2016*, pages 55–64.

Stephen Guo, Ming-Wei Chang, and Emre Kiciman. 2013. To link or not to link? a study on end-to-end tweet entity linking. In *NAACL-HLT 2013*.

Xianpei Han, Le Sun, and Jun Zhao. 2011. Collective entity linking in web text: a graph-based method. In *Proceeding of the SIGIR 2011*, pages 765–774.

Zhengyan He, Shujie Liu, Mu Li, Ming Zhou, Longkai Zhang, and Houfeng Wang. 2013. Learning entity representation for entity disambiguation. In *Proceedings of ACL 2013*.

Benjamin Heinzerling, Michael Strube, and Chin-Yew Lin. 2017. Trust, but verify better entity linking through automatic verification. EACL.

Ralf Herbrich, Tom Minka, and Thore Graepel. 2006. Trueskill^tm: A bayesian skill rating system. In *In Proceedings of NIPS 2006.*, pages 569–576.

Johannes Hoffart, Mohamed Amir Yosef, Ilaria Bordino, Hagen Fürstenau, Manfred Pinkal, Marc Spaniol, Bilyana Taneva, Stefan Thater, and Gerhard Weikum. 2011. Robust disambiguation of named entities in text. In *Proceedings of EMNLP 2011*.

Hongzhao Huang, Yunbo Cao, Xiaojiang Huang, Heng Ji, and Chin-Yew Lin. 2014. Collective tweet wikification based on semi-supervised graph regularization. In *Proceedings of ACL 2014*.

Heng Ji and Ralf Grishman. 2008. Refining event extraction through cross-document inference. In *Proceedings of ACL 2008*.

Guillaume Lample, Miguel Ballesteros, Sandeep Subramanian, Kazuya Kawakami, and Chris Dyer. 2016. Neural architectures for named entity recognition. In *In Proceedings of NAACL-HLT 2016*, pages 260–270.

Xiaohua Liu, Yitong Li, Haocheng Wu, Ming Zhou, Furu Wei, and Yi Lu. 2013. Entity linking for tweets. In *ACL (1)*, pages 1304–1311.

Zhengdong Lu and Hang Li. 2013. A deep architecture for matching short texts. In *In Proceedings of NIPS 2006.*, pages 1367–1375.

Gang Luo, Xiaojiang Huang, Chin-Yew Lin, and Zaiqing Nie. Joint entity recognition and disambiguation. In *Proceedings of the 2015 Conference on Empirical Methods in Natural Language Processing, EMNLP 2015, Lisbon, Portugal, September 17-21, 2015*.

Edgar Meij, Wouter Weerkamp, and Maarten de Rijke. 2012. Adding semantics to microblog posts. In *Proceedings of the WSDM, 2012*, pages 563–572.

Tomas Mikolov, Ilya Sutskever, Kai Chen, Greg S Corrado, and Jeff Dean. 2013. Distributed representations of words and phrases and their compositionality. In C. J. C. Burges, L. Bottou, M. Welling, Z. Ghahramani, and K. Q. Weinberger, editors, *Advances in Neural Information Processing Systems 26*, pages 3111–3119.

David N. Milne and Ian H. Witten. 2008. Learning to link with wikipedia. In *Proceedings of CIKM 2008*.

Feng Nie, Yunbo Cao, Jinpeng Wang, Chin-Yew Lin, and Rong Pan. 2018. Mention and entity description co-attention for entity disambiguation. In *Proceedings of the Thirty-Second AAAI Conference on Artificial Intelligence, New Orleans, Louisiana, USA, February 2-7, 2018*.

Michael Schuhmacher and Simone Paolo Ponzetto. 2014. Knowledge-based graph document modeling. In *Proceedings of CIKM 2014*, pages 543–552.

Yaming Sun, Lei Lin, Duyu Tang, Nan Yang, Zhenzhou Ji, and Xiaolong Wang. 2015. Modeling mention, context and entity with neural networks for entity disambiguation. In *Proceedings of IJCAI 2015*.

Katrin Weller, Aba-Sah Dadzie, and Danica Radovanovic. 2016. Making sense of microposts (#microposts2016) social sciences track. In *Proceedings of the 6th Workshop on 'Making Sense of Microposts' co-located with the 25th International World Wide Web Conference (WWW 2016), Montréal, Canada, April 11, 2016.*, pages 29–32.

Chenyan Xiong, Zhuyun Dai, Jamie Callan, Zhiyuan Liu, and Russell Power. 2017a. End-to-end neural ad-hoc ranking with kernel pooling. In *Proceedings of SIGIR 2017*, pages 55–64.

Chenyan Xiong, Russell Power, and Jamie Callan. 2017b. Explicit semantic ranking for academic search via knowledge graph embedding. In *Proceedings of the 26th International Conference on World Wide Web, WWW 2017, Perth, Australia, April 3-7, 2017*, pages 1271–1279.

Matthew D Zeiler. 2012. Adadelta: an adaptive learning rate method.

Zhicheng Zheng, Fangtao Li, Minlie Huang, and Xiaoyan Zhu. 2010. Learning to link entities with knowledge base. In *NAACL-HLT 2010*.

Adversarial Over-Sensitivity and Over-Stability Strategies for Dialogue Models

Tong Niu and **Mohit Bansal**
UNC Chapel Hill
{tongn, mbansal}@cs.unc.edu

Abstract

We present two categories of model-agnostic adversarial strategies that reveal the weaknesses of several generative, task-oriented dialogue models: *Should-Not-Change* strategies that evaluate over-sensitivity to small and semantics-preserving edits, as well as *Should-Change* strategies that test if a model is over-stable against subtle yet semantics-changing modifications. We next perform adversarial training with each strategy, employing a max-margin approach for negative generative examples. This not only makes the target dialogue model more robust to the adversarial inputs, but also helps it perform significantly better on the original inputs. Moreover, training on all strategies combined achieves further improvements, achieving a new state-of-the-art performance on the original task (also verified via human evaluation). In addition to adversarial training, we also address the robustness task at the model-level, by feeding it subword units as both inputs and outputs, and show that the resulting model is equally competitive, requires only 1/4 of the original vocabulary size, and is robust to one of the adversarial strategies (to which the original model is vulnerable) even without adversarial training.

1 Introduction

Adversarial evaluation aims at filling in the gap between potential train/test distribution mismatch and revealing how models will perform under real-world inputs containing natural or malicious noise. Recently, there has been substantial work on adversarial attacks in computer vision and NLP. Unlike vision, where one can simply add in imperceptible perturbations without changing an image's meaning, carrying out such subtle changes in text is harder since text is discrete in nature (Jia and Liang, 2017). Thus, some previous works have either avoided modifying original source inputs and only resorted to inserting distractive sentences (Jia and Liang, 2017), or have restricted themselves to introducing spelling errors (Belinkov and Bisk, 2018) and adding non-functioning tokens (Shalyminov et al., 2017). Furthermore, there has been limited adversarial work on generative NLP tasks, e.g., dialogue generation (Henderson et al., 2017), which is especially important because it is a crucial component of real-world virtual assistants such as Alexa, Siri, and Google Home. It is also a challenging and worthwhile task to keep the output quality of a dialogue system stable, because a conversation usually involves multiple turns, and a small mistake in an early turn could cascade into bigger misunderstanding later on.

Motivated by this, we present a comprehensive adversarial study on dialogue models – we not only simulate imperfect inputs in the real world, but also launch intentionally malicious attacks on the model in order to assess them on both over-sensitivity and over-stability. Unlike most previous works that exclusively focus on Should-Not-Change adversarial strategies (i.e., non-semantics-changing perturbations to the source sequence that *should not change* the response), we demonstrate that it is equally valuable to consider Should-Change strategies (i.e., semantics-changing, intentional perturbations to the source sequence that *should change* the response).

We investigate three state-of-the-art models on two task-oriented dialogue datasets. Concretely, we propose and evaluate five naturally motivated and increasingly complex Should-Not-Change and five Should-Change adversarial strategies on the VHRED (Variational Hierarchical Encoder-Decoder) model (Serban et al., 2017b) and the RL (Reinforcement Learning) model (Li et al., 2016) with the Ubuntu Dialogue Cor-

We publicly release all our code and data at https://github.com/WolfNiu/AdversarialDialogue

486

Proceedings of the 22nd Conference on Computational Natural Language Learning (CoNLL 2018), pages 486–496
Brussels, Belgium, October 31 - November 1, 2018. ©2018 Association for Computational Linguistics

pus (Lowe et al., 2015), and Dynamic Knowledge Graph Network with the Collaborative Communicating Agents (CoCoA) dataset (He et al., 2017).

On the Should-Not-Change side for the Ubuntu task, we introduce adversarial strategies of increasing linguistic-unit complexity – from shallow word-level errors, to phrase-level paraphrastic changes, and finally to syntactic perturbations. We first propose two rule-based perturbations to the source dialogue context, namely Random Swap (randomly transposing neighboring tokens) and Stopword Dropout (randomly removing stopwords). Next, we propose two data-level strategies that leverage existing parallel datasets in order to simulate more realistic, diverse noises: namely, Data-Level Paraphrasing (replacing words with their paraphrases) and Grammar Errors (e.g., changing a verb to the wrong tense). Finally, we employ Generative-Level Paraphrasing, where we adopt a neural model to automatically generate paraphrases of the source inputs.[1] On the Should-Change side for the Ubuntu task, we propose the Add Negation strategy, which negates the root verb of the source input, and the Antonym strategy, which changes verbs, adjectives, or adverbs to their antonyms. As will be shown in Section 6, the above strategies are effective on the Ubuntu task, but not on the collaborative-style, database-dependent Co-CoA task. Thus for the latter, we investigate additional Should-Change strategies including Random Inputs (changing each word in the utterance to random ones), Random Inputs with Entities (like Random Inputs but leaving mentioned entities untouched), and Normal Inputs with Confusing Entities (replacing entities in an agent's utterance with distractive ones) to analyze where the model's robustness stems from.

To evaluate these strategies, we first show that (1) both VHRED and the RL model are vulnerable to most Should-Not-Change and all Should-Change strategies, and (2) DynoNet's robustness to Should-Change inputs shows that it does not pay any attention to natural language inputs other than the entities contained in them. Next, observing how our adversarial strategies 'successfully' fool the target models, we try to expose

these models to such perturbation patterns early on during training itself, where we feed adversarial input context and ground-truth target pairs as training data. Importantly, we realize this adversarial training via a maximum-likelihood loss for Should-Not-Change strategies, and via a max-margin loss for Should-Change strategies. We show that this adversarial training can not only make both VHRED and RL more robust to the adversarial data, but also improve their performances when evaluated on the original test set (verified via human evaluation). In addition, when we train VHRED on all of the perturbed data from each adversarial strategy together, the performance on the original task improves even further, achieving the state-of-the-art result by a significant margin (also verified via human evaluation).

Finally, we attempt to resolve the robustness issue directly at the model-level (instead of adversarial-level) by feeding subword units derived from the Byte Pair Encoding (BPE) algorithm (Sennrich et al., 2016) to the VHRED model. We show that the resulting model not only reduces the vocabulary size by around 75% (thus trains much faster) and obtains results comparable to the original VHRED, but is also naturally (i.e., without requiring adversarial training) robust to the Grammar Errors adversarial strategy.

2 Tasks and Models

For a comprehensive study on dialogue model robustness, we investigate both semi-task-based troubleshooting dialogue (the Ubuntu task) and the new important paradigm of collaborative two-bot dialogue (the CoCoA task). The former focuses more on natural conversations, while the latter focuses more on the knowledge base. Consequently, the model trained on the latter tends to ignore the natural language context (as will be shown in Section 6.2) and hence requires a different set of adversarial strategies that can directly reveal this weakness (e.g., Random Inputs with Entities). Overall, adversarial strategies on Ubuntu and CoCoA reveal very different types of weaknesses of a dialogue model. We implement two models on the Ubuntu task and one on the Co-CoA task, each achieving state-of-the-art result on its respective task. Note that although we employ these two strong models as our testbeds for the proposed adversarial strategies, these adversarial strategies are not specific to the two models.

---

[1] A real example of Generative-Paraphrasing: context *"You can find xorg . conf in /etc/X11 . It 's not needed unless it is . ;-) You may need to create one yourself."* is paraphrased as *"You may find xorg . conf in /etc/X11 . It 's not necessary until it is . You may be required to create one ."*

2.1 Ubuntu Dialogue

Dataset and Task: The Ubuntu Dialogue Corpus (Lowe et al., 2015) contains 1 million 2-person, multi-turn dialogues extracted from Ubuntu chat logs, used to provide and receive technical support. We focus on the task of generating fluent, relevant, and goal-oriented responses.

Evaluation Method: The model is evaluated on F1's for both activities (technical verbs, e.g., "download", "install") and entities (technical nouns, e.g., "root", "web"). These metrics are computed by mapping the ground-truth and model responses to their corresponding activity-entity representations using the automatic procedure described in Serban et al. (2017a), who found that F1 is "particularly suited for the goal-oriented Ubuntu Dialogue Corpus" based on manual inspection of the extracted activities and entities. We also conducted human studies on the dialogue quality of generated responses (see Section 5 for setup and Section 6.1 for results).

Models: We reproduce the state-of-the-art Latent Variable Hierarchical Recurrent Encoder-Decoder (VHRED) model (Serban et al., 2016), and a Deep Reinforcement Learning based generative model (Li et al., 2016). For the VHRED model, we apply additive attention mechanism (Bahdanau et al., 2015) to the source sequence while keeping the remaining architecture unchanged. For the RL-based model, we adopt the mixed objective function (Paulus et al., 2018) and employ a novel reward: during training, for each source sequence S, we sample a response G on the decoder side, feed the encoder with a random source sequence S_R drawn from the train set, and use $-\log P(G|S_R)$ as the reward. Intuitively, if S_R stands a high chance of generating G (which corresponds to a large negative reward), it is very likely that G is dull and generic.

2.2 Collaborative Communicating Agents

Dataset and Task: The collaborative CoCoA[2] dialogue task involves two agents that are asymmetrically primed with a private Knowledge Base (KB), and engage in a natural language conversation to find out the unique entry shared by the two KBs. For a bot-bot chat of the CoCoA task, a bot is allowed one of the two actions each turn: performing an UTTERANCE action, where it generates an utterance, or making a SELECT action, where

it chooses an entry from the KB. Note that each bot's SELECT action is visible to the other bot, and each is allowed to make multiple SELECT actions if the previous guess is wrong.

Evaluation Method: One of the major metrics is Completion Rate, the percentage of two bots successfully finishing the task.

Models: We focus on DynoNet, the best-performing model for the CoCoA task (He et al., 2017). It consists of a dynamic knowledge graph, a graph embedding over the entity nodes, and a Seq2seq-based utterance generator.

3 Adversarial Strategies

3.1 Adversarial Strategies on Ubuntu

For Ubuntu, we introduce adversarial strategies of increasing linguistic-unit complexity – from shallow word-level errors such as Random Swap and Stopword Dropout, to phrase-level paraphrastic changes, and finally to syntactic Grammar Errors.

Should-Not-Change Strategies

(1) Random Swap: Swapping adjacent words occurs often in the real world, e.g., transposition of words is one of the most frequent errors in manuscripts (Headlam, 1902; Marqués-Aguado, 2014); it is also frequently seen in blog posts.[3] Thus, being robust to swapping adjacent words is useful for chatbots that take typed/written text as inputs (e.g., virtual customer support on a airline/bank website). Even for speech-based conversations, non-native speakers can accidentally swap words due to habits formed in their native language (e.g., SVO in English vs. SOV in Hindi, Japanese, and Korean). Inspired by this, we also generate globally contiguous but locally "time-reversed" text, where positions of neighboring words are swapped (e.g., *"I don't want you to go"* to *"I don't want to you go"*).

(2) Stopword Dropout: Stopwords are the most frequent words in a language. The most commonly-used 25 words in the Oxford English corpus make up one-third of all printed material in English, and these words consequently carry less information than other words do in a sentence.[4]

---

[2] https://stanfordnlp.github.io/cocoa/

[3] E.g., *"he would give to it me"* in https://talk.drugabuse.com/threads/his-behavior-this-week.4347/

[4] One could also use closed-class words (prepositions, determiners, coordinators, and pronouns), but we opt for stopwords because a majority of stopwords are indeed closed-class words, and secondly, closed-class words usually require a very accurate POS-tagger, which is not available for low-resource or noisy domains and languages (e.g., Ubuntu).

Inspired by this observation, we propose randomly dropping stopwords from the inputs (e.g., *"Ben ate the carrot"* to *"Ben ate carrot"*).

(3) Data-level Paraphrasing: We repurpose PPDB 2.0 (Pavlick et al., 2015) and replace words and phrases in the original inputs with their paraphrases (e.g., *"She bought a bike"* to *"She purchased a bicycle"*).

(4) Generative-level Paraphrasing: Although Data-level Paraphrasing provides us with semantic-preserving inputs most of the time, it still suffers from the fact that the validity of a paraphrase depends on the context, especially for words with multiple meanings. In addition, simply replacing word-by-word does not lead to new compositional sentence-level paraphrases, e.g., *"How old are you"* to *"What's your age"*. We thus also experiment with generative-level paraphrasing, where we employ the Pointer-Generator Networks (See et al., 2017), and train it on the recently published paraphrase dataset ParaNMT-5M (Wieting and Gimpel, 2017) which contains 5 millions paraphrase pairs.

(5) Grammar Errors: We repurpose the AESW dataset (Daudaravicius, 2015), text extracted from $9,919$ published journal articles with data before/after language editing. This dataset was used for training models that identify and correct grammar errors. Based on the corrections in the edits, we build a look-up table to replace each correct word/phrase with a wrong one (e.g., *"He doesn't like cakes"* to *"He don't like cake"*).

Should-Change Strategies

(1) Add Negation: Suppose we add negation to the source sequence of some task-oriented model — from *"I want some coffee"* to *"I don't want some coffee"*. A proper response to the first utterance could be *"Sure, I will bring you some coffee"*, but for the second one, the model should do anything but bring some coffee. We thus assume that if we add negation to the root verb of each source sequence and the response is unchanged, the model must be ignoring important linguistic cues like negation. Hence this qualifies as a Should-Change strategy, i.e., if the model is robust, it should change the response.

(2) Antonym: We change words in utterances to their antonyms to apply more subtle meaning changes (e.g., *"You need to install Ubuntu"* to *"You need to uninstall Ubuntu"*).[5]

---

[5]Note that Should-Change strategies may lead to contexts

3.2 Adversarial Strategies on CoCoA

We applied all the above successful strategies used for the Ubuntu task to the UTTERANCE actions in a bot-bot-chat setting for the CoCoA task, but found that none of them was effective on DynoNet. This is surprising considering that the model's language generation module is a traditional Seq2seq model. This observation motivated us to perform the following analysis. The high performance of bot-bot chat may have stemmed from two sources: information revealed in an utterance, or entries directly disclosed by a SELECT action.

To investigate which part the model relies on more, we experiment with different Should-Change strategies which introduce obvious perturbations that have minimal word or semantic meaning overlap with the original source inputs:

(1) Random Inputs: Turn both bots' utterances into random inputs. This aims at investigating how much the model depends on the SELECT action.

(2) Random Inputs with Kept Entities: Replace each bot's utterance with random inputs, but keep the contained entities untouched. This further investigates how much entities alone contribute to the final performance.

(3) Confusing Entity: Replace entities mentioned in bot A's utterances with entities that are present in bot B's KB but not in their shared entry (and vice versa). This aims at coaxing bot B into believing that the mentioned entities come from their shared entry. By intentionally making the utterances misleading, we expect DynoNet's performance to be lower — hence this qualifies as a Should-Change strategy.

4 Adversarial Training

To make a model robust to an adversarial strategy, a natural approach is exposing it to the same pattern of perturbation during training (i.e., *adversarial training*). This is achieved by feeding adversarial inputs as training data. For each strategy, we report results under three train/test combinations: (1) trained with normal inputs, tested on adversarial inputs (*N-train + A-test*), which evaluates whether the adversarial strategy is effective at

---

that do not correspond to any legitimate task completion action, but the purpose of such a strategy is to make sure that the model at least should not respond the same way as it responded to the original context, i.e., even for the no-action state, the model should respond with something different like *"Sorry, I cannot help with that."* Our semantic similarity results in Table 4 capture this intuition directly.

fooling the model and exposing its robustness issues; (2) trained with adversarial inputs, tested on adversarial inputs (*A-train + A-test*), which next evaluates whether adversarial training made the model more robust to that adversarial attack; and (3) trained with adversarial inputs, tested on normal inputs (*A-train + N-test*), which finally evaluates whether the adversarial training also makes the model perform equally or better on the original normal inputs. Note that (3) is important, because one should not make the model more robust to a strategy at the cost of lower performance on the original data; also when (3) improves the performance on the original inputs, it means adversarial training successfully teaches the model to recognize and be robust to a certain type of noise, so that the model performs better when encountering similar patterns during inference. Also note that we use perturbed train set for adversarial training, and perturbed test set for adversarial testing. There is thus no overlap between the two sets.

4.1 Adversarial Training for Should-Not-Change Strategies

For each Should-Not-Change strategy, we take an already trained model from a certain checkpoint,[6] and train it on the adversarial inputs with maximum likelihood loss for K epochs (Shalyminov et al., 2017; Belinkov and Bisk, 2018; Jia and Liang, 2017; Iyyer et al., 2018). By feeding "adversarial source sequence + ground-truth response pairs" as regular positive data, we teach the model that these pairs are also valid examples despite the added perturbations.

4.2 Adversarial Training for Should-Change Strategies

For Should-Change strategies, we want the F1's to be lower with adversarial inputs after adversarial training, since this shows that the model becomes sensitive to subtle yet semantic-changing perturbations. This cannot be achieved by naively training on the perturbed inputs with maximum likelihood loss, because the "perturbed source sequence + ground-truth response pairs" for Should-Change strategies are negative examples which we need to train the model to avoid from generating. Inspired by Mao et al. (2016) and Yu et al. (2017), we instead use a linear combination of maximum likeli-

Model	Activity F1	Entity F1
LSTM	1.18	0.87
HRED	4.34	2.22
VHRED	4.63	2.53
VHRED (w/ attn.)	**5.94**	3.52
Reranking-RL	5.67	**3.73**

Table 1: F1 results of previous works as compared to our models. LSTM, HRED and VHRED are results reported in Serban et al. (2017a). VHRED (w/ attn.) and Reranking-RL are our results. Top results are bolded.

hood loss and max-margin loss:

$$L = L_{\text{ML}} + \alpha L_{\text{MM}}$$
$$L_{\text{ML}} = \sum_i \log P(t_i|s_i)$$
$$L_{\text{MM}} = \sum_i \max\left(0, M + \log P(t_i|a_i) - \log P(t_i|s_i)\right)$$

where L_{ML} is the maximum likelihood loss, L_{MM} is the max-margin loss, α is the weight of the max-margin loss (set to 1.0 following Yu et al. (2017)), M is the margin (tuned be to 0.1), and t_i, s_i and a_i are the target sequence, normal input, and adversarial input, respectively.[7]

5 Experimental Setup

In addition to datasets, tasks, models and evaluation methods introduced in Section 2, we present training details in this section (see Appendix for a comprehensive version).

Models on Ubuntu: We implemented VHRED and Reranking-RL in TensorFlow (Abadi et al., 2016) and employed greedy search for inference. As shown in Table 1, for both models we obtained Activity and Entity F1's higher than the VHRED results reported in Serban et al. (2017a). Hence, each of these two implementations serves as a solid baseline for adversarial testing and training.

Should-Not-Change Strategies on Ubuntu: For Random Swap, we allow up to 1 swap of neighboring words per 4 words in each utterance. For Stopword Dropout, we allow up to 8 words to be dropped in each turn. For Data-level Paraphrasing, we use the small version of PPDB 2.0. For Generative-level Paraphrasing, we use the publicly available Pointer-Generator Networks code (See Appendix for some random samples of the generated paraphrases).[8] For Grammar Errors, in addition to those extracted from the AESW dataset,

---

[6]We do not train from scratch because each model (for each strategy) takes several days to converge.

[7]Please refer to supp. about greedy sampling based max-margin setup and CoCoA discussion for adversarial training.

[8]`https://github.com/becxer/pointer-generator`

Strategy Name	N-train + A-test	A-train + A-test	A-train + N-test	N-train + N-test
Normal Input	-	-	-	5.94, 3.52
Random Swap	6.10*, 3.42	6.47*, 3.64*	6.42*, 3.74*	-
Stopword Dropout	5.49*, 3.44	6.23*, 3.82*	6.29*, 3.71*	-
Data-Level Para.	5.38*, 3.18*	6.39*, 3.83*	6.32*, 3.87*	-
Generative-Level Para.	4.25*, 2.48*	5.89 , 3.60	6.11*, 3.66*	-
Grammar Errors	5.60*, 3.09*	5.93 , 3.67*	6.05 , 3.69*	-
All Should-Not-Change	-	-	6.74*, 3.97*	-
Add Negation	6.06 , 3.42	5.01*, 3.12*	6.07 , 3.46	-
Antonym	5.85 , 3.56	5.43*, 3.43	5.98 , 3.56	-

Table 2: Activity and Entity F1 results of adversarial strategies on the **VHRED** model. Numbers marked with * are stat. significantly higher/lower than their counterparts obtained with Normal Input (upper-right corner of table).

we also add a heuristic where an inflected verb is replaced with its respective infinitive form, and a plural noun with its singular form. Note that for all strategies we only keep an adversarial token if it is within the original vocabulary set.

Should-Change Strategies on Ubuntu: For Add Negation, we negate the first verb in each utterance. For Antonym, we modify the first verb, adjective or adverb that has an antonym.

Human Evaluation: We also conducted human studies on MTurk to evaluate adversarial training (pairwise comparison for dialogue quality) and generative paraphrasing (five-point Likert scale). The utterances were randomly shuffled to anonymize model identity, and we used MTurk with US-located human evaluators with approval rate $> 98\%$, and at least $10,000$ approved HITs. Results are presented in Section 6.1. Note that the human studies and automatic evaluation are complementary to each other: while MTurk annotators are good at judging how natural and coherent a response is, they are usually not experts in the Ubuntu operating system's technical details. On the other hand, automatic evaluation focuses more on the technical side (i.e., whether key activities or entities are present in the response).

Model on CoCoA: We adopted the publicly available code from He et al. (2017),[9] and used their already trained DynoNet model.

6 Results

6.1 Adversarial Results on Ubuntu

Result Interpretation For Table 2 and 3 with Should-Not-Change strategies, lower is better in the first column (since a successful adversarial testing strategy will be effective at fooling the model), while higher is better in the second column (since successful adversarial training should bring the performance back up). However, for Should-Change strategies, the reverse holds.[10] Lastly, in the third column, higher is better since we want the adversarially trained model to perform better on the original source inputs.

Results on Should-Not-Change Strategies Table 2 and 3 present the adversarial results on F1 scores of all our strategies for VHRED and Reranking-RL, respectively. Table 2 shows that VHRED is robust to none of the Should-Not-Change strategies other than Random Swap, while Table 3 shows that Reranking-RL is robust to none of the Should-Not-Change strategies other than Stopword Dropout. For each effective strategy, at least one of the F1's decreases statistically significantly[11] as compared to the same model fed with normal inputs. Next, all adversarial trainings on Should-Not-Change strategies not only make the model more robust to adversarial inputs (each *A-train + A-test* F1 is stat. significantly higher than that of *N-train + A-test*) , but also make them perform better on normal inputs (each *A-train + N-test* F1 is stat. significantly higher than that of *N-train + N-test*, except for Grammar Errors's Activity F1). Motivated by the success in adversarial training on each strategy alone, we also experimented with training on all Should-Not-Change strategies combined, and obtained F1's stat. significantly higher than any single strategy (the *All Should-Not-Change* row in Table 2), except that *All-Should-Not-Change*'s Entity F1 is stat. equal to that of Data-Level Paraphrasing, showing that these strategies are able to compensate for each other to further improve performance. An inter-

---

[10]Higher is better in the first column, because this shows that the model is not paying attention to important semantic changes in the source inputs (and is maintaining its original performance); while lower is better in the second column, since we want the model to be more sensitive to such changes after adversarial training.

[11]We obtained stat. significance via the bootstrap test (Noreen, 1989; Efron and Tibshirani, 1994) with 100K samples, and consider $p < 0.05$ as stat. significant.

Strategy Name	N-train + A-test	A-train + A-test	A-train + N-test	N-train + N-test
Normal Input	-	-	-	5.67, 3.73
Random Swap	5.49*, 3.56*	6.20*, 4.28*	6.36*, 4.39*	-
Stopword Dropout	5.51*, 4.09*	-	-	-
Data-Level Para.	5.28*, 3.07*	5.53*, 3.69	5.79*, 3.87*	-
Generative-Level Para.	4.47*, 2.63*	5.30*, 3.35*	5.86*, 3.90*	-
Grammar Errors	5.33*, 3.25*	5.55*, 3.92*	5.93*, 4.04*	-
Add Negation	5.61 , 3.79	4.92*, 2.78*	6.10*, 3.93*	-
Antonym	5.68 , 3.70	5.30*, 2.95*	5.80*, 3.71	-

Table 3: Activity and Entity F1 results of adversarial strategies on the **Reranking-RL** model. Numbers marked with * are stat. significantly higher/lower than their counterparts obtained with Normal Input (upper-right corner).

Strategy Name	VHRED		Reranking-RL	
	Cont.	Resp.	Cont.	Resp.
Random Swap	1.00	0.71	1.00	0.86
Stopword Dropout	0.61	0.50	0.76	0.68
Data-Level Para.	0.96	0.58	0.96	0.74
Gen.-Level Para.	0.70	0.40	0.76	0.55
Grammar Err.	0.96	0.58	0.97	0.74
Add Negation	0.96	0.69	0.97	0.81
Antonym	0.98	0.66	0.98	0.74

Table 4: Textual similarity of adversarial strategies on the VHRED and Reranking-RL models. "Cont." stands for "Context", and "Resp." stands for "Response".

Compared to Baseline	Win(%)	Tie(%)	Loss(%)
Random Swap	49	19	32
Stopword Dropout	45	19	36
Data-Level Para.	37	22	41
Generative-Level Para.	41	26	33
Grammar Errors	41	29	30
All Should-Not-Change	49	22	28
Add Negation	34	25	41
Antonym	40	29	31

Table 5: Human evaluation results on comparison between VHRED baseline trained on normal inputs vs. VHRED trained on each Should-Not-Change strategy (incl. one with all Should-Not-Change strategies combined) and each Should-Change strategy for Ubuntu.

	Pointer-Generator	ParaNMT-5M
Avg. Score	3.26	3.54

Table 6: Human evaluation scores on paraphrases generated by Pointer-Generator Networks and ground-truth pairs from ParaNMT-5M.

esting strategy to note is Random Swap: although it itself is not effective as an adversarial strategy for VHRED, training on it does make the model perform better on normal inputs.

Results on Should-Change Strategies Table 2 and 3 show that Add Negation and Antonym are both successful Should-Change strategies, because no change in *N-train + A-test* F1 is stat. significant compared to that of *N-train + N-test*, which shows that both models are ignoring the semantic-changing perturbations to the inputs. From the last two rows of *A-train + A-test* column in each table, we also see that adversarial training successfully brings down both F1's (stat. significantly) for each model, showing that the model becomes more sensitive to the context change.

Semantic Similarity In addition to F1, we also follow Serban et al. (2017a) and employ cosine similarity between average embeddings of normal and adversarial inputs/responses (proposed by Liu et al. (2016)) to evaluate how much the inputs/responses change in semantic meaning (Table 4). This metric is useful in three ways. Firstly, by comparing the two columns of context similarity, we can get a general idea of how much change is perceived *by each model*. For example, we can see that Stopword Dropout leads to more evident changes from VHRED's perspective than from Reranking-RL's. This also agrees with the F1 results in Table 2 and 3, which indicate

that Reranking-RL is much more robust to this strategy than VHRED is. The high context similarity of Should-Change strategies shows that although we have added "not" or replaced antonyms in every utterance of the source inputs, from the model's point of view the context has not changed much in meaning. Secondly, for each Should-Not-Change strategy, the cosine similarity of context is much higher than that of response, indicating that responses change more significantly in meaning than their corresponding contexts. Lastly, The high semantic similarity for Generative Paraphrasing also partly shows that the Pointer-Generator model in general produces faithful paraphrases.

Human Evaluation As introduced in Section 5, we performed two human studies on adversarial training and Generative Paraphrasing. For the first study, Table 5 indicates that models trained on each adversarial strategy (as well as on all Should-Not-Change strategies combined) indeed on average produced better responses, and mostly agrees with the adversarial training results in Table 2.[12]

---

[12]Note that human evaluation does not show improvements with the Data-Level-Paraphrasing and Add-Negation strate-

Context	Response
N: ... you could save your ubuntu files and reinstall Windows , then install ubuntu as a dual boot option __eou__ __eot__ aight buddy , so how do i get that **unknown** space back__eou__ **Random Swap:** ... you could your save ubuntu and files Windows reinstall , then install ubuntu as dual a option boot __eou__ __eot__ aight buddy , so do how i that get space **unknown** back __eou__	**NN:** you can use the Live CD , you can install Ubuntu on the same partition as the Windows partition __eou__ **NA:** I am using ubuntu . __eou__ **AA:** you can use Windows XP on the Windows partition , and then install Ubuntu on the same drive __eou__

Table 7: VHRED output example before and after adversarial training on the Random Swap strategy.

For the second study, Table 6 shows that on average the generated paraphrase has roughly the same semantic meaning with the original utterance, but may sometimes miss some information. Its quality is also close to that of the ground-truth in ParaNMT-5M dataset.

Output Examples of Generated Responses
We present a selected example of generated responses before and after adversarial training on the Random Swap strategy with the VHRED model in Table 7 (more examples in Appendix on all strategies with both models). First of all, we can see that it is hard to differentiate between the original and the perturbed context (*N-context* and *A-context*) if one does not look very closely. For this reason, the model gets fooled by the adversarial strategy, i.e., after adversarial perturbation, the *N-train + A-test* response (NA-Response) is worse than that of *N-train + N-test* (NN-Response). However, after our adversarial training phase, *A-train + A-test* (AA-Response) becomes better again.

6.2 Adversarial Results on CoCoA

Table 8 shows the results of Should-Change strategies on DynoNet with the CoCoA task. The Random Inputs strategy shows that even without communication, the two bots are able to locate their shared entry 82% of the time by revealing their own KB through SELECT action. When we keep the mentioned entities untouched but randomize all other tokens, DynoNet actually achieves state-of-the-art Completion Rate, indicating that the two agents are paying zero attention to each other's utterances other than the entities contained in them. This is also why we did not apply Add Negation and Antonym to DynoNet — if Random Inputs does not work, these two strategies will also make no difference to the performance (in other words Random Inputs subsumes the other two Should-

Strategy	Completion Rate	Num. of Turns
Norm. Inputs	0.94	16.06
Rand. Inputs	0.82	22.87
Rand. w/ Entity	0.95	17.19
Confusing Entity	0.77	24.11

Table 8: Adversarial Results on DynoNet.

Change strategies). We can also see that even with the Normal Inputs with Confusing Entities strategy, DynoNet is still able to finish the task 77% of the time, and with only slightly more turns. This again shows that the model mainly relies on the SELECT action to guess the shared entry.

7 Byte-Pair-Encoding VHRED

Although we have shown that adversarial training on most strategies makes the dialogue model more robust, generating such perturbed data is not always straightforward for diverse, complex strategies. For example, our data-level and generative-level strategies all leverage datasets that are not always available to a language. We are thus motivated to also address the robustness task on the model-level, and explore an extension to the VHRED model that makes it robust to Grammar Errors even without adversarial training.

Model Description: We performed Byte Pair Encoding (BPE) (Sennrich et al., 2016) on the Ubuntu dataset.[13] This algorithm encodes rare/unknown words as sequences of subword units, which helps segmenting words with the same lemma but different inflections (e.g., "showing" to "show + ing", and "cakes" to "cake + s"), making the model more likely to be robust to grammar errors such as verb tense or plural/singular noun confusion. We experimented BPE with 5K merging operations, and obtained a vocabulary size of 5121.

Results: As shown in Table 9, BPE-VHRED achieved F1's (5.99, 3.66), which is stat. equal to (5.94, 3.52) obtained without BPE. To our best knowledge, we are the first to apply BPE to a gen-

gies, though the latter does agree with F1 trends. Overall, we provide both human and F1 evaluations because they are complementary at judging naturalness/coherence vs. key Ubuntu technical activities/entities.

---

[13] We employed code released by the authors on `https://github.com/rsennrich/subword-nmt`

	VHRED	BPE-VHRED
Normal Input	5.94, 3.52	5.99, 3.66
Grammar Errors	5.60, 3.09	5.86, 3.54

Table 9: Activity, Entity F1 results of VHRED model vs. BPE-VHRED model tested on normal inputs.

erative dialogue task. Moreover, BPE-VHRED achieved (5.86, 3.54) on Grammar Errors based adversarial test set, which is stat. equal to the F1's when tested with normal data, indicating that BPE-VHRED is more robust to this adversarial strategy than VHRED is, since the latter had (5.60, 3.09) when tested with perturbed data, where both F1's are stat. signif. lower than when fed with normal inputs. Moreover, BPE-VHRED reduces the vocabulary size by 15K, corresponding to 4.5M fewer parameters. This makes BPE-VHRED train much faster. Note that BPE only makes the model robust to one type of noise (i.e. Grammar Errors), and hence adversarial training on other strategies is still necessary (but we hope that this encourages future work to build other advanced models that are naturally robust to diverse adversaries).

8 Related Works

Model-Dependent vs. Model-Agnostic Strategies: Many adversarial strategies have been applied to both Computer Vision (Biggio et al., 2012; Szegedy et al., 2013; Goodfellow et al., 2015; Mei and Zhu, 2015; Papernot et al., 2016; Narodytska and Kasiviswanathan, 2017; Liu et al., 2017; Carlini and Wagner, 2017; Papernot et al., 2017; Mironenco et al.; Wong, 2017; Gao et al., 2018) and NLP (Jia and Liang, 2017; Zhao et al., 2018; Belinkov and Bisk, 2018; Shalyminov et al., 2017; Mironenco et al.; Iyyer et al., 2018). Previous works have distinguished between model-aware strategies, where the adversarial algorithms have access to the model parameters, and model-agnostic strategies, where the adversary does not have such information (Papernot et al., 2017; Liu et al., 2017; Narodytska and Kasiviswanathan, 2017). We however, observed that within the model-agnostic category, there are two subcategories. One is *half-model-agnostic*, where although the adversary has no access to the model parameters, it is allowed to probe the target model and observe its output as a way to craft adversarial inputs (Biggio et al., 2012; Szegedy et al., 2013; Goodfellow et al., 2015; Mei and Zhu, 2015; Papernot et al., 2017; Mironenco et al.). On the other hand, a *pure-model-agnostic* adversary, such

as works by Jia and Liang (2017) and Belinkov and Bisk (2018), does not have any access to the model outputs when creating adversarial inputs, and is thus more generalizable across models/tasks. We adopt the pure-model-agnostic approach, only drawing inspiration from real-world noise, and testing them on the target model.

Adversarial in NLP: Text-based adversarial works have targeted both classification models (Weston et al., 2016; Jia and Liang, 2017; Wong, 2017; Liang et al., 2017; Samanta and Mehta, 2017; Shalyminov et al., 2017; Gao et al., 2018; Iyyer et al., 2018) and generative models (Hosseini et al., 2017; Henderson et al., 2017; Mironenco et al.; Zhao et al., 2018; Belinkov and Bisk, 2018). To our best knowledge, our work is the first to target generative goal-oriented dialogue systems with several new adversarial strategies in both Should-Not-Change and Should-Change categories, and then to fix the broken models through adversarial training (esp. using max-margin loss for Should-Change), and also achieving model robustness without using any adversarial data.

9 Conclusion

We first revealed both the over-sensibility and over-stability of state-of-the-art models on Ubuntu and CoCoA dialogue tasks, via Should-Not-Change and Should-Change adversarial strategies. We then showed that training on adversarial inputs not only made the models more robust to the perturbations, but also helped them achieve new state-of-the-art performance on the original data (with further improvements when we combined strategies). Lastly, we also proposed a BPE-enhanced VHRED model that not only trains faster with comparable performance, but is also robust to Grammar Errors even without adversarial training, motivating that if no strong adversary-generation tools (e.g., paraphraser) are available (esp. in low-resource domains/languages), we should try alternative model-robustness architectural changes.

Acknowledgments

We thank the anonymous reviewers for their helpful comments and discussions. This work was supported by DARPA (YFA17-D17AP00022), Facebook ParlAI Research Award, Google Faculty Research Award, Bloomberg Data Science Research Grant, and Nvidia GPU awards. The views contained in this article are those of the authors and not of the funding agency.

References

Martín Abadi, Paul Barham, Jianmin Chen, Zhifeng Chen, Andy Davis, Jeffrey Dean, Matthieu Devin, Sanjay Ghemawat, Geoffrey Irving, Michael Isard, et al. 2016. Tensorflow: A system for large-scale machine learning. In *OSDI*, volume 16, pages 265–283.

Dzmitry Bahdanau, Kyunghyun Cho, and Yoshua Bengio. 2015. Neural machine translation by jointly learning to align and translate. In *Proceedings of ICLR*.

Yonatan Belinkov and Yonatan Bisk. 2018. Synthetic and natural noise both break neural machine translation. In *Proceedings of ICLR*.

Battista Biggio, Blaine Nelson, and Pavel Laskov. 2012. Poisoning attacks against support vector machines. In *Proceedings of ICML*.

Nicholas Carlini and David Wagner. 2017. Adversarial examples are not easily detected: Bypassing ten detection methods. In *Proceedings of the 10th ACM Workshop on Artificial Intelligence and Security*, pages 3–14. ACM.

Vidas Daudaravicius. 2015. Automated evaluation of scientific writing data set (version 1.2)[data file]. *VTeX, Vilnius, Lithuania*.

Bradley Efron and Robert J. Tibshirani. 1994. *An introduction to the bootstrap*. CRC press.

Ji Gao, Jack Lanchantin, Mary Lou Soffa, and Yanjun Qi. 2018. Black-box generation of adversarial text sequences to evade deep learning classifiers. In *Deep Learning and Security Workshop*.

Ian J. Goodfellow, Jonathon Shlens, and Christian Szegedy. 2015. Explaining and harnessing adversarial examples. In *Proceedings of ICLR*.

He He, Anusha Balakrishnan, Mihail Eric, and Percy Liang. 2017. Learning symmetric collaborative dialogue agents with dynamic knowledge graph embeddings. In *Proceedings of ACL*.

W. Headlam. 1902. Transposition of words in mss. *The Classical Review*, 16(5):243–256.

Peter Henderson, Koustuv Sinha, Nicolas Angelard-Gontier, Nan Rosemary Ke, Genevieve Fried, Ryan Lowe, and Joelle Pineau. 2017. Ethical challenges in data-driven dialogue systems. *arXiv preprint arXiv:1711.09050*.

Hossein Hosseini, Sreeram Kannan, Baosen Zhang, and Radha Poovendran. 2017. Deceiving google's perspective api built for detecting toxic comments. *arXiv preprint arXiv:1702.08138*.

Mohit Iyyer, John Wieting, Kevin Gimpel, and Luke Zettlemoyer. 2018. Adversarial example generation with syntactically controlled paraphrase networks. In *Proceedings of NAACL*.

Robin Jia and Percy Liang. 2017. Adversarial examples for evaluating reading comprehension systems. In *Proceedings of EMNLP*.

Jiwei Li, Will Monroe, Alan Ritter, Michel Galley, Jianfeng Gao, and Dan Jurafsky. 2016. Deep reinforcement learning for dialogue generation. In *Proceedings of EMNLP*.

Bin Liang, Hongcheng Li, Miaoqiang Su, Pan Bian, Xirong Li, and Wenchang Shi. 2017. Deep text classification can be fooled. *arXiv preprint arXiv:1704.08006*.

Chia-Wei Liu, Ryan Lowe, Iulian V. Serban, Michael Noseworthy, Laurent Charlin, and Joelle Pineau. 2016. How not to evaluate your dialogue system: An empirical study of unsupervised evaluation metrics for dialogue response generation. In *Proceedings of EMNLP*.

Yanpei Liu, Xinyun Chen, Chang Liu, and Dawn Song. 2017. Delving into transferable adversarial examples and black-box attacks. In *Proceedings of ICLR*.

Ryan Lowe, Nissan Pow, Iulian Serban, and Joelle Pineau. 2015. The ubuntu dialogue corpus: A large dataset for research in unstructured multi-turn dialogue systems. *arXiv preprint arXiv:1506.08909*.

Junhua Mao, Jonathan Huang, Alexander Toshev, Oana Camburu, Alan L. Yuille, and Kevin Murphy. 2016. Generation and comprehension of unambiguous object descriptions. In *Proceedings of the IEEE conference on computer vision and pattern recognition*, pages 11–20.

Teresa Marqués-Aguado. 2014. Errors, corrections and other textual problems in three copies of a middle english antidotary. *Nordic Journal of English Studies*, 13(1):53–77.

Shike Mei and Xiaojin Zhu. 2015. Using machine teaching to identify optimal training-set attacks on machine learners. In *Proceedings of AAAI*, pages 2871–2877.

Mircea Mironenco, Dana Kianfar, Ke Tran, Evangelos Kanoulas, and Efstratios Gavves. Examining cooperation in visual dialog models. In *Proceedings of NIPS*.

Nina Narodytska and Shiva Prasad Kasiviswanathan. 2017. Simple black-box adversarial perturbations for deep networks. In *Proceedings of CVPR*.

Eric W. Noreen. 1989. *Computer-intensive methods for testing hypotheses*. Wiley New York.

Nicolas Papernot, Patrick McDaniel, Ian Goodfellow, Somesh Jha, Z. Berkay Celik, and Ananthram Swami. 2017. Practical black-box attacks against machine learning. In *Proceedings of the 2017 ACM on Asia Conference on Computer and Communications Security*, pages 506–519. ACM.

Nicolas Papernot, Patrick McDaniel, Somesh Jha, Matt Fredrikson, Z. Berkay Celik, and Ananthram Swami. 2016. The limitations of deep learning in adversarial settings. In *Security and Privacy (EuroS&P), 2016 IEEE European Symposium on*, pages 372–387. IEEE.

Romain Paulus, Caiming Xiong, and Richard Socher. 2018. A deep reinforced model for abstractive summarization. In *Proceedings of ICLR*.

Ellie Pavlick, Pushpendre Rastogi, Juri Ganitkevitch, Benjamin Van Durme, and Chris Callison-Burch. 2015. Ppdb 2.0: Better paraphrase ranking, fine-grained entailment relations, word embeddings, and style classification. In *Proceedings of the 53rd Annual Meeting of the Association for Computational Linguistics and the 7th International Joint Conference on Natural Language Processing (Volume 2: Short Papers)*, volume 2, pages 425–430.

Suranjana Samanta and Sameep Mehta. 2017. Towards crafting text adversarial samples. *arXiv preprint arXiv:1707.02812*.

Abigail See, Peter J. Liu, and Christopher D. Manning. 2017. Get to the point: Summarization with pointer-generator networks. In *Proceedings of ACL*.

Rico Sennrich, Barry Haddow, and Alexandra Birch. 2016. Neural machine translation of rare words with subword units. In *Proceedings of ACL*.

Iulian Vlad Serban, Tim Klinger, Gerald Tesauro, Kartik Talamadupula, Bowen Zhou, Yoshua Bengio, and Aaron C. Courville. 2017a. Multiresolution recurrent neural networks: An application to dialogue response generation. In *AAAI*, pages 3288–3294.

Iulian Vlad Serban, Alessandro Sordoni, Yoshua Bengio, Aaron C. Courville, and Joelle Pineau. 2016. Building end-to-end dialogue systems using generative hierarchical neural network models. In *AAAI*, pages 3776–3784.

Iulian Vlad Serban, Alessandro Sordoni, Ryan Lowe, Laurent Charlin, Joelle Pineau, Aaron C. Courville, and Yoshua Bengio. 2017b. A hierarchical latent variable encoder-decoder model for generating dialogues. In *AAAI*, pages 3295–3301.

Igor Shalyminov, Arash Eshghi, and Oliver Lemon. 2017. Challenging neural dialogue models with natural data: Memory networks fail on incremental phenomena. In *Proceedings of SemDial*.

Christian Szegedy, Wojciech Zaremba, Ilya Sutskever, Joan Bruna, Dumitru Erhan, Ian Goodfellow, and Rob Fergus. 2013. Intriguing properties of neural networks. *arXiv preprint arXiv:1312.6199*.

Jason Weston, Antoine Bordes, Sumit Chopra, Alexander M Rush, Bart van Merriënboer, Armand Joulin, and Tomas Mikolov. 2016. Towards ai-complete question answering: A set of prerequisite toy tasks. In *Proceedings of ICLR*.

John Wieting and Kevin Gimpel. 2017. Pushing the limits of paraphrastic sentence embeddings with millions of machine translations. *arXiv preprint arXiv:1711.05732*.

Catherine Wong. 2017. Dancin seq2seq: Fooling text classifiers with adversarial text example generation. *arXiv preprint arXiv:1712.05419*.

Licheng Yu, Hao Tan, Mohit Bansal, and Tamara L. Berg. 2017. A joint speakerlistener-reinforcer model for referring expressions. In *Computer Vision and Pattern Recognition (CVPR)*, volume 2.

Zhengli Zhao, Dheeru Dua, and Sameer Singh. 2018. Generating natural adversarial examples. In *Proceedings of ICLR*.

Improving Response Selection in Multi-turn Dialogue Systems by Incorporating Domain Knowledge

Debanjan Chaudhuri
Smart Data Analytics Group
University of Bonn & Fraunhofer IAIS
Germany
`chaudhur@cs.uni-bonn.de`

Agustinus Kristiadi
Smart Data Analytics Group
University of Bonn
Germany
`kristiadi@uni-bonn.de`

Jens Lehmann
Smart Data Analytics Group
University of Bonn & Fraunhofer IAIS
Germany
`jens.lehmann@cs.uni-bonn.de`

Asja Fischer
Department of Mathematics
Ruhr University Bochum
Germany
`asja.fischer@rub.de`

Abstract

Building systems that can communicate with humans is a core problem in Artificial Intelligence. This work proposes a novel neural network architecture for response selection in an end-to-end multi-turn conversational dialogue setting. The architecture applies context level attention and incorporates additional external knowledge provided by descriptions of domain-specific words. It uses a bi-directional Gated Recurrent Unit (GRU) for encoding context and responses and learns to attend over the context words given the latent response representation and vice versa. In addition, it incorporates external domain specific information using another GRU for encoding the domain keyword descriptions. This allows better representation of domain-specific keywords in responses and hence improves the overall performance. Experimental results show that our model outperforms all other state-of-the-art methods for response selection in multi-turn conversations.

1 Introduction

In a conversation scenario, a dialogue system can be applied to the task of freely generating a new response or to the task of selecting a response from a set of candidate responses based on the previous utterances, i.e. the context of the dialogue. The former is known as *generative* dialogue system while the latter is called *retrieval-based* (or response selection) dialogue system.

Both approaches can be realized using a modular architecture, where each module is responsible for a certain task such as natural language understanding, dialogue state-tracking, natural language

Context
Utterance 1:
My networking card is not working on my Ubuntu, can somebody help me?
Utterance 2:
What's your kernel version? Run *uname* -r or *sudo dpkg* -l |*grep* linux-headers |*grep* ii |*awk* '{*print* \$3}' and paste the output here.
Utterance 3:
It's 2.8.0-30-generic.
Utterance 4:
Your card is not supported in that kernel. You need to upgrade, that's like decade old kernel!
Utterance 5:
Ok how do I install the new kernel??
Response
Just do *sudo apt-get* upgrade, that's it.

Table 1: Illustration of a multi-turn conversation with domain specific words (UNIX commands) in italics.

generation, etc., or can be trained in an end-to-end manner optimized on a single objective function.

Previous work, belonging to the latter category, by Lowe et al. (2015a) applied neural networks to multi-turn response selection in conversations by encoding the utterances in the context as well as the possible responses with a Long Short-term Memory (LSTM) (Hochreiter and Schmidhuber, 1997). Based on the context and response encodings, the neural network then estimates the probability for each response to be the correct one given the context. More recently, a lot of enhanced architectures have been proposed that build on the

497

Proceedings of the 22nd Conference on Computational Natural Language Learning (CoNLL 2018), pages 497–507
Brussels, Belgium, October 31 - November 1, 2018. ©2018 Association for Computational Linguistics

general idea of encoding response and context first and performing some embedding-based matching after (Yan et al., 2016; Zhou et al., 2016; An et al., 2018; Dong and Huang, 2018).

Although such approaches result in efficient text-pair matching capabilities, they fail to attend over logical consistencies for longer utterances in the context, given the response. Moreover, in domain specific scenarios, a system's ability to incorporate additional domain knowledge can be very beneficial, e.g. for the example shown in Table 1.

In this paper, we propose a novel neural network architecture for multi-turn response-selection that extends the model proposed by Lowe et al. (2015a). Our major contributions are: (1) a neural network paradigm that is able to attend over important words in a context utterance given the response encoding (and vice versa), (2) an approach to incorporate additional domain knowledge into the neural network by encoding the description of domain specific words with a GRU and using a bilinear operation to merge the resulting domain specific representations with the vanilla word embeddings, and (3) an empirical evaluation on a publicly available multi-turn dialogue corpus showing that our system outperforms all other state-of-the-art methods for response selection in a multi-turn setting.

2 Related work

Recently, human-computer conversations have attracted increasing attention in the research community and dialogue systems have become a field of research on its own. The conversation models proposed in early studies (Walker et al., 2001; Oliver and White, 2004; Stent et al., 2002) were designed for catering to specific domains only, e.g. for performing restaurant bookings, and required substantial rule-based strategy building and human efforts in the building process. With the advancements in machine learning, there have been more and more studies on conversational agents which are based on data-driven approaches. Data-driven dialogue systems can chiefly be realized by two types of architectures: (1) pipeline architectures, which follow a modular pattern for modelling the dialogues, where each component is trained/created separately to perform a specific sub-task, and (2) end-to-end architectures, which consist of a single trainable module for modelling the conversations.

Task-oriented dialogue systems, which are designed to assist users in achieving specific goals, were mainly realized by pipeline architectures. Recently however, there have been more and more works on end-to-end dialogue systems because of the limitations of the former modular architectures, namely, the credit assignment problem and inter-component dependency, as for example described by Zhao and Eskenazi (2016). Wen et al. (2017) and Bordes et al. (2017) proposed encoder-decoder-based neural networks for modeling task oriented dialogues. Moreover, Zhao and Eskenazi (2016) proposed an end-to-end reinforcement learning-based system for jointly learning to perform dialogue state-tracking (Williams et al., 2013) and policy learning (Baird, 1995).

Since task oriented systems primarily focus on completing a specific task, they usually do not allow free flowing, articulate conversations with the user. Therefore, there has been considerable effort to develop non-goal driven dialogue systems, which are able to converse with humans on an open domain (Ritter et al., 2011). Such systems can be modeled using either generative architectures, which are able to freely generate responses to user queries, or retrieval-based systems, which pick a response suitable to a context utterance out of a provided set of responses. Retrieval-based systems are therefore more limited in their output while having the advantage of producing more informative, constrained, and grammatically correct responses (Ji et al., 2014).

2.1 Generative models

Ritter et al. (2011) were the first to formulate the task of automatic response generation as phrase-based statistical machine translation, which they tackled with n-gram-based language models. Later approaches (Shang et al., 2015; Vinyals and Le, 2015; Luong et al., 2015) applied Recurrent Neural Network (RNN)-based encoder-decoder architectures. However, dialogue generation is considerably more difficult than language translation because of the wide possibility of responses in interactions. Also, for dialogues, in order to generate a suitable response at a certain time-step, knowing only the previous utterance is often not enough and the ability to leverage the context from the sequence of previous utterances is required. To overcome such challenges, a hierarchical RNN encoder-decoder-based system has been proposed by Serban et al. (2016) for leveraging contextual information in conversations.

2.2 Retrieval-based models

Earlier works on retrieval-based systems focused on modeling short-text, single-turn dialogues. Hao et al. (2013) introduced a data set for this task and proposed a response selection system which is based on information retrieval techniques like the vector space model and semantic matching. Ji et al. (2014) suggested to apply a deep neural network for matching contexts and responses, while Wu et al. (2016) proposed a topic aware convolutional neural tensor network for answer retrieval in short-text scenarios.

More recently, there has been a lot of focus on developing retrieval-based models for multi-turn dialogues which is more challenging as the models need to take into account long-term dependencies in the context. Lowe et al. (2015a), introduced the Ubuntu Dialogue Corpus (UDC), which is the largest freely available multi-turn dialogue data set. Moreover, the authors proposed to leverage RNNs, e.g. LSTMs, to encode both the context and the response, before computing the score of the pair based on the similarity of the encodings (w.r.t. a certain measure). This class of methods is referred to as dual encoder architectures. Shortly after, Kadlec et al. (2015) investigated the performance of dual encoders with different kind of encoder networks, such as convolutional neural networks (CNNs) and bi-directional LSTMs. Yan et al. (2016) followed a different approach and trained a single CNN to map a context-response pair to the corresponding matching score.

Later on, various extensions of the dual encoder architecture have been proposed. Zhou et al. (2016) employed two encoders in parallel, one working on word- the other on utterance-level. Wu et al. (2017) proposed the Sequential Matching Network (SMN), where the candidate response is matched with every utterance in the context separately, based on which a final score is computed. The Cross Convolution Network (CNN) (An et al., 2018) extends the dual encoder with a cross convolution operation. The latter is a dot product between the embeddings of the context and response followed by a max-pooling operation. Both of the outputs are concatenated and fed into a fully-connected layer for similarity matching. Moreover, An et al. (2018) improve the representation of rare words by learning different embeddings for them from the data. Handling rare words has also been studied by Dong and Huang (2018), who proposed to handle Out-of-Vocabulary (OOV) words by using both pre-trained word embeddings and embeddings from task-specific data.

Furthermore, many models targeting response selection along with other sentence pair scoring tasks such as paraphrasing, semantic text scoring, and recognizing textual entailment have been proposed. Baudiš et al. (2016) investigated a stacked RNN-CNN architecture and attention-based models for sentence-pair scoring. Match-SRNN (Wan et al., 2016) employs a spatial RNN to capture local interactions between sentence pairs. Match-LSTM (Wang and Jiang, 2016) improves its matching performance by using LSTM-based, attention-weighted sentence representations. QA-LSTM (Tan et al., 2016) uses a simple attention mechanism and combines the LSTM encoder with a CNN.

Incorporating unstructured domain knowledge into dialogue system has initially been studied by Lowe et al. (2015b) and followed by Xu et al. (2016), who incorporated a loosely-structured knowledge base into a neural network using a special gating mechanism. They created the knowledge base from domain-specific data, however their model is not able to leverage any external domain knowledge.

3 Background

In this section, we will explain the task at hand and give a brief introduction to the neural network architectures our proposed model is based on.

3.1 Problem definition

Let the data set $\mathcal{D} = \{(c_i, r_i, y_i)\}_{i=1}^{M}$ be a set of M triples consisting of context c_i, response r_i, and ground truth label y_i. Each context is a sequence of utterances, that is $c_i = \{u_{il}\}_{l=1}^{L}$, where L is the maximum context length. We define an utterance as a sequence of words $\{w_t\}_{t=1}^{T}$. Thus, c_i can also be viewed as a sequence of words by concatenating all utterances in c_i. Each response r_i is an utterance and $y_i \in \{0, 1\}$ is the corresponding label of the given triple which takes a value of 1 if r_i is the correct response for c_i and 0 otherwise. The goal of retrieval-based dialogue systems is then to learn a predictive distribution $p(y|c, r, \boldsymbol{\theta})$ parameterized by $\boldsymbol{\theta}$. That is, given a context c and response r, we would like to infer the probability of r being a response to context c.

3.2 RNNs, BiRNNs and GRUs

Recurrent neural networks are one of the most popular classes of models for processing sequences of words $W = \{w_t\}_{t=1}^T$ with arbitrary length $T \in \mathbb{N}$, e.g. utterances or sentences. Each word w_t is first mapped onto its vector representation $\mathbf{w}_t$ (also referred to as word embedding), which serves as input to the RNN at time step t. The central element of RNNs is the recurrence relation of its hidden units, described by

$$\overrightarrow{\mathbf{h}}_t = f(\overrightarrow{\mathbf{h}}_{t-1}, \mathbf{w}_t | \phi) \ , \tag{1}$$

where ϕ are the parameters of the RNN and f is some nonlinear function. Accordingly, the state $\overrightarrow{\mathbf{h}}_t$ of the hidden units at time step t depends on the state $\overrightarrow{\mathbf{h}}_{t-1}$ in the previous time step and the t-th word in the sequence. This way, the hidden state $\overrightarrow{\mathbf{h}}_T$ obtained after T updates contains information about the whole sequence W, and can thus be regarded as an embedding of the sequence.

The RNN architecture can also be altered to take into account dependencies coming from both the past and the future by adding an additional sub-RNN that moves backward in time, giving rise to the name bi-directional RNN (biRNN). To achieve this, the network architecture is extended by an additional set of hidden units. The states $\overleftarrow{\mathbf{h}}_t$ of those hidden units are updated based on the current input word and the hidden state from the next time step. That is for $t = 1, \ldots, T - 1$:

$$\overleftarrow{\mathbf{h}}_{T-t} = f(\overleftarrow{\mathbf{h}}_{T-t+1}, \mathbf{w}_{T-t} | \phi) \ . \tag{2}$$

Here, the words are processed in reverse order, i.e. $w_T, \ldots, w_1$, such that $\overleftarrow{\mathbf{h}}_T$ (analogous to $\overrightarrow{\mathbf{h}}_T$ in the forward directed RNN) contains information about the whole sequence. At the t-th time step, the model's hidden representation of the sequence is then usually obtained by the concatenation of the hidden states from the forward and the backward RNN, i.e. by $\mathbf{h}_t = [\overrightarrow{\mathbf{h}}_t, \overleftarrow{\mathbf{h}}_t]$ and the embedding of the whole sequence W is given by $\mathbf{h}^W = [\overrightarrow{\mathbf{h}}_T, \overleftarrow{\mathbf{h}}_T]$.

Modeling very long sequences with RNNs is hard: Bengio et al. (1994) showed that RNNs suffer from vanishing and exploding gradients, which makes training over long-term dependency difficult. Such problems can be addressed by augmenting the RNN with additional gating mechanisms,

as it is done in LSTMs and the Gated Recurrent Unit (GRU) (Cho et al., 2014). These mechanisms allow the RNN to learn how much to update the hidden state flexibly in each step and help the RNN to deal with the vanishing gradient problem in long sequences better than vanilla RNNs. The gating mechanism of GRUs is motivated by that of LSTMs, but is much simpler to compute and implement. It contains two gates, namely the reset and update gate, whose states at time t are denoted by $\mathbf{z_t}$ and $\mathbf{r_t}$, respectively. Formally, a GRU is defined by the following update equations

$$\begin{aligned}
\mathbf{z}_t &= \sigma(\mathbf{W}_z \mathbf{x}_t + \mathbf{U}_z \mathbf{h}_{t-1}) \ , \\
\mathbf{r}_t &= \sigma(\mathbf{W}_r \mathbf{x}_t + \mathbf{U}_r \mathbf{h}_{t-1}) \ , \\
\tilde{\mathbf{h}}_t &= \tanh(\mathbf{W}_h \mathbf{x}_t + \mathbf{U}_h \mathbf{r}_i \odot \mathbf{h}_{t-1}) \ , \\
\mathbf{h}_t &= \mathbf{z}_t \odot \tilde{\mathbf{h}}_t + (1 - \mathbf{z}_t) \odot \mathbf{h}_{t-1} \ ,
\end{aligned}$$

where $\mathbf{x}_t$ is the input (corresponding to $\mathbf{w}_t$ in our setting) and the set of weight matrices $\phi = \{\mathbf{W}_z, \mathbf{U}_z, \mathbf{W}_r, \mathbf{U}_r, \mathbf{W}_h, \mathbf{U}_h\}$ constitute the learnable model parameters.

3.3 Dual Encoder

Recurrent neural networks and their variants have been used in many applications in the field of natural language processing, including retrieval-based dialogue systems. In this area the dual encoder (DE) (Lowe et al., 2015a) became a popular model. It uses a single RNN encoder to transform both context and response into low dimensional vectors and computes their similarity. More formally, let $\mathbf{h}^\mathbf{c}$ and $\mathbf{h}^\mathbf{r}$ be the encoded context and response, respectively. The probability of r being the correct response for c is then computed by the DE as

$$p(y|c, r, \boldsymbol{\theta}) = \sigma((\mathbf{h}^\mathbf{c})^{\mathrm{T}} \mathbf{M} \mathbf{h}^\mathbf{r} + b) \ , \tag{3}$$

where $\boldsymbol{\theta} = \{\phi, \mathbf{M}, b\}$ (recall, that ϕ is the set of parameters of the encoder RNN that outputs $\mathbf{h}^\mathbf{c}$ and $\mathbf{h}^\mathbf{r}$) is the set of parameters of the full model and σ is the sigmoid function. Note, that the same RNN is used to encode both context and response.

In summary, this approach can be described as first creating latent representations of context and response in the same vector space and then using the similarity between these latent embeddings (as induced by matrix $\mathbf{M}$ and bias b) for estimating the probability of the the response being the correct one for the given context.

4 Model description

Our model extends the DE described in Section 3.3 by two attention mechanisms which make the context encoding response-aware and vice versa. Furthermore, we augment the model with a mechanism for incorporating external knowledge to improve the handling of rare words. Both extensions are described in detail in the following subsections.

4.1 Attention augmented encoding

As described above, in the DE context and response are encoded independently from each other based on the same RNN. Instead of simply taking the final hidden state $\mathbf{h}^c$ (and $\mathbf{h}^r$) of the RNN as context (and response) encoding, we propose to use a response-aware attention mechanism to calculate the context embedding and vice versa.

Subsequently, we will describe this mechanism formally. Recall that a context c can be seen as sequence of words $\{w_t^c\}_{t=1}^T$ where all utterances are concatenated and T is the total number of words in the context. Given this sequence, the RNN (in our experiments a bi-directional GRU) produces a sequence of hidden states $\mathbf{h}_1^c, \ldots, \mathbf{h}_T^c$ and an encoding of the whole context sequence $\mathbf{h}^c$ as described in Section 3.2. Analogously, we get $\mathbf{h}_1^r, \ldots, \mathbf{h}_{T'}^r$ and $\mathbf{h}^r$ for a response consisting of a sequence of words $\{w_t^r\}_{t=1}^{T'}$, where T' is the total number of words in the response.

For calculating the response-aware context encoding, we first estimate attention weights α_t^c for the hidden state $\mathbf{h}_t^c$ in each time step, depending on the response encoding $\mathbf{h}^r$:

$$\alpha_t^c \propto \exp((\mathbf{h}_t^c)^\mathrm{T}\mathbf{W}_c\mathbf{h}^r) \ , \tag{4}$$

where $\mathbf{W}_c$ is a learnable parameter matrix. The response-aware context embedding then is given by

$$\hat{\mathbf{h}}^c = \sum_{t=1}^T \alpha_t^c \mathbf{h}_t^c \ . \tag{5}$$

Intuitively this means, that depending on the response we focus on different parts of the context sequence, for judging on how well the response matches the context. This may resemble human focus.

Similarly, we calculate the context-aware re-

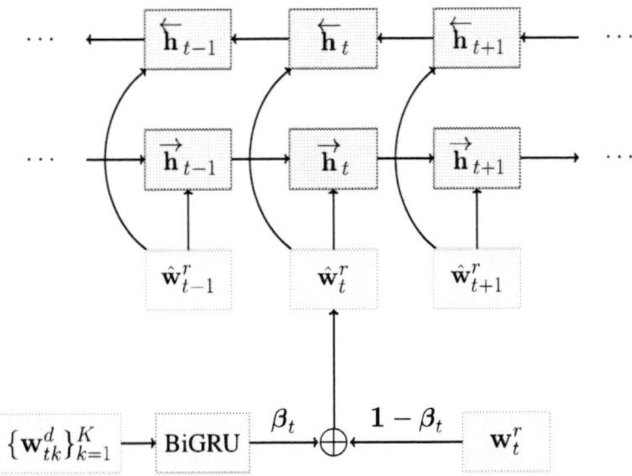

Figure 1: Our proposed way to incorporate domain knowledge into the model. β_t and $1 - \beta_t$ represent the (multiplicative) weights for the description embedding and the word embedding respectively. The resulting combination, $\hat{\mathbf{w}}_t^r$ acts as an input of the encoder.

sponse encoding by

$$\hat{\mathbf{h}}^r = \sum_{t=1}^T \alpha_t^r \mathbf{h}_t^r \ , \tag{6}$$

with attention weights

$$\alpha_t^r \propto \exp((\mathbf{h}_t^r)^\mathrm{T}\mathbf{W}_r\mathbf{h}^c) \ . \tag{7}$$

The two attention-weighted encodings (for response and context, respectively) then replace the vanilla encodings in equation (3), that is

$$p(y|c, r, \boldsymbol{\theta}) = \sigma((\hat{\mathbf{h}}^c)^\mathrm{T}\mathbf{M}\,\hat{\mathbf{h}}^r + b) \ . \tag{8}$$

4.2 Incorporating domain keyword descriptions

Bahdanau et al. (2018) proposed a method for learning embeddings for OOV words based on external dictionary definitions. They learn these description embeddings of words using an LSTM for encoding the corresponding definition. If a particular word included in the dictionary also appears in the corpus' vocabulary (for which vanilla word embeddings are given), they add the word embedding and the description embedding together. Otherwise, in the case of OOV words, they use solely the description embedding in place of the missing word embedding. Inspired by this approach, we use a similar technique to incorporate domain keyword descriptions into word embeddings.

If a word w_t^r in the response utterance is in the set of domain keywords $\mathcal{K}$, we firstly extract its description. The description of w_t^r is a sequence of words $\{w_{tk}^d\}_{k=1}^K$, which is projected onto sequence of embeddings $\{\mathbf{w}_{tk}^d\}_{k=1}^K$. This sequence is encoded using another bi-directional GRU to obtain a vector representation $\mathbf{h}_t^d$ of the same dimension as the vanilla word embeddings. If w_t^r is not in $\mathcal{K}$, we simply set $\mathbf{h}_t^d$ to zero. We call $\mathbf{h}_t^d$ the *description embedding*.

Some domain specific words might also happen to be common words. For instance, in the case of the UDC's vocabulary, there exist tokens such as *shutdown* [1] or *who* [2], which are ambiguous, i.e., although they are valid UNIX commands, they are also common words in natural language. The description embeddings of domain specific words can be simply added to the vanilla word embeddings as suggested by Bahdanau et al. (2018). However, it might be advantageous if the model can determine itself whether to treat the current word as a domain specific word, a common word, or something in between, depending on the context. For instance, if the context is mainly talking about system users, then *who* is most likely a UNIX keyword. Therefore, we propose a more flexible way to combine the description embedding $\mathbf{h}_t^d$ and the word embedding $\mathbf{w}_t^r$, that is, we define the final word embedding to be a convex combination of both, and let the combination coefficients be given by a function of $\mathbf{h}_t^d$ and the context embedding $\hat{\mathbf{h}}^c$. Intuitively, this allows the model to flexibly focus on the description or the vanilla embedding, in dependence on the context and the description. Formally, the combination coefficients $\boldsymbol{\beta}_t$ of t-th word in the response is given by

$$\boldsymbol{\beta}_t \propto \exp(\mathbf{U}^{\mathsf{T}}\hat{\mathbf{h}}^c + \mathbf{V}^{\mathsf{T}}\mathbf{w}_t^r) \ , \qquad (9)$$

where $\mathbf{U}$ and $\mathbf{V}$ are learnable parameter matrices. Note that $\boldsymbol{\beta}_t$ is a vector of the same dimension as the embeddings. The final embedding of w_t^r (which serves as input to the response encoder) is then the weighted sum

$$\hat{\mathbf{w}}_t^r = \boldsymbol{\beta}_t \odot \mathbf{h}_t^d + (1 - \boldsymbol{\beta}_t) \odot \mathbf{w}_t^r \ , \qquad (10)$$

where $\odot$ denotes the element wise multiplication.

5 Experiment

5.1 Ubuntu multi-turn dialogue corpus

Extending the work of Uthus and Aha (2013), Lowe et al. (2015a) introduced a version of the Ubuntu chat log conversations which is the largest

---

[1] UNIX command for system shutdown.
[2] UNIX command to get a list of currently logged-in users.

publicly available multi-turn, dyadic, and domain-specific dialogue data set. The chats are extracted from Ubuntu related topic specific chat rooms in the Freenode Internet Relay Chat (IRC) network. Usually, experienced users address a problem of someone by suggesting a potential solution and a *name mention* of the addressed user. A conversation between a pair of users often stops when the problem has been solved. However, they might continue having a discussion which is not related to the topic.

A preprocessed version of the above corpus and the needed vocabulary are provided by Wu et al. (2017). The preprocessing consisted of replacing numbers, URLs, and system paths with special placeholders as suggested by Xu et al. (2016). No additional preprocessing is performed by us. The data set consists of 1 million training triples, 500k validation triples, and 500k test triples. One half of the 1 million training triples are positive (triples with $y = 1$, i.e. the provided response fits the context) the other half negative (triples with $y = 0$). In contrast, in the validation and test set, for every context c_i, there exists one positive triple providing the ground-truth response to c_i and nine negative triples with unbefitting responses. Thus, in these sets, the ratio between positive and negative triples per context is 1:9 which makes evaluating the model with information retrieval metrics such as Recall@k possible (see Section 6).

5.2 Model hyperparameters

We chose a word embedding dimension of 200 as done by Wu et al. (2017). We use fastText (Bojanowski et al., 2016) to pre-train the word embeddings using the training set instead of using off-the-shelf word embeddings, following Wu et al. (2017). We set the hidden dimension of our GRU to be 300, as in the work of Lowe et al. (2015a). We restricted the sequence length of a context by a maximum of 320 words, and that of the response by 160. Because of the resulting size of the model and limited GPU memory, we had to use a smaller batch size of 32. We optimize the binary cross entropy loss of our model with respect to the training data using Adam (Kingma and Ba, 2015) with an initial learning rate of 0.0001. We train our model for a maximum of 20 epochs as according to our experience, this is more than enough to achieve convergence. The training is stopped when the validation recall does not increase after three sub-

Model	$R_2@1$	$R_{10}@1$	$R_{10}@3$	$R_{10}@5$
DE-RNN (Kadlec et al., 2015)	0.768	0.403	0.547	0.819
DE-CNN (Kadlec et al., 2015)	0.848	0.549	0.684	0.896
DE-LSTM (Kadlec et al., 2015)	0.901	0.638	0.784	0.949
DE-BiLSTM (Kadlec et al., 2015)	0.895	0.630	0.780	0.944
MultiView (Zhou et al., 2016)	0.908	0.662	0.801	0.951
DL2R (Yan et al., 2016)	0.899	0.626	0.783	0.944
r-LSTM (Xu et al., 2016)	0.889	0.649	0.857	0.932
MV-LSTM (Wan et al., 2016)	0.906	0.653	0.804	0.946
Match-LSTM (Wang and Jiang, 2016)	0.904	0.653	0.799	0.944
QA-LSTM (Tan et al., 2016)	0.903	0.633	0.789	0.943
SMN_{dyn} (Wu et al., 2017)	0.926	0.726	0.847	0.961
CCN (An et al., 2018)	-	0.727	0.858	0.971
ESIM (Dong and Huang, 2018)	-	0.734	0.854	0.967
AK-DE-biGRU (Ours)	**0.933**	**0.747**	**0.868**	**0.972**

Table 2: Evaluation results of our models compared to various baselines on Ubuntu Dialogue Corpus.

sequent epochs. The test set is evaluated on the model with the best validation recall.

For the implementation, we use PyTorch (Paszke et al., 2017). We train the model end-to-end with a single 12GB GPU. The implementation[3] of our models along with the additional domain knowledge base[4] are publicly available.

6   Results

Following Lowe et al. (2015a) and Kadlec et al. (2015), we use the Recall@k evaluation metric, where $R_n@k$ corresponds to the fraction of of examples for which the correct response is under the k best out of a set of n candidate responses, which were ranked according to there their probabilities under the model.

In our evaluation specifically, we use $R_2@1$, $R_{10}@1$, $R_{10}@3$, and $R_{10}@5$.

6.1   Comparison against baselines

We compare our model, which we refer to as *Attention and external Knowledge augmented DE with bi-directional GRU* (**AK-DE-biGRU**), against models previously tested on the same data set: the basic DE models analyzed by Lowe et al. (2015a) and Kadlec et al. (2015) using different encoders, such as convolutional neural network (**DE-CNN**), LSTM (**DE-LSTM**) and

bi-directional LSTM (**DE-BiLSTM**); the **Multi-View**, **DL2R** and **r-LSTM** models proposed by Zhou et al. (2016), Yan et al. (2016) and Xu et al. (2016), respectively; architectures for advanced context and response matching, namely **MV-LSTM** (Wan et al., 2016), **Match-LSTM** (Wang and Jiang, 2016), and **QA-LSTM** (Tan et al., 2016); architectures processing the context utterances individually, namely $\textbf{SMN}_{\textbf{dyn}}$ (Wu et al., 2017) and **CCN**; and we also use recently proposed **ESIM** (Dong and Huang, 2018) as a baseline.

The results are reported in Table 2. Our model outperforms all other models used as baselines. The largest improvement of our model compared to the best of the baselines (i.e. ESIM in general and SMN_{dyn} for $R_2@1$ metric) are with respect to the $R_{10}@1$ and $R_{10}@3$ metric, where we observed absolute improvements of 0.013 and 0.014 corresponding to 1.8% and 1.6% relative improvement , respectively. For $R_2@1$ and $R_{10}@5$ we observed more modest improvements of 0.007 (0.8%) and 0.005 (0.5%), respectively. Our results are significantly better with $p < 10^{-6}$ for a one-sample one-tailed t-test compared to the best baseline (ESIM), on $R_{10}@1$, $R_{10}@3$, $R_{10}@5$ metrics, using the outcome of 15 independent experiments. The variance between different trials is smaller than 0.001 for all evaluation metrics.

[3]https://github.com/SmartDataAnalytics/AK-DE-biGRU.
[4]Command descriptions scraped from Ubuntu man pages.

Model	$R_{10}@1$	$R_{10}@3$	$R_{10}@5$
DE-GRU	0.685	0.831	0.960
DE-biGRU	0.678	0.813	0.956
A-DE-GRU	0.712	0.845	0.964
A-DE-biGRU	0.739	0.864	0.968
AK$_+$-DE-biGRU	0.743	0.867	0.969
AK-DE-biGRU$_{w2v}$	0.745	0.866	0.970
AK-DE-biGRU	**0.747**	**0.868**	**0.972**

Table 3: Ablation study with different settings.

6.2 Ablation study

Our model differs in various ways from the vanilla DE: it uses a GRU instead of an LSTM for the encoding, introduces an attention mechanism for the encoding of the context and another for the encoding of the response, and incorporates additional knowledge in the response encoding process.

To analyze the effect of these components on the over all performance, we analyzed different model variants: a DE using a GRU or a bidirectional GRU as encoder (**DE-GRU** and **DE-biGRU**, respectively) and both of these models with attention augmented encoding for embedding both context and response (**A-DE-GRU** and **A-DE-biGRU**, respectively). We also tested the effects of using a simple addition instead of the weighted summation given in equation (10) for merging the word embedding with the desciption embedding (**AK$_+$-DE-biGRU**). Finally, we investigated a version of our model (**AK-DE-biGRU$_{w2v}$**) where we used pre-trained word2vec embeddings, as done by Wu et al. (2017), instead of learning our own word embeddings from the data set.

The results of the study are presented in Table 3. With the basic models, i.e. DE-GRU and DE-biGRU, as baselines, we observed around 4% and 9% improvement on $R_{10}@1$ when incorporating the attention mechanism (A-DE-GRU and A-DE-biGRU, respectively).

When domain knowledge is incorporated by simple addition (as in the work of Bahdanau et al. (2018)), i.e. in AK$_+$-DE-biGRU, we noticed 0.5% further improvement. Note however, that the results are not as good as when using the proposed weighted addition. Finally, using our method of incorporating domain knowledge in combination with embeddings trained from scratch with fastText (Bojanowski et al., 2016), the performance gets 0.3% better than when using pre-

Example Response Utterances

gui for shutdown try typing *sudo shutdown* -h now

sudo apt-get install qt4-designer there could be some qt dev packages too but i think the above will install them as dependencies

certainly won n't make a difference i m sure but maybe try *sudo shutdown* -r now shutdown works just fine graphical and command line

pci can you put the output of *lspci* on __url__ and give me the link please

i do n't see a line in xorg conf for hsync and vsync do you get the same you d create it i m looking at gentoo and ubuntu forums a sec

can be many reasons of *traceroute* __url__ you will not get a complete result

Table 4: Visualization of attention weight in utterance samples, darker shade means higher attention weight.

trained word2vec embeddings. In total, compared to the DE-biGRU baseline, our model (AK-DE-biGRU) achieves 10% of improvement in terms of the $R_{10}@1$ metric. Thus, the results clearly suggest that both the attention mechanism and the incorporation of domain knowledge, are effective approaches for improving the dual encoder architecture. Curiously, we noticed that for the baseline models, using a GRU as the encoder is better than using a biGRU. This finding is in line with the results from Kadlec et al. (2015) reported in Table 2. However, the table is turned when augmenting the models with an attention mechanism where the biGRU-based model outperforms the one with the GRU. This observation motivates us to consider a biGRU instead of a GRU in our final model.

6.3 Visualizing response attentions

To further investigate the results given by our model, we qualitatively inspected several samples of response utterances and their attention weights, as shown in Table 4. We noticed that our model learned to focus on technical terms, such as *lspci*,

Context utterances
Utterance 1: Ubuntu <version>
Utterance 2: hi all sony vaio fx120 will not turn off when shutting down, any ideas? btw acpi =o ff in boot parameters anything else i should be trying?
Utterance 3: how are you shutting down i.e. terminal or gui?

Table 5: Sample context utterances from UDC's test set whose correct response is the first utterance in Table 4.

shutdown, and *traceroute*. We also observed that the model is able to capture contextual importance, i.e. it is able to focus on context relevant words. For example, given the context in Table 5 and the correct response in the first row of Table 4, one can see the attention on the word *shutdown*, where it gets a lower weight when used as a common word in the first occurance than as a UNIX command in the second. [5]

6.4 Error analysis

We qualitatively analyzed the errors our method made. We observed that our model's predictions are biased toward high information utterances. That is, we observed for some examples that the correct response is generic (i.e. has low information), our model chooses a non-generic response, as shown in Table 6. Furthermore, we computed the average utterance information content (the entropy) for both the correct and predicted responses, based on Xu and Reitter (2018), where we obtained 9.25 bits and 9.34 bits, respectively. This quantitatively indicates that our model is slightly biased toward high information responses.

7 Conclusion and future work

We presented a novel model which extends the dual encoder architecture for multi-turn response selection by incorporating external domain knowledge and attention augmented encoding. Our experimental results demonstrate that our model outperformed other state-of-the-art methods for response selection in a multi-turn dialogue setting, and that the attention mechanism and incorporating additional domain knowledge are indeed effective approaches for improving the response se-

Examples of model error:
Correct: ok will do :), nope. **Predicted**: __url__ if you go down to the bottom of that tutorial i also have a post there that is a bit more detailed about my problem poster name is trent
Correct: hmm! ok **Predicted**: as did i w/ fbsd ... just check out the livecd for a bit
Correct: okay thank you a thread i hope :) **Predicted**: hmm ok because im not sure about iwconfig and wpa but we can give it a try do gksudo gedit __path__ then add a record like this __url__
Correct: right .. it is, it exists i verified **Predicted**: i want to connect to your computer remotely if you allow me to so i can fix the problem for you just follow the following procedure.
Correct: roger .. lemme check, got it ... thanks dude :) **Predicted**: just click the partition and then click the blue text next to mount point or you can simply navigate to that path

Table 6: Examples on the error our model made. We observed that our model's predictions are biased towards non-generic responses.

lection performance of the dual encoder architecture. Further improvement might be made by also considering domain knowledge in the context and by improving the handling of OOV words, e.g. by widening our domain specific word vocabulary and handling generic OOV words such as typos.

References

Guozhen An, Mehrnoosh Shafiee, and Davood Shamsi. 2018. Improving retrieval modeling using cross convolution networks and multi frequency word embedding. *arXiv preprint arXiv:1802.05373*.

Dzmitry Bahdanau, Tom Bosc, Stanisław Jastrzebski, Edward Grefenstette, Pascal Vincent, and Yoshua Bengio. 2018. Learning to compute word embeddings on the fly.

Leemon Baird. 1995. Residual algorithms: Reinforcement learning with function approximation. In *Machine Learning Proceedings 1995*, pages 30–37. Elsevier.

Petr Baudiš, Jan Pichl, Tomáš Vyskočil, and Jan Šedivỳ. 2016. Sentence pair scoring: Towards unified framework for text comprehension. *arXiv preprint arXiv:1603.06127.*

Yoshua Bengio, Patrice Simard, and Paolo Frasconi. 1994. Learning long-term dependencies with gradient descent is difficult. *IEEE transactions on neural networks*, 5(2):157–166.

Piotr Bojanowski, Edouard Grave, Armand Joulin, and Tomas Mikolov. 2016. Enriching word vectors with subword information. *arXiv preprint arXiv:1607.04606.*

Antoine Bordes, Y-Lan Boureau, and Jason Weston. 2017. Learning end-to-end goal-oriented dialog. In *Proceedings of the 3rd International Conference for Learning Representations.*

Kyunghyun Cho, B van Merrienboer, Caglar Gulcehre, F Bougares, H Schwenk, and Yoshua Bengio. 2014. Learning phrase representations using rnn encoder-decoder for statistical machine translation. In *Conference on Empirical Methods in Natural Language Processing (EMNLP 2014).*

Jianxiong Dong and Jim Huang. 2018. Enhance word representation for out-of-vocabulary on ubuntu dialogue corpus. *arXiv preprint arXiv:1802.02614.*

Wang Hao, Lu Zhengdong, Li Hang, et al. 2013. A dataset for research on short-text conversation. In *Proceed-ings of the 2013 Conference on Empirical Methods in Natural Language Processing*, pages 935–945.

Sepp Hochreiter and Jürgen Schmidhuber. 1997. Long short-term memory. *Neural computation*, 9(8):1735–1780.

Zongcheng Ji, Zhengdong Lu, and Hang Li. 2014. An information retrieval approach to short text conversation. In *Proceedings of International Conference on Computation and Language.*

Rudolf Kadlec, Martin Schmid, and Jan Kleindienst. 2015. Improved deep learning baselines for ubuntu corpus dialogs. In *NIPS on Machine Learning for Spoken Language Understanding.*

Diederik P Kingma and Jimmy Ba. 2015. Adam: A method for stochastic optimization. In *Proceedings of the 3rd International Conference for Learning Representations.*

Ryan Lowe, Nissan Pow, Iulian Serban, and Joelle Pineau. 2015a. The ubuntu dialogue corpus: A large dataset for research in unstructured multi-turn dialogue systems. In *Proceedings of SIGDIAL.*

Ryan Lowe, Nissan Pow, IV Serban, Laurent Charlin, and Joelle Pineau. 2015b. Incorporating unstructured textual knowledge sources into neural dialogue systems. In *Neural Information Processing Systems Workshop on Machine Learning for Spoken Language Understanding.*

Minh-Thang Luong, Ilya Sutskever, Quoc V Le, Oriol Vinyals, and Wojciech Zaremba. 2015. Addressing the rare word problem in neural machine translation. In *Proceeding of Association for Computational Linguistics.*

Johanna Moore Mary Ellen Foster Oliver and Lemon Michael White. 2004. Generating tailored, comparative descriptions in spoken dialogue.

Adam Paszke, Sam Gross, Soumith Chintala, Gregory Chanan, Edward Yang, Zachary DeVito, Zeming Lin, Alban Desmaison, Luca Antiga, and Adam Lerer. 2017. Automatic differentiation in pytorch.

Alan Ritter, Colin Cherry, and William B Dolan. 2011. Data-driven response generation in social media. In *Proceedings of the conference on empirical methods in natural language processing*, pages 583–593. Association for Computational Linguistics.

Iulian Vlad Serban, Alessandro Sordoni, Yoshua Bengio, Aaron C Courville, and Joelle Pineau. 2016. Building end-to-end dialogue systems using generative hierarchical neural network models. In *AAAI*, volume 16, pages 3776–3784.

Lifeng Shang, Zhengdong Lu, and Hang Li. 2015. Neural responding machine for short-text conversation. In *Proceedings of 53rd Annual Meeting of the Association for Computational Linguistics.*

Amanda Stent, Marilyn A Walker, Steve Whittaker, and Preetam Maloor. 2002. User-tailored generation for spoken dialogue: An experiment. In *Seventh International Conference on Spoken Language Processing.*

Ming Tan, Cicero dos Santos, Bing Xiang, and Bowen Zhou. 2016. Lstm-based deep learning models for non-factoid answer selection. In *Proceedings of the 4rd International Conference for Learning Representations.*

David C Uthus and David W Aha. 2013. Extending word highlighting in multiparticipant chat. In *FLAIRS Conference.*

Oriol Vinyals and Quoc Le. 2015. A neural conversational model. In *International Conference on Machine Learning: Deep Learning Workshop.*

Marilyn A Walker, Rebecca Passonneau, and Julie E Boland. 2001. Quantitative and qualitative evaluation of darpa communicator spoken dialogue systems. In *Proceedings of the 39th Annual Meeting on Association for Computational Linguistics*, pages 515–522. Association for Computational Linguistics.

Shengxian Wan, Yanyan Lan, Jun Xu, Jiafeng Guo, Liang Pang, and Xueqi Cheng. 2016. Match-srnn: Modeling the recursive matching structure with spatial rnn. In *Proceedings of the Twenty-Fifth International Joint Conference on Artificial Intelligence.*

Shuohang Wang and Jing Jiang. 2016. Learning natural language inference with lstm. In *Proceedings of NAACL-HLT 2016*.

Tsung-Hsien Wen, David Vandyke, Nikola Mrksic, Milica Gasic, Lina M Rojas-Barahona, Pei-Hao Su, Stefan Ultes, and Steve Young. 2017. A network-based end-to-end trainable task-oriented dialogue system. In *European Chapter of the Association for Computational Linguistics*.

Jason Williams, Antoine Raux, Deepak Ramachandran, and Alan Black. 2013. The dialog state tracking challenge. In *Proceedings of the SIGDIAL 2013 Conference*, pages 404–413.

Yu Wu, Wei Wu, Zhoujun Li, and Ming Zhou. 2016. Topic augmented neural network for short text conversation. *CoRR abs/1605.00090*.

Yu Wu, Wei Wu, Chen Xing, Ming Zhou, and Zhoujun Li. 2017. Sequential matching network: A new architecture for multi-turn response selection in retrieval-based chatbots. In *Proceedings of the 55th Annual Meeting of the Association for Computational Linguistics (Volume 1: Long Papers)*, volume 1, pages 496–505.

Yang Xu and David Reitter. 2018. Information density converges in dialogue: Towards an information-theoretic model. *Cognition*, 170:147–163.

Zhen Xu, Bingquan Liu, Baoxun Wang, Chengjie Sun, and Xiaolong Wang. 2016. Incorporating loose-structured knowledge into lstm with recall gate for conversation modeling. *arXiv preprint arXiv:1605.05110*.

Rui Yan, Yiping Song, and Hua Wu. 2016. Learning to respond with deep neural networks for retrieval-based human-computer conversation system. In *Proceedings of the 39th International ACM SIGIR conference on Research and Development in Information Retrieval*, pages 55–64. ACM.

Tiancheng Zhao and Maxine Eskenazi. 2016. Towards end-to-end learning for dialog state tracking and management using deep reinforcement learning. In *Proceedings of SIGDIAL*.

Xiangyang Zhou, Daxiang Dong, Hua Wu, Shiqi Zhao, Dianhai Yu, Hao Tian, Xuan Liu, and Rui Yan. 2016. Multi-view response selection for human-computer conversation. In *Proceedings of the 2016 Conference on Empirical Methods in Natural Language Processing*, pages 372–381.

The Lifted Matrix-Space Model for Semantic Composition

WooJin Chung[1]
woojin@nyu.edu

Sheng-Fu Wang[1]
shengfu.wang@nyu.edu

Samuel R. Bowman[1,2]
bowman@nyu.edu

[1]Dept. of Linguistics
New York University
10 Washington Place
New York, NY 10003

[2]Center for Data Science
New York University
60 Fifth Avenue
New York, NY 10011

Abstract

Tree-structured neural network architectures for sentence encoding draw inspiration from the approach to semantic composition generally seen in formal linguistics, and have shown empirical improvements over comparable sequence models by doing so. Moreover, adding multiplicative interaction terms to the composition functions in these models can yield significant further improvements. However, existing compositional approaches that adopt such a powerful composition function scale poorly, with parameter counts exploding as model dimension or vocabulary size grows. We introduce the Lifted Matrix-Space model, which uses a global transformation to map vector word embeddings to matrices, which can then be composed via an operation based on matrix-matrix multiplication. Its composition function effectively transmits a larger number of activations across layers with relatively few model parameters. We evaluate our model on the Stanford NLI corpus, the Multi-Genre NLI corpus, and the Stanford Sentiment Treebank and find that it consistently outperforms TreeLSTM (Tai et al., 2015), the previous best known composition function for tree-structured models.

1 Introduction

Contemporary theoretical accounts of natural language syntax and semantics consistently hold that sentences are tree-structured, and that the meaning of each node in each tree is calculated from the meaning of its child nodes using a relatively simple *semantic composition* process which is applied recursively bottom-up (Chierchia and McConnell-Ginet, 1990; Dowty, 2007). In tree-structured recursive neural networks (TreeRNN; Socher et al., 2010), a similar procedure is used to build representations for sentences for use in natural language understanding tasks, with distributed representations for words repeatedly fed through a neural

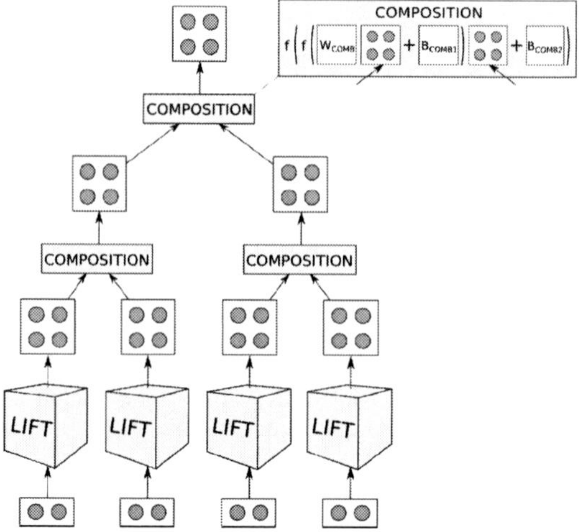

Figure 1: The Lifted Matrix-Space model in schematic form. Words are stored as vectors and projected into matrix space by the LIFT layer. A parametric COMPOSITION function combines pairs of these matrices using multiplicative interactions.

network *composition function* according to a binary tree structure supplied by a parser. The success of a tree-structured model largely depends on the design of its composition function.

It has been repeatedly shown that a composition function that captures multiplicative interactions between the two items being composed yields better results (Rudolph and Giesbrecht, 2010; Socher et al., 2012, 2013) than do otherwise-equivalent functions based on simple linear interactions. This paper presents a novel model which advances this line of research, the Lifted Matrix-Space model. We utilize a tensor-parameterized LIFT layer that learns to produce matrix representations of words that are dependent on the content of pre-trained word embedding vectors. Composition of two matrix representations is carried out by a composition layer, into which the two matrices are sequentially

Proceedings of the 22nd Conference on Computational Natural Language Learning (CoNLL 2018), pages 508–518
Brussels, Belgium, October 31 - November 1, 2018. ©2018 Association for Computational Linguistics

fed. Figure 1 illustrates the model design.

Our model was inspired by Continuation Semantics (Barker and Shan, 2014; Charlow, 2014), where each symbolic representation of words is converted to a higher-order function. There is a consensus in linguistic semantics that a subset of natural language expressions correspond to higher-order functions. Inspired by the works in programming language theory, Continuation Semantics takes a step further and claims that all expressions have to be converted into a higher-order function before they participate in semantic composition. The theory bridges a gap between linguistic semantics and programming language theory, and reinterprets various linguistic phenomena from the view of computation. While we do not directly implement Continuation Semantics, we follow its rough contours: We convert low-level representations (vectors) to higher-order functions (matrices), and composition only takes place between the higher-order functions.

A number of models have been developed to capture the multiplicative interactions between distributed representations. While having a similar objective, the proposed model requires fewer model parameters than the predecessors because it does not necessarily learn each word matrix representation separately, and the number of parameters for the composition function is not proportional to the cube of the hidden state dimension. Because of this, it can be trained with larger vocabularies and more hidden state activations than was possible with its predecessors.

We evaluate our model primarily on the task of *natural language inference* (NLI; MacCartney, 2009). The task consists in determining the inferential relation between a given pair of sentences. It is a principled and widely-used evaluation task for natural language understanding, and knowing the inferential relations is closely related to understanding the meaning of an expression (Chierchia and McConnell-Ginet, 1990). While other tasks such as question answering or machine translation require a model to learn task-specific behavior that goes beyond understanding sentence meaning, NLI results highlight sentence understanding performance in isolation. We also include an evaluation on sentiment classification for comparison with some earlier work.

We find that our model outperforms existing approaches to tree-structured modeling on all three tasks, though it does not set the state of the art on any of them, falling behind other types of complex model. We nonetheless expect that this method will be a valuable ingredient in future models for sentence understanding and a valuable platform for research of compositionality in learned representations.

2   Related work

Composition functions for tree-structured models have been thoroughly studied in recent years (Mitchell and Lapata, 2010; Baroni and Zamparelli, 2010; Zanzotto et al., 2010; Socher et al., 2011). While this line of research has been successful, the majority of the existing models ultimately rely on the additive linear combination of vectors. The Tree-structured recursive neural networks (TreeRNN) of Socher et al. (2010) compose two child node vectors $\vec{h}_l$ and $\vec{h}_r$ using this method:

$$(1) \quad \vec{h} = tanh(W \begin{bmatrix} \vec{h}_l \\ \vec{h}_r \end{bmatrix} + \vec{b})$$

where $\vec{h}_l$, $\vec{h}_r$, $\vec{h}$, $\vec{b} \in \mathbb{R}^{d \times 1}$, and $W \in \mathbb{R}^{d \times 2d}$. Throughout this paper, d stands for the number of activations of a given model.

However, there is no reason to believe that the additive linear combination of vectors is adequate for modeling semantic composition. Formal work in linguistic semantics has shown that many linguistic expressions are well-represented as functions. Accordingly, composing two meanings typically require feeding an argument into a function (function application; Heim and Kratzer, 1998). Such an operation involves a complex interaction between the two meanings, but the classic TreeRNN does not supply any additional means to capture the interaction.

Rudolph and Giesbrecht (2010) report that matrix multiplication, as opposed to element-wise addition, is more suitable for semantic composition. Their Compositional Matrix-Space model (CMS) represents words and phrases as matrices, and they are composed via a simple matrix multiplication:

$$(2) \quad P = AB$$

where $A, B, P \in \mathbb{R}^{d \times d}$ are matrix representations of the word embeddings. They provide a formal proof that element-wise addition/multiplication of vectors can be subsumed under matrix multiplication. Moreover, they claim that the order-sensitivity of matrix multiplication is adequate for capturing the semantic composition because natural language is order-sensitive.

However, as Socher et al. (2012) note, CMS loses syntactic information during composition due to the associative character of matrix multiplication. For instance, the following two tree structures in (3) are syntactically distinct, but CMS would produce the same result for both structures because its mode of composition is associative.

(3) a.   A   B   C   b.   A   B   C

CMS cannot distinguish the meaning of the two tree structures and invariably produces ABC (a sequence of matrix multiplications). Therefore, the information on syntactic constituency would be lost. This makes the model less desirable for handling semantic composition of natural language expressions for two reasons: First, the principle of compositionality is violated. Much of the success of the tree-structured models can be credited to the shared hypothesis that the meaning of every tree node is derived from the meanings of its child nodes. Abandoning this principle of compositionality gives up the advantage. Second, it cannot handle structural ambiguities exemplified in (4).

(4) John saw a man with binoculars.

(5) a.

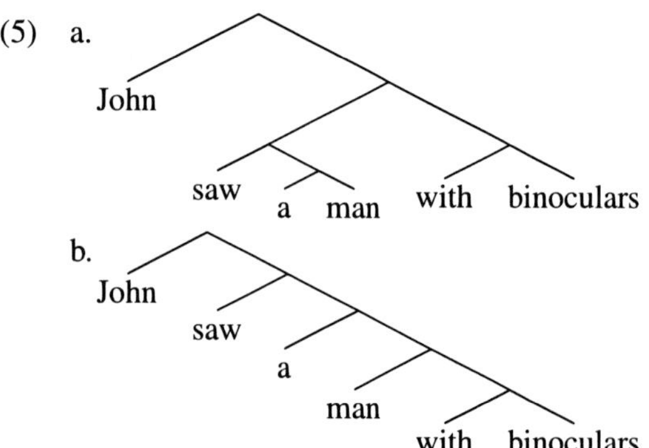

The sentence has two interpretations that can be disambiguated with the following paraphrases: (i) John saw a man via binoculars, and (ii) John saw a man who has binoculars. The common syntactic analysis of the ambiguity is that the prepositional phrase *with binoculars* can attach to two different locations. If it attaches to the verb phrase *saw a man*, the first interpretation arises. On the other hand, if it attaches to the noun *man*, the second interpretation is given. However, if the structural information is lost, we would have no way to disambiguate the two readings.

Socher et al.'s (2012) Matrix-Vector RNN (MV-RNN) is another attempt to capture the multiplicative interactions between two vectors, while conforming to the principle of compositionality. They hypothesize that representing operators as matrices can better reflect operator semantics. For each lexical item, a matrix (trained parameter) is assigned in addition to the pre-trained word embedding vector. The model aims to assign the right matrix representations to operators while assigning an identity matrix to words with no operator meaning. One step of semantic composition is defined as follows:

$$(6) \quad \vec{h} = f(B\vec{a}, A\vec{b}) = g\left(W \begin{bmatrix} B\vec{a} \\ A\vec{b} \end{bmatrix}\right)$$

$$(7) \quad H = f_M(A, B) = W_M \begin{bmatrix} A \\ B \end{bmatrix}$$

where $\vec{a}, \vec{b}, \vec{h} \in \mathbb{R}^{d \times 1}$, $A, B, H \in \mathbb{R}^{d \times d}$, and W, $W_M \in \mathbb{R}^{d \times 2d}$.

MV-RNN is computationally costly as it needs to learn an additional $d \times d$ matrix for each lexical item. It is empirically known that the size of the vocabulary is roughly proportional to the size of the corpus (Heaps' law; Herdan, 1960), therefore the number of model parameters increases as the corpus gets bigger. This makes the model less ideal for handling a large corpus: having a huge number of parameters causes a problem both for memory usage and for learning efficiency.

Chen et al. (2013) and Socher et al. (2013) present the recursive neural tensor network (RNTN) which reduces the computational complexity of MV-RNN, while capturing the multiplicative interactions between child vectors. The model introduces a third-order tensor V which interacts with the child node vectors as follows:

$$(8) \quad \vec{h} = tanh\left(W \begin{bmatrix} \vec{h}_l \\ \vec{h}_r \end{bmatrix} + \vec{b} + \vec{h}_l^T \mathbf{V} \vec{h}_r\right)$$

where $\vec{h}_l, \vec{h}_r, \vec{b} \in \mathbb{R}^{d \times 1}$, $\mathbf{W} \in \mathbb{R}^{d \times 2d}$, and $\mathbf{V} \in \mathbb{R}^{d \times d \times d}$. RNTN improves on MV-RNN in that its parameter size is not proportional to the size of the corpus. However, the addition of the third-order tensor $\mathbf{V}$ of dimension $d \times d \times d$ still requires proportionally more parameters.

The last composition function relevant to this paper is the Tree-structured long short-term memory networks (TreeLSTM; Tai et al., 2015; Zhu et al., 2015; Le and Zuidema, 2015), particularly the version over a constituency tree. It is an

Model	Params.	Associative	Multiplicative	Activation size w.r.t. TreeRNN
TreeRNN/LSTM	$O(d \times d)$	No	No	1
CMS	$O(V \times d \times d)$	Yes	Yes	$1/V$
MV-RNN	$O(V \times d \times d)$	No	Yes	$1/V$
RNTN	$O(d \times d \times d)$	No	Yes	$1/d$
LMS (this work)	$O(d \times d_{emb})$	No	Yes	$1/d_{emb}$

Table 1: Summary of the models. *Params.* is the number of model parameters (not counting pretrained word vectors), d is the number of activations at each tree node, d_{emb} is the dimension of the word embeddings, and V is the size of the vocabulary. *Associative* and *Multiplicative* indicate whether composition is associative and whether it includes multiplicative interactions between inputs, respectively. *Activation size w.r.t. TreeRNN* shows how activation sizes scale with respect to TreeRNN when all of the models have the same parameter count.

extension of TreeRNN which adapts long short-term memory (LSTM; Hochreiter and Schmidhuber, 1997) networks. It shares the advantage of LSTM networks in that it prevents the vanishing gradient problem (Hochreiter et al., 2001).

Unlike TreeRNN, the output hidden state $\vec{h}$ of TreeLSTM is not directly calculated from the hidden states of its child nodes, $\vec{h}_l$ and $\vec{h}_r$. Rather, each node in TreeLSTM maintains a cell state $\vec{c}$ that keeps track of important information of its child nodes. The output hidden state $\vec{h}$ is drawn from the cell state $\vec{c}$ by passing it through an output gate $\vec{o}$.

The cell state is calculated in three steps: (i) Compute a new candidate $\vec{g}$ from $\vec{h}_l$ and $\vec{h}_r$. TreeLSTM selects which values to take from the new candidate $\vec{g}$ by passing it through an input gate $\vec{i}$. (ii) Choose which values to forget from the cell states of the child nodes, $\vec{c}_l$ and $\vec{c}_r$. For each child node, an element-wise product ($\odot$) between its cell state and the forget gate (either $\vec{f}_l$ and $\vec{f}_r$, depending on the child node) is calculated. (iii) Lastly, sum up the results from (i) and (ii).

$$(9) \quad \vec{g} = tanh\left(W \begin{bmatrix} \vec{h}_l \\ \vec{h}_r \end{bmatrix} + \vec{b}\right)$$

$$(10) \quad \begin{bmatrix} \vec{i} \\ \vec{f}_l \\ \vec{f}_r \\ \vec{o} \end{bmatrix} = \begin{bmatrix} \sigma \\ \sigma \\ \sigma \\ \sigma \end{bmatrix} \left(W \begin{bmatrix} \vec{h}_l \\ \vec{h}_r \end{bmatrix} + \vec{b}\right)$$

$$(11) \quad \vec{c} = \vec{f}_l \odot \vec{c}_l + \vec{f}_r \odot \vec{c}_r + \vec{i} \odot \vec{g}$$

$$(12) \quad \vec{h} = \vec{o} \odot tanh(\vec{c})$$

TreeLSTM achieves the state-of-the-art performance among the tree-structured models in various tasks, including natural language inference and sentiment classification. However, there are non-tree-structured models on the market that outperform TreeLSTM. Our goal is to design a stronger composition function that enhances the performance of tree-structured models. We develop a composition function that captures the multiplicative interaction between distributed representations. At the same time, we improve on the predecessors in terms of scalability, making the model more suitable for larger datasets.

To recapitulate, TreeRNN and TreeLSTM reflect the principle of compositionality but cannot capture the multiplicative interaction between two expressions. In contrast, CMS incorporates multiplicative interaction but violates the principle of compositionality. MV-RNN is compositional and also captures the multiplicative interaction, but it requires a learned $d \times d$ matrix for each vocabulary item. RNTN is also compositional and incorporates multiplicative interaction, but it requires less parameters than MV-RNN. Nevertheless, it requires significantly more parameters than TreeRNN or TreeLSTM. Table 1 is an overview of the discussed models.

Other interesting works enrich semantic composition with additional context such as grammatical roles or function/argumenthood (Clark et al., 2008; Erk and Padó, 2008; Grefenstette et al., 2014; Asher et al., 2016; Weir et al., 2016).

3 The Lifted Matrix-Space model

3.1 Base model

We present the Lifted Matrix-Space model (LMS) which renders semantic composition in a novel way. Our model consists of three subparts: the LIFT layer, the composition layer, and the TreeLSTM wrapper. The LIFT layer takes a word embedding vector and outputs a corresponding $\sqrt{d} \times \sqrt{d}$ matrix (eq. 13).

$$(13) \quad H = tanh(\mathbf{W}_{\text{LIFT}}\vec{c} + B_{\text{LIFT}})$$

where $\vec{c} \in \mathbb{R}^{d_{emb} \times 1}$, $B_{\text{LIFT}} \in \mathbb{R}^{\sqrt{d} \times \sqrt{d}}$, and $\mathbf{W}_{\text{LIFT}} \in \mathbb{R}^{\sqrt{d} \times \sqrt{d} \times d_{emb}}$. The resulting H matrix serves as an input for the composition layer.

Given the matrix representations of two child nodes, H_l and H_r, the composition layer first takes H_l and returns a hidden state $H_{inner} \in \mathbb{R}^{\sqrt{d} \times \sqrt{d}}$ (eq. 14). Since H_{inner} is also a matrix, it can function as the weight matrix for H_r. The composition layer multiplies H_{inner} with H_r, adds a bias, and feeds the result into a non-linear activation function (eq. 15). This yields $H_{cand} \in \mathbb{R}^{\sqrt{d} \times \sqrt{d}}$, which for the base model is the output of semantic composition.

$$(14) \quad H_{inner} = tanh(W_{\text{COMB}} H_l + B_{\text{COMB}1})$$

$$(15) \quad H_{cand} = tanh(H_{inner} H_r + B_{\text{COMB}2})$$

As in CMS, the primary mode of semantic composition is matrix multiplication. However, LMS improves on CMS in that it avoids associativity. LMS differs from MV-RNN in that it does not learn a $d \times d$ matrix for each vocabulary item. Compared to RNTN, LMS transmits a larger number of activations across layers, given the same parameter count. In both models, the size of the third-order tensor is the dominant factor in determining the number of model parameters. The parameter count of LMS is approximately proportional to the number of activations (d), but the parameter count of RNTN is approximately proportional to the cube of the number of activations (d^3). Therefore, LMS can transmit the same number of activations with fewer model parameters.

3.2 LMS augmented with LSTM components

We augment the base model with LSTM components (LMS-LSTM) to circumvent the problem of long-term dependencies. As in the case of TreeL-STM, we additionally manage cell states ($\vec{c_l}, \vec{c_r}$). Since the LSTM components operate on vectors, we reshape H_{cand}, H_l, and H_r into $d \times 1$ column vectors respectively, and produce $\vec{g}$, $\vec{h_l}$, and $\vec{h_r}$. The output of the LSTM components are calculated based on these vectors, and is reshaped back to a $\sqrt{d} \times \sqrt{d}$ matrix (eq. 22).

$$(16) \quad \vec{g} = \text{VECTORIZE}(H_{cand})$$

$$(17) \quad \vec{h_l} = \text{VECTORIZE}(H_l)$$

$$(18) \quad \vec{h_r} = \text{VECTORIZE}(H_r)$$

$$(19) \quad \begin{bmatrix} \vec{i} \\ \vec{f_l} \\ \vec{f_r} \\ \vec{o} \end{bmatrix} = \begin{bmatrix} \sigma \\ \sigma \\ \sigma \\ \sigma \end{bmatrix} \left(W \begin{bmatrix} \vec{h_l} \\ \vec{h_r} \end{bmatrix} + B \right)$$

$$(20) \quad \vec{c} = \vec{f_l} \odot \vec{c_l} + \vec{f_r} \odot \vec{c_r} + \vec{i} \odot \vec{g}$$

$$(21) \quad \vec{h} = \vec{o} \odot tanh(\vec{c})$$

$$(22) \quad H = \text{TO-MATRIX}(\vec{h})$$

3.3 Simplified variants

We implement two LMS-LSTM variants with a simpler composition function as an ablation study. The first variant replaces the equations in (14) and (15) with a single equation (eq. 23), which does not utilize a weight matrix. It simply multiplies the matrix representations of two child nodes $H_l, H_r \in \mathbb{R}^{\sqrt{d} \times \sqrt{d}}$, adds a bias $B_{\text{COMB}} \in \mathbb{R}^{\sqrt{d} \times \sqrt{d}}$, and feeds the result into a non-linear activation function.

$$(23) \quad H_{cand} = tanh(H_l H_r + B_{\text{COMB}})$$

The second variant is more complex than the first, in a way that a weight matrix $W_{\text{COMB}} \in \mathbb{R}^{\sqrt{d} \times \sqrt{d}}$ is added to the equation (eq. 24). But unlike the full LMS-LSTM which has two *tanh* layers, it only utilizes one.

$$(24) \quad H_{cand} = tanh(W_{\text{COMB}} H_l H_r + B_{\text{COMB}})$$

4 Experiments

4.1 Implementation details

As our interest is in the performance of composition functions, we compare LMS-LSTM with TreeLSTM, the previous best known composition function for tree-structured models. To allow for efficient batching, we use the SPINN-PI-NT approach (Bowman et al., 2016), which implements standard TreeLSTM using stack and buffer data structures borrowed from parsing, rather than tree structures. We implement our model by replacing SPINN-PI-NT's composition function with ours and adding the LIFT layer.

We use the 300D reference GloVe vectors (840B token version; Pennington et al., 2014) for word representations. We fine-tune the word embeddings for improved results. We follow Bowman et al. (2016) and other prior work in our use of an MLP with product and difference features to classify pairs of sentences.

$$(25) \quad \vec{x}_{classifier} = \begin{bmatrix} \vec{h}_{premise} \\ \vec{h}_{hypothesis} \\ \vec{h}_{premise} - \vec{h}_{hypothesis} \\ \vec{h}_{premise} \odot \vec{h}_{hypothesis} \end{bmatrix}$$

The feature vector is fed into an MLP that consists of two ReLU neural network layers and a softmax layer. In both models, the objective function is a sum of a cross-entropy loss function and an L2 regularization term. Both models use the Adam optimizer (Kingma and Ba, 2014). Dropout (Srivastava et al., 2014) is applied to the classifier and to the word embeddings. The MLP layer also utilizes Layer Normalization (Ba et al., 2016).[1]

4.2 Datasets

We first train and test our models on the *Stanford Natural Language Inference corpus* (SNLI; Bowman et al., 2015). The SNLI corpus contains 570,152 pairs of natural language sentences that are labeled for *entailment*, *contradiction*, and *neutral*. It consists of sentences that were written and validated by humans. Along with the MultiNLI corpus introduced below, it is two orders of magnitude larger than other human-authored resources for NLI tasks. The following example illustrates the general format of the corpus.

(26) **PREMISE:** A soccer game with multiple males playing.
HYPOTHESIS: Some men are playing a sport.
LABEL: Entailment

We test our models on the *Multi-Genre Natural Language Inference corpus* (MultiNLI; Williams et al., 2017). The corpus consists of 433k pairs of examples, and each pair is labeled for *entailment*, *contradiction*, and *neutral*. MultiNLI has the same format as SNLI, so it is possible to train on both datasets at the same time (as we do when testing on MultiNLI). Two notable features distinguish MultiNLI from SNLI: (i) It is collected from ten distinct genres of spoken and written English. This makes the dataset more representative of human language use. (ii) The examples in MultiNLI are considerably longer than the ones in SNLI. These two features make MultiNLI classification fairly more difficult than SNLI. The pair of sentences in (27) is an illustrative example. The sen-

tences are from the section of the corpus that is transcribed verbatim from telephone speech.

(27) **GENRE:** Telephone speech
PREMISE: Yes now you know if if everybody like in August when everybody's on vacation or something we can dress a little more casual or
HYPOTHESIS: August is a black out month for vacations in the company.
LABEL: Contradiction

The MultiNLI training set consists of five different genres of spoken and written English, the *matched* test set contains sentence pairs from only those five genres, and the *mismatched* test set contains sentence pairs from additional genres.

We also experiment on the Stanford Sentiment Treebank (SST; Socher et al., 2013), which is constructed by extracting movie review excerpts written in English from `rottentomatoes.com`, and labeling them with Amazon Mechanical Turk. Each example in SST is paired with a parse tree, and each node of the tree is tagged with a fine-grained sentiment label (5 classes).

5 Results and Analysis

Table 2 summarizes the results on SNLI and MultiNLI classification. We use the same preprocessing steps for all results we report, including loading the parse trees supplied with the datasets. Dropout rate, size of activations, number and size of MLP layers, and L2 regularization term are tuned using repeated random search. MV-RNN and RNTN introduced in the earlier sections are extremely expensive in terms of computational resources, and training the models with comparative hyperparameter settings quickly runs out of memory on a high-end GPU. We do not include them in the comparison for this reason. TreeLSTM performs the best with one MLP layer, while LMS-LSTM displays the best performance with two MLP layers. The difference in parameter count is largely affected by this choice, and in principle one model does not demand notably more computational resources than the other.

On the SNLI test set, LMS-LSTM has an additional 1.3% gain over TreeLSTM. Also, both of the simplified variants of LMS-LSTM outperform TreeLSTM, but by a smaller margin. On the MultiNLI test sets, LMS-LSTM scores 1.3% higher on the matched test set and 1.9% higher on the mismatched test set.

---

[1] The source code and the checkpoints for the models trained for the NLI tasks are available at `https://github.com/nyu-mll/spinn`.

Model	Params.	S tr.	S te.	M tr.	M te. mat.	M te. mism.
Baselines						
CBOW (Williams et al., 2017)	–	–	80.6	–	65.2	64.6
BiLSTM (Williams et al., 2017)	2.8m	–	81.5	–	67.5	67.1
Shortcut-Stacked BiLSTM (Nie and Bansal, 2017)	34.7m	–	86.1	–	74.6	73.6
DIIN (Gong et al., 2018)	–	–	**88.0**	–	**78.8**	**77.8**
Existing Tree-Structured Model Runs						
300D TreeLSTM (Bowman et al., 2016)	3.4m	84.4	80.9	–	–	–
300D SPINN-PI (Bowman et al., 2016)	3.7m	89.2	83.2	–	–	–
Our Experiments						
441D LMS (base)	2.0(+11.6m)	79.7	76.5	–	–	–
441D LMS-LSTM (simplified, $-W_{\mathrm{COMB}}$, $-tanh$)	3.3(+11.6)m	90.5	84.1	–	–	–
324D LMS-LSTM (simplified, $-tanh$)	2.2(+11.6)m	92.5	84.5	–	–	–
700D TreeLSTM	2.0(+11.6)m	89.5	83.6	–	–	–
576D LMS-LSTM (full)	4.6(+11.6)m	86.0	<u>84.9</u>	–	–	–
700D TreeLSTM	4.6(+30.2)m	–	–	78.9	70.0	69.7
576D LMS-LSTM (full)	5.9(+30.2)m	–	–	80.5	<u>71.3</u>	<u>71.6</u>

Table 2: Results on NLI classification with sentence-to-vector encoders. *Params.* is the approximate number of model parameters, and the numbers in parentheses indicate the parameters contributed by word embeddings. *S tr.*, and *S te.* are the class accuracies (%) on SNLI train set and test set, respectively. *M tr.*, *M te. mat.*, and *M te. mism.* are the class accuracies (%) on MultiNLI train set, matched test set, and mismatched test set, respectively. Underlining marks the best result among tree-structured models.

We cite the state-of-the-art results of non-tree-structured models, although these models are only relevant for our absolute performance numbers. The Shortcut-Stacked sentence encoder achieves the state-of-the-art result among non-attention-based models, outperforming LMS-LSTM. While this paper focuses on the design of the composition function, we expect that adding depth along the lines of Irsoy and Cardie (2014) and shortcut connections to LMS-LSTM would offer comparable results. Gong et al.'s (2018) attention-based Densely Interactive Inference Network (DIIN) displays the state-of-the-art performance among all models. Applying various attention mechanisms to tree-structured models is left for future research.

We inspect the performance of the models on certain subsets of the MultiNLI corpus that manifest linguistically difficult phenomena, which was categorized by Williams et al. (2017). The phenomena include pronouns, quantifiers (e.g., *every, each, some*), modals (e.g., *must, can*), negation, wh-terms (e.g., *who, where*), belief verbs (e.g., *believe, think*), time terms (e.g., *then, today*), discourse markers (e.g., *but, thus*), presupposition triggers (e.g., *again, too*), and so on. In linguistic semantics, these phenomena are known to involve complex interactions that are more intricate than a simple merger of concepts. For instance, modals express possibilities or necessities that are

	LMS-LSTM		TreeLSTM	
Phenomenon	**Mat.**	**Mismat.**	**Mat.**	**Mismat.**
Pronoun	**72.0**	**71.6**	69.6	70.3
Quantifier	**72.2**	**71.7**	69.9	70.5
Modal	**70.6**	**70.8**	69.8	69.2
Negation	**72.3**	**74.1**	70.3	72.4
Wh-term	**70.5**	**69.7**	68.6	68.6
Belief verb	**70.1**	**70.1**	68.4	68.7
Time term	**70.0**	**71.1**	67.3	69.4
Discourse mark.	**68.8**	**68.8**	67.0	67.0
Presup. triggers	**71.5**	**71.9**	69.1	69.9
Compr./Supr.	**69.0**	67.5	67.0	67.1
Conditionals	**69.7**	**71.3**	68.2	70.5
Tense match	**73.3**	**72.5**	71.0	71.2
Interjection	**69.7**	**74.3**	**69.7**	72.5
Adj/Adv	**72.6**	**72.0**	70.3	70.7
Determiner	**72.4**	**72.1**	70.3	70.8
Length 0-10	**72.8**	**72.8**	69.8	72.7
Length 11-14	**72.6**	**72.8**	72	70.5
Length 15-19	**71.0**	**70.8**	69.3	68.3
Length 20+	**75.2**	68.2	69.8	**69.0**

Table 3: MultiNLI development set classification accuracies (%), classified using the tags introduced in Williams et al. (2017).

beyond "here and now". One can say 'John might be home' to convey that there is a possibility that John is home. The utterance is perfectly compatible with a situation in which John is in fact at school, so modals like *might* let us reason about things that are potentially false in the real world. We use the same code as Williams et al. (2017) to

Model	Test
Baselines	
MV-RNN (Socher et al., 2013)	44.4
RNTN (Socher et al., 2013)	45.7
Deep RNN (Irsoy and Cardie, 2014)	49.8
TreeLSTM (Tai et al., 2015)	51.0
TreeBiGRU w/ attention	52.4
(Kokkinos and Potamianos, 2017)	
Our Experiments	
312D TreeLSTM	48.9
144D LMS-LSTM	50.1

Table 4: Five-way test set classification accuracies (%) on the Stanford Sentiment Treebank.

Category	# of samples	Ratio (%)
NP	63346	43.31
VP	30534	20.08
PP	25624	17.98
ROOT	18267	12.49
S	4863	3.06
SBAR	2004	1.20
ADVP	1136	0.27
ADJP	408	0.13
Etc.	160	1.45

Table 5: Syntactic category distribution of SNLI development set, classified using the tags introduced in Bowman et al. (2015).

categorize the data to make fair comparisons.

In addition to the categories offered by Williams et al. (2017), we inspect whether sentences containing adjectives/adverbs affect the performance of the models. Baroni and Zamparelli (2010) show that adjectives are better represented as matrices, as opposed to vectors. We also inspect whether the presence of a determiner in the hypothesis that refers back to a salient referent in the premise affects the model performance. Determiners are known to encode intricate properties in linguistic semantics and have been one of the major research topics (Elbourne, 2005; Charlow, 2014). Lastly, we examine whether the performance of the models varies with respect to sentence length, as longer sentences are harder to comprehend.

Table 3 summarizes the result of the inspection on linguistically difficult phenomena. We see gains uniformly across the board, but with particularly clear gains on negation (+2% on the matched set/+1.7% on the mismatched set), quantifiers (+2.3%/+1.2%), time terms (+2.7%/+1.7%), tense matches (+2.3%/+1.3%), adjectives/adverbs (+2.3%/+1.3%), and longer sentences (length 15-19: +1.7%/+2.5%; length 20+: +5.4%/-0.8%).

Table 4 summarizes the results on SST classification, particularly on the fine-grained task with 5 classes. While our implementation does not exactly reproduce Tai et al.'s (2015) TreeLSTM results, a comparison between our trained TreeLSTM and LMS-LSTM is consistent with the patterns seen in NLI tasks.

We examine how well the constituent representations produced by LMS-LSTM and TreeLSTM encode syntactic category information. As mentioned earlier, there is a consensus in linguistic semantics that semantic composition involves func-tion application (i.e., feeding an argument to a function) which goes beyond a simple merger of two concepts. Given that the syntactic category of a node determines whether the node serves as a function or an argument in semantic composition, we hypothesize that the distributed representation of each node would encode syntactic category information if the models learned how to do function application. To assess the quality of the representations, we first split the SNLI development set into training and test sets. From the training set, we extract the hidden state of every constituent (i.e., phrase) produced by the best performing models. For each of the models, we train linear classifiers that learn to do the following two tasks: (i) 3-way classification, which trains and tests exclusively on noun phrases, verb phrases, and prepositional phrases, and (ii) 19-way classification, which trains and tests on all 19 category labels attested in the SNLI development set. The distribution of the 19 category labels is provided in Table 5. We opt for a linear classifier to keep the classification process simple, so that we can properly assess the quality of the constituent representations.

Table 6 summarizes the results on the syntactic category classification task. As a baseline, we train a bag-of-words (BOW) model which produces the hidden state of a given phrase by summing the GloVe embeddings of the words of the phrase. We train and test on the hidden states produced by BOW as well. The hidden state representations produced by LMS-LSTM yield the best results on both 3-way and 19-way classification tasks. Comparing LMS-LSTM and TreeLSTM representations, we see a 5.1% gain on the 3-way classification and a 5.5% gain on the 19-way classification.

Model	3-way		19-way	
	Train	**Test**	**Train**	**Test**
300D BOW	86.4	85.6	82.7	82.1
700D TreeLSTM	93.2	91.2	90.0	86.6
576D LMS-LSTM	97.3	**96.3**	94.0	**92.1**

Table 6: Syntactic category classification accuracies (%) on SNLI development set, classified using the tags introduced in Bowman et al. (2015).

Figure 2 depicts the corresponding confusion matrices for the 19-way classification task. We show the most frequent eight classes due to space limitations. We observe notable gains on adverbial phrases (ADVP; +24%), adjectival phrases (ADJP; +12%), verb phrases (VP; +9%), and clauses introduced by subordinate conjunction (SBAR; +9%). We also observe a considerable gain on non-terminal declarative clauses (S; +9%), although the absolute number is fairly low compared to other categories. While we do not have a full comprehension of the drop in classification accuracy, we speculate that the ambiguity of infinitival clauses and gerund phrases is one of the culprits. As exemplified in (28) and (29) respectively, infinitival clauses and gerund phrases are not only labeled as a VP but also as an S in the SNLI dataset. Given that our experiment is set up in a way that each constituent is assigned exactly one category label, a good number of infinitival clauses and gerund phrases that are labeled as an S could have been classified as a VP, resulting in a drop in classification accuracy. On the other hand, VP constituents are less affected by the ambiguity because the majority of them are neither an infinitival clause nor a gerund phrase, as shown in (30).

(28)   A dog carries a snowball [S [VP to give it to his owner]]

(29)   Two women are embracing while [S [VP holding to-go packages after just eating lunch]]

(30)   A few people [VP are [VP catching fish]]

With the exclusion of non-terminal declarative clauses, the categories we see notable gains are known to play the role of a function in semantic composition. On the other hand, both models are efficient in identifying noun phrases (NP), which are typically arguments of a function in semantic composition. We speculate that the results are indicative of LMS-LSTM's ability to identify func-

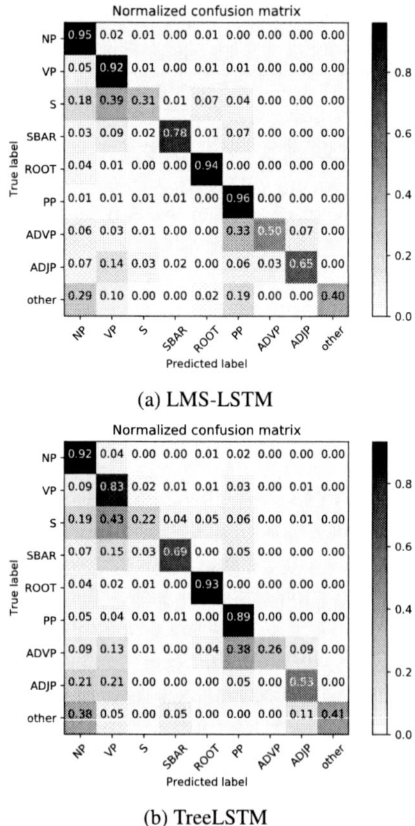

(a) LMS-LSTM

(b) TreeLSTM

Figure 2: Confusion matrices of LMS-LSTM and TreeLSTM for 19-way linear classification.

tions and arguments, and this hints that the model is learning to do function application.

6   Conclusion

In this paper, we propose a novel model for semantic composition that utilizes matrix multiplication. Experimental results indicate that, while our model does not reach the state of the art on any of the three datasets under study, it does substantially outperform all known tree-structured models, and lays a strong foundation for future work on tree-structured compositionality in artificial neural networks.

Acknowledgments

We thank NVIDIA Corporation for the donation of the Titan X Pascal GPU used for this research. This project has benefited from financial support to SB by Google, Tencent Holdings, and Samsung Research.

References

Nicholas Asher, Tim Van de Cruys, Antoine Bride, and Márta Abrusán. 2016. Integrating type theory and distributional semantics: a case study on adjective–noun compositions. *Computational Linguistics*, 42(4):703–725.

Jimmy Lei Ba, Jamie Ryan Kiros, and Geoffrey E. Hinton. 2016. Layer Normalization. *arXiv:1607.06450*.

Chris Barker and Chung-chieh Shan. 2014. *Continuations and natural language*, volume 53. Oxford studies in theoretical linguistics.

Marco Baroni and Roberto Zamparelli. 2010. Nouns are vectors, adjectives are matrices: Representing adjective-noun constructions in semantic space. In *Proceedings of the 2010 Conference on Empirical Methods in Natural Language Processing (EMNLP)*, pages 1183–1193.

Samuel R. Bowman, Gabor Angeli, Christopher Potts, and Christopher D. Manning. 2015. A large annotated corpus for learning natural language inference. In *Proceedings of the 2015 Conference on Empirical Methods in Natural Language Processing (EMNLP)*.

Samuel R. Bowman, Jon Gauthier, Abhinav Rastogi, Raghav Gupta, Christopher D. Manning, and Christopher Potts. 2016. A fast unified model for parsing and sentence understanding. In *Proceedings of the 54th Annual Meeting of the Association for Computational Linguistics*.

Simon Charlow. 2014. *On the semantics of exceptional scope*. Ph.D. thesis, New York University.

Danqi Chen, Richard Socher, Christopher D. Manning, and Andrew Y. Ng. 2013. Learning new facts from knowledge bases with neural tensor networks and semantic word vectors. In *Proceedings of workshop at ICLR*, pages 1–4.

Gennaro Chierchia and Sally McConnell-Ginet. 1990. *Meaning and grammar: An introduction to semantics*. MIT Press, Cambridge, MA.

Stephen Clark, Bob Coecke, and Mehrnoosh Sadrzadeh. 2008. A compositional distributional model of meaning. In *Proceedings of the Second Quantum Interaction Symposium (QI-2008)*, pages 133–140.

David Dowty. 2007. Compositionality as an empirical problem. In *Direct Compositionality*. Oxford University Press.

Paul D. Elbourne. 2005. *Situations and individuals*, volume 90. Mit Press Cambridge, MA.

Katrin Erk and Sebastian Padó. 2008. A structured vector space model for word meaning in context. In *Proceedings of the Conference on Empirical Methods in Natural Language Processing (EMNLP)*, pages 897–906.

Yichen Gong, Heng Luo, and Jian Zhang. 2018. Natural language inference over interaction space. *ICLR 2018*.

Edward Grefenstette, Mehrnoosh Sadrzadeh, Stephen Clark, Bob Coecke, and Stephen Pulman. 2014. Concrete sentence spaces for compositional distributional models of meaning. In *Computing meaning*, pages 71–86. Springer.

Irene Heim and Angelika Kratzer. 1998. *Semantics in Generative Grammar*. Blackwell Publishers.

Gustav Herdan. 1960. *Type-token mathematics*. Mouton.

Sepp Hochreiter, Yoshua Bengio, Paolo Frasconi, and Jürgen Schmidhuber. 2001. Gradient flow in recurrent nets: the difficulty of learning long-term dependencies. *A Field Guide to Dynamical Recurrent Networks*, pages 237–243.

Sepp Hochreiter and Jürgen Schmidhuber. 1997. Long short-term memory. *Neural Computation*, 9(8):1–32.

Ozan Irsoy and Claire Cardie. 2014. Deep recursive neural networks for compositionality in language. In *Proceedings of Advances in Neural Information Processing Systems*, pages 2096–2104.

Diederik Kingma and Jimmy Ba. 2014. Adam: A Method for Stochastic Optimization. *The International Conference on Learning Representations*, pages 1–13.

Filippos Kokkinos and Alexandros Potamianos. 2017. Structural Attention Neural Networks for improved sentiment analysis. *arXiv:1701.01811*.

Phong Le and Willem Zuidema. 2015. Compositional Distributional Semantics with Long Short Term Memory. *arXiv:1503.02510*.

Bill MacCartney. 2009. *Natural language inference*. Ph.D. thesis, Stanford University.

Jeff Mitchell and Mirella Lapata. 2010. Composition in distributional models of semantics. *Cognitive Science*, 34(8):1388–1429.

Yixin Nie and Mohit Bansal. 2017. Shortcut-stacked sentence encoders for multi-domain inference. In *Proceedings of the 2nd Workshop on Evaluating Vector Space Representations for NLP*, pages 41–45.

Jeffrey Pennington, Richard Socher, and Christopher D. Manning. 2014. Glove: Global vectors for word representation. In *Proceedings of the 2014 Conference on Empirical Methods in Natural Language Processing (EMNLP)*, pages 1532–1543.

Sebastian Rudolph and Eugenie Giesbrecht. 2010. Compositional matrix-space models of language. In *Proceedings of the 48th Annual Meeting of the Association for Computational Linguistics (ACL)*, pages 907–916.

Richard Socher, Brody Huval, Christopher D. Manning, and Andrew Y. Ng. 2012. Semantic compositionality through recursive matrix-vector spaces. In *Proceedings of the 2012 joint conference on Empirical Methods in Natural Language Processing and Computational Natural Language Learning*, pages 1201–1211.

Richard Socher, Cliff C. Lin, Christopher D. Manning, and Andrew Y. Ng. 2011. Parsing natural scenes and natural language with recursive neural networks. In *Proceedings of the 28th international conference on machine learning (ICML)*, pages 129–136.

Richard Socher, Christopher D. Manning, and Andrew Y. Ng. 2010. Learning continuous phrase representations and syntactic parsing with recursive neural networks. *Proceedings of the NIPS-2010 Deep Learning and Unsupervised Feature Learning Workshop*, pages 1–9.

Richard Socher, Alex Perelygin, Jean Wu, Jason Chuang, Christopher D. Manning, Andrew Y. Ng, and Christopher Potts. 2013. Recursive Deep Models for Semantic Compositionality over a Sentiment treebank. In *Proceedings of the 2013 Conference on Empirical Methods in Natural Language Processing (EMNLP)*, pages 1631–1642.

Nitish Srivastava, Geoffrey E. Hinton, Alex Krizhevsky, Ilya Sutskever, and Ruslan Salakhutdinov. 2014. Dropout: a simple way to prevent neural networks from overfitting. *Journal of Machine Learning Research*, 15(1):1929–1958.

Kai Sheng Tai, Richard Socher, and Christopher D. Manning. 2015. Improved semantic representations from tree-structured long short-term memory networks. In *Proceedings of ACL*, pages 1556–1566.

David Weir, Julie Weeds, Jeremy Reffin, and Thomas Kober. 2016. Aligning packed dependency trees: a theory of composition for distributional semantics. *Computational Linguistics*, 42(4):727–761.

Adina Williams, Nikita Nangia, and Samuel R. Bowman. 2017. A Broad-Coverage Challenge Corpus for Sentence Understanding through Inference. *arXiv:1704.05426*.

Fabio Massimo Zanzotto, Ioannis Korkontzelos, Francesca Fallucchi, and Suresh Manandhar. 2010. Estimating linear models for compositional distributional semantics. In *Proceedings of the 23rd International Conference on Computational Linguistics*, pages 1263–1271.

Xiaodan Zhu, Parinaz Sobhani, and Hongyu Guo. 2015. Long Short-Term Memory Over Tree Structures. In *Proc. of ICML*, pages 1604–1612.

End-to-End Neural Entity Linking

Nikolaos Kolitsas *
ETH Zürich
nikos_kolitsas@hotmail.com

Octavian-Eugen Ganea *
ETH Zürich
octavian.ganea@inf.ethz.ch

Thomas Hofmann
ETH Zürich
thomas.hofmann@inf.ethz.ch

Abstract

Entity Linking (EL) is an essential task for semantic text understanding and information extraction. Popular methods separately address the Mention Detection (MD) and Entity Disambiguation (ED) stages of EL, without leveraging their mutual dependency. We here propose the first neural end-to-end EL system that jointly discovers and links entities in a text document. The main idea is to consider all possible spans as potential mentions and learn contextual similarity scores over their entity candidates that are useful for both MD and ED decisions. Key components are context-aware mention embeddings, entity embeddings and a probabilistic mention - entity map, without demanding other engineered features. Empirically, we show that our end-to-end method significantly outperforms popular systems on the Gerbil platform when enough training data is available. Conversely, if testing datasets follow different annotation conventions compared to the training set (e.g. queries/ tweets vs news documents), our ED model coupled with a traditional NER system offers the best or second best EL accuracy.

1 Introduction and Motivation

Towards the goal of automatic text understanding, machine learning models are expected to accurately extract potentially ambiguous mentions of entities from a textual document and link them to a knowledge base (KB), e.g. Wikipedia or Freebase. Known as entity linking, this problem is an essential building block for various Natural Language Processing tasks, e.g. automatic KB construction, question-answering, text summarization, or relation extraction.

An EL system typically performs two tasks: i) Mention Detection (MD) or Named Entity Recog-

1) MD may split a larger span into
two mentions of less informative entities:
B. Obama's wife gave a speech [...]
Federer's coach [...]
2) MD may split a larger span into
two mentions of incorrect entities:
Obama Castle was built in 1601 in Japan.
The Kennel Club is UK's official kennel club.
A bird dog is a type of gun dog or hunting dog.
Romeo and Juliet by Shakespeare [...]
Natural killer cells are a type of lymphocyte
Mary and Max, the 2009 movie [...]
3) MD may choose a shorter span,
referring to an incorrect entity:
The Apple is played again in cinemas.
The New York Times is a popular newspaper.
4) MD may choose a longer span,
referring to an incorrect entity:
Babies Romeo and Juliet were born hours apart.

Table 1: Examples where MD may benefit from ED and viceversa. Each wrong MD decision (underlined) can be avoided by proper context understanding. The correct spans are shown in blue.

nition (NER) when restricted to named entities – extracts entity references in a raw textual input, and ii) Entity Disambiguation (ED) – links these spans to their corresponding entities in a KB. Until recently, the common approach of popular systems Ceccarelli et al. (2013); van Erp et al. (2013); Piccinno and Ferragina (2014); Daiber et al. (2013); Hoffart et al. (2011); Steinmetz and Sack (2013) was to solve these two sub-problems independently. However, the important dependency between the two steps is ignored and errors caused by MD/NER will propagate to ED without possibility of recovery Sil and Yates (2013); Luo et al. (2015). We here advocate for models that address the end-to-

---

*Equal contribution.

Proceedings of the 22nd Conference on Computational Natural Language Learning (CoNLL 2018), pages 519–529
Brussels, Belgium, October 31 - November 1, 2018. ©2018 Association for Computational Linguistics

end EL task, informally arguing that humans understand and generate text in a similar joint manner, discussing about entities which are gradually introduced, referenced under multiple names and evolving during time Ji et al. (2017). Further, we emphasize the importance of the mutual dependency between MD and ED. First, numerous and more informative linkable spans found by MD obviously offer more contextual cues for ED. Second, finding the true entities appearing in a specific context encourages better mention boundaries, especially for multi-word mentions. For example, in the first sentence of Table 1, understanding the presence of the entity `Michelle Obama` helps detecting its true mention *"B. Obama's wife"*, as opposed to separately linking *B. Obama* and *wife* to less informative concepts.

We propose a simple, yet competitive, model for end-to-end EL. Getting inspiration from the recent works of Lee et al. (2017) and Ganea and Hofmann (2017), our model first generates all possible spans (mentions) that have at least one possible entity candidate. Then, each mention - candidate pair receives a context-aware compatibility score based on word and entity embeddings coupled with a neural attention and a global voting mechanisms. During training, we enforce the scores of gold entity - mention pairs to be higher than all possible scores of incorrect candidates or invalid mentions, thus jointly taking the ED and MD decisions.

Our contributions are:

- We address the end-to-end EL task using a simple model that conditions the "linkable" quality of a mention to the strongest context support of its best entity candidate. We do not require expensive manually annotated negative examples of non-linkable mentions. Moreover, we are able to train competitive models using little and only partially annotated documents (with named entities only such as the CoNLL-AIDA dataset).

- We are among the first to show that, with one single exception, engineered features can be fully replaced by neural embeddings automatically learned for the joint MD & ED task.

- On the Gerbil[1] benchmarking platform, we empirically show significant gains for the end-to-end EL task when test and training data

<hr>

[1] `http://gerbil.aksw.org/gerbil/`

come from the same domain. Morever, when testing datasets follow different annotation schemes or exhibit different statistics, our method is still effective in achieving state-of-the-art or close performance, but needs to be coupled with a popular NER system.

2 Related Work

With few exceptions, MD/NER and ED are treated separately in the vast EL literature.

Traditional NER models usually view the problem as a word sequence labeling that is modeled using conditional random fields on top of engineered features Finkel et al. (2005) or, more recently, using bi-LSTMs architectures Lample et al. (2016); Chiu and Nichols (2016); Liu et al. (2017) capable of learning complex lexical and syntactic features.

In the context of ED, recent neural methods He et al. (2013); Sun et al. (2015); Yamada et al. (2016); Ganea and Hofmann (2017); Le and Titov (2018); Yang et al. (2018); Radhakrishnan et al. (2018) have established state-of-the-art results, outperforming engineered features based models. Context aware word, span and entity embeddings, together with neural similarity functions, are essential in these frameworks.

End-to-end EL is the realistic task and ultimate goal, but challenges in joint NER/MD and ED modeling arise from their different nature. Few previous methods tackle the joint task, where errors in one stage can be recovered by the next stage. One of the first attempts, Sil and Yates (2013) use a popular NER model to over-generate mentions and let the linking step to take the final decisions. However, their method is limited by the dependence on a good mention spotter and by the usage of hand-engineered features. It is also unclear how linking can improve their MD phase. Later, Luo et al. (2015) presented one of the most competitive joint MD and ED models leveraging semi-Conditional Random Fields (semi-CRF). However, there are several weaknesses in this work. First, the mutual task dependency is weak, being captured only by type-category correlation features. The other engineered features used in their model are either NER or ED specific. Second, while their probabilistic graphical model allows for tractable learning and inference, it suffers from high computational complexity caused by the usage of the cartesian product of all possible document span segmentations, NER categories and entity assignments. Another approach is J-NERD Nguyen et al. (2016) that addresses the end-to-end task using only engineered features and a probabilistic graphical model on top of sentence parse trees.

3 Neural Joint Mention Detection and Entity Disambiguation

We formally introduce the tasks of interest. For EL, the input is a text document (or a query or tweet) given as a sequence $D = \{w_1, \ldots, w_n\}$ of words from a dictionary, $w_k \in \mathcal{W}$. The output of an EL model is a list of mention - entity pairs $\{(m_i, e_i)\}_{i \in \overline{1,T}}$, where each mention is a word subsequence of the input document, $m = w_q, \ldots, w_r$, and each entity is an entry in a knowledge base KB (e.g. Wikipedia), $e \in \mathcal{E}$. For the ED task, the list of entity mentions $\{m_i\}_{i=\overline{1,T}}$ that need to be disambiguated is additionally provided as input. The expected output is a list of corresponding annotations $\{e_i\}_{i=\overline{1,T}} \in \mathcal{E}^T$.

Note that, in this work, we only link mentions that have a valid gold KB entity, setting referred in Röder et al. (2017) as *InKB* evaluation. Thus, we treat mentions referring to entities outside of the KB as "non-linkable". This is in line with few previous models, e.g. Luo et al. (2015); Ganea and Hofmann (2017); Yamada et al. (2016). We leave the interesting setting of discovering out-of-KB entities as future work.

We now describe the components of our neural end-to-end EL model, depicted in Figure 1. We aim for simplicity, but competitive accuracy.

Word and Char Embeddings. We use pre-trained Word2Vec vectors Mikolov et al. (2013). In addition, we train character embeddings that capture important word lexical information. Following Lample et al. (2016), for each word independently, we use bidirectional LSTMs Hochreiter and Schmidhuber (1997) on top of learnable char embeddings. These character LSTMs do not extend beyond single word boundaries, but they share the same parameters. Formally, let $\{z_1, \ldots, z_L\}$ be the character vectors of word w. We use the forward and backward LSTMs formulations defined recursively as in Lample et al. (2016):

$$h_t^f = FWD - LSTM(h_{t-1}^f, z_t) \qquad (1)$$
$$h_t^b = BKWD - LSTM(h_{t+1}^b, z_t)$$

Then, we form the character embedding of w is $[h_L^f; h_1^b]$ from the hidden state of the forward LSTM

corresponding to the last character concatenated with the hidden state of the backward LSTM corresponding to the first character. This is then concatenated with the pre-trained word embedding, forming the context-independent word-character embedding of w. We denote the sequence of these vectors as $\{v_k\}_{k \in \overline{1,n}}$ and depict it as the first neural layer in Figure 1.

Mention Representation. We find it crucial to make word embeddings aware of their local context, thus being informative for both mention boundary detection and entity disambiguation (leveraging contextual cues, e.g. "newspaper"). We thus encode context information into words using a bi-LSTM layer on top of the word-character embeddings $\{v_k\}_{k \in \overline{1,n}}$. The hidden states of forward and backward LSTMs corresponding to each word are then concatenated into *context-aware word embeddings*, whose sequence is denoted as $\{x_k\}_{k \in \overline{1,n}}$.

Next, for each possible mention, we produce a fixed size representation inspired by Lee et al. (2017). Given a mention $m = w_q, \ldots, w_r$, we first concatenate the embeddings of the first, last and the "soft head" words of the mention:

$$g^m = [x_q; x_r; \hat{x}^m] \qquad (2)$$

The soft head embedding $\hat{x}^m$ is built using an attention mechanism on top of the mention's word embeddings, similar with Lee et al. (2017):

$$\alpha_k = \langle \boldsymbol{w}_\alpha, x_k \rangle$$
$$a_k^m = \frac{\exp(\alpha_k)}{\sum_{t=q}^r \exp(\alpha_t)} \qquad (3)$$
$$\hat{x}^m = \sum_{k=q}^r a_k^m \cdot v_k$$

However, we found the soft head embedding to only marginally improve results, probably due to the fact that most mentions are at most 2 words long. To learn non-linear interactions between the component word vectors, we project g^m to a final mention representation with the same size as entity embeddings (see below) using a shallow feedforward neural network FFNN (a simple projection layer):

$$x^m = \text{FFNN}_1(g^m) \qquad (4)$$

Entity Embeddings. We use fixed continuous entity representations, namely the pre-trained entity embeddings of Ganea and Hofmann (2017),

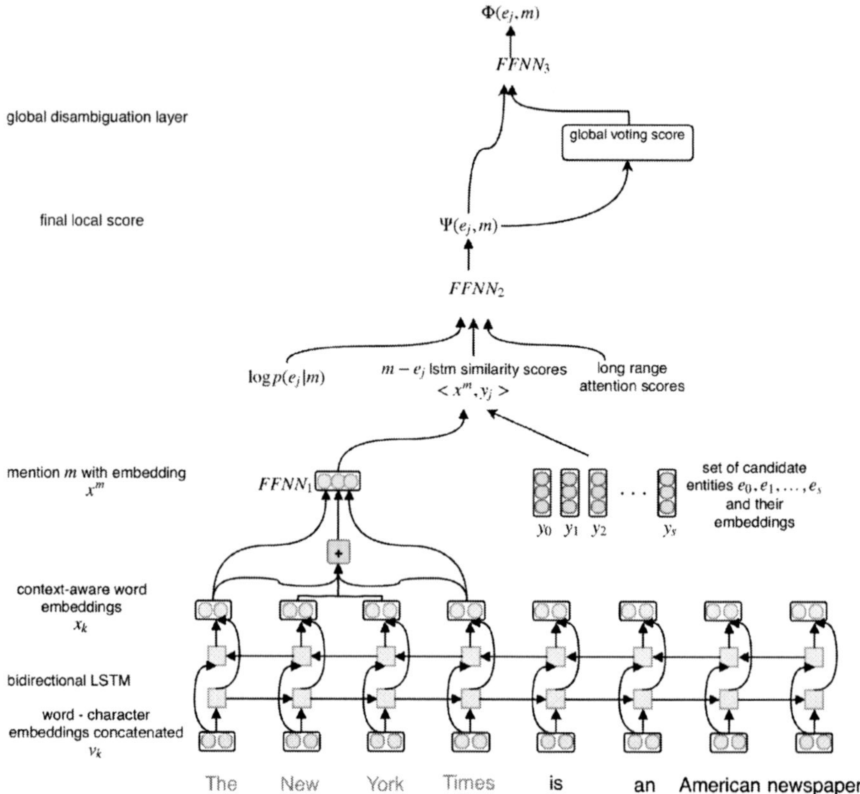

Figure 1: Our global model architecture shown for the mention *The New York Times*. The final score is used for both the mention linking and entity disambiguation decisions.

due to their simplicity and compatibility with the pre-trained word vectors of Mikolov et al. (2013). Briefly, these vectors are computed for each entity in isolation using the following exponential model that approximates the empirical conditional word-entity distribution $\hat{p}(w|e)$ obtained from co-occurrence counts.

$$\frac{\exp(\langle x_w, y_e \rangle)}{\sum_{w' \in \mathcal{W}} \exp(\langle x_{w'}, y_e \rangle)} \approx \hat{p}(w|e) \qquad (5)$$

Here, x_w are fixed pre-trained word vectors and y_e is the entity embedding to be trained. In practice, Ganea and Hofmann (2017) re-write this as a max-margin objective loss.

Candidate Selection. For each span m we select up to s entity candidates that might be referred by this mention. These are top entities based on an empirical probabilistic entity - map $p(e|m)$ built by Ganea and Hofmann (2017) from Wikipedia hyperlinks, Crosswikis Spitkovsky and Chang and YAGO Hoffart et al. (2011) dictionaries. We denote by $C(m)$ this candidate set and use it both at training and test time.

Final Local Score. For each span m that can possibly refer to an entity (i.e. $|C(m)| \geq 1$) and for each of its entity candidates $e_j \in C(m)$, we compute a similarity score using embedding dot-product that supposedly should capture useful information for both MD and ED decisions. We then combine it with the log-prior probability using a shallow FFNN, giving the context-aware entity - mention score:

$$\Psi(e_j, m) = \text{FFNN}_2([\log p(e_j|m); \langle x^m, y_j \rangle])$$
$$(6)$$

Long Range Context Attention. In some cases, our model might be improved by explicitly capturing long context dependencies. To test this, we experimented with the attention model of Ganea and Hofmann (2017). This gives one context embedding per mention based on informative context words that are related to at least one of the candidate entities. We use this additional context embedding for computing dot-product similarity with any of the candidate entity embeddings. This value is fed as additional input of FFNN_2 in Eq. 6. We refer to this model as *long range context attention*.

Training. We assume a corpus with documents and gold entity - mention pairs $\mathcal{G} = \{(m_i, e_i^*)\}_{i=\overline{1,K}}$ is available. At training time, for each input document we collect the set M of all (potentially overlapping) token spans m for which $|C(m)| \geq 1$. We then train the parameters of our model using the following minimization procedure:

$$\theta^* = \arg\min_{\theta} \sum_{m \in M} \sum_{e \in C(m)} V(\Psi_{\theta}(e, m)) \quad (7)$$

where the violation term V enforces the scores of gold pairs to be linearly separable from scores of negative pairs, i.e.

$$V(\Psi(e, m)) = \quad (8)$$
$$\begin{cases} \max(0, \gamma - \Psi(e, m)), & \text{if}(e, m) \in \mathcal{G} \\ \max(0, \Psi(e, m)), & \text{otherwise} \end{cases}$$

Note that, in the absence of annotated negative examples of "non-linkable" mentions, we assume that all spans in M and their candidates that do not appear in $\mathcal{G}$ should not be linked. The model will be enforced to only output negative scores for all entity candidates of such mentions.

We call *all spans training* the above setting. Our method can also be used to perform ED only, in which case we train only on gold mentions, i.e. $M = \{m | m \in \mathcal{G}\}$. This is referred as *gold spans training*.

Inference. At test time, our method can be applied for both *EL* and *ED only* as follows. First, for each document in our validation or test sets, we select all possibly linkable token spans, i.e. $M = \{m | |C(m)| \geq 1\}$ for EL, or the input set of mentions $M = \{m | m \in \mathcal{G}\}$ for ED, respectively. Second, the best linking threshold δ is found on the validation set such that the micro F1 metric is maximized when only linking mention - entity pairs with Ψ score greater than δ. At test time, only entity - mention pairs with a score higher than δ are kept and sorted according to their Ψ scores; the final annotations are greedily produced based on this set such that only spans not overlapping with previously selected spans (of higher scores) are chosen.

Global Disambiguation Our current model is "local", i.e. performs disambiguation of each candidate span independently. To enhance it, we add an extra layer to our neural network that will promote coherence among linked and disambiguated entities inside the same document, i.e. the *global disambiguation layer*. Specifically, we compute a "global" mention-entity score based on which we produce the final annotations. We first define the set of mention-entity pairs that are allowed to participate in the global disambiguation voting, namely those that already have a high local score:

$$V_G = \{(m, e) | m \in M, e \in C(m), \Psi(e, m) \geq \gamma'\}$$

Since we initially consider all possible spans and for each span up to s candidate entities, this filtering step is important to avoid both undesired noise and exponential complexity for the EL task for which M is typically much bigger than for ED. The final "global" score $G(e_j, m)$ for entity candidate e_j of mention m is given by the cosine similarity between the entity embedding and the normalized average of all other voting entities' embeddings (of the other mentions m').

$$V_G^m = \{e | (m', e) \in V_G \wedge m' \neq m\}$$
$$y_G^m = \sum_{e \in V_G^m} y_e$$
$$G(e_j, m) = \cos(y_{e_j}, y_G^m)$$

This is combined with the local score, yielding

$$\Phi(e_j, m) = \text{FFNN}_3([\Psi(e_j, m); G(e_j, m)])$$

The final loss function is now slightly modified. Specifically, we enforce the linear separability in two places: in $\Psi(e, m)$ (exactly as before), but also in $\Phi(e, m)$, as follows

$$\theta^* = \arg\min_{\theta} \quad (9)$$
$$\sum_{d \in D} \sum_{m \in M} \sum_{e \in C(m)} V(\Psi_{\theta}(e, m)) + V(\Phi_{\theta}(e, m))$$

The inference procedure remains unchanged in this case, with the exception that it will only use the $\Phi(e, m)$ global score.

Coreference Resolution Heuristic. In a few cases we found important to be able to solve simple coreference resolution cases (e.g. "Alan" referring to "Alan Shearer"). These cases are difficult to handle by our candidate selection strategy. We thus adopt the simple heuristic descried in Ganea and Hofmann (2017) and observed between 0.5% and 1% improvement on all datasets.

F1@MA F1@MI	AIDA A	AIDA B	MSNBC	OKE-2015	OKE-2016	N3-Reuters-128	N3-RSS-500	Derczynski	KORE50
FREME	23.6	23.8	15.8	26.1	22.7	26.8	32.5	31.4	12.3
	37.6	36.3	19.9	31.6	28.5	30.9	27.8	18.9	14.5
FOX	54.7	58.1	11.2	53.9	49.5	52.4	35.1	42.0	28.3
	58.0	57.0	8.3	56.8	50.5	53.3	33.8	38.0	30.8
Babelfy	41.2	42.4	36.6	39.3	37.8	19.6	32.1	28.9	52.5
	47.2	48.5	39.7	41.9	37.7	23.0	29.1	29.8	55.9
Entityclassifier.eu	43.0	42.9	41.4	29.2	33.8	24.7	23.1	16.3	25.2
	44.7	45.0	42.2	29.5	32.5	27.9	22.7	16.9	28.0
Kea	36.8	39.0	30.6	44.6	46.3	17.5	22.7	31.3	41.0
	40.4	42.3	30.9	46.2	46.4	18.1	20.5	26.5	46.8
DBpedia Spotlight	49.9	52.0	42.4	42.0	41.4	21.5	26.7	33.7	29.4
	55.2	57.8	40.6	44.4	43.1	24.8	27.2	32.2	34.9
AIDA	68.8	71.9	62.7	58.7	0.0	42.6	42.6	40.6	49.6
	72.4	72.8	65.1	63.1	0.0	46.4	42.4	32.6	55.4
WAT	69.2	70.8	62.6	53.2	51.8	45.0	45.3	44.4	37.3
	72.8	73.0	64.5	56.4	53.9	49.2	42.3	38.0	49.6
Best baseline	**69.2**	**71.9**	**62.7**	**58.7**	**51.8**	**52.4**	**45.3**	**44.4**	**52.5**
	72.8	**73.0**	**65.1**	**63.1**	**53.9**	**53.3**	**42.4**	**38.0**	**55.9**
base model	86.6	81.1	64.5	54.3	43.6	47.7	44.2	43.5	34.9
	89.1	80.5	65.7	58.2	46.0	49.0	38.8	38.1	42.0
base model + att	86.5	81.9	69.4	56.6	49.2	48.3	46.0	47.9	36.0
	88.9	82.3	69.5	60.7	51.6	51.1	40.5	42.3	42.2
base model + att + global	86.6	82.6	73.0	56.6	47.8	45.4	43.8	43.2	26.2
	89.4	82.4	72.4	61.9	52.7	50.3	38.2	34.1	35.2
ED base model + att + global using Stanford NER mentions	75.7	73.3	71.1	62.9	57.1	54.2	45.9	48.8	40.3
	80.3	74.6	71.0	66.9	58.4	54.6	42.2	42.3	46.0

Table 2: EL strong matching results on the Gerbil platform. Micro and Macro F1 scores are shown. We highlight the best and second best models, respectively. Training was done on AIDA-train set.

4   Experiments

Datasets and Metrics.   We used Wikipedia 2014 as our KB. We conducted experiments on the most important public EL datasets using the Gerbil platform Röder et al. (2017). Datasets' statistics are provided in Tables 5 and 6 (Appendix). This benchmarking framework offers reliable and trustable evaluation and comparison with state of the art EL/ED methods on most of the public datasets for this task. It also shows how well different systems generalize to datasets from very different domains and annotation schemes compared to their training sets. Moreover, it offers evaluation metrics for the end-to-end EL task, as opposed to some works that only evaluate NER and ED separately, e.g. Luo et al. (2015).

As previously explained, we do not use the NIL mentions (without a valid KB entity) and only compare against other systems using the InKB metrics.

For training we used the biggest publicly available EL dataset, AIDA/CoNLL Hoffart et al. (2011), consisting of a training set of 18,448 linked mentions in 946 documents, a validation set of 4,791 mentions in 216 documents, and a test set of 4,485 mentions in 231 documents.

We report micro and macro InKB F1 scores for both EL and ED. For EL, these metrics are computed both in the *strong matching* and *weak matching* settings. The former requires exactly predicting the gold mention boundaries and their entity annotations, whereas the latter gives a perfect score to spans that just overlap with the gold mentions and are linked to the correct gold entities.

Baselines.   We compare with popular and state-of-the-art EL and ED public systems, e.g. WAT Piccinno and Ferragina (2014), Dbpedia Spotlight Mendes et al. (2011), NERD-ML van Erp et al. (2013), KEA Steinmetz and Sack (2013), AIDA Hoffart et al. (2011), FREME, FOX Speck and Ngomo (2014), PBOH Ganea et al. (2016) or Babelfy Moro et al. (2014). These are integrated within the Gerbil platform. However, we did not compare with Luo et al. (2015) and other models outside Gerbil that do not use end-to-end EL metrics.

Training Details and Model Hyper-Parameters. We use the same model hyper-parameters for both EL and ED training. The only difference between the two settings is the span set M : EL uses *all spans training*, whereas ED uses *gold spans training* settings as explained before.

Our pre-trained word and entity embeddings are

solved % / matched gold entity % / position of ground truth in $p(e\|m)$	Number of mentions	ED Global model	ED Base + Att model	ED Base model	EL Global model	EL Base + Att model	EL Base model	EL Global -$\log p(e\|m)$
1	3390	98.8	98.6	98.3	96.7	96.6	96.2	93.3
		98.8	98.9	98.8	99.0	98.6	99.0	96.7
2	655	89.9	88.1	88.5	86.8	86.8	85.0	86.9
		89.9	88.5	88.9	90.8	90.8	88.4	89.8
3	108	83.3	81.5	75.9	79.1	80.2	74.8	84.3
		84.3	82.4	78.7	84.5	84.7	81.1	88.9
4-8	262	78.2	76.3	74.8	69.5	68.8	68.7	78.9
		78.2	79.0	76.0	78.2	78.7	76.0	83.5
9+	247	59.9	53.4	53.0	47.8	46.2	50.4	62.7
		63.6	60.7	58.7	58.2	59.4	54.8	67.5

Table 3: AIDA A dataset: Gold mentions are split by the position they appear in the $p(e|m)$ dictionary. In each cell, the upper value is the percentage of the gold mentions that were annotated with the correct entity (recall), whereas the lower value is the percentage of gold mentions for which our system's highest scored entity is the ground truth entity, but that might not be annotated in the end because its score is below the threshold δ.

300 dimensional, while 50 dimensional trainable character vectors were used. The char LSTMs have also hidden dimension of 50. Thus, word-character embeddings are 400 dimensional. The contextual LSTMs have hidden size of 150, resulting in 300 dimensional context-aware word vectors. We apply dropout on the concatenated word-character embeddings, on the output of the bidirectional context LSTM and on the entity embeddings used in Eq. 6. The three FFNNs in our model are simple projections without hidden layers (no improvements were obtained with deeper layers). For the *long range context attention* we used a word window size of K = 200 and keep top R = 10 words after the hard attention layer (notations from Ganea and Hofmann (2017)). We use at most $s = 30$ entity candidate per mention both at train and test time. γ is set to 0.2 without further investigations. γ' is set to 0, but a value of 0.1 was giving similar results.

For the loss optimization we use Adam Kingma and Ba (2014) with a learning rate of 0.001. We perform early stopping by evaluating the model on the AIDA validation set each 10 minutes and stopping after 6 consecutive evaluations with no significant improvement in the macro F1 score.

Results and Discussion. The following models are used.

i) **Base model**: only uses the mention local score and the log-prior. It does not use long range attention, nor global disambiguation. It does not use the head attention mechanism.

ii) **Base model + att**: the Base Model plus Long Range Context Attention.

ii) **Base model + att + global**: our Global Model (depicted in figure 1)

iv) **ED base model + att + global Stanford NER**: our ED Global model that runs on top of the detected mentions of the Stanford NER system Finkel et al. (2005).

EL strong and weak matching results are presented in Tables 2 and 7 (Appendix).

We first note that our system outperforms all baselines on the end-to-end EL task on both AIDA-A (dev) and AIDA-B (test) datasets, which are the biggest EL datasets publicly available. Moreover, we surpass all competitors on both EL and ED by a large margin, at least 9%, showcasing the effectiveness of our method. We also outperform systems that optimize MD and ED separately, including our *ED base model + att + global Stanford NER*. This demonstrates the merit of joint MD + ED optimization.

In addition, one can observe that weak matching EL results are comparable with the strong matching results, showcasing that our method is very good at detecting mention boundaries.

At this point, our main goal was achieved: if enough training data is available with the same characteristics or annotation schemes as the test data, then our joint EL offers the best model. This is true not only when training on AIDA, but also for other types of datasets such as queries (Table 11) or tweets (Table 12). However, when testing data

---

1) Annotated document:

SOCCER - SHEARER NAMED AS [1 [ENGLAND] CAPTAIN]. LONDON 1996-08-30 The world 's costliest footballer Alan Shearer was named as the new England captain on Friday. The 26-year-old, who joined Newcastle for 15 million pounds sterling, takes over from Tony Adams, who led the side during the European championship in June, and former captain David Platt. Adams and Platt are both injured and will miss England 's opening [3[World Cup]] qualifier against Moldova on Sunday. Shearer takes the captaincy on a trial basis, but new coach Glenn Hoddle said he saw no reason why the former Blackburn and Southampton skipper should not make the post his own. "I 'm sure Alan is the man for the job, " Hoddle said. [...] I spoke to Alan he was up for it [...]. Shearer 's Euro 96 striking partner [...].

Analysis:

[1 is considered a false negative and the ground truth is the entity England_national_football_team. Our annotation was for the span "ENGLAND CAPTAIN" and wrongly linked to the England_cricket_team. [3 The ground truth here is 1998_FIFA_World_Cup whereas our model links it to FIFA_World_Cup. [2,4,5 are correctly solved due to our coreference resolution heuristic.

---

2) Annotated document:

N. Korea urges S. Korea to return war veteran. SEOUL 1996-08-31 North Korea demanded on Saturday that South Korea return a northern war veteran who has been in the [1 South] since the 1950-53 war, Seoul 's unification ministry said. " ...I request the immediate repatriation of Kim In-so to North Korea where his family is waiting, " [1 North Korean] Red Cross president Li Song-ho said in a telephone message to his southern couterpart, [2 Kang Young-hoon]. Li said Kim had been critically ill with a cerebral haemorrhage. The message was distributed to the press by the South Korean unification ministry. Kim, an unrepentant communist, was captured during the [2 [3 Korean] War] and released after spending more than 30 years in a southern jail. He submitted a petition to the International Red Cross in 1993 asking for his repatriation. The domestic Yonhap news agency said the South Korean government would consider the northern demand only if the [3 North] accepted Seoul 's requests, which include regular reunions of families split by the [4 [4 Korean] War]. Government officials were not available to comment. South Korea in 1993 unconditionally repatriated Li In-mo, a nothern partisan seized by the [5 South] during the war and jailed for more than three decades.

Analysis:

[1, [3, and [5 cases illustrate the main source of errors. These are false negatives in which our model has the correct ground truth entity pair as the highest scored one for that mention, but since it is not confident enough (score $< \gamma$) it decides not to annotate that mention. In this specific document these errors could probably be avoided easily with a better coreference resolution mechanism.

[3 and [4 cases illustrate that the gold standard can be problematic. Specifically, instead of annotating the whole span *Korean War* and linking it to the war of 1950, the gold annotation only include *Korean* and link it to the general entity of *Korea_(country)*.

[2 is correctly annotated by our system but it is not included in the gold standard.

Table 4: Error analysis on a sample document. Green corresponds to true positive (correctly discovered and annotated mention), red to false negative (ground truth mention or entity that was not annotated) and orange to false positive (incorrect mention or entity annotation).

has different statistics or follows different conventions than the training data, our method is shown to work best in conjunction with a state-of-the-art NER system as it can be seen from the results of our **ED base model + att + global Stanford NER** for different datasets in Table 2. It is expected that such a NER system designed with a broader generalization scheme in mind would help in this case, which is confirmed by our results on different datasets.

While the main focus of this paper is the end-to-end EL and not the ED-only task, we do show ED results in Tables 8 and 9. We observe that our models are slightly behind recent top performing systems, but our unified EL - ED architecture has to deal with other challenges, e.g. being able to exchange global information between many more mentions at the EL stage, and is thus not suitable for expensive global ED strategies. We leave bridging this gap for ED as future work.

Additional results and insights are shown in the Appendix.

Ablation study   Table 3 shows an ablation study of our method. One can see that the $\log p(e|m)$ prior is very helpful for correctly linking unambiguous mentions, but is introducing noise when gold entities are not frequent. For this category of rare entities, removing this prior completely will result in a significant improvement, but this is not a practical choice since the gold entity is unknown at test time.

Error Analysis.   We conducted a qualitative experiment shown in Table 4. We showcase correct annotations, as well as errors done by our system on the AIDA datasets. Inspecting the output annotations of our EL model, we discovered the remarkable property of not over-generating incorrect mentions, nor under-generating (missing) gold spans. We also observed that additional mentions generated by our model do correspond in the majority of time to actual KB entities, but are incorrectly forgotten from the gold annotations.

5   Conclusion

We presented the first neural end-to-end entity linking model and show the benefit of jointly optimizing entity recognition and linking. Leveraging key components, namely word, entity and mention embeddings, we prove that engineered features can be almost completely replaced by modern neural networks. Empirically, on the established Gerbil benchmarking platform, we exhibit state-of-the-art performance for EL on the biggest public dataset, AIDA/CoNLL, also showing good generalization ability on other datasets with very different characteristics when combining our model with the popular Stanford NER system.

Our code is publicly available[2].

References

David Carmel, Ming-Wei Chang, Evgeniy Gabrilovich, Bo-June Paul Hsu, and Kuansan Wang. 2014. Erd'14: entity recognition and disambiguation challenge. In *ACM SIGIR Forum*, volume 48, pages 63–77. ACM.

Diego Ceccarelli, Claudio Lucchese, Salvatore Orlando, Raffaele Perego, and Salvatore Trani. 2013. Dexter: an open source framework for entity linking. In *Proceedings of the sixth international workshop on Exploiting semantic annotations in information retrieval*, pages 17–20. ACM.

Jason PC Chiu and Eric Nichols. 2016. Named entity recognition with bidirectional lstm-cnns. *Transactions of the Association for Computational Linguistics*, 4:357–370.

Marco Cornolti, Paolo Ferragina, Massimiliano Ciaramita, Stefan Rüd, and Hinrich Schütze. 2016. A piggyback system for joint entity mention detection and linking in web queries. In *Proceedings of the 25th International Conference on World Wide Web*, pages 567–578. International World Wide Web Conferences Steering Committee.

Joachim Daiber, Max Jakob, Chris Hokamp, and Pablo N Mendes. 2013. Improving efficiency and accuracy in multilingual entity extraction. In *Proceedings of the 9th International Conference on Semantic Systems*, pages 121–124. ACM.

Leon Derczynski, Diana Maynard, Giuseppe Rizzo, Marieke van Erp, Genevieve Gorrell, Raphaël Troncy, Johann Petrak, and Kalina Bontcheva. 2015. Analysis of named entity recognition and linking for tweets. *Information Processing & Management*, 51(2):32–49.

MGJ van Erp, G Rizzo, and R Troncy. 2013. Learning with the web: Spotting named entities on the intersection of nerd and machine learning. In *CEUR workshop proceedings*, pages 27–30.

Jenny Rose Finkel, Trond Grenager, and Christopher Manning. 2005. Incorporating non-local information into information extraction systems by gibbs sampling. In *Proceedings of the 43rd annual meeting on association for computational linguistics*, pages 363–370. Association for Computational Linguistics.

Octavian-Eugen Ganea, Marina Ganea, Aurelien Lucchi, Carsten Eickhoff, and Thomas Hofmann. 2016. Probabilistic bag-of-hyperlinks model for entity linking. In *Proceedings of the 25th International Conference on World Wide Web*, pages 927–938. International World Wide Web Conferences Steering Committee.

Octavian-Eugen Ganea and Thomas Hofmann. 2017. Deep joint entity disambiguation with local neural attention. In *Proceedings of the 2017 Conference on Empirical Methods in Natural Language Processing*, pages 2619–2629.

___
[2] `https://github.com/dalab/end2end_neural_el`

Zhengyan He, Shujie Liu, Mu Li, Ming Zhou, Longkai Zhang, and Houfeng Wang. 2013. Learning entity representation for entity disambiguation. In *Proceedings of the 51st Annual Meeting of the Association for Computational Linguistics (Volume 2: Short Papers)*, volume 2, pages 30–34.

Sepp Hochreiter and Jürgen Schmidhuber. 1997. Long short-term memory. *Neural computation*, 9(8):1735–1780.

Johannes Hoffart, Stephan Seufert, Dat Ba Nguyen, Martin Theobald, and Gerhard Weikum. 2012. Kore: keyphrase overlap relatedness for entity disambiguation. In *Proceedings of the 21st ACM international conference on Information and knowledge management*, pages 545–554. ACM.

Johannes Hoffart, Mohamed Amir Yosef, Ilaria Bordino, Hagen Fürstenau, Manfred Pinkal, Marc Spaniol, Bilyana Taneva, Stefan Thater, and Gerhard Weikum. 2011. Robust disambiguation of named entities in text. In *Proceedings of the Conference on Empirical Methods in Natural Language Processing*, pages 782–792. Association for Computational Linguistics.

Yangfeng Ji, Chenhao Tan, Sebastian Martschat, Yejin Choi, and Noah A Smith. 2017. Dynamic entity representations in neural language models. In *Proceedings of the 2017 Conference on Empirical Methods in Natural Language Processing*, pages 1830–1839.

Diederik P Kingma and Jimmy Ba. 2014. Adam: A method for stochastic optimization. *arXiv preprint arXiv:1412.6980*.

Guillaume Lample, Miguel Ballesteros, Sandeep Subramanian, Kazuya Kawakami, and Chris Dyer. 2016. Neural architectures for named entity recognition. In *Proceedings of NAACL-HLT*, pages 260–270.

Phong Le and Ivan Titov. 2018. Improving entity linking by modeling latent relations between mentions. *arXiv preprint arXiv:1804.10637*.

Kenton Lee, Luheng He, Mike Lewis, and Luke Zettlemoyer. 2017. End-to-end neural coreference resolution. In *Proceedings of the 2017 Conference on Empirical Methods in Natural Language Processing*, pages 188–197.

Liyuan Liu, Jingbo Shang, Frank Xu, Xiang Ren, Huan Gui, Jian Peng, and Jiawei Han. 2017. Empower sequence labeling with task-aware neural language model. *arXiv preprint arXiv:1709.04109*.

Gang Luo, Xiaojiang Huang, Chin-Yew Lin, and Zaiqing Nie. 2015. Joint entity recognition and disambiguation. In *Proceedings of the 2015 Conference on Empirical Methods in Natural Language Processing*, pages 879–888.

Pablo N Mendes, Max Jakob, Andrés García-Silva, and Christian Bizer. 2011. Dbpedia spotlight: shedding light on the web of documents. In *Proceedings of the 7th international conference on semantic systems*, pages 1–8. ACM.

Tomas Mikolov, Ilya Sutskever, Kai Chen, Greg S Corrado, and Jeff Dean. 2013. Distributed representations of words and phrases and their compositionality. In *Advances in neural information processing systems*, pages 3111–3119.

Andrea Moro, Alessandro Raganato, and Roberto Navigli. 2014. Entity linking meets word sense disambiguation: a unified approach. *Transactions of the Association for Computational Linguistics*, 2:231–244.

Dat Ba Nguyen, Martin Theobald, and Gerhard Weikum. 2016. J-nerd: joint named entity recognition and disambiguation with rich linguistic features. *Transactions of the Association for Computational Linguistics*, 4:215–229.

Andrea Giovanni Nuzzolese, Anna Lisa Gentile, Valentina Presutti, Aldo Gangemi, Darío Garigliotti, and Roberto Navigli. 2015. Open knowledge extraction challenge. In *Semantic Web Evaluation Challenge*, pages 3–15. Springer.

Francesco Piccinno and Paolo Ferragina. 2014. From tagme to wat: a new entity annotator. In *Proceedings of the first international workshop on Entity recognition & disambiguation*, pages 55–62. ACM.

Priya Radhakrishnan, Partha Talukdar, and Vasudeva Varma. 2018. Elden: Improved entity linking using densified knowledge graphs. In *Proceedings of the 2018 Conference of the North American Chapter of the Association for Computational Linguistics: Human Language Technologies, Volume 1 (Long Papers)*, volume 1, pages 1844–1853.

Giuseppe Rizzo, Marieke van Erp, and Raphaël Troncy. Benchmarking the extraction and disambiguation of named entities on the semantic web.

Michael Röder, Ricardo Usbeck, and Axel-Cyrille Ngonga Ngomo. 2017. Gerbil–benchmarking named entity recognition and linking consistently. *Semantic Web*, (Preprint):1–21.

Avirup Sil and Alexander Yates. 2013. Re-ranking for joint named-entity recognition and linking. In *Proceedings of the 22nd ACM international conference on Conference on information & knowledge management*, pages 2369–2374. ACM.

René Speck and Axel-Cyrille Ngonga Ngomo. 2014. Ensemble learning for named entity recognition. In *International semantic web conference*, pages 519–534. Springer.

Valentin I Spitkovsky and Angel X Chang. A cross-lingual dictionary for english wikipedia concepts.

Nadine Steinmetz and Harald Sack. 2013. Semantic multimedia information retrieval based on contextual descriptions. In *Extended Semantic Web Conference*, pages 382–396. Springer.

Yaming Sun, Lei Lin, Duyu Tang, Nan Yang, Zhenzhou Ji, and Xiaolong Wang. 2015. Modeling mention, context and entity with neural networks for entity disambiguation. In *Twenty-Fourth International Joint Conference on Artificial Intelligence*.

Ikuya Yamada, Hiroyuki Shindo, Hideaki Takeda, and Yoshiyasu Takefuji. 2016. Joint learning of the embedding of words and entities for named entity disambiguation. In *Proceedings of The 20th SIGNLL Conference on Computational Natural Language Learning*, pages 250–259.

Yi Yang, Ozan Irsoy, and Kazi Shefaet Rahman. 2018. Collective entity disambiguation with structured gradient tree boosting. In *Proceedings of the 2018 Conference of the North American Chapter of the Association for Computational Linguistics: Human Language Technologies, Volume 1 (Long Papers)*, volume 1, pages 777–786.

---

[3]`https://github.com/dice-group/gerbil/issues/98`

Modelling Salient Features as Directions in Fine-Tuned Semantic Spaces

Thomas Ager
School of CS & Informatics
Cardiff University, UK
agert@cardiff.ac.uk

Ondřej Kuželka
Dept. of Computer Science
KU Leuven, Belgium
ondrej.kuzelka@kuleuven.be

Steven Schockaert
School of CS & Informatics
Cardiff University, UK
schockaerts1@cardiff.ac.uk

Abstract

In this paper we consider semantic spaces consisting of objects from some particular domain (e.g. IMDB movie reviews). Various authors have observed that such semantic spaces often model salient features (e.g. how scary a movie is) as directions. These feature directions allow us to rank objects according to how much they have the corresponding feature, and can thus play an important role in interpretable classifiers, recommendation systems, or entity-oriented search engines, among others. Methods for learning semantic spaces, however, are mostly aimed at modelling similarity. In this paper, we argue that there is an inherent trade-off between capturing similarity and faithfully modelling features as directions. Following this observation, we propose a simple method to fine-tune existing semantic spaces, with the aim of improving the quality of their feature directions. Crucially, our method is fully unsupervised, requiring only a bag-of-words representation of the objects as input.

1 Introduction

Vector space representations, or 'embeddings', play a crucial role in various areas of natural language processing. For instance, word embeddings (Mikolov et al., 2013; Pennington et al., 2014) are routinely used as representations of word meaning, while knowledge graph embeddings (Bordes et al., 2013) are used to find plausible missing information in structured knowledge bases, or to exploit such knowledge bases in neural network architectures. In this paper we focus on domain-specific semantic spaces, i.e. vector space representations of the objects of a single domain, as opposed to the more heterogeneous setting of e.g. word embeddings.

Such domain-specific semantic spaces are used, for instance, to represent items in recommender systems (Vasile et al., 2016; Liang et al., 2016; Van Gysel et al., 2016), to represent entities in semantic search engines (Jameel et al., 2017; Van Gysel et al., 2017), or to represent examples in classification tasks (Demirel et al., 2017). In many semantic spaces it is possible to find directions that correspond to salient features from the considered domain. For instance, Gupta et al. (2015) found that features of countries, such as their GDP, fertility rate or even level of CO_2 emissions, can be predicted from word embeddings using a linear regression model. Similarly, in (Kim and de Marneffe, 2013) directions in word embeddings were found that correspond to adjectival scales (e.g. bad < okay < good < excellent) while Rothe and Schütze (2016) found directions indicating lexical features such as the frequency of occurrence and polarity of words. Finally, Derrac and Schockaert (2015) found directions corresponding to properties such as 'Scary', 'Romantic' or 'Hilarious' in a semantic space of movies.

In our work, we focus on improving the representation of these *feature directions* in domain-specific semantic spaces. Such feature directions are useful in a wide variety of applications. The most immediate example is perhaps that they allow for a natural way to implement critique-based recommendation systems, where users can specify how their desired result should relate to a given set of suggestions (Viappiani et al., 2006). For instance, Vig et al. (2012) propose a movie recommendation system in which the user can specify that they want to see suggestions for movies that are "similar to this one, but scarier". If the property of being scary is adequately modelled as a direction in a semantic space of movies, such critiques can be addressed in a straightforward way. Similarly, in (Kovashka et al., 2012) a system was developed that can find "shoes like these but shinier", based on a semantic space representation

530

Proceedings of the 22nd Conference on Computational Natural Language Learning (CoNLL 2018), pages 530–540
Brussels, Belgium, October 31 - November 1, 2018. ©2018 Association for Computational Linguistics

that was derived from visual features. Semantic search systems can use such directions to interpret queries involving gradual and possibly ill-defined features, such as "*popular* holiday destinations in Europe" (Jameel et al., 2017). While features such as popularity are typically not encoded in traditional knowledge bases, they can often be represented as semantic space directions. As another application, feature directions can also be used in interpretable classifiers. For example, Derrac and Schockaert (2015) learned rule based classifiers from rankings induced by the feature directions. Along similar lines, in this paper we will use shallow decision trees to evaluate the quality of our feature directions.

In the aforementioned applications, feature directions are typically emerging from vector space representations that have been learned with a similarity-centred objective, i.e. the main consideration when learning these representations is that similar objects should be represented as similar vectors. An important observation is that such spaces may not actually be optimal for modelling feature directions. To illustrate why this can be the case, Figure 1 shows a toy example in which basic geometric shapes are embedded in a two-dimensional space. Within this space, we can identify directions which encode how light an object is and how closely its shape resembles a square. While most of the shapes embedded in this space are grey-scale circles and squares, one of the shapes embedded in this space is a red triangle, which is a clear outlier. If this space is learned with a similarity-centred objective, the representation of the triangle will be far from all the other shapes. However, this means that outliers like this will often take up extreme positions in the rankings induced by the feature directions, and may thus lead us to incorrectly assume that they have certain features. In this example, the triangle would incorrectly be considered as the shape which most exhibits the features "light" and "square". In contrast, if we had learned the representation with the knowledge that it should model these two features rather than similarity, this triangle would have ended up closer to the bottom-left corner.

Unfortunately, we usually have no *a priori* knowledge of which are the most salient features. In this paper, we therefore suggest the following fully unsupervised strategy. First, we learn

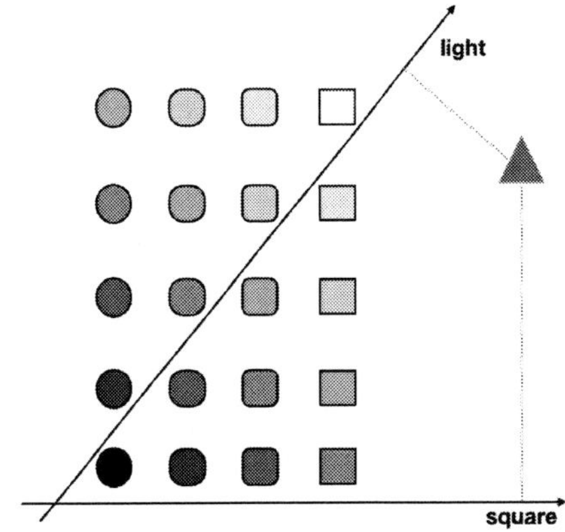

Figure 1: Toy example showing the effect of outliers in a two-dimensional embedding of geometric shapes.

a semantic space from bag-of-words representations of the considered objects, using a standard similarity-centric method. Using the method from (Derrac and Schockaert, 2015), we subsequently determine the most salient features in the considered domain, and their corresponding directions. Finally, we fine-tune the semantic space and the associated feature directions, modelling the considered features in a more faithful way. This last step is the main contribution of this paper. All code and hyperparameters are available online[1].

2   Related Work

Topic models.   The main idea underlying our method is to learn a representation in terms of salient features, where each of these features is described using a cluster of natural language terms. This is somewhat similar to Latent Dirichlet Allocation (LDA), which learns a representation of text documents as multinomial distributions over latent topics, where each of these topics corresponds to a multinomial distribution over words (Blei et al., 2003). Topics tend to correspond to salient features, and are typically labelled with the most probable words according to the corresponding distribution. However, while LDA only uses bag-of-words (BoW) representations, our focus is specifically on identifying and improving features that are modelled as directions in semantic spaces. One advantage of using vector spaces is that they offer more flexibility in how addi-

---

[1]`https://github.com/ThomasAger/`
`Modelling-Salient-Features-as-`
`Directions-in-Fine-Tuned-Semantic-Spaces`

tional information can be taken into account, e.g. they allow us to use neural representation learning methods to obtain these spaces. Many extensions of LDA have been proposed to incorporate additional information as well, e.g. aiming to avoid the need to manually specify the number of topics (Teh et al., 2004), modelling correlations between topics (Blei and Lafferty, 2005), or by incorporating meta-data such as authors or time stamps (Rosen-Zvi et al., 2004; Wang and McCallum, 2006). Nonetheless, such techniques for extending LDA offer less flexibility than neural network models, e.g. for exploiting numerical attributes or visual features.

Fine-tuning embeddings. Several authors have looked at approaches for adapting word embeddings. One possible strategy is to change how the embedding is learned in the first place. For example, some approaches have been proposed to learn word embeddings that are better suited at capturing sentiment Tang et al. (2016), or to learn embeddings that are optimized for relation extraction Hashimoto et al. (2015). Other approaches, however, start with a pre-trained embedding, which is then modified in a particular way. For example, in (Faruqui et al., 2015) a method is proposed to bring the vectors of semantically related words, as specified in a given lexicon, closer together. Similarly Yu et al. (2017) propose a method for refining word vectors to improve how well they model sentiment. In (Labutov and Lipson, 2013) a method is discussed to adapt word embeddings based on a given supervised classification task.

Semantic spaces. Within the field of cognitive science, feature representations and semantic spaces both have a long tradition as alternative, and often competing representations of semantic relatedness (Tversky, 1977). Conceptual spaces (Gärdenfors, 2004) to some extent unify these two opposing views, by representing objects as points in vector spaces, one for each facet (e.g. color, shape, taste in a conceptual space of fruit), such that the dimensions of each of these vector spaces correspond to primitive features. The main appeal of conceptual spaces stems from the fact that they allow a wide range of cognitive and linguistic phenomena to be modelled in an elegant way. The idea of learning semantic spaces with accurate feature directions can be seen as a first step towards methods for learning conceptual space representations from data, and thus towards the use of more

cognitively plausible representations of meaning in computer science. Our method also somewhat relates to the debates in cognitive science on the relationship between similarity and rule based processes (Hahn and Chater, 1998), in the sense that it allows us to explicitly link similarity based categorization methods (e.g. an SVM classifier trained on semantic space representations) with rule based categorization methods (e.g. the decision trees that we will learn from the feature directions).

3 Identifying Feature Directions

We assume that a domain-specific semantic space is given, and that for each of the objects which are modelled in this space, we also have a BoW representation. Our overall aim is to find directions in the semantic space that model salient features of the considered domain. For example, given a semantic space of movies, we would like to find a direction that models the extent to which each movie is scary, among others. Such a direction would then allow us to rank movies from the least scary to the most scary. We will refer to such directions as *feature directions*. Formally, each feature direction will be modelled as a vector v_f. However, we refer to *directions* rather than *vectors* to emphasize their intended ordinal meaning: feature directions are aimed at ranking objects rather than e.g. measuring degrees of similarity. In particular, if o is the vector representation of a given object then we can think of the dot product $v_f \cdot o$ as the value of object o for feature f, and in particular, we take $v_f \cdot o_1 < v_f \cdot o_2$ to mean that o_2 has the feature f to a greater extent than o_1.

To identify feature directions, we use a variant of the unsupervised method proposed in (Derrac and Schockaert, 2015), which we explain in this section. In Section 4, we will then introduce our approach for fine-tuning the semantic space and associated feature directions.

Step 1: Generating candidate feature directions. Each feature will be associated with a cluster of words, which we can regard as a description of the intuitive meaning of that feature. Since we assume no *a priori* information about which words might describe features that can be modelled as directions in the vector space, the method initially considers all nouns and adjectives that are sufficiently frequent in the BoW representations of the objects as candidate feature labels. Then, for each considered word w, a logistic regression classifier

20 Newsgroups: Accuracy Scored	Movie Reviews: NDCG Scored	Place-types: Kappa Scored
{sins, sinful, jesus, moses}	{environmentalist, wildlife, ecological}	{smile, kid, young, female}
{hitters, catcher, pitching, batting}	{prophets, bibles, scriptures}	{rust, rusty, broken, mill}
{ink, printers, printer, matrix}	{assassinating, assasins, assasin}	{eerie, spooky, haunted, ghosts}
{jupiter, telescope, spacecraft, satellites}	{reanimated, undead, zombified}	{religious, christian, chapel, carved}
{firearm, concealed, handgun, handguns}	{ufos, ufo, extraterrestrial, extraterrestrials}	{fur, tongue, teeth, ears}
{escaped, terror, wounded, fled}	{swordsman, feudal, swordfight, swordplay}	{weeds, shed, dirt, gravel}
{cellular, phones, phone}	{scuba, divers, undersea}	{stonework, archway, brickwork}
{brake, steering, tires, brakes}	{regiment, armys, soliders, infantry}	{rails, rail, tracks, railroad}
{riders, rider, ride, riding}	{toons, animations, animating, animators}	{dirty, trash, grunge, graffiti}
{formats, jpeg, gif, tiff}	{fundamentalists, doctrine, extremists}	{tranquility, majestic, picturesque}
{physicians, treatments physician}	{semitic, semitism, judaism, auschwitz}	{monument, site, arch, cemetery}
{bacteria, toxic, biology, tissue}	{shipwrecked, ashore, shipwreck}	{journey, traveling, travelling}
{planets, solar, mars, planetary}	{planetary, earths, asteroid, spaceships}	{mother, mom, children, child}
{symptoms, syndrome, diagnosis}	{atheism, theological, atheists, agnostic}	{frost, snowy, icy, freezing}
{universities, nonprofit, institution}	{astronaut, nasa, spaceship, astronauts}	{colourful, vivid, artistic, vibrant}

Table 1: The first clustered words of features for three different domains and three different scoring types.

is trained to find a hyperplane H_w in the semantic space that separates objects which contain w in their BoW representation from those that do not. The vector v_w perpendicular to this hyperplane is then taken as the direction that models the word w.

Step 2: Filtering candidate feature directions. To determine whether the word w is likely to describe an important feature for the considered domain, we then evaluate the quality of the candidate feature direction v_w. For example, we can use the classification accuracy to evaluate the quality in terms of the corresponding logistic regression classifier: if this classifier is sufficiently accurate, it must mean that whether word w relates to object o (i.e. whether it is used in the description of o) is important enough to affect the semantic space representation of o. In such a case, it seems reasonable to assume that w describes an important feature for the given domain.

One problem with accuracy as a scoring function is that these classification problems are often very imbalanced. In particular, for very rare words, a high accuracy might not necessarily imply that the corresponding direction is accurate. For this reason, Derrac and Schockaert (2015) proposed to use Cohen's Kappa score instead. In our experiments, however, we found that accuracy sometimes yields better results, so rather than fix the scoring function, we keep this as a hyperparameter of the model that can be tuned.

In addition to accuracy and Kappa, we also consider Normalized Discounted Cumulative Gain (NDCG). This is a standard metric in information retrieval which evaluates the quality of a ranking w.r.t. some given relevance scores (Järvelin and Kekäläinen, 2002). In our case, the rankings of the objects o are those induced by the dot products $v_w \cdot o$ and the relevance scores are determined by the Pointwise Positive Mutual Information (PPMI) score $ppmi(w, o)$, of the word w in the BoW representation of object o where $ppmi(w, o) = \max\left(0, \log\left(\frac{p_{wo}}{p_{w*} \cdot p_{*o}}\right)\right)$, and

$$p_{wo} = \frac{n(w, o)}{\sum_{w'} \sum_{o'} n(w', o')}$$

where $n(w, o)$ is the number of occurrences of w in the BoW representation of object o, $p_{w*} = \sum_{o'} p_{wo'}$ and $p_{*o} = \sum_{w'} p_{w'o}$. In principle, we may expect that accuracy and Kappa are best suited for binary features, as they rely on a hard separation in the space between objects that have the word in their BoW representation and those that do not, while NDCG should be better suited for gradual features. In practice, however, we could not find such a clear pattern in the differences between the words chosen by these metrics despite often finding different words.

Step 3: clustering candidate feature directions. As the final step, we cluster the best-scoring candidate feature directions v_w. Each of these clusters will then define one of the feature directions to be used in applications. The purpose of this clustering step is three-fold: it will ensure that the feature directions are sufficiently different (e.g. in a space of movies there is little point in having *funny* and *hilarious* as separate features), it will make the features easier to interpret (as a cluster of terms is more descriptive than an individual term), and it will alleviate sparsity issues when we want to relate features with the BoW representation, which will play an important role for the fine-tuning method described in the next section.

As input to the clustering algorithm, we consider the N best-scoring candidate feature directions v_w, where N is a hyperparameter. To cluster these N vectors, we have followed the approach proposed in (Derrac and Schockaert, 2015), which we found to perform slightly better than K-means. The main idea underlying their approach is to select the cluster centers such that (i) they are among the top-scoring candidate feature directions, and (ii) are as close to being orthogonal to each other as possible. We refer to (Derrac and Schockaert, 2015) for more details. The output of this step is a set of clusters $C_1, ..., C_K$, where we will identify each cluster C_j with a set of words. We will furthermore write v_{C_j} to denote the centroid of the directions corresponding to the words in the cluster C_j, which can be computed as $v_{C_j} = \frac{1}{|C_j|} \sum_{w_l \in C_j} v_l$ provided that the vectors v_w are all normalized. These centroids $v_{C_1}, ..., v_{C_k}$ are the feature directions that are identified by our method.

Table 1 displays some examples of clusters that have been obtained for three of the datasets that will be used in the experiments, modelling respectively movies, place-types and newsgroup postings. For each dataset, we used the scoring function that led to the best performance on development data(see Section 5). Only the first four words whose direction is closest to the centroid v_C are shown.

4 Fine-Tuning Feature Directions

To illustrate that the method from Section 3 can produce sub-optimal directions, the second column of Table 2 shows the top-ranked objects for some feature directions in the semantic space of place-types. For the feature represented by the cluster {*steep, climb, slope*}, the top ranked object *mountain* is clearly relevant. However, the next two objects — *landscape* and *national park* — are not directly related to this feature. Intuitively,

they are ranked highly because of their similarity to *mountain* in the vector space. Similarly, for the second feature, *building* is ranked highly because of its similarity to *skyscraper*, despite intuitively not having this feature. Finally, *fence* received a high rank for several features, mostly because it is an outlier in the space.

To improve the directions and address these problems, we propose a method for fine-tuning the semantic space representations and corresponding feature directions. The main idea is to use the BoW representations of the objects as a kind of weak supervision signal: if an object should be ranked highly for a given feature, we would expect the words describing that feature to appear frequently in its description. In particular, for each feature f we determine a total ordering $\preccurlyeq_f$ such that $o \preccurlyeq_f o'$ iff the feature f is more prominent in the BoW representation of object o' than in the BoW representation of o. We will refer to $\preccurlyeq_f$ as the *target ranking* for feature f. If the feature directions are in perfect agreement with this target ranking, it would be the case that $o \preccurlyeq o'$ iff $v_C \cdot o \leq v_C \cdot o'$. Since this will typically not be the case, we subsequently determine *target values* for the dot products $v_C \cdot o$. These target values represent the minimal way in which the dot products need to be changed to ensure that they respect the target ranking. Finally, we use a simple feedforward neural network to adapt the semantic space representations o and feature directions v_C to make the dot products $v_C \cdot o$ as close as possible to these target values.

4.1 Generating Target Rankings

Let $C_1, ..., C_K$ be the clusters that were found using the method from Section 3. Each cluster C_i typically corresponds to a set of semantically related words $\{w_1, ..., w_n\}$, which describe some salient feature from the considered domain. From the BoW representations of the objects, we can now define a ranking that reflects how strongly each object is related to the words from this cluster. To this end, we represent each object as a bag of clusters (BoC) and then compute PPMI scores over this representation. In particular, for a cluster $C = \{w_1, ..., w_m\}$, we define $n(C, o) = \sum_{i=1}^{m} n(w_i, o)$. In other words, $n(C, o)$ is the total number of occurrences of words from cluster C in BoW representation of o. We then write $ppmi(C, o)$ for the PPMI score corresponding to

Feature direction	Highest ranking objects	Highest fine-tuned ranking objects
{steep, climb, slope}	mountain, landscape, national park	ski slope, steep slope, slope
{illuminated, illumination, skyscraper}	building, city, skyscraper	tall building, office building, large building
{play, kid, kids}	school, field, fence	college classroom, classroom, school
{spooky, creepy, scary}	hallway, fence, building	hospital room, hospital ward, patient room
{amazing, dream, awesome}	fence, building, beach	hotel pool, resort, beach resort
{pavement, streetlight, streets}	sidewalk, fence, building	overpass road, overpass, road junction
{dead, hole, death}	fence, steps, park	grave, cemetery, graveyard
{spire, belltower, towers}	building, arch, house	bell tower, arch, religious site
{stones, moss, worldheritage}	landscape, fence, steps	ancient site, ancient wall, tomb
{mosaic, tile, bronze}	building, city, steps	cathedral, church, religious site

Table 2: Comparing the highest ranking place-type objects in the original and fine-tuned space.

this BoC representation, which is evaluated in the same way as $ppmi(C, o)$, but using the counts $n(C, o)$ rather than $n(w, o)$. The target ranking for cluster C_i is then such that o_1 is ranked higher than o_2 iff $ppmi(C_i, o_1) > ppmi(C_i, o_2)$. By computing PPMI scores w.r.t. clusters of words, we alleviate problems with sparsity and synonymy, which in turn allows us to better estimate the intensity with which a given feature applies to the object. For instance, an object describing a violent movie might not actually mention the word 'violent', but would likely mention at least some of the words from the same cluster (e.g. 'bloody' 'brutal' 'violence' 'gory'). Similarly, this approach allows us to avoid problems with ambiguous word usage; e.g. if a movie is said to contain 'violent language', it will not be identified as violent if other words related to this feature are rarely mentioned.

4.2 Generating Target Feature Values

Finding directions in a vector space that induce a set of given target rankings is computationally hard[2]. Therefore, rather than directly using the target rankings from Section 4.1 to fine-tune the semantic space, we will generate target values for the dot products $v_{C_j} \cdot o_i$ from these target rankings. One straightforward approach would be to use the PPMI scores $ppmi(C_j, o_i)$. However these target values would be very different from the initial dot products, which among others means that too much of the similarity structure from the initial vector space would be lost. Instead, we will use isotonic regression to find target values $\tau(C_j, o_i)$ for the dot product $v_{C_j} \cdot o_i$, which respect the ranking induced by the PPMI scores, but otherwise remain as close as possible to the initial dot prod-

---

[2]It is complete for the complexity class $\exists \mathbb{R}$, which sits between NP and PSPACE (Schockaert and Lee, 2015).

ucts.

Let us consider a cluster C_j for which we want to determine the target feature values. Let $o_{\sigma_1}, ..., o_{\sigma_n}$ be an enumeration of the objects such that $ppmi(C_j, o_{\sigma_i}) \leq ppmi(C_j, o_{\sigma_{i+1}})$ for $i \in \{1, ..., n - 1\}$. The corresponding target values $\tau(C_j, o_i)$ are then obtained by solving the following optimization problem:

Minimize: $\displaystyle\sum_i (\tau(C_j, o_i) - v_{C_j} \cdot o_i)^2$

Subject to:
$$\tau(C_j, o_{\sigma_1}) \leq \tau(C_j, o_{\sigma_2}) \leq ... \leq \tau(C_j, o_{\sigma_n})$$

4.3 Fine-Tuning

We now use the target values $\tau(C_j, o_i)$ to fine-tune the initial representations. To this end, we use a simple neural network architecture with one hidden layer. As inputs to the network, we use the initial vectors $o_1, ..., o_n \in \mathbb{R}^k$. These are fed into a layer of dimension l:

$$h_i = f(W o_i + b)$$

where W is an $l \times k$ matrix, $b \in \mathbb{R}^l$ is a bias term, and f is an activation function. After training the network, the vector h_i will correspond to the new representation of the ith object. The vectors h_i are finally fed into an output layer containing one neuron for each cluster:

$$g_i = D h_i$$

where D is a $K \times l$ matrix. Note that by using a linear activation in the output layer, we can interpret the rows of the matrix D as the K feature directions, with the components of the vector $g_i = (g_i^1, ..., g_i^K)$ being the corresponding dot products.

20 Newsgroups	F1 D1	F1 D3	F1 DN
FT MDS	**0.50**	**0.47**	**0.44**
MDS	0.44	0.42	0.43
FT PCA	0.40	0.36	0.34
PCA	0.25	0.27	0.36
FT Doc2Vec	0.44	0.42	0.41
Doc2Vec	0.29	0.34	0.44
FT AWV	0.47	0.45	0.40
AWV	0.41	0.38	0.43
FT AWVw	0.41	0.41	0.43
AWVw	0.38	0.40	0.43
LDA	0.40	0.37	0.35

Table 3: Results for 20 Newsgroups.

As the loss function for training the network, we use the squared error between the outputs g_i^j and the corresponding target values $\tau(C_j, o_i)$, i.e.:

$$\mathcal{L} = \sum_i \sum_j (g_i^j - \tau(C_j, o_i))^2$$

The effect of this fine-tuning step is illustrated in the right-most column of Table 2, where we can see that in each case the top ranked objects are now more closely related to the feature, despite being less common, and outliers such as 'fence' no longer appear.

5 Evaluation

To evaluate our method, we consider the problem of learning interpretable classifiers. In particular, we learn decision trees which are limited to depth 1 and 3, which use the rankings induced by the feature directions as input. This allows us to simultaneously assess to what extent the method can identify the right features and whether these features are modelled well using the learned directions. Note that depth 1 trees are only a single direction and a cut-off, so to perform well, the method needs to identify a highly relevant feature to the considered category. Depth 3 decision trees are able to model categories that can be characterized using at most three feature directions.

5.1 Experimental set-up

Datasets. We evaluate our method on four datasets. First, we used the *movies* and *place-types* datasets from (Derrac and Schockaert, 2015), which are available in preprocessed form[3]. The

former describes 15000 movies, using a BoW representation that was obtained by combining reviews from several sources. However, 1022 duplicate movies were found in the data, which we removed. The associated classification tasks are to predict the movie genres according to IMDB (23 classes), predicting IMDB plot keywords such as 'suicide', 'beach' or 'crying' (100 classes) and predicting age rating certificates such as 'UK-15' 'UK-18' or 'USA-R' (6 classes). All tasks are evaluated as binary classification tasks. We randomly split the datasets into 2/3 for training and 1/3 for testing. The place-types dataset was obtained by associating each place-type with the bag of tags that have been used to describe places of that type on Flickr. It contains BoW represenations for 1383 different place-types. The classification problems for this dataset involve predicting whether a place-type belongs to a given category in three different taxonomies: Geonames (7 classes), Foursquare (9 classes) and OpenCYC (20 classes). Since many of these categories are very small, for this dataset we have used 5-fold cross validation.

The remaining two datasets are standard datasets for document classification: *20 newsgroups* and the *IMDB sentiment* dataset. For the 20 newsgroups dataset, the standard[4] split was used where 11314 of the 18446 documents are used for training. Headers, footers and quote metadata were removed using scikit-learn[5]. The associated classification problem is to predict which newsgroup a given post was submitted to (20 classes). The IMDB sentiment dataset contains a total of 50000 documents, and it is split into 25000 documents for training and 25000 for testing. For the newsgroups and sentiment datasets, we used stopwords from the NLTK python package (Loper and Bird, 2002). For these datasets, we used all (lowercased) tokens and retained numbers, rather than only using nouns and adjectives. The associated classification problem is to predict the sentiment of the review (positive or negative).

Semantic Spaces. We will consider semantic spaces that have been learned using a number of different methods. First, following (Derrac and Schockaert, 2015), we use Multi-Dimensional Scaling (MDS) to learn semantic spaces from the angular differences between the PPMI weighted

---

[3] http://www.cs.cf.ac.uk/
semanticspaces/

[4] http://qwone.com/~jason/20Newsgroups/
[5] http://scikit-learn.org/stable/
datasets/twenty_newsgroups.html

Movie Reviews											
Genres	D1	D3	DN	**Keywords**	D1	D3	DN	**Ratings**	D1	D3	DN
FT MDS	**0.57**	**0.56**	0.51	FT MDS	**0.33**	**0.33**	0.24	FT MDS	**0.49**	**0.51**	**0.46**
MDS	0.40	0.49	**0.52**	MDS	0.31	0.32	**0.25**	MDS	0.46	0.49	**0.46**
FT AWV	0.42	0.42	0.39	FT AWV	0.25	0.25	0.15	FT AWV	0.47	0.44	0.39
AWV	0.35	0.44	0.43	AWV	0.26	0.21	0.19	AWV	0.44	0.48	0.41
LDA	0.52	0.51	0.45	LDA	0.22	0.19	0.18	LDA	0.48	0.48	0.41
Place-types											
Geonames	D1	D3	DN	**Foursquare**	D1	D3	DN	**OpenCYC**	D1	D3	DN
FT MDS	0.32	0.31	0.24	FT MDS	0.41	0.44	0.41	FT MDS	0.35	0.36	0.30
MDS	0.32	0.31	0.21	MDS	0.38	0.42	0.42	MDS	0.35	0.36	0.29
FT AWV	0.31	0.29	0.23	FT AWV	0.39	0.42	0.41	FT AWV	0.37	**0.37**	0.28
AWV	0.28	0.28	0.22	AWV	0.32	0.37	0.31	AWV	0.33	0.35	0.26
LDA	**0.34**	**0.32**	**0.27**	LDA	**0.55**	**0.48**	**0.47**	LDA	**0.40**	0.36	**0.31**

Table 4: The results for Movie Reviews and Place-Types on depth-1, depth-3 and unbounded trees.

IMDB Sentiment	D1	D3	DN
FT PCA	0.78	0.80	0.79
PCA	0.76	**0.82**	**0.80**
FT AWV	0.72	0.76	0.71
AWV	0.74	0.76	0.71
LDA	**0.79**	0.80	0.79

Table 5: Results for IMDB Sentiment.

BoW vectors. We also consider PCA, which directly uses the PPMI weighted BoW vectors as input, and which avoids the quadratic complexity of the MDS method. As our third method, we consider Doc2vec, which is inspired by the Skip-gram model (Le and Mikolov, 2014). Finally, we also learn semantic spaces by averaging word vectors, using a pre-trained GloVe word embeddings trained on the Wikipedia 2014 + Gigaword 5 corpus[6]. While simply averaging word vectors may seem naive, this was found to be a competitive approach for unsupervised representations in several applications (Hill et al., 2016). We consider two variants, In the first variant (denoted by AWV), we simply average the vector representations of the words that appear at least twice in the BoW representation, or at least 15 times in the case of the movies dataset. The second variant (denoted by AWVw) uses the same words, but weights the vectors by PPMI score. As a comparison method, we also include results for LDA.

Methodology. As candidate words for learning the initial directions, we only consider sufficiently frequent words. The thresholds we used are 100 for the movies dataset, 50 for the place-types, 30 for 20 newsgroups, and 50 for the IMDB sentiment dataset. We used the logistic regression implementation from scikit-learn to find the directions. We deal with class imbalance by weighting the positive instances higher.

For hyperparameter tuning, we take 20% of the data from the training split as development data. We choose the hyperparameter values that maximize the F1 score on this development data. As candidate values for the number of dimensions of the vector spaces we used $\{50, 100, 200\}$. The number of directions to be used as input to the clustering algorithm was chosen from $\{500, 1000, 2000\}$. The number of clusters was chosen from $\{k, 2k\}$, with k the chosen number of dimensions. For the hidden layer of the neural network, we fixed the number of dimensions as equal to the number of clusters. As the scoring metric for the dimensions, we considered accuracy, Kappa and NDCG. In all experiments, we used 300 epochs, a minibatch size of 200, and the tanh activation function for the hidden layer of the neural network. We train the network using Ada-Grad (Duchi et al., 2011), with default values, and the model was implemented in the Keras library. As the performance of LDA can be sensitive to the number of topics and other parameters, we tuned the number of topics from $\{50, 100, 200, 400\}$, the topic word prior from $\{0.1, 0.01, 0.001\}$ and the document topic prior $\{0.1, 0.01, 0.001\}$.

[6]https://nlp.stanford.edu/projects/glove/

To learn the decision trees, we use the scikit-learn implementation of CART, which allows us to limit the depth of the trees. To mitigate the effects of class imbalance, the less frequent class was given a higher weight during training.

5.2 Results

Table 3 shows the results for the 20 newsgroups dataset, where we use FT to indicate the results with fine-tuning[7]. We can see that the fine-tuning method consistently improves the performance of the depth-1 and depth-3 trees, often in a very substantial way. After fine-tuning, the results are also consistently better than those of LDA. For the unbounded trees (DN), the differences are small and fine-tuning sometimes even makes the results worse. This can be explained by the fact that the fine-tuning method specializes the space towards the selected features, which means that some of the structure of the initial space will be distorted. Unbounded decision trees are far less sensitive to the quality of the directions, and can even perform reasonably on random directions. Interestingly, depth-1 trees achieved the best overall performance, with depth-3 trees and especially unbounded trees overfitting. Since MDS and AWV perform best, we have only considered these two representations (along with LDA) for the remaining datasets, except for the IMDB Sentiment dataset, which is too large for using MDS.

The results for the movies and place-types datasets are shown in Table 4. For the MDS representations, the fine-tuning method again consistently improved the results for D1 and D3 trees. For the AWV representations, the fine-tuning method was also effective in most cases, although there are a few exceptions. What is noticeable is that for movie genres, the improvement is substantial, which reflects the fact that genres are a salient property of movies. For example, the decision tree for the genre 'Horror' could use the feature direction for $\{gore, gory, horror, gruesome\}$. Some of the other datasets refer to more specialized properties, and the performance of our method then depends on whether it has identified features that relate to these properties. It can be expected that a supervised variant of this method would perform consistently better in such cases.

After fine-tuning, the MDS based representation outperforms LDA on the movies dataset, but not for the place-types. This is a consequence of the fact that some of the place-type categories refer to very particular properties, such as geological phenomena, which may not be particularly dominant among the Flickr tags that were used to generate the spaces. In such cases, using a BoW based representation may be more suitable.

Finally, the results for IMDB Sentiment are shown in Table 5. In this case, the fine-tuning method fails to make meaningful improvements, and in some cases actually leads to worse results. This can be explained from the fact that the feature directions which were found for this space are themes and properties, rather than aspects of binary sentiment evaluation. The fine-tuning method aims to improve the representation of these properties, possibly at the expense of other aspects.

6 Conclusions

We have introduced a method to identify and model the salient features from a given domain as directions in a semantic space. Our method is based on the observation that there is a trade-off between accurately modelling similarity in a vector space, and faithfully modelling features as directions. In particular, we introduced a post-processing step, modifying the initial semantic space, which allows us to find higher-quality directions. We provided qualitative examples that illustrate the effect of this fine-tuning step, and quantitatively evaluated its performance in a number of different domains, and for different types of semantic space representations. We found that after fine-tuning, the feature directions model the objects in a more meaningful way. This was shown in terms of an improved performance of low-depth decision trees in natural categorization tasks. However, we also found that when the considered categories are too specialized, the fine-tuning method was less effective, and in some cases even led to a slight deterioration of the results. We speculate that performance could be improved for such categories by integrating domain knowledge into the fine-tuning method.

Acknowledgments

This work has been supported by ERC Starting Grant 637277.

---

[7]Since the main purpose of this first experiment was to see whether fine-tuning improved consistently across a broad set of representations, here we considered a slightly reduced pool of parameter values for hyperparameter tuning.

References

David M. Blei and John D. Lafferty. 2005. Correlated topic models. In *Advances in Neural Information Processing Systems 18*, pages 147–154.

David M. Blei, Andrew Y. Ng, Michael I. Jordan, and John Lafferty. 2003. Latent dirichlet allocation. *Journal of Machine Learning Research*, 3:2003.

Antoine Bordes, Nicolas Usunier, Jason Weston, and Oksana Yakhnenko. 2013. Translating embeddings for modeling multi-relational data. In *In Advances in Neural Information Processing Systems 26. Curran Associates, Inc*, pages 2787–2795.

Berkan Demirel, Ramazan Gokberk Cinbis, and Nazli Ikizler-Cinbis. 2017. Attributes2classname: A discriminative model for attribute-based unsupervised zero-shot learning. In *IEEE International Conference on Computer Vision*, pages 1241–1250.

J. Derrac and S. Schockaert. 2015. Inducing semantic relations from conceptual spaces: a data-driven approach to plausible reasoning. *Artificial Intelligence*, pages 74–105.

John Duchi, Elad Hazan, and Yoram Singer. 2011. Adaptive Subgradient Methods for Online Learning and Stochastic Optimization. *Journal of Machine Learning Research*, 12:2121–2159.

Manaal Faruqui, Jesse Dodge, Sujay Kumar Jauhar, Chris Dyer, Eduard Hovy, and Noah A Smith. 2015. Retrofitting word vectors to semantic lexicons. In *Proceedings of the 2015 Conference of the North American Chapter of the Association for Computational Linguistics: Human Language Technologies*, pages 1606–1615.

Peter Gärdenfors. 2004. *Conceptual Spaces: The Geometry of Thought*. MIT press.

Abhijeet Gupta, Gemma Boleda, Marco Baroni, and Sebastian Pad. 2015. Distributional vectors encode referential attributes. In *Proceedings of the 2015 Conference on Empirical Methods in Natural Language Processing*.

Ulrike Hahn and Nick Chater. 1998. Similarity and rules: distinct? exhaustive? empirically distinguishable? *Cognition*, 65:197 – 230.

Kazuma Hashimoto, Pontus Stenetorp, Makoto Miwa, and Yoshimasa Tsuruoka. 2015. Task-oriented learning of word embeddings for semantic relation classification. *CoRR*, abs/1503.00095.

Felix Hill, Kyunghyun Cho, and Anna Korhonen. 2016. Learning distributed representations of sentences from unlabelled data. In *Proceedings of the 2016 Conference of the North American Chapter of the Association for Computational Linguistics: Human Language Technologies*, pages 1367–1377.

Shoaib Jameel, Zied Bouraoui, and Steven Schockaert. 2017. Member: Max-margin based embeddings for entity retrieval. In *Proceedings of the 40th International ACM SIGIR Conference on Research and Development in Information Retrieval*, pages 783–792.

Kalervo Järvelin and Jaana Kekäläinen. 2002. Cumulated gain-based evaluation of IR techniques. *ACM Transactions on Information Systems*, 20(4):422–446.

Joo-Kyung Kim and Marie-Catherine de Marneffe. 2013. Deriving adjectival scales from continuous space word representations. In *Proceedings of the 2013 Conference on Empirical Methods in Natural Language Processing*, pages 1625–1630. ACL.

Adriana Kovashka, Devi Parikh, and Kristen Grauman. 2012. Whittlesearch: Image search with relative attribute feedback. In *IEEE Conference on Computer Vision and Pattern Recognition*, pages 2973–2980.

Igor Labutov and Hod Lipson. 2013. Re-embedding words. In *Proceedings of the 51st Annual Meeting of the Association for Computational Linguistics*, pages 489–493.

Quoc V. Le and Tomas Mikolov. 2014. Distributed representations of sentences and documents. In *Proceedings of the 31th International Conference on Machine Learning*, pages 1188–1196.

Dawen Liang, Jaan Altosaar, Laurent Charlin, and David M Blei. 2016. Factorization meets the item embedding: Regularizing matrix factorization with item co-occurrence. In *Proceedings of the 10th ACM Conference on Recommender Systems*, pages 59–66.

Edward Loper and Steven Bird. 2002. NLTK: The natural language toolkit. In *Proceedings of the ACL-02 Workshop on Effective Tools and Methodologies for Teaching Natural Language Processing and Computational Linguistics*, pages 63–70.

Tomas Mikolov, Ilya Sutskever, Kai Chen, Greg Corrado, and Jeffrey Dean. 2013. Distributed representations of words and phrases and their compositionality. In *Proceedings of the 26th International Conference on Neural Information Processing Systems - Volume 2*, NIPS'13, pages 3111–3119, USA. Curran Associates Inc.

Jeffrey Pennington, Richard Socher, and Christopher Manning. 2014. Glove: Global vectors for word representation. In *Proceedings of the 2014 Conference on Empirical Methods in Natural Language Processing (EMNLP)*, pages 1532–1543. Association for Computational Linguistics.

Michal Rosen-Zvi, Thomas Griffiths, Mark Steyvers, and Padhraic Smyth. 2004. The author-topic model for authors and documents. In *Proceedings of the 20th Conference on Uncertainty in Artificial Intelligence*, UAI '04, pages 487–494, Arlington, Virginia, United States. AUAI Press.

Sascha Rothe and Hinrich Schütze. 2016. Word embedding calculus in meaningful ultradense subspaces. In *ACL (2)*. The Association for Computer Linguistics.

Steven Schockaert and Jae Hee Lee. 2015. Qualitative reasoning about directions in semantic spaces. In *Proceedings of the Twenty-Fourth International Joint Conference on Artificial Intelligence*, pages 3207–3213. AAAI Press.

Duyu Tang, Furu Wei, Bing Qin, Nan Yang, Ting Liu, and Ming Zhou. 2016. Sentiment embeddings with applications to sentiment analysis. *IEEE Transactions on Knowledge and Data Engineering*, 28:496–509.

Yee Whye Teh, Michael I. Jordan, Matthew J. Beal, and David M. Blei. 2004. Sharing clusters among related groups: Hierarchical dirichlet processes. In *Proceedings of the 17th International Conference on Neural Information Processing Systems*, NIPS'04, pages 1385–1392, Cambridge, MA, USA. MIT Press.

Amos Tversky. 1977. Features of similarity. *Psychological review*, 84:327–352.

Christophe Van Gysel, Maarten de Rijke, and Evangelos Kanoulas. 2016. Learning latent vector spaces for product search. In *Proceedings of the 25th ACM International on Conference on Information and Knowledge Management*, pages 165–174.

Christophe Van Gysel, Maarten de Rijke, and Evangelos Kanoulas. 2017. Structural regularities in text-based entity vector spaces. In *Proceedings of the ACM SIGIR International Conference on Theory of Information Retrieval*, pages 3–10.

Flavian Vasile, Elena Smirnova, and Alexis Conneau. 2016. Meta-prod2vec: Product embeddings using side-information for recommendation. In *Proceedings of the 10th ACM Conference on Recommender Systems*, pages 225–232.

Paolo Viappiani, Boi Faltings, and Pearl Pu. 2006. Preference-based search using example-critiquing with suggestions. *Journal of Artificial Intelligence Research*, 27:465–503.

Jesse Vig, Shilad Sen, and John Riedl. 2012. The tag genome: Encoding community knowledge to support novel interaction. *ACM Transactions on Interactive Intelligent Systems*, 2(3):13:1–13:44.

Xuerui Wang and Andrew McCallum. 2006. Topics over time: a non-markov continuous-time model of topical trends. In *Proceedings of the 12th ACM SIGKDD international conference on Knowledge discovery and data mining*, pages 424–433. ACM.

Liang-Chih Yu, Jin Wang, K Robert Lai, and Xuejie Zhang. 2017. Refining word embeddings for sentiment analysis. In *Proceedings of the 2017 Conference on Empirical Methods in Natural Language Processing*, pages 534–539.

Model Transfer with Explicit Knowledge of the Relation between Class Definitions

Hiyori Yoshikawa and **Tomoya Iwakura**
Fujitsu Laboratories Ltd., Kanagawa, Japan
`{y.hiyori, iwakura.tomoya}@jp.fujitsu.com`

Abstract

This paper investigates learning methods for multi-class classification using labeled data for the *target* classification scheme and another labeled data for a similar but different classification scheme (*support* scheme). We show that if we have prior knowledge about the relation between support and target classification schemes in the form of a *class correspondence table*, we can use it to improve the model performance further than the simple multi-task learning approach. Instead of learning the individual classification layers for the support and target schemes, the proposed method converts the class label of each example on the support scheme into a set of candidate class labels on the target scheme via the class correspondence table, and then uses the candidate labels to learn the classification layer for the target scheme. We evaluate the proposed method on two tasks in NLP. The experimental results show that our method effectively learns the target schemes especially for the classes that have a tight connection to certain support classes.

1 Introduction

Machine learning based methods have shown high performance in many NLP tasks, which typically are formulated as some kinds of classification problems. Although there has been a remarkable progress in methods utilizing unlabeled resources, many tasks still require a large amount (at least thousands, in some cases millions or billions) of high quality labeled data to achieve high accuracy.

For many tasks, however, classification schemes vary depending on fields of application or other factors, and large and high quality labeled data following a single scheme is insufficient. Named entity recognition (NER) (Nadeau and Sekine, 2007) and text classification (TC) (Joachims, 1998) are typical examples that allow variable

classification schemes. For example, there are two kinds of NE type definitions for Japanese NER: IREX (Sekine and Isahara, 2000) with eight entity types and Sekine's extended NE (ENE) hierarchy with 200 entity types (Sekine et al., 2002). These two schemes are relevant but not in complete correspondence, *i.e.*, a class in ENE is not necessarily a proper subclass of a class in IREX and vice versa. For example, entities with `LOCATION` type in IREX are (a subtype of) `LOCATION` or `FACILITY` in ENE, while some entities with `FACILITY` type in ENE can also be `ORGANIZATION` in IREX. It is also the case that a classification scheme for an existing model is revised. In the case of news categolization, for example, a new category such as `world cup` would be added at a certain point of time; or the articles about eSports would newly categorised the existing `sports` category.

To obtain labeled data following the desired scheme, it is often required to create them almost from scratch or modify existing annotation because the existing data follow partly different schemes. However, the annotation processes to create such on-demand labeled data usually take too much cost to obtain enough data.

This paper addresses the methods to utilize the existing large amount of labeled data with a different classification scheme (*support scheme*) to learn a good model for the *target scheme* with a small amount of corresponding labeled data. One possible solution is the multi-task learning approach (Caruana, 1997) in which the model for each classification scheme is learned while sharing the model parameters for the input representation. A drawback of typical multi-task approaches is that they cannot exploit relation between two schemes directly, even if we know it in advance. The problem becomes critical when it is required to *preserve* the classification performance on the

Proceedings of the 22nd Conference on Computational Natural Language Learning (CoNLL 2018), pages 541–550
Brussels, Belgium, October 31 - November 1, 2018. ©2018 Association for Computational Linguistics

classes that are tightly connected to those of the support scheme. This corresponds to the following practical situation. We have a model working on some systems, and are required to modify it to adapt to a new classification scheme given only a small amount of examples related to the change of the scheme. It is also required that the performance of the retrained model is almost unchanged for the input examples that is not related to the change of the scheme. In the simple multi-task learning, the classification layer for the target scheme is learned only from the small labeled data for the target scheme. Such small data are often insufficient to learn *existing* classes in spite of the shared input representation.

In this paper, we propose a method to exploit the relation between the two classification schemes which is given in the form of a class correspondence table described in Section 3. Instead of learning the individual classification layers for the support and target schemes, the proposed method converts the class label of each example on the support scheme into a set of candidate class labels on the target scheme via the class correspondence table, and then uses it to learn the classification layer for the target scheme using the *learning with multiple labels* framework (Jin and Ghahramani, 2002). The difference from the typical multi-task learning methods is that the large amount of labeled data on the support scheme are directly used to learn the classification layer for the target scheme. It enables the model to learn the target scheme while preserving the performance on those classes which are tightly connected to the support scheme effectively. We conduct experiments for two tasks in NLP to verify the effectiveness of our proposed method.

The contribution of this paper is as follows.

- We propose a method to utilize the known relation of the two classification schemes by using the relation as an explicit constraint.

- We evaluated the proposed method on two task with public data and original but reproducible classification schemes.

The proposed method has the following advantages.

- We can utilize the prior knowledge on the relation between the support and the target classification schemes to effectively constrain the model.

- The method can learn the classes existing in the support scheme, even when the target labeled data contain few or no examples on these classes.

- It can also be used for such tasks in which the output is structured and difficult to be separated, *e.g.*, NER.

- The proposed method can be applied to the most of current neural network based models which output a probability distribution and take loss to update parameters with learning method such as SGDs. There is no need to violate the original network architecture.

2 Preliminaries

2.1 Problem Settings

The goal is to learn a classification scheme (*target scheme*) $f_\mathrm{T} : \mathcal{X} \to \mathcal{Y}_\mathrm{T}$ for a certain input space $\mathcal{X}$ (*e.g.*, sentences) and a set of class labels $\mathcal{Y}_\mathrm{T}$. We assume that the model to learn takes an input $x \in \mathcal{X}$ and predicts a probability distribution $p_\mathrm{T}(y|x; \theta_\mathrm{T})$ over $\mathcal{Y}_\mathrm{T}$, where θ_T represents the model parameters to learn. We focus on the situation that we have only a small amount of labeled data $D_\mathrm{T} = \{(x_i, y_i)\}_{i=1}^{N_\mathrm{T}}$. Instead, we have a large amount of labeled data $D_\mathrm{S} = \{(x_i, y_i)\}_{i=1}^{N_\mathrm{S}}$, where x_i is from the same input space $\mathcal{X}$ and the same domain distribution but y_i is from a different set of class labels $\mathcal{Y}_\mathrm{S}$. We denote $f_\mathrm{S} : \mathcal{X} \to \mathcal{Y}_\mathrm{S}$ by the classification scheme (*support scheme*) followed by D_S. In addition, we have prior knowledge about the relation between these two schemes f_S and f_T. We introduce the relation formally in Section 3.

In general, we can assume multiple support and target schemes. But this paper describes the cases of a single support scheme and a single target scheme for simplicity. Note that the formulation in the following can be extended to multi-support and multi-target cases straightforwardly.

2.2 Multi-task Learning

We first review simple multi-task learning on two tasks, which we use as a baseline as well as the basis of the proposed method.

In multi-task learning, the probability ditributions on both $\mathcal{Y}_\mathrm{S}$ and $\mathcal{Y}_\mathrm{T}$ are learned simultaneously with sharing a part of their model parameters. Let θ_R denote the shared part, θ_CT the part specific to the target model , and θ_CS the parameters specific to the support model. Then the probability distributions on the support and the target schemes can be written as $p_S(y|x; \theta_R, \theta_{CS})$ and $p_T(y|x; \theta_R, \theta_{CT})$, respectively.

For training, the following loss function is minimized:

$$L_{MT} = L_T + \lambda L_S, \tag{1}$$

where

$$L_T = -\frac{1}{N_T} \sum_{(x,y) \in D_T} \log p_T(y|x; \theta_R, \theta_{CT}), \tag{2}$$

$$L_S = -\frac{1}{N_S} \sum_{(x,y) \in D_S} \log p_S(y|x; \theta_R, \theta_{CS}), \tag{3}$$

and λ is a real-valued hyperparameter for specifying the weight of the support loss.

2.3 Learning with Multiple Labels

In learning with multiple labels (LwML) framework, each training example (x, Y) consists of an input x and a set of candidate labels Y instead of a single true label. It is assumed that the only one label in Y is correct for x, and the objective is to learn a classifier that maps inputs to the correct labels. To deal with the problem, the loss fucntion consists of the likelihood for the predicted distribution to be high within the candidate label set:

$$l_{ML}(x, Y, p) = \log \sum_{y \in Y} p(y|x). \tag{4}$$

3 Proposed Methods

In this section, we introduce relations between schemes in the form of *class correspondence table*, and how it is used for training a classifier for the target scheme.

3.1 Class Correspondence Table

We suppose that the two schemes introduced in Section 2.1 have a strong relation in that for an input x, the candidates for its class on the target scheme can be limited by its class on the support scheme. Here we give examples for two scheme sets introduced in Section 1. For Japanese NE type definitions, an entity with LOCATION type in IREX definition can be (a subtype of) LOCATION or FACILITY in ENE, but it cannot be other type such as PERSON, DISEASE or COLOR. For

news categolization, sports category in the target scheme comes only from sports and the categories which include articles about eSports in the support scheme.

Formally, we consider the following *class correspondence table*. The class correspondence table $\mathcal{T}$ is a map from a class in $\mathcal{Y}_S$ to a set of classes in $\mathcal{Y}_T$. It functions as a constraint on the target scheme f_T. Namely, the class $y_T = f_T(x)$ must be a member of $\mathcal{T}(y_S)$, where $y_S = f_S(x)$.

There are some possible ways to construct a class correspondence table. One is to define it by hands. For example, if the ontology related to the classification scheme is known, it is straightforward to define the class correspondence table according to the ontology. Another way is to define it from data. First, we apply the model learned for the support scheme to the examples in the labeled data for the target scheme. Then, we obtain pairs of labels on the support and the target schemes. The class correspondence table can be defined by allowing the pair that appears in the dataset at a certain frequency. While the method can automatically define the relation, there is a risk to drop the possible relation that is not found in the given dataset, or because of the insufficient model accuracy. We propose a model to alleviate the problem in Section 3.3.

3.2 Multi-Task Learning with Multiple Candidate Labels

For training, the following loss function is minimized:

$$L_{CS} = L_T + \lambda L_{SCS}, \tag{5}$$

where

$$L_{SCS} = -\frac{1}{N_S} \cdot$$
$$\sum_{(x,y) \in D_S} l_{ML}(x, \mathcal{T}(y), p_T(y|x; \theta_R, \theta_{CT})), \tag{6}$$

with a real-valued hyperparameter λ. The first term corresponds to the loss from the target dataset, and the second for the support dataset in the form of LwML with candidate classes given by the class correspondence table. Compared with the simple multi-task learning, our method trains only θ_T (*i.e.* θ_R and θ_{CT}) and does not require the parameters specific to support scheme. We call this model as **Class Shift constraint (CS)** model.

To get an intuition, let us see the special cases. If the support scheme is equal to the target scheme and the class correspondence is identity, then the loss (5) behaves just like a single-task learning with labeled data consisting of the support and the target data. If the class correspondence table allows all class shift for all classes in the support scheme, then L_{SCS} is always zero and so the support dataset has completely no effect on training.

3.3 Combination with Simple Multi-Task Learning

While CS model can exploit the prior knowledge about class correspondence, it has a potential problem that the class correspondence table can work inadequately. For example, if we construct the class correspondence table from some data automatically, there can be some overlooked relation because they just do not exist in the given data.

To overcome this problem, we propose an extention of the CS model which relaxes the class shift constraint by combining it with the loss from the simple multi-task learning:

$$L_{MTCS} = L_T + \lambda \left\{ \mu L_{SCS} + (1 - \mu) L_S \right\}, \quad (7)$$

with an additional hyperparameter $\mu \in [0, 1]$. We call this model as **Multi-Task with Class Shift constraint (MTCS)** model.

3.4 Training

For the following experiments with neural-based models, we adopt training by stochastic gradient descent (SGD) with mini-batches. For each iteration, we sample b examples from each of the support and the target labeled data, where b is the mini-batch size. Then the loss is calculated by (5) or (7) for the batch.

We suppose that the model is trained with a large amount of labeled data on the support scheme. When such labeled data is unavailable, however, it is possible to obtain pseudo-labeled data by applying the model for the support scheme to unlabeled data, and use them to train the model for the target scheme.

4 Experiments

We evaluated the proposed method on two tasks: named entity recognition (NER) and text classification (TC).

To examine the effectiveness of the proposed method, we adopted datasets that are not only large but also accompanied with well-organized ontology. We defined the target schemes following the exsiting shared tasks, while we defined different support schemes according to their ontology so that the labels correspond to the different level or granularity in the same ontology. By doing so, we can compare the proposed method with an ideal settings where all data is labeled according to the target scheme, which can be seen as an upper bound.

4.1 Named Entity Recognition (NER) task

We conducted NER task on GENIA corpus. GENIA corpus (Kim et al., 2003) was developed as a resource for text mining in biomedical literature. It contains annotated text for 2,000 Medline abstracts, and the annotated information includes term annotation for entities related to biological components such as proteins, genes and cells.

As described in (Kim et al., 2003), the entities are annotated according to hierarchical ontology, and have 36 types. BioNLP / JNLPBA shared task (Kim et al., 2004) is organized by GENIA project as well. The task is to extract named entities of 5 types, which is defined by integrating the above 36 types following the ontology.

We used the JNLPBA definition as the target scheme, and made another definition for the support scheme. We show the class correspondence in Table 1. Note that the O (no tag) class in the target scheme corresponds to Nucleic_acid and O classes in the support scheme. It means that the shift from the support scheme to the target scheme involves both class subdivision and integration. We also note that we follow BIOES (Collobert et al., 2011) representation to convert the NE tags into the word-level class labels. It means that each NE class (say XXX) except O corresponds to 4 word-level classes (S-XXX, B-XXX, I-XXX, and E-XXX). We construct the class correspondence table by associating the labels with same prefix for each corresponding label pair. For instance, if a class XXX in the support scheme corresponds to the label YYY in the target scheme, the word-level class label S-XXX corresponds to S-YYY, and so on. This setting is based on a strong assumption that the modification of the tagging scheme does not change the range of named entity mentions. As it is not always true, the relaxed formulation (7) is expected to work better.

We created the NER input for the support

Support scheme	Target scheme	Original GENIA ontology
`Nucleic_acid`	DNA	DNA (5 types)
	RNA	RNA (5 types)
	O (no tag)	`polynucleotide, nucleotide`
`Protein`	`Protein`	`protein` (7 types)
`O` (no tag)	`Cell_type`	`cell_type`
	`Cell_line`	`cell_line`
	O (no tag)	others (15 types) + no tag

Table 1: Class correspondence table for NER task.

Support		
Sentences		14838
Types	`Nucleic_acid`	6954
	`Protein`	26777

Target	Train	Dev	Test
Sentences	2966	742	3856
Types	DNA	1868	412	1056
	RNA	206	50	118
	`Protein`	3634	1257	5067
	`Cell_type`	887	241	1921
	`Cell_line`	635	176	500

Table 2: Data statistics of NER task.

scheme from the original GENIA corpus. For tokenization we used NLTK (Bird et al., 2009), and then broke tokens at the start and the end of the entity mentions. Since the task does not allow overlap of entity mentions, we chose the shortest mentions and discarded longer ones when mentions are nested in the original corpus. We used JNLPBA dataset as the input for the target scheme. Table 2 shows the statistics of the dataset.

4.2 Text Classification (TC) task

For TC, we used DBpedia ontology classification dataset created by (Zhang et al., 2015). Each sample in the dataset consists of the description text and the class of a DBpedia (Lehmann et al., 2015) entry. The entries are chosen from 14 ontology classes. We use these classes as the target scheme, and defined the support scheme by integrating the categories into 5 classes. The class correspondence is shown in Table 3. Table 4 shows the statistics of the dataset.

4.3 Baseline Methods

We compare the following methods with the proposed methods CS and MTCS described in Section 3.

- **Target Only** trains a model with only labeled data on the target scheme.

- **Finetune** method first trains a model with labeled data on the support scheme. Then, the model for the target scheme is trained for another set of labeled data with the shared part θ_R of the parameters initialized with the value trained on the support data (Razavian et al., 2014).

- **MT** is the multi-task learning method described in Section 2.2.

- **ALL Target** represents training on an ideal situation that all training examples are labeled according to the target scheme. The total number of training examples of each task is the sum of the number of labeled data for the support and the target schemes.

We also initialized model parameters for MT, CS and MTCS with the Finetune method.

4.4 Models and Training Settings

For NER, we used the model similar to the one described in (Ma and Hovy, 2016) with the same network parameters, except that we used the sum of word-level loss as in (Collobert and Weston, 2008) instead of the structural loss[1][2], mainly because of the computation time. As a result, the model is trained as a simple word-level label classification.

For TC, we used a simple softmax model which is similar to fastText (Grave et al., 2017) model with the same network parameters except we use pretrained word embeddings; we use simple softmax instead of hierarchical softmax; and only bag-of-words features are used to construct input representation.

---

[1]It is reported that its performance is competitive to the structural loss (Chiu and Nichols, 2016).

[2]The training of CRF with multiple label candidates can be found in (Tsuboi et al., 2008).

Support scheme	Target scheme
`Org`	`Company, EducationalInstitution`
`Artist`	`Artist`
`Non-artist`	`Athlete, OfficeHolder`
`Work`	`Album, Film, WrittenWork`
`Other`	`MeanOfTransportation, Building, NaturalPlace, Village, Animal, Plant`

Table 3: Class correspondence table for TC task.

Support		
Sentences		500000
Types	`Org`	70688
	`Artist`	35419
	`Non_artist`	70544
	`Work`	106162
	`Other`	212187

Target (14 classes)	Train	Dev	Test
Sentences	5000	60000	70000
Sentences / class (ave.)	357.1	4285.7	5000

Table 4: Data statistics of TC task. We show only the average number of sentences per class for target since the data is highly balanced.

Hyperparameter	NER	TC
dropout rate	0.5	0.5
batch size	10	10
initial learning rate	0.1	0.075
learning rate decay	0.1	0.05
gradient clipping	0.5	0.5
λ (MT)	1.0	1.25
λ (CS)	1.0	1.0
λ (MTCS)	1.5	1.25
μ (MTCS)	0.5	0.6

Table 5: Hyperparameter settings.

For both models, all parameters except the softmax layers on the top are shared. We implemented these models using DyNet (Neubig et al., 2017) library.

The models are trained by SGD with mini-batches as mentioned in Section 3.4, and some optimization techniques are used including dropout, learning rate decay and gradient clipping following (Ma and Hovy, 2016). The result of hyperparameter tuning on development data is described in Table 5.

We used pretrained word embeddings from

Method	NER (F1)	TC (Acc.)
Target Only	66.02	93.29
Finetune	68.29	94.71
MT	68.73	94.91
CS	**68.73**	**95.81**
MTCS	**69.12**	**95.67**
All Target	72.23	96.81

Table 6: Results for NER and TC task.

PMC open access subset (commercial use version)[3] for NER and from Wikipedia dump $(2010/10/11)$[4] for TC.

4.5 Experimental Results

All of the following results are averaged over five runs.

Table 6 shows the F1 scores for NER task and accuracy scores for TC task. For NER, the performance of CS is competitive to MT, but by combining them (MTCS) we had the improved performance. On the other hand, for TC task CS outperforms MT in a certain degree. The effect of their combination of (MTCS) is limited on this task.

We also evaluated the effect of the class shift constraint when the amount of labeled data for the target scheme is quite small. Figure 1 and Figure 2 show how the scores improve as the size of the labeled data for the target scheme increases. We can see that the advantage of CS and MTCS methods are significant especially when the size of the labeled data for the target scheme is very small.

Next, we evaluated how the models *preserve* the classification performance on the classes that are tightly connected to some classes in the support scheme. We first trained a model on the support scheme (*support model*) using the labeled data for the support scheme. Next we transfer the model for the target scheme with the labeled data

---

[3]https://www.ncbi.nlm.nih.gov/pmc/tools/openftlist/
[4]https://dumps.wikimedia.org/backup-index.html

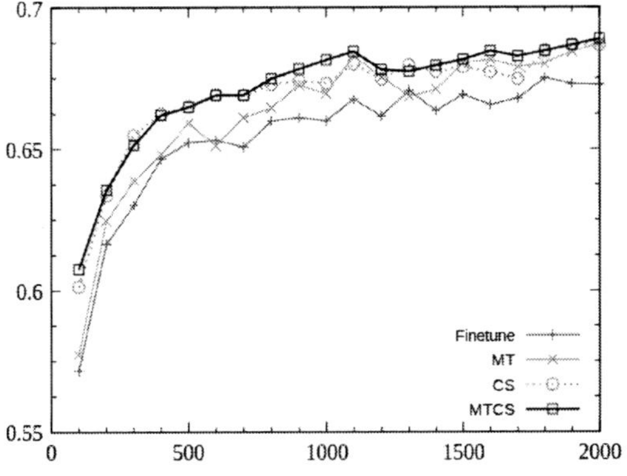

Figure 1: F1 scores with different data size on target scheme for NER task.

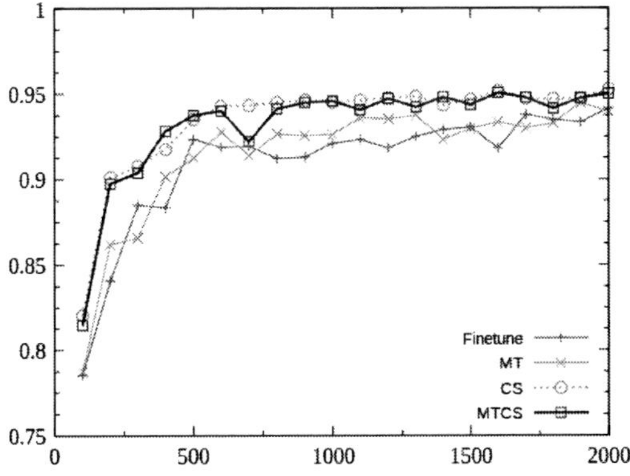

Figure 2: Accuracy scores with different data size on target scheme for TC task.

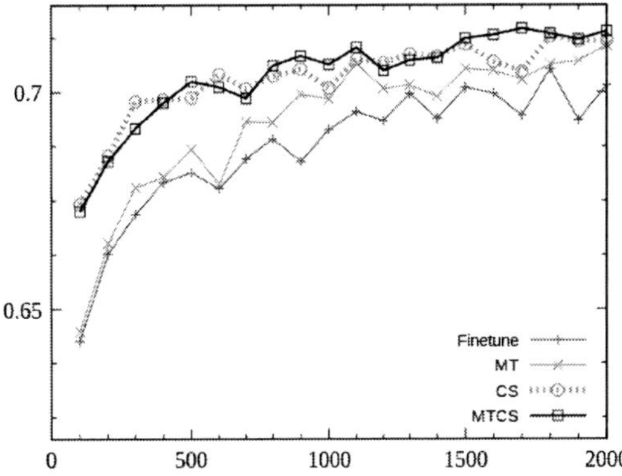

Figure 3: F1 scores with different data size on the target scheme for `Protein` class in NER task.

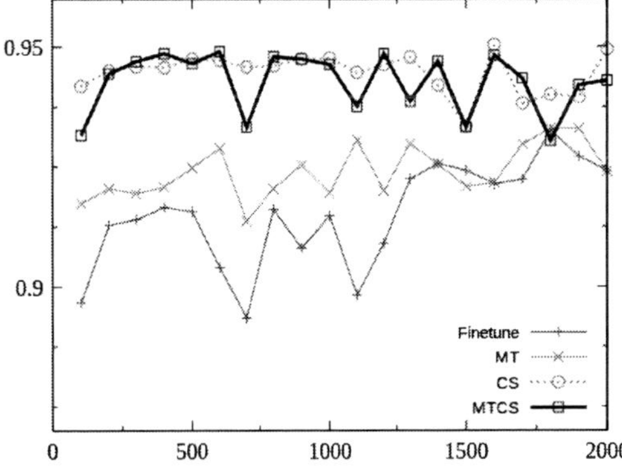

Figure 4: Accuracy scores with different data size on the target scheme for `Artist` class in TC task.

for the target scheme using Finetune, MT, CS, or MTCS. Then, test data are labeled by both the support model and the transferred model. By doing so, we can compare the classification performance of the support model and the transferred models on the *unchanged* classes for these tasks, namely `Protein` for NER and `Artist` for TC. We first check the performance of the transferred models on these classes with the small size of labeled data for the target schemes. Figure 3 and Figure 4 show the results. Compared to Finetune and MT, the performance of CS and MTCS is high even when the size of labeled data for the target scheme is very small. It suggests that the proposed methods effectively use the knowledge from support models for recognizing these classes. Table 7 shows the number of examples that are correctly classified by the transferred models out of those correctly classified by the support model. For NER task, the support model extracted 3193 out of 5067 `Protein` mentions correctly. For TC task, the support model categorized 4534 out of 5000 text with `Artist` labels correctly. We can see that the proposed methods succeed to prevent performance deterioration more effectively than Finetune and MT.

5 Related Work

Improving model performance with knowledge from other models or data sources is one of the central research topics in machine learning.

Domain adaptation methods utilize training data that have the same class definition but they come from different domains (Daumé III, 2007; Dai et al., 2007; Crammer and Mansour, 2012). These methods focus on the change of input distribution,

Method	NER-Protein	TC-Artist
Finetune	0.928 (2963)	0.966 (4380)
MT	0.933 (2979)	0.980 (4445)
CS	**0.956 (3053)**	**0.991 (4495)**
MTCS	**0.955 (3051)**	**0.989 (4486)**

Table 7: The proportion of performance preservation from the support model on unchanged classes. The numbers in the brackets represent the number of examples correctly classified by both the support and the target models.

not the classicication scheme.

Multi-task learning approaches with nerual networks often achieve this by sharing input representation among different tasks. The objectives of jointly learned tasks are often different and the mapping from the shared representation to the output for each task is learned independently (Liu et al., 2015; Hashimoto et al., 2017). Therefore, the relation between classification schemes is not directly considered.

Some studies focus on adding model capabilities to handle new tasks without storing all training data for old tasks. The central issue is to avoid catastrophic forgetting (Li and Hoiem, 2017), and several approaches have been explored (Lopez-Paz et al., 2017; Kirkpatrick et al., 2017; Triki et al., 2017). As with standard multi-task learning, many studies in this line assume different tasks with task-specific output models. iCaRL (Rebuffi et al., 2017) assumes a different problem named class-incremental learning. A stream of new class examples is observed and the model is required at any time to perform as a multi-class classifier on the classes observed so far. However, modifying the classification scheme on observed samples is not considered in this framework.

Knowledge distillation (Hinton et al., 2015) is another topic of knowledge transfer, which can be used to simplify a large complex classification model such as ensemble model by letting a simple model imitate the output distributions of the complex model instead of predicted labels. It is also used for preventing catastrophic forgetting in continual learning (Rebuffi et al., 2017; Shmelkov et al., 2017).

Learning with Hierarchy and Exclusion (HEX) graph (Deng et al., 2014) is a promising method utilizing pre-defined relationship between class labels. HEX graph can express exclusion and sub-sumption relations between class labels. Despite that it is originally used for a different kind of problems (multi-class classification which allows multiple labels for an input), it is possible to solve our problem setting in this framework. In fact, we can construct a HEX graph by assigning exclusive edges to all class pairs within the same scheme and to class pairs from different schemes which do not correspond in the class correspondence table. One of the main advantages of our method is the computational cost. Inference with HEX graph is sometimes computationally prohibitive depending on the graph structure, while inference with our model is not affected by the structure of the class correspondence table. In addition, HEX graph approach requires parameters of both support and target classes even at inference. Hence it is not suitable if the classification scheme can change many times.

Another related framework is semi-supervised learning, which use both labeled and unlabeled data. The approaches include use of classifiers trained with automatically generated training data from unlabeled data (Ando and Zhang, 2005), use of automatically labeled data (Suzuki and Isozaki, 2008), language model (Peters et al., 2017, 2018) trained from unlabeled data, and so on. In discriminative models, knowledge from unlabled data is often incorporated in the models as improved input representation or additional features. Since our method does not restrict input representation, such semi-supervised methods can be easily combined.

6 Conclusion

We have proposed a training method for the setting where we have only a small amount of labeled data for the target scheme, but have access to a large amount of labeled data for a related support scheme with the class correspondence table. The experimental results on a named entity recognition task and a text classification task showed that our proposed methods outperform finetune and simple multi-task learning methods.

Although the experiment for NER task showed that MTCS model has potential to work with a possibly incomplete class correspondence table, further experiments are necessary to verify its effectiveness on automatically generated class correspondence tables. Future work also includes applying our method to improve models learned from a single corpus by combining other corpora with different schemes, experiments on multi-support and multi-target settings, and extensions to the case where input domain of labeled data for support and target schemes are different.

References

Rie Kubota Ando and Tong Zhang. 2005. A high-performance semi-supervised learning method for text chunking. In *Proc. of ACL*, pages 1–9.

Steven Bird, Ewan Klein, and Edward Loper. 2009. *Natural Language Processing with Python*, 1st edition. O'Reilly Media, Inc.

Rich Caruana. 1997. Multitask learning. *Machine learning*, 28(1):41–75.

Jason Chiu and Eric Nichols. 2016. Named entity recognition with bidirectional LSTM-CNNs. *Transactions of the Association for Computational Linguistics*, 4:357–370.

Ronan Collobert and Jason Weston. 2008. A unified architecture for natural language processing: Deep neural networks with multitask learning. In *Proc. of ICML*, pages 160–167.

Ronan Collobert, Jason Weston, Léon Bottou, Michael Karlen, Koray Kavukcuoglu, and Pavel Kuksa. 2011. Natural language processing (almost) from scratch. *Journal of Machine Learning Research*, 12(Aug):2493–2537.

Koby Crammer and Yishay Mansour. 2012. Learning multiple tasks using shared hypotheses. In *Proc. of NIPS*, pages 1484–1492.

Wenyuan Dai, Qiang Yang, Gui-Rong Xue, and Yong Yu. 2007. Boosting for transfer learning. In *Proc. of ICML*, pages 193–200.

Hal Daumé III. 2007. Frustratingly easy domain adaptation. In *Proc. of ACL*, pages 256–263.

Jia Deng, Nan Ding, Yangqing Jia, Andrea Frome, Kevin Murphy, Samy Bengio, Yuan Li, Hartmut Neven, and Hartwig Adam. 2014. Large-scale object classification using label relation graphs. In *Proc. of ECCV*, pages 48–64.

Edouard Grave, Tomas Mikolov, Armand Joulin, and Piotr Bojanowski. 2017. Bag of tricks for efficient text classification. In *Proc. of EACL*, pages 427–431.

Kazuma Hashimoto, Yoshimasa Tsuruoka, Richard Socher, et al. 2017. A joint many-task model: Growing a neural network for multiple nlp tasks. In *Proc. of EMNLP*, pages 1923–1933.

Geoffrey Hinton, Oriol Vinyals, and Jeffrey Dean. 2015. Distilling the knowledge in a neural network. In *NIPS Deep Learning and Representation Learning Workshop*.

Rong Jin and Zoubin Ghahramani. 2002. Learning with multiple labels. In *Proc. of NIPS*, pages 921–928.

Thorsten Joachims. 1998. Text categorization with support vector machines: Learning with many relevant features. In *Proc. of ECML*, pages 137–142.

Jin-Dong Kim, Tomoko Ohta, Yuka Tateisi, and Jun'ichi Tsujii. 2003. GENIA corpus – a semantically annotated corpus for bio-textmining. *Bioinformatics*, 19(Supplement 1):i180–i182.

Jin-Dong Kim, Tomoko Ohta, Yoshimasa Tsuruoka, Yuka Tateisi, and Nigel Collier. 2004. Introduction to the bio-entity recognition task at jnlpba. In *Proc. of JNLPBA*, pages 70–75.

James Kirkpatrick, Razvan Pascanu, Neil Rabinowitz, Joel Veness, Guillaume Desjardins, Andrei A Rusu, Kieran Milan, John Quan, Tiago Ramalho, Agnieszka Grabska-Barwinska, et al. 2017. Overcoming catastrophic forgetting in neural networks. *Proc. of the National Academy of Sciences U.S.A.*

Jens Lehmann, Robert Isele, Max Jakob, Anja Jentzsch, Dimitris Kontokostas, Pablo N Mendes, Sebastian Hellmann, Mohamed Morsey, Patrick Van Kleef, Sören Auer, et al. 2015. DBpedia–a large-scale, multilingual knowledge base extracted from Wikipedia. *Semantic Web*, 6(2):167–195.

Zhizhong Li and Derek Hoiem. 2017. Learning without forgetting. *IEEE Transactions on Pattern Analysis and Machine Intelligence*.

Xiaodong Liu, Jianfeng Gao, Xiaodong He, Li Deng, Kevin Duh, and Ye-Yi Wang. 2015. Representation learning using multi-task deep neural networks for semantic classification and information retrieval. In *Proc. of NAACL*, pages 912–921.

David Lopez-Paz et al. 2017. Gradient episodic memory for continual learning. In *Proc. of NIPS*, pages 6467–6476.

Xuezhe Ma and Eduard Hovy. 2016. End-to-end sequence labeling via bi-directional LSTM-CNNs-CRF. In *Proc. of ACL*, pages 1064–1074.

David Nadeau and Satoshi Sekine. 2007. A survey of named entity recognition and classification. *Lingvisticae Investigationes*, 30(1):3–26.

Graham Neubig, Chris Dyer, Yoav Goldberg, Austin Matthews, Waleed Ammar, Antonios Anastasopoulos, Miguel Ballesteros, David Chiang, Daniel Clothiaux, Trevor Cohn, Kevin Duh, Manaal Faruqui, Cynthia Gan, Dan Garrette, Yangfeng Ji, Lingpeng Kong, Adhiguna Kuncoro, Gaurav Kumar, Chaitanya Malaviya, Paul Michel, Yusuke Oda, Matthew Richardson, Naomi Saphra, Swabha Swayamdipta, and Pengcheng Yin. 2017. DyNet: The dynamic neural network toolkit. *arXiv preprint arXiv:1701.03980*.

Matthew Peters, Waleed Ammar, Chandra Bhagavatula, and Russell Power. 2017. Semi-supervised sequence tagging with bidirectional language models. In *Proc. of ACL*, pages 1756–1765.

Matthew E. Peters, Mark Neumann, Mohit Iyyer, Matt Gardner, Christopher Clark, Kenton Lee, and Luke Zettlemoyer. 2018. Deep contextualized word representations. In *Proc. of NAACL*.

Ali Sharif Razavian, Hossein Azizpour, Josephine Sullivan, and Stefan Carlsson. 2014. CNN features off-the-shelf: An astounding baseline for recognition. In *Proc. of CVPR workshops*, pages 806–813.

Sylvestre-Alvise Rebuffi, Alexander Kolesnikov, and Christoph H. Lampert. 2017. iCaRL: Incremental classifier and representation learning. pages 5533–5542.

Satoshi Sekine and Hitoshi Isahara. 2000. IREX: IR & IE evaluation project in japanese. In *Proc. of LREC*, pages 1977–1980.

Satoshi Sekine, Kiyoshi Sudo, and Chikashi Nobata. 2002. Extended named entity hierarchy. In *Proc. of LREC'02*.

Konstantin Shmelkov, Cordelia Schmid, and Karteek Alahari. 2017. Incremental learning of object detectors without catastrophic forgetting. In *2017 IEEE International Conference on Computer Vision (ICCV)*, pages 3420–3429.

Jun Suzuki and Hideki Isozaki. 2008. Semi-supervised sequential labeling and segmentation using gigaword scale unlabeled data. In *Proc. of ACL*, pages 665–673.

Amal Rannen Triki, Rahaf Aljundi, Matthew B. Blaschko, and Tinne Tuytelaars. 2017. Encoder based lifelong learning. *Proc. of ICCV*, pages 1329–1337.

Yuta Tsuboi, Hisashi Kashima, Shinsuke Mori, Hiroki Oda, and Yuji Matsumoto. 2008. Training conditional random fields using incomplete annotations. In *Proc. of COLING*, pages 897–904.

Xiang Zhang, Junbo Zhao, and Yann LeCun. 2015. Character-level convolutional networks for text classification. In *Proc. of NIPS*, pages 649–657.

Aiming to Know You Better Perhaps Makes Me a More Engaging Dialogue Partner

Yury Zemlyanskiy
University of Southern California
Los Angeles, CA 90089
`yury.zemlyanskiy@usc.edu`

Fei Sha
Netflix
Los Angeles, CA 90028
`fsha@netflix.com`[*]

Abstract

There have been several attempts to define a plausible motivation for a chit-chat dialogue agent that can lead to engaging conversations. In this work, we explore a new direction where the agent specifically focuses on discovering information about its interlocutor. We formalize this approach by defining a quantitative metric. We propose an algorithm for the agent to maximize it. We validate the idea with human evaluation where our system outperforms various baselines. We demonstrate that the metric indeed correlates with the human judgments of engagingness.

1 Introduction

There has been a significant progress in creating end-to-end data-driven dialogue systems (Ritter et al., 2011; Vinyals and Le, 2015; Serban et al., 2017; Shang et al., 2015; Sordoni et al., 2015). The general scheme is to view dialogues as a sequence transduction process. This process is then modeled with the sequence-to-sequence (SEQ2SEQ) neural network (Sutskever et al., 2014) whose parameters are fit on large dialogue corpora such as OpenSubtitles (Tiedemann, 2009). What is especially appealing about these systems is that they do not require hand-crafted rules to generate reasonable responses in the open-domain dialogue (i.e., chit-chat) setting.

An important goal of such systems is to be able to have a meaningful and engaging conversation with a real person. Despite the progress, however, this goal remains elusive — current systems often generate generic and universally applicable responses (to any questions) such as *"I do not know"*. While such responses are reasonable in isolation, collectively too many of them are per-

ceived as dull and repetitive (Sordoni et al., 2015; Serban et al., 2017; Li et al., 2016a,b).

It remains open what metrics to use to optimize a data-driven model to produce highly engaging dialogues (Liu et al., 2016). Li et al. (2016b,a) propose to use several heuristic criteria: how easy to answer the utterance with non-generic response, how grammatical the response is, etc. Zhang et al. (2018) suggests to use pre-defined facts about the conversation agents as the context for the dialogue. Specifically, conditioning on those facts (called "memories" in their approach), the dialogue becomes "personalized", purposefully coherent and is perceived being more engaging.

In this paper, we investigate a different approach which leverages the following intuition: an engaging dialogue between two agents is a conversation that is focused and intends to **_discover_** information with the goal of increased understanding of each other. In other words, discovering implies asking engaging and inquisitive questions that are not meant to be answered with dull responses.

How do we use these intuitions to build engaging dialogue chatbots? Imagine a dialogue between a chatbot and a human. The human has facts about herself and is willing to share with the chatbot. The chatbot has only a vague idea what those facts might be – for instance, it knows out of 100 possible ones, 3 of them are true. The chatbot's initial utterance could be random as it has no knowledge of what the 3 are. However, the chatbot wants to be engaging so it constantly selects utterances so that it can use them to identify those 3 facts. This is in spirit analogous to a (job) interview: the HR representative (i.e., our interviewer "chatbot") is trying to figure out the personality characteristics (i.e., "facts") of the applicant (i.e., the "human" interviewee). A successful interview implies that the HR representative was able to get as much information about the applicant as possi-

---

[*]*On leave from U. of Southern California (feisha@usc.edu)*

Proceedings of the 22nd Conference on Computational Natural Language Learning (CoNLL 2018), pages 551–561
Brussels, Belgium, October 31 - November 1, 2018. ©2018 Association for Computational Linguistics

ble within a limited amount of time, while dull and repetitive questions are avoided at all cost. In other words, the amount of gathered information can be seen as a proxy measure to the engagingness of the dialogue.

We have implemented such an "interview" setting to validate our intuitions. First, we have developed a metric called DISCOVERYSCORE that can measure how much information has been gathered by the chit-chat bot after a dialogue. During a dialogue, we show how this metric can be used to guide the chatbot's generation of responses at its turns — these responses are selected so that they lead to the highest expected DISCOVERYSCORE. To identify such responses, the chit-chat chatbot needs to simulate how its human counterpart would react. To this end, we have proposed an improved version of the personalized chatbot (Zhang et al., 2018) and use it as the chit-chat bot's model of the human. Finally, we perform human studies on the Amazon Mechanical Turk platform and demonstrate the positive correlation between DISCOVERYSCORE and the engagingness scores assessed by human evaluators on our chit-chat bot.

The rest of the paper is organized as the follows. We discuss briefly the related work in Section 2. In Section 3, we then describe various components in our approach: the metric DISCOVERYSCORE for assessing how engaging an dialogue is, a chatbot model that is used in our study, and a response selection procedure for our chatbot to yield engaging conversations. We report empirical studies in Section 4 and conclude in Section 5.

2 Related Work

One of the biggest challenges for chit-chat bots is the lack of the exact objective for models to optimize. This stands in stark contrast to task-oriented dialogue systems (Wen et al., 2016; Su et al., 2016b).

Several heuristic criteria are proposed in (Li et al., 2016a,b) as objectives to optimize. Asghar et al. (2017) proposes humans-in-the-loop to select the best response out of a few generated candidates. Cheng et al. (2018) uses an additional input signal – the specificity level of a response, which is estimated by certain heuristics at training time and can be varied during evaluation.

Another way to address the lack of the explicit objective function is to predict many possible responses at once. Zhou et al. (2017) maps the input message to the distribution over intermediate factors, each of which produces a different response. Similarly, (Zhao et al., 2017; Shen et al., 2018; Gu et al., 2018) use variants of *variational autoencoder*. These approaches are complementary to defining the objective for dialogue models, as an external reward can further guide the response generation and simplify learning such one-to-many mappings.

Liu et al. (2016) hypothesizes that creating a perfect metric for automatic evaluation (so it can be used to optimize a dialogue model to be more engaging, at least in principle) is as hard as creating human-like dialogue system itself. The authors also note that some of the common automatic evaluation metrics (of generated texts) like BLEU, METEOR or ROGUE correlate poorly with human judgments of engagingness. Lowe et al. (2017) suggests a metric ADEM, which is trained to mimic human evaluators. While it's shown to have better correlation with the scores assigned by humans, it also gives preference to safer and generic responses.

In our work, we propose to measure how much information the chit-chat bot has gathered about its human counterpart as a proxy to the engagingness of the dialogue. To the best of our knowledge, this metric has not been explored actively in the design of chit-chat bots.

To apply the metric to generate engaging utterances, the chit-chat bot needs to have a model of how the human partner will respond to its utterances. To this end, we have used the chit-chat bot developed in (Zhang et al., 2018) as a base model and improved upon it. That bot, called PROFILE-MEMORY, has a set of memories (basically, factual sentences) defining its persona and can output personalized utterances using those memories. Note that in (Zhang et al., 2018) PROFILEMEMORY is used as a chit-chat bot to generate contextualized dialogue (so as to be engaging). In our work, however, we use it and its improved version as a model of how humans might chat. Our chit-chat bots can be any existing ones (such as a vanilla SEQ2SEQ model without persona) or another PROFILEMEMORY with its own persona that is different from what humans might have. The key difference is that our chit-chat bot generates utterances to elicit human counterparts to reveal about themselves while PROFILEMEMORY in its original work generates utterances to tell stories about itself.

Similar ideas have been explored in cognitive research. Rothe et al. (2016) analyzed how people ask questions to elicit information about the world within a *Battleship* game (Gureckis and Markant, 2009). In particular, they proposed to evaluate questions based on *Expected Information Gain* (Oaksford and Chater, 1994), which is built on the similar principles as DISCOVERYSCORE.

3 Method

In the following section, we describe in details our approach for designing engaging chit-chat bots. We start by describing the main idea, followed by discussing each component in our approach.

3.1 Main Idea

The main idea behind our approach is that the chit-chat bot stays in "discovery" mode. Its main goal is to identify key aspects of its human counterpart. Algorithmically, it chooses utterances to elicit responses from the human so that the responses increase its understanding of the human.

More formally, imagine each human is characterized by a collection of K facts $F = \{z_1, z_2, \ldots, z_K\}$, where z_1 is *I was born in Russia*, z_2 is *My favorite vegetable is carrot*, and z_K is *I like to swim*. The chit-chat bot has access to a universal set of all candidate facts $\mathcal{U}$, and F is just a subset of $\mathcal{U}$. However, the bot does not know the precise composition of F at the beginning of the conversation. Its goal is to identify the subset (or to reduce the uncertainty about it). With a bit abuse of terminology, we call F the personality of the human or the persona.

We denote a dialogue as a sequence of sentences $h_N = [s_1, t_1, ..., s_N, t_N]$ where s_n denotes the sentences by the chit-chat bot and t_n denotes the ones by the human.

3.2 A Metric for Measuring Engagingness

The chit-chat bot assumes that the human's response t is generated probabilistically when it is the human's turn to respond to the chit-chat bot's utterance s

$$P(t \mid s, F) = \sum_{z \in F} P(t \mid s, z) P(z \mid s, F) \quad (1)$$

Intuitively, the human first decides on which fact z she plans to use (ie, which information she wants to reveal) and based on the fact and the chit-chat bot's question, she provides an answer.

The goal of the *discovery oriented* chit-chat is to maximize the mutual information between the dialogue and the revealed personality

$$\mathcal{I}(F; h_N) = \mathbb{H}[P(F)] - \mathbb{H}[P(F \mid h_N)] \quad (2)$$

where $\mathbb{H}[\cdot]$ stands for the entropy of the distribution. Maximizing the mutual information is equivalent to minimizing the uncertainty about F after a dialogue. Intuitively, the chit-chat bot aims to discover the maximum amount of knowledge about the human. We thus term this quantity as the DISCOVERYSCORE.

For simplicity, we assume a uniform prior on which F is. Thus, the key quantity to compute is the entropy of the posterior probability. We proceed in two steps.

Calculating the posterior probability We assume that every human's response t_n is independent from the previous dialogue history, conditioned on the immediately previous message, and chatbot's question s_n is independent unconditionally. Thus, the posterior can be computed recursively:

$$P(F \mid h_N) \approx$$
$$P(F \mid h_{N-1}) \sum_{f \in F} P(z_N = f \mid s_N, t_N) \quad (3)$$

where z_N is the fact used in the Nth turn. The "single-turn" posterior for the specific fact f is computed as (we have dropped the subscript N to be cleaner)

$$P(z = f \mid s, t) =$$
$$\frac{P(t \mid s, z = f) P(z = f \mid s)}{\sum_{f' \in \mathcal{U}} P(t \mid s, z = f') P(z = f' \mid s)} \quad (4)$$

We will make a further simplifying assumption that $P(z = f' \mid s)$ is uniform[1] and compute the

---

[1] This is only an approximation: the human will respond to "what kind of food do you like?" with any facts that relate to food but definitely not to geographical locations, sports, etc. However, this assumption is not as damaging as long as $P(t \mid s, z = f)$ is almost zero for the z that $P(z = f \mid s)$ should be ignored – the multiplication would result in zero anyway. Since z refers to the fact, $P(t|s, z = f)$ being almost zero reduces to suggest that for a response t, there are just only a very limited number of s (questions) and facts that can be used to generate that response. For example, a response *"I lived in Russia as a child"* can only be elicited from *"Where did you spend your childhood?"* (as question) and *"I was born in Russia"* (as a fact). For any other question and fact pair (such as *"Where did you spend your childhood?"*,

posterior approximately

$$P(z = f \mid s, t) \approx \frac{P(t \mid s, z = f)}{\sum_{f' \in \mathcal{U}} P(t \mid s, z = f')} \quad (5)$$

Substituting this into the expression for $P(F \mid h_N)$, we obtain

$$P(F \mid h_N) \approx$$
$$P(F \mid h_{N-1}) \frac{\sum_{f \in F} P(t_N \mid s_N, z_N = f)}{\sum_{f \in \mathcal{U}} P(t_N \mid s_N, z_N = f)} \quad (6)$$

Acute readers might have identified this as a form of Bayesian belief update, incorporating new evidence at time N. The likelihood $P(t_N \mid s_N, z_N = f)$ depends on how to model how the human generates responses. It is sufficient to note that this probability can be computed conveniently by personalized chatbot models. We postpone the details to the next section.

Calculating the entropy We make an assumption that the number of facts K assigned to the human is known in advance. Therefore, we can consider only probabilities $P(F \mid h_N)$, where F is of a particular known size.

$$P(F \mid h_N, |F| = K) = \frac{P(F \mid h_N)}{\sum\limits_{F' \subset \mathcal{U}, |F'| = K} P(F' \mid h_N)}$$
$$(7)$$

The entropy of distribution $P(F \mid h_N, |F| = K)$ can be computed directly by enumerating all possible combinations of K facts.

3.3 ChatBot Models

In our work, there are two types of chatbot models. The first one is the chit-chat bot who will respond to messages from the human conversation partner. While we can use any existing chatbot models, the key ingredient to our approach is to respond so that the expected gain of knowledge on the human is increased. However, since the chit-chat bot cannot inquire the human with "if I answer you this, would I gain knowledge?", it has to estimate the gain in knowledge from its model of the human. The second type of model addresses the aspect of modeling the human. In particular, among the 3 models described below, all 3 can be used as the chit-chat bot models and only PROFILEMEMORY and PROFILEMEMORY$^+$ can be used as the model of humans[2].

SEQ2SEQ dialogue model This basic model maps an input message t to a vector representation using the encoder LSTM layer and uses it as an initial state h_0^d for the decoder LSTM layer. The decoder predicts a response s sequentially, word by word via softmax. Both the encoder and the decoder share the same input embeddings table.

PROFILEMEMORY model PROFILEMEMORY (Zhang et al., 2018) is built on top of SEQ2SEQ and uses exactly the same architecture for the encoder. Additionally, it has a list of memory slots (called *profile memory*) and each slot stores a fact, represented by a sentence. Each fact is encoded into a single vector representation using the weighted average of its word embeddings where the embeddings table is shared with the encoder and the decoder. In this work, we call the profile memory as the personality.

The decoder is an LSTM layer with attention over the encoded memories. In essence, the attention mechanism computes a weight for each fact and a weighted sum of the facts form a context vector. The context vector and the hidden states are combined as inputs to a softmax layer to generate words sequentially. For details, please consult (Zhang et al., 2018)

PROFILEMEMORY$^+$ model The PROFILE-MEMORY has a weakness that is especially critical to our intent of using it as a model of the human. It has to apply attention at every step, even when responding to messages which are not relevant to any of the facts. Thus it always reveals something about the personality (unless the attention is uniform, generally hard to achieve in practice). To address this issue, we enhance the model with a *DefaultFact*, which does not correspond to any real sentence. It does have a vector representation (as other facts do) except the representation is learned during the training. An advantage is that the *DefaultFact* allows to efficiently train on the dialogue datasets without profile memories, such as OpenSubtitles – intuitively it is the bucket for "all other facts" that the dialogue does not explicitly refer to.

---

and *"I like apples"*), the response would be unlikely. We believe this is largely due to the experimental/data design that has ensured facts are being largely non-overlapping for each personality and the dialogues are in general centered around the facts. We leave to future work on how to refine this approximation.

[2]In our empirical studies, we use PROFILEMEMORY$^+$ most of the time as it is more powerful than the other two.

3.4 Dialoguing with Intent to Discover

As a metric, DISCOVERYSCORE can only be computed over and assess a finished dialogue. How can we leverage it to encourage the chit-chat bot to be more engaging? In what follows, we describe one of the most important components in our approach.

Instead of using the standard maximum a posterior inference for the typical SEQ2SEQ (and its variants) to generate a sentence, we proceed in two steps to identify the best utterance that has the potential to yield high DISCOVERYSCORE. The first step is to generate a large set of candidate utterances (for example, using beam search). The second step is to re-rank these utterances. We describe the second step in details as the first step is fairly standard.

At the Nth turn of the dialogue, the chit-chat bot has access to the dialogue history h_{N-1} and an estimate of the human's personality $P(F \mid h_{N-1})$. Let s be a sentence from the chatbot's candidate set. Since the bot has a model of the human, it can predict the human's response t as

$$t \sim P(\cdot \mid h_{N-1}, s, F) = P(\cdot \mid s, F) \quad (8)$$

where F is used to instantiate the model's memory/facts/personality – in other words, we query the model to see what kind of utterances the human might respond with.

The value of a possible response s, i.e, the expected DISCOVERYSCORE assuming s and t completes the dialogue with $h_N = [h_{N-1}, s, t]$, is then given by

$$V(s) = \mathbb{E}_{F \sim P(\cdot|h_{N-1})} \mathbb{E}_{t \sim P(\cdot|s,F)} \mathcal{I}(F; h_N) \quad (9)$$

Note that the first expectation is needed as the bot has uncertainty of what personality the human is. In practice, we compute this for each s from the candidate set by sampling F and t. We then select the optimal utterance that maximize the value

$$s_N = \arg\max_s V(s) \quad (10)$$

4 Experiments

We evaluate empirically the proposed approach in several aspects. First, we investigate the effectiveness of the proposed PROFILEMEMORY$^+$ model. This model is especially used to model human interlocutors so that it can be used by the chit-chat bot to estimate how an utterance could elicit the human partner to reveal key facts about her (cf. Section 3.4). Secondly, we investigate whether the proposed metric DISCOVERYSCORE correlates with the engagingness score of a dialogue assessed by human evaluators.

4.1 Evaluating PROFILEMEMORY$^+$

We contrast PROFILEMEMORY$^+$ to SEQ2SEQ and PROFILEMEMORY. We show that not only PROFILEMEMORY$^+$ is a stronger model for personalized chit-chat but also PROFILEMEMORY$^+$ does not reveal its personality easily. Being discreet is a highly desirable property when the model is used to simulate the human participating in the dialogue; when the facts are easily revealed, then the chit-chat bot can use generic or irrelevant questions to identify the personality thus the dialogue does not become engaging.

4.1.1 As a stronger personalized chatbot

Datasets We train all three models on the original PersonaChat dataset (Zhang et al., 2018) and the Year 2009 version of the OpenSubtitles corpus (Tiedemann, 2009). The PersonaChat data set, which consists of crowdsourced 9000 dialogues (123,000 message-response pairs in total) between two people with randomly assigned personas/personalities. There are total 1155 personalities and each personality is defined by 3 to 5 memories (facts such as *"I was born in Russia"* or *"I like to swim"*). 968 dialogues are set aside for validation and 1000 for testing. We report the perplexity of our models on this test data set. The OpenSubtitles corpus has 322,000 dialogues (1.2 million message-response pairs). During training, we augment samples from OpenSubtitles with random personas, which forces PROFILEMEMORY$^+$ to actively prioritize *DefaultFact* over these fake facts.

Implementation Details Similarly to (Zhang et al., 2018), we use a single layer LSTM for both the encoder and the decoder with hidden size of 1024 for all models. The word embeddings are of size 300 and are initialized with GloVe word vectors (Pennington et al., 2014). All models are trained for 20 epochs to maximize the likelihood of the data by using SGD with momentum with batch size 128. Learning rate is reduced by a factor of 4 if the validation perplexity has increased compared to the previous epoch. We found that *general* post-attention (Luong et al., 2015) over

Model	Datasets	Perplexity
SEQ2SEQ	P	38.08
PROFILEMEMORY	P	34.54
SEQ2SEQ	P	31.538
SEQ2SEQ	P+O	30.022
PROFILEMEMORY	P	28.406
PROFILEMEMORY	P+O	27.373
PROFILEMEMORY$^+$	P	28.098
PROFILEMEMORY$^+$	P+O	**26.807**

Table 1: Perplexity on PersonaChat test dialogues by 3 different models. For datasets, P stands for PersonaChat and O for OpenSubtitles. The first two rows are reported by (Zhang et al., 2018). The rests are from our implementation.

encoded memories gives better performance than pre-attention. Weights for encoding memories are being learned during training and are initialized with 0.01 for the top 100 frequent words, and with 1 for others. We found that this simple initialization procedure outperforms the one suggested in (Zhang et al., 2018).

Results The perplexity on the test dialogues by all of the models is contrasted in Table 1. The first two rows are previously reported in (Zhang et al., 2018). The rest results are from models implemented by us.

Our re-implementation of SEQ2SEQ and PROFILEMEMORY show better performance than what are reported in (Zhang et al., 2018), likely due to the difference in the amount of data used for training[3] , as well as model architecture (post- instead of pre-attention) and optimization procedure (e.g., SGD vs. ADAM).

Including additional data such as OpenSubtitles, in general, improves performance. Our PROFILEMEMORY$^+$ performs better than PROFILEMEMORY. This is the benefit of having *Default-Fact* (cf. Section 3.3) which re-directs the attention by the messages and responses that are not related to the real personality away it. On the other end, in PROFILEMEMORY, the attention has to select a real personality no matter what the messages or responses are.

4.1.2 As a discreet chatbot

Since we intend to use a personalized chatbot such as PROFILEMEMORY and PROFILEMEMORY$^+$ as a model of the human interlocutor, we would want the model to behave intelligently: when given an

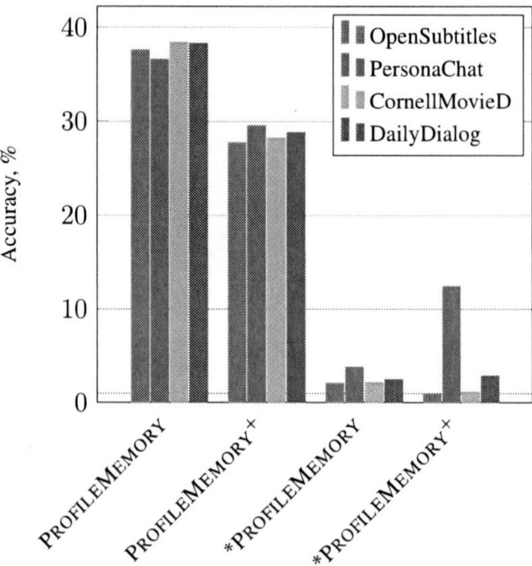

Figure 1: Average accuracies of utterances sampled from different corpora (PersonaChat, OpenSubtitles, CornellMovieDialog, DailyDialog) in revealing the personality of the human interlocutor modeled by personalized chatbots (cf. Section 4.1.2). PROFILEMEMORY and PROFILEMEMORY$^+$ have been trained on PersonaChat data set, while *PROFILEMEMORY and *PROFILEMEMORY$^+$ have been trained on both PersonaChat and OpenSubtitles.

Top 5 sentences, accuracy 29-32%
Tell me about it! What do you do for fun?
Nice! what is it that you do?
In a cabin, all by myself, hoping my grandkids will visit. any you?
You should give it a try! what do you do with your weekends?
Wow cool. what do you do in your spare time. i work on art projects.

Bottom 5 sentences (sampled), accuracy 0%
How come you were rejected?
So he can stay put
Spending the night pondering life.
Hence the fact that she survived.
Maybe she just needs a friend?

Table 2: Examples of sentences from PersonaChat dataset with the highest and the worst accuracies in revealing a personality of PROFILEMEMORY$^+$ model (trained jointly on PersonaChat and OpenSubtitles). We expect human to reply to such utterances with something which will more likely (correspondingly, less likely) reveal her personality. Note, that we don't predict human's personality from the presented utterances alone. Rather, these are considered good (correspondingly, bad) questions to get to know your interlocutor better.

---

[3]Zhang et al. (2018) only modeled the second person in dialogues, which reduces the training data by half.

irrelevant message, the model should not reveal its personality. When given a relevant message, the model reveals its personality. We can expect a similar behavior from a real human, which might reply with *"I don't know"* or *"I don't understand"*, when the question is irrelevant to them. In other words, we want to avoid simulating dialogues like this – Chatbot: *"Hmm... Thank you."*, Human (Simulation): *"I was born in Russia"*. With this adversity, the chit-chat bot has to ask meaningful and relevant questions if its goal is to discover the personality of the human interlocutor.

Experiment setup We randomly sample 100 memories/facts (out of total 5709) from the PersonaChat dataset. For simplicity, we assume the model of the human interlocutor has a simple personality, denoted by one of the 100 facts. We assign this single personality to each of the PROFILEMEMORY and PROFILEMEMORY$^+$ models trained on either the PersonalChat dataset or jointly with the OpenSubtitles dataset. So there are 4 variants in total.

We then construct a simple 2-turn dialogue, where the model is given a probing message and the model responses with a sampled utterance. We use the DISCOVERYSCORE (cf. Section 3.2) to measure how much the dialogue reveals a personality. We then select the personality that maximizes the revealing. If the selected personality is the true personality, we consider the lead message is able to accurately predict the personality. We then average all probing messages to compute the averaged accuracy.

For probing messages, we use sentences from 4 different datasets - PersonaChat, OpenSubtitles, CornellMovieDialogCorpus (Danescu-Niculescu-Mizil and Lee, 2011) and DailyDialog (Li et al., 2017). Our expectation is that an ideal model won't reveal its personality when asked a random question from OpenSubtitles or CornellMovieDialogCorpus, since most of the time it's completely irrelevant lines from a movie script. DailyDialog contains more casual conversations, so some of them we expect to be useful. Of course, the accuracy of random sentences from PersonaChat should be the highest on average, since the corpus was collected with the intent to get to know each other better.

Results The averaged accuracies from the different corpora are shown in Figure 1.

For PROFILEMEMORY$^+$ trained only on PersonaChat data, all types of sentences have similar effectiveness in predicting personality. However, after joint learning with OpenSubtitles, only sentences from PersonaChat (which are most relevant to personalities) are able to predict noticeably accurate than other sentences.

As an illustration, examples of the sentences from PersonaChat with the best and the worst accuracy are presented in the Table 2, for the PROFILEMEMORY$^+$ trained both on PersonaChat and OpenSubtitles.

These findings, together with the superior modeling ability (cf. Section 4.1.1 and Table 1), have validated the usage of PROFILEMEMORY$^+$ trained additionally on OpenSubtitles as a proper model for human interlocutors.

4.2 Human Evaluation

We report human evaluations to show that (1) DISCOVERYSCORE can be used to measure how engaging the conversation is. (2) the dialogue's quality can be increased by choosing a response with the highest expected future DISCOVERYSCORE (cf. Section 3.4).

Setup We use "The Conversational Intelligence Challenge 2"[4] evaluation procedure provided in ParlAI framework (Miller et al., 2017). We use around 200 Amazon Mechanical Turkers for human evaluation. The same procedure is also used in (Zhang et al., 2018).

During an evaluation round, a Turker is assigned a random persona (with 3-5 profile facts) from the PersonaChat dataset. Each Turker is paired with a chatbot – we experiment with several models including SEQ2SEQ and PROFILEMEMORY trained on PersonaChat and PROFILEMEMORY$^+$ model trained on both PersonaChat and OpenSubtitles. The chatbot can also adopt personal facts, but only PROFILEMEMORY and PROFILEMEMORY$^+$ are able to utilize it. Every evaluation dialogue has at least 6 turns per participant.

After the dialogue the Turker is asked to evaluate its interlocutor (i.e., the chatbot) by how fluent, engaging and consistent it is on a 1 to 5 scale (5 being the best). Our primary focus is engagingness score and we will show in below that it correlates well with the DISCOVERYSCORE we proposed. The Turker is also asked to guess the chatbot's persona out of two given persona candidates

ChatBot Model	Fluency	Engagingness	Consistency	Persona Detection, %
SEQ2SEQ	3.90 (1.24)	3.52 (1.44)	3.77 (1.32)	57.14
+ BeamSearch	4.25 (1.13)	3.51 (1.11)	3.92 (1.27)	47.41
+ BeamSearch + Re-ranking	4.64 (0.67)	**3.92** (1.14)	4.03 (1.16)	48.65
PROFILEMEMORY	4.13 (1.04)	3.62 (1.48)	3.92 (1.29)	68.57
+ BeamSearch	4.54 (0.82)	3.92 (1.09)	4.28 (1.11)	60.58
+ BeamSearch + Re-ranking	4.25 (0.97)	**4.10** (1.10)	4.22 (1.06)	70.00
PROFILEMEMORY$^+$	4.03 (1.22)	3.70 (1.22)	3.79 (1.34)	78.89
+ BeamSearch	4.59 (0.84)	3.73 (1.44)	4.16 (1.20)	61.22
+ BeamSearch + Re-ranking	4.41 (1.05)	**4.27** (1.07)	3.99 (1.26)	69.89

Table 3: Human evaluation results of various dialogues models. Every model is evaluated by its fluency, engagingness and consistency on a scale from 1 to 5. Persona Detection corresponds to how accurate a human can guess the chatbot's personality thus demonstrating how well a model utilizes the assigned persona (note, it's **not** related to DISCOVERYSCORE). Numbers in parenthesis correspond to standard deviation.

Engagingness	Average DISCOVERYSCORE	% of questions	Average Length
1	2.578 (1.697)	37.6	8.04
2	2.776 (1.923)	48.4	8.53
3	2.634 (1.837)	53.0	8.29
4	2.977 (2.044)	65.6	7.92
5	3.196 (1.682)	55.6	8.68

Table 4: Average DISCOVERYSCORE over dialogues grouped by corresponding engagingness score in different tiers. Numbers in parenthesis correspond to standard deviation.

(each with 3-5 profile facts). This metric is called "Persona Detection" and demonstrates how well the model is utilizing the assigned persona. Naturally, we expect SEQ2SEQ-based chatbots to have Persona Detection rate around 50% since they are not using provided persona at all. Each chatbot model is evaluated on at least 100 dialogues.

Response generation We experimented with both the greedy decoding (which is default) and the beam search (with 100 beam size) for text generation.

DISCOVERYSCORE-based re-ranking As described in Section 3.4, we use DISCOVERYSCORE-based re-ranking to select the response with the intent to discover the personality of the human participant. Concretely, the chatbot is given a set of 30 facts from PersonaChat data set, which does include the true facts. The chatbot is also told that the human has only 3 facts in her personality. This is mainly for computational efficiency.

The re-ranking takes place in two steps. First, the chatbot generates 100 response candidates. For every candidate, it performs 10 simulated di-

alogues with the PROFILEMEMORY$^+$ model as a proxy for the human interlocutor. Finally, it selects the response with the highest expected DISCOVERYSCORE.

Results The evaluation results are presented in the Table 3. The results clearly demonstrate that the DISCOVERYSCORE-oriented re-ranking makes conversations more engaging for all type of the chatbot models.

When re-ranking is used, many human evaluators provided a feedback stating that the model was acting "genuinely interested" and asked a lot of questions. In contrast, modeling without re-ranking had a lower engagingness score precisely because of the lack of questions.

Persona Detection score indicates that PROFILEMEMORY$^+$ is doing a better job in modeling a persona. We also see a decrease in this metric when we combine PROFILEMEMORY$^+$ with the re-ranking procedure, which is likely caused by the chatbot asking more questions than revealing itself personality.

Example dialogues between human and two PROFILEMEMORY$^+$ models with and without DISCOVERYSCORE-based re-ranking are given in

ChatBot's Persona	Human's Persona
I will graduate from college in two years.	I play piano.
My parents are divorced.	I have a ten year old son.
I could not live without my dog, Bart.	I graduated high school in 1986.
I am very popular and have a lot of friends.	I hope to become a music teacher after retirement.
I am an excellent student.	

[Human]: Hi! How are you doing?
PROFILEMEMORY$^+$: I am good how are you
DISCOVERYSCORE: I am well, thank you. How are you?

[Human]: I'm doing okay
PROFILEMEMORY$^+$: Okay.
DISCOVERYSCORE: Ok. What do you do for work?

[Human]: I'm working in some local company. How about you?
PROFILEMEMORY$^+$: I am a stay at home mom
DISCOVERYSCORE: I am a college student. Do you have any hobbies?

[Human]: I'm a musician, I'm playing piano from time to time.
PROFILEMEMORY$^+$: What city are you from?
DISCOVERYSCORE: That is cool. Do you have any hobbies?

[Human]: Not really. But I hope to become a music teacher soon. What are your hobbies?
PROFILEMEMORY$^+$: What kind of music do you like?
DISCOVERYSCORE: I like to spend time with my friends and family. You?

Table 5: Examples of the dialogue between human and chatbots: PROFILEMEMORY$^+$ model conducts only beam size for best response and DISCOVERYSCORE additionally uses DISCOVERYSCORE-based re-ranking.

the Table 5.

DISCOVERYSCORE as a proxy for Engagingness We group all the dialogues between chatbots and humans by the assigned engagingness score and compute the average DISCOVERYSCORE, average length of utterances and average percentage of generated questions - see Table 4. Interestingly enough, there is no obvious correlation between how engaging the dialogue has been perceived and simple metrics like the length of the response or the number of asked questions. On the other hand, it is strongly correlated with DISCOVERYSCORE, indicating that it indeed can be used as one of the automatic metrics for dialogues quality.

5 Conclusion & Future Work

We introduce a new metric DISCOVERYSCORE to assess the engagingness of a dialogue based on the intuition that the more interested the chatbot is in its interlocutor the more engaging the dialog becomes. We propose an improved PROFILEMEMORY$^+$ model, which achieves state-of-the-art perplexity results on the PersonaChat dataset. One appealing property of the model is that it doesn't reveal assigned personality upon irrelevant questions. We demonstrate how it can be used to estimate the expected DISCOVERYSCORE by running simulations with the model as a human substitute. A re-ranking method that uses such estimates allows us to significantly improve the dialogue engagingness score over several baselines, which we demonstrate with human evaluations.

We hope to continue exploring DISCOVERYSCORE in more general settings with richer, more complicated personalization or when profile information is not explicitly defined.

Acknowlegements

We appreciate the feedback from the reviewers. This work is partially supported by USC Graduate Fellowships, NSF IIS-1065243, 1451412, 1513966/1632803/1833137, 1208500, CCF-1139148, a Google Research Award, an Alfred P. Sloan Research Fellowship, gifts from Facebook and Netflix, and ARO# W911NF-12-1-0241 and W911NF-15-1-0484.

References

Nabiha Asghar, Pascal Poupart, Xin Jiang, and Hang Li. 2017. Deep active learning for dialogue generation. In *Proceedings of the 6th Joint Conference* on Lexical and Computational Semantics, *SEM @ACM 2017, Vancouver, Canada, August 3-4, 2017, pages 78–83. Association for Computational Linguistics.

Regina Barzilay and Min-Yen Kan, editors. 2017. *Proceedings of the 55th Annual Meeting of the Association for Computational Linguistics, ACL 2017, Vancouver, Canada, July 30 - August 4, Volume 1: Long Papers*. Association for Computational Linguistics.

Xueqi Cheng, Jun Xu, Jiafeng Guo, Yanyan Lan, Ruqing Zhang, and Yixing Fan. 2018. Learning to control the specificity in neural response generation. In *Proceedings of the 56th Annual Meeting of the Association for Computational Linguistics, ACL 2018, Melbourne, Australia, July 15-20, 2018, Volume 1: Long Papers*, pages 1108–1117. Association for Computational Linguistics.

Cristian Danescu-Niculescu-Mizil and Lillian Lee. 2011. Chameleons in imagined conversations: A new approach to understanding coordination of linguistic style in dialogs. In *Proceedings of the Workshop on Cognitive Modeling and Computational Linguistics, ACL 2011*.

Xiaodong Gu, Kyunghyun Cho, JungWoo Ha, and Sunghun Kim. 2018. Dialogwae: Multimodal response generation with conditional wasserstein auto-encoder. *CoRR*, abs/1805.12352.

Todd M Gureckis and Douglas B. Markant. 2009. Active Learning Strategies in a Spatial Concept Learning Game. *Proceedings of the 31st Annual Conference of the Cognitive Science Society*.

Jiwei Li, Michel Galley, Chris Brockett, Jianfeng Gao, and Bill Dolan. 2016a. A diversity-promoting objective function for neural conversation models. In *NAACL HLT 2016, The 2016 Conference of the North American Chapter of the Association for Computational Linguistics: Human Language Technologies, San Diego California, USA, June 12-17, 2016*, pages 110–119. The Association for Computational Linguistics.

Jiwei Li, Will Monroe, Alan Ritter, Dan Jurafsky, Michel Galley, and Jianfeng Gao. 2016b. Deep reinforcement learning for dialogue generation. In (Su et al., 2016a), pages 1192–1202.

Yanran Li, Hui Su, Xiaoyu Shen, Wenjie Li, Ziqiang Cao, and Shuzi Niu. 2017. Dailydialog: A manually labelled multi-turn dialogue dataset. In *Proceedings of the Eighth International Joint Conference on Natural Language Processing, IJCNLP 2017, Taipei, Taiwan, November 27 - December 1, 2017 - Volume 1: Long Papers*, pages 986–995. Asian Federation of Natural Language Processing.

Chia-Wei Liu, Ryan Lowe, Iulian Serban, Michael Noseworthy, Laurent Charlin, and Joelle Pineau. 2016. How NOT to evaluate your dialogue system: An empirical study of unsupervised evaluation metrics for dialogue response generation. In (Su et al., 2016a), pages 2122–2132.

Ryan Lowe, Michael Noseworthy, Iulian Vlad Serban, Nicolas Angelard-Gontier, Yoshua Bengio, and Joelle Pineau. 2017. Towards an automatic turing test: Learning to evaluate dialogue responses. In (Barzilay and Kan, 2017), pages 1116–1126.

Thang Luong, Hieu Pham, and Christopher D. Manning. 2015. Effective approaches to attention-based neural machine translation. In *Proceedings of the 2015 Conference on Empirical Methods in Natural Language Processing, EMNLP 2015, Lisbon, Portugal, September 17-21, 2015*, pages 1412–1421. The Association for Computational Linguistics.

Alexander H. Miller, Will Feng, Dhruv Batra, Antoine Bordes, Adam Fisch, Jiasen Lu, Devi Parikh, and Jason Weston. 2017. Parlai: A dialog research software platform. In *Proceedings of the 2017 Conference on Empirical Methods in Natural Language Processing, EMNLP 2017, Copenhagen, Denmark, September 9-11, 2017 - System Demonstrations*, pages 79–84. Association for Computational Linguistics.

Mike Oaksford and Nick Chater. 1994. A rational analysis of the selection task as optimal data selection. *Psychological Review*, 101(4):608–631.

Jeffrey Pennington, Richard Socher, and Christopher D. Manning. 2014. Glove: Global vectors for word representation. In *Proceedings of the 2014 Conference on Empirical Methods in Natural Language Processing, EMNLP 2014, October 25-29, 2014, Doha, Qatar, A meeting of SIGDAT, a Special Interest Group of the ACL*, pages 1532–1543. ACL.

Alan Ritter, Colin Cherry, and William B. Dolan. 2011. Data-driven response generation in social media. In *Proceedings of the 2011 Conference on Empirical Methods in Natural Language Processing, EMNLP 2011, 27-31 July 2011, John McIntyre Conference Centre, Edinburgh, UK, A meeting of SIGDAT, a Special Interest Group of the ACL*, pages 583–593. ACL.

Anselm Rothe, Brenden M. Lake, and Todd M. Gureckis. 2016. Asking and evaluating natural language questions. In *Proceedings of the 38th Annual Meeting of the Cognitive Science Society, Recogbizing and Representing Events, CogSci 2016, Philadelphia, PA, USA, August 10-13, 2016*. cognitivesciencesociety.org.

Iulian Vlad Serban, Alessandro Sordoni, Ryan Lowe, Laurent Charlin, Joelle Pineau, Aaron C. Courville, and Yoshua Bengio. 2017. A hierarchical latent variable encoder-decoder model for generating dialogues. In (Singh and Markovitch, 2017), pages 3295–3301.

Lifeng Shang, Zhengdong Lu, and Hang Li. 2015. Neural responding machine for short-text conversation. In *Proceedings of the 53rd Annual Meeting of the Association for Computational Linguistics and the 7th International Joint Conference on Natural Language Processing of the Asian Federation of Natural Language Processing, ACL 2015, July 26-31, 2015, Beijing, China, Volume 1: Long Papers*, pages 1577–1586. The Association for Computer Linguistics.

Xiaoyu Shen, Hui Su, Shuzi Niu, and Vera Demberg. 2018. Improving variational encoder-decoders in dialogue generation. In *Proceedings of the Thirty-Second AAAI Conference on Artificial Intelligence, New Orleans, Louisiana, USA, February 2-7, 2018*. AAAI Press.

Satinder P. Singh and Shaul Markovitch, editors. 2017. *Proceedings of the Thirty-First AAAI Conference on Artificial Intelligence, February 4-9, 2017, San Francisco, California, USA*. AAAI Press.

Alessandro Sordoni, Michel Galley, Michael Auli, Chris Brockett, Yangfeng Ji, Margaret Mitchell, Jian-Yun Nie, Jianfeng Gao, and Bill Dolan. 2015. A neural network approach to context-sensitive generation of conversational responses. In *NAACL HLT 2015, The 2015 Conference of the North American Chapter of the Association for Computational Linguistics: Human Language Technologies, Denver, Colorado, USA, May 31 - June 5, 2015*, pages 196–205. The Association for Computational Linguistics.

Jian Su, Xavier Carreras, and Kevin Duh, editors. 2016a. *Proceedings of the 2016 Conference on Empirical Methods in Natural Language Processing, EMNLP 2016, Austin, Texas, USA, November 1-4, 2016*. The Association for Computational Linguistics.

Pei-Hao Su, Milica Gasic, Nikola Mrksic, Lina Maria Rojas-Barahona, Stefan Ultes, David Vandyke, Tsung-Hsien Wen, and Steve J. Young. 2016b. Continuously learning neural dialogue management. *CoRR*, abs/1606.02689.

Ilya Sutskever, Oriol Vinyals, and Quoc V. Le. 2014. Sequence to sequence learning with neural networks. In *Advances in Neural Information Processing Systems 27: Annual Conference on Neural Information Processing Systems 2014, December 8-13 2014, Montreal, Quebec, Canada*, pages 3104–3112.

Jörg Tiedemann. 2009. News from OPUS – a collection of multilingual parallel corpora with tools and interfaces. In *Proceedings of Recent Advances in Natural Language Processing (RANLP)*, volume 5, pages 237–248.

Oriol Vinyals and Quoc V. Le. 2015. A neural conversational model. *CoRR*, abs/1506.05869.

Tsung-Hsien Wen, Milica Gasic, Nikola Mrksic, Lina Maria Rojas-Barahona, Pei-Hao Su, Stefan Ultes, David Vandyke, and Steve J. Young. 2016. A network-based end-to-end trainable task-oriented dialogue system. *CoRR*, abs/1604.04562.

Saizheng Zhang, Emily Dinan, Jack Urbanek, Arthur Szlam, Douwe Kiela, and Jason Weston. 2018. Personalizing dialogue agents: I have a dog, do you have pets too? *CoRR*, abs/1801.07243.

Tiancheng Zhao, Ran Zhao, and Maxine Eskénazi. 2017. Learning discourse-level diversity for neural dialog models using conditional variational autoencoders. In (Barzilay and Kan, 2017), pages 654–664.

Ganbin Zhou, Ping Luo, Rongyu Cao, Fen Lin, Bo Chen, and Qing He. 2017. Mechanism-aware neural machine for dialogue response generation. In (Singh and Markovitch, 2017), pages 3400–3407.

Neural Maximum Subgraph Parsing
for Cross-Domain Semantic Dependency Analysis

Yufei Chen♠, Sheng Huang♠, Fang Wang♠, Weiwei Sun♠♡ and Xiaojun Wan♠
♠ Institute of Computer Science and Technology, Peking University
♠ The MOE Key Laboratory of Computational Linguistics, Peking University
♡ Center for Chinese Linguistics, Peking University
`{yufei.chen,huangsheng,foundwang,ws,wanxiaojun}@pku.edu.cn`

Abstract

We present experiments for cross-domain semantic dependency analysis with a neural Maximum Subgraph parser. Our parser targets 1-endpoint-crossing, pagenumber-2 graphs which are a good fit to semantic dependency graphs, and utilizes an efficient dynamic programming algorithm for decoding. For disambiguation, the parser associates words with BiLSTM vectors and utilizes these vectors to assign scores to candidate dependencies. We conduct experiments on the data sets from SemEval 2015 as well as Chinese CCGBank. Our parser achieves very competitive results for both English and Chinese. To improve the parsing performance on cross-domain texts, we propose a data-oriented method to explore the linguistic generality encoded in English Resource Grammar, which is a precision-oriented, hand-crafted HPSG grammar, in an implicit way. Experiments demonstrate the effectiveness of our data-oriented method across a wide range of conditions.

1 Introduction

Semantic Dependency Parsing (SDP) is defined as the task of recovering sentence-internal bilexical semantic dependency structures, which encode predicate–argument relationships for all content words. Such sentence-level semantic analysis of text is concerned with the characterization of events and is therefore important to understand the essential meaning of a natural language sentence. With the advent of many supporting resources, SDP has become a well-defined task with a substantial body of work and comparative evaluation. (Almeida and Martins, 2015; Du et al., 2015a; Zhang et al., 2016; Peng et al., 2017; Wang et al., 2018). Two SDP shared tasks have been run as part of the 2014 and 2015 International Workshops on Semantic Evaluation (SemEval) (Oepen et al., 2014, 2015).

There are two key dimensions of the data-driven dependency parsing approach: decoding and disambiguation. Existing decoding approaches to syntactic or semantic analysis into bilexical dependencies can be categorized into two dominant types: transition-based (Zhang et al., 2016; Wang et al., 2018) and graph-based, i.e., Maximum Subgraph (Kuhlmann and Jonsson, 2015; Cao et al., 2017a) approaches. For disambiguation, while early work on dependency parsing focused on global linear models, e.g., structured perceptron (Collins, 2002), recent work shows that deep learning techniques, e.g., LSTM (Hochreiter and Schmidhuber, 1997), is able to significantly advance the state-of-the-art of the parsing accuracy. From the above two perspectives, i.e., the decoding and disambiguation frameworks, we find that what is still underexploited is neural Maximum Subgraph parsing for highly constrained graph classes, e.g., noncrossing graphs. In this paper, we fill this gap in the literature by developing a neural Maximum Subgraph parser.

Previous work showed that the 1-endpoint-crossing, pagenumber-2 (1EC/P2) graphs are an appropriate graph class for modeling semantic dependency structures (Cao et al., 2017a). In this paper, we build a parser that targets 1EC/P2 graphs. Based on an efficient first-order Maximum Subgraph decoder, we implement a data-driven parser that scores arcs based on stacked bidirectional-LSTM (BiLSTM) together with a multi-layer perceptron. Using the benchmark data sets from SemEval 2015 Task 18 (Oepen et al., 2015), our parser gives very competitive results for English semantic parsing. To test the ability for cross-lingual parsing, we also conduct experiments on the Chinese CCGBank (Tse and Curran, 2010) and Enju HPSGBank (Yu et al., 2010) data. Our parser plays equally well for Chinese, resulting in an error reduction of 23.5% and 9.4% over the best

562

Proceedings of the 22nd Conference on Computational Natural Language Learning (CoNLL 2018), pages 562–572
Brussels, Belgium, October 31 - November 1, 2018. ©2018 Association for Computational Linguistics

published result reported in Zhang et al. (2016) and Du et al. (2015b).

Most studies on semantic parsing focused on the in-domain setting, meaning that both training and testing data are drawn from the same domain. Even a data-driven parsing system achieves a high in-domain accuracy, it usually performs rather poorly on the out-of-domain data (Oepen et al., 2015). How to build robust semantic dependency parsers that can learn across domains remains an under-addressed problem. To improve the cross-domain parsing performance, we propose a data-oriented model to explore the linguistic generality encoded in a hand-crafted, domain-independent, linguistically-precise English grammar, namely English Resource Grammar (ERG; Flickinger, 2000). In particular, we introduce a cost-sensitive training model to learn cross-domain semantic information implicitly encoded in WikiWoods (Flickinger et al., 2010), i.e., a corpus that collects the wikipedia[1] texts as well as their automatic syntactico-semantic annotations produced by ERG. Evaluation demonstrates the usefulness of the imperfect annotations automatically created by ERG.

Our parser is available at `https://github.com/draplater/msg-parser`.

2 Semantic Dependency Parsing

2.1 Semantic Dependency Analysis

SDP is the task of mapping a natural language sentence into a formal meaning representation in the form of a dependency graph. Figure 1 shows an Minimal Recursion Semantics (MRS; Copestake et al., 2005) reduced semantic dependency analysis (Ivanova et al., 2012). In this example, the semantic analysis is represented as a labeled directed graph in which the vertices are tokens in the sentence. The graph abstracts away from syntactic analysis (e.g., the complementizer—*that*—and passive construction are excluded) and includes most semantically relevant non-anaphoric local (e.g., from "wants" to "Mark") and long-distance (e.g., from "buy" to "company") dependencies. The arc labels encode linguistically-motivated, broadly-applicable semantic relations that are grounded under the type-driven semantics. It is worth noting that semantic dependency graphs are not necessarily trees: (1) a token may be multiply headed because a word can be the arguments

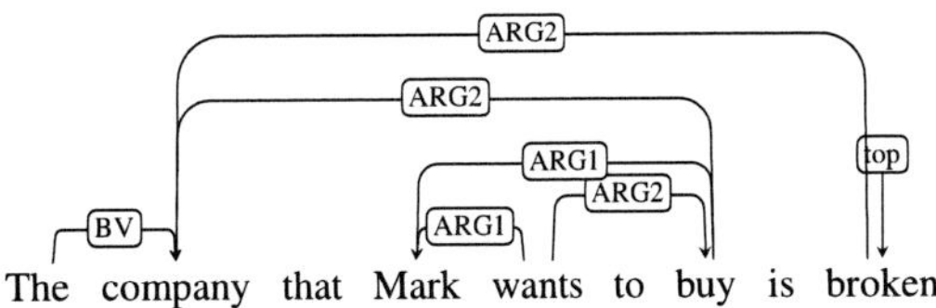

Figure 1: A fragment of a semantic dependency graph.

of more than one predicate; (2) cycles are allowed if the direction of arcs are not taken into account.

2.2 Previous Work

Some recent work on parsing targets the graph-structured semantic representations that are more general than the tree representation. Existing approaches can be categorized into two dominant types: the transition-based (Zhang et al., 2016; Wang et al., 2018) and graph-based, i.e., Maximum Subgraph (Kuhlmann and Jonsson, 2015; Cao et al., 2017a), approaches. Previous investigations on transition-based string-to-semantic-graph parsing adopt many ideas from syntactic string-to-tree parsing, such as how to handle crossing arcs and how to perform neural disambiguation. Zhang et al. (2016) introduced two transition systems that can generate arbitrary graphs and augmented them into practical semantic dependency parsers with a structured perceptron model. Wang et al. (2018) evaluated the effectiveness of deep learning techniques for transition-based SDP.

Kuhlmann and Jonsson (2015) proposed to formulate SDP as the search for the maximum subgraphs for some particular graph classes. This proposal is called Maximum Subgraph parsing, which is a generalization of the graph-based parsing framework for syntactic parsing. For arbitrary graphs, Du et al. (2015a) proved that the second-order Maximum Subgraph problem is an NP-hard problem. Nevertheless, Almeida and Martins (2015) and Du et al. (2015a) showed that dual decomposition is a practical technique to solve the problem. Considering more restricted graph classes, Kuhlmann and Jonsson (2015) introduced a dynamic programming algorithem for parsing to noncrossing graphs. Cao et al. (2017a; 2017b) showed that 1EC/P2 graphs are more suitable for describing semantic graphs than the noncrossing graphs, and they also allow low-degree dynamic programming algorithms for decoding.

---

[1] `https://www.wikipedia.org`

3   A Neural Maximum Subgraph Parser

3.1   Maximum Subgraph Parsing

Usually, syntactic dependency analysis employs the *tree*-shaped representation. Dependency parsing, thus, can be formulated as the search for a maximum spanning tree (MST) from an arc-weighted (complete) graph. For SDP where the target representation are no longer trees, Kuhlmann and Jonsson (2015) proposed to generalize the MST model to other types of subgraphs. In general, dependency parsing is formulated as the search for Maximum Subgraph regarding to a particular graph class, viz. $\mathcal{G}$: Given a graph $G = (V, A)$, find a subset $A' \subseteq A$ with maximum total weight such that the induced subgraph $G' = (V, A')$ belongs to $\mathcal{G}$. Formally, we have the following optimization problem:

$$
\begin{aligned}
G'(s) &= \arg \max_{H \in \mathcal{G}(s,G)} \text{SCORE}(H) \\
&= \arg \max_{H \in \mathcal{G}(s,G)} \sum_{p \text{ in } H} \text{SCOREPART}(s, p)
\end{aligned}
\tag{1}
$$

Here, $\mathcal{G}(s, G)$ is the set of all graphs that belong to $\mathcal{G}$ and are compatible with s and G. For parsing, G is usually a complete graph. $\text{SCOREPART}(s, p)$ evaluates whether a small subgraph p of a candidate graph H is a good partial analysis for sentence s.

For some graph classes and some types of score functions, there exists efficient algorithms for solving (1). For example, when $\mathcal{G}$ is the set of noncrossing graphs and SCOREPART is limited to handle individual dependencies, (1) can be solved in cubic-time (Kuhlmann and Jonsson, 2015).

3.2   Parsing to 1EC/P2 Graphs

Previous work showed that the Maximum Subgraph framework is not only elegant in theory but also effective in practice (Kuhlmann and Jonsson, 2015; Cao et al., 2017a,b). In particular, 1EC/P2 graphs are an appropriate graph class for modeling semantic dependency structures (Cao et al., 2017a). Figure 2 presents an example to illustrate the 1-endpoint-crossing property, while Figure 3 shows a case for pagenumber-2. Below we present the formal description of the two properties that are adopted from Pitler et al. (2013) and Kuhlmann and Jonsson (2015) respectively.

Figure 2: (a, c)'s crossing edges (b, d) and (b, e) share an endpoint b.

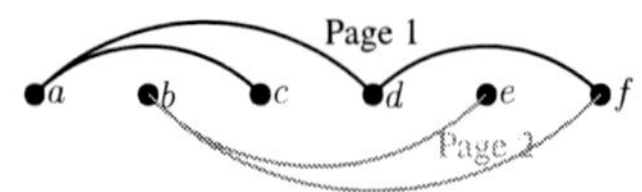

Figure 3: A pagenumber-2 graph. The upper and the lower figures represent two half-planes respectively.

Definition 1 *A dependency graph is 1-Endpoint-Crossing if for any edge e, all edges that cross e share an endpoint p named pencil point.*

Definition 2 *A pagenumber-k graph means it consists at most k half-planes, and arcs on each half-plane are noncrossing.*

If $\mathcal{G}$ is the set of 1-endpoint-crossing graphs or more restricted 1EC/P2 graphs, the optimization problem (1) in the first-order case can be solved in quintic-time (Cao et al., 2017a) by using dynamic programming. Furthermore, ignoring one linguistically-rare structure in 1EC/P2 graphs descreases the complexity to $O(n^4)$ (Cao et al., 2017a). In this paper, we implement Cao et al. Cao et al. (2017a)'s algorithm as the basis of our parser.

3.3   Disambiguation with an LSTM

3.3.1   The Architecture

A semantic graph mainly consists of two parts: the structural part and the label part. The former describes the predicate–argument relation in the sentence, and the latter describes the type of this relation. In our model, the structural part and the label part are regarded as independent of each other. We use a coarse-to-fine strategy: finding the maximum unlabeled subgraph first and assigning a label for every edge in this subgraph then. The motivation is to avoid the calculation of a number of unnecessary label scores in order to improve the processing efficiency.

Following Kiperwasser and Goldberg (2016)'s successful experience on syntactic tree parsing and Peng et al. (2017)'s experience on semantic graph parsing, we employ a stacked bidirectional-LSTM (BiLSTM) based model to assign scores. In our system, the BiLSTM vectors associated with the input words are utilized to calculate scores for the

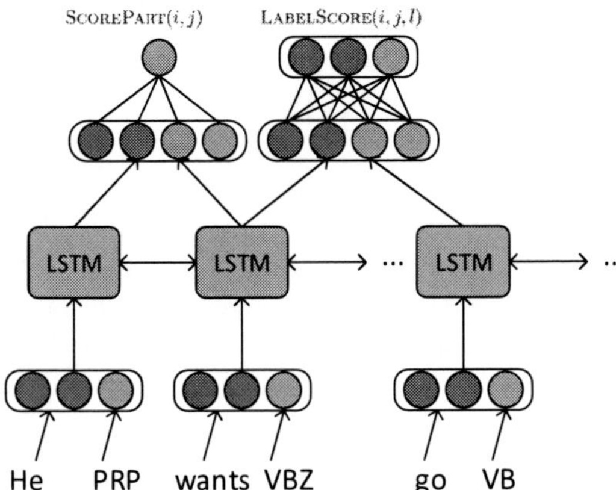

Figure 4: The architecture of the network when processing *He wants to go*. The upper-left nonlinear transform is used for edge scoring while the upper right one is used for label scoring.

candidate dependencies as well as their relation types. Figure 4 shows the architecture of our system.

3.3.2 Dense Representations

We use words as well as POS tags as clues for scoring an individual arc. In particular, we transform all of them into continuous and dense vectors. Inspired by Costa-jussà and Fonollosa (2016)'s work, we utilize character-based embedding for low-frequency words, i.e., words that appear more than k times in the training data, and word-based embeddings for other words. The word-based embedding module applies the common lookup-table mechanism, while the character-based word embedding w_i is implemented by extracting the features (denoted as $c_1, c_2, \ldots, c_n$) within a character-based BiLSTM:

$$x_1 : x_n = \mathrm{BiLSTM}(c_1 : c_n)$$

$$w_i = x_1 + x_n$$

3.3.3 Lexical Feature Extractor

The concatenation of word embedding w_i and POS-tag embedding p_i of each word in specific sentence is used as the input of BiLSTMs to extract context-related feature vectors r_i for each position i.

$$a_i = w_i \oplus p_i$$

$$r_1 : r_n = \mathrm{BiLSTM}(a_1 : a_n)$$

3.3.4 Factorized Scoring

In our first order model, the SCORE function evaluates the preference of a semantic dependency graph by considering every bilexical relation in this graph one by one. In particular, the corresponding SCOREPART function assigns a score to a candidate arc between word i and word j using a non-linear transform from the two feature vectors, viz. r_i and r_j, associated to the two words:

$$\mathrm{SCOREPART}(i, j) =$$
$$W_2 \cdot \mathrm{ReLU}(W_{1,1} \cdot r_i + W_{1,2} \cdot r_j + b)$$

The assignment task for dependency labels can be regarded as a classification task. Our label scoring process is similar to the prediction of dependencies:

$$\mathrm{LABEL}(i, j) = \arg\max$$
$$W_2 \cdot \mathrm{ReLU}(W_{1,1} \cdot r_i + W_{1,2} \cdot r_j + b) + b_2$$

We can see here the two *local* score functions explicitly utilize the positions of a semantic head and a semantic dependent. It is similar to the first-order factorization as defined in a number of linear parsing models, e.g., the models defined by Martins and Almeida (2014) and Cao et al. (2017a).

3.3.5 Training

In order to update graphs which achieve high model scores but are actually wrong, we use a margin-based approach to compute loss from the gold graph G^* and the best prediction $\hat{G}$ under current model. We define the *loss* term as:

$$\max(0, \Delta(G^*, \hat{G}) - \mathrm{SCORE}(G^*) + \mathrm{SCORE}(\hat{G}))$$

The margin objective Δ measures the similarity between the gold graph G^* and the prediction $\hat{G}$. Follow Peng et al. (2017)'s approach, we define Δ as weighted Hamming to trade off between precision and recall.

4 Cross-Domain Parsing with a Precision Grammar and a Data-Oriented Model

4.1 Precision Grammar-Guided Parsing

Semantic dependency graphs like Minimal Recursion Semantics (MRS) reduced analysis (dubbed DM) and Head-driven Phrase Structure Grammar (HPSG) grounded predicate–argument analysis (dubbed PAS) are derived from the linguistic analysis licensed by a deep linguistic grammar.

They are parallel with the deep syntactic analysis, and the semantic construction process of them is strictly compositional. Another type of domain-independent, sentence-level semantic annotations are based on annotators' reflection of the meanings of particular natural language sentences. No syntactic constraints on linguistic signals are introduced explicitly introduced. A representative example is Abstract Meaning Representation (AMR; Banarescu et al., 2013).

Different from data-driven syntactic parsing, semantic parsing for the first type of annotation can leverage a precision grammar-guided model. Such a model applies a rich set of precise linguistic rules to constrain their search for a preferable syntactic or semantic analysis. In recent years, several of these linguistically motivated parsing systems achieved high performances that are comparable or even superior to the treebank-based purely data-driven parsers. For example, using ERG (Flickinger, 2000), which provides precise linguistic analyses for a broad range of phenomena, as the the core engine, PET[2] (Callmeier, 2000) and ACE[3] produce better results than all existing data-driven semantic parsers for sentences that can be parsed by ERG.

The main weakness of the precision grammar-guided parsers is their robustness with respect to both coverage and efficiency. Even for treebanking on the newswire data, i.e., the Wall Street Journal data from Penn TreeBank, ERG lacks analyses for c.a. 11% sentences (Oepen et al., 2015). For the texts from the web, e.g., tweets, this problem is much more serious. Moreover, checking all linguistic constraints makes a grammar-guided parser too slow for many realistic NLP applications. On the contrary, light-weight, data-driven parsers usually have complementary strengthes in terms of both coverage and efficiency.

4.2 The Parser-Oriented Model

Intuitively, a hand-crafted precision grammar, e.g., ERG, reflects highly generalized properties of a particular language and is thus highly resilient to domain shifts. Accordingly, one should expect that a precision grammar-guided parser which guarantees the a rich set of domain-independent linguistic constraints to be met can be more robust to domain shifts than a purely data-driven parser.

In related work for syntactic parsing, Ivanova et al. (2013) showed that the ERG-based parser was more robust to domain variation than several representative data-driven parsers.

Zhang and Wang (2009) proposed to derive features from syntactic parses generated by PET to assist a data-driven dependency tree parser and observed some encouraging results for cross-domain evaluation. However, there are at least two drawbacks of their ERG-guided parser based method:

1. A considerable number of sentences cannot benefit from ERG since PET may produce no analysis.

2. This method fails to take parsing efficiency into account.

4.3 Our Data-Oriented Model

In this paper, we introduce a new data-oriented strategy to consume a precision grammar. The key idea is to take a grammar as an imperfect annotator: We let a precision grammar-guided parser parse large-scale raw texts in an *offline* way, and then utilize the automatically generated analysis as imperfect training data. Because we only need raw texts to be parsed once, even if this process takes much time, it is still reasonable. A grammar-guided parser cannot parse a considerable portion of data, but this will not cause serious problems because we can take an enormous amount of sentences as annotation candidates. Just considering the wikipedia, we can collect at least dozens of millions of comparatively high-quality sentences.

An essential problem of this method is that such imperfect annotations bring in annotation errors which may hurt parser training. To deal with this problem, we adopted a cost-sensitive training method to train our model on the extended training data. In each epoch, we trained on imperfect corpus first and then on gold-standard corpus. When processing an imperfect sentence, we do not take a loss into consideration if the loss of this sentence is too small. In particular, if a loss of a bilexical relation between two tokens is less than 0.05, we would exclude the loss. As for label assigning, we exclude losses less than 0.5. These threshold numbers are tuned on the development data.

---

[2]http://pet.opendfki.de/
[3]http://sweaglesw.org/linguistics/ace/

	System		DM			PAS			PSD		
			LP	LR	LF	LP	LR	LF	LP	LR	LF
IN-DOMAIN	Du et al.	ensemble	90.93	87.32	89.09	92.90	89.67	91.26	78.60	72.93	75.66
	Almeida and Martins	single	89.84	86.64	88.21	91.87	89.92	90.88	78.62	74.23	76.36
	Peng et al.	single	--	--	89.4	--	--	92.2	--	--	**77.6**
	Peng et al.	multitask	--	--	90.4	--	--	92.7	--	--	78.5
	Wang et al.	single	--	--	89.3	--	--	91.4	--	--	76.1
	Wang et al.	ensemble	--	--	90.3	--	--	91.7	--	--	78.6
	Ours	single	90.74	90.40	**90.57**	92.26	92.43	**92.35**	76.42	76.33	76.38
	Ours (E[3])	ensemble	92.17	91.35	91.76	93.50	92.98	93.24	78.83	77.07	77.95
	Ours ([E10])	ensemble	92.81	91.65	**92.23**	93.91	93.22	**93.56**	79.33	78.00	**78.66**
OUT-OF-DOMAIN	Du et al.	ensemble	84.29	79.53	81.84	89.47	85.10	87.23	77.36	69.61	73.28
	Almeida and Martins	single	84.81	78.90	81.75	88.52	85.30	86.88	78.68	71.31	74.82
	Peng et al.	single	--	--	84.5	--	--	88.3	--	--	75.3
	Peng et al.	multitask	--	--	85.3	--	--	89.0	--	--	**76.4**
	Wang et al.	single	--	--	83.2	--	--	87.2	--	--	73.2
	Wang et al.	ensemble	--	--	84.9	--	--	87.6	--	--	75.9
	Ours	single	85.70	85.02	**85.37**	89.11	88.85	**88.98**	73.54	73.19	73.36
	Ours (E[3])	ensemble	87.65	86.24	86.94	90.72	89.31	90.01	76.10	73.83	74.95
	Ours (E[10])	ensemble	88.13	86.37	**87.24**	91.19	89.50	**90.34**	76.75	74.48	75.60

Table 1: Labeled F_1 on the test data from SemEval 2015.

Hyper-parameter	Val
Randomly-initialized word embedding dimension	100
Pre-trained word embedding dimension	100
Randomly-initialized character embedding dimension	100
Character LSTM layers for each direction	2
Randomly-initialized POS-Tag embedding dimension	50
POS-Tag dropout	0.5
Batch size	32
BiLSTM dimension for each direction	150
BiLSTM layers	5
MLP hidden layers	1
MLP hidden layer dimension	100

Table 2: Hyper-parameter setting of our model.

5 Experiments

5.1 Set-up for the Baseline System

To evaluate neural Maximum Subgraph parsing in practice, we first conduct experiments on the three English data sets, namely DM, PAS and PSD[4], which are from the SemEval 2015 Task18 (Oepen et al., 2015). We use the "standard" training, validation, and test splits to facilitate comparisons. In other words, the data splitting policy follows the shared task. In addition to English parsing, we consider Chinese SDP and use two data sets: (1) Chinese PAS data provided by SemEval 2015, and (2) Chinese CCGBank (Tse and Curran, 2010) to evaluate the cross-lingual ability of our model. All the SemEval data sets are publicly available from

LDC (Oepen et al., 2016).

We use DyNet[5] to implement our neural models. We use the automatic batch technique (Neubig et al., 2017) in DyNet to perform mini-batch gradient descent training. The batch size is 32. The detailed network hyper-parameters are summarized in Table 2. We use the same pre-trained word embedding as Kiperwasser and Goldberg (2016).

5.2 Main Results of English Parsing

Table 1 lists the parsing accuracy of our system as well as the best published results in the literature for comparison. Results from other papers are of different yet representative decoding or disambiguation frameworks. Du et al. (2015a)'s and Almeida and Martins (2015)'s parsers use global linear models to perform disambiguation. These systems obtained the best parsing accuracy for the SemEval 2015 shared task. Peng et al. (2017)'s and Wang et al. (2018)'s parsers utilize neural models, LSTMs in particular, to score either arcs or transitions. Our single models get the highest scores on not only in-domain but also out-of-domain test sets for the DM and PAS data sets, and they obtain comparable results with the state-of-art parser on the PSD data set. Comparing our results to the results obtained by parsers based on linear models, we can see the effectiveness of the BiLSTM based disambiguation model. The preci-

---

[4] DM, PAS and PSD are short for DeepBank, Enju HPS-GBank and Prague Dependency Treebank.

[5] https://github.com/clab/dynet

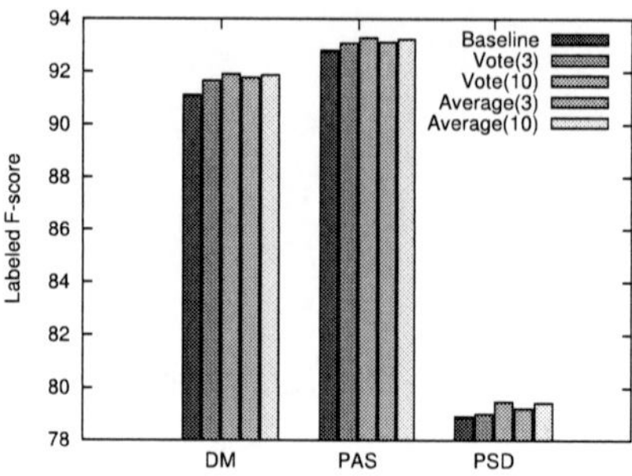

Figure 5: Labeled F_1 relative to different ensemble methods. Results are obtained on the development data.

sion of the two linear model-based parsers is comparable or even superior to our neural parser, but the recall is far behind.

5.3 Model Ensemble

Ensemble methods have been shown very helpful to boost the accuracy of neural network based parsing. We evaluate two ensemble methods, voting and score averaging. In the voting method, each model parses the sentence to graph respectively. An edge will exist on the combined graph only if more than half output graphs of these models contain this edge. The label of this edge will be the most common label. In the score averaging method, we use averaged score parts to get a maximum graph and classify labels.

We choose 3/10 kind of different initial parameters to train models for ensemble. Figure 5 shows the result of the two ensemble methods. The averaging method has slightly better performance on the 3 datasets. The performance of this method on test data is shown on Table 1.

5.4 Data for Cross-Domain Experiments

Since around 2001, the ERG has been accompanied by syntactico-semantic annotations, where for each sentence an annotator has selected the intended analysis among all alternatives licensed by the grammar. This derived resource, namly Redwoods[6] (Oepen et al., 2002; Flickinger et al., 2017), is a collection of hand-annotated corpora and consists of data sets from several distinct domains. Redwoods also includes (re)treebanking results of the first 22 sections of the venerable Wall Street Journal (WSJ) text and the section of Brown Corpus in the Penn Treebank (Marcus et al., 1993). The WSJ part is also known as Deep-

---

[6]http://moin.delph-in.net/RedwoodsTop

Bank (Flickinger et al., 2012). The Brown corpus part is used as the out-of-domain test data by SemEval 2015. The DM data sets for both SemEval 2014 and 2015 SDP shared tasks are based on the RedWoods corpus.

Besides gold standard annoations, Flickinger et al. (2010) built the WikiWoods corpus[7], which provides automatically created annotations for the texts from wikipedia. The annotations are disambiguated using the MaxEnt model trained using redwoods without DeepBank. We use a small portion of Wikiwoods, which contains 857,329 sentences in total.

To evaluate the (positive) impact of ERG on out-of-domain parsing, we conduct experiments on the DM data. The first group of experiments are designed to be comparable with the results obtained by various participant systems of SemEval 2015. The detailed data set-up is as follows:

- **Test Data**. We use the Brown corpus section which is provided by SemEval 2015.

- **Training Data**. We use three data sets for training: (1) DeepBank, (2) RedWoods and (3) a small portion of WikiWoods reparsed using the MaxEnt model trained on Deep-Bank. We denote this reparsed WikiWoods as WikiWoods-ACE, since the HPSG analysis is provided by the ACE parser. To extract the semantic dependency graph, we use the pydelphin tool[8].

For the second group of experiments, we use the section *wsj21* from the DeepBank as test data, which is the official in-domain test of the SemEval 2015. The training data includes the "RedWoods minus DeepBank" annotations (RedwoodsWOD for short) as well as the official WikiWoods annotations. Note that the MaxEnt model used to obtain the official WikiWoods annotations are compatible with RedwoodswWOD. Due to the diversity of the RedwoodsWOD and DeepBank sentences, this set-up can also be viewed as an out-of-domain evaluation.

5.5 Results of Cross-Domain Parsing

Table 3 summarizes experimental results for different cross-domain evaluation set-ups. For the

---

[7]http://moin.delph-in.net/WikiWoods
[8]https://github.com/delph-in/pydelphin

Training Data		LP	LR	LF
IN-DOMAIN (SEMEVAL)				
DeepBank	S	90.74	90.40	90.57
Redwoods	S	91.50	90.57	91.03
DeepBank+WikiWoods-ACE	S	91.93	90.72	91.32
DeepBank+WikiWoods-ACE	E[3]	92.73	91.48	92.11
OUT-OF-DOMAIN (SEMEVAL)				
DeepBank	S	85.70	85.02	85.37
Redwoods	S	86.28	84.85	85.56
DeepBank+WikiWoods-ACE	S	88.30	86.42	87.35
DeepBank+WikiWoods-ACE	E[3]	89.53	87.57	88.54
OUT-OF-DOMAIN (REDWOODSWOD)				
DeepBank	S	90.74	90.40	90.57
RedwoodsWOD	S	81.40	78.99	80.18
RedwoodsWOD+WikiWoods	S	84.05	79.86	81.90
RedwoodsWOD+WikiWoods	E[3]	84.84	81.02	82.88

Table 3: Labeled F_1 on the DM test sets. "S" denotes single model, while "E[3]" denotes ensemble model with 3 sub-models.

first group of experiments, we test the parser using different training data sets. The baseline utilizes the WSJ portion only. While more reliable training data is added, the performances increase consistently. We notice that the improvement extending the training data from DeepBank to Redwoods is quite limited for the out-of-domain evaluation. One reason is that the amount of enlarged gold standard annotations is still limited: The DeepBank training data contains 35,656 sentences (838,374 tokens, i.e., roughly words), while the additional training data contains 35,950 sentences (538,659 tokens). For comparison, we select 480,564 sentences (5,346,703 tokens) from WikiWoods to train another model, and leave out other parts of Redwoods. The performance improvement is more remarkable when providing more data, even though such data contains annotation errors. For the second group of experiments, we use the RedwoodsWOD sentences for training and the DeepBank WSJ sentences for evaluation. For this set-up, consistent improvements of the parser quality are observed.

5.6 Results of Chinese Parsing

To test the ability for cross-lingual parsing, we conduct experiments on HPSG and CCG grounded semantic analyses respectively. The HPSG grounded analysis is provided by SemEval 2015 and the underlying framework is the same to the English PAS data. The CCG grounded analysis is from Chinese CCGBank. We use the same set-up as Zhang et al. (2016). Both data sets are transformed from Chinese TreeBank with two rich sets of heuristic rules (Yu et al., 2010; Tse and Curran, 2010). Table 4 and 5 presents all results. Our parser significantly outperforms Zhang et al. (2016)'s Zhang et al. (2016) system on Chinese CCGBank, which achieved best reported performance.

Chinese POS tagging has a great impact on parsing. In this paper, we consider two POS taggers: a symbol-refined generative HMM tagger (SR-HMM) (Huang et al., 2009) and a BiLSTM-CRF model when assisting Chinese SDG. For the neural tagging model, in addition to a BiLSTM layer for encoding words, we set a BiLSTM layer for encoding characters, which supports us to derive character-level representations for all words. In particular, vectors from the character-level LSTM is concatenated with the pre-trained word embedding before feeding into the other word-level BiLSTM network to capture contextual information. The final module of our CRF tagger is a linear chain CRF which scores the output sequence by factoring it in local tag bi-grams. From Table 5, we can see that POS information is very important to Chinese SDP. This phenomenon is consist with Chinese syntactic parsing, including both constituency and dependency parsing. Mandarin Chinese is recognized as a morphology-poor language: POS tags are defined mainly according to words' distributional rather than morphological properties. The LSTM-based tagger can leverage

Model	LP	LR	LF
Peking	84.75	82.15	83.43
Ours	85.49	84.11	84.79

Table 4: Labeled F_1 on the test set of SemEval 2015 for Chinese. "Peking" is the participant system that obtained the best parsing accuracy for Chinese in SemEval 2015.

Model	POS	LP	LR	LF
ZDSW	Gold	82.09	81.81	81.95
Ours	Gold	86.37	86.00	86.19
	SR-HMM	80.19	80.53	80.37
	BiLSTM-CRF	81.13	81.74	81.43

Table 5: Labeled F_1 on the test set of Chinese CCGBank. "ZDSW" is the system that obtained the best parsing accuracy on the Chinese CCGBank data in the literature.

the power of the RNN architecture to learn non-local dependencies and thus benefit our semantic dependency parser a lot.

6 Conclusion

Parsing sentences to linguistically-rich semantic representations is a key goal of Natural Language Understanding. We introduce a new parser for semantic dependency analysis, which combines two promising parsing techniques, i.e., decoding based on Maximum Subgraph algorithms and disambiguation based on BiLSTMs. To our knowledge, this is the first neural Maximum Subgraph parser. Our parser significantly improves state-of-the-art accuracy on three out of total four data sets from SemEval 2015 for English/Chinese parsing and the CCGBank data for Chinese parsing. We also propose a new data-oriented method to leverage ERG, a linguistically-motivated, hand-crafted grammar, to improve cross-domain performance. Experiments demonstrate the effectiveness of taking ERG as an imperfect annotator. We think this method can be re-used for other types of data-driven semantic parsing models.

Acknowledgement

This work was supported by the National Natural Science Foundation of China (61772036, 61331011) and the Key Laboratory of Science, Technology and Standard in Press Industry (Key Laboratory of Intelligent Press Media Technology). We thank the anonymous reviewers for their helpful comments. Weiwei Sun is the corresponding author.

References

C. Mariana S. Almeida and T. André F. Martins. 2015. Lisbon: Evaluating TurboSemanticParser on Multiple Languages and Out-of-Domain Data. *Proceedings of SemEval 2015*.

Laura Banarescu, Claire Bonial, Shu Cai, Madalina Georgescu, Kira Griffitt, Ulf Hermjakob, Kevin Knight, Philipp Koehn, Martha Palmer, and Nathan Schneider. 2013. Abstract Meaning Representation for Sembanking. In *Proceedings of the 7th Linguistic Annotation Workshop and Interoperability with Discourse*, pages 178–186, Sofia, Bulgaria. Association for Computational Linguistics.

Ulrich Callmeier. 2000. Pet. a platform for experimentation with efficient hpsg processing techniques. *Journal of Natural Language Engineering*, 6(1):99–108.

Junjie Cao, Sheng Huang, Weiwei Sun, and Xiaojun Wan. 2017a. Parsing to 1-endpoint-crossing, pagenumber-2 graphs. In *Proceedings of the 55th Annual Meeting of the Association for Computational Linguistics (Volume 1: Long Papers)*, pages 2110–2120, Vancouver, Canada. Association for Computational Linguistics.

Junjie Cao, Sheng Huang, Weiwei Sun, and Xiaojun Wan. 2017b. Quasi-second-order parsing for 1-endpoint-crossing, pagenumber-2 graphs. In *Proceedings of EMNLP 2017*. Association for Computational Linguistics.

Michael Collins. 2002. Discriminative training methods for hidden markov models: Theory and experiments with perceptron algorithms. In *Proceedings of the 2002 Conference on Empirical Methods in Natural Language Processing*, pages 1–8. Association for Computational Linguistics.

Ann Copestake, Dan Flickinger, Carl Pollard, and Ivan A. Sag. 2005. Minimal Recursion Semantics: An introduction. *Research on Language and Computation*, pages 281–332.

Marta R. Costa-jussà and José A. R. Fonollosa. 2016. Character-based neural machine translation. In *Proceedings of the 54th Annual Meeting of the Association for Computational Linguistics (Volume 2: Short Papers)*, pages 357–361, Berlin, Germany.

Yantao Du, Weiwei Sun, and Xiaojun Wan. 2015a. A data-driven, factorization parser for CCG dependency structures. In *Proceedings of the 53rd Annual Meeting of the Association for Computational Linguistics and the 7th International Joint Conference on Natural Language Processing (Volume 1: Long Papers)*, pages 1545–1555, Beijing, China. Association for Computational Linguistics.

Yantao Du, Fan Zhang, Xun Zhang, Weiwei Sun, and Xiaojun Wan. 2015b. Peking: Building semantic dependency graphs with a hybrid parser. In *Proceedings of the 9th International Workshop on Semantic Evaluation (SemEval 2015)*, pages 927–931, Denver, Colorado. Association for Computational Linguistics.

Dan Flickinger. 2000. On building a more efficient grammar by exploiting types. *Nat. Lang. Eng.*, 6(1):15–28.

Dan Flickinger, Stephan Oepen, and Emily M. Bender. 2017. *Sustainable Development and Refinement of Complex Linguistic Annotations at Scale*. Springer Netherlands, Dordrecht.

Dan Flickinger, Stephan Oepen, and Gisle Ytrestøl. 2010. Wikiwoods: Syntacto-semantic annotation for English wikipedia. In *Proceedings of the Seventh International Conference on Language Resources and Evaluation (LREC'10)*, Valletta, Malta. European Language Resources Association (ELRA).

Daniel Flickinger, Yi Zhang, and Valia Kordoni. 2012. Deepbank: A dynamically annotated treebank of the wall street journal. In *Proceedings of the Eleventh International Workshop on Treebanks and Linguistic Theories*, pages 85–96.

Sepp Hochreiter and Jürgen Schmidhuber. 1997. Long Short-Term Memory. *Neural Comput.*, 9(8):1735–1780.

Zhongqiang Huang, Vladimir Eidelman, and Mary Harper. 2009. Improving a simple bigram hmm part-of-speech tagger by latent annotation and self-training. In *Proceedings of Human Language Technologies: The 2009 Annual Conference of the North American Chapter of the Association for Computational Linguistics, Companion Volume: Short Papers*, pages 213–216, Boulder, Colorado. Association for Computational Linguistics.

Angelina Ivanova, Stephan Oepen, Rebecca Dridan, Dan Flickinger, and Lilja Øvrelid. 2013. On different approaches to syntactic analysis into bi-lexical dependencies. an empirical comparison of direct, PCFG-based, and HPSG-based parsers. In *Proceedings of The 13th International Conference on Parsing Technologies (IWPT-2013)*, pages 63–72, Nara, Japan.

Angelina Ivanova, Stephan Oepen, Lilja Øvrelid, and Dan Flickinger. 2012. Who did what to whom? A contrastive study of syntacto-semantic dependencies. In *Proceedings of the Sixth Linguistic Annotation Workshop*, pages 2–11, Jeju, Republic of Korea.

Eliyahu Kiperwasser and Yoav Goldberg. 2016. Simple and accurate dependency parsing using bidirectional LSTM feature representations. *Transactions of the Association for Computational Linguistics*, 4:313–327.

Marco Kuhlmann and Peter Jonsson. 2015. Parsing to noncrossing dependency graphs. *Transactions of the Association for Computational Linguistics*, 3:559–570.

Mitchell P. Marcus, Mary Ann Marcinkiewicz, and Beatrice Santorini. 1993. Building a large annotated corpus of English: the penn treebank. *Computational Linguistics*, 19(2):313–330.

André F. T. Martins and Mariana S. C. Almeida. 2014. Priberam: A turbo semantic parser with second order features. In *Proceedings of the 8th International Workshop on Semantic Evaluation (SemEval 2014)*, pages 471–476, Dublin, Ireland. Association for Computational Linguistics and Dublin City University.

Graham Neubig, Yoav Goldberg, and Chris Dyer. 2017. On-the-fly operation batching in dynamic computation graphs. In *Advances in Neural Information Processing Systems*.

Stephan Oepen, Marco Kuhlmann, Yusuke Miyao, Daniel Zeman, Silvie Cinková, Dan Flickinger, Jan Hajič, Angelina Ivanova, and Zdeňka Urešová. 2016. Semantic Dependency Parsing (SDP) graph banks release 1.0 LDC2016T10. Web Download.

Stephan Oepen, Marco Kuhlmann, Yusuke Miyao, Daniel Zeman, Silvie Cinková, Dan Flickinger, Jan Hajic, and Zdenka Uresová. 2015. Semeval 2015 task 18: Broad-coverage semantic dependency parsing. In *Proceedings of the 9th International Workshop on Semantic Evaluation (SemEval 2015)*.

Stephan Oepen, Marco Kuhlmann, Yusuke Miyao, Daniel Zeman, Dan Flickinger, Jan Hajic, Angelina Ivanova, and Yi Zhang. 2014. Semeval 2014 task 8: Broad-coverage semantic dependency parsing. In *Proceedings of the 8th International Workshop on Semantic Evaluation (SemEval 2014)*, pages 63–72, Dublin, Ireland. Association for Computational Linguistics and Dublin City University.

Stephan Oepen, Kristina Toutanova, Stuart Shieber, Christopher Manning, Dan Flickinger, and Thorsten Brants. 2002. The lingo redwoods treebank motivation and preliminary applications. In *Proceedings of the 19th International Conference on Computational Linguistics - Volume 2*, COLING '02, pages 1–5, Stroudsburg, PA, USA. Association for Computational Linguistics.

Hao Peng, Sam Thomson, and Noah A. Smith. 2017. Deep multitask learning for semantic dependency parsing. In *Proceedings of the 55th Annual Meeting of the Association for Computational Linguistics (Volume 1: Long Papers)*, pages 2037–2048, Vancouver, Canada. Association for Computational Linguistics.

Emily Pitler, Sampath Kannan, and Mitchell Marcus. 2013. Finding optimal 1-endpoint-crossing trees. *TACL*, 1:13–24.

Daniel Tse and James R. Curran. 2010. Chinese CCGbank: extracting CCG derivations from the penn Chinese treebank. In *Proceedings of the 23rd International Conference on Computational Linguistics*

(Coling 2010), pages 1083–1091, Beijing, China. Coling 2010 Organizing Committee.

Yuxuan Wang, Wanxiang Che, Jiang Guo, and Ting Liu. 2018. A neural transition-based approach for semantic dependency graph parsing. In *Proceedings of the Thirty-Second AAAI Conference on Artificial Intelligence*.

Kun Yu, Miyao Yusuke, Xiangli Wang, Takuya Matsuzaki, and Junichi Tsujii. 2010. Semi-automatically developing Chinese hpsg grammar from the penn Chinese treebank for deep parsing. In *Coling 2010: Posters*, pages 1417–1425, Beijing, China. Coling 2010 Organizing Committee.

Xun Zhang, Yantao Du, Weiwei Sun, and Xiaojun Wan. 2016. Transition-based parsing for deep dependency structures. *Computational Linguistics*, 42(3):353–389.

Yi Zhang and Rui Wang. 2009. Cross-domain dependency parsing using a deep linguistic grammar. In *Proceedings of the Joint Conference of the 47th Annual Meeting of the ACL and the 4th International Joint Conference on Natural Language Processing of the AFNLP*, pages 378–386, Suntec, Singapore. Association for Computational Linguistics.

From Random to Supervised: A Novel Dropout Mechanism Integrated with Global Information

Hengru Xu[1,†]   **Shen Li[2,†]**   **Renfen Hu[3]**   **Si Li[1]**   **Sheng Gao[1,‡]**

[1]{xuhengru, lisi, gaosheng}@bupt.edu.cn
[2]shen@deeplycurious.ai
[3]irishere@mail.bnu.edu.cn
[1] SICE, Beijing University of Post and Telecommunication
[2] Deeplycurious.ai
[3] Institute of Chinese Information Processing, Beijing Normal University

Abstract

Dropout is used to avoid overfitting by randomly dropping units from the neural networks during training. Inspired by dropout, this paper presents GI-Dropout, a novel dropout method integrating with global information to improve neural networks for text classification. Unlike the traditional dropout method in which the units are dropped randomly according to the same probability, we aim to use explicit instructions based on global information of the dataset to guide the training process. With GI-Dropout, the model is supposed to pay more attention to inapparent features or patterns. Experiments demonstrate the effectiveness of the dropout with global information on seven text classification tasks, including sentiment analysis and topic classification.

1 Introduction

Recently, neural networks have achieved remarkable results in natural language processing (NLP). Convolutional Neural Network (CNN) and Recurrent Neural Network (RNN) are two popular types of neural network architectures and both of them are widely applied to various NLP tasks. CNN is known for its strong ability in extracting position-invariant features and RNN is highlighted in modeling sequences (Yin et al., 2017). In sentence classification tasks, models based on CNN or RNN aim to represent sentences as appropriate embeddings, which are supposed to encode semantic features for the classification.

However, with the consideration of computational complexity and spatial limitation, neural networks are often trained via mini-batch in which global information is gathered implicitly rather than explicitly. To facilitate the learning process, Li et al. (2017) extract global semantic features from the training dataset, and encode them into CNN filters with a novel initialization mechanism. This approach gains significant improvements in sentiment analysis and topic classification tasks.

Unlike most of machine learning methods, the advantage of neural networks is extracting features with less need of feature engineering. In general, the stronger ability of a model to learn features automatically, the better performance it will achieve. However, during the training process, neural networks tend to focus on some distinctive words or phrases but ignore other noteworthy patterns, which may result in overfitting, especially in a small dataset. To avoid this problem, dropout is proposed (Hinton et al., 2012; Srivastava et al., 2014). The key idea of dropout is to randomly drop units from the neural network during training and use a smaller weight of these units in the test.

Inspired by the above works, we propose a novel dropout method guided by global information (GI-Dropout). In our method, we force the model to pay more attention to features that are inapparent or with low frequency by dropping words that are prominent and easy to learn. Unlike the traditional dropout method where neurons are dropped randomly with the same probability, we encode global information into dropout. Specifically, we drop words based on their importance which are calculated from training data via a novel Naïve Bayes (NB) weighting technique.

With this dropout method, neural networks tend to extract not only the obvious features but also the unobvious features which are also helpful for the classification. By integrating our method into a classic CNN model for text classification (Kim, 2014) and a novel self-attentive RNN (Lin et al., 2017), we observe significant improvements in

---

† Hengru Xu and Shen Li contributed equally to this work.
‡ Corresponding author.

Proceedings of the 22nd Conference on Computational Natural Language Learning (CoNLL 2018), pages 573–582
Brussels, Belgium, October 31 - November 1, 2018. ©2018 Association for Computational Linguistics

various benchmarks.[1] The advantages of our approach are as follows:

1. Global information is directly obtained from the training data without any external resources;

2. GI-Dropout is simple but effective, and could be easily applied to other DNN models;

3. The computation brought by our method is relatively small, resulting in little additional training cost.

2 Related Work

Recently, neural networks dominate the state-of-the-art results on a wide range of NLP tasks. For text classification, Kim (2014) proposes a classical one-layer CNN which is very efficient for feature extraction, and it is considered as a strong baseline for various sentiment and topic classification tasks. Following this work, Yin and Schütze (2015) introduce multichannel variable-size convolution, and Zhang et al. (2016b) exploit different pre-trained word embeddings (e.g. word2vec and GloVe). Zhang and Wallace (2017) improve the CNN model by optimizing hyper-parameters and provide a detailed sensitivity analysis.

RNNs also achieve comparable performance in this area. Tang et al. (2015) show that gated RNN performs well on document-level sentiment classification. Lin et al. (2017) propose a enhanced model to extract an interpretable sentence embedding by introducing self-attention mechanism and yields a significant performance gain compared with other sentence embedding methods.

Yin et al. (2017) make a systematic comparison of CNNs and RNNs, showing that both of the networks can provide complementary information for text classification tasks, while which architecture performs better depends on how important it is to semantically understand the global/long-range semantics.

To improve the semantic understanding abilities of the models, some works aim to encode prior knowledge into the networks. For example, Hu et al. (2016) present a framework that encapsulates the logical structured knowledge into a neural network. Li et al. (2017) encode global semantic features into the convolutional filters instead of

initializing them randomly, which helps the filters focus on learning useful n-grams.

Another effective method to facilitate learning process is to exploit dropout mechanism. Apparently, if a model pays too much attention to a few distinct patterns, it can easily give rise to an overfitting, especially in a small dataset. Hinton et al. (2012) introduce Binary (regular) Dropout, showing that it can prevent co-adaptation of neurons by randomly dropping units from the neural networks during training, so as to reduce overfitting. Later Srivastava et al. (2014) show that multiplying outputs of the neurons by a random variable drawn from Gaussian distributions works as well, or perhaps better than regular dropout. Ba and Frey (2013) present standout, an adaptive dropout method, where each variable's dropout probability is calculated by a binary belief network, which can be trained jointly with the neural networks. Kingma et al. (2015) introduce variational dropout, a generalization of Gaussian dropout where the dropout rates are also learned during training.

The existing dropout methods are often based on mathematics or learned jointly with the downstream task, where global information is not explicitly utilized. Different from previous works, we focus on how to utilize global information to help model training via dropout. As depicted in Figure 3, GI-Dropout is introduced at the beginning of the baseline models, which is different from prior dropout methods which aim at controlling units in the networks rather than input words in the texts.

In this work, we use the global information to guide dropout method by dropping words based on their importance. Hence, neural networks are able to extract not only the obvious features but also the unobvious features which are also helpful for the classification.

3 Our method

The intuition behind our method is straightforward. Since neural networks aim to capture semantic features and classify sentences by the features, we encourage models to share more attention to unobvious features by dropping words according to their importance. Some features are so distinctive that model can learn them easily. However, a sentence may have more than one feature that can contribute to class prediction. For

---

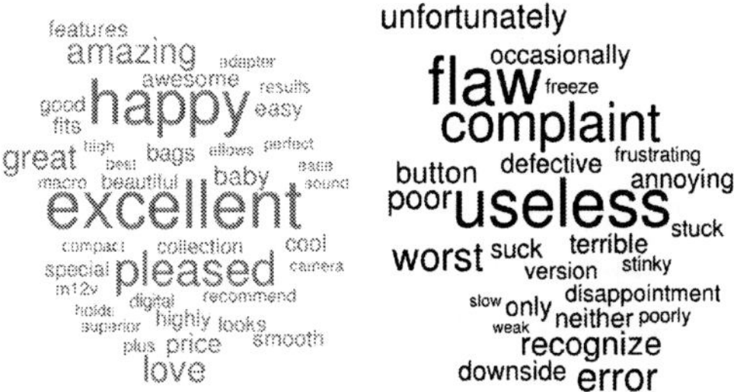

Figure 1: Top 30 key words of each class in Customer Review dataset

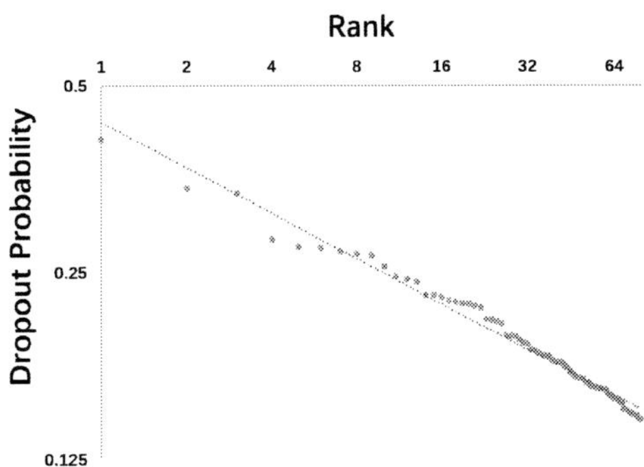

Figure 2: GI-Dropout probability and rank in SST-1 with $\beta = 0.95$.

instance, in "The story is sad and very boring", "boring" is of strong polarity and indicates negative emotion. Neural networks may not be sensitive to other features like "sad" which is also helpful for the sentiment classification, due to the very strong impact of "boring". In GI-Dropout, a word of higher importance score has greater possibility to be dropped. Thus, models are forced to learn unobvious features and will achieve better performance in prediction.

3.1 Importance Score

Firstly, we compute an importance score for each word. Intuitively, word "unique" is much more important than "movie" for determining polarities of reviews. Naïve Bayes (NB) weighting is an effective technique for determining the importance of words (Martineau and Finin, 2009; Wang and Manning, 2012; Li et al., 2017). The NB weight r of word w in class c is calculated as follows:

$$r_c^w = \frac{(n_c^w + \alpha)/\, \|n_c\|_1}{(n_{\bar{c}}^w + \alpha)/\, \|n_{\bar{c}}\|_1} \quad (1)$$

where n_c^w is the count of word w in class c, $n_{\bar{c}}^w$ is the count of word w in the other classes, $\|n_c\|_1$ is the count of all the word occurrences in class c, $\|n_{\bar{c}}\|_1$ is the count of all the word occurrences in the other classes, α is a smoothing parameter and is set as 1 in this paper.

To avoid low-frequency words being recognized as important words, we propose an improved NB weighting method based on (1):

$$r_c^w = \frac{(n_c^w + \alpha)/\, \|n_c\|_1}{(n_{\bar{c}}^w + \alpha)/\, \|n_{\bar{c}}\|_1} \times \log_\beta n_c^w \quad (2)$$

where $\log_\beta n_c^w$ is introduced as a frequency factor. The base β is a hyperparameter.

For positive class in movie review dataset (MR), the scores of words like "unique" and "warm"

should be large since they appear much more frequently in positive texts than in negative texts. As for neutral words like "the" and "movie", their scores should be small. For a word w, we select the max score of it as its importance score:

$$r^w = max(r_{c_0}^w, r_{c_1}^w, ..., r_{c_n}^w) \quad (3)$$

In Figure 1, we show top 30 key words of each class in customer review dataset (CR). We aim to drop these key words with higher probabilities and encourage the model to pay more attention to other unobvious features.

3.2 Dropout Probability

As shown in 3.1, we compute words importance scores with the whole training data. It is a simple yet effective way to represent the global information. After obtaining the scores, we compress them into $[0, 1)$. The GI-Dropout probability of word w is:

$$p(r) = \frac{e^r - 1}{e^r + 1} \quad (4)$$

where r is the importance score of w calculated via (2). A word would not be ignored when its probability is 0.

The β in (2) is a key parameter. As shown in Figure 2, after tuning β, the GI-Dropout probability of a word and its probability rank follow Zipf's Law. Zipf (1935) states that given a sample of words, the frequency of any word is inversely proportional to its rank in the frequency table. Replacing the frequency with GI-Dropout probability, we can get a variant of Zipf's Law. The experiments will show that setting β to this value in SST-1 is not a coincidence.

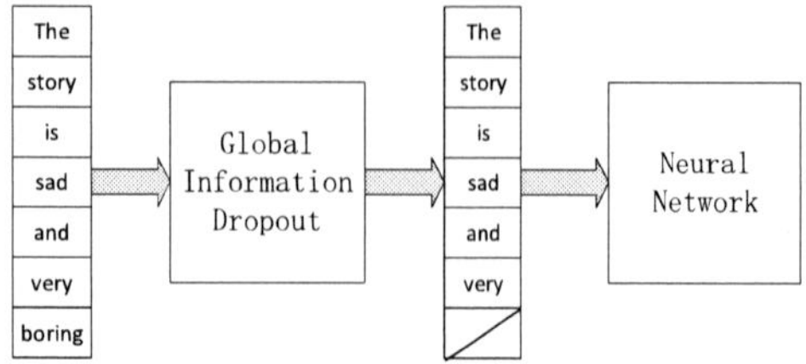

Figure 3: GI-Dropout. In this case, the word embedding of "boring" is dropped and set to zero vector while "sad" is not.

3.3 GI-Dropout Method

As illustrated in Figure 3, we implement a GI-Dropout layer before the neural network. Models without our dropout method can be viewed as the special case in which all the words are not dropped in GI-Dropout layer, i.e. dropout probabilities of all words are 0.

In this paper, every word in training data has a score to measure its importance via the novel NB weighting method, as well as a dropout probability calculated by the proposed scale function. During training, the words will be dropped according to their dropout probabilities.

The way to implement our dropout method is very straightforward. In embedding layer, we get the word embedding e_i of word w_i after looking it up in the embedding table. After that, this word can be dropped according to its GI-Dropout possibility. For word w_i, we set the e_i to zero vector if it needs to be dropped. Through this method, the neural network will not learn features from words whose embeddings are zero vectors. It is worth noted that the dropout probabilities of words differ from each other, which is different from the traditional dropout method where all the neurons are dropped according to the same probability. The dropout probabilities which are encoded with global information, guide the model to share attention to unobvious patterns.

In traditional dropout method, all the neurons are used in testing, but their weights are scaled down by a factor p (same with p in training) since a part of units emit nothing to the next layer during training. While in our method, during evaluation and testing, dropout probabilities of all the words are set to 0 so as to use all the patterns, and scaling is not needed.

Dataset	c	l	N	V	Test
MR	2	20	10662	18765	CV
SST-1	5	18	11855	17836	2210
SST-2	2	19	9613	16185	1821
Subj	2	23	10000	21323	CV
TREC	6	10	5952	9592	500
CR	2	19	3775	5340	CV
MPQA	2	3	10606	6246	CV

Table 1: Datasets summary. c: Number of target classes. l: Average sentence length. N: Dataset size. V: Vocabulary size. Test: Test set size (CV means there is no standard train/test split and thus 10-fold CV is used).

4 Experiments

CNN-non-static proposed by Kim (2014) is considered as a very strong baseline in sentence classification. Self-attentive RNN proposed by Lin et al. (2017) also achieves outstanding performance in many sentence classification tasks. We adopt these two models to evaluate GI-dropout.

4.1 Datasets

Following (Kim, 2014), we evaluate the performance of the proposed approach on various datasets. We use the same seven datasets with (Kim, 2014), including both sentiment analysis and topic classification tasks:

MR: Movie reviews sentiment datasets[2].

SST-1: Stanford Sentiment Treebank with 5 sentiment labels (Socher et al., 2013)[3]. The data consists of phrases-level and sentence-level instances. To keep same with (Kim, 2014), we train the model on both phrases and sentences but only test on sentences.

SST-2: SST-1 data with binary labels.

Subj: Subjective or objective classification dataset (Pang and Lee, 2005).

TREC: 6-class question classification dataset (Li and Roth, 2002) [4].

CR: Customer products review dataset (Hu and Liu, 2004) [5].

---

[2]https://www.cs.cornell.edu/people/pabo/movie-review-data/

[3]http://nlp.stanford.edu/sentiment/

[4]http://cogcomp.cs.illinois.edu/Data/QA/QC/

[5]http://www.cs.uic.edu/liub/FBS/sentiment-analysis.html

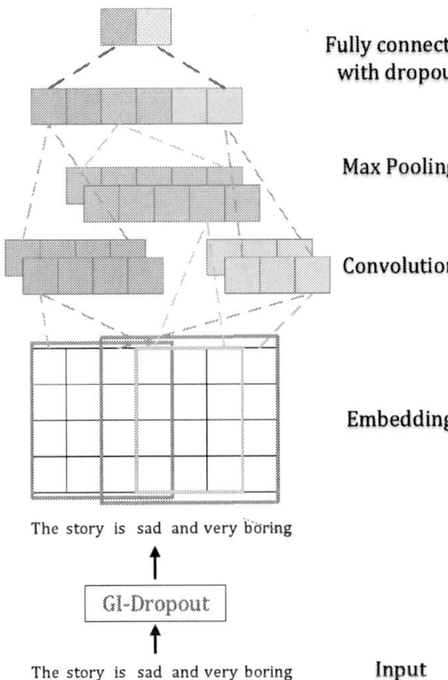

Figure 4: CNN architectures with GI-Dropout.

MPQA: Opinion polarity detection dataset (Wiebe et al., 2005).

The statistics of the datasets can be seen in Table 1.

4.2 CNN Model

CNNs use filters to capture semantic features of n-grams. After that, max-pooling is introduced to force the network to capture the most useful local features produced by convolutional layers (Collobert et al., 2011). A simple CNN model in (Kim, 2014) consists of the embedding layer, one convolution and pooling layer, and one fully connected layer. Four model variations are provided in (Kim, 2014), and we choose the CNN-non-static model as our baseline. The hyperparameters of the CNN are described in Table 2. The architecture of the model integrated with GI-Dropout is shown in Figure 4.

4.3 Self-attentive RNN Model

Long Short-Term Memory (LSTM) is a specific recurrent neural network (RNN) architecture which is good at modeling temporal sequences and

Parameters	Values
Word embeddings	GoogleNews-negative300 [6]
Fine-tune	Yes
Convolution	1-d
Filter size	[3, 4, 5]
Filter numbers	300
Activation function	ReLU
Pooling method	max-over-time
MLP dropout rate	0.5

Table 2: CNN configuration.

can capture long-range dependencies (Sak et al., 2014). Attention mechanism, first proposed in (Bahdanau et al., 2014), has become an integral part of sequence modeling. The self-attentive RNN proposed by Lin et al. (2017) consists of a bidirectional LSTM (biLSTM) and the self-attention mechanism. Self-attention mechanism is used to replace the max pooling or averaging step after the biLSTM. Multiple hops of attention are performed to extract semantic features in different aspects of the sentence.

In brief, suppose we have a sentence of n tokens, and let the hidden unit number for each unidirectional LSTM be u. After the biLSTM layer, we can get H, which have the size of n-by-$2u$. The attention mechanism takes the whole LSTM hidden states H as input, and outputs a vector of weights a,

$$a = softmax(w_{s2} \tanh(W_{s1} H^T)) \qquad (5)$$

where W_{s1} is a weight matrix with a shape of d_a-by-$2u$, and W_{s2} is a vector of parameters with size d_a which is a hyperparameter.

To extract r different aspects of the sentence, Lin et al. (2017) present multiple hops of attention, i.e. extend the w_{s2} into a r-by-d_a matrix and note it as W_{s2}. In the end, the annotation vector a becomes annotation matrix A.

$$A = softmax(W_{s2} \tanh(W_{s1} H^T)) \qquad (6)$$

The sentence embedding is:

$$M = AH \qquad (7)$$

Then the paper uses two layer 2-layer MLP with ReLU activation function to predict the label of

---

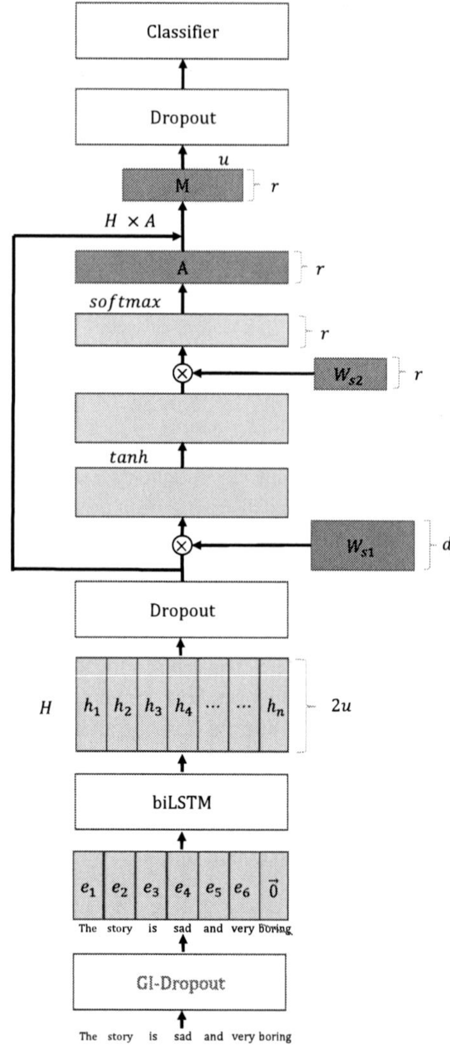

Figure 5: Self-attentive RNN architectures.

the sentence. Besides, a penalization term is introduced to encourage the diversity of summation weight vectors across different hops of attention.

Since Lin et al. (2017) do not provide source codes, we reproduce the model and integrate dropout layers into the model as shown in Figure 5. We perform a grid search to get the best baseline hyperparameters with which the model can achieve the state-of-the-art accuracy in most of the datasets. This model uses a bidirectional LSTM with 300 dimensions of hidden states in each direction. In self attention part, d_a is 350 and the coefficient of the penalization term is 1. r is set to 4 considering the size of datasets and the length

Parameters	Values
Word embeddings	Glove-300 [7]
Fine-tune	Yes
biLSTM hidden units	300
d_a	350
r	4
MLP Activation	ReLU
MLP dropout rate	0.5

Table 3: Self-attentive RNN configuration.

of texts. We also use a 2-layer ReLU output MLP with 2000 hidden units. During training we use a 0.5 dropout rate on the MLP. The hyperparameters are described in Table 3.

4.4 Experiment Settings

We apply our method to two baseline models. For fair comparison, we use the same hyperparameters settings with two baselines for training and testing. For datasets that do not have test sets, we split them for cross-validation with fixed random seeds. We train all the models using early stopping and set timedelay to 10.

4.5 Effectiveness of GI-Dropout

Results on 7 datasets are listed in Table 4. Experiments show that the models with GI-Dropout outperform both CNN and self-attentive RNN baselines by a significant margin.

To test whether global information makes key contribution, we conduct another experiment in which all words are dropped according to the same probability at the GI-Dropout layer. Grid search method is used to find the best result which is listed in "Dropout-same-prob" row.

The one-layer CNN provides a very strong baseline. The first line is the result of CNN-non-static model in (Kim, 2014). We reproduce the experiment results in "CNN-baseline" row.

Table 4 shows that by simply dropping all the words according to the same probability, the model gains slight improvements against CNN baseline on all the datasets except in MPQA. Similarly, it achieves improvements compared with RNN baseline on most datasets.

---

[7] A widely used publicly available 300-dimension word embeddings (Pennington et al., 2014).

Model	MR	SST-1	SST-2	Subj	TREC	CR	MPQA
CNN-non-static	81.5	48.0	87.2	93.4	93.6	84.3	89.5
CNN-reproduce	81.4	47.8	87.5	93.0	92.4	84.3	89.6
CNN-Dropout-same (p)	81.5(0.1)	48.5(0.1)	87.6(0.1)	93.5(0.2)	92.9(0.1)	84.5(0.5)	87.4(0.1)
CNN-GI-Dropout (β)	**81.9**(0.87)	**49.0**(0.95)	**88.1**(0.98)	**93.4**(0.91)	**93.2**(0.83)	**85.1**(0.87)	**89.8**(0.98)
RNN-baseline	82.1	49.7	89.7	93.6	92.6	84.1	89.6
RNN-Dropout-same (p)	82.2(0.2)	51.9(0.1)	90.1(0.1)	93.9(0.1)	93.4(0.2)	84.2(0.1)	**89.7**(0.1)
RNN-GI-Dropout (β)	**82.5**(0.87)	**54.1**(0.95)	**90.4**(0.95)	**94.2**(0.98)	**94.8**(0.95)	**84.7**(0.91)	**89.7**(0.98)
MVCNN	-	49.6	<u>89.4</u>	93.9	-	-	-
MGNC-CNN	-	48.7	88.3	<u>94.1</u>	95.5	-	-
CNN-Rule	81.7	-	89.3	-	-	85.3	-
Semantic-CNN	82.1	50.8	89.0	93.7	94.4	<u>86.0</u>	<u>89.3</u>
combine-skip	76.5	-	-	93.6	92.2	80.1	87.1
DSCNN	<u>82.2</u>	50.6	88.7	93.9	<u>95.6</u>	-	-
Paragraph Vector	74.8	48.7	87.8	90.5	91.8	78.1	74.2
NBSVM	79.4	-	-	93.2	-	81.8	86.3
Tree LSTM	-	<u>51.0</u>	88.0	-	-	-	-

Table 4: Effectiveness of GI-Dropout. Dropout-same means dropping units with the same probability. Results also include: MVCNN (Yin and Schütze, 2015), MGNC-CNN (Zhang et al., 2016b), CNN-Rule (Hu et al., 2016), Semantic-CNN (Li et al., 2017), combine-skip (Kiros et al., 2015), combine-skip (Kiros et al., 2015), DSCNN (Zhang et al., 2016a), Paragraph Vector (Le and Mikolov, 2014), NBSVM (Wang and Manning, 2012) and Tree LSTM (Tai et al., 2015).

β	CNN	RNN
$0.98\ (10^{-0.01})$	48.8	51.9
$0.95\ (10^{-0.02})$	**49.0**	**54.1**
$0.91\ (10^{-0.04})$	48.0	51.8
$0.87\ (10^{-0.06})$	48.1	52.4
$0.83\ (10^{-0.08})$	47.4	51.4

Table 5: β and accuracy in SST-1.

Top-k	CNN baseline	GI-Dropout in CNN
0	87.5	88.1
50	87.1	87.9
100	86.7	87.9
200	86.1	87.5
500	84.7	86.6
1000	81.7	84.0

Table 6: Accuracy decline when removing top-k apparent words in SST-2.

By integrating our GI-Dropout mechanism, the model further improves the performance significantly on both CNN and RNN models. Compared with Dropout-same, there is a clear advantage that results on all of the datasets have been improved.

With the comparison between GI-Dropout and Dropout-same, we are convinced that GI-Dropout benefits from global information which provides explicit semantic information to guide the training process.

Even when compared with other models with complex architectures, GI-Dropout models achieve the best accuracy on most datasets, especially in SST-1 and SST-2.

4.6 Further Analysis of Our Method

With GI-Dropout, we drop words according to their importance scores. The higher score of a word, the greater chance it is to be ignored. We further analyze why GI-Dropout works so well, and the relationship between β and accuracy.

GI-dropout helps models to learn inapparent features. To test whether the method indeed helps models to learn the inapparent features, we conduct experiments where the top-k apparent words (with highest important scores) were removed from test cases in SST-2. Results are shown in Table 6. We can observe that the CNN baseline model is more sensitive to the apparent features and GI-dropout can still have relatively good results even when we remove top 1000 apparent words. Thus, the model is supposed to pay more attention to the inapparent features with the help of GI-Dropout.

GI-dropout helps models to reduce the overfitting for the apparent features. The frequent words can easily induce the model to focus on limited features and activate a part of units with large score. This can be seen by analyzing the cases which the proposed model makes a correct prediction and the baseline makes a incorrect prediction:

(1) *provide -lrb- s -rrb- nail-biting suspense and credible characters <u>without</u> relying on technology-of-the-moment technique or **pretentious**[8] dialogue.*

(2) *the screenplay <u>sabotages</u> the movie's **strengths** at almost every juncture.*

(3) *this is <u>cool</u>, <u>slick</u> stuff, ready to <u>quench</u> the thirst of an audience that **misses** the summer blockbusters.*

The baseline model is prone to focus only on the prominent features, e.g. the **"pretentious"** (negative) in case (1), **"strengths"** (positive) in case(2) and **"miss"** (negative) in case (3), and then make wrong predictions. Even though there are some important words indicating the opposite polarity, e.g. **"without"** in case (1), **"sabotages"** in case (2) , **"cool"**, **"slick"** and **"quench"** in case (3), the model can not make use of these features efficiently.

By integrating our GI-dropout method, the model can learn not only the obvious features, e.g. **"strengths"**, but also the less obvious features e.g. **"sabotages"**. Thus, it makes correct predictions in all the above cases.

The relationship between β and accuracy. Another thing should be noticed is the value of β in Equation 2. As shown in Figure 2, the probability of a word and its rank follow Zipf's Law when β is 0.95 in SST-1. Actually, for each dataset, there is an appropriate β value for Equation 2 that can approximate the dropout probability and its rank with a Zipfian distribution. We assume that the β setting in accord with Zipf's Law could have an important positive effect on the model perfor-

mance. To examine this hypothesis, we further test the influences of different β values on the CNN and RNN model. As expected, Table 5 shows that the models achieve the best results for both CNN and RNN in SST-1 with β setting to 0.95.

5 Conclusion

This paper proposes GI-Dropout, a novel dropout method which utilizes global information and guides neural networks to extract not only obvious features but also unobvious features.

This idea is inspired by dropout in which units are dropped randomly in training according to the same probability. Unlike traditional dropout method, we aim to use global information to guide our dropout based on the importance of the words.

By integrating this mechanism, we encode global information explicitly into model via a novel Naïve Bayes Weighting method. We discover that model can be sensitive to some inapparent patterns, which is of great help to the classification. Experimental results demonstrate the effectiveness of GI-Dropout on multiple text classification tasks. In addition, our method requires few external resources and relatively small calculation. It is simple but effective and could be easily applied to other NLP tasks.

Acknowledgments

This work was supported by National Natural Science Foundation of China (No. 61702047), Beijing Natural Science Foundation (No. 4174098), the Fundamental Research Funds for the Central Universities (No. 2017RC02), National Social Science Fund of China (No. 18CYY029) and China Postdoctoral Science Foundation funded project (No. 2018M630095).

References

Jimmy Ba and Brendan Frey. 2013. Adaptive dropout for training deep neural networks. In C. J. C. Burges, L. Bottou, M. Welling, Z. Ghahramani, and K. Q. Weinberger, editors, *Advances in Neural Information Processing Systems 26*, pages 3084–3092. Curran Associates, Inc.

Dzmitry Bahdanau, Kyunghyun Cho, and Yoshua Bengio. 2014. Neural machine translation by jointly learning to align and translate. *arXiv preprint arXiv:1409.0473*.

Ronan Collobert, Jason Weston, Léon Bottou, Michael Karlen, Koray Kavukcuoglu, and Pavel Kuksa.

---

[8]Words in **bold** denote the apparent features with high importance scores, e.g. "pretentious" appears 159 times in **positive** texts and 5 in **negative** texts. Words with <u>underline</u> represent unobvious features that also contribute to the class prediction.

2011. Natural language processing (almost) from scratch. *Journal of Machine Learning Research*, 12(Aug):2493–2537.

Geoffrey E Hinton, Nitish Srivastava, Alex Krizhevsky, Ilya Sutskever, and Ruslan R Salakhutdinov. 2012. Improving neural networks by preventing co-adaptation of feature detectors. *arXiv preprint arXiv:1207.0580*.

Minqing Hu and Bing Liu. 2004. Mining and summarizing customer reviews. In *Proceedings of the tenth ACM SIGKDD international conference on Knowledge discovery and data mining*, pages 168–177. ACM.

Zhiting Hu, Xuezhe Ma, Zhengzhong Liu, Eduard Hovy, and Eric Xing. 2016. Harnessing deep neural networks with logic rules. In *Proceedings of the 54th Annual Meeting of the Association for Computational Linguistics (Volume 1: Long Papers)*, volume 1, pages 2410–2420.

Yoon Kim. 2014. Convolutional neural networks for sentence classification. *arXiv preprint arXiv:1408.5882*.

Diederik P Kingma, Tim Salimans, and Max Welling. 2015. Variational dropout and the local reparameterization trick. In C. Cortes, N. D. Lawrence, D. D. Lee, M. Sugiyama, and R. Garnett, editors, *Advances in Neural Information Processing Systems 28*, pages 2575–2583. Curran Associates, Inc.

Ryan Kiros, Yukun Zhu, Ruslan R Salakhutdinov, Richard Zemel, Raquel Urtasun, Antonio Torralba, and Sanja Fidler. 2015. Skip-thought vectors. In *Advances in neural information processing systems*, pages 3294–3302.

Quoc Le and Tomas Mikolov. 2014. Distributed representations of sentences and documents. In *International Conference on Machine Learning*, pages 1188–1196.

Shen Li, Zhe Zhao, Tao Liu, Renfen Hu, and Xiaoyong Du. 2017. Initializing convolutional filters with semantic features for text classification. In *Proceedings of the 2017 Conference on Empirical Methods in Natural Language Processing*, pages 1884–1889.

Xin Li and Dan Roth. 2002. Learning question classifiers. In *Proceedings of the 19th international conference on Computational linguistics-Volume 1*, pages 1–7. Association for Computational Linguistics.

Zhouhan Lin, Minwei Feng, Cicero Nogueira dos Santos, Mo Yu, Bing Xiang, Bowen Zhou, and Yoshua Bengio. 2017. A structured self-attentive sentence embedding. *arXiv preprint arXiv:1703.03130*.

Justin Martineau and Tim Finin. 2009. Delta tfidf: An improved feature space for sentiment analysis.

Tomas Mikolov, Ilya Sutskever, Kai Chen, Greg S Corrado, and Jeff Dean. 2013. Distributed representations of words and phrases and their compositionality. In *Advances in neural information processing systems*, pages 3111–3119.

Bo Pang and Lillian Lee. 2005. Seeing stars: Exploiting class relationships for sentiment categorization with respect to rating scales. In *Proceedings of the 43rd annual meeting on association for computational linguistics*, pages 115–124. Association for Computational Linguistics.

Jeffrey Pennington, Richard Socher, and Christopher Manning. 2014. Glove: Global vectors for word representation. In *Proceedings of the 2014 conference on empirical methods in natural language processing (EMNLP)*, pages 1532–1543.

Haşim Sak, Andrew Senior, and Françoise Beaufays. 2014. Long short-term memory recurrent neural network architectures for large scale acoustic modeling. In *Fifteenth annual conference of the international speech communication association*.

Richard Socher, Alex Perelygin, Jean Wu, Jason Chuang, Christopher D Manning, Andrew Ng, and Christopher Potts. 2013. Recursive deep models for semantic compositionality over a sentiment treebank. In *Proceedings of the 2013 conference on empirical methods in natural language processing*, pages 1631–1642.

Nitish Srivastava, Geoffrey Hinton, Alex Krizhevsky, Ilya Sutskever, and Ruslan Salakhutdinov. 2014. Dropout: A simple way to prevent neural networks from overfitting. *The Journal of Machine Learning Research*, 15(1):1929–1958.

Kai Sheng Tai, Richard Socher, and Christopher D Manning. 2015. Improved semantic representations from tree-structured long short-term memory networks. In *Proceedings of the 53rd Annual Meeting of the Association for Computational Linguistics and the 7th International Joint Conference on Natural Language Processing (Volume 1: Long Papers)*, volume 1, pages 1556–1566.

Duyu Tang, Bing Qin, and Ting Liu. 2015. Document modeling with gated recurrent neural network for sentiment classification. In *Proceedings of the 2015 conference on empirical methods in natural language processing*, pages 1422–1432.

Sida Wang and Christopher D Manning. 2012. Baselines and bigrams: Simple, good sentiment and topic classification. In *Proceedings of the 50th Annual Meeting of the Association for Computational Linguistics: Short Papers-Volume 2*, pages 90–94. Association for Computational Linguistics.

Janyce Wiebe, Theresa Wilson, and Claire Cardie. 2005. Annotating expressions of opinions and emotions in language. *Language resources and evaluation*, 39(2-3):165–210.

Wenpeng Yin, Katharina Kann, Mo Yu, and Hinrich Schütze. 2017. Comparative study of cnn and rnn for natural language processing. *arXiv preprint arXiv:1702.01923*.

Wenpeng Yin and Hinrich Schütze. 2015. Multichannel variable-size convolution for sentence classification. In *Proceedings of the Nineteenth Conference on Computational Natural Language Learning*, pages 204–214.

Rui Zhang, Honglak Lee, and Dragomir Radev. 2016a. Dependency sensitive convolutional neural networks for modeling sentences and documents. In *Proceedings of NAACL-HLT*, pages 1512–1521.

Ye Zhang, Stephen Roller, and Byron C Wallace. 2016b. Mgnc-cnn: A simple approach to exploiting multiple word embeddings for sentence classification. In *Proceedings of NAACL-HLT*, pages 1522–1527.

Ye Zhang and Byron Wallace. 2017. A sensitivity analysis of (and practitioners guide to) convolutional neural networks for sentence classification. In *Proceedings of the Eighth International Joint Conference on Natural Language Processing (Volume 1: Long Papers)*, volume 1, pages 253–263.

George K Zipf. 1935. The psychology of language. *NY Houghton-Mifflin*.

Sequence to Sequence Mixture Model for Diverse Machine Translation

Xuanli He   **Gholamreza Haffari**
Monash University, Australia
{xuanli.he1, gholamreza.haffari}@monash.edu

Mohammad Norouzi
Google Brain
mnorouzi@google.com

Abstract

Sequence to sequence (SEQ2SEQ) models often lack diversity in their generated translations. This can be attributed to the limitation of SEQ2SEQ models in capturing lexical and syntactic variations in a parallel corpus resulting from different styles, genres, topics, or ambiguity of the translation process. In this paper, we develop a novel sequence to sequence mixture (S2SMIX) model that improves both translation diversity and quality by adopting a committee of specialized translation models rather than a single translation model. Each mixture component selects its own training dataset via optimization of the marginal log-likelihood, which leads to a soft clustering of the parallel corpus. Experiments on four language pairs demonstrate the superiority of our mixture model compared to a SEQ2SEQ baseline with standard or diversity-boosted beam search. Our mixture model uses negligible additional parameters and incurs no extra computation cost during decoding.

1 Introduction

Neural sequence to sequence (SEQ2SEQ) models have been remarkably effective machine translation (MT) (Sutskever et al., 2014; Bahdanau et al., 2015). They have revolutionized MT by providing a unified end-to-end framework, as opposed to the traditional approaches requiring several sub-models and long pipelines. The neural approach is superior or on-par with statistical MT in terms of translation quality on various MT tasks and domains e.g. (Wu et al., 2016; Hassan et al., 2018).

A well recognized issue with SEQ2SEQ models is the lack of diversity in the generated translations. This issue is mostly attributed to the decoding algorithm (Li et al., 2016), and recently to the model (Zhang et al., 2016; Schulz et al., 2018a). The former direction has attempted to design diversity encouraging decoding algorithm,

particularly beam search, as it generates translations sharing the majority of their tokens except a few trailing ones. The latter direction has investigated modeling enhancements, particularly the introduction of continuous latent variables, in order to capture lexical and syntactic variations in training corpora, resulted from the inherent ambiguity of the human translation process.[1] However, improving the translation diversity and quality with SEQ2SEQ models is still an open problem, as the results of the aforementioned previous work are not fully satisfactory.

In this paper, we develop a novel sequence to sequence mixture (S2SMIX) model that improves both translation quality and diversity by adopting a committee of specialized translation models rather than a single translation model. Each mixture component selects its own training dataset via optimization of the marginal log-likelihood, which leads to a soft clustering of the parallel corpus. As such, our mixture model introduces a conditioning global discrete latent variable for each sentence, which leads to grouping together and capturing variations in the training corpus. We design the architecture of S2SMIX such that the mixture components share almost all of their parameters and computation.

We provide experiments on four translation tasks, translating from English to German/French/Vietnamese/Spanish. The experiments show that our S2SMIX model consistently outperforms strong baselines, including SEQ2SEQ model with the standard and diversity encouraged beam search, in terms of both translation diversity and quality. The benefits of our mixture model comes with negligible additional parameters and no extra computation at inference time, compared to the vanilla SEQ2SEQ model.

---

[1] For a given source sentence, usually there exist several valid translations.

Proceedings of the 22nd Conference on Computational Natural Language Learning (CoNLL 2018), pages 583–592
Brussels, Belgium, October 31 - November 1, 2018. ©2018 Association for Computational Linguistics

2   Attentional Sequence to Sequence

An attentional sequence to sequence (SEQ2SEQ) model (Sutskever et al., 2014; Bahdanau et al., 2015) aims to directly model the conditional distribution of an output sequence $\mathbf{y} \equiv (y_1, \dots, y_T)$ given an input $\mathbf{x}$, denoted $P(\mathbf{y} \mid \mathbf{x})$. This family of autoregressive probabilistic models decomposes the output distribution in terms of a product of distributions over individual tokens, often ordered from left to right as,

$$P_\theta(\mathbf{y} \mid \mathbf{x}) \;=\; \prod_{t=1}^{|\mathbf{y}|} P_\theta(y_t \mid \mathbf{y}_{<t}, \mathbf{x}) \,, \qquad (1)$$

where $\mathbf{y}_{<t} \equiv (y_1, \dots, y_{t-1})$ denotes a prefix of the sequence $\mathbf{y}$, and θ denotes the tunable parameters of the model.

Given a training dataset of input-output pairs, denoted by $\mathcal{D} \equiv \{(\mathbf{x}, \mathbf{y}^*)_d\}_{d=1}^{D}$, the *conditional log-likelihood* objective, predominantly used to train SEQ2SEQ models, is expressed as,

$$\ell_{\mathrm{CLL}}(\theta) = \sum_{(\mathbf{x},\mathbf{y}^*)\in\mathcal{D}} \sum_{t=1}^{|\mathbf{y}^*|} \log P_\theta(y_t^* \mid \mathbf{y}_{<t}^*, \mathbf{x}) \,. \quad (2)$$

A standard implementation of the SEQ2SEQ model is composed of an encoder followed by a decoder. The encoder transforms a sequence of source tokens denoted $(x_1, \dots, x_N)$, into a sequence of hidden states denoted $(\mathbf{h}_1, \dots, \mathbf{h}_N)$ via a recurrent neural network (RNN). Attention provides an effective mechanism to represent a soft alignment between the tokens of the input and output sequences (Bahdanau et al., 2015), and more recently to model the dependency among the output variables (Vaswani et al., 2017).

In our model, we adopt a bidirectional RNN with LSTM units (Hochreiter and Schmidhuber, 1997). Each hidden state $\mathbf{h}_n$ is the concatenation of the states produced by the forward and backward RNNs, $\mathbf{h}_n = [\mathbf{h}_{\rightarrow n}, \mathbf{h}_{n\leftarrow}]$. Then, we use a two-layer RNN decoder to iteratively emit individual distributions over target tokens $(y_1, \dots, y_T)$. At time step t, we compute the hidden representations of an output prefix $\mathbf{y}_{\leq t}$ denoted $\mathbf{s}_t^1$ and $\mathbf{s}_t^2$ based on an embedding of y_t denoted $\mathrm{M}[y_t]$, previous representations $\mathbf{s}_{t-1}^1, \mathbf{s}_{t-1}^2$, and a context vector $\mathbf{c}_t$ as,

$$\mathbf{s}_t^1 = \mathrm{LSTM}(\mathbf{s}_{t-1}^1, \mathrm{M}[y_t]; \mathbf{c}_t) \,, \quad (3)$$

$$\mathbf{s}_t^2 = \mathrm{LSTM}(\mathbf{s}_{t-1}^2, \mathbf{s}_t^1; \mathbf{c}_t) \,, \qquad (4)$$

$$P_\theta(y_{t+1} \mid \mathbf{y}_{\leq t}, \mathbf{x}) = \mathrm{softmax}(W\mathbf{s}_t^2 + W'\mathbf{c}_t) \,, \quad (5)$$

where M is the embedding table, and W and W' are learnable parameters. The context vector $\mathbf{c}_t$ is computed based on the input and attention,

$$e_{t,n} = \mathbf{v}^\top \tanh(W_h \mathbf{h}_n + W_s \mathbf{s}_{t-1}^1 + \mathbf{b}_a) \,, \quad (6)$$

$$\mathbf{a}_t = \mathrm{softmax}(\mathbf{e}_t) \,, \qquad (7)$$

$$\mathbf{c}_t = \sum_n a_{t,n}\, \mathbf{h}_n \,, \qquad (8)$$

where W_h, W_s, $\mathbf{b}_a$, and $\mathbf{v}$ are learnable parameters, and $\mathbf{a}_t$ is the attention distribution over the input tokens at time step t. The decoder utilizes the attention information to decide which input tokens should influence the next output token y_{t+1}.

3   Sequence to Sequence Mixture Model

We develop a novel *sequence to sequence mixture* (S2SMIX) model that improves both translation quality and diversity by adopting a committee of specialized translation models rather than a single translation model. Each mixture component selects its own training dataset via optimization of the marginal log-likelihood, which leads to a soft clustering of the parallel corpus. We design the architecture of S2SMIX such that the mixture components share almost all of their parameters except a few conditioning parameters. This enables a direct comparison against a SEQ2SEQ baseline with the same number of parameters.

Improving translation diversity within SEQ2SEQ models has received considerable recent attention (*e.g.*, Vijayakumar et al. (2016); Li et al. (2016)). Given a source sentence, human translators are able to produce a set of diverse and reasonable translations. However, although beam search for SEQ2SEQ models is able to generate various candidates, the final candidates often share majority of their tokens, except a few trailing ones. The lack of diversity within beam search raises an issue for possible re-ranking systems and for scenarios where one is willing to show multiple translation candidates to the user. Prior work attempts to improve translation diversity by incorporating a diversity penalty during beam search (Vijayakumar et al., 2016; Li et al., 2016). By contrast, our S2SMIX model naturally incorporates diversity both during training and inference.

The key difference between the SEQ2SEQ and S2SMIX models lies in the formulation of the conditional probability of an output sequence $\mathbf{y}$ given an input $\mathbf{x}$. The S2SMIX model represents $P_\theta(\mathbf{y} \mid$

$\mathbf{x}$) by marginalizing out a discrete latent variable $z \in \{1, \dots, K\}$, which indicates the selection of the mixture component, *i.e.*,

$$P_\theta(\mathbf{y} \mid \mathbf{x}) = \sum_{z=1}^{K} P_\theta(\mathbf{y} \mid \mathbf{x}, z) \, P(z \mid \mathbf{x}), \qquad (9)$$

where K is the number of mixture components. For simplicity and to promote diversity, we assume that the mixing coefficients follow a uniform distribution such that for all $z \in \{1, \dots, K\}$,

$$P(z \mid \mathbf{x}) = 1/K. \qquad (10)$$

For the family of S2SMIX models with uniform mixing coefficients (10), the conditional log-likelihood objective (2) can be re-expressed as:

$$\ell_{\mathrm{CLL}}(\theta) = \mathrm{constant} +$$
$$\sum_{(\mathbf{x},\mathbf{y}^*)\in\mathcal{D}} \log \sum_{z=1}^{K} \exp \underbrace{\sum_{t=1}^{|\mathbf{y}^*|} \log P_\theta(y_t^* \mid \mathbf{y}_{<t}^*, \mathbf{x}, z)}_{P_\theta(\mathbf{y}\mid\mathbf{x},z)},$$
$$(11)$$

where $\log(1/K)$ terms were excluded because they offset the objective by a constant value. Such a constant has no impact on learning the parameters θ. One can easily implement the objective in (11) using automatic differentiation software such as tensorflow (Abadi et al., 2016), by adopting a LogSumExp operator to aggregate the loss of the individual mixture components. When the number of components K is large, computing the terms $P_\theta(y_t^* \mid \mathbf{y}_{<t}^*, \mathbf{x}, z)$ for all values of $z \in \{1, \dots, K\}$ can require a lot of GPU memory. To mitigate this issue, we will propose a memory efficient formulation in Section 3.3 inspired by the EM algorithm.

3.1 S2SMIX Architecture

We design the architecture of the S2SMIX model such that individual mixture components can share as many parameters and as much computation as possible. Accordingly, all of the mixture components share the same encoder, which requires processing the input sentence only once. We consider different ways of injecting the conditioning signal into the decoder. As depicted in Figure 1, we consider different ways of injecting the conditioning on z into our two-layer decoder. These different variants require additional lookup tables denoted $\mathrm{M}_1, \mathrm{M}_2$, or M_b.

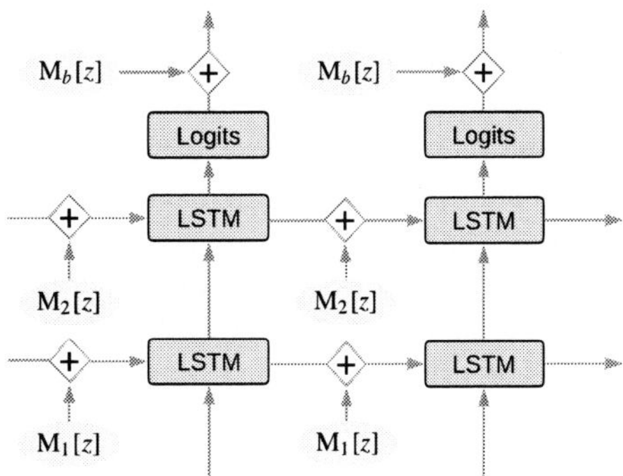

Figure 1: An illustration of a two-layer LSTM decoder with different ways of injecting the conditioning signal.

When we incorporate the conditioning on z into the LSTM layers, each lookup table (*e.g.*, M_1 and M_2) has K rows and D_{LSTM} columns, where D_{LSTM} denotes the number of dimensions of the LSTM states (512 in our case). We combine the state of the LSTM with the conditioning signal via simple addition. Then the LSTM update equations take the form,

$$\mathbf{s}_t^i = \mathrm{LSTM}(\mathbf{s}_{t-1}^i + \mathrm{M}_i[z], \, \mathrm{input}), \qquad (12)$$

for $i \in \{1, 2\}$. We refer to the addition of the conditioning signal to the bottom and top LSTM layers of the decoder as *bt* and *tp* respectively. Note that in the bt configuration, the attention mask depends on the indicator variable z, whereas in the tp configuration that attention mask is shared across different mixture components.

We also consider incorporating the conditioning signal into the softmax layer to bias the selection of individual words in each mixture component. Accordingly, the embedding table M_b has K rows and D_{vocab} entries, and the logits from (5) are added to the corresponding row of M_b as,

$$P_\theta(y_{t+1} \mid \mathbf{y}_{\leq t}, \mathbf{x}, z) = \mathrm{softmax}(\mathrm{logits} + \mathrm{M}_b[z]). \qquad (13)$$

We refer to this configuration as *sf* and to the configuration that includes all of the conditioning signals as *all*.

3.2 Separate Beam Search per Component

At the inference stage, we conduct a separate beam search per mixture component. Performing beam search independently for each component encourages diversity among the translation candidates as different mixture components often prefer certain phrases and linguistic structures over each other. Let $\hat{\mathbf{y}}_z$ denote the result of the beam search for a mixture component z. The final output of our model, denoted $\hat{\mathbf{y}}$ is computed by selecting the translation candidate with the highest probability under the corresponding mixture component, *i.e.*,

$$\hat{\mathbf{y}} = \operatorname*{argmax}_{1 \leq z \leq K} \log P_\theta(\hat{\mathbf{y}}_z \mid \mathbf{x}, z) . \qquad (14)$$

In order to accurately estimate the conditional probability of each translation candidate based on (9), one needs to evaluate each candidate using all of the mixture components. However, this process considerably increases the inference time and latency. Instead, we approximate the probability of each candidate by only considering the mixture component based on which the candidate translation has been decoded, as outlined in (14). This approximation also encourages the diversity as we emphasized in this work.

Note that we have K mixture components and a beam search of b per component. Overall, this requires processing $K \times b$ candidates. Accordingly, we compare our model with a SEQ2SEQ model using the same beam size of $K \times b$.

3.3 Memory Efficient Formulation

In this paper, we adopt a relatively small number of mixture components (up to 16), but to encompass various clusters of linguistic content and style, one may benefit from a large number of components. Based on our experiments, the memory footprint of a S2SMIX with K components increases by about K folds, partly because the softmax layers take a big fraction of the memory. To reduce the memory requirement for training our model, inspired by prior work on EM algorithm (Neal and Hinton, 1998), we re-express the gradient of the conditional log-likelihood objective in (11) *exactly* as,

$$\frac{d}{d\theta}\ell_{\text{CLL}}(\theta) =$$

$$\sum_{(\mathbf{x},\mathbf{y}^*)\in\mathcal{D}} \sum_{z=1}^{K} P(z \mid \mathbf{x}, \mathbf{y}^*)\frac{d}{d\theta}\log P_\theta(\mathbf{y}^* \mid \mathbf{x}, z) ,$$

$$(15)$$

where with uniform mixing coefficients, the posterior distribution $P(z \mid \mathbf{x}, \mathbf{y}^*)$ takes the form,

$$P(z \mid \mathbf{x}, \mathbf{y}) = \frac{\exp \ell_z(\mathbf{y} \mid \mathbf{x})}{\sum_k \exp \ell_k(\mathbf{y} \mid \mathbf{x})} , \qquad (16)$$

where $\ell_z(\mathbf{y} \mid \mathbf{x}) = \log P_\theta(\mathbf{y} \mid \mathbf{x}, z)$.

Based on this formulation, one can compute the posterior distribution in a few forward passes, which require much less memory. Then, one can draw one or a few Monte Carlo (MC) samples from the posterior to obtain an unbiased estimate of the gradient in (15). As shown in algorithm 1, the training procedure is divided into two parts. For each minibatch we compute the component-specific log-loss for different mixture components in the first stage. Then, we exponentiate and normalize the losses as in (16) to obtain the posterior distribution. Finally, we draw one sample from the posterior distribution per input-output example, and optimize the parameters according to the loss of such a component. These two stages are alternated until the model converges. We note that this algorithm follows an *unbiased* stochastic gradient of the marginal log likelihood.

Algorithm 1 Memory efficient S2SMIX

    Initialize a computational graph: cg
    Initialize a optimizer: opt
    repeat
        draw a random minibatch of the data
        empty list Γ
        for $z = 1$ **to** K **do**
            $\ell_z :=$ cg.forward(minibatch, z)
            $\Gamma :=$ add $\exp(\ell_z)$ to Γ
        end for
        $\Gamma :=$ normalize(Γ)
        $\tilde{z} :=$ sample(Γ)
        $\ell :=$ cg.forward(minibatch, $\tilde{z}$)
        opt.gradient_descent(ℓ)
    until converge

---

4 Experiments

Dataset. To assess the effectiveness of the S2SMIX model, we conduct a set of translation experiments on TEDtalks on four language pairs: English→French (en-fr), English→German (en-de), English→Vietnamese (en-vi), and English→Spanish (en-es).

We use IWSLT14 dataset[2] for en-es, IWSLT15

---

[2]https://sites.google.com/site/iwsltevaluation2014/home

Data	en-fr	en-de	en-vi	en-es
Train	208,719	189,600	133,317	173,601
Dev	5,685	6,775	1,553	5,401
Test	2,762	2,762	1,268	2,504

Table 1: Statistics of all language pairs for IWSLT data after preprocessing

dataset for en-vi, and IWSLT16 dataset[3] for en-fr and en-de. We pre-process the corpora by Moses tokenizer[4], and preserve the true case of the text. For en-vi, we use the pre-processed corpus distributed by Luong and Manning (2015)[5]. For training and dev sets, we discard all of the sentence pairs where the length of either side exceeds 50 tokens. The number of sentence pairs of different language pairs after preprocessing are shown in Table 1. We apply byte pair encoding (BPE) (Sennrich et al., 2016) to handle rare words on en-fr, en-de and en-es, and share the BPE vocabularies between the encoder and decoder for each language pair.

Implementation details. All of the models use a one-layer bidirectional LSTM encoder and a two-layer LSTM decoder. Each LSTM layer in the encoder and decoder has a 512 dimensional hidden state. Each input word embeddings is 512 dimensional as well. We adopt the Adam optimizer (Kingma and Ba, 2014). We adopt dropout with a 0.2 dropout rate. The minibatch size is 64 sentence pairs. We train each model 15 epochs, and select the best model in terms of the perplexity on the dev set.

Diversity metrics. Having more diversity in the candidate translations is one of the major advantages of the S2SMIX model. To quantify diversity within a set $\{\hat{\mathbf{y}}_m\}_{m=1}^M$ of translation candidates, we propose to evaluate average pairwise BLEU between pairs of sentences according to

$$\text{div\_bleu} \equiv 100 - \frac{\sum_{i=1}^{M} \sum_{j=i+1}^{M} \text{BLEU}(\hat{\mathbf{y}}_i, \hat{\mathbf{y}}_j)}{M(M-1)/2} \quad (17)$$

As an alternative metric of diversity within a set $\{\hat{\mathbf{y}}_m\}_{m=1}^M$ of translations, we propose a metric based on the fraction of the n-grams that are

[3] https://sites.google.com/site/iwsltevaluation2016
[4] https://github.com/moses-smt/mosesdecoder
[5] https://nlp.stanford.edu/projects/nmt

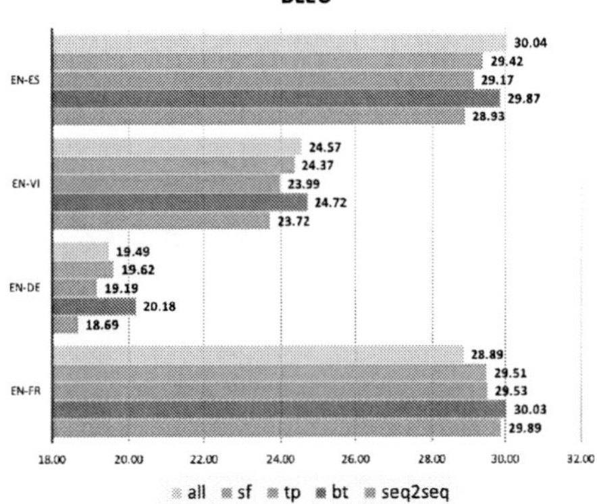

Figure 2: BLEU scores of the different variants of S2SMIX model and SEQ2SEQ model.

not shared among the translations, *i.e.,*

$$\text{div\_ngram} \equiv 1 - \frac{\left|\cap_{m=1}^{M}\text{ngrams}(\hat{\mathbf{y}}_m)\right|}{\left|\cup_{m=1}^{M}\text{ngrams}(\hat{\mathbf{y}}_m)\right|} \quad (18)$$

where $\text{ngram}(\mathbf{y})$ returns the set of unique n-grams in a sequence $\mathbf{y}$. We report average div_bleu and average div_ngram across the test set for the translation candidates found by beam search. We measure and report bigram diversity in the paper and report unigram diversity in the supplementary material.

4.1 Experimental results

S2SMIX configuration. We start by investigating which of the ways of injecting the conditioning signal into the S2SMIX model is most effective. As seen in Section 3, the mixture components can be built by adding component-specific vectors to the logits (sf), the top LSTM layer (tp) or the bottom LSTM layer (bt) in the decoder, or all of them (all). Figure 2 shows the BLEU score of these variants on the translation tasks across four different language pairs. We observe that adding a component-specific vector to the recurrent cells in the bottom layer of the decoder is the most effective, and results in BLEU scores superior or on-par with the other variants across the four language pairs.

Therefore, we use this model variant in all experiments for the rest of the paper.

Furthermore, Table 2 shows the number of parameters in each of the variants as well as the base SEQ2SEQ model. We confirm that the mixture model variants introduce negligible number

	en-fr	en-de	en-vi	en-es
SEQ2SEQ	173.22	173.78	112.76	173.21
S2SMIX-4				
bt	173.23	173.79	112.77	173.22
tp	173.23	173.79	112.77	173.22
sf	173.70	174.27	112.88	173.70
all	173.72	174.29	112.90	173.72

Table 2: Size of the parameters (MB) for the base SEQ2SEQ model and the variants of S2SMIX with four mixtures.

	beam	en-fr	en-de	en-vi	en-es
	4	30.26	19.52	24.82	29.40
SEQ2SEQ	8	30.18	19.77	23.55	29.76
	16	27.63	19.13	19.05	28.19
	1	30.61	20.18	25.16	31.17
S2SMIX-4	2	31.22	20.71	25.28	31.47
	4	31.97	21.08	25.36	31.21

Table 3: BLEU scores of different systems over different search space.

	en-fr	en-de	en-vi	en-es
BLEU				
SEQ2SEQ-d	29.85	19.18	24.62	29.72
S2SMIX-4	30.61	20.18	25.16	31.17
DIV_BLEU				
SEQ2SEQ-d	20.43	22.66	14.51	18.83
S2SMIX-4	34.85	47.85	37.40	38.31

Table 4: S2SMIX with 4 components vs SEQ2SEQ endowed with the beam-diverse decoder (Li et al., 2016) with the beam size of 4.

of new parameters compared to the base SEQ2SEQ model. Specifically, only up to 0.002% increase in the parameter size are introduced, across all of the language pairs and mixture model variants.

S2SMIX vs. SEQ2SEQ. We compare our mixture model against a vanilla SEQ2SEQ model both in terms of translation quality and diversity. To be fair, we compare models with the same number of beams during inference, *e.g.,* we compare vanilla SEQ2SEQ using a beam size of 8 with S2SMIX-4 with 4 component and a beam size of 2 per component.

As an effective regularization strategy, we adopt label smoothing to strengthen generalisation performance (Szegedy et al., 2016; Pereyra et al., 2017; Edunov et al., 2018). Unlike conventional cross-entropy loss, where the probability mass for the ground truth word y is set to 1 and $q(y') = 0$ for $y' \neq y$, we smooth this distribution as:

$$q(y) = 1 - \epsilon, \tag{19}$$
$$q(y') = \frac{\epsilon}{V - 1} \tag{20}$$

where ϵ is a smoothing parameter, and V is the vocabulary size. In our experiments, ϵ is set to 0.1.

Table 3 shows the results across four language pairs. Each row in the top part should be compared with the corresponding row in the bottom part for a fair comparison in terms of the effective beam size. Firstly, we observe that increasing the beam size deteriorates the BLEU score for the SEQ2SEQ model. Similar observations have been made in the previous work (Tu et al., 2017). This behavior is in contrast to our S2SMIX model where increasing the beam size improves the BLEU score, except en-es, which demonstrates a decreasing trend when beam size increases from 2 to 4. Secondly, our S2SMIX models outperform their SEQ2SEQ counterparts in all settings with the same number of bins.

Figure 3 shows the diversity comparison between the S2SMIX model and the vanilla SEQ2SEQ model where the number of decoding beams is 8. The diversity metrics are bigram and BLEU diversity as defined earlier in the section. Our S2SMIX models significantly dominate the SEQ2SEQ model across language pairs in terms of the diversity metrics, while keeping the translation quality high (c.f. the BLEU scores in Table 3).

We further compare against the SEQ2SEQ model endowed with the beam-diverse decoder (Li et al., 2016). This decoder penalizes sibling hypotheses generated from the same parent in the search tree, according to their ranks in each decoding step. Hence, it tends to rank high those hypotheses from different parents, hence encouraging diversity in the beam.

Table 4 presents the BLEU scores as well as the diversity measures. As seen, the mixture model significantly outperforms the SEQ2SEQ endowed with the beam-diverse decoder, in terms of the diversity in the generated translations. Furthermore, the mixture model achieves up to 1.7 BLEU score improvements across three language pairs.

	en-fr		en-de		en-vi		en-es	
	BLEU	time	BLEU	time	BLEU	time	BLEU	time
S2SMIX-4	30.61	1.25	20.18	1.33	25.16	1.14	31.17	1.30
MC sampling:								
S2SMIX-4	30.43	1.67	19.74	1.67	24.93	1.58	31.27	1.67
S2SMIX-8	30.66	2.08	20.41	2.05	24.86	2.00	31.44	2.06
S2SMIX-16	30.74	3.10	20.43	2.88	24.90	2.83	30.82	3.02

Table 5: BLEU scores using greedy decoding and training time based on the original log-likelihood objective and online EM coupled with gradient estimation based on a single MC sample. The training time is reported by taking the average running time of one minibatch update across a full epoch.

Large mixture models. Memory limitations of the GPU may make it difficult to increase the number of mixture components beyond a certain amount. One approach is to decrease the number of sentence pairs in a minibatch, however, this results in a substantial increase in the training time. Another approach is to resort to MC gradient estimation as discussed in Section 3.3.

The top-part of Table 5 compares the models trained by online EM vs the original log-likelihood objective, in terms of the BLEU score and the training time. As seen, the BLEU score of the EM-trained models are on-par with those trained on the log-likelihood objective. However, online EM leads to up to 35% increase in the training time for S2SMIX-4 across four different language pairs, as we first need to do a forward pass on the minibatch in order to form the lower bound on the log-likelihood training objective.

The bottom-part of Table 5 shows the effect of online EM coupled with sampling only one mixture component to form a stochastic approximation to the log-likelihood lower bound. For each minibatch, we first run a forward pass to compute the probability of each mixture component given each sentence pair in the minibatch. We then sample a mixture component for each sentence-pair to form the approximation of the log-likelihood lower bound for the minibatch, which is then optimized using back-propagation. As we increase the number of mixture components from 4 to 8, we see about 0.7 BLEU score increase for en-de; while there is no significant change in the BLEU score for en-fr, en-vi and en-es.

Increasing the number of mixture components further to 16 does not produce gains on these datasets. Time-wise, training with online EM coupled with 1-candidate sampling should be significantly faster that the vanilla online EM and the

original likelihood objective in principle, as we need to perform the backpropagation only for the selected mixture component (as opposed to all mixture components). Nonetheless, the additional computation due to increasing the number of mixtures from 4 to 8 is about 26%, which increases to about 55% when going from 8 to 16 mixture components.

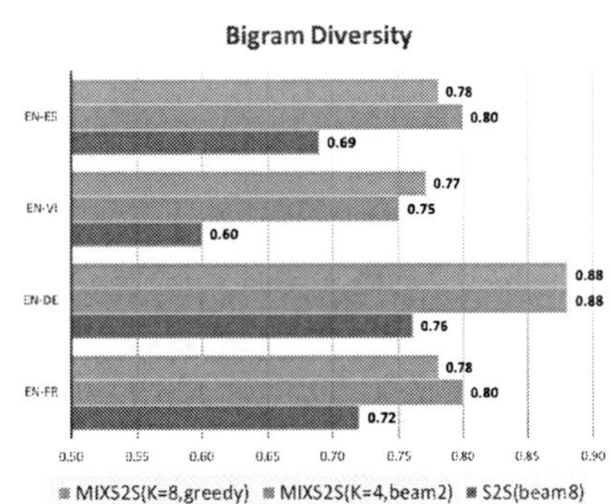

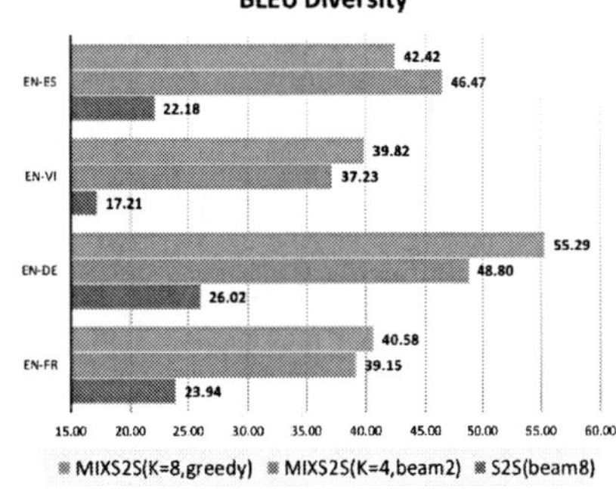

Figure 3: Diversity bigram (top) and BLEU (bottom) for the SEQ2SEQ model vs S2SMIX models, with the number of decoding beams set to 8.

4.2 Qualitative Analysis

Finally, we would like to demonstrate that our S2SMIX does indeed encourage diversity and im-

Source	And this information is stored for at least six months in Europe , up to two years .
Reference	Và những thông tin này được lưu trữ trong ít nhất sáu tháng ở châu Âu , cho tới tận hai năm .
SEQ2SEQ	
	Và thông tin này được lưu trữ trong ít sáu tháng ở Châu Âu , hai năm tới .
	Và thông tin này được lưu trữ trong ít sáu tháng ở Châu Âu , trong hai năm tới .
	Và thông tin này được lưu trữ trong ít sáu tháng ở Châu Âu , hai năm tới
	Và thông tin này được lưu trữ trong ít sáu tháng ở Châu Âu , trong hai năm tới
S2SMIX	
	Và thông tin này được lưu trữ trong ít nhất 6 tháng ở châu Âu , đến 2 năm .
	Và thông tin này được lưu trữ trong ít nhất 6 tháng ở châu Âu , lên tới hai năm .
	Và thông tin này được lưu trữ trong ít nhất 6 tháng ở châu Âu , trong vòng hai năm .
	Và thông tin này được lưu trữ trong ít nhất 6 tháng ở châu Âu , lên tới hai năm

Table 6: <u>Words</u> indicate diversity compared with the references, while red words denote translation improvement.

prove the translation quality. As shown in Table 6, compared with SEQ2SEQ, which mistranslates the second clause, our S2SMIX is not only capable of generating a group of correct translation, but also emitting synonyms for different mixture components. We provide more examples in the supplementary material.

5 Related Work

Obviously, different domains aim at different readers, thus they exhibit distinctive genres compared to other domains. A well-tuned MT system cannot directly apply to new domains; otherwise, translation quality will degrade. Based on this factor, out-domain adaptation has been widely studied for MT, ranging from data selection (Li et al., 2010; Wang et al., 2017), tuning (Luong and Manning, 2015; Farajian et al., 2017) to domain tags (Chu et al., 2017). Similarly, in-domain adaptation is also a compelling direction. Normally, to train an universal MT system, the training data consist of gigantic corpora covering numerous and various domains.This training data is naturally so diverse that Mima et al. (1997) incorporated extra-linguistic information to enhance translation quality. Michel and Neubig (2018) argue even without explicit signals (gender, politeness etc.), they can handle domain-specific information via annotation of speakers, and easily gain quality improvement from a larger number of domains. Our approach is considerably different from the previous work. We remove any extra annotation, and treat domain-related information as latent variables, which are learned from corpus.

Prior to our work, diverse generation has been studied in image captioning, as some of the training set are comprised of images paired with multiple reference captions. Some work puts their efforts on decoding stages, and form a group of beam search to encourage diversity (Vijayakumar et al., 2016), while others pay more attention to adversarial training (Shetty et al., 2017; Li et al., 2018). Within translation, our method is similar to Schulz et al. (2018b), where they propose a MT system armed with variational inference to account for translation variations. Like us, their diversified generation is driven by latent variables. Albeit the simplicity of our model, it is effective and able to accommodate variation or diversity. Meanwhile, we propose several diversity metrics to perform quantitative analysis.

Finally, Yang et al. (2018) proposes a mixture of softmaxes to enhance the expressiveness of language model, which demonstrate the effectiveness of our S2SMIX model under the matrix factorization framework.

6 Conclusions and Future Work

In this paper, we propose a sequence to sequence mixture (S2SMIX) model to improve translation diversity within neural machine translation via incorporating a set of discrete latent variables. We propose a model architecture that requires negligible additional parameters and no extra computation at inference time. In order to address prohibitive memory requirement associated with large mixture models, we augment the training procedure by computing the posterior distribution followed by Monte Carlo sampling to estimate the gradients. We observe significant gains both in terms of BLEU scores and translation diversity with a mixture of 4 components. In the future, we intend to replace the uniform mixing coefficients with learnable parameters, since different components should not necessarily make an equal contribution to a given sentence pair. Moreover, we will consider applying our S2SMIX model to other NLP problems in which diversity plays an important role.

7 Acknowledgements

We would like to thank Quan Tran, Trang Vu and three anonymous reviewers for their valuable comments and suggestions. This work was supported by the Multi-modal Australian ScienceS Imaging and Visualisation Environment (MASSIVE)[6], and in part by an Australian Research Council grant (DP160102686).

References

Martín Abadi, Ashish Agarwal, Paul Barham, Eugene Brevdo, Zhifeng Chen, Craig Citro, Gregory S. Corrado, Andy Davis, Jeffrey Dean, Matthieu Devin, Sanjay Ghemawat, Ian J. Goodfellow, Andrew Harp, Geoffrey Irving, Michael Isard, Yangqing Jia, Rafal Józefowicz, Lukasz Kaiser, Manjunath Kudlur, Josh Levenberg, Dan Mané, Rajat Monga, Sherry Moore, Derek Gordon Murray, Chris Olah, Mike Schuster, Jonathon Shlens, Benoit Steiner, Ilya Sutskever, Kunal Talwar, Paul A. Tucker, Vincent Vanhoucke, Vijay Vasudevan, Fernanda B. Viégas, Oriol Vinyals, Pete Warden, Martin Wattenberg, Martin Wicke, Yuan Yu, and Xiaoqiang Zheng. 2016. Tensorflow: Large-scale machine learning on heterogeneous distributed systems. *arXiv:1603.04467*.

Dzmitry Bahdanau, Kyunghyun Cho, and Yoshua Bengio. 2015. Neural machine translation by jointly learning to align and translate. *ICLR*.

Chenhui Chu, Raj Dabre, and Sadao Kurohashi. 2017. An empirical comparison of simple domain adaptation methods for neural machine translation. *CoRR*, abs/1701.03214.

Sergey Edunov, Myle Ott, Michael Auli, David Grangier, and Marc'Aurelio Ranzato. 2018. Classical structured prediction losses for sequence to sequence learning. *In Proceedings of NAACL-HLT 2018.*

M Amin Farajian, Marco Turchi, Matteo Negri, and Marcello Federico. 2017. Multi-domain neural machine translation through unsupervised adaptation. In *Proceedings of the Second Conference on Machine Translation*, pages 127–137.

Hany Hassan, Anthony Aue, Chang Chen, Vishal Chowdhary, Jonathan Clark, Christian Federmann, Xuedong Huang, Marcin Junczys-Dowmunt, William Lewis, Mu Li, et al. 2018. Achieving human parity on automatic chinese to english news translation. *arXiv:1803.05567*.

Sepp Hochreiter and Jürgen Schmidhuber. 1997. Long short-term memory. *Neural computation*, 9(8):1735–1780.

Diederik P. Kingma and Jimmy Ba. 2014. Adam: A method for stochastic optimization. *CoRR*, abs/1412.6980.

Dianqi Li, Xiaodong He, Qiuyuan Huang, Ming-Ting Sun, and Lei Zhang. 2018. Generating diverse and accurate visual captions by comparative adversarial learning. *arXiv preprint arXiv:1804.00861*.

Jiwei Li, Will Monroe, and Dan Jurafsky. 2016. A simple, fast diverse decoding algorithm for neural generation. *CoRR*, abs/1611.08562.

Mu Li, Yinggong Zhao, Dongdong Zhang, and Ming Zhou. 2010. Adaptive development data selection for log-linear model in statistical machine translation. In *Proceedings of the 23rd International Conference on Computational Linguistics*, pages 662–670. Association for Computational Linguistics.

Minh-Thang Luong and Christopher D Manning. 2015. Stanford neural machine translation systems for spoken language domains. In *IWSLT*.

Paul Michel and Graham Neubig. 2018. Extreme adaptation for personalized neural machine translation. In *In Proceedings of the 56th Annual Meeting of the Association for Computational Linguistics (ACL)*, Melbourne, Australia.

Hideki Mima, Osamu Furuse, and Hitoshi Iida. 1997. Improving performance of transfer-driven machine translation with extra-linguistic informatioon from context, situation and environment. In *IJCAI (2)*, pages 983–989.

Radford M Neal and Geoffrey E Hinton. 1998. A view of the em algorithm that justifies incremental, sparse, and other variants. *Learning in graphical models*.

Gabriel Pereyra, George Tucker, Jan Chorowski, Łukasz Kaiser, and Geoffrey Hinton. 2017. Regularizing neural networks by penalizing confident output distributions. *arXiv preprint arXiv:1701.06548*.

Philip Schulz, Wilker Aziz, and Trevor Cohn. 2018a. A stochastic decoder for neural machine translation. *CoRR*, arXiv:1805.10844.

Philip Schulz, Wilker Aziz, and Trevor Cohn. 2018b. A stochastic decoder for neural machine translation. In *In Proceedings of the 56th Annual Meeting of the Association for Computational Linguistics (ACL)*, Melbourne, Australia.

---

[6]https://www.massive.org.au/

Rico Sennrich, Barry Haddow, and Alexandra Birch. 2016. Neural machine translation of rare words with subword units. In *Proceedings of the 54th Annual Meeting of the Association for Computational Linguistics (Volume 1: Long Papers)*, volume 1, pages 1715–1725.

Rakshith Shetty, Marcus Rohrbach, Lisa Anne Hendricks, Mario Fritz, and Bernt Schiele. 2017. Speaking the same language: Matching machine to human captions by adversarial training. In *In Proceedings of the IEEE International Conference on Computer Vision (ICCV)*.

Ilya Sutskever, Oriol Vinyals, and Quoc V. Le. 2014. Sequence to sequence learning with neural networks. *NIPS*.

Christian Szegedy, Vincent Vanhoucke, Sergey Ioffe, Jon Shlens, and Zbigniew Wojna. 2016. Rethinking the inception architecture for computer vision. In *Proceedings of the IEEE conference on computer vision and pattern recognition*, pages 2818–2826.

Zhaopeng Tu, Yang Liu, Lifeng Shang, Xiaohua Liu, and Hang Li. 2017. Neural machine translation with reconstruction. *AAAI*.

Ashish Vaswani, Noam Shazeer, Niki Parmar, Jakob Uszkoreit, Llion Jones, Aidan N Gomez, Łukasz Kaiser, and Illia Polosukhin. 2017. Attention is all you need. *NIPS*.

Ashwin K Vijayakumar, Michael Cogswell, Ramprasath R Selvaraju, Qing Sun, Stefan Lee, David Crandall, and Dhruv Batra. 2016. Diverse beam search: Decoding diverse solutions from neural sequence models. *arXiv preprint arXiv:1610.02424*.

Rui Wang, Masao Utiyama, Lemao Liu, Kehai Chen, and Eiichiro Sumita. 2017. Instance weighting for neural machine translation domain adaptation. In *Proceedings of the 2017 Conference on Empirical Methods in Natural Language Processing*, pages 1482–1488.

Yonghui Wu, Mike Schuster, Zhifeng Chen, Quoc V Le, Mohammad Norouzi, Wolfgang Macherey, Maxim Krikun, Yuan Cao, Qin Gao, Klaus Macherey, et al. 2016. Google's neural machine translation system: Bridging the gap between human and machine translation. *arXiv:1609.08144*.

Zhilin Yang, Zihang Dai, Ruslan Salakhutdinov, and William W. Cohen. 2018. Breaking the softmax bottleneck: A high-rank RNN language model. In *International Conference on Learning Representations*.

Biao Zhang, Deyi Xiong, Jinsong Su, Hong Duan, and Min Zhang. 2016. Variational neural machine translation. *CoRR*, arXiv:1605.07869.

Author Index